PRENTICE HALL

LITERATURE

THE BRITISH TRADITION

PRENTICE HALL
LITERATURE

COPPER

BRONZE

SILVER

GOLD

PLATINUM

THE AMERICAN EXPERIENCE

THE BRITISH TRADITION

WORLD MASTERPIECES

PRENTICE HALL

LITERATURE

THE BRITISH TRADITION

FOURTH EDITION

A HIGHLAND COTTAGE
Myles Birket Foster

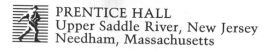
PRENTICE HALL
Upper Saddle River, New Jersey
Needham, Massachusetts

PRENTICE HALL
Simon & Schuster Education Group
A VIACOM COMPANY

STAFF CREDITS FOR PRENTICE HALL LITERATURE

Editorial: Ellen Bowler, Douglas McCollum, Philip Fried, Kelly Ackley, Eric Hausmann, Lauren Weidenman

Multicultural/ESL: Marina Liapunov, Barbara T. Stone

Marketing: Mollie Ledwith, Belinda Loh

National Language Arts Consultants: Ellen Lees Backstrom, Ed.D., Craig A. McGhee, Karen Massey, Vennisa Travers, Gail Witt

Permissions: Doris Robinson

Design: AnnMarie Roselli, Gerry Schrenk, Laura Bird

Media Research: Libby Forsyth, Suzi Myers, Martha Conway

Production: Suse Bell, Gertrude Szyferblatt

Computer Test Banks: Greg Myers, Suzi Myers

Pre-Press Production: Kathryn Dix, Paula Massenaro, Carol Barbara

Print and Bind: Rhett Conklin, Matt McCabe

ACKNOWLEDGMENTS

Grateful acknowledgment is made to the following for permission to reprint copyrighted material:

Edward Arnold (Publishers) Ltd.
"The Helping Hand" from *The Life to Come and Other Stories* by E. M. Forster. Copyright © 1972 The Trustees of the Late E. M. Forster. Reprinted by permission.

Curtis Brown Ltd, London
"Naming of Parts" from *A Map of Verona* by Henry Reed, 1946, copyright Henry Reed. Reprinted by permission of Curtis Brown Ltd, London.

Jonathan Clowes Ltd., London, on behalf of Doris Lessing
Excerpt from "The Small Personal Voice" from *A Small*
Personal Voice: Essays, Reviews, Interviews by Doris Lessing. Copyright © 1957 by Doris Lessing. Reprinted by permission of Jonathan Clowes Ltd., London, on behalf of Doris Lessing.

Doubleday & Company, Inc.
"The Lagoon" from *Tales of Unrest* by Joseph Conrad (Doubleday, Page & Company). Reprinted by permission of Doubleday & Company, Inc.

Dutton Signet, a division of Penguin Books USA, Inc.
From BEOWULF by Burton Raffel, translator, translated by Burton Raffel. Translation copyright © 1963 by Burton Raffel. Afterword © 1963 by New American Library. Used by permission.

(Continued on page 1238.)

CONTENTS

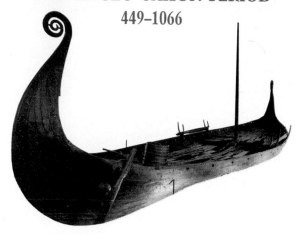

THE ENGLISH RENAISSANCE
1485–1625

THE SEVENTEENTH CENTURY
1625–1660

The Schools of Donne and Jonson   357

The Puritan Age   403

THE ROMANTIC AGE
1798–1832

THE VICTORIAN AGE
1833–1901

THE TWENTIETH CENTURY
1901 TO PRESENT

Prose   825

PRENTICE HALL

LITERATURE
THE BRITISH TRADITION

There is always one moment . . . when the door opens and lets the future in.

—Graham Greene

BAYEUX (bā yō') TAPESTRY: NORMAN CAVALRY CHARGE AT THE SHIELDWALL AT THE BATTLE OF HASTINGS

THE ANGLO-SAXON PERIOD
449–1066

When Angles and Saxons came hither from the east,
Sought Britain over the broad-spreading sea,
Haughty war-smiths overcame the Britons,
Valiant earls got for themselves a home.

from *The Anglo-Saxon Chronicle*

The passage on the previous page comes from a modern translation of *The Anglo-Saxon Chronicle,* an early record of English history. It tells of the attacks staged by warriors from what are now Denmark and Germany on the rock-bound coast of Britain during the fifth century. Most of the fierce "war-smiths" identified themselves as Angles and Saxons, though some belonged to a smaller tribe, the Jutes. At first these pirates sailed their shallow boats across the "broad-spreading" North Sea to raid Britain's low-lying eastern coast. By A.D. 449, however, their raids had turned into a full-scale invasion.

The arrival of the Anglo-Saxons in Britain signaled the beginning of the English language. The "war-smiths" soon drove native Britons from the eastern, central, and southern portions of their island. Those areas became known as "Angles' land," or England. The closely related Germanic languages spoken by the conquering tribes developed into a new language called "Angle-ish," or English. Although that language would change a great deal over the centuries, it was the precursor of the English we speak today. As the language took shape, so did the literature of England, Ireland, Scotland, and Wales.

To put these early times into historical perspective, we must first examine the people whom the Angles and Saxons conquered, the settlers of Britain before 449.

Britain Before the Anglo-Saxons

Who were the earliest inhabitants of the British Isles? The answer is not entirely clear, for some of them arrived in Britain in the dim recesses before recorded time. Among them were Iberians from present-day Spain and Portugal, who brought late Stone Age weapons to Britain's shores. The last, and by far the most important, of the early conquerors were the Celts, a people from southern Europe who had gradually migrated west. Between 800 and 600 B.C., two groups of Celts invaded the British Isles.

Arrival of the Celts

One group, who called themselves Brythons (now spelled "Britons"), settled on the largest

island, Britain. The other, known as Gaels, settled on the second largest island, known to us as Ireland. Gaels and Britons spoke different but related languages of the Celtic family. Celtic languages had nothing in common with the Germanic ones later associated with the Angles and Saxons.

The Celts were farmers and hunters. They organized themselves into tightly knit clans, each with a fearsome loyalty to its chieftain. When these clans fell into argument with one another, they often looked to a class of priests known as Druids to settle their disputes. Druids presided over religious rituals and also memorized and recited long, heroic poems that preserved the people's myths about the past. Some of the poems may have

INSIGNIA OF THE ROMAN CIVIL GOVERNOR OF THE FIVE BRITISH PROVINCES
Page from an early 15th-century copy of a 4th-century list of Imperial Magistrates

included fables about such leaders as Old King Cole of the nursery rhyme and King Lear of Shakespeare's tragic play.

The Roman Conquest

The next conquerors of Britain were the far more sophisticated Romans. In 55 B.C. and again the next year, the Roman general Julius Caesar made hasty invasions. Although he barely penetrated the island, he quickly declared it conquered and returned to what is now France to work on his memoirs. The true conquest of Britain occurred nearly one hundred years later during the reign of the Roman emperor Claudius. Disciplined Roman legions spread out over the island, establishing camps, which soon grew into towns.

The Romans transplanted many comforts of their urban, Mediterranean culture to the distant, rain-drenched north. In perhaps their greatest contribution, they constructed a system of well-paved roads through the woodland wilderness, highways that continued to serve the island for centuries.

The Roman rule of Britain lasted for more than 300 years. It ended only when northern European tribes invaded Italy and increased pressure on Rome itself. The last Roman legions departed from Britain to defend Rome in A.D. 407. By that time, some of their towns were already falling to ruin, and the Britons faced a new set of invaders.

The Anglo-Saxon Conquest

As we have seen, the next invaders were the Anglo-Saxons. Who were these ancient people? Lacking authentic first-hand accounts from the period, historians simply have to guess. Some Anglo-Saxons appear to have been deep-sea fishermen, already accustomed to marauding coasts along the Baltic Sea. Others seem to have been farmers, perhaps seeking soil richer than the sandy or marshy land at home. Ferocious as the Angles and Saxons may have been, they did not perform their piracy merely for plunder—at least not for long. They sought and won territory, apparently by rowing their shallow boats up river into the British heartland and then building camps and waging war on the Britons. Gradually, the newcomers gained the upper hand over the island's settlers and took over more and more of what today is England.

Early Anglo-Saxon Life

The first Angles, Saxons, and Jutes transferred to England their highly organized tribal units. Each tribe was ruled by a king, chosen by a *witan,* or council of elders. Invading groups set up numerous small kingdoms, and at first the various kingdoms fought frequently. As time went on, however, many of these tribal differences faded. Anglo-Saxon kingdoms traded with one another. Men married women from different tribes. Kingdoms gradually absorbed one another until seven larger ones remained. As previously mentioned, all this intermingling produced a new language. We call it Anglo-Saxon or Old English to distinguish it from our modern form.

The Anglo-Saxons brought to Britain their own pagan beliefs. In the world of the sixth century, the ever-present dangers of death by accident or warfare had led these people to take a rather grim view of life. In fact, the early Anglo-Saxons believed that every human life was in the hands of fate. Their attitude was sharply different from the Christian belief in the freedom of an individual to determine his or her own path.

The early Anglo-Saxons worshiped ancient Germanic gods. They included Tiu, god of war and the sky; Woden, chief of the gods; and Fria, Woden's wife and goddess of the home. These gods were abandoned with the coming of Christianity. Even so, their names survive in our words *Tuesday, Wednesday,* and *Friday.*

In terror of the Anglo-Saxons, the Britons retreated to the edges of their island—and beyond. Some went to the southwestern tip (Cornwall), or the hilly western region (Wales), of Britain. Still others joined the Gaels of Ireland. This group then traveled back to Britain and settled in the northern part of the island, Scotland. In all these areas, people spoke Celtic languages—

The Anglo-Saxon Period
(A.D. 449– A.D. 1066)

St. Augustine

Charles Martel
Battling
the Moors

A Viking Sword

| 300 | 450 | 600 |

BRITISH EVENTS

- Romans withdraw from Britain.
    - St. Patrick begins missionary work in Ireland.
        - Anglo-Saxon invasion.

- Death of the legendary hero King Arthur.
    - St. Augustine founds Christian monastery at Canterbury, Kent.

- Synod of Whitby establishes Roman Church in England.
    - **Bede** completes *A History of the English Church and People.*

WORLD EVENTS

- Western Europe: Fall of Western Roman Empire.
    - Italy: Theodoric the Great establishes Ostrogothic kingdom.
        - France: Clovis, King of Franks, converts to Christianity.
            - Eastern Europe: Plague kills half the population.
                - Mexico: Toltecs defeat Mayas.
                - Japan: Buddhism introduced.
                    - China: Beginning of book printing.

- Middle East: Jerusalem conquered by Arabs.
    - Egypt: Library at Alexandria destroyed.
        - Spain: Seville conquered by Moors.
            - France: Charles Martel defeats Moors.

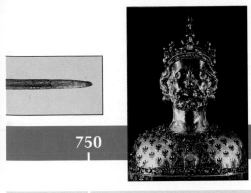

King
Charlemagne

Danes
Attacking
A British
Town

The Coronation
of William
the Conqueror

750

900

1050

- Surviving version of *Beowulf* composed.
  - Vikings attack Lindisfarne.
    - Scottish Ruler Kenneth MacAlprin unites Scots and Picts.
      - Truce with Danes divides England between Saxon rule in south and Danish rule in east and north.

- Howel the Good unites kingdom of Wales.
  - Saxon monks copy Old English poems into *Exeter Book*.
    - English defeated by Danes at Battle of Maldon.
    - Brian Boru unites Kingdom of Ireland.
      - Duncan I inherits Scottish throne.
      - Macbeth murders Duncan I.
        - Edward the Confessor becomes king of Saxons.

- Normans defeat Saxons; William the Conqueror becomes king of England.

- France: Charlemagne becomes king.
  - Peru: Incas build city of Machu Picchu.
    - Persia: Algebra devised.
      - France: Einhard writes *Life of Charlemagne*.
        - Russia: Nation founded by Vikings.
          - North Atlantic: Vikings discover Iceland.

- Western Europe: Feudalism developed.
  - France: Normans establish Normandy.
    - Greenland: Eric the Red establishes first Viking colony.
      - North America: Viking explorer Leif Ericson explores Canadian coast.
      - Middle East: Moslems destroy Holy Sepulcher in Jerusalem.
        - Spain: Birth of El Cid, national hero who fought Moors.

- Italy: Normans conquer Sicily.

SAXONS, JUTES, AND ANGLES ARRIVING IN BRITAIN BY SEA
English manuscript illumination

northern Britain in the hope of winning souls for the faith. In their travels, they won acceptance among many Scots and some Saxons and Angles. Their conversions led, in turn, to the establishment of monasteries in the north.

Meanwhile, the Roman Church had reorganized itself and was beginning to send missionaries throughout Europe. In 597, the Roman cleric Saint Augustine (not the early Christian Church father) arrived in southeast England and quickly converted King Ethelbert of Kent to Christianity. Augustine set up a monastery at Canterbury in Kent and began preaching his faith to other rulers in southern England. To win over a kingdom, Augustine and his followers needed only to convert the king, who would then make Christianity the religion of his realm. By the year 650, they had largely succeeded.

The new religion had a profound effect on Anglo-Saxon civilization. No longer could ruling warlords indulge themselves in the belief that they had descended from pagan gods. No longer could freemen think it permissible to treat their wives or children or slaves with cruelty. Christian clerics were able to end old feuds by denouncing revenge and calling upon a higher law. By providing counsel to quarreling rulers, the Church promoted peace and played a major role in unifying the English people.

Cornish, Welsh, and Irish and Scottish Gaelic. All but the Cornish language are still spoken today.

The Coming of Christianity

During the fourth century, the Romans had accepted Christianity and introduced it to Britain. A century later, when the Celts fled the Anglo-Saxons, they took their Christian faith with them. After Rome fell to barbarian tribes in A.D. 476, communications weakened between Celtic and Roman Christians. While the Roman Church was recovering from political chaos, the Celtic Christian Church continued to thrive. In 563, a group of Irish monks set sail in tiny skiffs for the west coast of Scotland. A soldier and abbot named Columba, along with some monks, moved across

Christianity and Literature

The Church also brought to England two elements of civilization that had been missing since the departure of the Romans: education and written literature. Christian leaders established schools at Canterbury and York and supervised the preservation of learning in the island's monasteries. Within their secluded halls, monks often worked as scribes, recording and duplicating *manuscripts,* or books written by hand. At first they worked only in Latin, the language of Church scholarship. Often several monks labored for years to complete a single manuscript. These volumes were elaborately painted and illuminated in gold and silver.

From such monastic training emerged a Northumbrian monk later considered the "father of English history." Today we know him as the Venerable Bede (673–735). Bede was a master of thorough research, tracking down information by studying earlier documents and interviewing people who had witnessed or taken part in past events. His most famous volume was *A History of the English Church and People,* a monumental work that offers the clearest account we have of early Anglo-Saxon times.

Although Christianity did indeed temper Anglo-Saxon civilization, it did not destroy the northerners' spirit. Glimpses of an earlier world lived on in the fragments of epics such as *Beowulf,* a long narrative poem that depicted great battles between Anglo-Saxon warriors and superhuman monsters. The Anglo-Saxons remained a hardy group. Now they were about to come face to face with a new peril—invasion by the Vikings.

The First Danish Invasion

Between the ninth and twelfth centuries, a great restlessness overtook the region of northern Europe known as Scandinavia. Besct with a rising population and limited farmland, the people of Norway, the Norse, and of Denmark, the Danes, took to the seas. In some of their most adventurous voyages, the Vikings (warriors) carried their piracy to the British Isles. The Norse set their sights on Northumbria, Scotland, Wales, and Ireland, whereas the Danes targeted eastern and southern England.

Viking invaders sacked and plundered monasteries, destroyed manuscripts, and stole sacred religious objects. They burned entire communities and put villagers to the sword. Wherever the Vikings went, the sight of their square-sailed ships stirred specters of terror and destruction. One Anglo-Saxon prayer of the day reflected the fear that the Danish pirates inspired: "From the fury of the Northmen, O Lord, deliver us."

Although the English fought back valiantly, the Danes made broad inroads. By the middle of the ninth century, most of northern, eastern, and central England had fallen to the invaders. They called their territory the Danelaw. Only the Saxon kingdom of Wessex managed to fight the Danes to a standstill.

Alfred the Great

In 871, a king ascended to the Wessex throne who would become the only ruler in England's history ever to be honored with the epithet "the Great." His name was Alfred, and he earned the title partly by resisting further Danish encroachment. Under a truce concluded in 886, England was formally divided: the Saxons acknowledged Danish rule in the east and north, but the Danes agreed to respect Saxon rule in the south. As the king of a much-expanded Wessex, Alfred the Great became a national hero.

Alfred's achievements went far beyond the field of battle, however. Not only was he instrumental in preserving the remnants of pre-Danish civilization in Britain, but he encouraged a rebirth of learning and education. To make literature and other documents more accessible, he oversaw translations of Bede's *History* and other works from Latin into Anglo-Saxon, the everyday language of the people. In this way he fostered the growth of the English language and its literature. He also began to keep records of English history in the *Anglo-Saxon Chronicle,* one of our principal sources of information on early English life.

Gradually the Danes became more peaceful, and old animosities subsided. Even before their arrival in England, many Danes had been accustomed to the merchant's trade, however crudely it may have existed in northern Europe at the time. Now they built their Danelaw communities not only as military fortresses but as trading centers, and one result was the growth of English towns.

Like the Anglo-Saxons, the Danes spoke a Germanic language, so they were able to communicate easily with the English. In fact, many Norse words slowly crept into the English vocabulary. The word *law* is Danish, for example. Its use reflected the Danes' interest in legal procedures.

The Second Danish Invasion and the Norman Conquest

The peace and stability that began with Alfred's reign lasted more than a century. Immigration from Scandinavia dwindled, and the descendants of Alfred the Great were able to regain much

EDWARD THE CONFESSOR SPEAKS TO HAROLD OF WESSEX
Detail from the Bayeux Tapestry

conquered territory. Toward the close of the tenth century, however, a new series of onslaughts began as more Danes from Europe attempted to recapture and widen the Danelaw. Once they had succeeded, they forced the Saxon witan to select a succession of Danish kings.

Then, in 1042, the line of succession returned to a descendant of Alfred the Great. This king, Edward, had gained the title "the Confessor" because he was a deeply religious Christian. He had spent many of his early years in Normandy, a region once settled by Scandinavians and now a part of France. Norman on his mother's side, Edward had developed a close friendship with his cousin William, Normandy's ruler. Once Edward took the English throne, his association with the Normans further weakened Saxon power. His death in 1066 led directly to a Norman conquest of England and brought to an end the Anglo-Saxon period of literature, as we shall see in the next unit.

Anglo-Saxon Literature

Scholars now believe that the literature of the British Isles began with Celtic Druids. These priests assumed the function of storytellers, reciting poems about Celtic leaders and their heroic deeds. In the same way, Anglo-Saxon literature began not with books, but with spoken verse and incantations. Their purpose was to pass along tribal history and values to a population that mostly could not read or write.

To be sure, some Anglo-Saxons were familiar with the written word. In the third century in northern Europe, they had devised an alphabet of letters called *runes*. When they came to Britain, they brought this alphabet with them and used it until the Latin alphabet we have today superseded it. Runes were used chiefly for inscriptions on important buildings, on statues, and the like.

The reciting of poems often occurred on ceremonial occasions such as the celebration of a military victory. A warrior's comrades would gather in his hall or castle, and the performance would begin. The performers were usually professional minstrels, known as *scops,* and their assistants, called *gleemen.* The scops and gleemen recited for hours and, in some instances, even for days.

Scholars now suppose that these recitations took place to the accompaniment of a harp. The poems followed a set formula of composition, which probably made them easier to memorize. A formal, rigid pattern of word stresses gave the lyrics a terse, sing-song effect. A mid-line pause, called a *caesura,* occurred in many lines. Another part of the pattern was *alliteration,* the repetition of sounds, especially initial consonant sounds.

Types of Anglo-Saxon Verse

Only about 30,000 lines of Anglo-Saxon verse still exist. Almost all of it is found in four works dating from about A.D. 975 to 1050. The early verse falls mainly into two categories. One is heroic poetry, which recounts the achievements of warriors involved in great battles. The other is elegiac poetry, sorrowful laments that mourn the deaths of loved ones and the loss of the past.

Copied many years after their composition, the poems have obviously undergone many changes. Later scops may have adapted them, and so may have monastic scribes. Nevertheless, pagan elements remain, particularly in the ever-present sense of an ominous fate, or *wyrd.* Consider, for example, these lines from one of the elegiac poems, "The Wanderer":

"He who shall muse   on these mold-
    ering ruins,
And deeply ponder   this darkling life,
Must brood on old legends   of battle

and bloodshed,
And heavy the mood   that troubles his
        heart: . . .

The Beowulf Legend

Of the heroic poetry, the most important work is *Beowulf,* the story of a great pagan warrior renowned for his courage, strength, and dignity. *Beowulf* is an *epic,* a long heroic poem. Because it is the first such work to be composed in the English language, it is considered the national epic of England.

Like most Anglo-Saxon poets, the author of *Beowulf* is unknown. Although versions of the poem were probably recited as early as the sixth century, the text that we have today was composed in the eighth century and not written down until the eleventh. Thus, the poem includes many references to Christian ideas and Latin classics. Clearly evident in *Beowulf,* however, are the values of a warrior society, especially such values as dignity, bravery, and prowess in battle:

And Beowulf was ready, firm with our
        Lord's
High favor and his own bold courage
        and strength.

Emphasis on such values did not disappear in Christian times. It appeared in later Anglo-Saxon poems such as *The Battle of Maldon,* which commemorates a great military defeat by the Danes.

Among the few known poets of the Christian era, two are worthy of mention—Caedmon and Cynewulf. Caedmon, who apparently lived in the seventh century, is mentioned in Bede's *History.* The poet's only authenticated verse consists of a few lines that Bede recorded, called "Caedmon's Hymn." Nevertheless, the term *Caedmonian verse* is often used to identify other early Christian poetry in English. Scholars believe that Cynewulf lived around the turn of the ninth century. He is known because he "signed" his name, spelling it out in runes, on four poems that survive today.

Anglo-Saxon Prose

Before the reign of Alfred the Great, all important prose written in the British Isles was composed in Latin. The monks who transcribed these works regarded the vernacular, the language of the common people, as a "vulgar tongue." The greatest of England's Latin scholars was the Venerable Bede, as mentioned earlier. His *History* gives an account of England from the Roman invasion to his own time.

Bede's *History* concerns itself mostly with northern England, but it is not simply the story of Northumbria or the people who settled there. The monk couples his view of the Roman Church as a universal force with a distinctly nationalistic view of a unified English people. Although Bede wrote in Latin, his *History* may nevertheless be considered the first truly English prose work. From it we derive much of what we know about early Anglo-Saxon times.

Bede's successor as the leading English scholar was Alcuin (735–804), another monk who, like Bede, won fame throughout Europe. Trained at York, Alcuin traveled widely in Europe and eventually headed the palace school of the powerful European emperor Charlemagne. By the time of his death, Alcuin had produced many major works in philosophy, religion, and Latin grammar.

Alfred the Great and His Successors

Historians usually credit Alfred the Great with having changed the course of British literature. The spur he gave to the English language was evident in its more widespread use among scholars after his death. Of these scholars, the foremost were Aelfric and Wulfstan, who both flourished during the tenth century. Aelfric, a monk of Wessex, wrote many works in the vernacular, including a series of *homilies,* or sermons, based on Bible stories. Though in prose, these sermons employ a great deal of the sort of alliteration more commonly associated with Anglo-Saxon poetry. Wulfstan, an archbishop of York, also wrote several sermons in Old English, including a famous speech on the devastation of the Danish raids.

After the Normans occupied England, they gradually transformed the English that the Anglo-Saxons spoke. Old English, or Anglo-Saxon, evolved into what we now call Middle English, whose literature we will explore in the next unit.

Quotations by Prominent Figures of the Period

I sing of myself, a sorrowful woman.
>   **Anonymous,** "A Wife's Lament," translated by Kemp Malone

This tale is true, and mine. It tells
How the sea took me, swept me back
And forth, in sorrow and fear and pain.
>   **Anonymous,** "The Seafarer," translated by Burton Raffel

It is better never to begin a good work than, having begun
it, to stop.
>   **Bede,** *A History of the English Church and People*

Out from the marsh, from the foot of misty
Hills and bogs, bearing God's hatred,
Grendel came.

Beowulf spoke, in spite of the swollen
Livid wound, knowing he'd unwound
His strings of days on earth. . . .

                              My days
Have gone by as fate willed, waiting
For its word to be spoken.
>   **Anonymous,** *Beowulf,* translated by Burton Raffel

Light was first
Through the Lord's word
Named day:
Beauteous, bright creation!
>   **Caedmon,** *Creation: The First Day,* translated by Benjamin Thorpe

And those people should not be listened to who keep saying
the voice of the people is the voice of God, since the
riotousness of the crowd is always very close to madness.
>   **Alcuin** in a letter to Charlemagne

Alcuin was my name; learning I loved.
>   **Alcuin** in his own epitaph

Thought shall be harder, heart the keener, courage the
greater, as our might lessens.
>   **Anonymous,** *The Battle of Maldon,* translated by R. K. Gordon

READING CRITICALLY

The Literature of 449–1066

When you read literature, it is important to investigate its historical context. Doing so will help you to understand the writer's ideas and techniques.

HISTORICAL CONTEXT In 449 the island of Britain was invaded by warlike Germanic peoples known as Angles and Saxons. These invaders brought with them their pagan beliefs and traditions, which appear in Anglo-Saxon poetry and legends. They also brought with them a grim, fatalistic view of the world. These Germanic invaders were followed by Roman missionaries, who converted Britain to Christianity. During this time, different kinds of literature developed, including the oral poetry of the Anglo-Saxons and written historical and religious prose. The literature of the time shows both pagan and Christian influences.

LITERARY MOVEMENTS Very few people were able to read during this period. Therefore, an oral tradition flourished. The Anglo-Saxons were fond of poetry, which was developed and passed on by *scops,* or poet-singers. Eventually, some of this oral literature was written down by monks in monasteries, who are largely responsible for having preserved oral material.

WRITERS' TECHNIQUES Because most literature was oral, it was composed in such a way that it was easily memorized. Lines of poetry with regular rhythms were easier to remember than was prose. Poets used alliteration for the same reason. In addition, Anglo-Saxon poets were fond of the kenning, a compound metaphorical name for something, such as "whale's home" for the sea. The Anglo-Saxon poetry that has been preserved illustrates these techniques.

GUIDE FOR INTERPRETING

The Seafarer

Composed by an unknown poet, "The Seafarer" was discovered in a collection of manuscripts now called *The Exeter Book.* Given to Exeter Cathedral by the eleventh-century Bishop Leofric, *The Exeter Book* was probably compiled during the reign of Alfred the Great, between 871 and 899. We do not know why the particular works in *The Exeter Book* were gathered together, nor can we say for certain that "The Seafarer" was meant to be read apart from the rest.

Literary Forms

Anglo-Saxon Lyric Poetry. "The Seafarer" is usually called an elegy, or a mournful, contemplative poem, but it can also be considered part of the medieval literary genre called *planctus,* meaning "complaint." What distinguishes *planctus* from elegy is a fictional speaker and a subject that may be a loss other than death. The emotions expressed by the speakers in both types of poetry are strong. Several other Anglo-Saxon works in *The Exeter Book,* including "The Wanderer" (page 53), are lyric or elegiac poems.

Some scholars believe "The Seafarer" employs two speakers: one who makes a personal "complaint" and a second who comments on the condition described by the first. The second part of the poem, beginning at line 64, is different in tone from the first, and it emphasizes man's relationship with the divine rather than one man's personal plight. The religious content of "The Seafarer" adds richness and complexity to its lyric style.

Primary Source

The critic Rosemary Woolf has written about the clever use of imagery in "The Seafarer."

> The poet seems in fact to have given an individual twist to the traditional images of man as an exile . . . and of life as a sea-voyage. According to his stylized figurative pattern the man who lives a life on land is always in a state of security and contentment: he is therefore mindless of the Christian image of man as an exile; . . . The sea, however, is always a place of isolation and hardship: the man, therefore, who chooses to be literally what in Christian terms he is figuratively, must forsake the land and live upon the sea.

Focus

The Dark Ages were a time of great turmoil and uncertainty. The Anglo-Saxons wrote about their woes to help make sense of them. How do people today deal with a sense of loss or alienation? Write about some things that people do to encourage themselves.

The Seafarer

translated by Burton Raffel

This tale is true, and mine. It tells
How the sea took me, swept me back
And forth in sorrow and fear and pain,
Showed me suffering in a hundred ships,
In a thousand ports, and in me. It tells   5
Of smashing surf when I sweated in the cold
Of an anxious watch, perched in the bow
As it dashed under cliffs. My feet were cast
In icy bands, bound with frost,
With frozen chains, and hardship groaned   10
Around my heart. Hunger tore
At my sea-weary soul. No man sheltered
On the quiet fairness of earth can feel
How wretched I was, drifting through winter
On an ice-cold sea, whirled in sorrow,   15
Alone in a world blown clear of love,
Hung with icicles. The hailstorms flew.
The only sound was the roaring sea,
The freezing waves. The song of the swan
Might serve for pleasure, the cry of the sea-fowl,   20
The death-noise of birds instead of laughter,
The mewing of gulls instead of mead.
Storms beat on the rocky cliffs and were echoed
By icy-feathered terns and the eagle's screams;
No kinsman could offer comfort there,   25
To a soul left drowning in desolation.
     And who could believe, knowing but
The passion of cities, swelled proud with wine
And no taste of misfortune, how often, how wearily,
I put myself back on the paths of the sea.   30
Night would blacken; it would snow from the north;
Frost bound the earth and hail would fall,
The coldest seeds. And how my heart
Would begin to beat, knowing once more
The salt waves tossing and the towering sea!   35
The time for journeys would come and my soul
Called me eagerly out, sent me over
The horizon, seeking foreigners' homes.

SHIPS WITH THREE MEN, FISH
Bodleian Library, Oxford

But there isn't a man on earth so proud,
40 So born to greatness, so bold with his youth,
Grown so brave, or so graced by God,
That he feels no fear as the sails unfurl,
Wondering what Fate has willed and will do.
No harps ring in his heart, no rewards,
45 No passion for women, no worldly pleasures,
Nothing, only the ocean's heave;
But longing wraps itself around him.
Orchards blossom, the towns bloom,
Fields grow lovely as the world springs fresh,
50 And all these admonish that willing mind
Leaping to journeys, always set
In thoughts traveling on a quickening tide.
So summer's sentinel, the cuckoo, sings
In his murmuring voice, and our hearts mourn
55 As he urges. Who could understand,
In ignorant ease, what we others suffer
As the paths of exile stretch endlessly on?
        And yet my heart wanders away,
My soul roams with the sea, the whales'
60 Home, wandering to the widest corners
Of the world, returning ravenous with desire,
Flying solitary, screaming, exciting me
To the open ocean, breaking oaths
On the curve of a wave.
        Thus the joys of God
65 Are fervent with life, where life itself
Fades quickly into the earth. The wealth
Of the world neither reaches to Heaven nor remains.
No man has ever faced the dawn
Certain which of Fate's three threats
70 Would fall: illness, or age, or an enemy's
Sword, snatching the life from his soul.
The praise the living pour on the dead
Flowers from reputation: plant
An earthly life of profit reaped
75 Even from hatred and rancor, of bravery
Flung in the devil's face, and death
Can only bring you earthly praise
And a song to celebrate a place
With the angels, life eternally blessed
80 In the hosts of Heaven.
        The days are gone
When the kingdoms of earth flourished in glory;
Now there are no rulers, no emperors,
No givers of gold, as once there were,

When wonderful things were worked among them
85   And they lived in lordly magnificence.
Those powers have vanished, those pleasures are dead.
The weakest survives and the world continues,
Kept spinning by toil. All glory is tarnished.
The world's honor ages and shrinks,
90   Bent like the men who mold it. Their faces
Blanch as time advances, their beards
Wither and they mourn the memory of friends.
The sons of princes, sown in the dust.
The soul stripped of its flesh knows nothing
95   Of sweetness or sour, feels no pain,
Bends neither its hand nor its brain. A brother
Opens his palms and pours down gold
On his kinsman's grave, strewing his coffin
With treasures intended for Heaven, but nothing
100   Golden shakes the wrath of God
For a soul overflowing with sin, and nothing
Hidden on earth rises to Heaven.
                We all fear God. He turns the earth,
He set it swinging firmly in space,
105   Gave life to the world and light to the sky.
Death leaps at the fools who forget their God.
He who lives humbly has angels from Heaven
To carry him courage and strength and belief.
A man must conquer pride, not kill it,
110   Be firm with his fellows, chaste for himself,
Treat all the world as the world deserves,
With love or with hate but never with harm,
Though an enemy seek to scorch him in hell,
Or set the flames of a funeral pyre
115   Under his lord. Fate is stronger
And God mightier than any man's mind.
Our thoughts should turn to where our home is,
Consider the ways of coming there,
Then strive for sure permission for us
120   To rise to that eternal joy,
That life born in the love of God
And the hope of Heaven. Praise the Holy
Grace of Him who honored us,
Eternal, unchanging creator of earth. Amen.

RESPONDING TO THE SELECTION

Your Response

1. Do you agree that "Fate is stronger . . . than any man's mind"? Why or why not?

Recalling

2. What are three images the poet uses in the first stanza to convey his sense of isolation?
3. (a) What happens to "fools who forget their God"? (b) What happens to those who "live humbly"?

Interpreting

4. How might you explain the mixed feelings about the sea that the poet seems to feel?
5. Pagans in Anglo-Saxon England—that is, non-Christians—felt themselves at the mercy of forces utterly beyond their control, whereas Christians put their trust in salvation and heaven. In what way do lines 39 through 43 show the influence of both beliefs?
6. Explain lines 66 and 67: "The wealth / Of the world neither reaches to Heaven nor remains."
7. "The Seafarer" is a poem of contrasts. What contrast is implied in lines 80 through 102?
8. What does the poet mean by the word *home* in line 117?

Applying

9. Explain how a person can dislike something as much as the sailor dislikes life at sea and yet keep going back to it.

ANALYZING LITERATURE

Understanding Anglo-Saxon Poetry

A **lyric poem** is one that expresses intense personal emotions. "The Seafarer" mixes pagan with Christian beliefs and expresses sorrow for something lost or past. At times the poet's feelings seem to border on despair.

1. What deep personal feelings does the poet express in the first part of "The Seafarer" that show this to be a lyric poem?
2. "The Seafarer" has two distinct parts, the second of which begins at line 64. What are some of the strong emotions expressed in the second part of the poem?

CRITICAL THINKING AND READING

Comparing and Contrasting Attitudes

To **compare** two ideas or attitudes is to point out similarities. To **contrast** them is to point out differences.

Explain what accounts for the poet's state of mind at the beginning of the poem and at the end.

THINKING AND WRITING

Writing About Anglo-Saxon Beliefs

"The Seafarer" is not an easy poem to understand. One critic has said that almost any theory can explain its meaning. What is *your* theory? What main idea do you think the poet intends to convey? In your prewriting, list the various thoughts and feelings the poet expresses in the poem. Use these notes as the basis for a thesis statement in which you summarize what you think is the main idea of the poem. In writing a first draft, support your thesis statement with evidence from the poem. When you revise, be sure you have made clear the reasons for your conclusion.

LEARNING OPTION

Language. Old English is the English language as it existed from about the year 500 to about 1150. Our language has changed so much since then that Anglo-Saxon poems like "The Seafarer" must be translated, just as if they were written in a foreign language. Here are lines 42 and 43 from "The Seafarer" in Old English:

> þæt he a his sæfore   sorge næbbe.
> to hwon hine Dryhten   gedon wille.

Some Old English words such as *tree, sleep,* and *winter* are still in common use. Others appear in dictionaries but are seldom used anymore. Find the meanings of the following words: *churl, thane, tor, yare, yclept.* Then write a sentence using each word and try to make the meaning of the word clear in context.

BEOWULF

700 [?]

Composed by an unknown poet who lived more than twelve hundred years ago, *Beowulf* marks the beginning of English literature. Minstrels called scops recited this poem to audiences in England for about three hundred years before it was first written down. Only one original manuscript of the complete 3,128-line poem survives, but *Beowulf* is in no danger of becoming extinct. Not only does it have lasting historical importance as a record of the Angles, Saxons, and Jutes in England, but it also tells a hair-raising tale that has electrified readers and listeners through the centuries.

Beowulf, a Geat from a region that is today southern Sweden, sets sail from his homeland to try to free Danish King Hrothgar's great banquet hall, Herot, of a monster that has been ravaging it for twelve years. This monster, Grendel, is a terrifying swampland creature of enormous size whose eyes burn "with a gruesome light." The struggle between Beowulf, a young adventurer eager for fame, and Grendel, a fierce and bloodthirsty foe, is the first of three mortal battles in the long poem. The first battle is the one described in this book. The second struggle pits Beowulf against Grendel's "water-hag" mother, and the third, fifty years later, against a dragon.

Although the action takes place in sixth-century Scandinavia, the poem is unmistakably English. Recited originally in Old English, *Beowulf* is based on legends and chronicles of the various Northern Europeans who migrated to England.

GUIDE FOR INTERPRETING

from Beowulf

Literary Forms

Anglo-Saxon Epic Poetry. An epic is a long narrative poem, sometimes developed orally, that celebrates the deeds of a legendary or heroic figure. A few epics predate the Anglo-Saxon *Beowulf,* including the Greek *Iliad* and *Odyssey* by Homer and the Roman *Aeneid* by Virgil. Typically, an epic features a hero who is larger than life and concerns eternal human problems such as the struggle between good and evil. An epic is presented in a serious manner, often through the use of elevated language. The hero of an epic represents widespread national, cultural, or religious values.

Beowulf is one of the oldest European epics. Its hero, Beowulf, embodies the highest ideals of his time and place: loyalty, valor, selflessness, and a sense of justice. He represents good, whereas Grendel represents evil. Throughout *Beowulf* there is a prevailing yet somewhat uneasy blend of Christian ethics and pagan morality. Against a backdrop of gloom that reflects the Anglo-Saxons' stoic acceptance of fate, the story applauds the highest virtues of human nature—courage, generosity, faithfulness. Despite its blood and horror, *Beowulf* is a deeply idealistic narrative.

Anglo-Saxon epic poetry, of which *Beowulf* is the greatest example, has certain distinctive features. One is the two-part line. Each line is separated by a pause, known as a *caesura,* and there are generally two strong beats per part. Another feature is the *kenning,* a colorful, indirect way of naming something: The sea is a *whalepath;* a battle is *spear play;* the sun is the *candle of the skies.*

Commentary

Beowulf belongs to the present as well as to the past. Perhaps the most popular contemporary works it inspired are a series of epics about the fantasy world of Middle Earth. Beginning in 1937 with *The Hobbit,* Oxford don J.R.R. Tolkien wove imaginative tales about good and evil. The enthusiastic response to his trilogy *The Lord of the Rings* (1954–55)—*The Fellowship of the Ring, The Two Towers,* and *The Return of the King*—prompted him to continue the saga in *The Silmarillion* (1977), an account of the origins of Middle Earth. Tolkien, however, was originally far more famous for completely changing the way we interpret *Beowulf.* In his 1936 article "Beowulf: The Monsters and the Critics," he saw *Beowulf* as poetry rather than history, and modern *Beowulf* scholarship began.

Focus

At the time *Beowulf* was composed, the ideals of the Anglo-Saxons included loyalty, valor, selflessness, and a sense of justice. Those are still highly regarded ideals, but others exist. List four other ideals that are important to Americans today.

from Beowulf

translated by Burton Raffel

The selection opens during an evening of celebration at Herot, the banquet hall of the Danish king Hrothgar (hroth' gär). Outside in the darkness, however, lurks the monster Grendel, a murderous creature who poses a great danger to the people inside the banquet hall.

The Wrath of Grendel

A powerful monster, living down
In the darkness, growled in pain, impatient
As day after day the music rang
Loud in that hall,[1] the harp's rejoicing

5 Call and the poet's clear songs, sung
Of the ancient beginnings of us all, recalling
The Almighty making the earth, shaping
These beautiful plains marked off by oceans,
Then proudly setting the sun and moon

10 To glow across the land and light it;
The corners of the earth were made lovely with trees
And leaves, made quick with life, with each
Of the nations who now move on its face. And then
As now warriors sang of their pleasure:

15 So Hrothgar's men lived happy in his hall
Till the monster stirred, that demon, that fiend,
Grendel, who haunted the moors, the wild
Marshes, and made his home in a hell
Not hell but earth. He was spawned in that slime,

20 Conceived by a pair of those monsters born
Of Cain,[2] murderous creatures banished
By God, punished forever for the crime
Of Abel's death. The Almighty drove
Those demons out, and their exile was bitter,

25 Shut away from men; they split
Into a thousand forms of evil—spirits
And fiends, goblins, monsters, giants,
A brood forever opposing the Lord's
Will, and again and again defeated.

30 Then, when darkness had dropped, Grendel
Went up to Herot, wondering what the warriors
Would do in that hall when their drinking was done.

1. hall: Herot.

2. Cain: The oldest son of Adam and Eve, who murdered his brother Abel.

THE DRAGON FOR "THE HIGH KINGS"
George Sharp

He found them sprawled in sleep, suspecting
Nothing, their dreams undisturbed. The monster's
35 Thoughts were as quick as his greed or his claws:
He slipped through the door and there in the silence
Snatched up thirty men, smashed them
Unknowing in their beds and ran out with their bodies,
The blood dripping behind him, back
40 To his lair, delighted with his night's slaughter.
        At daybreak, with the sun's first light, they saw
How well he had worked, and in that gray morning
Broke their long feast with tears and laments
For the dead. Hrothgar, their lord, sat joyless
45 In Herot, a mighty prince mourning
The fate of his lost friends and companions,
Knowing by its tracks that some demon had torn
His followers apart. He wept, fearing
The beginning might not be the end. And that night
50 Grendel came again, so set
On murder that no crime could ever be enough,
No savage assault quench his lust
For evil. Then each warrior tried
To escape him, searched for rest in different
55 Beds, as far from Herot as they could find,
Seeing how Grendel hunted when they slept.
Distance was safety; the only survivors
Were those who fled him. Hate had triumphed.
        So Grendel ruled, fought with the righteous,
60 One against many, and won; so Herot
Stood empty, and stayed deserted for years,
Twelve winters of grief for Hrothgar, king
Of the Danes, sorrow heaped at his door
By hell-forged hands. His misery leaped
65 The seas, was told and sung in all
Men's ears: how Grendel's hatred began,
How the monster relished his savage war
On the Danes, keeping the bloody feud
Alive, seeking no peace, offering
70 No truce, accepting no settlement, no price
In gold or land, and paying the living
For one crime only with another. No one
Waited for reparation from his plundering claws:
That shadow of death hunted in the darkness,
75 Stalked Hrothgar's warriors, old
And young, lying in waiting, hidden
In mist, invisibly following them from the edge
Of the marsh, always there, unseen.
        So mankind's enemy continued his crimes,

80　Killing as often as he could, coming
　　Alone, bloodthirsty and horrible. Though he lived
　　In Herot, when the night hid him, he never
　　Dared to touch king Hrothgar's glorious
　　Throne, protected by God—God,
85　Whose love Grendel could not know. But Hrothgar's
　　Heart was bent. The best and most noble
　　Of his council debated remedies, sat
　　In secret sessions, talking of terror
　　And wondering what the bravest of warriors could do.
90　And sometimes they sacrificed to the old stone gods,
　　Made heathen vows, hoping for Hell's
　　Support, the Devil's guidance in driving
　　Their affliction off. That was their way,
　　And the heathen's only hope, Hell
95　Always in their hearts, knowing neither God
　　Nor His passing as He walks through our world, the Lord
　　Of Heaven and earth; their ears could not hear
　　His praise nor know His glory. Let them
　　Beware, those who are thrust into danger,
100　Clutched at by trouble, yet can carry no solace
　　In their hearts, cannot hope to be better! Hail
　　To those who will rise to God, drop off
　　Their dead bodies and seek our Father's peace!

The Coming of Beowulf

　　　　So the living sorrow of Healfdane's son[3]
105　Simmered, bitter and fresh, and no wisdom
　　Or strength could break it: that agony hung
　　On king and people alike, harsh
　　And unending, violent and cruel, and evil.
　　　　In his far-off home Beowulf, Higlac's[4]
110　Follower and the strongest of the Geats—greater
　　And stronger than anyone anywhere in this world—
　　Heard how Grendel filled nights with horror
　　And quickly commanded a boat fitted out,
　　Proclaiming that he'd go to that famous king,
115　Would sail across the sea to Hrothgar,
　　Now when help was needed. None
　　Of the wise ones regretted his going, much
　　As he was loved by the Geats: the omens were good,
　　And they urged the adventure on. So Beowulf
120　Chose the mightiest men he could find,
　　The bravest and best of the Geats, fourteen
　　In all, and led them down to their boat;
　　He knew the sea, would point the prow
　　Straight to that distant Danish shore.

3. Healfdane's (hä′ alf den′nəz) **son:** Hrothgar.

4. Higlac's (hig′ laks): Higlac was the king of the Geats (gā′ ats) and Beowulf's feudal lord and uncle.

ARTHUR GOING TO AVALON FOR "THE HIGH KINGS" (detail)
George Sharp

125   Then they sailed, set their ship
Out on the waves, under the cliffs.
Ready for what came they wound through the currents,
The seas beating at the sand, and were borne
In the lap of their shining ship, lined
130 With gleaming armor, going safely
In that oak-hard boat to where their hearts took them.
The wind hurried them over the waves,
The ship foamed through the sea like a bird
Until, in the time they had known it would take,
135 Standing in the round-curled prow they could see
Sparkling hills, high and green,
Jutting up over the shore, and rejoicing
In those rock-steep cliffs they quietly ended
Their voyage. Jumping to the ground, the Geats
140 Pushed their boat to the sand and tied it
In place, mail shirts and armor rattling
As they swiftly moored their ship. And then
They gave thanks to God for their easy crossing.
     High on a wall a Danish watcher
145 Patrolling along the cliffs saw
The travelers crossing to the shore, their shields
Raised and shining; he came riding down,
Hrothgar's lieutenant, spurring his horse,
Needing to know why they'd landed, these men
150 In armor. Shaking his heavy spear
In their faces he spoke:
                       "Whose soldiers are you,
You who've been carried in your deep-keeled ship
Across the sea-road to this country of mine?
Listen! I've stood on these cliffs longer
155 Than you know, keeping our coast free
Of pirates, raiders sneaking ashore
From their ships, seeking our lives and our gold.
None have ever come more openly—
And yet you've offered no password, no sign
160 From my prince, no permission from my people for your
    landing
Here. Nor have I ever seen,
Out of all the men on earth, one greater
Than has come with you; no commoner carries
Such weapons, unless his appearance, and his beauty,
165 Are both lies. You! Tell me your name,
And your father's; no spies go further onto Danish
Soil than you've come already. Strangers,
From wherever it was you sailed, tell it,
And tell it quickly, the quicker the better,
170 I say, for us all. Speak, say
Exactly who you are, and from where, and why."

Their leader answered him, Beowulf unlocking
Words from deep in his breast:
                                        "We are Geats,
Men who follow Higlac. My father
175 Was a famous soldier, known far and wide
As a leader of men. His name was Edgetho.
His life lasted many winters;
Wise men all over the earth surely
Remember him still. And we have come seeking
180 Your prince, Healfdane's son, protector
Of this people, only in friendship: instruct us,
Watchman, help us with your words! Our errand
Is a great one, our business with the glorious king
Of the Danes no secret; there's nothing dark
185 Or hidden in our coming. You know (if we've heard
The truth, and been told honestly) that your country
Is cursed with some strange, vicious creature
That hunts only at night and that no one
Has seen. It's said, watchman, that he has slaughtered
190 Your people, brought terror to the darkness. Perhaps
Hrothgar can hunt, here in my heart,
For some way to drive this devil out—
If anything will ever end the evils
Afflicting your wise and famous lord.
195 Here he can cool his burning sorrow.
Or else he may see his suffering go on
Forever, for as long as Herot towers
High on your hills."
                            The mounted officer
Answered him bluntly, the brave watchman:
200   "A soldier should know the difference between words
And deeds, and keep that knowledge clear
In his brain. I believe your words, I trust in
Your friendship. Go forward, weapons and armor
And all, on into Denmark. I'll guide you
205 Myself—and my men will guard your ship,
Keep it safe here on our shores,
Your fresh-tarred boat, watch it well,
Until that curving prow carries
Across the sea to Geatland a chosen
210 Warrior who bravely does battle with the creature
Haunting our people, who survives that horror
Unhurt, and goes home bearing our love."
        Then they moved on. Their boat lay moored,
Tied tight to its anchor. Glittering at the top
215 Of their golden helmets wild boar heads gleamed,
Shining decorations, swinging as they marched,
Erect like guards, like sentinels, as though ready

To fight. They marched, Beowulf and his men
And their guide, until they could see the gables
220 Of Herot, covered with hammered gold
And glowing in the sun—that most famous of all dwellings,
Towering majestic, its glittering roofs
Visible far across the land.
Their guide reined in his horse, pointing
225 To that hall, built by Hrothgar for the best
And bravest of his men; the path was plain,
They could see their way . . .

*Beowulf and his men arrive at Herot and are about to be
escorted in to see King Hrothgar.*

Beowulf arose, with his men
230 Around him, ordering a few to remain
With their weapons, leading the others quickly
Along under Herot's steep roof into Hrothgar's
Presence. Standing on that prince's own hearth,
Helmeted, the silvery metal of his mail shirt
235 Gleaming with a smith's high art, he greeted
The Danes' great lord:

"Hail, Hrothgar!
Higlac is my cousin[5] and my king; the days
Of my youth have been filled with glory. Now Grendel's
Name has echoed in our land: sailors
240 Have brought us stories of Herot, the best
Of all mead-halls, deserted and useless when the moon
Hangs in skies the sun had lit,
Light and life fleeing together.
My people have said, the wisest, most knowing
245 And best of them, that my duty was to go to the Danes'
Great king. They have seen my strength for themselves,
Have watched me rise from the darkness of war,
Dripping with my enemies' blood. I drove
Five great giants into chains, chased
250 All of that race from the earth. I swam
In the blackness of night, hunting monsters
Out of the ocean, and killing them one
By one; death was my errand and the fate
They had earned. Now Grendel and I are called
255 Together, and I've come. Grant me, then,
Lord and protector of this noble place,
A single request! I have come so far,
Oh shelterer of warriors and your people's loved friend,
That this one favor you should not refuse me—
260 That I, alone and with the help of my men,
May purge all evil from this hall. I have heard,
Too, that the monster's scorn of men

5. cousin: Here, used as a general term for relative.

Is so great that he needs no weapons and fears none.
Nor will I. My lord Higlac
265 Might think less of me if I let my sword
Go where my feet were afraid to, if I hid
Behind some broad linden[6] shield: my hands
Alone shall fight for me, struggle for life
Against the monster. God must decide
270 Who will be given to death's cold grip.
Grendel's plan, I think, will be
What it has been before, to invade this hall
And gorge his belly with our bodies. If he can,
If he can. And I think, if my time will have come,
275 There'll be nothing to mourn over, no corpse to prepare
For its grave: Grendel will carry our bloody
Flesh to the moors, crunch on our bones
And smear torn scraps of our skin on the walls
Of his den. No, I expect no Danes
280 Will fret about sewing our shrouds, if he wins.
And if death does take me, send the hammered
Mail of my armor to Higlac, return
The inheritance I had from Hrethel, and he
From Wayland.[7] Fate will unwind as it must!''

6. linden: A very sturdy type of wood.

7. Wayland: From Germanic folklore, an invisible blacksmith.

The Battle with Grendel

That night Beowulf and his men take the places of Hrothgar and the Danes inside Herot. While his men sleep, Beowulf lies awake, eager to meet with Grendel.

285   Out from the marsh, from the foot of misty
Hills and bogs, bearing God's hatred,
Grendel came, hoping to kill
Anyone he could trap on this trip to high Herot.
He moved quickly through the cloudy night,
290 Up from his swampland, sliding silently
Toward that gold-shining hall. He had visited Hrothgar's
Home before, knew the way—
But never, before nor after that night,
Found Herot defended so firmly, his reception
295 So harsh. He journeyed, forever joyless,
Straight to the door, then snapped it open,
Tore its iron fasteners with a touch
And rushed angrily over the threshold.
He strode quickly across the inlaid
300 Floor, snarling and fierce: his eyes
Gleamed in the darkness, burned with a gruesome
Light. Then he stopped, seeing the hall
Crowded with sleeping warriors, stuffed
With rows of young soldiers resting together.

305 And his heart laughed, he relished the sight,
Intended to tear the life from those bodies
By morning; the monster's mind was hot
With the thought of food and the feasting his belly
Would soon know. But fate, that night, intended
310 Grendel to gnaw the broken bones
Of his last human supper. Human
Eyes were watching his evil steps,
Waiting to see his swift hard claws.
Grendel snatched at the first Geat
315 He came to, ripped him apart, cut
His body to bits with powerful jaws,
Drank the blood from his veins and bolted
Him down, hands and feet; death
And Grendel's great teeth came together,
320 Snapping life shut. Then he stepped to another
Still body, clutched at Beowulf with his claws,
Grasped at a strong-hearted wakeful sleeper
—And was instantly seized himself, claws
Bent back as Beowulf leaned up on one arm.
325   That shepherd of evil, guardian of crime,
Knew at once that nowhere on earth
Had he met a man whose hands were harder;
His mind was flooded with fear—but nothing
Could take his talons and himself from that tight
330 Hard grip. Grendel's one thought was to run
From Beowulf, flee back to his marsh and hide there:
This was a different Herot than the hall he had emptied.
But Higlac's follower remembered his final
Boast and, standing erect, stopped
335 The monster's flight, fastened those claws
In his fists till they cracked, clutched Grendel
Closer. The infamous killer fought
For his freedom, wanting no flesh but retreat,
Desiring nothing but escape; his claws
340 Had been caught, he was trapped. That trip to Herot
Was a miserable journey for the writhing monster!
    The high hall rang, its roof boards swayed,
And Danes shook with terror. Down
The aisles the battle swept, angry
345 And wild. Herot trembled, wonderfully
Built to withstand the blows, the struggling
Great bodies beating at its beautiful walls;
Shaped and fastened with iron, inside
And out, artfully worked, the building
350 Stood firm. Its benches rattled, fell
To the floor, gold-covered boards grating
As Grendel and Beowulf battled across them.

Hrothgar's wise men had fashioned Herot
To stand forever; only fire,
355 They had planned, could shatter what such skill had put
Together, swallow in hot flames such splendor
Of ivory and iron and wood. Suddenly
The sounds changed, the Danes started
In new terror, cowering in their beds as the terrible
360 Screams of the Almighty's enemy sang
In the darkness, the horrible shrieks of pain
And defeat, the tears torn out of Grendel's
Taut throat, hell's captive caught in the arms
Of him who of all the men on earth
365 Was the strongest.
               That mighty protector of men
Meant to hold the monster till its life
Leaped out, knowing the fiend was no use
To anyone in Denmark. All of Beowulf's
Band had jumped from their beds, ancestral
370 Swords raised and ready, determined
To protect their prince if they could. Their courage
Was great but all wasted: they could hack at Grendel

MULTICULTURAL CONNECTION

Monsters Around the World

Most of us are familiar with Dracula, Frankenstein's monster, and King Kong, but monsters go back a lot further in history. Almost all cultures tell stories of fantastic creatures that both frighten and fascinate us.

Monsters in early civilizations. Where did these stories come from? Some may have been inspired by unfamiliar animals. Sea mammals like the manatee, for instance, may have given rise to stories of mermaids and mermen. Other creatures may have been invented to explain the creation of the world, natural phenomena, or the struggle between good and evil.

Among the world's earliest monsters were the winged bull of Babylon, the dragon, and the griffin—a creature with the body and hind legs of a lion and the head, wings, and claws of an eagle. In ancient Greek mythology, many monsters were half human and half beast: the harpy, a bird with a woman's head; the sphinx, a winged lion with a woman's head; the centaur, half man, half horse; and the Minotaur, half man, half bull.

Monsters in Native American folklore. Native American folklore is filled with monsters who lived long ago. Examples include Fire-Moccasins, who sets fire everywhere he steps, and Burr-Woman, who clings to a person's back and won't let go. In many tales, a hero must kill the creatures to save his people. For instance, the Jicarilla Apache folk hero Killer-of-Enemies slays a giant elk, a rock monster, and a monster eagle!

Monsters today. Even in today's scientific world, some people believe in monsters. They report sightings of the Loch Ness monster, the hairy giant called Bigfoot or Sasquatch, and Yeti, a mysterious creature thought to live high in the Himalayas.

Exploring on Your Own

Research more about monsters in the folklore section of your library or read about the world's most famous man-made monster in Mary Shelley's novel *Frankenstein.*

From every side, trying to open
A path for his evil soul, but their points
375 Could not hurt him, the sharpest and hardest iron
Could not scratch at his skin, for that sin-stained demon
Had bewitched all men's weapons, laid spells
That blunted every mortal man's blade.
And yet his time had come, his days
380 Were over, his death near; down
To hell he would go, swept groaning and helpless
To the waiting hands of still worse fiends.
Now he discovered—once the afflictor
Of men, tormentor of their days—what it meant
385 To feud with Almighty God: Grendel
Saw that his strength was deserting him, his claws
Bound fast, Higlac's brave follower tearing at
His hands. The monster's hatred rose higher,
But his power had gone. He twisted in pain,
390 And the bleeding sinews deep in his shoulder
Snapped, muscle and bone split
And broke. The battle was over, Beowulf

HEAD OF CARVED POST FROM THE SHIP BURIAL AT OSEBERG

HELMET
Statens Historiska Museet, Stockholm
Werner Forman Archive

GOLDEN HORN
National Museet Copenhagen

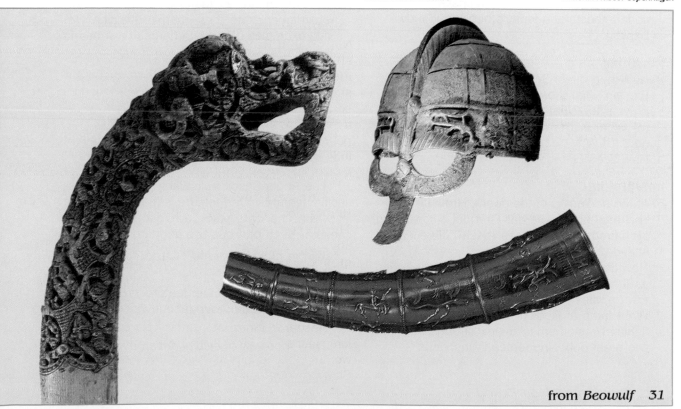

from *Beowulf* 31

Had been granted new glory: Grendel escaped,
But wounded as he was could flee to his den,
395　His miserable hole at the bottom of the marsh,
Only to die, to wait for the end
Of all his days. And after that bloody
Combat the Danes laughed with delight.
He who had come to them from across the sea,
400　Bold and strong-minded, had driven affliction
Off, purged Herot clean. He was happy,
Now, with that night's fierce work; the Danes
Had been served as he'd boasted he'd serve them; Beowulf,
A prince of the Geats, had killed Grendel,
405　Ended the grief, the sorrow, the suffering
Forced on Hrothgar's helpless people
By a bloodthirsty fiend. No Dane doubted
The victory, for the proof, hanging high
From the rafters where Beowulf had hung it, was the
　　monster's
410　Arm, claw and shoulder and all.

▮ RESPONDING TO THE SELECTION

Your Response

1. How do you think Grendel compares to the fictional monsters in today's books and movies? Explain.

Recalling

2. (a) When does Grendel first go to Herot? (b) Explain what the warriors are doing when he arrives. (c) What does he do to them?
3. (a) What is Beowulf's plan for fighting Grendel? (b) Why does he choose this plan?
4. How does Grendel die?

Interpreting

5. At the beginning of the poem, Hrothgar's warriors are happy, whereas Grendel is consumed by hatred. What causes these differences in attitude?
6. How does Beowulf's remark, "Fate will unwind as it must," reflect the Anglo-Saxons' attitude toward fate?
7. What traits of Beowulf and Grendel raise the fight between them to an epic struggle between two great opposing forces in the world?

Applying

8. Beowulf is thought to be a perfect hero for his time. (a) What qualities should a modern hero have? (b) In what situations might a modern hero demonstrate these heroic qualities? (c) Give examples of modern heroes or of heroic behavior.

▮ ANALYZING LITERATURE

Understanding the Anglo-Saxon Epic

An **epic** is a long narrative poem, presented in an elevated style, that celebrates episodes in a people's heroic tradition.

The Anglo-Saxon epic *Beowulf* has two distinctive features. One feature is the two-part line in which the two parts are separated by a caesura. Each part has two strong beats.

Till the *mon*ster *stirred* / that *de*mon, that *fiend*

The kenning is another feature in *Beowulf*. A kenning is a colorful, roundabout way of naming something.

That *shepherd of evil, guardian of crime*

1. What are the two parts and the four strong beats in each of the following lines?

   As day after day the music rang
   Loud in that hall, the harp's rejoicing

2. In addition to the example given, find another kenning in Beowulf.
3. Explain why you do or do not find the use of kenning effective.

CRITICAL THINKING AND READING

Making Inferences About Ideals

An **inference** is a conclusion you reach based on various details in a work of literature. The hero in an epic embodies the highest ideals of the times. The Anglo-Saxon epic *Beowulf* reflects the values of the plundering Anglo-Saxon warriors. Beowulf himself is a fighting man, eager to take on challenging personal encounters for a good cause.

From Beowulf's description of his previous heroic feats (lines 247–254), you can infer that his listeners respected and admired the qualities that enabled Beowulf to accomplish such deeds. In addition, you can infer that they believed that such qualities enabled Beowulf to take on the evil Grendel.

1. In what specific way does Beowulf demonstrate loyalty to his lord and king?
2. In what specific ways does he demonstrate his valor?
3. In lines 378–380, Grendel realizes that he has been beaten:

Now he discovered—once the afflictor
Of men, tormentor of their days—what it meant
To feud with Almighty God.

What inference about Anglo-Saxon beliefs can you make from these lines?

THINKING AND WRITING

Writing About Character Traits

Write a composition for your classmates in which you tell the incidents in *Beowulf* from Grendel's point of view. Begin by jotting down notes about Grendel's thoughts and feelings during his final, fatal visit to Hrothgar's hall. Then, arrange these notes in a logical order to create a working outline. Next, write a draft, keeping in mind that you are giving Grendel's version of events, not your own or Beowulf's. Finally, revise your draft, improving your content and organization and correcting any errors you find in grammar or mechanics.

LEARNING OPTIONS

1. **Art.** Create a brief comic book that features the adventures of Beowulf. Use a comic-book character such as Superman as the model for your hero. Illustrate episodes from the poem or make up new adventures. Make sure, however, that your hero has character traits that are consistent with Beowulf's.
2. **Performance.** Present a dramatic reading of "The Battle with Grendel." Divide this section of the poem among several classmates, giving each approximately a dozen lines to read aloud. Select logical places for making the transitions from speaker to speaker (sometimes within a printed line). Practice your dramatic reading, paying close attention to the action and emotions being expressed. During the reading, be guided by punctuation rather than by line breaks. For your performance you may wish to use costumes and props that reflect the historical context of the poem.

GUIDE FOR INTERPRETING

from Beowulf

Writers' Techniques

Pagan and Christian Elements. The eighth-century poet who composed *Beowulf* lived in a civilization that had become Christian only a hundred or so years earlier. It is not surprising, therefore, that for the characters and events of his story, he drew upon pagan legends and folk tales. The magnificent monsters of *Beowulf,* for example, are derived from the trolls of Scandinavian mythology, who were shadowy creatures that lurked around waterfalls or caves.

However, the Christian beliefs of the poets of England also pervade the poem. For example, the poet disguises the true lineage of Grendel and his mother, giving them instead a biblical origin:

> . . . He [Grendel] was spawned in that slime,
> Conceived by a pair of those monsters born
> Of Cain, murderous creatures banished
> By God, punished forever for the crime
> Of Abel's death . . .

In battling Grendel, Beowulf is not only a brave pagan warrior but also a Christian hero challenging the forces of evil, the first such hero in a line that includes Sir Galahad of the Round Table and the legendary Saint George, dragon slayer and patron saint of England.

The combat with Grendel's mother, described on the following pages, also reflects the weaving together of pagan and Christian elements. The creature's underwater lair and the magic sword found by the hero are familiar elements in pagan folk tales. However, in *Beowulf* God plays a role in the battle: "and Holy/God, who sent him victory, gave judgment/For truth and right . . ."

Commentary

The Christian influence on the poem is not limited to specific references to the Bible and God. As Charles W. Kennedy points out, the spirit of the newly victorious religion is evident throughout the epic: ". . . *Beowulf* is a tale of the pagan past in which the endurance, the loyalty, the courage, and the strength of the heroic age are tempered by union with Christian virtues. . . ." Alert readers will find this "welding of pagan heroism with Christian virtue" in the depiction of Beowulf as a young warrior and an aging king.

Focus

In his battle with Grendel's mother and later with a dragon, Beowulf faces the possibility of failure. Briefly describe a time when you had to confront the possibility of failure. Tell how you struggled with this feeling and overcame it.

from Beowulf

translated by Burton Raffel

*Hrothgar and his host celebrate Beowulf's victory over the
monster Grendel. That night, however, Grendel's mother
kidnaps and kills Hrothgar's closest friend and carries off
the claw that Beowulf tore from her child. The next day
the horrified king tells Beowulf about the two monsters
and their underwater lair.*

The Monsters' Lair

"I've heard that my people, peasants working
In the fields, have seen a pair of such fiends
Wandering in the moors and marshes, giant
Monsters living in those desert lands.

415 And they've said to my wise men that, as well as they
could see,
One of the devils was a female creature.
The other, they say, walked through the wilderness
Like a man—but mightier than any man.
They were frightened, and they fled, hoping to find
help

420 In Herot. They named the huge one Grendel:
If he had a father no one knew him,
Or whether there'd been others before these two,
Hidden evil before hidden evil.
They live in secret places, windy

425 Cliffs, wolf-dens where water pours
From the rocks, then runs underground, where mist
Steams like black clouds, and the groves of trees
Growing out over their lake are all covered
With frozen spray, and wind down snaclike

430 Roots that reach as far as the water
And help keep it dark. At night that lake
Burns like a torch. No one knows its bottom,
No wisdom reaches such depths. A deer,
Hunted through the woods by packs of hounds,

435 A stag with great horns, though driven through the
forest
From faraway places, prefers to die
On those shores, refuses to save its life
In that water. It isn't far, nor is it
A pleasant spot! When the wind stirs

440 And storms, waves splash toward the sky,
    As dark as the air, as black as the rain
    That the heavens weep. Our only help,
    Again, lies with you. Grendel's mother
    Is hidden in her terrible home, in a place
445 You've not seen. Seek it, if you dare! Save us,
    Once more, and again twisted gold,
    Heaped-up ancient treasure, will reward you
    For the battle you win!''

The Battle with Grendel's Mother

*Beowulf resolves to kill the "lady monster." Arriving at
the lake under which she lives, Beowulf and his
companions see serpents in the water and sea beasts on
the rocks. The young hero kills one of the beasts with an
arrow and then prepares to fight with Grendel's mother.*

Then Edgetho's brave son[1] spoke:

"Remember,

450 Hrothgar, Oh knowing king, now
    When my danger is near, the warm words we uttered,
    And if your enemy should end my life
    Then be, oh generous prince, forever
    The father and protector of all whom I leave
455 Behind me, here in your hands, my belovèd
    Comrades left with no leader, their leader
    Dead. And the precious gifts you gave me,
    My friend, send them to Higlac. May he see
    In their golden brightness, the Geats' great lord
460 Gazing at your treasure, that here in Denmark
    I found a noble protector, a giver
    Of rings whose rewards I won and briefly
    Relished. And you, Unferth,[2] let
    My famous old sword stay in your hands:
465 I shall shape glory with Hrunting, or death
    Will hurry me from this earth!''

As his words ended
    He leaped into the lake, would not wait for anyone's
    Answer; the heaving water covered him
    Over. For hours he sank through the waves;
470 At last he saw the mud of the bottom.
    And all at once the greedy she-wolf
    Who'd ruled those waters for half a hundred
    Years discovered him, saw that a creature
    From above had come to explore the bottom
475 Of her wet world. She welcomed him in her claws,
    Clutched at him savagely but could not harm him,

1. Edgetho's brave son:
Beowulf. Elsewhere he is
identified by such phrases
as "the Geats' proud
prince" and "the Geats'
brave prince." These
different designations add
variety and interest to the
poem.

2. Unferth: A Danish
warrior who had
questioned Beowulf's
bravery before the battle
with Grendel.

Tried to work her fingers through the tight
Ring-woven mail on his breast, but tore
And scratched in vain. Then she carried him, armor
480 And sword and all, to her home; he struggled
To free his weapon, and failed. The fight
Brought other monsters swimming to see
Her catch, a host of sea beasts who beat at
His mail shirt, stabbing with tusks and teeth
485 As they followed along. Then he realized, suddenly,
That she'd brought him into someone's battle-hall,
And there the water's heat could not hurt him,
Nor anything in the lake attack him through
The building's high-arching roof. A brilliant
490 Light burned all around him, the lake
Itself like a fiery flame.
                        Then he saw
The mighty water witch and swung his sword,
His ring-marked blade, straight at her head;
The iron sang its fierce song,
495 Sang Beowulf's strength. But her guest
Discovered that no sword could slice her evil
Skin, that Hrunting could not hurt her, was useless
Now when he needed it. They wrestled, she ripped
And tore and clawed at him, bit holes in his helmet,
500 And that too failed him; for the first time in years
Of being worn to war it would earn no glory;
It was the last time anyone would wear it. But
    Beowulf
Longed only for fame, leaped back
Into battle. He tossed his sword aside,
505 Angry; the steel-edged blade lay where
He'd dropped it. If weapons were useless he'd use
His hands, the strength in his fingers. So fame
Comes to the men who mean to win it
And care about nothing else! He raised
510 His arms and seized her by the shoulder; anger
Doubled his strength, he threw her to the floor.
She fell, Grendel's fierce mother, and the Geats'
Proud prince was ready to leap on her. But she rose
At once and repaid him with her clutching claws,
515 Wildly tearing at him. He was weary, that best
And strongest of soldiers; his feet stumbled
And in an instant she had him down, held helpless.
Squatting with her weight on his stomach, she drew
A dagger, brown with dried blood, and prepared
520 To avenge her only son. But he was stretched
On his back, and her stabbing blade was blunted
By the woven mail shirt he wore on his chest.

SLAYING OF A BULL ON THE BASE OF A
CAULDRON (CELTIC ARTIFACT, 100 B.C.)
National Museum, Copenhagen

The hammered links held; the point
Could not touch him. He'd have traveled to the bottom
   of the earth,
525 Edgetho's son, and died there, if that shining
Woven metal had not helped—and Holy
God, who sent him victory, gave judgment
For truth and right, Ruler of the Heavens,
Once Beowulf was back on his feet and fighting.

530   Then he saw, hanging on the wall, a heavy
Sword, hammered by giants, strong
And blessed with their magic, the best of all weapons
But so massive that no ordinary man could lift
Its carved and decorated length. He drew it
535 From its scabbard, broke the chain on its hilt,
And then, savage, now, angry
And desperate, lifted it high over his head
And struck with all the strength he had left,
Caught her in the neck and cut it through,
540 Broke bones and all. Her body fell
To the floor, lifeless, the sword was wet
With her blood, and Beowulf rejoiced at the sight.
   The brilliant light shone, suddenly,
As though burning in that hall, and as bright as
   Heaven's
545 Own candle, lit in the sky. He looked
At her home, then following along the wall
Went walking, his hands tight on the sword,
His heart still angry. He was hunting another
Dead monster, and took his weapon with him
550 For final revenge against Grendel's vicious
Attacks, his nighttime raids, over
And over, coming to Herot when Hrothgar's
Men slept, killing them in their beds,
Eating some on the spot, fifteen
555 Or more, and running to his loathsome moor
With another such sickening meal waiting
In his pouch. But Beowulf repaid him for those visits,
Found him lying dead in his corner,
Armless, exactly as that fierce fighter
560 Had sent him out from Herot, then struck off
His head with a single swift blow. The body
Jerked for the last time, then lay still.
   The wise old warriors who surrounded Hrothgar,
Like him staring into the monsters' lake,
565 Saw the waves surging and blood
Spurting through. They spoke about Beowulf,
All the graybeards, whispered together

**CELTIC FIGURE FROM THE SIDE OF A
BOWL FROM A BURIAL MOUND (NORWAY,
9TH CENTURY)**

And said that hope was gone, that the hero
Had lost fame and his life at once, and would never
570 Return to the living, come back as triumphant
As he had left; almost all agreed that Grendel's
Mighty mother, the she-wolf, had killed him.
The sun slid over past noon, went further
Down. The Danes gave up, left
575 The lake and went home, Hrothgar with them.
The Geats stayed, sat sadly, watching,
Imagining they saw their lord but not believing
They would ever see him again.

                  —Then the sword
Melted, blood-soaked, dripping down
580 Like water, disappearing like ice when the world's
Eternal Lord loosens invisible
Fetters and unwinds icicles and frost
As only He can, He who rules
Time and seasons, He who is truly
585 God. The monsters' hall was full of
Rich treasures, but all that Beowulf took
Was Grendel's head and the hilt of the giants'
Jeweled sword; the rest of that ring-marked
Blade had dissolved in Grendel's steaming
590 Blood, boiling even after his death.
And then the battle's only survivor
Swam up and away from those silent corpses;
The water was calm and clean, the whole
Huge lake peaceful once the demons who'd lived in it
595 Were dead.
      Then that noble protector of all seamen
Swam to land, rejoicing in the heavy
Burdens he was bringing with him. He
And all his glorious band of Geats
Thanked God that their leader had come back
   unharmed;
600 They left the lake together. The Geats
Carried Beowulf's helmet, and his mail shirt.
Behind them the water slowly thickened
As the monsters' blood came seeping up.
They walked quickly, happily, across
605 Roads all of them remembered, left
The lake and the cliffs alongside it, brave men
Staggering under the weight of Grendel's skull,
Too heavy for fewer than four of them to handle—
Two on each side of the spear jammed through it—
610 Yet proud of their ugly load and determined
That the Danes, seated in Herot, should see it.
Soon, fourteen Geats arrived

DETAIL OF A DRAGON HEAD ON THE
MAMMEN HORSE COLLAR (VIKING
ARTIFACT, 10TH CENTURY)
National Museum, Denmark

At the hall, bold and warlike, and with Beowulf,
Their lord and leader, they walked on the mead-hall
615 Green. Then the Geats' brave prince entered
Herot, covered with glory for the daring
Battles he had fought; he sought Hrothgar
To salute him and show Grendel's head.
He carried that terrible trophy by the hair,
620 Brought it straight to where the Danes sat,
Drinking, the queen among them. It was a weird
And wonderful sight, and the warriors stared.

The Last Battle

*After being honored by Hrothgar, Beowulf and his fellow
Geats return home. He is welcomed by the king, his uncle
Higlac, and later becomes king himself when Higlac and
his son have died. Beowulf rules Geatland for fifty years.
Then a dragon menaces his kingdom. Although he is an
old man, Beowulf determines to slay the beast. Before
going into battle, he tells the men who have accompanied
him about the history of the royal house and his exploits
in its service.*

    And Beowulf uttered his final boast:
    "I've never known fear, as a youth I fought
625 In endless battles. I am old, now,
But I will fight again, seek fame still,
If the dragon hiding in his tower dares
To face me."
                    Then he said farewell to his followers,
Each in his turn, for the last time:
630   "I'd use no sword, no weapon, if this beast
Could be killed without it, crushed to death
Like Grendel, gripped in my hands and torn

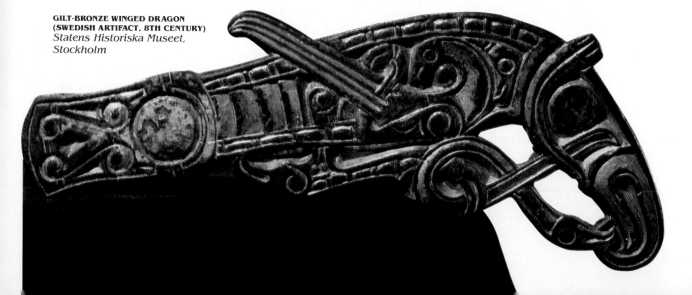

**GILT-BRONZE WINGED DRAGON
(SWEDISH ARTIFACT, 8TH CENTURY)**
*Statens Historiska Museet,
Stockholm*

Limb from limb. But his breath will be burning
Hot, poison will pour from his tongue.
635 I feel no shame, with shield and sword
And armor, against this monster: when he comes to
   me
I mean to stand, not run from his shooting
Flames, stand till fate decides
Which of us wins. My heart is firm,
640 My hands calm: I need no hot
Words. Wait for me close by, my friends.
We shall see, soon, who will survive
This bloody battle, stand when the fighting
Is done. No one else could do
645 What I mean to, here, no man but me
Could hope to defeat this monster. No one
Could try. And this dragon's treasure, his gold
And everything hidden in that tower, will be mine
Or war will sweep me to a bitter death!"
650   Then Beowulf rose, still brave, still strong,
And with his shield at his side, and a mail shirt on
   his breast,
Strode calmly, confidently, toward the tower, under
The rocky cliffs: no coward could have walked there!
And then he who'd endured dozens of desperate
655 Battles, who'd stood boldly while swords and shields
Clashed, the best of kings, saw
Huge stone arches and felt the heat
Of the dragon's breath, flooding down
Through the hidden entrance, too hot for anyone
660 To stand, a streaming current of fire
And smoke that blocked all passage. And the Geats'
Lord and leader, angry, lowered
His sword and roared out a battle cry,
A call so loud and clear that it reached through
665 The hoary rock, hung in the dragon's
Ear. The beast rose, angry,
Knowing a man had come—and then nothing
But war could have followed. Its breath came first.
A steaming cloud pouring from the stone,
670 Then the earth itself shook. Beowulf
Swung his shield into place, held it
In front of him, facing the entrance. The dragon
Coiled and uncoiled, its heart urging it
Into battle. Beowulf's ancient sword
675 Was waiting, unsheathed, his sharp and gleaming
Blade. The beast came closer; both of them
Were ready, each set on slaughter. The Geats'
Great prince stood firm, unmoving, prepared

Behind his high shield, waiting in his shining

680 Armor. The monster came quickly toward him,
Pouring out fire and smoke, hurrying
To its fate. Flames beat at the iron
Shield, and for a time it held, protected
Beowulf as he'd planned; then it began to melt,

685 And for the first time in his life that famous prince
Fought with fate against him, with glory
Denied him. He knew it, but he raised his sword
And struck at the dragon's scaly hide.
The ancient blade broke, bit into

690 The monster's skin, drew blood, but cracked
And failed him before it went deep enough, helped
    him
Less than he needed. The dragon leaped
With pain, thrashed and beat at him, spouting
Murderous flames, spreading them everywhere.

695 And the Geats' ring-giver did not boast of glorious
Victories in other wars: his weapon
Had failed him, deserted him, now when he needed it
Most, that excellent sword. Edgetho's
Famous son stared at death,

700 Unwilling to leave this world, to exchange it
For a dwelling in some distant place—a journey
Into darkness that all men must make, as death
Ends their few brief hours on earth.
    Quickly, the dragon came at him, encouraged

705 As Beowulf fell back; its breath flared,
And he suffered, wrapped around in swirling
Flames—a king, before, but now
A beaten warrior. None of his comrades
Came to him, helped him, his brave and noble

710 Followers; they ran for their lives, fled
Deep in a wood. And only one of them
Remained, stood there, miserable, remembering,
As a good man must, what kinship should mean.

    His name was Wiglaf, he was Wexstan's son

715 And a good soldier; his family had been Swedish,
Once. Watching Beowulf, he could see
How his king was suffering, burning. Remembering
Everything his lord and cousin had given him,
Armor and gold and the great estates

720 Wexstan's family enjoyed, Wiglaf's
Mind was made up; he raised his yellow
Shield and drew his sword—an ancient
Weapon that had once belonged to Onela's
Nephew, and that Wexstan had won, killing

725 The prince when he fled from Sweden, sought safety
With Herdred, and found death.[3] And Wiglaf's father
Had carried the dead man's armor, and his sword,
To Onela, and the king had said nothing, only
Given him armor and sword and all,

730 Everything his rebel nephew had owned
And lost when he left this life. And Wexstan
Had kept those shining gifts, held them
For years, waiting for his son to use them,
Wear them as honorably and well as once

735 His father had done; then Wexstan died
And Wiglaf was his heir, inherited treasures
And weapons and land. He'd never worn
That armor, fought with that sword, until Beowulf
Called him to his side, led him into war.

740 But his soul did not melt, his sword was strong;
The dragon discovered his courage, and his weapon,
When the rush of battle brought them together.
    And Wiglaf, his heart heavy, uttered
The kind of words his comrades deserved:

745 "I remember how we sat in the mead-hall, drinking
And boasting of how brave we'd be when Beowulf
Needed us, he who gave us these swords
And armor: all of us swore to repay him,
When the time came, kindness for kindness

750 —With our lives, if he needed them. He allowed us to
    join him,
Chose us from all his great army, thinking
Our boasting words had some weight, believing
Our promises, trusting our swords. He took us
For soldiers, for men. He meant to kill

755 This monster himself, our mighty king,
Fight this battle alone and unaided,
As in the days when his strength and daring dazzled
Men's eyes. But those days are over and gone
And now our lord must lean on younger

760 Arms. And we must go to him, while angry
Flames burn at his flesh, help
Our glorious king! By almighty God,
I'd rather burn myself than see
Flames swirling around my lord.

765 And who are we to carry home
Our shields before we've slain his enemy
And ours, to run back to our homes with Beowulf
So hard-pressed here? I swear that nothing
He ever did deserved an end

770 Like this, dying miserably and alone,
Butchered by this savage beast: we swore

3. Onela's/Nephew . . . found death: When Onela seized the throne of Sweden, his two nephews sought shelter with the king of Geatland, Herdred. Wiglaf's father, Wexstan, killed the older nephew for Onela.

GILT-SILVER BROOCH FROM GOTLAND (PRE-VIKING SCANDINAVIA)
Statens Historiska Museet, Stockholm

That these swords and armor were each for us all!"
    Then he ran to his king, crying encouragement
As he dove through the dragon's deadly fumes.

The Spoils

*Together, Wiglaf and Beowulf kill the dragon, but the old
king is mortally wounded. As a last request, Beowulf asks
Wiglaf to bring him the treasure that the dragon was
guarding.*

775   Then Wexstan's son went in, as quickly
As he could, did as the dying Beowulf
Asked, entered the inner darkness
Of the tower, went with his mail shirt and his sword.
Flushed with victory he groped his way,
780 A brave young warrior, and suddenly saw
Piles of gleaming gold, precious
Gems, scattered on the floor, cups
And bracelets, rusty old helmets, beautifully
Made but rotting with no hands to rub
785 And polish them. They lay where the dragon left
    them;
It had flown in the darkness, once, before fighting
Its final battle. (So gold can easily
Triumph, defeat the strongest of men,
No matter how deep it is hidden!) And he saw,
790 Hanging high above, a golden
Banner, woven by the best of weavers
And beautiful. And over everything he saw
A strange light, shining everywhere,
On walls and floor and treasure. Nothing
795 Moved, no other monsters appeared;
He took what he wanted, all the treasures
That pleased his eye, heavy plates
And golden cups and the glorious banner,
Loaded his arms with all they could hold.
800 Beowulf's dagger, his iron blade,
Had finished the fire-spitting terror
That once protected tower and treasures
Alike; the gray-bearded lord of the Geats
Had ended those flying, burning raids
805 Forever.
        Then Wiglaf went back, anxious
To return while Beowulf was alive, to bring him
Treasure they'd won together. He ran,
Hoping his wounded king, weak
And dying, had not left the world too soon.

**SILVER PENDANT SHOWING THE HELMET
OF THE VENDEL (EARLY VIKING PERIOD,
10TH CENTURY)**
*Statens Historiska Museet,
Stockholm*

THE OSEBERG SHIP (VIKING ARTIFACT, C. A.D. 850)
Viking Ship Museum, Bygdoy, Oslo

810   Then he brought their treasure to Beowulf, and found
      His famous king bloody, gasping
      For breath. But Wiglaf sprinkled water
      Over his lord, until the words
      Deep in his breast broke through and were heard.
815   Beholding the treasure he spoke, haltingly:
        "For this, this gold, these jewels, I thank
      Our Father in Heaven, Ruler of the Earth—
      For all of this, that His grace has given me,
      Allowed me to bring to my people while breath
820   Still came to my lips. I sold my life
      For this treasure, and I sold it well. Take
      What I leave, Wiglaf, lead my people,
      Help them; my time is gone. Have
      The brave Geats build me a tomb,
825   When the funeral flames have burned me, and build
        it
      Here, at the water's edge, high
      On this spit of land, so sailors can see
      This tower, and remember my name, and call it
      Beowulf's tower, and boats in the darkness

from *Beowulf*   **45**

830 And mist, crossing the sea, will know it."
    Then that brave king gave the golden
Necklace from around his throat to Wiglaf,
Gave him his gold-covered helmet, and his rings,
And his mail shirt, and ordered him to use them well:
835   "You're the last of all our far-flung family.
Fate has swept our race away,
Taken warriors in their strength and led them
To the death that was waiting. And now I follow
    them."
    The old man's mouth was silent, spoke
840 No more, had said as much as it could;
He would sleep in the fire, soon. His soul
Left his flesh, flew to glory.

The Farewell

*Wiglaf denounces the soldiers who deserted Beowulf in
his combat with the dragon. The Geats burn their king's
body on a great funeral pyre and bitterly lament his death.*

        Then the Geats built the tower, as Beowulf
Had asked, strong and tall, so sailors
845 Could find it from far and wide; working
For ten long days they made his monument,
Sealed his ashes in walls as straight
And high as wise and willing hands
Could raise them. And the riches he and Wiglaf
850 Had won from the dragon, rings, necklaces,
Ancient, hammered armor—all
The treasures they'd taken were left there, too,
Silver and jewels buried in the sandy
Ground, back in the earth, again
855 And forever hidden and useless to men.
And then twelve of the bravest Geats
Rode their horses around the tower,
Telling their sorrow, telling stories
Of their dead king and his greatness, his glory,
860 Praising him for heroic deeds, for a life
As noble as his name. So should all men
Raise up words for their lords, warm
With love, when their shield and protector leaves
His body behind, sends his soul
865 On high. And so Beowulf's followers
Rode, mourning their beloved leader,
Crying that no better king had ever
Lived, no prince so mild, no man
So open to his people, so deserving of praise.

RESPONDING TO THE SELECTION

Your Response

1. Do you think that Beowulf grows in stature as a hero? Explain.

Recalling

2. Briefly summarize the battle between Beowulf and Grendel's mother.
3. Describe what happens when Beowulf attempts to fight the dragon alone.

Interpreting

4. Critics have praised the *Beowulf* poet's skill at describing various settings. (a) Find a passage in which the poet displays this skill. (b) Explain what makes the description so effective.
5. (a) Compare and contrast the three battles described in these excerpts. (b) In what ways are all three battles different versions of the poem's main conflict?
6. (a) Identify the figure of speech that the poet uses in lines 578–583. (b) Explain how the figure of speech adds to the meaning of the poem.

Applying

7. Many critics claim that *Beowulf* contains themes that are relevant to modern life. Do you agree or disagree? Why?

ANALYZING LITERATURE

Tracing Pagan and Christian Elements

In *Beowulf* we can see evidence of the Anglo-Saxon warrior culture, with its stress on heroism, and Christianity's emphasis on brotherly love and God's compassion. For example, in the combat with the dragon, Beowulf seeks "fame" like any self-respecting warrior. As he is dying, however, he thanks "Our Father in Heaven" for the opportunity to give his people the treasure.

1. Reread the tribute to Beowulf in the last eight lines of the poem. Identify pagan and Christian influences in the qualities for which the king is praised. Give reasons for your conclusions.
2. A prominent Germanic pagan belief is that fame is the only thing that will survive a human's death. (a) What evidence do you find in this poem of the importance placed on public esteem or reputation? (b) What value do you feel contemporary society places on fame?
3. The poem contains many references to the blind and mysterious power of *Wyrd,* or Fate, as in line 836. Do such references suggest pagan or Christian influence? Explain.

THINKING AND WRITING

Responding to Criticism

Burton Raffel, who wrote this translation, remarked that, "of all the many-sided excellences of *Beowulf,*" one of the most satisfying "is the poet's insight into people." Respond to this observation, expressing your agreement or disagreement. First, gather evidence. Identify instances in which the poet does or does not show insight into human nature. Then, write a thesis statement setting forth your point of view. Support this statement with references to specific passages in the poem. As you revise your essay, see whether you can find other passages that support your thesis. Remember that descriptions of action can reveal character as effectively as direct statements.

LEARNING OPTION

Art. Sculpt a model of Grendel's mother or the dragon. First, review the details the poet uses to describe the monster. Then, choose materials (such as clay, papier-mâché, or plaster) that you think would be appropriate. Create some sketches of how your monster will look. Finally, construct your monster. Ask your classmates to compare your model with their mental images of the monster. How similar are they? In what ways do they differ?

COMPARING TRANSLATIONS

Beowulf

TRANSLATION: "A THANKLESS AND DESOLATE UNDERTAKING"

The twentieth-century poet Ezra Pound once remarked that "all translation is a thankless, or at least most apt to be a thankless and desolate undertaking." Although translating *Beowulf* has proven to be an especially challenging task, an impressive number of scholars have tried their hands at it. Currently, well over half a dozen translations of *Beowulf* are in print, and a score of others are available in libraries. But judging from the problems these scholars encountered—and the criticism they received—Pound may well have had a point about the translator's task!

THE DISASTROUS FATE OF THE *BEOWULF* MANUSCRIPT

Most translators of *Beowulf* start with the *Beowulf* manuscript. This manuscript, however, is far from perfect. It represents the work of two tenth-century scribes copying from an older manuscript. However, the text is in prose, not verse. It contains spotty punctuation and vowel markings, apparently resulting from the uncertainty of the unlearned scribes. In addition, the manuscript is damaged—a disastrous fire in 1731 scorched the manuscript, hastening its disintegration. It was sheer good fortune that Danish scholar Thorkelin made the first translation in 1787 before the manuscript crumbled further. Subsequent work showed that letters visible when Thorkelin worked have become illegible or even disappeared completely. Although steps were taken to preserve the manuscript from further harm, precious passages had already been lost forever.

THE PECULIAR PROBLEMS OF TRANSLATING *BEOWULF*

Aside from the dilemma of working with a damaged text, *Beowulf* presents special problems for the translator. Most notable is the metrical puzzle, for the form of Old English verse is very different from that of modern poetry. Most poetry composed after the Norman Conquest in 1066 depends on the regular pattern of stressed and unstressed syllables. Old English poetry, in contrast, is held together by four stresses and alliteration. If this dilemma is not enough to give pause to even the most determined translator, consider *Beowulf's* content. How can a translator make the remote, unfamiliar past of a long-gone civilization come alive for today's readers?

THE KENNEDY VERSUS RAFFEL TRANSLATIONS

Of all the translations now available, scholars generally agree that Charles Kennedy and Burton Raffel have produced the most useful works. That's about all they agree on, however, for each translator has his staunch defenders—and detractors.

Kennedy called his 1940 poetic translation an example of "authentic modern verse." However, he has been criticized for using such artificial expressions as "Lo! I ween" and "smote him sore." But critics

Manuscript page from BEOWULF
The British Museum

have condemned the modern idiom Raffel used in his 1963 version as "too physical," and panned the entire work for creating "a new art rather than making available the old."

THE CASE OF THE FIRST THREE LINES

Openings set the stage for what's to follow. Which of the following two openings do you think best captures the excitement and grandeur of *Beowulf*?

Kennedy's translation

Lo! we have listened to many a lay
Of the Spear-Danes' fame, their splendor of old,
Their mighty princes, and martial deeds!

Raffel's translation

HEAR ME! We've heard of Danish heroes,
Ancient kings and the glory they cut
For themselves, swinging mighty swords!

What difference in tone do you detect between Kennedy's literal translation of the Old English "lā" into "lo" and Raffel's use of the more modern phrase "Hear me"? Is Kennedy's translation more dignified? Is Raffel's more assertive? Why might Kennedy have used the alliterative *l* (lo, listened, and *lay*) but Raffel the *h* (hear, heard, heroes) in the same first line? Why do you think Kennedy translated the original as "splendor of old" but Raffel used "glory they cut"? Notice how Raffel used *enjambment*, running the second line into the third, to set a swing to the passage, while Kennedy used a list to create a feeling of nobility and stateliness.

That two scholars can produce such different versions of only three lines shows the challenges and excitement of translation!

CROSS CURRENTS

Beowulf and John Gardner's *Grendel*

Let's face it—against heroic Beowulf, evil Grendel just didn't stand a chance. And if Beowulf didn't kill the monster, the bad press surely would have! This situation changed recently, however, when contemporary novelist John Gardner decided to tell the monster's side of the story in his novel *Grendel*. And what a story it is! *Newsweek* called Gardner's *Grendel* "a marvelous novel, absolutely marvelous: witty, intelligent, delightful."

BEOWULF BECOMES *GRENDEL*?

How much of the Anglo-Saxon tale of *Beowulf* did Gardner use in his novel? Is *Grendel* simply the Beowulf legend retold from the monster's point of view? Let's start with the form of each. *Beowulf* can be divided into four parts: the episode with Grendel, the battle with Grendel's mother, the return voyage, and the dragon fight. Each part ends before the next begins, and Beowulf rules successfully for fifty years between the dragon fight and his victory over Grendel and his mother. The order of events in *Grendel* is very different, however. The novel begins with the monster attacking Hrothgar's meadhall and men, and ends right after the fight with Beowulf, as Grendel is about to die. This particular section is only about a quarter of the Anglo-Saxon poem. There is also a difference in characters. Although both Grendel's mother and the dragon appear in *Grendel*, Gardner gives each new roles.

A MONSTER WITH A NAPKIN TUCKED UNDER HIS CHIN

The main difference between the Anglo-Saxon poem and the modern "retelling,"
however, lies in the development of Grendel as a character. In *Beowulf*, the monster is static, his actions predictable. In *Grendel*, the monster is dynamic, his awareness growing as the action unfolds. Compare Grendel's attack in this excerpt from Gardner's novel to lines 285–324 of the poem (pages 28–29).

"I am swollen with excitement, bloodlust and joy and a strange fear that mingle in my chest like the twisting rage of a bone-fire," Grendel begins. "I step onto the brightly shining floor and angrily advance onto them. They're all asleep, the whole company! I can hardly believe my luck and my wild heart laughs, but I let out no sound. Swiftly, softly, I will move from bed to bed and destroy them all, swallow every man. I am blazing, half-crazy with joy. For pure, mad prank, I snatch a cloth from the nearest table and tie it around my neck to make a napkin. I delay no longer. I seize up a sleeping man, tear at him hungrily, bite through his bone-locks and suck hot, slippery blood. He goes down in huge morsels, head, chest, hips, legs, even the hands and feet. My face and arms are wet, matted. The napkin is sopping. The dark floor steams. I move on at once and I reach for another one . . . and I seize a wrist. A shock goes through me. Mistake!"

A monster tying a napkin around his neck? This is not the Grendel we've encountered in *Beowulf*! Gardner's use of the first-person point of view helps him remake Grendel from the Anglo-Saxon incarnation of blind evil, unthinking and senseless, into a conscious, rational force.

BEOWULF TAUNTS GRENDEL

Gardner plays equally sly tricks with Beowulf. In place of the noble hero of Anglo-Saxon lore we get a man who is strangely mechanical, even mad. Beowulf taunts Grendel as he kills him, demanding songs that amount to the playground surrender of ''enough.'' See how Grendel describes it in this passage:

> And now something worse. He's whispering—spilling words like showers of sleet, his mouth three inches from my ear. I will not listen. I continue whispering. As long as I whisper to myself I need not hear. His syllables lick at me, chilly fire . . . I do not listen. I am sick at heart. I have been betrayed by talk like that. ''Mama!'' I bawl . . . And still he whispers.
>
> Grendel, Grendel! You make the world by whispers, second by second. Are you blind to that? Whether you make it a grave or a garden of roses is not the point. Feel the wall: is it not hard? He smashes me against it, breaks open my forehead. Hard, yes! . . . Now sing of walls! Sing!
>   I howl.
>   Sing!
>   ''I'm singing!''
>   Sing words! Sing raving hymns!
>   ''You're crazy! Ow!''

GRENDEL (Frontispiece from BEOWULF)
Patten Wilson
The British Library

>   Sing!
>   ''I sing of walls,'' I howl. ''Hooray for the hardness of walls!''

AN EXTRAORDINARY ACHIEVEMENT

What *The New York Times* called John Gardner's ''extraordinary achievement'' is far more than *Beowulf* retold from Grendel's view. It's a funny, intriguing, and ultimately touching examination of the way we look at monsters, heroes, and the world we create with both.

GUIDE FOR INTERPRETING

The Wanderer

Literary Elements

The Theme of Exile. *Exile* means "separation or banishment from one's native country, region, or home." The theme of exile recurs throughout world literature—the medieval Italian poet Dante wrote *Divine Comedy* after being banished from his beloved city of Florence—but this theme is expressed with memorable sadness and pain in Anglo-Saxon poetry.

We cannot understand what exile meant to an Anglo-Saxon warrior until we understand what he meant by "home." While we identify ourselves as citizens of a certain country, an Anglo-Saxon warrior viewed himself as the follower of a particular lord or king. The notion of loyalty toward one's country, called patriotism today, did not exist. It was the lord himself who commanded allegiance, and of course there were many lords in what is now called England. The Anglo-Saxon word for "lord," *hlaford,* came from the word *hlafweard,* which means "guardian of the loaf." The lord was the dispenser of bread and the source of sustenance. He was also the dispenser of the booty won in raids and skirmishes, or a "gold-lord." Perhaps even more important, he guaranteed the security of his followers in a dangerous and uncertain world. In return, he expected loyalty in war. His followers would form his great shield-wall in the thick of battle.

The most important symbol of home was the mead-hall (mead was an alcoholic beverage made of fermented honey and water), where the lord and his followers shared the warmth of fire, the comfort of food and drink, and the pleasures of hearing poetry recited. The pleasures of poetry were especially welcome when the *scop* praised the heroism of the listening warriors. Because we tend to identify home with individual families living in a house or an apartment, it is useful to keep in mind the image of the mead-hall while reading "The Wanderer." Enlivened with a feeling of fellowship, the mead-hall was smoky, noisy, smelly, and crowded. It was home.

Imagine what it meant for a warrior to lose his lord and his place in the mead-hall. The Anglo-Saxon exile was indeed a *wraecca,* a word meaning "wretch, stranger, unhappy man, and wanderer."

Focus

Suppose that you were forced to leave your home for an indefinite period of time. List some of the things that you would miss the most. What effect would the loss of these things eventually have on you?

The Wanderer

translated by Charles W. Kennedy

**RECONSTRUCTED HELMET, SUTTON HOO
SHIP BURIAL (A.D. 7TH CENTURY)**

Oft to the wanderer,   weary of exile,
Cometh God's pity,   compassionate love,
Though woefully toiling   on wintry seas
With churning oar   in the icy wave,
5   Homeless and helpless   he fled from fate.
Thus saith the wanderer   mindful of misery,
Grievous disasters,   and death of kin:
   "Oft when the day broke,   oft at the dawning,
Lonely and wretched   I wailed my woe.
10 No man is living,   no comrade left,
To whom I dare fully   unlock my heart.
I have learned truly   the mark of a man
Is keeping his counsel   and locking his lips,
Let him think what he will!   For, woe of heart
15 Withstandeth not fate;   a failing spirit
Earneth no help.   Men eager for honor
Bury their sorrow   deep in the breast.
   "So have I also,   often in wretchedness
Fettered[1] my feelings,   far from my kin,
20 Homeless and hapless,[2]   since days of old,
When the dark earth   covered my dear lord's face,
And I sailed away   with sorrowful heart,
Over wintry seas,   seeking a gold-lord,
If far or near   lived one to befriend me
25 With gift in the mead-hall   and comfort for grief.
   "Who bears it, knows   what a bitter companion,
Shoulder to shoulder,   sorrow can be,
When friends are no more.   His fortune is exile,
Not gifts of fine gold;   a heart that is frozen,
30 Earth's winsomeness[3] dead.   And he dreams of the hall-men,
The dealing of treasure,   the days of his youth,

---

1. Fettered (Fet' ərd): Chained, restrained.
2. hapless (hap' lis): Unlucky.
3. winsomeness (win' səm nəs): Pleasantness,
delightfulness.

When his lord bade welcome   to wassail[4] and feast.
But gone is that gladness,   and never again
Shall come the loved counsel   of comrade and king.
35   "Even in slumber   his sorrow assaileth,
And, dreaming he claspeth   his dear lord again,
Head on knee, hand on knee,   loyally laying,
Pledging his liege[5]   as in days long past.
Then from his slumber   he starts lonely-hearted,
40   Beholding gray stretches   of tossing sea,
Sea-birds bathing,   with wings outspread,
While hailstorms darken,   and driving snow.
Bitterer then   is the bane of his wretchedness,
The longing for loved one: his grief is renewed.
45   The forms of his kinsmen   take shape in the silence;
In rapture he greets them;   in gladness he scans
Old comrades remembered.   But they melt into air
With no word of greeting   to gladden his heart.
Then again surges   his sorrow upon him;
50   And grimly he spurs   his weary soul
Once more to the toil   of the tossing sea.
   "No wonder therefore,   in all the world,
If a shadow darkens   upon my spirit
When I reflect   on the fates of men—
55   How one by one   proud warriors vanish
From the halls that knew them,   and day by day
All this earth ages   and droops unto death.
No man may know wisdom   till many a winter
Has been his portion.   A wise man is patient,
60   Not swift to anger,   nor hasty of speech,
Neither too weak,   nor too reckless, in war,
Neither fearful nor fain,[6]   nor too wishful of wealth,
Nor too eager in vow—   ere he know the event.
A brave man must bide[7]   when he speaketh his boast
65   Until he know surely   the goal of his spirit.
   "A wise man will ponder   how dread is that doom
When all this world's wealth   shall be scattered and waste

---

4. wassail (wăs′ əl): A toast in drinking a person's
health, or a celebration at which such toasts are
made.
5. liege (lēj): Loyalty.
6. fain (făn): An archaic word meaning "eager"; in
this context it means "too eager."
7. bide (bīd): Wait.

Iuitas syrie que nunc tyrus dicit̄. olim serra uocabat̄ a pisce quodam qui illic abundabat. quem sua lingua sar apellāt ex quo diruatū est huī similitudinis pisciculos sardas. sardinas q̄ uocari.

SERRA FLYING OVER A BOAT: ILLUMINA-TION FROM AN ENGLISH BESTIARY (C. 1185)

As now, over all,   through the regions of earth,
Walls stand rime-covered[8]   and swept by the winds.

70 The battlements crumble,   the wine-halls decay;
Joyless and silent   the heroes are sleeping
Where the proud host fell   by the wall they defended.
Some battle launched   on their long, last journey;
One a bird bore   o'er the billowing sea;

75 One the gray wolf slew;   one a grieving earl
Sadly gave   to the grave's embrace.
The Warden of men   hath wasted this world
Till the sound of music   and revel is stilled,
And these giant-built structures   stand empty of life.

80   "He who shall muse   on these moldering ruins,
And deeply ponder   this darkling life,
Must brood on old legends   of battle and bloodshed,
And heavy the mood   that troubles his heart:
'Where now is the warrior?   Where is the war horse?

85 Bestowal of treasure,   and sharing of feast?
Alas! the bright ale-cup,   the byrny-clad[9] warrior,
The prince in his splendor   —those days are long sped
In the night of the past,   as if they never had been!'
And now remains only,   for warriors' memorial,

90 A wall wondrous high   with serpent shapes carved.
Storms of ash-spears   have smitten the earls,
Carnage of weapon,   and conquering fate.
   "Storms now batter   these ramparts of stone;
Blowing snow   and the blast of winter

95 Enfold the earth;   night-shadows fall
Darkly lowering,   from the north driving
Raging hail   in wrath upon men.
Wretchedness fills   the realm of earth,
And fate's decrees   transform the world.

100 Here wealth is fleeting,   friends are fleeting,
Man is fleeting,   maid is fleeting;
All the foundation of earth   shall fail!"
   Thus spake the sage   in solitude pondering.
Good man is he   who guardeth his faith.

105 He must never too quickly   unburden his breast
Of its sorrow, but eagerly   strive for redress;
And happy the man   who seeketh for mercy
From his heavenly Father,   our fortress and strength.

---

8. rime (rīm) **-covered:** Covered with frost.
9. byrny (bər' nē) **-clad:** Dressed in a coat of
chain-mail armor.

RESPONDING TO THE SELECTION

Your Response

1. Can you identify with the feelings expressed in "The Wanderer?" Why or why not?

Recalling

2. (a) What event causes the wanderer to go into exile? (b) What is the goal of his search?
3. Identify a brief passage in which he expresses his outlook on life.

Interpreting

4. "The Wanderer" has been called an elegy, meaning a poem of mourning and lament. (a) Identify three vivid details that you feel evoke a mood of mourning and lament. (b) Explain why these details are effective.
5. How does the poet's use of repetition contribute to the mood?
6. Explain the wanderer's attitude toward wisdom. Find details to support your answer.
7. **Tone** refers to a writer's attitude toward the subject or theme. (a) Choose two adjectives to describe the tone of this poem. (b) Give reasons for your choices.

Applying

8. What does this poem suggest about the role of women in the Anglo-Saxon world?
9. What would a modern wanderer be like? Briefly describe the causes of such a person's exile and the goal of his or her search.

ANALYZING LITERATURE

Understanding Exile

As a poem about exile and the loss of one's home, "The Wanderer" works primarily through contrast. For instance, the vivid dream image in which the wanderer once again clasps his king, "Head on knee, hand on knee," contrasts with the waking image of the monotonous "gray stretches" of sea and the "Seabirds . . . with wings outspread." The first image conveys closeness and enfolded intimacy, while the second communicates the far-flung emptiness of exile and desolation.

1. Identify two other pairs of contrasting images in the poem and explain how they contribute to the theme of exile.
2. In addition to using contrasting images, the poet juxtaposes his personal experience with broad generalities about human life. Would the poem be more effective or less effective if the poet's generalizations (lines 100–103) preceded his account of his exile? Why?

CRITICAL THINKING AND READING

Appreciating a Poem's Structure

Critics often seek to understand a poem by analyzing its structure, or the major units of meaning into which it is divided. "The Wanderer," for example, is framed by opening (lines 1–5) and closing (lines 104–108) passages that refer to God's "pity" and "mercy." These religious invocations are clearly different from the soliloquy in the rest of the poem. The body of the poem itself, however, can also be divided into distinct parts.

1. Identify the units of meaning into which you think the poem should be divided. Indicate the lines where each begins and ends.
2. Explain why you divided the poem as you did. Consider such factors as a change in pronouns or a shift from an individual's experience to generalities.

THINKING AND WRITING

Responding to Criticism

The scholar Michael Alexander argues that the mournful mood of "The Wanderer" is not diminished by the more comforting religious passages that appear at the beginning and end of the poem. Write an essay in which you agree or disagree with this assertion. Begin by identifying the passages and phrases that contribute most to the poem's mood. Then write a thesis statement expressing your opinion of Alexander's critical comment. In revising your work, test your thesis by rereading the poem several times and being receptive to the mood it evokes in you.

BEDE

673–735

Much of what the world knows about England before A.D. 700 is based on a history written in Latin by a Benedictine monk, Bede, who is often called the father of English history. Bede was the most learned scholar of his day not only in England but in all of Western Europe. Although he wrote forty books on a variety of subjects, his reputation would be secure on the basis of a single book—his *Historia Ecclesiastica Gentis Anglorum,* or, in English, *A History of the English Church and People.*

Bede was born in Wearmouth (now the city of Sunderland) on the northeast coast of England. As a child of seven, he entered the nearby monastic school of Jarrow on the river Tyne. A diligent student, he took full advantage of the library at Jarrow, in time becoming a priest, teacher, and scholar at the monastery. He remained at Jarrow for the rest of his life.

A contemporary of the unknown author of *Beowulf,* Bede was fascinated by a broad range of ideas. His writings summarize much of the thought and learning of his time. As the earliest important English prose writer, he concentrated on the Bible but did not neglect science and history. One of his innovations was the dating of events from the birth of Christ, a system that other scholars began to follow. It was through Bede's work that the Christian chronology in use today became common throughout Europe.

Bede had a deep love for his native island and its people, which led him to write his *History of the English Church and People.* In working on his history, Bede gathered information from many kinds of documents, interviewed knowledgeable monks, and, in general, proceeded very much like a modern historian, although he accepted as fact some miracles that a modern historian would not.

In the *History,* Bede describes the conquests of the Anglo-Saxon tribes and the fortunes of the various small fiefdoms that spread across the land. His primary concern, however, was the expansion of Christianity and the growth of the Church in England. He wrote in Latin, the language of scholarship in his age. There are several surviving manuscripts, however, that have the Old English text in addition to Bede's Latin version. He became famous throughout the land as one of the most learned scholars of his age, despite the fact that he never ventured beyond Northumbria.

In the century after his death, King Alfred translated Bede's history from Latin into English. In the same century, the word *Venerable* was first applied to his name to honor his wisdom and achievements. The honor was well deserved. The Venerable Bede was largely responsible for what is sometimes called the Christian renaissance in eighth-century England.

GUIDE FOR INTERPRETING

from A History of the English Church and People

Writers' Techniques

Historical Writing. A history is a factual narrative or record of past events. Unless a historian has actually observed the events being described, he or she must rely on outside sources. These sources include testimony from living witnesses, accounts in letters or memoirs, and records from courts, businesses, churches, armies, or other groups. Today's historian has libraries of books, newspapers, and films to consult, as well as unwritten records, such as buildings, artwork, and various physical remains of bygone days. An enormous amount of historical material exists.

That was not the case in Bede's time. English monastic libraries had modest collections of documents that Bede read, cross-checked, and evaluated. He made excellent use of the limited resources of his time. Bede was an innovator among historical writers, and if he sometimes accepted unlikely tales as truth, he did so far less often than did most scholars of his era.

Focus

If you were writing a history of your community, you would have to find and use a number of different sources. List at least five specific sources that might be helpful.

Primary Source

Joseph Addison wrote, "The end of a man's life is often compared to the winding up of a well-written play, where the principal persons still act in character, whatever the fate is which they undergo." Bede's death was certainly in character, and it became the subject of historical writing in the hands of Cuthbert, a former student: "At the ninth hour, Bede said to me, 'I have a few valuables in my cask—pepper, vestments, and incense. Run quickly and bring the priests of our monastery, so that I may share among them little gifts, such as God has granted me.' And I did so with trembling. When they were all present, he addressed each and every one, urging them, imploring them they should say prayers and masses for him—which they freely promised. But they all kept weeping and sorrowing, especially because he said they must not think to see his face much longer in this world. But they rejoiced because he said, 'It is time for me, if my Maker sees fit, to be freed from the flesh and go to Him who made me out of nothing, at the time when I was nothing. I have lived a long time, and my merciful Judge has ordered my life well. . . . This and much else he said for our instruction, and passed his last day happily until evening . . . upon the floor of his little cell, chanting . . . his spirit passed from the body."

from # A History of the English Church and People

Bede translated by Leo Sherley-Price

The Situation of Britain and Ireland: Their Earliest Inhabitants

Britain, formerly known as Albion, is an island in the ocean, facing between north and west, and lying at a considerable distance from the coasts of Germany, Gaul, and Spain, which together form the greater part of Europe. It extends 800 miles northwards, and is 200 in breadth, except where a number of promontories stretch farther, the coastline round which extends to 3,675 miles. To the south lies Belgic Gaul,[1] from the nearest shore of which travelers can see the city known as Rutubi Portus, which the English have corrupted to Reptacestir.[2] The distance from there across the sea to Gessoriacum,[3] the nearest coast of the Morini, is 50 miles or, as some write it, 450 furlongs. On the opposite side of Britain, which lies open to the boundless ocean, lie the isles of the Orcades.[4] Britain is rich in grain and timber; it has good pasturage for cattle and draft animals,[5] and vines are cultivated in various localities. There are many land and sea birds of various species, and it is well known for its plentiful springs and rivers abounding in fish. There are salmon and eel fisheries, while seals, dolphins, and sometimes whales are caught. There are also many varieties of shellfish, such as mussels, in which are often found excellent pearls of several colors: red, purple, violet, and green, but mainly white. Cockles are abundant, and a beautiful scarlet dye is extracted from them which remains unfaded by sunshine or rain; indeed, the older the cloth, the more beautiful its color. The country has both salt and hot springs, and the waters flowing from them provide hot baths, in which the people bathe separately according to age and sex. As Saint Basil says: "Water receives its heat when it flows across certain metals, and becomes hot, and even scalding." The land has rich veins of many metals, including copper, iron, lead, and silver. There is also much black jet[6] of fine quality, which sparkles in firelight. When burned, it drives away snakes, and, like amber, when it is warmed by friction, it clings to whatever is applied to it. In old times, the country had twenty-eight noble cities, and innumerable castles, all of which were guarded by walls, towers, and barred gates.

Since Britain lies far north toward the pole, the nights are short in summer, and at midnight it is hard to tell whether the evening twilight still lingers or whether dawn is approaching; for in these northern latitudes the sun does not remain long below the horizon at night. Consequently both sum-

---

1. Belgic Gaul: France.
2. Reptacestir: Richborough, part of the city of Sandwich.
3. Gessoriacum: Boulogne, France.
4. Orcades: The Orkney Isles.
5. draft animals: Animals used for pulling loads.

---

6. jet *n.*: A type of coal.

mer days and winter nights are long, and when the sun withdraws southwards, the winter nights last eighteen hours. In Armenia,[7] Macedonia,[8] and Italy, and other countries of that latitude, the longest day lasts only fifteen hours and the shortest nine.

At the present time there are in Britain, in harmony with the five books of the divine law, five languages and four nations —English, British, Scots, and Picts. Each of these have their own language, but all are united in their study of God's truth by the fifth, Latin, which has become a common medium through the study of the scriptures. The original inhabitants of the island were the Britons, from whom it takes its name, and who, according to tradition, crossed into Britain from Armorica,[9] and occupied the southern parts. When they had spread northwards and possessed the greater part of the islands, it is said that some Picts from Scythia[10] put to sea in a few long ships and were driven by storms around the coasts of Britain, arriving at length on the north

---

7. Armenia: Now part of the Soviet Union.
8. Macedonia: Now a region divided among Greece, Yugoslavia, and Bulgaria.

9. Armorica: Brittany, France.
10. Scythia (sith' ē ə): An ancient region in southeastern Europe.

from *A History of the English Church and People* 61

MONKS
Bodleian Library, Oxford

coast of Ireland. Here they found the nation of the Scots, from whom they asked permission to settle, but their request was refused. Ireland is the largest island after Britain, and lies to the west. It is shorter than Britain to the north, but extends far beyond it to the south towards the northern coasts of Spain, although a wide sea separates them. These Pictish seafarers, as I have said, asked for a grant of land to make a settlement. The Scots replied that there was not room for them both, but said: "We can give you good advice. There is another island not far to the east, which we often see in the distance on clear days. Go and settle there if you wish; should you meet resistance, we will come to your help." So the Picts crossed into Britain, and began to settle in the north of the island, since the Britons were in possession of the south. Having no women with them, these Picts asked wives of the Scots, who consented on condition that, when any dispute arose, they should choose a king from the female royal line rather than the male. This custom continues among the Picts to this day. As time went on, Britain received a third nation, that of the Scots, who migrated from Ireland under their chieftain Reuda, and by a combination of force and treaty, obtained from the Picts the settlements that they still hold. From the name of this chieftain, they are still known as Dalreudians, for in their tongue *dal* means a division.

Ireland is broader than Britain, and its mild and healthy climate is superior. Snow rarely lies longer than three days, so that there is no need to store hay in summer for winter use or to build stables for beasts. There are no reptiles, and no snake can exist there, for although often brought over from Britain, as soon as the ship nears land, they breathe its scented air and die. In fact, almost everything in this isle enjoys immunity to poison, and I have heard that folk suffering from snakebite have drunk water in which scrapings from the leaves of books from Ireland had been steeped, and that this remedy checked the spreading poison and reduced the swelling. The island abounds in milk and honey, and there is no lack of vines, fish, and birds, while deer and goats are widely hunted. It is the original home of the Scots, who, as already mentioned, later migrated and joined the Britons and Picts in Britain. There is a very extensive arm of the sea, which originally formed the boundary between the Britons and the Picts. This runs inland from the west for a great distance as far as the strongly fortified British city of Alcuith.[11] It was to the northern shores of this firth that the Scots came and established their new homeland.

---

11. Alcuith (al kü′ əth): Dumbarton, Scotland.

RESPONDING TO THE SELECTION

Your Response

1. Do you find Bede's history of England more appealing than a standard history textbook? Why or why not?

Recalling

2. What countries formed the greater part of Europe at the time of Bede's history?
3. (a) In Bede's time, what were the four nations in Britain? (b) What united them?

Interpreting

4. What does the explanation about scarlet dye imply about the lifestyle of the people?
5. Bede states that Britain once "had twenty-eight noble cities . . . guarded by walls, towers, and barred gates." What does this statement suggest about the political situation at the time?
6. What is one unlikely tale that Bede includes in his history?

Applying

7. If you wanted to read a reliable history of early England, why would you probably choose something other than Bede's work? What kind of source might you choose?

ANALYZING LITERATURE

Understanding Historical Writing

A history provides factual information about the past. This information comes from a variety of sources, including books and other printed materials, public records, and personal letters, memoirs, and interviews. A good historian does more than just list facts, however. Bede presents his facts as part of an understandable whole.

1. Accuracy is very important in historical writing. Read the quotation from the Scots on page 62. (a) Do you think the statement is an exact quotation? (b) If not, does it cast doubt on the accuracy of Bede's history? Explain.
2. Bede sometimes relies on people's oral statements for his information. On page 62 he makes a specific reference to such a source. What is it?

CRITICAL THINKING AND READING

Making Inferences About Attitudes

Bede's history reflects his own attitudes and those of the people he is writing about. Since these attitudes tend to be revealed indirectly, you must make inferences, or draw conclusions about them. For example, Bede states that the people of England are "united in their study of God's truth." From this statement you can infer that religion played an important role in the life of the people.

1. From Bede's comments on page 62, what do you think was the general attitude in Britain toward snakes?
2. Do you think the Picts and Scots got along well with each other? Cite the evidence on which you base your inference.

THINKING AND WRITING

Writing a Critical Review

Give your opinion of this excerpt from Bede's history. First, jot down your answers to the following questions: Does the history seem accurate? Is it clearly written? What do you find to be its most striking fact? Next, write a topic sentence that states your opinion clearly. Then, write a draft, using examples to support your opinion. Finally, revise your draft, making sure that its sentences are in logical order.

LEARNING OPTION

Cross-curricular Connection. Investigate the history of illuminated manuscripts—the colorful, ornate, handmade illustrated books created before the printing press was invented. Where were they first made? Who made them? What media were used to create them? What purposes did the elaborate calligraphic designs and illustrations serve? Find several examples of illuminated manuscripts from various time periods and bring them to class. Give a brief explanation about the background of each.

THE CHANGING ENGLISH LANGUAGE

Old English 449–1066

"ENGLISC"

The story of English is the story of roamings and settling, invasions and war. What we call *Anglo-Saxon* or *Old English* developed through the contributions of many different peoples, including the Jutes (from Danish Jutland), the Saxons (from the region of Germany still called Lower Saxony), and scatterings of other groups. Old English began with the *Angles*, a people who originated in a section of Denmark still called *Angeln*, a word that means "an angle in the coast." The Celts called their German conquerors *Saxons* but by degrees the terms *Anglii* and *Anglia* entered their speech. Soon, people were referring to their language as *Englisc* and themselves as *Angelcynn;* literally, the relatives (*cynn* as "kin") of the Angles. By A.D. 1000 they called their country *Englaland*.

THE HUNDRED MOST COMMON WORDS

The Anglo-Saxons were farmers—when they were not at war—and they soon settled down and took over all the good farming country, chasing the Celts to the hilltops or to Wales and Ireland. Although more than half the vocabulary of modern English is borrowed from other languages, and more than half the words of Old English (some say as much as 85 percent) have vanished, the language of these Anglo-Saxon farmers became the basis of modern English. Of the hundred most common words in our speech today, every one derives from Old English; of the next hundred, eighty-three are native. Some Old English words hardly need translation—*mann* and *hus* for example—although of

course we spell them differently today (*man* and *house*). It is nearly impossible to write a modern English sentence without using a wealth of Old English vocabulary. All the words in Roosevelt's famous comforting phrase—"The only thing we have to fear is fear itself"—come from Old English. Francis Scott Key used words derived from Old English in 1814 when he saw the flag waving over Fort McHenry: "Oh say, can you see, by the dawn's early light, what so proudly we hailed at the twilight's last gleaming?" "Proudly" is the only non-native word, and it was borrowed nearly a thousand years ago!

RIDDLES

The Anglo-Saxons delighted in word play, riddles, and ambiguity in language. Few people could read or write, and so they had to rely on their memories. As a result, the Anglo-Saxons developed their oral tradition very fully. They liked stating their ideas in subtle, original ways and especially admired poems that went in circles. This love of word play, which characterizes English to the present, can be seen especially in *The Exeter Book of Riddles*, a collection of Old English verse. Can you solve this one-line riddle? "On the way a miracle: water becomes bone." Ice!

THE INFLUENCE OF CHRISTIANITY

Although the English people already knew about *heofon* (heaven), *synne* (sin) and *hel* (hell), the language received a huge boost in A.D. 597, when Christianity arrived with its enormous Latin vocabulary, more than 400 words of which survive to this day. For example, the Latin *evangelium* (good news) became the English *god-spell*, which has become the modern word *gospel*. Even more important, words from Latin gave English speakers the ability to express abstract thoughts, including such concepts as *angel* and *discipline*. Further, Old English rejuvenated itself by giving new meaning to old words. *God, heaven,* and *hell* all assumed deeper meanings upon the arrival of Christianity.

THE VIKINGS SIMPLIFY ENGLISH

Superior numbers and literacy assured the victory of English over Danish, but the Danes left a lasting influence on English nonetheless. First, they contributed at least 900 words, such as *husbondi* (*housemaster* or *husband*) and *syster* (sister). Second, the Danes added pronouns to English, filling a real linguistic need. Most important, before the arrival of the Danes, Old English conveyed meaning through word endings rather than word order. The Danes simplified language by eliminating this practice, called inflection, although the process would not be completed until Middle English developed.

THE SPELLING DILEMMA

Written English presented a problem that still confounds us today: spelling. Almost all writing is based on symbols that stand for the sounds of the language they record. The early scribes used the Roman alphabet to record Old English. The Roman alphabet did a fine job of representing the sounds of Latin, for which it had been created. But Old English included a number of

decidedly un-Roman sounds, such as the sound we now write as *TH*. The scribes solved the problem by borrowing two symbols from the runic alphabet, þ and ð. Unfortunately, they used the two symbols interchangeably. This continued with other sounds, and spelling problems abounded.

So begun, English would continue to develop over the next four hundred years, becoming ever richer and more flexible.

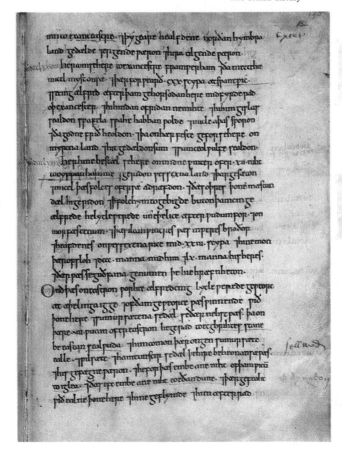

YOUR WRITING PROCESS

WRITING ABOUT A MODERN HERO

Beowulf is adventurous, strong, and aggressive—qualities that Anglo-Saxons obviously considered "heroic." Has the nature of heroism changed since the poem was written? To answer this question, think about a person that you regard as a modern hero and the reasons for your choice.

> **Focus**
>
> **Assignment:** Write an introduction to a book about a modern hero or heroine.
> **Purpose:** To summarize the person's accomplishments and encourage readers to finish the book.
> **Audience:** High-school students.

Prewriting

1. Brainstorm possibilities with a partner. With a partner, brainstorm to compile a list of modern heroes. Don't rule anyone out. You might browse through the biography section in a library or flip through news magazines for ideas.

2. What makes a hero? Do some freewriting to answer this question. Let your mind wander. If you get stuck, just rewrite the question until your mind starts working again.

> **Student Model**
>
> What makes a hero? You don't have to be a man! Beowulf seems so violent. Maybe heroes today are nonviolent, like Martin Luther King, Jr., but what about The Terminator? Sports heroes—Magic Johnson, Bo Jackson. I'd like to write about a female, but who? What makes a hero? Seems like they do something for others—unselfish. Altruistic—is that the right word? Do heroes have to be famous? I hope not.

3. Research. Narrow your choices to two or three; then do some preliminary research. Try biographies and recent magazine articles. Talk to others. Then make your choice.

Drafting

1. Write a catchy introduction. Intrigue your readers with an anecdote, capture their attention with a description, or provoke them with a question. Find a unique and enticing way to begin. Remember, however, that you may not discover the best beginning until you have actually started writing.

2. Include quotations. Try to find quotations by or about your subject to give your draft validity and immediacy.

> ### Student Model
>
> When I asked my mother to name her heroes, she quickly replied, "Gloria Steinem. She's a model for an entire generation of women. She's had her ups and downs, but she's encouraged all of us." I'd never heard of Gloria Steinem, but once I started reading and listening, I was convinced that she is a heroine of our time.

3. Try allusions. Sometimes, an effective way to make a point is to make an allusion, that is, a reference to literature, history, or popular culture. For example, the phrase "a twentieth-century Beowulf" might be a provocative way to describe an Arnold Schwarzenegger character.

Revising and Editing

1. Introduce sentence variety. Have you used long sentences to convey complex and interwoven images and ideas and short, simple sentences for rhythm and emphasis?

> ### Student Model
>
> **Before:** *Ms.* magazine was co-founded by Gloria Steinem in 1972. It quickly became a forum for feminist voices. It tried to give a voice to American women who were caught between traditional roles and the sexual revolution.
>
> **After:** By the 1970's, American women were caught between traditional roles and new aspirations. They needed a voice. They needed a forum. Gloria Steinem gave them both. How? She gave them *Ms.* magazine.

2. Peer editing. Don't count on yourself to be objective about your writing. Enlist a trusted peer editor to read critically and answer questions like the following:
- What is the strongest part of this draft? The weakest?
- Based on this essay, what three words would you use to describe the subject?
- Do you consider the subject heroic? Why or why not?

3. Scrutinize verbs. Pay close attention to verbs; they carry your sentences. Make sure they are lively and active. Also make sure you use a consistent and simple tense.

Writer's Hint

Use as few words as possible to make your point. For example, weed out adverbs whenever you can. Often, they can be deleted from phrases like "*simply* beautiful" or "*completely* alone."

Options for Publishing
- Mail your essay to someone in another town who shares your admiration for this man or woman.
- If your hero is alive, mail a copy of your essay to him or her with a letter explaining your assignment.
- Combine your essays into a classroom display of Modern Heroes that includes photographs of the various subjects.

PILGRIMS TO CANTERBURY: DETAIL OF AN ENGLISH ILLUMINATED MANUSCRIPT, *c.*1400

THE MEDIEVAL PERIOD
1066–1485

A Knyght ther was, and that a worthy man
That fro the tyme that he first bigan
To riden out, he loved chivalrie,
Trouthe and honour, fredom and curteisie

Geoffrey Chaucer

The famous description on the preceding page comes from an English literary masterpiece, *The Canterbury Tales,* by Geoffrey Chaucer (1340–1400). The passage reflects many of the ideas and attitudes held by Europeans during the fourteenth century. In these years, knights lived by the code of chivalry, which stressed truth, honor, and courtesy off the battlefield and valor on it. The Roman Catholic Church had become the only force uniting most of Western Europe. Religion pervaded daily life, and to be a devout Christian—a worthy man—was important not only to knights but to all members of English society.

During these years, the English language changed from its Anglo-Saxon form to one called Middle English, far more familiar to modern readers. Looking at Chaucer's words above, we can readily recognize their modern English counterparts—"knyght" is *knight,* "ther" is *there,* "fro" is *from,* "riden" is *ride,* "chivalrie" is *chivalry,* and so on. The change from Old English to Middle English took place gradually. Yet this change can be traced to one riveting event—the Norman invasion of 1066.

The Norman Conquest

The Normans, or "north men," were descendants of Vikings who had invaded the coast of France in the ninth century. Over the years, these people had adopted many French ways. They had become devout Christians. They had accustomed themselves to speaking a dialect of the French language. They had also organized themselves according to the French political and economic system of the times—feudalism.

William, Duke of Normandy, had family ties to Edward the Confessor, the English king. When Edward died in 1066, the Saxon witan—the council of elders—chose Harold II as king. William of Normandy, meanwhile, claimed that Edward had promised him the throne. William thereupon led a few thousand Norman and French troops across the English Channel to assert his claim by force.

He met King Harold at the Battle of Hastings near a seaside village in southern England. Harold was killed, and William emerged victorious. He then headed for London, brutally crushing all resistance. At Westminster Abbey on Christmas Day, William "the Conqueror" took the throne of England as King William I.

Over the next five years, William consolidated his victory. He suppressed the Anglo-Saxon nobility and confiscated their lands. He saw to it that Normans controlled government at all levels. The Normans conducted their business in Norman French or Latin. They gradually remade England along feudal lines.

The Rise of Feudalism

Feudalism had taken root on the European continent at a time when no central government was strong enough to keep order. Under the circumstances, nobles had to rely on their own warriors for help. The system they created was an exchange of property for personal service. The person who granted the property was the lord or overlord. The person who received it was the vassal. The vassal promised service to his lord in a ceremony called the act of homage. At the same time, the vassal usually pledged his faithfulness by taking the Christian vow of fealty.

In theory, all the land belonged to the ruler. The king kept some of it for his personal use, granted some to the church, and parceled out the rest among his powerful supporters. He gave these supporters noble titles—usually "Baron"—and the special privileges that went with them. The parcels of land granted to the barons were known as fiefs.

As a vassal of his overlord, each baron was obliged to pay certain fees or taxes. He was also expected to supply a specified number of knights, or professional soldiers, should the king require them. In return for their services, knights usually received smaller parcels of land, called manors. The peasants who worked these manors were the lowest class in the feudal system, the serfs. Manors became the basic community of the feudal system. Most were self-sufficient, using their own craftsmen to provide nearly all their needs.

In the eleventh century, Europe had no nation-states with firm political boundaries. William and the Norman kings who followed him—

A BAILIFF SUPERVISING THE HARVEST
English manuscript illumination
Early 14th century

William II, Henry I, and Stephen of Blois—held feudal domains in both England and France. Since they had two realms, Norman kings had far wider responsibilities than Saxon kings had faced. The situation also meant that English barons dissatisfied with their overlord could cross the English Channel and stir up trouble on the other side.

A Shifting Language

Like a great many of history's conquerors, the Normans thought themselves vastly superior to the people they had conquered. The invaders treated the Saxons and Danes as not quite human and sniffed at their language as unworthy of respect. The Normans substituted their dialect of French in the law courts as well as in the conduct of business in general. To this day, French words such as *bail* and *sergeant* remain embedded in the language of English law.

Traces of Norman discrimination against the Saxons have lingered for centuries. Sir Walter Scott, in his nineteenth-century novel *Ivanhoe,* noted one aspect of Norman superiority. In the field, he wrote, a domestic animal is often referred to by its Saxon name—swine, sheep, or ox. When the same animal appears on a dinner table, however, it takes a French name—pork, mutton, or beef. In other words, the raising of farm animals was considered a Saxon activity, whereas the more elegant pursuit, dining, befitted the Normans.

Reign of the Plantagenets

Although Norman influence continued for centuries, Norman rule ended in 1154 when Henry Plantagenet, Count of Anjou, came to the throne as Henry II. Henry founded the royal house of Plantagenet, otherwise known as the Angevin (from Anjou) line of English monarchs. A strongly committed ruler, Henry established a record as one of England's ablest kings. He had an avid interest in government and a keen understanding of the law.

Henry II and the Church

Henry's concern with legal matters led him into direct conflict with the Church. By the twelfth century, the Church had grown ever more powerful, obtaining the authority to put clergymen on trial in Church-run courts. Henry sought to curb some abuses connected with this privilege. When the archbishop's seat at Canterbury fell vacant, he appointed his friend Thomas Becket to the position, expecting Becket to go along with royal policy. Instead, Becket defied the king and appealed to the Pope. The Pope sided with Becket, provoking Henry to rage.

Some of Henry's knights misunderstood the royal wrath. In 1170, four of them went to Canterbury and murdered Becket in his cathedral. Henry quickly condemned the crime and tried to atone for it by making a holy journey, or pilgrimage, to Becket's tomb. Thereafter a pilgrimage to Becket's shrine at Canterbury became a common English means of showing religious devotion. The characters in Chaucer's *The Canterbury Tales,* for example, make just such a pilgrimage.

Origins of Constitutional Government

The next king, Richard I, spent most of his reign staging military expeditions overseas. His activities proved costly, and his successor, King John, inherited the debts. John tried to raise money by ordering new taxes on the barons and saved money by curtailing services such as the sending of judges to local districts to settle quarrels. The barons resisted these measures, bringing England to the edge of civil war. To avert further trouble, King John at last agreed to certain of the

The Medieval Period (A.D. 1066– A.D. 1485)

The Murder of Thomas Becket

Genghis Kahn

King John Signs the Magna Carta

1060   **1140**   **1220**

BRITISH EVENTS

- Saxons defeated at Hastings.
  - Canterbury becomes England's religious center.
    - Construction on Tower of London begins.
      - Henry I becomes king.
        - First recorded miracle play performed at Dunstable.
          - Oxford becomes a center for learning.

- Thomas Becket, Archbishop of Canterbury, murdered.
  - Henry II conquers southeastern Ireland.
    - Glass windows first used in private homes.
      - Beginning of legendary era of Robin Hood.
        - King John forced to sign Magna Carta.
          - First Newgate Prison built in London.

- First coal mined at Newcastle.
  - First commoners allowed in Parliament.
    - Edward I becomes king.
      - Cambridge University founded.
        - England conquers Wales.
          - Edward I assembles Model Parliament.

WORLD EVENTS

- Europe and Middle East: First Crusade begins.
  - France: *Song of Roland* written.
    - Portugal: Alfonso VII defeats Moors.

- Spain: First paper manufactured.
  - Italy: Tower of Pisa built.
    - Europe and Middle East: Third Crusade begins.
      - Austria: Duke Leopold imprisons Richard I of England.
        - Iceland: *Elder Edda,* a collection of Norse myths and legends, first appears.
          - China: Mongol leader Genghis Khan captures Peking.

- Italy: First known sonnet appears.
  - Europe: Pope Gregory IX establishes Inquisition.
    - Eastern Europe: Mongols withdraw from Poland and Hungary.
      - China: Marco Polo visits court of Kublai Khan.
        - Europe and Middle East: End of Crusades.
          - South Pacific: Moas, large flightless birds, become extinct.

Roger Bacon

Black Death
Sweeps
Through England

Printer's Device
Used by Caxton

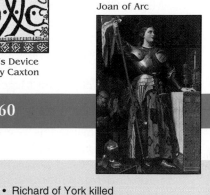
Joan of Arc

1300   **1380**   **1460**

- Beginning of Hundred Years' War with France.
  - Black death begins sweeping through England.
    - Bible first translated into English.
      - Surviving version of *Sir Gawain and the Green Knight* written.

- Peasants' Revolt.
  - **Chaucer** begins writing *The Canterbury Tales*.

- *The Second Shepherds' Play* first performed.

- Richard of York killed at Battle of Wakefield.
  - **Thomas Malory** writes *Morte d' Arthur*.
    - William Caxton builds first English printing press.

- Beginning of Wars of the Roses.

- Italy: Dante begins writing *The Divine Comedy*.
  - Africa: Mali Empire reaches its zenith.
    - Mexico: Aztecs establish Mexico City.
      - India: Bubonic plague begins.
        - Italy: Petrarch crowned poet laureate in Rome.
          - France: English defeat French at Crécy.

- Italy: Beginning of Medici rule.
  - France: Joan of Arc leads French in breaking Siege of Orleans.
    - Peru: Inca Empire reaches its zenith.

- North America: Iroquois nations unite.
  - France: Hundred Years' War with England ends.
    - Germany: First Gutenberg Bible printed.

- France: François Villon publishes *Grand Testament*.
  - Portugal: John II refuses to finance Columbus.
    - Italy: Botticelli paints *Birth of Venus*.

barons' conditions by putting his seal to the Magna Carta (Latin for "Great Charter").

In this document, the king promised not to tax land without first meeting with the barons. He also said he would choose as his officers only those "who know the law of the realm and mean to observe it well." The Magna Carta produced no radical changes in government. Yet many historians believe that the document's restrictions on royal power marked the beginning of constitutional government in England.

Constitutional government continued to develop under subsequent kings. During the reign of Henry III, the Great Council of barons who advised the king came to be called Parliament. Henry's successor, Edward I, became the first king to summon a Parliament partly elected by "free men"—a term that included some ordinary townspeople as well as barons. By the end of the thirteenth century, then, Parliament had already been established as a cornerstone of government in the British Isles.

The Growth of Towns

It was no accident that some members of Parliament now represented townspeople. In the thirteenth century, towns were becoming increasingly important in English life. The Crusades, a series of religious wars in the eleventh to thirteenth centuries, had stimulated trade between Europe and the Middle East. As trade expanded, so did Europe's trading centers. The largest of these centers in England was London, originally built by the Romans. Four times more populous than any other English community, London had already achieved status as a city.

In London and elsewhere, townspeople organized themselves into guilds, or associations, of various sorts. The two most significant types were merchant guilds and craft guilds. Merchant guilds were formed in an effort to promote business within a town, often at the expense of other towns nearby. As these guilds became more powerful, some of them virtually took over town governments. Craft guilds, like our modern labor unions, sought to protect the interests of workers such as weavers, carpenters, and tanners. They also tried to assure the quality of the work these craftspeople produced. Such organizations operated in a world in which advancement was tightly controlled. A young person typically entered a craft as an apprentice, or beginner, and worked his way up the ladder, sometimes reaching the highest rung as master craftsman.

The growth of towns meant that wealth was no longer restricted to land ownership, which remained a privilege of the nobility. Unfortunately, it also meant that people lived much closer together, often under conditions that were far from sanitary. When infectious diseases came to England, they spread havoc in the towns. The worst epidemic, a great plague called the Black Death, swept the island in 1348 and 1349, killing a third of the population.

FOUR KINGS OF ENGLAND
13th-century manuscript

The Later Middle Ages

By the time of the Black Death, England had already passed into the period known as the Later Middle Ages. This period lasted from the beginning of the fourteenth century to the end of the fifteenth. During these years, the house of Lancaster replaced the Plantagenets on the throne, only to be replaced in turn by the house of York. The Lancastrian kings were Henry IV, Henry V, and Henry VI, all of whom later became central figures in the historical dramas of Shakespeare.

During the Later Middle Ages, the feudal system went into a steep decline. As new towns appeared, feudal notions of land tenure seemed more and more outdated. After the Black Death swept across England, a massive labor shortage increased the value of a peasant's work. More and more landowners began paying their farmers in cash, giving these workers a greater sense of freedom. Along with freedom went frustration, as peasants began complaining about discriminatory laws and onerous taxation. Finally, in 1381, peasants in southern England staged a revolt, demanding, among other things, an end to serfdom. Although the revolt was eventually crushed, many of its causes continued, and so did the peasants' discontent.

An Attack on the Church

At about the time of the peasants' revolt, other complaints were being directed at the church. They came from an outspoken scholar, John Wycliffe (c. 1320–1384), who thought that religion had traveled far from its roots. Wycliffe opposed all forms of wealth among the clergy. He showed only scorn for monks, calling them men with "red and fat cheeks and great bellies." He believed that all religious authority sprang from the Bible, not from the Church.

Wycliffe directed the translation of the Bible into English in the hope of making it more accessible to the people. He also helped to organize an order of "poor priests" known as Lollards. Eventually, the archbishop of Canterbury moved against the Lollards as heretics, people who attack Church doctrine and undermine Church authori-

FUNERAL OF A PLAGUE VICTIM
Trinity Chapel Window
Canterbury Cathedral, 14th century

ty. Yet the Lollards continued to spread Wycliffe's teachings for a number of years after the scholar's death.

Wars of the Roses

Just as the English Middle Ages had opened with a struggle for power, they closed with a similar conflict. This one began in 1453, when King Henry VI suffered the first of many bouts of madness. Parliament appointed his cousin Richard of York as temporary head of government. When Henry recovered briefly, Richard was forced from office, and Henry returned to the throne. Richard would not depart without a fight, however. The resulting civil war became known as the first War of the Roses, for it pitted the house of York, whose symbol was a white rose, against the house of Lancaster, whose symbol was a red rose.

In 1461, a Yorkist victory put Richard's son, Edward, on the throne. As Edward IV, he ruled England until his death in 1483, when his eldest son, still a boy, became Edward V. Soon afterward, Edward V and his brother died mysteriously in the Tower of London while under the supposed protection of their uncle, Richard of Gloucester. Richard, accused by many people of these "Tower murders," then proclaimed himself King Richard III.

Two years later, Henry Tudor, a distant cousin and supporter of the Lancastrian kings, led a rebellion against the unpopular King Richard and

KING HENRY VII OF ENGLAND, 1505
Michiel Sittow

killed him. Tudor, crowned Henry VII, later married Richard's niece. By doing so, he united the houses of York and Lancaster and ended the Wars of the Roses. By the time Henry had established a new royal line, the house of Tudor, the English Middle Ages had ended.

Chivalry and Romance

Most societies have lived by a well-established set of ideals, and England of the Middle Ages was no exception. One set of standards by which people measured themselves during these years was the code of knightly behavior known as chivalry. The idea of chivalry first arose on the European continent at the time of the Crusades. Although the Crusades often involved brutality and bloodshed, they encouraged warriors to search for higher rules of conduct.

At first the code dealt mainly with loyalty and valor, both on and off the battlefield. By the thirteenth century, however, chivalry had grown considerably more complex. Every knight was supposed to pledge his service to a lady. He might also be expected to joust for his lady's favor or to rescue maidens in distress.

French poets known as troubadours popularized this tradition in songs of gallant knights. Originally these songs were written in Romance, or Roman-influenced, languages rather than Latin, and so they were called romances. At the French court, it became important for knights to treat ladies with a respect that bordered on reverence. Gradually the same ideal took root in the English court.

The Legend of King Arthur

One example illustrating the development of chivalry originated with the Celts. For centuries after their defeat by the Anglo-Saxons, the Celts had told stories of a great hero, King Arthur. Inasmuch as historians cannot say for certain whether Arthur actually lived or not, tales about him are considered legends, a blend of fiction and fact. When the Normans were battling the Anglo-Saxons, they became interested in the old Celtic legends. In about 1136, a Welsh-born scholar, Geoffrey of Monmouth (c. 1100–1154), drew upon his knowledge of Celtic legends and his readings of Bede to produce a *History of the Kings of Britain.* This fanciful history, though written in Latin, quickly popularized the early Celtic king.

Because of the Normans' French ties, the tales of Arthur spread not only in England but also in France. There they were influenced by other romances, often involving the French hero Charlemagne. New versions of the Arthur legend, though usually set in the past, began to depict Arthur as more modern in his practices. His Knights of the Round Table became paragons of chivalry, as adept in courtly love as they were in fighting battles. The legend also inspired *Sir Gawain and the Green Knight,* a fourteenth-century narrative poem by an anonymous author. In the poem an Arthurian knight, Sir Gawain, displays all the virtues of chivalry in his battles with the Green Knight, a supernatural figure.

SIR GALAHAD, 1864
Dante Gabriel Rossetti

Arthurian romance reached its height with *Morte d' Arthur (The Death of Arthur)*, a fifteenth-century prose work by Sir Thomas Malory (d. 1471). Translating from French sources, Malory created the most complete Middle English compilation of the various legends involving Arthur and his court. *Morte d' Arthur* was printed in twenty-one volumes.

Learning and Literature

Although the Normans and French eventually had great influence on English letters, that development did not begin in 1066. To the contrary, the Norman invasion put a temporary halt to scholarship and literature in the British Isles. After the turbulence of conquest subsided, however, England experienced a "little renaissance," a small rebirth of learning, in the twelfth century. Although monasteries continued their scholastic traditions, new centers of learning emerged. Scholars flocked to the religious community at Oxford to hear lectures by noted visitors; then colleges were built to house the scholars, and the first English university was born. A second university at Cambridge followed some years later.

Probably the most famous scholar that Oxford produced in the Middle Ages was Roger Bacon (c. 1214–1294), a scientist and mathematician now considered the father of English philosophy. A member of the Franciscan brotherhood, Bacon created his *Opus Majus* (Major Work), a Latin study of science, grammar, mathematics, and philosophy, at the request of the Pope. Later, however, the Church condemned Bacon as a heretic. The scholar died in obscurity, probably at Oxford, but his ideas were taken up a century later by another Franciscan, William of Ockham (d. 1349). Like Bacon, Ockham attempted to use a scientific approach in exploring the universe; he, too, was accused of heresy.

While Latin remained the language of Church and university scholarship, Norman French was frequently used in government. Both languages contributed to what came to be called Middle English. Latin literature gradually gave way to literature written in the vernacular, or the language of the people. The use of the vernacular increased after 1380, when John Wycliffe began directing the English translation of the Bible. Wycliffe's work proved a major advance for literature, inasmuch as it encouraged more people to learn to read.

Another important invention of the period, printing from movable type, also encouraged literacy. In 1454, a German silversmith, Johann Gutenberg, perfected a process with individual metal letters that could be used again and again. Printing spread rapidly from Germany to other parts of Europe, and further improvements were made. In 1476, a London merchant, William Caxton (c. 1422–1491) set up the first movable-type press in England. This invention meant that English literature no longer needed to be hand copied by church scribes. Now it could be produced far more quickly and made available to a much wider circle of readers.

Poetry of the English Middle Ages

One of Caxton's first projects was the printing of *The Canterbury Tales*. His enthusiasm for this verse showed the importance that he and others placed on poetry in general. Two key poets of the period, William Langland and Geoffrey Chaucer, lived during the Later Middle Ages. Their writings reveal the changes that were taking place in the English language and in society as a whole.

**JOHANN GUTENBERG EXAMINING THE
FIRST PROOF OF HIS PRINTED BIBLE**
After the painting by J.L.G. Ferris

Geoffrey Chaucer

The towering figure of Middle English verse is Geoffrey Chaucer. In many estimates, he ranks second only to Shakespeare as England's greatest writer. Chaucer owed much of his early sophistication to his training as an attendant to King Edward III. The poet also traveled widely and familiarized himself with important Italian poets, including Dante and Petrarch.

Chaucer's major works include a number of narrative poems, such as the verse romance *Troilus and Criseyde* (1372–1386) and several shorter poems. Yet his finest achievement was *The Canterbury Tales,* a series of verse stories told by different pilgrims on their way to the tomb of Thomas Becket. The pilgrims represent many walks of life—a knight, a squire, a clerk, a friar, a nun, a miller, a merchant, and so on. In Chaucer's deft hands, each storyteller emerges as a vivid personality in his or her own right. Some of the tales have religious themes; others are humorous or satiric. All in all, they provide a remarkable portrait of life in the Later Middle Ages.

Lyrics and Ballads

Europeans of the Middle Ages had a fondness for a harplike instrument called the lyre. In palaces and castles, poets often strummed lyres as they recited their verse. From this custom English lyric poetry developed.

Lyric poems of this period fall into two main categories, secular and religious. The usual topics of the secular poetry are love or nature; many of them celebrate the renewal of spring or the joys of summer:

> Summer is icumen in;
> Lhude° sing cuccu!   °Loudly

Religious lyrics might consist of a hymn praising God or a prayer of supplication. One of the most famous religious lyrics in Middle English celebrates the Virgin Mary:

> I syng of myden
>   That is makeles;°   °matchless
> Kyng of alle kynges
>   To here son che ches.°   °she chose

Another includes the Latin line *Timor mortis conturbat me* ("The fear of death disturbs me") to

William Langland

Scholars know very little about the poet they usually call William Langland. He appears to have come from western England and to have been a country boy. In his masterpiece, *Piers Plowman,* he followed a tradition of the Middle Ages by writing in the form of an allegory, a work in which most of the characters, settings, and events are arranged in a symbolical pattern. He also took a typically Anglo-Saxon delight in alliteration.

Like John Wycliffe, Langland was greatly concerned with the ways the wealthy oppress the poor. He left little doubt that his sympathies went out to those who had been treated harshly by the world. His most vivid writing concerned events he may have witnessed—tavern squabbles, for instance, or the misery of people suffering from the plague. Some scholars judge *Piers Plowman* to convey the deepest feelings of any poem in all of English literature.

teach the lesson that in the midst of life there is death:

> In what state that ever I be,
> > *Timor mortis conturbat me.*
> As I me walked in on° morning   °one
> I hard a birde both wepe and synge;
> This was the tenor of her talkynge:
> > *Timor mortis conturbat me.*

Another popular poetic form was the ballad, a folk song that told a story. Experts find most surviving ballads impossible to date. Those from the Scottish border probably arose long after the Middle Ages, and those from before 1485 have most likely changed a good deal over the centuries.

One surviving series of ballads concerns Robin Hood, a legendary hero who may have existed around the turn of the thirteenth century. Robin, an outlaw, lives in the woods with his band of "merrye" men, robbing from the rich and helping the poor. He and his lady friend, Maid Marian, eventually became part of traditional May Day festivities. These folk celebrations honoring the coming of spring took place each year on the first day of May.

Drama of the Middle Ages

The theater of William Shakespeare had its roots in the dramas of the Middle Ages. During early Norman times, the Church often sponsored plays as part of religious services. In time, these plays moved from the church to the churchyard and then to the marketplace. The earliest dramas were miracle plays, in England sometimes also called mystery plays. They retold stories from the Bible or dealt with some aspect of the lives of saints.

Over the years, the theater gained in popularity among English townspeople. Several communities became famous for performing a particular series of plays, or cycle, which presented a Biblical history of humankind. York, the religious capital of northern England, had one of the largest cycles. Chester and Wakefield also staged multi-play productions. Clergymen usually wrote the plays, and actors performed them on wagons or fixed scaffolds. Each of the town's craft guilds would take turns producing one play.

PAGE FROM THE LANSDOWNE MS. OF CHAUCER'S *CANTERBURY TALES*

During the turbulent years of the fifteenth century, a new kind of drama arose—the morality play. Morality plays depicted the life of an ordinary person, sometimes from birth to death. Along the way, the hero meets characters who symbolize abstract qualities, such as Vice or Virtue. The purpose of these allegorical dramas was to teach a moral lesson.

The most famous surviving morality play is *Everyman,* which had its origin in the Netherlands and was not adapted for English audiences until about 1500. By that time, Middle English was giving way to modern English, the form of the language we speak today. Even so, *Everyman* is usually studied as part of Middle English literature, for it is one of the most powerful examples of the kinds of morality plays performed in the Later Middle Ages.

Subsequent generations of writers owe a great debt to the literature of the English Middle Ages. In Chaucer, the era produced the first major writer in English to be known and respected for his craft. With works such as *Everyman,* the period produced the foundations of the great English dramatic tradition. In addition, the romantic adventures of King Arthur and his knights became a source to which future writers would turn again and again.

Quotations by Prominent Figures of the Period

Manners maketh man.
    William of Wykeham, Motto of two colleges at Oxford

It behooves us to place the foundations of knowledge in mathematics.
    Roger Bacon, *Opus Majus*

Who pulleth out this sword of this stone and anvil, is rightwise king born of all England.
    Sir Thomas Malory, *Morte d'Arthur*

In a somer seson whan soft was the sonne
Who will bell the cat?
    William Langland, *Piers Plowman*

A foule may ek° a wys-man often gide.°   °also   °guide
    Geoffrey Chaucer, *Troilus and Criseyde*

Looke who that is moost vertuous alway.
Pryvee° and apert, and most entendeth ay   °private, secret
To do the gentil dedes that he kan;
Tak him for the grettest gentil man.
    Geoffrey Chaucer, "The Wife of Bath's Tale," *The Canterbury Tales*

Pacience is an heigh vertu, certeyn.
    Geoffrey Chaucer, "The Franklin's Tale," *The Canterbury Tales*

When captains couragious, whom death could not daunte
Did march to the seige of the city of Gaunt,
They mustered their soldiers by two and by three
And the foremost in battle was Mary Ambree.
    Anonymous, "Mary Ambree"

Come listen to me, you gallants so free,
    All you that loves mirth to hear,
And I will you tell of a bold outlaw
    That lived in Nottinghamshire.
    Anonymous, "Robin Hood and Allen a Dale"

READING CRITICALLY

The Literature of 1066–1485

When you read literature, it is important to place it in historical context. Doing so will help you to understand influences on the writer's ideas and techniques.

HISTORICAL CONTEXT In 1066 the Normans conquered England by defeating the Anglo-Saxons at the Battle of Hastings. Although many Anglo-Saxon traditions and attitudes survived the invasion, the Normans dramatically changed English life by introducing a social, economic, and political system called feudalism. Under this system land was divided among noble overlords. Controlling large, self-sufficient feudal manors, the overlords were served by knights, who provided protection; and serfs, who farmed the land and herded animals. Although it was an ideal that few of them may have actually attained, the knights tried to live according to the code of chivalry, which required them to be honorable, courteous, brave, and skillful. Toward the later part of this period, guns were replacing swords, and the feudal order was being replaced by the aristocratic code.

LITERARY MOVEMENTS The concept of chivalry played an important role in shaping the literature of the Medieval Period. When chivalry was joined with such fantastic elements as giants, wizards, sorcerers, and dragons, the form of literature known as the romance was created. Filled with fantasy, adventure, and courtly love, romances were one of the most popular literary forms of the period. Apart from romantic literature, most of the literature of the period reflected the influence of religion. This influence is most noticeable in the two forms of drama that were popular during the period: mystery plays and morality plays.

WRITERS' TECHNIQUES Although the first printing press was established toward the end of the Medieval Period, much of the literature of the period was composed orally. Folk ballads were sung or recited by common people and passed down from generation to generation. These ballads, along with most other medieval literature, were written in verse and told a story. Toward the end of the period, however, a number of writers began to work in prose.

English and Scottish Folk Ballads

Long before most people in Britain could read or write, they were familiar with the stories told in ballads. A **ballad** is a narrative poem, usually brief, that is meant to be sung. When the writer is unknown, the ballad is called a **folk** ballad, or sometimes a **popular** or **traditional** ballad. Such ballads as "Barbara Allan" have been recited, chanted, or sung from their earliest appearance up to the present day.

No one knows when the first folk ballads appeared in Britain, but it was probably during the twelfth century. Because the ballads were unwritten, they were passed along orally for many centuries. Most of the earliest ballads we know date from about the fifteenth century. At that time no one paid much attention to them as literature. Not until 1765, with the publication of Bishop Thomas Percy's *Reliques of Ancient English Poetry,* did ballads come to be recognized as a fascinating part of Britain's literary heritage.

Sir Walter Scott, the author of *Ivanhoe,* was one of a number of famous writers whose interest in old ballads was sparked by Percy's *Reliques.* Scott often traveled to the Scottish-English border region to collect material on the subject. His *Minstrelsy of the Scottish Border,* published in 1803, is a pioneer work of scholarship on the background and variations of Scottish ballads.

The four ballads in this unit originated in the wild, rugged border country between England and Scotland. They were sung in the Scots dialect. As they were passed along from person to person, place to place, and generation to generation, these ballads acquired new words and new verses. There is no such thing as a standard version of a folk ballad, because every balladeer feels free to make alterations. Literally hundreds of versions of "Barbara Allan" have appeared in print.

Many ballads handed down to us in English have counterparts in other languages. This is because the incidents they describe are shared by much of European folklore. Both "Barbara Allan" and "The Twa Corbies" are found in other languages, for example, as is "Sir Patrick Spens," although not in its present form.

Folk ballads, with their familiar melodies, are truly songs of the people. Later writers, including Sir Walter Scott, produced literary ballads in imitation of the traditional ones. But few literary ballads have had the power of the old folk ballads to capture and hold the imagination.

Sir Patrick Spens; Get Up and Bar the Door; The Twa Corbies; Barbara Allan

Literary Forms

Folk Ballad. It is not surprising that folk ballads appeared on the rugged English-Scottish border. Folk ballads typically originated in areas in which a formal, written literature had yet to develop or where people's lives did not permit books and reading.

A folk ballad usually presents a single dramatic episode. It is told impersonally, through action and dialogue, with very little characterization, description, or motivation. The story seems to be simple and direct, yet because it often begins in the middle and lacks transitions, it can convey an air of mystery. Ballads deal with many subjects: adventure, love, jealousy, heroism, disaster, revenge. A few folk ballads are humorous.

Most ballads have quatrains, or four-line stanzas, in which the second and fourth lines rhyme. Often there are eight syllables in the first and third lines and six syllables in the second and fourth lines. Ballads frequently have a refrain—a regularly repeated phrase or line at the end of a stanza, or sometimes a separate repeated stanza. The general effect is musical, as you would expect in poems meant to be sung.

Focus

Most popular music has a brief life span. Songs from a few years ago tend to sound dated and sentimental to listeners today. Yet folk ballads have been sung for centuries and in some places are still performed for appreciative audiences. Why? What is it that can make a song so enduring? Write about the qualities that you think help a song become a long-lasting popular classic.

Primary Source

One of the most enduring modern ballads is "Taxi," Harry Chapin's haunting lament of lost love and opportunity. The story begins with the chance meeting between a down-and-out taxi driver and his seemingly successful former girlfriend:

> It was raining hard in 'Frisco.
> I needed one more fare to make my night.
> A lady up ahead waved to flag me down.
> She got in at the light.

"Through the too many miles and the too little smiles," the narrator remembers their dreams. By the end of the song, he realizes that neither he nor his former love is happy. What other modern ballads do you know that are meant to be sung?

Sir Patrick Spens

This version of "Sir Patrick Spens" is in the original Middle English.

The king sits in Dumferling[1] toune,
    Drinking the blude-reid wine:
"O whar will I get guid sailor,
    To sail this schip of mine?"

5 Up and spak an eldern knicht,
    Sat at the kings richt kne:
"Sir Patrick Spens is the best sailor,
    That sails upon the se."

The king has written a braid letter,
10   And signd it wi his hand,
And sent it to Sir Patrick Spens,
    Was walking on the sand.

The first line that Sir Patrick red,
    A loud lauch lauchèd he;
15 The next line that Sir Patrick red,
    The teir blinded his ee.

"O wha is this has don this deid,
    This ill deid don to me,
To send me out this time o' the yeir,
20   To sail upon the se!

"Mak hast, mak hast, my mirry men all
    Our guid schip sails the morne:"
"O say na sae, my master deir,
    For I feir a deadlie storme.

25 "Late, late yestreen I saw the new moone,
    Wi the auld moone in hir arme,
And I feir, I feir, my deir master,
    That we will cum to harme."

O our Scots nobles wer richt laith
30   To weet their cork-heild schoone,
Bot lang owre a' the play wer playd,
    Thair hats they swam aboone.

MEDIEVAL BARON DINING; FROM BREVIARIUM GRIMARI, 15TH CENTURY

---

1. Dumferling: A town in Scotland near Edinburgh.

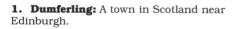

Sir Patrick Spens

This version of "Sir Patrick Spens" is in modern English.

The king sits in Dumferling town,
    Drinking the blood-red wine:
"O where will I get a good sailor,
    To sail this ship of mine?"

5 Up and spoke an ancient knight,
    Sat at the king's right knee:
"Sir Patrick Spens is the best sailor,
    That sails upon the sea."

The king has written a broad letter,
10   And signed it with his hand,
And sent it to Sir Patrick Spens,
    Was walking on the sand.

The first line that Sir Patrick read,
    A loud laugh laughed he;
15 The next line that Sir Patrick read,
    The tear blinded his eye.

"O who is this has done this deed,
    This ill deed done to me,
To send me out this time of the year,
20   To sail upon the sea!

"Make haste, make haste, my merry men all
    Our good ship sails the morn:"
"O say not so, my master dear,
    For I fear a deadly storm.

25 "Late, late yesterday evening I saw the new moon,
    With the old moon in her arm,
And I fear, I fear, my dear master,
    That we will come to harm."

O our Scots nobles were right loath
30   To wet their cork-heeled shoes,
But long before the play were played,
    Their hats they swam above.

O lang, lang may their ladies sit,
    Wi thair fans to their hand,
35 Or eir they se Sir Patrick Spens
    Cum sailing to the land.

O lang, lang may the ladies stand,
    Wi thair gold kems in their hair,
Waiting for thar ain deir lords,
40   For they'll se thame na mair.

Half owre, half owre to Aberdour,[1]
    It's fiftie fadom deip,
And thair lies guid Sir Patrick Spens,
    Wi the Scots lords at his feit.

---

1. Aberdour: A town near Edinburgh.

RESPONDING TO THE SELECTION

Your Response

1. How would you have responded to the king's request?

Recalling

2. What problem does the king face at the beginning of the ballad?
3. How does Sir Patrick Spens react to the king's letter?

Interpreting

4. Why do you think the king's wine is described as "blood-red"?
5. Why does Sir Patrick Spens view the king's request as an "ill deed"?
6. In the seventh stanza, why does the sailor think the voyage is ill-fated?
7. (a) What happens to the Scots lords who dislike the idea of getting their "cork-heeled shoes" wet? (b) How do you know? (c) How is this outcome ironic?
8. In what way does Sir Patrick Spens seem to embody medieval ideals of duty?

Applying

9. Sir Patrick Spens does his duty despite his serious—and well-founded—misgivings. What might he have done to avoid sailing? How wise would such a course of action have been?

ANALYZING LITERATURE

Understanding Folk Ballads

"Sir Patrick Spens," like most folk ballads, is short and deals with a single episode. Abrupt transitions and the absence of characterization and description force the audience to make assumptions about characters, places, and events. Dialogue moves the story along.

1. (a) How many characters are directly quoted in the poem? (b) Who are they?
2. What are some of the missing details in "Sir Patrick Spens" that, if included, would make the ballad easier to understand?

LEARNING OPTIONS

1. **Performance.** Like popular music, folk ballads were created to be performed before an audience. With a small group of classmates, plan a performance of "Sir Patrick Spens." Individual students can create music, play instruments, and sing various parts of the ballad. If you wish, make up additional stanzas to extend the story.

O long, long may their ladies sit,
    With their fans into their hand,
35 Or ever they see Sir Patrick Spens
        Come sailing to the land.

O long, long may the ladies stand,
    With their gold combs in their hair,
Waiting for their own dear lords,
40   For they'll see them no more.

Halfway over, halfway over to Aberdour,
    It's fifty fathoms deep
And there lies good Sir Patrick Spens,
    With the Scots lords at his feet.

---

2. **Language.** A current version of a centuries-old ballad like "Sir Patrick Spens" looks quite different from the way it looked when it first appeared in print. Not only is the old Scots dialect unfamiliar to most modern readers, so is much of the spelling and vocabulary of the standard English of that period. Write a brief note to the king from Sir Patrick Spens, explaining why an immediate sea voyage is not a good idea. Use Old English spellings from the ballad for at least a dozen words in your note.

MULTICULTURAL CONNECTION

Ballads Across the Oceans

How ballads were made. The word *ballad* comes from an Old French term meaning "to dance"; scholars used to think that ballads were created spontaneously during village festivals to accompany folk dancing. Historians now think that ballads were written by individuals, and then picked up and sung by musicians, bards, and other members of the community. They were particularly popular in the British Isles, Denmark, France, Germany, Greece, and Russia, as well as in Spain where they were known as "romances."

Ballads in different countries. Ballad forms vary from country to country. Most ballads are short, have repeating lines or refrains, and describe a single memorable situation or conflict. Ballads from England, Scandinavia, and Hungary have rhymed stanzas, whereas those of Russia and the Balkans do not. Spanish ballads have assonant rhyme—vowel sounds that are alike—and lines of sixteen syllables, divided in half by a rhythmic pause.

American ballads. Many American ballads recount the lives of everyday folk heros such as the outlaw Jesse James, the railroad engineer Casey Jones, and the doomed lovers Frankie and Johnny. American folk singers like Johnny Cash and Bob Dylan have continued the ballad tradition in many of their songs.

Exploring on Your Own

Find a ballad that you particularly like. Read it aloud in class, acting out the parts of the various characters.

Get Up
and Bar the Door

It fell about the Martinmas[1] time,
    And a gay time it was then,
When our goodwife got puddings to make,
    She's boild them in the pan.

5 The wind sae cauld blew south and north.
    And blew into the floor;
Quoth our goodman to our goodwife,
    "Gae out and bar the door."

"My hand is in my hussyfskap,[2]
10   Goodman, as ye may see;
An it should nae be barrd this hundred year,
    It's no be barrd for me."[3]

They made a paction[4] tween them twa.
    They made it firm and sure.
15 That the first word whaeer shoud speak,
    Shoud rise and bar the door.

Then by there came two gentlemen,
    At twelve o'clock at night,
And they could neither see house nor hall,
20   Nor coal nor candlelight.

"Now whether is this a rich man's house,
    Or whether it is a poor?"
But neer a word wad ane o' them[5] speak,
    For barring of the door.

25 And first they[6] ate the white puddings,
    And then they ate the black:
Tho muckle[7] thought the goodwife to hersel,
    Yet neer a word she spake.

Then said the one unto the other,
30   "Here, man, take ye my knife;
Do ye tak aff the auld man's beard,
    And I'll kiss the goodwife."

1. **Martinmas time:**
November 11.

2. **hussyfskap:** Household
duties.

3. **"it should . . . me":** It
will not be barred in a
hundred years if it has to
be barred by me."
4. **paction:** Agreement.

5. **them:** The man and
his wife.

6. **they:** The strangers.

7. **muckle:** Much.

"But there's nae water in the house,
    And what shall we do than?"
35 "What ails ye at the pudding broo,[8]
    That boils into[9] the pan?"

O up then started our goodman,
    An angry man was he:
"Will ye kiss my wife before my een,
40   And scad[10] me wi pudding bree?"[11]

Then up and started our goodwife,
    Gied three skips on the floor:
"Goodman, you've spoken the foremost word;
    Get up and bar the door."

8. "What . . . broo:
"What's the matter with
pudding water?
9. into: In.

10. scad: Scald.
11. bree: Broth.

▌R ESPONDING TO THE SELECTION

Your Response

1. What does this ballad say to you about male-female relationships?

Recalling

2. What agreement do the husband and wife reach about barring the door?
3. To whom does the word *one* refer in line 29?
4. What do the two strangers plan to do to (a) the goodman? (b) the goodwife?
5. (a) Who wins the battle of wills between husband and wife? (b) How?

Interpreting

6. Why does the goodman want the door barred?
7. When do the goodman and his wife first become aware of the presence of the strangers?
8. In lines 25–29 the goodwife is thinking to herself. What might she be thinking?
9. What do you think the stranger means when he suggests taking "aff the auld man's beard"?
10. What serious point does this humorous ballad make?

Applying

11. Can people be hurt by stubbornness—their own or someone else's? Explain your answer.

▌L EARNING OPTIONS

1. **Cross-curricular Connection.** Some holidays celebrated in England are unfamiliar to most Americans. One of them is Martinmas, a festival often mentioned in Middle English literature such as "Get Up and Bar the Door." Find out about the origin and celebration of Martinmas. Whom does it honor and why? How is the holiday celebrated? Be prepared to present your findings orally in class.
2. **Performance.** In a group of three, prepare and deliver a dramatic reading of this ballad. One student should read the part of the goodwife and one the part of the goodman. The third should serve as narrator, reading the remaining lines. Use appropriate inflection to convey the humor of the poem and the characters of the goodman and goodwife.

The Twa Corbies[1]

1. **Twa Corbies:** Two ravens.

As I was walking all alane,
I heard twa corbies making a mane.[2]
The tane unto the tither did say,
"Whar sall we gang and dine the day?"

2. **mane:** Moan.

5   "In behint yon auld fail dyke,[3]
I wot[4] there lies a new-slain knight;
And naebody kens[5] that he lies there
But his hawk, his hound, and his lady fair.

3. **fail dyke:** Bank of earth.
4. **wot:** know.
5. **kens:** knows.

"His hound is to the hunting gane,
10 His hawk to fetch the wild-fowl hame,
His lady's ta'en anither mate,
So we may mak our dinner sweet.

"Ye'll sit on his white hause-bane,[6]
And I'll pike out his bonny blue e'en;[7]
15 Wi' ae lock o' his gowden hair
We'll theek[8] our nest when it grows bare.

6. **hause-bane:** Neck-bone.
7. **e'en:** Eyes.

8. **theek:** Thatch.

"Mony a one for him maks mane,
But nane sall ken whar he is gane.
O'er his white banes, when they are bare,
20 The wind sall blaw for evermair."

R ESPONDING TO THE SELECTION

Your Response

1. What message about human life does this ballad express to you? Explain.

Recalling

2. (a) Where is the knight lying? (b) In what condition is he?
3. Who besides the ravens knows what has happened to the knight?
4. What does one of the ravens suggest doing with the knight's golden hair?

Interpreting

5. (a) How would you describe the tone of the ballad? (b) How does the tone add to the ballad's impact?
6. What effect would be lost if the incident were described by a human speaker rather than depicted as a conversation between two ravens?

Applying

7. Stories told from the point of view of an animal are unusual but by no means rare. Can you recall other stories that present the viewpoint of an animal?

Barbara Allan

It was in and about the Martinmas time,[1]
    When the green leaves were a-fallin';
That Sir John Graeme in the West Country
    Fell in love with Barbara Allan.

5 He sent his man down through the town
    To the place where she was dwellin':
"O haste and come to my master dear,
    Gin[2] ye be Barbara Allan."

O slowly, slowly rase[3] she up,
10   To the place where he was lyin',
And when she drew the curtain by:
    "Young man, I think you're dyin'."

"O it's I'm sick, and very, very sick,
    And 'tis a' for Barbara Allan."
15 "O the better for me ye sal[4] never be,
    Though your heart's blood were a-spillin'.

"O dinna ye mind,[5] young man," said she,
    "When ye the cups were fillin',
That ye made the healths gae round and round,
20   And slighted Barbara Allan?"

He turned his face unto the wall,
    And death with him was dealin':
"Adieu, adieu, my dear friends all,
    And be kind of Barbara Allan."

25 And slowly, slowly rase she up,
    And slowly, slowly left him;
And sighing said she could not stay,
    Since death of life had reft[6] him.

She had not gane a mile but twa,[7]
30   When she heard the dead-bell knellin',
And every jow[8] that the dead-bell ga'ed[9]
    It cried, "Woe to Barbara Allan!"

"O mother, mother, make my bed,
    O make it soft and narrow:
35 Since my love died for me today,
    I'll die for him tomorrow."

1. **Martinmas time:** November 11.

2. **gin:** If.

3. **rase:** Rose.

4. **sal:** Shall.

5. **dinna ye mind:** Don't you remember.

6. **reft:** Deprived.

7. **not . . . twa:** Gone but two miles.

8. **jow:** Stroke.
9. **ga'ed:** Made.

VERONICA VERONESE
Dante Gabriel Rossetti
Delaware Art Museum

Your Response

1. Do you find bittersweet songs like this one appealing? Why or why not?

Recalling

2. Why does Sir John Graeme want Barbara Allan to visit him?
3. According to Sir John, why is he "sick, and very, very sick"?
4. What reason does Barbara Allan give for acting unconcerned about his plight?
5. (a) When does Barbara Allan admit how she feels about Sir John? (b) How does she feel?

Interpreting

6. (a) At what point does the ballad make you critical of Barbara Allan? (b) When does it make you sympathize with her?
7. One critic thinks that Sir John acts "like a spineless lover who gave up the ghost without a struggle." How would you answer that criticism?

Applying

8. "Barbara Allan," like most ballads, leaves out things you might like to know. If you were adding a stanza to it (not necessarily at the end), what information would you include?

CRITICAL THINKING AND READING

Interpreting Symbols in Folk Ballads

Ballads are generally concise and direct, but sometimes their words and phrases function as symbols, thereby suggesting more than is immediately evident. A **symbol** is a word, person, or object that stands for something beyond itself. For example, the events in "Barbara Allan" (as well as in "Get Up and Bar the Door") occur "about the Martinmas time." Martinmas, a Christian festival on November 11 in honor of St. Martin, gradually came to symbolize both revelry and a warm break in the autumn weather. A balladeer, by making use of a well-understood symbol like Martinmas, could add meaning to a brief story without adding an excessive number of words.

1. The literal meaning of line 18, "When ye the cups were fillin'," is that Sir John was filling people's glasses with drinks. What is the symbolic meaning?
2. When Barbara Allan asks her mother to "make my bed . . . soft and narrow," in lines 33 and 34, what kind of "bed" is probably being symbolized?

THINKING AND WRITING

Writing About a Folk Ballad

Choose one of the four folk ballads you have read. Reread it until you are sure you understand it fully. Take notes. Write the first draft of a composition that explains the events in the ballad, noting any details that are implied but not directly stated. Point out the literary techniques—such as rhyme, dialogue, repetition—that heighten the dramatic effect of the ballad. Go over your first draft carefully, and make any changes needed. Then write the final draft.

LEARNING OPTION

Speaking and Listening. "Barbara Allan," sometimes called "Bawbie Allan," "Bonnie Barbara Allan," or a similar title, is one of the most widely recorded ballads in history. It was brought to America in the earliest days of settlement. Today there are many recorded American versions as well as many English and Scottish versions of the song.

As a class project, find at least three recorded versions of "Barbara Allan" and bring them to class. Play them all, noting the differences in wording from one recording to another. Explain which version you prefer and why.

GUIDE FOR INTERPRETING

1375[?]

Audiences in the Middle Ages enjoyed tales of adventure and fantasy featuring heroes and rogues, magicians and monsters. One of the finest of these medieval romances, *Sir Gawain and the Green Knight,* was written by an unknown bard who lived at the time of Chaucer. "Master Anonymous," as the *Gawain* poet has been called, tells an unforgettable tale about one of the legendary knights of King Arthur's Round Table.

Although the poet is unknown, the *Gawain* manuscript (of which the British Museum owns the only copy) suggests something of its creator's background. The poet probably lived in northwestern England, judging by the poem's dialect and by its old-fashioned alliterative verse, neither of which reflects the fashion in Chaucer's London. Nevertheless, the poet is familiar with life at court and, like Chaucer, may have been connected to an aristocratic household. The poet also seems to have read widely in Latin and French as well as in English.

Sir Gawain's plot elements date back many centuries. In ancient vegetation myths, beheading is a ritual death intended to ensure the return of spring and the growth of new crops. More in line with Sir Gawain's adventure, a ninth-century Irish narrative recounts a beheading contest as the supreme test of courage. Twelfth-century French romances tell a similar tale, whereas the temptations faced by young Gawain may owe something to early French stories.

Arthurian legends, popular throughout Europe, developed orally over a long period of time. Despite this lengthy tradition, *Sir Gawain* is an original and masterful work. Not only is it excitingly told, but the poet introduces a high degree of realism into the setting. Most medieval romances take place with Camelot shimmering in the bright days of spring or summer. This poem does not. Sir Gawain's adventures occur in the bleakness of winter, with the chill desolation a fitting backdrop to the hero's trials. Nor is the hero himself without fault, as he is in so many other tales of knights and ladies. Sir Gawain is admirable but not invulnerable, which lends psychological truth to this medieval story. As one critic put it, the hero "gains in human credibility what he loses in ideal perfection."

from Sir Gawain and the Green Knight

Literary Forms

Medieval Romance. From the twelfth to the fifteenth century, medieval romances were the popular literature of England. Based on the feudal ideal of chivalry and imbued with adventure, love, and the supernatural, medieval romances typically feature kings, knights, and damsels in distress. The earliest romances were always in verse, but later ones were sometimes in prose.

The enduring popularity of these tales of romance stems in part from their glamorous portrayal of castle life—the festivals, the feasts, the knights in armor, the courtly love. Medieval romances were for many generations the stock in trade of professional storytellers, some of whom were employed in noble households, while others made the rounds of modest inns and taverns. As literacy increased, the status of the minstrel declined, but the romances, preserved in written form, continue to have appeal even today.

Of all the medieval romances, the best known are those about King Arthur and his Knights of the Round Table. Arthur, who may have been a Welsh chieftain in the fifth or sixth century, is the central figure in early Arthurian romances. In later ones, King Arthur's knights, such as Sir Gawain and Sir Lancelot, assume the principal roles.

Focus

In a few sentences, comment on the following statement by Charles Kingsley, nineteenth-century English historian and writer: "Some say that the spirit of chivalry is past, that the spirit of romance is dead. The age of chivalry is never past, so long as there is a wrong left unredressed on earth."

Primary Source

Many authors have retold the Arthurian legend, perhaps the most spellbinding of all medieval romances. One of the most famous versions is T. H. White's *The Once and Future King.* Here, White describes some of the glories of the age:

> For there, under the window in Arthur's Gramarye, the sun's rays flamed from a hundred jewels of stained glass in monasteries and convents, or danced from the pinnacles of cathedrals and castles, which their builders had actually loved. . . . Think of the glass itself, with its five grand colors stained right through. It was rougher than ours, thicker, fitted in smaller pieces. . . . Picture the insides of those ancient churches, . . . insides blazing with color, plastered with frescoes in which all the figures stood on tiptoe, fluttering with tapestry or with brocades from Bagdad.

from Sir Gawain and the Green Knight

translated by Marie Borroff

The work begins at the start of a New Year's Eve feast at King Arthur's Court in Camelot. Before anyone has started eating, the festivities are interrupted by an immense green knight who suddenly appears at the hall door. The knight rides a green horse and is armed with a gigantic ax.

This horseman hurtles in, and the hall enters;
Riding to the high dais,[1] recked he no danger;
Not a greeting he gave as the guests he o'erlooked,
Nor wasted his words, but "Where is," he said,
5 "The captain of this crowd? Keenly I wish
To see that sire with sight, and to himself say my say."
      He swaggered all about
      To scan the host so gay;
      He halted, as if in doubt
10   Who in that hall held sway.

There were stares on all sides as the stranger spoke,
For much did they marvel what it might mean
That a horseman and a horse should have such a hue,
Grow green as the grass, and greener, it seemed.
15 Then green fused on gold more glorious by far.
All the onlookers eyed him, and edged nearer,
And awaited in wonder what he would do,
For many sights had they seen, but such a one never,
So that phantom and fairy the folk there deemed it,
20 Therefore chary[2] of answer was many a champion bold,
And stunned at his strong words stone-still they sat
In a swooning silence in the stately hall.
As all were slipped into sleep, so slackened their speech
  apace.
      Not all, I think, for dread,
25   But some of courteous grace
      Let him who was their head
      Be spokesman in that place.

Then Arthur before the high dais that entrance beholds,
And hailed him, as behooved, for he had no fear,

1. dais (dā' is) *n.*: Platform.

2. chary (cher' ē) *adj.*: Not giving freely.

FROM THE ROMANCE OF KING ARTHUR
AND HIS KNIGHTS OF THE ROUND TABLE
Arthur Rackham

30   And said "Fellow, in faith you have found fair welcome;
       The head of this hostelry Arthur am I;
       Leap lightly down, and linger, I pray,
       And the tale of your intent you shall tell us after."
       "Nay, so help me," said the other, "He that on high sits,
35   To tarry here any time, 'twas not mine errand;
       But as the praise of you, prince, is puffed up so high,
       And your court and your company are counted the best,
       Stoutest under steel-gear on steeds to ride,
       Worthiest of their works the wide world over,
40   And peerless to prove in passages of arms,
       And courtesy here is carried to its height,
       And so at this season I have sought you out.
       You may be certain by the branch that I bear in hand
       That I pass here in peace, and would part friends,
45   For had I come to this court on combat bent,
       I have a hauberk[3] at home, and a helm beside,
       A shield and a sharp spear, shining bright,
       And other weapons to wield, I ween well, to boot,
       But as I willed no war, I wore no metal.
50   But if you be so bold as all men believe,
       You will graciously grant the game that I ask by right."
           Arthur answer gave
           And said, "Sir courteous knight,
           If contest here you crave,
55   You shall not fail to fight."

       "Nay, to fight, in good faith, is far from my thought;
       There are about on these benches but beardless children,
       Were I here in full arms on a haughty[4] steed,
       For measured against mine, their might is puny.
60   And so I call in this court for a Christmas game,
       For 'tis Yule, and New Year, and many young bloods about;
       If any in this house such hardihood claims,
       Be so bold in his blood, his brain so wild,
       As stoutly to strike one stroke for another,
65   I shall give him as my gift this gisarme[5] noble,
       This ax, that is heavy enough, to handle as he likes,
       And I shall bide the first blow, as bare as I sit.
       If there be one so wilful my words to assay,
       Let him leap hither lightly, lay hold of this weapon;
70   I quitclaim it forever, keep it as his own,
       And I shall stand him a stroke, steady on this floor,
       So you grant me the guerdon to give him another, sans
         blame.[6]
           In a twelvemonth[7] and a day
           He shall have of me the same;
75   Now be it seen straightway
           Who dares take up the game."

3. hauberk (hô′ bərk) *n.*: Coat of armor.

4. haughty (hôt′ ē) *adj.*: Lofty.

5. gisarme (gi zärm′) *n.*: Battle-ax.

6. I . . . blame: I will stand firm while he strikes me with the ax provided that you reward me with the opportunity to do the same to him without being blamed for it.

7. twelvemonth: A year.

If he astonished them at first, stiller were then
All that household in hall, the high and the low;
The stranger on his green steed stirred in the saddle,
80 And roisterously his red eyes he rolled all about,
Bent his bristling brows, that were bright green,
Wagged his beard as he watched who would arise.
When the court kept its counsel he coughed aloud,
And cleared his throat coolly, the clearer to speak:
85 "What, is this Arthur's house," said that horseman then,
"Whose fame is so fair in far realms and wide?
Where is now your arrogance and your awesome deeds,
Your valor and your victories and your vaunting words?
Now are the revel and renown of the Round Table
90 Overwhelmed with a word of one man's speech,
For all cower and quake, and no cut felt!"
With this he laughs so loud that the lord grieved;
The blood for sheer shame shot to his face, and pride.
   With rage his face flushed red,
95   And so did all beside.
   Then the king as bold man bred
   Toward the stranger took a stride.

And said, "Sir, now we see you will say but folly,
Which whoso has sought, it suits that he find.
100 No guest here is aghast of your great words.
Give to me your gisarme, in God's own name,
And the boon you have begged shall straight be granted."
He leaps to him lightly, lays hold of his weapon;
The green fellow on foot fiercely alights.
105 Now has Arthur his ax, and the haft grips,
And sternly stirs it about, on striking bent.
The stranger before him stood there erect,
Higher than any in the house by a head and more;
With stern look as he stood, he stroked his beard,
110 And with undaunted countenance drew down his coat,
No more moved nor dismayed for his mighty dints
Than any bold man on bench had brought him a drink of
 wine.
   Gawain by Guenevere
   Toward the king doth now incline:
115   "I beseech, before all here,
   That this melee may be mine."

"Would you grant me the grace," said Gawain to the king,
"To be gone from this bench and stand by you there,
If I without discourtesy might quit this board,
120 And if my liege lady[8] misliked it not,
I would come to your counsel before your court noble.

8. liege (lēj) **lady:**
Guenevere, the wife of the
lord, Arthur, to whom
Gawain is bound to give
service and allegiance.

For I find it not fit, as in faith it is known,
When such a boon is begged before all these knights,
Though you be tempted thereto, to take it on yourself
125 While so bold men about upon benches sit,
That no host under heaven is hardier of will,
Nor better brothers-in-arms where battle is joined;
I am the weakest, well I know, and of wit feeblest;
And the loss of my life would be least of any;
130 That I have you for uncle is my only praise;
My body, but for your blood, is barren of worth;
And for that this folly befits not a king,
And 'tis I that have asked it, it ought to be mine,
And if my claim be not comely let all this court judge in
    sight."
135   The court assays the claim,
                And in counsel all unite
                To give Gawain the game
                And release the king outright.

Then the king called the knight to come to his side,
140 And he rose up readily, and reached him with speed,
Bows low to his lord, lays hold of the weapon,
And he releases it lightly, and lifts up his hand,
And gives him God's blessing, and graciously prays
That his heart and his hand may be hardy both.
145 "Keep, cousin," said the king, "what you cut with this day,
And if you rule it aright, then readily, I know,
You shall stand the stroke it will strike after."
Gawain goes to the guest with gisarme in hand,
And boldly he bides there, abashed not a whit.
150 Then hails he Sir Gawain, the horseman in green:
"Recount we our contract, ere you come further.
First I ask and adjure you, how you are called
That you tell me true, so that trust it I may."
"In good faith," said the good knight, "Gawain am I
155 Whose buffet befalls you,[9] whate'er betide after,   **9. Whose . . . you:** Whose
And at this time twelvemonth take from you another   blow you will receive.
With what weapon you will, and with no man else alive."
                The other nods assent:
                "Sir Gawain, as I may thrive,
160   I am wondrous well content
                That you this dint[10] shall drive."   **10. dint:** Blow.

"Sir Gawain," said the Green Knight, "By God, I rejoice
That your fist shall fetch this favor I seek,
And you have readily rehearsed, and in right terms,
165 Each clause of my covenant with the king your lord,

Save that you shall assure me, sir, upon oath,
That you shall seek me yourself, wheresoever you deem
My lodgings may lie, and look for such wages[11]
As you have offered me here before all this host."

11. wages: A blow.

170 "What is the way there?" said Gawain, "Where do you
   dwell?"
I heard never of your house, by Him that made me,
Nor I know you not, knight, your name nor your court.
But tell me truly thereof, and teach me your name,
And I shall fare forth to find you, so far as I may,
175 And this I say in good certain, and swear upon oath."
"That is enough in New Year, you need say no more,"
Said the knight in the green to Gawain the noble,
"If I tell you true, when I have taken your knock,
And if you handily have hit, you shall hear straightway
180 Of my house and my home and my own name;
Then follow in my footsteps by faithful accord.
And if I spend no speech, you shall speed the better:
You can feast with your friends, nor further trace my
   tracks.[12]

          Now hold your grim tool steady
185   And show us how it hacks."
          "Gladly, sir; all ready,"
          Says Gawain; he strokes the ax.

**12. If I tell
you . . . tracks** (lines
178–183): The Green
Knight tells Gawain that he
will let him know where he
lives after he has taken the
blow. If he is unable to
speak following the blow,
there will be no need for
Gawain to know.

The Green Knight upon ground girds him with care:
Bows a bit with his head, and bares his flesh:
190 His long lovely locks he laid over his crown,
Let the naked nape for the need be shown.
Gawain grips to his ax and gathers it aloft—
The left foot on the floor before him he set—
Brought it down deftly upon the bare neck,
195 That the shock of the sharp blow shivered the bones
And cut the flesh cleanly and clove it in twain,[13]
That the blade of bright steel bit into the ground.
The head was hewn off and fell to the floor;
Many found it at their feet, as forth it rolled;
200 The blood gushed from the body, bright on the green,
Yet fell not the fellow, nor faltered a whit,
But stoutly he starts forth upon stiff shanks,
And as all stood staring he stretched forth his hand,
Laid hold of his head and heaved it aloft,
205 Then goes to the green steed, grasps the bridle,
Steps into the stirrup, bestrides his mount,
And his head by the hair in his hand holds,
And as steady he sits in the stately saddle
As he had met with no mishap, nor missing were his head.

13. clove it in twain: Split
it in two.

210 His bulk about he haled,
  That fearsome body that bled;
  There were many in the court that quailed
  Before all his say was said.

  For the head in his hand he holds right up;
215 Toward the first on the dais directs he the face,
  And it lifted up its lids, and looked with wide eyes,
  And said as much with its mouth as now you may hear:
  "Sir Gawain, forget not to go as agreed,
  And cease not to seek till me, sir, you find,
220 As you promised in the presence of these proud knights.
  To the Green Chapel come, I charge you, to take
  Such a dint as you have dealt—you have well deserved
  That your neck should have a knock on New Year's morn.
  The Knight of the Green Chapel I am well-known to many,
225 Wherefore you cannot fail to find me at last;
  Therefore come, or be counted a recreant knight."
  With a roisterous rush he flings round the reins,
  Hurtles out at the hall door, his head in his hand,
  That the flint fire flew from the flashing hooves.
230 Which way he went, not one of them knew
  Nor whence he was come in the wide world so fair.
    The king and Gawain gay
    Make a game of the Green Knight there,
    Yet all who saw it say
235   'Twas a wonder past compare.

  Though high-born Arthur at heart had wonder,
  He let no sign be seen, but said aloud
  To the comely queen, with courteous speech,
  "Dear dame, on this day dismay you no whit;
240 Such crafts are becoming at Christmastide,
  Laughing at interludes, light songs and mirth,
  Amid dancing of damsels with doughty knights.
  Nevertheless of my meat now let me partake,
  For I have met with a marvel, I may not deny."
245 He glanced at Sir Gawain, and gaily he said,
  "Now, sir, hang up your ax, that has hewn enough,"
  And over the high dais it was hung on the wall
  That men in amazement might on it look,
  And tell in true terms the tale of the wonder.
250 Then they turned toward the table, those two together,
  The good king and Gawain, and made great feast,
  With all dainties double, dishes rare,
  With all manner of meat and minstrelsy both,
  Such happiness wholly had they that day in hold.

255   Now take care, Sir Gawain,
        That your courage wax not cold
        When you must turn again
        To your enterprise foretold.

The following November, Sir Gawain sets out to fulfill his promise to the Green Knight. For weeks he travels alone through the cold, threatening woods of North Wales. Then, after he prays for shelter, he comes upon a wondrous castle on Christmas Eve, where he is greeted warmly by the lord of the castle and his lady. Sir Gawain inquires about the location of the Green Chapel, and the lord assures him that it is nearby and promises to provide him with a guide to lead him there on New Year's Day. Before the lord and Sir Gawain retire for the night, they agree to exchange whatever they receive during the next three days. Sir Gawain keeps his pledge for the first two days, but on the third day he does not give the lord the magic green girdle that the lady gives him because she promises that the girdle will protect him from any harm. The next day, Gawain sets out for the Green Chapel. His guide urges him not to proceed, but Gawain refuses to take this advice. He feels that it would be dishonorable not to fulfill his pledge. He is determined to accept his fate; however, he does wear the magic green girdle that the lady had given him.

SIR GAWAIN AND THE GREEN KNIGHT
The Bodleian Library, Oxford

He puts his heels to his horse, and picks up the path;
260 Goes in beside a grove where the ground is steep,
Rides down the rough slope right to the valley;
And then he looked a little about him—the landscape was
    wild,
And not a soul to be seen, nor sign of a dwelling,
But high banks on either hand hemmed it about,
265 With many a ragged rock and rough-hewn crag;
The skies seemed scored by the scowling peaks.
Then he halted his horse, and hoved there a space,
And sought on every side for a sight of the Chapel,
But no such place appeared, which puzzled him sore,
270 Yet he saw some way off what seemed like a mound,
A hillock high and broad, hard by the water,
Where the stream fell in foam down the face of the steep
And bubbled as if it boiled on its bed below.
The knight urges his horse, and heads for the knoll;
275 Leaps lightly to earth; loops well the rein
Of his steed to a stout branch, and stations him there.
He strides straight to the mound, and strolls all about,
Much wondering what it was, but no whit the wiser;
It had a hole at one end, and on either side,
280 And was covered with coarse grass in clumps all without,
And hollow all within, like some old cave,
Or a crevice of an old crag—he could not discern aright.
          "Can this be the Chapel Green?
          Alack!" said the man, "Here might
285   The devil himself be seen
          Saying matins[14] at black midnight!"

"Now by heaven," said he, "it is bleak hereabouts;
This prayer house is hideous, half covered with grass!
Well may the grim man mantled in green
290 Hold here his orisons,[15] in hell's own style!
Now I feel it is the Fiend, in my five wits,
That has tempted me to this tryst,[16] to take my life;
This is a Chapel of mischance, may the mischief take it!
As accursed a country church as I came upon ever!"
295 With his helm on his head, his lance in his hand,
He stalks toward the steep wall of that strange house.
Then he heard, on the hill, behind a hard rock,
Beyond the brook, from the bank, a most barbarous din:
Lord! it clattered in the cliff fit to cleave it in two,
300 As one upon a grindstone ground a great scythe!
Lord! it whirred like a mill-wheel whirling about!
Lord! it echoed loud and long, lamentable to hear!
Then "By heaven," said the bold knight, "That business up
    there
Is arranged for my arrival, or else I am much misled.

14. matins *n.*: Morning prayers.

15. orisons *n.*: Prayers.

16. tryst (trist) *n.*: Meeting.

305   Let God work! Ah me!
                All hope of help has fled!
                Forfeit my life may be
                But noise I do not dread.''

Then he listened no longer, but loudly he called,
310   "Who has power in this place, high parley to hold?
For none greets Sir Gawain, or give him good day;
If any would a word with him, let him walk forth
And speak now or never, to speed his affairs.''
"Abide,'' said one on the bank above over his head,
315   "And what I promised you once shall straightway be
      given.''
Yet he stayed not his grindstone, nor stinted its noise,
But worked awhile at his whetting before he would rest,
And then he comes around a crag, from a cave in the rocks,
Hurtling out of hiding with a hateful weapon,
320   A Danish ax[17] devised for that day's deed,
With a broad blade and bright, bent in a curve,
Filed to a fine edge—four feet it measured
By the length of the lace that was looped round the haft.
And in form as at first, the fellow all green,
325   His lordly face and his legs, his locks and his beard,
Save that firm upon two feet forward he strides,
Sets a hand on the ax-head, the haft to the earth;
When he came to the cold stream, and cared not to wade,
He vaults over on his ax, and advances amain
330   On a broad bank of snow, overbearing and brisk of mood.
          Little did the knight incline
          When face to face they stood;
          Said the other man, "Friend mine,
          It seems your word holds good!''

335   "God love you, Sir Gawain!'' said the Green Knight then,
"And well met this morning, man, at my place!
And you have followed me faithfully and found me betimes,
And on the business between us we both are agreed:
Twelve months ago today you took what was yours,
340   And you at this New Year must yield me the same.
And we have met in these mountains, remote from all eyes:
There is none here to halt us or hinder our sport;
Unhasp your high helm, and have here your wages;
Make no more demur than I did myself
345   When you hacked off my head with one hard blow.''
"No, by God,'' said Sir Gawain, "that granted me life,
I shall grudge not the guerdon,[18] grim though it prove;
And you may lay on as you like till the last of my part be
      paid.''

17. Danish ax: A long-bladed ax.

18. guerdon: Reward.

350   He proffered, with good grace,
            His bare neck to the blade,
            And feigned a cheerful face:
            He scorned to seem afraid.

Then the grim man in green gathers his strength,
355 Heaves high the heavy ax to hit him the blow.
With all the force in his frame he fetches it aloft,
With a grimace as grim as he would grind him to bits;
Had the blow he bestowed been as big as he threatened,
A good knight and gallant had gone to his grave.
360 But Gawain at the great ax glanced up aside
As down it descended with death-dealing force,
And his shoulders shrank a little from the sharp iron.
Abruptly the brawny man breaks off the stroke,
And then reproved with proud words that prince among
    knights.
365 "You are not Gawain the glorious," the green man said,
"That never fell back on field in the face of the foe,
And now you flee for fear, and have felt no harm:
Such news of that knight I never heard yet!
I moved not a muscle when you made to strike,
370 Nor caviled at the cut in King Arthur's house;
My head fell to my feet, yet steadfast I stood,
And you, all unharmed, are wholly dismayed—
Wherefore the better man I, by all odds, must be."
          Said Gawain, "Strike once more;
375   I shall neither flinch nor flee;
          But if my head falls to the floor
          There is no mending me!"

"But go on, man, in God's name, and get to the point!
Deliver me my destiny, and do it out of hand,
380 For I shall stand to the stroke and stir not an inch
Till your ax has hit home—on my honor I swear it!"
"Have at thee then!" said the other, and heaves it aloft,
And glares down as grimly as he had gone mad.
He made a mighty feint, but marred not his hide;
385 Withdrew the ax adroitly before it did damage.
Gawain gave no ground, nor glanced up aside,
But stood still as a stone, or else a stout stump
That is held in hard earth by a hundred roots.
Then merrily does he mock him, the man all in green:
390 "So now you have your nerve again, I needs must strike;
Uphold the high knighthood that Arthur bestowed,
And keep your neck-bone clear, if this cut allows!"
Then was Gawain gripped with rage, and grimly he said.

"Why, thrash away, tyrant, I tire of your threats;
395 You make such a scene, you must frighten yourself."
Said the green fellow, "In faith, so fiercely you speak
That I shall finish this affair, nor further grace allow."
        He stands prepared to strike
        And scowls with both lip and brow;
400   No marvel if the man mislike
        Who can hope no rescue now.

He gathered up the grim ax and guided it well:
Let the barb at the blade's end brush the bare throat;
He hammered down hard, yet harmed him no whit
405 Save a scratch on one side, that severed the skin;
The end of the hooked edge entered the flesh,
And a little blood lightly leapt to the earth.
And when the man beheld his own blood bright on the
    snow,
He sprang a spear's length with feet spread wide,
410 Seized his high helm, and set it on his head,
Shoved before his shoulders the shield at his back,
Bares his trusty blade, and boldly he speaks—
Not since he was a babe born of his mother
Was he once in this world one half so blithe—
415 "Have done with your hacking—harry me no more!
I have borne, as behooved, one blow in this place;
If you make another move I shall meet it midway
And promptly, I promise you, pay back each blow with
    brand.
        One stroke acquits me here;
420   So did our covenant stand
        In Arthur's court last year—
        Wherefore, sir, hold your hand!"

He lowers the long ax and leans on it there,
Sets his arms on the head, the haft on the earth,
425 And beholds the bold knight that bides there afoot,
How he faces him fearless, fierce in full arms,
And plies him with proud words—it pleases him well.
Then once again gaily to Gawain he calls,
And in a loud voice and lusty, delivers these words:
430 "Bold fellow, on this field your anger forbear!
No man has made demands here in manner uncouth,
Nor done, save as duly determined at court.
I owed you a hit and you have it; be happy therewith!
The rest of my rights here I freely resign.
435 Had I been a bit busier, a buffet, perhaps,
I could have dealt more directly; and done you some harm.

First I flourished with a feint, in frolicsome mood,
And left your hide unhurt—and here I did well
By the fair terms we fixed on the first night;
440 And fully and faithfully you followed accord:
Gave over all your gains as a good man should.
A second feint, sir, I assigned for the morning
You kissed my comely wife—each kiss you restored.
For both of these there behooved but two feigned blows by
    right.
445   True men pay what they owe;
            No danger then in sight.
            You failed at the third throw,
            So take my tap, sir knight.

"For that is my belt about you, that same braided girdle,
450 My wife it was that wore it; I know well the tale,
And the count of your kisses and your conduct too,
And the wooing of my wife—it was all my scheme!
She made trial of a man most faultless by far
Of all that ever walked over the wide earth;
455 As pearls to white peas, more precious and prized,
So is Gawain, in good faith, to other gay knights.
Yet you lacked, sir, a little in loyalty there,
But the cause was not cunning, nor courtship either,
But that you loved your own life; the less, then, to blame."
460 The other stout knight in a study stood a long while,
So gripped with grim rage that his great heart shook.
All the blood of his body burned in his face
As he shrank back in shame from the man's sharp speech.
The first words that fell from the fair knight's lips:
465 "Accursed be a cowardly and covetous heart!
In you is villainy and vice, and virtue laid low!"
Then he grasps the green girdle and lets go the knot,
Hands it over in haste, and hotly he says:
"Behold there my falsehood, ill hap betide it!
470 Your cut taught me cowardice, care for my life,
And coveting came after, contrary both
To largesse and loyalty belonging to knights.
Now am I faulty and false, that fearful was ever
Of disloyalty and lies, bad luck to them both! and greed.
475   I confess, knight, in this place,
            Most dire is my misdeed;
            Let me gain back your good grace,
            And thereafter I shall take heed."

Then the other laughed aloud, and lightly he said,
480 "Such harm as I have had, I hold it quite healed.

GAWAIN RECEIVING THE GREEN GIRDLE
Woodcut by Fritz Kredel from Gardner
The Complete Works of the Gawain Poet, 1965
The University of Chicago

from *Sir Gawain and the Green Knight* **109**

You are so fully confessed, your failings made known,
And bear the plain penance of the point of my blade,
I hold you polished as a pearl, as pure and as bright
As you had lived free of fault since first you were born.
485 And I give you, sir, this girdle that is gold-hemmed
And green as my garments, that, Gawain, you may
Be mindful of this meeting when you mingle in throng
With nobles of renown—and known by this token
How it chanced at the Green Chapel, to chivalrous knights.
490 And you shall in this New Year come yet again
And we shall finish out our feast in my fair hall, with
    cheer.''

Commentary

Humorist Samuel Clemens took a lighter look at the King Arthur legend in his 1889 novel, *A Connecticut Yankee in King Arthur's Court.* A Hartford munitions maker, clunked on the head ''during a misunderstanding conducted with crowbars,'' wakes up to find himself in Camelot, England, in the year 513. ''The Boss,'' as he comes to be called, has opinions on everything. Here he discusses the proper medieval attire for following Sir Gawaine:

''I was to have an early breakfast, and start at dawn, for that was the usual way; but I had the demon's own time with my armor, and this delayed me a little. It is troublesome to get into, and there is so much detail. First you wrap a layer or two of blanket around your body, for a sort of cushion and to keep off the cold iron; then you put on your sleeves and a shirt of chain mail—these are made of small steel links woven together, and they form a fabric so flexible that if you toss your shirt onto the floor, it slumps into a pile like a peck of wet fishnet; it is very heavy and is nearly the most uncomfortablest material in the world for a nightshirt . . . then you put on your shoes—flat-boats roofed over the interleaving bands of steel . . . and you begin to feel crowded; then you hitch onto the breastplate the half-petticoat of broad overlapping bands of steel which hangs down in front but is scalloped out behind you so you can sit down, and isn't any real improvement on an inverted coalscuttle, either for looks or for wear, or to wipe your hands on; next you belt on your sword; then you put your stove-pipe joints onto your arms, your iron gauntlets onto your hands, your iron rat-trap onto your head . . . This is no time to dance. Well, a man that is packed away like that is a nut that isn't worth the cracking, there is so little of the meat, when you get down to it, by comparison to the shell.'' Imagine getting on the horse!

RESPONDING TO THE SELECTION

Your Response

1. Do you think King Arthur should have allowed Sir Gawain to accept the Green Knight's challenge? Why or why not?

Recalling

2. The Green Knight's challenge has two parts. (a) What is Sir Gawain to do immediately? (b) What is he to do a year later?
3. What does Sir Gawain do at the Green Chapel to cause the Green Knight to question his valor?
4. Why does the Green Knight only scratch Sir Gawain with his ax?

Interpreting

5. The Green Knight laughs at the members of the Round Table in line 92. Why?
6. When Sir Gawain sees the Green Chapel, who does he think the Green Knight may be?
7. In lines 465–477 why is Sir Gawain upset?

Applying

8. What modern occupation do you think comes closest to matching the duties and ideals of the Knights of the Round Table? Explain your answer.

ANALYZING LITERATURE

Understanding Medieval Romances

Most medieval romances:
- Embody the ideals of chivalry
- Are set in a remote time or place
- Emphasize rank and social distinctions
- Convey a sense of the supernatural
- Present a hero engaged in pure adventure
- Have a loose structure, lacking in unity
- Include love as a major plot element
- Feature spontaneous, unmotivated fighting.

1. Which of these characteristics does *Sir Gawain and the Green Knight* NOT display?

2. In medieval romances a hero seldom admits failure. Does Sir Gawain follow this tradition? Explain.

CRITICAL THINKING AND READING

Making Inferences About Chivalry

Human actions and motivations reflect the ideals of the society in which people live. Today a community leader might laugh off the kind of challenge the Green Knight hurls at King Arthur. You can infer from the way Arthur and Sir Gawain react, however, that in the age of chivalry one took seriously such challenges to one's courage.

1. What ideals of medieval society can you infer from Sir Gawain's offer to accept the challenge made to Arthur?
2. What ideals can you infer from Sir Gawain's distress at the end of the poem, even after he has withstood the blow of the ax?

THINKING AND WRITING

Evaluating the Medieval Romance

One of the world's most famous novels, *Don Quixote* by Miguel de Cervantes, satirizes medieval romances like *Sir Gawain and the Green Knight*. What aspects of the medieval romance do you think Cervantes may have felt deserved satire? Jot down your answers to this question, and then arrange them in a logical order for development in an essay. Write the essay. Make any revisions that seem necessary.

LEARNING OPTION

Cross-curricular Connection. Find a piece of instrumental music that you think accurately reflects a scene or setting in *Sir Gawain and the Green Knight*. The music you select should match the tone and mood of the writing. Play a recording of the music in class or, if possible, perform it yourself on a musical instrument.

GEOFFREY CHAUCER

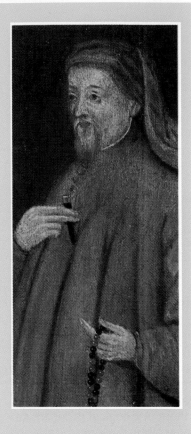

1343[?]–1400

In his own lifetime, Geoffrey Chaucer was considered the greatest English poet, and the centuries have not dimmed his reputation. With the single exception of William Shakespeare, no English writer has surpassed Chaucer's achievements. His unfinished masterpiece, *The Canterbury Tales,* ranks as one of the world's finest works of literature. It also provides the best contemporary picture we have of fourteenth-century England.

Although the exact date of Geoffrey Chaucer's birth is unknown, official records furnish many details of his active life as a public servant. His father was a well-to-do wine merchant in London, a man with sufficient influence to secure young Geoffrey a position as page in a household connected to that of King Edward III. As a page Chaucer's duties were humble, but the job provided him an opportunity to observe the ruling aristocracy, thus broadening his knowledge of the various classes of society. In 1359, while serving in the English army in France, he was captured and held prisoner. The king paid a £16 (sixteen pounds) ransom for his release. In 1366 Chaucer married a lady-in-waiting to the queen. His marriage to Philippa Pan lasted until her death in 1387. Scholars believe that Chaucer and his wife had three children. Their eldest, Thomas, was apparently ambitious and advanced higher in the world than his father had. Little is known about a son, probably called Lewis, and a daughter called Elizabeth.

Throughout his life Chaucer served in key government positions. He was a controller of customs, a justice of the peace, and a one-term member of Parliament. He spent time in France and Italy on diplomatic missions, served as a supervisor of construction and repairs at Westminster Abbey and the Tower of London, and late in life, acted as a subforester of the king's forest.

It might seem that Chaucer had little time for writing, but in fact he was able to produce a great deal. He began writing poetry in his twenties and continued to do so for the rest of his life. Moreover, as he grew older, his literary works showed increasing depth and sophistication. In *Troilus and Criseyde,* a long poem dealing with themes from classical antiquity, he displays the dramatic flair and penetrating insight into human character that are his hallmarks. *The Canterbury Tales,* of which only twenty-four of the projected 124 tales were completed, shows Chaucer's absolute mastery of the storyteller's art.

Chaucer was the first person to be buried in what is now the Poet's Corner of Westminster Abbey.

THE CANTERBURY TALES

People in medieval England sometimes made pilgrimages to sacred shrines. One such shrine was the cathedral in Canterbury, a town about fifty miles southeast of London, where archbishop Thomas à Becket had been murdered in 1170. The pilgrims often traveled in groups for companionship and protection. Chaucer's masterpiece, *The Canterbury Tales,* introduces a group of "nine and twenty" pilgrims, one of whom is Chaucer himself. These pilgrims appear first at the Tabard Inn in Southwark, near London, and later on the road to Canterbury.

The Canterbury Tales is a frame story; that is, a story that includes, or frames, another story or stories. Chaucer's frame is the pilgrimage, which he originally planned as a round trip but which remained incomplete at his death. Within this frame are the twenty-four individual stories the pilgrims tell. Chaucer did not invent the frame-story device. The same structural scheme had been used centuries earlier in *The Thousand and One Nights,* and Boccaccio, an Italian contemporary of Chaucer, used it in the *Decameron,* published about 1350.

Chaucer's handling of his pilgrimage frame is brilliant. The stories are mostly familiar ones, superbly retold. Perhaps even more impressive than the stories are the storytellers. Chaucer's pilgrims, all of whom are introduced briefly in his Prologue, are memorable, vividly drawn individuals whose personalities are unique but whose character traits are universal. The pilgrims interact with one another; clashes erupt among them as one pilgrim takes offense at another's tale and proceeds to retaliate with his or her own story.

By using the vehicle of the pilgrimage, Chaucer brings together people from the three main segments of medieval society—the church, the court, and the common people. His pilgrims are drawn from the class structure of feudalism (a knight, a squire, a reeve, for example) as well as from the more open classes in the emerging cities (a merchant, an innkeeper) and the powerful, hierarchical church of the time (a nun, a friar, a pardoner). Chaucer's interest in all these people and the shrewd but affectionate pictures he draws of them make them stand out in such distinct detail that they seem real, alive, and almost modern in their foibles and concerns.

Chaucer wrote only the "Tale of Melibeus" and the "Parson's Tale" in prose. With the exception of the "Monk's Tale," he told his story in either rhymed couplets or in stanzas of seven lines. His use of iambic pentameter couplets was a forerunner of the heroic couplets perfected in the 1700's by Alexander Pope.

GUIDE FOR INTERPRETING

The Prologue *from* The Canterbury Tales

Writers' Techniques

Characterization. Characterization refers to the personality of a fictional character as well as to the methods by which a writer creates that personality. Writers use a number of methods of characterization. Sometimes a writer makes a direct statement about a person: "Phil was hard to get to know, but those who knew him liked him." More often an author reveals character in an indirect way, through action, thoughts, and dialogue: "I should really study harder," Joan thought, laying the novel aside. "If I did, I could probably pass the test." Character can also be revealed through comments about the person by others in the story: "He's the kind of guy," said Linda, "who thinks football is the most important thing in life." A character's physical appearance and habits can help to reveal personality: "Doris wore the same threadbare dress she had worn to the party, but today she stood straighter, her shoulders squared." In defining a character, a writer will often combine these techniques to create a lifelike picture.

Focus

Jot down a few notes for a physical description of a fictional character. Choose a name for your character. Then note the following details: (1) facial features, (2) typical expression, (3) body structure, (4) typical posture, (5) clothing, (6) physical surroundings. Try to list details that not only describe the character but help to reveal personality.

Primary Source

What was it like to live during the Middle Ages? In *The Life and Times of Chaucer,* the contemporary writer John Gardner creates a vivid picture.

> But in small things, too, we might be bothered, at least at first, by life in the Middle Ages—for instance, by Chaucer's annoying habit (or any other well-educated man's) of always reading to himself aloud, never silently, "barking on books," as one fifteenth-century playwright puts it; or, to speak of things less petty, we might be bothered by the general manners of the better class of people in the fourteenth century. They ate with their fingers, except for the occasional employment of a knife or soup spoon, and even the fingers of courtly ladies were not impeccably clean.

The Prologue

Geoffrey Chaucer
translated by Nevill Coghill

   Whan that Aprill with his shourës sootë
The droghte of March hath percëd to the rootë
And bathëd every veyne in swich licour
Of which vertu engendrëd is the flour,
5 Whan Zephirus eek with his sweetë breeth
Inspirëd hath in every holt and heeth
The tendrë croppës, and the yongë sonnë
Hath in the Ram his half cours y-ronnë,
And smalë fowelës maken melodyë
10 That slepen al the nyght with open eye,
So priketh hem Nature in hir corages,
Than longen folk to goon on pilgrymages,
And palmeres for to seken straungë strondës,
To fernë halwës kouthe in sondry londës.
15 And specially, from every shirës endë
Of Engelond, to Caunterbury they wendë,
The holy, blisful martir for to seke
That hem hath holpen whan that they were seekë.

   When in April the sweet showers fall
And pierce the drought of March to the root, and all
The veins are bathed in liquor of such power
As brings about the engendering of the flower,
5 When also Zephyrus[1] with his sweet breath
Exhales an air in every grove and heath
Upon tender shoots, and the young sun
His half-course in the sign of the Ram[2] has run,
And the small fowl are making melody
10 That sleep away the night with open eye
(So nature pricks them and their heart engages)
Then people long to go on pilgrimages
And palmers[3] long to seek the stranger strands[4]
Of far-off saints, hallowed in sundry lands,
15 And specially, from every shire's end
In England, down to Canterbury they wend
To seek the holy blissful martyr,[5] quick
To give his help to them when they were sick.

1. Zephyrus (zef′ ər əs):
The west wind.

2. Ram: Aries, the first
sign of the zodiac. The
pilgrimage began on April
11, 1387.

3. palmers: Pilgrims who
wore two crossed palm
leaves to show that they
had visited the Holy Land.

4. strands: Shores.

5. martyr: St. Thomas à
Becket, the Archbishop of
Canterbury, who was
murdered in the
Canterbury Cathedral in
1170.

THE TABARD INN
Arthur Szyk for the Canterbury Tales

It happened in that season that one day
20 In Southwark[6], at The Tabard,[7] as I lay
Ready to go on pilgrimage and start
For Canterbury, most devout at heart,
At night there came into that hostelry
Some nine and twenty in a company
25 Of sundry folk happening then to fall
In fellowship, and they were pilgrims all
That towards Canterbury meant to ride.

6. Southwark (suth′ ərk):
A suburb of London at the time.
7. The Tabard (ta′ bərd):
An inn.

The rooms and stables of the inn were wide;
They made us easy, all was of the best.

30 And shortly, when the sun had gone to rest,
By speaking to them all upon the trip
I soon was one of them in fellowship
And promised to rise early and take the way
To Canterbury, as you heard me say.

35   But nonetheless, while I have time and space,
Before my story takes a further pace,
It seems a reasonable thing to say
What their condition was, the full array
Of each of them, as it appeared to me

40 According to profession and degree,
And what apparel they were riding in;
And at a Knight I therefore will begin.
There was a *Knight,* a most distinguished man,
Who from the day on which he first began

45 To ride abroad had followed chivalry,
Truth, honor, generousness and courtesy.
He had done nobly in his sovereign's war
And ridden into battle, no man more,
As well in Christian as heathen places,

50 And ever honored for his noble graces.
When we took Alexandria,[8] he was there.
He often sat at table in the chair
Of honor, above all nations, when in Prussia.
In Lithuania he had ridden, and Russia,

55 No Christian man so often, of his rank.
When, in Granada, Algeciras sank
Under assault, he had been there, and in
North Africa, raiding Benamarin;
In Anatolia he had been as well

60 And fought when Ayas and Attalia fell,
For all along the Mediterranean coast
He had embarked with many a noble host.
In fifteen mortal battles he had been
And jousted for our faith at Tramissene

65 Thrice in the lists, and always killed his man.
This same distinguished knight had led the van
Once with the Bey of Balat, doing work
For him against another heathen Turk;
He was of sovereign value in all eyes.

70 And though so much distinguished, he was wise
And in his bearing modest as a maid.
He never yet a boorish thing had said
In all his life to any, come what might;
He was a true, a perfect gentle-knight.

8. Alexandria: The site of one of the campaigns fought by Christians against groups who posed a threat to Europe during the fourteenth century. The place names that follow refer to other battlesites in these campaigns, or crusades.

75   Speaking of his equipment, he possessed
        Fine horses, but he was not gaily dressed.
        He wore a fustian[9] tunic stained and dark
        With smudges where his armor had left mark;
        Just home from service, he had joined our ranks
80   To do his pilgrimage and render thanks.
            He had his son with him, a fine young *Squire,*
        A lover and cadet, a lad of fire
        With locks as curly as if they had been pressed.
        He was some twenty years of age, I guessed.
85   In stature he was of a moderate length,
        With wonderful agility and strength.
        He'd seen some service with the cavalry
        In Flanders and Artois and Picardy[10]
        And had done valiantly in little space
90   Of time, in hope to win his lady's grace.
        He was embroidered like a meadow bright
        And full of freshest flowers, red and white.
        Singing he was, or fluting all the day;
        He was as fresh as is the month of May.
95   Short was his gown, the sleeves were long and wide;
        He knew the way to sit a horse and ride.
        He could make songs and poems and recite,
        Knew how to joust and dance, to draw and write.
        He loved so hotly that till dawn grew pale
100   He slept as little as a nightingale.
        Courteous he was, lowly and serviceable,
        And carved to serve his father at the table.
            There was a *Yeoman*[11] with him at his side,
        No other servant; so he chose to ride.
105   This Yeoman wore a coat and hood of green,
        And peacock-feathered arrows, bright and keen
        And neatly sheathed, hung at his belt the while
        —For he could dress his gear in yeoman style,
        His arrows never drooped their feathers low—
110   And in his hand he bore a mighty bow.
        His head was like a nut, his face was brown.
        He knew the whole of woodcraft up and down.
        A saucy brace[12] was on his arm to ward
        It from the bow-string, and a shield and sword
115   Hung at one side, and at the other slipped
        A jaunty dirk,[13] spear-sharp and well-equipped.
        A medal of St. Christopher[14] he wore
        Of shining silver on his breast, and bore
        A hunting-horn, well slung and burnished clean,
120   That dangled from a baldric[15] of bright green.
        He was a proper forester I guess.

9. fustian (fus' chən): A coarse cloth of cotton and linen.

10. Flanders . . . Picardy: Regions in Belgium and France.

11. *Yeoman* (yō' mən) *n.*: Attendant.

12. brace: Bracelet.

13. dirk *n.*: A short, straight dagger.
14. St. Christopher: The patron saint of forests and travelers.
15. baldric *n.*: A belt worn over one shoulder and across the chest to support a sword.

There also was a *Nun*, a Prioress.[16]
Her way of smiling very simple and coy.
Her greatest oath was only "By St. Loy!"[17]
125 And she was known as Madam Eglantyne.
And well she sang a service,[18] with a fine
Intoning through her nose, as was most seemly,
And she spoke daintily in French, extremely,
After the school of Stratford-atte-Bowe;[19]
130 French in the Paris style she did not know.
At meat her manners were well taught withal;
No morsel from her lips did she let fall,
Nor dipped her fingers in the sauce too deep;
But she could carry a morsel up and keep
135 The smallest drop from falling on her breast.
For courtliness she had a special zest,
And she would wipe her upper lip so clean
That not a trace of grease was to be seen
Upon the cup when she had drunk; to eat,
140 She reached a hand sedately for the meat.
She certainly was very entertaining,
Pleasant and friendly in her ways, and straining
To counterfeit a courtly kind of grace,
A stately bearing fitting to her place,
145 And to seem dignified in all her dealings.
As for her sympathies and tender feelings,
She was so charitably solicitous
She used to weep if she but saw a mouse
Caught in a trap, if it were dead or bleeding.
150 And she had little dogs she would be feeding
With roasted flesh, or milk, or fine white bread.
And bitterly she wept if one were dead
Or someone took a stick and made it smart;
She was all sentiment and tender heart.
155 Her veil was gathered in a seemly way,
Her nose was elegant, her eyes glass-gray;
Her mouth was very small, but soft and red,
Her forehead, certainly, was fair of spread,
Almost a span[20] across the brows, I own;
160 She was indeed by no means undergrown.
Her cloak, I noticed, had a graceful charm.
She wore a coral trinket on her arm,
A set of beads, the gaudies[21] tricked in green,
Whence hung a golden brooch of brightest sheen
165 On which there first was graven a crowned A,
And lower, *Amor vincit omnia.*[22]
 Another *Nun*, the chaplain at her cell,
Was riding with her, and *three Priests* as well.

16. Prioress *n.*: In an abbey, the nun ranking just below the abbess.
17. St. Loy: St. Eligius, patron saint of goldsmiths and courtiers.
18. service: Daily prayer.

19. Stratford-atte-Bowe: A nunnery near London.

THE YEOMAN
Arthur Szyk for the Canterbury Tales

20. span: Nine inches.

21. gaudies: Large green beads that marked certain prayers on a set of prayer beads.
22. *Amor vincit omnia* (ä môr′ wink′ it ôm′ nē ä): "Love conquers all" (Latin).

A *Monk* there was, one of the finest sort
170 Who rode the country; hunting was his sport.
A manly man, to be an Abbot able;
Many a dainty horse he had in stable.
His bridle, when he rode, a man might hear
Jingling in a whistling wind as clear,
175 Aye, and as loud as does the chapel bell
Where my lord Monk was Prior of the cell.
The Rule of good St. Benet or St. Maur[23]
As old and strict he tended to ignore;
He let go by the things of yesterday
180 And took the modern world's more spacious way.
He did not rate that text at a plucked hen
Which says that hunters are not holy men
And that a monk uncloistered is a mere
Fish out of water, flapping on the pier,
185 That is to say a monk out of his cloister.
That was a text he held not worth an oyster;
And I agreed and said his views were sound;
Was he to study till his head went round
Poring over books in cloisters? Must he toil
190 As Austin[24] bade and till the very soil?
Was he to leave the world upon the shelf?
Let Austin have his labor to himself.
      This Monk was therefore a good man to horse;
Greyhounds he had, as swift as birds, to course.
195 Hunting a hare or riding at a fence
Was all his fun, he spared for no expense.
I saw his sleeves were garnished at the hand
With fine gray fur, the finest in the land,
And on his hood, to fasten it at his chin
200 He had a wrought-gold cunningly fashioned pin;
Into a lover's knot it seemed to pass.
His head was bald and shone like looking-glass;
So did his face, as if it had been greased.
He was a fat and personable priest;
205 His prominent eyeballs never seemed to settle.
They glittered like the flames beneath a kettle;
Supple his boots, his horse in fine condition.
He was a prelate fit for exhibition,
He was not pale like a tormented soul.
210 He liked a fat swan best, and roasted whole.
His palfrey[25] was as brown as is a berry.
      There was a *Friar*, a wanton[26] one and merry,
A Limiter,[27] a very festive fellow.
In all Four Orders[28] there was none so mellow
215 So glib with gallant phrase and well-turned speech.

23. St. Benet or St. Maur: St. Benedict, author of monastic rules, and St. Maurice, one of his followers. Benet and Maur are French versions of Benedict and Maurice.

24. Austin: English version of St. Augustine, who criticized lazy monks.

25. palfrey: Saddle horse.
26. wanton: Jolly.
27. Limiter: A friar who is given begging rights for a certain limited area.
28. Four Orders: There were four orders of friars who supported themselves by begging: Dominicans, Franciscans, Carmelites, and Augustinians.

THE MONK
Arthur Szyk for the Canterbury Tales

He'd fixed up many a marriage, giving each
Of his young women what he could afford her.
He was a noble pillar to his Order.
Highly beloved and intimate was he
220 With County folk within his boundary,
And city dames of honor and possessions;
For he was qualified to hear confessions,
Or so he said, with more than priestly scope;
He had a special license from the Pope.
225 Sweetly he heard his penitents at shrift[29]
With pleasant absolution, for a gift.
He was an easy man in penance-giving
Where he could hope to make a decent living;
It's a sure sign whenever gifts are given
230 To a poor Order that a man's well shriven,[30]
And should he give enough he knew in verity
The penitent repented in sincerity.
For many a fellow is so hard of heart
He cannot weep, for all his inward smart.
235 Therefore instead of weeping and of prayer
One should give silver for a poor Friar's care.
He kept his tippet[31] stuffed with pins for curls,
And pocket-knives, to give to pretty girls.
And certainly his voice was gay and sturdy,
240 For he sang well and played the hurdy-gurdy.[32]
At sing-songs he was champion of the hour.
His neck was whiter than a lily-flower
But strong enough to butt a bruiser down.
He knew the taverns well in every town
245 And every innkeeper and barmaid too
Better than lepers, beggars and that crew,
For in so eminent a man as he
It was not fitting with the dignity
Of his position, dealing with a scum
250 Of wretched lepers; nothing good can come
Of dealings with the slum-and-gutter dwellers,
But only with the rich and victual-sellers.
But anywhere a profit might accrue
Courteous he was and lowly of service too.
255 Natural gifts like his were hard to match.
He was the finest beggar of his batch,
And, for his begging-district, payed a rent;
His brethren did no poaching where he went.
For though a widow mightn't have a shoe,
260 So pleasant was his holy how-d'ye-do
He got his farthing from her just the same
Before he left, and so his income came

29. shrift: Confession.

30. well shriven: Absolved of his sins.

31. tippet: Hood.

32. hurdy-gurdy: A stringed instument played by cranking a wheel.

To more than he laid out. And how he romped,
Just like a puppy! He was ever prompt
265   To arbitrate disputes on settling days
(For a small fee) in many helpful ways,
Not then appearing as your cloistered scholar
With threadbare habit hardly worth a dollar,
But much more like a Doctor or a Pope.
270   Of double-worsted was the semi-cope[33]
Upon his shoulders, and the swelling fold
About him, like a bell about its mold
When it is casting, rounded out his dress.
He lisped a little out of wantonness
275   To make his English sweet upon his tongue.
When he had played his harp, or having sung,
His eyes would twinkle in his head as bright
As any star upon a frosty night.
This worthy's name was Hubert, it appeared.
280   There was a *Merchant* with a forking beard
And motley dress; high on his horse he sat,
Upon his head a Flemish[34] beaver hat
And on his feet daintily buckled boots.
He told of his opinions and pursuits
285   In solemn tones, and how he never lost.
The sea should be kept free at any cost
(He thought) upon the Harwich-Holland range,[35]
He was expert at currency exchange.
This estimable Merchant so had set
290   His wits to work, none knew he was in debt,
He was so stately in negotiation,
Loan, bargain and commercial obligation.
He was an excellent fellow all the same;
To tell the truth I do not know his name.
295   An *Oxford Cleric*, still a student though,
One who had taken logic long ago,
Was there; his horse was thinner than a rake,
And he was not too fat, I undertake,
But had a hollow look, a sober stare;
300   The thread upon his overcoat was bare.
He had found no preferment in the church
And he was too unworldly to make search
For secular employment. By his bed
He preferred having twenty books in red
305   And black, of Aristotle's[36] philosophy,
To having fine clothes, fiddle or psaltery.[37]
Though a philosopher, as I have told,
He had not found the stone for making gold.[38]
Whatever money from his friends he took

33. semi-cope: Cape.

34. Flemish: From Flanders.

35. Harwich-Holland range: The North Sea between England and Holland.

36. Aristotle's (ar′ is tot′ əlz): Referring to the Greek philosopher (384–322 B.C.).

37. psaltery (sôl′ tər ē): An ancient stringed instrument.

38. stone . . . gold: At the time alchemists believed that a "philosopher's stone" existed that could turn base metals into gold.

THE STUDENT
Arthur Szyk for the Canterbury Tales

310   He spent on learning or another book
       And prayed for them most earnestly, returning
       Thanks to them thus for paying for his learning.
       His only care was study, and indeed
       He never spoke a word more than was need,
315   Formal at that, respectful in the extreme,
       Short, to the point, and lofty in his theme.
       The thought of moral virtue filled his speech
       And he would gladly learn, and gladly teach.
           A *Sergeant at the Law* who paid his calls,
320   Wary and wise, for clients at St. Paul's[39]
       There also was, of noted excellence.
       Discreet he was, a man to reverence,
       Or so he seemed, his sayings were so wise.
       He often had been Justice of Assize
325   By letters patent, and in full commission.
       His fame and learning and his high position
       Had won him many a robe and many a fee.
       There was no such conveyancer[40] as he;
       All was fee-simple[41] to his strong digestion,
330   Not one conveyance could be called in question.
       Nowhere there was so busy a man as he;
       But was less busy than he seemed to be.
       He knew of every judgment, case and crime
       Recorded, ever since King William's time.
335   He could dictate defenses or draft deeds;
       No one could pinch a comma from his screeds,
       And he knew every statute off by rote.
       He wore a homely parti-colored coat
       Girt with a silken belt of pin-stripe stuff;
340   Of his appearance I have said enough.
           There was a *Franklin*[42] with him, it appeared;
       White as a daisy-petal was his beard.
       A sanguine man, high-colored and benign,
       He loved a morning sop[43] of cake in wine.
345   He lived for pleasure and had always done,
       For he was Epicurus'[44] very son,
       In whose opinion sensual delight
       Was the one true felicity in sight.
       As noted as St. Julian[45] was for bounty
350   He made his household free to all the County.
       His bread, his ale were the finest of the fine
       And no one had a better stock of wine.
       His house was never short of bake-meat pies,
       Of fish and flesh, and these in such supplies
355   It positively snowed with meat and drink
       And all the dainties that a man could think.

39. St. Paul's: A London cathedral near which lawyers often met to discuss their cases.

40. conveyancer: One who draws up documents for transferring ownership of property.

41. fee-simple: Restricted ownership.

42. *Franklin:* Wealthy landowner.

43. sop: Piece.

44. Epicurus' (ep' i kyoor' əs): Referring to a Greek philosopher (342?–370 B.C.) who believed that happiness is the most important goal in life.

45. St. Julian: Patron saint of hospitality.

According to the seasons of the year
Changes of dish were ordered to appear.
He kept fat partridges in coops, beyond,
360 Many a bream and pike were in his pond.
Woe to the cook whose sauces had no sting
Or who was unprepared in anything!
And in his hall a table stood arrayed
And ready all day long, with places laid.
365 As Justice at the Sessions[46] none stood higher;
He often had been Member for the Shire.[47]
A dagger and a little purse of silk
Hung at his girdle, white as morning milk.
As Sheriff he checked audit, every entry.
370 He was a model among landed gentry.

A *Haberdasher*, a *Dyer*, a *Carpenter*,
A *Weaver* and a *Carpet-maker* were
Among our ranks, all in the livery
Of one impressive guild-fraternity.
375 They were so trim and fresh their gear would pass
For new. Their knives were not tricked out with brass
But wrought with purest silver, which avouches
A like display on girdles and on pouches.
Each seemed a worthy burgess,[48] fit to grace
380 A guild-hall with a seat upon the dais.
Their wisdom would have justified a plan
To make each one of them an alderman;
They had the capital and revenue,
Besides their wives declared it was their due.
385 And if they did not think so, then they ought;
To be called "*Madam*" is a glorious thought,
And so is going to church and being seen
Having your mantle carried like a queen.

They had a *Cook* with them who stood alone
390 For boiling chicken with a marrow-bone,
Sharp flavoring-powder and a spice for savor.
He could distinguish London ale by flavor,
And he could roast and seethe and broil and fry,
Make good thick soup and bake a tasty pie.
395 But what a pity—so it seemed to me,
That he should have an ulcer on his knee.
As for blancmange,[49] he made it with the best.

There was a *Skipper* hailing from far west;
He came from Dartmouth, so I understood.
400 He rode a farmer's horse as best he could,
In a woolen gown that reached his knee.
A dagger on a lanyard[50] falling free
Hung from his neck under his arm and down.
The summer heat had tanned his color brown,

46. Sessions: Court sessions.
47. Member . . . Shire: Parliamentary representative for the county.

48. burgess: A member of a legislative body.

49. blancmange (blə mänj'): At the time, a creamy chicken dish.

50. lanyard: A loose rope around the neck.

405 And certainly he was an excellent fellow.
 Many a draught of vintage, red and yellow,
 He'd drawn at Bordeaux, while the trader snored.
 The nicer rules of conscience he ignored.
 If, when he fought, the enemy vessel sank,
410 He sent his prisoners home; they walked the plank.
 As for his skill in reckoning his tides,
 Currents and many another risk besides,
 Moons, harbors, pilots, he had such dispatch
 That none from Hull to Carthage was his match.
415 Hardy he was, prudent in undertaking;
 His beard in many a tempest had its shaking,
 And he knew all the havens as they were
 From Gottland to the Cape of Finisterre,
 And every creek in Brittany and Spain;
420 The barge he owned was called *The Maudelayne.*
　　 A *Doctor* too emerged as we proceeded;
 No one alive could talk as well as he did
 On points of medicine and of surgery,
 For, being grounded in astronomy,
425 He watched his patient's favorable star
 And, by his Natural Magic, knew what are
 The lucky hours and planetary degrees
 For making charms and magic effigies.
 The cause of every malady you'd got
430 He knew, and whether dry, cold, moist or hot;[51]
 He knew their seat, their humor and condition.
 He was a perfect practicing physician.
 These causes being known for what they were,
 He gave the man his medicine then and there.
435 All his apothecaries[52] in a tribe
 Were ready with the drugs he would prescribe,
 And each made money from the other's guile;
 They had been friendly for a goodish while.
 He was well-versed in Esculapius[53] too
440 And what Hippocrates and Rufus knew
 And Dioscorides, now dead and gone,
 Galen and Rhazes, Hali, Serapion,
 Averroes, Avicenna, Constantine,
 Scotch Bernard, John of Gaddesden, Gilbertine.[54]
445 In his own diet he observed some measure;
 There were no superfluities for pleasure,
 Only digestives, nutritives and such.
 He did not read the Bible very much.
 In blood-red garments, slashed with bluish-gray
450 And lined with taffeta,[55] he rode his way;
 Yet he was rather close as to expenses
 And kept the gold he won in pestilences.

51. The cause . . . hot: It was believed that the body was composed of four "humors" (cold and dry, hot and moist, hot and dry, cold and moist) and that diseases resulted from a disturbance of one of these "humors."

52. apothecaries (ə päth′ ə ker′ ēz): Persons who prepared drugs.

53. Esculapius (es′ kyoo lā′ pē əs): In Roman mythology, the god of medicine and healing.

54. Hippocrates . . . Gilbertine: Famous physicians and medical authorities.

55. taffeta (taf′ i tə): A fine silk fabric.

Gold stimulates the heart, or so we're told.
He therefore had a special love of gold.

455   A worthy *woman* from beside *Bath*[56] city
Was with us, somewhat deaf, which was a pity.
In making cloth she showed so great a bent
She bettered those of Ypres and of Ghent.[57]
In all the parish not a dame dared stir
460 Towards the altar steps in front of her,
And if indeed they did, so wrath was she
As to be quite put out of charity.
Her kerchiefs were of finely woven ground;[58]
I dared have sworn they weighed a good ten pound,
465 The ones she wore on Sunday, on her head.
Her hose were of the finest scarlet red
And gartered tight; her shoes were soft and new.
Bold was her face, handsome, and red in hue.
A worthy woman all her life, what's more
470 She'd had five husbands, all at the church door,
Apart from other company in youth;
No need just now to speak of that, forsooth.
And she had thrice been to Jerusalem,
Seen many strange rivers and passed over them;
475 She'd been to Rome and also to Boulogne,
St. James of Compostella and Cologne,[59]
And she was skilled in wandering by the way.
She had gap-teeth, set widely, truth to say.
Easily on an ambling horse she sat
480 Well wimpled[60] up, and on her head a hat
As broad as is a buckler[61] or a shield;
She had a flowing mantle that concealed
Large hips, her heels spurred sharply under that.
In company she liked to laugh and chat
485 And knew the remedies for love's mischances,
An art in which she knew the oldest dances.

    A holy-minded man of good renown
There was, and poor, the *Parson* to a town,
Yet he was rich in holy thought and work.
490 He also was a learned man, a clerk,
Who truly knew Christ's gospel and would preach it
Devoutly to parishioners, and teach it.
Benign and wonderfully diligent,
And patient when adversity was sent
495 (For so he proved in great adversity)
He much disliked extorting tithe[62] or fee,
Nay rather he preferred beyond a doubt
Giving to poor parishioners round about
From his own goods and Easter offerings.
500 He found sufficiency in little things.

56. *Bath:* An English resort city.

57. **Ypres** (ē′ prə) **and of Ghent** (gent): Flemish cities known for wool making.

58. ground: A composite fabric.

59. Jerusalem . . . Rome . . . Boulogne . . . St. James of Compostella . . . Cologne: Famous pilgrimage sites at the time.

60. wimpled: Wearing a scarf covering the head, neck, and chin.

61. buckler: A small, round shield.

62. tithe (tīth): One tenth of a person's income, paid as a tax to support the church.

Wide was his parish, with houses far asunder,
Yet he neglected not in rain or thunder,
In sickness or in grief, to pay a call
  On the remotest, whether great or small,
505 Upon his feet, and in his hand a stave.
This noble example to his sheep he gave,
First following the word before he taught it,
And it was from the gospel he had caught it.
This little proverb he would add thereto
510 That if gold rust, what then will iron do?
For if a priest be foul in whom we trust
No wonder that a common man should rust;
And shame it is to see—let priests take stock—
A soiled shepherd and a snowy flock.
515 The true example that a priest should give
Is one of cleanness, how the sheep should live.
He did not set his benefice to hire[63]
And leave his sheep encumbered in the mire
Or run to London to earn easy bread
520 By singing masses for the wealthy dead,
Or find some Brotherhood and get enrolled.
He stayed at home and watched over his fold
So that no wolf should make the sheep miscarry.
He was a shepherd and no mercenary.
525 Holy and virtuous he was, but then
Never contemptuous of sinful men,
Never disdainful, never too proud or fine,
But was discreet in teaching and benign.
His business was to show a fair behavior
530 And draw men thus to Heaven and their Savior,
Unless indeed a man were obstinate;
And such, whether of high or low estate,
He put to sharp rebuke to say the least.
I think there never was a better priest.
535 He sought no pomp or glory in his dealings,
No scrupulosity had spiced his feelings.
Christ and His Twelve Apostles and their lore
He taught, but followed it himself before.
    There was a *Plowman* with him there, his brother.
540 Many a load of dung one time or other
He must have carted through the morning dew.
He was an honest worker, good and true,
Living in peace and perfect charity,
And, as the gospel bade him, so did he,
545 Loving God best with all his heart and mind
And then his neighbor as himself, repined
At no misfortune, slacked for no content,
For steadily about his work he went

THE WIFE OF BATH
Arthur Szyk for the Canterbury Tales

63. set . . . hire: Pay
someone else to perform
his parish duties.

To thrash his corn, to dig or to manure
550 Or make a ditch; and he would help the poor
For love of Christ and never take a penny
If he could help it, and, as prompt as any,
He paid his tithes in full when they were due
On what he owned, and on his earnings too.
555 He wore a tabard[64] smock and rode a mare.
    There was a *Reeve*,[65] also a *Miller*, there,
A College *Manciple*[66] from the Inns of Court,
A papal *Pardoner*[67] and, in close consort,
A Church-Court *Summoner*,[68] riding at a trot,
560 And finally myself—that was the lot.
    The *Miller* was a chap of sixteen stone,[69]
A great stout fellow big in brawn and bone.
He did well out of them, for he could go
And win the ram at any wrestling show.
565 Broad, knotty and short-shouldered, he would boast
He could heave any door off hinge and post,
Or take a run and break it with his head.
His beard, like any sow or fox, was red
And broad as well, as though it were a spade;
570 And, at its very tip, his nose displayed
A wart on which there stood a tuft of hair.
Red as the bristles in an old sow's ear.
His nostrils were as black as they were wide.
He had a sword and buckler at his side,
575 His mighty mouth was like a furnace door.
A wrangler and buffoon, he had a store
Of tavern stories, filthy in the main.
His was a master-hand at stealing grain.
He felt it with his thumb and thus he knew
580 Its quality and took three times his due—
A thumb of gold, by God, to gauge an oat!
He wore a hood of blue and a white coat.
He liked to play his bagpipes up and down
And that was how he brought us out of town.
585 The *Manciple* came from the Inner Temple;
All caterers might follow his example
In buying victuals; he was never rash
Whether he bought on credit or paid cash.
He used to watch the market most precisely
590 And go in first, and so he did quite nicely.
Now isn't it a marvel of God's grace
That an illiterate fellow can outpace
The wisdom of a heap of learned men?
His masters—he had more than thirty then—
595 All versed in the abstrusest legal knowledge,
Could have produced a dozen from their College

64. tabard: A loose jacket.

65. *Reeve*: An estate manager.

66. *Manciple*: A buyer of provisions.

67. *Pardoner*: One who dispenses papal pardons.

68. *Summoner*: One who serves summonses to church courts.

69. sixteen stone: 224 pounds. A stone equals 14 pounds.

Fit to be stewards in land and rents and game
To any Peer in England you could name,
And show him how to live on what he had
600 Debt-free (unless of course the Peer were mad)
Or be as frugal as he might desire,
And they were fit to help about the Shire
In any legal case there was to try;
And yet this Manciple could wipe their eye.

605   The *Reeve* was old and choleric and thin;
His beard was shaven closely to the skin,
His shorn hair came abruptly to a stop
Above his ears, and he was docked on top
Just like a priest in front; his legs were lean,
610 Like sticks they were, no calf was to be seen.
He kept his bins and garners[70] very trim;
No auditor could gain a point on him.
And he could judge by watching drought and rain
The yield he might expect from seed and grain.
615 His master's sheep, his animals and hens,
Pigs, horses, dairies, stores and cattle-pens
Were wholly trusted to his government.
And he was under contract to present
The accounts, right from his master's earliest years.
620 No one had ever caught him in arrears.
No bailiff, serf or herdsman dared to kick,
He knew their dodges, knew their every trick;
Feared like the plague he was, by those beneath.
He had a lovely dwelling on a heath,
625 Shadowed in green by trees above the sward.[71]
A better hand at bargains than his lord,
He had grown rich and had a store of treasure
Well tucked away, yet out it came to pleasure
His lord with subtle loans or gifts of goods,
630 To earn his thanks and even coats and hoods.
When young he'd learnt a useful trade and still
He was a carpenter of first-rate skill.
The stallion-cob he rode at a slow trot
Was dapple-gray and bore the name of Scot.
635 He wore an overcoat of bluish shade
And rather long; he had a rusty blade
Slung at his side. He came, as I heard tell,
From Norfolk, near a place called Baldeswell.
His coat was tucked under his belt and splayed.
640 He rode the hindmost of our cavalcade.
     There was a *Summoner* with us in the place
Who had a fire-red cherubinnish face,[72]
For he had carbuncles. His eyes were narrow,
He was as hot and lecherous as a sparrow.

70. garners *n.*: Buildings for storing grain.

71. sward *n.*: Turf.

72. fire–red . . . face: In the art of the Middle Ages, the faces of cherubs, or angels, were often painted red.

645   Black, scabby brows he had, and a thin beard.
            Children were afraid when he appeared.
            No quicksilver, lead ointments, tartar creams,
            Boracic, no, nor brimstone, so it seems,
            Could make a salve that had the power to bite,
650   Clean up or curve his whelks of knobby white.
            Or purge the pimples sitting on his cheeks.
            Garlic he loved, and onions too, and leeks,
            And drinking strong wine till all was hazy.
            Then he would shout and jabber as if crazy,
655   And wouldn't speak a word except in Latin
            When he was drunk, such tags as he was pat in;
            He only had a few, say two or three,
            That he had mugged up out of some decree;
            No wonder, for he heard them every day.
660   And, as you know, a man can teach a jay
            To call out "Walter" better than the Pope.
            But had you tried to test his wits and grope
            For more, you'd have found nothing in the bag.
            Then *"Questio quid juris"*[73] was his tag.
665   He was a gentle varlet and a kind one,
            No better fellow if you went to find one.
            He would allow—just for a quart of wine—
            Any good lad to keep a concubine
            A twelvemonth and dispense it altogether!
670   Yet he could pluck a finch to leave no feather:
            And if he found some rascal with a maid
            He would instruct him not to be afraid
            In such a case of the Archdeacon's curse
            (Unless the rascal's soul were in his purse)
675   For in his purse the punishment should be.
            "Purse is the good Archdeacon's Hell," said he.
            But well I know he lied in what he said;
            A curse should put a guilty man in dread,
            For curses kill, as shriving brings, salvation.
680   We should beware of excommunication.
            Thus, as he pleased, the man could bring duress
            On any young fellow in the diocese.
            He knew their secrets, they did what he said.
            He wore a garland set upon his head
685   Large as the holly-bush upon a stake
            Outside an ale-house, and he had a cake,
            A round one, which it was his joke to wield
            As if it were intended for a shield.
                He and a gentle *Pardoner* rode together,
690   A bird from Charing Cross of the same feather,
            Just back from visiting the Court of Rome.
            He loudly sang *"Come hither, love, come home!"*

73. *"Questio quid juris":* "The question is, what is the point of the law?" (Latin).

The Summoner sang deep seconds to this song,
No trumpet ever sounded half so strong.
695 This Pardoner had hair as yellow as wax,
Hanging down smoothly like a hank of flax.
In driblets fell his locks behind his head
Down to his shoulders which they overspread;
Thinly they fell, like rat-tails, one by one.
700 He wore no hood upon his head, for fun;
The hood inside his wallet had been stowed,
He aimed at riding in the latest mode;
But for a little cap his head was bare
And he had bulging eyeballs, like a hare.
705 He'd sewed a holy relic on his cap;
His wallet lay before him on his lap,
Brimful of pardons come from Rome all hot.
He had the same small voice a goat has got.
His chin no beard had harbored, nor would harbor,
710 Smoother than ever chin was left by barber.
I judge he was a gelding, or a mare.
As to his trade, from Berwick down to Ware
There was no pardoner of equal grace,
For in his trunk he had a pillowcase
715 Which he asserted was Our Lady's veil.
He said he had a gobbet[74] of the sail
Saint Peter had the time when he made bold
To walk the waves, till Jesu Christ took hold.
He had a cross of metal set with stones
720 And, in a glass, a rubble of pigs' bones.
And with these relics, any time he found
Some poor up-country parson to astound,
On one short day, in money down, he drew
More than the parson in a month or two,
725 And by his flatteries and prevarication
Made monkeys of the priest and congregation.
But still to do him justice first and last
In church he was a noble ecclesiast.
How well he read a lesson or told a story!
730 But best of all he sang an Offertory,[75]
For well he knew that when that song was sung
He'd have to preach and tune his honey-tongue
And (well he could) win silver from the crowd.
That's why he sang so merrily and loud.
735   Now I have told you shortly, in a clause,
The rank, the array, the number and the cause
Of our assembly in this company
In Southwark, at that high-class hostelry
Known as *The Tabard*, close beside *The Bell*.
740 And now the time has come for me to tell

74. gobbet: Piece.

75. Offertory: The song that accompanies the collection of the offering at a church service.

How we behaved that evening; I'll begin
After we had alighted at the inn,
Then I'll report our journey, stage by stage,
All the remainder of our pilgrimage.
745 But first I beg of you, in courtesy,
Not to condemn me as unmannerly
If I speak plainly and with no concealings
And give account of all their words and dealings,
Using their very phrases as they fell.
750 For certainly, as you all know so well,
He who repeats a tale after a man
Is bound to say, as nearly as he can,
Each single word, if he remembers it,
However rudely spoken or unfit,
755 Or else the tale he tells will be untrue,
The things invented and the phrases new.
He may not flinch although it were his brother,
If he says one word he must say the other.
And Christ Himself spoke broad[76] in Holy Writ,
760 And as you know there's nothing there unfit,
And Plato[77] says, for those with power to read,
"The word should be as cousin to the deed."
Further I beg you to forgive it me
If I neglect the order and degree
765 And what is due to rank in what I've planned.
I'm short of wit as you will understand.
    Our *Host* gave us great welcome; everyone
Was given a place and supper was begun.
He served the finest victuals you could think,
770 The wine was strong and we were glad to drink.
A very striking man our Host withal,
And fit to be a marshal in a hall.
His eyes were bright, his girth a little wide;
There is no finer burgess in Cheapside.[78]
775 Bold in his speech, yet wise and full of tact,
There was no manly attribute he lacked,
What's more he was a merry-hearted man.
After our meal he jokingly began
To talk of sport, and, among other things
780 After we'd settled up our reckonings,
He said as follows: "Truly, gentlemen,
You're very welcome and I can't think when
—Upon my word I'm telling you no lie—
I've seen a gathering here that looked so spry,
785 No, not this year, as in this tavern now.
I'd think you up some fun if I knew how.
And, as it happens, a thought has just occurred
And it will cost you nothing, on my word.

76. broad: Bluntly.

77. Plato: A Greek philosopher (427?–347? B.C.).

78. Cheapside: A district in London.

You're off to Canterbury—well, God speed!
790 Blessed St. Thomas answer to your need!
And I don't doubt, before the journey's done
You mean to while the time in tales and fun.
Indeed, there's little pleasure for your bones
Riding along and all as dumb as stones.
795 So let me then propose for your enjoyment,
Just as I said, a suitable employment.
And if my notion suits and you agree
And promise to submit yourselves to me
Playing your parts exactly as I say
800 Tomorrow as you ride along the way,
Then by my father's soul (and he is dead)
If you don't like it you can have my head!
Hold up your hands, and not another word."
    Well, our consent of course was not deferred,
805 It seemed not worth a serious debate;
We all agreed to it at any rate
And bade him issue what commands he would.
"My lords," he said, "now listen for your good,
And please don't treat my notion with disdain.
810 This is the point. I'll make it short and plain.
Each one of you shall help to make things slip
By telling two stories on the outward trip
To Canterbury, that's what I intend,
And, on the homeward way to journey's end
815 Another two, tales from the days of old;
And then the man whose story is best told,
That is to say who gives the fullest measure
Of good morality and general pleasure,
He shall be given a supper, paid by all,
820 Here in this tavern, in this very hall,
When we come back again from Canterbury.
And in the hope to keep you bright and merry
I'll go along with you myself and ride
All at my own expense and serve as guide.
825 I'll be the judge, and those who won't obey
Shall pay for what we spend upon the way.
Now if you all agree to what you've heard
Tell me at once without another word,
And I will make arrangements early for it."
830   Of course we all agreed, in fact we swore it
Delightedly, and made entreaty too
That he should act as he proposed to do,
Become our Governor in short, and be
Judge of our tales and general referee,
835 And set the supper at a certain price.
We promised to be ruled by his advice

Come high, come low; unanimously thus
We set him up in judgment over us.
More wine was fetched, the business being done;

840 We drank it off and up went everyone
To bed without a moment of delay.
        Early next morning at the spring of day
Up rose our Host and roused us like a cock,
Gathering us together in a flock,

845 And off we rode at slightly faster pace
Than walking to St. Thomas' watering-place;[79]
And there our Host drew up, began to ease
His horse, and said, "Now, listen if you please,
My lords! Remember what you promised me.

850 If evensong and matins will agree[80]
Let's see who shall be first to tell a tale.
And as I hope to drink good wine and ale
I'll be your judge. The rebel who disobeys,
However much the journey costs, he pays.

855 Now draw for cut and then we can depart;
The man who draws the shortest cut shall start."

79. St. Thomas' watering-place: A brook two miles from the inn.

80. If evensong . . . agree: If what you said last night holds true this morning.

Primary Source

Seventeenth-century poet and dramatist John Dryden called Chaucer the "father of English poetry," a ranking still considered valid today. Dryden held Chaucer in the "same degree of veneration as the Grecians held Homer or the Romans held Virgil," and found in his work "a perpetual fountain of good sense." Writing about a hundred years later, poet and essayist Samuel Taylor Coleridge found: " . . . unceasing delight in Chaucer. His cheerfulness is especially delicious to me in my old age. How exquisitely tender he is, and yet how perfectly free from the least touch of sickly melancholy or morbid drooping. The sympathy of the poet with the subjects of his poetry is particularly remarkable in Shakespeare and Chaucer; but what Shakespeare effects by a strong act of imagination and mental changing, Chaucer does without any effort, merely by the inborn kindly joyousness of his nature. How well we seem to know Chaucer! How absolutely nothing do we know of Shakespeare!"

RESPONDING TO THE SELECTION

Your Response

1. Which pilgrim would you most like to meet? Why?

Recalling

2. What does Chaucer say that people long to do when spring comes?
3. Which pilgrim is described as being (a) "modest as a maid"? (b) "all sentiment and tender heart"? (c) "a very festive fellow"?
4. Which pilgrim is described as having (a) "a special love of gold"? (b) "gap-teeth"? (c) "a store of tavern stories"?
5. What entertainment on the journey does the host propose?

Interpreting

6. Chaucer pokes gentle fun at some of the pilgrims. What is his opinion of the Nun's singing voice and of her French?
7. Although the Friar and the Parson are both religious men, they are very different. What are some of the ways in which they differ?
8. What, if anything, does Chaucer seem to dislike about (a) the Skipper? (b) the Doctor?

Applying

9. If Chaucer were writing *The Canterbury Tales* today, what three kinds of pilgrims do you think he might consider adding to the group?

ANALYZING LITERATURE

Understanding Characterization

Chaucer sometimes makes direct statements about a character: "He was an honest worker, good and true." More often he reveals character indirectly, often through action: "She used to weep if she but saw a mouse/Caught in a trap." There is not much dialogue in the Prologue, but Chaucer frequently uses physical appearance to suggest character. Compare the appearance of the Miller ("A great stout fellow big in brawn and bone") with that of the Reeve ("old and choleric and thin"). Their looks match their personalities.

1. What nouns does Chaucer use to characterize the Squire?
2. How does Chaucer mainly characterize (a) the Doctor? (b) the Host?

CRITICAL THINKING AND READING

Making Inferences About Characters

If you are to understand fictional characters fully, you must make inferences about them. You must draw conclusions based on what the writer has told you about their actions, thoughts, words, and appearance. When Chaucer writes of the Parson, "That if gold rust, what will iron do?" you can infer that the Parson realizes he should be a model of behavior for his parishioners. What can you infer about the Pardoner from the information in lines 670–675?

THINKING AND WRITING

Writing a Pilgrim's Tale

Now that you know something about each of Chaucer's pilgrims, choose one and study his or her sketch carefully. When you are sure you understand the pilgrim's character, write a tale that he or she might tell. You may modernize the tale, if you wish, setting it in the present. But make sure the message of the tale fits the character of the pilgrim.

LEARNING OPTIONS

1. **Art.** In paintings, drawings, a collage, or another form of art, create portraits of several of the pilgrims. Pay close attention to the details that Chaucer uses to describe the pilgrims. If you wish, find out more about the medieval attire these individuals might have worn.
2. **Cross-curricular Connection.** Create a diagram that shows the different segments of medieval society—the church, the court, common people—and the types of individuals found in each. Include people like those depicted in the Prologue.

ONE WRITER'S PROCESS

Geoffrey Chaucer and The Canterbury Tales

PREWRITING

Why Did He Write the Tales? No one knows for sure what prompted Chaucer to begin work on *The Canterbury Tales*. Some believe that Chaucer himself may have participated in a pilgrimage to Canterbury. Whether or not this is true, he certainly had the opportunity to observe from his window in London many other pilgrims starting their journey.

An Ambitious Plan Chaucer lived such a long time ago that it should not surprise us that no original notes or plans for *The Canterbury Tales* have survived. From the Prologue, however, we do know the scope of the task that Chaucer set for himself. Each of thirty pilgrims was to tell four tales, which means that at some point he intended to write at least 120 tales! This is an ambitious plan by anyone's standards, and since *The Canterbury Tales* remained unfinished at the time of his death, we will never find out if Chaucer ever reconsidered his plan.

DRAFTING

A Writing "Technology" Different From Ours It is almost certain that none of the surviving manuscripts of *The Canterbury Tales* is written in Chaucer's own hand. A common practice for a fourteenth-century man of letters of Chaucer's stature was to employ a professional scribe to write down his words for him. Chaucer even composed a short poem, "Chaucers Wordes unto Adam, His Owne Scriveyn," to address one such copyist. The following lines from the poem suggest that Chaucer was not altogether satisfied with his scribe's efforts: "So ofte a-daye I mot thy werk renewe,/It to correcte and eek to rubbe and scrape."

REVISING

A Continuing Process While we do not have a great deal of information regarding Chaucer's methods of revision, there is evidence to suggest that Chaucer did revise individual tales. Some scholars believe that a few of the tales were written singly at an earlier time in Chaucer's career and then reworked to fit into the frame story of the pilgrimage. In addition, several manuscripts of *The Canterbury Tales* contain corrections and deletions, and there is reason to believe that a number of these may have been made under Chaucer's own supervision.

PUBLISHING

Did Chaucer Receive Patronage? Chaucer probably did not receive any substantial gifts from the nobility specifically meant to support this writing. Like many authors today, Chaucer earned his living through hard work—he was a skillful civil servant—and then retired to his private world of books and reading.

How Publishing Differed Two crucial factors made publishing in Chaucer's time much different from publishing today. One factor was the continuing strength of the oral tradition. Today, when television and other mass media are so powerful, the oral tradition has become less common. Most of us no longer spend very much time reading aloud or telling stories. In Chaucer's time, however, that tradition was much stronger. Chaucer himself sometimes seems uncertain as to whether he is writing for an immediate audience that will *hear* his works read or for a larger and more remote audience that will read them in manuscript (printing had not yet been invented). In general, he seems to have thought that his earlier poems would be read aloud and that *The Canterbury Tales* would be read in manuscript.

The second factor is that English was not securely established as the language of publication. Recall that in 1066, the Normans had invaded England and brought the French language with them. In Chaucer's time, English was making a strong comeback, but it still had to compete with Latin and French. Latin was preferred for theological writings, and French was used for civil record-keeping and documents of state. French literature also remained popular with royalty and the higher nobility. However, among the minor nobility and Chaucer's fellow civil servants, a new audience for English literary works was beginning to emerge.

Who Was Chaucer's Audience? Chaucer's immediate audience consisted of those whose social rank was similar to his own. Among this audience was a group of educated women who served the ladies of the court. To better appreciate the small size of Chaucer's circle, we should remember that the plague of 1348–1349 had reduced the population of England to 3.5 million and that the English nobility numbered about 10,000! London, the center of Chaucer's activities, had a population of just 40,000.

A Growing Audience By the fifteenth century, however, Chaucer's readership was growing rapidly. In the first years of that century, some high-quality manuscripts of *The Canterbury Tales* were prepared for the nobility. Ironically, the relatively large number of lower quality manuscripts—on paper rather than vellum or parchment—that soon followed indicates that Chaucer was winning widespread acceptance.

THINKING ABOUT THE PROCESS

1. Publishing has changed considerably from Chaucer's time to our own. Do you think it will change in the immediate future? Explain.
2. **Cross-curricular Connection.** Investigate how manuscripts were prepared before the invention of printing and share your findings with the class.

GUIDE FOR INTERPRETING

The Nun's Priest's Tale

The Mock-Heroic Style. Writers use a mock-heroic style when they write about trivial matters in a manner that would be more appropriate for great and important events. The disparity between content and style results in comic effects. For example, imagine describing a vain young man in front of his mirror as if he were participating in a solemn, religious ritual: "With total devotion and concentration and hardly breathing at all, Tom carefully applied the comb to the curl that had violated the upper part of his ear. . . ."

In "The Nun's Priest's Tale," Chaucer uses the mock-heroic style to transform a popular animal fable into a masterpiece of comedy. He describes the barnyard interactions of animals as if he were writing an epic poem. Among the elements he borrows from epic writing are the hero's elaborate boasts, the vivid accounts of battles, and the intervention of supernatural forces. To make his tale even more ridiculous, he includes barnyard debates about controversial issues of the day: fate versus free will, and woman as the source of man's misfortune. The contrast between these lofty concerns and the animal debaters is ludicrous but appealing.

Chaucer casts a rooster and hen as his romantic leads, presenting them as if they were the lord and lady of a castle. As master of all he surveys, the rooster Chanticleer is pompous, naive, and thoroughly charming. He struts and preaches, displaying his male ego and sprinkling his conversation with learned classical allusions. Meanwhile, his hen-wife Pertelote is a comically practical heroine. She gives her lord and master advice about his health and, for all his strutting, wields emotional power over him.

The mock-heroic style works best when ridicule is tempered with affection. Chaucer certainly succeeds in this respect. His fondness for his characters, even at their most absurd, comes through in the pleasant and cheerful tone of the tale.

Think about the many little things you do every day: brushing your teeth, tying your shoe laces, opening a box of cereal. Use the mock-heroic style to describe a trivial chore or activity that is part of your daily routine. Remember to stress the contrast between style and subject matter in order to heighten the humor. When you have finished, exchange descriptions with a classmate.

The Nun's Priest's Tale

Geoffrey Chaucer

Once, long ago, there dwelt a poor old widow
In a small cottage, by a little meadow
Beside a grove and standing in a dale.
This widow-woman of whom I tell my tale
5   Since the sad day when last she was a wife
Had led a very patient, simple life.
Little she had in capital or rent,
But still, by making do with what God sent,
She kept herself and her two daughters going.
10 Three hefty sows—no more—were all her showing,
Three cows as well; there was a sheep called Molly.
   Sooty her hall, her kitchen melancholy,
And there she ate full many a slender meal;
There was no *sauce piquante*[1] to spice her veal,
15 No dainty morsel ever passed her throat,
According to her cloth she cut her coat.
Repletion[2] never left her in disquiet
And all her physic was a temperate diet,
Hard work for exercise and heart's content.
20 And rich man's gout did nothing to prevent
Her dancing, apoplexy[3] struck her not;
She drank no wine, nor white nor red had got.
Her board was mostly served with white and black,
Milk and brown bread, in which she found no lack;
25 Broiled bacon or an egg or two were common,
She was in fact a sort of dairy-woman.
   She had a yard that was enclosed about
By a stockade and a dry ditch without,
In which she kept a cock called Chanticleer.
30 In all the land for crowing he'd no peer;
His voice was jollier than the organ blowing
In church on Sundays, he was great at crowing.
Far, far more regular than any clock
Or abbey bell the crowing of this cock.
35 The equinoctial wheel and its position[4]
At each ascent he knew by intuition;
At every hour—fifteen degrees of movement—
He crowed so well there could be no improvement.

1. sauce piquante
(pē′ kȯnt): French for a
pleasantly sharp sauce,
used for fancy and
expensive meals.
2. Repletion (ri plē′ shȯn)
n.: The state of having
eaten too much.

3. apoplexy: An old-
fashioned term for a
stroke.

**4. equinoctial . . .
position:** Chaucer and his
contemporaries accounted
for changes in the
positions of stars and
planets by imagining that
the heavens circled the
earth once a day, moving
fifteen degrees each hour.

His comb was redder than fine coral, tall
40 And battlemented like a castle wall,
His bill was black and shone as bright as jet,
Like azure were his legs and they were set
On azure toes with nails of lily white,
Like burnished gold his feathers, flaming bright.
45   This gentlecock was master in some measure
Of seven hens, all there to do his pleasure.
They were his sisters and his paramours,
Colored like him in all particulars;
She with the loveliest dyes upon her throat
50 Was known as gracious Lady Pertelote.
Courteous she was, discreet and debonair,
Companionable too, and took such care
In her deportment, since she was seven days old
She held the heart of Chanticleer controlled,
55 Locked up securely in her every limb;
O such happiness his love to him!
And such a joy it was to hear them sing,
As when the glorious sun began to spring,
In sweet accord *My love is far from land*[5]
60 —For in those far off days I understand
All birds and animals could speak and sing.
    Now it befell, as dawn began to spring,
When Chanticleer and Pertelote and all
His wives were perched in this poor widow's hall
65 (Fair Pertelote was next him on the perch),
This Chanticleer began to groan and lurch
Like someone sorely troubled by a dream,
And Pertelote who heard him roar and scream
Was quite aghast and said, "O dearest heart,
70 What's ailing you? Why do you groan and start?
Fie, what a sleeper! What a noise to make!"
"Madam," he said, "I beg you not to take
Offense, but by the Lord I had a dream
So terrible just now I had to scream;
75 I still can feel my heart racing from fear.
God turn my dream to good and guard all here.
And keep my body out of durance vile![6]
I dreamt that roaming up and down a while
Within our yard I saw a kind of beast,
80 A sort of hound that tried or seemed at least
To try and seize me . . . would have killed me dead!
His color was a blend of yellow and red,
His ears and tail were tipped with sable fur
Unlike the rest; he was a russet cur.
85 Small was his snout, his eyes were glowing bright.

5. *My love is far from land:* The refrain of a popular song.

6. durance vile: Long imprisonment.

**ENGLISH TRAVELERS SETTING FORTH
FROM THE CANTERBURY TALES**
The British Library

It was enough to make one die of fright.
That was no doubt what made me groan and swoon."
　　"For shame," she said, "you timorous poltroon![7]
Alas, what cowardice! By God above,

90　You've forfeited my heart and lost my love.
I cannot love a coward, come what may.
For certainly, whatever we may say,
All women long—and O that it might be!—
For husbands tough, dependable and free,

95　Secret, discreet, no niggard,[8] not a fool
That boasts and then will find his courage cool
At every trifling thing. By God above,
How dare you say for shame, and to your love,
That anything at all was to be feared?

100　Have you no manly heart to match your beard?
And can a dream reduce you to such terror?
Dreams are a vanity, God knows, pure error.
Dreams are engendered in the too-replete
From vapors in the belly, which compete

105　With others, too abundant, swollen tight.
　　"No doubt the redness in your dream tonight
Comes from the superfluity and force
Of the red choler in your blood. Of course.
That is what puts a dreamer in the dread

110　Of crimsoned arrows, fires flaming red,
Of great red monsters making as to fight him,
And big red whelps and little ones to bite him;
Just so the black and melancholy vapors
Will set a sleeper shrieking, cutting capers

115　And swearing that black bears, black bulls as well,
Or blackest fiends are haling him to Hell.
And there are other vapors that I know
That on a sleeping man will work their woe,
But I'll pass on as lightly as I can.

120　"Take Cato[9] now, that was so wise a man,
Did he not say, 'Take no account of dreams'?
Now, sir," she said, "on flying from these beams,
For love of God do take some laxative;
Upon my soul that's the advice to give

125　For melancholy choler; let me urge
You free yourself from vapors with a purge.
And that you may have no excuse to tarry
By saying this town has no apothecary,
I shall myself instruct you and prescribe

130　Herbs that will cure all vapors of that tribe,
Herbs from our very farmyard! You will find
Their natural property is to unbind

7. poltroon (päl trōōn′)
n.: Coward.

8. niggard: Stingy
person.

9. Cato: A Roman
statesman and philosopher
(95–46 B.C.) with a
reputation for wisdom.

And purge you well beneath and well above.
Now don't forget it, dear, for God's own love!
135 Your face is choleric and shows distension;
Be careful lest the sun in his ascension
Should catch you full of humors,[10] hot and many.
And if he does, my dear, I'll lay a penny
It means a bout of fever or a breath
140 Of tertian ague.[11] You may catch your death.
        "Worms for a day or two I'll have to give
As a digestive, then your laxative.
Centaury, fumitory, caper-spurge
And hellebore will make a splendid purge;
145 And then there's laurel or the blackthorn berry,
Ground-ivy too that makes our yard so merry;
Peck them right up, my dear, and swallow whole.
Be happy, husband, by your father's soul!
Don't be afraid of dreams. I'll say no more."
150   "Madam," he said, "I thank you for your lore,
But with regard to Cato all the same,
His wisdom has, no doubt, a certain fame,
But though he said that we should take no heed
Of dreams, by God in ancient books I read
155 Of many a man of more authority
Than ever Cato was, believe you me,
Who say the very opposite is true
And prove their theories by experience too.
Dreams have quite often been significations
160 As well of triumphs as of tribulations
That people undergo in this our life.
This needs no argument at all, dear wife,
The proof is all too manifest indeed.
    "One of the greatest authors one can read
165 Says thus: there were two comrades once who went
On pilgrimage, sincere in their intent.
And as it happened they had reached a town
Where such a throng was milling up and down
And yet so scanty the accommodation,
170 They could not find themselves a habitation,
No, not a cottage that could lodge them both.
And so they separated, very loath,
Under constraint of this necessity
And each went off to find some hostelry,
175 And lodge whatever way his luck might fall.
    "The first of them found refuge in a stall
Down in a yard with oxen and a plow.
His friend found lodging for himself somehow
Elsewhere, by accident or destiny,

10. **humors:** People in Chaucer's time believed that bodily fluids called humors were responsible for one's health and disposition. An excess of the fluid called yellow bile resulted in a choleric, or quick-tempered, personality. In lines 108 and 125, Chaucer seems to use the word *choler* as a synonym for the term *humor.*

11. **tertian ague** (tur′ shən ā′ gyoo): A malarial fever.

180 Which governs all of us and equally.
   "Now it so happened, long ere it was day,
  This fellow had a dream, and as he lay
  In bed it seemed he heard his comrade call,
  'Help! I am lying in an ox's stall
185 And shall tonight be murdered as I lie.
  Help me, dear brother, help or I shall die!
  Come in all haste!' Such were the words he spoke;
  The dreamer, lost in terror, then awoke.
  But once awake he paid it no attention,
190 Turned over and dismissed it as invention,
  It was a dream, he thought, a fantasy.
  And twice he dreamt this dream successively.
   "Yet a third time his comrade came again,
  Or seemed to come, and said, 'I have been slain.
195 Look, look! my wounds are bleeding wide and deep,
  Rise early in the morning, break your sleep

And go to the west gate. You there shall see
A cart all loaded up with dung,' said he,
'And in that dung my body has been hidden.
200 Boldly arrest that cart as you are bidden.
It was my money that they killed me for.'
   "He told him every detail, sighing sore,
And pitiful in feature, pale of hue.
This dream, believe me, Madam, turned out true;
205 For in the dawn, as soon as it was light,
He went to where his friend had spent the night
And when he came upon the cattle-stall
He looked about him and began to call.
   "The innkeeper, appearing thereupon,
210 Quickly gave answer, 'Sir, your friend has gone.
He left the town a little after dawn.'
The man began to feel suspicious, drawn
By memories of his dream—the western gate,
The dung-cart—off he went, he would not wait,
215 Towards the western entry. There he found,
Seemingly on its way to dung some ground,
A dung-cart loaded on the very plan
Described so closely by the murdered man.
So he began to shout courageously
220 For right and vengeance on the felony,
'My friend's been killed! There's been a foul attack,
He's in that cart and gaping on his back!
Fetch the authorities, get the sheriff down
—Whosever job it is to run the town—
225 Help! My companion's murdered, sent to glory!'
   "What need I add to finish off the story?
People ran out and cast the cart to ground,
And in the middle of the dung they found
The murdered man. The corpse was fresh and new.
230   "O blessed God, that art so just and true,
Thus thou revealest murder! As we say,
'Murder will out.' We see it day by day.
Murder's a foul, abominable treason,
So loathsome to God's justice, to God's reason,
235 He will not suffer its concealment. True,
Things may lie hidden for a year or two,
But still 'Murder will out,' that's my conclusion.
   "All the town officers in great confusion
Seized on the carter and they gave him hell,
240 And then they racked the innkeeper as well,
And both confessed. And then they took the wrecks
And there and then they hanged them by their necks.
   "By this we see that dreams are to be dreaded.

And in the self-same book I find embedded,
245 Right in the very chapter after this
(I'm not inventing, as I hope for bliss)
The story of two men who started out
To cross the sea—for merchandise no doubt—
But as the winds were contrary they waited.
250 It was a pleasant town, I should have stated,
Merrily grouped about the haven-side.
A few days later with the evening tide
The wind veered round so as to suit them best;
They were delighted and they went to rest
255 Meaning to sail next morning early. Well,
To one of them a miracle befell.
    "This man as he lay sleeping, it would seem,
Just before dawn had an astounding dream.
He thought a man was standing by his bed
260 Commanding him to wait, and thus he said:
'If you set sail tomorrow as you intend
You will be drowned. My tale is at an end.'
    "He woke and told his friend what had occurred
And begged him that the journey be deferred
265 At least a day, implored him not to start.
But his companion, lying there apart,
Began to laugh and treat him to derision.[12]
'I'm not afraid,' he said, 'of any vision,
To let it interfere with my affairs;
270 A straw for all your dreamings and your scares.
Dreams are just empty nonsense, merest japes;[13]
Why, people dream all day of owls and apes,
All sorts of trash that can't be understood,
Things that have never happened and never could.
275 But as I see you mean to stay behind
And miss the tide for wilful sloth of mind,
God knows I'm sorry for it, but good day!'
And so he took his leave and went his way.
    "And yet, before they'd covered half the trip
280 —I don't know what went wrong—there was a rip
And by some accident the ship went down,
Her bottom rent,[14] all hands aboard to drown
In sight of all the vessels at her side,
That had put out upon the self-same tide.
285   "So, my dear Pertelote, if you discern
The force of these examples, you may learn
One never should be careless about dreams,
For, undeniably, I say it seems
That many are a sign of trouble breeding.
290   "Now, take St. Kenelm's life which I've been reading;

12. derision (di rizh′ ən)
n.: Contempt or ridicule.

13. japes: Jokes.

14. Rent: Torn.

He was Kenulphus' son, the noble King
Of Mercia. Now, St. Kenelm dreamt a thing
Shortly before they murdered him one day.
He saw his murder in a dream, I say.
295 His nurse expounded it and gave her reasons
On every point and warned him against treasons
But as the saint was only seven years old
All that she said about it left him cold.
He was so holy how could visions hurt?
300   "By God, I willingly would give my shirt
To have you read his legend as I've read it;
And, Madam Pertelote, upon my credit,
Macrobius wrote of dreams and can explain us
The vision of young Scipio Africanus,[15]
305 And he affirms that dreams can give a due
Warnings of things that later on come true.
        "And then there's the Old Testament—a manual
Well worth your study; see the *Book of Daniel.*
Did Daniel think a dream was vanity?
310 Read about Joseph too and you will see
That many dreams—I do not say that all—
Give cognizance of what is to befall.
        "Look at Lord Pharaoh, king of Egypt! Look
At what befell his butler and his cook.
315 Did not their visions have a certain force?
But those who study history of course
Meet many dreams that set them wondering.
        "What about Croesus too, the Lydian king,
Who dreamt that he was sitting in a tree,
320 Meaning he would be hanged? It had to be.
        "Or take Andromache, great Hector's wife;[16]
The day on which he was to lose his life
She dreamt about, the very night before,
And realized that if Hector went to war
325 He would be lost that very day in battle.
She warned him; he dismissed it all as prattle
And sallied forth to fight, being self-willed,
And there he met Achilles and was killed.
The tale is long and somewhat overdrawn,
330 And anyhow it's very nearly dawn,
So let me say in very brief conclusion
My dream undoubtedly foretells confusion,
It bodes me ill, I say. And, furthermore,
Upon your laxatives I set no store,
335 For they are venomous. I've suffered by them
Often enough before and I defy them.
        "And now, let's talk of fun and stop all this.

15. Scipio Africanus
(sip′ ē ō af′ ri kā′ nəs):
A famous Roman general
(237–183 B.C.).

16. Andromache (an
dräm′ ə kē) **. . . wife:** She
was the wife of the
greatest warrior in Troy,
Hector, at the time of the
Trojan War.

Dear Madam, as I hope for Heaven's bliss,
Of one thing God has sent me plenteous grace,
340   For when I see the beauty of your face,
That scarlet loveliness about your eyes,
All thought of terror and confusion dies.
For it's as certain as the Creed, I know,
Mulier est hominis confusio
345   (A Latin tag, dear Madam, meaning this:
'Woman is man's delight and all his bliss'),
For when at night I feel your feathery side,
Although perforce I cannot take a ride
Because, alas, our perch was made too narrow,
350   Delight and solace fill me to the marrow
And I defy all visions and all dreams!"
    And with that word he flew down from the beams,
For it was day, and down his hens flew all,
And with a chuck he gave the troupe a call
355   For he had found a seed upon the floor.
Royal he was, he was afraid no more.
He feathered Pertelote in wanton play
And trod her twenty times ere prime of day.
Grim as a lion's was his manly frown
360   As on his toes he sauntered up and down;
He scarcely deigned to set his foot to ground
And every time a seed of corn was found
He gave a chuck, and up his wives ran all.
Thus royal as a prince who strides his hall
365   Leave we this Chanticleer engaged on feeding
And pass to the adventure that was breeding.
    Now when the month in which the world began,
March, the first month, when God created man,
Was over, and the thirty-second day
370   Thereafter ended, on the third of May
It happened that Chanticleer in all his pride,
His seven wives attendant at his side,
Cast his eyes upward to the blazing sun,
Which in the sign of *Taurus* then had run
375   His twenty-one degrees and somewhat more,
And knew by nature and no other lore
That it was nine o'clock. With blissful voice
He crew triumphantly and said, "Rejoice,
Behold the sun! The sun is up, my seven.
380   Look, it has climbed forty degrees in heaven,
Forty degrees and one in fact, by this.
Dear Madam Pertelote, my earthly bliss,
Hark to those blissful birds and how they sing!
Look at those pretty flowers, how they spring!

385 Solace and revel fill my heart!'' He laughed.
     But in that moment Fate let fly her shaft;
Ever the latter end of joy is woe,
God knows that worldly joy is swift to go.
A rhetorician[17] with a flair for style
390 Could chronicle this maxim in his file
Of Notable Remarks with safe conviction.
Then let the wise give ear; this is no fiction
My story is as true, I undertake,
As that of good Sir Lancelot du Lake[18]
395 Who held all women in such high esteem.
Let me return full circle to my theme.
     A coal-tipped fox of sly iniquity[19]
That had been lurking round the grove for three
Long years, that very night burst through and passed
400 Stockade and hedge, as Providence forecast,
Into the yard where Chanticleer the Fair
Was wont, with all his ladies, to repair.
Still, in a bed of cabbages, he lay
Until about the middle of the day
405 Watching the cock and waiting for his cue,
As all these homicides so gladly do
That lie about in wait to murder men.
O false assassin, lurking in thy den!
O new Iscariot, new Ganelon!
410 And O Greek Sinon,[20] thou whose treachery won
Troy town and brought it utterly to sorrow!
O Chanticleer, accursed be that morrow
That brought thee to the yard from thy high beams!
Thou hadst been warned, and truly, by thy dreams

17. rhetorician (ret' ə rish' ən) *n.*: A person skilled in public speaking or writing.

18. Sir Lancelot du Lake: The most celebrated of King Arthur's knights of the Round Table.

19. iniquity (i nik' wi tē) *n.*: Wickedness.

20. Iscariot . . . Ganelon . . . Sinon: Each of these men was famous for betrayal. Judas Iscariot betrayed Jesus Christ; Ganelon betrayed Charlemagne's greatest knight, Roland; and Sinon convinced King Priam to bring the Trojan horse, filled with Greek troops, into Troy.

THE NUN'S PRIEST DETAIL FROM THE ELLESMERE MANUSCRIPT
The Huntington Library, San Marino, California

The Nun's Priest's Tale 151

415   That this would be a perilous day for thee.
       But that which God's foreknowledge can foresee
    Must needs occur, as certain men of learning
    Have said. Ask any scholar of discerning;
    He'll say the Schools are filled with altercation
420   On this vexed matter of predestination[21]
    Long bandied by a hundred thousand men.
    How can I sift it to the bottom then?
    The Holy Doctor St. Augustine shines
    In this, and there is Bishop Bradwardine's
425   Authority, Boethius'[22] too, decreeing
    Whether the fact of God's divine foreseeing
    Constrains me to perform a certain act
    —And by "constraint" I mean the simple fact
    Of mere compulsion by necessity—
430   Or whether a free choice is granted me
    To do a given act or not to do it
    Though, ere it was accomplished, God foreknew it,
    Or whether Providence is not so stringent
    And merely makes necessity contingent.
435   But I decline discussion of the matter;
    My tale is of a cock and of the clatter
    That came of following his wife's advice
    To walk about his yard on the precise
    Morning after the dream of which I told.
440   O woman's counsel is so often cold!
    A woman's counsel brought us first to woe,
    Made Adam out of Paradise to go
    Where he had been so merry, so well at ease.
    But, for I know not whom it may displease
445   If I suggest that women are to blame,
    Pass over that; I only speak in game.
    Read the authorities to know about
    What has been said of women; you'll find out.
    These are the cock's words, and not mine, I'm giving;
450   I think no harm of any woman living.
     Merrily in her dust-bath in the sand
    Lay Pertelote. Her sisters were at hand
    Basking in sunlight. Chanticleer sang free,
    More merrily than a mermaid in the sea
455   (For *Physiologus*[23] reports the thing
    And says how well and merrily they sing).
    And so it happened as he cast his eye
    Towards the cabbage at a butterfly
    It fell upon the fox there, lying low.
460   Gone was all inclination then to crow.
    "Cok cok," he cried, giving a sudden start,

21. predestination (prē des' tə nā' shən) *n.*: The idea that God arranges beforehand everything that will happen.

22. Bishop Bradwardine's . . . Boethius' (bō ē' thē əs): Bishop Bradwardine was a well-known theologian of Chaucer's time. Boethius (A.D. 480–524) was a famous Roman philosopher.

23. *Physiologus*: A book on nature written in Latin meter.

As one who feels a terror at his heart,
For natural instinct teaches beasts to flee
The moment they perceive an enemy,
465 Though they had never met with it before.
       This Chanticleer was shaken to the core
And would have fled. The fox was quick to say
However, "Sir! Whither so fast away?
Are you afraid of me, that am your friend?
470 A fiend, or worse, I should be, to intend
You harm, or practice villainy upon you;
Dear sir, I was not even spying on you!
Truly I came to do no other thing
Than just to lie and listen to you sing.
475 You have as merry a voice as God has given
To any angel in the courts of Heaven;
To that you add a musical sense as strong
As had Boethius who was skilled in song.
My Lord your Father (God receive his soul!),
480 Your mother too—how courtly, what control!—
Have honored my poor house, to my great ease;
And you, sir, too, I should be glad to please.
For, when it comes to singing, I'll say this
(Else may these eyes of mine be barred from bliss),
485 There never was a singer I would rather
Have heard at dawn than your respected father.
All that he sang came welling from his soul
And how he put his voice under control!
The pains he took to keep his eyes tight shut
490 In concentration—then the tip-toe strut,
The slender neck stretched out, the delicate beak!
No singer could approach him in technique
Or rival him in song, still less surpass.
I've read the story in *Burnel the Ass*,[24]
495 Among some other verses, of a cock
Whose leg in youth was broken by a knock
A clergyman's son had given him, and for this
He made the father lose his benefice.
But certainly there's no comparison
500 Between the subtlety of such an one
And the discretion of your father's art
And wisdom. Oh, for charity of heart,
Can you not emulate your sire and sing?"
       This Chanticleer began to beat a wing
505 As one incapable of smelling treason,
So wholly had this flattery ravished reason.
Alas, my lords! there's many a sycophant[25]
And flatterer that fill your courts with cant

CHAUCER RECITING *TROILUS & CRESSIDA* BEFORE A COURT GATHERING (frontispiece)
Corpus Christi College

24. *Burnel the Ass*: A twelfth-century poem in which a rooster gains revenge after being mistreated by a priest's son.

25. sycophant (sik′ ə fənt) *n.*: A person who seeks favor by flattering influential people.

And give more pleasure with their zeal forsooth
510 Than he who speaks in soberness and truth.
Read what *Ecclesiasticus*[26] records
Of flatterers. 'Ware treachery, my lords!
    This Chanticleer stood high upon his toes,
He stretched his neck, his eyes began to close,
515 His beak to open; with his eyes shut tight
He then began to sing with all his might.
    Sir Russel Fox then leapt to the attack,
Grabbing his gorge he flung him o'er his back
And off he bore him to the woods, the brute,
520 And for the moment there was no pursuit.
    O Destiny that may not be evaded!
Alas that Chanticleer had so paraded!
Alas that he had flown down from the beams!
O that his wife took no account of dreams!
525 And on a Friday too to risk their necks!
O Venus, goddess of the joys of sex,
Since Chanticleer thy mysteries professed
And in thy service always did his best,
And more for pleasure than to multiply
530 His kind, on thine own day is he to die?
    O Geoffrey, thou my dear and sovereign master[27]
Who, when they brought King Richard to disaster
And shot him dead, lamented so his death,
Would that I had thy skill, thy gracious breath,
535 To chide a Friday half so well as you!
(For he was killed upon a Friday too.)
Then I could fashion you a rhapsody
For Chanticleer in dread and agony.
    Sure never such a cry or lamentation

CHAUCER'S CANTERBURY PILGRIMS
William Blake
The Huntington Library, San Marino, California

540   Was made by ladies of high Trojan station,
       When Ilium fell and Pyrrhus with his sword
       Grabbed Priam by the beard, their king and lord,
       And slew him there as the *Aeneid* tells,[28]
       As what was uttered by those hens. Their yells
545   Surpassed them all in palpitating fear
       When they beheld the rape of Chanticleer.
       Dame Pertelote emitted sovereign shrieks
       That echoed up in anguish to the peaks
       Louder than those extorted from the wife
550   Of Hasdrubal,[29] when he had lost his life
       And Carthage all in flame and ashes lay.
       She was so full of torment and dismay
       That in the very flames she chose her part
       And burnt to ashes with a steadfast heart.
555   O woeful hens, louder your shrieks and higher
       Than those of Roman matrons when the fire
       Consumed their husbands, senators of Rome,
       When Nero burnt their city and their home,
       Beyond a doubt that Nero was their bale![30]
560   Now let me turn again to tell my tale;
       This blessed widow and her daughters two
       Heard all these hens in clamor and halloo
       And, rushing to the door at all this shrieking,
       They saw the fox towards the covert streaking
565   And, on his shoulder, Chanticleer stretched flat.
       "Look, look!" they cried, "O mercy, look at that!
       Ha! Ha! the fox!" and after him they ran,
       And stick in hand ran many a serving man,
       Ran Coll our dog, ran Talbot, Bran and Shaggy,
570   And with a distaff in her hand ran Maggie,
       Ran cow and calf and ran the very hogs
       In terror at the barking of the dogs;
       The men and women shouted, ran and cursed,
       They ran so hard they thought their hearts would burst,
575   They yelled like fiends in Hell, ducks left the water
       Quacking and flapping as on point of slaughter,
       Up flew the geese in terror over the trees,
       Out of the hive came forth the swarm of bees;
       So hideous was the noise—God bless us all,
580   Jack Straw and all his followers in their brawl[31]
       Were never half so shrill, for all their noise,
       When they were murdering those Flemish boys,
       As that day's hue and cry upon the fox.
       They grabbed up trumpets made of brass and box,
585   Of horn and bone, on which they blew and pooped,
       And therewithal they shouted and they whooped

28. Sure never . . . Aeneid tells: A reference to the destruction of Troy as described in the Roman poet Virgil's *Aeneid*.

29. Hasdrubal (haz′ droo bəl): A Carthaginian general.

30. bale: Evil, harm.

31. Jack Straw . . . brawl: Jack Straw was one of the leaders of the Peasants' Revolt (1381).

So that it seemed the very heavens would fall.
   And now, good people, pay attention all.
See how Dame Fortune quickly changes side
590 And robs her enemy of hope and pride!
This cock that lay upon the fox's back
In all his dread contrived to give a quack
And said, "Sir Fox, if I were you, as God's
My witness, I would round upon these clods
595 And shout, 'Turn back, you saucy bumpkins all!
A very pestilence upon you fall!
Now that I have in safety reached the wood
Do what you like, the cock is mine for good;
I'll eat him there in spite of every one.'"
600   The fox replying, "Faith, it shall be done!"
Opened his mouth and spoke. The nimble bird,
Breaking away upon the uttered word,
Flew high into the tree-tops on the spot.
And when the fox perceived where he had got,
605 "Alas," he cried, "alas, my Chanticleer,
I've done you grievous wrong, indeed I fear
I must have frightened you; I grabbed too hard
When I caught hold and took you from the yard.
But, sir, I meant no harm, don't be offended,
610 Come down and I'll explain what I intended;
So help me God I'll tell the truth—on oath!"
"No," said the cock, "and curses on us both,
And first on me if I were such a dunce
As let you fool me oftener than once.
615 Never again, for all your flattering lies,
You'll coax a song to make me blink my eyes;
And as for those who blink when they should look,
God blot them from his everlasting Book!"
"Nay, rather," said the fox, "his plagues be flung
620 On all who chatter that should hold their tongue."
   Lo, such it is not to be on your guard
Against the flatterers of the world, or yard,
And if you think my story is absurd,
A foolish trifle of a beast and bird,
625 A fable of a fox, a cock, a hen,
Take hold upon the moral, gentlemen.
   St. Paul himself, a saint of great discerning,
Says that all things are written for our learning;
So take the grain and let the chaff be still.
630 And, gracious Father, if it be thy will
As saith my Savior, make us all good men,
And bring us to his heavenly bliss.
                    Amen.

RESPONDING TO THE SELECTION

Your Response

1. In what part of the tale do you think Chaucer's mock-heroic style is most effective? Why?

Recalling

2. Which physical features of Chanticleer and Pertelote are presented as especially attractive?
3. What is Pertelote's advice to Chanticleer when he tells her his dream?
4. How does the fox capture Chanticleer? How does Chanticleer escape?

Interpreting

5. (a) Compare and contrast the methods of argument that Pertelote and Chanticleer use to defend their interpretations of dreams. (b) What are the fallacies in each argument?
6. The first story that Chanticleer tells has the three-part structure typical of medieval tales: an exposition describing the characters and setting, a complication or problem, and a climax. Does "The Nun's Priest's Tale" as a whole follow this pattern? Why or why not?
7. (a) What is the moral of this fable? (b) How seriously do you think the narrator takes this moral? Explain.
8. What does this tale suggest about its teller, the nun's priest?

Applying

9. What does this tale reveal about the concerns of people in medieval times? Do we share similar concerns today? Explain.

ANALYZING LITERATURE

Understanding the Mock-Heroic Style

Chaucer uses the **mock-heroic style** in "The Nun's Priest's Tale," portraying the domestic animals in a barnyard as if they were the heroes and heroines of a great epic. He describes Chanticleer, for example, in terms that seem more appropriate for a mighty warrior: "His comb was red-der than fine coral, tall/And battlemented like a castle wall/ . . . Like burnished gold his feathers, flaming bright."

1. Epic heroes are often boastful. (a) How does the narrator portray Chanticleer's boastfulness through his words and behavior? (b) Why does this boastfulness strike a humorous note?
2. Which words and phrases in the description of Pertelote would be more suitable for a noble lady than for a hen?
3. Epics often depict the intervention of gods or goddesses in the affairs of humans. Where does Chaucer imitate this convention?

CRITICAL THINKING AND READING

Understanding Courtly Love

According to the tradition of courtly love popular in medieval times, a knight and a noble lady could only experience love at a distance. The goal was not marriage, or even physical contact, but admiration from afar. The lady's role was to believe in the knight's heroism and to inspire him with a token of her love, like a scarf or belt. His role was to show courage and total devotion.

Does the romance between Pertelote and Chanticleer follow the rules of courtly love? Why or why not?

THINKING AND WRITING

Writing a Beast Fable

The beast epic and fable were very popular during the medieval period. Write your own beast fable in which you use the mock-heroic style that characterizes "The Nun's Priest's Tale." Select a situation or theme that your classmates will recognize, and decide on the moral lesson that your story will illustrate. Then choose appropriate animal characters. Before writing, briefly outline the exposition, complication, and climax of your tale. As you write, remember to describe the activities of your beasts in lofty, mock-heroic terms. Test the success of your fable by reading it aloud to a group of classmates.

GUIDE FOR INTERPRETING

The Pardoner's Tale *from* The Canterbury Tales

Writers' Techniques

Exemplum. An anecdote is a brief account of an incident or event. Although "The Pardoner's Tale" may seem rather long for an anecdote, it is a special kind of anecdote—a 238-line anecdote within a sermon, something the Pardoner would have called an *exemplum,* or example. While anecdotes are often personal or biographical, the *exemplum* in "The Pardoner's Tale" is intended to establish the truth of a moral.

The idea for "The Pardoner's Tale" did not originate with Chaucer; it goes back to antiquity. The Pardoner uses this simple but powerful anecdote as an *exemplum* to prove the maxim, *"Radix malorum est cupiditas,"* or "Greed is the root of all evil."

Focus

You have heard many sayings similar to "Greed is the root of all evil." List at least five such sayings. Try to think of ones for which a good *exemplum* might be written.

Primary Source

In "The Pardoner's Tale," Chaucer drew from traditional stories, such as this *exemplum* on swearing by Thomas of Cantimpre, written before 1263.

In the city of Louvain, within the boundaries of Brabant we saw a noble and worthy citizen who, rising to go to matins on the holy night of Good Friday, passed in front of a tavern in which dissolute young men were sitting, playing at dice and vying with one another in blasphemies and oaths. Continuing on his way, this citizen found men in the street near the tavern who were making a loud lamentation over a certain stranger who was badly wounded and bleeding. When he asked the men who had inflicted these wounds they answered: 'Those young men who are playing dice.' Entering the tavern, the citizen upbraided the young men for playing on that night and asked them sternly why they had so cruelly beaten the stranger who had been with them. Much astonished, the young men denied that anyone had come in since they had sat down, and protested that they had wounded no one either by word or blow. Going forth quickly with the citizen, they sought for the bleeding stranger but could not find him. Having now recovered their senses, each of them realized that by their terrible oaths they had again insulted the Lord Christ and by their taunts had crucified him afresh.

from The Pardoner's Tale

Geoffrey Chaucer

translated by Nevill Coghill

During their journey to Canterbury, each of the pilgrims tells a tale. After the Knight, the Miller, the Reeve, the Nun, and the narrator have finished, the Pardoner entertains the others with a tale that supports his claim that "greed is the root of all evil."

It's of three rioters I have to tell
Who long before the morning service bell[1]
Were sitting in a tavern for a drink.
And as they sat, they heard the hand-bell clink
5 Before a coffin going to the grave;
One of them called the little tavern-knave[2]
And said "Go and find out at once—look spry!—
Whose corpse is in that coffin passing by;
And see you get the name correctly too."
10 "Sir," said the boy, "no need, I promise you;
Two hours before you came here I was told.
He was a friend of yours in days of old,
And suddenly last night, the man was slain,
Upon his bench, face up, dead drunk again.
15 There came a privy[3] thief, they call him Death,
Who kills us all round here, and in a breath
He speared him through the heart, he never stirred.
And then Death went his way without a word.
He's killed a thousand in the present plague,[4]
20 And, sir, it doesn't do to be too vague
If you should meet him; you had best be wary.
Be on your guard with such an adversary,
Be primed to meet him everywhere you go,
That's what my mother said. It's all I know."
25 The publican[5] joined in with, "By St. Mary.
What the child says is right; you'd best be wary,
This very year he killed, in a large village
A mile away, man, woman, serf at tillage,[6]
Page in the household, children—all there were.
30 Yes, I imagine that he lives round there.
It's well to be prepared in these alarms,
He might do you dishonor." "Huh, God's arms!"

1. long before . . . bell: Long before 9:00 A.M.

2. tavern-knave: Serving boy.

3. privy: Secretive.

4. plague: The Black Death, which killed over a third of the population of England in 1348 and 1349.

5. publican: Innkeeper.

6. tillage: Plowing.

The rioter said, "Is he so fierce to meet?
I'll search for him, by Jesus, street by street.
35   God's blessed bones! I'll register a vow!
Here, chaps! The three of us together now,
Hold up your hands, like me, and we'll be brothers
In this affair, and each defend the others,
And we will kill this traitor Death, I say!
40   Away with him as he has made away
With all our friends. God's dignity! To-night!"
     They made their bargain, swore with appetite,
These three, to live and die for one another
As brother-born might swear to his born brother.
45   And up they started in their drunken rage
And made towards this village which the page
And publican had spoken of before.
Many and grisly were the oaths they swore,
Tearing Christ's blessed body to a shred;[7]
50   "If we can only catch him, Death is dead!"
     When they had gone not fully half a mile,
 Just as they were about to cross a stile,
They came upon a very poor old man
Who humbly greeted them and thus began,
55   "God look to you, my lords, and give you quiet!"
To which the proudest of these men of riot
Gave back the answer, "What, old fool? Give place!
Why are you all wrapped up except your face?
Why live so long? Isn't it time to die?"
60   The old, old fellow looked him in the eye
And said, "Because I never yet have found,
Though I have walked to India, searching round
Village and city on my pilgrimage,
One who would change his youth to have my age.
65   And so my age is mine and must be still
Upon me, for such time as God may will.
     "Not even Death, alas, will take my life;
So, like a wretched prisoner at strife
Within himself, I walk alone and wait
70   About the earth, which is my mother's gate,
Knock-knocking with my staff from night to noon
And crying, 'Mother, open to me soon!
Look at me, mother, won't you let me in?
See how I wither, flesh and blood and skin!
75   Alas! When will these bones be laid to rest?
Mother, I would exchange—for that were best—
The wardrobe in my chamber, standing there
So long, for yours! Aye, for a shirt of hair[8]
To wrap me in!' She has refused her grace,
80   Whence comes the pallor of my withered face.

7. Tearing . . . shred:
Their oaths included
expressions such as "God's
arms" (line 32) and "God's
blessed bones" (line 35).

8. shirt of hair: Here, a
shroud.

"But it dishonored you when you began
To speak so roughly, sir, to an old man,
Unless he had injured you in word or deed.
It says in holy writ, as you may read,
85 'Thou shalt rise up before the hoary head
And honor it,' And therefore be it said
'Do no more harm to an old man than you,
Being now young, would have another do
When you are old'—if you should live till then.
90 And so may God be with you, gentlemen,
For I must go whither I have to go."
     "By God," the gambler said, "you shan't do so,
You don't get off so easy, by St. John!
I heard you mention, just a moment gone,
95 A certain traitor Death who singles out
And kills the fine young fellows hereabout.
And you're his spy, by God! You wait a bit.
Say where he is or you shall pay for it,
By God and by the Holy Sacrament!
100 I say you've joined together by consent
To kill us younger folk, you thieving swine!"
     "Well, sirs," he said, "if it be your design
To find out Death, turn up this crooked way
Towards that grove. I left him there today
105 Under a tree, and there you'll find him waiting.
He isn't one to hide for all your prating.
You see that oak? He won't be far to find.
And God protect you that redeemed mankind,
Aye, and amend you!" Thus that ancient man.
110   At once the three young rioters began
To run, and reached the tree, and there they found
A pile of golden florins[9] on the ground,

9. florins: Coins.

New-coined, eight bushels of them as they thought.
No longer was it Death those fellows sought,
115 For they were all so thrilled to see the sight,
The florins were so beautiful and bright,
That down they sat beside the precious pile.
The wickedest spoke first after a while.
"Brothers," he said, "you listen to what I say.
120 I'm pretty sharp although I joke away.
It's clear that Fortune has bestowed this treasure
To let us live in jollity and pleasure.
Light come, light go! We'll spend it as we ought.
God's precious dignity! Who would have thought
125 This morning was to be our lucky day?
     "If one could only get the gold away,
Back to my house, or else to yours, perhaps—
For as you know, the gold is ours, chaps—
We'd all be at the top of fortune, hey?

130 But certainly it can't be done by day.
     People would call us robbers—a strong gang,
     So our own property would make us hang.
     No, we must bring this treasure back by night
     Some prudent way, and keep it out of sight.
135 And so as a solution I propose
     We draw for lots and see the way it goes.
     The one who draws the longest, lucky man,
     Shall run to town as quickly as he can
     To fetch us bread and wine—but keep things dark—
140 While two remain in hiding here to mark
     Our heap of treasure. If there's no delay,
     When night comes down we'll carry it away,

THE PARDONER
Arthur Szyk for the Canterbury Tales

All three of us, wherever we have planned."
He gathered lots and hid them in his hand
145 Bidding them draw for where the luck should fall.
It fell upon the youngest of them all,
And off he ran at once towards the town.
As soon as he had gone, the first sat down
And thus began a parley[10] with the other:
150 "You know that you can trust me as a brother;
Now let me tell you where your profit lies;
You know our friend has gone to get supplies
And here's a lot of gold that is to be
Divided equally amongst us three.
155 Nevertheless, if I could shape things thus
So that we shared it out—the two of us—
Wouldn't you take it as a friendly turn?"
"But how!" the other said with some concern,
"Because he knows the gold's with me and you;
160 What can we tell him? What are we to do?'
"Is it a bargain," said the first, "or no?
For I can tell you in a word or so
What's to be done to bring the thing about."
"Trust me," the other said, "you needn't doubt
165 My word. I won't betray you, I'll be true."
"Well," said his friend, "you see that we are two,
And two are twice as powerful as one.
Now look; when he comes back, get up in fun
To have a wrestle; then, as you attack,
170 I'll up and put my dagger through his back
While you and he are struggling, as in game;
Then draw your dagger too and do the same.
Then all this money will be ours to spend,
Divided equally of course, dear friend.
175 Then we can gratify our lusts and fill
The day with dicing at our own sweet will."
Thus these two miscreants[11] agreed to slay
The third and youngest, as you heard me say.
The youngest, as he ran towards the town,
180 Kept turning over, rolling up and down
Within his heart the beauty of those bright
New florins, saying, "Lord, to think I might
Have all that treasure to myself alone!
Could there be anyone beneath the throne
185 Of God so happy as I then should be?"
And so the Fiend,[12] our common enemy,
Was given power to put it in his thought
That there was always poison to be bought,
And that with poison he could kill his friends.

10. parley (pär′ lē): Discussion.

11. miscreants (mis′ krē ɔnts): Villains.

12. Fiend: Satan.

190 To men in such a state the Devil sends
Thoughts of this kind, and has a full permission
To lure them on to sorrow and perdition;[13]
For this young man was utterly content
To kill them both and never to repent.

195   And on he ran, he had no thought to tarry,
Came to the town, found an apothecary
And said, "Sell me some poison if you will,
I have a lot of rats I want to kill
And there's a polecat too about my yard
200 That takes my chickens and it hits me hard;
But I'll get even, as is only right,
With vermin that destroy a man by night."
  The chemist answered, "I've a preparation
Which you shall have, and by my soul's salvation
205 If any living creature eat or drink
A mouthful, ere he has the time to think,
Though he took less than makes a grain of wheat,
You'll see him fall down dying at your feet;
Yes, die he must, and in so short a while
210 You'd hardly have the time to walk a mile,
The poison is so strong, you understand."
  This cursed fellow grabbed into his hand
The box of poison and away he ran
Into a neighboring street, and found a man
215 Who lent him three large bottles. He withdrew
And deftly poured the poison into two.
He kept the third one clean, as well he might,
For his own drink, meaning to work all night
Stacking the gold and carrying it away.
220 And when this rioter, this devil's clay,
Had filled his bottles up with wine, all three,
Back to rejoin his comrades sauntered he.
  Why make a sermon of it? Why waste breath?
Exactly in the way they'd planned his death
225 They fell on him and slew him, two to one.
Then said the first of them when this was done,
"Now for a drink. Sit down and let's be merry,
For later on there'll be the corpse to bury."
And, as it happened, reaching for a sup,
230 He took a bottle full of poison up
And drank; and his companion, nothing loth,
Drank from it also, and they perished both.
  There is, in Avicenna's long relation[14]
Concerning poison and its operation,
235 Trust me, no ghastlier section to transcend
What these two wretches suffered at their end.
Thus these two murderers received their due,
So did the treacherous young poisoner too.

13. perdition:
Damnation.

14. Avicenna's (aʹ və senʹ əz) **long relation:** A book on medicines written by Avicenna (980–1037), an Arab physician, which contains a chapter on poisons.

RESPONDING TO THE SELECTION

Your Response

1. Were you surprised at the fate of the three rioters? Why or why not?

Recalling

2. What do the three rioters pledge to do?
3. (a) What does the old man tell the rioters they will find under a tree? (b) What do they actually find there?
4. How do the two rioters decide to increase their share of the gold? Explain their plan.

Interpreting

5. In line 39, Death is presented as a traitor. Do you think this description is appropriate? Explain your answer.
6. Do the rioters keep the pledge they made in the tavern? Why or why not?
7. Does the old man know that in directing the three rioters to the oak tree he is sending them to their deaths? Explain.

Applying

8. What person in the news today, or in the recent past, has shown character traits similar to those of the Pardoner?

ANALYZING LITERATURE

Understanding an Anecdote (Exemplum)

"The Pardoner's Tale" is an *exemplum,* a brief moral story that the Pardoner tells the pilgrims. In medieval times an *exemplum* was often included in a sermon.

1. How does the young rioter's dialogue with the chemist help to characterize both the rioter and his two companions?
2. What moral does this *exemplum* establish?
3. In what ways does "The Pardoner's Tale" differ from a short story?

CRITICAL THINKING AND READING

Making Inferences

In the Prologue Chaucer makes the point that he is reporting the pilgrims' tales, "using their very phrases." Therefore, although the narrator of *The Canterbury Tales* is Chaucer, the narrator of each individual tale is a particular pilgrim. You can make judgments about the Pardoner based on his narration. Since Chaucer has already commented in the Prologue on the Pardoner's character, you have a chance to compare Chaucer's view of the Pardoner with the Pardoner's view of himself.

1. Does the topic the Pardoner chooses for his *exemplum* reflect his own interests? Explain.
2. Considering Chaucer's Prologue, how seriously do you think the Pardoner takes his moral that "Greed is the root of evil"? Explain.

THINKING AND WRITING

Writing an Analysis

Write an essay analyzing "The Pardoner's Tale." An analysis is not a plot summary; it is an explanation of how the various elements in a literary work fit together. In analyzing Chaucer's tale, consider at least three of these elements: characters, plot, dialogue, moral, rhyme scheme, similes, symbolism.

LEARNING OPTION

Speaking and Listening. After the Norman Conquest of England in 1066, there were two languages in daily use, the French of the invaders and the Old English of the natives. As time passed, the English language began to change. By about 1150, the changes in English were notable enough for later scholars to identify the beginning of a new period. Middle English lasted from 1150 to 1500.

You will find Middle English easier to read than Old English, but it differs from the English we use today. In Middle English, every syllable is pronounced: *bathed* is /bath'ed/; *soote* is /sō'tə/. Some consonants that today are silent were sounded in Middle English: *k* in *k*nyght; *g* in *g*nawe; *l* in fo*l*k; *gh* in drou*gh*te. Keeping these basic rules of pronunciation in mind, read aloud lines 1–18 on page 115 with a small group of classmates.

CROSS CURRENTS

Travel Writing

Travel became important during the Middle Ages and many travelers—both fictional and real-life—kept records of their journeys. Chaucer's pilgrims set off for Canterbury, King Arthur and his knights encountered strange creatures on their quests, and the real-life Marco Polo visited the court of Kublai Khan.

Writing about travel has been important throughout the ages and across cultures. For example, traveling along the Silk Road to India in the year 648, Prince Tripitaka stopped at the oasis of Kharashahr to describe an unusual custom. "The children born of common parents," he wrote, "have their heads flattened by the pressure of a wooden board." Not all travel diaries note such remarkable customs, but then again, not all travelers encounter waters "bluish-black in color, salty and bitter in taste" in whose depths "dragons and fishes swim together; scaly monsters rise to the surface,

WORLD MAP: CATHAY AND THE EMPIRE OF THE GREAT KHAN, 1459
Mauro
Biblioteca Nazionale Marciana, Venice

and passing travelers pray to them for good fortune."

EDUCATIONAL ACCOUNTS?

Whether the things travelers encounter on their journeys are exciting or commonplace, an astonishing number of people are moved to record their voyages in diaries. Many justify their accounts by claiming that travel is educational. E. S. Bates, for example, describes the "educational" sights people saw on the Continent in the 1600's:

> Torture accompanying execution was common, and branding and mutilation things that no traveller could well avoid seeing. But none seemed to want to avoid them: Evelyn [author of a famous diary] went to the Chatelet prison at Paris to look on while a prisoner underwent legal torture. The only occasions that seem to have struck them as too horrible was when the headsman bungled matters: a Dutchman at Paris saw one try sixteen times and then have to be assisted.

It appears that education, like beauty, may be in the eye of the beholder!

DIGNITY AND DECORUM

A travel diary allows one to record one's thoughts after the fact, and still maintain one's dignity. Few people were as famous for their dignity as Queen Victoria of England. Notice how she maintained her pride even as her carriage tumbled over, spilling her and Princess Alice to the ground.

A MEDIEVAL VIEW OF THE UNIVERSE
Ronald Sheridan Ancient Art and Architecture Collection

There was an awful pause, during which Alice said: "We are upsetting." In another moment—during which I had time to reflect whether we should be killed or not, and thought there were still things I had not settled and wanted to—the carriage turned over on its side, and we were all precipitated to the ground!

According to Victoria's account, she "precipitated" from the carriage. No "fall" or "drop" here!

"OPEN THE HEART'S STORE"

A travel diary gives us a way to say that this is what I, not the camera, saw. This is how Clara Milburn, an ordinary English-woman, voiced it in her travel diary: "There is so much background, one can't be dull, but can just open the heart's store, look round the shelves, take down the memory and live it over again. Grand!"

SIR THOMAS MALORY

1405[?]–1471

Who was the real Thomas Malory? Was he a Welshman whose name comes from "Maleor," a portion of Flintshire county in North Wales? Was he Thomas Malory of Hutton Conyers in Yorkshire? Or was he Thomas Malory of Newbold Revell in Warwickshire? The identity of the author of *Morte d'Arthur* is still a mystery, and speculation among literary scholars and historians leads only to a composite portrait, pieced together from the most reliable bits of evidence. This is appropriate when we consider that a large part of the task of writing *Morte d'Arthur* involved gathering bits of information about another figure whose identity is steeped in mystery: the legendary King Arthur himself.

"Syr Thomas Maleore knyght" is how the author's name appears in the first printings of *Morte d'Arthur.* It is generally accepted that during the Wars of the Roses (the bloody conflict between two factions of royalty that marred the latter half of the fifteenth century in England) this knight, a supporter of the House of Lancaster, was imprisoned at least once. His arrest in 1451 for vandalizing a monastery in Lincolnshire marked the beginning of what may have been a long battle with authorities loyal to the House of York. A number of crimes are attributed to him, although he denied them all. He was accused of twice looting the Abbey of Coombe, extorting money from a number of people, setting an ambush with intent to murder, raiding cattle, and various other crimes. He was even charged with breaking out of jail and once escaped custody by swimming a moat! It is not certain to what extent the charges were justified; nevertheless, Malory spent the greater portion of his later years in prison. Some combination of presumed or real criminal behavior and the making of powerful enemies kept him there. Existing records indicate that "Thomas Malorie, knight" was excluded from four general pardons granted by Yorkist King Edward IV to Lancastrian political prisoners.

It was in prison that Malory began writing *Morte d'Arthur.* How it was possible for him to compile and give order to a collection of French, English, and Latin tales about King Arthur and the Knights of the Round Table while incarcerated is not clear. As a knight, he was probably granted access to books, some of which may well have been the Arthurian texts that he translated and adapted. It is thought that Malory completed *Morte d'Arthur* in prison and may even have died there. His great prose work was given its name and published posthumously in 1485 by William Caxton, the man who established the first printing press in England.

GUIDE FOR INTERPRETING

from Morte d'Arthur

Historical Context

Arthurian Legend. It is ironic that so much material has been written about King Arthur when there is no proof whatsoever that a Celtic chieftain named Arthur ever truly existed. An important stimulus for the enormous wealth of Arthurian literature has been the fact that he *may* have existed. Not knowing for sure that an actual Arthur performed the deeds attributed to him has inspired many creative people, Malory among them, to endow the character with almost supernatural valor, integrity, and wisdom.

Where did the legend come from? Several early sources refer to a warrior-king named Arthur who lived, fought, and died in the years immediately following the withdrawal of Roman troops from Britain, at about the middle of the fifth century. The most reliable of these sources is a book called *On the Ruin and Conquest of Britain,* written in the 540's by a British cleric named Gildas, who may have interviewed people who were alive when Arthur was. Though Gildas does not mention Arthur by name, he describes a warrior who led the Britons against invading Anglo-Saxons in the Battle of Badon Hill, bringing peace to Britain for forty years.

Other accounts appear in the ninth century, when Arthur was already a folk hero. One, the *Annals of Wales,* places the Battle of Badon Hill between the years 490 and 516. Nennius's *History of the Britons* chronicles twelve battles allegedly fought by Arthur. Written about 830, it locates Arthur in the north of England, near the city of Carlisle at the Scottish border, and dates the battles in the latter part of the sixth century. This suggests that he fought not Anglo-Saxons but rival British chieftains who were seeking supremacy in one of the last outposts of Roman civilization.

Arthur's fame spread quickly. In fact, Sir Thomas Malory's *Morte d'Arthur* is drawn from tales written in France, where Arthur was a particularly popular figure. Malory's work, in turn, was the primary basis for many subsequent versions, including the 1960 Lerner and Lowe musical play, *Camelot.*

Primary Source

Early British historians attributed tremendous powers to Arthur, their national hero. Nennius, a Welsh historian, tells us that "The twelfth battle was on Badon Hill, in which nine hundred and sixty men fell in one day from one attack by Arthur, and no one killed them but himself alone." It seems he was no ordinary man.

Focus

Think about legendary people in our time who have accomplished difficult or important tasks. Write about the qualities and traits these people displayed that may have helped them to persevere.

from Morte d'Arthur

Sir Thomas Malory

This selection begins after King Arthur has traveled to France at the insistence of his nephew, Gawain, to besiege his former friend and knight, Lancelot, for his involvement with Queen Guenevere. However, the king's attempts to punish are halfhearted, and he is soon forced to abandon them altogether when he learns that his nephew, Mordred, has seized control of England. Arthur leads his forces back to England, and Mordred attacks them upon their landing. Gawain is killed in the fighting, but before he dies, he manages to send word to Lancelot that Arthur is in need of assistance.

So upon Trinity Sunday at night King Arthur dreamed a wonderful dream, and in his dream him seemed[1] that he saw upon a chafflet[2] a chair, and the chair was fast to a wheel, and thereupon sat King Arthur in the richest cloth of gold that might be made. And the King thought there was under him, far from him, an hideous deep black water, and therein was all manner of serpents, and worms, and wild beasts, foul and horrible. And suddenly the King thought that the wheel turned upside down, and he fell among the serpents, and every beast took him by a limb. And then the King cried as he lay in his bed, "Help, help!"

And then knights, squires, and yeomen awaked the King, and then he was so amazed that he wist[3] not where he was. And then so he awaked until it was nigh day, and then he fell on slumbering again, not sleeping nor thoroughly waking. So the King seemed[4] verily that there came Sir Gawain unto him with a number of fair ladies with him. So when King Arthur saw him, he said, "Welcome, my sister's son. I weened ye had been dead. And now I see thee on-live, much am I beholden unto Almighty Jesu. Ah, fair nephew and my sister's son, what been these ladies that hither be come with you?"

"Sir," said Sir Gawain, "all these be ladies for whom I have foughten for when I was man living. And all these are those that I did battle for in righteous quarrels, and God hath given them that grace, at their great prayer, because I did battle for them for their right, that they should bring me hither unto you. Thus much hath given me leave God, for to warn you of your death. For and ye fight as tomorn[5] with Sir Mordred, as ye both have assigned, doubt ye not ye must be slain, and the most party of your people on both parties. And for the great grace and goodness that Almighty Jesu hath unto you, and for pity of you and many more other good men there shall be slain, God hath sent me to you of his special grace to give you warning that in no wise ye do battle as tomorn, but that ye take a treaty for a month from today. And proffer you largely,[6] so that tomorn ye put in a delay. For within a month shall come Sir Lancelot with all his noble knights and rescue you worshipfully and slay Sir Mordred and all that ever will hold with him."

Then Sir Gawain and all the ladies vanished. And anon the King called upon his knights, squires, and yeomen, and charged

---

1. **him seemed:** It seemed to him.
2. **chafflet:** Platform.
3. **wist:** Knew.

4. **the King seemed:** It seemed to the King.
5. **and . . . tomorn:** If you fight tomorrow.
6. **proffer you largely:** Make generous offers.

them wightly[7] to fetch his noble lords and wise bishops unto him. And when they were come the King told them of his avision,[8] that Sir Gawain had told him and warned him that, and he fought on the morn, he should be slain. Then the King commanded Sir Lucan the Butler and his brother Sir Bedivere the Bold, with two bishops with them, and charged them in any wise to take a treaty for a month from today with Sir Mordred. "And spare not: proffer him lands and goods as much as ye think reasonable."

So then they departed and came to Sir Mordred where he had a grim host of an hundred thousand, and there they entreated Sir Mordred long time. And at the last Sir Mordred was agreed for to have Cornwall and Kent by King Arthur's days, and after that, all England, after the days of King Arthur.

Then were they condescended[9] that King Arthur and Sir Mordred should meet betwixt both their hosts, and each of them should bring fourteen persons. And so they came with this word unto Arthur. Then said he, "I am glad that this is done," and so he went into the field.

And when King Arthur should depart, he warned all his host that, and they see any sword drawn, "Look ye come on fiercely and slay that traitor Sir Mordred, for I in no wise trust him." In like wise Sir Mordred warned his host that "And ye see any manner of sword drawn, look that ye come on fiercely, and so slay all that ever before you standeth, for in no wise I will not trust for this treaty." And in the same wise said Sir Mordred unto his host, "For I know well my father will be avenged upon me."

And so they met as their pointment[10] was and were agreed and accorded thoroughly. And wine was fetched and they drank together. Right so came an adder out of a little heathbush, and it stung a knight in the foot. And so when the knight felt him so stung, he looked down and saw the adder. And anon he drew his sword to slay the adder, and thought none other harm. And when the host on both parties saw that sword drawn, then they blew beams,[11] trumpets, and horns, and shouted grimly. And so both hosts dressed them together. And King Arthur took his horse and said, "Alas, this unhappy day!" and so rode to his party, and Sir Mordred in like wise.

And never since was there never seen a more dolefuller battle in no Christian land, for there was but rushing and riding, lunging and striking; and many a grim word was there spoken of either to other, and many a deadly stroke. But ever King Arthur rode throughout the battle[12] of Sir Mordred many times and did full nobly, as a noble king should do, and at all times he fainted never. And Sir Mordred did his devoir that day and put himself in great peril.

And thus they fought all the long day, and never stinted[13] till the noble knights were laid to the cold earth. And ever they fought still till it was near night, and by then was there an hundred thousand laid dead upon the down. Then was King Arthur wood-wroth[14] out of measure when he saw his people so slain from him. And so he looked about him and could see no more of all his host, and good knights left no more on-live, but two knights: the t'one was Sir Lucan the Butler and the other his brother Sir Bedivere. And yet they were full sore wounded.

"Jesu, mercy," said the King, "where are all my noble knights become? Alas that ever I should see this doleful day! For now," said King Arthur, "I am come to mine end. But would to God," said he, "that I wist now where were that traitor Sir Mordred that has caused all this mischief."

---

7. wightly: Quickly.
8. avision: Dream.
9. condescended: Agreed.
10. pointment: Arrangement.

11. beams: A type of trumpet.
12. battle: Battalion.
13. stinted: Stopped.
14. wood-wroth: Wild with rage.

Then King Arthur looked about and was ware where stood Sir Mordred leaning upon his sword among a great heap of dead men.

"Now give me my spear," said King Arthur unto Sir Lucan, "for yonder I have espied the traitor that all this woe hath wrought."

"Sir, let him be," said Sir Lucan, "for he is unhappy. And if ye pass this unhappy day ye shall be right well revenged upon him. And, good lord, remember ye of your night's dream, and what the spirit of Sir Gawain told you tonight, and yet God of his great goodness hath preserved you hitherto. And for God's sake, my lord, leave off by this, for, blessed be God, ye have won the field: for yet we been here three on-live, and with Sir Mordred is not one on-live. And therefore if ye leave off now, this wicked day of destiny is past."

"Now, tide[15] me death, tide me life," said the King, "now I see him yonder alone, he shall never escape mine hands. For at a better avail shall I never have him."

"God speed you well!" said Sir Bedivere.

Then the King got his spear in both his hands and ran toward Sir Mordred, crying and saying, "Traitor, now is thy deathday come!"

And when Sir Mordred saw King Arthur he ran until him with his sword drawn in his hand, and there King Arthur smote Sir Mordred under the shield, with a thrust of his spear, throughout the body more than a fathom. And when Sir Mordred felt that he had his death's wound, he thrust himself with the might that he had up to the burr[16] of King Arthur's spear, and right so he smote his father King Arthur with his sword holden in both his hands, upon the side of the head, that the sword pierced the helmet and the casing of the brain. And therewith Sir Mordred dashed down stark dead to the earth.

And noble King Arthur fell in a swough to the earth, and there he swooned often-times, and Sir Lucan and Sir Bedivere oft-times heaved him up. And so, weakly betwixt them, they led him to a little chapel not far from the seaside, and when the King was there, him thought him reasonably eased. Then heard they people cry in the field. "Now go thou, Sir Lucan," said the King, "and do me to wit[17] what betokens that noise in the field."

So Sir Lucan departed, for he was grievously wounded in many places. And so as he walked he saw and harkened by the moon-light how that pillagers and robbers were come into the field to pill and to rob many a full noble knight of brooches and bracelets and of many a good ring and many a rich jewel. And who that were not dead all out there they slew them for their harness and their riches. When Sir Lucan understood this work, he came to the King as soon as he might and told him all what he had heard and seen. "Therefore by my read,"[18] said Sir Lucan, "it is best that we bring you to some town."

"I would it were so," said the King, "but I may not stand, my head works so. Ah, Sir Lancelot," said King Arthur, "this day have I sore missed thee. And alas that ever I was against thee, for now have I my death, whereof Sir Gawain me warned in my dream."

Then Sir Lucan took up the King the t'one party[19] and Sir Bedivere the other party; and in the lifting up the King swooned and in the lifting Sir Lucan fell in a swoon that part of his guts fell out of his body, and therewith the noble knight's heart burst. And when the King awoke he beheld Sir Lucan how he lay foaming at the mouth and part of his guts lay at his feet.

"Alas," said the King, "this is to me a full heavy sight to see this noble duke so die for my sake, for he would have helped me that had more need of help than I. Alas that he would not complain him for his heart was

---

15. **tide:** Befall.
16. **burr:** Hand guard.

17. **me to wit:** Let me know.
18. **read:** Advice.
19. **party:** Side.

so set to help me. Now Jesu have mercy upon his soul."

Then Sir Bedivere wept for the death of his brother.

"Now leave this mourning and weeping, gentle knight," said the King, "for all this will not avail me. For wit thou well, and I might live myself, the death of Sir Lucan would grieve me evermore. But my time passeth on fast," said the King. "Therefore," said King Arthur unto Sir Bedivere, "take thou here Excalibur my good sword and go with it to yonder water's side; and when thou comest there I charge thee throw my sword in that water and come again and tell me what thou sawest there."

"My lord," said Sir Bedivere, "your commandment shall be done, and I shall lightly[20] bring you word again."

So Sir Bedivere departed. And by the way he beheld that noble sword, that the pommel and the haft[21] was all precious stones. And then he said to himself, "If I throw this rich sword in the water, thereof shall never come good, but harm and loss." And then Sir Bedivere hid Excalibur under a tree. And so, as soon as he might, he came again unto the King and said he had been at the water and had thrown the sword into the water.

"What saw thou there?" said the King.

"Sir," he said, "I saw nothing but waves and winds."

"That is untruly said of thee," said the King. "And therefore go thou lightly again and do my commandment; as thou art to me loved and dear, spare not, but throw it in."

Then Sir Bedivere returned again and took the sword in his hand. And yet him thought sin and shame to throw away that noble sword. And so eft[22] he hid the sword and returned again and told the King that he had been at the water and done his commandment.

"What sawest thou there?" said the King.

THE NINE HEROES TAPESTRIES: CHRISTIAN HEROES: ARTHUR (detail)
Probably Nicolas Bataille, Paris
The Metropolitan Museum of Art

"Sir," he said, "I saw nothing but waters wap and waves wan."[23]

"Ah, traitor unto me and untrue," said King Arthur, "now hast thou betrayed me twice. Who would have weened that thou that has been to me so loved and dear, and thou art named a noble knight, and would betray me for the riches of this sword. But now go again lightly, for thy long tarrying putteth me in great jeopardy of my life, for I have taken cold. And but if thou do now as I bid thee, if ever I may see thee I shall slay thee mine own hands, for thou wouldest for my rich sword see me dead."

Then Sir Bedivere departed and went to the sword and lightly took it up, and so he went to the water's side; and there he bound the girdle about the hilts, and threw the sword as far into the water as he might. And there came an arm and an hand above the water and took it and clutched it, and shook it thrice and brandished; and then vanished

---

20. lightly: Quickly.
21. pommel . . . haft: Hilt and hand guard.
22. eft: Again.

23. waters . . . wan: Waters lap and waves grow dark.

away the hand with the sword into the water. So Sir Bedivere came again to the King and told him what he saw.

"Alas," said the King, "help me hence, for I dread me I have tarried overlong."

Then Sir Bedivere took the King upon his back and so went with him to that water's side. And when they were at the water's side, even fast[24] by the bank floated a little barge with many fair ladies in it; and among them all was a queen; and all they had black hoods, and all they wept and shrieked when they saw King Arthur.

"Now put me into that barge," said the King; and so he did softly. And there received him three ladies with great mourning, and so they set them down. And in one of their laps King Arthur laid his head, and then the queen said, "Ah, my dear brother, why have ye tarried so long from me? Alas, this wound on your head hath caught overmuch cold." And anon they rowed fromward the land, and Sir Bedivere beheld all tho ladies go froward him.

Then Sir Bedivere cried and said, "Ah, my lord Arthur, what shall become of me, now ye go from me and leave me here alone among mine enemies?"

"Comfort thyself," said the King, "and do as well as thou mayest, for in me is no trust for to trust in. For I must into the vale of Avilion[25] to heal me of my grievous wound. And if thou hear nevermore of me, pray for my soul."

But ever the queen and ladies wept and shrieked, that it was pity to hear. And as soon as Sir Bedivere had lost sight of the barge he wept and wailed, and so took the forest and went all that night.

And in the morning he was ware, betwixt two bare woods, of a chapel and an hermitage. Then was Sir Bedivere glad, and thither he went, and when he came into the chapel he saw where lay an hermit groveling on all fours, close thereby a tomb was new dug. When the hermit saw Sir Bedivere he knew him well, for he was but little tofore Bishop of Canterbury, that Sir Mordred put to flight.

"Sir," said Sir Bedivere, "what man is there here interred that you pray so fast for?"

"Fair son," said the hermit. "I wot not verily but by guessing. But this same night, at midnight, here came a number of ladies and brought here a dead corpse and prayed me to inter him. And here they offered an hundred tapers, and gave me a thousand gold coins."

"Alas," said Sir Bedivere, "that was my lord King Arthur, which lieth here buried in this chapel."

Then Sir Bedivere swooned, and when he awoke he prayed the hermit that he might abide with him still, there to live with fasting and prayers:

"For from hence will I never go," said Sir Bedivere, "by my will, but all the days of my life here to pray for my lord Arthur."

"Sir, ye are welcome to me," said the hermit, "for I know you better than ye think that I do: for ye are Sir Bedivere the Bold, and the full noble duke Sir Lucan the Butler was your brother."

Then Sir Bedivere told the hermit all as you have heard tofore, and so he stayed with the hermit that was beforehand Bishop of Canterbury. And there Sir Bedivere put upon him poor clothes, and served the hermit full lowly in fasting and in prayers.

Thus of Arthur I find no more written in books that been authorized, neither more of the very certainty of his death heard I nor read, but thus was he led away in a ship wherein were three queens; that one was King Arthur's sister, Queen Morgan le Fay, the other was the Queen of North Galis, and the third was the Queen of the Waste Lands.

Now more of the death of King Arthur could I never find, but that these ladies brought him to his grave, and such one was interred there which the hermit bare witness that was once Bishop of Canterbury. But yet the hermit knew not in certain that he was verily the body of King Arthur; for

---

24. fast: Close.
25. Avilion: A legendary island.

this tale Sir Bedivere, a knight of the Table Round, made it to be written.

Yet some men say in many parts of England that King Arthur is not dead, but carried by the will of our Lord Jesu into another place; and men say that he shall come again, and he shall win the Holy Cross. Yet I will not say that it shall be so, but rather I would say: here in this world he changed his life. And many men say that there is written upon the tomb this:

HIC IACET ARTHURUS, REX
QUONDAM, REXQUE FUTURUS[26]

---

26. Hic ... futurus: Here lies Arthur, who was once king and king will be again.

RESPONDING TO THE SELECTION

Your Response

1. Do you think King Arthur should have required Sir Bedivere to throw the noble sword Excalibur into the water? Why or why not?

Recalling

2. What warning does King Arthur receive in his dream?
3. (a) How does Arthur slay Mordred? (b) What does Mordred do just before he dies?
4. (a) What does Sir Bedivere learn on the morning after the battle? (b) What does he decide to do as a result of his discovery?

Interpreting

5. (a) How would you characterize Arthur? (b) How would you characterize Mordred?
6. What do you think are Sir Bedivere's reasons for twice failing to obey Arthur's request to throw Excalibur into the water?
7. What is ironic, or unexpected, about the way the battle begins?
8. How does the ending add to the mysterious, magical quality of the tale?

Applying

9. Why do you think the legend of King Arthur has retained its popularity for so long?

ANALYZING LITERATURE

Recognizing Legends

Legends are anonymous traditional stories popularly believed to be based on history. Generally, legends reflect the attitudes and values of the society that created them, and the heroes of legends usually possess qualities that the people of that society consider admirable. Legends also often involve evil characters who possess qualities considered undesirable.

1. What qualities does King Arthur possess that would have been considered admirable during medieval times?
2. What qualities does Mordred possess that would be considered undesirable?

THINKING AND WRITING

Writing About Legends

Although legends are often based on actual events, they usually involve characters with superhuman powers and contain fantastic events. Choose a folk hero from this or another culture. What superior qualities is he or she reputed to have had? What fantastic tasks did he or she accomplish? Write a brief paper comparing this hero to Arthur as he is portrayed in this excerpt from Malory's *Morte d'Arthur*. When you revise, make sure you have used clear transitions to make your comparisons.

LEARNING OPTION

Cross-curricular Connection. Explore methods of combat in the medieval era. How did armor and its use develop over time? What sorts of weaponry were common? What technologies did strategists in medieval wars have at their disposal? Prepare a brief oral report with illustrations for the class.

GUIDE FOR INTERPRETING

1475[?]

English theater began with what are called miracle plays, sometimes referred to as mystery plays. The aim of a miracle play is to dramatize an incident from the Bible. Morality plays, which came later, deal with the human struggle between virtue and vice. They feature characters that represent abstract concepts such as Beauty, Good Deeds, Knowledge, and Death. The most famous and sophisticated of the morality plays is *Everyman,* written by an unknown playwright.

The English theater originated in the medieval church. To make religious services more meaningful and impressive, the clergy began inserting bits of dialogue into the mass. These miniature dramas, much expanded, became miracle plays. The plays moved outdoors, lost their direct connection with the church, and became a popular form of entertainment. The miracle plays were performed on wagons that moved from place to place within a town or city. Each wagon stopped at designated stations and presented the same play at each. A viewer could sometimes see as many as fifty miracle plays by staying in one place throughout the day and watching as the procession of wagons passed by.

Morality plays such as *Everyman* grew out of these miracle plays and also out of medieval allegories, not all of them English, in which the characters are abstractions—Fear, Courtesy, Greed, Delight, and so on. *Everyman* resembles an earlier Dutch morality play, *Elckerlijk,* and because the subject matter of the two plays, the summoning of death, is so common, both may come from a single source. The theme of *Everyman* is the salvation of the soul as death approaches. When Everyman is summoned by Death, he finds that none of his friends and relatives—Fellowship, Cousin, Kindred, or Goods—will keep him company. As he makes his descent into the grave, only Good Deeds will go with him.

This play has enjoyed extraordinary success since its appearance in the fifteenth century. The allegory has been translated into many languages, has been used by later writers as the basis of their plays, and has often been performed, both as an academic revival and as a commercial production, on the twentieth-century stage.

from Everyman

Literary Forms

Morality Play. Medieval morality plays have a singleness of purpose—to dramatize the conflict between the power of good and evil for control of one's soul. Although the plays are intended to entertain audiences, they also seek to teach strict lessons of right and wrong. Essentially religious, morality plays are allegories in which characters appear as abstract virtues and vices. By their very nature, the characters are one-dimensional, lacking the complexity found in characters in more sophisticated drama. The plays were originally produced for a middle-class town audience, many of whose members could neither read nor write. The authors of most of the plays are unknown. This may seem strange because *Everyman* and other moralities came into being at a time when records were kept. A main reason for the anonymity of writers is (as the morality plays teach) that worldly ambition counted for little in the Church-dominated culture of that era. Lack of credit for individual achievement was the order of the day. No one knows, for instance, who designed the magnificent Gothic cathedrals or created the stained glass and statues that adorn them. The medieval architect and sculptor, like the medieval playwright, worked primarily for the glory of God.

Commentary

Four different copies of *Everyman* survive—two whole, one damaged, one fragmentary. It is thought that all four texts were printed between 1508 and 1537. The text used most often now, known as the Britwell copy, is the one reprinted in 1904. The title page of this slender volume is printed with the well-known woodcut of Everyman. In this picture he sports a small, round hat with a feather sticking jauntily out of the brim and a short open cape with broad lapels. He holds his hands up sadly, palms turned outward. His expression is upset as he turns toward the skeletal, eerie figure of Death, who is sternly summoning him. The background is dotted with what look like graveyard crosses; Death holds what appears to be a huge scroll, probably the list of those to be summoned next. If you were preparing an edition of *Everyman,* what cover illustration would you provide?

Focus

Assume you are writing a play to dramatize a principle such as "Honesty is the best policy" or "Haste makes waste." Write the principle. Then list at least five characters you would cast in the play. Give them abstract names like Deceit or Punctuality.

from Everyman

Here beginneth a treatise[1] how the High Father of Heaven sendeth DEATH *to summon every creature to come and give account of their lives in this world, and is in manner of a moral play.*

[*Enter* MESSENGER.]

MESSENGER. I pray, you all give your audience,
    And hear this matter with reverence,
    By figure[2] a moral play.
    The Summoning of Everyman called it is,
5   That of our lives and ending shows
    How transitory we be all day.[3]
    The matter is wonder precious,
    But the intent of it is more gracious
    And sweet to bear away.
10   The story saith: Man, in the beginning
    Look well, and take good heed to the ending,
    Be you never so gay.
    You think sin in the beginning full sweet,
    Which in the end causeth the soul to weep,
15   When the body lieth in clay.
    Here shall you see how fellowship and jollity,
    Both strength, pleasure, and beauty,
    Will fade from thee as flower in May.
    For ye shall hear how our Heaven-King
20   Calleth Everyman to a general reckoning.
    Give audience and hear what he doth say.

[*Exit* MESSENGER. *Enter* GOD.]

GOD. I perceive, here in my majesty,
    How that all creatures be to me unkind,[4]
    Living without dread in worldly prosperity.
25   Of ghostly[5] sight the people be so blind,
    Drowned in sin, they know me not for their God.
    In worldly riches is all their mind:
    They fear not of my righteousness the sharp rod;
    My law that I showed when I for them died
30   They forget clean, and shedding of my blood red.
    I hanged between two,[6] it cannot be denied:
    To get them life I suffered to be dead.
    I healed their feet, with thorns hurt was my head.
    I could do no more than I did, truly—
35   And now I see the people do clean forsake me.

1. **treatise:** Narrative.

2. **by figure:** In form.

3. **all day:** Always.

4. **unkind:** Thoughtless.

5. **ghostly:** Spiritual.

6. **two:** The two thieves between whom Christ was crucified.

They use the seven deadly sins damnable,
As pride, coveitise,[7] wrath, and gluttony
Now in the world be made commendable.
And thus they leave of angels the heavenly company.

40 Every man liveth so after his own pleasure,
And yet of their life they be nothing sure.
I see the more that I them forbear,
The worse they be from year to year:
All that liveth appaireth[8] fast.

45 Therefore I will, in all the haste,
Have a reckoning of every man's person.
For, and[9] I leave the people thus alone
In their life and wicked tempests,
Verily they will become much worse than beasts;

50 For now one would by envy another up eat.
Charity do they all clean forgeet.
I hoped well that every man
In my glory should make his mansion,
And thereto I had them all elect.[10]

55 But now I see, like traitors deject,[11]
They thank me not for the pleasure that I to[12] them
    meant,
Nor yet for their being that I them have lent.
I proffered the people great multitude of mercy,
And few there be that asketh it heartily.[13]

60 They be so cumbered[14] with worldly riches
That needs on them I must do justice—
On every man living without fear.
Where art thou, Death, thou mighty messenger?

[*Enter* DEATH.]

DEATH. Almighty, God, I am here at your will,
65 Your commandment to fulfull.
GOD. Go thou to Everyman,
And show him, in my name,
A pilgrimage he must on him take,
Which he in no wise may escape;

70 And that he bring with him a sure reckoning
Without delay or any tarrying.
DEATH. Lord, I will in the world go run over all,[15]
And cruelly out-search both great and small.

[*Exit* GOD.]

Everyman will I beset that liveth beastly
75 Out of God's laws, and dreadeth not folly.
He that loveth riches I will strike with my dart,
His sight to blind, and from heaven to depart[16]—
Except that Almsdeeds[17] be his good friend—
In hell for to dwell, world without end.

7. coveitise: Avarice.

8. appaireth:
Degenerates.

9. and: If.

10. elect: Chosen.
11. deject: Abased.
12. to: For.

13. heartily: Sincerely.
14. cumbered:
Encumbered.

15. over all: Everywhere.

16. depart: Separate.
17. Almsdeeds: Deeds of
mercy; good deeds.

80 Lo, yonder I see Everyman walking:
Full little he thinketh on my coming;
His mind is on fleshly lusts and his treasure,
And great pain it shall cause him to endure
Before the Lord, Heaven-King.

[*Enter* EVERYMAN.]

85 Everyman, stand still! Whither art thou going
Thus gaily? Hast thou thy Maker forgeet?
EVERYMAN. Why askest thou?
Why wouldest thou weet?[18]

18. **weet:** Know.

DEATH. Yea, sir, I will show you:
In great haste I am sent to thee
From God out of his majesty.
EVERYMAN. What! sent to me?
DEATH. Yea, certainly.
Though thou have forgot him here,
95 He thinketh on thee in the heavenly sphere,
As, ere we depart, thou shalt know.
EVERYMAN. What desireth God of me?
DEATH. That shall I show thee:
A reckoning he will needs have
100 Without any longer respite.
EVERYMAN. To give a reckoning longer leisure I crave.
This blind[19] matter troubleth my wit.

19. **blind:** Unexpected.

DEATH. On thee thou must take a long journay:
Therefore thy book of count[20] with thee thou bring,

20. **count:** Accounts.

105 For turn again thou cannot by no way.
And look thou be sure of thy reckoning,
For before God thou shalt answer and shew
Thy many bad deeds and good but a few—
How thou hast spent thy life and in what wise,
110 Before the Chief Lord of Paradise.
Have ado that we were in that way,[21]
For weet thou well thou shalt make none attornay.[22]

21. **Have ado . . . way:** Let us get started.
22. **none attornay:** None appear in your place.

EVERYMAN. Full unready I am such reckoning to give.
I know thee not. What messenger art thou?
115 **DEATH.** I am Death that no man dreadeth,[23]
For every man I 'rest,[24] and no man spareth;
For it is God's commandment
That all to me should be obedient.

23. **that no man dreadeth:** That fears no one.
24. **'rest:** Arrest.

EVERYMAN. O Death, thou comest when I had thee least in mind.
120 In thy power it lieth me to save:
Yet of my good[25] will I give thee, if thou will be kind,
Yea, a thousand pound shalt thou have—
And defer this matter till another day.

25. **good:** Goods.

DEATH. Everyman, it may not be, by no way.

125   I set nought by[26] gold, silver, nor riches,
      Nor by pope, emperor, king, duke, nor princes,
      For, and I would receive gifts great,
      All the world I might get.
      But my custom is clean contrary:
130   I give thee no respite. Come hence and not tarry!
      EVERYMAN. Alas, shall I have no longer respite?
      I may say Death giveth no warning.
      To think on thee it maketh my heart sick,
      For all unready is my book of reckoning.
135   But twelve year and I might have a biding,[27]
      My counting-book I would make so clear
      That my reckoning I should not need to fear.
      Wherefore, Death, I pray thee, for God's mercy,
      Spare me till I be provided of remedy.
140   **DEATH.** Thee availeth not to cry, weep, and pray;
      But haste thee lightly[28] that thou were gone that journay,
      And prove[29] thy friends, if thou can.
      For weet thou well the tide[30] abideth no man,
      And in the world each living creature
145   For Adam's sin must die of nature.[31]
      EVERYMAN. Death, if I should this pilgrimage take
      And my reckoning surely make,
      Show me, for saint[32] charity,
      Should I not come again shortly?
150   **DEATH.** No, Everyman. And thou be once there,
      Thou mayst never more come here,
      Trust me verily.
      EVERYMAN. O gracious God in the high seat celestial,
      Have mercy on me in this most need!
155   Shall I have company from this vale terrestrial
      Of mine acquaintance that way me to lead?
      DEATH. Yea, if any be so hardy
      That would go with thee and bear thee company.
      Hie[33] thee that thou were gone to God's magnificence,
160   Thy reckoning to give before his presence.
      What, weenest[34] thou thy life is given thee,
      And thy worldly goods also?
      EVERYMAN. I had weened so, verily.
      DEATH. Nay, nay, it was but lent thee.
165   For as soon as thou art go,
      Another a while shall have it and then go therefro,
      Even as thou hast done.
      Everyman, thou art mad! Thou hast thy wits[35] five,
      And here on earth will not amend thy live![36]
170   For suddenly I do come.
      EVERYMAN. O wretched caitiff! Whither shall I flee
      That I might 'scape this endless sorrow?

26. set nought by: Care nothing for.

27. twelve year . . . biding: If I might have a twelve-year delay.

28. lightly: Quickly.
29. prove: Test.
30. tide: Time.

31. of nature: Naturally.

32. saint: Holy.

33. Hie: Hasten.

34. weenest: Suppose.

35. wits: Senses.
36. thy live: In thy life.

Now, gentle Death, spare me till tomorrow,
That I may amend me
175   With good advisement.[37]
  DEATH. Nay, thereto I will not consent,
    Nor no man will I respite,
    But to the heart suddenly I shall smite,
    Without any advisement.
180   And now out of thy sight I will me hie:
    See thou make thee ready shortly,
    For thou mayst say this is the day
    That no man living may 'scape away.
  [*Exit* DEATH.]

37. advisement: Preparation.

Everyman calls on Fellowship, Cousin, Kindred, and Goods (his friends, relatives, and wealth) to accompany him on his journey, but they all refuse and desert him. Everyman then summons his Good Deeds and Knowledge, and Knowledge leads him to Confession, who comforts him. Following his meeting with Confession, Everyman is assisted by Good Deeds, Knowledge, Beauty, Strength, Five-Wits (Five Senses), and Discretion (the attributes that make up an integrated person) in making up his book of accounts. Then each one, except for Good Deeds and Knowledge, leaves him as he makes final preparations for his journey to the grave.

  EVERYMAN. O Jesu, help, all hath forsaken me!
185   **GOOD DEEDS.** Nay, Everyman, I will bide with thee:
    I will not forsake thee indeed;
    Thou shalt find me a good friend at need.
  EVERYMAN. Gramercy,[38] Good Deeds! Now may I true friends see.
    They have forsaken me every one—
190   I loved them better than my Good Deeds alone.
    Knowledge, will ye forsake me also?
  KNOWLEDGE. Yea, Everyman, when ye to Death shall go,
    But not yet, for no manner of danger.
  EVERYMAN. Gramercy, Knowledge, with all my heart!
195   **KNOWLEDGE.** Nay, yet will I not from hence depart
    Till I see where ye shall become.[39]
  EVERYMAN. Methink, alas, that I must be gone
    To make my reckoning and my debts pay,
    For I see my time is nigh spent away.
200   Take example, all ye that this do hear or see,
    How they that I best loved do forsake me,
    Except my Good Deeds that bideth truly.
  GOOD DEEDS. All earthly things is but vanity.

38. Gramercy: Good thanks.

39. where ye shall become: What shall become of you.

Beauty, Strength, and Discretion do man forsake,
205 Foolish friends and kinsmen that fair spake—
All fleeth save Good Deeds, and that am I.
EVERYMAN. Have mercy on me, God most mighty,
And stand by me, thou mother and maid, holy Mary!
GOOD DEEDS. Fear not: I will speak for thee.
210 **EVERYMAN.** Here I cry God mercy!
GOOD DEEDS. Short our end, and 'minish our pain.[40]
Let us go, and never come again.
EVERYMAN. Into thy hands, Lord, my soul I commend:
Receive it, Lord, that it be not lost.
215 As thou me boughtest,[41] so me defend,
And save me from the fiend's boast,
That I may appear with that blessed host
That shall be saved at the day of doom.
In manus tuas, of mights most,
220 Forever *commendo spiritum meum.*[42]

[EVERYMAN *and* GOOD DEEDS *descend into the grave.*]

KNOWLEDGE. Now hath he suffered that we all shall endure,
The Good Deeds shall make all sure.
Now hath he made ending,
Methinketh that I hear angels sing
225 And make great joy and melody
Where Everyman's soul received shall be.
ANGEL. [*within*] Come, excellent elect spouse to Jesu![43]
Here above thou shalt go
Because of thy singular virtue.
230 Now the soul is taken the body fro,
Thy reckoning is crystal clear:
Now shalt thou into the heavenly sphere—
Unto the which all ye shall come
That liveth well before the day of doom.

[*Enter Doctor.*[44]]

235 **DOCTOR.** This memorial[45] men may have in mind:
Ye hearers, take it of worth, old and young,
And forsake Pride, for he deceiveth you in the end.
And remember Beauty, Five-Wits, Strength, and
  Discretion,
They all at the last do Everyman forsake,
240 Save his Good Deeds there doth he take—
But beware, for and they be small,
Before God he hath no help at all—
None excuse may be there for Everyman.
Alas, how shall he do than?[46]
245 For after death amends may no man make,
For then mercy and pity doth him forsake.

40. Short . . . pain: Make our death quick and diminish our pain.

41. boughtest: Redeemed.

42. *In manus . . . meum:* "Into thy hands, O greatest of powers, I commend my spirit forever." (Latin)

43. spouse to Jesu: Everyman's soul is referred to as the bride of Jesus.

44. doctor: A learned theologian.
45. memorial: Reminder.

46. than: Then.

If his reckoning be not clear when he doth come,
God will say, "*Ite, maledicti, in ignem eternum!*"[47]
And he that hath his account whole and sound,
250   High in heaven he shall be crowned,
Unto which place God bring us all thither,
That we may live body and soul togither.
Thereto help, the Trinity!
Amen, say ye, for saint charity.

47. *Ite . . . eternum*: "Depart, ye cursed, into everlasting fire." (Latin)

THE OLD MAN AND DEATH, C.1774
Joseph Wright of Derby
Wadsworth Atheneum, Hartford

Your Response

1. Do you agree with God's assessment of humanity in the play? Why or why not?

Recalling

2. On what mission does God send Death?
3. What does Everyman request when he first learns the purpose of Death's visit?
4. (a) How does Good Deeds respond to Everyman's plea for companionship? (b) How does Knowledge respond?

Interpreting

5. What is God's main complaint about the way people on earth are behaving?
6. Death repeatedly refuses to give Everyman any additional time. Why?
7. What does Death tell Everyman about the ownership of worldly goods?

Applying

8. How do you account for the fact that stage productions of *Everyman* have continued to be successful up to the present day?

ANALYZING LITERATURE

Understanding a Morality Play

The basic question in a morality play is "What must I do to be saved?" A struggle occurs between good and evil for the possession of one's soul. The characters are abstractions: Death, Pride, Strength, Beauty, Knowledge. *Everyman's* plot is restricted to the last part of a typical morality play—the arrival of Death.

1. Find two places in *Everyman* (not at the very beginning or end) where a line or lines directly express the play's message. Write the lines.
2. Which characters represent categories of people rather than abstract qualities?

CRITICAL THINKING AND READING

Interpreting Names as Symbols

The name of a character in literature can be used as a symbol. A **symbol** is a word, person, or object that stands for something more than just itself. For example, a star can stand for achievement, but the word *star* can also be used as a character's name for the same purpose—e.g., Brenda Starr. In *Everyman,* a character is simply called Achievement. Achievement, however, can also be suggested by a name like Mark Winner. Choose two of the following fictional names and make them into appropriate morality play names. (Example: Mr. Bumble = Stupidity) (1) Mr. Gradgrind (2) Holly Golightly (3) Jack Armstrong (4) Lady Sneerwell (5) Tess Truehart (6) Flem Snopes (7) Daddy Warbucks.

THINKING AND WRITING

Discussing a Morality Play

Write an essay in which you discuss the playwright's answer in *Everyman* to the morality play question about the conduct of life. Give your opinion of the play's effectiveness. Is the play dramatic? Persuasive? Would it be better if Everyman escaped Death? Explain. When you revise, make sure you supply adequate support for your opinion.

LEARNING OPTION

Performance. When you act in a play, it is important to understand your part as the playwright intended it to be. This requires going beyond a mere reading of lines. What is the character's function in the play? What is his or her personality and motivation?

Go to the library and borrow a recording of a play for which you can also borrow the text. Choose a scene and read it a few times. Then, listen to the professional actor read it. Note the stresses, the pauses, and the emotions. Compare the professional performance with your own.

Next, with one or two classmates, select a passage from *Everyman,* choose parts, and read the passage until its meaning becomes completely clear. Make sure you know how you want to say every word. If possible, practice with a tape recorder. Then perform the passage in class.

THE CHANGING ENGLISH LANGUAGE

Middle English 1066–1485

THE NORMAN CONQUEST

In the long run, the Norman Conquest may have benefited the English language; in the short run, it was a disaster. As Normans took over the country, so they took over the language, replacing English with French. Norman clergymen ruled the English church, Norman clerks ran the English government, Norman merchants regulated English commerce—and they all spoke French. In effect, the Norman conquest transformed England virtually overnight into a bilingual country. While most of the English still spoke English at home and among themselves, to survive many learned to understand French, if not to speak it. Likewise, many of the French-speaking upper classes understood English, even if they could not speak it.

The immediate changes in English reflect the influence of the conquerors on the conquered. The English lived in a humble *cot* (cottage); the Normans, in a French *maneir* (manor or mansion) or *castel.* The English

did the *werc;* the Normans relished the *leisir* and *profit.* Life for the Normans was *asie;* for the English, *hard.* In writing, Latin became the language of business. In 1154, the English monks abandoned their work on the *Anglo-Saxon Chronicle* and a great silence fell on English writing. The victory of Norman French seemed complete. Had things continued in this way, England might well have assumed the language of its conquerors.

Why did English survive? First, English was simply too well rooted to die. It was one thing for writing, controlled by a small group of educated clerks, to adopt Latin and French; it was quite another for the established daily speech of regular people to change. Second, the two cultures quickly intermarried. Thus, as early as 1177, a chronicler could write that "the two nations have become so mixed that it is scarcely possible today, speaking of free men, to tell who is English, who is of Norman race." Third, around 1200 King John lost nearly all of his land in France to the French crown. In effect, this forced the Norman lords to make up their minds whether to be French or English.

Bayeux Tapestry—Normans Attack the English

ENGLISH MAKES A COMEBACK

The appearance of church sermons, prayers, and carols in English in the early part of the thirteenth century heralded the recovery of the language. English words began to sneak into Latin documents. By 1300 almost everyone in England spoke English, but only a few also spoke French. A poet of the age, writing in English, was able to report that:

Lewede men cune Ffrensch non
Among an hondryd, unne pis on.

**Beginning of prologue to the CANTERBURY TALES
15th-Century Manuscript**

(Of French the common men know none/Among a hundred, scarcely one.)

Anti-French sentiment during the Hundred Years' War with France (1337–1453) greatly encouraged people to speak English rather than French. The Black Death, by causing so many deaths in monasteries and churches, gave rise to a new generation of non-French and -Latin speakers who took over as abbots and prioresses.

MIDDLE ENGLISH

English had survived, but it had changed. It had become what scholars now call Middle English, a term coined in the nineteenth century to describe English from 1150 to 1500. The category is somewhat artificial, though, for much of what has come to be called Middle English is simply a written record of what had already happened to the spoken language. Therefore, while spoken English had almost certainly shed most of its inflections (word changes that indicate meaning) by 1066, it was not until the language was written down that these changes were recorded. Another important simplification in the language was the adoption of prepositions to replace the Old English word endings, a process that we know began earlier. Still another key change was the loss of grammatical gender in the vast majority of words. Today we use gender in a few pronouns, such as *he* and *she* for male and female people and *it* to refer to everything else. Further, words were no longer formed in the Old English style, by adding complex prefixes and suffixes. To some extent this was replaced by the use of Latin prefixes (*dis-*, *trans-*, and *re-*). Overall, these changes resulted in a vast simplification of the language.

GEOFFREY CHAUCER

Chaucer's career illustrates the triumph of English. By deliberately writing in English, he represented the rebirth of English as a national language. His work integrates the changes English had undergone in the preceding centuries—the richness of Middle English, Latinized and Frenchified by Christianity and conquest.

THE TRIUMPH OF ENGLISH

Seventeen years after Chaucer's death, Henry V became the first English king since Harold to use English in his official documents, including his will. In 1415 Henry crossed the Channel to fight the French. In the first letter he dictated in France, he decided to write in English. This national statement indicates a turning point. English had triumphed.

YOUR WRITING PROCESS

WRITING A SATIRIC PORTRAIT

"Satire is a sort of glass, wherein beholders do generally discover everybody's face but their own."

Jonathan Swift

Many writers, like Chaucer, have created portraits of their society by satirizing various personality types. Even a high school, which is a society of students, teachers, and others, can be depicted satirically. To find out how important issues in a society can be addressed humorously, and beneficially, through satire, try writing a gently satiric portrait of a type of student in your school.

> **Focus**
>
> **Assignment:** Write a satirical character sketch of a type of student in your school.
> **Purpose:** To illustrate the imperfections in a high school society in a humorous way.
> **Audience:** Your fellow students and your teacher.

Prewriting

1. Identify personality types. Think about and discuss with your classmates types of students in your school. You may want to use a sunburst diagram to identify these types.

Student Model

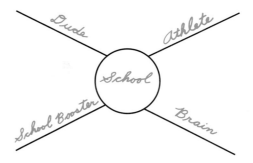

2. Which traits can you satirize? Work with a group of classmates to list the traits of the character type you have chosen to satirize. Don't restrict yourself to personality traits. Include details of dress and speech as well.

3. Choose a format. Decide if you want to write your character sketch in prose or verse. It is probably easier to write one in prose but a sketch in verse might be more memorable.

4. Give your character a suitable name. You may simply want to base the name on your character's primary trait, for example, "The Brain." You may, however, want to give your character an imaginative name that suggests his or her primary traits. For instance, you might call an athletic type "Hank the Hulk."

Drafting

1. Refer to your list of traits. For help during the drafting stage, look at the list of traits you created. Remember that satirists use exaggeration to make their points. How can you exaggerate your character's traits so that they will seem slightly absurd?

2. Be aware of your tone. Although you exaggerate, you should avoid a mean or spiteful tone. By keeping your satire affectionate, you will be able to instruct and entertain your audience without offending anyone.

3. Include examples of your character's speech. Portions of your sketch may include a monologue spoken by your character. Showing how your character speaks will help round out your sketch.

Student Model

Last night I went over to Wayne Dude's house. He was wearing a rock concert t-shirt as usual, and I heard a lot of noise in the background. "Hi," he said when I appeared at the door. "I'm your excellent host Wayne. Word! There are a lot of gnarly dudes here and nobody's lame. So come in and we'll just party on, party on. Chill!"

---

4. Remember your audience. Make sure you take into account that your sketch will be read by your teacher and fellow students alike. Your material should be suitable for your entire audience.

Revising and Proofreading

1. Ask a classmate to read and comment on your draft. Have this reader answer questions like the following:
- Do you recognize the character type I have described?
- Have I captured the way in which this type of character speaks and behaves?
- Is my tone humorous without being insulting?

2. Proofread your sketches. Make sure that the final version of your character sketch is free of errors in grammar, usage, spelling, and punctuation.

Writer's Tip
Recall how Chaucer uses key details of dress to characterize the various types of people he is satirizing.

Options for Publishing
- Find a fellow student who has satirized the same personality type and exchange portraits with each other.
- Contribute your satire to a class book of satiric sketches entitled *Modern Canterbury Tales.*
- Illustrate your sketch with an exaggerated drawing, or caricature, that will add to the satire. Then read your satire aloud to the class and show them the caricature.

Grammar Tip
Remember to use a comma, question mark, or exclamation mark after a quoted sentence that comes before an interrupting expression. Example: "You are an adult," warned my mother. "You must be responsible for your own actions."

QUEEN ELIZABETH AND SIR WALTER RALEIGH
Charles Edouard Boutibonne

THE ENGLISH RENAISSANCE
1485–1625

This royal throne of kings, this sceptered isle,
This earth of majesty, this seat of Mars,
This other Eden, demi-paradise,
This fortress built by Nature for herself
Against infection and the hand of war,
This happy breed of men, this little world,
This precious stone set in the silver sea,
Which serves it in the office of a wall,
Or as a moat defensive to a house,
Against the envy of less happier lands,
This blessed plot, this earth, this realm, this England.

William Shakespeare

The ending of the Wars of the Roses and the founding of the Tudor dynasty in 1485 opened a new era in English life. Monarchs assured stability by increasing their own power and undercutting the strength of the nobles. At the same time, they dramatically changed England's religious practices. They also helped to transform England from a small, insular nation into one of the world's great powers. In this way the English people gained a new pride and sense of nationhood, clearly reflected in the patriotic lines by William Shakespeare (1564–1616) on the previous page.

The Coming of the Renaissance

The Renaissance was a flowering of literary, artistic, and intellectual development that began in Italy in the fourteenth century. The movement was inspired by the arts and scholarship of ancient Greece and Rome, which were rediscovered during the Crusades. Classical learning lived again as new generations of scholars and artists explored and extended the achievements of the ancients. Among the key characteristics of the Renaissance were:

- The religious devotion of the Middle Ages, with its emphasis on the afterlife, gave way to a new interest in the human being's place here on Earth.

- Universities introduced a new curriculum called the humanities, which included history, geography, poetry, and modern languages.

- The invention of printing from movable type made books available to more people than ever before. A German printer, Johann Gutenberg, published a Bible in the 1450's that is believed to be the first book printed in the new manner.

- While scholars used Greek and Latin to study the ancients and students learned those languages in school, more and more writers began working in the vernacular—the local language. In England, the English language shed some of its regional differences and became increasingly standardized.

The Slow Spread of Renaissance Ideas

The Renaissance did not jump the Channel into England until the final two decades of the fifteenth century. At that time, Renaissance ideas had already been spreading across the European continent for more than a century. Because the Renaissance began in Italy, many of the leading Renaissance figures were Italian. Among them were the poet Dante Alighieri (1265–1321), author of *The Divine Comedy;* Francesco Petrarca, known as Petrarch (1304–1374), who wrote lyric poetry in a new fourteen-line form called the sonnet; and the painter, sculptor, architect, engineer, and scientist Leonardo da Vinci (1452–1519). Because of the scope of his interests and talents, Da Vinci typifies what we call the Renaissance man—a person of broad education and interests whose curiosity knew no bounds.

The Age of Exploration

The Renaissance thirst for knowledge had many practical consequences, one of which was a great burst of exploration. The Crusades had opened routes to Asia, but the merchants of the Italian city-states quickly monopolized trade over the new routes by sea and land. Seeking their own path to the riches of Asia, navigators representing Portugal and Spain began seeking an all-sea route. Aided by the development of the compass and by advances in astronomy, which freed them from the need to cling closely to the ocean's shores, these navigators ventured far and wide. Their explorations culminated in Columbus's arrival in the New World in 1492. Soon, European powers were establishing colonies in the Americas and extracting great wealth from the new lands.

England's participation in this Age of Exploration began in 1497, when the Italian-born explorer John Cabot, sailing for an English company, reached Newfoundland (an island off the east coast of what is now Canada) and perhaps also the mainland. Cabot thus laid the basis for future English claims in North America. However, English leaders would not exploit those claims until near the end of the English Renaissance.

The Protestant Reformation

Hand in hand with commercial expansion came a growing sense of nationalism, which, along with the new Renaissance spirit, led many Europeans to question the universal authority of the Roman Catholic Church. Many people had grievances against the Church. Some objected to the sale of indulgences—remissions of punishment for sins, for which people made payments that often went straight into the pockets of corrupt Church officials. Critics also objected to other forms of payment to the Church, viewing them as a form of taxation. Other people argued that Church leaders played favorites by supporting Mediterranean powers against more northerly countries. Still others—scholars who were influenced by the growth of independent thinking in the universities—questioned Church teachings and the Church hierarchy.

One critical scholar was the great Dutch thinker Desiderius Erasmus (1466–1536), whose edition of the New Testament raised serious questions about standard Church interpretations of the Bible. Erasmus studied and taught in England. Through his friendship with such English writers as Thomas More (1478–1535), Erasmus focused attention on issues of morality and religion, which remained as central concerns of the English Renaissance, often overshadowing the artistic concerns that dominated the Italian Renaissance.

Although Erasmus himself remained a Roman Catholic, he helped to pave the way for a split in the Roman Church that began in 1517, when a German monk named Martin Luther (1483–1546) nailed a list of dissenting beliefs (his *Ninety-five Theses*) to the door of a German church. Luther's protest was aimed only at reforming the Roman Catholic Church, but it ended by dividing that Church and introducing a new Christian denomination known as Protestantism. The process that Luther started has come to be called the Protestant Reformation.

Fueled by political discontent, the Protestant Reformation swept through much of Europe. It led to frequent wars between European nations whose rulers had opposing religious beliefs. Protestants and Catholics both suffered persecution, depending on where they happened to live and which religion their ruler supported. Protestants themselves were divided, and in Germany the followers of Luther (called Lutherans) persecuted the followers of another Protestant reformer, John Calvin of Geneva. Calvin's ideas (called Calvinism) found a foothold in Switzerland, England, and Scotland, however, and helped bring about the establishment of the Puritan and Presbyterian sects.

England Under the Tudors

The Tudor dynasty ruled England from 1485 to 1603. Looking back, we see this period as a time of stability and economic expansion. English wool growers were finding new markets abroad. English investors were forming trading companies to tap the riches of far-off places like India. London had grown into a metropolis of more than 180,000 people. However, those who lived in Tudor times often saw economic changes as a threat to the old familiar ways, and memories of the Wars of the Roses caused many people to fear new outbreaks of civil strife.

Henry VII and Henry VIII

The first Tudor monarch, Henry VII, inherited an England that had been depleted and exhausted by years of civil war. By the time he died in 1509, he had rebuilt the nation's treasury and established law and order. In doing so, he had restored the prestige of the monarchy and had set the stage for his successors.

Henry VII was succeeded by his handsome and athletic son, Henry VIII. Like his father, Henry VIII was a practicing Catholic. He even wrote a book against Luther, for which a grateful Pope granted him the title "Defender of the Faith."

Henry VIII's relationship with the Pope did not last, however. Because his marriage with Catherine of Aragon had not produced a son, Henry tried to obtain an annulment from the Pope so that he could marry Anne Boleyn. When the Pope refused, Henry remarried anyway. This defiance of

The English Renaissance
(A.D. 1485– A.D. 1625)

Columbus
Sets Sail
From Spain

Francisco Pizarro

Queen Elizabeth I

| 1500 | 1525 | 1550 |

BRITISH EVENTS

- *Everyman* first performed.
  - First masque performed.
    - Thomas More publishes *Utopia*.
      - Bowling becomes popular in London.

- Henry VIII issues Act of Supremacy.
  - Church of England established.
    - Thomas More executed.
      - John Knox leads Calvinist reformation in Scotland.
        - Henry VIII dies.
          - *The Book of Common Prayer* issued.

- Elizabeth I becomes queen.
  - Thomas Tallis publishes English cathedral music.
    - More than 20,000 Londoners die in plague.

WORLD EVENTS

- Columbus lands in New World.
  - North America: John Cabot explores northeastern coast.
    - Africa: Vasco da Gama rounds Cape of Good Hope.
      - Italy: Leonardo da Vinci paints *Mona Lisa*.
        - Italy: Michelangelo paints ceiling of Sistine Chapel.
          - Japan: Ports opened to European ships.
            - North America: Ponce de León explores Florida.
              - Africa: Algiers and Tunisia founded.
                - Magellan sails around the world.

- Italy: Pope Leo X excommunicates Martin Luther.
  - Poland: Copernicus completes treatise on astronomy.
    - Peru: Pizarro conquers Incas.
    - France: Rabelais publishes *Gargantua and Pantagruel*, Book 1.
      - Spain: St. Ignatius Loyola founds Jesuit brotherhood.

- Italy: Cellini completes bronze statue of Perseus.
  - India: Akbar the Great comes to power.
    - Malta: Knights of St. John fight off Turkish invasion.
      - Belgium: Bruegel paints *The Wedding Dance*.
        - South America: 2,000,000 Indians die of typhoid.
          - Brazil: Rio de Janeiro founded by Portuguese.

William
Shakespeare

Globe Theater

The Pilgrims Land
at Plymouth Rock

1575   **1600**   **1625**

- Francis Drake returns from circumnavigating the globe.
  - **Sir Philip Sidney** writes *Astrophel and Stella.*
    - Mary, Queen of Scots executed.
      - English Navy defeats Spanish Armada.
        - **Edmund Spenser** publishes *The Faerie Queene,* Part I.
          - **Shakespeare** writes *Romeo and Juliet.*
            - Globe Theater opens.

- East India Company founded.
  - Elizabeth I dies; James I becomes king.
    - **Shakespeare's** *Macbeth* first performed.
      - **Ben Jonson** publishes *Volpone.*
        - King James Bible published.
          - Francis Bacon publishes *Novum Organum.*
            - First patent laws passed.

- James I dies.

- France: Montaigne's *Essays* published.
  - Italy: Pope Gregory XIII introduces new calendar.
    - South America: Sir Walter Raleigh explores Orinoco River.

- Spain: Cervantes publishes Part I of *Don Quixote.*
  - North America: British colony established at Jamestown.
    - Italy: Galileo builds first telescope.
      - North America: French colony of Quebec established.
        - Germany: Kepler proposes laws of planetary motion.
          - North America: Pilgrims land at Plymouth Rock.

papal authority led to an open break with the Roman Catholic Church. Under the Act of Supremacy (1534), the king assumed full control of the Church in England and severed all ties with Rome. Henry became supreme head of the new Church of England (or Anglican Church). He seized the Catholic Church's English property and dissolved the powerful monasteries, selling some of their lands to benefit the royal treasury and granting the rest as gifts to loyal friends.

Although the Protestant Reformation was not directly responsible for Henry's break with Rome, it helped to pave the way. Many people in England had resented Roman dominance, and the break helped to stir new feelings of national pride. Henry used ruthless measures to suppress opposition among monks, friars, and a few others. He even had his former friend and leading advisor, Thomas More, executed, because More had refused to renounce his faith.

Henry married six times in all. His first two marriages produced two daughters, Mary and Elizabeth. His third wife, Jane Seymour, bore a son, Edward, who was but a frail child when Henry died in 1547.

Edward VI and Mary I

Henry VIII's son, Edward VI, became king at the age of nine and died at the age of fifteen. During his brief reign, a series of parliamentary acts were instituted that dramatically changed the nation's religious practices. English replaced Latin in church ritual, and the Anglican prayer book, *The Book of Common Prayer,* became required in public worship. By Edward's death in 1553, England was well on its way to becoming a Protestant nation.

Roman Catholicism made a turbulent comeback, however, when Edward's half-sister, Mary, took the throne. Mary I was herself Catholic, and she restored Roman practices to the Church of England. She also restored the authority of the Pope over the English Church and insisted on marrying her Spanish cousin, Philip II, thus seeming to make England a minor appendage to the powerful Spanish state. In a time of growing national feeling, many people found these acts extremely unpatriotic. People were also disturbed by Mary's violent repression of Protestants. Ordering the execution of nearly 300 Protestants, she earned the nickname Bloody Mary and strengthened anti-Catholic sentiment within England.

Elizabeth I

When Mary I died after a five-year reign, her half-sister, Elizabeth I, came to the throne. She would be the last of the Tudors, dying unmarried and childless, after a long and successful reign.

Strong and clever, Elizabeth was probably England's ablest monarch since William the Conqueror. She received a Renaissance education and read widely in the Greek and Latin classics. She became a great patron of the arts, gathering around her a flock of courtiers that included most of the best writers of her day. Many of the era's greatest literary works bear a dedication to the queen, and the word *Elizabethan* has come to signify the English Renaissance at its height.

Elizabeth also put an end to the religious turmoil that had existed during Mary I's reign. She reestablished the monarch's supremacy in the Church of England and restored *The Book of Common Prayer,* and she instituted a policy of religious moderation that enjoyed great popular support, although it failed to please many devout Catholics and Protestants.

Often working with England's Catholic factions were France and Spain, Europe's strongest powers at the start of Elizabeth's reign. Both nations sought to dominate England, but each was anxious that the other should not. Elizabeth and her counselors adroitly played one side against the other, dangling offers of marriage to the queen as bait. Elizabeth's clever maneuvering of French and Spanish royalty allowed England a period of peace during which commercial and maritime interests prospered.

If Elizabeth had one outstanding problem, it was her Catholic cousin Mary Stuart, queen of Scotland by birth and (as great-granddaughter of Henry VII) next in line for the throne of England. Because Catholics did not recognize Henry VIII's marriage to Elizabeth's mother, Anne Boleyn, they considered Mary Stuart the queen of England. As a prisoner in England for nineteen years,

Mary became the center of numerous Catholic plots against Elizabeth. While punishing the plotters, Elizabeth let her royal cousin live. Finally, however, a court convicted Mary of plotting to murder Elizabeth, and Parliament insisted on Mary's execution. Mary went to the block in 1587, a Catholic martyr. Her famous motto, "In my end is my beginning," took on new meaning when her death led Catholic Spain to declare war on England.

Defeat of the Spanish Armada

The quarrels between Spain and England went beyond the execution of Mary. Spain rejected most English claims to territory in the Americas and resented the fact that English adventurers, known as privateers, had been attacking and plundering Spanish ships. In theory, privateers like John Hawkins and Francis Drake operated on their own, but in reality they acted on the authority of Queen Elizabeth.

Spain's King Philip II, already infuriated by the sea pirates, considered Mary's execution the last straw. He prepared a Spanish fleet, or armada, of 130 warships and sent it to attack England. In an eight-day battle in the English Channel in 1588, English sailors outfought and outmaneuvered the Spanish fleet. The defeat of the Spanish armada marked the decline of Spain and the emergence of England as a great sea power.

THE LAUNCHING OF FIRESHIPS AGAINST THE SPANISH ARMADA (detail)
National Maritime Museum, Greenwich, England

Stuarts and Puritans

The English Renaissance continued after Elizabeth died in 1603, although a new dynasty—the Stuarts—came to the throne of England. Determined that the end of the Tudor line should not bring a dispute over the throne and a return of civil strife, Elizabeth named Scotland's King James VI as her successor. James's claim to England's throne rested on his descent from King Henry VII through his mother, Mary Stuart, Elizabeth's old antagonist. Unlike Mary, however, James was a Protestant.

The years of the new Stuart king (1603–1625), who became England's James I, are sometimes described as the Jacobean era, from *Jacobus,* the Latin word for *James.* On the surface, the era seemed to be merely an extension of the Elizabethan age. Like his predecessor, James I was a strong supporter of the arts. He also took measures to further England's position as a world power, sponsoring the establishment of England's first successful American colony—Jamestown, Virginia.

During James's reign, however, a conflict began developing that would later erupt into war. Guided by the medieval idea of the "divine right of kings," James I often treated the Parliament with contempt. He and Parliament became involved in a power struggle, quarreling over taxes and foreign wars. James I also persecuted the Puritans, who were strongly represented in the House of Commons. Prompted by James's religious intolerance, a group of Puritans migrated to America and established the Plymouth Colony in 1620.

Achievements of the English Renaissance

The Elizabethan Age produced an explosion of cultural energy. English architects designed and constructed beautiful mansions. Composers turned out new hymns to fit the Anglican service and popularized the English madrigal, a love song sung without musical accompaniment, often by several harmonizing voices. Painters and sculptors were busy, too. While the Renaissance masters

QUEEN ELIZABETH I, c. 1588
by or after George Gower

generally were not English, some—like the German artist Hans Holbein the Younger (1497?–1543), court painter to Henry VIII—did move to England.

Meanwhile, the Renaissance spurred the growth of English educational institutions. Instead of depending on tutors, wealthy families began sending their sons to public schools (that is, schools outside the home—they were actually what Americans call private secondary schools). At the same time, the universities at Oxford and Cambridge were improved and expanded.

Literature in Early Tudor Times

The years from 1485 to 1558 served as a prelude to the great age of Elizabethan literature. Many major writers, such as Thomas More, continued to work in Latin. More's *Utopia* (1516) is a powerful vision of a society free of medieval superstition and prejudice. With increasing frequency, writers were using the vernacular—English. The poet Thomas Wyatt (1503–1542), who had traveled widely on the continent, introduced the sonnet to England. Wyatt translated or adapted many of the sonnets of the Italian Renaissance

poet Petrarch. A second early Tudor poet, Henry Howard, Earl of Surrey (1517–1547), experimented with the sonnet form and was the first to use blank verse, the unrhymed ten-syllable lines that would later be the tool of the great Elizabethan dramatists.

Elizabethan Poetry

During the lengthy reign of Elizabeth I, English literature came of age. Many of the most significant literary developments came in the area of poetry. Favoring lyric poetry, rather than the narrative poems favored by their medieval predecessors, the Elizabethan poets perfected the sonnet and began experimenting with other poetic forms.

One of the most popular literary forms during the Elizabethan age was the sonnet cycle, a series of sonnets that fit loosely together to form a story. The first of the great Elizabethan sonnet cycles was *Astrophel and Stella* by Philip Sidney (1554–1586). As a member of a poetry club called Areopagus, Sidney also helped to adapt classical verse forms to fit the English language.

Another major Elizabethan poet was Edmund Spenser (1552?–1599). Spenser wrote intricate verse filled with rich imagery. Although Spenser wrote many fine sonnets, his most famous work, *The Faerie Queene,* is an imaginative epic, or long heroic poem, dedicated to Queen Elizabeth. Spenser wrote his epic in complex nine-line units, now called Spenserian stanzas.

Christopher Marlowe (1564–1593), a noted playwright, was also a gifted lyric poet. Marlowe helped popularize pastoral verse, which idealizes the rustic simplicity of rural life, in such poems as "The Passionate Shepherd to His Love."

Marlowe's poem inspired Sir Walter Raleigh (1552?–1618) to write a famous response, "The Nymph's Reply to the Shepherd." Poet, historian, courtier, soldier, and explorer, Raleigh was a typical Renaissance man whose adventurous life mirrored the restless spirit of his day.

Another brilliant lyric poet, William Shakespeare, brought the Elizabethan sonnet to new heights. In composing his sonnets, Shakespeare changed the pattern and rhyme scheme of the Petrarchan, or Italian, sonnet, employing a form now known as the English, or Shakespearean, sonnet.

Elizabethan Drama

During the Elizabethan age, English drama also came into full bloom. Playwrights turned away from religious subjects and began writing more complex and sophisticated plays. Drawing upon the classical models of ancient Greece and Rome, writers reintroduced tragedies—plays in which disaster befalls a hero or heroine—and comedies—originally, plays in which a humorous situation leads to a happy resolution. Playwrights also began writing their plays in carefully crafted blank verse, using rich language, filled with vivid imagery.

Since Elizabethan dramas were almost entirely in verse, it is not surprising that many of the age's best poets were also its leading playwrights. Christopher Marlowe became the first major Elizabethan dramatist in the 1580's, writing such plays as *Tamburlaine the Great* and *The Tragical History of Doctor Faustus*. Had Marlowe lived past the age of thirty, he might well have rivaled Shakespeare as England's greatest playwright.

Shakespeare began his involvement with the theater as an actor. By 1592, he was a popular playwright, his works even having been performed at Elizabeth's court. After the Globe Theater was built in 1599, many of Shakespeare's plays were performed there. Shakespeare wrote thirty-seven plays, among them many of the greatest plays of all time. He wrote nine tragedies, including *Romeo and Juliet, Hamlet,* and *Macbeth;* several comedies, including *The Merchant of Venice* and *A Midsummer Night's Dream;* ten histories, including *Richard II, Richard III,* and *Henry V;* and a number of plays often classified as "romances" or "tragic comedies." Filled with powerful and beautiful language, his plays display his deep understanding of human nature and his compassion for all types and classes of people. Because of their eloquent language and their depth and complexity, Shakespeare's plays have retained their popularity for centuries. The seventeenth-century writer Ben Jonson said of Shakespeare: "He was not of an age but for all time."

Elizabethan and Jacobean Prose

Prose took a back seat to poetry and drama in the English Renaissance. Scholars still preferred to write in Latin, and their English prose had a Latin flavor. Because they used long words and ornate sentences, their work is often difficult to read today.

Several Elizabethan poets contributed major works of prose, however. Philip Sidney's *Defence of Poesie* (about 1582) is one of the earliest works of English literary criticism. Thomas Nashe's *The Unfortunate Traveler* (1594), a fictional tale, was a forerunner of the novel. Another important work of prose, *History of the World,* was written by Walter Raleigh during his years of confinement in the Tower of London (for allegedly plotting against James I).

Perhaps the leading prose writer of the English Renaissance was Francis Bacon, a high government official under James I. "I have taken all knowledge to be my province," Bacon wrote, and his literary output reflects his scholarship in many fields. His greatest work, the *Novum Organum* (1620), written in Latin, made major contributions to natural science and philosophy. Bacon is also known for his formal essays—short prose works focusing on single topics. His essays, including "Of Studies" and "Of Ambition," highlight the rational detachment of his clever, inquiring mind.

The most monumental prose achievement of the entire English Renaissance is undoubtedly the English translation of the Bible commissioned by King James on the advice of Protestant clergymen. Fifty-four scholars labored for three years to bring this magnificent work to fruition. The King James Bible, or Authorized Version, is among the most widely quoted and influential works in the English language.

The English Renaissance moved England out of its medieval past and into the modern world. No writers since have surpassed the literary achievements of Shakespeare or the majestic language of the King James Bible. These provide the standard against which all English literature has been judged right down to the present time.

BRITISH VOICES

Quotations by Prominent Figures of the Period

They (in Utopia) wonder much to hear that gold, which in itself is so useless a thing, should be everywhere so much esteemed.

Sir Thomas More, *Utopia*

I know I have the body of a weak and feeble woman, but I have the heart and stomach of a king, and of a king of England too.

Elizabeth I in a speech to the troops on the approach of the Armada

Was this the face that launched a thousand ships,
And burnt the topless towers of Ilium?

Christopher Marlowe, *The Tragical History of Doctor Faustus*

Now is the winter of our discontent
Made glorious summer by this sun of York.

William Shakespeare, *Richard III*

The quality of mercy is not strained,
It droppeth as the gentle rain from heaven
Upon the place beneath: it is twice blessed;
It blesseth him that gives and him that takes. . . .

William Shakespeare, *The Merchant of Venice*

The fault, dear Brutus, is not in our stars,
But in ourselves, that we are underlings.

William Shakespeare, *Julius Caesar*

Something is rotten in the state of Denmark.

William Shakespeare, *Hamlet*

The world's mine oyster.

William Shakespeare, *The Merry Wives of Windsor*

Of one that loved not wisely but too well.

William Shakespeare, *Othello*

How sharper than a serpent's tooth it is
To have a thankless child!

William Shakespeare, *King Lear*

READING CRITICALLY

The Literature of 1485–1625

When you read literature, it is important to place it in its historical context. Doing so will help you understand influences on a writer's ideas and techniques.

HISTORICAL CONTEXT During the years from 1485 to 1625, English life changed dramatically. The feudal system disappeared, and overseas commerce transformed England into a wealthy and powerful nation. The English navy became one of the world's strongest military forces, and through exploration and colonization, Britain developed into a large, rapidly expanding empire. Religious life in England also underwent a major transformation during this period. Refusing to accept the Pope's decision not to allow him to divorce his wife, King Henry VIII severed the country's connection with the Roman Catholic Church and established the Church of England, appointing himself as the church's leader.

LITERARY MOVEMENTS It was during this period that English literature came into full bloom. A cultural movement known as the Renaissance swept through the European continent, eventually making its way into England. Responding to this movement, Queen Elizabeth I actively supported education, science, and the arts. Her support helped to generate a tremendous amount of literary activity. Influenced by the classical works of ancient Rome and Greece, writers explored new literary forms and created some of the finest works the country has ever produced.

WRITERS' TECHNIQUES The most significant developments of the period were in the areas of poetry and drama. Turning away from the long narrative poems of the Middle Ages, poets introduced a new poetic form, the lyric, into English literature. Lyrics are short, tightly structured poems in which the speaker generally focuses on conveying his or her thoughts or feelings. During this period lyrics were usually written in sonnet form, and they frequently dealt with the subject of love. Sonnets were often written in sequences and were generally filled with energetic, musical language. Dramas during this period were also known for their beautiful language. Written in carefully crafted verse, these dramas delve into complex characters and themes, frequently offering important insights about human nature.

SIR PHILIP SIDNEY

1554–1586

Sir Philip Sidney wrote the first great sonnet sequence in English, *Astrophel and Stella*. Before Sidney, Sir Thomas Wyatt and the Earl of Surrey had written excellent sonnets, but Sidney was the first to write a series of sonnets linked by subject matter and theme. In addition, his *The Defence of Poesie* marks the beginning of English literary criticism.

Sidney was born at Penshurst, the country home of his aristocratic family. After studying at Oxford and Cambridge, he traveled extensively in Europe. Back in England, he became a favorite at court, where his charm, intelligence, and good judgment were recognized and admired. In 1581 he made the acquaintance of Penelope Devereux, the daughter of Lord Essex. She was then thirteen. They became engaged, but the engagement was later broken off and Penelope became the wife of Lord Rich. She is the Stella of *Astrophel and Stella*.

In 1580 he fell out of favor with the court for writing a letter to Queen Elizabeth urging her not to marry the Duke of Anjou. He then retired to his sister's home, where he wrote part of *Arcadia*, a pastoral romance. Eventually he regained his status with the queen and was knighted in 1583. In 1586 during a military engagement against the Spanish Catholics in Holland, Sidney was wounded. As he lay on the ground, he refused the water offered him, insisting that it be given to another wounded soldier. Twenty-six days later Sidney died, to the great grief of his country.

As the nephew of the influential Earl of Leicester and the son of the highly respected Elizabethan statesman Sir Henry Sidney, young Philip had been groomed for success since childhood. Yet, throughout his life he carried himself with modesty. Former schoolmate Fulke Greville captured Sidney's innate dignity in a line from the biography he wrote twenty-five years after his friend's death: "though I . . . knew him from a child, yet I never knew him other than a man—with such staidness of mind, lovely and familiar gravity, as carried grace and reverence above greater years."

During his life Sir Philip Sidney was widely revered as a courtier, soldier, scholar, and poet—a model gentleman of the English Renaissance. Today he is acknowledged as the first important English literary critic. He is also recognized as the poet who inspired the sonnet sequences of later Renaissance poets and as the author of a number of eloquent sonnets that stand with the best poetry of this period.

GUIDE FOR INTERPRETING

Sonnet 31; Sonnet 39

Literary Forms

The Sonnet Sequence. A sonnet sequence is a group of sonnets linked by theme or subject. The form was brought to perfection by the fourteenth-century Italian poet Petrarch, whose *Sonnets to Laura* directly or indirectly inspired the sequences of later poets.

Again and again certain conventions appear in sonnet sequences: The lady is golden-haired, with cheeks like roses or lilies. She is proud. She cruelly rebuffs her poet-lover. The lover is unfailingly faithful. He fears her scorn and rejection but hopes for her love. Hence he describes himself as alternately freezing and burning. He is like a ship tossed by the sea. He calls upon sleep to ease his cares. Through his poetry his lady will be given eternal fame.

The widespread reliance of English Renaissance poets on such Petrarchan conventions makes their poetry seem somewhat artificial. In real life love is seldom as it is depicted in these poems. Nevertheless, the sonnet sequences were enormously popular in their day, and the best of them are still read today.

Focus

Do any love stories of today (in books, films, and TV shows) make use of widely recurring conventional ideas about men, women, and the course of love? List as many as you can recall.

Primary Source

In Sonnet 31 the speaker refers to "wit." This was one of the most important qualities of a Renaissance courtier and writer. Although the speaker here refers to intelligence rather than humor, Sonnet 31—as with much of Sidney's work—is shot through with clever, often humorous wordplays. J.C.A. Rathmell believes that Sidney's poetry "is characterized by the frequent appearance of a sly and subtle wit that is always threatening into question, albeit affectionately, the heroic and romantic values it ostensibly celebrates." Although Sidney's sonnets can be marred by over-elaboration, he continues, "what is immediately discernible, however, is his critical awareness of these elements in his work and his readiness to subject them to a good-humored scrutiny . . . an often disconcertingly dry and caustic wit are crucial components of Sidney's style, and it is their alliance with other quite contrary elements—vulnerability, sensibility, and a lingering attachment to the old high ways of romance and chivalry—that combine to make his writing so distinctive, and so winning." What examples of wit can you find in life today?

Sonnet 31

Sir Philip Sidney

With how sad steps, O Moon, thou climb'st the skies!
   How silently, and with how wan a face!
   What, may it be that even in heavenly place
That busy archer[1] his sharp arrows tries?
5 Sure, if that long-with-love-acquainted eyes
   Can judge of love, thou feel'st a lover's case.
   I read it in thy looks, thy languished grace,
To me, that feel the like, thy state descries.[2]
   Then even of fellowship, O Moon, tell me
10   Is constant love deemed there but want of wit?[3]
Are beauties there as proud as here they be?
Do they above love to be loved, and yet
   Those lovers scorn whom that love doth possess?
   Do they call virtue there ungratefulness?

---

1. busy archer: Cupid, the Roman god of love.
2. descries: Reveals.
3. wit: Intelligence.

RESPONDING TO THE **S**ELECTION

Your Response

1. Do you think the speaker's complaints about love are fair and accurate? Why or why not?

Recalling

2. What four lover's complaints are expressed in the sestet?
3. Describe the appearance of the moon.

Interpreting

4. What is the connection between the appearance of the moon and the thoughts the speaker utters?
5. Paraphrase lines 3–4 and lines 5–8.
6. Judging by what is said in the sonnet, what do you infer about the speaker's relationship with his lady?

Applying

7. How would you answer the speaker's question to the moon: "O Moon, tell me/Is constant love deemed there but want of wit"? How is constancy in love viewed in the modern world? Explain your answer.

SHEPHERDS UNDER A FULL MOON
Samuel Palmer
Ashmolean Museum, Oxford

Primary Source

London in Sidney's day held little of the beauties of nature that he described in his sonnets. Here is how Alfred H. Bill describes what the city was like when Sidney was a teenager:

"There were the aisles of the cathedral, filled with bargaining hucksters and strutting loungers. The streets were thronged with grave merchants, apprentices dodging on their errands, groups of idle serving men badged with blue and gold, whose swords and bucklers might clash at any moment in some bloody outbreak of their noble masters' rivalry at court. Gallants swaggered through the press, so extravagant in the width of their ruffs and the lengths of their swords and daggers that a law had to be passed to regulate them . . . There was the stirring of cutpurses at night. There were stage plays; and even a sensitive boy had been so toughened by the brutal sights common at the time that he could look on at a bull-baiting or a bear-baiting with as much enjoyment as one of the present day gets out of a boxing match. Criminals were strung up publicly and as nearly as might be on the scene of their wrong-doing. Dead pirates clanked on their chains in the gallows on the river-bank. With a litte luck one might see at Tyburn the ghastly business of a traitor's disembowelment alive. The heads and quarters of such, all shiny-black with the tar that preserved them from the weather, decorated the spikes above London Bridge and Temple Bar."

From this description, what picture do you get of London in Sidney's day? Would you have like to have lived there? Why or why not?

Sonnet 39

Sir Philip Sidney

Come sleep, O sleep, the certain knot of peace,
The baiting place[1] of wit, the balm of woe,
The poor man's wealth, the prisoner's release,
The indifferent judge between the high and low;

5   With shield of proof[2] shield me from out the prease[3]
Of those fierce darts Despair at me doth throw:
O make in me those civil wars to cease;
I will good tribute pay, if thou do so.
Take thou of me smooth pillows, sweetest bed,

10 A chamber deaf to noise, and blind to light,
A rose garland, and a weary head:
And if these things, as being thine by right,
Move not thy heavy grace, thou shalt in me,
Livelier then elsewhere, Stella's image see.

---

1. baiting place: A place for refreshment.
2. proof: Proven strength.
3. prease: Crowd.

Commentary

"Come sleep," the speaker cries in the first line of Sonnet 39. But what exactly causes sleep? And what purpose does it serve? Scientists have made enormous strides in identifying the chemicals our brain releases to make us sleep and have described several kinds of sleep. D-sleep, for example, is so called because people awakened during this stage often report that they have been *d*reaming. S-sleep, in contrast, seems not to be marked by dreaming, although it is also a deep stage of sleep.

Despite this progress in understanding the nature of sleep, no one is really sure what function sleep provides. Some scientists claim that sleep has no biological function at all—that it is simply a sort of habit! Others, however, believe that sleep does indeed play a very important role in our survival. We experience more S-sleep after exercise, during periods of starvation, and at other times of metabolic stress, for example. This suggests that S-sleep most likely helps rebuild the body and the brain. D-sleep appears to function in much the same way, but on a more complex level, restoring the higher-level brain functions.

The need for sleep varies tremendously. An infant sleeps sixteen to eighteen hours a day, at least half of which is D-sleep. A teenager, though, sleeps only seven to eight hours, of which one and a half hours are spent in D-sleep. You've probably heard stories of people who do not need sleep, but such reports are unproven; everyone needs at least four or five hours of sleep a night.

Your Response

1. From what kind of situation do you think the speaker is seeking sleep as a means of escape? Explain.

Recalling

2. What six benefits does the speaker attribute to sleep in lines 1–4?

Interpreting

3. Literally, what are the fierce darts that Despair hurls (line 6)?
4. What might the metaphor "civil wars" (line 7) signify?
5. In what sense could sleep see Stella's image in the speaker?
6. Why is the speaker addressing sleep?

Applying

7. What psychological truth about people's desire for sleep is the basis for the speaker's calling upon sleep?

A NALYZING LITERATURE

Understanding a Sonnet Sequence

The names Astrophel and Stella mean "star-lover" and "star." Since it is known that Sidney's sequence of 108 sonnets plus eleven songs deals with his love for Penelope Devereux, we know that Astrophel represents Sidney and Stella represents Penelope. The 108 sonnets do not present a love story in narrative form. Rather, they offer reflections on the course of Astrophel's love. A reader, however, can detect the story that underlies the sequence.

Since *Astrophel and Stella* makes extensive use of the love-poem conventions present in Petrarch's *Sonnets to Laura,* the sequence seems to mix the artificial and the real, convention and sincerity. In the best of Sidney's poems, the Petrarchan conventions produce an effect of courtly grace and charm, while allowing the lover's real feelings to show through.

1. Do Sidney's two sonnets seem to you primarily sincere or primarily artificial? Give reasons for your opinion.
2. Why do you suppose a poet would decide to use an elaborate set of conventional ideas and images in love poetry, rather than write of love in a realistic way?

T HINKING AND WRITING

Writing a Letter of Response

If Stella had received Sonnets 31 and 39 as a gift from Sidney, how might she have responded to them? What might she have said to him in a letter acknowledging that she had received and read the sonnets? Write the letter you think Stella might have written.

First, reread the material in the Guide for Reading to review the way ladies were depicted in sonnet sequences. Then, decide what Stella would have said in her letter. Assume that she "got the message" Sidney's poems contain. How would she have expressed her thanks for the poems? How would she have responded to the poems' implications about her and her treatment of Astrophel? When you revise your letter, try to match the courtly, Petrarchan style of Sidney's sonnets.

L EARNING OPTIONS

1. **Cross-curricular Connection.** The commentary on page 206 discusses scientific theories about sleep. Do your own research on this topic. What are the biological and psychological functions of sleep? Why do we dream? Summarize your findings in an oral or written report.
2. **Speaking and Listening.** Many writers have expressed original thoughts about sleep. Use a dictionary of quotations to find three observations about sleep that you consider to be especially insightful and well expressed. Share your quotations orally with the class.

CHRISTOPHER MARLOWE

1564–1593

Though not the first English poet to write in blank verse (unrhymed iambic pentameter), Christopher Marlowe's brilliant use of it in his plays established it as the preeminent meter for verse drama and ultimately for epic poetry in English. Marlowe wrote one of the world's immortal tragedies, *Dr. Faustus,* as well as several other notable plays and poems.

Born in Canterbury, Marlowe was the son of a shoemaker. He went to Cambridge University on a scholarship usually awarded to students studying for the ministry. However, he spent much of his time writing plays and serving as a government agent. He never took holy orders. He is, indeed, reputed to have been an atheist, or at least to have held highly unorthodox religious views.

While at Cambridge, Marlowe wrote *Tamburlaine,* the play that made the public aware of his dazzling abilities. It dramatizes the exploits of a fourteenth-century Scythian shepherd who conquered much of the known world. As Marlowe portrays him, Tamburlaine personifies energy and ambition. He is a dynamic character well served by the dramatist's powerful blank verse. In the remaining six years of his life, Marlowe wrote five more plays, including *Dr. Faustus* and a sequel to *Tamburlaine.* On May 30, 1593, he was stabbed to death in a tavern. His murder may have been the result of a fight over the bill, or it may have been a political assassination.

Was Marlowe a spy? Hints that he may have been for a time a spy for Queen Elizabeth's secret service rest on an astonishing letter the Queen's Privy council wrote to the authorities at Cambridge in June of 1587. The letter seeks to suppress rumors that Marlowe planned to go to Rheims. "It was not in her Majesty's pleasure that anyone employed as he had been in matters touching the benefit of his country should be defamed by those who are ignorant in the affairs he went about," they wrote. Such official concern for a young divinity student suggests that Marlowe had performed an unusual service for the government.

Marlowe's fame rests primarily on his plays, especially on his "mighty line," as Ben Jonson described his dramatic blank verse. *Dr. Faustus* has been a classic of dramatic literature for four hundred years. However, Marlowe's nondramatic poetry alone would be enough to secure him a permanent place in English literature. His *Hero and Leander* is one of the finest narrative poems ever written in English, and "The Passionate Shepherd to His Love" is one of the best known and most popular lyrics of the English Renaissance.

GUIDE FOR INTERPRETING

from The Tragical History of the Life and Death of Doctor Faustus

Historical Context

The Faust Legend. The Faust legend is one of the most important of western civilization. Numerous writers have seen it as a profound revelation of the consequences of aspiring to rise above the human condition.

The legend derives from the life and activities of an actual German scholar and magician, Johann Faust (or Faustus), who lived from about 1480 to 1540. He traveled widely, performed magic, and died under mysterious circumstances. Many Germans of the time considered him a fraud, but Martin Luther, the founder of Protestantism, believed that he had satanic powers. Even during Faust's life he was the subject of legends. According to many of them, he had sold his soul to the devil for youth, knowledge, and magical powers.

In 1587 a crude, unreliable biography of Faust appeared. The unknown author had incorporated into it many legends of other magicians. The biography concludes with Faust going to hell at the end of his life. This volume appeared in an English translation titled *The History of the Damnable Life and Deserved Death of Doctor John Faustus*. It is the immediate source of Marlowe's play, which was probably written in 1588.

Commentary

What effect did *The Tragical History of the Life and Death of Doctor Faustus* have on Elizabethan audiences? Witches and devils were very real to Elizabethans, and when Faustus signed his soul away, their blood froze. Indeed, Elizabethans often attributed to witchcraft any unexplained occurrence. Many legends sprang up about performances of *Doctor Faustus*. One story concerns a performance of the play in Exeter. As Faustus summoned the devils, the actors counted one more devil than the scene called for and feared that Satan himself was in their midst. Terrified, they stopped the play, the audience ran from their seats, and the actors bolted from town early the next morning.

Focus

Think of an experience you would anticipate with dread—for example, a test of some kind, a visit to a doctor or dentist, or a confrontation. What would be your thoughts and feelings beforehand? Write a monologue that presents the thoughts that pass through your mind. Try to write the monologue in a way that expresses your feelings without actually naming them.

The Tragical History of the Life and Death of Doctor Faustus

from

Christopher Marlowe

Early in the play, Dr. Faustus, the main character, contracts his soul to the devil for special powers of the mind. Now, facing death, he makes a desperate attempt to repent and save his soul.

FAUST. Ah, Faustus,
  Now hast thou but one bare hour to live
  And then thou must be damned perpetually!
  Stand still, you ever-moving spheres of heaven,
5 That time may cease and midnight never come;
  Fair Nature's eye, rise, rise again, and make
  Perpetual day; or let this hour be but
  A year, a month, a week, a natural day,
  That Faustus may repent and save his soul!
10 *O lente lente currite noctis equi.*[1]
  The stars move still,[2] time runs, the clock will strike,
  The devil will come, and Faustus must be damned.
  O, I'll leap up to my God! Who pulls me down?
  See, see, where Christ's blood streams in the firmament!
15 One drop would save my soul—half a drop! ah, my Christ!
  Rend not my heart for naming of my Christ;
  Yet will I call on him—O, spare me, Lucifer!
  Where is it now? 'Tis gone; and see where God
  Stretcheth out his arm and bends his ireful brows.
20 Mountains and hills, come, come and fall on me
  And hide me from the heavy wrath of God,
  No, no—
  Then will I headlong run into the earth:
  Earth, gape! O no, it will not harbor me.
25 You stars that reigned at my nativity,
  Whose influence hath allotted death and hell,
  Now draw up Faustus like a foggy mist

---

1. O lente . . . equi: "Slowly, slowly run, O horses of the night," adapted from a line in Ovid's *Amores.*
2. still: Always.

FAUST CONJURING UP THE DEVIL (WOODCUT)
Artist Unknown

Into the entrails of yon laboring cloud
That when you vomit forth into the air,
30   My limbs may issue from your smoky mouths,
So that my soul may but ascend to heaven.

[*The watch strikes.*]

Ah, half the hour is past; 'twill all be past anon.
O God,
If thou wilt not have mercy on my soul,
35   Yet for Christ's sake whose blood hath ransomed me
Impose some end to my incessant pain:
Let Faustus live in hell a thousand years,
A hundred thousand, and at last be saved!
O, no end is limited to damnèd souls!

from *The Tragical History of Doctor Faustus*   211

40   Why wert thou not a creature wanting soul?
        Or why is this immortal that thou hast?
        Ah, Pythagoras' *metempsychosis*[3]—were that true,
        This soul should fly from me, and I be changed
        Unto some brutish beast. All beasts are happy,
45   For when they die
        Their souls are soon dissolved in elements,
        But mine must live still to be plagued in hell.
        Cursed be the parents that engendered me!
        No, Faustus, curse thyself, curse Lucifer
50   That hath deprived thee of the joys of heaven.

[*The clock strikes twelve.*]

    It strikes, it strikes! Now, body, turn to air
    Or Lucifer will bear thee quick[4] to hell!

[*Thunder and lightning.*]

    O soul, be changed to little water drops
    And fall into the ocean, ne'er be found.
55   My God, my God, look not so fierce on me!

[*Enter* DEVILS.]

    Adders and serpents, let me breathe awhile!
    Ugly hell, gape not—come not, Lucifer—
    I'll burn my books—ah, Mephistophilis!

[*Exit* DEVILS *with* FAUSTUS.]

----

3. metempsychosis: The supposed passing of the soul at death into another body; from the philosophy of Pythagoras, an ancient Greek philosopher and mathematician, who lived in the sixth century B.C.
4. quick: Alive.

RESPONDING TO THE SELECTION

Your Response
1. If you were facing death, how would you feel? How would your response compare with Faustus's?

Recalling
2. What vain hopes and longings pass through Faustus's mind as midnight approaches?
3. Why does Faustus want to be changed into a beast?

Interpreting
4. Explain his exclamation "O, I'll leap up to my God! Who pulls me down? / See, see, where Christ's blood streams in the firmament!"
5. What does Faustus request of the stars in lines 25–31?
6. Paraphrase lines 40–46.
7. Analyze Marlowe's poetic technique in the excerpt. How does he convey Faustus's terror and despair?

Applying
8. Can you imagine another situation that would cause someone to feel terror and despair equal to Faustus's? Explain why you do or do not think that Faustus's terror and despair are unsurpassable.

ANALYZING LITERATURE

Understanding Historical Context
Marlowe's *Dr. Faustus* is the first great literary treatment of the Faust legend. Since then, a number of major writers have used the legend as the basis for literary works. The greatest of these is Goethe's poetic drama *Faust*.

The importance of the Faust legend is that it illustrates what some thinkers see as an enduring impulse in Western civilization from the Renaissance to the present: the drive to go beyond ordinary bounds of knowledge and power, even at the cost of one's own soul.

1. What impression do you get of Faustus's character and personality from his speech?
2. What moral values and attitudes does the speech implicity uphold?
3. Name one character from history who could be termed "Faustian." Explain the similarity between this character and Faust.
4. Explain why the quest for knowledge would be a popular theme during the English Renaissance.

LEARNING OPTIONS

1. **Cross-curricular Connection.** Investigate the life of the historical Johann Faust (or Faustus). Why did he become the subject of so many legends? Consult encyclopedias, histories of the Renaissance period, critical works on the Faust story, and other sources to find information. Present your findings in either a written or oral report.
2. **Speaking and Listening.** The Faust legend has inspired many composers as well as writers. Locate a recording of at least one musical work—opera, oratorio, stage music, or symphony—that is based on the story of Faust. Listen to the recording by yourself. Write down your responses to it. Then read any notes accompanying the recording and gather any other information about the composer you can find. Bring the recording to class and share your personal responses and the information about the composer in a brief introduction to the music. Play the recording (or a portion of it) for the class, and ask for responses from other students.

GUIDE FOR INTERPRETING

The Passionate Shepherd to His Love

Literary Forms

Pastoral Poetry. A lyric poem expresses personal thoughts and feelings. As the word *iyric* suggests, such a poem may have some of the characteristics of a song. It is often brief and written in rhymed verse with a pronounced rhythm. In fact, many lyric poems, such as the one you are about to read, have been set to music. Ballads, sonnets, odes, songs, and elegies are some of the more common types of lyric poetry.

"The Passionate Shepherd to His Love" is one of the most famous examples of pastoral poetry. A **pastoral poem** is a lyric that celebrates the beauty and pleasures of country life. Pastoral poetry often makes use of a number of traditional conventions. The speaker is frequently a shepherd. He either addresses or speaks about a shepherdess or other country maiden with whom he is in love. The world of nature is idealized. The goodness and happiness of a life in harmony with such a world are valued above all else. Pastoral poetry was especially popular during the English Renaissance, but the tradition extends from the classical era of Greece and Rome to the present.

Focus

Think of the most appealing country place you know. If you wanted to persuade a friend to visit the place, which features would you mention? List five or six and briefly describe them.

Primary Source

Perhaps because of his own experience wrestling with words, Renaissance critic, university president, and baseball commissioner A. Bartlett Giamatti had this to say about Marlowe's use of language: "Renaissance man felt he had the power to transform himself because he had the power of language. Words were units of energy. Through words man could assume forms and aspire to shapes and states otherwise beyond his reach." But "words, like men, were fallen; . . . they contained, as we do, shapes of evil within them. Fallen words . . . are unstable elements; thus they are, as we are, such dangers to us. As we must always check that impulse to deformation in ourselves, so we must constantly be aware of the beast in language—Spenser calls it the Blatant Beast, whose rabid bite is vicious slander—and we must know that when we unleash a word and let it soar, we run the risk of loosing an evil force as well, one that we cannot control. We, as men using words, must stay within our limits, or what we master may master and misshape us." What power does language give you? What limits does it impose on you?

The Passionate Shepherd to His Love

Christopher Marlowe

Come live with me, and be my love,
And we will all the pleasures prove[1]
That hills and valleys, dales and fields,
And all the craggy mountains yields.

5   And we will sit upon the rocks,
Seeing the shepherds feed their flocks,
By shallow rivers, to whose falls
Melodious birds sing madrigals.

---

1. prove: Experience.

THE HIRELING SHEPHERD
William Holman Hunt
The Manchester City Art Galleries

And I will make thee beds of roses,
10 And a thousand fragrant posies,
A cap of flowers and a kirtle[2]
Embroidered all with leaves of myrtle;

A gown made of the finest wool,
Which from our pretty lambs we pull;
15 Fair lined slippers for the cold,
With buckles of the purest gold;

A belt of straw and ivy buds,
With coral clasps and amber studs;
And if these pleasures may thee move,
20 Come live with me, and be my love.

The shepherd swains shall dance and sing
For thy delight each May morning;
If these delights thy mind may move,
Then live with me, and be my love.

---

2. kirtle: Skirt.

◼ RESPONDING TO THE SELECTION

Your Response
1. Do you think the shepherd makes a persuasive case to his love? Why or why not?

Recalling
2. Describe the kind of life the shepherd is offering his love.

Interpreting
3. How realistic is his representation of the kind of life he and his love will lead? Explain.

Applying
4. If a poet of today were to write a contemporary version of this poem, how might the details differ from Marlowe's?

◼ ANALYZING LITERATURE

Appreciating Pastoral Poems
A **pastoral poem** idealizes the rustic life. Such poetry often contains an implied contrast between the good life of nature and the corrupt life of a court or city.
1. Read Marlowe's poem aloud. What qualities of it might inspire someone to set it to music?
2. Since a shepherd, not Marlowe, is the speaker, in what sense can the poem be said to express personal thoughts and feelings?
3. Would you infer from "The Passionate Shepherd to His Love" that Marlowe's Elizabethan readers valued the pastoral life because England was becoming more urbanized? Why or why not?

A WRITER RESPONDS

"**T**he Passionate Shepherd to His Love" has received a lot of attention from other writers. In his play The Merry Wives of Windsor, Shakespeare had a character sing a few lines from it. Other poets have actually written responses to the invitation made in Marlowe's poem. Among them were John Donne ("The Bait"), Robert Herrick ("To Phyllis, to Love and Live with Him") and, in the twentieth century, C. Day Lewis ("Song").

The most famous and—some have argued—the best response was written by Sir Walter Raleigh in 1600. Though today we remember Raleigh as a courtier and as the founder of the colony of Virginia, his contemporaries greatly respected his talents as a poet. Raleigh's life came to a tragic end when he was imprisoned and executed for treason in 1618. Since few of his poems were published during his life, we are fortunate that "The Nymph's Reply to the Shepherd" has survived.

The Nymph's Reply to the Shepherd
Sir Walter Raleigh

If all the world and love were young,
and truth in every shepherd's tongue
These pretty pleasures might me move
To live with thee, and be thy love.

Time drives the flocks from field to fold,
When rivers rage and rocks grow cold,
and Philomel[1] becometh dumb,
the rest complains of cares to come.

The flowers do fade, and wanton fields
to wayward winter reckoning yields:
A honey tongue, a heart of gall,
Is fancy's spring, but sorrow's fall.

Thy gowns, thy shoes, thy beds of roses,
Thy cap, thy kirtle[2], and thy posies
Soon break, soon wither, soon forgotten,
In folly ripe, in reason rotten.

Thy belt of straw and ivy buds,
Thy coral clasps and amber studs,
All these in me no means can move
To come to thee and be thy love.

But could youth last and love still breed,
Has joy no date[3] nor age no need,
Then these delights my mind might move,
To live with thee and be thy love.

---

1. Philomel: The nightingale.

2. kirtle: Skirt.   **3. date:** Ending.

LEARNING OPTION

Writing. Write a response of your own to Marlowe's poem, either in prose or poetry. You may want to model your poem on Marlowe's or Raleigh's. Do you consider the Shepherd's invitation at all enticing, or do you view it with as much skepticism as the speaker in "The Nymph's Reply . . ." does? You may use humor to make your point, but keep the tone of your response consistent throughout.

EDMUND SPENSER

1552–1599

Edmund Spenser, the "poet's poet," is one of the very greatest poets of the English Renaissance. An imaginative experimenter, he invented what became known as the Spenserian stanza and the Spenserian sonnet, new verse forms that exerted a powerful influence on the poets who followed him.

Unlike many poets of the time, Edmund Spenser was born into a working-class family. His father was a clothmaker, and Edmund attended the Merchant Taylors' School on a scholarship for a poor man's son. He went on to Cambridge University as a "sizar," a student who was required to work his way through school. During Spenser's first year at Cambridge, his earliest poems were published.

Graduating with an M.A. degree in 1576, Spenser served in a variety of positions with wealthy noblemen, including that of secretary to the Earl of Leicester, a favorite of Queen Elizabeth I. While in Leicester's service, he became friends with Sir Philip Sidney, and the two of them formed the core of a select literary group.

In 1580 Spenser took a position as secretary to the Lord Deputy of Ireland. Thereafter he spent most of his life in Ireland, acquiring Kilcolman Castle, an Irish estate, where he did much of his writing. Sir Walter Raleigh visited him at Kilcolman Castle and was so impressed by Spenser's unfinished *The Faerie Queene* that he persuaded Spenser to take the first three books to London for publication.

The Faerie Queene established Spenser's reputation as the leading poet of his day. This great work, intentionally written in an archaic style, combines two literary forms, the romance and the epic, in an allegory about "the twelve moral virtues." Dedicated to Queen Elizabeth I, *The Faerie Queene* brought Spenser a small pension but no position at court.

In 1595 Spenser married Elizabeth Boyle, whom his sonnet sequence *Amoretti* commemorates. *Amoretti,* which means "little cupids" or "little love poems," is unique in the English Renaissance for being addressed to the poet's wife.

Irish rebels destroyed Spenser's castle during an uprising, and Spenser returned to London. He died on January 13, 1599, and is buried in what is now the Poet's Corner of Westminster Abbey.

GUIDE FOR INTERPRETING

from The Faerie Queene; Sonnet 1; Sonnet 26; Sonnet 75

Writers' Techniques

Spenserian Poetry. Edmund Spenser had a lifelong interest in theories of poetry, and he is recognized as one of the great innovators in English verse forms. Two of his innovations are especially notable.

When Spenser wrote *The Faerie Queene,* he created a new type of stanza that was later named for him. A Spenserian stanza consists of nine lines, the first eight of which are in iambic pentameter. The ninth line has two additional syllables and is called an *alexandrine*. The rhyme scheme of a Spenserian stanza is *ababbcbcc*.

Although most sonnets follow either the Petrarchan or the Shakespearean form, there is a third type called the Spenserian sonnet. A Spenserian sonnet has fourteen lines, but its rhyme scheme differs from that of other sonnets. The rhyme scheme is *abab bcbc cdcd ee*. Often there is no break in a Spenserian sonnet between the octave (first eight lines) and sestet (last six lines).

Focus

Spenser intended *The Faerie Queene,* a lengthy allegory, to consist of twelve books, but he completed only six. In each, a hero representing a moral virtue was to have a series of adventures, fighting off such enemies as Envy, Pride, and Despair. Among the virtues in Spenser's plan are Holiness, Friendship, Justice, and Courtesy. All twelve books were to be unified by the presence of the legendary Prince Arthur and of Gloriana, who represents Queen Elizabeth I. Select either a virtue, such as truth or honesty, or a fault, such as pride or envy, and write about it.

Primary Source

Even in Elizabethan days, poets had trouble getting paid. *The Oxford Book of Literary Anecdotes* records the following event:

Queen Elizabeth ordered that Spenser be given one hundred pounds in payment for some poems he had written in her honor. Lord Treasurer Burleigh objected to the payment, scorning Spenser's work with the comment, "What, all this for a song?" The Queen replied, "Then give him a reason" [for not being paid]. After waiting some time and receiving neither reason nor money, Spenser decided to remind the Queen of her promise. He sent her the following poem: "I was promised on a time/To have reason for my rhyme./From that time, unto this season,/I received nor rhime, nor reason."

The paper produced the intended effect, and the Queen, after sharply criticizing the Treasurer, immediately ordered that Spenser be paid the hundred pounds she had promised.

from The Faerie Queene

Edmund Spenser

This excerpt from Spenser's epic, The Faerie Queene, *is a description of the Redcrosse Knight, the hero of Book 1, who represents the virtue of holiness.*

A Gentle Knight was pricking[1] on the plaine,
Ycladd in mightie armes[2] and silver shielde,
Wherein old dints of deepe wounds did remaine,
The cruell markes of many a bloudy fielde;
5   Yet armes till that time did he never wield:[3]
His angry steede did chide his foming bitt,
As much disdayning to the curbe to yield:
Full jolly[4] knight he seemd, and faire did sitt,
As one for knightly giusts[5] and fierce encounters fitt.

---

1. pricking: Cantering.
2. armes: Armor.
3. Wherein . . . wield: The knight wears the armor of the Christian man, which bears the dents of every Christian's fight against evil. However, Redcrosse is wearing the armor for the first time.
4. jolly: Gallant.
5. giusts: Jousts.

■ RESPONDING TO THE SELECTION

Your Response

1. What effect do the archaic spellings in these lines have on you? Explain.

Recalling

2. (a) What is the knight wearing? (b) What is he carrying? (c) What is he doing?

Interpreting

3. What is strange about the knight's armor?
4. The knight is described as gentle and jolly (gallant). What one adjective do you think might sum up the knight's character?

Applying

5. If you were to pick a character to represent the moral virtue of truth, what kind of person would you choose?

■ ANALYZING LITERATURE

Understanding the Spenserian Stanza

The first eight lines of a Spenserian stanza are in iambic pentameter, ten syllables with a pattern of alternating stressed and unstressed syllables. The ninth line, called the alexandrine, has two additional syllables.

1. Choose three lines of the stanza from *The Faerie Queene,* and mark them for stressed and unstressed syllables and for feet. Use ∪ to indicate an unstressed syllable and / to indicate a stressed syllable.
2. What is the rhyme scheme of this stanza?

Sonnet 1

Edmund Spenser

Happy ye leaves when as those lily hands,
which hold my life in their dead doing[1] might,
Shall handle you and hold in love's soft bands,
Like captives trembling at the victor's sight,
5   And happy lines, on which with starry light,
Those lamping[2] eyes will deigne sometimes to look
And read the sorrows of my dying spright,[3]
Written with tears in heart's close[4] bleeding book.
And happy rhymes bathed in the sacred brook
10 Of Helicon[5] whence she derived is,
When ye behold that angel's blessed look,
My soul's long lacked food, my heaven's bliss.
Leaves, lines, and rhymes, seek her to please alone,
Whom if ye please, I care for other none.

---

1. doing: Killing.
2. lamping: Flashing.
3. spright: Spirit.
4. close: Secret.
5. sacred . . . Helicon: From Greek mythology, the Hippocrene, the fountain from which the waters of poetic inspiration flowed, located on Mt. Helicon, the sacred home of the Muses.

RESPONDING TO THE SELECTION

Your Response
1. Do you think the speaker's beloved will be pleased by this tribute? Why or why not?

Recalling
2. What three listeners does the speaker address in Sonnet 1?

Interpreting
3. Who is "she" in line 10 and "her" in line 13?
4. What are the listeners asked to do?
5. (a) To what objects does Spenser give human qualities? (b) How does Spenser tie this personification to the main idea of the sonnet?

Applying
6. What animal would you choose to personify pride? Why?

ANALYZING LITERATURE

Understanding the Spenserian Sonnet
The rhyme scheme of a Spenserian sonnet differs from that of the more familiar Petrarchan sonnet. The Spenserian rhyme scheme is *abab bcbc cdcd ee*. Does this rhyme scheme seem easier or harder for a poet to work with? Explain.

LEARNING OPTION

Cross-curricular Connection. Find out more about Mt. Helicon in Greece. What does its name mean? Who were the Muses in Greek mythology, and why are they associated with this mountain? Present your findings to the class.

Sonnet 26

Edmund Spenser

Sweet is the rose, but grows upon a briar;
Sweet is the juniper, but sharp his bough;
Sweet is the eglantine,[1] but pricketh near;
Sweet is the fir bloom, but his branches rough;
5   Sweet is the cypress, but his rynd is tough,
Sweet is the nut, but bitter is his pill;[2]
Sweet is the broom flower, but yet sour enough;
And sweet is moly, but his root is ill.
So every sweet with sour is tempered still,[3]
10 That maketh it be coveted the more:
For easy things that may be got at will,
Most sorts of men do set but little store.
Why then should I account of little pain,
That endless pleasure shall unto me gain.

---

1. eglantine: A European rose with hooked spines.
2. pill: Shell.
3. still: Always.

RESPONDING TO THE SELECTION

Your Response

1. Do you agree with what the speaker says about the connection between "sweet and sour" in life? Why or why not?

Recalling

2. According to Spenser, what is the effect of tempering every "sweet with sour"?

Interpreting

3. What is the effect of the repetition in lines 1–8?
4. How would you express in today's English what Spenser says in the closing couplet?

Applying

5. List other situations in life in which the sweet is offset by the sour.
6. Find information on the Chinese principle of *yin* and *yang.*

LEARNING OPTION

Writing. The vocabulary and sentence structure in Spenser's sonnets are considerably different from what a poet would use today. Rewrite all or part of Sonnet 26, using straightforward, contemporary English. If you wish, duplicate the meter and rhyme scheme of the original. Share your "translation" with the class.

Sonnet 75

Edmund Spenser

One day I wrote her name upon the strand,[1]
But came the waves and washèd it away:
Again I wrote it with a second hand,
But came the tide, and made my pains his prey.

5 "Vain man," said she, "that dost in vain assay,
A mortal thing so to immortalize,
For I myself shall like to this decay,
And eek[2] my name be wipèd out likewise."
"Not so," quod[3] I, "let baser things devise.

10 To die in dust, but you shall live by fame:
My verse your virtues rare shall eternize,
And in the heavens write your glorious name.
Where whenas death shall all the world subdue,
Our love shall live, and later life renew."

---

1. strand: Beach.
2. eek: Also.
3. quod: Said.

RESPONDING TO THE SELECTION

Your Response

1. Whose point of view—the speaker's or his lady's—do you think is closer to the truth? Why?

Recalling

2. What two events occur twice in the first quatrain of Sonnet 75?
3. (a) Who begins speaking in line 5? (b) Who begins speaking in line 9?

Interpreting

4. (a) Why does the poet believe his love's name will not be washed away by the tide? (b) Has time proven him right?

Applying

5. How do the three sonnets from Spenser's *Amoretti*—1, 26, and 75—fit the definition of a sonnet sequence?

THINKING AND WRITING

Comparing and Contrasting Sonnets

Reread Sonnet 26 and Sonnet 75, noting their similarities and differences. Write a composition in which you compare and contrast the form, tone, and meaning of the two sonnets. Begin with a chart:

	Form	Tone	Meaning
Sonnet 26			
Sonnet 75			

Use the chart as a basis for writing the first draft of your composition. Remember that to **compare** means "to examine similarities"; to **contrast** means "to discuss differences." When you have finished, read your first draft carefully for organization, content, grammar, mechanics, and style. Revise it as necessary.

WILLIAM SHAKESPEARE

1564–1616

Because of his profound understanding of the many aspects of human nature, his compassion for all types and classes of people, and the power and beauty of his language, William Shakespeare is generally regarded as the greatest writer of English literature. More than 350 years after his death, Shakespeare's plays continue to be read widely and produced frequently throughout the world. His plays have the same powerful impact on audiences today that they had when they were first staged.

Shakespeare was born in a small country town, Stratford-on-Avon, in April (probably April 23) 1564. His father was a successful businessman who held a number of positions in the town government. Presumably educated at the Stratford grammar school, Shakespeare acquired a basic understanding of Latin, but he did not attend a university. Shakespeare married Anne Hathaway in 1582, and the couple had a daughter, Susanna, in 1583 and twins, Hamnet and Judith, in 1585. Very little is known about Shakespeare's life from the date the twins were born to his appearance in a London acting company seven years later.

By that time, however, he had already developed a reputation as an actor and had written several plays. It was not unusual for members of theater companies to do a number of different jobs, from writing to acting to designing costumes to taking care of advertising, theater arrangements, and finances. By 1594 Shakespeare was a part owner and the principal playwright of the Lord Chamberlain's Men, one of the most successful theater companies in London. In 1599 the company built the famous Globe Theater, where most of Shakespeare's plays were performed. When James I became king in 1603, following Queen Elizabeth I's death, he took control of the Lord Chamberlain's Men and renamed the company The King's Men. In about 1610 Shakespeare retired to Stratford, though he continued to write plays. Six years later, on April 23, he died and was buried in Holy Trinity Church in Stratford.

Because Shakespeare wrote his plays to be performed, not published, no one knows exactly when each of the plays was written. However, through extensive research, scholars have been able to chart several periods in Shakespeare's development as a playwright. During his early years (through most of the 1590's), Shakespeare wrote a number of comedies (including *The Comedy of Errors, Love's Labor's Lost, The Merchant of Venice,* and *A Midsummer Night's Dream*), several histories (including *Richard II, Richard III,* and

Henry IV), and two tragedies (Titus Andronicus and Romeo and Juliet). Shakespeare then wrote several of his finest romantic comedies (As You Like It, Twelfth Night, and Much Ado About Nothing) just before the turn of the century. During the first decade of the seventeenth century, Shakespeare created his greatest tragedies (Hamlet, Othello, King Lear, Macbeth, Antony and Cleopatra, and Coriolanus). Finally, toward the end of his life, Shakespeare wrote several plays referred to as romances or tragicomedies (The Winter's Tale, Cymbeline, and The Tempest).

In addition to his thirty-seven plays, Shakespeare wrote 154 sonnets and two narrative poems. He probably worked on his sonnets from 1592 through 1598, a time when sonneteering was in vogue in London. It is likely that he wrote many of them in 1592, when the London theater was closed because of a plague.

Below is a list of Shakespeare's poems and plays in roughly chronological order.

Poems
Venus and Adonis
The Rape of Lucrece
Sonnets
The Phoenix and the Turtle

Plays
The Comedy of Errors
Love's Labor's Lost
1 Henry VI
2 Henry VI
3 Henry VI
Richard III
Titus Andronicus
The Taming of the Shrew
The Two Gentlemen of Verona
Romeo and Juliet
Richard II
A Midsummer Night's Dream
The Life and Death of King John
The Merchant of Venice
1 Henry IV
2 Henry IV
Much Ado About Nothing
Henry V
Julius Caesar

As You Like It
Twelfth Night
Hamlet
The Merry Wives of Windsor
Troilus and Cressida
All's Well That Ends Well
Othello
Measure for Measure
King Lear
Macbeth
Antony and Cleopatra
Timon of Athens
Coriolanus
Pericles
Cymbeline
The Winter's Tale
The Tempest
Henry VIII

GUIDE FOR INTERPRETING

Sonnet 29; Sonnet 73; Sonnet 116; Sonnet 130

Writers' Techniques

Shakespearean Sonnet During the Elizabethan period, the sonnet sequence, a group of sonnets unified by a common theme, became a popular literary form. Shakespeare's 154 sonnets, like those in other sonnet sequences, are numbered and fit loosely together to form a story. Most of the sonnets are addressed to a handsome, talented young man, urging him at first to marry and have children who can carry on his talents. The speaker also warns the young man about the destructive powers of time, age, and moral weakness. Midway through the sequence, the sonnets focus on a rival poet who has also addressed poems to the young man. Twenty-five of the later sonnets are addressed to a "dark lady," who is romantically involved with both the speaker and the young man. These later sonnets focus on the grief she causes by her betrayal of the speaker.

Scholars fiercely debate the identity of the young man (Mr. W.H.), the dark lady, and the rival poet to whom the sonnets are addressed. Leading candidates for the role of Mr. W.H. are Henry Wriothesley, third earl of Southampton, to whom Shakespeare dedicated his narrative poems, and William Herbert, third earl of Pembroke. Those favoring Southampton claim Mrs. John Davenant was the dark lady, but the Pembroke side believes it was Mary Fitton, a woman of doubtful reputation. The many nominees for the rival poet include Edmund Spenser, Christopher Marlowe, Ben Jonson, and John Donne, all Shakespeare's contemporaries—but even Chaucer, who had been dead for 200 years, has been proposed!

William Shakespeare did not invent what is now called the Shakespearean sonnet (Sir Thomas Wyatt and the Earl of Surrey did), but he is its greatest master. A Shakespearean sonnet, fourteen lines in iambic pentameter, consists of three quatrains and a rhyming couplet. The usual rhyme scheme is *abab cdcd efef gg*. Shakespeare's sonnets ordinarily present a problem or premise in the first twelve lines and offer a solution or conclusion (sometimes a statement of the theme) in the final couplet.

Focus

Shakespeare's sonnets reflect on various aspects of life, such as personal relationships, the passing of time, and the relationship between human beings and nature. Jot down your thoughts on three aspects of life that you might consider writing about in a sonnet. Then list some of the ideas and emotions you associate with each one.

Sonnet 29

William Shakespeare

When in disgrace with fortune and men's eyes,
I all alone beweep my outcast state,
And trouble deaf heaven with my bootless[1] cries,
And look upon myself and curse my fate,
5 Wishing me like to one more rich in hope,
Featured like him, like him with friends possessed,
Desiring this man's art, and that man's scope,
With what I most enjoy contented least.
Yet in these thoughts myself almost despising,
10 Haply I think on thee, and then my state,
Like to the lark at break of day arising
From sullen earth, sings hymns at heaven's gate;
    For thy sweet love remembered such wealth brings
    That then I scorn to change my state with kings.

---

1. bootless: Futile.

RESPONDING TO THE SELECTION

Your Response
1. What experiences have made you feel "wealthy"? Explain.

Recalling
2. With whom or what is the speaker in disfavor?
3. What are three things the speaker wishes for?

Interpreting
4. How would you describe the mood (a) of the first eight lines of this sonnet? (b) of the last six lines?
5. Why is the comparison with the lark an appropriate one for the speaker to make?
6. How do the last two lines summarize the theme of the sonnet?

Applying
7. If you were to give this sonnet a title, what would it be?

ANALYZING LITERATURE

Understanding Shakespearean Sonnets
Sonnet 29 is a Shakespearean sonnet consisting of three quatrains and a couplet. It has the usual rhyme scheme of such a sonnet, *abab cdcd efef gg.* In a Shakespearean sonnet, the poet typically presents a problem or premise in the first twelve lines followed by a solution or conclusion in the last two. In Sonnet 29, however, a change in direction occurs at line 9, as it does in a Petrarchan sonnet.

1. Each of the first two quatrains expresses a distinct but related thought. In your own words, what are these two thoughts?
2. What rhyming words represent (a) the *b*'s in the rhyme scheme? (b) The *e*'s? (c) The *g*'s?
3. How does the thought expressed in the last two lines of the sonnet relate to what is said in the first eight lines?
4. What is your reaction to this sonnet's theme?

THE SONNET
William Mulready
Victoria & Albert Museum Trustees

Sonnet 73

William Shakespeare

That time of year thou mayst in me behold
When yellow leaves, or none, or few, do hang
Upon those boughs which shake against the cold,
Bare ruined choirs where late the sweet birds sang.
5 In me thou see'st the twilight of such day
As after sunset fadeth in the west,
Which by and by black night doth take away,
Death's second self that seals up all in rest.
In me thou see'st the glowing of such fire,
10 That on the ashes of his youth doth lie,
As the deathbed whereon it must expire,
Consumed with that which it was nourished by.[1]
    This thou perceivest, which makes thy love more
        strong,
    To love that well which thou must leave ere long.

---

1. Consumed . . . by: Choked by the ashes of that which fueled its flame.

▌RESPONDING TO THE SELECTION

Your Response

1. Do you agree with the speaker's claim that the nearness of death makes "love more strong"? Why or why not?

Recalling

2. To what season of the year does the speaker compare himself?
3. To what time of day does the speaker compare himself?
4. What comparison does the speaker make in the third quatrain?

Interpreting

5. How does the speaker resemble the three things to which he compares himself?

6. In the "bare ruined choirs" of line 4, the word *choirs* refers literally to the loft where church singers perform. What does it mean as Shakespeare uses it here?
7. Explain the meaning of "Death's second self" in line 8.
8. How does the thought in the final couplet relate to the rest of the sonnet?

Applying

9. Many people regret growing old. How do you think the speaker in this sonnet feels about it? Support your answer with details from the sonnet.

Sonnet 116

William Shakespeare

Let me not to the marriage of true minds
Admit impediments.[1] Love is not love
Which alters when it alteration finds,
Or bends with the remover to remove.
5   O, no! It is an ever-fixèd mark
That looks on tempests and is never shaken;
It is the star to every wandering bark,[2]
Whose worth's unknown, although his height be taken.
Love's not Time's fool, though rosy lips and cheeks
10   Within his bending sickle's compass come;
Love alters not with his brief hours and weeks,
But bears it out even to the edge of doom.[3]
     If this be error, and upon me proved,
     I never writ, nor no man ever loved.

---

1. impediments: Reasons why a marriage should not be allowed to take place.
2. star . . . bark: The star that guides every wandering ship; the North Star.
3. doom: Judgment Day.

RESPONDING TO THE SELECTION

Your Response

1. Besides true love, what other human qualities or ideals might be considered unalterable?

Recalling

2. According to the speaker, what are three things that love is not?
3. To what is love compared in the second quatrain?

Interpreting

4. What are the points of similarity between true love and the North Star?

5. The speaker notes that "Love's not Time's fool." (a) What does he mean? (b) How does this idea fit in with the central theme of the sonnet?
6. Ordinarily, the final couplet in a Shakespearean sonnet offers a summary or solution. This final couplet is a bit different. What point does it make about the content of the rest of the sonnet?

Applying

7. What is your opinion of the speaker's concept of true love? Explain your answer.

Sonnet 130

William Shakespeare

My mistress' eyes are nothing like the sun;
Coral is far more red than her lips' red;
If snow be white, why then her breasts are dun;
If hairs be wires, black wires grow on her head.
5   I have seen roses damasked,[1] red and white,
But no such roses see I in her cheeks;
And in some perfumes is there more delight
Than in the breath that from my mistress reeks.[2]
I love to hear her speak. Yet well I know
10 That music hath a far more pleasing sound.
I grant I never saw a goddess go;[3]
My mistress, when she walks, treads on the ground.
    And yet, by heaven, I think my love as rare
    As any she belied with false compare.

---

1. damasked: Variegated.
2. reeks: Emanates.
3. go: Walk.

RESPONDING TO THE SELECTION

Your Response

1. Do you find Sonnet 130 humorous? Why or why not?

Recalling

2. What is less than perfect about the mistress's (a) lips? (b) cheeks? (c) breath? (d) voice?

Interpreting

3. Sonnet 130 is often called an anti-Petrarchan sonnet. What do you think is meant by anti-Petrarchan?
4. There are indications even before the final couplet that the speaker loves his mistress despite her supposed imperfections. What is one such indication?

Applying

5. Would you like to have this kind of sonnet written about you, or would you prefer the more traditional kind with its idealized comparisons? Give your reasons.

THINKING AND WRITING

Comparing and Contrasting Sonnets

Choose the Shakespeare sonnet you like best. Then choose a sonnet by either Sidney or Spenser. Write an essay in which you compare and contrast the form, tone, and meaning of the two sonnets. Set up a chart for taking notes. Write the first draft of your essay, keeping in mind that to **compare** means "to examine similarities;" to **contrast** means "to discuss differences."

As you write, try to incorporate direct quotations from the sonnets into your paper. When you have finished your first draft, reread it, paying special attention to the way you have punctuated direct quotations. Make any changes needed before completing your final draft. Then share it with your classmates.

CROSS CURRENTS

The Elizabethan World View

ORDER IN THE LAND

The Elizabethans viewed the world as an ordered, rational place. Each person occupied a specific rung on the social ladder. With each rank came responsibilities to those above and below in the chain. Everyone understood and accepted this hierarchy, and it was constantly reinforced in daily life.

Fol.50. THE FIRST BOOKE OF THE

Hic canet errantē Lunam,Soliſq; labores
Arcturūq;,pluuiaſq; hyad.geinoſq; triões

THE PRIMUM MOBILE from THE COSMOGRAPHICAL GLASSE, 1559
from William Cuningham
The Huntington Library, San Marino, California

On Sunday, during compulsory services at the Established Church of England, for example, ministers explained that "Every degree of people . . . hath appointed to them, their duty and order. Some are in high degree, some are in low, some kings and princes, some inferiors and subjects. Almighty God hath created and appointed all things . . . in a most excellent and perfect order."

This sort of ranking extended to everything in the universe; each element, creature, and spiritual being occupied a fixed place in the universe.

HEAVENLY BODIES

This divinely directed order began with the heavens themselves. To the Elizabethans the entire universe was enclosed by a sphere called the *primum mobile*. Beneath it lay the fixed stars. Next came the planets, whose motion was directed by the *primum mobile*. While opinion differed on exactly how many planets made up the universe—was it nine? Ten? Eleven?—no one with any sense doubted that these spheres circled around a fixed Earth. Copernicus had a wild idea that the sun, not the Earth, was the center of the universe. He even went so far as to claim that the Earth was actually in motion, not fixed in place!

The angels too obeyed a strict hierarchy. The three different classes ranged from the highest, the Seraphs, to the lowest, the angels. Shakespeare commented on this order in *Troilus and Cressida* when Ulysses remarked that "The heavens themselves, the planets, and this center/Observe degree, priority, and place."

THE GREAT CHAIN OF BEING

Heaven and its inhabitants were linked to the rest of the universe through a concept called The Great Chain of Being. It stretched from the humblest thing in the universe all the way up to God, and the order of each world was reflected in all others. England's rulers, for example, were ranked in an order that corresponded to the order of the rest of creation. The sovereign was analogous to fire, the chief element; the sun, the chief planet; and the eagle, the chief bird, for instance.

Naturally, humans, with their superior intellect, were superior to the other worlds. A woman in *The Comedy of Errors* points this out while lecturing to her sister:

> The beasts, the fishes, and the
>   winged fowl,
> Are their males' subjects and at
>   their controls.
> Man, more divine, the master of all
>   these,
> Lord of the wide world and wilde
>   watery seas,
> Endued with intellectual sense and
>   souls,
> Of more preeminence than fish and
>   fowls,
> Are masters to their females, and
>   their lords;
> Then let your will attend on their
>   accords.

Although her sister resents being told she ought to be submissive to men, the Elizabethans saw the dominance of the man within the family as a model for the broader world order.

FATHER KNOWS BEST

As the king ruled over the kingdom, so the man of the family ruled over his wife and children. He had absolute right to dispose of his daughters in marriage, for example. Old Capulet would be considered an extremely considerate father to the Elizabethans, for when the question of Juliet's marriage to Paris is first discussed, he is willing to let her refuse. It is not until she defies him that he gives commands. Children were brought up to fear and respect their parents. They called their father "Sir" and stood in his presence. The power and authority of the father was recognized as part of the social order.

DRESS FOR SUCCESS

This rigid hierarchy was even seen in the clothing laws, which decreed who was allowed to wear what. Clothing Acts were passed to halt the "intolerable abuse and unmeasurable disorder" caused by the poorer people dressing as their betters. No one under the rank of knight, for example, could wear velvet cloaks or silk stockings; only countesses and higher appeared in purple silk; gold and silver cloth were allowed only for nobles. But most people ignored the laws, much to the dismay of the lawmakers.

THE LINKS WEAKEN

Dramatic advances in knowledge prompted some to stress the old idea of hierarchy, but the quickening pace, combined with the avalanche of invention and discovery, relentlessly undermined the previously accepted notions of order.

GUIDE FOR INTERPRETING

Tell Me Where Is Fancy Bred; It Was a Lover and His Lass; Fear No More the Heat o' the Sun

Writers' Techniques

Shakespearean Songs. Music and song were important aspects of life during the English Renaissance. Serenades, street songs, pastoral invitations, nonsense songs, ballads—all were popular at every level of English society. Shakespeare included 124 songs in his plays. The songs serve specific purposes in the plays in which they appear; they were not added merely to capitalize on the appeal of music. Although Shakespeare's songs were sung on stage as part of the productions, none of the original printed versions of the plays includes the music. As a consequence, much of the original music has been lost. Nevertheless, the lyrics can be enjoyed as poems without music. They can also be appreciated outside the context of the plays. William Shakespeare, unparalleled playwright and poet, was also one of England's great songwriters.

Focus

Take the lyrics of a popular song and rewrite them in your own way. Your song can be as playful or as serious as you wish.

Primary Source

> But supper being ended, and Musicke bookes, according to the custome being brought to the table; the mistresse of the house presented mee with a part, earnestly requesting mee to sing. But when after manie excuses, I protested unfainedly that I could not: everie one began to wonder. Yea, some whispered to others, demaunding how I was brought up . . .

Few of us today have been embarrassed by being unable to sing unfamiliar music at the dinner table! Yet young people in Shakespeare's day were expected to be able to do just that, according to Elizabethan composer Thomas Morely's account of how a young man of his acquaintance came to study music. Young men learned Latin, Greek, and French in school, but music was not taught in the classroom, for there was no need to teach music in a country where "every christening, wedding, and funeral went to the strains of flutes and trumpets and the sound of drums and singing; where May Day games and the feast of St. Nicholas resounded with music, and travelers reported everywhere the beautiful playing of violas and pandoras and that 'even in small villages the musicians wait on you for a small fee.'" At what occasions do we expect music now? How do we learn music today?

Tell Me Where Is Fancy¹ Bred

William Shakespeare

This song is sung in The Merchant of Venice *(Act III, Scene ii) while Bassanio is trying to choose among the caskets of gold, silver, and lead, knowing that only by making the correct choice will he be able to win Portia as his wife.*

Tell me where is fancy bred,
Or in the heart or in the head?
How begot, how nourishèd?
    Reply, reply.
5 It is engendered in the eyes,
With gazing fed; and fancy dies
In the cradle where it lies.
    Let us all ring fancy's knell:
I'll begin it—Ding, dong, bell.
10 Ding, dong, bell.

---

1. Fancy: Love.

RESPONDING TO THE SELECTION

Your Response

1. To what sort of music can you imagine these words sung? Explain.

Recalling

2. What two possible sources of fancy are mentioned at the beginning of the song?
3. Where does the reply to the two questions place the origin of fancy?

Interpreting

4. The word *fancy* is central to the meaning of the poem. It means "love," to be sure, but a superficial kind of love—a love based only on outward appearances. Why is this distinction important?
5. What is it that helps fancy flourish?
6. Why do you think the speaker says that fancy dies in the cradle?
7. What does it mean to "ring fancy's knell"?

Applying

8. Bassanio must choose the correct one of three caskets if he is to win Portia. Two of the caskets are of glittering gold and silver; one is of plain lead. Bassanio chooses the lead casket. Using the words of the song as clues, tell why you think he makes that choice.

It Was a Lover and His Lass

William Shakespeare

This song, from As You Like It *(Act V, Scene iii), is sung by two pages to Touchstone, a clown, and Audrey, a country maid, on the day before their marriage.*

It was a lover and his lass,
    With a hey, and a ho, and a hey nonino,
That o'er the green cornfield did pass
    In the springtime, the only pretty ringtime,[1]
5 When birds do sing, hey ding a ding, ding.
Sweet lovers love the spring.

Between the acres of the rye,
    With a hey, and a ho, and a hey nonino,
These pretty country folks would lie,
10   In the springtime, the only pretty ringtime,
When birds do sing, hey ding a ding, ding.
Sweet lovers love the spring.

This carol they began that hour,
    With a hey, and a ho, and a hey nonino,
15 How that life was but a flower
    In the springtime, the only pretty ringtime,
When birds do sing, hey ding a ding, ding.
Sweet lovers love the spring.

And therefore take the present time,
20   With a hey, and a ho, and a hey nonino,
For love is crownèd with the prime
    In the springtime, the only pretty ringtime,
When birds do sing, hey ding a ding, ding.
Sweet lovers love the spring.

---

1. ringtime: Wedding season.

THE WOODCUTTER COURTING THE MILKMAID
Thomas Gainsborough
Woburn Abbey

RESPONDING TO THE SELECTION

Your Response

1. Do you agree with the poet's attitude toward springtime? Why or why not?

Recalling

2. To what do lovers compare life?

Interpreting

3. Why do you think springtime is called "the only pretty ringtime"?
4. What does the song advise about love?

Applying

5. Love songs have always been popular. What modern love song do you think comes closest to having the same message as "It Was a Lover and His Lass"?

CRITICAL THINKING AND READING

Finding Details That Develop Mood

The **mood** of a piece of writing is the atmosphere or emotion it conveys. Mood can be created through descriptive details and word choice. For example, a dark sky, rolling thunder, and howling wind can create an eerie mood. Such words as *shivering, aghast, oppressive,* and *helplessness* can add to it.

1. How would you describe the mood in this song?
2. (a) What descriptive details help convey the mood? (b) What words help convey it?

Fear No More the Heat o' the Sun

William Shakespeare

This song, from Cymbeline *(Act IV, Scene ii), is a lament
for Imogen, the heroine, who is supposed to be dead.*

Fear no more the heat o' the sun,
    Nor the furious winter's rages;
Thou thy worldly task hast done,
    Home art gone, and ta'en thy wages.
5 Golden lads and girls all must,
As[1] chimney sweepers, come to dust.

Fear no more the frown o' the great;
    Thou art past the tyrant's stroke;
Care no more to clothe and eat;
10   To thee the reed is as the oak:
The scepter, learning, physic,[2] must
All follow this, and come to dust.

Fear no more the lightning flash,
    Nor the all-dreaded thunder stone;[3]
15 Fear not slander, censure rash;
    Thou hast finished joy and moan:
All lovers young, all lovers must
Consign to thee, and come to dust.

No exorciser harm thee!
20 Nor no witchcraft charm thee!
Ghost unlaid forbear thee!
Nothing ill come near thee!
Quiet consummation have;
And renownèd be thy grave!

---

1. As: Like.
2. scepter, learning, physic: Kings, scholars, doctors.
3. thunder stone: At the time it was believed that the sound of
thunder was caused by falling meteorites.

Your Response

1. Do you think this song is effectively consoling? Why or why not?

Recalling

2. What are five aspects of life that the deceased no longer has to worry about?

Interpreting

3. In the last stanza, what do the three concerns mentioned have in common?
4. Judging by what the deceased need no longer fear, what kind of life do you think she had?

Applying

5. If this song were to be sung today, where would you be most likely to hear it? Explain your answer.

ANALYZING LITERATURE

Understanding Shakespeare's Songs

The songs in Shakespeare's plays are functional; that is, each serves a specific purpose. In "Fear No More the Heat o' the Sun," the purpose is to convince the audience to look upon Imogen's death as a release from the pain and sorrow of life. The details in the song all stress the idea that Imogen has no further need to fear these troubling aspects of existence.

1. What are some of the details that support the purpose of the song?
2. Suppose the lament were to take exactly the opposite approach—with the details chosen to emphasize life's vanished joys. What might some of the specific details be?

THINKING AND WRITING

Writing About Shakespeare's Songs

Write an essay about Shakespeare's songs, commenting on their themes, tone, and language. Begin by rereading the songs and taking notes on them. Then write a thesis sentence that states the main idea you intend to develop. In writing your first draft, try to work in appropriate quotations from the songs. Reread the first draft, making sure the essay is logically developed and reads smoothly. Write a final draft incorporating all changes and corrections.

Commentary

In the United States it is hard to find an inn in the thirteen original states dating back to the Revolutionary period that doesn't claim "Washington Slept Here." In England a similar situation exists in regard to Shakespeare. Although there is a lack of sure information about Shakespeare's life, traditions about the poet have become attached to places and objects. For example, tradition identifies the pew in Stratford's Guild Chapel in which Shakespeare worshipped. In 1877 the head of the grammar school proudly displayed Shakespeare's desk to visitors.

"William was a studious lad and selected that corner of the room so that he might not be disturbed by the other boys," he said, with no proof whatsoever to back up his claim. Although Shakespeare left no personal papers behind, tradition has identified and enshrined an absurd assortment of his personal effects: his pencil-case, walking stick, gloves, brooch, table, spoon, and wooden salt cellars. The owner of the Shakespeare Hotel proudly showed off Shakespeare's clock before selling it at public auction in 1880; not to be bested, the nearby Falcon Inn boasted the shovel-board at which he played.

THE ELIZABETHAN THEATER

English drama came of age during the reign of Elizabeth I, developing into a sophisticated and very popular art form. Although playwrights like Shakespeare were mainly responsible for the great theatrical achievements of the time, the importance of actors, audiences, and theater buildings should not be underestimated.

Before the reign of Elizabeth I, theater companies traveled about the country putting on plays wherever they could find an audience, often performing in the open courtyards of inns. Spectators watched either from the ground or from balconies or galleries above.

England's First Playhouse

When Shakespeare was twelve years old, an actor named James Burbage built London's first theater, called simply The Theater, just beyond the city walls in Shoreditch. Actors—even prominent and well-to-do actors like Burbage—occupied an anomalous place in London society. They were frowned upon by the city fathers but were wildly popular with the common people, who clamored to see them perform in plays. Though actors were considered rogues and vagabonds by some, they were held in sufficient repute to be called on frequently to perform at court. A man like Burbage enjoyed a reputation somewhat like a rock star's today.

In 1572 an act of Parliament required theater companies to operate under the patronage of a respectable person or organization, and two years later a London ordinance imposed a number of licensing restrictions on theatrical groups and productions. Burbage's acting company enjoyed the patronage of the Earl of Leicester, but it was Burbage himself who financed the new theater.

The Globe Theater

In 1597 the city fathers closed down The Theater, so Burbage and his men dismantled it and hauled it in pieces across the Thames to Southwark. It took them six months to rebuild it, and when they did they renamed it The Globe.

Scholars disagree about what The Globe actually looked like, since there are no surviving drawings or detailed written descriptions. Shakespeare refers to the building in *Henry V* as "this wooden O," so we have a sense that it was round or octagonal. It is presumed that an important influence on the design of the theater was the bear-baiting and bull-baiting rings built in Southwark. These "sports" arenas were circular, open to the sky, and had galleries all around.

The building had to have been small enough to ensure that the actors would be heard, but we know that performances could draw audiences as large as 2500 to 3000 people. These truly packed houses must have been quite uncomfortable at times, especially when you consider that people didn't bathe or change their clothes

very often! Those who paid an admission price of a penny (a not inconsiderable sum of money then) stood throughout the performance. Some of the audience even sat in a gallery *behind* the performers. Their seats were the second most expensive in the house, and though they saw only the actors' backs and probably couldn't hear very well, they were content to be seen by the other members of the audience.

Actors of the period had none of the elaborate technology that helps modern actors. There were no sets or lighting at The Globe. Plays were performed in the bright afternoon sunlight, and a playwright's words alone had to create moods like the one in the eerie first scene of *Macbeth*. Holding an audience spellbound was made even more difficult by the fact that most of them were eating and drinking throughout the performance.

The Globe met its demise when a cannon was fired as part of a performance of *King Henry VIII* and the flaming wadding landed on the theater's thatched roof. Everyone escaped unharmed, but The Globe burned to the ground. By then, however, other theaters had been built, and the men (and boys, who played all the women's roles) who continued to act in them were able to convey for many other audiences the power of Shakespeare's plays.

The Tragedy of Macbeth

Macbeth is one of Shakespeare's great tragedies, a compelling and timeless drama about the success, treachery, and disintegration of a brave but flawed human being. Its diagnosis of evil is as apt today as it was when The King's Men first presented the play.

Shakespeare completed *Macbeth* in 1606, not long after the appearance of his other great tragedies—*Hamlet, Othello,* and *King Lear.* Intended as a tribute to King James I, *Macbeth* may have been first performed before the royal family at Hampton Court, a palace twelve miles from the center of London. King James, who already wore the crown of Scotland when he ascended the throne of England, would have found *Macbeth* especially intriguing. The play is set in Scotland in the eleventh century, when James's family, the Stuarts, first came to the Scottish throne. One of the strongest and most virtuous characters in the play, Banquo, is said to have been the father of the first of the Stuart kings.

Shakespeare derived the basic plot for *Macbeth* from an account of eleventh-century Scottish history in Raphael Holinshed's *Chronicles of England, Scotland, and Ireland.* In writing his play, Shakespeare altered and expanded Holinshed's history, reshaped the personalities, and invented some new characters.

The central character in *Macbeth,* as in other Elizabethan (and Greek) tragedies, is a tragic hero, a person of high rank and personal quality. Because of a fatal weakness, a tragic flaw, the hero becomes involved in a series of events that lead to his eventual downfall and destruction.

At the beginning of Shakespeare's play, the hero, Macbeth, is pictured as courageous, trustworthy, and loyal. By the end of the play, his ambition has driven him to commit a series of horrendous acts that, once begun, he is powerless to stop. While the audience is repelled by Macbeth's actions, it also pities him, understanding Macbeth's anguish and knowing how easy it is to fall prey to uncontrolled ambition or greed.

The temptations Macbeth faces are ones that have confronted people throughout time. These universal lures—along with Shakespeare's suspense-filled plot, superbly drawn characters, and masterly use of language—have contributed to the play's continuing popularity from Elizabethan days to the present.

The Whole Play

A great play like *Macbeth* weaves a variety of elements into a unified whole. No matter how impressive the individual speeches or how memorable the incidents, the play must be judged on its total effect. If the playwright has successfully blended plot, character, setting, atmosphere, diction, and imagery—and if the actors have then captured the entire rich tapestry on stage—the result is an intensely satisfying drama.

Plot

Basic to every plot is conflict, or struggle. External conflict occurs when a character struggles against another person or an outside force. In *Macbeth* there is external conflict between Macbeth and Macduff. Internal conflict is that which occurs within the mind of a character. Macbeth's agonizing over whether or not to kill Duncan is an example of internal conflict.

Character

Nothing is more important in a work of literature than the portrayal of character. *Macbeth* is a masterpiece of characterization. Macbeth, the tragic hero, is shown as being destroyed because of a tragic flaw.

Setting

Setting is the time and place in which the events in a literary work take place. The general setting of *Macbeth* is Scotland (and briefly England) in the tenth and eleventh centuries. Specific scenes are set at Inverness, on a desolate heath, in the royal palace at Forres, and so on. Because of the limited scenery in Elizabethan drama, Shakespeare often has his characters describe their surroundings.

Atmosphere

The atmosphere in *Macbeth* is one of doom and foreboding. Much of the action takes place in foul weather or in the "thick night" of darkened castles. The witches and apparitions cast a pall whenever they appear. Except for the porter's brief speech, there is little in the play resembling lightheartedness.

Diction

The term *diction* has two meanings. It can mean the pronunciation of words by an actor or other speaker. It can also mean the writer's choice of words, which in a play are delivered by the actors. A writer chooses words with care, making sure they are appropriate to the character, theme, and atmosphere of the literary work. For example, King Duncan in *Macbeth* uses language suitable for a king, while the porter speaks in a more earthy style.

Imagery

Imagery is usually visual, but it can evoke responses from any of the senses. Images, wrote one critic, like those of ". . . pouring the sweet milk of concord into hell; of the earth shaking in fever; . . . of the tale told by an idiot . . . —all keep the imagination moving 'on a wild and violent sea.' . . ."

GUIDE FOR INTERPRETING

Writers' Techniques

The Tragedy of Macbeth, Act I

Blank Verse. Like all of Shakespeare's plays, *Macbeth* is written mainly in blank verse. **Blank verse** is composed of unrhymed lines of iambic pentameter. Iambic pentameter has five feet, or beats, per line, and every other syllable is stressed. The following two lines are an example of blank verse from Act I of *Macbeth*.

```
  U   /  U   /  U / U  /    U    /
Your face my thane, is as a book where men
  U  /   U    /  U  / U /  U  /
May read strange manners. To beguile the time,
```

Blank verse, which was introduced into English literature by the Earl of Surrey, can be stately and dignified, but it can also produce an effect of smooth, natural speech more effectively than most other metrical patterns. It is one of the most flexible and versatile verse forms, a favorite not only of the poets during the English Renaissance, but of many later poets.

Focus

Because of its versatility, blank verse can be used to reproduce all kinds of speech. Listen carefully to a discussion, or think of a conversation you have recently had. Reshape that speech into dialogue written in blank verse. Try to make it sound as natural as possible.

Commentary

Unlike many of Shakespeare's other plays, *Macbeth* is relatively easy to date. Most scholars believe its subject and themes were sparked by the notorious Gunpowder Plot of 1605. By writing *Macbeth,* Shakespeare probably capitalized on the sympathy generated by the failed conspiracy to kill James I and the Parliament. The plot originated with a group of Catholics seeking revenge against James's severe anti-Catholic laws. With the help of soldier of fortune Guy Fawkes, the rebels planned to blow up Parliament. They rented a cellar directly beneath the House of Lords in which to stockpile thirty-six barrels of gunpowder. Fawkes was to ignite the gunpowder on November 5 and then escape to Flanders. One of the rebels, however, exposed the plot, and Fawkes was arrested as he emerged from the cellar. After officials found fuses hidden on his person he was tortured on the rack until he confessed and revealed his associates, nearly all of whom were hanged with him on January 31, 1606. The Gunpowder Plot is celebrated in Great Britain on November 5, when people hang effigies of Guy Fawkes.

The Tragedy of Macbeth

William Shakespeare

CHARACTERS

Duncan, King of Scotland

Malcolm
Donalbain } his sons

Macbeth
Banquo
Macduff
Lennox
Ross } noblemen of Scotland
Menteith
Angus
Caithness

Fleance, son to Banquo
Siward, Earl of Northumberland,
  general of the English forces
Young Siward, his son

Seyton, an officer attending on Macbeth
Son to Macduff
An English Doctor
A Scottish Doctor
A Porter
An Old Man
Three Murderers
Lady Macbeth
Lady Macduff
A Gentlewoman attending
  on Lady Macbeth
Hecate
Witches
Apparitions
Lords, Officers, Soldiers, Attend-
  ants, and Messengers

Setting: Scotland; England

Act I

Scene i. *An open place.*
[*Thunder and lightning. Enter* THREE WITCHES.]

> **FIRST WITCH.** When shall we three meet again?
>   In thunder, lightning, or in rain?
>
> **SECOND WITCH.** When the hurlyburly's done,
>   When the battle's lost and won.
>
> 5   **THIRD WITCH.** That will be ere the set of sun.
>
> **FIRST WITCH.** Where the place?
>
> **SECOND WITCH.**   Upon the heath.
>
> **THIRD WITCH.** There to meet with Macbeth.

THE THREE WITCHES
Henry Fuseli
Courtauld Institute Galleries, London

FIRST WITCH. I come, Graymalkin.[1]

SECOND WITCH. Paddock[2] calls.

THIRD WITCH.   Anon![3]

10   **ALL.** Fair is foul, and foul is fair.
        Hover through the fog and filthy air.   [*Exit.*]

1. Graymalkin: The first witch's helper, a gray cat.
2. Paddock: The second witch's helper, a toad.
3. Anon: At once.

Scene ii. *A camp near Forres, a town in northeast Scotland.*
[*Alarum within.*[1] *Enter* KING DUNCAN, MALCOLM, DONALBAIN, LENNOX, *with* ATTENDANTS, *meeting a bleeding* CAPTAIN.]

    KING. What bloody man is that? He can report,
        As seemeth by his plight, of the revolt
        The newest state.

1. Alarum within: Trumpet call offstage.

MALCOLM.   This is the sergeant[2]
Who like a good and hardy soldier fought
'Gainst my captivity. Hail, brave friend!
Say to the king the knowledge of the broil[3]
As thou didst leave it.

CAPTAIN.   Doubtful it stood,
As two spent swimmers, that do cling together
And choke their art.[4] The merciless Macdonwald—
Worthy to be a rebel for to that
The multiplying villainies of nature
Do swarm upon him—from the Western Isles[5]
Of kerns and gallowglasses[6] is supplied;
And fortune, on his damnèd quarrel[7] smiling,
Showed like a rebel's whore:[8] but all's too weak:
For brave Macbeth—well he deserves that name—
Disdaining fortune, with his brandished steel,
Which smoked with bloody execution,
Like valor's minion[9] carved out his passage
Till he faced the slave;
Which nev'r shook hands, nor bade farewell to him,
Till he unseamed him from the nave to th' chops,[10]
And fixed his head upon our battlements.

KING. O valiant cousin! Worthy gentleman!

CAPTAIN. As whence the sun 'gins his reflection[11]
Shipwracking storms and direful thunders break,
So from that spring whence comfort seemed to come
Discomfort swells. Mark, King of Scotland, mark:
No sooner justice had, with valor armed,
Compelled these skipping kerns to trust their heels
But the Norweyan lord,[12] surveying vantage,[13]
With furbished arms and new supplies of men,
Began a fresh assault.

KING.   Dismayed not this
Our captains, Macbeth and Banquo?

CAPTAIN.   Yes;
As sparrows eagles, or the hare the lion.
If I say sooth,[14] I must report they were
As cannons overcharged with double cracks;[15]
So they doubly redoubled strokes upon the foe.
Except[16] they meant to bathe in reeking wounds,
Or memorize another Golgotha,[17]
I cannot tell—
But I am faint; my gashes cry for help.

5
10
15
20
25
30
35
40

2. sergeant: Officer.

3. broil: Battle.

4. choke their art: prevent each other from swimming.

5. Western Isles: The Hebrides, off Scotland.
6. Of kerns and gallowglasses: With lightly armed Irish foot soldiers and heavily armed soldiers.
7. damnèd quarrel: Accursed cause.
8. Showed . . . whore: Falsely appeared to favor Macdonwald.
9. minion: Favorite.
10. unseamed . . . chops: Split him open from the navel to the jaws.

11. 'gins his reflection: Rises.

12. Norweyan lord: King of Norway.
13. surveying vantage: Seeing an opportunity.

14. sooth: Truth.
15. cracks: Explosives.
16. except: Unless.
17. memorize . . . Golgotha (gol' gə thə): Make the place as memorable for slaughter as Golgotha, the place where Christ was crucified.

KING. So well thy words become thee as thy wounds;
They smack of honor both. Go get him surgeons.

[*Exit* CAPTAIN, *attended.*]

[*Enter* ROSS *and* ANGUS.]

Who comes here?

45   **MALCOLM.**   The worthy Thane[18] of Ross.

LENNOX. What a haste looks through his eyes! So
    should he look
That seems to[19] speak things strange.

ROSS.   God save the king!

KING. Whence cam'st thou, worthy Thane?

ROSS.   From Fife, great King;
Where the Norweyan banners flout the sky
50   And fan our people cold.
Norway[20] himself, with terrible numbers,
Assisted by that most disloyal traitor
The Thane of Cawdor, began a dismal[21] conflict;
Till that Bellona's bridegroom, lapped in proof,[22]
55   Confronted him with self-comparisons,[23]
Point against point, rebellious arm 'gainst arm,
Curbing his lavish[24] spirit: and, to conclude,
The victory fell on us.

KING.   Great happiness!

ROSS.   That now
Sweno, the Norways' king, craves composition;[25]
60   Nor would we deign him burial of his men
Till he disbursèd, at Saint Colme's Inch,[26]
Ten thousand dollars to our general use.

KING. No more that Thane of Cawdor shall deceive
Our bosom interest:[27] go pronounce his present[28]
    death,
65   And with his former title greet Macbeth.

ROSS. I'll see it done.

KING. What he hath lost, noble Macbeth hath won.

[*Exit.*]

Scene iii. *A heath near Forres.*
[*Thunder. Enter the* THREE WITCHES.]

FIRST WITCH. Where hast thou been, sister?

SECOND WITCH. Killing swine.[1]

THIRD WITCH. Sister, where thou?

---

18. Thane: A Scottish title of nobility.

19. seems to: Seems about to.

20. Norway: The King of Norway.
21. dismal: Threatening.
22. Bellona's . . . proof: Macbeth is called the mate of Bellona, the goddess of war, clad in tested armor.
23. self-comparisons: Counter movements.
24. lavish: Insolent.

25. composition: Terms of peace.
26. St. Colme's Inch: Island near Edinburgh, Scotland.

27. our bosom interest: My heart's trust.
28. present: Immediate.

1. Killing swine: It was commonly believed that witches killed domestic animals.

FIRST WITCH. A sailor's wife had chestnuts in her lap,
And mounched, and mounched, and mounched.
5   "Give me," quoth I.
"Aroint thee,[2] witch!" the rump-fed ronyon[3] cries.
Her husband's to Aleppo[4] gone, master o' th' Tiger:
But in a sieve[5] I'll thither sail,
And, like a rat without a tail,[6]
10 I'll do, I'll do, and I'll do.

SECOND WITCH. I'll give thee a wind.

FIRST WITCH. Th' art kind.

THIRD WITCH. And I another.

FIRST WITCH. I myself have all the other;
15   And the very ports they blow,[7]
All the quarters that they know
I' th' shipman's card.[8]
I'll drain him dry as hay:
Sleep shall neither night nor day
20 Hang upon his penthouse lid;[9]
He shall live a man forbid:[10]
Weary sev'nights[11] nine times nine
Shall he dwindle, peak,[12] and pine:
Though his bark cannot be lost,
25 Yet it shall be tempest-tossed.
Look what I have.

SECOND WITCH. Show me, show me.

FIRST WITCH. Here I have a pilot's thumb,
Wracked as homeward he did come.
              [Drum within.]

30 **THIRD WITCH.** A drum, a drum!
Macbeth doth come.

ALL. The weird[13] sisters, hand in hand,
Posters[14] of the sea and land,
Thus do go about, about:
35 Thrice to thine, and thrice to mine,
And thrice again, to make up nine.
Peace! The charm's wound up.

[Enter MACBETH *and* BANQUO.*]*

MACBETH. So foul and fair a day I have not seen.

BANQUO. How far is 't called to Forres? What are these
40 So withered, and so wild in their attire,
That look not like th' inhabitants o' th' earth,
And yet are on 't? Live you, or are you aught

2. Aroint thee: Be off.
3. rump-fed ronyon: Fat-rumped, scabby creature.
4. Aleppo: A trading center in Syria.
5. sieve: It was commonly believed that witches often sailed in sieves.
6. rat . . . tail: According to popular belief, witches could assume the form of any animal, but the tail would always be missing.
7. they blow: To which the winds blow.
8. card: Compass.

9. penthouse lid: Eyelid.
10. forbid: Cursed.
11. sev'nights: Weeks.
12. peak: Waste away.

13. weird: Destiny-serving.
14. Posters: Swift travelers.

That man may question? You seem to understand
        me,
    By each at once her choppy[15] finger laying
45 Upon her skinny lips. You should be women,
    And yet your beards forbid me to interpret
    That you are so.

MACBETH.   Speak, if you can: what are you?

FIRST WITCH. All hail, Macbeth! Hail to thee, Thane of
        Glamis!

SECOND WITCH. All hail, Macbeth! Hail to thee, Thane of
        Cawdor!

THIRD WITCH. All hail, Macbeth, that shalt be King
50   hereafter!

BANQUO. Good sir, why do you start, and seem to fear
    Things that do sound so fair? I' th' name of truth,
    Are you fantastical,[16] or that indeed
    Which outwardly ye show? My noble partner
55 You greet with present grace[17] and great prediction
    Of noble having[18] and of royal hope,
    That he seems rapt withal:[19] to me you speak not.
    If you can look into the seeds of time,
    And say which grain will grow and which will not,
60 Speak then to me, who neither beg nor fear
    Your favors nor your hate.

FIRST WITCH. Hail!

SECOND WITCH. Hail!

THIRD WITCH. Hail!

65 **FIRST WITCH.** Lesser than Macbeth, and greater.

SECOND WITCH. Not so happy,[20] yet much happier.

THIRD WITCH. Thou shalt get kings, though thou be
        none.
    So all hail, Macbeth and Banquo!

FIRST WITCH. Banquo and Macbeth, all hail!

70 **MACBETH.** Stay, you imperfect[21] speakers, tell me more:
    By Sinel's[22] death I know I am Thane of Glamis;
    But how of Cawdor? The Thane of Cawdor lives,
    A prosperous gentleman; and to be King
    Stands not within the prospect of belief,
75 No more than to be Cawdor. Say from whence
    You owe[23] this strange intelligence?[24] Or why
    Upon this blasted heath you stop our way
    With such prophetic greeting? Speak, I charge you.
                            [WITCHES *vanish.*]

15. choppy: chapped.

16. fantastical: Imaginary.
17. grace: Honor.
18. having: Possession.
19. rapt withal: Entranced by it.

20. happy: Fortunate.

21. imperfect: Incomplete.
22. Sinel's (si′ nəlz): Macbeth's father's.

23. owe: Own.
24. intelligence: Information.

MACBETH AND THE WITCHES
Clarkson Stanfield
Leicestershire Museums

BANQUO. The earth hath bubbles as the water has,
  And these are of them. Whither are they vanished?

MACBETH. Into the air, and what seemed corporal[25] melted
  As breath into the wind. Would they had stayed!

BANQUO. Were such things here as we do speak about?
  Or have we eaten on the insane root[26]
  That takes the reason prisoner?

MACBETH. Your children shall be kings.

BANQUO.   You shall be King.

MACBETH. And Thane of Cawdor too. Went it not so?

BANQUO. To th' selfsame tune and words. Who's here?

[*Enter* ROSS *and* ANGUS.]

ROSS. The King hath happily received, Macbeth,
  The news of thy success; and when he reads[27]
  Thy personal venture in the rebels' fight,
  His wonders and his praises do contend
  Which should be thine or his.[28] Silenced with that,
  In viewing o'er the rest o' th' selfsame day,
  He finds thee in the stout Norweyan ranks,
  Nothing afeard of what thyself didst make,
  Strange images of death.[29] As thick as tale
  Came post with post,[30] and every one did bear
  Thy praises in his kingdom's great defense,
  And poured them down before him.

ANGUS.   We are sent
  To give thee, from our royal master, thanks;
  Only to herald thee into his sight,
  Not pay thee.

ROSS. And for an earnest[31] of a greater honor,
  He bade me, from him, call thee Thane of Cawdor;
  In which addition,[32] hail, most worthy Thane!
  For it is thine.

BANQUO. [*Aside*] What, can the devil speak true?

MACBETH. The Thane of Cawdor lives: why do you
  dress me
  In borrowed robes?

ANGUS.   Who was the thane lives yet,
  But under heavy judgment bears that life
  Which he deserves to lose. Whether he was
  combined[33]

80

85

90

95

100

105

110

25. corporal: Real.

26. insane root: Henbane or hemlock, believed to cause insanity.

27. reads: Considers.
28. His wonders . . . his: His admiration contends with his desire to praise you.
29. Nothing . . . death: Killing, but not being afraid of being killed.
30. As thick . . . post: As fast as could be counted came messenger after messenger.

31. earnest: Pledge.

32. In which addition: With this new title.

33. combined: Allied.

With those of Norway, or did line³⁴ the rebel
With hidden help and vantage,³⁵ or that with both
He labored in his country's wrack,³⁶ I know not;

115 But treasons capital, confessed and proved,
Have overthrown him.

MACBETH.   [*Aside*] Glamis, and Thane of Cawdor:
The greatest is behind.³⁷ [*To* ROSS *and* ANGUS]
     Thanks for your pains.
[*Aside to* BANQUO] Do you not hope your children
     shall be kings,
When those that gave the Thane of Cawdor to me
Promised no less to them?

120 **BANQUO.** [*Aside to* MACBETH] That, trusted home,³⁸
Might yet enkindle you unto³⁹ the crown,
Besides the Thane of Cawdor. But 'tis strange:
And oftentimes, to win us to our harm,
The instruments of darkness tell us truths,

125 Win us with honest trifles, to betray 's
In deepest consequence.
Cousins,⁴⁰ a word, I pray you.

MACBETH.   [*Aside*] Two truths are told,
As happy prologues to the swelling act
Of the imperial theme.⁴¹—I thank you,
     gentlemen.—

130 [*Aside*] This supernatural soliciting
Cannot be ill, cannot be good. If ill,
Why hath it given me earnest of success,
Commencing in a truth? I am Thane of Cawdor:
If good, why do I yield to that suggestion⁴²

135 Whose horrid image doth unfix my hair
And make my seated⁴³ heart knock at my ribs,
Against the use of nature?⁴⁴ Present fears
Are less than horrible imaginings.
My thought, whose murder yet is but fantastical

140 Shakes so my single⁴⁵ state of man that function
Is smothered in surmise, and nothing is
But what is not.

BANQUO.   Look, how our partner's rapt.
MACBETH. [*Aside*] If chance will have me King, why,
     chance may crown me,
Without my stir.

BANQUO.   New honors come upon him,
Like our strange⁴⁶ garments, cleave not to their
145   mold
But with the aid of use.

34. line: support.
35. vantage: Assistance.
36. wrack: Ruin.

37. behind: Still to come.

38. home: fully.
39. enkindle you unto: Encourage you to hope for.

40. Cousins: Often used as a term of courtesy between fellow noblemen.

41. swelling . . . theme: Stately idea that I will be King.

42. suggestion: Thought of murdering Duncan.
43. seated: Fixed.
44. Against . . . nature: In an unnatural way.

45. single: Unaided, weak.

46. strange: New.

MACBETH. [*Aside*] Come what come may,
Time and the hour runs through the roughest day.

BANQUO. Worthy Macbeth, we stay upon your leisure.[47]

MACBETH. Give me your favor.[48] My dull brain was
    wrought
150   With things forgotten. Kind gentlemen, your pains
    Are registered where every day I turn
    The leaf to read them. Let us toward the King.
    [*Aside to* BANQUO] Think upon what hath chanced,
        and at more time,
    The interim having weighed it,[49] let us speak
    Our free hearts[50] each to other.

155 **BANQUO.**   Very gladly.

MACBETH. Till then, enough. Come, friends.   [*Exit.*]

Scene iv. *Forres. The palace.*

[*Flourish.*[1] *Enter* KING DUNCAN, LENNOX, MALCOLM, DONALBAIN, *and*
ATTENDANTS.]

KING. Is execution done on Cawdor? Are not
    Those in commission[2] yet returned?

MALCOLM.   My liege,
    They are not yet come back. But I have spoke
    With one that saw him die, who did report
5   That very frankly he confessed his treasons,
    Implored your Highness' pardon and set forth
    A deep repentance: nothing in his life
    Became him like the leaving it. He died
    As one that had been studied[3] in his death,
10   To throw away the dearest thing he owed[4]
    As 'twere a careless[5] trifle.

KING.   There's no art
    To find the mind's construction[6] in the face:
    He was a gentleman on whom I built
    An absolute trust.

[*Enter* MACBETH, BANQUO, ROSS, *and* ANGUS.]

             O worthiest cousin!
15   The sin of my ingratitude even now
    Was heavy on me: thou art so far before,
    That swiftest wing of recompense is slow
    To overtake thee. Would thou hadst less deserved,
    That the proportion both of thanks and payment
20   Might have been mine![7] Only I have left to say,
    More is thy due than more than all can pay.

**47. stay upon your lei-
sure:** Await your conve-
nience.
48. favor: Pardon.

49. The interim . . . it:
When we have had time to
think about it.
50. Our free hearts: Our
minds freely.

1. Flourish: Trumpet
fanfare.

2. in commission: Commissioned to oversee the
execution.

3. studied: Rehearsed.
4. owed: Owned.
5. careless: Worthless.

6. mind's construction:
A person's character.

7. Would . . . mine: If
you had been less worthy,
my thanks and payment
could have exceeded the rewards you deserve.

MACBETH. The service and the loyalty I owe,
In doing it, pays itself.[8] Your Highness' part
Is to receive our duties: and our duties
25 Are to your throne and state children and servants;
Which do but what they should, by doing every thing
Safe toward[9] your love and honor.

KING.   Welcome hither.
I have begun to plant thee, and will labor
To make thee full of growing. Noble Banquo,
30 That hast no less deserved, nor must be known
No less to have done so, let me enfold thee
And hold thee to my heart.

BANQUO.   There if I grow,
The harvest is your own.

KING.   My plenteous joys,
Wanton[10] in fullness, seek to hide themselves
35 In drops of sorrow. Sons, kinsmen, thanes,
And you whose places are the nearest, know,
We will establish our estate upon
Our eldest, Malcolm,[11] whom we name hereafter
The Prince of Cumberland: which honor must
40 Not unaccompanied invest him only,
But signs of nobleness, like stars, shall shine
On all deservers. From hence to Inverness,[12]
And bind us further to you.

MACBETH. The rest is labor, which is not used for you.[13]
45 I'll be myself the harbinger,[14] and make joyful
The hearing of my wife with your approach;
So, humbly take my leave.

KING.   My worthy Cawdor!

MACBETH. [*Aside*] The Prince of Cumberland! That is a
step
On which I must fall down, or else o'erleap,
50 For in my way it lies. Stars, hide your fires;
Let not light see my black and deep desires:
The eye wink at the hand;[15] yet let that be
Which the eye fears, when it is done, to see.   [*Exit.*]

KING. True, worthy Banquo; he is full so valiant,
55 And in his commendations I am fed;
It is a banquet to me. Let's after him,
Whose care is gone before to bid us welcome.
It is a peerless kinsman.   [*Flourish. Exit.*]

8. pays itself: Is its own reward.

9. Safe toward: With sure regard for.

10. Wanton: Unrestrained.

11. Establish . . . Malcolm: Make Malcolm the heir to my throne.

12. Inverness: Macbeth's castle.

13. The rest . . . you: Anything not done for you is laborious.
14. harbinger: An advance representative of the army or royal party who makes arrangements for a visit.

15. wink at the hand: Be blind to the hand's deed.

Scene v. *Inverness. Macbeth's* castle.
[*Enter* MACBETH'S WIFE, *alone, with a letter.*]

LADY MACBETH. [*Reads*] "They met me in the day of
success; and I have learned by the perfect'st report
they have more in them than mortal knowledge.
When I burned in desire to question them fur-
5 ther, they made themselves air, into which they vanished. Whiles I stood rapt in the wonder of it, came
missives[1] from the King, who all-hailed me 'Thane
of Cawdor'; by which title, before, these weird sisters
saluted me, and referred me to the coming on
10 of time, with 'Hail, King that shalt be!' This have I
thought good to deliver thee,[2] my dearest partner of
greatness, that thou mightst not lose the dues of
rejoicing, by being ignorant of what greatness is
promised thee. Lay it to thy heart, and farewell."

15 Glamis thou art, and Cawdor, and shalt be
What thou art promised. Yet do I fear thy nature;
It is too full o' th' milk of human kindness
To catch the nearest[3] way. Thou wouldst be great,
Art not without ambition, but without
20 The illness[4] should attend it. What thou wouldst
    highly,
That wouldst thou holily; wouldst not play false,
And yet wouldst wrongly win. Thou'dst have, great
    Glamis,
That which cries "Thus thou must do" if thou have
    it;
And that which rather thou dost fear to do
25 Than wishest should be undone.[5] Hie thee hither,
That I may pour my spirits in thine ear,
And chastise with the valor of my tongue
All that impedes thee from the golden round[6]
Which fate and metaphysical aid doth seem
To have thee crowned withal.

[*Enter* MESSENGER.]

30   What is your tidings?
MESSENGER. The King comes here tonight.

LADY MACBETH.   Thou'rt mad to say it!
Is not thy master with him, who, were't so,
Would have informed for preparation?

MESSENGER. So please you, it is true. Our thane is
    coming.
35 One of my fellows had the speed of him,[7]
Who, almost dead for breath, had scarcely more
Than would make up his message.

1. **missives:** Messengers.

2. **deliver thee:** Report to you.

3. **nearest:** Quickest.

4. **illness:** Wickedness.

5. **that which . . . undone:** What you are afraid of doing you would not wish undone once you have done it.
6. **round:** Crown.

7. **had . . . him:** Overtook him.

LADY MACBETH. Give him tending;
He brings great news. [*Exit* MESSENGER.]
The raven himself is hoarse
That croaks the fatal entrance of Duncan
40 Under my battlements. Come, you spirits
That tend on mortal[8] thoughts, unsex me here,
And fill me, from the crown to the toe, top-full
Of direst cruelty! Make thick my blood,
Stop up th' access and passage to remorse[9]
45 That no compunctious visitings of nature[10]
Shake my fell[11] purpose, nor keep peace between
Th' effect[12] and it! Come to my woman's breasts,
And take my milk for gall,[13] you murd'ring minis-
ters,[14]
Wherever in your sightless[15] substances
50 You wait on[16] nature's mischief! Come, thick night,
And pall[17] thee in the dunnest[18] smoke of hell,
That my keen knife see not the wound it makes,
Nor heaven peep through the blanket of the dark,
To cry "Hold, hold!"

[*Enter* MACBETH.]

Great Glamis! Worthy Cawdor!
Greater than both, by the all-hail hereafter!
55 Thy letters have transported me beyond
This ignorant[19] present, and I feel now
The future in the instant.[20]

MACBETH. My dearest love,
Duncan comes here tonight.

LADY MACBETH. And when goes hence?

MACBETH. Tomorrow, as he purposes.

LADY MACBETH. O, never
60 Shall sun that morrow see!
Your face, my Thane, is as a book where men
May read strange matters. To beguile the time,[21]
Look like the time; bear welcome in your eye,
Your hand, your tongue: look like th' innocent flower,
65 But be the serpent under 't. He that's coming
Must be provided for: and you shall put
This night's great business into my dispatch;[22]
Which shall to all our nights and days to come
Give solely sovereign sway and masterdom.

MACBETH. We will speak further.

70 **LADY MACBETH.** Only look up clear.[23]
To alter favor ever is to fear.[24]
Leave all the rest to me. [*Exit.*]

---

8. mortal: Deadly.
9. remorse: Compassion.
10. compunctious . . . nature: Natural feelings of pity.
11. fell: Savage.
12. effect: Fulfillment.
13. milk for gall: Kindness in exchange for bitterness.
14. ministers: Agents.
15. sightless: Invisible.
16. wait on: Assist.
17. pall: Enshroud.
18. dunnest: Darkest.

19. ignorant: Unknowing.
20. instant: Present.

21. beguile the time: Deceive the people tonight.

22. dispatch: Management.

23. look up clear: Appear innocent.
24. To alter . . . fear: To show a disturbed face will arouse suspicion.

Scene vi. *Before Macbeth's castle.*

[*Hautboys.*[1] *Torches.* **Enter** KING DUNCAN, MALCOLM, DONALBAIN, BANQUO, LENNOX, MACDUFF, ROSS, ANGUS, *and* ATTENDANTS.]

KING. This castle hath a pleasant seat;[2] the air
    Nimbly and sweetly recommends itself
    Unto our gentle[3] senses.

BANQUO.   This guest of summer,
    The temple-haunting martlet,[4] does approve[5]
5   By his loved mansionry[6] that the heaven's breath
    Smells wooingly here. No jutty,[7] frieze,
    Buttress, nor coign of vantage,[8] but this bird
    Hath made his pendent bed and procreant cradle.[9]
    Where they most breed and haunt,[10] I have observed
    The air is delicate.

[*Enter* LADY MACBETH.]

10 KING.   See, see, our honored hostess!
    The love that follows us sometime is our trouble,
    Which still we thank as love. Herein I teach you
    How you shall bid God 'ield us for your pains
    And thank us for your trouble.[11]

LADY MACBETH.   All our service
15   In every point twice done, and then done double,
    Were poor and single business[12] to contend
    Against those honors deep and broad wherewith
    Your Majesty loads our house: for those of old,
    And the late dignities heaped up to them,
    We rest your hermits.[13]

20 KING.   Where's the Thane of Cawdor?
    We coursed[14] him at the heels, and had a purpose
    To be his purveyor:[15] but he rides well,
    And his great love, sharp as his spur, hath holp[16] him
    To his home before us. Fair and noble hostess,
    We are your guest tonight.

25 LADY MACBETH.   Your servants ever
    Have theirs, themselves, and what is theirs, in
        compt,[17]
    To make their audit at your Highness' pleasure,
    Still[18] to return your own.

KING.   Give me your hand.
    Conduct me to mine host: we love him highly,
30   And shall continue our graces towards him.
    By your leave, hostess.   [*Exit.*]

---

1. **Hautboys:** Oboes announcing the arrival of royalty.
2. **seat:** Location.
3. **gentle:** Soothed.
4. **temple-haunting martlet:** The martin, a bird that usually nests in churches. In Shakespeare's time *martin* was a slang term for a person who is easily deceived.
5. **approve:** Show.
6. **mansionry:** Nests.
7. **jutty:** Projection.
8. **coign of vantage:** Advantageous corner.
9. **procreant** (prō′ krē ənt) **cradle:** Nest where the young are hatched.
10. **haunt:** Visit.
11. **The love . . . trouble:** Though my visit inconveniences you, you should ask God to reward me for coming, because it was my love for you that prompted my visit.
12. **single business:** Feeble service.
13. **rest your hermits:** Remain your dependents bound to pray for you. Hermits were often paid to pray for another person's soul.
14 **coursed:** Chased.
15. **purveyor:** Advance supply officer.
16. **holp:** Helped.
17. **compt:** Trust.
18. **Still:** Always.

Scene vii. *Macbeth's castle.*

[Hautboys. Torches. Enter a SEWER,[1] *and diverse* SERVANTS *with dishes and service over the stage. Then enter* MACBETH.*]*

MACBETH. If it were done[2] when 'tis done, then 'twere
    well
    It were done quickly. If th' assassination
    Could trammel up the consequence, and catch,
    With his surcease, success;[3] that but this blow
5   Might be the be-all and the end-all—here,
    But here, upon this bank and shoal of time,
    We'd jump the life to come.[4] But in these cases
    We still have judgment here; that we but teach
    Bloody instructions, which, being taught, return
10   To plague th' inventor: this even-handed[5] justice
    Commends[6] th' ingredients of our poisoned chalice[7]
    To our own lips. He's here in double trust:
    First, as I am his kinsman and his subject,
    Strong both against the deed; then, as his host,
15   Who should against his murderer shut the door,
    Not bear the knife myself. Besides, this Duncan
    Hath borne his faculties[8] so meek, hath been
    So clear[9] in his great office, that his virtues
    Will plead like angels trumpet-tongued against
20   The deep damnation of his taking-off;
    And pity, like a naked newborn babe,
    Striding the blast, or heaven's cherubin[10] horsed
    Upon the sightless couriers[11] of the air,
    Shall blow the horrid deed in every eye,
25   That tears shall drown the wind. I have no spur
    To prick the sides of my intent, but only
    Vaulting ambition, which o'erleaps itself
    And falls on th' other—

[Enter LADY MACBETH.*]*

                How now! What news?

LADY MACBETH. He has almost supped. Why have you
    left the chamber?

MACBETH. Hath he asked for me?

30 **LADY MACBETH.**   Know you not he has?

MACBETH. We will proceed no further in this business:
    He hath honored me of late, and I have bought[12]
    Golden opinions from all sorts of people,
    Which would be worn now in their newest gloss,
    Not cast aside so soon.

35 **LADY MACBETH.**   Was the hope drunk

1. sewer: Chief butler.

2. done: Over and done with.

3. If . . . success: If the assassination could be done successfully and without consequence.
4. We'd . . . come: I would risk life in the world to come.

5. even-handed: Impartial.
6. commends: Offers.
7. chalice: Cup.

8. faculties: Powers.
9. clear: Blameless.

10. cherubin: Angels.
11. sightless couriers: Unseen messengers (the wind).

12. bought: Acquired.

Wherein you dressed yourself? Hath it slept since?
And wakes it now, to look so green and pale
At what it did so freely? From this time
Such I account thy love. Art thou afeard
40 To be the same in thine own act and valor
As thou art in desire? Wouldst thou have that
Which thou esteem'st the ornament of life,[13]
And live a coward in thine own esteem,
Letting "I dare not" wait upon[14] "I would,"
Like the poor cat i' th' adage?[15]

45 **MACBETH.**   Prithee, peace!
I dare do all that may become a man;
Who dares do more is none.

LADY MACBETH.   What beast was 't then
That made you break[16] this enterprise to me?
When you durst do it, then you were a man;
50 And to be more than what you were, you would
Be so much more the man. Nor time nor place
Did then adhere,[17] and yet you would make both.
They have made themselves, and that their[18] fitness
    now
Does unmake you. I have given suck, and know
55 How tender 'tis to love the babe that milks me:
I would, while it was smiling in my face,
Have plucked my nipple from his boneless gums,
And dashed the brains out, had I so sworn as you
Have done to this.

MACBETH.   If we should fail?

LADY MACBETH.   We fail?
60 But[19] screw your courage to the sticking-place[20]
And we'll not fail. When Duncan is asleep—
Whereto the rather shall his day's hard journey
Soundly invite him—his two chamberlains
Will I with wine and wassail[21] so convince,[22]
65 That memory, the warder of the brain,
Shall be a fume, and the receipt of reason
A limbeck only:[23] when in swinish sleep
Their drenchèd natures lies as in a death,
What cannot you and I perform upon
70 Th' unguarded Duncan, what not put upon
His spongy[24] officers, who shall bear the guilt
Of our great quell?[25]

MACBETH.   Bring forth men-children only;
For thy undaunted mettle[26] should compose
Nothing but males. Will it not be received,
75 When we have marked with blood those sleepy two

13. ornament of life: The crown.

14. wait upon: Follow.
15. poor . . . adage: From an old proverb about a cat who wants to eat fish but is afraid of getting its paws wet.

16. break: Reveal.

17. Did then adhere: Was then suitable (for the assassination).
18. that their: Their very.

19. But: Only.
20. sticking-place: The notch that holds the bowstring of a taut crossbow.

21. wassail: Carousing.
22. convince: Overpower.

23. That . . . only: That memory, the guardian of the brain, will be confused by the fumes of the drink, and the reason become like a still, distilling confused thoughts.
24. spongy: Sodden.
25. quell: Murder.

26. mettle: Spirit.

SCENE FROM MACBETH
Cattermole
By permission of The Folger Shakespeare Library

MULTICULTURAL CONNECTION

Shakespeare in Translation

Translated into many languages. You might say that Shakespeare is the second most popular author of all time. Only the Bible has been translated into more languages. Shakespeare is especially admired in the former Soviet Union, where his work has been translated into twenty-eight of the languages spoken in that part of the world.

Operas and films. Of course, there is more than one way to translate a play. In Italy, composer Guiseppe Verdi turned three of Shakespeare's plays into operas: *Macbeth,* *Otello* (*Othello*), and *Falstaff* (based on *The Merry Wives of Windsor*). When the Japanese film director Akira Kurosawa turned *Macbeth* into a film called *Throne of Blood*, he set the story in medieval Japan and made the Scottish king a samurai lord.

The ultimate compliment, though, goes beyond adaptation to outright adoption. Shakespeare became so popular in the United Arab Republic that in 1964 one critic was moved to claim that the playwright had actually been an Arab named Shayk al-Subair.

Listening and Sharing

Listen to parts of Verdi's opera *Macbeth* with your classmates and discuss how Verdi captures the mood of the play.

Macbeth, Act 1, Scene i   261

Of his own chamber, and used their very daggers,
That they have done 't?

LADY MACBETH.   Who dares receive it other,[27]
As we shall make our griefs and clamor roar
Upon his death?

     27. **other:** Otherwise.

MACBETH.   I am settled, and bend up
80   Each corporal agent to this terrible feat.
Away, and mock the time[28] with fairest show:
False face must hide what the false heart doth know.

                                 [*Exit.*]

     28. **mock the time:** Mislead the world.

RESPONDING TO THE SELECTION

Your Response

1. Do you find the developments in Macbeth's character believable? Why or why not?
2. Do you think the witches' predictions will come true? Why or why not?

Recalling

3. (a) What does the Captain tell King Duncan about Macbeth's battlefield deeds? (b) What does the King learn from Ross about the Thane of Cawdor's activities? (c) What reward for victory does Macbeth receive almost immediately from the King?
4. What do the three witches predict (a) for Macbeth? (b) for Banquo?
5. (a) What happens to the Thane of Cawdor? (b) Why, despite the witches' predictions, does Macbeth have reason to doubt he will succeed Duncan as king?
6. (a) How does Lady Macbeth first learn of the witches' predictions regarding Macbeth? (b) What in Macbeth's personality does she fear may thwart his ambition?
7. (a) What action does Lady Macbeth plan to take during the King's visit? (b) How does she intend to accomplish it? (c) How does she

advise Macbeth to act in King Duncan's presence?

Interpreting

8. Both the witches and Macbeth make statements about "foul" and "fair." (a) What are two possible meanings for the witches' words? (b) What does Macbeth mean by his remark?
9. Macbeth and Banquo respond differently to the witches' predictions. (a) After becoming Thane of Cawdor, how does Macbeth react to the thought of becoming king? (b) How does Banquo view the witches' predictions?
10. In Scene vi, what is the irony in the description of the air surrounding Macbeth's castle?
11. Why is Macbeth indecisive about killing the King?
12. How does Lady Macbeth's understanding of her husband's character help her to convince him that the murder plot should be carried out?

Applying

13. How do you think that Macbeth should have answered Lady Macbeth when, speaking of the planned murder, she said, "What beast was't then / That made you break this enterprise to me?"

ANALYZING LITERATURE

Understanding Blank Verse

Most of the lines in Shakespeare's plays are written in **blank verse**, or unrhymed iambic pentameter. Each line has ten syllables, with the stress falling on every second syllable.

ᵁ / ᵁ / ᵁ / ᵁ / ᵁ /
The King hath happily received, Macbeth,

ᵁ / ᵁ / ᵁ / ᵁ / ᵁ /
The news of thy success; and when he reads

Blank verse approximates the rhythm of spoken conversation. To keep the lines from becoming monotonous, Shakespeare sometimes varies the pattern of unstressed and stressed syllables or writes a shorter or longer line. Pauses at different places in the lines also help to prevent a singsong rhythm from developing.

1. Scansion is the analysis of verse according to its meter. Write the following lines, marking stressed and unstressed syllables.

   But here, upon this bank and shoal of
      time,
   We'd jump the life to come. But in these
      cases

2. What variation does the second line show?
3. Find two successive lines in Act 1 that are in perfect iambic pentameter. Write them, and mark the stressed and unstressed syllables.

CRITICAL THINKING AND READING

Making Inferences About Characters

When you read or see a play by Shakespeare, you must make inferences about the major characters. You have to draw your own conclusions about their personalities and motivations. Since Shakespeare's characters are complex, you should avoid hasty conclusions. For instance, Macbeth at first appears to be brave, resolute, and loyal. But later in Act I you begin to see him in a different light. Always wait until you have sufficient evidence before making inferences about an important Shakespearean character.

1. In Scene iii, from line 70 to the end, Shakespeare presents a vivid picture of Macbeth. Based on the accumulating evidence, what inferences can you draw about Macbeth's character?
2. What can you infer about Banquo from the more limited evidence in Scene iii, lines 120–126?

THINKING AND WRITING

Comparing and Contrasting Characters

Write a composition in which you compare and contrast the character of Macbeth with that of Lady Macbeth. Find at least two passages spoken by each character that illustrate and support the points you intend to make. Include these in your first draft. When you revise, make sure the quoted passages fit logically into what you have written.

LEARNING OPTIONS

1. **Speaking and Listening.** Choose a passage of about ten lines from Act I of *Macbeth*. Review it until you understand it fully. Then practice reading it aloud. When reading blank verse, allow the meaning of the passage—and its punctuation—to guide you. Stop at the end of a line only when the punctuation calls for it. When you are ready, read the passage to the class in such a way that the meaning comes through clearly to your audience.
2. **Cross-curricular Connection.** The setting of *Macbeth* has an important influence on the atmosphere in Act I. Find out more about the highlands of Scotland. What is the terrain like? What are the prevailing weather patterns? What kinds of plant and animal life are found there? Prepare a brief presentation for the class, using paintings or photographs as illustrations.

GUIDE FOR INTERPRETING

Macbeth, Act II

Writers' Techniques

Atmosphere. The atmosphere in a work of literature is its general mood or feeling. Atmosphere can often be described in one word: *fateful,* for example, or *melancholy* or *cheerful.* A writer creates atmosphere mainly through setting, word choice, and selection of specific details. Since realistic scenery was minimal and since lighting could not be controlled on the Elizabethan stage, Shakespeare often had to rely on dialogue to describe settings. His precise wording and choice of details help build the prevailing mood in each play. A great deal of the atmosphere in *Macbeth* and other Elizabethan plays depends on speech—on what the characters say. Shakespeare, like most great writers, is a master at creating atmosphere.

Focus

Choose an adjective that describes mood—*lively, dismal,* or *scary,* for example—and freewrite a passage that creates the intended atmosphere. Choose words that help to emphasize the mood. You may find it helpful to look in a thesaurus.

Primary Source

Nineteenth-century Shakespearean scholar A. C. Bradley commented on the central effect of atmosphere in *Macbeth.*

> A Shakespearean tragedy, as a rule, has a special tone or atmosphere of its own, quite as perceptible, however difficult to describe. The effect of this atmosphere is marked with unusual strength in *Macbeth.* It is due to a variety of influences . . . so that, acting and reacting, they form a whole; and the desolation of the blasted heath, the design of the Witches, the guilt in the hero's soul, the darkness of the night, seem to emanate from one and the same source. . . . Darkness, we may even say blackness, broods over this tragedy. It is remarkable that almost all the scenes which at once recur to the memory take place either at night or in some dark spot. The vision of the dagger, the murder of Duncan, the sleepwalking of Lady Macbeth, are all night scenes. The witches dance in the thick air of a storm, or, 'black and midnight hags' receive Macbeth in a cavern. The blackness of the night is to the hero a thing of fear, even of horror; and that which he feels becomes the spirit of the play . . . The atmosphere of *Macbeth* is not that of unrelieved blackness . . . it is really the impression of a black night broken by flashes of light and color, sometimes vivid and even glaring.

Act II

Scene i. *Inverness. Court of Macbeth's castle.*
[*Enter* BANQUO, *and* FLEANCE, *with a torch before him.*]

BANQUO. How goes the night, boy?

FLEANCE. The moon is down; I have not heard the clock.

BANQUO. And she goes down at twelve.

FLEANCE.   I take't, 'tis later, sir.

BANQUO. Hold, take my sword. There's husbandry[1] in
    heaven.
5   Their candles are all out. Take thee that[2] too.
  A heavy summons[3] lies like lead upon me,
  And yet I would not sleep. Merciful powers,
  Restrain in me the cursèd thoughts that nature
  Gives way to in repose!

[*Enter* MACBETH, *and a* SERVANT *with a torch.*]

                      Give me my sword!
10   Who's there?

MACBETH. A friend.

BANQUO. What, sir, not yet at rest? The King's a-bed:
  He hath been in unusual pleasure, and
  Sent forth great largess to your offices:[4]
15   This diamond he greets your wife withal,
  By the name of most kind hostess; and shut up[5]
  In measureless content.

MACBETH.   Being unprepared,
  Our will became the servant to defect,
  Which else should free have wrought.[6]

BANQUO.   All's well.
20   I dreamt last night of the three weird sisters:
  To you they have showed some truth.

MACBETH.   I think not of them.
  Yet, when we can entreat an hour to serve,
  We would spend it in some words upon that business,
  If you would grant the time.

BANQUO.   At your kind'st leisure.

25 **MACBETH.** If you shall cleave to my consent, when 'tis,[7]
  It shall make honor for you.

---

1. **husbandry:** Thrift.

2. **that:** Probably his sword belt.
3. **summons:** Weariness.

4. **largess . . . offices:** Gifts to your servants' quarters.
5. **shut up:** Retired.

6. **Being . . . wrought:** Because we did not have enough time to prepare, we were unable to entertain as lavishly as we wanted to.

7. **cleave . . . 'tis:** Join my cause when the time comes.

BANQUO.   So[8] I lose none
In seeking to augment it, but still keep
My bosom franchised[9] and allegiance clear,
I shall be counseled.

MACBETH.   Good repose the while!

30 **BANQUO.** Thanks, sir. The like to you!

[*Exit* BANQUO *with* FLEANCE.]

MACBETH. Go bid thy mistress, when my drink is ready,
She strike upon the bell. Get thee to bed.

[*Exit* SERVANT.]

Is this a dagger which I see before me,
The handle toward my hand? Come, let me clutch
        thee.
35 I have thee not, and yet I see thee still.
Art thou not, fatal vision, sensible[10]
To feeling as to sight, or art thou but
A dagger of the mind, a false creation,
Proceeding from the heat-oppressèd brain?
40 I see thee yet, in form as palpable
As this which now I draw.
Thou marshal'st[11] me the way that I was going;
And such an instrument I was to use.
Mine eyes are made the fools o' th' other senses,
45 Or else worth all the rest. I see thee still;
And on thy blade and dudgeon[12] gouts[13] of blood,
Which was not so before. There's no such thing.
It is the bloody business which informs[14]
Thus to mine eyes. Now o'er the one half-world
50 Nature seems dead, and wicked dreams abuse[15]
The curtained sleep; witchcraft celebrates
Pale Hecate's offerings;[16] and withered murder,
Alarumed by his sentinel, the wolf,
Whose howl's his watch, thus with his stealthy pace,
With Tarquin's[17] ravishing strides, towards his de-
55   sign
Moves like a ghost. Thou sure and firm-set earth,
Hear not my steps, which way they walk, for fear
Thy very stones prate of my whereabout,
And take the present horror from the time,
60 Which now suits with it.[18] Whiles I threat, he lives:
Words to the heat of deeds too cold breath gives.

[*A bell rings.*]

I go, and it is done: the bell invites me.
Hear it not, Duncan, for it is a knell
That summons thee to heaven, or to hell.   [*Exit.*]

---

8. So: Provided that.

9. bosom franchised: Heart free (from guilt).

10. sensible: Able to be felt.

11. marshal'st: Leads.

12. dudgeon: Wooden hilt.
13. gouts: Large drops.
14. informs: Takes shape.
15. abuse: Deceive.

16. Hecate's (hĕk′ə tēz) **offerings:** Offerings to Hecate, the Greek goddess of witchcraft.
17. Tarquin's: Of Tarquin, a Roman tyrant.

18. take . . . it: Remove the horrible silence which suits this moment.

ELLEN TERRY AS LADY MACBETH
John Singer Sargent
Tate Gallery, on Loan to National Portrait Gallery, London

Scene ii. *Macbeth's castle.*

[*Enter* LADY MACBETH.]

> **LADY MACBETH.** That which hath made them drunk hath
>   made me bold;
> What hath quenched them hath given me fire. Hark!
>   Peace!
> It was the owl that shrieked, the fatal bellman,
> Which gives the stern'st good-night.[1] He is about it.
> 5   The doors are open, and the surfeited grooms[2]
> Do mock their charge with snores. I have drugged
>   their possets,[3]
> That death and nature do contend about them,
> Whether they live or die.

1. bellman . . . good-night: It was customary for a bell to be rung at midnight outside a condemned person's cell on the night before an execution.

2. surfeited grooms: Overfed servants.

3. possets: Warm bedtime drinks.

MACBETH. [*Within*] Who's there? What, ho?

LADY MACBETH. Alack, I am afraid they have awaked
10   And 'tis not done! Th' attempt and not the deed
    Confounds⁴ us. Hark! I laid their daggers ready;
    He could not miss 'em. Had he not resembled
    My father as he slept, I had done 't.

4. Confounds: Ruins.

[*Enter* MACBETH.]

                     My husband!

MACBETH. I have done the deed. Didst thou not hear a
    noise?

LADY MACBETH. I heard the owl scream and the crickets
15   cry.
    Did not you speak?

MACBETH.   When?

LADY MACBETH.   Now.

MACBETH.   As I descended?

LADY MACBETH. Ay.

MACBETH. Hark!
    Who lies i' th' second chamber?

LADY MACBETH.   Donalbain.

20 **MACBETH.** This is a sorry⁵ sight.

5. sorry: Miserable.

LADY MACBETH. A foolish thought, to say a sorry sight.

MACBETH. There's one did laugh in 's sleep, and one
    cried "Murder!"
    That they did wake each other. I stood and heard
    them.
    But they did say their prayers, and addressed them
    Again to sleep.

25 **LADY MACBETH.** There are two⁶ lodged together.

6. two: Malcolm and Donalbain, Duncan's sons.

MACBETH. One cried "God bless us!" and "Amen" the
    other,
    As they had seen me with these hangman's hands:
    List'ning their fear, I could not say "Amen,"
    When they did say "God bless us!"

LADY MACBETH.   Consider it not so deeply.

MACBETH. But wherefore could not I pronounce
30   "Amen"?
    I had most need of blessing, and "Amen"
    Stuck in my throat.

LADY MACBETH.   These deeds must not be thought
    After these ways; so, it will make us mad.

MACBETH. Methought I heard a voice cry "Sleep no more!
35   Macbeth does murder sleep"—the innocent sleep,
    Sleep that knits up the raveled sleave[7] of care,
    The death of each day's life, sore labor's bath,
    Balm of hurt minds, great nature's second course,[8]
    Chief nourisher in life's feast—

LADY MACBETH.   What do you mean?

40   **MACBETH.** Still it cried "Sleep no more!" to all the house:
    "Glamis hath murdered sleep, and therefore Cawdor
    Shall sleep no more: Macbeth shall sleep no more."

LADY MACBETH. Who was it that thus cried? Why, worthy
        Thane,
    You do unbend[9] your noble strength, to think
45   So brainsickly of things. Go get some water,
    And wash this filthy witness[10] from your hand.
    Why did you bring these daggers from the place?
    They must lie there: go carry them, and smear
    The sleepy grooms with blood.

MACBETH.   I'll go no more.
50   I am afraid to think what I have done;
    Look on 't again I dare not.

LADY MACBETH.   Infirm of purpose!
    Give me the daggers. The sleeping and the dead
    Are but as pictures. 'Tis the eye of childhood
    That fears a painted devil. If he do bleed,
55   I'll gild[11] the faces of the grooms withal,
    For it must seem their guilt.   [Exit. Knock within.]

MACBETH.   Whence is that knocking?
    How is 't with me, when every noise appalls me?
    What hands are here? Ha! They pluck out mine eyes!
    Will all great Neptune's ocean wash this blood
60   Clean from my hand? No; this my hand will rather
    The multitudinous seas incarnadine,[12]
    Making the green one red.

[Enter LADY MACBETH.]

LADY MACBETH. My hands are of your color, but I shame
    To wear a heart so white. [Knock.] I hear a knocking
65   At the south entry. Retire we to our chamber.
    A little water clears us of this deed:
    How easy is it then! Your constancy
    Hath left you unattended.[13] [Knock.] Hark! more
        knocking.

7. knits . . . sleave:
Straightens out the tangled threads.
8. second course: The main course; sleep.

9. unbend: Relax.

10. witness: Evidence.

11. gild: Paint.

12. incarnadine (in kär′ nə din): Redden.

13. Your constancy . . . unattended: Your firmness of purpose has left you.

Get on your nightgown, lest occasion call us
70 And show us to be watchers.[14] Be not lost
So poorly in your thoughts.

MACBETH. To know my deed, 'twere best not know
myself. [*Knock.*]
Wake Duncan with thy knocking! I would thou
couldst!   [*Exit.*]

14. watchers: Up late.

Scene iii. *Macbeth's castle.*
[*Enter a* PORTER.[1] *Knocking within.*]

PORTER. Here's a knocking indeed! If a man were porter
of hell gate, he should have old[2] turning the key.
[*Knock.*] Knock, knock, knock! Who's there, i' th'
name of Beelzebub?[3] Here's a farmer, that
5 hanged himself on th' expectation of plenty.[4] Come
in time! Have napkins enow[5] about you; here you'll
sweat for 't. [*Knock.*] Knock, knock! Who's there, in
th' other devil's name? Faith, here's an equivocator,
that could swear in both the scales against
10 either scale;[6] who committed treason enough for
God's sake, yet could not equivocate to heaven. O,
come in, equivocator. [*Knock.*] Knock, knock, knock!
Who's there? Faith, here's an English tailor come
hither for stealing out of a French hose:[7]
15 come in, tailor. Here you may roast your goose.[8]
[*Knock.*] Knock, knock; never at quiet! What are you?
But this place is too cold for hell. I'll devil-porter it no
further. I had thought to have let in some of all
professions that go the primrose way to th'
20 everlasting bonfire. [*Knock.*] Anon, anon! [*Opens an
entrance.*] I pray you, remember the porter.

[*Enter* MACDUFF *and* LENNOX.]

MACDUFF. Was it so late, friend, ere you went to bed,
That you do lie so late?

PORTER. Faith, sir, we were carousing till the second
25 cock:[9] and drink, sir, is a great provoker of three
things.

MACDUFF. What three things does drink especially
provoke?

PORTER. Marry, sir, nose-painting, sleep, and urine.
30 Lechery, sir, it provokes and unprovokes; it provokes
the desire, but it takes away the performance: therefore much drink may be said to be an equivocator with lechery: it makes him and it mars him: it

1. porter: Doorkeeper.

2. should have old:
Would have plenty of.
3. Beelzebub (bē el' zə
bub): The chief devil.
4. A farmer . . . plenty:
A farmer who hoarded
grain, hoping that the prices would come up as a re-
sult of a bad harvest.
5. enow: Enough.
**6. an equivocator . . .
scale:** A liar who could
make two contradictory
statements and swear that
both were true.
7. stealing . . . hose:
Stealing some cloth from
the hose while making
them.
8. goose: Pressing iron.

9. second cock: 3:00
A.M.

35 sets him on and it takes him off; it per-
suades him and disheartens him; makes him stand
to and not stand to; in conclusion, equivocates him
in a sleep, and giving him the lie, leaves him.

MACDUFF. I believe drink gave thee the lie[10] last night.

PORTER. That it did, sir, i' the very throat on me: but I
40 requited him for his lie, and, I think, being too strong
for him, though he took up my legs some-
time, yet I make a shift to cast[11] him.

MACDUFF. Is thy master stirring?

[*Enter* MACBETH.]

Our knocking has awaked him; here he comes.

LENNOX. Good morrow, noble sir.

45 **MACBETH.**   Good morrow, both.

MACDUFF. Is the king stirring, worthy Thane?

MACBETH.   Not yet.

MACDUFF. He did command me to call timely[12] on him:
I have almost slipped the hour.

MACBETH.   I'll bring you to him.

MACDUFF. I know this is a joyful trouble to you;
50 But yet 'tis one.

MACBETH. The labor we delight in physics pain.[13]
This is the door.

MACDUFF.   I'll make so bold to call,
For 'tis my limited service.[14]   [*Exit* MACDUFF.]

LENNOX. Goes the king hence today?

MACBETH.   He does: he did appoint so.

55 **LENNOX.** The night has been unruly. Where we lay,
Our chimneys were blown down, and, as they say,
Lamentings heard i' th' air, strange screams of
    death,
And prophesying with accents terrible
Of dire combustion[15] and confused events
60 New hatched to th' woeful time: the obscure bird[16]
Clamored the livelong night. Some say, the earth
Was feverous and did shake.

MACBETH.   'Twas a rough night.

LENNOX. My young remembrance cannot parallel
A fellow to it.

10. gave thee the lie: Laid you out.

11. cast: Vomit.

12. timely: Early.

13. labor . . . pain: Labor that we enjoy cures discomfort.

14. limited service: Assigned duty.

15. combustion: Confusion.
16. obscure bird: Bird of darkness, the owl.

LADY MACBETH SEIZING THE DAGGERS
Henry Fuseli
The Tate Gallery, London

[*Enter* MACDUFF.]

65   **MACDUFF.** O horror, horror, horror! Tongue nor heart
       Cannot conceive nor name thee.

       MACBETH AND LENNOX.   What's the matter?

       MACDUFF. Confusion[17] now hath made his masterpiece.
       Most sacrilegious murder hath broke ope
       The Lord's anointed temple,[18] and stole thence
       The life o' th' building.

70   **MACBETH.**   What is 't you say? The life?

       LENNOX. Mean you his Majesty?

       MACDUFF. Approach the chamber, and destroy your
       sight

17. Confusion: Destruction.

18. The Lord's anointed temple: The King's body.

With a new Gorgon:[19] do not bid me speak;
See, and then speak yourselves. Awake, awake!

[*Exit* MACBETH *and* LENNOX.]

75   Ring the alarum bell. Murder and Treason!
Banquo and Donalbain! Malcolm! Awake!
Shake off this downy sleep, death's counterfeit,
And look on death itself! Up, up, and see
The great doom's image![20] Malcolm! Banquo!
80   As from your graves rise up, and walk like sprites,[21]
To countenance[22] this horror. Ring the bell.

[*Bell rings. Enter* LADY MACBETH.]

LADY MACBETH. What's the business,
That such a hideous trumpet calls to parley[23]
The sleepers of the house? Speak, speak!

MACDUFF.   O gentle lady,
85   'Tis not for you to hear what I can speak:
The repetition, in a woman's ear,
Would murder as it fell.

[*Enter* BANQUO.]

                          O Banquo, Banquo!
Our royal master's murdered.

LADY MACBETH.   Woe, alas!
What, in our house?

BANQUO.   Too cruel anywhere.
90   Dear Duff, I prithee, contradict thyself,
And say it is not so.

[*Enter* MACBETH, LENNOX, *and* ROSS.]

MACBETH. Had I but died an hour before this
      chance,
I had lived a blessèd time; for from this instant
There's nothing serious in mortality:[24]
95   All is but toys.[25] Renown and grace is dead,
The wine of life is drawn, and the mere lees[26]
Is left this vault[27] to brag of.

[*Enter* MALCOLM *and* DONALBAIN.]

DONALBAIN. What is amiss?

MACBETH.   You are, and do not know 't.
The spring, the head, the fountain of your blood
100   Is stopped; the very source of it is stopped.

MACDUFF. Your royal father's murdered.

MALCOLM.   O, by whom?

19. Gorgon: Medusa, a mythological monster whose appearance was so ghastly that those who looked at it turned to stone.

20. great doom's image: Likeness of Judgment Day.
21. sprites: Spirits.
22. countenance: Be in keeping with.

23. parley: A war conference.

24. serious in mortality: Worthwhile in mortal life.
25. toys: Trifles.
26. lees: Dregs.
27. vault: World.

LENNOX. Those of his chamber, as it seemed, had
    done 't:
    Their hands and faces were all badged[28] with blood;
    So were their daggers, which unwiped we found
105   Upon their pillows. They stared, and were distracted.
    No man's life was to be trusted with them.

28. badged: Marked.

MACBETH. O, yet I do repent me of my fury,
    That I did kill them.

MACDUFF.   Wherefore did you so?

MACBETH. Who can be wise, amazed, temp'rate and
    furious,
110   Loyal and neutral, in a moment? No man.
    The expedition[29] of my violent love
    Outrun the pauser, reason. Here lay Duncan,
    His silver skin laced with his golden blood,
    And his gashed stabs looked like a breach in nature
115   For ruin's wasteful entrance: there, the murderers,
    Steeped in the colors of their trade, their daggers
    Unmannerly breeched with gore.[30] Who could
    refrain,
    That had a heart to love, and in that heart
    Courage to make 's love known?

29. expedition: Haste.

30. breeched with gore:
Covered with blood.

LADY MACBETH.   Help me hence, ho!

MACDUFF. Look to the lady.

MALCOLM. [*Aside to* DONALBAIN] Why do we hold our
120   tongues,
    That most may claim this argument for ours?[31]

31. That most . . . ours:
Who are the most con-
cerned with this topic.

DONALBAIN. [*Aside to Malcolm*] What should be spoken
    here,
    Where our fate, hid in an auger-hole,[32]
    May rush, and seize us? Let's away:
    Our tears are not yet brewed.

32. auger-hole: Tiny hole,
an unsuspected place be-
cause of its size.

125   **MALCOLM.** [*Aside to* DONALBAIN] Nor our strong sorrow
    Upon the foot of motion. [33]

BANQUO.   Look to the lady.
             [LADY MACBETH *is carried out.*]
    And when we have our naked frailties hid,[34]
    That suffer in exposure, let us meet
    And question[35] this most bloody piece of work,
130   To know it further. Fears and scruples[36] shake us.
    In the great hand of God I stand, and thence
    Against the undivulged pretense[37] I fight
    Of treasonous malice.

**33. Our tears . . .
motion:** We have not yet
had time for tears nor to
turn our sorrow into ac-
tion.
34. when . . . hid: When
we have put on our clothes.
35. question: Investigate.
36. scruples: Doubts.

37. undivulged pretense:
Hidden purpose.

MACDUFF.   And so do I.

ALL. So all.

MACBETH. Let's briefly[38] put on manly readiness,
    And meet i' th' hall together.

38. **briefly:** Quickly.

135 **ALL.** Well contented.

[Exit all but MALCOLM *and* DONALBAIN.]

MALCOLM. What will you do? Let's not consort with
    them.
    To show an unfelt sorrow is an office[39]
    Which the false man does easy. I'll to England.

39. **office:** Function.

DONALBAIN. To Ireland, I; our separated fortune
140   Shall keep us both the safer. Where we are
    There's daggers in men's smiles; the near in blood,
    The nearer bloody.[40]

40. **the near . . .
bloody:** The closer we are
in blood relationship to
Duncan, the greater our
chance of being murdered.

MALCOLM. This murderous shaft that's shot
    Hath not yet lighted,[41] and our safest way
    Is to avoid the aim. Therefore to horse;
145   And let us not be dainty of leave-taking,
    But shift away. There's warrant[42] in that theft
    Which steals itself[43] when there's no mercy left.

[Exit.]

41. **lighted:** Reached its
target.
42. **warrant:** Justification
43. **that theft . . . itself:**
stealing away.

Scene iv. *Outside Macbeth's castle.*
[Enter ROSS *with an* OLD MAN.]

OLD MAN. Threescore and ten I can remember well:
    Within the volume of which time I have seen
    Hours dreadful and things strange, but this sore[1]
      night
    Hath trifled former knowings.

1. **sore:** Grievous.

ROSS. Ha, good father,
5   Thou seest the heavens, as troubled with man's act,
    Threatens his bloody stage. By th' clock 'tis day,
    And yet dark night strangles the traveling lamp:[2]
    Is 't night's predominance, or the day's shame,
    That darkness does the face of earth entomb,
    When living light should kiss it?

2. **traveling lamp:** The
sun.

10 **OLD MAN.** 'Tis unnatural,
    Even like the deed that's done. On Tuesday last
    A falcon, tow'ring in her pride of place,[3]
    Was by a mousing owl hawked at and killed.

3. **tow'ring . . . place:**
Soaring at its summit.

ROSS. And Duncan's horses—a thing most strange
    and certain—
15   Beauteous and swift, the minions of their race,
    Turned wild in nature, broke their stalls, flung out,
    Contending 'gainst obedience, as they would make
    War with mankind.

OLD MAN.   'Tis said they eat[4] each other.   **4. eat:** Ate.

ROSS. They did so, to th' amazement of mine eyes,
That looked upon 't.

[*Enter* MACDUFF.]

20   Here comes the good Macduff.
How goes the world, sir, now?

MACDUFF.   Why, see you not?

ROSS. Is 't known who did this more than bloody deed?

MACDUFF. Those that Macbeth hath slain.

ROSS.   Alas, the day!
What good could they pretend? [5]   **5. pretend:** Hope for.

MACDUFF.   They were suborned:[6]   **6. suborned:** Bribed.
25   Malcolm and Donalbain, the king's two sons,
Are stol'n away and fled, which puts upon them
Suspicion of the deed.

ROSS.   'Gainst nature still.
Thriftless ambition, that will ravin up[7]   **7. ravin up:** Devour
Thine own life's means! Then 'tis most like   greedily.
30   The sovereignty will fall upon Macbeth.

MACDUFF. He is already named, and gone to Scone[8]   **8. Scone** (sko͞on): Where
To be invested.   Scottish kings were
                                    crowned.

ROSS.   Where is Duncan's body?

MACDUFF. Carried to Colmekill,
The sacred storehouse of his predecessors
And guardian of their bones.

35   **ROSS.**   Will you to Scone?

MACDUFF. No, cousin, I'll to Fife. [9]   **9. Fife:** Where Macduff's
                                    castle is located.

ROSS.   Well, I will thither.

MACDUFF. Well, may you see things well done there.
    Adieu,
Lest our old robes sit easier than our new!

ROSS. Farewell, father.

40   **OLD MAN.** God's benison[10] go with you, and with those   **10. benison:** Blessing.
That would make good of bad, and friends of foes!
                                    [*Exit.*]

RESPONDING TO THE SELECTION

Your Response

1. Who do you think bears the greater responsibility for the murder of King Duncan—Macbeth or Lady Macbeth? Explain.

Recalling

2. (a) Why, according to Lady Macbeth, did she not kill the King herself? (b) What does Macbeth do with the daggers after the murder? (c) Why does this bother Lady Macbeth? (d) What action does she take?

3. (a) What does the drunken porter imagine he is doing in response to the knocking at the door? (b) What does Macbeth wish the knocking could do? (c) Who is doing the knocking? Why?

4. (a) Who first learns that a murder has taken place? (b) What action does Macbeth take against the grooms? (c) Why do Malcolm and Donalbain leave Macbeth's castle?

5. (a) Who does Macduff say has killed King Duncan? Why do Malcolm and Donalbain fall under suspicion, according to Macduff?

Interpreting

6. What does Macbeth mean by saying he has "murdered sleep"?

7. What is ironic about Lady Macbeth's remark "A little water clears us of this deed"?

8. (a) Why do you think critics consider the porter's speech to be comic relief? (b) How do the porter's comments on the people arriving at "hell gate" mirror Macbeth's dilemma?

9. What do you think causes Lady Macbeth to faint?

10. (a) Why does Ross have doubts about accepting the grooms as the murderers? (b) Why is Macduff concerned that "our old robes" may fit "easier than our new"?

Applying

11. In his soliloquy in Scene i, Macbeth speaks of "vaulting ambition." (a) How can vaulting ambition bring with it great success? (b) How can it bring with it destruction?

ANALYZING LITERATURE

Understanding Atmosphere

Atmosphere is the general mood or feeling in a literary work. In *Macbeth* the murder of the King occurs on an unusually dark, moonless night. The blackness of the night, which is conveyed through dialogue, matches the blackness of the deed. The grim, foreboding atmosphere reinforces the emotional states of the characters.

1. What is eerie about Macbeth's soliloquy in Scene i?

2. Reread Lennox's description of the night, Scene iii, lines 43–50. How does this description add to the atmosphere of the scene?

3. (a) How do the strange natural occurrences mentioned in Scene iv affect the atmosphere? (b) How do they relate to the night's events at Inverness Castle?

CRITICAL THINKING AND READING

Interpreting Symbols

A **symbol** is a word, person, object, or action that stands for something beyond itself. A flag, for example, is more than a piece of cloth; it stands for a country, its people, its ideals. Similarly, the ringing of the bell in Scene i is more than just a sound. It symbolizes an imminent death, much like the bell announcing an execution at London's Newgate prison or the small bell that was rung outside a condemned person's cell at midnight to urge repentance.

1. In Scene ii, Lady Macbeth compares an owl's shriek to the "fatal bellman." How does this comparison extend the symbol of the bell?

2. Blood and water function as symbols in Scene ii, lines 44–68. (a) What does each symbolize? (b) What indication is there that Macbeth is less impressed by this symbolism than his wife is?

3. It has been suggested that the Old Man in Scene iv is a symbol for the people of Scotland. What is there about the Old Man that makes this suggestion plausible?

GUIDE FOR INTERPRETING

Macbeth, Act III

Writers' Techniques

Irony. In general, irony is a contrast between what is said and what is meant or between what is expected and what occurs. There are three kinds of irony in literature, all of which occur in *Macbeth*.

Dramatic irony exists when the words or acts of a character in a play carry a meaning the character does not understand but the audience does. An example of dramatic irony occurs in *Macbeth* at the beginning of Act I, Scene vi, when Banquo and Duncan discuss the pleasant and delicate air as they arrive at Inverness. The audience knows, but Banquo and Duncan do not, that a murderous plot is being hatched behind the castle walls.

Situational irony occurs when the expected results of an action or situation differ from the actual results.

Verbal irony exists when a speaker says one thing and means the opposite. In a famous speech in Shakespeare's *Julius Caesar,* for example, when Mark Antony says of the assassins of Caesar, "So are they all, all honorable men," he means exactly the opposite of what he says. To him, the assassins are *not* honorable men. Antony's words are therefore verbal irony.

Commentary

The Elizabethans believed that ghosts of dead people could return to earth. Spirits could appear to whomever they wanted, whenever they wanted, so that one person in a crowd might see a ghost while the others did not. Ghosts were especially likely to return when they were troubled. In Shakespeare's plays, ghosts often return to haunt a murderer. Although clergymen preached that the belief in ghosts was wicked and sinful, people remained convinced that ghosts were real, and well-equipped Elizabethan households boasted a stockpile of charms to ward off ghosts.

Perhaps William Shakespeare had his country folks' belief in ghosts in mind when he chose this epitaph for his own grave:

> Good friend, for Jesus' sake forbare
> To dig the dust encloséd here.
> Blest be the man that spares these stones,
> And curst be he that moves my bones.

Focus

At this point in *Macbeth,* you know a great deal about the major characters—more, in fact, than they know about themselves. Based on your knowledge, take notes on what you think will happen to the following characters by the end of the play: Macbeth, Lady Macbeth, Banquo, Macduff.

Act III

Scene i. *Forres. The palace.*
[*Enter* BANQUO.]

    BANQUO. Thou hast it now: King, Cawdor, Glamis, all,
    As the weird women promised, and I fear
    Thou play'dst most foully for 't. Yet it was said
    It should not stand¹ in thy posterity,

5   But that myself should be the root and father
    Of many kings. If there come truth from them—
    As upon thee, Macbeth, their speeches shine—
    Why, by the verities on thee made good,
    May they not be my oracles as well

10   And set me up in hope? But hush, no more!

[*Sennet*² *sounded. Enter* MACBETH *as King,* LADY MACBETH, LENNOX, ROSS, LORDS, *and* ATTENDANTS.]

    MACBETH. Here's our chief guest.

    LADY MACBETH.   If he had been forgotten,
    It had been as a gap in our great feast,
    And all-thing³ unbecoming.

    MACBETH. Tonight we hold a solemn⁴ supper, sir,
    And I'll request your presence.

15   **BANQUO.**   Let your Highness
    Command upon me, to the which my duties
    Are with a most indissoluble tie
    For ever knit.

    MACBETH. Ride you this afternoon?

    BANQUO.   Ay, my good lord.

20   **MACBETH.** We should have else desired your good advice
    (Which still hath been both grave and prosperous⁵)
    In this day's council; but we'll take tomorrow.
    Is 't far you ride?

    BANQUO. As far, my lord, as will fill up the time
25   'Twixt this and supper. Go not my horse the better,⁶
    I must become a borrower of the night
    For a dark hour or twain.

    MACBETH.   Fail not our feast.

    BANQUO. My lord, I will not.

    MACBETH. We hear our bloody cousins are bestowed
30   In England and in Ireland, not confessing
    Their cruel parricide, filling their hearers
    With strange invention.⁷ But of that tomorrow,

1. stand: Continue.

2. Sennet: Trumpet call.

3. all-thing: Altogether.

4. solemn: Ceremonious.

5. grave and prosperous: Weighty and profitable.

6. Go not . . . better: Unless my horse goes faster than I expect.

7. invention: Lies.

When therewithal we shall have cause of state
Craving us jointly.[8] Hie you to horse. Adieu,
35   Till you return at night. Goes Fleance with you?

BANQUO. Ay, my good lord: our time does call upon 's.

MACBETH. I wish your horses swift and sure of foot,
And so I do commend you to their backs.
Farewell.   *[Exit* BANQUO.*]*
40   Let every man be master of his time
Till seven at night. To make society
The sweeter welcome, we will keep ourself
Till suppertime alone. While[9] then, God be with you!

        [Exit LORDS *and all but* MACBETH *and a* SERVANT.*]*

Sirrah,[10] a word with you: attend those men
45   Our pleasure?

ATTENDANT. They are, my lord, without the palace gate.

MACBETH. Bring them before us.   *[Exit* SERVANT.*]*
To be thus[11] is nothing, but[12] to be safely thus—
Our fears in Banquo stick deep,
50   And in his royalty of nature reigns that
Which would be feared. 'Tis much he dares;
And, to[13] that dauntless temper of his mind,
He hath a wisdom that doth guide his valor
To act in safety. There is none but he
55   Whose being I do fear: and under him
My genius is rebuked,[14] as it is said
Mark Antony's was by Caesar. He chid[15] the sisters,
When first they put the name of King upon me,
And bade them speak to him; then prophetlike
60   They hailed him father to a line of kings.
Upon my head they placed a fruitless crown
And put a barren scepter in my gripe,[16]
Thence to be wrenched with an unlineal hand,
No son of mine succeeding. If 't be so,
65   For Banquo's issue have I filed[17] my mind;
For them the gracious Duncan have I murdered;
Put rancors in the vessel of my peace
Only for them, and mine eternal jewel[18]
Given to the common enemy of man,[19]
70   To make them kings, the seeds of Banquo kings!
Rather than so, come, fate, into the list,
And champion me to th' utterance![20] Who's there?

[Enter SERVANT *and* TWO MURDERERS.*]*

Now go to the door, and stay there till we call.
                     [Exit SERVANT.*]*
Was it not yesterday we spoke together?

8. cause . . . jointly:
Matters of state demanding
our joint attention.

9. While: Until.

10. Sirrah: A common address to an inferior.

11. thus: King.
12. but: Unless.

13. to: Added to.

14. genius is rebuked:
Guardian spirit is cowed.
15. chid: Scolded.

16. gripe: Grip.

17. filed: Defiled.

18. eternal jewel: Soul.
19. common . . . man:
The Devil.

20. champion me to th' utterance: Fight against me to the death.

MURDERERS. It was, so please your Highness.

75   **MACBETH.**   Well then, now
      Have you considered of my speeches? Know
      That it was he in the times past, which held you
      So under fortune,[21] which you thought had been
      Our innocent self: this I made good to you
      In our last conference; passed in probation[22] with
80   you,
      How you were born in hand,[23] how crossed, the
        instruments,
      Who wrought with them, and all things else that
        might
      To half a soul[24] and to a notion[25] crazed
      Say "Thus did Banquo."

  FIRST MURDERER.   You made it known to us.

85   **MACBETH.** I did so; and went further, which is now
      Our point of second meeting. Do you find
      Your patience so predominant in your nature,
      That you can let this go? Are you so gospeled,[26]
      To pray for this good man and for his issue,
90   Whose heavy hand hath bowed you to the grave
      And beggared yours for ever?

  FIRST MURDERER.   We are men, my liege.

  MACBETH. Ay, in the catalogue ye go for[27] men;
      As hounds and greyhounds, mongrels, spaniels,
        curs,
      Shoughs, water-rugs[28] and demi-wolves, are clept[29]
95   All by the name of dogs: the valued file[30]
      Distinguishes the swift, the slow, the subtle,
      The housekeeper, the hunter, every one
      According to the gift which bounteous nature
      Hath in him closed,[31] whereby he does receive
100   Particular addition,[32] from the bill
      That writes them all alike: and so of men.
      Now if you have a station in the file,[33]
      Not i' th' worst rank of manhood, say 't,
      And I will put that business in your bosoms
105   Whose execution takes your enemy off,
      Grapples you to the heart and love of us,
      Who wear our health but sickly in his life,[34]
      Which in his death were perfect.

  SECOND MURDERER.   I am one, my liege,
      Whom the vile blows and buffets of the world
110   Hath so incensed that I am reckless what
      I do to spite the world.

---

21. held . . . fortune: Kept you from good fortune.

22. passed in probation: Reviewed the proofs.

23. born in hand: Deceived.

24. half a soul: A halfwit.

25. notion: Mind.

26. gospeled: Ready to forgive.

27. go for: Pass as.

28. Shoughs (shuks), **water-rugs:** Shaggy dogs, long-haired dogs.

29. clept: Called.

30. valued file: Classification by valuable traits.

31. closed: Enclosed.

32. addition: Distinction (to set it apart from other dogs).

33. file: Ranks.

34. wear . . . life: Are sick as long as he lives.

FIRST MURDERER.   And I another
So weary with disasters, tugged with fortune,
That I would set[35] my life on any chance,
To mend it or be rid on 't.

MACBETH.   Both of you
Know Banquo was your enemy.

115   **BOTH MURDERERS.**   True, my lord.

MACBETH. So is he mine, and in such bloody distance[36]
That every minute of his being thrusts
Against my near'st of life:[37] and though I could
With barefaced power sweep him from my sight
120   And bid my will avouch[38] it, yet I must not,
For certain friends that are both his and mine,
Whose loves I may not drop, but wail his fall[39]
Who I myself struck down: and thence it is
That I to your assistance do make love,
125   Masking the business from the common eye
For sundry weighty reasons.

SECOND MURDERER.   We shall, my lord,
Perform what you command us.

FIRST MURDERER.   Though our lives—

MACBETH. Your spirits shine through you. Within this
        hour at most
I will advise you where to plant yourselves,
130   Acquaint you with the perfect spy o' th' time,
The moment on 't;[40] for 't must be done tonight,
And something[41] from the palace; always thought[42]
That I require a clearness:[43] and with him—
To leave no rubs[44] nor botches in the work—
135   Fleance his son, that keeps him company,
Whose absence is no less material to me
Than is his father's, must embrace the fate
Of that dark hour. Resolve yourselves apart:[45]
I'll come to you anon.

MURDERERS.   We are resolved, my lord.

140   **MACBETH.** I'll call upon you straight.[46] Abide within.
It is concluded: Banquo, thy soul's flight,
If it find heaven, must find it out tonight.   [*Exit.*]

Scene ii. *The palace.*
[*Enter* MACBETH'S LADY *and a* SERVANT.]

LADY MACBETH. Is Banquo gone from court?

SERVANT. Ay, madam, but returns again tonight.

35. set: Risk.

36. distance: Disagreement.

37. near'st of life: Most vital parts.

38. avouch: Justify.

39. wail his fall: (I must) bewail his death.

40. the perfect . . . on 't: The exact information of the exact time.
41. something: Some distance.
42. thought: Remembered.
43. clearness: Freedom from suspicion.
44. rubs: Flaws.
45. Resolve yourselves apart: Make your own decision.

46. straight: Immediately.

LADY MACBETH. Say to the King, I would attend his
    leisure
    For a few words.

SERVANT.   Madam, I will.   *[Exit.]*

LADY MACBETH.   Nought's had, all's spent,
5   Where our desire is got without content:
    'Tis safer to be that which we destroy
    Than by destruction dwell in doubtful joy.

[Enter MACBETH.*]*

    How now, my lord! Why do you keep alone,
    Of sorriest fancies your companions making,
10   Using those thoughts which should indeed have died
    With them they think on? Things without all remedy
    Should be without regard: what's done is done.

MACBETH. We have scotched[1] the snake, not killed it:
    She'll close[2] and be herself, whilst our poor malice
15   Remains in danger of her former tooth.[3]
    But let the frame of things disjoint,[4] both the worlds[5]
        suffer,
    Ere we will eat our meal in fear, and sleep
    In the affliction of these terrible dreams
    That shake us nightly: better be with the dead,
20   Whom we, to gain our peace, have sent to peace,
    Than on the torture of the mind to lie
    In restless ecstasy.[6] Duncan is in his grave;
    After life's fitful fever he sleeps well.
    Treason has done his worst: nor steel, nor poison,
25   Malice domestic, foreign levy,[7] nothing,
    Can touch him further.

LADY MACBETH.   Come on.
    Gentle my lord, sleek o'er your rugged looks;
    Be bright and jovial among your guests tonight.

MACBETH. So shall I, love; and so, I pray, be you:
30   Let your remembrance apply to Banquo;
    Present him eminence,[8] both with eye and tongue:
    Unsafe the while, that we must lave[9]
    Our honors in these flattering streams
    And make our faces vizards[10] to our hearts,
    Disguising what they are.

35 **LADY MACBETH.**   You must leave this.

MACBETH. O, full of scorpions is my mind, dear wife!
    Thou know'st that Banquo, and his Fleance, lives.

LADY MACBETH. But in them nature's copy's not eterne.[11]

1. **scotched:** Wounded.
2. **close:** Heal.
3. **in . . . tooth:** In as much danger as before.
4. **frame of things disjoint:** Universe collapse.
5. **both the worlds:** Heaven and earth.

6. **ecstasy:** Frenzy.

7. **Malice . . . levy:** Civil and foreign war.

8. **Present him eminence:** Honor him.
9. **Unsafe . . . lave:** We are unsafe as long as we have to wash.
10. **vizards** (viz′ ərdz): Masks.

11. **nature's . . . eterne:** Nature's lease is not eternal.

BANQUO AT THE GATE, WOOD ENGRAVING AFTER SIR JOHN GILBERT

MACBETH. There's comfort yet; they are assailable.
40   Then be thou jocund. Ere the bat hath flown
        His cloistered flight, ere to black Hecate's summons
        The shard-borne[12] beetle with his drowsy hums
        Hath rung night's yawning peal, there shall be done
        A deed of dreadful note.

LADY MACBETH.   What's to be done?

45 **MACBETH.** Be innocent of the knowledge, dearest
            chuck,[13]
        Till thou applaud the deed. Come, seeling[14] night,
        Scarf up[15] the tender eye of pitiful day,
        And with thy bloody and invisible hand
        Cancel and tear to pieces that great bond[16]
50   Which keeps me pale! Light thickens, and the crow
        Makes wing to th' rooky[17] wood.
        Good things of day begin to droop and drowse,
        Whiles night's black agents to their preys do rouse.
        Thou marvel'st at my words: but hold thee still;
55   Things bad begun make strong themselves by ill:
        So, prithee, go with me.   [*Exit.*]

12. shard-borne: Borne on scaly wings.

13. chuck: A term of endearment.
14. seeling: Eye-closing. Falconers sometimes sewed a hawk's eyes closed in order to train it.
15. Scarf up: Blindfold.
16. great bond: Between Banquo and fate.
17. rooky: Full of rooks, or crows.

Scene iii. *Near the palace.*

[*Enter* THREE MURDERERS.]

FIRST MURDERER. But who did bid thee join with us?

THIRD MURDERER.   Macbeth.

SECOND MURDERER. He needs not our mistrust; since he
delivers
Our offices[1] and what we have to do
To the direction just.[2]

FIRST MURDERER.   Then stand with us.
5   The west yet glimmers with some streaks of day.
Now spurs the lated traveler apace
To gain the timely inn, and near approaches
The subject of our watch.

THIRD MURDERER.   Hark! I hear horses.

BANQUO. [*Within*] Give us a light there, ho!

SECOND MURDERER.   Then 'tis he. The rest
10 That are within the note of expectation[3]
Already are i' th' court.

FIRST MURDERER.   His horses go about.[4]

THIRD MURDERER. Almost a mile: but he does usually—
So all men do—from hence to th' palace gate
Make it their walk.

[*Enter* BANQUO *and* FLEANCE, *with a torch.*]

SECOND MURDERER. A light, a light!

THIRD MURDERER.   'Tis he.

15 **FIRST MURDERER.**   Stand to 't.

BANQUO. It will be rain tonight.

FIRST MURDERER.   Let it come down.

[*They set upon* BANQUO.]

BANQUO. O, treachery! Fly, good Fleance, fly, fly, fly!
                              [*Exit* FLEANCE.]

                    Thou mayst revenge. O slave! [*Dies.*]

THIRD MURDERER. Who did strike out the light?

FIRST MURDERER.   Was't not the way?[5]

20 **THIRD MURDERER.** There's but one down; the son is fled.

SECOND MURDERER. We have lost best half of our affair.

FIRST MURDERER. Well, let's away and say how much is
done.   [*Exit.*]

---

1. offices: Duties.
2. direction just: Exact detail.

3. within . . . expectations: On the list of expected guests.
4. His . . . about: His horses have been taken to the stable.

5. way: Thing to do.

Scene iv. *The palace.*
[*Banquet prepared. Enter* MACBETH, LADY MACBETH, ROSS, LENNOX,
LORDS, *and* ATTENDANTS.]

MACBETH. You know your own degrees;[1] sit down:
    At first and last, the hearty welcome.

LORDS. Thanks to your Majesty.

MACBETH. Ourself will mingle with society[2]
5   And play the humble host.
    Our hostess keeps her state,[3] but in best time
    We will require[4] her welcome.

LADY MACBETH. Pronounce it for me, sir, to all our
      friends,
    For my heart speaks they are welcome.

[*Enter* FIRST MURDERER.]

MACBETH. See, they encounter thee with their hearts'
10   thanks.
    Both sides are even: here I'll sit i' th' midst:
    Be large in mirth; anon we'll drink a measure[5]
    The table round. [*Goes to* MURDERER] There's blood
      upon thy face.

MURDERER. 'Tis Banquo's then.

15 MACBETH. 'Tis better thee without than he within.[6]
    Is he dispatched?

MURDERER. My lord, his throat is cut; that I did for him.

MACBETH. Thou art the best o' th' cutthroats.
    Yet he's good that did the like for Fleance;
20   If thou didst it, thou art the nonpareil.[7]

MURDERER. Most royal sir, Fleance is 'scaped.

MACBETH. [*Aside*] Then comes my fit again: I had else
      been perfect,
    Whole as the marble, founded as the rock,
    As broad and general as the casing[8] air:
25   But now I am cabined, cribbed, confined, bound in
    To saucy[9] doubts and fears.—But Banquo's safe?

MURDERER. Ay, my good lord: safe in a ditch he bides,
    With twenty trenchèd[10] gashes on his head,
    The least a death to nature.[11]

MACBETH.   Thanks for that.
    [*Aside*] There the grown serpent lies; the worm
30   that's fled

1. degrees: Ranks. At
state banquets guests were
seated according to rank.

2. society: The company.

3. keeps her state: Remains seated on her
throne.
4. require: Request.

5. measure: Toast.

6. thee . . . within: You
outside than he inside.

7. nonpareil: Without
equal.

8. as . . . casing: As unrestrained as the surrounding.
9. saucy: Insolent.

10. trenchèd: Trenchlike.
11. nature: Natural life.

Hath nature that in time will venom breed,
No teeth for th' present. Get thee gone. Tomorrow
We'll hear ourselves[12] again.   [*Exit* MURDERER.]

LADY MACBETH.   My royal lord,
You do not give the cheer.[13] The feast is sold
35   That is not often vouched, while 'tis a-making,
'Tis given with welcome.[14] To feed were best at home;
From thence, the sauce to meat is ceremony;[15]
Meeting were bare without it.

[*Enter the* GHOST OF BANQUO, *and sits in* MACBETH'*s place.*]

MACBETH.   Sweet remembrancer!
Now good digestion wait on appetite,
And health on both!

40   **LENNOX.**   May 't please your Highness sit.

MACBETH. Here had we now our country's honor roofed,[16]
Were the graced person of our Banquo present—
Who may I rather challenge for unkindness
Than pity for mischance![17]

ROSS.   His absence, sir,
Lays blame upon his promise. Please 't your
45   Highness
To grace us with your royal company?

MACBETH. The table's full.

LENNOX.   Here is a place reserved, sir.

MACBETH. Where?

LENNOX. Here, my good lord. What is 't that moves your
Highness?

MACBETH. Which of you have done this?

50   **LORDS.**   What, my good lord?

MACBETH. Thou canst not say I did it. Never shake
Thy gory locks at me.

ROSS. Gentlemen, rise, his Highness is not well.

LADY MACBETH. Sit, worthy friends. My lord is often thus,
55   And hath been from his youth. Pray you, keep seat.
The fit is momentary; upon a thought[18]
He will again be well. If much you note him,
You shall offend him and extend his passion.[19]
Feed, and regard him not.—Are you a man?

60   **MACBETH.** Ay, and a bold one, that dare look on that
Which might appall the devil.

12. hear ourselves: Talk
it over.

13. give the cheer: Make
the guests feel welcome.

**14. The feast . . .
welcome:** The feast at
which the host fails to
make the guests feel wel-
come while the food is
being prepared is no more
than a bought dinner.

15. From . . . ceremony:
Ceremony adds a pleasant
flavor to the food.

16. our . . . roofed: The
most honorable men in the
country under one roof.

17. Who . . . mischance:
Whom I hope I may re-
proach for being absent
due to discourtesy rather
than pity because he has
had an accident.

18. upon a thought: In a
moment.

19. passion: Suffering.

LADY MACBETH.   O proper stuff!
This is the very painting of your fear.
This is the air-drawn dagger which, you said,
Led you to Duncan. O, these flaws[20] and starts,
65 Impostors to true fear, would well become
A woman's story at a winter's fire,
Authorized[21] by her grandam. Shame itself!
Why do you make such faces? When all's done,
You look but on a stool.

MACBETH.   Prithee, see there!
70 Behold! Look! Lo! How say you?
Why, what care I? If thou canst nod, speak too.
If charnel houses[22] and our graves must send
Those that we bury back, our monuments
Shall be the maws of kites.[23]   [*Exit* GHOST.]

LADY MACBETH.   What, quite unmanned in folly?

MACBETH. If I stand here, I saw him.

75 **LADY MACBETH.**   Fie, for shame!

MACBETH. Blood hath been shed ere now, i' th' olden
          time,
Ere humane statute purged the gentle weal;[24]
Ay, and since too, murders have been performed
Too terrible for the ear. The times has been
80 That, when the brains were out, the man would die,
And there an end; but now they rise again,
With twenty mortal murders on their crowns,[25]
And push us from our stools. This is more strange
Than such a murder is.

LADY MACBETH.   My worthy lord,
Your noble friends do lack you.

85 **MACBETH.**   I do forget.
Do not muse at me, my most worthy friends;
I have a strange infirmity, which is nothing
To those that know me. Come, love and health to all!
Then I'll sit down. Give me some wine, fill full.

[*Enter* GHOST.]

90 I drink to th' general joy o' th' whole table,
And to our dear friend Banquo, whom we miss;
Would he were here! To all and him we thirst,[26]
And all to all.

LORDS.   Our duties, and the pledge.

20. flaws: Gusts of wind; outbursts of emotion.

21. Authorized: Vouched for.

22. charnel houses: Vaults containing human bones dug up in making new graves.
23. our . . . kites: Our tombs shall be the bellies of birds of prey.

24. Ere . . . weal: Before humane laws civilized the state and made it gentle.

25. mortal . . . crowns: Deadly wounds on their heads.

26. thirst: Drink.

MACBETH. Avaunt![27] and quit my sight! Let the earth
  hide thee!
95 Thy bones are marrowless, thy blood is cold;
  Thou hast no speculation[28] in those eyes
  Which thou dost glare with.

LADY MACBETH.   Think of this, good peers,
  But as a thing of custom, 'tis no other.
  Only it spoils the pleasure of the time.

100 **MACBETH.** What man dare, I dare.
  Approach thou like the rugged Russian bear,
  The armed rhinoceros, or th' Hyrcan[29] tiger;
  Take any shape but that,[30] and my firm nerves
  Shall never tremble. Or be alive again,
105 And dare me to the desert[31] with thy sword.
  If trembling I inhabit[32] then, protest me
  The baby of a girl. Hence, horrible shadow!
  Unreal mock'ry, hence!   [*Exit* GHOST.]
     Why, so: being gone,
  I am a man again. Pray you, sit still.

LADY MACBETH. You have displaced the mirth, broke the
110 good meeting,
  With most admired[33] disorder.

MACBETH.   Can such things be,
  And overcome us[34] like a summer's cloud,
  Without our special wonder? You make me strange
  Even to the disposition that I owe,[35]
115 When now I think you can behold such sights,
  And keep the natural ruby of your cheeks,
  When mine is blanched with fear.

ROSS.   What sights, my lord?

LADY MACBETH. I pray you, speak not: He grows worse
  and worse;
  Question enrages him: at once, good night.
120 Stand not upon the order of your going,[36]
  But go at once.

LENNOX. Good night; and better health
  Attend his Majesty!

LADY MACBETH. A kind good night to all!
     [*Exit* LORDS.]

MACBETH. It will have blood, they say: blood will have
  blood.
  Stones have been known to move and trees to
  speak;

27. Avaunt: Be gone!

28. speculation: sight.

29. Hyrcan (hər′ kən):
From Hyrcania, a province
of the ancient Persian and
Macedonian empires south
of the Caspian Sea.
30. that: Banquo's shape.
31. desert: A place where
neither of us could escape.
32. inhabit: Remain indoors.

33. admired: Amazing.

34. overcome us: Come
over us.

35. disposition . . . owe:
My own nature.

36. Stand . . . going: Do
not wait to depart in order
of rank.

125   Augures and understood relations[37] have
        By maggot-pies and choughs[38] and rooks brought
          forth
        The secret'st man of blood.[39] What is the night?

LADY MACBETH. Almost at odds[40] with morning, which is
        which.

MACBETH. How say'st thou, that Macduff denies his
        person
        At our great bidding?

130 LADY MACBETH.   Did you send to him, sir?

MACBETH. I hear it by the way, but I will send:
        There's not a one of them but in his house
        I keep a servant fee'd.[41] I will tomorrow,
        And betimes[42] I will, to the weird sisters:
135   More shall they speak, for now I am bent[43] to know
        By the worst means the worst. For mine own good
        All causes shall give way. I am in blood
        Stepped in so far that, should I wade no more,
        Returning were as tedious as go o'er.
140   Strange things I have in head that will to hand,
        Which must be acted ere they may be scanned.[44]

LADY MACBETH. You lack the season of all natures,[45]
        sleep.

MACBETH. Come, we'll to sleep. My strange and self-
        abuse[46]
        Is the initiate fear that wants hard use.[47]
145   We are yet but young in deed.   [*Exit.*]

Scene v. *A witches' haunt.*

[*Thunder. Enter the* THREE WITCHES, *meeting* HECATE.]

FIRST WITCH. Why, how now, Hecate! you look angerly.

HECATE. Have I not reason, beldams[1] as you are,
        Saucy and overbold? How did you dare
        To trade and traffic with Macbeth
5   In riddles and affairs of death;
        And I, the mistress of your charms,
        The close contriver[2] of all harms,
        Was never called to bear my part,
        Or show the glory of our art?
10   And, which is worse, all you have done
        Hath been but for a wayward son,
        Spiteful and wrathful; who, as others do,
        Loves for his own ends, not for you.
        But make amends now: get you gone,

37. Augures and understood relations: Omens and the relationship between the omens and what they represent.
38. maggot-pies and choughs (*ch*ufs): Magpies and crows.
39. man of blood: Murderer.
40. at odds: Disputing.

41. fee'd: Paid to spy.
42. betimes: Quickly.
43. bent: Determined.

44. scanned: Examined.

45. season . . . natures: Preservative of all living creatures.
46. My . . . self-abuse: My strange delusion.
47. initiate . . . use: Beginner's fear that will harden with experience.

1. beldams: Hags.

2. close contriver: secret inventor.

15 And at the pit of Acheron[3]
Meet me i' th' morning: thither he
Will come to know his destiny.
Your vessels and your spells provide,
Your charms and everything beside.
20 I am for th' air; this night I'll spend
Unto a dismal and a fatal end:
Great business must be wrought ere noon.
Upon the corner of the moon
There hangs a vap'rous drop profound;
25 I'll catch it ere it come to ground:
And that distilled by magic sleights[4]
Shall raise such artificial sprites[5]
As by the strength of their illusion
Shall draw him on to his confusion.[6]
30 He shall spurn fate, scorn death, and bear
His hopes 'bove wisdom, grace, and fear:
And you all know security[7]
Is mortals' chiefest enemy.

[*Music and a song.*]

Hark! I am called; my little spirit, see,
35 Sits in a foggy cloud and stays for me.   [*Exit.*]

[*Sing within,* "Come away, come away," *etc.*]

FIRST WITCH. Come, let's make haste; she'll soon be back
again.   [*Exit.*]

Scene vi. *The palace.*
[*Enter* LENNOX *and another* LORD.]

LENNOX. My former speeches have but hit[1] your
thoughts,
Which can interpret farther.[2] Only I say
Things have been strangely borne.[3] The gracious
Duncan
Was pitied of Macbeth: marry, he was dead.
5 And the right-valiant Banquo walked too late;
Whom, you may say, if 't please you, Fleance killed,
For Fleance fled. Men must not walk too late.
Who cannot want the thought,[4] how monstrous
It was for Malcolm and for Donalbain
10 To kill their gracious father? Damnèd fact![5]
How it did grieve Macbeth! Did he not straight,
In pious rage, the two delinquents tear,
That were the slaves of drink and thralls[6] of sleep?
Was not that nobly done? Ay, and wisely too;
15 For 'twould have angered any heart alive
To hear the men deny 't. So that I say

3. Acheron (ak′ ə ron′):
Hell; in Greek mythology
the river of Hades.

4. sleights: Devices.

5. artificial sprites: Spirits created by magic.

6. confusion: Ruin.

7. security: Overconfi-
dence.

1. hit: Coincided.

2. Which . . . farther:
From which you can draw
your own conclusions.
3. borne: Managed.

4. cannot . . . thought:
Can fail to think.

5. fact: Deed.

6. thralls: slaves.

He has borne all things well: and I do think
That, had he Duncan's sons under his key—
As, an 't[7] please heaven, he shall not—they should
find
20   What 'twere to kill a father. So should Fleance.
But, peace! for from broad[8] words, and 'cause he
failed
His presence at the tyrant's feast, I hear,
Macduff lives in disgrace. Sir, can you tell
Where he bestows himself?

LORD.   The son of Duncan,
25   From whom this tyrant holds the due of birth,[9]
Lives in the English court, and is received
Of the most pious Edward[10] with such grace
That the malevolence of fortune nothing
Takes from his high respect.[11] Thither Macduff
30   Is gone to pray the holy King, upon his aid[12]
To wake Northumberland and warlike Siward;[13]
That by the help of these, with Him above
To ratify the work, we may again
Give to our tables meat, sleep to our nights,
35   Free from our feasts and banquets bloody knives,
Do faithful homage and receive free honors:[14]
All which we pine for now. And this report
Hath so exasperate the King that he
Prepares for some attempt of war.

LENNOX.   Sent he to Macduff?

40 **LORD.** He did: and with an absolute "Sir, not I,"
The cloudy[15] messenger turns me his back,
And hums, as who should say "You'll rue the time
That clogs[16] me with this answer."

LENNOX.   And that well might
Advise him to a caution, t' hold what distance
45   His wisdom can provide. Some holy angel
Fly to the court of England and unfold
His message ere he come, that a swift blessing
May soon return to this our suffering country
Under a hand accursed!

LORD.   I'll send my prayers with him.
                      [*Exit.*]

7. an 't: If it.

8. broad: Unguarded.

9. due of birth: Birthright, claim to the throne.
10. Edward: Edward the Confessor, King of England 1042–1066.
11. with . . . respect: Does not diminish the high respect he is given.
12. upon his aid: To aid Malcolm.
13. To . . . Siward: To call to arms the commander of the English forces, the Earl of Northumberland, and his son Siward.
14. free honors: Honors given to free men.

15. cloudy: Disturbed.

16. clogs: Burdens.

RESPONDING TO THE SELECTION

Your Response

1. Lennox seems to see through Macbeth's deception. What would you do if you were Lennox?

Recalling

2. (a) In Scene i, what are Banquo's thoughts about the witches' prophecies? (b) What are Macbeth's thoughts about the prophecies?
3. (a) What two people are the murderers told to kill? (b) Why is it necessary to kill both?
4. What goes wrong with the murderers' plans?
5. (a) Why does Macbeth want to see the witches again? (b) What does Lady Macbeth think Macbeth needs most?
6. (a) In Scene vi, what reason does Lennox give for Macduff's being in disgrace? (b) What is Macduff trying to accomplish in England?

Interpreting

7. Macbeth's soliloquy in Scene i shows that his attitude toward those who stand in his way has changed. Recall the soliloquy prior to Duncan's murder. What change or changes have occurred?
8. How does Macbeth's technique of persuading the murderers resemble Lady Macbeth's earlier method of persuading Macbeth?
9. How has the relationship between Macbeth and Lady Macbeth changed?
10. Events at the banquet show that Macbeth can no longer pretend to be innocent. What evidence is there that he will continue to kill those who threaten him?

Applying

11. By the end of Act III, Macbeth is in desperate trouble. What advice would you give him concerning his best course of action?

ANALYZING LITERATURE

Understanding Irony

In verbal irony there is a contrast between what is said and what is meant. An example of verbal irony occurs in Act III, Scene i, when Macbeth says to Banquo, "Here's our chief guest," knowing that Banquo will be murdered on his orders before the great feast begins.

1. What three additional examples of verbal irony can you find in the conversation in Scene i between Macbeth and Banquo?
2. In Scene vi, Lennox appears to accept Macbeth's version of the various murders. (a) How can you tell from what Lennox says that he does not really believe in Macbeth's innocence? (b) What are three examples of verbal irony in Lennox's opening speech?

CRITICAL THINKING AND READING

Interpreting Connotative Meanings

The **connotation** of a word is its associated meanings. For instance, the denotation, or literal meaning, of the word *home* is "the place where one lives." The associations of *home* give the word its connotative meanings: "warmth, love, peace." Shakespeare often chose words for their connotative meanings.

1. When the ghost of Banquo exits (Scene iv, line 108), Macbeth says, "I am a man again." What are the connotative meanings of *man*?
2. When Macbeth is talking to the murderers (Scene i, lines 90–91), he says, "Whose heavy hand hath bowed you to the grave / And *beggared* yours forever?" What are the connotative meanings of *beggared*?

THINKING AND WRITING

Who Is the Third Murderer?

Shakespeare never reveals the identity of the third murderer. Who do you think he or she might be? Write an essay supporting your theory. Reread Scene iii carefully. Then build a case, using details from the play to support it. Use the process of elimination to exonerate some of the characters. Remember, though, that the third murderer may have been sent by someone—even the witches—for a specific purpose (perhaps the killing of Banquo or the escape of Fleance). In revising, make sure to leave no gaps in logic in your argument.

GUIDE FOR INTERPRETING

Macbeth, Act IV

Writers' Techniques

Plot Development. The plot of a literary work is the sequence of related events that create and then resolve a conflict. Conflict is the struggle, or interplay of forces, that takes place within the story. The main character may be in conflict with another person, with a value system, with fate, or with nature. Certain background information is necessary for an understanding of the action. This information is called exposition, and it usually appears early in the story. The plot movement at the beginning is one of rising action toward a climax. The climax, or crisis, is the peak of tension, a dramatic turning point. In a tragedy like *Macbeth,* the climax often occurs near the middle of the play. Then comes a period of falling action, which, in tragedy, shows the downfall of the tragic hero. The falling action leads finally to the resolution, or *denouement,* the point at which the conflict ends and the outcome is made clear.

Focus

Plot is closely intertwined with character. Indeed, in a work of literary merit, you will find that character largely drives the plot, not the other way around. Make some notes analyzing the character of Macbeth. List his virtues as well as his faults, for the complexity of Macbeth's character lies at the heart of his difficulties.

Commentary

Although Shakespeare began with Holinshed's account of two different murders, he transformed these historical tales into an entirely original plot. The first influence was the story of Duncan's assassination (c. 1040) by Macbeth and several rebels—including the treacherous Banquo, whose character Shakespeare obviously changed. He combined this with the earlier murder of another Scottish monarch, King Duff. As in *Macbeth,* King Duff was murdered on orders from his host for the evening; unlike the murder of Duncan in *Macbeth,* King Duff was killed by servants. The Bard also used parts of Holinshed's tale of King Kenneth. He transferred an inability to sleep and a terrifying guilt at being part of a murder from King Kenneth to Lady Macbeth but discarded the specifics of the murder itself and the mysterious voice promising divine punishment. He also compressed the events of Macbeth's seventeen-year reign into as many weeks. Finally, two of the greatest scenes in *Macbeth* are both original to Shakespeare. Both have to do with guilt: the banquet scene (III, iii) and the sleepwalking scene (V, i). Many critics feel that Shakespeare's most brilliant invention in the play is the banquet scene, which draws the plot together by dramatizing many of the ideas previously implied.

Act IV

Scene i. *A witches' haunt.*
[*Thunder. Enter the* THREE WITCHES.]

FIRST WITCH. Thrice the brinded[1] cat hath mewed.

SECOND WITCH. Thrice and once the hedge-pig[2] whined.

THIRD WITCH. Harpier[3] cries. 'Tis time, 'tis time.

FIRST WITCH. Round about the caldron go:
5　　In the poisoned entrails throw.
　　Toad, that under cold stone
　　Days and nights has thirty-one
　　Swelt'red venom sleeping got,[4]
　　Boil thou first i' th' charmèd pot.

10　**ALL.** Double, double, toil and trouble;
　　Fire burn and caldron bubble.

SECOND WITCH. Fillet of a fenny snake,
　　In the caldron boil and bake;
　　Eye of newt and toe of frog,
15　　Wool of bat and tongue of dog,
　　Adder's fork[5] and blindworm's[6] sting,
　　Lizard's leg and howlet's[7] wing,
　　For a charm of pow'rful trouble,
　　Like a hell-broth boil and bubble.

20　**ALL.** Double, double, toil and trouble;
　　Fire burn and caldron bubble.

THIRD WITCH. Scale of dragon, tooth of wolf,
　　Witch's mummy, maw and gulf[8]
　　Of the ravined[9] salt-sea shark,
25　　Root of hemlock digged i' th' dark,
　　Liver of blaspheming Jew,
　　Gall of goat, and slips of yew
　　Slivered in the moon's eclipse,
　　Nose of Turk and Tartar's lips,[10]
30　　Finger of birth-strangled babe
　　Ditch-delivered by a drab,
　　Make the gruel thick and slab:[11]
　　Add thereto a tiger's chaudron,[12]
　　For th' ingredient of our caldron.

35　**ALL.** Double, double, toil and trouble;
　　Fire burn and caldron bubble.

SECOND WITCH. Cool it with a baboon's blood,
　　Then the charm is firm and good.

[*Enter* HECATE *and the other* THREE WITCHES.]

1. **brinded:** Striped.

2. **hedge-pig:** Hedgehog.

3. **Harpier:** One of the spirits attending the witches.

4. **Swelt'red . . . got:** Venom sweated out while sleeping.

5. **fork:** Forked tongue.
6. **blindworm's:** Small, limbless lizard's.
7. **howlet's:** A small owl's.

8. **maw and gulf:** Stomach and gullet.
9. **ravined:** Ravenous.

10. **blaspheming Jew . . . Tartar's lips:** For many in Shakespeare's audience, the words "Jew," "Turk," and "Tartar" evoked stereotypical enemies of Christianity.
11. **slab:** sticky.
12. **chaudron** (shô′ drən): Entrails.

HECATE. O, well done! I commend your pains;
40   And every one shall share i' th' gains:
    And now about the caldron sing,
    Like elves and fairies in a ring,
    Enchanting all that you put in.

[*Music and a song:* "Black Spirits," *etc. Exit* HECATE
and the other THREE WITCHES.]

SECOND WITCH. By the pricking of my thumbs,
45   Something wicked this way comes:
    Open, locks,
    Whoever knocks!

[*Enter* MACBETH.]

MACBETH. How now, you secret, black, and midnight
    hags!
    What is 't you do?

ALL.   A deed without a name.

50 **MACBETH.** I conjure you, by that which you profess,
    Howe'er you come to know it, answer me:
    Though you untie the winds and let them fight
    Against the churches; though the yesty[13] waves
    Confound[14] and swallow navigation up;
55   Though bladed corn be lodged[15] and trees blown
    down;
    Though castles topple on their warders' heads;
    Though palaces and pyramids do slope[16]
    Their heads to their foundations; though the treas-
    ure
    Of nature's germens[17] tumble all together,
60   Even till destruction sicken, answer me
    To what I ask you.

FIRST WITCH.   Speak.

SECOND WITCH.   Demand.

THIRD WITCH.   We'll answer.

FIRST WITCH. Say, if th' hadst rather hear it from our
    mouths,
    Or from our masters?

MACBETH.   Call' em, let me see 'em.

FIRST WITCH. Pour in sow's blood, that hath eaten
65   Her nine farrow;[18] grease that's sweaten
    From the murderer's gibbet[19] throw
    Into the flame.

ALL.   Come, high or low,

13. yesty: Foamy.
14. Confound: Destroy.
15. lodged: Beaten down.

16. slope: Bend.

17. nature's germens: Seeds of all life.

18. farrow: Young pigs.
19. gibbet (jib' it): Gallows.

Thyself and office[20] deftly show!

[*Thunder.* FIRST APPARITION: *an Armed Head.*[21]]

MACBETH. Tell me, thou unknown power—

FIRST WITCH.   He knows thy thought:
70   Hear his speech, but say thou nought.

FIRST APPARITION. Macbeth! Macbeth! Macbeth! Beware
        Macduff!
      Beware the Thane of Fife. Dismiss me: enough.
                                    [*He descends.*]

MACBETH. Whate'er thou art, for thy good caution
        thanks:
      Thou hast harped[22] my fear aright. But one word
        more—

FIRST WITCH. He will not be commanded. Here's
75   another,
      More potent than the first.

[*Thunder.* SECOND APPARITION: *a Bloody Child.*[23]]

SECOND APPARITION. Macbeth! Macbeth! Macbeth!

MACBETH. Had I three ears, I'd hear thee.

SECOND APPARITION. Be bloody, bold, and resolute! Laugh
        to scorn
80   The pow'r of man, for none of woman born
      Shall harm Macbeth.   [*Descends.*]

MACBETH. Then live, Macduff: what need I fear of thee?
      But yet I'll make assurance double sure,
      And take a bond of fate.[24] Thou shalt not live;
85   That I may tell pale-hearted fear it lies,
      And sleep in spite of thunder.

[*Thunder.* THIRD APPARITION: *a Child Crowned, with a
tree in his hand.*[25]]

                                    What is this,
      That rises like the issue of a king,
      And wears upon his baby-brow the round
      And top of sovereignty? [26]

ALL.   Listen, but speak not to 't.

90 **THIRD APPARITION.** Be lion-mettled, proud, and take no
        care
      Who chafes, who frets, or where conspirers are:
      Macbeth shall never vanquished be until
      Great Birnam Wood to high Dunsinane Hill
      Shall come against him.   [*Descends.*]

20. office: Function.

21. an Armed Head: A
symbol of Macduff.

22. harped: Hit upon.

23. a Bloody Child: A
symbol of Macduff at birth.

24. take . . . fate: Get a
guarantee from fate (by killing Macduff).

25. a Child . . . hand: A
symbol of Malcolm.

26. top of sovereignty:
Crown.

MACBETH.   That will never be.
95   Who can impress[27] the forest, bid the tree
        Unfix his earth-bound root? Sweet bodements,[28]
            good!
        Rebellious dead, rise never, till the Wood
        Of Birnam rise, and our high-placed Macbeth
        Shall live the lease of nature,[29] pay his breath
100   To time and mortal custom.[30] Yet my heart
        Throbs to know one thing. Tell me, if your art
        Can tell so much: shall Banquo's issue ever
        Reign in this kingdom?

ALL.   Seek to know no more.

MACBETH. I will be satisfied. Deny me this,
105   And an eternal curse fall on you! Let me know.
        Why sinks that caldron? And what noise is this?
[*Hautboys.*]

FIRST WITCH. Show!

SECOND WITCH. Show!

THIRD WITCH. Show!

110 **ALL.** Show his eyes, and grieve his heart;
        Come like shadows, so depart!

[*A show of eight* KINGS *and* BANQUO, *last* KING *with a glass*[31] *in his hand.*]

MACBETH. Thou art too like the spirit of Banquo. Down!
        Thy crown does sear mine eyelids. And thy hair,
        Thou other gold-bound brow, is like the first.
115   A third is like the former. Filthy hags!
        Why do you show me this? A fourth! Start, eyes!
        What, will the line stretch out to th' crack of doom?
        Another yet! A seventh! I'll see no more.
        And yet the eighth appears, who bears a glass
120   Which shows me many more; and some I see
        That twofold balls and treble scepters[32] carry:
        Horrible sight! Now I see 'tis true;
        For the blood-boltered[33] Banquo smiles upon me,
        And points at them for his.[34] What, is this so?

125 **FIRST WITCH.** Ay, sir, all this is so. But why
        Stands Macbeth thus amazedly?
        Come, sisters, cheer we up his sprites,
        And show the best of our delights:
        I'll charm the air to give a sound,
130   While you perform your antic round,[35]
        That this great king may kindly say
        Our duties did his welcome pay.

27. impress: Force into service.
28. bodements: Prophecies.

29. lease of nature: Natural lifespan.
30. mortal custom: Natural death.

31. glass: Mirror.

32. twofold . . . scepters: Coronation emblems and insignia of the kingdoms of England, Scotland, and Ireland, united in 1603 when James VI of Scotland became James I of England.
33. blood-boltered: With his hair matted with blood.
34. his: His descendants.
35. antic round: Grotesque circular dance.

[*Music.* THE WITCHES *dance, and vanish.*]

MACBETH. Where are they? Gone? Let this pernicious
   hour
  Stand aye accursèd in the calendar!
  Come in, without there!

[*Enter* LENNOX.]

135 **LENNOX.**   What's your Grace's will?

MACBETH. Saw you the weird sisters?

LENNOX.   No, my lord.

MACBETH. Came they not by you?

LENNOX.   No indeed, my lord.

MACBETH. Infected be the air whereon they ride,
  And damned all those that trust them! I did hear
140 The galloping of horse. Who was 't came by?

Macbeth, Act IV, Scene i 299

LENNOX. 'Tis two or three, my lord, that bring you word
Macduff is fled to England.

MACBETH.   Fled to England?

LENNOX. Ay, my good lord.

MACBETH. [*Aside*] Time, thou anticipat'st[36] my dread
exploits.
145 The flighty purpose never is o'ertook
Unless the deed go with it.[37] From this moment
The very firstlings of my heart[38] shall be
The firstlings of my hand. And even now,
To crown my thoughts with acts, be it thought and
done:
150 The castle of Macduff I will surprise;
Seize upon Fife; give to th' edge o' th' sword
His wife, his babes, and all unfortunate souls
That trace[39] him in his line. No boasting like a fool;
This deed I'll do before this purpose cool:
155 But no more sights!—Where are these gentlemen?
Come, bring me where they are.   [*Exit.*]

Scene ii. *Macduff's castle.*
[*Enter* MACDUFF'S WIFE, *her* SON, *and* ROSS.]

LADY MACDUFF. What had he done, to make him fly the
land?

ROSS. You must have patience, madam.

LADY MACDUFF.   He had none:
His flight was madness. When our actions do not,
Our fears do make us traitors.

ROSS.   You know not
5 Whether it was his wisdom or his fear.

LADY MACDUFF. Wisdom! To leave his wife, to leave his
babes,
His mansion and his titles,[1] in a place
From whence himself does fly? He loves us not;
He wants the natural touch:[2] for the poor wren,
10 The most diminutive of birds, will fight,
Her young ones in her nest, against the owl.
All is the fear and nothing is the love;
As little is the wisdom, where the flight
So runs against all reason.

ROSS.   My dearest coz,[3]
15 I pray you, school[4] yourself. But, for your husband,
He is noble, wise, judicious, and best knows

36. anticipat'st: Foretold.

37. The flighty . . . it:
The fleeting plan is never
fulfilled unless it is carried
out at once.
38. firstlings . . . heart:
First thoughts, impulses.

39. trace: Succeed.

1. titles: possessions.

2. wants . . . touch:
Lacks natural affection.

3. coz: Cousin.
4. school: Control.

The fits o' th' season.[5] I dare not speak much further:
But cruel are the times, when we are traitors
And do not know ourselves;[6] when we hold rumor
20   From what we fear,[7] yet know not what we fear,
But float upon a wild and violent sea
Each way and move. I take my leave of you.
Shall not be long but I'll be here again.
Things at the worst will cease, or else climb upward
25   To what they were before. My pretty cousin,
Blessing upon you!

LADY MACDUFF. Fathered he is, and yet he's fatherless.

ROSS. I am so much a fool, should I stay longer,
It would be my disgrace and your discomfort.[8]
I take my leave at once.   [Exit ROSS.]

30   LADY MACDUFF.   Sirrah, your father's dead;
And what will you do now? How will you live?

SON. As birds do, mother.

LADY MACDUFF.   What, with worms and flies?

SON. With what I get, I mean; and so do they.

LADY MACDUFF. Poor bird! thou'dst never fear the net nor
lime,[9]
35   The pitfall nor the gin.[10]

SON. Why should I, mother? Poor birds they are not set
for.
My father is not dead, for all your saying.

LADY MACDUFF. Yes, he is dead: how wilt thou do for a
father?

SON. Nay, how will you do for a husband?

40   LADY MACDUFF. Why, I can buy me twenty at any market.

SON. Then you'll buy 'em to sell[11] again.

LADY MACDUFF. Thou speak'st with all thy wit, and yet
i' faith,
With wit enough for thee.[12]

SON. Was my father a traitor, mother?

45   LADY MACDUFF. Ay, that he was.

SON. What is a traitor?

LADY MACDUFF. Why, one that swears and lies.[13]

SON. And be all traitors that do so?

5. fits o' th' season: Disorders of the time.

6. when . . . ourselves: When we are treated as traitors but do not know of any treason.

7. when . . . fear: Believe rumors based on our fears.

8. It . . . discomfort: I would disgrace myself and embarrass you by weeping.

9. lime: Birdlime, a sticky substance smeared on branches to catch birds.
10. gin: Trap.

11. sell: Betray.

12. for thee: For a child.

13. swears and lies: Takes an oath and breaks it.

WOOD ENGRAVING AFTER SIR JOHN GILBERT

LADY MACDUFF. Every one that does so is a traitor, and
must be hanged.

50   **SON.** And must they all be hanged that swear and lie?

LADY MACDUFF. Every one.

SON. Who must hang them?

LADY MACDUFF. Why, the honest men.

SON. Then the liars and swearers are fools; for there are
55   liars and swearers enow[14] to beat the honest men
    and hang up them.

LADY MACDUFF. Now, God help thee, poor monkey! But
    how wilt thou do for a father?

SON. If he were dead, you'd weep for him. If you would
60   not, it were a good sign that I should quickly have a
    new father.

LADY MACDUFF. Poor prattler, how thou talk'st!

[*Enter a* MESSENGER.]

MESSENGER. Bless you, fair dame! I am not to you known,
    Though in your state of honor I am perfect.[15]
65   I doubt[16] some danger does approach you nearly:
    If you will take a homely[17] man's advice,
    Be not found here; hence, with your little ones.
    To fright you thus, methinks I am too savage;
    To do worse to you were fell[18] cruelty,
70   Which is too nigh your person. Heaven preserve you!
    I dare abide no longer.   [*Exit* MESSENGER.]

LADY MACDUFF.   Whither should I fly?
    I have done no harm. But I remember now
    I am in this earthly world, where to do harm
    Is often laudable, to do good sometime
75   Accounted dangerous folly. Why then, alas,
    Do I put up that womanly defense,
    To say I have done no harm?—What are these faces?

[*Enter* MURDERERS.]

MURDERER. Where is your husband?

LADY MACDUFF. I hope, in no place so unsanctified
    Where such as thou mayst find him.

80 **MURDERER.**   He's a traitor.

SON. Thou li'st, thou shag-eared[19] villain!

MURDERER.   What, you egg!

[*Stabbing him.*]

Young fry[20] of treachery!

SON.   He has killed me, mother:
    Run away, I pray you! [*Dies.*]

[*Exit* LADY MACDUFF *crying "Murder!"*
followed by MURDERERS.]

---

14. enow: Enough.

15. in . . . perfect: I am
fully informed of your honorable rank.
16. doubt: Fear.
17. homely: Simple.

18. fell: Fierce.

19. shag-eared: Hairy-eared.

20. fry: Offspring.

Scene iii. *England. Before the King's palace.*
[*Enter* MALCOLM *and* MACDUFF.]

MALCOLM. Let us seek out some desolate shade, and there
    Weep our sad bosoms empty.

MACDUFF.   Let us rather
    Hold fast the mortal[1] sword, and like good men
    Bestride our down-fall'n birthdom.[2] Each new morn
5   New widows howl, new orphans cry, new sorrows
    Strike heaven on the face, that it resounds
    As if it felt with Scotland and yelled out
    Like syllable of dolor. [3]

MALCOLM.   What I believe, I'll wail;
    What know, believe; and what I can redress,
10   As I shall find the time to friend,[4] I will.
    What you have spoke, it may be so perchance.
    This tyrant, whose sole[5] name blisters our tongues,
    Was once thought honest:[6] you have loved him well;
    He hath not touched you yet. I am young; but something
    thing
15   You may deserve of him through me;[7] and wisdom[8]
    To offer up a weak, poor, innocent lamb
    T' appease an angry god.

MACDUFF. I am not treacherous.

MALCOLM.   But Macbeth is.
    A good and virtuous nature may recoil
20   In an imperial charge.[9] But I shall crave your pardon;
    That which you are, my thoughts cannot
        transpose:[10]
    Angels are bright still, though the brightest[11] fell:
    Though all things foul would wear[12] the brows of
        grace,
    Yet grace must still look so. [13]

MACDUFF.   I have lost my hopes.

MALCOLM. Perchance even there where I did find my
25   doubts.
    Why in that rawness[14] left you wife and child,
    Those precious motives, those strong knots of love,
    Without leave-taking? I pray you,
    Let not my jealousies[15] be your dishonors.
30   But mine own safeties.[16] You may be rightly just
    Whatever I shall think.

MACDUFF.   Bleed, bleed, poor country:
    Great tyranny, lay thou thy basis sure,

---

1. mortal: Deadly.

2. Bestride . . . birthdom: Protectively stand over our native land.

3. Like . . . dolor: A similar cry of anguish.

4. to friend: Be friendly.

5. sole: Very.

6. honest: Good.

7. deserve . . . me: Earn by betraying me to Macbeth.

8. wisdom: It is wise.

9. recoil . . . charge: Give way to a royal command.

10. transpose: Transform.

11. the brightest: Lucifer.

12. would wear: Desire to wear.

13. so: Like itself.

14. rawness: Unprotected state or condition.

15. jealousies: Suspicions.

16. safeties: Protections.

For goodness dare not check thee: wear thou thy
    wrongs:
The title is affeered.[17] Fare thee well, lord:
35   I would not be the villain that thou think'st
For the whole space that's in the tyrant's grasp
And the rich East to boot.

MALCOLM.   Be not offended:
I speak not as in absolute fear of you.
I think our country sinks beneath the yoke;
40   It weeps, it bleeds, and each new day a gash
Is added to her wounds. I think withal
There would be hands uplifted in my right;[18]
And here from gracious England[19] have I offer
Of goodly thousands: but, for all this,
45   When I shall tread upon the tyrant's head,
Or wear it on my sword, yet my poor country
Shall have more vices than it had before,
More suffer, and more sundry ways than ever,
By him that shall succeed.

MACDUFF.   What should he be?

50   **MALCOLM.** It is myself I mean, in whom I know
All the particulars of vice so grafted[20]
That, when they shall be opened,[21] black Macbeth
Will seem as pure as snow, and the poor state
Esteem him as a lamb, being compared
With my confineless harms. [22]

55   **MACDUFF.**   Not in the legions
Of horrid hell can come a devil more damned
In evils to top Macbeth.

MALCOLM.   I grant him bloody,
Luxurious,[23] avaricious, false, deceitful,
Sudden,[24] malicious, smacking of every sin
60   That has a name: but there's no bottom, none,
In my voluptuousness: your wives, your daughters,
Your matrons and your maids, could not fill up
The cistern of my lust, and my desire
All continent impediments[25] would o'erbear,
65   That did oppose my will. Better Macbeth
Than such an one to reign.

MACDUFF.   Boundless intemperance
In nature[26] is a tyranny; it hath been
Th' untimely emptying of the happy throne,
And fall of many kings. But fear not yet
70   To take upon you what is yours: you may
Convey[27] your pleasures in a spacious plenty,

17. affeered: Legally confirmed.

18. in my right: On behalf of my claim.
19. England: The King of England.

20. grafted: Implanted.
21. opened: In bloom.

22. confineless harms: Unbounded evils.

23. luxurious: Lecherous.
24. Sudden: Violent.

25. continent impediments: Restraints.

26. nature: Man's nature.

27. Convey: Secretly manage.

And yet seem cold, the time you may so hoodwink.
We have willing dames enough. There cannot be
That vulture in you, to devour so many
As will to greatness dedicate themselves,
Finding it so inclined.

MALCOLM.   With this there grows
In my most ill-composed affection[28] such
A stanchless[29] avarice that, were I King,
I should cut off the nobles for their lands,
Desire his jewels and this other's house:
And my more-having would be as a sauce
To make me hunger more, that I should forge
Quarrels unjust against the good and loyal,
Destroying them for wealth.

MACDUFF.   This avarice
Sticks deeper, grows with more pernicious root
Than summer-seeming[30] lust, and it hath been
The sword of[31] our slain kings. Yet do not fear.
Scotland hath foisons[32] to fill up your will
Of your mere own.[33] All these are portable,[34]
With other graces weighed.

MALCOLM. But I have none: the king-becoming graces,
As justice, verity, temp'rance, stableness,
Bounty, perseverance, mercy, lowliness,
Devotion, patience, courage, fortitude,
I have no relish of them, but abound
In the division of each several crime,[35]
Acting it many ways. Nay, had I pow'r, I should
Pour the sweet milk of concord into hell,
Uproar the universal peace, confound[36]
All unity on earth.

MACDUFF.   O Scotland, Scotland!

MALCOLM. If such a one be fit to govern, speak:
I am as I have spoken.

MACDUFF.   Fit to govern!
No, not to live. O nation miserable!
With an untitled[37] tyrant bloody-sceptered,
When shalt thou see thy wholesome days again,
Since that the truest issue of thy throne[38]
By his own interdiction[39] stands accursed,
And does blaspheme his breed?[40] Thy royal father
Was a most sainted king: the queen that bore thee,
Oft'ner upon her knees than on her feet,
Died[41] every day she lived. Fare thee well!
These evils thou repeat'st upon thyself

28. affection: Character.
29. stanchless: Never-ending.

30. summer-seeming: Summerlike.
31. of: That killed.
32. foisons (foi′ zənz): Plenty.
33. mere own: Own property.
34. portable: Bearable.

35. division . . . crime: Variations of each kind of crime.

36. confound: Destroy.

37. untitled: Having no right to the throne.
38. truest . . . throne: Child of the true king.
39. interdiction: Exclusion.
40. blaspheme his breed: Slander his ancestry.
41. Died: Prepared for heaven.

Hath banished me from Scotland. O my breast,
Thy hope ends here!

MALCOLM.   Macduff, this noble passion,
115 Child of integrity, hath from my soul
     Wiped the black scruples, reconciled my thoughts
     To thy good truth and honor. Devilish Macbeth
     By many of these trains⁴² hath sought to win me
     Into his power; and modest wisdom⁴³ plucks me
120 From over-credulous haste: but God above
     Deal between thee and me! For even now
     I put myself to thy direction, and
     Unspeak mine own detraction,⁴⁴ here abjure
     The taints and blames I laid upon myself,
125 For⁴⁵ strangers to my nature. I am yet
     Unknown to woman, never was forsworn,
     Scarcely have coveted what was mine own,
     At no time broke my faith, would not betray
     The devil to his fellow, and delight
130 No less in truth than life. My first false speaking
     Was this upon myself. What I am truly,
     Is thine and my poor country's to command:
     Whither indeed, before thy here-approach,
     Old Siward, with ten thousand warlike men,
135 Already at a point,⁴⁶ was setting forth.
     Now we'll together, and the chance of goodness
     Be like our warranted quarrel!⁴⁷ Why are you silent?

MACDUFF. Such welcome and unwelcome things at once
     'Tis hard to reconcile.

[*Enter a* DOCTOR.]

MALCOLM. Well, more anon. Comes the King forth, I pray
140   you?

DOCTOR. Ay, sir. There are a crew of wretched souls
     That stay⁴⁸ his cure: their malady convinces
     The great assay of art;⁴⁹ but at his touch,
     Such sanctity hath heaven given his hand,
     They presently amend.⁵⁰

145 MALCOLM.   I thank you, doctor.
                              [*Exit* DOCTOR.]

MACDUFF. What's the disease he means?

MALCOLM.   'Tis called the evil:⁵¹
     A most miraculous work in this good King,
     Which often since my here-remain in England
     I have seen him do. How he solicits heaven,
150 Himself best knows: but strangely-visited people,

42. **trains:** Enticements.
43. **modest wisdom:** Prudence.

44. **detraction:** Slander.

45. **For:** As.

46. **at a point:** Prepared.

47. **the chance . . . quarrel:** May our chance of success equal the justice of our cause.

48. **stay:** Wait for.
49. **convinces . . . art:** Defies the efforts of medical science.
50. **presently amend:** Immediately recover.

51. **evil:** Scrofula (skrof′ yə lə), a skin disease called "the king's evil" because it was believed that it could be cured by the king's touch.

All swoll'n and ulcerous, pitiful to the eye,
The mere[52] despair of surgery, he cures,
Hanging a golden stamp[53] about their necks,
Put on with holy prayers: and 'tis spoken,
155 To the succeeding royalty he leaves
The healing benediction. With this strange virtue
He hath a heavenly gift of prophecy,
And sundry blessings hang about his throne
That speak him full of grace.

[*Enter* ROSS.]

MACDUFF.   See, who comes here?

160 **MALCOLM.** My countryman; but yet I know him not.

MACDUFF. My ever gentle[54] cousin, welcome hither.

MALCOLM. I know him now: good God, betimes[55] remove
The means that makes us strangers!

ROSS.   Sir, amen.

MACDUFF. Stands Scotland where it did?

ROSS.   Alas, poor country!
165 Almost afraid to know itself! It cannot
Be called our mother but our grave, where nothing[56]
But who knows nothing is once seen to smile;
Where sighs and groans, and shrieks that rent the
air,
Are made, not marked, where violent sorrow seems
170 A modern ecstasy.[57] The dead man's knell
Is there scarce asked for who,[58] and good men's lives
Expire before the flowers in their caps,
Dying or ere they sicken.

MACDUFF.   O, relation
Too nice,[59] and yet too true!

MALCOLM.   What's the newest grief?

175 **ROSS.** That of an hour's age doth hiss the speaker;[60]
Each minute teems[61] a new one.

MACDUFF.   How does my wife?

ROSS. Why, well.

MACDUFF.   And all my children?

ROSS.   Well too.

MACDUFF. The tyrant has not battered at their peace?

ROSS. No; they were well at peace when I did leave 'em.

52. mere: Utter.
53. stamp: Coin.

54. gentle: Noble.

55. betimes: Quickly.

56. nothing: No one.

57. modern ecstasy: Ordinary emotion.
58. The dead . . . who: People can no longer keep track of Macbeth's victims.

59. nice: Exact.

60. That . . . speaker: The report of the grief of an hour ago is hissed as stale news.
61. teems: Gives birth to.

180   **MACDUFF.** Be not a niggard of your speech: how goes 't?

    ROSS. When I came hither to transport the tidings,
        Which I have heavily borne, there ran a rumor
        Of many worthy fellows that were out;[62]
        Which was to my belief witnessed[63] the rather,
185   For that I saw the tyrant's power[64] afoot.
        Now is the time of help. Your eye in Scotland
        Would create soldiers, make our women fight,
        To doff[65] their dire distresses.

    MALCOLM.   Be 't their comfort
        We are coming thither. Gracious England hath
190   Lent us good Siward and ten thousand men;
        An older and a better soldier none
        That Christendom gives out.

    ROSS.   Would I could answer
        This comfort with the like! But I have words
        That would be howled out in the desert air,
        Where hearing should not latch[66] them.

195   **MACDUFF.**   What concern they?
        The general cause or is it a fee-grief[67]
        Due to some single breast?

    ROSS.   No mind that's honest
        But in it shares some woe, though the main part
        Pertains to you alone.

    MACDUFF.   If it be mine,
200   Keep it not from me, quickly let me have it.

    ROSS. Let not your ears despise my tongue for ever,
        Which shall possess them with the heaviest sound
        That ever yet they heard.

    MACDUFF.   Humh! I guess at it.

    ROSS. Your castle is surprised; your wife and babes
205   Savagely slaughtered. To relate the manner,
        Were, on the quarry[68] of these murdered deer,
        To add the death of you.

    MALCOLM.   Merciful heaven!
        What, man! Ne'er pull your hat upon your brows;
        Give sorrow words. The grief that does not speak
210   Whispers the o'er-fraught[69] heart and bids it break.

    MACDUFF. My children too?

    ROSS.   Wife, children, servants, all
        That could be found.

62. out: In rebellion.
63. witnessed: Confirmed.
64. power: Army.

65. doff: Put off.

66. latch: Catch.

67. fee-grief: Personal grief.

68. quarry: Heap of game slain in a hunt.

69. o'er-fraught: Overburdened.

MACDUFF.   And I must be from thence!
My wife killed too?

ROSS.   I have said.

MALCOLM.   Be comforted.
Let's make us med'cines of our great revenge,
215   To cure this deadly grief.

MACDUFF. He has no children. All my pretty ones?
Did you say all? O hell-kite![70] All?
What, all my pretty chickens and their dam
At one fell swoop?

MALCOLM. Dispute it[71] like a man.

220   **MACDUFF.**   I shall do so;
But I must also feel it as a man.
I cannot but remember such things were,
That were most precious to me. Did heaven look on,
And would not take their part? Sinful Macduff,
225   They were all struck for thee! Naught[72] that I am,
Not for their own demerits but for mine
Fell slaughter on their souls. Heaven rest them now!

MALCOLM. Be this the whetstone of your sword. Let grief
Convert to anger; blunt not the heart, enrage it.

230   **MACDUFF.** O, I could play the woman with mine eyes,
And braggart with my tongue! But, gentle heavens,
Cut short all intermission; front to front[73]
Bring thou this fiend of Scotland and myself;
Within my sword's length set him. If he 'scape,
Heaven forgive him too!

MALCOLM.   This time goes manly.
Come, go we to the King. Our power is ready;
Our lack is nothing but our leave.[74] Macbeth
Is ripe for shaking, and the pow'rs above
Put on their instruments.[75] Receive what cheer you
    may.
240   The night is long that never finds the day.   [*Exit.*]

---

70. hell-kite: Hellish bird of prey.

71. Dispute it: Counter your grief.

72. Naught: Wicked.

73. front to front: Face to face.

74. Our . . . leave: We need only to take our leave.
75. Put . . . instruments: Urge us onward as their agents.

Your Response

1. Do you think Macduff should be held responsible for the deaths in his family? Why or why not?

Recalling

2. (a) What does the first apparition tell Macbeth? (b) How does the prophecy of the second apparition seem to contradict that of the first? (c) What does the third apparition promise?
3. (a) What question do the witches refuse to answer? (b) What vision do they parade before Macbeth?
4. (a) In his conversation with Macduff, why does Malcolm pretend to have all of Macbeth's vices and more? (b) What convinces Malcolm that Macduff is trustworthy?
5. (a) What good news about "gracious England" does Ross bring Malcolm? (b) What bad news does Ross bring Macduff?

Interpreting

6. Why does Macbeth readily accept the predictions made by the second and third apparitions?
7. (a) In the witches' procession of kings, why do some kings carry double and triple scepters? (b) Why does Banquo carry a mirror?
8. (a) What is Macbeth's reason for killing Macduff's wife and child? (b) How do these murders differ from the previous ones?
9. How would you describe Macbeth's character at this point in the play?
10. How is Malcolm's character revealed in the dialogue with Macduff in Scene iii?
11. Based on Macduff's reaction to the murder of his wife and son, how would you describe Macduff's character?

Applying

12. In staging *Macbeth,* some producers eliminate Scene ii, the murder of Lady Macduff and her son. (a) What reasons do you think they give for doing so? (b) What is your reaction to that kind of cut?

ANALYZING LITERATURE

Understanding Plot Development

Plot is a series of related incidents progressing through a period of rising action to a climax.

1. How do the apparitions' prophecies in Scene i prepare the audience for the plot developments to follow?
2. By the end of Act IV, the character of each major living participant—Macbeth, Lady Macbeth, Malcolm, Macduff, even Ross—has been made clear. How has this portrayal of character laid the groundwork for later events?

CRITICAL THINKING AND READING

Reading Between the Lines

In a play as carefully crafted as *Macbeth,* there are very few insignificant lines. For instance, in Act IV when one of the witches says, "'Tis time, 'tis time," the reader should think, "Time for what? Time for the witches to exact their price from Macbeth?"

Even today, critics have differing opinions about the character of Ross, a man who can be evaluated only by reading between the lines. What is your opinion of Ross's character—is he a toadying politician, a loyal Scot, or something else? Defend your assessment.

THINKING AND WRITING

Writing About Macbeth's Tragic Flaw

Macbeth is a tragic hero, a person of high rank who is brought to eventual ruin by a flaw in his character. Macbeth's tragic flaw is his ambition, which leads him into a series of bloody and increasingly indefensible acts. Write a composition in which you relate Macbeth's character to the plot development of the play. First, make some notes on how Macbeth's personality and motivations get him into trouble and prevent him from getting out. Then, write a first draft. When you revise, make sure each of your major points ties Macbeth's character to a plot element.

GUIDE FOR INTERPRETING

Writers' Techniques

Macbeth, Act V

Theme. The theme of a literary work is its central idea, an idea that can usually be expressed as a general statement about life. Every element in a work of literature—plot, character, setting, and so on—contributes to the theme. In many works of literature, including *Macbeth,* the theme pertains not only to the lives of the characters on stage but also, and more importantly, to the lives of the members of the audience. Sometimes it is possible to state a theme in one sentence, although complex literary works may require a lengthier explanation. A theme may be directly stated, but more commonly it is implied.

Focus

Jot down a few lines from Act V of *Macbeth* (and perhaps from earlier acts) that seem to imply the theme of the play. While the theme is not directly stated, the dialogue gives many indications that you will find helpful. Remember that the theme cannot be expressed in a single word or phrase. It requires at least a complete sentence and often more.

Primary Source

The theme of *Macbeth* is reinforced by the imagery of blood that permeates the play. Critic Mark Von Doren claimed,

> Never in a play has there been so much of this substance, and never has it been so sickening . . . The second scene opens with a messenger running in to Duncan red with wounds. And blood darkens every scene thereafter. It is not bright red, nor does it run freely and wash away . . . It is so real that we see, feel, and smell it on everything. And it sticks. "This is a sorry sight," says Macbeth as he comes from Duncan's murder, staring at his hands. He had not thought there would be so much blood on them, or that it would stay like that. Lady Macbeth is for washing the "filthy witness" off, but Macbeth knows that all great Neptune's oceans will not make him clean; rather his hand, plunged into the green, will make it all one red. The blood of the play is everywhere physical in its looks and gross in its quantity.

Act V

Scene i. *Dunsinane. In the castle.*
[*Enter a* DOCTOR OF PHYSIC *and a* WAITING-GENTLEWOMAN.]

DOCTOR. I have two nights watched with you, but can perceive no truth in your report. When was it she last walked?

5   **GENTLEWOMAN.** Since his Majesty went into the field.[1] I have seen her rise from her bed, throw her nightgown upon her, unlock her closet,[2] take forth paper, fold it, write upon 't, read it, afterwards seal it, and again return to bed; yet all this while in a most fast sleep.

10   **DOCTOR.** A great perturbation in nature, to receive at once the benefit of sleep and do the effects of watching![3] In this slumb'ry agitation, besides her walking and other actual performances, what, at any time, have you heard her say?

  GENTLEWOMAN. That, sir, which I will not report after
15   her.

  DOCTOR. You may to me, and 'tis most meet[4] you should.

  GENTLEWOMAN. Neither to you nor anyone, having no witness to confirm my speech.

[*Enter* LADY MACBETH, *with a taper.*]

  Lo you, here she comes! This is her very guise,[5]
20   and, upon my life, fast asleep! Observe her; stand close.[6]

  DOCTOR. How came she by that light?

  GENTLEWOMAN. Why, it stood by her. She has light by her continually. 'Tis her command.

25   **DOCTOR.** You see, her eyes are open.

  GENTLEWOMAN. Ay, but their sense[7] are shut.

  DOCTOR. What is it she does now? Look, how she rubs her hands.

  GENTLEWOMAN. It is an accustomed action with her, to
30   seem thus washing her hands: I have known her continue in this a quarter of an hour.

  LADY MACBETH. Yet here's a spot.

  DOCTOR. Hark! She speaks. I will set down what comes from her, to satisfy[8] my remembrance the more
35   strongly.

---

1. field: Battlefield.

2. closet: Chest.

3. effects of watching: Deeds of one awake.

4. meet: Suitable.

5. guise: Custom.

6. close: Hidden.

7. sense: Powers of sight.

8. satisfy: Support.

MRS. SIDDONS AS LADY MACBETH
G. H. Harlow
Garrick Club

LADY MACBETH. Out, damned spot! Out, I say! One: two: why, then 'tis time to do 't. Hell is murky. Fie, my lord, fie! A soldier, and afeard? What need we fear who knows it, when none can call our pow'r to

40   accompt?[9] Yet who would have thought the old man to have had so much blood in him?

DOCTOR. Do you mark that?

9. to accompt: Into account.

LADY MACBETH. The Thane of Fife had a wife. Where is she now? What, will these hands ne'er be clean? No more o' that, my lord, no more o' that! You mar all with this starting.

DOCTOR. Go to, go to! You have known what you should not.

GENTLEWOMAN. She has spoke what she should not, I am sure of that. Heaven knows what she has known.

LADY MACBETH. Here's the smell of the blood still. All the perfumes of Arabia will not sweeten this little hand. Oh, oh, oh!

DOCTOR. What a sigh is there! The heart is sorely charged.[10]

10. **charged:** Burdened.

GENTLEWOMAN. I would not have such a heart in my bosom for the dignity[11] of the whole body.

11. **dignity:** Worth.

DOCTOR. Well, well, well—

GENTLEWOMAN. Pray God it be, sir.

DOCTOR. This disease is beyond my practice. Yet I have known those which have walked in their sleep who have died holily in their beds.

LADY MACBETH. Wash your hands; put on your night-gown; look not so pale! I tell you yet again, Banquo's buried. He cannot come out on 's[12] grave.

12. **on 's:** Of his.

DOCTOR. Even so?

LADY MACBETH. To bed, to bed! There's knocking at the gate. Come, come, come, come, give me your hand! What's done cannot be undone. To bed, to bed, to bed! [*Exit* LADY MACBETH.]

DOCTOR. Will she go now to bed?

GENTLEWOMAN. Directly.

DOCTOR. Foul whisp'rings are abroad. Unnatural deeds
Do breed unnatural troubles. Infected minds
To their deaf pillows will discharge their secrets.
More needs she the divine than the physician.
God, God forgive us all! Look after her;
Remove from her the means of all annoyance,[13]
And still keep eyes upon her. So good night.
My mind she has mated[14] and amazed my sight:
I think, but dare not speak.

13. **annoyance:** Injury.

14. **mated:** Baffled.

GENTLEWOMAN. Good night, good doctor.
[*Exit.*]

Scene ii. *The country near Dunsinane.*
[*Drum and colors. Enter* MENTEITH, CAITHNESS, ANGUS, LENNOX, SOLDIERS.]

MENTEITH. The English pow'r[1] is near, led on by
    Malcolm,
His uncle Siward and the good Macduff.
Revenges burn in them; for their dear causes
Would to the bleeding and the grim alarm
Excite the mortified man.[2]

5   ANGUS.   Near Birnam Wood
Shall we well meet them; that way are they coming.

CAITHNESS. Who knows if Donalbain be with his
    brother?

LENNOX. For certain, sir, he is not. I have a file[3]
Of all the gentry: there is Siward's son,
10 And many unrough[4] youths that even now
Protest[5] their first of manhood.

MENTEITH.   What does the tyrant?

CAITHNESS. Great Dunsinane he strongly fortifies.
Some say he's mad; others, that lesser hate him,
Do call it valiant fury: but, for certain,
15 He cannot buckle his distempered cause
Within the belt of rule.[6]

ANGUS.   Now does he feel
His secret murders sticking on his hands;
Now minutely revolts upbraid his faith-breach.[7]
Those he commands move only in command,
20 Nothing in love. Now does he feel his title
Hang loose about him, like a giant's robe
Upon a dwarfish thief.

MENTEITH.   Who then shall blame
His pestered[8] senses to recoil and start,
When all that is within him does condemn
Itself for being there?

25 CAITHNESS.   Well, march we on,
To give obedience where 'tis truly owed.
Meet we the med'cine of the sickly weal,[9]
And with him pour we, in our country's purge,
Each drop of us.[10]

LENNOX.   Or so much as it needs
30 To dew the sovereign flower and drown the weeds.[11]
Make we our march towards Birnam.
                    [*Exit, marching.*]

---

1. **pow'r:** Army.

2. **Would . . . man:** Would incite a dead man to join the bloody and grim call to arms.

3. **file:** List.

4. **unrough:** Beardless.
5. **Protest:** Assert.

6. **rule:** Self-control.

7. **minutely . . . faith-breach:** Every minute revolts rebuke his disloyalty.

8. **pestered:** Tormented.

9. **med'cine . . . weal:** Malcolm and his supporters are "the med'cine" that will heal "the sickly" commonwealth.
10. **Each . . . us:** Every last drop of our blood.

11. **dew . . . weeds:** Water the royal flower (Malcolm) and drown the weeds (Macbeth).

Scene iii. *Dunsinane. In the castle.*
[*Enter* MACBETH, DOCTOR, *and* ATTENDANTS.]

MACBETH. Bring me no more reports; let them fly all![1]
    Till Birnam Wood remove to Dunsinane
    I cannot taint[2] with fear. What's the boy Malcolm?
    Was he not born of woman? The spirits that know
5   All mortal consequences[3] have pronounced me thus:
    "Fear not, Macbeth; no man that's born of woman
    Shall e'er have power upon thee." Then fly, false
       thanes,
    And mingle with the English epicures.[4]
    The mind I sway[5] by and the heart I bear
10   Shall never sag with doubt nor shake with fear.

[*Enter* SERVANT.]

    The devil damn thee black, thou cream-faced loon.[6]
    Where got'st thou that goose look?

SERVANT. There is ten thousand—

MACBETH.   Geese, villain?

SERVANT.   Soldiers, sir.

MACBETH. Go prick thy face and over-red thy fear.
15   Thou lily-livered boy. What soldiers, patch?[7]
    Death of thy soul! Those linen[8] cheeks of thine
    Are counselors to fear. What soldiers, whey-face?

SERVANT. The English force, so please you.

MACBETH. Take thy face hence.   [*Exit* SERVANT.]
              Seyton!—I am sick at heart.
20   When I behold—Seyton, I say!—This push[9]
    Will cheer me ever, or disseat[10] me now.
    I have lived long enough. My way of life
    Is fall'n into the sear,[11] the yellow leaf,
    And that which should accompany old age,
25   As honor, love, obedience, troops of friends,
    I must not look to have; but, in their stead,
    Curses not loud but deep, mouth-honor, breath,
    Which the poor heart would fain deny, and dare not.
    Seyton!

[*Enter* SEYTON.]

SEYTON. What's your gracious pleasure?

30 MACBETH.   What news more?

SEYTON. All is confirmed, my lord, which was reported.

---

1. **let . . . all:** Let them all desert me!

2. **taint:** Become infected

3. **mortal consequences:** Future human events.

4. **epicures:** Gluttons.
5. **sway:** Move.

6. **loon:** Fool.

7. **patch:** Fool.
8. **linen:** Pale as linen.

9. **push:** Effort.
10. **disseat:** Unthrone.

11. **the sear:** A withered state.

MACBETH. I'll fight, till from my bones my flesh be
    hacked.
    Give me my armor.

SEYTON.   'Tis not needed yet.

MACBETH. I'll put it on.
35   Send out moe[12] horses, skirr[13] the country round.
    Hang those that talk of fear. Give me mine armor.
    How does your patient, doctor?

DOCTOR.   Not so sick, my lord,
    As she is troubled with thick-coming fancies
    That keep her from her rest.

MACBETH.   Cure her of that.
40   Canst thou not minister to a mind diseased,
    Pluck from the memory a rooted sorrow,
    Raze out[14] the written troubles of the brain,
    And with some sweet oblivious antidote
    Cleanse the stuffed bosom of that perilous stuff
    Which weighs upon the heart?

45 **DOCTOR.**   Therein the patient
    Must minister to himself.

MACBETH. Throw physic[15] to the dogs, I'll none of it.
    Come, put mine armor on. Give me my staff.
    Seyton, send out.—Doctor, the thanes fly from
    me.—
50   Come, sir, dispatch. If thou couldst, doctor, cast
    The water[16] of my land, find her disease
    And purge it to a sound and pristine health,
    I would applaud thee to the very echo,
    That should applaud again.—Pull 't off,[17] I say.—
55   What rhubarb, senna, or what purgative drug,
    Would scour these English hence? Hear'st thou of
    them?

DOCTOR. Ay, my good lord; your royal preparation
    Makes us hear something.

MACBETH.   Bring it[18] after me.
    I will not be afraid of death and bane[19]
60   Till Birnam Forest come to Dunsinane.

DOCTOR. [*Aside*] Were I from Dunsinane away and clear,
    Profit again should hardly draw me here.   [*Exit.*]

Scene iv. Country near Birnam Wood.
[*Drum and colors. Enter* MALCOLM, SIWARD, MACDUFF, SIWARD's SON,
MENTEITH, CAITHNESS, ANGUS, *and* SOLDIERS, *marching.*]

---

12. moe: More.
13. skirr: Scour.

14. Raze out: Erase.

15. physic: Medicine.

16. cast the water: Diagnose the illness.

17. Pull 't off: Pull off a piece of armor which has been put on incorrectly in Macbeth's haste.

18. it: His armor.
19. bane: Destruction.

MALCOLM. Cousins, I hope the days are near at hand
That chambers will be safe.[1]

MENTEITH.   We doubt it nothing.

SIWARD. What wood is this before us?

MENTEITH.   The Wood of Birnam.

MALCOLM. Let every soldier hew him down a bough
5   And bear 't before him. Thereby shall we shadow[2]
The numbers of our host, and make discovery[3]
Err in report of us.

SOLDIERS.   It shall be done.

SIWARD. We learn no other but the confident tyrant
Keeps still in Dunsinane, and will endure
Our setting down before 't.[4]

10   MALCOLM.   'Tis his main hope,
For where there is advantage to be given
Both more and less[5] have given him the revolt,
And none serve with him but constrainèd things
Whose hearts are absent too.

MACDUFF.   Let our just censures
15   Attend the true event,[6] and put we on
Industrious soldiership.

SIWARD.   The time approaches,
That will with due decision make us know
What we shall say we have and what we owe.[7]
Thoughts speculative their unsure hopes relate,
20   But certain issue strokes must arbitrate:[8]
Towards which advance the war.[9] [*Exit, marching.*]

Scene v. *Dunsinane. Within the castle.*
[*Enter* MACBETH, SEYTON, *and* SOLDIERS, *with drum and colors.*]

MACBETH. Hang out our banners on the outward walls.
The cry is still "They come!" Our castle's strength
Will laugh a siege to scorn. Here let them lie
Till famine and the ague[1] eat them up.
5   Were they not forced[2] with those that should be ours,
We might have met them dareful,[3] beard to beard,
And beat them backward home.
                        [*A cry within of women.*]
                                What is that noise?

SEYTON. It is the cry of women, my good lord.   [*Exit.*]

1. **That . . . safe:** That people will be safe in their own homes.

2. **shadow:** Conceal.
3. **discovery:** Those who see us.

4. **setting down before 't:** Laying siege to it.

5. **more and less:** People of high and low rank.

6. **our . . . event:** True judgment await the actual outcome.

7. **owe:** Own.

8. **strokes . . . arbitrate:** Fighting must decide.
9. **war:** Army.

1. **ague:** Fever.
2. **forced:** Reinforced.
3. **dareful:** Boldly.

MACBETH. I have almost forgot the taste of fears:

10 The time has been, my senses would have cooled
To hear a night-shriek, and my fell[4] of hair
Would at a dismal treatise[5] rouse and stir
As life were in 't. I have supped full with horrors.
Direness, familiar to my slaughterous thoughts,
Cannot once start[6] me.

[*Enter* SEYTON.]

15   Wherefore was that cry?

SEYTON. The Queen, my lord, is dead.

MACBETH. She should[7] have died hereafter;
There would have been a time for such a word.[8]
Tomorrow, and tomorrow, and tomorrow
20 Creeps in this petty pace from day to day,
To the last syllable of recorded time;
And all our yesterdays have lighted fools
The way to dusty death. Out, out, brief candle!
Life's but a walking shadow, a poor player
25 That struts and frets his hour upon the stage
And then is heard no more. It is a tale
Told by an idiot, full of sound and fury
Signifying nothing.

[*Enter a* MESSENGER.]

Thou com'st to use thy tongue; thy story quickly!

30 **MESSENGER.** Gracious my lord,
I should report that which I say I saw,
But know not how to do 't.

MACBETH.   Well, say, sir.

MESSENGER. As I did stand my watch upon the hill,
I looked toward Birnam, and anon, methought,
The wood began to move.

35 **MACBETH.**   Liar and slave!

MESSENGER. Let me endure your wrath, if 't be not so.
Within this three mile may you see it coming;
I say a moving grove.

MACBETH.   If thou speak'st false,
Upon the next tree shalt thou hang alive,
40 Till famine cling[9] thee. If thy speech be sooth,[10]
I care not if thou dost for me as much.
I pull in resolution, and begin
To doubt th' equivocation of the fiend
That lies like truth: "Fear not, till Birnam Wood

4. fell: Scalp.
5. treatise: Story.

6. start: Startle.

7. should: Inevitably would.
8. word: Message.

9. cling: Wither.
10. sooth: Truth.

45	Do come to Dunsinane!" And now a wood
	Comes toward Dunsinane. Arm, arm, and out!
	If this which he avouches[11] does appear,
	There is nor flying hence nor tarrying here.
	I 'gin to be aweary of the sun,
50	And wish th' estate o' th' world were now undone.
	Ring the alarum bell! Blow wind, come wrack!
	At least we'll die with harness[12] on our back. [*Exit.*]

11. avouches: Asserts.

12. harness: Armor.

Scene vi. *Dunsinane. Before the castle.*
[*Drum and colors. Enter* MALCOLM, SIWARD, MACDUFF, *and their army, with boughs.*]

MALCOLM. Now near enough. Your leavy[1] screens throw
    down,
And show like those you are. You, worthy uncle,
Shall, with my cousin, your right noble son,
Lead our first battle.[2] Worthy Macduff and we
5 Shall take upon 's what else remains to do,
According to our order.[3]

1. leavy: Leafy.

2. battle: Battalion.

3. order: Plan.

SIWARD.   Fare you well.
Do we but find the tyrant's power[4] tonight,
Let us be beaten, if we cannot fight.

4. power: Forces.

MACDUFF. Make all our trumpets speak; give them all
    breath,
10 Those clamorous harbingers of blood and death.
               [*Exit. Alarums continued.*]

Scene vii. *Another part of the field.*
[*Enter* MACBETH.]

MACBETH. They have tied me to a stake; I cannot fly,
But bearlike I must fight the course.[1] What's he
That was not born of woman? Such a one
Am I to fear, or none.

1. bearlike . . . course: Like a bear chained to a stake being attacked by dogs, I must fight until the end.

[*Enter* YOUNG SIWARD.]

YOUNG SIWARD. What is thy name?

5 MACBETH.   Thou'lt be afraid to hear it.

YOUNG SIWARD. No; though thou call'st thyself a hotter
    name
Than any is in hell.

MACBETH.   My name's Macbeth.

YOUNG SIWARD. The devil himself could not pronounce a
    title
More hateful to mine ear.

MACBETH.   No, nor more fearful.

YOUNG SIWARD. Thou liest, abhorrèd tyrant; with my
10   sword
      I'll prove the lie thou speak'st.
              [*Fight, and* YOUNG SIWARD *slain.*]

MACBETH.   Thou wast born of woman.
      But swords I smile at, weapons laugh to scorn,
      Brandished by man that's of a woman born.   [*Exit.*]

[*Alarums. Enter* MACDUFF.]

MACDUFF. That way the noise is. Tyrant, show thy face!
15   If thou be'st slain and with no stroke of mine,
      My wife and children's ghosts will haunt me still.
      I cannot strike at wretched kerns, whose arms
      Are hired to bear their staves.[2] Either thou, Macbeth,
      Or else my sword, with an unbattered edge,
20   I sheathe again undeeded.[3] There thou shouldst be;
      By this great clatter, one of greatest note
      Seems bruited.[4] Let me find him, Fortune!
      And more I beg not.   [*Exit. Alarums.*]

[*Enter* MALCOLM *and* SIWARD.]

SIWARD. This way, my lord. The castle's gently
        rend'red:[5]
25   The tyrant's people on both sides do fight;
      The noble thanes do bravely in the war;
      The day almost itself professes yours,
      And little is to do.

MALCOLM.   We have met with foes
      That strike beside us.[6]

SIWARD.   Enter, sir, the castle.
                    [*Exit. Alarum.*]

Scene viii. *Another part of the field.*
[*Enter* MACBETH.]

MACBETH. Why should I play the Roman fool, and die
      On mine own sword?[1] Whiles I see lives,[2] the gashes
      Do better upon them.

[*Enter* MACDUFF.]

MACDUFF.   Turn, hell-hound, turn!

MACBETH. Of all men else I have avoided thee.
5   But get thee back! My soul is too much charged
      With blood of thine already.

MACDUFF.   I have no words:
      My voice is in my sword, thou bloodier villain
      Than terms can give thee out![3]
           [*Fight. Alarum.*]

2. **staves:** Spears.

3. **undeeded:** Unused.

4. **bruited:** Reported.

5. **gently rend'red:** Easily surrendered.

6. **strike . . . us:** Deliberately miss us.

1. **play . . . sword:** Die like Brutus or Cassius, who killed themselves with their own swords in the moment of defeat.
2. **Whiles . . . lives:** So long as I see living men.

3. **terms . . . out:** Words can describe you.

MACBETH.   Thou losest labor:
As easy mayst thou the intrenchant[4] air
10 With thy keen sword impress[5] as make me bleed:
Let fall thy blade on vulnerable crests;
I bear a charmèd life, which must not yield
To one of woman born.

MACDUFF.   Despair thy charm,
And let the angel[6] whom thou still hast served
15 Tell thee, Macduff was from his mother's womb
Untimely ripped.[7]

MACBETH. Accursèd be that tongue that tells me so,
For it hath cowed my better part of man![8]
And be these juggling fiends no more believed,
20 That palter[9] with us in a double sense;
That keep the word of promise to our ear,
And break it to our hope. I'll not fight with thee.

MACDUFF. Then yield thee, coward,
And live to be the show and gaze o' th' time:[10]
25 We'll have thee, as our rarer monsters[11] are,
Painted upon a pole,[12] and underwrit,
"Here may you see the tyrant."

MACBETH.   I will not yield,
To kiss the ground before young Malcolm's feet,
And to be baited with the rabble's curse.
30 Though Birnam Wood be come to Dunsinane,
And thou opposed, being of no woman born,
Yet I will try the last. Before my body
I throw my warlike shield. Lay on, Macduff;
And damned be him that first cries "Hold, enough!"
                         [*Exit, fighting. Alarums.*]

[*Re-enter fighting, and* MACBETH *slain. Exit* MACDUFF, *with*
MACBETH. *Retreat and flourish.*[13] *Enter, with drum and
colors,* MALCOLM, SIWARD, ROSS, THANES, *and* SOLDIERS.]

35 **MALCOLM.** I would the friends we miss were safe arrived.

SIWARD. Some must go off;[14] and yet, by these I see,
So great a day as this is cheaply bought.

MALCOLM. Macduff is missing, and your noble son.

ROSS. Your son, my lord, has paid a soldier's debt:
40 He only lived but till he was a man;
The which no sooner had his prowess confirmed
In the unshrinking station[15] where he fought,
But like a man he died.

SIWARD.   Then he is dead?

---

4. intrenchant: Incapable of being cut.
5. impress: Make a dent in.

6. angel: Fallen angel, fiend.

7. his . . . ripped: Macduff's mother died before giving birth to him.

8. better . . . man: Courage.
9. palter: Juggle.

10. gaze o' th' time: Spectacle of the age.
11. monsters: Freaks.
12. Painted . . . pole: Pictured on a banner stuck on a pole by a showman's booth.

13. Retreat and flourish: Trumpet call to withdraw and fanfare.

14. go off: Die.

15. unshrinking station: Place where he stood firmly.

ROSS. Ay, and brought off the field. Your cause of sorrow
45 Must not be measured by his worth, for then
    It hath no end.

SIWARD.   Had he his hurts before?

ROSS. Ay, on the front.

SIWARD.   Why then, God's soldier be he!
    Had I as many sons as I have hairs,
    I would not wish them to a fairer death:
    And so his knell is knolled.

50 **MALCOLM.**   He's worth more sorrow,
    And that I'll spend for him.

SIWARD.   He's worth no more:
    They say he parted well and paid his score:
    And so God be with him! Here comes newer comfort.

[*Enter* MACDUFF, *with* MACBETH'S *head.*]

MACDUFF. Hail, King! for so thou art: behold, where
        stands
55 Th' usurper's cursèd head. The time is free.[16]
    I see thee compassed with thy kingdom's pearl,[17]
    That speak my salutation in their minds,
    Whose voices I desire aloud with mine:
    Hail, King of Scotland!

ALL.   Hail, King of Scotland!

[*Flourish.*]

60 **MALCOLM.** We shall not spend a large expense of time
    Before we reckon with your several loves,[18]
    And make us even with you.[19] My thanes and kins-
        men,
    Henceforth be earls, the first that ever Scotland
    In such an honor named. What's more to do,
65 Which would be planted newly with the time[20]—
    As calling home our exiled friends abroad
    That fled the snares of watchful tyranny,
    Producing forth the cruel ministers
    Of this dead butcher and his fiendlike queen,
70 Who, as 'tis thought, by self and violent hands
    Took off her life—this, and what needful else
    That calls upon us, by the grace of Grace
    We will perform in measure, time, and place:[21]
    So thanks to all at once and to each one,
    Whom we invite to see us crowned at Scone.

                    [*Flourish. Exit all.*]

16. The . . . free: Our country is liberated.
17. compassed . . . pearl: Surrounded by the noblest people in the kingdom.

18. reckon . . . loves: Reward each of you for your devotion.
19. make . . . you: Pay what we owe you.

20. What's . . . time: What remains to be done at the beginning of this new age.

21. in measure . . . place: Fittingly at the appropriate time and place.

Your Response

1. Does the ending of the play satisfy you? Why or why not? If not, how would you change it?
2. Why do you think *Macbeth* continues to appeal to audiences after nearly four hundred years?

Recalling

3. (a) While Lady Macbeth is sleepwalking, to what three prior events does she refer? (b) To which event does she keep coming back?
4. (a) What news does Seyton bring Macbeth in Scene v? (b) What in the messenger's report makes Macbeth fear that the apparitions' second prophecy is coming true?
5. (a) In Scene viii why does Macbeth tell Macduff he does not wish to fight him? (b) What does Macduff tell Macbeth concerning the apparitions' third prophecy?
6. (a) Whom does Macbeth kill in the encounter with the English forces? (b) Whom does Macduff kill? (c) At the end of the play, who is to be crowned King of Scotland?

Interpreting

7. Why do you think it is an "accustomed action" for Lady Macbeth to wash her hands while sleepwalking?
8. (a) Why does Macbeth remain confident of surviving the battle with Malcolm's army despite his own troops' desertion? (b) Judging by the way Macbeth behaves in Scene iii, describe his state of mind.
9. What changes in his personality is Macbeth describing in Scene v, lines 9–14?
10. Why does Macbeth say, "She should have died hereafter," upon learning of the death of Lady Macbeth?
11. Macbeth, mad and murderous though he is, shows certain admirable traits to the very end. What are some of his better traits?

Applying

12. If Macbeth had defeated Malcolm's forces and remained King of Scotland, what actions do you think he would have taken in regard to (a) Malcolm? (b) the rebellious Scottish lords? (c) the witches?

ANALYZING LITERATURE

Understanding Theme

Theme is the central or dominating idea in a literary work. In a tragedy the theme is based on the actions of a tragic hero—a basically moral person, often of noble stature, whose downfall usually results from a bad choice. The bad choice stems from a tragic flaw in the hero's character.

1. What is the tragic flaw in Macbeth's character? Support your answer.
2. What is the theme of *Macbeth?* State the theme in the form of a universal truth, not restricted to Macbeth's tragic flaw and its consequences.
3. What events in Act V show Macbeth's downfall to be complete and irreversible?

LEARNING OPTIONS

1. **Performance.** With a group of classmates, perform a scene from *Macbeth.* Choose a director, assign the roles, and prepare props and costumes. In rehearsing the scene, focus on conveying the meaning and emotion of the dialogue and creating the appropriate atmosphere. If you wish, include sound effects and music in your performance.
2. **Speaking and Listening.** *Macbeth,* like other Shakespeare plays, has been used as the basis for the libretto, or script, of an opera. The Italian composer Giuseppe Verdi (1813–1901) wrote his *Macbeth* in 1847. Find a recording, videotape, or laserdisc of this opera. Listen to it or watch it in its entirety. Then choose an excerpt in which you think the music enhances the dramatic action particularly well. Before playing the excerpt in class, give a brief introductory statement about Verdi's work and explain why you chose the scene you did. Play the excerpt and be prepared to answer questions from your classmates.

ONE WRITER'S PROCESS

William Shakespeare and Macbeth

PREWRITING

History in the Making When William Shakespeare wrote his plays, the language and themes which we find so "elevated" today were actually geared for the entertainment of the average sixteenth-century person. In some plays, he made political history his subject matter, knowing that it would probably engage the interest of most theatergoers.

Courting Patronage Shakespeare wrote at a time when patronage, or support of the arts by wealthy individuals, was imperative; without it, there would have been no money to build theaters or to stage performances. In order to court that patronage, a playwright often found it necessary to flatter the patron in some way or, at least, to avoid offending the patron with material that could be found tactless or tasteless. As a result, many of Shakespeare's plays reflect what was the current "politically correct" thinking in order to ensure continued support of his theater company and career as a playwright.

When King James I succeeded to the throne of England in 1603 following the death of Queen Elizabeth I, he adopted Shakespeare's acting company, The Lord Chamberlain's Men, and renamed them The King's Men. It is quite likely that Shakespeare wrote *Macbeth* in 1605–1606 to please King James, his new patron.

DRAFTING

Finding a Good Story The story upon which *Macbeth* is based comes from Holinshed's *Chronicles of England, Scotland, and Ireland.* Shakespeare had used this book for other plot ideas, such as the story lines of *King Lear* and *Richard II.* The original Macbeth was a Scottish thane, or prince, named Mackbeth, who killed the reigning king, Duncane, in order to become king himself. Mackbeth was later killed by Duncane's son Malcolme Cammore.

Shakespeare loved a good story of murder and revenge; he had already used such plots in *Hamlet* and *Julius Caesar.* In writing the story of Macbeth, Shakespeare chose to present King James with a cautionary tale of two good kings (Duncan and Malcolm), and a wicked king (Macbeth). Shakespeare was, in effect, warning James to be cautious about those he chose to serve under him at court.

Adapting Information Shakespeare also found in the *Chronicles* mention of a man named Banquho, a friend of Mackbeth's, who "gathered the finances due to the king." He learned that Banquho's descendants did in fact come to rule Scotland many years later. Banquho had been with Mackbeth when he met the three witches—"women in strange and wild apparell"—who foretold Banquho's future, saying that his descendants would govern Scotland. Shakespeare used this information in the play, creating the plot line in which Macbeth and Banquo meet the three witches and in which Macbeth deems it necessary to kill Banquo to prevent his heirs from taking the throne.

To Please a King It is interesting to note that the return of Banquo's ghost at the banquet (Act III, scene iv) does not really advance the primary plot of the play. After all, it is not Banquo's descendants but Duncan's son Malcolm who will unseat Macbeth. The ghost of Duncan would perhaps have been a more appropriate warning presence. Some critics suggest that Shakespeare was keenly aware of the birthright and lineal descent of

King James I, which relied upon the Stuart succession of kings: James was the ninth Stuart king. Banquo, not Duncan or Malcolm, was the progenitor of the Stuart line and the ancestor of King James. In the scene in which a parade of eight kings passes before Macbeth and Banquo's ghost, and Banquo points to them as "his," Shakespeare was presenting King James's forebears. The importance of Banquo in the play, therefore, probably resulted from Shakespeare's desire to please his royal patron.

Political and Economic Realities Some have argued that by insinuating Banquo into the heart of *Macbeth* in this way, Shakespeare was flattering King James I at the expense of the sound structure of the play, which should have centered around Duncan's ghost. If the argument is true, this is a good example of how the political and economic realities of life influenced a writer's choice of subject matter and the way he chose to develop it.

REVISING AND EDITING

Comments From a Friendly Rival We know very little about Shakespeare's method of revising. However, Ben Jonson, a friendly rival of Shakespeare's, once complained that his fellow playwright did not revise enough: "I remember, the players have often mentioned it as an honour to Shakespeare, that in his writing (whatever he penned) he never blotted out [a] line. My answer hath been, would he had blotted a thousand." This tantalizing fragment evokes a picture of Shakespeare as a flawless writing machine. If the anecdote is true, however, it might also mean that Shakespeare did a lot of revising in his head.

PUBLISHING

The Playwrights' Dilemma By 1592, Shakespeare had made his mark as a playwright. However, none of his plays had yet come out in print. At the time, authors had little control over their work once it left their hands; they were not protected by copyright laws. Playwrights, of all writers, had least to say about what happened to their work. Their audience was the theatergoing public, not a reading public. When they sold a play to a theatrical company, it became the company's property. As long as the play was still being performed on stage, the theater company did everything it could to prevent the play from appearing in print, because once it was published, anyone could produce it on stage.

Belated Publishing For these reasons, only about half of Shakespeare's plays appeared in print during his lifetime. The first collection of his plays, known as the First Folio, appeared seven years after his death. It included better versions of plays that had been printed illegally, together with many plays that had never before appeared in print, including *Macbeth*. Surprising as it sounds, Shakespeare never read a book by Shakespeare!

THINKING ABOUT THE PROCESS

1. How was publishing in Shakespeare's time different from publishing today?
2. **Brainstorming** Create a plot summary for a play based on either a current or historical political event. What details of the event might be difficult to stage? How would you alter the events to make them more stageworthy?

The supernatural, intrigue, murder, madness—these and other elements in The Tragedy of Macbeth *have guaranteed audiences at its performances for almost four hundred years. While scholars may assure us it is an outstanding example of Elizabethan tragedy written in blank verse, Shakespeare's play about the quest for power in the Scottish Middle Ages is—first and foremost—vigorously entertaining.*

The vitality of a play is experienced primarily in the theater, where actors gain much of their inspiration from the presence of an audience. After the curtain falls, however, a play lives on as average theatergoers and professional critics alike assimilate and judge it. As early as the eighteenth century, drama criticism had begun to blossom as a literary genre. Of the works popular at the time, Shakespeare's plays received a lion's share of critical attention.

William Hazlitt (1778–1830), one of the most outspoken critics in the Romantic era, recorded his thoughts about Shakespeare and other dramatists in essay form. Initially unsuccessful as a writer, Hazlitt was surprised and delighted when, soon after taking a job as a reporter for a London newspaper in 1812, he developed a faithful readership. Five years later, he was able to publish his essays as a book, Characters of Shakespeare's Plays. *The following is an excerpt from the essay "Macbeth."*

from Macbeth

William Hazlitt

"The poet's eye in a fine
* frenzy rolling*
Doth glance from heaven to
* earth, from earth to heaven;*
And as imagination bodies forth
The forms of things
* unknown, the poet's pen*
Turns them to shape, and
* gives to airy nothing*
A local habitation and a name."[1]

---

1. "The poet's eye . . . name": From Shakespeare's *A Midsummer Night's Dream,* Act V, Scene i.

Macbeth and *Lear*, *Othello* and *Hamlet*, are usually reckoned Shakespeare's four principal tragedies. *Lear* stands first for the profound intensity of the passion; *Macbeth* for the wildness of the imagination and the rapidity of the action; *Othello* for the progressive interest and powerful alternations of feeling; *Hamlet* for the refined development of thought and sentiment. If the force of genius shown in each of these works is astonishing, their variety is not less so. They are like different creations of the same mind, not one of which has the slightest reference to the rest. This distinctness and originality is indeed the necessary consequence of truth and nature. Shakespeare's genius alone appeared to possess the resources of nature. He is "your only *tragedy maker*." His plays have the force of things upon the mind. What he represents is brought home to the bosom as a part of our experience, implanted in the memory as if we had known the places, persons, and things of which he treats. *Macbeth* is like a record of a preternatural and tragical event. It has the rugged severity of an old chronicle with all that the imagination of the poet can engraft upon traditional belief. The castle of Macbeth, round which "the air smells wooingly," and where "the temple-haunting martlet builds," has a real subsistence in the mind; the Weird Sisters meet us in person on "the blasted heath"; the "air-drawn dagger" moves slowly before our eyes; the "gracious Duncan," the "blood-boltered Banquo" stand before us; all that passed through the mind of Macbeth passes, without the loss of a tittle,[2] through ours. All that could actually take place, and all that is only possible to be conceived, what was said and what was done, the workings of passion, the spells of magic, are brought before us with the same absolute truth and vividness.

Shakespeare excelled in the openings of his plays: that of *Macbeth* is the most striking of any. The wildness of the scenery, the sudden shifting of the situations and characters, the bustle, the expectations excited, are equally extraordinary. From the first entrance of the Witches and the description of them when they meet Macbeth:

> *What are these*
> *So wither'd and so wild*
> *in their attire,*
> *That look not like the*

---

2. **tittle** *n.:* A very small particle.

> *inhabitants of th' earth*
> *And yet are on't?*

the mind is prepared for all that follows.

This tragedy is alike distinguished for the lofty imagination it displays, and for the tumultuous vehemence of the action; and the one is made the moving principle of the other. The overwhelming pressure of preternatural agency urges on the tide of human passion with redoubled force. Macbeth himself appears driven along by the violence of his fate like a vessel drifting before a storm: he reels to and fro like a drunken man; he staggers under the weight of his own purposes and the suggestions of others; he stands at bay with his situation; and from the superstitious awe and breathless suspense into which the communications of the Weird Sisters throw him is hurried on with daring impatience to verify their predictions, and with impious and bloody hand to tear aside the veil which hides the uncertainty of the future. He is not equal to the struggle with fate and conscience. He now "bends up each corporal instrument to the terrible feat"; at other times his heart misgives him, and he is cowed and abashed by his success. "The deed, no less than the attempt, confounds him." His mind is assailed by the stings of remorse, and full of "preternatural solicitings." His speeches and soliloquies are dark riddles on human life, baffling solution, and entangling him in their labyrinths. In thought he is absent and perplexed, sudden and desperate in act, from a distrust of his own resolution. His energy springs from the anxiety and agitation of his mind. His blindly rushing forward on the objects of his ambition and revenge, or his recoiling from them, equally betrays the harassed state of his feelings. This part of his character is admirably set off by being brought in connection with that of Lady Macbeth, whose obdurate strength of will and masculine firmness give her the ascendancy over her husband's faltering virtue. She at once seizes on the opportunity that offers for the accomplishment of all their wished-for greatness, and never flinches from her object till all is over. The magnitude of her resolution almost covers the magnitude of her guilt. She is a great bad woman, whom we hate, but whom we fear more than we hate. She does not excite our loathing and abhorrence like Regan and Goneril.[3] She is only wicked to gain a great end and is perhaps more distinguished by her commanding presence of mind and inexorable self-will, which do not suffer her to be diverted from a bad purpose, when once formed, by weak and womanly regrets, than by the hardness of her heart or want of natural affections. The impression which her lofty determination of character makes on the mind of Macbeth is well described where he exclaims:

> Bring forth men children only;
> For thy undaunted mettle should
>   compose
> Nothing but males!

Nor do the pains she is at to "screw his courage to the sticking-place," the reproach to him, not to be "lost so poorly in himself," the assurance that "a little water clears them of this deed," show anything but her greater consistency in depravity. Her strong-nerved ambition furnishes ribs of steel to "the sides of his intent"; and she is herself wound up to the execution of her baneful project with the same unshrinking fortitude in crime, that in other circumstances she would probably have shown patience in suffering. The deliberate sacrifice of all other considerations to the gaining "for their future days and nights sole sovereign sway

and masterdom," by the murder of Duncan, is gorgeously expressed in her invocation on hearing of "his fatal entrance under her battlements":

>   Come all you spirits
> That tend on mortal
>   thoughts, unsex me here:
> And fill me, from the
>   crown to th' toe, top-full
> Of direst cruelty; make
>   thick my blood,
> Stop up the access and
>   passage to remorse,
> That no compunctious
>   visitings of nature
> Shake my fell purpose,
>   nor keep peace between
> The effect and it. Come to
>   my woman's breasts,
> And take my milk for gall,
>   you murthering ministers,
> Wherever in your
>   sightless substances
> You wait on nature's
>   mischief. Come, thick
>   night!
> And pall thee in the
>   dunnest smoke of hell,
> That my keen knife see
>   not the wound it makes,
> Nor heav'n peep through
>   the blanket of the dark,
> To cry, hold, hold!

When she first hears that "Duncan comes there to sleep" she is so overcome by the news, which is beyond her utmost expectations, that she answers the messenger, "Thou 'rt mad to say it"; and on receiving her husband's account of the predictions of the Witches, conscious of his instability of purpose, and that her presence is necessary to goad him on to the consummation of his promised greatness, she exclaims:

---

3. Regan and Goneril: King Lear's evil daughters in Shakespeare's *King Lear.*

Hie thee hither,
That I may pour my
  spirits in thine ear,
And chastise with the
  valor of my tongue
All that impedes thee
  from the golden round,
Which fate and
  metaphysical aid doth seem
To have thee crowned withal.

This swelling exultation and keen spirit of triumph, this uncontrollable eagerness of anticipation, which seems to dilate her form and take possession of all her faculties, this solid, substantial flesh and blood display of passion, exhibit a striking contrast to the cold, abstracted, gratuitous, servile malignity of the Witches, who are equally instrumental in urging Macbeth to his fate for the mere love of mischief, and from a disinterested delight in deformity and cruelty. They are hags of mischief, obscene panders to iniquity, malicious from their impotence of enjoyment, enamored of destruction, because they are themselves unreal, abortive, half-existences, who become sublime from their exemption from all human sympathies and contempt for all human affairs, as Lady Macbeth does by the force of passion! Her fault seems to have been an excess of that strong principle of self-interest and family aggrandizement, not amenable to the common feelings of compassion and justice, which is so marked a feature in barbarous nations and times. A passing reflection of this kind, on the resemblance of the sleeping king to her father, alone prevents her from slaying Duncan with her own hand. . . .

Macbeth (generally speaking) is done upon a stronger and more systematic principle of contrast than any other of Shakespeare's plays. It moves upon the verge of an abyss, and is a constant struggle between life and death. The action is desperate and the reaction is dreadful. It is a huddling together of fierce extremes, a war of opposite natures which of them shall destroy the other. There is nothing but what has a violent end or violent beginnings. The lights and shades are laid on with a determined hand; the transitions from triumph to despair, from the height of terror to the repose of death, are sudden and startling; every passion brings in its fellow-contrary, and the thoughts pitch and jostle against each other as in the dark. The whole play is an unruly chaos of strange and forbidden things, where the ground rocks under our feet. Shakespeare's genius here took its full swing, and trod upon the farthest bounds of nature and passion.

LEARNING OPTION

Writing. Think about the books you have recently read and the plays or films you have recently seen. Choose one that you would feel confident reviewing for your friends. As you organize your thoughts, ask yourself the following: Do I feel strongly enough about the work to write an interesting review? Who will read this review? What facts will they need to know about the book, play, or film? What opinions do I have about its execution? What details can I use to support my opinions? Take notes while you are gathering your ideas. Then write the review, making sure it presents a clear expression of your opinions. Ask a classmate to read your draft and, when you revise, incorporate his or her comments.

The King James Bible

1611

King James I, son of Mary Queen of Scots, ascended the English throne upon the death of Queen Elizabeth I. One of the first demands the new king faced was that of the Puritans for a uniform English version of the Bible. At the Hampton Court Conference in 1604, James accepted their demand. He commissioned fifty-four English scholars and clergymen to compare all extant texts of the Bible and to produce a definitive English edition. They succeeded perhaps beyond their expectations. The King James Version of the Holy Bible, published in 1611, has been called "the only classic ever created by a committee." From its earliest appearance until the present day it has been regarded as one of the great works of English literature.

The Bible, a collection of books developed over a period of more than twelve hundred years, consists of two main parts, the Old Testament and the New Testament. The Old Testament was originally written in Hebrew, the New Testament in Greek. In A.D. 382, St. Jerome began to translate the Bible into Latin, and his translation, called the Vulgate Version, remained the standard Bible in the West for centuries. An English reformer, John Wyclif, along with his followers, produced the first English translation from Latin in the late 1300's.

It was the Reformation in the 1500's, however—and the growing use of Gutenberg's movable type—that increased the demand for a Bible in the vernacular, or common language of the people. William Tyndale, a Protestant chaplain and tutor, decided to prepare a new English translation from Hebrew and Greek. Faced with clerical opposition at home, he went to Germany, where he translated and printed the New Testament in English. Arrested for heresy while at work on the Old Testament, Tyndale was executed near Brussels, Belgium, in 1536. The importance of Tyndale's New Testament is that the King James committee, impressed by its diction and rhythm, followed it more closely than any other translation in working on their 1611 masterpiece.

Other Bibles preceded the King James Version. None had the immense impact of the King James or Authorized Version, which in fact was never officially "authorized." It won its acceptance through use. Generations of people in Great Britain and the United States grew up reading its text and adding its wisdom to the common store of knowledge. Hundreds of expressions—"swords into plowshares," "fat of the land," "out of the mouths of babes"—are familiar to nearly every English-speaking person, while the magnificent rhythms of the Bible have influenced English prose and poetry throughout its history.

GUIDE FOR INTERPRETING

Psalm 23; The Parable of the Prodigal Son; I Corinthians 13

Literary Forms

Psalm and Parable. The Bible, particularly the Old Testament, contains a wide variety of literary forms in both prose and poetry. Many of them are already familiar to you, but two may not be. A psalm is a song or lyric poem in praise of God. Psalms were originally meant to be sung to the accompaniment of a stringed instrument. Today the word *psalm* generally refers to one of the 150 poetic pieces in the Old Testament Book of Psalms. Although the Hebrew authors of the psalms are mostly unknown, King David is often credited with having composed a few of them. The subject matter of the psalms varies widely. Some are hymns for public worship; others tell of historical events; still others portray everyday life in the Holy Land.

A parable is a short, simple story, usually about a common kind of occurrence, from which a moral or religious lesson can be drawn. Some parables, such as that of the unproductive vineyard, appear in the Old Testament. In the New Testament, Jesus often answers a question by telling a brief story based on an experience familiar to his listeners. Among the best known New Testament parables are those of the good Samaritan, the mustard seed, and the prodigal son.

Commentary

The King James Bible was published the same year that Shakespeare began his last play, *The Tempest*. While both works are masterpieces of the English language, there is one significant difference between them—words. Shakespeare used a stunning range of words in *The Tempest* (as well as in his other works). The authors of the King James Bible, in contrast, used but 8,000 different words to convey their message. Noting this contrast moved one critic to remark that "from that day to this, the Shakespearean cornucopia and the biblical iron rations represent, as it were, the North and South poles of the language, reference points for writers and speakers throughout the world, from the Shakespearean splendor of a Joyce or Dickens to the biblical rigor of a Bunyan or Hemingway."

Focus

Think of an incident that would make a good parable. It should be an everyday occurrence whose outcome conveys a moral lesson. Jot down some notes about what happened. Indicate why you think the incident you have chosen fits the requirements for a parable.

Psalm 23

The Lord is my shepherd; I shall not want.

He maketh me to lie down in green pastures: he leadeth me
    beside the still waters.

He restoreth my soul: he leadeth me in the paths of
    righteousness for his name's sake.

Yea, though I walk through the valley of the shadow of
    death, I will fear no evil: for thou art with me; thy rod and
    thy staff they comfort me.

5   Thou preparest a table before me in the presence of mine
    enemies; thou anointest my head with oil; my cup
    runneth over.

Surely goodness and mercy shall follow me all the days of
    my life: and I will dwell in the house of the Lord forever.

■R ESPONDING TO THE SELECTION

Your Response

1. Do you think the image of a shepherd is effective in this psalm? Why or why not?

Recalling

2. In the first part of the psalm, what images convey the idea of the Lord as a shepherd?
3. At what point does the psalmist change from speaking of the Lord as a shepherd to viewing Him as a host preparing a feast?

Interpreting

4. Why would the Lord's (shepherd's) rod and staff comfort the psalmist (sheep)?
5. Why is it significant that the table is prepared "in the presence of mine enemies"?

Applying

6. Two years before the King James Bible appeared, the Douay Version, an English translation from Latin, was published in France. Following are the last three lines of Psalm 23 in the Douay Bible. What stylistic features of the King James Version distinguish it from the Douay Version?

Thou hast fatted my head with oil,
    and my chalice inebriating how
    goodly is it!
And thy mercy shall follow me
    all the days of my life
And that I may dwell in the house
    of the Lord in longitude of days.

■A NALYZING LITERATURE

Recognizing a Psalm

A **psalm** is a sacred song or lyric poem. The psalms in the Book of Psalms, originally in Hebrew, were meant to be sung to the accompaniment of a stringed instrument. Since none of the Bible translations really advanced that purpose, the paraphrasing of psalms into metrical verse began during the Reformation. This rephrasing, which permitted the psalms to be sung by congregations, emphasized the lyrical nature of the original compositions.

What qualities of Psalm 23 make it especially lyrical?

Luke 15:11-32

The Parable of the Prodigal Son

A certain man had two sons. And the younger of them said to his father, "Father, give me the portion of goods that falleth to me." And he divided unto them his living.

And not many days after the younger son gathered all together, and took his journey into a far country, and there wasted his substance with riotous living. And when he had spent all, there arose a mighty famine in that land; and he began to be in want. And he went and joined himself to a citizen of that country; and he sent him into his fields to feed swine. And he would fain[1] have filled his belly with the husks that the swine did eat and no man gave unto him.

And when he came to himself, he said, "How many hired servants of my father's have bread enough and to spare, and I perish with hunger! I will arise and go to my father, and will say unto him, "Father, I have sinned against heaven, and before thee, and am no more worthy to be called thy son. Make me as one of thy hired servants.""

And he arose, and came to his father. But when he was yet a great way off, his father saw him, and had compassion and ran, and fell on his neck, and kissed him. And the son said unto him, "Father, I have sinned against heaven, and in thy sight, and am no more worthy to be called thy son."

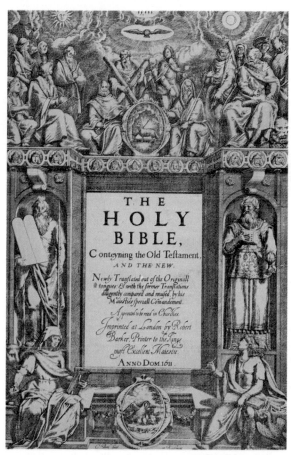

KING JAMES BIBLE, 1611
Title page of the New Testament
The Folger Shakespeare Library

---

1. fain *adv.*: Gladly.

But the father said to his servants, "Bring forth the best robe, and put it on him; and put a ring on his hand, and shoes on his feet; and bring hither the fatted calf, and kill it; and let us eat, and be merry: for this my son was dead, and is alive again; he was lost, and is found." And they began to be merry.

Now his elder son was in the field; and as he came and drew nigh to the house, he heard music and dancing. And he called one of the servants, and asked what these things meant. And he said unto him, "Thy brother is come; and thy father hath killed the fatted calf, because he hath received him safe and sound."

And he was angry, and would not go in: therefore came his father out, and entreated him. And he answering said to his father, "Lo, these many years do I serve thee, neither transgressed I at any time thy commandment; and yet thou never gavest me a kid, that I might make merry with my friends; but as soon as this thy son was come, which hath devoured thy living, thou hast killed for him the fatted calf."

And he said unto him, "Son, thou art ever with me, and all that I have is thine. It was meet[2] that we should make merry, and be glad: for this thy brother was dead, and is alive again; and was lost, and is found."

---

2. **meet** *adj.*: Fitting.

■R ESPONDING TO THE SELECTION

Your Response
1. What would you have done if you were the father in this parable? Explain.

Recalling
2. What happens to the younger son's money?
3. (a) Why does the younger son decide to return home? (b) What does he intend to say to his father?
4. How does the father react to the return of his younger son?
5. (a) Why is the older son angry? (b) How does his father answer the complaint?

Interpreting
6. From the limited evidence given in the parable, how repentant do you think the younger son is?
7. Why is the father happy rather than unhappy at the sight of his younger son?

8. To what extent do you think the older son is justified in being angry at the treatment given his brother?

Applying
9. A parable is meant to teach a moral or spiritual lesson. What lesson do you draw from this one?
10. Sometimes this parable is called "The Parable of the *Lost* Son." How might that title affect your reaction to it?

■L EARNING OPTIONS

1. **Writing.** This parable is narrated in the third person. Write a first-person version of the parable, telling the story from the point of view of one of the three main characters.
2. **Art.** Draw or paint a scene of your choice from the parable. Try to express the emotions of the characters in your rendering.

I Corinthians 13

Though I speak with the tongues of men and of angels, and have not charity, I am become as sounding brass, or a tinkling cymbal. And though I have the gift of prophecy, and understand all mysteries, and all knowledge; and though I have all faith, so that I could remove mountains, and have not charity, I am nothing. And though I bestow all my goods to feed the poor, and though I give my body to be burned, and have not charity, it profiteth me nothing. Charity suffereth long, and is kind; charity envieth not; charity vaunteth not itself, is not puffed up, doth not behave itself unseemly, seeketh not her own, is not easily provoked, thinketh no evil; rejoiceth not in iniquity, but rejoiceth in the truth; beareth all things, believeth all things, hopeth all things, endureth all things. Charity never faileth: but whether there be prophecies, they shall fail; whether there be tongues, they shall cease; whether there be knowledge, it shall vanish away. For we know in part, and we prophesy in part. But when that which is perfect is come, then that which is in part shall be done away. When I was a child, I spake as a child, I understood as a child, I thought as a child: but when I became a man, I put away childish things. For now we see through a glass darkly; but then face to face: now I know in part; but then shall I know even as also I am known. And now abideth faith, hope, charity, these three; but the greatest of these is charity.

RESPONDING TO THE SELECTION

Your Response

1. How does Paul's definition of charity, or love, compare with your own?

Recalling

2. In each of the first three sentences, the apostle Paul mentions some impressive personal achievements. (a) What are they? (b) In each case, if he lacks charity, what is the result?

3. The sentence beginning "Charity suffereth long" describes the nature of charity. (a) What does charity do? (b) What does it not do?

Interpreting

4. This passage is a letter to the Corinthians. In it Paul advises them to prepare for the coming perfect times with God. What analogy does he use to make his point clear?

5. Knowing what Paul means by "charity" is vital to an understanding of the passage. He does *not* mean "human kindness" or "doing good." What does the word *charity* mean, as Paul uses it? Context clues can help, but you may also need to consult a dictionary.

6. (a) Find two uses of parallelism. (b) Does the use of parallelism make the writing more effective or less effective? Explain.

Applying

7. The apostle Paul is giving advice to the Corinthians on how to live a spiritual life. How, if at all, do you think it would be possible to know whether or not a person is following Paul's advice concerning charity?

THE CHANGING ENGLISH LANGUAGE

Shakespearean English 1485–1625

A BLOODLESS INVASION

After the Normans invaded England in 1066, there were no more major assaults by foreign armies, but there did come another kind of invasion—the onslaught of European culture.

Throughout the reign of the Tudors, England quarreled with her neighbors on the continent. Henry VIII severed allegiance with Rome. His daughter Elizabeth constantly sparred with the superpowers of the day, France and Spain. Through these skirmishes came the increasing interchange of words. Sailors returning from France brought cargo in the holds and *bigot* and *detail* on their lips. From Italy came *cupola* and *stucco;* the Dutch countries contributed *smuggle* and *reef.* Spenser's poetry even contains slang from the sailors who defeated the Armada!

WHAT SHALL WE CALL IT?

When they weren't off negotiating, exploring, or trading, the English were inventing and discovering wondrous new things, which all had to be named. From physics came *paradox* and *chronology;* from biology, *skeleton.* Through Vesalius's work with anatomy, we learned how *strenuous* activity could be. Soon people needed an *encyclopedia* to learn about *gravity!*

LATIN AND GREEK ENTER THE MIX

The renewed focus on scholarship also helped the English language to grow. This interest in learning sparked a new class of scholars who were concerned with the refinement of writing style. Such writers as Thomas More and Francis Bacon rebelled against what they saw as the awkwardness of English. Bacon, for example, preferred to write in Latin, which was still the language of scholarship. English, he sneered, will "play the bankrupts with books." When forced to write in English, these men decorated their sentences with Latinate words they had gleaned from classical texts. From Latin they took *agile, capsule, habitual,* for instance; from Greek, *catastrophe, lexicon,* and *thermometer.*

A RETURN TO BASICS?

Not everyone was enthusiastic about the deluge of new words pouring into the language. Elizabeth's subjects felt as proud of their native tongue as they did of their land—and took both very seriously. Thomas Chaloner is often cited for his attack on writers who "serche . . . out of some rotten Pamphlet foure or fyve disused woords of antiquitee, therewith to darken the sence unto the reader." But others endorsed the importation of foreign terms: "Seeing that we borrow (and not shamefully) from the Dutch, the Breton, the Roman, the Dane, and French, Italian, and Spaniard, how can our stock be other than exceeding plentiful?" The battle between these two camps spilled over onto the stage. One of Ben Jonson's plays shows a poet cleansed of such borrowed Latin words as *retrograde* and *inflate.* Despite such protests, this mix of domestic and foreign words resulted in a language that one critic has called "of unsurpassed richness and beauty, which, however, defies all the rules."

AND NOW TO THOSE RULES . . .

This rich influx of foreign words into English did have its drawbacks, however—chief among them, the matter of consistent rules for the different parts of speech. During the Renaissance, almost any English word could be used as almost every part of speech. Adverbs could become verbs, for example, and nouns could become adjectives; nouns and adjectives could even take the place of verbs and adverbs. In Elizabethan English you could *happy* your friend, *malice* or *foot* your enemy, or *fall* an axe on his neck. Words could be spelled any number of different ways—even within the same sentence! Nouns didn't have to match their verbs. The order of words in a sentence was up for grabs as well: Objects could come before verbs and adjectives could come after nouns, for example. Despite the linguistic model of Latin, the order of the day was disorder. In general, people felt that it was more important for language to be strong and interesting than logical.

IT LOOKS FAMILIAR . . .

Since the language of the Renaissance was shaped to appeal to listeners, why does it seem hard to understand today? It is simply that language changes. As it grew during the Renaissance, so it has developed through the centuries, and many words used in the past have long been discarded, replaced by terms that describe our life now. Someone from the Renaissance who arrived in America today would be baffled by *television* and *computer,* as we are by their *chopine* (a high-heeled shoe) and *kecksey* (a

wild plant). Even more perilous are the words that look familiar—those we think we know but that mean something entirely different today. For example, when someone in a Shakespearean play remarks, "I love not the *humor* of it," he is talking about the general tone of a situation, not its amusing aspects.

But it is only through such change that language remains fascinating—even challenging—and always alive.

Letter from Patent granted by Elizabeth I to Francis Drake

YOUR WRITING PROCESS

WRITING A LEGAL ARGUMENT

Macbeth killed the king. There is no real argument there. However, was he a victim of circumstances beyond his control? Also, what about Lady Macbeth? Is she innocent because she didn't hold the knife, or is she as guilty as her husband? What would you tell a jury if you were prosecuting or defending one of these characters?

Focus

Assignment: Write a closing legal argument either for or against Macbeth or Lady Macbeth.
Purpose: To persuade a jury to condemn or be merciful to either defendant.
Audience: A jury of Elizabethan men and women.

Prewriting

1. Freewrite to choose. Do some freewriting about each character: Is she or he without doubt guilty, or were there extenuating circumstances? Test each theory to see which one elicits the strongest opinion and the most logical support. It may help to make a second choice, too, just in case you change your mind.

Student Model

Sure Macbeth killed Duncan, but just look at how he was pushed into it. The witches filled his head with notions of grandeur, and his wife criticized his lack of ambition. He believed so strongly that he should become king that it was like a kind of madness. It seemed that he lost his own will. Maybe that is the definition of madness.

2. Scan the play for evidence. Once you have chosen a position, scan the play scene by scene for evidence.
3. Write a thesis statement. Write one sentence that summarizes your argument; be sure it says more than "Macbeth is guilty." Show why or how you reached your conclusion. This statement will govern your entire speech. Of course, it can evolve and develop focus during the rest of your writing process.

4. Outline your argument. A formal speech such as this will profit by a fairly formal outline. Lead your audience, point by point, down a road to which your thesis statement is the only logical conclusion.

Drafting

1. Appeal to emotion and intellect. Juries vote with both their heads and their hearts; don't limit your persuasion to one or the other. Appeal to both logic and emotion.

> **Student Model**
>
> In her own words, Lady Macbeth looks like an innocent flower, but she is the serpent herself. Her speech is full of *s*'s; you can almost hear her hiss.

2. Remember your audience. You are appealing to a jury of Elizabethan men and women. Skim the introduction to this unit for information that might help you find ways to fire their interest. For example, which of their beliefs about royalty might be relevant to your argument?

3. Say it with style. How you say it can be as important as what you say. Say it with gusto or pizazz. Whisper, shout, question, or warn. Use description, narration, quotation, or explanation. Whatever method you choose, make sure it is appropriate, consistent, and emphatic.

Revising and Editing

1. Pair up with the opposition. Find a peer who has taken the opposite position about the same character. Read each other's drafts and offer suggestions. Try to address each other's arguments in your own speeches as you revise.

2. Avoid *and* and *so*. Look carefully at your conjunctions, especially *and* and *so,* the two most commonly used. As you revise, eliminate *ands* by specifying the relationships between ideas.

> **Student Model**
>
> Lady Macbeth practically confesses to the crime and when she says, "What's done cannot be undone!"

Writer's Hint

Linear sentences unfold in the natural subject-verb-object order. They are predictable. On the other hand, periodic sentences withhold their meanings until the end (or period) is reached. Using both will give your writing variety and zest.

Options for Publishing

• Find someone who has taken the opposing position. Read your arguments aloud to a jury of twelve classmates and have them reach a verdict.

• Collect all of the arguments written in class and share them with another class that is studying *Macbeth*. Ask them to choose their favorites.

Reviewing Your Writing Process

1. Which of the prewriting steps helped you the most in drafting your argument? Explain.

2. Did arguing the case for or against one of the characters give you a better appreciation of the play? Why or why not?

THE THAMES AT WESTMINSTER STAIRS
Claude de Jongh, c. 1631 or 1637
Yale Center for British Art, Paul Mellon Collection

THE SEVENTEENTH CENTURY

1625–1660

During the time men live without a common power to keep them all in awe, they are in that condition which is called war, and such a war as is of every man against every man. . . . In such condition there is no place for industry, because the fruit thereof is uncertain, and consequently no culture of the earth; no navigation, nor use of the commodities that may be imported by sea; no commodious building; . . . no arts; no letters; no society; and, which is worst of all, continual fear, and danger of violent death; and the life of man, solitary, poor, nasty, brutish, and short.

Thomas Hobbes

In the preceding passage, Thomas Hobbes pictures the terrible condition of people who lived before there were kings to bring order to society. Without rulers to keep people "in awe," Hobbes insisted, society would dissolve in chaos, and life would be "poor, nasty, brutish, and short." Hobbes claimed he was writing about a "state of nature" that existed before the dawn of history. But, in 1651, he had good reason to worry about the breakdown of society. The English had shocked the world by beheading their king in 1649 and abolishing the monarchy. Perhaps England had not quite reverted to the state of nature Hobbes imagined, but Hobbes, like many conservatives, believed that the violence would continue until the English again had "a common power to keep them all in awe."

It is difficult to believe that civil war followed so closely on the Golden Age of Elizabeth, with its triumphant defeat of the Spanish Armada and its brilliant literary achievements. Looking back, we see the English Renaissance as a time of unsurpassed accomplishments, but to people at the time, the age was one of frightening doubts as well as great expectations.

In science, philosophy, religion, and politics, long-held beliefs and ideas were discredited. The Ptolemaic worldview—according to which Earth is the center of a finite universe—was giving way to the Copernican theory of an infinite universe in which the Earth is merely one planet in one of countless solar systems, and not even at the center of its own solar system. William Gilbert's studies of magnetism and William Harvey's discovery of the circulation of the blood opened new realms to human imagination as well as to human understanding. Sir Francis Bacon's writings popularized a reliance on observation and experimentation, as opposed to ancient authority, in scientific and intellectual pursuits. And, later in the century, Sir Isaac Newton created the classical physics that remained unchallenged until our own century. The triumph of the modern scientific spirit in the seventeenth century is symbolized by the establishment of the Royal Society in 1662.

Moreover, religious and political grievances, masked by the brilliance of Elizabeth I, began to emerge in the reign of the first Stuart king, James I. During the reign of Charles I, they led to a full-scale civil war. The Civil War unleashed new forces in English society, challenging the most basic ideas of order, even the monarchy itself. It swept away the rigid structure of the old society, in which the court was the center of political power and literary activity. In its place grew a new, competitive society, with a looser social structure and greater freedom in religion and politics.

The Roots of Civil Conflict

The roots of the religious and political conflicts that underlay the Civil War stretched back many years. Under Elizabeth, the Anglican Church held to a middle course between Catholicism and Calvinism. Puritans still worshiped and held positions in the Anglican Church, even though they disagreed with some of the Church's practices. That situation started to change after James I became king in 1603. James made no secret of his hostility toward Calvinism. He used his power as head of the Anglican Church to dismiss Puritan clergymen.

Charles I

In 1625, Charles I inherited all the religious problems his father had faced—and made them worse. He was married to the sister of the king of France, a Catholic. That fact alone alarmed the people of England, most of whom were firmly Protestant.

Like his father, Charles had little love for Puritans. The king wholeheartedly supported Archbishop Laud, the reactionary leader of the anti-Puritans. Laud insisted that clergymen "conform," or observe all the church ceremonies, including those the Puritans disliked. In this way, Laud pulled the Anglican Church back toward Catholicism. Laud retreated so far from Protestantism, in fact, that the Pope offered to make him a Catholic bishop. Laud refused, but many Protestants still saw him as a Catholic in all but name.

PORTRAIT OF CHARLES I
Anthony Van Dyck
The Louvre, Paris

Money Troubles

Charles I was like his father in another way. He was determined, in the words of Charles Dickens, "to be a high and mighty king not to be called to account by anybody." This attitude put Charles on a collision course with Parliament, and the crash came quickly over a basic question: money.

Charles had instigated wars against Spain and France and needed money to fight both enemies. Under English law, the money had to be granted to him by Parliament. But Parliament supported neither venture, and the king had to turn elsewhere. From his wealthy subjects Charles extorted loans by threatening them with prison. Charles lost popularity with commoners by pressing the poor into service as soldiers and sailors.

The king's abuse of his power angered many subjects. When Parliament met in 1628, its members boldly stood up to the king by passing the Petition of Right. This document spelled out the basic rights of Englishmen—at the time women had no political rights. Charles unhappily accepted the Petition of Right in order to get approval for

The Seventeenth Century

(A.D. 1625 – A.D. 1660)

New Amsterdam

Sir Francis Bacon

Execution of Charles I

1625   **1635**   **1645**

BRITISH EVENTS

- Full-bottomed wigs come into fashion.
  - Sir Francis Bacon publishes *The New Atlantis.*
    - William Harvey explains blood circulation.
      - **John Donne's** *Poems* published.
      - **George Herbert's** *The Temple* published.
        - Covent Garden Market opens.

- Public mail service established.
  - Charles I summons Long Parliament.
  - **John Milton** publishes *Lycidas.*
    - **John Donne's** *Devotions Upon Emergent Occasions* published.
      - English Civil War begins.
      - Puritans close theaters.

- **John Suckling** publishes *Fragmenta Aurea.*
  - First newspaper ad appears.
    - George Fox founds Society of Friends (Quakers).
  - **Robert Herrick** publishes *Hesperides.*
    - Charles I beheaded.
    - **Richard Lovelace** publishes *Lucasta.*

WORLD EVENTS

- North America: Dutch found New Amsterdam.
  - France: Beginning of public advertising.
  - North America: William Bradford begins writing *Of Plymouth Plantation.*
  - Boston founded by John Winthrop.

- North America: Rhode Island founded by Roger Williams.
  - Japan: All Europeans expelled.
    - India: English settlement established at Madras.
      - North America: *Bay Psalm Book* published in Massachusetts.
      - Italy: First European cafe opens in Venice.
        - Holland: Rembrandt paints *Night Watch.*
          - China: Ming Dynasty ends.

- North America: Massachusetts establishes free public schools.

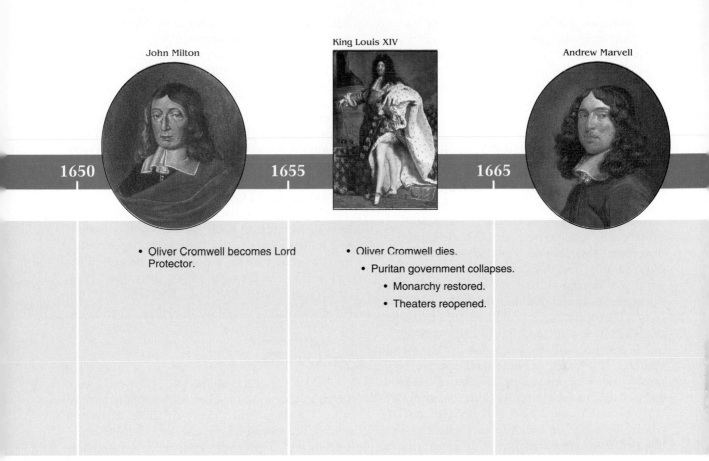

John Milton

King Louis XIV

Andrew Marvell

1650

1655

1665

- Oliver Cromwell becomes Lord Protector.

- Oliver Cromwell dies.
  - Puritan government collapses.
    - Monarchy restored.
    - Theaters reopened.

- North America: Anne Bradstreet's collection of poems *The Tenth Muse Lately Sprung Up in America* published.
  - North America: William Bradford finishes *Of Plymouth Plantation*.
    - France: Louis XIV becomes king.

- France: First stockings manufactured.
  - France: Molière publishes *The Flying Doctor*.
    - South Africa: First Dutch settlers arrive.

new revenues. He soon showed that he had no intention of abiding by it. When leaders of Parliament protested, Charles had them arrested and then dissolved Parliament. For the next eleven years, Charles ruled without so much as calling Parliament into session.

Conflict With the Puritans

Many English subjects were disgusted with Charles, but none more so than the Puritans. The king's ally, Archbishop Laud, had stepped up his persecution of these Calvinist "dissenters." In brutal public ceremonies, Puritan leaders had their noses slit, their cheeks branded, and their ears cropped off. The Puritans often displayed such faith and resolve during these mutilations that they won the hearts of onlookers. "The more I am beaten down, the more I am lifted up!" exclaimed one Puritan as a torturer finished his work.

It was no accident that Laud and the "High Church" Anglicans supported the king, while most Puritans opposed him. The Puritan religious outlook had implications for politics. Radical Puritans wanted to do away with bishops and the whole hierarchy of the Anglican Church. They believed that each congregation, or group of worshipers, had the right to choose its own minister. As you can see, this belief resembled democracy in politics.

Most Puritans were dead set against the idea of a king's "divine right" to rule, on which Charles I insisted. One Puritan put the matter plainly: "A King is a thing men have made for their own sakes." It was only a short step further to the idea that men could *un*make a king. James I had understood this danger and summed it up in the curt phrase, "No bishop, no king."

The Long Parliament

The policies of Charles and Archbishop Laud were unpopular enough in England. But when the king and the archbishop tried to force conformity on Scottish Calvinists, the Scots rose up in defiance. In 1639, King Charles had to lead an army north to put down the rebellion. With the war stalemated, Charles returned to London, once again desperate for funds.

Parliament, however, was in no mood to grant the king's request without guarantees in return. Among other things, Parliament demanded the trial of Laud and Thomas Wentworth, the hated leader of the king's army. Both were tried and later executed. The legislators also insisted on reforms to limit the power of the king. As the session went on in the stormy atmosphere of London, one demand led to another. At last, in 1642, Parliament condemned Charles as a tyrant.

Charles struck back by sending armed men into Parliament to seize the opposition leaders. The leaders escaped, and Parliament began raising its own army. Charles fled north, rallying loyalists to his side. For the next eleven years, the "Long Parliament" ruled England. The Civil War had begun.

The Civil War

When war came, the people of England were forced to choose sides. The king's supporters were called Cavaliers, since many of these aristocrats were skilled horsemen, or cavalry. They generally lived in the countryside. Parliament drew its followers from London and the towns, where Puritanism ran strong. Because these austere Calvinists cut their hair short, they were known as Roundheads.

The same grit Puritans had shown under the torturer's hand made them fierce enemies. The dour Puritan leader Oliver Cromwell took charge of Parliament's forces. He drilled them into an unparalleled fighting machine called the New Model Army. At the Battle of Marston Moor, the New Model Army showed the power of its training. The next year, in 1645, Cromwell's troops defeated a Cavalier army and captured Charles I.

Meanwhile, a battle of another kind was going on in Parliament. There, members of the different Protestant factions were struggling for power. Gradually, the most radical Puritans won out. In 1648, they shut the doors on moderate members. Then the radicals brought Charles I to trial. With no moderates to oppose them, the radical Puri-

EXECUTION OF CHARLES I AT WHITEHALL, LONDON, JANUARY 30, 1649
Colored woodcut from contemporary ballad-sheet

tans found the king guilty of treason. Charles I was beheaded on January 30, 1649. Parliament, or the few members who remained, declared that the monarchy was over and that England was a republic.

From Commonwealth to Protectorate

The monarchy was gone, but what would replace it? Oliver Cromwell became leader of the new English Commonwealth, as the new government was called. Cromwell, ruling with the radicals left in Parliament, faced the hopeless task of uniting a nation divided not into two but numerous factions. Many subjects had turned against

Parliament after the execution of Charles I. A popular poem of the time lamented:

> On Tuesday last his Grace,
> Cheerfully, cheerfully,
> Went to his dying place,
>   to end all strife,
> Where many a weeping eye,
> With groans unto the skie,
> To see his Majesty,
> There end his life.

Discontent among the English people was fueled by the severe policies of the Puritans. They outlawed gambling, horse racing, newspapers, fancy clothes, public dancing, and theater. Cromwell faced perils from outside England, too. In Scotland, rebels rallied to Charles II, son of the executed king. In Ireland, Catholics had risen against Protestant landowners. Cromwell himself led the force that savagely repressed that rebellion. In addition, England was at war against Spain and Holland.

These disorders forced Cromwell to give up even the pretense of republican government. In 1653, he dissolved Parliament and named himself Lord Protector. He ruled as a virtual dictator until his death in 1658, when his son became Lord Protector. By then the English people were thoroughly sick of the endless taxations, violence, and disorder. Parliament reconvened and asked Charles II to become king. In 1660, the monarchy was restored. Though Cromwell inspired as much

fear and hatred as love and reverence, he always remained true to his own high moral purposes. The measures he resorted to as ruler of England were stern and painful, yet they were probably necessary to achieve order in such a troubled, disorderly period of English history.

Literature of a Turbulent Age

The reign of Charles I and the Interregnum, or period between reigns, that followed were a time of intense religious and political conflict. Under Charles I, the court remained the center of literary life. Poets upheld the traditional courtly values of loyalty to crown and church and the strict code of honor. Not surprisingly, the poets often fought on the side of the king.

The literature of the turbulent years from 1625 to 1660 in part continues the styles of the Renaissance and in part reflects changing conditions. Although Ben Jonson and others wrote plays that were more popular than Shakespeare's, the period is not remembered for its drama. Rather, it is an age that produced some of the best-loved poems in English—Jonson's crystalline lyrics and dignified longer poems modeled after classical precedents; John Donne's brilliant, intellectually ingenious amorous and religious verses; and Andrew Marvell's lyrics combining the classical polish of Jonson and the intellectual brilliance of Donne. Appropriate to a society cleft by civil war, the literature of the age had another side. The Puritan writers John Milton and John Bunyan produced deeply religious works very much different in style and substance from those of Jonson, Donne, and their followers.

CONTEMPORARY PORTRAIT OF OLIVER CROMWELL
Unknown Artist

Jonson's Life

The most influential writer of the early 1600's was Ben Jonson. Jonson's life is a mirror of the tensions of his time. Jonson rose from humble origins—his stepfather was a bricklayer. The family lived near Westminster Abbey, however, and Jonson was lucky enough to attend its school. There he read the Greek and Latin authors that shaped so much of his own later writing. Although he hoped to attend college, the young Jonson found himself laying bricks. But he refused to give up his ambitions. One friend described him as having "a trowel in his hand . . . and a book in his pocket."

Jonson set down his trowel to become a soldier, and later turned up as an actor in London. One of his earliest works, a satirical play, was condemned as slanderous and landed Jonson in jail. A later play was well received, but Jonson had little chance to bask in the praise. He argued with an actor, killed him in a duel, and was once again imprisoned. There Jonson converted to Catholicism, though he later returned to the Anglican Church—another sign of the changeable times he lived in.

Ultimately, Jonson became a great favorite of James I and was friendly with many noblemen and with other writers—including Shakespeare, who acted in one of Jonson's earliest plays and is the subject of one of his finest poems. By the 1620's, Jonson was the best-known poet in a city of poets. As one admirer said, Jonson was the "fairest light in no darke time."

The Schools of Jonson and Donne

Jonson's Work

In Jonson's life we can see the turmoil of his age—violence, persecution, religious conflict. But in his writing Jonson strove for the perfection and harmony he found in his beloved classical authors, turning away from the ornate style of Elizabethan times. Although Jonson was steeped in, and greatly influenced by, the classics, he was not an imitator. He created his own voice, which people of the time recognized as distinctively modern and strong.

Jonson took seriously the role of poet. He believed, in fact, that no other profession could compare to it. Poets, he wrote, encourage "young men to all good disciplines, inflame grown men to all great virtues, [and] keep old men in their best

and supreme state." A person could not be "the good poet without first being a good man," he asserted. Jonson lived up to this moral duty in several ways: by giving good advice in some poems; by honoring worthy men and women in others; and, in his plays, by satirizing corruption and immorality.

John Donne

The other great poet of the early 1600's was John Donne (1572?–1631). Whereas Jonson did all he could to raise the prestige of poets, and personally oversaw the printing of his poems, Donne never tried to make writing a career. His

BEN JONSON

poems, in fact, were not published until two years after his death. But manuscripts of his work circulated at court, and his witty, cerebral poems created a widely admired style in English literature: metaphysical poetry.

Donne's life, like Jonson's, reflected the turbulent age. Donne was raised a Roman Catholic. After studying at Oxford, he traveled abroad, fighting against the Spanish in the 1590's. As a young man, Donne took an active part in the life of the court and composed many fine love poems. (According to Ben Jonson, Donne wrote "all his best pieces ere he was twenty-five.") Later, Donne turned to the Protestant faith. In 1615, he was ordained as an Anglican minister. His sermons in St. Paul's Cathedral, which often lasted for hours, held hundreds of listeners at rapt attention. They are among the finest prose works of the century. After the death of his wife, Donne withdrew from society. In contrast to the fervent love poems of his youth, Donne's later poetry expresses intense religious feeling, often penitential in character. Given Donne's evolution from courtier to minister, it is not surprising that his poetry often embodies the conflict between the spirit and the world.

More than any other poet, Donne is associated with the metaphysical school of poetry. Metaphysical poetry is characterized by an unusual degree of intellectualism. Even in his love poems, Donne will base his images and figures of speech on material drawn from law, medieval theology and philosophy, natural science, metallurgy, medicine, astronomy, old legends, and other sources that more conventional poets seldom made use of. Moreover, Donne's poems are frequently structured like ingenious, subtle arguments involving complicated—and often witty—reasoning. Finally, they often employ a type of metaphor termed a *conceit*. A conceit is a comparison in which the subject is likened to something that would never normally be associated with it. In Donne's most famous conceit, for example, he likens his and his beloved's souls to the legs of a geometrician's compass:

> If they be two, they are two so
> As stiff twin compasses are two;

> Thy soul, the fixed foot, makes no show
> To move, but doth if the other do.
> And though it in the center sit,
>   Yet, when the other far doth roam,
> It leans and hearkens after it,
>   And grows erect as that comes home.

The Sons of Ben

Jonson and Donne were the dominant poets of their age. Later poets of the seventeenth century are usually classified as being disciples of either Jonson or Donne. Like all such categorizations, these are only partly correct. The "Sons of Ben"

JOHN DONNE

were also influenced by Donne's work, and the "School of Donne" did read and admire Ben Jonson. The basic distinction is useful nonetheless.

Among the best-known Sons of Ben were Robert Herrick, Sir John Suckling, and Richard Lovelace. These Sons of Ben are also called Cavalier poets, since they are identified with the king's cause. Robert Herrick (1591–1674) was probably closest to Jonson in style and temperament. Although he lived through the Civil War and Interregnum, Herrick's poetry gives little evidence of these worldly disturbances. He concentrated instead on things that could not be touched by war: "I sing of Brooks, of Blossomes, Birds, and Bowers;/Of April, May, of June and July-Flowers." Herrick, who became an Anglican minister, also wrote graceful religious poems.

Sir John Suckling (1609–1642), an admirer of Jonson's style but not of his moral severity, was also influenced by Donne's early love poems. Suckling, the perfect courtier, was everything the Puritans despised. A gambler, cardsharp, and pleasure seeker, he is remembered today for his love poems. In 1639, Suckling marched north with Charles I to put down the Scottish rebellion. He fled England two years later after becoming involved in a political intrigue and died in France at a young age.

Richard Lovelace (1618–1657) was, like Suckling, a luminary of Charles I's court. A strikingly handsome man, Lovelace wrote about themes near the heart of the Cavaliers: honor, bravery, true love, and stoical resolve. Lovelace also fought for the king's cause and went to prison for it. It was there that he wrote many of his finest poems.

The School of Donne

The most notable followers of John Donne were George Herbert (1593–1633) and Andrew Marvell (1621–1678). Herbert's mother was a friend of Donne's, and in many ways the life of Herbert parallels Donne's. He keenly felt the tension between religious and worldly drives. At first intending to enter the Church, Herbert was tempted for a time to enjoy the sparkling life at the court of James I. Later Herbert became an Anglican deacon and gave himself to the care of his parish. Like Donne, Herbert excelled at the conceit and the other stylistic features of metaphysical poetry. However, Herbert's best poems are almost all religious lyrics. When read together, in his volume *The Temple,* they reveal a greater range of religious feelings than are found in Donne's religious verse.

Andrew Marvell was born later than the other metaphysical and Cavalier poets and is in many ways a figure of transition. Marvell was still a young man when the Civil War began and had little connection with the court. In fact, for three years Marvell tutored the daughter of a Puritan leader. Later Marvell became a colleague of John

GEORGE HERBERT

Milton, the greatest of the Puritan poets. When the monarchy was restored in 1660, Marvell used his influence at court to prevent Milton's execution for treason.

Marvell's best lyrics blend the metaphysical brilliance of Donne and Herbert and the classical finish of Jonson and Herrick. They offer observations on nature, love, and God that, at first, seem urbane and conventional but, on closer inspection, prove profound and problematical. His best-known poem, "To His Coy Mistress," is one of the very best lyrics in English literature.

The Puritan Writers

So far we have been looking at poets connected with the court of the Stuarts. But perhaps the greatest poet of the seventeenth century was a Puritan, not a Cavalier: John Milton. The Puritan movement also produced the best-selling prose writer of the century, John Bunyan. Only the Bible sold more copies than Bunyan's religious narrative *The Pilgrim's Progress.*

John Milton

In John Milton (1608–1674), the streams of the Renaissance and the Reformation flow together. Like Ben Jonson, he was a learned disciple of the Greek and Latin authors. But unlike Elizabethan humanists and the Cavalier poets, Milton was a profound Calvinist who studied the Old Testament in Hebrew.

Milton was born in London to a prosperous middle-class family. He got a good basic education, studied at Cambridge, and spent six years after college reading and studying on his own. In the 1640's, Milton was working as a private tutor in London. As the battle between Charles I and Parliament grew hotter, Milton began writing political pamphlets for the Roundhead cause. His part in the "pamphlet wars" produced *Areopagitica,* a ringing call for freedom of the press.

Milton supported the Commonwealth and Protectorate and even defended the execution of Charles I. As Cromwell's rule turned to a dictatorship, however, Milton lost hope in the possibility of forming a just society on Earth. Milton, who went completely blind by 1652, set about composing an epic that would offer a poetic explanation as to why God allows suffering and unhappiness in this world.

Paradise Lost, published in 1667, reflects Milton's humanistic love of poetry and his Puritan devotion to God. In Book I of *Paradise Lost,* Milton voices his poetic ambition: to create "things unattempted yet in Prose or Rhyme." A few lines later he asserts his religious aim: to "justify the ways of God to men." The poem is both a heroic epic that recounts the expulsion of Adam and Eve from Eden and a vindication of God's wisdom.

John Bunyan

After decades of political activity, Milton concluded that the best humans could hope for was to lead their individual lives blamelessly. That was the premise that John Bunyan began with. Unlike Milton, Bunyan had little education beyond reading the Bible, but what his reading and studies lacked in variety they made up for in profundity. A tinker by trade, Bunyan wandered from town to town in rural England, preaching wherever people would listen. After the restoration of Charles II, Bunyan was imprisoned, and it was there he wrote *The Pilgrim's Progress.*

The simplicity of the work in form and style was no small factor in its success. The allegory tells the story of a man who flees sin to lead a holy life. In his "apology" for the work Bunyan tells his readers:

> This book will make a traveller of thee,
> If by its counsel thou wilt ruled be;
> It will direct thee to the Holy Land,
> If thou wilt its directions understand.

Bunyan and Milton produced the greatest literary works of the Puritan revolution. The Commonwealth had failed, but left behind a new culture that was neither courtly nor Puritan. The next age would belong to professional writers, journalists, and playwrights, not to courtly poets or Puritan proselytizers. The revolution that had begun in the mid-seventeenth century would continue in the eighteenth.

BRITISH VOICES

Quotations by Prominent Figures of the Period

No man is an Island, entire of itself;. . . any man's death diminishes me, because I am involved in Mankind; and therefore never send to know for whom the bell tolls; it tolls for thee.
   John Donne, "Meditation XVII"

Art hath an enemy called Ignorance.
   Ben Jonson, "Every Man Out of His Humor"

Drink to me only with thine eyes
And I will pledge with mine.
   Ben Jonson, "To Celia"

Gather ye rosebuds while ye may,
Old Time is still a-flying.
   Robert Herrick, "To the Virgins, to Make Much of Time"

They also serve who only stand and wait.
   John Milton, "Sonnet: On His Blindness"

But at my back I always hear
Time's winged chariot hurrying near.
   Andrew Marvell, "To His Coy Mistress"

I have laid aside business, and gone a-fishing.
   Izaak Walton, *The Compleat Angler*

Stone walls do not a prison make,
   Nor iron bars a cage.
   Richard Lovelace, "To Althea, from Prison"

READING CRITICALLY

The Literature of 1625–1660

When you read literature, it is important to place it in its historical context. Doing so will help you to understand influences on the writer's ideas and techniques.

HISTORICAL CONTEXT During the years from 1625 to 1660, England suffered from tremendous political and religious unrest. Shortly after Charles I inherited the throne in 1625, he became involved in a power struggle with the Parliament, whose members strongly objected to his efforts to limit Parliamentary authority. Charles I's continuing suppression of Puritans also aroused a great deal of anger among certain members of the Parliament, many of whom were Puritans. This controversy resulted in a civil war that began in 1642 and brought about the temporary downfall of the monarchy in 1649. Oliver Cromwell, a Puritan member of Parliament, ruled the nation for nine years before dying in 1658 and leaving the country in the hands of his son, Richard. Richard proved to be an ineffective ruler, however, and in 1660 the monarchy was restored.

LITERARY MOVEMENTS The writers of this period can be divided essentially into two groups: the metaphysical poets and the Sons of Ben. A group consisting of John Donne and several of his followers, the metaphysical poets are known for their intellectual verse filled with complex, elaborate, and striking comparisons. In contrast, the Sons of Ben, led by the influential poet Ben Jonson, are known for their precise, witty, and elegant poetry. However, John Milton, probably the most significant writer of the period, did not fit into either of these categories. Drawing upon a variety of literary traditions, Milton produced a range of different types of works.

WRITERS' TECHNIQUES Among the metaphysical poets, the conceit, an especially striking type of metaphor, was a popular literary device. Influenced by the works of the ancient Greeks and Romans, the Sons of Ben relied on classical poetic forms and often used allusions in their works. Milton made extensive use of both metaphors and allusions.

The Schools of
Donne and Jonson

GREENWICH PALACE FROM THE NORTHEAST WITH A MAN-OF-WAR AT ANCHOR (detail) *c.* 1630
National Maritime Museum

JOHN DONNE

1572(?)–1631

John Donne's reputation has changed over time. He was very popular during his own lifetime, but his writings went out of favor soon after his death. At the beginning of the twentieth century, however, interest in his works revived. Now Donne occupies a major position in literature. Modern critics place him with William Shakespeare and John Milton at the very pinnacle of English poetry.

Donne was raised by his widowed mother, who was a devout Catholic and a member of the family of St. Thomas More. At the time, being Catholic was difficult, for Roman Catholics were severely discriminated against in Queen Elizabeth's England. Indeed, Donne later recanted his Catholicism and joined the Anglican Church. Scholars are divided as to his motives. They wonder whether he experienced a genuine conversion or made a shrewd move to try to gain advancement in court society.

Donne's life is generally described as falling into two parts. The first is often thought of as the "wild youth of Jack Donne, ambitious man about town." Bright, clever, and charming, Donne was welcomed into the most exclusive court circles and served as private secretary to one of the Queen's highest-ranking officials. He was so charming that he wooed and won the hand in marriage of Anne More, his employer's niece.

As with his religious conversion, some scholars have questioned Donne's motives. Cynics thought that through this marriage Donne had made a shrewd move to advance his career. However, things did not work out that way. Because of the opposition of Anne's father, Donne's marriage ruined his chances for advancement. As a consequence, the devoted couple and their many children experienced seventeen years of poverty, illness, and despair. During these years Donne eked out a living as a writer of religious tracts and as the temporary secretary of several aristocrats. He also became, during this difficult period, one of the most widely read and influential poets of the age.

Later Donne was ordained and made dean of St. Paul's Cathedral in London. This began the second part of his life, which has been described as the "sacred calling of Dr. John Donne, Dean of St. Paul's." From this time until his death, Donne was the most popular preacher in England; his meditations and sermons were published during his life and went through several editions.

We should not, however, overemphasize the differences between the younger and older Donne. All of his writings, whether on love or faith, were written with the same intensity and wit.

GUIDE FOR INTERPRETING

Song, Holy Sonnet 10, Holy Sonnet 14

Donne was a leading writer of what has come to be called metaphysical poetry because of its concern with philosophical and religious issues. This kind of poetry is characterized by the extensive use of paradoxes and conceits.

Paradox. In literature, a paradox is an apparent self-contradiction that reveals a kind of truth. One of the most famous literary paradoxes can be found in Donne's "Holy Sonnet 14": "Take me to You, imprison me, for I, / Except You enthral me, never shall be free." Finding "freedom" in prison or in slavery would seem to many people a contradiction. But here, "prison" and "enthral" (enslave) are metaphors for submissive devotion to God, which to the deeply religious person represents true freedom.

Metaphysical Conceit. A conceit is an extended, fanciful metaphor that makes a surprising or unexpected comparison. In the sixteenth century, the Elizabethans were delighted by long, elaborate conceits, as in Sir Philip Sidney's comparison of the moon with a languishing lover in "Sonnet 31." The metaphysical poets, such as John Donne and Andrew Marvell, wrote ingenious, often shocking conceits in which very dissimilar objects are compared.

Sir George More was so furious that his seventeen-year-old daughter Anne married John Donne against his wishes that he not only threw her and his son-in-law out of his home, but convinced Lord Chancellor Egerton to fire Donne from his position as Secretary to the Great Seal and arranged to have the young poet imprisoned. Donne and his wife found sanctuary in a house in Pyrford, but they were still near Anne's father, who lived in Surrey. Legend has it that one of the first actions Donne took upon his arrival in Pyrford was to write the following lines on a pane of glass in his new home:

John Donne

An Donne

Undone.

Was Donne really "undone"? According to what he says in "Song," what did he lose—and what did he win?

Write a short composition in which you use metaphors to describe an unusual experience you have had. Find objects, ideas, or common experiences that you can compare with your own experience and explain the connections.

Song

John Donne

Sweetest love, I do not go,
    For weariness of thee,
Nor in hope the world can show
    A fitter love for me;
5   But since that I
Must die at last, 'tis best
To use[1] myself in jest,
      Thus by feigned[2] deaths to die.

Yesternight the sun went hence,
10   And yet is here today;
He hath no desire nor sense,
    Nor half so short a way;
      Then fear not me,
But believe that I shall make
15 Speedier journeys, since I take
      More wings and spurs than he.

O how feeble is man's power,
    That if good fortune fall,
Cannot add another hour,
20   Nor a lost hour recall!
      But come bad chance,
And we join to it our strength,
And we teach it art and length,
    Itself o'er us to advance.

25 When thou sigh'st, thou sigh'st not wind,
    But sigh'st my soul away;
When thou weep'st, unkindly kind,
    My life's blood doth decay.
      It cannot be
30 That thou lovest me as thou say'st,
If in thine my life thou waste,
    That art the best of me.

---

1. use: Condition.
2. feigned: Imagined.

Let not thy divining heart
    Forethink me any ill,
35   Destiny may take thy part,
    And may thy fears fulfill;
    But think that we
    Are but turned aside to sleep.
    They who one another keep
40   Alive, ne'r parted be.

RESPONDING TO THE SELECTION

Your Response

1. Do you agree with what the speaker says about good fortune and bad fortune in stanza 3? Why or why not?

Recalling

2. What are the speaker's reasons for leaving his beloved?
3. What does the speaker say happens when "bad chance" comes (lines 21–24)?
4. How does the speaker suggest that his beloved think of their parting?

Interpreting

5. To what is the sun in stanza 2 compared?
6. (a) Of what is the speaker trying to convince his beloved? (b) How would you outline the speaker's argument?
7. What is the tone of the poem? Is it angry, beseeching, reassuring, uncertain, mocking?

Applying

8. The speaker in this poem resorts to exaggeration as an instrument of persuasion. Do you think that exaggerating in order to win is a valid persuasive technique? Explain your answer.
9. Although this is a love poem, it is cast in the form of an argument. Why is that appropriate?

ANALYZING LITERATURE

Understanding Paradox

A paradox is an apparent self-contradiction that reveals a truth. A very well known one is the statement of Jesus in Matthew 16:25, "For whosoever will save his life shall lose it." A related paradox can be found in Donne's Holy Sonnet 10: ". . . poor death, nor yet canst thou kill me." In this example the speaker says death cannot kill him because as a devout Christian he will have eternal life. Our very puzzlement adds zest to our understanding once we have figured out the meaning of the paradox, which is why religious leaders and writers so often employ them.

Donne's "Song" contains a couple of paradoxes. Explain why the following quote is a paradox, what it means, and how it works in the poem: "When thou weep'st, unkindly kind" (line 27).

LEARNING OPTION

Writing. Imagine you were the person addressed by the speaker in "Song." How would you react to the speaker's argument? Would you find his words consoling? Write a brief poem in which you answer the speaker's argument, either accepting or rejecting it. Choose a poetic form and style that are fitting for the thoughts and feelings you want to express. If you wish, use the style and tone that Donne uses in "Song."

Holy Sonnet 10

John Donne

Death be not proud, though some have called thee
Mighty and dreadful, for thou art not so;
For those whom thou think'st thou dost overthrow,
Die not, poor death, nor yet canst thou kill me.
5   From rest and sleep, which but thy pictures[1] be,
Much pleasure; then from thee much more must flow,
And soonest our best men with thee do go,
Rest of their bones, and soul's delivery[2]
Thou art slave to fate, chance, kings, and desperate men,
10   And dost with poison, war, and sickness dwell,
And poppy,[3] or charms can make us sleep as well
And better than thy stroke; why swell'st[4] thou then?
One short sleep past, we wake eternally,
And death shall be no more; Death, thou shalt die.

---

1. pictures: Images.
2. And . . . delivery: Our best men go with you to rest their bones
and find freedom for their souls.
3. poppy: Opium.
4. swell'st: Swell with pride.

RESPONDING TO THE SELECTION

Your Response

1. Do you find the speaker's ideas about death convincing? Why or why not?

Recalling

2. Why does the speaker say in lines 5–8 that death is pleasant?
3. How does the speaker characterize death in lines 9–12?
4. Why does the speaker say that death shall be no more?

Interpreting

5. (a) What does the speaker mean when he says in lines 3–4, "For those whom thou think'st thou dost overthrow, / Die not, poor death, nor yet canst thou kill me"? (b) In what way is this meaning reinforced by the last two lines?
6. (a) What does the paradox "Death, thou shalt die" mean? What makes it paradoxical? (b) In what way does the final paradox serve as the conclusion to the argument of the poem?

Applying

7. In the poem the speaker gives human characteristics to death. This is called *personification.* Death has often been personified in art and literature, sometimes as the grim reaper carrying a scythe, at other times as an angel with black wings and a net, and at still other times as a fierce horseman whose head is a

SIR THOMAS ASTON AT THE DEATHBED OF HIS WIFE
John Souch
Manchester City Art Galleries

skull. Think of other ways you have seen death personified in literature or art. Discuss with your classmates what each of these images implies about our attitudes toward death. How does Donne's poem address these attitudes?

ANALYZING LITERATURE

Understanding Metaphysical Conceit

The term *conceit* comes from the Italian word *concetto,* meaning "conception." Metaphysical poets often worked out complex, farfetched con-

ceits, and Donne's are among the best of them. Sometimes a metaphysical conceit is an elaborate image; sometimes it can be just a line or two. What is essential to all metaphysical conceits, however, is the startling conjunction of dissimilar concepts, ideas, images, or objects. The underlying conceit of "Holy Sonnet 10" is the likening of death to a proud but ultimately ineffectual tyrant.

1. What are the images in the poem that illustrate the conceit?
2. How do they relate with each other to form a single image of a powerless Death?

Holy Sonnet 14

John Donne

Batter my heart, three-personed God;[1] for You
As yet but knock, breathe, shine, and seek to mend;
That I may rise, and stand, o'erthrow me, and bend
Your force, to break, blow, burn and make me new.
5 I, like an usurped town, to another due,
   Labor to admit You, but O, to no end,
Reason Your viceroy[2] in me, me should defend,
But is captived, and proves weak or untrue.
Yet dearly I love You, and would be loved fain,
10 But am betrothed unto Your enemy.
Divorce me, untie, or break that knot again;
Take me to You, imprison me, for I,
Except You enthral[3] me, never shall be free,
Nor ever chaste, except You ravish me.

---

1. three-personed God: The Trinity:
the Father, the Son, and the Holy Ghost.
2. viceroy: Deputy.
3. enthral: Enslave.

Primary Source

The great critic and writer Samuel Johnson was the first to identify—and indict—the metaphysical poets. His discussion appeared in 1779 in his *Lives of the English Poets*. He explains:

"About the beginning of the seventeenth century appeared a race of writers that may be termed the metaphysical poets . . . (They) were men of learning, and to show their learning was their whole endeavor; but, unluckily resolving to show it in rhyme, instead of writing poetry, they only wrote verses, and, very often, such verses as stood the trial of the finger better than of the ear; for the modulation was so imperfect that they were only found to be verses by counting the syllables.

"Their thoughts are often new, but seldom natural; they are not obvious, but neither are they just; and the reader, far from wondering that he missed them, wonders more frequently by what perverseness of industry they were ever found. . . .

"The most heterogeneous ideas are yoked by violence together; nature and art are ransacked for illustrations, comparisons, and allusions; their learning instructs, and their subtilty surprises; but the reader commonly thinks his improvement dearly bought, and, though he sometimes admires, is seldom pleased . . .

"From this account of their compositions it will be readily inferred that they were not successful in representing or moving the affections . . . Their wish was only to say what they hoped had never been said before."

Your Response

1. What images, lines, or ideas in this poem do you find most striking? Explain.

Recalling

2. In the first four lines, what does the speaker ask God to do?
3. (a) To what does the speaker compare himself in line 5? (b) Of what does the speaker complain in lines 6–8? (c) How is reason characterized in lines 7 and 8?
4. (a) How does the speaker describe his condition in lines 9–10? (b) What does the speaker ask God to do in lines 11–12?

Interpreting

5. In line 2, why does the speaker complain of God's gentleness? Why does the speaker want God to treat him violently?
6. (a) What are the paradoxes in lines 3, 13, and 14? (b) What do they mean? (c) How do they affect you, the reader?
7. Who is the "enemy" to whom the speaker is "betrothed"?
8. What is the tone in this poem?

Applying

9. In the poem the speaker wants to be overwhelmed with emotion. There are many instances when a person might want to experience a deep emotion. What are some of these instances?

CRITICAL THINKING AND READING

Following an Argument

Metaphysical poets were said to combine "passion with reason." Reason is the chief tool of philosophy, and arguments are the chief tools of reason. A philosophical argument—which is much different from the shouting match we usually think of—is a logical or reasonable demonstration of how certain facts or ideas can or must lead to a conclusion. When you say, "I believe such and such because of this, that, and the other," you are offering an *argument* for your beliefs.

But of course, few if any literary works display their arguments as bluntly as we have just done. For example, if we think of "Holy Sonnet 14" as an argument—rather than as a prayer or an appeal, which is another way to view the poem—then we might ask why the speaker is saying, in effect, "God, please beat down my resistance so that I can worship you." After reflection, we might come up with the proposition that "Suffering overwhelms doubt and leads to the love of God."

Reread "Holy Sonnet 14" and support the proposition with images and metaphors from the poem. First, state the proposition or thesis; then give the evidence that supports the proposition. Finally, restate the proposition as a conclusion in such a way as to indicate it follows from the evidence.

THINKING AND WRITING

Writing a Philosophical Argument

Take your argument—thesis or proposition, supporting evidence, and conclusion—for Donne's poem and discuss it in a 500-word composition. Make sure you express your opinion of Donne's argument. Include in your discussion evidence supporting your opinion.

Working with Donne's poem, write your own philosophical argument. For example, "Holy Sonnet 14" might suggest questions about the difficulty of making a commitment or of feeling an attachment to a transcendent or abstract idea. Freewrite, exploring your answer to this question. After you have arrived at an answer to your question, take that as your thesis or proposition. Develop supporting evidence; take into account opposing views, if there are any; answer them; and present your conclusion. When you revise, keep in mind that when writing an argumentative essay, you have to persuade your readers that your views are correct. Are your supporting details arranged so that they will have a powerful effect? Have you provided enough support? Proofread your essay and prepare a final draft.

GUIDE FOR INTERPRETING

Meditation 17

Writers' Techniques

Theme. The central or main idea of a literary work is its theme. In some works the theme is stated directly. For example, in Sonnet 116 Shakespeare expresses his theme directly with the words "Love alters not." More often, though, the theme of a literary work is presented indirectly. An example of this can be found in John Donne's "Song." We can say the theme of the poem is something like: "Separation may seem like death, but it is really more like sleep, and lovers would suffer less if they viewed their separation this way."

Works of literature often have more than one theme. When they do, there is usually one dominant or principal idea and several secondary or subordinate ones. For example, the major theme of *Macbeth* is the effects of ruthless ambition. This is not, however, the only theme in the play. To it can be added as secondary themes: cruelty by rulers causes rebellion; illegitimate power will be overthrown; and evil deeds bring their own punishment.

No matter the kind of writing, themes arise from the elements of the work. In a poem, for example, metaphor, image, and choice of words frequently develop the theme; in a play or novel, plot, character, and dialogue usually illustrate the theme; and in an essay, subordinate ideas and the ways in which language is used.

Commentary

In 1940 Ernest Hemingway sparked a run on copies of "Meditation 17" when he used a phrase from it as the title for his best-selling novel, *For Whom the Bell Tolls*. To underscore the parallel between the theme of Donne's meditation and that of his book, Hemingway also quoted a portion of the meditation on the book's inside front cover. Hemingway used the theme of Donne's "Meditation 17" as a call for personal involvement in the Spanish Civil War, the subject of his novel.

Publishers rushed to reissue "Meditation 17." The Oxford Press reported that all its editions of Donne's poetry sold out, while "fifteen hundred sheets [of 'Meditation 17'] ordered by Random House were bombed out of existence."

What do you think there was in Donne's theme in "Meditation 17" that captured the mood of the war years?

Focus

Jot down ideas as they come to you while reading Donne's meditation. Then assign numbers to your ideas according to their importance to you. Make number one your main theme.

Meditation 17

John Donne

Nunc lento sonitu dicunt, Morieris.

(Now, this bell tolling softly for another, says to me, Thou must die.)

Perchance he for whom this bell tolls may be so ill as that he knows not it tolls for him; and perchance I may think myself so much better than I am as that they who are about me and see my state may have caused it to toll for me, and I know not that. The church is catholic, universal, so are all her actions; all that she does belongs to all. When she baptizes a child, that action concerns me; for that child is thereby connected to that head which is my head too, and ingrafted into that body[1] whereof I am a member. And when she buries a man, that action concerns me: all mankind is of one author and is one volume; when one man dies, one chapter is not torn out of the book, but translated[2] into a better language; and every chapter must be so translated. God employs several translators; some pieces are translated by age, some by sickness, some by war, some by justice; but God's hand is in every translation, and his hand shall bind up all our scattered leaves again for that library where every book shall lie open to one another. As therefore the bell that rings to a sermon calls not upon the preacher only, but upon the congregation to come, so this bell calls us all; but how much more me, who am brought so near the door by this sickness. There was a contention as far as a suit[3] (in which both piety and dignity, religion and estimation,[4] were mingled) which of the religious orders should ring to prayers first in the morning; and it was determined that they should ring first that rose earliest. If we understand aright the dignity of this bell that tolls for our evening prayer, we would be glad to make it ours by rising early, in that application, that it might be ours as well as his whose indeed it is. The bell doth

---

3. suit: Lawsuit.
4. estimation: Self-esteem.

1. body: The Church
2. translated: Carried across on a spiritual level from one sphere to another.

toll for him that thinks it doth; and though it intermit again, yet from that minute that that occasion wrought upon him, he is united to God. Who casts not up his eye to the sun when it rises? but who takes off his eye from a comet when that breaks out? Who bends not his ear to any bell which upon any occasion rings? but who can remove it from that bell which is passing a piece of himself out of this world? No man is an island, entire of itself; every man is a piece of the continent, a part of the main.[5] If a clod be washed away by the sea, Europe is the less, as well as if a promontory were, as well as if a manor of thy friend's or of thine own were. Any man's death diminishes me because I am involved in mankind, and therefore never send to know for whom the bell tolls; it tolls for thee. Neither can we call this a begging of misery or a borrowing of misery, as though we were not miserable enough of ourselves but must fetch in more from the next house, in taking upon us the misery of our neighbors. Truly it were an excusable covetousness if we did; for affliction is a treasure, and scarce any man hath enough of it. No man hath affliction enough that is not matured and ripened by it, and made fit for God by that affliction. If a man carry treasure in bullion, or in a wedge of gold, and have none coined into current money, his treasure will not defray him as he travels. Tribulation is treasure in the nature of it, but it is not current money in the use of it, except we get nearer and nearer our home, heaven, by it. Another man may be sick too, and sick to death, and this affliction may lie in his bowels as gold in a mine and be of no use to him; but this bell that tells me of his affliction digs out and applies that gold to me, if by this consideration of another's danger, I take mine own into contemplation and so secure myself by making my recourse to my God, who is our only security.

---

5. **main:** Mainland.

Primary Source

Poet and critic T. S. Eliot ignited a literary bonfire in 1921 when he set about establishing Donne as the speaker for the twentieth-century mood. Eliot believed that:

"In the seventeenth century a dissociation of sensibility set in, from which we have never recovered; and this dissociation . . . was aggravated by the influence of the two most poweful poets of the century, Milton and Dryden.

"Each of these men performed certain poetic functions so magnificently well that the magnitude of the effect concealed the absence of others. The language went on and in some respects improved; the best verse of Collins, Gray, Johnson, and even Goldsmith satisfies some of our fastidious demands better than that of Donne or Marvell or King. But while the language became more refined, the feeling became more crude. The feeling, the sensibility, expressed in the 'Country Churchyard' is cruder than that in 'Coy Mistress' . . .

"We can only say that it appears likely that poetry in our civilization, as it exists at present, must be *difficult*. Our civilization comprehends great variety and complexity, and this variety and complexity, playing upon a refined sensibility, must produce more . . . complex results. The poet must become more and more comprehensive, more allusive, more indirect, in order to force, to dislocate if necessary, language into his meaning."

His remarks set the standard for a generation of students: Donne soared; Milton and Dryden plummeted.

GEORGE HERBERT

1593–1633

Herbert was born to a wealthy and influential aristocratic family. Instead of becoming a high-ranking official at the English court, however, he became a country parson at one of the smallest rural churches in England. There he served the poor and wrote the poems that gained him fame.

Like many wealthy young men, George Herbert first looked toward worldly success. He served as spokesman for Cambridge University, usually a steppingstone to high public office, and became a favorite of King James I. It was during this period of great promise that Herbert also served for two years as a Member of Parliament. With the deaths of his mother and several patrons, he withdrew from London. In 1630 he accepted a parish assignment in a remote part of England. For the remaining three years of his life, he devoted himself to his church: He restored the church buildings at his own expense, tended to his parishioners, performed music for his congregation, and composed devotional poems.

In many ways, Herbert's poetry shows the influence of John Donne. This is understandable, since Donne was older and a good family friend. Herbert's temperament, however, was very different from that of his doubt-ridden, anxious mentor. The poetry Herbert wrote is graceful, pious verse intended to instill devotion by giving pleasure. As he himself put it: "A verse may find him who a sermon flies, / And turn delight into a sacrifice."

Herbert organized his poems in a particular sequence and called his collection *The Temple*. Just before his death, he sent the manuscript of *The Temple* to a profoundly religious friend named Nicholas Ferrar with a special request. If Ferrar found the poems worthy, then he should have them published; if not, they should be burned. Fortunately, Ferrar found the poems worthy. *The Temple,* as it turned out, was enormously popular throughout the seventeenth century.

Herbert had carefully given his collection of 160 very different poems a unifying concept. Taken together, the poems represent the experience of attending church. *The Temple* opens with the rather long poem "The Church Porch" and then, in a wide variety of verse forms, represents parts of a church building, religious services, sacred objects, and private devotions. We can glimpse the large assortment of forms and themes present in Herbert's work by examining the poems reprinted in this volume.

RESPONDING TO THE SELECTION

Your Response

1. Do you agree or disagree with Donne's statement that "affliction is a treasure"? Explain.

Recalling

2. Why does Donne say the tolling bell applies to him as well as to others?
3. Why does Donne say that contemplation of the tolling bell brings one close to God?

Interpreting

4. To what do the metaphors "chapter," "book," "language," and "translated" refer?
5. What is meant by "No man is an island entire of itself; every man is a piece of the continent"?

Applying

6. At the beginning of the Second World War, Donne's phrase "No man is an island" became widely used as a slogan by those fighting Nazi Germany. It served to explain why Great Britain went to war in defense of Poland and France, and why the United States helped Britain in its most difficult times. How does this meaning of the phrase compare with the meaning intended by Donne?
7. What is Donne's attitude toward death in "Meditation 17"? How does it compare with his view of death in "Holy Sonnet 10"?

ANALYZING LITERATURE

Recognizing Themes

Themes are the central ideas of literary works. Some works have several themes in the same piece, one dominant and others subordinate. The subordinate ideas usually play a supporting role by backing up or reinforcing the main idea.

1. In the following list of ideas from "Meditation 17," which one is central and which are secondary?
   a. Death comes to everyone.

b. There is life after death.
c. All humans share the same experiences.
d. Contemplation of another's death and suffering can prepare one for life after death.
e. By empathizing with another's suffering, we recognize our common humanity.
f. No individual exists alone.

2. Explain how the secondary ideas support the main one, and show how Donne's theme controls the other ideas.

CRITICAL THINKING AND READING

Arguing Through Analogy

An **analogy** is a comparison that shows the resemblance between two or more things, ideas, or people. For example, one might draw an analogy between a teacher, who takes students through the difficulties of a subject, and a guide, who takes travelers over some difficult or dangerous terrain.

Analogies are often used to explain complicated ideas or argue difficult points. As a rule, an analogy compares an unusual or abstract concept to something familiar or concrete. A frequent analogy, for example, is the comparison of the effect of a person's attractiveness to the action of a magnet on metal, as when we talk of an individual's "magnetism."

To "prove" that there is an afterlife and that death is not final, Donne draws an analogy. What is that analogy? How does this analogy contribute to the overall argument of "Meditation 17"?

THINKING AND WRITING

Writing About the Theme of a Work

Take the idea that you chose in Analyzing Literature as central to "Meditation 17" and discuss how Donne developed it. Show how he hammered away at certain ideas through repetition. Also show how one idea supported another in almost pyramidal fashion, with Donne's main theme at the apex.

GUIDE FOR INTERPRETING

Virtue, Easter Wings

Writers' Techniques

Emblematic Images. Emblems usually were pictures accompanied by mottoes or labels and by poems that connected or explained the pictures and the mottoes. In some instances the poem itself was shaped so as to serve as picture, motto, and explanation. Verses of this type are called *emblematic images* or *emblem poems*. George Herbert's "Easter Wings" is such a poem.

Emblem poems were written so that visual image and verbal image could reinforce one another. "Easter Wings," for example, is about the resurrection of the spirit and how angelic wings may well help the troubled soul to rise and take flight. When this poem was first published, it was printed on its side. In this way, the poem *looked* as if an angel or bird were flying, wings spread apart.

Shaped poems have been produced intermittently since ancient times. An ancient Roman, writing about a sea fight, positioned the lines of his poems so that they made pictures of ships at battle. Shaped poems were not produced after the classical period until their popular revival at the beginning of the Renaissance. One Renaissance poet wrote a drinking song shaped like a bottle. Other poets wrote their verses so as to make shapes of crosses, altars, hearts, tears, and so forth. Shaped poems are still being written today, and they often still serve as emblems.

Focus

Write the name of a picture that appeals to you. For example, you might choose the painting *Mona Lisa* by Leonardo da Vinci, or the photograph of the Beatles dressed as *Sergeant Pepper's Lonely Hearts Club Band*. Use the name as the motto and write a short comment for both motto and picture.

Primary Source

What kind of preacher was Herbert? Were his sermons full of the clever wordplays that characterize his verse? One source tells us that Herbert delivered his first sermon "after a most florid manner, both with great learning and eloquence," but promised that "since Almighty God does not intend to lead men to heaven by hard questions, he would not therefore fill their heads with unnecessary notions; but that for their sakes, his language and his expressions should be more plain and practical in his future sermons. . . . He often tells them, that sermons are dangerous things, that none goes out of church as he came in, but either better or worse; that none is careless before his Judge, and that the word of God shall judge us. By these and other means the parson procures attention; but the character of his sermon is holiness; he is not witty, or learned, or eloquent, but holy."

Virtue

George Herbert

Sweet day, so cool, so calm, so bright,
The bridal of the earth and sky;
The dew shall weep thy fall tonight;
     For thou must die.

5 Sweet rose, whose hue angry and brave[1]
Bids the rash gazer wipe his eye:
Thy root is ever in its grave,
     And thou must die.

Sweet spring, full of sweet days and roses,
10 A box where sweets[2] compacted lie;
My music shows ye have your closes,[3]
     And all must die.

Only a sweet and virtuous soul,
Like seasoned timber, never gives;
15 But though the whole world turn to coal,[4]
     Then chiefly lives.

---

1. angry and brave: Red (the hue of anger) and splendid.
2. sweets: Perfumes.
3. closes: The concluding sounds.
4. turn to coal: Be reduced to cinder and ash by the fires of the
Last Judgment (see II Peter 3:10).

RESPONDING TO THE SELECTION

Your Response
1. Do you agree that the virtuous soul need not fear death? Why or why not?

Recalling
2. In the first three stanzas of "Virtue," what happens to "sweet day," "sweet rose," and "sweet spring"?
3. In the last stanza, what happens to the "sweet and virtuous soul"?

Interpreting
4. (a) What do the last lines of each of the four stanzas say? (b) How is the last line in the fourth stanza different from the other three? (c) When combined, what additional meaning do they gain?
5. How does Herbert express the thought that all of nature dies but the soul lives eternally?
6. (a) Mark the rhyme scheme of the poem. (b) What rhyming sound is most often repeated? (c) What rhyming sound replaces this in the last stanza? (d) In what way does the rhyme emphasize the theme or main point of the poem?

Applying

7. Basically, this poem says that the virtuous soul need not fear death. What other poem in this book imparts a similar message?

ANALYZING LITERATURE

Understanding Emblematic Images

Although emblematic images are usually associated with pictures and shaped verse, it is sometimes possible to see a kind of emblematic impulse in more traditionally formed poems. To see the emblematic image in a poem such as "Virtue," for example, we need to probe the meaning of the word *emblem.* The word comes from Latin and means "inlaid." (In mosaic, little pieces of stone are laid together according to a pattern that forms an image.) From this use it came to mean "symbol," one thing standing for another.

In early Renaissance emblems, poems were written to comment on or explain pictorial symbols. After a while, poems and pictures became separated and the reader of an emblematic poem had to imagine the symbolic picture to which it related.

Explain how the day, the rose, and spring are alike. Then explain what "seasoned timber" represents and how it relates to the day, the rose, and spring. Describe a pictorial image you think this poem might fit.

Easter Wings

George Herbert

   Lord, who createdst man in wealth and store,[1]
     Though foolishly he lost the same,
       Decaying more and more,
         Till he became
5   Most poor:
         With thee
       O let me rise
     As larks, harmoniously,
   And sing this day thy victories:
10 Then shall the fall further the flight in me.

   My tender age in sorrow did begin.
     And still with sickness and shame
       Thou didst so punish sin,
         That I became
15   Most thin.
         With thee
       Let me combine
     And feel this day thy victory:
   For, if I imp[2] my wing on thine,
Affliction shall advance the flight in me.

---

1. store: Abundance.
2. imp: Graft.

RESPONDING TO THE SELECTION

Your Response

1. How might a "fall further the flight" in someone?

Recalling

2. At the end of the poem, why does the speaker say he wants to "combine" with God? In what way does this echo lines 6–10?

Interpreting

3. (a) In line 11, what does the speaker mean when he says, "My tender age in sorrow did begin"? Why should he have begun in sorrow? (b) How does this line echo lines 1–5?

4. In what way is line 10 a paradox?

5. How are the title and shape of the poem appropriate to its theme?

Applying

6. George Herbert was sickly as a child and remained in frail health throughout his rather short life. He also moved from the pomp of the royal court to the poverty of a rural church. In what way are these personal experiences reflected in "Easter Wings"?

CRITICAL THINKING AND READING

Analyzing Herbert's Style

The word *style* refers to the characteristic way in which an individual does something, such as dressing, swimming, painting a picture, or writing a poem. In literature, style refers specifically to the way a writer uses language.

When we analyze a literary style, we examine the writer's characteristic choice of words, use of figures of speech, arrangement of sentences, organization of paragraphs, and, in poetry, treatment of rhythm and rhyme. Sometimes we also look at an author's use of certain literary devices—such as paradox, imagery, or symbolism—and his or her preference for certain subjects or themes. John Donne, for example, seems to prefer themes that reflect anxiety, uncertainty, or suffering. He often uses exaggerated language when treating these difficult matters, thereby creating discomfort and heightening the emotional response to his writing. Donne's style could thus be described as highly provocative.

George Herbert stands in marked contrast to Donne. The poems Herbert wrote tend to make the reader feel comfortable, perhaps even soothed, as if listening to the gentle murmur of continuous prayer. Herbert's diction, or vocabulary, is essentially quiet, never clangorous as is Donne's on many occasions. Even when dealing with so potentially traumatic a subject as the Fall of Man or his own approaching death, Herbert's words are mild, almost as if spoken in a whisper.

Reread "Easter Wings" and look closely at the way Herbert uses language. For example, notice the way he uses rhyme (in Herbert's day, "poor" rhymed with "more" and "store"). Describe Herbert's style in this poem and show how it complements his main idea. In addition to his use of rhyme, take into account his choice of words, his changes in line lengths, and his treatment of metaphors and similes.

THINKING AND WRITING

Writing About Emblematic Images

Properly speaking, an emblem consisted of a picture, a motto, and a poem. Over time, however, many poems were written so that they formed their own picture, as in "Easter Wings," or they were written to explain or comment on a picture in the poet's mind, as might be said of "Virtue."

Choose a poem in this book and describe the picture that could accompany the poem today. Relate specific details from the poem to your description. When you revise, make sure you have provided enough support for your choice of emblem.

LEARNING OPTION

Writing. Shaped poems, also called *concrete poems,* are still popular today. Write your own shaped poem. First, think of a subject that you can represent in a simple graphic form. Then, write the poem, perhaps describing the object with various kinds of figurative language or sound devices. Next, experiment with the lines of your poem to "mold" them into the shape. Should some lines be broken in different places? How should the lines be arranged on the page? When you revise, consider whether your poem could be called an emblem. Make sure everything about it contributes to the effect you desire.

ANDREW MARVELL

1621–1678

Although seemingly relaxed in style, Andrew Marvell's poetry and politics were actually quite tough. Beneath his graceful lyrics lie somber ideas and rigorous structures. Alongside his ready adaptability resided a firm attachment to his friends and beliefs.

Marvell was the son of a Puritan minister who was appointed to a church in Hull, a small town on the Humber River in northern England. There young Andrew remained until he entered Cambridge University at the age of twelve. While at Cambridge, he wrote several poems in Greek and Latin that were published by the university in a volume dedicated to King Charles I. After his father's death, Marvell traveled in Europe, where he learned to speak several other languages.

During his stay in Europe, the English Parliament, dominated by Puritans, rebelled against the king. On first returning to England, Marvell established friendships with royalist supporters of Charles I. At this time he wrote several verses commemorating these friends, among whom was the poet Richard Lovelace. Somewhat later he was hired by Lord Fairfax, the commanding general of the antiroyalist Parliamentary army, to teach his daughter foreign languages. Marvell held this position for about two years, during which time he may have written most of the poems for which he is now famous.

Several years later, Marvell became tutor to the ward of Oliver Cromwell, leader of the Puritan rebellion and ruler of England. Shortly afterward Marvell served as unofficial court poet to Cromwell himself. Obviously capable, Marvell gained the attention and sponsorship of the great English poet John Milton, who was at the time Latin Secretary to Cromwell's Council of State. Several years later Marvell became Milton's assistant. During this period Marvell wrote several political and commemorative poems.

In 1659, after Cromwell's death and shortly before the monarchy was restored, Marvell was elected the Member of Parliament from Hull. He was regularly returned to Parliament until his death, almost twenty years later. It is believed that while a member, he was mainly responsible for saving Milton from a long imprisonment and possible death sentence.

Marvell showed an extraordinary ability to adjust to the realities of his time. He also displayed, however, an equal firmness of principle. After the Restoration of Charles II, Marvell wrote political satires and prose pamphlets attacking the abuses of monarchy and defending democratic concepts.

GUIDE FOR INTERPRETING

To His Coy Mistress, The Picture of Little T. C. in a Prospect of Flowers

Writers' Techniques

Couplets and Quatrains. Two of the most common structural elements in poetry are couplets and quatrains. Two lines that rhyme are called a *couplet,* and four lines that rhyme in various ways are called a *quatrain*. Here is an example of a couplet and a quatrain. The verses are by Andrew Marvell, who used these forms in an early poem that he wrote as a debate between the Soul and Pleasure.

Quatrain:

PLEASURE

Wilt thou all the glory crave	*a*
That war or peace commend?	*b*
Half the world shall be thy slave,	*a*
The other half thy friend.	*b*

Couplet:

SOUL

What friends, if to my self untrue!	*c*
What slaves, unless I captive you!	*c*

Although both the couplet and the quatrain are often used as complete stanzas by themselves, they are also frequently used as parts of longer stanzas.

Focus

Write two lines that rhyme, then write several more rhyming pairs of lines. If four of these rhyming lines seem related, perhaps because they deal with the same subject or central idea, put them together. Then write four new lines in which the rhymes alternate. You might then have one quatrain rhyming *a b a b* and another rhyming *a a b b*.

Primary Source

Charles II decided to show his respect for Marvell's wit and intelligence as well as buy his allegiance. He sent a messenger who told Marvell that the king would grant him a favor. When Marvell refused, the messenger offered a thousand gold pieces. With a smile Marvell replied, "Surely, my good Lord, you do not mean to treat me ludicrously by these munificent offers, which seem to interpret a poverty on my part. Pray, my Lord Treasurer, do these apartments wear in the least the air and mark of need? And as for my living, that is plentiful and good, which you shall have from the mouth of the servant. —Pray, what had I to dinner yesterday? —'A shoulder of mutton, sir.'" The messenger left with a smile, and Marvell went to ask his bookseller for a loan.

Can you see Marvell's independent streak in these poems?

To His Coy Mistress

Andrew Marvell

Had we but world enough, and time,
This coyness lady were no crime.
We would sit down, and think which way
To walk, and pass our long love's day.
5 Thou by the Indian Ganges' side
Should'st rubies find; I by the tide
Of Humber[1] would complain. I would
Love you ten years before the Flood,
And you should if you please refuse
10 Till the conversion of the Jews.[2]
My vegetable love should grow
Vaster than empires, and more slow;
An hundred years should go to praise
Thine eyes, and on thy forehead gaze;
15 Two hundred to adore each breast,
But thirty thousand to the rest;
An age at least to every part,
And the last age should show your heart.
For, lady, you deserve this state,[3]
20 Nor would I love at lower rate.
     But at my back I always hear
Time's winged chariot hurrying near:
And yonder all before us lie
Deserts of vast eternity.
25 Thy beauty shall no more be found,
Nor, in thy marble vault, shall sound
My echoing songs; then worms shall try
That long-preserved virginity,
And your quaint honor turn to dust,
30 And into ashes all my lust:
The grave's a fine and private place,
But none I think do there embrace.
     Now therefore, while the youthful hew
Sits on thy skin like morning dew,
35 And while thy willing soul transpires[4]
At every pore with instant fires,

---

1. Humber: River flowing through Hull, Marvell's home town.
2. conversion of the Jews: According to Christian tradition, the Jews were to be converted immediately before the Last Judgment.
3. state: Dignity.
4. transpires: Breathes out.

Now let us sport us while we may,
And now, like amorous birds of prey,
Rather at once our time devour
40 Than languish in his slow-chapped[5] power.
Let us roll all our strength, and all
Our sweetness, up into one ball,
And tear our pleasures with rough strife
Thorough[6] the iron gates of life:
45 Thus, though we cannot make our sun
Stand still, yet we will make him run.

----

5. slow-chapped: Slow-jawed.
6. thorough: Through.

RESPONDING TO THE SELECTION

Your Response

1. What is your attitude toward the speaker in this poem? How would you respond to him?

Recalling

2. According to line 1 of "To His Coy Mistress," under what conditions would the lady's coyness not be a crime?
3. In lines 3–7, what would the lady and the speaker each do, separately and together?
4. In lines 21–24, what does the speaker hear at his back, and what lies before him and the lady?
5. In what place does the action described in lines 25–32 occur?
6. In lines 33–40, why does the speaker urge the lady to act "now"?
7. In conclusion (lines 41–46), what does the speaker say that he and the lady should do?

Interpreting

8. If you had to state the speaker's objections to the lady's resistance in one sentence, what would that sentence be?
9. Since time is central to the poem, how is it expressed? Point to the word pictures or images and to the comparisons or metaphors that stand for and represent time.

Applying

10. The lines "But at my back I always hear / Time's winged chariot hurrying near" have a great depth of meaning. What modern experience might these lines express?

ANALYZING LITERATURE

Recognizing Couplets and Quatrains

Couplets are two lines that rhyme, and quatrains are four lines that rhyme in various ways. One of the ways to make a quatrain is to join two couplets that deal with one idea, word picture, or comparison. This is sometimes done in long poems, although the quatrain may thus be "hidden."

There are indeed several hidden quatrains in this poem made up entirely of couplets. For example, look at lines 21–24.

These four lines make a single unit, a quatrain. The preceding lines all deal with praising the beauty of the lady; the following lines describe what happens to the body after death. By contrast, this quatrain deals directly with the experience of time.

Find at least one other hidden quatrain. Explain how Marvell's ideas, word pictures, and comparisons are developed through couplets.

The Picture of Little T. C. in a Prospect[1] of Flowers

Andrew Marvell

   See with what simplicity
   This nymph begins her golden days!
   In the green grass she loves to lie,
   And there with her fair aspect tames
5   The wilder flowers and gives them names,
   But only with the roses plays,
        And them does tell
   What color best becomes them, and what smell.
   Who can foretell for what high cause
10   This darling of the gods was born!
   Yet this is she whose chaster laws
   The wanton love shall one day fear,
   And, under her command severe
   See his bow broke and ensigns[2] torn.
15   Happy who can
   Appease this virtuous enemy of man!
   O then let me in time compound
   And parley with those conquering eyes
   Ere they have tried their force to wound,
20   Ere, with their glancing wheels, they drive
   In triumph over hearts that strive,
   And them that yield but more despise:
        Let me be laid,
   Where I may see thy glories from some shade.
25   Meantime, whilst every verdant[3] thing
   Itself does at thy beauty charm,
   Reform the errors of the spring;
   Make that the tulips may have share
   Of sweetness, seeing they are fair;
30   And roses of their thorns disarm:
        But most procure

---

1. **prospect:** Landscape.
2. **ensigns:** Flags.
3. **verdant** *adj.*: Green.

That violets may a longer age endure.
But O, young beauty of the woods,
Whom nature courts with fruits and flowers,
35 Gather the flowers, but spare the buds,
Lest Flora[4] angry at thy crime
To kill her infants in their prime,
Do quickly make th' example yours;
        And ere we see,
40 Nip in the blossom all our hopes and thee.

---

4. Flora: The Roman goddess of flowers.

RESPONDING TO THE SELECTION

Your Response

1. How does your idea of a perfect "golden day" in nature compare with the speaker's?

Recalling

2. What is the nymph doing in stanza 1?
3. Why does the speaker, in stanza 3, want to converse with "those conquering eyes"?
4. What is asked for in the fourth stanza?
5. Of what is the "young beauty" warned in the last stanza?

Interpreting

6. Nymphs are pretty young nature goddesses from classical mythology. They were often depicted in art and literature as rejecting ardent lovers, many of whom were gods. What details in the poem identify little T.C. with a wood nymph?
7. The speaker at first addresses someone outside the poem, then suddenly shifts and directly addresses little T.C. Where in the poem does this shift occur? What word signals the shift?

Applying

8. Each stanza of this poem ends in a couplet, two lines that rhyme. What other poems that you have read in this book end their stanzas with couplets?
9. In a sense, "The Picture of Little T. C. in a Prospect of Flowers" can be thought of as an emblem poem, such as George Herbert might have written. Emblems were pictures with mottoes and poems. What sort of picture do you think would be appropriate for this poem?

THINKING AND WRITING

Comparing and Contrasting Styles

A literary style is a distinctive use of language. Individual writers have their own style, but sometimes groups of writers also share a common style. The metaphysical poets were such a group. Among the stylistic traits shared by these poets were a fondness for conceits (extended, farfetched comparisons), paradoxes (apparent contradictions), arguments (efforts at persuasion), and obscure bits of knowledge. Choose two metaphysical writers. List the characteristics of their style. Write an essay comparing and contrasting their styles. When you revise, make sure you have included details from their poems to support your ideas.

BEN JONSON

1572–1637

From bricklayer to literary dictator, Ben Jonson's rise in stature is a true "rags to riches" tale. Not only did his life have mythic proportions, but his physique did too. He was a large man with boundless energy and enormous courage. A friend of Shakespeare and Donne, Jonson was also their chief rival in drama and lyric. In addition, Jonson was a classical scholar, an astute critic, a superb prose stylist, a skillful translator, and the chief arbiter of taste for an entire generation of writers.

Adopted when an infant by a bricklayer, Jonson worked for his stepfather while attending the equivalent of high school under one of the leading teachers of the age. Too poor to pursue his education further, Jonson enlisted in the army and fought in the wars for Dutch independence from Spain. At one point, he fought in single combat the champion of the enemy before the massed armies of Holland and Spain. Jonson won.

After returning to England, Jonson went on the stage as an actor. His early years in the theater were stormy ones: He was jailed one time for taking part in a "seditious and slanderous" play; another time he was almost hanged for killing a fellow actor in a duel; and still later he was suspected of taking part in a plot on the life of King James I. Despite the turbulence of his life, however, Jonson learned his stagecraft well and became a major dramatist in his own right. His first play featured William Shakespeare acting in a major role, and his later plays were performed by the chief acting companies of the day, including Shakespeare's.

Jonson was so successful that he was granted a handsome pension by King James I and treated as if he were poet laureate of England. Over many years he had written masques—elaborate entertainments—for the royal court, where he was a favorite writer. During these years he was enormously influential, functioning as virtual dictator over the literary efforts of the day.

A number of the brightest and best of the young court writers flocked about Jonson and called themselves the "Sons of Ben" or "Tribe of Ben." Among the outstanding Sons of Ben can be counted Robert Herrick and John Suckling. Although not himself one of the "Sons," Richard Lovelace was also much influenced by Jonson. Indeed, Jonson's direct influence extended beyond these poets to the end of the seventeenth century and into the eighteenth. It is still felt today. What Jonson said of Shakespeare can be said of Jonson as well: "He was not of an age, but for all time."

GUIDE FOR INTERPRETING

On My First Son; Song: To Celia; To the Memory of My Beloved Master, William Shakespeare

Writers' Techniques

Apostrophe. An apostrophe is a figure of speech in which an abstract idea or quality, a place or inanimate thing, or a dead or absent person is addressed as if present and able to hear and understand what is said. Ben Jonson used an apostrophe when he directly addressed William Shakespeare, who had been dead for several years, in his poem "To the Memory of My Beloved Master, William Shakespeare."

Apostrophes were first written by the ancient Greeks and Romans. Here is the opening line to Homer's *Odyssey:*

Tell me, Muse, of the man of many ways. . . .

Although it is rare to find a modern poet apostrophizing, it does sometimes occur. Dylan Thomas apostrophized part of his anatomy in his poem "All All and All the Dry World's Lever."

Know, O my bone, the jointed lever.

For the most part, though, use of the apostrophe today sounds old-fashioned, which brings to mind an ancient Roman apostrophe.

O time! O custom!

Focus

Often people have unfinished conversations with others, conversations that they complete later by "addressing" the other person mentally. Complete an unfinished conversation.

Primary Source

Few comments have been as controversial as Jonson's remarks about Shakespeare: "I remember, the players have often mentioned it as an honor to Shakespeare, that in his writing . . . he never blotted out a line. My answer hath been, would he had blotted a thousand. Which they thought was a malevolent speech. . . . And to justify mine own candor (for I loved the man, and do honor his memory, on this side of idolatry, as much as any). He was (indeed) honest, and of an open, and free nature: he had an excellent fancy; brave notions, and gentle expressions. . . . But he redeemed his vices, with his virtues. There was ever more in him to be praised, than to be pardoned." How do you think Jonson really felt about Shakespeare? As you read, look for the feelings Jonson expresses about the person in each poem.

On My First Son

Ben Jonson

Farewell, thou child of my right hand,[1] and joy;
    My sin was too much hope of thee, loved boy,
Seven years thou wert lent to me, and I thee pay,
    Exacted by thy fate, on the just[2] day.
5 O, could I lose all father,[3] now. For why
    Will man lament the state he should envy?
To have so soon scaped world's, and flesh's rage,
    And, if no other misery, yet age?
Rest in soft peace, and, asked, say here doth lie
10   Ben Jonson his best piece of poetry.
For whose sake, henceforth, all his vows be such,
    As what he loves may never like too much.

---

1. child . . . hand: The literal translation of the Hebrew name Benjamin. Jonson's son was born in 1596 and died in 1603.
2. just: Exact.
3. lose . . . father: Give up all thoughts of being a father.

RESPONDING TO THE SELECTION

Your Response

1. Do you think the speaker is wise in not wanting to love anything so strongly again? Explain.

Recalling

2. What is the epitaph Jonson has composed for his son in lines 9–12? What vow does Jonson make as part of the epitaph?

Interpreting

3. How would you explain the "sin" Jonson attributes to himself in line 2? What details in the poem support this reading?
4. Why does Jonson say in line 6 that an early death is enviable?

Applying

5. Compare Jonson's poem on his son's death with Donne's meditation and sonnet. Does Jonson express as much anguish or suffering as Donne?

ANALYZING LITERATURE

Understanding Apostrophes

The apostrophe is a literary convention that allows an author to bring vividly to the mind of a reader the subject of the apostrophe. It endows that subject with a degree of life it might not otherwise have and thereby makes it easier for the reader to share the writer's emotion.

1. To whom is this poem addressed?
2. What question does Jonson ask in lines 5–8?
3. Explain how the device of the apostrophe allows him to clearly express his emotions.

Song: To Celia

Ben Jonson

Drink to me only with thine eyes,
And I will pledge with mine;
Or leave a kiss but in the cup,
And I'll not look for wine.
5   The thirst that from the soul doth rise,
Doth ask a drink divine:
But might I of Jove's[1] nectar sup,
I would not change for thine.

I sent thee late[2] a rosy wreath,
10   Not so much honoring thee,
As giving it a hope, that there
It could not withered be.
But thou thereon did'st only breathe,
And sent'st it back to me;
15   Since when it grows and smells, I swear,
Not of itself, but thee.

---

1. Jove's: Jupiter's. In Roman mythology, Jupiter
is the ruler of the gods.
2. late: Recently.

RESPONDING TO THE SELECTION

Your Response

1. How might you respond differently to this poem
if it were sung rather than read silently?

Recalling

2. In lines 5–8, what does the speaker say the
soul requires, and what substitutes does it
desire?
3. (a) Why, according to lines 11–12, did the
speaker send the "rosy wreath" to Celia?
(b) In lines 14–16, what does the speaker say
happened to the wreath?

Interpreting

4. The speaker says a number of times that he
prefers expressions of love to drink, whether
wine or nectar. (a) What does love give him
that drink cannot? (b) In which lines does he
say this?

Applying

5. Many of Jonson's songs were updated versions of classical Latin and Greek poems. If
you were asked to update "Song: To Celia,"
how would you do so?
6. In your opinion, why has this song been so
popular through the centuries?

To the Memory of My Beloved Master, William Shakespeare

Ben Jonson

To draw no envy, Shakespeare, on thy name,
Am I thus ample[1] to thy book and fame:
While I confess thy writings to be such
As neither man nor Muse can praise too much.
5 'Tis true, and all men's suffrage.[2] But these ways
Were not the paths I meant unto thy praise:
For silliest[3] ignorance on these may light,
Which, when it sounds at best, but echoes right;
Or blind affection,[4] which doth ne'er advance
10 The truth, but gropes, and urgeth all by chance;
Or crafty malice, might pretend this praise,
And think to ruin, where it seemed to raise . . .
But thou art proof against them, and indeed
Above the ill fortune of them, or the need.
15 I, therefore will begin. Soul of the age!
The applause! delight! the wonder of our stage!
My Shakespeare, rise; I will not lodge thee by
Chaucer, or Spenser, or bid Beaumont[5] lie
A little further, to make thee a room:
20 Thou art a monument, without a tomb,
And art alive still, while thy book doth live,
And we have wits to read, and praise to give.

---

1. ample: Liberal.
2. suffrage: Agreement.
3. silliest: Simplest.
4. blind affection: Prejudice.
5. Beaumont: Francis Beaumont (1584–1616), a playwright who was one of Shakespeare's contemporaries. Chaucer, Spenser, and Beaumont were buried in Westminster Abbey; Shakespeare was buried in Stratford. Jonson believes that it is proper for Shakespeare to be buried apart from these other important writers.

SHAKESPEARE AND BEN JONSON AT CHESS
Karel van Mander

That I not mix thee so, my brain excuses,
I mean with great, but disproportioned[6] Muses;
25 For, if I thought my judgment were of years,
I should commit thee surely with thy peers,
And tell, how far thou didst our Lyly outshine,
Or sporting Kyd, or Marlowe's[7] mighty line.
And though thou hadst small[8] Latin, and less Greek,
30 From thence to honor thee, I would not seek
For names; but call forth thund'ring Aeschylus,
Euripides, and Sophocles to us,
Paccuvius, Accius,[9] him of Cordova dead,[10]
To life again, to hear thy buskin[11] tread,
35 And shake a stage: Or, when thy socks[12] were on,

---

6. disproportioned: Not comparable.
7. Lyly . . . Kyd . . . Marlowe: Elizabethan playwrights who influenced Shakespeare.
8. small: A limited knowledge of.
9. Aeschylus (es′ kə ləs)**, Euripides** (yoo rip′ ə dēz′) **. . . Sophocles** (sof′ ə klēz′) **. . . Paccuvius** (pə kōō′ vē əs)**, Accius** (ak′ ē əs): Classical Greek and Roman tragic playwrights.
10. him . . . dead: Classical Roman playwright, Seneca, born in Cordova, Spain.
11. buskin: Symbolizes tragedy. Tragic actors wore shoes with thick "buckskin" soles.
12. socks: Symbolize comedy. Comic actors wore thin-soled shoes called "socks."

Leave thee alone, for the comparison
Of all, that insolent Greece, or haughty Rome
Sent forth, or since did from their ashes come.
Triumph, my Britain, thou hast one to show,
40 To whom all scenes[13] of Europe homage owe.
He was not of an age, but for all time!
And all the Muses still were in their prime,
When like Apollo[14] he came forth to warm
Our ears, or like a Mercury[15] to charm!
45 Nature herself was proud of his designs,
And joyed to wear the dressing of his lines!
Which were so richly spun, and woven so fit,[16]
As, since, she will vouchsafe no other wit.
The merry Greek, tart Aristophanes,
50 Neat Terence, witty Plautus,[17] now not please,
But antiquated, and deserted lie
As they were not of Nature's family.
Yet must I not give Nature all; thy art,
My gentle Shakespeare, must enjoy a part.
55 For though the poet's matter nature be,
His art doth give the fashion.[18] And, that he
Who casts[19] to write a living line, must sweat,
(Such as thine are) and strike the second heat
Upon the Muse's anvil; turn the same,
60 (And himself with it) that he thinks to frame,
Or for the laurel[20] he may gain a scorn;
For a good poet's made, as well as born.
And such wert thou. Look how the father's face
Lives in his issue, even so, the race
65 Of Shakespeare's mind, and manners brightly shines
In his well torned, and true filèd[21] lines;
In each of which, he seems to shake a lance,[22]
As brandished at the eyes of ignorance.

---

13. scenes: Stages.
14. Apollo: In Greek and Roman mythology, the god of light, music, and poetry.
15. Mercury: In Roman mythology, the messenger of the gods and the god of cleverness.
16. fit: Appropriately.
17. Aristophanes (ar′ is tof′ ə nēz′) **. . . Terence** (ter′ əns)
. . . Plautus (plô′ təs): Classical Greek and Roman comic playwrights.
18. fashion: Form.
19. casts: Undertakes.
20. laurel: Fame.
21. true filèd: Accurately polished.
22. shake a lance: A pun on Shakespeare's name.

Sweet swan of Avon![23] what a sight it were
70   To see thee in our waters yet appear,
And make those flights upon the banks of Thames
That so did take Eliza and our James![24]
But stay, I see thee in the hemisphere
Advanced, and made a constellation there!
75   Shine forth, thou star of poets, and with rage[25]
Or influence, chide, or cheer the drooping stage,
Which, since thy flight from hence, hath mourned like
    night,
And despairs day, but for thy volume's light.

---

23. Avon: The river on which Shakespeare's home town, Stratford, is located.
24. Eliza . . . James: Queen Elizabeth I and King James I.
25. rage: Poetic inspiration.

RESPONDING TO THE SELECTION

Your Response

1. Who is your favorite writer? Why? How do your reasons compare with Jonson's ideas?

Recalling

2. According to lines 1–12, what are the wrong reasons for praising Shakespeare?
3. According to the final two lines, how has the stage been affected by Shakespeare's death?

Interpreting

4. What does Jonson mean when he comments that Shakespeare was "not of an age, but for all time"?
5. What is the meaning of the metaphor in lines 57–59?
6. (a) What does this poem reveal about Jonson's attitude toward Shakespeare? (b) What does it reveal about his attitudes concerning the art of writing?
7. How does your awareness of the meaning of the allusions contribute to your overall understanding of Jonson's poem?

8. How do Jonson's allusions reflect his interest in classical Greek and Roman literature?

Applying

9. In this poem Jonson expresses the idea that a writer can be immortalized through his or her work. Explain whether or not you agree with this suggestion.

THINKING AND WRITING

Writing a Letter

Write a letter to Ben Jonson in which you tell him whether you agree with the attitudes he expresses concerning Shakespeare and the art of writing. Reread the poem, focusing on Jonson's attitudes. Brainstorm about your own attitudes on these subjects. Then express your opinions in a personal letter. Use an informal, conversational writing style, but be sure to support your opinions. When you revise, make sure you have not included any unnecessary information. Proofread your letter and prepare a final draft.

ROBERT HERRICK

1591–1674

Called the greatest songwriter of the English language, Herrick wrote verses that often please the ear more than the mind. Although he lived through one of the most controversial periods of English history, little of this is reflected in his poetry. His poems are light, whimsical, highly polished, and extremely artificial. They are also a joy to read and hear.

Born to a wealthy goldsmith in London who died when Robert was young, Herrick was apprenticed to his even wealthier uncle, who was also a goldsmith. Although there are no records of his early education, Herrick went up to Cambridge when he was 22 and graduated when he was 29 with a master's degree. Shortly afterward he was ordained a minister and served as a chaplain with English troops fighting in France. On his return from France, he was assigned a rural parish in southwestern England. At first unhappy at his "internal exile," Herrick soon adjusted to the lovely countryside and the easy life of a country parson. There he wrote his charming verse that celebrated equally the passage of time, the beauty of nature, the joys of love, the pleasures of paganism, and the modesty of Christian devotion.

Although not politically active, Herrick was evicted from his parish by triumphant Puritans after the final defeat of Charles I. Returning to his native and much-loved London, Herrick published his poems in a single, thick little volume with two titles: *Hesperides* and *Noble Numbers. Hesperides,* which is the classical Greek name for a mythological garden at the western edge of the world, contained Herrick's secular poems, for which he is best known today. *Noble Numbers* contained his religious verse. Published at a politically turbulent time in London, Herrick's light and graceful poems were ignored by his contemporaries. Interest in them was revived in the nineteenth century, and they are highly regarded today.

With the Restoration in 1660, Herrick went back to his parish in the west country and remained there until his death. When he was young, he had been one of the most ardent disciples of Ben Jonson. From the older poet, Herrick had learned the virtues of a light touch, of a polished surface, and of a restrained manner. He carried his lessons well into his exile, where he sang "of brooks, of blossoms, birds, and bowers: / Of April, May, of June, and July flowers."

GUIDE FOR INTERPRETING

An Ode for Him;
To the Virgins, to Make Much of Time

Writers' Techniques

Symbols. A symbol stands for something other than itself, while at the same time making us aware of itself. For example, although we realize that the American flag is a piece of cloth, we also recognize that it stands for the United States, its system of government, and the kinds of freedom that are enjoyed here. Writers often use symbols because they are such economical ways of expressing complex ideas. For example, the rose is used frequently to express the idea of the swift passage of time and the short duration of beauty and freshness. Feasts or meals often symbolize sharing, affection, community, and close companionship. The rose and the feast are central symbols in the following two poems by Herrick.

Commentary

In "To the Virgins, to Make Much of Time," Herrick advises young women to marry while they can. How does Herrick's advice relate to the reality of marriage-making in the seventeenth century?

Marriages were essentially economic, not romantic, affairs. In most cases, the parents made all the arrangements. A daughter would almost always agree to marry the man that her parents had selected, for she was usually still a teenager and had been brought up to expect her parents to select her husband. Often, as with the very wealthy, the negotiations for marriage began when the prospective brides were still infants. Sometimes, however, girls flatly refused to accept their parents' choices.

Fourteen-year-old Mary Boyle, the daughter of the Earl of Cork, stood her ground against the match her parents had arranged. In turning down James Hamilton, she wrote, "My aversion for him was extraordinary. I could never be brought by fair means or foul to it." Dorothy Osborn was equally determined to marry for love rather than for social and economic advantage. Although the family estates were ruined by the Civil War, her father's health was declining, and her mother was dead, she steadily refused the stream of prospective husbands that her brother provided. "I am certain," she wrote, "I could not love the most perfect person in the world unless I did first believe he had a passion for me."

In light of the realities of seventeenth-century marriages, why do you think Herrick advises women to marry young?

Focus

Write the name of an object, such as a flag, a flower, a football, a catcher's mitt, a sewing needle, or a rolling pin. First, describe the object as it actually exists: the way it looks and what it is used for. Then, write down all the associations you make with the object.

An Ode for Him (Ben Jonson)

Robert Herrick

<blockquote>

Ah Ben!
Say how, or when
Shall we thy guests
Meet at those lyric feasts,
5   Made at the Sun,
The Dog, the Triple Tun?[1]
Where we such clusters had,
As made us nobly wild, not mad;
And yet each verse of thine
10 Outdid the meat, outdid the frolic wine.

My Ben
Or[2] come again:
Or send to us,
Thy wits great overplus;
15   But teach us yet
Wisely to husband[3] it;
Lest we that talent spend:
And having once brought to an end
That precious stock; the store
20 Of such a wit the world should have no more.

</blockquote>

---

1. Sun . . . Dog . . . Triple Tun: The names of taverns where "The Tribe of Ben" (see p. 382) would gather.

2. or: Either.

3. husband: Conserve.

Your Response

1. Has someone been a great source of inspiration in your life? Explain.

Recalling

2. What question is asked in the first six lines?
3. (a) In lines 11–16, what does the speaker ask of Ben? (b) In lines 17–20, what risks does the speaker describe if Ben does not respond?

Interpreting

4. In what way were the speaker and others Ben Jonson's guests?
5. The tone of this poem is melancholy. What words, phrases, and thoughts contribute to setting this melancholy tone?

Applying

6. "An Ode for Him" is a poem praising Ben Jonson. Today there are many occasions on which we speak words of praise. What are those occasions, and how would you express yourself on such occasions?

CRITICAL THINKING AND READING

Knowing Differences Among Synonyms

A **synonym** is a word that has the same or a similar meaning as another word. Sometimes, several words are synonyms, such as *error, mistake, slipup,* and *blunder.* They all mean "incorrectness" or "inaccuracy," but there are slight differences among them. *Error* often implies that the incorrectness has serious ramifications, as when we say, "That was an error in judgment." In contrast, a mistake is often less serious.

We might use the word *slipup* if we felt a mistake was the result of carelessness. A slipup is usually even less serious than a mistake. On the other hand, *blunder* implies greater ramifications than *slipup* or *mistake.* The senses of *stupidity, clumsiness,* and *sloppiness* are part of the meaning of *blunder.*

If we were to arrange our three synonyms according to how close in meaning they are to the word *error,* we would put them in the following order:

error, (1) mistake, (2) blunder, and (3) slipup. Do the same with the following words taken from "An Ode for Him." Look up the synonyms in a dictionary, number them according to how close in meaning they are to the main word, and explain how they differ from one another.

1. *feast:* meal, banquet, religious celebration
2. *wild:* uncivilized, uncontrolled, impassioned
3. *teach:* guide, train, instruct

THINKING AND WRITING

Writing About Synonyms

Imagine that you are writing a letter to a friend explaining how you arranged the synonyms. In your letter, answer the following questions. What was the basis for the order in which you placed the synonyms? Did you first look in a dictionary to find out what the words mean? Did you try to make up sentences to fit the definitions? Did you try out the definitions and sentences on people you know? What was their reaction? Did you check out the order of the synonyms with these people? How did they react to that? Did they confirm your judgment? If not, what did you do? At the end of your letter, ask your friend what he or she thinks the order of the synonyms should be and why. Revise your letter and prepare a final draft.

To the Virgins, to Make Much of Time

Robert Herrick

Gather ye rosebuds while ye may,
    Old time is still a-flying;
And this same flower that smiles today
    Tomorrow will be dying.

5   The glorious lamp of heaven, the sun,
    The higher he's a-getting,
The sooner will his race be run,
    And nearer he's to setting.

That age is best which is the first,
10   When youth and blood are warmer;
But being spent, the worse, and worst
    Times still succeed the former.

Then be not coy, but use your time,
    And, while ye may, go marry;
15 For, having lost but once your prime,
    You may forever tarry.[1]

---

1. tarry (tar′ē) *v.*: Delay.

■ RESPONDING TO THE SELECTION

Your Response

1. Do you agree with the speaker's claim that youth is the best time of life? Why or why not?

Recalling

2. In stanza 1, why does the speaker advise the girls to gather the rosebuds while they may?
3. According to the third stanza, what is the best age, and what happens when it is passed?

4. In stanza 4, why does the speaker suggest that the young girls stop delaying and marry?

Interpreting

5. The central theme or idea of this poem is the swift passage of time. What images express this theme?

Applying

6. This poem is in one sense advice to young women to marry while still young. In what way

THREE LADIES ADORNING A TERM OF HYMEN
Sir Joshua Reynolds
The Tate Gallery, London

does it also express the "carpe diem" or "seize the day" tradition? Why do you think this tradition was so popular during the seventeenth century?

 ANALYZING LITERATURE

Understanding Symbols

Symbols are taken for what they are and, at the same time, stand for something else. The po-

ets of the sixteenth and seventeenth centuries loved playing with the conventions of their art. One of the most popular conventions of the period was to combine images of swiftly passing time with an urgent expression of love. Robert Herrick was one of the most successful players of this conventional game.

1. Point to all the symbols of time in "To the Virgins, to Make Much of Time."
2. How do these symbols work together to suggest "blossoming youth" and "decaying age"?

BIOGRAPHIES

Sir John Suckling (1609–1642)
Richard Lovelace (1618–1657)

The works of Suckling and Lovelace have been linked together as the prime examples of the lyrics known as *Cavalier poetry*. Both poets wrote a light and easy kind of verse associated with the court of Charles I. Both affected a tone of gentlemanly nonchalance in their poems; both were courtiers under Charles.

Suckling came from an extremely wealthy family and used up his inheritance by living extravagantly. At one point he hired one hundred fighting men, dressed them up in fancy uniforms, went off to fight for the king in Scotland, and was roundly beaten. When he was not engaged in futile fights, he wasted his wealth in gambling. However, he was also a serious patron of many excellent poets, wrote four plays that were spectacularly staged and published at his own exorbitant cost, and composed the delicate lyrics that have gained him fame for more than 300 years. As Parliament rebelled against King Charles I and gained control of the government, Suckling joined in a conspiracy to free a Royalist leader from the Tower of London. The plot was exposed and Suckling fled to France. There he died impoverished and in despair.

Also from an extremely wealthy family, Lovelace was the pretty boy of Cavalier poetry. He was so handsome that the king and queen ordered that he be granted a master's degree before he completed his studies at Oxford. He was, however, also talented. While at Oxford he wrote a play, painted some fine pictures, and performed credibly on several musical instruments. Perhaps because he was so attractive, Lovelace was chosen by the Royalists to present to Parliament a demand for the restoration of the king's right to absolute authority. Lovelace was immediately arrested. While imprisoned, he wrote "To Althea" as a justification for siding with the king even though it meant being confined in jail. After his release from prison, he rejoined Charles's forces in the civil war and spent most of his fortune to help equip the king's army. Upon Charles's defeat in 1645, Lovelace went to France and fought against Holland. Returning to England some while later, he was once again imprisoned by the Puritans. It was during this second imprisonment that he prepared for publication the volume of poems that included "To Lucasta." Although no one knows for certain, it is believed that he died in poverty.

GUIDE FOR INTERPRETING

The Constant Lover; Song; To Lucasta, on Going to the Wars; To Althea, from Prison

Writers' Techniques

Tone. In literature, tone refers to the attitude expressed by an author toward his or her subject or audience. A writer's attitude is conveyed through language, characterization, setting, point of view, and details of appearance, voice, location, and the like. Whether in prose or poetry, recognizing the writer's tone is essential to an understanding of the work. Without this recognition, we cannot tell if an author is serious or playful, mocking or admiring, angry or joking, laughing or crying. Very often the tone of a piece of writing can shift from one attitude to another.

Focus

Describe the way you feel about something. Your subject can be either serious or trivial. Do not say directly how you feel; do not say, "I am angry," "I am amused," "I am proud," or "I am sorry." The important thing is that you reveal how you feel through the words and details you use in your writing.

Primary Source

A man investigating prison conditions in the seventeenth century wrote, "Lord Bless me! What a Sight is here! I do not think there had been so much cruelty in the Hearts of Englishmen, to use Englishmen in this manner." What he saw was appalling indeed.

Prisoners were herded together, without privacy or comfort. They slept on piles of straw, usually directly on the cold ground. Since there was no indoor plumbing, bathing was virtually impossible. A few prisons had fireplaces, and jailers might provide coals for a fee, but more than a century later the majority of English prisons still did not have heating or baths. Prisoners were given only a quarter of a loaf of bread daily, supplemented by what their family and friends could supply. Scores perished from jail fever. For this, prisoners paid five pounds a year!

Because jailers had to pay a tax on windows, fresh air was scarcer than water and heat. One eyewitness wrote, "The most pernicious infection next to the plague is the smell of a jail, whereof we have had, in our time, experience once or twice." One visitor protected himself by "smelling to vinegar, while I was in those places, and changing my apparel afterwards."

How does the tone of "To Althea, from Prison" reflect prison life in the seventeenth century?

The Constant Lover

Sir John Suckling

Out upon it! I have loved
    Three whole days together;
And am like to love three more,
    If it prove fair weather.

5 Time shall molt away his wings,
    Ere he shall discover
In the whole wide world again
    Such a constant lover.

But the spite on 't is, no praise
10   Is due at all to me:
Love with me had made no stays,
    Had it any been but she.

Had it any been but she,
    And that very face,
15 There had been at least ere this
    A dozen dozen in her place.

THE INTERRUPTED SLEEP
François Boucher
The Metropolitan Museum of Art

⬛ RESPONDING TO THE SELECTION

Your Response

1. What is your opinion of this "constant lover"? Explain.

Recalling

2. According to lines 3 and 4, what conditions are necessary for the speaker to continue to love?
3. In the second stanza, how long will it be before Time will find a lover as faithful as the speaker?
4. According to stanza 3, why is praise not due the speaker?
5. In the last stanza, what reason does the speaker give for not leaving his lady for another "dozen dozen" women?

Interpreting

6. The poem is an elaborate compliment to a lady. What are the elements that contribute to this compliment?
7. When an inanimate object or an abstract idea, such as Time or Death, is given human characteristics, it is called *personification*. What is personified in stanza 2, and how does it work in the poem?
8. (a) What attitudes toward love and the woman are evident? (b) In what way is the word *constant* in the title ironic?

Applying

9. What qualities do you think characterize a constant lover?

Song

Sir John Suckling

FAIR IS MY LOVE
Edwin A. Abbey
The Harris Museum and Art Gallery, Preston

Why so pale and wan, fond lover?
    Prithee, why so pale?
Will, when looking well can't move her,
    Looking ill prevail?
5   Prithee, why so pale?

Why so dull and mute, young sinner?
    Prithee, why so mute?
Will, when speaking well can't win her,
    Saying nothing do't?
10   Prithee, why so mute?

Quit, quit, for shame; this will not move,
    This cannot take her.
If of herself she will not love,
    Nothing can make her:
15   The devil take her!

RESPONDING TO THE SELECTION

Your Response

1. Do you agree with the speaker's advice? Explain.

Recalling

2. In the first stanza of "Song," how does the lover look?
3. What is the question the speaker asks in the second stanza?

Interpreting

4. The third stanza is different from the two preceding ones. In what way is it different?
5. What has caused the "fond" lover to look and behave in the way described by the speaker?
6. What do you think is the lover's emotional state? Explain your answer.

Applying

7. This poem is in a sense an early example of advice to the lovelorn. If a good friend broke up with a loved one, what sort of advice would you give? What would you say and how would you say it?

THINKING AND WRITING

Writing About Tone

Write an essay in which you discuss the tone of Suckling's "Song." Imagine that you will deliver this paper to a scholarly audience. For this audience you will want to discuss the use of irony and wit as instruments for expressing the poet's attitude toward his subject.

GOING TO THE BATTLE
Edward Burne-Jones
Fitzwilliam Museum, Cambridge

To Lucasta, on Going to the Wars

Richard Lovelace

Tell me not, Sweet, I am unkind,
　　That from the nunnery
Of thy chaste breast, and quiet mind,
　　To war and arms I fly.

5　True, a new mistress now I chase,
　　The first foe in the field;
And with a stronger faith embrace
　　A sword, a horse, a shield.

Yet this inconstancy is such,
10　　As you too shall adore;
I could not love thee, Dear, so much,
　　Loved I not honor more.

RESPONDING TO THE SELECTION

Your Response
1. Do you find the speaker's reasoning convincing? Explain.

Recalling
2. In the second stanza, whom does the speaker chase, and what will he embrace?
3. According to the last stanza, why will the abandoned lady "adore" the speaker's "inconstancy"?

Interpreting
4. What is the "new mistress" the speaker refers to in the second stanza?
5. What do you believe is the "stronger faith" mentioned by the speaker in line 7?

6. What does the speaker mean when he says in lines 11–12, "I could not love thee, Dear, so much / Loved I not honor more"?
7. This poem is an argument made by the speaker to his lady love in an effort to convince her to accept his leaving her for war. What details in the poem support this interpretation?

Applying
8. If you were to leave a loved one to go off to fight, what would you say to convince that person to accept your departure?
9. In "Song" (page 360), John Donne also wrote an argument trying to persuade his beloved to accept his leaving her. Compare the poems by Donne and Lovelace. How do they differ? In what one respect are they similar?

To Althea, from Prison

Richard Lovelace

When love with unconfined wings
    Hovers within my gates,
And my divine Althea brings
    To whisper at the grates;
5 When I lie tangled in her hair
    And fettered to her eye,
The gods[1] that wanton[2] in the air
    Know no such liberty.

When flowing cups run swiftly round,
10   With no allaying Thames,[3]
Our careless heads with roses bound,
    Our hearts with loyal flames;
When thirsty grief in wine we steep,
    When healths[4] and drafts[5] go free,
15 Fishes that tipple in the deep,
    Know no such liberty.

When, like committed linnets,[6] I
    With shriller throat shall sing
The sweetness, mercy, majesty,
20   And glories of my King;
When I shall voice aloud how good
    He is, how great should be,
      Enlarged[7] winds that curl the flood,
      Know no such liberty.

---

1. gods: The word *gods* is replaced by *birds* in some versions of this poem.
2. wanton: Play.
3. cups . . . Thames (temz): Wine that has not been diluted by water (from the river Thames).
4. healths: Toasts.
5. drafts: Drinks.
6. committed linnets: Caged finches.
7. enlarged: Released.

25   Stone walls do not a prison make,
        Nor iron bars a cage;
    Minds innocent and quiet take
        That for an hermitage;
    If I have freedom in my love,
30   And in my soul am free,
    Angels alone that soar above,
        Enjoy such liberty.

RESPONDING TO THE SELECTION

Your Response

1. What is your definition of freedom? How does it compare with the speaker's?

Recalling

2. (a) According to lines 1–4, where is the god Love hovering? (b) Where is the "divine Althea" whispering?
3. (a) In lines 5–8, what does the speaker say gives him the greatest freedom? (b) What conditions does the speaker describe in the second stanza as yielding the greatest freedom?
4. (a) What, in the last stanza, does the speaker say is required to enable him to enjoy the maximum freedom? (b) What or who does the speaker say in the first three stanzas will experience no greater freedom than he? (c) To what does the speaker compare his freedom in the last stanza?

Interpreting

5. (a) The conditions for the speaker's freedom form a progressive movement in the first three stanzas. What is that movement? (b) Summarize the speaker's conception of freedom.
6. In seventeenth-century England, part of the conflict between King Charles I and his rebellious Parliament was over freedom. Charles wanted to rule by "divine right," which meant basically that he could do as he wished. Parliament wished to take that right away from him. To Charles, this meant a loss of freedom. The Puritans in Parliament, on the other hand, felt that Charles had tried to take away their freedom of religion. From their point of view, it was either his freedom or their freedom that was at stake.

(a) In what way does Lovelace's poem, "To Althea," reflect this issue? (b) Why does each stanza turn on the idea of "liberty"?
7. Some critics have called "To Althea" a love poem; others have said it was an expression of devotion to King Charles. Which interpretation do you believe is right and why?

Applying

8. The first two lines of the fourth stanza of "To Althea" are very famous. They have been repeated down through the ages, often by people who did not know their source. Aside from their poignancy, why, in your opinion, have these lines been so very popular?

LEARNING OPTION

Cross-curricular Connection. Investigate the conflict between King Charies I and the Puritans in Parliament over issues of political and religious freedom. Write a brief news report that dramatizes one aspect of the controversy. You may invent dialogue and details, but make sure that your report is, on the whole, historically accurate.

The Puritan Age

THE FARRIER'S SHOP, c. 1620–1687
Gael Barend
Guildhall Art Gallery, London

JOHN MILTON

1608–1674

Ranked with William Shakespeare and Geoffrey Chaucer as among the greatest poets of the English language, John Milton actually produced comparatively few poems. The major part of his life he spent either studying literature or writing political tracts. Yet *Paradise Lost* by itself would have been enough to earn him a place among the immortals of English literature.

Born in London to a middle-class family, Milton grew up in a highly cultured environment. His father was a composer and musician of considerable ability as well as a professional scribe or notary. Milton's father was also deeply religious and devoted to the Protestant cause. Educated first at home by tutors, Milton started his formal education in the equivalent of high school when he was about thirteen. While a student at this school, he mastered Greek, Latin, and Hebrew as well as several modern European languages. Then he went on to college.

It was while at Cambridge University that Milton decided to prepare himself for a career as a great poet ("God's poet," was how he described it). From this point until the English Civil War broke out, Milton devoted himself to a life of study. After earning his degrees from Cambridge, he withdrew to his father's house at Horton for five years, where he is reputed to have read everything that was written in the ancient and modern languages that he knew. It was during this long period of study that Milton wrote "L'Allegro," "Il Penseroso," and "Lycidas," which by themselves would have earned him a lasting position as a major poet. Following his stay at Horton, he went on the Grand European Tour for two years.

While Milton was in Europe, Parliament rebelled against King Charles I; learning of the revolt, Milton cut short his trip and rushed back to England. There he immediately took up the cudgels in defense of the Parliamentary and Puritan cause. It was in this role that he took part in the pamphlet war of the time and became a leading proponent of republican principles. As a result of his brilliant writings, Oliver Cromwell made Milton Latin Secretary of the Commonwealth. It was in this job that he went blind. Upon restoration of the monarchy, he was at first imprisoned and then released. Andrew Marvell, his former assistant and now Member of Parliament, may have argued in his behalf.

After Milton's release and the loss of most of his property, he withdrew into his blindness and poverty to write *Paradise Lost,* the greatest epic of the English language.

GUIDE FOR INTERPRETING

When I Consider How My Light Is Spent; On His Having Arrived at the Age of Twenty-Three

Writers' Techniques

The Italian Sonnet. The sonnet is one of the major forms of English poetry, but it was invented by the Italians in the thirteenth century. It was imported into England by Wyatt and Surrey in the middle of the sixteenth century. The Italian sonnet is a fourteen-line lyric poem. It is usually divided into two segments, an octave of eight lines and a sestet of six lines. According to the sonnet convention, the octave is supposed to present a situation or problem, and the sestet is supposed to offer an answer or response. The rhyme scheme also follows a fairly strict pattern. The octave rhymes *abbaabba,* and the sestet usually varies, although within a fairly narrow range. In English, sonnets, whether Italian or not, are written in ten-syllable lines, five beats to the line, with a stress pattern that goes like this:

$$\cup \quad / \quad \cup \quad / \quad \cup \quad / \cup \quad / \quad \cup \quad /$$
How soon hath Time, the subtle thief of youth,

Commentary

In "On His Having Arrived at the Age of Twenty-Three," Milton assesses his life. People completing their education today sometimes assess their lives as they prepare to embark on a career. Some people feel that they should already have accomplished more. Imagine how they would feel hearing the stories of child prodigies who have already achieved a lifetime of accomplishments before reaching their teens!

Wolfgang Amadeus Mozart (1756–1791), for example, began music lessons at age four, and by five was composing minuets. A year later his ability to sight-read music caused a sensation throughout Europe. He wrote his first symphony at eight; at twelve he wrote two operas and a mass. His achievements grew as he matured, and today, as then, he is considered a musical genius.

John Stuart Mill (1806–1873) was fluent in Greek at three, Latin at eight—not to mention his accomplishments in history and mathematics. By twelve he had read the classics in the original. He became an important theorist and writer in politics, economics, and philosophy who dedicated himself to justice and the public good.

According to the poem, how does Milton believe he will accomplish his goals?

Focus

Jot down some ideas on reaching whatever age you might now be—16, 17, 18. Try to include some ideas reflecting your view of your accomplishments to date and what you expect from the future.

When I Consider How My Light Is Spent

John Milton

When I consider how my light is spent
 Ere half my days, in this dark world and wide,
 And that one talent[1] which is death to hide,
 Lodged with me useless, though my soul more bent
5 To serve therewith my Maker, and present
 My true account, lest he returning chide;
 "Doth God exact day labor, light denied?"
 I fondly[2] ask; but Patience to prevent
That murmur, soon replies, "God doth not need
10 Either man's work or his own gifts; who best
 Bear his mild yoke, they serve him best. His state
Is kingly. Thousands[3] at his bidding speed
 And post[4] o'er land and ocean without rest:
 They also serve who only stand and wait."

---

1. talent: An allusion to the parable of the talents (Matthew 25:14-30).
2. fondly: Foolishly.
3. thousands: Thousands of angels.
4. post: Travel.

RESPONDING TO THE SELECTION

Your Response

1. How might you adjust to blindness? Compare your attitude to Milton's.

Recalling

2. According to lines 1–2, at what point in the speaker's life does his eyesight fail?
3. What three qualities does the second speaker attribute to God?

Interpreting

4. Why, in your opinion, might Milton have felt that his blindness made his talent useless?
5. Explain the last line of the poem: "They also serve who only stand and wait."
6. This sonnet, unlike most other sonnets, is like the dialogue in a play. How does this unusual formal arrangement affect your understanding of the poem?

Applying

7. Do you feel it is necessary for people to use their talents? Explain your answer.

ANALYZING LITERATURE

Understanding Italian Sonnets

The rhyme scheme of Milton's sonnet on his blindness is *abbaabba cdecde,* which is common to the Italian sonnet. To emphasize their rhyme scheme, most sonneteers end-stop their lines. When a natural pause occurs at the end of a line, the line is called *end-stopped.* An example of end stopping is the third line of Milton's "When I Consider . . ." This can be contrasted with the next line, the normal reading of which carries one over to the following or fifth line. This kind of carryover is called *enjambment* or a *run-on line.* Run-on lines tend to obscure end rhymes and thereby make the rhyme scheme more subtle than it might otherwise be. There are a number of run-on lines in Milton's poem.

Another characteristic of the sonnet is the change that takes place between the first eight lines, or octave, and the following six lines, or sestet. Most often the change is very subtle in the Italian sonnet. In Milton's "When I Consider . . ." it is very obvious.

1. Which rhyme sounds are end-stopped and which run on in the octave?

2. How many end-stopped lines are there in the sestet?

3. Did you read the run-on lines as if you were reading prose? Explain your answer.

4. Which seem more natural to you, the end-stopped lines or the run-on ones? Which seem more artificial?

5. What shift in tone do you notice between the octave and sestet when reading aloud? How do you account for this shift?

LEARNING OPTION

Speaking and Listening. Many books, both non-fiction and fiction, have been written by or about people who have overcome challenging physical conditions. Examples include *The Story of My Life* by Helen Keller; *It's Good to Be Alive* by Roy Campanella; *My Left Foot* by Christy Brown; *Sunrise at Campobello,* a play about Franklin D. Roosevelt by Dore Schary; and the play *Children of a Lesser God* by Mark Medoff. Read one of these books, watch a movie version of one of them, or choose another book with a similar theme. Share your impressions of the book or film orally with the class.

Primary Source

Milton's essay, "The Second Defense of the English People," written in 1654, offers an intriguing glimpse into his life. In the following excerpt, he discusses his childhood and describes what he sees as the cause for his later blindness:

"I will now mention who and whence I am. I was born at London, of an honest family; my father was distinguished by the undeviating integrity of his life; my mother, by the esteem in which she was held, and the alms which she bestowed. My father destined me from a child to the pursuits of literature; and my appetite for knowledge was so voracious, that, from twelve years of age, I hardly ever left my studies, or went to bed before midnight. This primarily led to my loss of sight. My eyes were naturally weak, and I was subject to frequent head-aches; which, however, could not chill the ardor of my curiosity, or retard the progress of my improvement."

On His Having Arrived at the Age of Twenty-Three

John Milton

How soon hath Time, the subtle thief of youth,
    Stolen on his wing my three and twentieth year!
    My hasting days fly on with full career,[1]
    But my late spring no bud or blossom showeth.
5 Perhaps my semblance might deceive[2] the truth,
    That I to manhood am arrived so near,
    And inward ripeness doth much less appear,
    That some more timely-happy spirits[3] endueth.[4]
    Yet be it less or more, or soon or slow,
10   It shall be still[5] in strictest measure even,
    To that same lot,[6] however mean or high,
Toward which Time leads me, and the will of Heaven;
    All is, if I have grace to use it so,
    As ever in my great Taskmaster's eye.

---

1. career: Speed.
2. deceive: Prove false.
3. timely-happy spirits: Other people who seem to be more accomplished poets at the age of twenty-three.
4. endueth: Endoweth.
5. still: Always.
6. lot: Fate.

MULTICULTURAL CONNECTION

Celebrating Birthdays

John Milton may have had mixed feelings about turning twenty-three, but how do people in different cultures today feel about birthdays?

In India, the birthday child remains the center of attention all day, does not have to go to school, and cannot be punished, regardless of his or her behavior. However, this royal treatment lasts only until a child's sixteenth birthday.

Adults are the ones who have the most elaborate birthday parties in China. This is part of the ancient Chinese tradition of revering age and wisdom.

A girl's fifteenth birthday is very important in Hispanic cultures. The occasion is celebrated with a large party and gifts to honor "la quinceañera" (the fifteen-year-old).

In Korea, the sixtieth birthday, called *hwan'gap,* is a festive occasion because it marks the completion of one full cycle of life and the beginning of another.

Sharing Your Experiences

What events in your own life marked your becoming a young adult? How were they celebrated? Discuss this with classmates.

RESPONDING TO THE SELECTION

Your Response

1. Have you ever felt the kind of dissatisfaction that the speaker feels about himself? Explain.

Recalling

2. According to the first line, who or what is the "subtle thief of youth"?
3. According to the second line, what was stolen?
4. In line 4, what is not shown?
5. In lines 5–6, what is the speaker's image that "might deceive the truth"?
6. According to lines 7–8, what does not appear that others seem to have?
7. According to lines 8–12, to what will the speaker's accomplishments eventually conform?
8. What, according to lines 13–14, is forever in the "great Taskmaster's eye"?

Interpreting

9. A metaphor is a comparison of two unlike things. In line 4, Milton uses two metaphors: one for the advanced stage of his youth, the other to represent the early or full development of his poetic ability. Which words are the metaphors?
10. Compare and contrast the concerns of the first four and second four lines of the poem.
11. Overall, what concerns the speaker in the first eight lines?
12. How do the last six lines answer the concern expressed in the first eight lines?

Applying

13. One reason Milton may have felt he hadn't achieved much is that he hadn't yet decided on a career. He had first thought of entering the church and becoming a minister, but by the time he was twenty-three had decided against it. How many people do you know who have made career decisions by the time they were twenty-three? Why do you think it is so difficult to do this?

THINKING AND WRITING

Comparing and Contrasting Sonnets

Write an essay comparing and contrasting Italian and English sonnets. Imagine you are writing this essay for your school newspaper.

The English sonnet, which is also commonly known as the Shakespearean sonnet, is markedly different from the Italian form. The sonnet was first developed by the Italians as a fourteen-line love poem with a strict rhyme scheme and structure. The structure is divided into an eight-line octave and a six-line sestet.

The English sonnet, which derives from the Italian, has an entirely different structure and rhyme scheme. The sonnet is divided into three four-line quatrains and a concluding two-line couplet. Each of these units has a different set of rhymes and a slightly different thought or image.

Use Shakespeare's Sonnet 73 (page 229) and Milton's "On His Having Arrived at the Age of Twenty-Three" as your models. Analyze the rhyme scheme in both poems, and explain the shifts in thought and image in both poems. Also describe the subjects of both poems. In what way are the subjects similar? How are they different? When you revise, make sure you have arranged your information in logical order. Proofread your essay and prepare a final draft.

LEARNING OPTION

Performance. Milton's sonnets lend themselves well to dramatic reading. Choose either "When I Consider How My Light Is Spent" or "On His Having Arrived at the Age of Twenty-Three" to interpret orally for the class. Review the lines carefully, making sure you fully understand them. Then practice reading the sonnet aloud, trying to express its meaning accurately through stresses, pauses, and appropriate tone. Consider playing recorded music during your performance.

GUIDE FOR INTERPRETING

from Paradise Lost

Epic Poetry. An epic is a long narrative poem written in an elevated style. It tells the story of a major cultural hero and reflects the values of the society in which it was produced. The early English epic *Beowulf* exhibits the values of the Anglo-Saxon warriors for whom it was composed. John Milton's epic *Paradise Lost* expresses the values of Christian England in the late seventeenth century. It also expresses, however, ideas that are so universal that the poem has become *the* epic of the English-speaking world.

Milton based his poem on the biblical story of Adam and Eve, and his style on the classical epics of ancient Greece and Rome. Like the *Aeneid,* the epic of classical Rome, Milton divided *Paradise Lost* into twelve books. He wrote the poem in blank verse, which no one writing in English had done before except in plays. Because the great epics of ancient Greece and Rome did not rhyme, Milton chose to use blank verse, which is unrhymed iambic pentameter.

Paradise Lost had to be licensed by the Archbishop of Canterbury before it could be published. As was the practice, the Archbishop passed the manuscript to a deputy. In this case the deputy was a chaplain named Tomkyns who had written pamphlets against the dissenters. Fortunately, Tomkyns did not wish to direct attention to himself and so chose to ignore anti-monarchical passages in the manuscript that might even have gotten Milton hanged. Tomkyns might also have thought that *Paradise Lost* was religious verse not likely to be read at court and therefore its contents were not important. He approved it.

After his manuscript was licensed by the Archbishop, Milton found a publisher for it in Aldersgate, which had not been destroyed in the recent Great Fire. The contract, still preserved in the national museum, records that the agreement was drawn up between the author "John Milton, gent. of the one parte, and Samuel Symons, printer, of the other parte." For his work Milton received five pounds down and was to receive a second five pounds each for the sale of the first, second, and third editions, respectively.

Milton earned only five more pounds for the sale of the first edition. All told, he received ten pounds for his masterpiece. Do you think the market for serious literature has changed?

Jot down all the information you remember of the biblical story of the fall of Adam and Eve.

from Paradise Lost

John Milton

Of man's first disobedience, and the fruit
Of that forbidden tree, whose mortal[1] taste
Brought death into the world, and all our woe,
With loss of Eden, till one greater Man[2]
5   Restore us, and regain the blissful seat,
Sing Heavenly Muse,[3] that on the secret top
Of Oreb, or of Sinai,[4] didst inspire
That shepherd, who first taught the chosen seed,
In the beginning how the Heavens and Earth
10 Rose out of Chaos: or if Sion hill[5]
Delight thee more, and Siloa's brook[6] that flowed
Fast[7] by the oracle of God, I thence
Invoke thy aid to my adventurous song,
That with no middle flight intends to soar
15 Above the Aonian mount,[8] while it pursues
Things unattempted yet in prose or rhyme.
And chiefly thou O Spirit,[9] that dost prefer
Before all temples the upright heart and pure,
Instruct me, for thou know'st; thou from the first
20 Wast present, and with mighty wings outspread
Dovelike sat'st brooding on the vast abyss
And mad'st it pregnant: what in me is dark
Illumine, what is low raise and support;
That to the height of this great argument[10]

---

1. mortal: Deadly.
2. one . . . Man: Christ.
3. Heavenly Muse: Urania, the muse of astronomy and sacred poetry in Greek mythology. Here, Milton associates Urania with the holy spirit that inspired Moses ("That shepherd,") to receive and interpret the word of God for the Jews ("the chosen seed"). To convey the message of God to his people, Moses wrote the first five books of the Bible, including Genesis. Genesis is the book on which *Paradise Lost* is based.
4. Oreb (ôr′ ĕb) **. . . Sinai** (sī′ nī′): Alternate names for the mountain where God communicated the laws to Moses.
5. Sion (sī′ ən) **hill:** The hill near Jerusalem on which the temple ("the oracle of God,") stood.
6. Siloa's (sī lō′ əz) **brook:** A stream near Sion hill.
7. fast: Close.
8. Aonian (ā ō′ nē ən) **Mount:** Mount Helicon in Greek mythology, home of the Muses. Milton is drawing a comparison between the epic he is now presenting and the epics written by the classical poets, Homer and Virgil.
9. Spirit: The Holy Spirit, the voice that provided inspiration for the Hebrew prophets.
10. argument: Theme.

25   I may assert Eternal Providence,
     And justify the ways of God to men.
           Say first, for Heaven hides nothing from thy view
     Nor the deep tract of Hell, say first what cause
     Moved our grand[11] parents in that happy state,
30   Favored of Heaven so highly, to fall off
     From their Creator, and transgress his will
     For[12] one restraint,[13] lords of the world besides?[14]
     Who first seduced them to that foul revolt?
     The infernal Serpent; he it was, whose guile
35   Stirred up with envy and revenge, deceived
     The mother of mankind, what time his pride
     Had cast him out from Heaven, with all his host
     Of rebel angels, by whose aid aspiring
     To set himself in glory above his peers,
40   He trusted to have equaled the Most High,
     If he opposed; and with ambitious aim
     Against the throne and monarchy of God
     Raised impious war in Heaven and battle proud
     With vain attempt. Him the Almighty Power
45   Hurled headlong flaming from the ethereal sky
     With hideous ruin and combustion down
     To bottomless perdition, there to dwell
     In adamantine[15] chains and penal fire.
     Who durst defy the Omnipotent to arms.
50   Nine times the space that measures day and night
     To mortal men, he with his horrid crew
     Lay vanquished, rolling in the fiery gulf,
     Confounded though immortal. But his doom
     Reserved him to more wrath; for now the thought
55   Both of lost happiness and lasting pain
     Torments him; round he throws his baleful eyes
     That witnessed[16] huge affliction and dismay,
     Mixed with obdurate pride and steadfast hate.
     At once as far as angels' ken,[17] he views
60   The dismal situation waste and wild:
     A dungeon horrible, on all sides round,
     As one great furnace flamed, yet from those flames
     No light, but rather darkness visible
     Served only to discover sights of woe,
65   Regions of sorrow, doleful shades, where peace

---

11. grand: First in importance and in time.
12. for: Because of.
13. one restraint: That Adam and Eve should not eat of the fruit of the tree of knowledge.
14. besides: In every other respect.
15. adamantine (ad′ ə man′ tēn) *adj*: Unbreakable.
16. witnessed: Gave evidence of.
17. ken: Can see.

And rest can never dwell, hope never comes
That comes to all; but torture without end
Still urges,[18] and a fiery deluge, fed
With ever-burning sulfur unconsumed:
70 Such place eternal justice had prepared
For these rebellious, here their prison ordained
In utter darkness, and their portion set
As far removed from God and light of Heaven
As from the center thrice to the utmost pole.[19]
75 O how unlike the place from whence they fell!
There the companions of his fall, o'erwhelmed
With floods and whirlwinds of tempestuous fire,
He soon discerns, and weltering by his side
One next himself in power, and next in crime,
80 Long after known in Palestine, and named
Beelzebub.[20] To whom the archenemy,
And thence in Heaven called Satan, with bold words
Breaking the horrid silence thus began:
    "If thou beest he; but O how fallen! how changed
85 From him, who in the happy realms of light
Clothed with transcendent brightness didst outshine
Myriads though bright: if he whom mutual league,
United thoughts and counsels, equal hope
And hazard in the glorious enterprise,
90 Joined with me once, now misery hath joined
In equal ruin: into what pit thou seest
From what height fallen, so much the stronger proved
He with his thunder:[21] and till then who knew
The force of those dire arms? Yet not for those,
95 Nor what the potent Victor in his rage
Can else inflict, do I repent or change,
Though changed in outward luster, that fixed mind
And high disdain, from sense of injured merit,
That with the Mightiest raised me to contend,
100 And to the fierce contention brought along
Innumerable force of spirts armed
That durst dislike his reign, and me preferring,
His utmost power with adverse power opposed
In dubious battle on the plains of Heaven,
105 And shook his throne. What though the field be lost?
All is not lost; the unconquerable will,

---

18. urges: Afflicts.
19. center . . . pole: Three times the distance from the center of the universe (earth) to the outermost sphere of the universe.
20. Beelzebub (bē el' zə bub'): Traditionally, the chief devil, or Satan. In this poem, Satan's chief lieutenant among the fallen angels.
21. He . . . thunder: God.

And study[22] of revenge, immortal hate,
And courage never to submit or yield:
And what is else not to be overcome?
110 That glory never shall his wrath or might
Extort from me. To bow and sue for grace
With suppliant knee, and deify his power
Who from the terror of this arm so late
Doubted[23] his empire, that were low indeed,
115 That were an ignominy and shame beneath
This downfall; since by fate the strength of gods
And this empyreal substance[24] cannot fail,
Since through experience of this great event,
In arms not worse, in foresight much advanced,
120 We may with more successful hope resolve
To wage by force or guile eternal war
Irreconcilable, to our grand Foe,
Who now triumphs, and in the excess of joy
Sole reigning holds the tyranny of Heaven."
125   So spake the apostate angel, though in pain,
Vaunting aloud, but racked with deep despair;
And him thus answered soon his bold compeer.[25]
    "O prince, O chief of many thronèd Powers,
That led the embattled Seraphim[26] to war
130 Under thy conduct, and in dreadful deeds
Fearless, endangered Heaven's perpetual King,
And put to proof his high supremacy,
Whether upheld by strength, or chance, or fate!
Too well I see and rue the dire event[27]
135 That with sad overthrow and foul defeat
Hath lost us Heaven, and all this mighty host
In horrible destruction laid thus low,
As far as gods and heavenly essences
Can perish: for the mind and spirit remains
140 Invincible, and vigor soon returns,
Though all our glory extinct, and happy state
Here swallowed up in endless misery.
But what if he our conqueror (whom I now
Of force[28] believe almighty, since no less
145 Than such could have o'erpowered such force as ours)
Have left us this our spirit and strength entire
Strongly to suffer and support our pains,

---

22. study: Pursuit.
23. doubted: Feared for.
24. empyreal (em pir′ ē əl) **substance:** The indestructible substance
of which Heaven, or the empyrean, is composed.
25. compeer: Comrade, equal.
26. Seraphim (sĕr′ ə fim): The highest order of angels.
27. event: Outcome.
28. of force: Necessarily.

That we may so suffice[29] his vengeful ire,
Or do him mightier service as his thralls
150 By right of war, whate'er his business be
Here in the heart of Hell to work in fire,
Or do his errands in the gloomy deep?
What can it then avail though yet we feel
Strength undiminished, or eternal being
155 To undergo eternal punishment?''
Whereto with speedy words the Archfiend replied:
    ''Fallen cherub, to be weak is miserable,
Doing or suffering:[30] but of this be sure,
To do aught[31] good never will be our task,
160 But ever to do ill our sole delight,
As being the contrary to his high will
Whom we resist. If then his providence
Out of our evil seek to bring forth good,
Our labor must be to pervert that end,
165 And out of good still[32] to find means of evil;
Which oft times may succeed, so as perhaps
Shall grieve him, if I fail not,[33] and disturb
His inmost counsels from their destined aim.
But see the angry Victor[34] hath recalled
170 His ministers of vengeance and pursuit
Back to the gates of Heaven: the sulfurous hail
Shot after us in storm, o'erblown hath laid
The fiery surge, that from the precipice
Of Heaven received us falling, and the thunder,
175 Winged with red lightning and impetuous rage,
Perhaps hath spent his shafts, and ceases now
To bellow through the vast and boundless deep.
Let us not slip[35] the occasion, whether scorn,
Or satiate[36] fury yield it from our Foe.
180 Seest thou yon dreary plain, forlorn and wild,
The seat of desolation, void of light,
Save what the glimmering of these livid flames
Casts pale and dreadful? Thither let us tend
From off the tossing of these fiery waves,
185 There rest, if any rest can harbor there,
And reassembling our afflicted powers,[37]
Consult how we may henceforth most offend

---

29. suffice: Satisfy.
30. doing or suffering: Whether one is active or passive.
31. aught: Anything.
32. still: Always.
33. if . . . not: Unless I am mistaken.
34. angry Victor: God.
35. slip: Fail to take advantage of.
36. satiate: Satisfied.
37. afflicted powers: Overthrown armies.

Our Enemy, our own loss how repair,
How overcome this dire calamity,
190 What reinforcement we may gain from hope,
If not what resolution from despair.''
    Thus Satan talking to his nearest mate,
With head uplift above the wave, and eyes
That sparkling blazed; his other parts besides,
195 Prone on the flood, extended long and large,

PARADISE LOST, 1688
From the British Library

Lay floating many a rood,[38] in bulk as huge
As whom the fables name of monstrous size,
Titanian, or Earthborn, that warred on Jove,
Briareos or Typhon,[39] whom the den
200 By ancient Tarsus[40] held, or that sea beast
Leviathan,[41] which God of all his works
Created hugest that swim the ocean stream:
Him haply slumbering on the Norway foam
The pilot of some small night-foundered skiff,
205 Deeming some island, oft, as seamen tell,
With fixed anchor in his scaly rind
Moors by his side under the lee, while night
Invests[42] the sea, and wished morn delays:
So stretched out huge in length the Archfiend lay
210 Chained on the burning lake, nor ever thence
Had risen or heaved his head, but that the will
And high permission of all-ruling Heaven
Left him at large to his own dark designs,
That with reiterated crimes he might
215 Heap on himself damnation, while he sought
Evil to others, and enraged might see
How all his malice served but to bring forth
Infinite goodness, grace and mercy shown
On man by him seduced, but on himself
220 Treble confusion, wrath and vengeance poured.
Forthwith upright he rears from off the pool
His mighty stature; on each hand the flames
Driven backward, slope their pointing spires, and rolled
In billows leave in the midst a horrid vale.
225 Then with expanded wings he steers his flight
Aloft, incumbent[43] on the dusky air
That felt unusual weight, till on dry land
He lights, if it were land that ever burned
With solid, as the lake with liquid fire;
230 And such appeared in hue, as when the force
Of subterranean wind transports a hill
Torn from Pelorus, or the shattered side

---

38. rood: An old unit of measure, equal to seven or eight yards.
39. Titanian (tī tā′ nē ən) **. . . Earthborn . . . Briareos** (brī är′ ē
əs) **. . . Typhon** (tī′ fən): In classical mythology, both the Titans, led
by Briareos, who had a hundred hands, and the Giants (Earthborn),
led by Typhon, a hundred-headed serpent monster, fought with Jove.
As punishment for their rebellion, both Briareos and Typhon were
thrown into the underworld.
40. Tarsus (tär′ səs): The capital of Cilicia (sə lish′ ə). Typhon is said
to have lived in Cilicia near Tarsus.
41. Leviathan (lə vī′ ə thən): A great sea monster.
42. invests: Covers.
43. incumbent: Lying.

Of thundering Etna,[44] whose combustible
And fueled entrails thence conceiving fire,
235 Sublimed[45] with mineral fury, aid the winds,
And leave a singed bottom all involved[46]
With stench and smoke: such resting found the sole
Of unblessed feet. Him followed his next mate,
Both glorying to have scaped the Stygian[47] flood
240 As gods, and by their own recovered strength,
Not by the sufferance[48] of supernal[49] power.
    "Is this the region, this the soil, the clime,"
Said then the lost Archangel, "this the seat
That we must change[50] for Heaven, this mournful gloom
245 For that celestial light? Be it so, since he
Who now is sovereign can dispose and bid
What shall be right: farthest from him is best,
Whom reason hath equaled, force hath made supreme
Above his equals. Farewell happy fields,
250 Where joy forever dwells. Hail horrors! Hail
Infernal world! and thou, profoundest Hell
Receive thy new possessor, one who brings
A mind not to be changed by place or time.
The mind is its own place, and in itself
255 Can make a Heaven of Hell, a Hell of Heaven.
What matter where, if I be still the same,
And what I should be, all but less than he
Whom thunder hath made greater? Here at least
We shall be free; the Almighty hath not built
260 Here for his envy, will not drive us hence:
Here we may reign secure, and in my choice
To reign is worth ambition though in Hell:
Better to reign in Hell than serve in Heaven.
But wherefore[51] let we then our faithful friends,
265 The associates and copartners of our loss
Lie thus astonished[52] on the oblivious[53] pool,
And call them not to share with us their part
In this unhappy mansion, or once more
With rallied arms to try what may be yet
270 Regained in Heaven, or what more lost in Hell?"

---

44. Pelorus (pə lôr′ əs) **. . . Etna:** Volcanic mountains in Sicily.
45. sublimed: Vaporized.
46. involved: Enveloped.
47. Stygian (stīj′ ē ən): Of the river Styx, which, in Greek mythology, encircled Hades, the home of the dead.
48. sufferance: Permission.
49. supernal: Heavenly.
50. change: Exchange.
51. wherefore: Why.
52. astonished: Stunned.
53. oblivious: Causing forgetfulness.

RESPONDING TO THE SELECTION

Your Response

1. What in Milton's description of Hell do you find most vivid? Explain.

Recalling

2. The first five lines of *Paradise Lost* allude to the biblical story of Adam and Eve and their expulsion from Paradise. What are the five elements of the story that Milton chooses to emphasize?

3. In lines 29–36, Milton fills out a bit of the story of Adam and Eve. What new element does he introduce here?

4. Lines 34–53 tell of another, earlier fall from grace. (a) Who fell that earlier time? (b) What caused that earlier fall?

5. Lines 59–74 describe Hell. What are its main features?

6. In lines 84–155 Satan addresses Beelzebub and speaks of eternal rebellion and war against God. (a) What are his motives for continuing the war? (b) Explain Beelzebub's advice.

7. From lines 193 to 209, Milton describes the size of Satan. To what creatures is Satan compared?

Interpreting

8. Throughout his invocation, from the first line to the twenty-sixth, Milton mixes references to the Hebrew Bible and classical mythology. What effect is created by Milton's combination of Hebrew and Greek-Roman elements?

9. In what ways are the Fall of Adam and Eve paralleled by the Fall of Satan and his cohorts? Point out the parallels in the poem.

10. Between lines 200 and 208, Milton uses an epic simile in which he compares Satan to the sea beast Leviathan. How does Milton convey the huge size of Leviathan?

11. From lines 242 until the end of this excerpt at line 270, Satan expresses simultaneously his despair at losing heaven and his resolve to glory in his lost condition. What words, phrases, and lines show Satan's feelings?

12. How would you describe Satan's character? Is he petty, mean, grand, self-pitying, heroic, stubborn, weak, or rebellious? You may combine several of these characterizations, but support your choices with references to the poem.

Applying

13. The eighteenth-century poet William Blake said "Milton was of the Devil's party." What do you think this statement means? Explain why you agree or disagree with this statement. Find evidence from the poem to support your answer.

ANALYZING LITERATURE

Understanding Epic Poetry

Epic poems express the values of their cultures through stories of heroes and villains in conflict. As in any other kind of story, the conflict is central and can be of many different kinds. Some conflicts are between characters, some are between a character and the environment, and some are within a character's mind.

The conflict in *Paradise Lost* is essentially between Satan and God, and the arena in which the struggle takes place is in the heart and mind first of Eve and then of Adam. The most illuminating insights into the struggle, however, come from the mind of Satan, which is always conscious of the beauty of goodness as it plans evil.

1. What causes Satan the greatest mental anguish?

2. How does he view Heaven? Contrast this to his view of Hell.

3. Interpret his statement, "The mind is its own place, and in itself / Can make a Heaven of Hell, a Hell of Heaven."

Views of Paradise

You're plodding through the gray slush, an icy wind tearing at your eyes. Your cheeks are flushed crimson, your fingers nearly frozen. Suddenly a car veers too close to the curb, an angry face glares out, and a blast of icy slush dives into your shoes. In desperation, your thoughts drift to a lush green garden overflowing with sweet fruit. Peace and freedom reign, as people live in harmony with each other and their animal companions. The birds sing lyrically, the flowers sway softly, and a fresh breeze wafts gently over all. Paradise!

The word *paradise* came from the Old Persian word *pairidaeza,* which meant a "walled enclosure, pleasure park, garden." Curiously, the description of paradise differs little among various cultures. Cross-culturally and throughout the ages, it is seen as a beautiful garden free from violence or pain.

CUNEIFORM TABLETS

An early account of paradise appears on tablets produced by the Sumer tribe in southern Mesopotamia around the year 5000 B.C. The inscription opens with praise for the plain of Babylon, called "Edinn." In this innocent, clean, and sun-filled land, gods are forever young, healthy, and amiable. The only thing lacking is water, but this is soon brought by the sun god Utu at the command of the water god Enki. Water completes paradise by creating a lush garden bursting with fruit.

THE GARDEN OF EDEN

In *Paradise Lost,* Milton gives the traditional description of the Garden of Eden. Again we have a garden: this time, an en-closed area on the top level of a steep hill whose sides are covered with rows of shrubs. The entire scene is illuminated by the glorious light of the sun. The image suggests the power of humanity as well as the beauty and security of paradise.

Milton's account owes much to the traditional seventeenth-century European gardens. These were private estates and parks, carefully and cleverly planted in geometrical patterns, and stocked for their wealthy owners. These lavish formal gardens were an idealized setting for thought and learning.

THE GOLDEN APPLES OF THE SUN

In Greek mythology, paradise is the garden of the Hesperides, the home of the daughters of Atlas, the evening star. Assisted by a dragon, the inhabitants guard the tree that gives the golden apples. The tree, with branches and leaves of gold, had been a wedding gift to the goddess Hera from Gaea, Mother Earth. The apples were so closely guarded that theft was thought impossible; in fact, one of the hero Hercules' twelve labors was to bring back the golden apples of the Hesperides.

AFRICAN, BUDDHIST, AND HINDU TALES OF PARADISE

Although every culture has a different word for "paradise," the tales are curiously alike. In African tales, for example, paradise is a beautiful garden with ample food and leisure. There is no death or disease. Humans live in harmony with animals, able to understand their language. But something happened that ended paradise, making life what it is today.

THE GARDEN OF EDEN
Erastus S. Field

To the Buddhists, India will become paradise when the next Buddha, called *Maitreya*, appears. Evil will vanish and people will be strong and healthy. The earth will effortlessly yield an abundance of rice. Calm, broad rivers will nourish a wonderful variety of fruits and flowers.

Perhaps the most striking example of paradise is the Hindu belief in the world ages, called *yugas*. There are four world ages in each cycle, all related to the ages of the life of the god Brahma. The *krtayuga* is the golden age, equivalent to paradise, where equality, prosperity, and fulfillment reign. This is followed by three ages of increasing decay, culminating in the dark age, when people and the world are at their worst. By some Buddhist accounts, we are now unfortunately in the dark age, slated to last 432,000 human years.

PARADISE ON EARTH?

People have long searched the four corners of the globe for paradise. The Guarani Indians of South America provide perhaps the best recorded instance of an actual quest. They believe that paradise really exists on earth, but that it is cleverly concealed. For more than 400 years, the tribe has conducted numerous voyages to find what they call the "land without evil."

Christopher Columbus claimed that the freshwater tides he found in the Gulf of Paria between Trinidad and the coast of South America originated in the four rivers that flow out of Eden. He took as proof the area's sweet climate, fragrant flowers, and lush vegetation. But paradise has also been "discovered" in less logical places, such as the North Pole!

JOHN BUNYAN

1628–1688

Perhaps the most widely read book by any English author, *The Pilgrim's Progress,* was written by an ill-educated traveling tinker, or mender of pots, pans, and other household utensils. John Bunyan's father had also been a tinker and had trained him in his craft. As a child John received some education at the local grammar school. After he was married, Bunyan further educated himself by reading the Bible and two religious tracts that his wife brought as a dowry. On the basis of this background he wrote a great many religious books and tracts, culminating in the most popular, *The Pilgrim's Progress.*

Born and raised near Bedford in central England, he left there at sixteen to join the Parliamentary army and did not return until a number of years later. At twenty-one he married, and at twenty-five he started to preach after several years of an intense spiritual struggle. Bunyan had joined a nonconformist sect and was an unlicensed preacher to its congregation at Bedford. Upon the restoration of the Stuart monarchy, Bunyan, as well as many other nonconformist preachers, was arrested. Refusing to renounce his faith, he remained imprisoned for twelve years, during which time he wrote a fairly large number of religious works. Upon his release as a result of a general amnesty, Bunyan returned to Bedford as a licensed preacher. Except for a short period during which he was imprisoned again, Bunyan remained in Bedford for the rest of his life. There he preached to his congregation and an increasing audience in the barn that served as his church and continued to work at his trade as a tinker. During his second imprisonment, Bunyan wrote the first part of *The Pilgrim's Progress.* Several years later he wrote the second part of this work and a number of other fairly successful books. Altogether Bunyan wrote and published nearly sixty works, yet at his death he was almost as poor as when he was born.

From the seventeenth century through the nineteenth, *The Pilgrim's Progress* was the most successful Christian text written by an Englishman. It was translated into well over 100 languages. Once you have read it, you can understand why the book was so popular. Bunyan was a superb storyteller. He wrote with humor; drew vivid, easily understandable characters; provided suspense and action; and sent a clear, unambiguous message. Moreover, his language, though simple and colloquial, is charged with echoes of the Bible. In essence, Bunyan's tale reflected the main cultural values of his audience.

GUIDE FOR INTERPRETING

from *The Pilgrim's Progress*

Writers' Techniques

Allegory. When the plot, characters, and setting of a story clearly represent abstract ideas, the narrative is called an **allegory.** An allegory can be prose or poetry. It operates on at least two levels: an on-the-surface level and a beneath-the-surface level.

The interest in allegory goes back very far in human history. In fact, the word itself comes from ancient Greece. However, allegory as a way of creating literature hit its stride in the Middle Ages. There are several kinds of allegories. *The Faerie Queene,* for example, is primarily a social allegory, although it has religious, moral, and political elements as well. *Everyman,* on the other hand, is almost entirely a moral allegory, and *The Pilgrim's Progress* is almost entirely a religious one.

The purpose of all allegory is to teach entertainingly. As Bunyan put it in his preface to *The Pilgrim's Progress:*

> [Fish] must be groped for, and tickled too,
> Or they will not be catch'd, whate'er you do.

To make their instruction clear, writers of allegories draw simple, one-dimensional characters and settings, which are then assigned the names of their governing traits. For example, *The Pilgrim's Progress* is an allegory of Christian redemption and salvation. The hero's name is Christian. He leaves the City of Destruction (this world) and goes toward the Celestial City (the place of salvation or heaven). Some of the characters he meets on his journey are Obstinate, Faithful, and Mr. Worldly Wiseman.

Focus

Jot down the character names for several traits, such as Happy, Dour, Mr. Cynic, or Miss Know-it-All. Then write little scenes in which these characters display their traits.

Primary Source

"Vanity Fair" is an allegorical version of a country fair. Fairs were common in Bunyan's day. A disgruntled seventeenth-century shopper, annoyed at the price and quality offered, reports that "There are (as I take it) few great towns in England that have not their weekly markets . . . where all manner of provisions for household is to be bought and sold, for ease and benefit of the country round about. . . . And, as these have been in times past erected for the benefit of the realm, so are they in many places too, too much abused: for the relief and ease of the buyer is not so much intended in them as the benefit of the seller. . . . For, in most of these markets, neither . . . bread nor . . . sweetness of grain are any whit looked unto, but each one suffered to sell or set up what and how himself listeth."

from The Pilgrim's Progress

John Bunyan

Vanity Fair

This is probably the best-known episode of The Pilgrim's Progress. *The book's hero, Christian, and his companion, Faithful, pass through the town of Vanity during the season of the local fair. Local fairs were an important British tradition, giving people the opportunity to buy wares sold by merchants from all over Europe. At the same time, these fairs involved a good deal of eating and drinking and offered a wide variety of entertainment. In this selection, Bunyan uses the fair to demonstrate how worldly attractions can corrupt religious life.*

Then I saw in my dream, that when they were got out of the wilderness, they presently saw a town before them, and the name of that town is Vanity; and at the town there is a fair kept, called Vanity Fair. It is kept all the year long. It beareth the name of Vanity Fair, because the town where it is kept, is lighter than vanity, and also, because all that is there sold, or that cometh thither, is vanity; as is the saying of the wise, "All that cometh is vanity" (Ecclesiastes 1:2, 14; 2:11, 7; 11:8; Isaiah 11:17).

This fair is no new-erected business, but a thing of ancient standing. I will show you the original of it.

Almost five thousand years ago, there were pilgrims walking to the Celestial City,[1] as these two honest persons are; and Beelzebub,[2] Apollyon,[3] and Legion,[4] with their companions, perceiving by the path that the pilgrims made, that their way to the city lay through this town of Vanity, they contrived here to set up a fair; a fair wherein should be sold all sorts of vanity, and that it should last all the year long. Therefore at this fair are all such merchandise sold as houses, lands, trades, places, honors, preferments,[5] titles, countries, kingdoms, lusts, pleasures, and delights of all sorts, as harlots, wives, husbands, children, masters, servants, lives, blood, bodies, souls, silver, gold, pearls, precious stones, and what not.

And moreover, at this fair there is at all times to be seen jugglings, cheats, games, plays, fools, apes, knaves, and rogues, and that of every kind.

Here are to be seen, too, and that for nothing, thefts, murders, adulteries, false swearers, and that of a blood-red color.

And as, in other fairs of less moment, there are the several rows and streets under

---

1. Celestial City: The source of salvation.
2. Beelzebub (bē el′ zə bub): Prince of the devils (Matthew 12:24).
3. Apollyon (a pol′ yən): The angel of the bottomless pit (Revelation 9:11).
4. Legion: The unclean spirit (Mark 5:9).

---

5. preferments: Appointments and promotions to political or ecclesiastical positions.

their proper names, where such and such wares are vended; so here likewise you have the proper places, rows, streets (namely, countries and kingdoms), where the wares of this fair are soonest to be found. Here is the Britain Row, the French Row, the Italian Row, the Spanish Row, the German Row, where several sorts of vanities are to be sold. But as in other fairs some one commodity is as the chief of all the fair, so the ware of Rome and her merchandise is greatly promoted in this fair; only our English nation, with some others, have taken a dislike thereat.

Now, as I said, the way to the Celestial City lies just through this town where this lusty[6] fair is kept; and he that would go to the city, and yet not go through this town, ''must needs go out of the world'' (I Corinthians 5 :10). The Prince of princes himself, when here, went through this town to his own country, and that upon a fair day too;[7] yea, and, as I think, it was Beelzebub, the

---

6. lusty: Merry.
7. The Prince . . . too: Refers to the temptation of Christ in the wilderness (Matthew 4:1—11).

PILGRIM'S PROGRESS
Angels/Pilgrim/Knight Figures
John Bunyan
The British Library

chief lord of this fair, that invited him to buy of his vanities; yea, would have made him lord of the fair, would he but have done him reverence as he went through the town. Yea, because he was such a person of honor, Beelzebub had him from street to street, and showed him all the kingdoms of the world in a little time, that he might, if possible, allure that Blessed One to cheapen[8] and buy some of his vanities; but he had no mind to the merchandise, and, therefore, left the town without laying out so much as one farthing upon these vanities. This fair, therefore, is an ancient thing of long standing, and a very great fair.

Now these pilgrims, as I said, must needs go through this fair. Well, so they did; but, behold, even as they entered into the fair, all the people in the fair were moved, and the town itself, as it were, in a hubbub about them, and that for several reasons: for

First, the pilgrims were clothed with such kind of raiment[9] as was diverse from the raiment of any that traded in that fair. The people, therefore, of the fair made a great gazing upon them: some said they were fools, some they were bedlams[10] and some they were outlandish men[11] (I Corinthians 2:7,8).

Secondly, and as they wondered at their apparel, so they did likewise at their speech; for few could understand what they said. They naturally spoke the language of Canaan,[12] but they that kept the fair were the men of this world; so that, from one end of the fair to the other, they seemed barbarians each to the other (Job 12:4; I Corinthians 4:9).

Thirdly, but that which did not a little amuse the merchandisers was that these pilgrims set very light by their wares; they

cared not so much as to look upon them; and if they called upon them to buy, they would put their fingers in their ears, and cry, "Turn away mine eyes from beholding vanity," and look upwards, signifying that their trade and traffic was in heaven (Psalms 129:37; Philippians 3:19, 20).

One chanced mockingly, beholding the carriages of the men, to say unto them, "What will ye buy?" But they, looking gravely upon him, said, "We buy the truth" (Proverbs 23:23). At that there was an occasion taken to despise the men the more; some mocking, some taunting, some speaking reproachfully, and some calling upon others to smite them. At last things came to a hubbub and great stir in the fair, insomuch that all order was confounded. Now was word presently brought to the great one of the fair, who quickly came down, and deputed some of his most trusty friends to take these men into examination, about whom the fair was almost overturned. So the men were brought to examination; and they that sat upon[13] them, asked them whence they came, whither they went, and what they did there, in such an unusual garb? The men told them that they were pilgrims and strangers in the world, and that they were going to their own country, which was the Heavenly Jerusalem (Hebrews 11:13–16); and that they had given no occasion to the men of the town, nor yet to the merchandisers, thus to abuse them, and to let[14] them in their journey, except it was for that, when one asked them what they would buy, they said they would buy the truth. But they that were appointed to examine them did not believe them to be any other than bedlams and mad, or else such as came to put all things into a confusion in the fair. Therefore they took them and beat them, and besmeared them with dirt, and then put them into the cage, that they might be made a spectacle to all the men of the fair.

---

8. cheapen: Ask the price of.
9. raiment: Clothing.
10. bedlams: Lunatics from Bethlehem Hospital, the insane asylum in London.
11. outlandish men: Foreigners.
12. Canaan: The Promised Land. The "language of Canaan" is the language of the Bible.

---

13. sat upon: Interrogated and tried them.
14. let: Hinder.

RESPONDING TO THE SELECTION

Your Response

1. If you had been accompanying the pilgrims, how might you have reacted to Vanity Fair? Explain.

Recalling

2. In *The Pilgrim's Progress,* on what path or route is the town of Vanity located?
3. What can be seen at the fair?
4. Which individuals *must* go through the town and hence through the fair as well?
5. What were the three reasons the two pilgrims caused such a stir at the fair?
6. What did the pilgrims say that led to their being examined by "the great one's trusty friends"?

Interpreting

7. Why do the travelers have to pass through the fair to reach their destination?
8. What does the fair represent?
9. Why were the pilgrims so uppity toward the inhabitants of the fair?

Applying

10. "Vanity Fair," as well as the whole of *The Pilgrim's Progress,* represents a level and type of writing that is no longer common. If you were to write something like "Vanity Fair" today, how would you go about it?

ANALYZING LITERATURE

Recognizing Allegory

Everything in an allegory is geared toward delivering a message. The plot, characters, dialogue, and setting all contribute to the same end—to make the author's ideas immediately understandable.

1. How does the allusion to the temptation of Jesus in the wilderness relate to the purpose of the fair at Vanity?
2. Why is the town and its fair astride the path the true Christian must follow?
3. Why is the fair run by Beelzebub?

4. In relation to Christian virtue, what does the fair represent?

CRITICAL THINKING AND READING

Identifying Effective Details

In an allegory the characters, setting, and plot have a symbolic as well as a literal meaning. The pilgrims in Bunyan's story, for instance, represent those who are trying to live a truly Christian life. Yet an allegory cannot be successful unless its details are vivid and memorable enough to engage readers in the literal events of the story. One such detail is the gibe that someone hurls at the pilgrims: "What will ye buy?" We can hear the sneering mockery in this almost casual insult.

1. Why was Bunyan's choice of a local fair as the setting for this episode an excellent means to interest his readers?
2. (a) Identify three details of Vanity Fair that are probably based on real fairs in Bunyan's time. (b) Give reasons for your choices.
3. In the final passage of this excerpt, Bunyan describes how the pilgrims are beaten and abused by the men of the town. Which details in this description are especially effective?
4. Think of another vivid detail Bunyan could have used to make his narrative even more interesting.

THINKING AND WRITING

Writing an Allegory for Today's World

Allegories generally use one-dimensional characters and situations to present clear ideas about religious, moral, political, or social issues. Write an allegory about the modern world for your fellow students. Remember, allegories are stories, and all stories have conflict. In allegories this conflict is between characters representing abstract ideas. You should have one central character that the reader can identify with. Do not forget to choose a particular point of view when writing your narrative. You may wish to use a first-person or third-person narrator, or you may wish to alternate between the two, as Bunyan did.

THE CHANGING ENGLISH LANGUAGE

New Worlds, New Words

The Renaissance had sparked the rebirth of spoken and written English. The language continued to grow and spread during the reign of James I. As the seventeenth century opened, English was poised on the edge of worldwide recognition.

The story of English in the seventeenth century is largely the story of the New World. Sparked by a combination of optimism, faith, and self-interest, thousands of people undertook the brutal voyage to America. Captain John Smith established the first permanent British colony in Jamestown, Virginia, in 1607; the Puritans anchored the Mayflower at Plymouth Bay in December 1620. With these voyages, the English language was planted—and took root—in an entirely new land.

Initially, the majority of people who braved the terrors of the unknown were Puritans from a section of England called East Anglia, the Puritan stronghold. Cromwell himself was from East Anglia and had trained his New Model Army there. Throughout the period Puritans from East Anglia would continue to pour into the New World, seeking to establish a stronghold of their faith and better their lot in life. As they brought their dreams across the ocean, so they brought their language.

SEVENTEENTH-CENTURY ENGLISH LINGERS TODAY

This mass immigration to the New World had an exciting effect on the English language. Thomas Jefferson commented on the results of this movement nearly 200 years after the first settlers established their fragile beachheads on the shores of the New World. "New circumstances," he said, "call for new words, new phrases, and the transfer of old words to new objects."

Even today, visitors from England can hear distinctive traces of seventeenth-century British speech in American English. To the ears of the British, these words

CAPTAIN JOHN SMITH

are clearly archaic. For example, today in American English we use *gotten*—a term commonplace in England until the late eighteenth century—in place of *got*. American speakers still use the term *mad* to mean "angry," another remnant of seventeenth-century English. In England today, *sick* means "nausea," not illness in general, as is the case in modern America, where we have retained the older definition. *Platter,* meaning "dish," is a commonplace term in America; it is largely unknown in contemporary England. Another frequently used American term carried over on those first ships is *I guess;* scholars have identified it as dating back as far as Chaucer's age. The English use *autumn* to refer to the season before winter; we interchange it with the seventeenth-century word *fall.*

YOU SAY POTATO . . .

And how did all this sound? Despite the growing discontent with monarchy in the beginning of the seventeenth century, the speech of the court still set the standard for "proper" spoken and written English throughout the land. The sound of this "standard English" was different enough from the speech of the villages to be discernible, however. A country visitor to the court was easily able to identify what he called a "true kynde of pronunciation," one of the first references to what was to become standard English. As we can tell from this remark, those who spoke in courtly tones thought themselves vastly superior to those who used country dialect. Another contemporary noted this elitist attitude when he wrote:

> There be gentlemen and other that speake, but specially write, as good Southerne as we of Middlesex or Surrey do, but not the common people or every shire, of whome the gentlemen, and also their learned clarkes, do for the most part condescend.

Since Johnson had yet to write his dictionary, people tended to spell words as they sounded, which offers us clues as to their pronunciation. From the above quotation, for example, we can see that *clerkes* was pronounced "clarkes" because of the way it was spelled. Many of the rhymes found in poetry of the age—such as "tea" with "tay," and "sea" with "say"—also offer hints. From these clues and others, scholars believe that seventeenth-century standard English most likely sounded like a combination of the Irish and West Country speech of today.

CALLS FOR LANGUAGE REFORM

Carried across the vast ocean by eager pilgrims, English took firm root in the fertile linguistic soil of the new land. But back home in England, many people were beginning to feel that language matters had gotten out of hand. English, perhaps like the bulk of English society itself, was willful and coarse. In the decades to come, writers and scholars would be increasingly concerned with reining in the unruly mother tongue.

YOUR WRITING PROCESS

WRITING A LETTER OF EVALUATION

Seventeenth-century poets were a varied and passionate lot. In addition, they were not shy about expressing their opinions of one another's work. Imagine that you are Ben Jonson, John Donne, John Milton, or Richard Lovelace. You have just read a new poem by one of your contemporaries, and you want to write the poet a letter, evaluating the poem.

> **Focus**
>
> **Assignment:** Write a letter in which one seventeenth-century poet discusses a poem written by another.
> **Purpose:** To evaluate the poem.
> **Audience:** A seventeenth-century poet.

Prewriting

1. Take your pick. Which poets made the strongest impressions? Which pairs of poets seemed most different? Which ones did you like most? Thinking about these questions will help you choose the poetic voice you would most like to adopt as well as the poet to whom you will write.

2. Incorporate key facts into your plan. Once you have chosen a pair of poets, read all the relevant biographical and historical material in this unit. Note differences, similarities, and connections in a chart like the one below.

Student Model

	DONNE	SUCKLING
Biography	1572–1631 wild youth; experienced a religious conversion and became a preacher; devoted to his wife and children	1609–1642 wealthy family; gambled and wasted money; fought on the Royalist side in France; died a poor man
Poems	wrote about love and religion; used elaborate metaphysical conceits; poems very intellectual	wrote about love; a light mocking tone; cynical; poems are brief, easier to understand than Donne's

3. Find your voice. Choose the poet whose voice you will adopt in the letter. Then do some freewriting in the voice of this poet.

4. Choose a poem. Once you have a sense of your poet's voice, choose a poem by the other poet to write about. Try to select a poem that will elicit a strong reaction.

Drafting

1. Plan before you draft. Don't ramble. Plan your evaluation so that it flows logically and coherently. Use a formal outline or a rough list to map out your draft.

2. Back up your broad judgments with specific support. Like any good evaluation, your writing should follow a pattern of broad judgments followed by a variety of relevant and specific support. Quote lines of poetry. Refer to specific facts. Choose specific words to make your points count.

3. Include the good, the bad, and the ugly. An evaluation can include both compliments and complaints. These poets are a dramatic and passionate group; allow them to be honest and bold!

Revising and Editing

1. Have you used figurative language? You are a poet. It stands to reason that you would use poetic language even in your prose. Try to make at least one of your points using a fresh and powerful simile, metaphor, or personification.

> ### Student Model
> Writing as Donne:
> To find the bottom of your poem, one does not have to look far. It is a puddle, Mr. Jonson, and great poems are wells.

2. Experiment with flourish and flair. Have fun with the voice you borrow. For example, if you want to be snide, you can make a comment like the following: "Good poetry is poetic, figurative, and somewhat elusive. Your poem, I fear, is not."

3. What works? What doesn't? Exchange letters with a classmate. Ask him or her whether a sentence is too long to read well or if a simile is effective. Also ask whether the letter reveals the standards behind the evaluation.

4. Proofread your letter. Have you used the correct form for a personal letter? Also, is your letter free of errors in grammar, usage, and mechanics? If you are commenting on another's work, you don't want your own writing criticized.

Writer's Hint
It is tempting to begin ten out of ten sentences with their subjects. By transferring modifying words and phrases to the beginnings of sentences, you can improve the variety and vividness of your style.

Options for Publishing
• Display your letter on a bulletin board along with a representative poem by each of the two poets.
• In pairs read letters aloud to your classmates: Jonson to Donne, then Donne to Jonson, for example.

Reviewing Your Writing Process
1. Did you find it difficult to write in the voice of a seventeenth-century poet? Why or why not?
2. Which editing tip helped you most as you revised your letter? Explain.

MORVILLE HALL, SHROPSHIRE
John Inigo Richards
Roy Miles Fine Paintings, London

THE RESTORATION AND THE EIGHTEENTH CENTURY

1660–1798

All Nature is but art, unknown to thee,
All chance, direction which thou canst not see;
All discord, harmony not understood;
All partial evil, universal good.

Alexander Pope

In 1660, England stood at the threshold of a new age. The religious conflicts that had brought on the Civil War had been settled, and a king once again sat on the throne. The people of England could look forward to a period of stability, order, and progress.

This happy prospect was reinforced by the ideas of a scientific revolution then sweeping Europe. From their close observation of nature, Isaac Newton and other scientists concluded that harmony and order underlay all the events in the world. They also believed that human beings were capable of discovering and understanding that order.

The Scientific Revolution ushered in a new era called the Age of Reason, or the Enlightenment. During the Enlightenment, confidence in human reason spread beyond the realm of science. In the verses quoted on page 433, for example, Alexander Pope asserted that everything in nature has a design and purpose. Disharmony is an illusion—no more than "harmony not understood." Like scientists, Pope believed, poets must struggle to see beneath the superficial chaos and grasp the underlying harmony of the world.

The Enlightenment thus put great emphasis on order, harmony, and stability. At the same time, however, it was an age that believed in progress, and progress meant change. Great changes indeed overtook England between 1660 and the late 1700's. As Parliament restricted the power of the monarch, England improved what was already an admirably democratic political system in Europe. Even more profound changes took place in the economic sphere. English merchants were accumulating great wealth, in part because of their trade with England's colonial empire. In the late 1700's, they began to invest in the first factories of the Industrial Revolution. By 1800, Britain had surpassed its ancient rival, France, as the foremost military and economic power in Europe.

From 1660 to the late 1700's, British literature continued to exhibit order and harmony in spite of, or perhaps because of, the rapid transformation of British society. Before discussing the literature of the period, however, it will be helpful to look in more detail at the political, social, and economic developments that took place in England from 1660 to the end of the 1700's.

The Growth of English Democracy

The Restoration of Monarchy

Soon after Oliver Cromwell's death, in 1658, Parliament offered the crown to the exiled son of Charles I. In 1660, he became Charles II. Most English people fervently hoped that the restoration of the House of Stuart would end the fighting between Puritans and Anglicans and between Parliament and the Crown.

The omens in the first years of Charles II's reign were not good. In 1665, a plague swept the city of London, killing 70,000 people. A year later, the Great Fire destroyed over half the city's houses. Yet these calamities were quickly overcome. London was rebuilt on a grander scale under the direction of the brilliant architect Christopher Wren (1632–1723). Profits from the global trade carried on by British merchants furthered London's growth.

Charles II had lived in Paris during Cromwell's Protectorship. In sharp contrast to the drab Puritan leaders, Charles II enjoyed elegance. His court copied the plush clothing, rich jewelry, and elaborate wigs of Paris. An avid patron of the arts, Charles also invited Italian composers and Dutch painters to live and work in London. In 1662, he advanced the scientific spirit of the age by chartering the Royal Society, devoted to the study of natural science.

Although some critics said Charles cared more about pleasure than power, he was a shrewd ruler. He kept his Catholic convictions to himself even while accepting money from the Catholic king of France. The problem of having a Catholic king rule a Protestant nation could not, however, be kept in check forever. After Charles II died, James, son of Charles I, became king. James II was a stubborn ruler and a devout Catholic. Trouble loomed when James appointed Catholics to high offices and dismissed Parliament for failing to obey his wishes.

A Glorious Revolution

The crisis came in 1688, when James II's wife gave birth to a son. To the people of England, this meant that another Catholic king would someday sit on the throne. Parliament reacted quickly. Several leaders invited Mary, the Protestant daughter of James II, to rule England jointly with her husband, William of Orange. William was a prince of Holland and a champion of Protestantism in Europe.

When William and Mary arrived in England, they were prepared to fight for the throne if necessary. But James, recalling the fate of his father, escaped to France. The people of England hailed the event as a "Glorious Revolution," since not a drop of blood had been shed. The next year, William and Mary agreed to respect a Bill of Rights passed by Parliament. Among other things, it guaranteed Parliament the right to approve all taxes and said that a king could not suspend the law. With the Bill of Rights, England attained a limited, or constitutional, monarchy. Although it was far from being a democracy in the modern sense, England was among the most democratic nations of Europe.

Political Parties Emerge

After William of Orange followed his wife Mary to the grave in 1702, Mary's sister Anne, a Protestant, became queen. Under Queen Anne, England grew stronger and more united. One important act of her reign was the joining of the realms of England and Scotland. The Act of Union, passed in 1707, created the nation of Great Britain, with a central government in London.

During Anne's reign, there was another important political development. Once again, France and Britain were at war. The war helped to crystallize two political factions in Parliament, the Tories and the Whigs. The Tories included aristocrats and lesser landowners. As a group, they were conservatives who were against the changes taking place in Britain. Most Tories opposed the war with France as a waste of tax money. Whigs, on the other hand, supported the war. Many Whigs came from Britain's growing class of merchants, who

QUEEN ANNE AND THE KNIGHTS OF THE GARTER, 1713 (detail)
Peter Angelis

made handsome profits supplying war goods. They also wanted Britain to crush France once and for all and become the undisputed trade leader of Europe. The split between Tories and Whigs would remain a basic fact of British politics for many decades.

Favoring the Tories, Queen Anne signed a treaty to end the war in 1713, the same year she fell ill. Earlier, Parliament had passed a law stipulating that only a Protestant could inherit the throne. When Anne died in 1714, the throne passed to a little-known relative of James I who ruled a small principality in Hanover, Germany.

A Cabinet and Prime Minister

The new king, George I, spoke no English and had little interest in the affairs of Britain. He seemed an unlikely figure to advance democracy in Britain, but in fact he did. George I relied on ministers, chosen from Parliament, to run the country. This group of ministers was called the cabinet, and the chief among them came to be known as the prime minister. Robert Walpole, a brilliant and energetic Whig, was the first man to unify the cabinet government in the person of the prime minister. Thus began the cabinet system still used in Britain today. Through the cabinet, Parliament gained a greater voice in the nation's policies.

The Restoration and the Eighteenth Century (A.D. 1660 – A.D. 1798)

John
Locke

The Great
Fire of London

Illustrations
From
*Gulliver's
Travels*

1650　　　　　　　**1680**　　　　　　　**1710**

BRITISH EVENTS

- **Samuel Pepys** begins *Diary.*
- Royal Society chartered.
- Drury Lane Theater opens.
- Great Fire of London.
- First cheddar cheese produced.
- **John Milton's** *Paradise Lost* published.
- **John Dryden** publishes *An Essay of Dramatic Poesy.*

- James II becomes king.
- Glorious Revolution.
- Bill of Rights becomes law.
- First daily newspaper begins publication.
- Great Britain created by Act of Union.
- First Copyright Act.
- First literary magazine, *The Tatler,* begins publication.

- **Alexander Pope** publishes *The Rape of the Lock.*
- George I becomes king.
- First organized cricket match takes place.
- **Daniel Defoe** publishes *Robinson Crusoe.*
- **Jonathan Swift** publishes *Gulliver's Travels.*
- William Hogarth paints *The Rake's Progress.*

WORLD EVENTS

- Holland: Rembrandt paints *The Syndics.*
- France: Louis XIV begins building palace at Versailles.
- North America: Britain seizes New Netherlands.
- Italy: Stradivari labels first violin.
- France: Molière's *Tartuffe* first performed.

- Dodo becomes extinct.
- China: All ports opened to foreign trade.
- India: Calcutta founded by British.
- Japan: Kabuki theater developed.
- Russia: Peter the Great begins building St. Petersburg.
- North America: La Salle explores Great Lakes.

- Holland: Fahrenheit constructs mercury thermometer.
- France: Louis XV succeeds to throne.
- Germany: Bach composes *Brandenburg Concertos.*
- Brazil: First coffee planted.
- Pacific: Behring explores Alaskan waters.
- Russia: Ballet school opens in St. Petersburg.

The Boston
Tea Party

Wolfgang
Amadeus
Mozart

The Storming
of the Bastille

1740   **1770**   **1800**

- Last Jacobite rebellion in Scotland.
  - Henry Fielding publishes *Tom Jones.*
    - **Thomas Gray** publishes "Elegy in a Country Churchyard."
      - **Samuel Johnson** publishes *Dictionary of the English Language.*
    - Britain enters Seven Years' War.
      - Oliver Goldsmith publishes *The Vicar of Wakefield.*

- Actress Sarah Siddons debuts at Drury Lane Theater.
  - **Robert Burns** publishes *Poems Chiefly in Scottish Dialect.*
    - **William Blake** publishes *Songs of Innocence.*
      - **James Boswell** publishes *The Life of Samuel Johnson.*
        - England goes to war with France.
          - Admiral Nelson defeats French at Aboukir Bay.

- Prussia: Frederick the Great succeeds to throne.
  - France: Montesquieu publishes *The Spirit of the Law.*
    - Portugal: Sign language invented.
      - North America: Benjamin Franklin invents lightning rod.
        - Canada: British troops capture Quebec.
          - North America: Stamp Act imposed.

- North America: Boston Tea Party.
  - France: Louis XVI succeeds to throne.
    - North America: American Revolution begins.
      - Peru: Rebellion against Spanish rule.
        - France: First school for the blind established.
          - Austria: Mozart's *Marriage of Figaro* first performed.
            - France: Revolution begins with storming of Bastille.
              - Africa: Mungo Park explores Niger River.

In 1760, another Hanoverian king came to the British throne. Born in Britain, George III thought of himself as an Englishman, not a German. He was a strong-willed man who took his mother seriously when she said, "George, be a king." Using his wealth and influence, the king packed Parliament with men loyal to him. He then set about pursuing his own policies. His strong-headed handling of the American colonies helped bring about the American Revolution.

The king's disastrous policies toward America angered Parliament. In 1783, a fiery twenty-four-year-old became prime minister. William Pitt, the youthful Tory leader, had great plans for reform of the British government. Before he had a chance to put them into effect, however, France erupted in revolution. Soon thereafter, Britain and France were at war again, putting off any chance of reform.

KING GEORGE III OF ENGLAND, c. 1760
Allan Ramsay

The Transformation of Britain's Economy

An Agricultural Revolution

After the Restoration, Britain's system of government became gradually more democratic. Gradual changes also occurred in the economic life of the nation.

In 1660, the vast majority of the British people were farmers. Most either rented their fields from a landlord or cultivated a patch of common land. By the late 1600's, however, new economic forces were changing life in the countryside. New farm tools made it possible for farmers to plant and harvest a much bigger crop. As a result, landlords began to fence in the land they had once rented out, hiring laborers to work the land for them.

Bigger, more efficient estates replaced the small holdings of earlier times. By the mid-1700's, British farms were producing much more food. With more food available, the population of the small island surged upward. Since fewer farmhands were needed, many people left the countryside. In the growing towns, they became the factory hands who ran the machines of the early Industrial Revolution.

The Industrial Age Dawns

The Industrial Revolution began in Britain. A series of British inventions after 1750 made the spinning and weaving of cloth much more efficient. At the same time, the steam engine was perfected and adapted to run a power loom. These machines were brought together in factories, which were soon producing vast quantities of cotton cloth. Merchants sold the goods all over the world, adding more gold to the nation's coffers.

Although the Industrial Revolution happened first in England, the nation did not become predominantly industrial until the 1800's. As late as the 1790's, a majority of British people still earned their living as farmers. Yet the economic changes of the 1700's had major significance. They profoundly affected ways of thinking about the world.

New Ideas for a New Age

The Enlightenment

In a sense, the Industrial Revolution began when British inventors found practical ways to apply the ideas of the Scientific Revolution. The Scientific Revolution led to other developments as well. Works by Enlightenment thinkers in many other fields can all be considered its offspring.

In 1687, Sir Isaac Newton published his monumental study of gravity and the movement of the planets. Popular awareness of Newton's achievement is reflected in this couplet from a poem by Alexander Pope:

> Nature and Nature's laws lay hid in
> night:
> God said, Let Newton be! and all was
> light.

Each breakthrough in astronomy, physics, and chemistry seemed to affirm the hope that human beings would someday perfect their knowledge of the world. Thinkers in other fields tried to make their studies as orderly and rational as the studies of a scientist. In *The Wealth of Nations,* for example, Adam Smith suggested that economic life is ruled by laws as discoverable as scientific laws.

One of the greatest figures of the Enlightenment was John Locke, a British philosopher and political theorist. After the Glorious Revolution, Locke brought the rationalism of the age to his study of government. Kings, said Locke, did not have a "divine right" to hold power. Rather, a monarch's authority came from the consent of the people. If the monarch abuses his subjects, they "are thereupon absolved from any further obedience." Locke's enlightened ideas about government helped shape the arguments of the American colonists during their disputes with George III.

The scientific advances of the Enlightenment established the basis for the new technology of the Industrial Revolution. But beyond that, a new confidence in human ability encouraged inventors to experiment with new devices, and capitalists to

SIR ISAAC NEWTON, c. 1726
Attributed to John Vanderbank

risk their money on untested ideas. Hence, the Industrial Revolution both grew out of and reinforced the new scientific spirit.

The Neoclassical Ideal

Everywhere they looked, the Enlightenment thinkers discerned what they took to be evidence of the world's harmony and order. When Alexander Pope and others sought kindred spirits in the past, they often found them among the writers of ancient Greece and Rome. In the works of Homer, Virgil, Horace, and other classical authors, Enlightenment thinkers and artists discovered harmony, restraint, and clarity—the very qualities they admired most.

English writers of the Enlightenment are often called *neoclassical* because they emulated classical styles. The features of neoclassicism are easy to identify. One feature is the frequent use of classical allusions—that is, references to the myths, gods, and heroes of ancient times. Another is an inclination to generalize about the world rather than to describe it from a particular individual's point of view. John Dryden, Alexander Pope, and Samuel Johnson often put their generalizations about the world in the form of *aphorisms*—short, quotable sentences, such as "The proper study of mankind is man." (See the quotations on page 443.)

One other feature of neoclassicism makes the work of Pope and others lively and amusing: a fondness for satire, the literary ridicule of the vices, follies, and stupidities of society. Such classical poets as Horace, Juvenal, and Martial provided the English poets of the eighteenth century with superb models of the genre.

Most of the satires of the time were mild and inoffensive, usually written in a formal, neoclassical style. Pope, for example, wrote a long poem, *The Dunciad,* in a high-flown, heroic style—but the poem is a satirical celebration of stupidity. Other satirists, such as Jonathan Swift, were less polite. His *Gulliver's Travels* includes savage attacks on lawyers, princes, and mankind in general. In *A Modest Proposal,* Swift suggests a way "for preventing the children of poor people in Ireland from being a burden to their parents or country." Swift's ironic solution—to eat them—is the modest proposal at the heart of a bitter satire directed against the English absentee landlords who were destroying Ireland.

The Literary World Expands

As Britain grew wealthier, more men and women could afford an education. The number of people who could read grew, as did the number who could spend money on books. This change had several results. Daily newspapers began to appear. The first real magazine, the *Gentleman's Magazine,* began publication in 1731. The first private lending libraries, which charged their members a fee, also opened in the mid-1700's.

In London, coffeehouses and clubs became popular places for middle-class men to stop in, read the newspapers, and chat about politics. Expanding literacy presented writers with a real opportunity. No longer did they have to rely on a few wealthy patrons for their livelihood. For the

first time, writers could at least survive on the money they made from their books and articles. The modern world of publishers, copyright laws, and royalties began to take shape in London during the 1700's.

Three Literary Ages

The literature of the Restoration and eighteenth century may be thought of as comprising three broad divisions, or "ages": the Age of Dryden, the Age of Pope and Swift, and the Age of Johnson.

The Age of Dryden

The Age of Dryden in literature extends from the year of the restoration of Charles II, 1660, to 1700, the year of Dryden's death. In history, this forty-year period is called the Restoration. Dryden, whose works included poems, plays, and essays, dominated the period. He was named poet laureate, England's official poet, by Charles II.

Among Dryden's most famous works are his satirical poems, especially *MacFlecknoe,* written in 1682. These satires included unflattering portraits of real people of his time. Although the poems employ lofty, heroic language, they actually ridicule their "heroes." For this reason, they are often called mock-heroic poems, or mock epics. Dryden also created several celebratory poems for royal and other public events. These poems, in true Enlightenment spirit, hail the achievements of humanity. A famous example is "A Song for St. Cecilia's Day," an ode in honor of music.

The Restoration was also noted for its plays, especially comedies. When he became king, Charles II reopened the London theaters, which the disapproving Puritans had closed. The Restoration theaters, fancier and more costly than those of Shakespeare's time, did a thriving business. Dryden himself wrote the best tragedy of the period. Entitled *All for Love,* it recounts the ill-fated romance of Antony and Cleopatra.

Prose writing also flourished in the Restoration. Dryden wrote a series of essays about drama that laid the foundation for British literary criticism. These, along with his translations of Plutarch's works and other prose compositions, represent what many literary historians consider the first modern prose. They are clear, plain, direct, colloquial in tone, and—for people of today—easy to read. Probably the most fascinating prose work of the period, however, was the diary kept by Samuel Pepys (1633–1703). Pepys kept his journal for nine years, beginning in 1660. With remarkable frankness he recorded the daily events in London during those turbulent years, including the deadly plague of 1665 and the Great Fire.

The Age of Pope and Swift

During the reign of Queen Anne in the early 1700's, one of the most admired writers in London was Alexander Pope. Pope's poetry is a shining example of neoclassical style, exhibiting wit, elegance, and moderation. All these qualities show forth in his most famous work, *The Rape of the Lock,* a mock-heroic poem that satirizes the absurdities of a war between the sexes.

Pope also had enormous influence as a literary critic. His principles found eloquent expression in *An Essay on Criticism,* a long verse essay in heroic couplets. Many well-known aphorisms can be traced to that work, including the following couplet:

> True wit is Nature to advantage
>   dress'd;
> What oft was thought, but ne'er so well
>   express'd.

Pope, a Tory, was a special favorite of Queen Anne. When George I came to power in 1714, the Tories fell out of favor, and Pope retired to his country house. There he wrote *An Essay on Man,* a long poem that asserts the essential order and goodness of the universe and the rightness of humanity's place in it.

Another Tory writer of the time was Jonathan Swift (1667–1745). Swift, a close friend of Pope's, wrote mild satires while Queen Anne reigned. After her death and the fall of the Tories, Swift grew increasingly bitter. The behavior of the rising merchants, whom he viewed as shameless money grubbers, enraged Swift. *Gulliver's Travels* and *A Modest Proposal* date from this later period. Swift stood apart from many of his contempor-

THE RAKE'S PROGRESS: NO. 5, THE MARRIAGE
William Hogarth

ies by his antagonism to the idea that human nature is essentially good. In his great satires, he presents the older view that human nature is deeply flawed, and that improvement must begin with a recognition of our intellectual and moral limitations.

One book that enjoyed a huge success at the time told about a shipwrecked British sailor struggling to survive on a deserted island. The work, *Robinson Crusoe,* has been called the first novel in English. It was such a success that its author, Daniel Defoe, immediately set to work on other novels. Defoe's experiments with the novel opened up a new form of fiction that, in the 1800's, would become the favorite reading matter of the middle classes.

England's first literary periodicals, *The Tatler* and *The Spectator,* also appeared in the early 1700's. Written by Joseph Addison (1672–1719) and Richard Steele (1672–1729), these one-page papers included crisply written reflective essays and news. The essays quickly became models for other prose writers.

The Age of Johnson

Alexander Pope died in 1744, and Jonathan Swift the following year. The dominant literary figure of the next generation was Samuel Johnson. Like many young writers after him, Johnson honed his writing style by working as a journalist. He later published his own magazine, *The Rambler.* Johnson also wrote poetry, literary criticism, and a novel. His most important work, however, was the *Dictionary of the English Language,* published in 1755. It was the first dictionary that could be considered a standard and authoritative reference work on English.

Samuel Johnson dominated his age not only by his writings but also by his conversation and acquaintanceships. A brilliant and inexhaustible talker, he was friendly with most of the writers, painters, and actors of his time. His wise advice helped nurture the careers of many younger talents.

One reason we know so much about Samuel Johnson is that one of those younger talents, James Boswell (1740–1795), wrote his biography. Boswell followed his friend and mentor from club to coffeehouse to dinner party, faithfully recording Johnson's comments and witticisms. The result, Boswell's *Life of Samuel Johnson,* was the first modern biography written in English. It gives a vivid portrait not only of Johnson but of life in London in the 1700's.

The Age of Johnson saw other literary accomplishments. On the stage, the Restoration tradition of satire was carried on by Oliver Goldsmith and other comic playwrights. Among the many important works of prose, Edward Gibbon's history of Rome stands out. Novelists, working in the tradition begun by Defoe, produced a spate of popular books. Among the best were Samuel Richardson's *Pamela* and *Clarissa,* Fanny Burney's *Evelina,* Henry Fielding's *Tom Jones* and *Joseph Andrews,* and Lawrence Sterne's *Tristram Shandy.*

The Eclipse of the Enlightenment

By 1750, Britain was launched on a course of rapid industrialization. In the new industrial towns, mills and factories belched smoke into the country air. Inside the factories, men, women, and children toiled at machines for twelve and fourteen hours a day. Every year more poor people crowded into the towns and cities, unable to find regular work and barely able to survive.

As a result of these changes, writers and intellectuals began to lose faith in the ability of human reason to solve every problem. The thinkers in the Age of Reason looked to science to make life better for humanity. Yet by the late 1700's, "progress" seemed to be bringing misery to millions.

As they began to doubt the basic assumptions of the Enlightenment, writers turned away from the standards of neoclassicism. Instead of using the impersonal, high-flown style of the early 1700's, some wrote in the common language of everyday life. Departing from the spirit of rationalism, they charged their poems with powerful emotions. Thomas Gray's *Elegy Written in a Country Churchyard,* completed in 1750, exemplifies the transition from the formal, classical poetic styles of the early eighteenth century to the more emotional manner of the Romantic era.

William Blake broke even more sharply with the ideas and attitudes of Pope and the neoclassicists. In simple language, he conveyed mystical ideas and biting attacks on what England was becoming. In one poem he derided those who held to a complacent faith in human rationality, while ignoring the spiritual side of human existence:

> You don't believe—I won't attempt to
>   make ye;
> You are asleep—I won't attempt to
>   wake ye.
> Sleep on! Sleep on! while in your pleas-
>   ant dreams
> Of Reason you may drink of Life's clear
>   streams.
> Reason and Newton, they are quite two
>   things;
> For so the swallow and the sparrow
>   sings.

The Age of Reason, with its unbounded faith in human intelligence, was coming to an end. New voices were being raised, and they no longer spoke in the clipped and polished language of rationalist neoclassicism. They would make the 1800's a new literary age.

BRITISH VOICES

Quotations by Prominent Figures of the Period

Errors, like straws, upon the surface flow;
He who would search for pearls must dive below.
   John Dryden, *All for Love*

Titles are shadow, crowns are empty things,
The good of subjects is the end of kings.
   Daniel Defoe, *The True-Born Englishman*

Satire is a sort of glass, wherein beholders do generally
discover everybody's face but their own.
   Jonathan Swift, "The Battle of the Books"

Proper words in proper places make the true definition of a
style.
   Jonathan Swift, "Letter to a Young Clergyman"

Sweet are the slumbers of the virtuous man.
   Joseph Addison, *Cato*

Reading is to the mind what exercise is to the body.
   Richard Steele, *The Tatler*

The noblest motive is the public good.
   Richard Steele, *The Spectator*

To err is human, to forgive divine.
   Alexander Pope, *An Essay on Criticism*

Fools rush in where angels fear to tread.
   Alexander Pope, *An Essay on Criticism*

When a man is tired of London, he is tired of life.
   Samuel Johnson, Quoted by James Boswell in *The Life of Samuel Johnson*

The paths of glory lead but to the grave.
   Thomas Gray, "Elegy Written in a Country Churchyard"

The best laid plans o' mice and men
Gang aft a-gley.
   Robert Burns, "To a Mouse"

READING CRITICALLY

The Literature of 1660–1798

When you read literature, it is important to place it in its historical context. Doing so will help you to see how it was shaped by the dominant attitudes of the period and to appreciate the techniques the writer used to convey these attitudes.

HISTORICAL CONTEXT In the years 1660 to 1798, English life was dominated by a desire for social and political stability. The nation had been severely shaken by the events of the civil war and the Puritan dictatorship and sought to reestablish a sense of order and security. Although the monarchy had been restored, the Parliament developed into the nation's supreme ruling force. Despite this shift in power, the English people generally remained complacent. The nation prospered financially, and its citizens tended to be patriotic and optimistic. This sense of optimism resulted in part from scientific and philosophical advances that helped create a belief that everything in the universe could be explained.

LITERARY MOVEMENTS The literature written between 1660 and 1798 generally reflects the faith in reason and the desire for stability that characterized English life at the time. Strongly influenced by the works of classical Greek and Roman authors, writers generally displayed their intelligence, education, and sense of discipline in their works. They also conveyed their faith in English traditions and captured the elegance of English aristocratic life at the time. Toward the end of the eighteenth century, however, some poets, who are often referred to as pre-Romantics, began to react against the emphasis on reason and the intellect.

WRITERS' TECHNIQUES During this period English prose flourished. Writers wrote formal essays on a variety of subjects, presenting logical, scientific arguments. The literary letter became a popular form, the first modern biography was written, and literary criticism and fiction flourished. In poetry, writers generally turned away from the lyric and wrote formally structured poems, often filled with classical allusions. Writers often displayed their wit by satirizing the society of their day in both poems and essays. The pre-Romantic poets, however, disregarded the tastes of the time and reestablished the lyric.

The Restoration

THE ELECTION—THE POLLING
William Hogarth
Sir John Soane's Museum, London

JOHN DRYDEN

1631–1700

John Dryden dominated the literary scene in the last quarter of the seventeenth century. The most accomplished poet of the period, he also ranks high in English letters as a dramatist, essayist, satirist, and critic. His versatility and professionalism helped to establish writing as a legitimate career in England. The poet T. S. Eliot has maintained that Dryden "is the ancestor of nearly all that is best in the poetry of the eighteenth century," while the poet Matthew Arnold observed, "Here at last we have the true English prose, a prose such as we would all gladly use if only we knew how."

Born at the vicarage of Aldwinkle All Saints, Northamptonshire, where his father was a country gentleman, young Dryden studied at Westminster School. He graduated from Trinity College, Cambridge, in 1654, and five years later published his first important poem, *Heroic Stanzas*. The poem commemorates the death of Oliver Cromwell, under whose protectorate Dryden seems to have held a minor political post. A year later, in *Astraea Redux,* he did a political about-face and hailed the return to the throne of King Charles II. While in his fifties, Dryden, who had once been a Puritan and then an Anglican, became a convert to Roman Catholicism.

Dryden first came to prominence as a playwright, producing blank-verse tragedies and comedies. He was appointed poet laureate in 1668, a position that was supposed to pay an annual salary of 200 pounds, but because of problems in the royal treasury, he received only half of that. His best play, *All for Love* (1677), is a rewriting of Shakespeare's *Antony and Cleopatra* in a clear, simple style. He displays his full power in *Absalom and Achitophel,* a political poem published in 1681. This poem was followed a year later by the equally impressive *The Medall,* also on politics.

After the Revolution of 1688, which brought the Protestants William and Mary to the English throne, Dryden lost his laureateship. He was replaced by Thomas Shadwell, whom Dryden had satirized a few years earlier in the poem *MacFlecknoe*. To compensate for his lost income, Dryden increased his output, translating classical writers and writing prologues and miscellaneous pieces. The last of these efforts, his *Fables, Ancient and Modern*—translations of Chaucer, Boccaccio, and Ovid—appeared the year he died.

As a writer, Dryden was uniquely a man of his era. He expressed himself on virtually every important issue of the day. His friend William Congreve, a fellow playwright, pays tribute to Dryden's talents, saying that "no man hath written in our language so much . . . and in so various manners so well. . . ."

GUIDE FOR INTERPRETING

from An Essay of Dramatic Poesy

Essay. An essay is a prose composition that expresses the writer's viewpoint on a limited topic. Essays vary in length from several paragraphs to the equivalent of an entire book. Modern essays are generally short, but in the eighteenth century, when the essay flourished as a popular literary form, essays were considerably longer. Dryden's complete essay on dramatic poesy—about thirty-five printed pages—is of average length for the time.

Essays can be classified as formal or informal. A *formal* essay is one that deals with a serious subject in a carefully organized and intellectual way. An *informal,* or *personal,* essay is lighter and less structured than a formal essay. It may be humorous, and—even though classified as nonfiction—it may stretch the truth considerably or abandon it entirely. An informal essay is generally written in a conversational tone, reflecting the personality of the author and displaying distinctly personal touches.

Writing style, as with style in fashion, changes through the years. Dryden's style of writing, however, has become "classic"—the standard by which we measure all other writing—because it is clear, direct, and elegant. To Samuel Johnson, for example, Dryden does not appear "to have any other art than that of expressing with clearness what he thinks with vigor. His style could not easily be imitated, either seriously or ludicrously; for, being always equable and always varied, it has no prominent or discriminative characters." What are the qualities of Dryden's style?

His sentences are basically subject-verb-object, with just enough variety to avoid monotony. Although his sentences are usually longer than was fashionable in the seventeenth century, they are not overly long when judged by earlier standards. Clear and concise, they have a conversational tone and do not contain excessive figurative language. What other elements of style can you find in the following essay that contribute to Dryden's concise, clear, and dignified writing?

When you read a work of fiction, what do you look for? An exciting plot? Well-developed, believable characters? Insights into human nature? List at least five characteristics that you think a work of fiction should have. Then make a second list in which you include the characteristics that detract from a work of fiction—for example, dull characters or an unbelievable plot.

from An Essay of Dramatic Poesy

John Dryden

Shakespeare and Ben Jonson Compared

To begin, then, with Shakespeare. He was the man who of all modern, and perhaps ancient poets, had the largest and most comprehensive soul. All the images of nature were still present to him, and he drew them, not laboriously, but luckily; when he describes anything, you more than see it, you feel it too. Those who accuse him to have wanted[1] learning, give him the greater commendation: he was naturally learned; he needed not the spectacles of books to read nature; he looked inwards, and found her there. I cannot say he is everywhere alike; were he so, I should do him injury to compare him with the greatest of mankind. He is many times flat, insipid; his comic wit degenerating into clenches,[2] his serious swelling into bombast. But he is always great, when some great occasion is presented to him; no man can say he ever had a fit subject for his wit, and did not then raise himself as high above the rest of poets,

Quantum lenta solent inter viburna cupressi[3]

The consideration of this made Mr. Hales of Eton say that there was no subject of which any poet ever writ, but he would produce it much better done in Shakespeare; and however others are now generally preferred before him, yet the age wherein he lived, which had contemporaries with him Fletcher[4] and Jonson, never equaled them to him in their esteem: and in the last king's court, when Ben's reputation was at highest, Sir John Suckling, and with him the greater part of the courtiers, set our Shakespeare far above him. . . .

As for Jonson, to whose character I am now arrived, if we look upon him while he was himself (for his last plays were but his dotages), I think him the most learned and judicious writer which any theater ever had. He was a most severe judge of himself, as well as others. One cannot say he wanted wit, but rather that he was frugal of it. In his works you find little to retrench[5] or alter. Wit, and language, and humor also in some measure, we had before him; but something of art was wanting to the drama till he came.

---

1. **wanted:** Lacked.
2. **clenches:** Puns.
3. ***Quantum . . . cupressi:*** As do cypresses among the bending shrubs. From Virgil's *Eclogues* 1:25.

4. **Fletcher:** John Fletcher (1579–1625), an Elizabethan playwright.
5. **retrench:** Delete.

from *An Essay of Dramatic Poesy* **449**

He managed his strength to more advantage than any who preceded him. You seldom find him making love in any of his scenes or endeavoring to move the passions; his genius was too sullen and saturnine[6] to do it gracefully, especially when he knew he came after those who had performed both to such a height. Humor was his proper sphere: and in that he delighted most to represent mechanic people.[7] He was deeply conversant in the ancients, both Greek and Latin, and he borrowed boldly from them: there is scarce a poet or historian among the Roman authors of those times whom he has not translated in *Sejanus* and *Catiline*.[8] But he has done his robberies so openly, that one may see he fears not to be taxed by any law. He invades authors like a monarch; and

what would be theft in other poets is only victory in him. With the spoils of these writers he so represents old Rome to us, in its rites, ceremonies, and customs, that if one of their poets had written either of his tragedies, we had seen less of it than in him. If there was any fault in his language, 'twas that he weaved it too closely and laboriously, in his serious plays; perhaps, too, he did a little too much Romanize our tongue, leaving the words which he translated almost as much Latin as he found them, wherein, though he learnedly followed the idiom of their language, he did not enough comply with the idiom of ours. If I would compare him with Shakespeare, I must acknowledge him the more correct poet, but Shakespeare the greater wit. Shakespeare was the Homer, or father of our dramatic poets; Jonson was the Virgil, the pattern of elaborate writing; I admire him, but I love Shakespeare. . . .

---

6. **saturnine:** Heavy.
7. **mechanic people:** Artisans.
8. ***Sejanus* and *Catiline*:** Two of Jonson's plays.

▌RESPONDING TO THE SELECTION

Your Response

1. Do you think Dryden is fair in his comparison of the two writers? Why or why not?

Recalling

2. How does Dryden respond to the criticism that Shakespeare lacked learning?
3. According to Dryden, what was missing from English drama before Ben Jonson started writing?
4. Far from accusing Jonson of theft, what does Dryden say about his borrowing from classical writers?

Interpreting

5. In your own words, what does Dryden mean by saying that Shakespeare "had the largest and most comprehensive soul"?

6. Dryden uses a Latin quotation from Virgil to describe Shakespeare's achievement. How does this quotation relate to the comment that immediately precedes it?
7. In what sense does Dryden mean that Shakespeare was not a "correct poet"?

Applying

8. Assume that the virtues of Shakespeare and Jonson represent the qualities Dryden admires in all writers. (a) What qualities would Dryden's perfect writer have? (b) What writer, in your opinion, comes closest to having those qualities? Explain the reasons for your choice.

▌ANALYZING LITERATURE

Understanding an Essay

An **essay** is a prose composition, usually short, that deals with one topic. Typically, the writer of an essay states his or her personal views on the topic. A formal essay is serious and dignified. An informal essay is lighter and more conversational. Dryden's "Essay of Dramatic Poesy," written more than 300 years ago, may not seem like an informal essay, but it is. It is written in the form of a conversation among four friends as they are boating on the Thames. One of them, named Neander, represents Dryden. He is the person speaking in the excerpt included in this book.

1. Two signs of informality in writing are (a) the occasional use of sentence fragments and (b) the occasional use of a conjunction to start a sentence. Find an example of each of these in the excerpt from Dryden's essay.
2. Compare Dryden's essay with Donne's "Meditation 17" (pages 367–368). What are three noticeable differences in prose style between the two? (In examining prose style, look at sentence structure, sentence length, rhetorical devices, word choice, and so on.)

CRITICAL THINKING AND READING

Charting an Analysis

Dryden's "An Essay of Dramatic Poesy" is an analysis of the literary merits of William Shakespeare and Ben Jonson. The essay contains a number of specific statements praising, criticizing, or comparing the two writers. List as many properties of a writer as you can find in Dryden's essay. These properties can be good or bad. Beside each property on your list, state in a phrase or short sentence how Dryden rates each writer. For example, you might list "Education" as a property. Your entry for Shakespeare might then read,

"Lacked formal education but was thoroughly self-educated."

Property	Shakespeare	Jonson
1. Education	Lacked formal education but was thoroughly self-educated	

If nothing is said about one of the two writers in regard to a particular property, write, "No comment." Complete your chart with a statement summarizing Dryden's overall opinion of Shakespeare and Jonson as writers.

THINKING AND WRITING

Writing an Evaluation of an Analysis

Review the chart you prepared on Shakespeare and Jonson. Also review the lists you made before reading. Use these materials as the basis for an essay in which you evaluate Dryden's analysis of the literary merits of Shakespeare and Jonson. Take into account your own opinion of Shakespeare and Jonson. Is Dryden fair to Shakespeare? Does Dryden overrate Jonson? Keep these and other questions in mind as you write the first draft. When you are ready to revise, reread the Dryden excerpt to be sure you are interpreting his opinions accurately. Be sure you have supported your own opinions well. Make any needed changes. Then write your final draft.

GUIDE FOR INTERPRETING

A Song for St. Cecilia's Day

Literary Forms

Ode. An ode is a lyric poem, usually rhymed, that addresses and praises a person, an object, or a quality. Most odes are dignified or exalted in subject matter and style. The word *ode* comes from a Greek word meaning "song." The earliest odes, dating back to ancient Greece, were elaborate chants with themes and responses sung by a divided choir. Pindar, a Greek poet of the fifth century B.C., refined the form, becoming one of its great masters. The form he devised has been considerably changed over the centuries. Although Dryden patterned his odes loosely on classical models, later writers varied the form in many ways. Once recognizable by its shape, the ode today is more a matter of tone and intention than structure.

Commentary

In his day it was common knowledge among literary circles that Dryden was a solemn, dignified person who was not much given to making amusing remarks. He admitted this himself on numerous occasions. One of his witty rejoinders, however, has been passed down.

According to many reports, he and his wife, Lady Elizabeth, do not seem to have been on very friendly terms with each other. If we trust the gossip of the day, the relationship got off to a rocky start because Dryden had been forced into marriage with the woman by one of her brothers. Regardless of the reason, the union was less than cordial.

One day, so the story goes, Lady Elizabeth began to feel more than usually neglected by her husband, who spent a great deal of time alone with his books and papers. Marching into the study, she burst out, "Lord, Mr. Dryden, how can you always be poring over those musty books? I wish I were a book, and then I should have more of your company." Dryden was ready with a quick answer. "Pray, my dear," he replied, "if you do become a book let it be an almanack, for then I shall change you every year."

What contrast do you see between "A Song for St. Cecilia's Day" and Dryden's domestic situation?

Focus

Jot down some thoughts on a person, thing, or event you think deserves to be honored. Then freewrite a short tribute, either in a paragraph or in a few lines of poetry, in which you make clear the qualities of the person, thing, or event that you believe justify the tribute.

A Song for St. Cecilia's Day[1]

John Dryden

1

From harmony, from heavenly harmony
    This universal frame[2] began;
    When Nature underneath a heap
    Of jarring atoms[3] lay,
5   And could not heave her head,
The tuneful voice was heard from high,
    "Arise, ye more than dead."

Then cold and hot and moist and dry[4]
    In order to their stations leap,
10   And Music's power obey.
From harmony, from heavenly harmony
    This universal frame began:
    From harmony to harmony
Through all the compass of the notes it ran,
15 The diapason[5] closing full in Man.

2

What passion cannot Music raise and quell?
    When Jubal[6] struck the corded shell,
    His listening brethren stood around,
    And, wondering, on their faces fell
20   To worship that celestial sound.

---

1. "A Song for St. Cecilia's Day" was composed for the Festival of St. Cecilia on November 22, 1687. According to legend, St. Cecilia was an early Christian martyr, who became the patron saint of music.
2. universal frame: The structure of the universe.
3. jarring atoms: The chaos that preceded the creation of the universe.
4. cold . . . dry: Earth, fire, water, and air, the four elements out of which everything was composed, according to the ancient Greeks.
5. diapason (dī′ ə pā′ zən): The entire range of tones on a musical scale. Dryden is also making reference to the Chain of Being, the ordered creation from inanimate nature up to man.
6. Jubal: In Genesis 4:21, Jubal is said to be the inventor of the lyre and the pipe.

THE MUSIC OF A BYGONE AGE
John Melhuish Strudwick

Less than a god they thought there could not dwell
Within the hollow of that shell
That spoke so sweetly, and so well.
What passion cannot Music raise and quell?

3

25 The trumpet's loud clangor
Excites us to arms
With shrill notes of anger
And mortal alarms.
The double double double beat
30 Of the thundering drum
Cries, "Hark! the foes come:
Charge, charge, 'tis too late to retreat."

4

The soft complaining flute
In dying notes discovers[7]
35 The woes of hopeless lovers,
Whose dirge is whispered by the warbling lute.

5

Sharp violins proclaim
Their jealous pangs and desperation.
Fury, frantic indignation,
40 Depth of pains and height of passion,
For the fair, disdainful dame.

6

But Oh! What art can teach,
What human voice can reach
The sacred organ's praise?
45 Notes inspiring holy love,
Notes that wing their heavenly ways
To mend the choirs above.

7

Orpheus[8] could lead the savage race,
And trees unrooted left their place,
50 Sequacious of the lyre:
But bright Cecilia raised the wonder higher:

---

7. discovers: Reveals.
8. Orpheus (ôr′ fē əs): In Greek mythology, a poet and musician whose magic musical powers enabled him to charm rocks, trees, and wild beasts by playing his lyre.

When to her organ vocal breath was given,
An angel heard, and straight appeared
    Mistaking earth for heaven.

GRAND CHORUS

55 *As from the power of sacred lays[9]*
        The spheres began to move.[10]
    And sung the great Creator's praise
        To all the blessed above;
        So when the last and dreadful hour
60 *This crumbling pageant[11] shall devour,*
    The trumpet shall be heard on high,[12]
    The dead shall live, the living die,
    And Music shall untune the sky.

---

9. lays: Songs.
10. spheres . . . move: According to legend, the celestial bodies
(spheres) were put into motion by angelic song. The motion of the
spheres was believed to produce harmonious music, a hymn of
"praise" for the "Creator," sung by the created.
11. pageant: The universe.
12. trumpet . . . high: From I Corinthians 15:52, the last trumpet
that will announce the Last Judgment, or the end of the universe.

Primary Source

For people in the eighteenth century,
music was a social as well as an
intellectual pastime. In the summer
concerts were offered in public gardens,
where people strolling among the
"regular rows of young trees" feasted on
fruit tarts, almond cheesecakes, and fine
Epping butter. Sometimes there were
fireworks as well, brilliant displays
"splendid beyond conception." The
following contemporary advertisement
promised exotically named fireworks as
well as music:

"Marybone Gardens.—This day,
June 2, will be performed a Concert of
Vocal and Instrumental Music. In the
course of which will be sung for the first
time this season an Entertainment of
Music called 'The MAGNET.' The Vocal
Parts by Mr. Reinhold, Miss Wilde, and
Miss Wewitzer. The celebrated Mons.
Ladell, Musician to the King of Portugal,
will perform a Concert on the German
Flute. Admittance Two Shillings and
Sixpence. The Doors will be opened at
Five o'clock. The Concert will begin at
Half Past Six o'clock . . . To-morrow Sig.
Torre's Second Exhibition; when he will
repeat the Forge of Vulcan, as it was
performed at the Marriage of his Royal
Highness the Count d'Artois.

"Marybone Gardens will open
To-morrow Evening immediately after
Five o'clock for Company to walk in.
Tea, Coffee, and other Refreshments
may be had at the Bar. To prevent
Improper company each Person to pay
sixpence at the Door."

Your Response

1. Does the power of music affect you as greatly as it did Dryden? Explain.

Recalling

2. In addition to the corded shell, what musical instruments are mentioned in the poem?
3. What does Dryden claim an angel did upon hearing Cecilia play the organ?
4. What instrument will announce Judgment Day?

Interpreting

5. The word *harmony* dominates the first stanza. What meaning, or meanings, does it have as Dryden uses it?
6. (a) What musical instrument does Dryden suggest is the most heavenly? (b) In view of the day the poem celebrates, why is this praise especially appropriate?
7. Why will music "untune the sky" in "the last and dreadful hour"?

Applying

8. Dryden is often called an "occasional" poet, because he wrote in response to major news events, literary developments, and, as in this poem, to celebrate special days. Occasional poetry is no longer popular. What do people do today to commemorate special events and heroes?

ANALYZING LITERATURE

Recognizing an Ode

An **ode** is a lyrical poem that pays homage to a person, thing, or quality. The earliest odes are from classical times, such as those of the Greek poet Pindar (522?–443 B.C.) and the Latin poet Horace (65–8 B.C.). The Pindaric, or Greek, ode, which is the ancestor of the odes written by Dryden, is composed of three-part stanzas called *triads*. Each triad is made up of a *strophe* (sung by one half the singers in a choir), an *antistrophe* (sung by the other half), and an *epode* (sung by

the entire choir). Dryden and other poets of the seventeenth century use much looser stanzaic structures than Pindar's, as do later writers.

1. In "A Song for St. Cecilia's Day," how many lines are (a) in each numbered stanza? (b) in the Grand Chorus?
2. (a) Which stanzas have regular patterns of rhyme? (b) What are these patterns? (Use *a, b, c,* and so on, to show patterns.)
3. Why do you think Dryden uses such an irregular stanza and rhyme scheme for his poem?

CRITICAL THINKING AND READING

Understanding the Effect of Sound

Dryden's words carry meaning not only in a lexical, or dictionary, sense but also through their sound. For example, in the third stanza, the word *shrill* echoes—that is, imitates the sound of—the insistent cry of the trumpet. The word *double,* while not in itself evocative of a drum, becomes so when repeated like a drumbeat—"double, double, double."

1. Which word in the third stanza besides *double* has a sound that echoes the pounding of the drum?
2. Which words in the fourth stanza have sounds that echo the melodic flute and lute?
3. Which sounds in the fifth stanza echo the piercing tone of the violin?

THINKING AND WRITING

Writing an Ode

Choose one of the following topics as the subject for an ode. You may decide on the number of stanzas and the length of lines, but try to follow at least two of the rhyme patterns used by Dryden in "A Song for St. Cecilia's Day." Also use as many echoic, or sound-imitative, devices as you can. Read your ode aloud to judge its effect. After revising, proofread it and prepare a final draft.

1. The United States
2. A season of the year
3. A brother or sister
4. Honesty

SAMUEL PEPYS

1633–1703

Samuel Pepys (pēps) is an unusual figure in English literature, not so much because his fame rests on a single work but rather because the one work, his *Diary,* was never intended for publication. This diary, which Pepys kept in shorthand and in his own private code, was not deciphered until the nineteenth century.

The man who painted this vivid portrait of seventeenth-century London was a "very worthy, industrious, and curious person," according to his friend John Evelyn. Born in London, the son of a tailor, Pepys studied at St. Paul's School and Magdalene (môd′ lən) College, Cambridge. Upon graduation in 1653, he became secretary to his influential cousin, Edward Montagu, later the Earl of Sandwich. Two years later he married Elizabeth St. Michel, a girl of fifteen. The *Diary* contains many details of their strife-ridden union, which survived Pepys countless infidelities and lasted until her early death in 1669.

Pepys began his career—and his diary—as a naval man in 1660, when he was appointed clerk of the king's ships and clerk of the privy seal. His advancement, as the *Diary* notes, was rapid, and with each new position Pepys grew richer. Yet his life was not without its tragedies. In the same year that his wife died, Pepys's failing eyesight caused him to stop keeping his diary. In 1679 he was imprisoned briefly in the Tower of London, accused of popery and treason, and in 1690 he once again spent time in prison on charges of intrigue.

The *Diary,* originally in six manuscript volumes, remained in cipher until 1819, when a student at Magdalene College, Cambridge, began transcribing it. Published in 1825, the *Diary* proved a fascinating mix of candid private revelations and keenly observed public scenes. The 1660's, during which the diary was kept, saw Pepys's personal rise from obscure clerk to highly regarded public servant. It also saw—and through Pepys's eyes modern readers can see—the coronation of King Charles II, London's devastating plague of 1665, and the Great Fire of 1666.

In the centuries since his death, some readers have dismissed Pepys as a shallow figure and his observations as mere gossip. But the Samuel Pepys who emerges from between the lines of the *Diary* is more than just a government careerist with a roving eye. He is a man of intelligence and great diplomacy, much admired by the people of his time. He is also a diarist of exceptional honesty and perception. Readers today who wish to know about life in seventeenth-century London are greatly in his debt.

GUIDE FOR INTERPRETING

from The Diary

Literary Forms

Diary. A diary is a personal, day-by-day record of events, experiences, and observations. Perhaps you think of a diary as simply a collection of notes about the small details in one's life, such as what the diarist had for breakfast. Many diaries fit that definition, but not all. The diaries that become literature are usually those that provide insights into important historical events or periods. *The Diary of Anne Frank,* for instance, gives readers a poignant glimpse of a young Jewish girl's ultimately futile attempt to escape Nazi persecution by hiding with her family in Nazi-occupied Netherlands in World War II. The events have an importance beyond Anne Frank's individual fate. Moreover, as with most diaries that are regarded as literature, it is exceptionally well written.

Commentary

Pepys's diary gives us firsthand information about life in London. As we know from Pepys's account, fire posed a considerable threat in the town and countryside. Once started, fires spread with terrible speed. Water could be obtained only with great difficulty through pumps and conduits. Homes in town were supplied by a huge waterwheel at London Bridge, but people in the country had to rely on well water or had to store rainwater in huge lead casks. By the beginning of the eighteenth century, with memories of the Great Fire still fresh, officials were taking stronger measures against the threat of fire.

In 1708, for example, an act was passed "for the better preventing of mischiefs that may happen by fire." Some shops carried rope ladders and other devices to help people escape from burning buildings. Most noteworthy, perhaps, was the establishment of the first insurance companies. These included the symbolically named Phoenix, The Friendly Society, and The Amicable Contributors. The firms all had offices in London coffeehouses, which were centers for the exchange of news and views, and meeting places for businessmen, wits, and idlers.

What evidence do you have from Pepys's account that adequate measures were not yet in place to combat the fires?

Focus

Write down some notes about an especially memorable event you have experienced. These notes can be in the form of a diary entry; they do not have to be written in grammatically complete sentences or arranged in an orderly sequence.

from The Diary

Samuel Pepys

The Plague

Sept. 3, 1665. (Lord's Day.) Church being done, my Lord Bruncker, Sir J. Minnes, and I up to the vestry[1] at the desire of the Justices of the Peace, Sir Theo. Biddulph and Sir W. Boreman and Alderman Hooker, in order to the doing something for the keeping of the plague from growing; but Lord! to consider the madness of the people of the town, who will (because they are forbid) come in crowds along with the dead corps[2] to see them buried; but we agreed on some orders for the prevention thereof.[3] Among other stories, one was very passionate, methought, of a complaint brought against a man in the town for taking a child from London from an infected house. Alderman Hooker told us it was the child of a very able citizen in Gracious Street, a saddler,[4] who had buried all the rest of his children of the plague, and himself and wife now being shut up and in despair of escaping, did desire only to save the life of this little child; and so prevailed to have it received stark-naked into the arms of a friend, who brought it (having put it into new fresh clothes) to Greenwich; where upon hearing the story, we did agree it should be permitted to be received and kept in the town. Thence with my Lord Bruncker to Captain Cocke's, where we mighty merry and supped, and very late I by water to Woolwich, in great apprehensions of an ague. . . .

Sept. 14, 1665. When I come home I spent some thoughts upon the occurrences of this day, giving matter for as much content on one hand and melancholy on another, as any day in all my life. For the first; the finding of my money and plate,[5] and all safe at London, and speeding in my business of money this day. The hearing of this good news to such excess, after so great a despair of my Lord's doing anything this year; adding to that, the decrease of 500 and more, which is the first decrease we have yet had in the sickness since it begun: and great hopes that the next week it will be greater. Then, on the other side, my finding that though the bill[6] in general is abated, yet the city within the walls is increased, and likely to continue so, and is close to our house there. My meeting dead corpses of the plague, carried to be buried close to me at noonday through the city in Fanchurch Street. To see a person sick of the sores, carried close by me by Grace church in a

---

1. vestry (ves' trē) *n.:* A church meeting room.
2. corps: corpses.
3. but we . . . thereof: Funeral processions were forbidden in London during the plague. However, the law was often ignored.
4. saddler *n.:* A person who makes, sells, and repairs saddles.
5. plate: Valuable serving dishes and flatware.
6. bill: Weekly list of burials.

hackney coach.[7] My finding the Angell Tavern at the lower end of Tower Hill, shut up, and more than that, the alehouse at the Tower Stairs, and more than that, the person was then dying of the plague when I was last there, a little while ago, at night, to write a short letter there, and I overheard the mistress of the house sadly saying to her husband somebody was very ill, but did not think it was of the plague. To hear that poor Payne, my waiter, hath buried a child, and is dying himself. To hear that a laborer I sent but the other day to Dagenhams, to know how they did there, is dead of the plague; and that one of my own watermen, that carried me daily, fell sick as soon as he had landed me on Friday morning last, when I had been all night upon the water (and I believe he did get his infection that day at Brainford), and is now dead of the plague. To hear that Captain Lambert and Cuttle are killed in the taking these ships; and that Mr. Sidney Montague is sick of a desperate fever at my Lady Carteret's, at Scott's Hall. To hear that Mr. Lewes hath another daughter sick. And, lastly, that both my servants, W. Hewer and Tom Edwards, have lost their fathers, both in St. Sepulcher's parish, of the plague this week, do put me into great apprehensions of melancholy, and with good reason. But I put off the thoughts of sadness as much as I can, and the rather to keep my wife in good heart and family also. After supper (having eat nothing all this day) upon a fine tench[8] of Mr. Shelden's taking, we to bed.

The Fire of London

Sept. 2, 1666. (Lord's day.) Some of our maids sitting up late last night to get things ready against our feast today, Jane called us up about three in the morning, to tell us of a great fire they saw in the city. So I rose and slipped on my night-gown, and went to her window, and thought it to be on the back side of Mark Lane at the farthest; but, being unused to such fires as followed, I thought it far enough off; and so went to bed again and to sleep. About seven rose again to dress myself, and there looked out at the window, and saw the fire not so much as it was and farther off. So to my closet to set things to rights after yesterday's cleaning. By and by Jane comes and tells me that she hears that above 300 houses have been burned down tonight by the fire we saw, and that it is now burning down all Fish Street, by London Bridge. So I made myself ready presently, and walked to the Tower,[9] and there got up upon one of the high places, Sir J. Robinson's little son going up with me; and there I did see the houses at that end of the bridge all on fire, and an infinite great fire on this and the other side the end of the bridge; which, among other people, did trouble me for poor little Michell and our Sarah on the bridge. So down, with my heart full of trouble, to the Lieutenant of the Tower, who tells me that it begun this morning in the King's baker's house in Pudding Lane, and that it hath burned St. Magnus's Church and most part of Fish Street already. So I down to the waterside, and there got a boat and through bridge, and there saw a lamentable fire. Poor Michell's house, as far as the Old Swan, already burned that way, and the fire running farther, that in a very little time it got as far as the steel yard, while I was there. Everybody endeavoring to remove their goods, and flinging into the river or bringing them into lighters that lay off; poor people staying in their houses as long as till the very fire touched them, and then running into boats, or clambering from one pair of stairs by the waterside to another. And among other things, the poor pigeons, I perceive, were loth to leave their houses, but hovered about the windows and balconies

---

7. hackney coach: A carriage for hire.
8. tench *n.*: A type of fish.

9. Tower: The Tower of London.

THE GREAT FIRE OF LONDON, 1666
The Museum of London

till they were, some of them burned, their wings, and fell down. Having stayed, and in an hour's time seen the fire rage every way, and nobody, to my sight, endeavoring to quench it, but to remove their goods, and leave all to the fire, and having seen it get as far as the steel yard, and the wind mighty high and driving it into the city; and everything, after so long a drought, proving combustible, even the very stones of churches, and among other things the poor steeple by which pretty Mrs.— lives, and whereof my old schoolfellow Elborough is parson, taken fire in the very top, and there burned till it fell down. I to Whitehall (with a gentleman with me who desired to go off from the Tower, to see the fire, in my boat), and there up to the King's closet in the chapel, where people come about me, and I did give them an account dismayed them all, and word was carried in to the King. So I was called for, and did tell the King and Duke of York

what I saw, and that unless his Majesty did command houses to be pulled down nothing could stop the fire. They seemed much troubled, and the King commanded me to go to my Lord Mayor from him, and command him to spare no houses, but to pull down before the fire every way. The Duke of York bid me tell him that if he would have any more soldiers he shall; and so did my Lord Arlington afterwards, as a great secret. Here meeting with Captain Cocke, I in his coach, which he lent me, and Creed with me to Paul's,[10] and there walked along Watling Street, as well as I could, every creature coming away loaden with goods to save, and here and there sick people carried away in beds. Extraordinary good goods carried in carts and on backs. At last met my Lord Mayor in Canning Street, like a man spent,

---

10. Paul's: St. Paul's Cathedral.

with a handkerchief about his neck. To the King's message he cried, like a fainting woman, "Lord! what can I do? I am spent: people will not obey me. I have been pulling down houses; but the fire overtakes us faster than we can do it." That he needed no more soldiers; and that, for himself, he must go and refresh himself, having been up all night. So he left me, and I him, and walked home, seeing people all almost distracted, and no manner of means used to quench the fire. The houses, too, so very thick thereabouts, and full of matter for burning, as pitch and tar, in Thames Street; and warehouses of oil, and wines, and brandy, and other things. Here I saw Mr. Isaake Houblon, the handsome man, prettily dressed and dirty, at his door at Dowgate, receiving some of his brothers' things, whose houses were on fire; and, as he says, have been removed twice already; and he doubts (as it soon proved) that they must be in a little time removed from his house also, which was a sad consideration. And to see the churches all filling with goods by people who themselves should have been quietly there at this time. By this time it was about twelve o'clock; and so home. Soon as dined, and walked through the city, the streets full of nothing but people and horses and carts loaden with goods, ready to run over one another, and removing goods from one burned house to another. They now removing out of Canning Street (which received goods in the morning) into Lumbard Street, and farther; and among others I now saw my little goldsmith, Stokes, receiving some friend's goods, whose house itself was burned the day after. I to Paul's Wharf, where I had appointed a boat to attend me, and took in Mr. Carcasse and his brother, whom I met in the street, and carried them below and above bridge to and again to see the fire, which was now got farther, both below and above, and no likelihood of stopping it. Met with the King and Duke of York in their barge, and with them to Queenhithe, and there called Sir Richard Browne

to them. Their order was only to pull down houses apace, and so below bridge at the waterside; but little was or could be done, the fire coming upon them so fast. Good hopes there was of stopping it at the Three Cranes above, and at Buttolph's Wharf below bridge, if care be used; but the wind carries it into the city, so as we know not by the waterside what it do there. River full of lighters and boats taking in goods, and good goods swimming in the water, and only I observed that hardly one lighter or boat in three that had the goods of a house in, but there was a pair of virginals[11] in it. Having seen as much as I could now, I away to Whitehall by appointment, and there walked to St. James's Park, and there met my wife and Creed and Wood and his wife, and walked to my boat; and there upon the water again, and to the fire up and down, it still increasing, and the wind great. So near the fire as we could for smoke; and all over the Thames, with one's face in the wind, you were almost burned with a shower of firedrops. This is very true; so as houses were burned by these drops and flakes of fire, three or four, nay, five or six houses, one from another. When we could endure no more upon the water, we to a little alehouse on the Bankside, over against the Three Cranes, and there stayed till it was dark almost, and saw the fire grow; and, as it grew darker, appeared more and more, and in corners and upon steeples, and between churches and houses, as far as we could see up the hill of the city, in a most horrid malicious bloody flame, not like the fine flame of an ordinary fire. Barbary and her husband away before us. We stayed till, it being darkish, we saw the fire as only one entire arch of fire from this to the other side the bridge, and in a bow up the hill for an arch of above a mile long: it made me weep to see it. The churches, houses, and all on fire and flaming at once; and a horrid noise the flames made, and the cracking of houses

---

11. **virginals** n.: Small, legless harpsichords.

at their ruin. So home with a sad heart, and there find everybody discoursing and lamenting the fire; and poor Tom Hater come with some of his few goods saved out of his house, which is burned upon Fish Street Hill. I invited him to lie at my house, and did receive his goods, but was deceived in his lying there, the news coming every moment of the growth of the fire; so as we were forced to begin to pack up our own goods, and prepare for their removal; and did by moonshine (it being brave dry, and moonshine, and warm weather) carry much of my goods into the garden, and Mr. Hater and I did remove my money and iron chests into my cellar, as thinking that the safest place. And got my bags of gold into my office, ready to carry away, and my chief papers of accounts also there, and my tallies into a box by themselves. So great was our fear, as Sir W. Batten hath carts come out of the country to fetch away his goods this night. We did put Mr. Hater, poor man, to bed a little; but he got but very little rest, so much noise being in my house, taking down of goods.

3rd. About four o'clock in the morning, my Lady Batten sent me a cart to carry away all my money, and plate, and best things, to Sir W. Rider's at Bednall Green. Which I did, riding myself in my nightgown in the cart; and, Lord! to see how the streets and the highways are crowded with people running and riding, and getting of carts at any rate to fetch away things. I find Sir W. Rider tired with being called up all night, and receiving things from several friends. His house full of goods, and much of Sir W. Batten's and Sir W. Pen's. I am eased at my heart to have my treasure so well secured. Then home, with much ado to find a way, nor any sleep all this night to me nor my poor wife.

RESPONDING TO THE SELECTION

Your Response

1. Does Pepys's *Diary* make the Great Fire of London seem real to you? Why or why not?

Recalling

2. In his entry for September 3, 1665, Pepys tells a story of a saddler's family. What is the story of the last living child?
3. (a) When does Pepys first learn of the Great Fire? (b) When Pepys looks out his window at seven in the morning on September 2, 1666, what does he observe about the fire?
4. (a) What does Pepys recommend to the King and the Duke of York? (b) What is the reply?
5. Summarize Pepys's actions on September 3, 1666.

Interpreting

6. In the entry for September 14, 1665, Pepys states that he has despaired "of my Lord's doing anything this year." (a) What does he mean by the statement? (b) What does it indicate about Pepys's beliefs?
7. On September 2, 1666, Pepys sees "the churches all filling with goods by people who themselves should have been quietly there at this time." (a) Why do you think people are storing goods in churches? (b) Why do you think they themselves should have been there at the time?
8. From the evidence of these diary entries, how would you describe Pepys's character and personality?

Applying

9. (a) In Pepys's London, which do you think was the greater disaster—the plague or the Great Fire? Explain. (b) What disasters in modern times, if any, compare with the London plague of 1665 and the Great Fire of 1666?

The Age of Pope and Swift

CONVERSATION IN A PARK
Thomas Gainsborough
The Louvre, Paris

DANIEL DEFOE

1660–1731

Although Daniel Defoe produced an impressive number of pamphlets, essays, and poems throughout his life, he was nearly sixty years old before he began writing the novels that established him as a writer of genius. Defoe's *Robinson Crusoe,* a book that recounts the mostly fictional adventures of a real person, marked the beginning of the modern English novel. Defoe's realistic, almost documentary narrative of a man marooned on a desert island was something new in English literature. It established a genre.

Defoe's interests were an odd mixture of business, politics, religion, and journalism. Born to a middle-class family named Foe (he added the "De" later), Defoe attended a school run by the Dissenters, a loosely knit group that refused to accept the principles set down by the Church of England. He considered entering the Presbyterian ministry but instead turned his attention to commerce. He invested heavily and not always wisely in a variety of ventures—a ship, diving bells, wines, civet cats. The scope of his activities is shown by the size of his debt: When he declared bankruptcy in 1692, he owed his creditors 17,000 pounds.

At that point, he turned to writing (and to patrons of his writing) to try to improve his fortunes. His pen, however, also got him into trouble. After enjoying brief success with *The True-Born Englishman* (1701), a defense of King William III against his detractors, he wrote an ill-advised satire, *The Shortest Way with the Dissenters* (1702), that landed him in jail and in the pillory. This pamphlet condemned the very religious group Defoe favored. Its irony amused neither the Dissenters nor members of the Church of England, but Defoe had enough popularity to attract cheering supporters rather than rock throwers at his pillory appearance.

Late in life Defoe turned to writing books that purported to be memoirs, among them *Robinson Crusoe* (1719) and *Moll Flanders* (1722). These books were not considered novels in the strict sense; they were sold as nonfiction. Although Defoe has been accused "of forging a story, and imposing it on the world for truth," these books are generally regarded as novels today—and as outstanding novels at that.

Defoe's journalistic talents served him well in writing *A Journal of the Plague Year* (1722). He studied official documents, interviewed survivors of the plague, and may have drawn upon his own memories as a young child. The vivid historical re-creation of the plague is a triumph of Defoe's energetic, detailed style in a genre that set English fiction upon a new path.

from A Journal of the Plague Year

Writers' Techniques

First-person Narrative. Fiction is written from one of two main points of view—first person or third person. The narrator's perspective can vary somewhat in each of them. A third-person narrator, for example, can be *omniscient* (all-knowing) or *limited* (restricted to the mind of one character). A first-person narrator ("I") can be a *participant* (directly involved in the action) or an *observer* (reporting on the actions of another, as Watson reports on Sherlock Holmes).

From a writer's standpoint, first-person narration imposes severe limitations. The narrator must be physically present at all times and involved in most of the important action. Everything must be observed through the eyes and mind of that narrator; there can be no omniscience, no multiple viewpoints. If the first-person narrator is a participant, the story will sound much like a personal memoir or an autobiography. If the writing is realistic and plausible, you may think (unless told otherwise) that you are reading nonfiction. In *A Journal of the Plague Year,* that is exactly what Defoe had in mind.

Focus

Choose an imaginary setting to describe, such as a new planet inhabited by an unfamiliar species or your own community at a time in the distant past or future. Using that setting, list some of the specific details you would include in a first-person narrative.

Primary Source

Plague struck with terrifying frequency, but it was only one of a series of epidemics that ravaged England in the seventeenth century. More frequent were outbreaks of smallpox, dysentery, and measles. Herbal and folk remedies were passed down through generations. Treatments varied from place to place, and both men and women took an active interest in doctoring.

To relieve measles, for example, people advised that a live sheep be laid on the bed of the afflicted one, "because these creatures are easily infected and draw the venom to themselves, by which means some ease may happen to the sick person." To treat plague, you were advised:

> "Take halfe a handfull of Rew, likewise of Mandragories, Featherfew, Sorrell Burnet, and a quantity of the Crops and rootes of Dragons, and wash them clean, and seeth them with a soft fire in running water for a potle to a quart, and then straine them together through a cleane cloth, and if it be bitter, put thereto a quantity of sugar-candy, and if this medicine be used before the Purples do arise, yee shall be whole by God's grace."

from A Journal of the Plague Year

Daniel Defoe

The face of London was now indeed strangely altered, I mean the whole mass of buildings, city, liberties, suburbs, Westminster, Southwark, and altogether; for as to the particular part called the city, or within the walls, that was not yet much infected.

THE DEAD CART
The British Library

But in the whole the face of things, I say, was much altered; sorrow and sadness sat upon every face; and though some parts were not yet overwhelmed, yet all looked deeply concerned; and as we saw it apparently coming on, so everyone looked on himself and his family as in the utmost danger. Were it possible to represent those times exactly to those that did not see them, and give the reader due ideas of the horror that everywhere presented itself, it must make just impressions upon their minds and fill them with surprise. London might well be said to be all in tears; the mourners did not go about the streets indeed, for nobody put on black or made a formal dress of mourning for their nearest friends; but the voice of mourning was truly heard in the streets. The shrieks of women and children at the windows and doors of their houses, where their dearest relations were perhaps dying, or just dead, were so frequent to be heard as we passed the streets, that it was enough to pierce the stoutest heart in the world to hear them. Tears and lamentations were seen almost in every house, especially in the first part of the visitation; for toward the latter end men's hearts were hardened, and death was so always before their eyes, that they did not so much concern themselves for the loss of their friends, expecting that themselves should be summoned the next hour. . . .

I went all the first part of the time freely

about the streets, though not so freely as to run myself into apparent danger, except when they dug the great pit in the churchyard of our parish of Aldgate. A terrible pit it was, and I could not resist my curiosity to go and see it. As near as I may judge, it was about forty feet in length, and about fifteen or sixteen feet broad, and, at the time I first looked at it, about nine feet deep; but it was said they dug it near twenty feet deep afterwards in one part of it, till they could go no deeper for the water; for they had, it seems, dug several large pits before this. For though the plague was long a-coming to our parish, yet, when it did come, there was no parish in or about London where it raged with such violence as in the two parishes of Aldgate and Whitechapel.

I say they had dug several pits in another ground, when the distemper began to spread in our parish, and especially when the dead carts began to go about, which was not, in our parish, till the beginning of August. Into these pits they had put perhaps fifty or sixty bodies each; then they made larger holes, wherein they buried all that the cart brought in a week, which, by the middle to the end of August, came to from 200 to 400 a week; and they could not well dig them larger, because of the order of the magistrates confining them to leave no bodies within six feet of the surface; and the water coming on at about seventeen or eighteen feet, they could not well, I say, put more in one pit. But now, at the beginning of September, the plague raging in a dreadful manner, and the number of burials in our parish increasing to more than was ever buried in any parish about London of no larger extent, they ordered this dreadful gulf to be dug, for such it was rather than a pit.

They had supposed this pit would have supplied them for a month or more when they dug it, and some blamed the churchwardens for suffering[1] such a frightful thing,

telling them they were making preparations to bury the whole parish, and the like; but time made it appear the churchwardens knew the condition of the parish better than they did, for the pit being finished the 4th of September, I think, they began to bury in it the 6th, and by the 20th, which was just two weeks, they had thrown into it 1114 bodies, when they were obliged to fill it up, the bodies being then come to lie within six feet of the surface. I doubt not but there may be some ancient persons alive in the parish who can justify the fact of this, and are able to show even in what place of the churchyard the pit lay better than I can. The mark of it also was many years to be seen in the churchyard on the surface, lying in length parallel with the passage which goes by the west wall of the churchyard out of Houndsditch, and turns east again into Whitechapel, coming out near the Three Nuns' Inn.

It was about the 10th of September that my curiosity led, or rather drove, me to go and see this pit again, when there had been near 400 people buried in it; and I was not content to see it in the daytime, as I had done before, for then there would have been nothing to have been seen but the loose earth; for all the bodies that were thrown in were immediately covered with earth by those they called the buriers, which at other times were called bearers; but I resolved to go in the night and see some of them thrown in.

There was a strict order to prevent people coming to those pits, and that was only to prevent infection. But after some time that order was more necessary, for people that were infected and near their end, and delirious also, would run to those pits, wrapped in blankets or rugs, and throw themselves in, and, as they said, bury themselves. I cannot say that the officers suffered any willingly to lie there; but I have heard that in a great pit in Finsbury, in the parish of Cripplegate, it lying open then to the fields, for it was not then walled about,

---

1. **suffering:** Allowing.

[some] came and threw themselves in, and expired there, before they threw any earth upon them; and that when they came to bury others, and found them there, they were quite dead, though not cold.

This may serve a little to describe the dreadful condition of that day, though it is impossible to say anything that is able to give a true idea of it to those who did not see it, other than this, that it was indeed very, very, very dreadful, and such as no tongue can express.

I got admittance into the churchyard by being acquainted with the sexton who attended, who, though he did not refuse me at all, yet earnestly persuaded me not to go, telling me very seriously, for he was a good, religious, and sensible man, that it was indeed their business and duty to venture, and to run all hazards, and that in it they might hope to be preserved; but that I had no apparent call to it but my own curiosity, which, he said, he believed I would not pretend was sufficient to justify my running that hazard. I told him I had been pressed in my mind to go, and that perhaps it might be an instructing sight, that might not be without its uses. "Nay," says the good man, "if you will venture upon that score, name of God go in; for, depend upon it, 't will be a sermon to you, it may be, the best that ever you heard in your life. 'T is a speaking sight," says he, "and has a voice with it, and a loud one, to call us all to repentance"; and with that he opened the door and said, "Go, if you will."

His discourse had shocked my resolution a little, and I stood wavering for a good while, but just at that interval I saw two links[2] come over from the end of the Minories, and heard the bellman, and then appeared a dead cart, as they called it, coming over the streets; so I could no longer resist my desire of seeing it, and went in. There was nobody, as I could perceive at first, in the church-yard, or going into it, but the buriers and the fellow that drove the cart, or rather led the horse and cart; but when they came up to the pit they saw a man go to and again,[3] muffled up in a brown cloak, and making motions with his hands under his cloak, as if he was in a great agony, and the buriers immediately gathered about him, supposing he was one of those poor delirious or desperate creatures that used to pretend, as I have said, to bury themselves. He said nothing as he walked about, but two or three times groaned very deeply and loud, and sighed as he would break his heart.

When the buriers came up to him they soon found he was neither a person infected and desperate, as I have observed above, or a person distempered in mind, but one oppressed with a dreadful weight of grief indeed, having his wife and several of his children all in the cart that was just come in with him, and he followed in an agony and excess of sorrow. He mourned heartily, as it was easy to see, but with a kind of masculine grief that could not give itself vent by tears; and calmly defying the buriers to let him alone, said he would only see the bodies thrown in and go away, so they left importuning him. But no sooner was the cart turned round and the bodies shot into the pit promiscuously, which was a surprise to him, for he at least expected they would have been decently laid in, though indeed he was afterwards convinced that was impracticable; I say, no sooner did he see the sight but he cried out aloud, unable to contain himself. I could not hear what he said, but he went backward two or three steps and fell down in a swoon. The buriers ran to him and took him up, and in a little while he came to himself, and they led him away to the Pie Tavern over against the end of Houndsditch, where, it seems, the man was known, and where they took care of him. He looked into the pit again as he went away,

---

2. **links:** Torches.

3. **to and again:** To and fro.

but the buriers had covered the bodies so immediately with throwing in earth, that though there was light enough, for there were lanterns, and candles in them, placed all night round the sides of the pit, upon heaps of earth, seven or eight, or perhaps more, yet nothing could be seen.

This was a mournful scene indeed, and affected me almost as much as the rest; but the other was awful and full of terror. The cart had in it sixteen or seventeen bodies; some were wrapped up in linen sheets, some in rags, some little other than naked, or so loose that what covering they had fell from them in the shooting out of the cart, and they fell quite naked among the rest; but the matter was not much to them, or the indecency much to anyone else, seeing they were all dead, and were to be huddled together into the common grave of mankind, as we may call it, for here was no difference made, but poor and rich went together; there was no other way of burials, neither was it possible there should, for coffins were not to be had for the prodigious numbers that fell in such a calamity as this.

RESPONDING TO THE SELECTION

Your Response

1. What detail in Defoe's description seemed most vivid to you? Explain.

Recalling

2. (a) Describe the great pit in the churchyard of Aldgate parish. (b) What was the purpose of the pit?
3. How many bodies does the narrator say were buried in the great pit between September 6 and September 20?
4. (a) What prompts the narrator to visit the pit? (b) Why does he go at night?
5. (a) What kind of person did the buriers at first suppose the man in the brown cloak to be? (b) Summarize the incident concerning the man in the brown cloak.

Interpreting

6. Why do you think the narrator describes the great pit in such a specific way?
7. Judging by the tone of this excerpt and the narrator's reason for visiting the pit, what kind of person do you think the narrator is?
8. Why does the sexton at the churchyard say that visiting the pit will "be a sermon to you . . . a voice . . . to call us all to repentance"?
9. What causes the "masculine grief" of the man in the brown cloak to turn suddenly to anguish?

Applying

10. Many writers have written fictional accounts of great disasters or have used fictional disasters as backgrounds for their stories. Why do you think disasters have this fictional appeal?

ANALYZING LITERATURE

Recognizing First-person Narrative

A **first-person narrative** is one told by an "I" narrator—a person present at the events being described. A first-person narrator can be either a participant in or an observer of the main action. Defoe's *A Journal of the Plague Year* claims to be a first-person narrative of a London resident, one "H. F.," written during the great plague of 1665. In reality, it is a fictional reconstruction written by Defoe more than fifty years later.

1. Why do you think Defoe chose a first-person narrator, an "eyewitness," to present this account of the plague year?
2. Defoe has been called the father of modern journalism. (a) If H. F.'s first-person account of the plague were true, what features would qualify it as good journalism? (b) What features would you not find in a current news story?

JONATHAN SWIFT

1667–1745

The life of Jonathan Swift is a tale of thwarted ambition coupled with brilliant literary achievement. In the Church of England and in British politics, he sometimes seemed on the verge of great success, only to have an unkind fate baffle his expectations. In literature, on the other hand, he achieved an almost unparalleled triumph with *Gulliver's Travels,* a book that can be read—and has been read since its publication—as a children's story, a fantasy, a parody of travel books, and a sophisticated satire of English politics.

Jonathan Swift was born in Dublin, Ireland, to English parents. His father died before he was born, and young Jonathan, through the assistance of relatives, attended Kilkenny Grammar School and Trinity College, Dublin. Later he joined the household of Sir William Temple, a retired diplomat, who lived at Moor Park, Surrey, England. Swift read, studied, and wrote for the next few years. Receiving none of the hoped-for political support from Sir William, he decided on a career in the church.

After Temple's death in 1699, Swift was given a small parish near London. The satirical writing he had done while in the Temple household was somewhat out of character for a clergyman, but its brilliance was widely acknowledged when it appeared as two separate books in 1704. Published anonymously, *A Tale of a Tub* satirizes excesses in religion and learning, while *The Battle of the Books* describes a comic encounter between ancient and modern literature.

Although *A Tale of a Tub* dashed his hopes for advancement to the rank of bishop in the Church of England, Swift remained a defender of the Anglican faith. In 1710, he changed his political allegiance from the conservative Whig party to the Tory party favored by Queen Anne. He benefited immediately from this switch. As the leading party writer for the government, he wrote many pamphlets and wielded considerable political influence. The glory was short-lived, however. Anne died in 1714; the Whigs regained power; and Swift, embittered, returned to Ireland as dean of St. Patrick's Cathedral, a position he would hold for more than thirty years.

Back in Ireland, he continued to write satires, including *Drapier's Letters* (1724) and *A Modest Proposal* (1729), which championed the Irish cause. With the publication of *Gulliver's Travels* (1726), he reached the height of his literary power. In his later years, he suffered what was probably Ménière's disease, marked by a serious loss of memory and balance. His death in 1745 deprived the world of one of its great writers—a generous and learned man who despised the fanaticism, selfishness, and pride of people in general but admired individual human beings.

GUIDE FOR INTERPRETING

from Gulliver's Travels

Writers' Techniques

Satire. Satire is writing that uses wit and humor to ridicule vices, follies, stupidities, and abuses. Irony is often an element in satire, as is sarcasm. Satire can take the form of prose, poetry, or drama. Satirists, by directing their barbs toward those they view as offenders, hope to improve the situation—to reform individuals, groups, or humanity as a whole. Satire may be gentle and amusing, or it may be cruel and even vicious. Whatever its tone, satire is usually subtle enough to require the reader to make at least a small mental leap to connect it with its target.

Focus

Think about current social or political problems or situations that might be suitable subjects for satire. Try to suggest at least two. Jot these ideas down. After each subject, give one aspect of it that is particularly open to ridicule.

Primary Source

The allure of distant lands is timeless. In Swift's day, as in our own, writers offered advice to would-be travelers. Perhaps these "Hints for Travellers," from the late seventeenth century, would have helped Gulliver in his voyages!

> In such a one going to travel; there is required–
> First. A competent age. That he be above eighteen or twenty years old: although the years of fourteen or fifteen are more proper for learning the true accent of any language . . .
> Secondly. That he hath the Latin tongue.
> Thirdly. That he be skillful in architecture: able so well to limn or paint, as to take in paper the situation of a castle or a city, or a platform [plan] of a fortification.
> Fourthly. That he be well grounded in the true religion: lest he be seduced and perverted.
> Fifthly. He should be first well acquainted with his own country, before he go abroad; as to the places and government.
> Sixthly. It were of use to inform himself, before he undertakes his voyage, by the best . . . map of . . . the country he goes to; both in itself, and relatively to the universe.
> Men that travel must be very cautious both of speech and demeanor. The Italian proverb saith, "For a man to travel safely through the world; it behoveth him to have a falcon's eye, an ass's ears, a monkey's face, a merchant's words, a camel's back, a hog's mouth, and a deer's feet."

from Gulliver's Travels

Jonathan Swift

In Gulliver's Travels, *Swift exposes the corruption and defects in England's political, social, and economic institutions. The work centers on the four imaginary voyages of Lemuel Gulliver, the narrator, a well-educated but unimaginative ship's surgeon. Each of these voyages takes Gulliver to a different remarkable and bizarre world. During his stays in these imaginary lands, Gulliver is led toward realizations about the flawed nature of the society from which he had come, and he returns to England filled with disillusionment.*

from A Voyage to Lilliput

After being shipwrecked, Gulliver swims to shore and drifts off to sleep. When he awakens, he finds that he has been tied down by the Lilliputians (lil' ə py̅o̅o̅' shənz), a race of people who are only six inches tall. Though he is held captive and his sword and pistols are taken from him, Gulliver gradually begins to win the Lilliputians' favor because of his mild disposition, and he is eventually granted his freedom. Through Gulliver's exposure to Lilliputian politics and court life, the reader becomes increasingly aware of the remarkable similarities between the English and Lilliputian affairs of state. The following excerpt begins during a discussion between the Lilliputian Principal Secretary of Private Affairs and Gulliver concerning the affairs of the Lilliputian empire.

We are threatened with an invasion from the island of Blefuscu,[1] which is the other great empire of the universe, almost as large and powerful as this of his Majesty. For as to what we have heard you affirm, that there are other kingdoms and states in the world, inhabited by human creatures as large as yourself, our philosophers are in much doubt, and would rather conjecture that you dropped from the moon, or one of the stars; because it is certain, that an hundred mortals of your bulk would, in a short time, destroy all the fruits and cattle of his Majesty's dominions. Besides, our histories of six thousand moons make no mention of any other regions, than the two great empires of Lilliput and Blefuscu. Which two mighty powers have, as I was going to tell you, been engaged in a most obstinate war for six and thirty moons past. It began upon the following occasion. It is allowed on all hands, that the primitive way of breaking eggs before we eat them, was upon the larger end; but his present Majesty's grandfather, while he was a boy, going to eat an egg, and breaking it according to the ancient practice, happened to cut one of his fingers. Whereupon the Emperor, his father, published an edict,

---

1. **Blefuscu:** Represents France.

commanding all his subjects, upon great penalties, to break the smaller end of their eggs. The people so highly resented this law that our histories tell us there have been six rebellions raised on that account; wherein one emperor lost his life, and another his crown.[2] These civil commotions were constantly fomented by the monarchs of Blefuscu; and when they were quelled, the exiles always fled for refuge to that empire. It is computed that eleven thousand persons have, at several times, suffered death rather than submit to break their eggs at the smaller end. Many hundred large volumes have been published upon this controversy; but the books of the Big-Endians have been long forbidden, and the whole party rendered incapable by law of holding employments.[3] During the course of these troubles, the emperors of Blefuscu did frequently expostulate by their ambassadors, accusing us of making a schism in religion, by offending against a fundamental doctrine of our great prophet Lustrog, in the fifty-fourth chapter of the *Brundecral* (which is their Alcoran[4]). This, however, is thought to be a mere strain upon the text, for the words are these: That all true believers shall break their eggs at the convenient end; and which is the convenient end, seems, in my humble opinion, to be left to every man's conscience, or at least in the power of the chief magistrate[5] to determine. Now the Big-Endian exiles have found so much credit in the Emperor of Blefuscu's court, and so much private assistance and encouragement from their party here at home, that a bloody war hath been carried on between the two empires for

six and thirty moons with various success; during which time we have lost forty capital ships, and a much greater number of smaller vessels, together with thirty thousand of our best seamen and soldiers; and the damage received by the enemy is reckoned to be somewhat greater than ours. However, they have now equipped a numerous fleet, and are just preparing to make a descent upon us; and his Imperial Majesty, placing great confidence in your valor and strength, hath commanded me to lay this account of his affairs before you.

I desired the Secretary to present my humble duty to the Emperor, and to let him know, that I thought it would not become me, who was a foreigner, to interfere with parties; but I was ready, with the hazard of my life, to defend his person and state against all invaders.

The empire of Blesfuscu is an island situated to the north-northeast side of Lilliput, from whence it is parted only by a channel of eight hundred yards wide. I had not yet seen it, and upon this notice of an intended invasion, I avoided appearing on that side of the coast, for fear of being discovered by some of the enemy's ships, who had received no intelligence of me, all intercourse between the two empires having been strictly forbidden during the war, upon pain of death, and an embargo laid by our Emperor upon all vessels whatsoever. I communicated to his Majesty a project I had formed of seizing the enemy's whole fleet; which, as our scouts assured us, lay at anchor in the harbor ready to sail with the first fair wind. I consulted the most experienced seamen upon the depth of the channel, which they had often plumbed, who told me, that in the middle at high water it was seventy *glumgluffs* deep (which is about six feet of European measure), and the rest of it fifty *glumgluffs* at most. I walked to the northeast coast over against Blefuscu, where, lying down behind a hillock, I took out my small pocket perspective-glass, and

---

2. It is allowed . . . crown: Here, Swift satirizes the dispute in England between the Catholics (Big-Endians) and Protestants (Little-Endians). King Henry VIII who "broke" with the Catholic church, King Charles I who "lost his life," and King James who lost his "crown" are each referred to in the passage.

3. the whole party . . . employments: The Test Act (1673) prevented Catholics from holding office.

4. Alcoran: Koran, the sacred book of the Moslems.

5. chief magistrate: Ruler.

viewed the enemy's fleet at anchor, consisting of about fifty men of war, and a great number of transports. I then came back to my house and gave order (for which I had a warrant) for a great quantity of the strongest cable and bars of iron. The cable was about as thick as packthread, and the bars of the length and size of a knitting-needle. I trebled the cable to make it stronger, and for the same reason I twisted three of the iron bars together, bending the extremities into a hook. Having thus fixed fifty hooks to as many cables, I went back to the northeast coast and, putting off my coat, shoes, and stockings, walked into the sea in my leathern jerkin, about half an hour before high water. I waded with what haste I could, and swam in the middle about thirty yards until I felt ground; I arrived at the fleet in less than half an hour. The enemy was so frightened when they saw me, that they leaped out of their ships, and swam to shore, where there

could not be fewer than thirty thousand souls. I then took my tackling, and, fastening a hook to the hole at the prow of each, I tied all the cords together at the end. While I was thus employed, the enemy discharged several thousand arrows, many of which struck in my hands and face and, besides the excessive smart, gave me much disturbance in my work. My greatest apprehension was for my eyes, which I should have infallibly lost, if I had not suddenly thought of an expedient. I kept among other little necessaries a pair of spectacles in a private pocket, which, as I observed before, had escaped the Emperor's searchers. These I took out and fastened as strongly as I could upon my nose and thus armed went on boldly with my work in spite of the enemy's arrows, many of which struck against the glasses of my spectacles, but without any other effect further than a little to discompose them. I had now fastened all the hooks

Illustration for Gulliver's Travels, *Willy Pogany*
The Donnell Library Children's Room, New York Public Library

and, taking the knot in my hand, began to pull; but not a ship would stir, for they were all too fast held by their anchors, so that the boldest part of my enterprise remained. I therefore let go the cord, and, leaving the hooks fixed to the ships, I resolutely cut with my knife the cables that fastened the anchors, receiving above two hundred shots in my face and hands; then I took up the knotted end of the cables to which my hooks were tied and, with great ease, drew fifty of the enemy's largest men-of-war after me.

The Blefuscudians, who had not the least imagination of what I intended, were at first confounded with astonishment. They had seen me cut the cables and thought my design was only to let the ships run adrift or fall foul on each other; but when they perceived the whole fleet, moving in order, and saw me pulling at the end, they set up such a scream of grief and despair that it is almost impossible to describe or conceive. When I had got out of danger, I stopped a while to pick out the arrows that stuck in my hands and face, and rubbed on some of the same ointment that was given me at my first arrival, as I have formerly mentioned. I then took off my spectacles, and, waiting about an hour until the tide was a little fallen, I waded through the middle with my cargo and arrived safe at the royal port of Lilliput.

The Emperor and his whole court stood on the shore expecting the issue of this great adventure. They saw the ships move forward in a large half-moon but could not discern me, who was up to my breast in water. When I advanced to the middle of the channel, they were yet more in pain, because I was under water to my neck. The Emperor concluded me to be drowned, and that the enemy's fleet was approaching in a hostile manner; but he was soon eased of his fears; for, the channel growing shallower every step I made, I came in a short time within hearing, and holding up the end of the cable by which the fleet was fastened, I cried in a loud voice, Long live the most puissant[6] Emperor of Lilliput! This great prince received me at my landing with all possible encomiums and created me a *Nardac* upon the spot, which is the highest title of honor among them.

His Majesty desired I would take some other opportunity of bringing all the rest of his enemy's ships into his ports. And so unmeasurable is the ambition of princes, that he seemed to think of nothing less than reducing the whole empire of Blefuscu into a province and governing it by a viceroy; of destroying the Big-Endian exiles and compelling that people to break the smaller end of their eggs, by which he would remain sole monarch of the whole world. But I endeavored to divert him from this design by many arguments drawn from the topics of policy as well as justice, and I plainly protested that I would never be an instrument of bringing a free and brave people into slavery. And when the matter was debated in council, the wisest part of the ministry were of my opinion.

This open bold declaration of mine was so opposite to the schemes and politics of his Imperial Majesty that he could never forgive me; he mentioned it in a very artful manner at council, where I was told that some of the wisest appeared, at least, by their silence, to be of my opinion; but others, who were my secret enemies, could not forbear some expressions, which by a sidewind reflected on me. And from this time began an intrigue between his Majesty and a junta of ministers maliciously bent against me, which broke out in less than two months and had like to have ended in my utter destruction. Of so little weight are the greatest services to princes when put into the balance with a refusal to gratify their passions.

from A Voyage to Brobdingnag

Gulliver's second voyage leads him to

---

6. puissant (py$\overline{oo}$′ i sənt): Powerful.

Brobdingnag (brob' ding nag'), an island located near Alaska that is inhabited by giants twelve times as tall as Gulliver. After being sold to the Queen of Brobdingnag, Gulliver describes the English social and political institutions to the king, who reacts to his description with contempt and disgust.

It is the custom that every Wednesday (which, as I have before observed, was their Sabbath), the King and Queen, with the royal issue of both sexes, dine together in the apartment of his Majesty, to whom I was now become a favorite; and at these times my little chair and table were placed at his left hand before one of the saltcellars. This prince took a pleasure in conversing with me, inquiring into the manners, religion, laws, government, and learning of Europe, wherein I gave him the best account I was able. His apprehension was so clear, and his judgment so exact, that he made very wise reflections and observations upon all I said. But I confess, that after I had been a little too copious in talking of my own beloved country, of our trade, and wars by sea and land, of our schisms in religion, and parties in the state, the prejudices of his education prevailed so far, that he could not forbear taking me up in his right hand, and stroking me gently with the other, after an hearty fit of laughing, asked me whether I were a Whig or a Tory.[7] Then turning to his first minister, who waited behind him with a white staff, near as tall as the mainmast of the *Royal Sovereign*,[8] he observed how contemptible a thing was human grandeur, which could be mimicked by such diminutive insects as I. And yet, said he, I dare engage, those creatures have their titles and distinctions of honor, they contrive little nests and burrows, that they call houses and cities; they make a figure in dress and equipage;[9] they

love, they fight, they dispute, they cheat, they betray. And thus he continued on, while my color came and went several times, with indignation to hear our noble country, the mistress of arts and arms, the scourge of France, the arbitress of Europe, the seat of virtue, piety, honor and truth, the pride and envy of the world, so contemptuously treated. . . .

He laughed at my odd kind of arithmetic (as he was pleased to call it) in reckoning the numbers of our people by a computation drawn from the several sects among us in religion and politics. He said he knew no reason why those who entertain opinions prejudicial to the public should be obliged to change or should not be obliged to conceal them. And, as it was tyranny in any government to require the first, so it was weakness not to enforce the second; for, a man may be allowed to keep poisons in his closets, but not to vend them about as cordials.

He observed, that among the diversions of our nobility and gentry[10] I had mentioned gaming.[11] He desired to know at what age this entertainment was usually taken up, and when it was laid down. How much of their time it employed; whether it ever went so high as to affect their fortunes. Whether mean vicious people by their dexterity in that art might not arrive at great riches, and sometimes keep our very nobles in dependence, as well as habituate them to vile companions, wholly take them from the improvment of their minds, and force them, by the losses they received, to learn and practice that infamous dexterity upon others.

He was perfectly astonished with the historical account I gave him of our affairs during the last century, protesting it was only an heap of conspiracies, rebellions, murders, massacres, revolutions, banishments, the very worst effects that avarice,

---

7. Whig . . . Tory: British political parties.
8. *Royal Sovereign*: One of the largest ships in the British Navy.
9. equipage (ek' wə pij): Horses and carriages.

10. gentry: The class of landowning people ranking just below the nobility.
11. gaming: Gambling.

faction, hypocrisy, perfidiousness, cruelty, rage, madness, hatred, envy, lust, malice, and ambition could produce.

His Majesty in another audience was at the pains to recapitulate the sum of all I had spoken; compared the questions he made with the answers I had given; then taking me into his hands, and stroking me gently, delivered himself in these words, which I shall never forget, nor the manner he spoke them in. "My little friend Grildrig, you have made a most admirable panegyric upon your country. You have clearly proved that ignorance, idleness, and vice are the proper ingredients for qualifying a legislator. That laws are best explained, interpreted, and applied by those whose interest and abilities lie in perverting, confounding, and eluding them. I observe among you some lines of an institution, which in its original might have been tolerable, but these half erased, and the rest wholly blurred and blotted by corruptions. It doth not appear from all you have said how any one perfection is required toward the procurement of any one station among you, much less that men are ennobled on account of their virtue, that priests are advanced for their piety or learning, soldiers for their conduct or valor, judges for their integrity, senators for the love of their country, or counselors for their wisdom. As for yourself, continued the King, who have spent the greatest part of your life in traveling, I am well disposed to hope you may hitherto have escaped many vices of your country. But, by what I have gathered from your own relation, and the answers I have with much pains wringed and extorted from you, I cannot but conclude the bulk of your natives to be the most pernicious race of little odious vermin that nature ever suffered to crawl upon the surface of the earth."

Nothing but an extreme love of truth could have hindered me from concealing this part of my story. It was in vain to discover my resentments, which were always turned into ridicule; and I was forced to rest with patience while my noble and most beloved country was so injuriously treated. I am heartily sorry as any of my readers can possibly be that such an occasion was given, but this prince happened to be so curious and inquisitive upon every particular that it could not consist either with gratitude or good manners to refuse giving him what satisfaction I was able. Yet thus much I may be allowed to say in my own vindication that I artfully eluded many of his questions and gave to every point a more favorable turn by many degrees than the strictness of truth would allow. For I have always borne that laudable partiality to my own country, which Dionysius Halicarnassensis[12] with so much justice recommends to an historian. I would hide the frailties and deformities of my political mother and place her virtues and beauties in the most advantageous light. This was my sincere endeavor in those many discourses I had with that mighty monarch, although it unfortunately failed of success.

But great allowances should be given to a king who lives wholly secluded from the rest of the world, and must therefore be altogether unacquainted with the manners and customs that most prevail in other nations: the want of which knowledge will ever produce many prejudices, and a certain narrowness of thinking, from which we and the politer countries of Europe are wholly exempted. And it would be hard indeed, if so remote a prince's notions of virtue and vice were to be offered as a standard for all mankind.

To confirm what I have now said, and further to show the miserable effects of a confined education, I shall here insert a passage which will hardly obtain belief. In hopes to ingratiate myself farther into his Majesty's favor, I told him of an invention discovered between three and four hundred

---

12. Dionysius (dī′ ə nis/h′ əs) **Halicarnassensis** (hal′ ə kär na sen′ sis): A Greek writer who lived in Rome and attempted to persuade the Greeks to submit to their Roman conquerors.

years ago, to make a certain powder, into an heap of which the smallest spark of fire falling, would kindle the whole in a moment, although it were as big as a mountain, and make it all fly up in the air together, with a noise and agitation greater than thunder. That a proper quantity of this powder rammed into an hollow tube of brass or iron, according to its bigness, would drive a ball of iron or lead with such violence and speed as nothing was able to sustain its force. That the largest balls, thus discharged, would not only destroy whole ranks of an army at once, but batter the strongest walls to the ground, sink down ships, with a thousand men in each, to the bottom of the sea; and when linked together by a chain, would cut through masts and rigging, divide hundreds of bodies in the middle, and lay all waste before them. That we often put this powder into large hollow balls of iron, and discharged them by an engine into some city we were besieging, which would rip up the pavement, tear the houses to pieces, burst and throw splinters on every side, dashing out the brains of all who came near. That I knew the ingredients very well, which were cheap, and common; I understood the manner of compounding them, and could direct his workmen how to make those tubes of a size proportionable to all other things in his Majesty's kingdom, and the largest need not be above two hundred foot long; twenty or thirty of which tubes, charged with the proper quantity of powder and balls, would batter down the walls of the strongest town in his dominions in a few hours, or destroy the whole metropolis, if ever it should pretend to dispute his absolute commands. This I humbly offered to his Majesty as a small tribute of acknowledgment in return of so many marks that I had received of his royal favor and protection.

The King was struck with horror at the description I had given of those terrible engines and the proposal I had made. He was amazed how so impotent and groveling an insect as I (these were his expressions) could entertain such inhuman ideas, and in so familiar a manner as to appear wholly unmoved at all the scenes of blood and desolation which I had painted as the common effects of those destructive machines; whereof he said some evil genius, enemy to mankind, must have been the first contriver. As for himself, he protested that although few things delighted him so much as new discoveries in art or in nature, yet he would rather lose half his kingdom than be privy to such a secret, which he commanded me, as I valued my life, never to mention any more.

Illustration for Gulliver's Travels, Willy Pogany
The Donnell Library
Children's Room, New York
Public Library

RESPONDING TO THE SELECTION

Your Response

1. If you were going to write a satire of modern life, what social or political situations would you choose as subjects? Explain.

Recalling

2. (a) Describe the conflict between Lilliput and Blefuscu over the breaking of eggs. (b) How many people have died as a result?
3. (a) What are some of the words the King of Brobdingnag uses to describe English history of the preceding hundred years? (b) How does he describe the English people?

Interpreting

4. Concerning the dispute between English Catholics and Protestants, what does Swift's attitude seem to be? Explain.
5. Why does Gulliver lose favor with the Lilliputian King in spite of having captured the Blefuscudian fleet?
6. If the views of the King of Brobdingnag represent Swift's own views, what is Swift's general opinion of recent English history and politics?
7. (a) Why do you think Gulliver supposes that his gunpowder proposal to the King of Brobdingnag will be regarded favorably? (b) How is it regarded? (c) Why?

Applying

8. Why do you think Swift makes one of the races of people Gulliver visits tiny and the other huge?

ANALYZING LITERATURE

Understanding Satire

Satire is writing in which wit and humor are used to expose and ridicule human vice and folly. Instead of praising the ideal, the satirist focuses on what is false, despicable, or foolish. Satire can be light and good-humored, or it can be bitter and unsparing. An important ingredient of much satire is *irony*—that is, a contrast between what is said and what is meant. For example, when Gulliver says that his "color came and went several times, with indignation to hear our noble country . . . the seat of virtue, piety, honor . . . the pride and envy of the world, so contemptuously treated," you can be quite sure that Swift is being ironic.

1. What is Swift satirizing in *Gulliver's Travels?*
2. Point out at least three examples of irony in the excerpts from *Gulliver's Travels*.

CRITICAL THINKING AND READING

Understanding Generalizations

A **generalization** is a conclusion based on accumulation of evidence. Evidence may include facts, statistics, and incidents. In "A Voyage to Brobdingnag," the King makes a number of generalizations about the English and other Europeans based on what Gulliver tells him.

1. What generalization does the King make after Gulliver has told him about European manners, religion, law, and learning? Is it a valid one in light of the information the King has? Explain.
2. After listening to Gulliver's historical account of "our affairs during the last century," what generalization does the King make about each of the following groups?
   a. legislators   c. soldiers   e. senators
   b. priests   d. judges
3. What broader generalization does the King make about *all* the groups listed above?

THINKING AND WRITING

Writing a New Adventure for Gulliver

In addition to Lilliput and Brobdingnag, Gulliver journeys to a place called Laputa and to the land of the Houyhnhnms. In Laputa, Swift's satire is directed against learned fools—impractical professors who, among other silly enterprises, are trying to extract sunshine from cucumbers. In the land of the Houyhnhnms, he encounters a race of noble, intelligent horses that are served by vile, human-like Yahoos. Create a fifth land for Gulliver to visit. In a brief account of a new voyage by Gulliver, give the land and its inhabitants names and characteristics. Include the truths about humans that Gulliver hears uttered in this strange land. When you revise, make sure you have told your tale in chronological order.

BIOGRAPHIES

Joseph Addison (1672–1719)
Sir Richard Steele (1672–1729)

Although great writing seldom results from a team effort, the collaboration of Joseph Addison and Richard Steele is an exception to the general rule. Addison and Steele's work on two precedent-setting periodicals, *The Tatler* and *The Spectator,* has earned both authors a permanent place in literary history.

The two men, born a few weeks apart, were opposites in many ways. Joseph Addison, dignified, shy, and rather cold, enjoyed a reputation as a Latin scholar. Richard Steele, energetic, witty, and outgoing, was a man-about-town. Nevertheless, for most of their lives they were close friends, temperamentally different but sharing similar aims and values. Addison, born in a village in Wiltshire, England, and Steele, born in Dublin, Ireland, met as classmates at the Charterhouse School in London. They then went on to Oxford, from which Addison graduated but Steele did not.

Instead, Steele took a commission in the army and immersed himself in the London literary scene. Steele had a tendency to live beyond his means, and in 1709, to earn some extra money, he started *The Tatler,* a periodical dealing with "gallantry, pleasure and entertainment." *The Tatler* proved highly popular in London coffeehouses, appearing three times a week from April 1709 to January 1711.

Since his undergraduate days, Addison had pursued a different path from that of Steele. An outstanding student, he became a Fellow of Magdalen College, Oxford, and was invited by John Dryden to do translations of Virgil. After four years of European study and travel, he produced a hugely successful epic poem, *The Campaign,* celebrating the Duke of Marlborough's victory at the Battle of Blenheim. In 1706 Addison was named undersecretary of state, and two years later was elected to the House of Commons, where he served until his death.

In 1709, while serving briefly as secretary to the Lord Lieutenant of Ireland, Addison began reading the newly published *Tatler.* Despite Steele's pen name, "Isaac Bickerstaff," Addison recognized the writing as that of his old friend, and he began to submit contributions, notes, and suggestions. *The Tatler,* mostly the work of Steele, was succeeded by *The Spectator,* issued daily except Sunday from March 1711 to December 1712, and revived briefly in 1714. *The Spectator* was mostly the work of Addison, although Steele contributed regularly.

GUIDE FOR INTERPRETING

Country Manners;
Thoughts in Westminster Abbey

Literary Forms

Informal Essay. An informal essay, like a formal essay, presents the observations and opinions of its author, but it does so in a more relaxed and conversational manner. It is sometimes called a *familiar* essay, a *personal* essay, or, when printed in a magazine or newspaper, a *periodical* essay. The eighteenth century was a time in which the formal essay flourished. The informal essay, introduced by the sixteenth-century French writer Michel de Montaigne, had a great influence on English writers through the vigorous translation of John Florio. An informal essay, less structured than a formal essay, is written in a personal, often anecdotal, sometimes humorous way.

The informal essays of Addison and Steele were published regularly in *The Tatler* and *The Spectator*. These two publications are notable for their wide-ranging, nonpolitical content and their graceful tone and style. Steele was the more imaginative writer, and Addison, the better craftsman. Both set a high standard for later periodical essayists and journalists.

Commentary

How were the periodicals of Addison and Steele different from the newspapers of the day? The newspapers recorded events; *The Spectator* and *The Tatler* transformed journalism into literature.

In earlier years, influential men employed writers to provide them with news of the court in their absence. By the beginning of the seventeenth century, this expanded into the news-book, sixteen pages of foreign news, much of it scurrilous, including torrents of abuse and outright lies. This led to years of suppression, but the pamphlets flourished, and by the middle of the century the newspaper was firmly entrenched. Advertisements appeared in 1655. These ads are amusing by today's standards; coffee, for instance, was promoted as "a simple Innocent thing incomparable good for those that are troubled with melancholy." By 1715 the newspaper was established, and the press was a power recognized by every political party.

Focus

Think of a topic on which opinion varies. It should be a topic about which you have strong opinions. Jot down notes about this topic. These notes should include support for your own viewpoint as well as evidence that helps to refute the opposing viewpoint. Save these notes for later use.

Country Manners

Joseph Addison

The Spectator, July 17, 1711

The first and most obvious reflections which arise in a man who changes the city for the country are upon the different manners of the people whom he meets with in those two different scenes of life. By manners I do not mean morals, but behavior and good breeding as they show themselves in the town and in the country.

And here, in the first place, I must observe a very great revolution that has happened in this article of good breeding. Several obliging deferences, condescensions, and submissions, with many outward forms and ceremonies that accompany them, were first of all brought up among the politer part of mankind, who lived in courts and cities and distinguished themselves from the rustic part of the species (who on all occasions acted bluntly and naturally) by such a mutual complaisance and intercourse of civilities. These forms of conversation by degrees multiplied and grew troublesome; the modish world found too great a constraint in them, and have therefore thrown most of them aside. Conversation was so encumbered with show and ceremony that it stood in need of a reformation to retrench its superfluities and restore its natural good sense and beauty. At present, therefore, an unconstrained carriage and a certain openness of behavior are the height of good breeding. The fashionable world is grown free and easy; our manners sit more loose upon us; nothing is so modish as an agreeable negligence. In a word, good breed-ing shows itself most where to an ordinary eye it appears the least.

If after this we look on the people of mode in the country, we find in them the manners of the last age. They have no sooner fetched themselves up to the fashion of a polite world, but the town has dropped them, and are nearer to the first stage of nature than to those refinements which formerly reigned in the court and still prevail in the country. One may now know a man that never conversed in the world by his excess of good breeding. A polite country squire[1] shall make you as many bows in half an hour as would serve a courtier[2] for a week. There is infinitely more to do about place and precedency in a meeting of justices' wives than in an assembly of duchesses.

This rural politeness is very troublesome to a man of my temper who generally takes the chair that is next me and walks first or last, in the front or in the rear, as chance directs. I have known my friend Sir Roger's dinner almost cold before the company could adjust the ceremonial and be prevailed upon to sit down; and have heartily pitied my old friend when I have seen him forced to pick and cull his guests, as they sat at the several parts of his table, that he might drink their healths according to their respective ranks and qualities. Honest Will Wimble, who I should have thought had

---

1. squire n.: A country gentleman or landed proprietor.
2. courtier (kôr′ tē ər) n.: An attendant at a royal court.

been altogether uninfected with ceremony, gives me abundance of trouble in this particular. Though he has been fishing all the morning, he will not help himself at dinner till I am served. When we are going out of the hall, he runs behind me; and last night, as we were walking in the fields, stopped short at a stile till I came up to it and, upon my making signs to him to get over, told me, with a serious smile, that sure I believed they had no manners in the country.

There has happened another revolution in the point of good breeding which relates to the conversation among men of mode and which I cannot but look upon as very extraordinary. It was certainly one of the first distinctions of a well-bred man to express everything that had the most remote appearance of being obscene in modest terms and distant phrases; whilst the clown, who had no such delicacy of conception and expression, clothed his ideas in those plain homely terms that are the most obvious and natural. This kind of good manners was perhaps carried to an excess so as to make conversation too stiff, formal, and precise; for which reason (as hypocrisy in one age is generally succeeded by atheism in another) conversation is in a great measure relapsed into the first extreme; so that at present several of our men of the town, and particularly those who have been polished in France, make use of the most coarse, uncivilized words in our language and utter themselves often in such a manner as a clown would blush to hear.

This infamous piece of good breeding, which reigns among the coxcombs[3] of the town, has not yet made its way into the country; and as it is impossible for such an irrational way of conversation to last long among a people that makes any profession of religion or show of modesty, if the country gentlemen get into it, they will certainly be left in the lurch. Their good breeding will come too late to them, and they will be thought a parcel of lewd clowns, while they fancy themselves talking together like men of wit and pleasure.

As the two points of good breeding, which I have hitherto insisted upon, regard behavior and conversation, there is a third which turns upon dress. In this too the country are very much behindhand. The rural beaus are not yet got out of the fashion that took place at the time of the Revolution[4] but ride about the country in red coats and laced hats; while the women in many parts are still trying to outvie one another in the height of their headdresses.

But a friend of mine, who is now upon the western circuit, having promised to give me an account of the several modes and fashions that prevail in the different parts of the nation through which he passes, I shall defer the enlarging upon this last topic till I have received a letter from him, which I expect every post.

---

3. coxcombs *n.*: Silly, vain men; dandies.
4. the Revolution: The "Glorious Revolution" of 1688, during which James II was expelled from the throne.

RESPONDING TO THE SELECTION

Your Response

1. Are manners more important or less important to you than they were to Joseph Addison? Explain.

Recalling

2. (a) What happened in the first "great revolution . . . of good breeding"? (b) Where did the revolution occur? (c) What brought about the change?
3. How did "country gentlemen" react to the change in city manners?
4. What annoys the writer about the behavior of (a) Sir Roger? (b) Honest Will Wimble?
5. (a) What did the second revolution in good breeding involve? (b) Where did it occur? (c) Why might its effects make "a clown . . . blush"?
6. (a) How has the country reacted to the revolution in conversation? (b) To what other area of good breeding may country gentlemen someday react?

Interpreting

7. Why do you think the country lags behind the city in manners?
8. Why would a city dweller who had once expected an "excess of good breeding" now be annoyed by it?
9. (a) To which group mentioned in the essay does the writer belong? (b) Why must he await a letter before he can comment on the fashion prevailing in the country?

Applying

10. In the United States today, what are the differences, if any, between country manners and city manners? Explain.
11. In nineteenth-century America, Walt Whitman wrote, "To the real artist in humanity, what are called bad manners are often the most picturesque and significant of all." How do you think Addison and Steele would have reacted to Whitman's comment? Explain your answer.

ANALYZING LITERATURE

Understanding the Informal Essay

As its name implies, an **informal essay** expresses the observations and opinions of its author in a personal, conversational way. The informal essay is less rigid than the formal essay. The views stated can be highly individual, even outrageous. Although Addison and Steele are seldom outrageous, they do express unequivocal, thought-provoking opinions.

1. For each of the three "points of good breeding" in "Country Manners," find one statement that you consider highly opinionated.
2. A personal essay shows clear signs of having been written by the specific individual whose opinions it expresses. What are three such signs in "Country Manners"?

THINKING AND WRITING

Writing an Informal Essay

Use the topic that you chose for Focus, page 483, or select a new topic on which opinions vary. Possible general topic areas include politics, sports, arts, and leisure. If you are using the topic you chose earlier, consult the notes you took. If not, begin by stating your opinion clearly in one sentence; then jot down notes before you start to write. When writing the first draft of your informal essay, use a personal, conversational style. In revising the first draft, pay close attention to tone. A good conversational style is friendly and down-to-earth but not overly clever.

LEARNING OPTION

Cross-curricular Connection. How did the city of London and the English countryside look in Addison's time? Find reproductions of several eighteenth-century English paintings. An artist to consider for city scenes is William Hogarth; for the countryside, try John Constable. Display the prints in class, and be prepared to answer questions about the paintings and the artists.

Thoughts in Westminster Abbey[1]

Joseph Addison

The Spectator, March 30, 1711

When I am in a serious humor, I very often walk by myself in Westminster Abbey; where the gloominess of the place, and the use to which it is applied, with the solemnity of the building, and the condition of the people who lie in it, are apt to fill the mind with a kind of melancholy, or rather thoughtfulness, that is not disagreeable. I yesterday passed a whole afternoon in the churchyard, the cloisters, and the church, amusing myself with the tombstones and inscriptions that I met with in those several regions of the dead. Most of them recorded nothing else of the buried person, but that he was born upon one day, and died upon another: the whole history of his life being comprehended in those two circumstances, that are common to all mankind. I could not but look upon these registers of existence, whether of brass or marble, as a kind of satire upon the departed persons; who had left no other memorial of them, but that they were born and that they died. They put me in mind of several persons mentioned in the battles of heroic poems, who have sounding names given them, for no other reason but that they may be killed, and are celebrated for nothing but being knocked on the head.

Upon my going into the church, I entertained myself with the digging of a grave; and saw in every shovelful of it that was thrown up, the fragment of a bone or skull intermixed with a kind of fresh moldering earth that some time or other had a place in the composition of a human body. Upon this I began to consider with myself what innumerable multitudes of people lay confused together under the pavement of that ancient cathedral; how men and women, friends and enemies, priests and soldiers, monks and prebendaries,[2] were crumbled amongst one another, and blended together in the same common mass; how beauty, strength, and youth, with old age, weakness, and deformity, lay undistinguished in the same promiscuous heap of matter.

After having thus surveyed this great magazine of mortality, as it were, in the lump; I examined it more particularly by the accounts which I found on several of the monuments which are raised in every quarter of that ancient fabric. Some of them were covered with such extravagant epitaphs that, if it were possible for the dead person to be acquainted with them, he would blush at the praises which his friends have bestowed upon him. There are others so excessively modest, that they deliver the character of the person departed in Greek or

---

1. Westminster Abbey: A famous church in Westminster, England, where English monarchs are crowned, and where English monarchs and many famous writers and statesmen are buried.

2. prebendaries (preb′ ən der′ ēz) *n.*: In the Church of England, honorary clergymen.

Hebrew, and by that means are not understood once in a twelvemonth. In the poetical quarter, I found there were poets who had no monuments, and monuments which had no poets. I observed, indeed, that the present war[3] had filled the church with many of these uninhabited monuments, which had been erected to the memory of persons whose bodies were perhaps buried in the plains of Blenheim,[4] or in the bosom of the ocean.

I could not but be very much delighted with several modern epitaphs, which are written with great elegance of expression and justness of thought, and therefore do honor to the living as well as to the dead. As a foreigner is very apt to conceive an idea of the ignorance or politeness of a nation, from the turn of their public monuments and inscriptions, they should be submitted to the perusal of men of learning and genius, before they are put in execution. Sir Cloudesly Shovel's[5] monument has very often given me great offense: instead of the brave rough English admiral, which was the distinguishing character of that plain gallant man, he is represented on his tomb by the figure of a beau, dressed in a long periwig,[6] and reposing himself upon velvet cushions under a canopy of state. The inscription is answerable to the monument; for instead of celebrating the many remarkable actions he had performed in the service of his country, it acquaints us only with the manner of his death, in which it was impossible for him to reap any honor. The Dutch,

---

3. the present war: The War of the Spanish Succession, in which England and several other European nations fought against an alliance led by the French and Spanish.
4. Blenheim (blen′ əm): Village in western Bavaria that was the site of an important battle (1704) during the War of the Spanish Succession.

5. Sir Cloudesly Shovel (1650–1707): English admiral and commander of the British fleet.
6. periwig (per′ ə wig′) n.: A type of wig often worn by men during the seventeenth and eighteenth centuries.

ST. EDMUND'S CHAPEL, WESTMINSTER ABBEY
John Fulleylove

whom we are apt to despise for want of genius, show an infinitely greater taste of antiquity and politeness in their buildings and works of this nature, than what we meet with in those of our own country. The monuments of their admirals, which have been erected at the public expense, represent them like themselves; and are adorned with rostral crowns and naval ornaments, with beautiful festoons of seaweed, shells, and coral.

But to return to our subject. I have left the repository of our English kings for the contemplation of another day, when I shall find my mind disposed for so serious an amusement. I know that entertainments of this nature are apt to raise dark and dismal thoughts in timorous minds and gloomy imaginations; but for my own part, though I am always serious, I do not know what it is to be melancholy; and can therefore take a view of nature in her deep and solemn scenes, with the same pleasure as in her most gay and delightful ones. By this means I can improve myself with those objects which others consider with terror. When I look upon the tombs of the great, every emotion of envy dies in me; when I read the epitaphs of the beautiful, every inordinate desire goes out; when I meet with the grief of parents upon a tombstone, my heart melts with compassion; when I see the tomb of the parents themselves, I consider the vanity of grieving for those whom we must quickly follow: when I see kings lying by those who deposed them, when I consider rival wits placed side by side, or the holy men that divided the world with their contests and disputes, I reflect with sorrow and astonishment on the little competitions, factions, and debates of mankind. When I read the several dates of the tombs, of some that died yesterday, and some six hundred years ago, I consider that great day when we shall all of us be contemporaries, and make our appearance together.

![R] ESPONDING TO THE SELECTION

Your Response

1. What are your thoughts and feelings when you visit monuments to famous people? Explain.

Recalling

2. (a) At what times does the author say he visits Westminster Abbey? (b) Why does he go then?
3. (a) Who was Sir Cloudsley Shovel? (b) What kind of man was he? (c) Why does the author object to Shovel's monument?

Interpreting

4. What two kinds of epitaphs seem to offend the author most?

5. The author states that some modern epitaphs "do honor to the living as well as to the dead." (a) What does he mean? (b) Why does he think proposed monuments and epitaphs should be reviewed by "men of learning and genius"?
6. What does the author mean by "that great day when we shall all of us be contemporaries"?

Applying

7. At the end of the essay the author lists a number of ironies he sees in Westminster Abbey. (a) Which of them seems the most poignant to you? (b) What ironies can you think of that might be added to the list?

CROSS CURRENTS

Literary Magazines Today

Editor Reginald Gibbons recently observed in the *Chicago Tribune*, "It's no accident that almost every writer of our century who is now regarded as the author of great and enduring work was first published in the little literary magazines, some of which, like T. S. Eliot's famous *Criterion*, had as few as 700 subscribers."

Many literary magazines from the early part of the twentieth century have passed into legend, but not before leaving an indelible mark on literature and culture. *The Masses, The Pagan, The Dial,* and *The Fugitive* published the early works of T. S. Eliot, Ezra Pound, Wallace Stevens, as well as many other landmark writers. The mass-market magazines, in contrast, published the long-forgotten verse of such authors as Anne Bunner and Fannie Stearns Davis. But before we can consider the effect of today's literary magazines, we have to be sure we know how to recognize one!

WHAT IS A LITERARY MAGAZINE?

The Council of Literary Magazines and Presses includes among its members 380 literary magazines. They define a literary magazine as "a noncommercial magazine in which fiction, poetry, or literary essay comprises at least 50% of the editorial material." Yet many of these journals are indeed published for a profit. *Granta,* for instance, is published by Penguin Books. This notable magazine, begun by students at Cambridge University in 1888, has showcased the work of A. A. Milne (of Winnie the Pooh fame), E. M. Forster, Sylvia Plath, Graham Greene, and Saul Bellow, to mention just a few. In a similar fashion, the publishing house of W. W. Norton supports the literary magazine *Antaeus,* and Vintage Books publishes *The Quarterly.*

According to this definition, mass-market literary magazines are an entirely different kettle of literature. Yet *The New Yorker, Atlantic, Harper's, The New York Review of Books, The Times Literary Supplement,* and *Partisan Review* devote the majority of their editorial space to publishing some of today's most important fiction, poetry, and literary essays. Twenty-five percent of the 155 short stories published in single volumes in 1987 were first published in *The New Yorker; The Atlantic* came in a laudable second. Virtually all the stories published in these magazines, however, were by already-famous writers.

But whether they are published for profit or not, literary magazines offer an astonishing diversity of style and content. At one end of the spectrum are the long-established publications such as *The Paris Review.* Founded as a journal where undiscovered writers could gain public notice, *The Paris Review* has enjoyed the same fate as many of its original contributors: It has gone mainstream. Now they publish the work of such well-known writers as Nadine Gordimer and John Irving. At the other end of the scale are such "hip lit" publications as *Bomb* and *Between C & D.* The latter, for example, has rejected the understated in favor of shock: The entire print run of 600 copies, printed directly from a home computer, is distributed with sprocket holes still attached and the pages connected in a single, long accordion of folded pages. The content is as offbeat as the style.

HOW ARE LITERARY MAGAZINES DISTRIBUTED?

How do people hear about literary magazines? Many are distributed through universities and colleges; others are publicized through word of mouth. A surprising number of literary magazines are distributed through bookstores. These include the more famous titles—*Antioch Review, VLS (Voice Literary Supplement), Yale Literary Magazine, Hudson Review, TriQuarterly, American Poetry Review, Hornbook, Paris Review, American Book Review, American Poetry Review,* and *October*—as well as the often colorfully named newer productions—*Coyote's Journal, Callaloo, Southpaw, Sulphur, Zyzzyva, Alcatraz, Imagine,* and *ACM (Another Chicago Magazine).*

Often, bookstores alert their customers to new literary magazines through poetry readings, book signings, and fancy receptions. Although literary magazines often sell only a handful of copies, they are surprisingly profitable to bookstore owners. Richard Bray, owner of Guild Books in Chicago, remarked, "We don't lose money on them. It's profitable from the standpoint that people who buy and browse these magazines are probably, more than any other category, book buyers. Just as magazines in general are a draw to help sell books, I'd say literary magazines are—and more so."

THE IMPORTANCE OF LITERARY MAGAZINES

Although the number of people reading literary magazines is limited, these publications nonetheless play a very significant role in the literary scene. They give famous writers a chance to take a chance and try a new writing style or topic, but, even more important, they allow readers to see new and unusual literary experiments by writers who are still developing a career. You might be the one to discover the next "classic" writer!

ALEXANDER POPE

1688–1744

From the age of eight or nine, Alexander Pope knew that he wanted to become not just a poet but a great poet. Before he was twenty-one, his *Essay on Criticism* had brought him to the attention of the leading literary figures of England. His satiric *The Rape of the Lock,* probably the best mock-epic poem in English, followed when he was twenty-four. Despite a crippling childhood disease and persistent ill health, Pope triumphantly achieved his boyhood ambition. A brilliant satirist in verse, he gave his name to the literary era (the Age of Pope and Swift) in which he lived and wrote.

Born into the Roman Catholic family of a London linen merchant, Pope had to struggle for position. After the expulsion of King James II, English Catholics could not legally vote, hold office, attend a university, or live within ten miles of London. To comply with the rule of residency, his family moved to Binfield, near Windsor Forest, a rural setting where Pope spent his formative years writing poetry, studying the classics, and becoming broadly self-educated. Pope's physical problems were as severe as his religious ones. Deformed by tuberculosis of the spine, Pope stood only about four and a half feet tall—"the little Alexander whom the women laugh at," he said—and he suffered from nervousness and excruciating headaches throughout his life. In 1718 Pope moved to a five-acre estate at Twickenham (twit' nam), a village on the Thames, where he lived until his death.

Although Pope, "the Wasp of Twickenham," is more often remembered for his quarrels than for his cordiality, he became friends, and remained so for life, with members of a Tory group that included Jonathan Swift, John Gay, and Lord Bolingbroke. Pope instigated the formation of the Scriblerus Club, the purpose of which was to ridicule what its members regarded as "false tastes in learning." The satiric emphasis of the club probably gave some impetus to the writing of Swift's *Gulliver's Travels,* Gay's *Beggar's Opera,* and Pope's *The Dunciad*—a "burlesque heroick" attack on Pope's literary enemies (most of whom are now forgotten).

In the 1730's Pope's writing became increasingly philosophical. He embarked on a massive work concerning morality and government, but completed only *An Essay on Man* and *Moral Essays*. Nevertheless, the entire body of his work is sufficient for critics today to accord him exceptionally high praise. The twentieth-century poet Edith Sitwell calls Pope "perhaps the most flawless artist our race has yet produced."

GUIDE FOR INTERPRETING

from The Rape of the Lock

Literary Forms

Mock Epic. A mock epic is a long, humorous narrative poem that treats a trivial subject in the grand, elevated style of a true epic such as the *Odyssey* or *Paradise Lost*. Sometimes called a *mock-heroic* poem, this literary form reached the height of its popularity in the eighteenth century. The *conventions,* or standard elements, of an epic require both the characters and the action to be of heroic proportions. The theme of a true epic concerns fundamental human problems. In a classical epic, gods and goddesses oversee and sometimes intervene in human affairs. When these conventions of an epic are satirically applied to a subject of little consequence, the result can be highly amusing.

Focus

Freewrite about an incident you have heard or read about that you think has been magnified beyond its importance. In your writing, carry the incident to an illogical extreme, as the writer of a mock epic would do.

Primary Source

Concerned that the publication of his poem could cause hard feelings, Pope wrote a dedication to Arabella Fermor, the model for Belinda, intended to coax her into a good mood.

> Madam,
> It will be in vain to deny that I have some Regard for this Piece, since I Dedicate it to You. Yet . . . it was intended only to divert a few young ladies, who have good Sense and good Humor enough, to laugh not only at their Sex's little unguarded Follies, but at their own. But as it was communicated with the Air of A Secret, it soon found its Way into the World. . . .
>
> As to the following Cantos, all the Passages in them are as Fabulous, as the Vision at the Beginning, or the Transformation at the end; (except the Loss of your Hair, which I always mention with Reverence). The Human Persons are as Fictitious as the Airy ones; and the Character of Belinda, as it is now manag'd, resembles you in nothing but in Beauty.
>
> If this Poem had as many Graces as there are in Your Person, or in Your Mind, yet I could never hope it would pass thro' the World half so Uncensured as You have done. But let its Fortune be what it will, mine is happy enough, to have given you this Occasion of assuring You that I am, with the truest Esteem . . . A. Pope

from The Rape of the Lock

Alexander Pope

The Rape of the Lock, a mock epic, or a humorous poem written in the style of and recalling situations from the famous epic poems of Homer, Virgil, and Milton, is based on an actual incident. When Lord Petre, a wealthy baron, cut a lock of hair from the head of the beautiful Arabella Fermor, a great quarrel developed between the lady's family and the family of Lord Petre. Following the incident, Pope's friend John Caryll suggested that Pope write a poem mocking the trivial incident to point out the absurdity of the families' reactions. In writing The Rape of the Lock, *however, Pope went far beyond the ridiculous incident that inspired it. The poem, filled with allusions to the great literary works of the past, is a poignant appraisal of the social manners and human behavior of the time.*

The first of the poem's five cantos opens with a formal statement of theme and an invocation to the Muse for poetic inspiration. Then Belinda, the poem's heroine, receives a warning from the sylph Ariel that a dreadful event will take place in her immediate future. In Canto II, during a boat ride on the Thames, an adventurous baron admires Belinda's hair and is determined to cut two bright locks from her head and keep them as a prize. Aware of the baron's desires, Ariel urges the spirits to protect Belinda.

Canto III

Close by those meads, forever crowned with flowers,
Where Thames with pride surveys his rising towers,
There stands a structure of majestic frame,[1]
Which from the neighboring Hampton takes its name.
5 Here Britain's statesmen oft the fall foredoom
Of foreign tyrants, and of nymphs at home;
Here thou, great Anna![2] whom three realms obey,

---

1. structure . . . frame: Hampton Court, a royal palace near London.
2. Anna: Queen Anne, who ruled England, Ireland, and Scotland from 1702 through 1714.

THE BARGE, 1895-96
Aubrey Beardsley

Dost sometimes counsel take—and sometimes tea.
  Hither the heroes and the nymphs resort,
10 To taste awhile the pleasures of a court;
  In various talk th' instructive hours they passed,
  Who gave the ball, or paid the visit last;
  One speaks the glory of the British Queen,
  And one describes a charming Indian screen;
15 A third interprets motions, looks, and eyes;
  At every word a reputation dies.

from *The Rape of the Lock*   495

Snuff, or the fan,[3] supply each pause of chat,
With singing, laughing, ogling, and all that.
      Meanwhile, declining from the noon of day,
20   The sun obliquely shoots his burning ray;
The hungry judges soon the sentence sign,
And wretches hang that jurymen may dine;
The merchant from th' Exchange[4] returns in peace,
And the long labors of the toilet[5] cease.
25   Belinda now, whom thirst of fame invites,
Burns to encounter two adventurous knights,
At omber[6] singly to decide their doom;
And swells her breast with conquests yet to come.
Straight the three bands prepare in arms to join,
30   Each band the number of the sacred nine.[7]
Soon as she spreads her hand, th' aerial guard
Descend, and sit on each important card:
First Ariel perched upon a Matadore,[8]
Then each, according to the rank they bore;
35   For sylphs, yet mindful of their ancient race,
Are, as when women, wondrous fond of place.
      Behold, four kings in majestry revered,
With hoary whiskers and a forky beard;
And four fair queens whose hands sustain a flower,
40   Th' expressive emblem of their softer power;
Four knaves in garbs succinct,[9] a trusty band,
Caps on their heads, and halberts[10] in their hand;
And particolored troops, a shining train,
Draw forth to combat on the velvet plain.
45   The skilful nymph reviews her force with care:
Let spades be trumps! she said, and trumps they were.
      Now move to war her sable Matadores,
In show like leaders of the swarthy Moors.
Spadillio[11] first, unconquerable Lord!
50   Led off two captive trumps, and swept the board.
As many more Manillio[12] forced to yield,
And marched a victor from the verdant field.[13]

---

3. snuff . . . fan: At the time, gentlemen commonly took snuff, and ladies usually carried a fan.

4. Exchange: The London financial center where merchants, bankers, and brokers conducted business.

5. toilet: Dressing tables.

6. omber: A popular card game.

7. sacred nine: A reference to the nine Muses of Greek mythology.

8. Matadore: A powerful card that could take a trick.

9. succinct (sək siŋkt′): Belted.

10. halberts: Long-handled weapons.

11. Spadillio: The ace of spades.

12. Manillio: The two of spades.

13. verdant field: The card table, covered with a green cloth.

Him Basto[14] followed, but his fate more hard
Gained but one trump and one plebeian card.
55   With his broad saber next, a chief in years,
The hoary majesty of spades appears,
Puts forth one manly leg, to sight revealed,
The rest, his many-colored robe concealed.
The rebel knave, who dares his prince engage,
60   Proves the just victim of his royal rage.
Even mighty Pam,[15] that kings and queens o'erthrew
And mowed down armies in the fights of loo,
Sad chance of war! now destitute of aid,
Falls undistinguished by the victor spade!
65   Thus far both armies to Belinda yield;
Now to the baron fate inclines the field.
His warlike Amazon her host invades,
Th' imperial consort of the crown of spades.
The club's black tyrant first her victim died,
70   Spite of his haughty mien, and barbarous pride.
What boots[16] the regal circle on his head,
His giant limbs, in state unwieldy spread;
That long behind he trails his pompous robe,
And, of all monarchs, only grasps the globe?
75   The baron now his diamonds pours apace;
Th' embroidered king who shows but half his face,
And his refulgent queen, with powers combined
Of broken troops an easy conquest find.
Clubs, diamonds, hearts, in wild disorder seen,
80   With throngs promiscuous strew the level green.
Thus when dispersed a routed army runs,
Of Asia's troops, and Afric's sable sons,
With like confusion different nations fly,
Of various habit, and of various dye,
85   The pierced battalions disunited fall,
In heaps on heaps; one fate o'erwhelms them all.
        The knave of diamonds tries his wily arts,
And wins (oh shameful chance!) the queen of hearts.
At this, the blood the virgin's cheek forsook,
90   A livid paleness spreads o'er all her look;
She sees, and trembles at th' approaching ill,
Just in the jaws of ruin, and codille.[17]
And now (as oft in some distempered state)
On one nice trick depends the general fate.

14. Basto: The ace of clubs.
15. Pam: The knave of clubs, the highest card in the game called "100."
16. what boots: Of what benefit is.
17. codille: A term meaning the defeat of a hand of cards.

95 An ace of hearts steps forth; the king unseen
   Lurked in her hand, and mourned his captive queen.
   He springs to vengeance with an eager pace,
   And falls like thunder on the prostrate ace.
   The nymph exulting fills with shouts the sky;
100 The walls, the woods, and long canals reply.
      Oh thoughtless mortals! ever blind to fate,
   Too soon dejected, and too soon elate.
   Sudden, these honors shall be snatched away,
   And cursed forever this victorious day.

THE RAPE OF THE LOCK, 1895–96
Aubrey Beardsley

105 For lo! the board with cups and spoons is crowned,
 The berries crackle, and the mill turns round;[18]
 On shining altars of Japan[19] they raise
 The silver lamp; the fiery spirits blaze;
 From silver spouts the grateful liquors glide,
110 While China's earth[20] receives the smoking tide.
 At once they gratify their scent and taste,
 And frequent cups prolong the rich repast.
 Straight hover round the fair her airy band;
 Some, as she sipped, the fuming liquor fanned,
115 Some o'er her lap their careful plumes displayed,
 Trembling, and conscious of the rich brocade.
 Coffee (which makes the politician wise,
 And see through all things with his half-shut eyes)
 Sent up in vapors to the baron's brain
120 New stratagems, the radiant lock to gain.
 Ah cease, rash youth! desist ere 'tis too late,
 Fear the just gods, and think of Scylla's fate![21]
 Changed to a bird, and sent to flit in air,
 She dearly pays for Nisus' injured hair!

125 But when to mischief mortals bend their will,
 How soon they find fit instruments of ill!
 Just then, Clarissa drew with tempting grace
 A two-edged weapon from her shining case:
 So ladies in romance assist their knight,
130 Present the spear, and arm him for the fight.
 He takes the gift with reverence, and extends
 The little engine[22] on his fingers' ends;
 This just behind Belinda's neck he spread,
 As o'er the fragrant steams she bends her head.
135 Swift to the lock a thousand sprites repair,
 A thousand wings, by turns, blow back the hair;
 And thrice they twitched the diamond in her ear;
 Thrice she looked back, and thrice the foe drew near.
 Just in that instant, anxious Ariel sought
140 The close recesses of the virgin's thought;
 As on the nosegay in her breast reclined,
 He watched th' ideas rising in her mind,
 Sudden he viewed, in spite of all her art,
 An earthly lover lurking at her heart.[23]

---

18. the berries . . . round: The coffee beans are ground in a hand mill at the table.
19. altars of Japan: Small imported lacquer tables.
20. China's earth: Earthenware cups imported from China.
21. Scylla's (sil′ əz) **fate:** Scylla, the daughter of King Nisus, was turned into a sea bird because she cut off the lock of her father's hair on which his safety depended and sent it to his enemy.
22. engine: Instrument.
23. earthly lover . . . heart: If in her heart Belinda wants the baron to succeed, they cannot protect her.

145   Amazed, confused, he found his power expired,
    Resigned to fate, and with a sigh retired.
          The peer now spreads the glittering forfex[24] wide,
    T' enclose the lock; now joins it, to divide.
    Even then, before the fatal engine closed,
150   A wretched sylph too fondly interposed;
    Fate urged the shears, and cut the sylph in twain,
    (But airy substance soon unites again).
    The meeting points the sacred hair dissever
    From the fair head, forever, and forever!
155   Then flashed the living lightning from her eyes,
    And screams of horror rend th' affrighted skies.
    Not louder shrieks to pitying heaven are cast,
    When husbands, or when lap dogs breathe their last;
    Or when rich China vessels fallen from high,
160   In glittering dust, and painted fragments lie!
          "Let wreaths of triumph now my temples twine,"
    The victor cried, "the glorious prize is mine!"
    While fish in streams, or birds delight in air,
    Or in a coach and six the British Fair,
165   As long as *Atalantis*[25] shall be read,
    Or the small pillow grace a lady's bed,
    While visits shall be paid on solemn days,
    When numerous wax lights in bright order blaze,
    While nymphs take treats, or assignations give,
170   So long my honor, name, and praise shall live!
    What time would spare, from steel receives its date,[26]
    And monuments, like men, submit to fate!
    Steel could the labor of the gods destroy,
    And strike to dust th' imperial towers of Troy;
175   Steel could the works of mortal pride confound,
    And hew triumphal arches to the ground.
    What wonder then, fair nymph! thy hairs should feel,
    The conquering force of unresisted steel?

from Canto V

In Canto IV, *after Umbriel, "a dusky, melancholy sprite," empties a bag filled with "the force of female lungs, sighs, sobs, and passions, and the war of tongues" onto Belinda's head, the lady erupts over the loss of her lock. Then she "bids her beau," Sir Plume, to "demand the precious hairs," but Plume is unable to persuade the baron to return the hair.*

---

24. forfex: Scissors.
25. *Atalantis:* A popular book of scandalous gossip.
26. receives its date: Is destroyed.

In the beginning of Canto V, *Clarissa, a level-headed nymph, tries to bring an end to the commotion, but rather than being greeted with applause, her speech is followed by a battle cry.*

"To arms, to arms!" the fierce virago[27] cries,
And swift as lightning to the combat flies.
All side in parties, and begin th' attack;
Fans clap, silks rustle, and tough whalebones crack;
5   Heroes' and heroines' shouts confusedly rise,
And bass and treble voices strike the skies.
No common weapons in their hands are found,
Like gods they fight, nor dread a mortal wound.
    So when bold Homer makes the gods engage,
10 And heavenly breasts with human passions rage;
'Gainst Pallas, Mars, Latona, Hermes[28] arms;
And all Olympus[29] rings with loud alarms:
Jove's[30] thunder roars, heaven trembles all around,
Blue Neptune[31] storms, the bellowing deeps resound;
15 Earth shakes her nodding towers, the ground gives way,
And the pale ghosts start at the flash of day!
    Triumphant Umbriel on a sconce's height[32]
Clapped his glad wings, and sat to view the fight;
Propped on their bodkin spears,[33] the sprites survey
20 The growing combat, or assist the fray.
    While through the press enraged Thalestris[34] flies,
And scatters death around from both her eyes,
A beau and witling[35] perished in the throng,
One died in metaphor, and one in song.
25 "O cruel nymph! a living death I bear,"
Cried Dapperwit, and sunk beside his chair.
A mournful glance Sir Fopling[36] upwards cast,
"Those eyes are made so killing"—was his last.

---

27. virago (və rā′ gō): Scolding woman.
28. Pallas . . . Hermes: Gods who directed the Trojan War. Pallas and Hermes supported the Greeks, while Mars and Latona sided with the Trojans.
29. Olympus: The mountain which was supposed to be the home of the gods.
30. Jove's: Referring to Jupiter, the ruler of the Gods in Roman mythology; identified with Zeus in Greek mythology.
31. Neptune: The Roman god of the sea; identified with Poseidon in Greek mythology.
32. sconce's height: A candleholder attached to the wall.
33. bodkin spears: Large needles.
34. Thalestris (thə lĕs′ trĭs): An Amazon (a race of female warriors supposed to have lived in Scythia) who played a role in the medieval tales of Alexander the Great.
35. witling: A person who fancies himself or herself a wit.
36. Dapperwit, Sir Fopling: Names of amusing characters in comedies of the time.

Thus on Maeander's[37] flowery margin lies
30   Th' expiring swan, and as he sings he dies.
        When bold Sir Plume had drawn Clarissa down,
Chloe[38] stepped in, and killed him with a frown;
She smiled to see the doughty hero slain,
But, at her smile, the beau revived again.
35   Now Jove suspends his golden scales in air,
Weighs the men's wits against the lady's hair;
The doubtful beam long nods from side to side;
At length the wits mount up, the hairs subside.
        See, fierce Belinda on the baron flies,
40   With more than usual lightning in her eyes;
Nor feared the chief th' unequal fight to try,
Who sought no more than on his foe to die.
But this bold lord with manly strength endued,
She with one finger and a thumb subdued:
45   Just where the breath of life his nostrils drew,
A charge of snuff the wily virgin threw;
The gnomes direct, to every atom just,
The pungent grains of titillating dust.
Sudden with starting tears each eye o'erflows,
50   And the high dome re-echoes to his nose.
        "Now meet thy fate," incensed Belinda cried,
And drew a deadly bodkin[39] from her side . . .
        "Boast not my fall," he cried, "insulting foe!
Thou by some other shalt be laid as low.
55   Nor think, to die dejects my lofty mind;
All that I dread is leaving you behind!
Rather than so, ah let me still survive,
And burn in Cupid's flames—but burn alive."
        "Restore the lock!" she cries; and all around
60   "Restore the lock!" the vaulted roofs rebound.
Not fierce Othello in so loud a strain
Roared for the handkerchief that caused his pain.[40]
But see how oft ambitious aims are crossed,
And chiefs contend till all the prize is lost!
65   The lock, obtained with guilt, and kept with pain,
In every place is sought, but sought in vain.
With such a prize no mortal must be blessed,
So Heaven decrees! with Heaven who can contest?

---

37. Maeander's: Referring to a river in Asia.
38. Chloe (klō′ ē): The heroine of the ancient Greek pastoral
romance, *Daphnis and Chloe.*
39. bodkin: An ornamental pin shaped like a dagger.
40. not . . . pain: In Shakespeare's *Othello,* the hero is convinced
that his wife is being unfaithful to him when she cannot find the
handkerchief that he had given her. Actually, the handkerchief had
been taken by the villain, Iago, who uses it as part of his evil plot.

THE BATTLE OF THE BEAUX AND BELLES
Aubrey Beardsley

Some thought it mounted to the lunar sphere,
70   Since all things lost on earth are treasured there.
There heroes' wits are kept in ponderous vases,
And beaux' in snuffboxes and tweezer cases.
There broken vows and deathbed alms are found,
And lovers' hearts with ends of riband bound . . .
75   But trust the Muse—she saw it upward rise,
Though marked by none but quick, poetic eyes . . .
A sudden star, it shot through liquid[41] air
And drew behind a radiant trail of hair . . .[42]
        Then cease, bright Nymph! to mourn thy ravished hair,
80   Which adds new glory to the shining sphere!
Not all the tresses that fair head can boast,
Shall draw such envy as the lock you lost.
For, after all the murders of your eye,[43]
When, after millions slain, yourself shall die;
85   When those fair suns shall set, as set they must,
And all those tresses shall be laid in dust,
This lock, the Muse shall consecrate to fame,
And midst the stars inscribe Belinda's name.

---

41. liquid: Clear.
42. trail of hair: The word "comet" comes from a Greek word meaning "long-haired."
43. murders . . . eye: Lovers struck down by her glances.

■ RESPONDING TO THE SELECTION

Your Response

1. Do you think Pope effectively satirizes his subject? Explain.

Recalling

2. (a) In what activity is Belinda engaged during the first half of Canto III? (b) What is the outcome?
3. (a) What is the "two-edged weapon" that Clarissa gives the baron? (b) How many times does the baron fail to get the lock of hair? (c) How does Belinda respond when he does get it? (d) How does the baron react?
4. (a) In Canto V, what noises accompany the attack that follows Belinda's cry of "To arms, to arms!"? (b) With what weapon does Belinda threaten the baron's life? (c) What does she demand that he do?
5. (a) Who has possession of the lock at the end of Canto V? (b) What do some people think has happened to it?

Interpreting

6. Why do you think Pope precedes the trivial episodes in Canto III with such a grisly image as "wretches hang that jurymen may dine"?
7. What similarity is there between Pope's description of the omber game and his description of the events following the theft of the lock?

8. Lines 79–88 in Canto V are "elegant spoofing" according to one critic. Yet in a sense Pope made the poem's extravagant claim come true. How did he do it?

Applying

9. Pope based *The Rape of the Lock* on an actual incident. What incident in the news today might provide the basis for a similar mock epic? (Your freewriting on page 493 may supply an answer to this question.)

ANALYZING LITERATURE

Understanding Mock Epic

A **mock epic** is a humorous narrative poem done in the manner of a true epic. It may resemble classical epics such as the *Odyssey* or the *Iliad*. It may contain elements of English epics such as *Beowulf* or *Paradise Lost*. Or, as in *The Rape of the Lock*, a mock epic may show traces of both types. In any case it will have characters who perform what appear to be heroic deeds. It may also contain references from mythology and include impossible or supernatural events.

1. (a) What are three trivial incidents in *The Rape of the Lock* that Pope presents in a heroic manner? (b) What are three characteristics of the heroic manner that the poem exhibits?
2. What are some of the mythical creatures, including deities and muses, mentioned in the poem? Try to find at least seven.

CRITICAL THINKING AND READING

Inferring the Author's Purpose

Up to a point, the author's purpose in writing *The Rape of the Lock* is evident. Pope is mocking the overwrought reaction of two noble families to a hair-cutting prank. In his own words, Pope is "using a vast force to lift a feather." But that is not his only intent. The author has a more serious purpose than just memorializing a silly in-

cident. To understand what it is, you have to read between the lines—to infer—what Pope believes about human behavior and social manners. The following lines from the poem give clues to the author's purpose. First, interpret the lines in your own words. Then, write a general statement expressing what you believe to be Pope's purpose in writing the poem.

1. "Oh thoughtless mortals! ever blind to fate,/Too soon dejected, and too soon elate." (Canto III, lines 101–102)
2. "But when to mischief mortals bend their will,/How soon they find fit instruments of ill!" (Canto III, lines 125–126)
3. "But see how oft ambitious aims are crossed,/And chiefs contend till all the prize is lost!" (Canto V, lines 63–64)

THINKING AND WRITING

Writing About Tone

Tone is sometimes easier to recognize than to describe. You can easily see that the tone of *The Rape of the Lock* is lofty and heroic. But which features of Pope's language lend the poem its distinctive tone? Ask yourself these questions, and jot down your answers.

1. How do the words in the poem differ from the words you use in ordinary speaking and writing? (Consider figurative as well as literal meanings of words.)
2. How does the arrangement of words differ from that in most sentences in everyday English? (Pay attention to inverted elements, modifier placement, parallelism, and so on.)
3. More broadly, what is the total effect of Pope's language? (Look at his overstatement, allusions, choice of details—indeed, anything that makes the poem high-flown and mock heroic.)

Use your answers to these questions to write a composition on the tone of *The Rape of the Lock*. Begin by stating what you believe the tone of the poem to be. Support that statement by citing examples and using quotations from the poem. Revise, checking especially organization and coherence.

GUIDE FOR INTERPRETING

from An Essay on Man

Writers' Techniques

Heroic Couplet. A heroic couplet is a rhyming pair of lines in iambic pentameter. Since it requires the clear thought and precise wording admired by classically inspired writers, it was a favorite verse form among Restoration and eighteenth-century poets. Dryden, Swift, and Pope are among the best-known users of the form. The heroic couplet, concise and quotable, is often used in satire. The following lines from Pope's *The Rape of the Lock* form a heroic couplet.

$$\cup \quad / \quad \cup / \quad \cup \quad / \quad \cup / \cup \quad /$$
He springs to vengeance with an eager pace,
$$\cup \quad / \quad \cup \quad / \quad \cup / \quad \cup \quad / \quad \cup \quad /$$
And falls like thunder on the prostrate ace.

Focus

Many of Pope's heroic couplets are closed couplets—that is, their two lines represent a complete thought.

> True wit is Nature to advantage dress'd,
> What oft was thought, but ne'er so well expressed.

That couplet, a complete thought, is from Pope's *Essay on Criticism*. Create a closed couplet; it must consist of two rhyming lines of ten syllables each, with the stress falling on every second syllable. As a closed couplet, it must make a complete, understandable statement, ideally in an effective and memorable way.

Primary Source

The form of the heroic couplet is easy to mock and makes Pope, because of his tendency to quarrel with others, an easy target as well. The following parody of Pope's style is an excerpt from *A Pipe of Tobacco* (1736) by Isaac Hawkins Browne.

The parody is agreeable and skillful and, though it lacks any bite, was very much admired in its own day, as was its author. Although sensitive about his work, Pope spoke highly of Browne and his parody, remarking: "Browne is an excellent copyist, and those who talk ill of him are very much in the wrong."

> . . . Nor less, the critic owns thy genial aid,
> While supperless he plies the piddling trade.
> What tho' to love and soft delights a foe,
> By ladies hated, hated by the beau,
> Yet social freedom, long to courts unknown,
> Fair health, fair truth, and virtue are thy own.
> Come to thy poet, come with healing wings,
> And let me taste thee unexcis'd by kings.

from An Essay on Man

Alexander Pope

An Essay on Man *is an examination of human nature, society, and morals. In describing the work, Pope comments that it is "a general map of man, marking out . . . the greater parts, their extent, their limits, and their connection." The following excerpt is from the second epistle, in which Pope attempts to show how it is possible for humanity to achieve a psychological harmony through self-understanding and self-love.*

Know then thyself, presume not God to scan;
The proper study of mankind is man.
Placed on this isthmus of a middle state,
A being darkly wise, and rudely great:
5 With too much knowledge for the skeptic side,
With too much weakness for the stoic's pride,
He hangs between; in doubt to act, or rest;
In doubt to deem himself a god, or beast;
In doubt his mind or body to prefer;
10 Born but to die, and reasoning but to err;
Alike in ignorance, his reason such,
Whether he thinks too little, or too much:
Chaos of thought and passion, all confused;
Still by himself abused, or disabused;
15 Created half to rise, and half to fall;
Great lord of all things, yet a prey to all;
Sole judge of truth, in endless error hurled:
The glory, jest, and riddle of the world!

RESPONDING TO THE SELECTION

Your Response

1. How does your own understanding of human nature compare with Pope's? Explain.

Recalling

2. What does Pope say should be the object of man's study?
3. According to Pope, what prevents man from being (a) a skeptic? (b) a stoic?

Interpreting

4. Pope writes that man stands on an "isthmus of a middle state." He describes the middle state in detail. In a single word, what is (a) at one end of the isthmus? (b) at the other end?
5. What do you think Pope means by the line "In doubt his mind or body to prefer"?
6. "Know then thyself," writes Pope. How can a person "in mindless error hurled" achieve that goal?

Applying

7. Most writers today reject the idea that literature should present an obvious moral. Pope believed just the opposite. He felt that poetry has a didactic, or instructional, role to play. What do you think?

ANALYZING LITERATURE

Understanding a Heroic Couplet

A **heroic couplet** is a pair of rhymed lines in iambic pentameter. An iamb is a metrical foot consisting of one short syllable followed by one long syllable or one unstressed syllable followed by one stressed syllable. The word *apply* (ə plī'), for instance, could function as an iamb:

$$\cup \ /$$
apply

1. Find one word that functions as an iamb in each of the following lines: 1, 2, 7, 8, 11.
2. Since it is a heroic couplet, lines 7–8 should rhyme, but they seem not to. (a) What explanation can you suggest for this apparent mistake? (Hint: Look up in a dictionary the pronunciation of the adjective *bestial*.) (b) Find five similarly nonrhyming pairs of words in *The Rape of the Lock*. How can you explain them?

CRITICAL THINKING AND READING

Generalizing

To some extent—except for stable religious convictions—each era sets its own moral and intellectual standards. What is viewed as acceptable in one century may seem outrageous in another. For example, the word *leg*, since it referred to a part of the human anatomy, was considered so scandalous by Victorians that even chairs and tables were said to have *limbs*. Today the word *leg* seems innocuous.

1. If Pope's observations represent the thought of his day, how did people in the eighteenth century view the relationship between the intellect and the emotions?
2. What differences, if any, do you see in that relationship today?

THINKING AND WRITING

Responding to Neoclassical Criticism

In the preface to his poem "Religio Laici," John Dryden offers his critical opinion of how poetry should be written:

> The expressions of a poem designed purely for instruction ought to be plain and natural, and yet majestic; for the poet is . . . a kind of lawgiver, and those three qualities which I have named are proper to the legislative style.

In an essay of no more than one page, state (1) whether you agree with Dryden as to how a poem "purely for instruction" should be written and (2) whether you think *An Essay on Man* (based on the excerpt you have read) has the three elements named. Draw freely from the poem to support your opinion. When you revise, make sure you have provided adequate support for your opinion.

The Age of Johnson

Oliver Goldsmith, James Boswell,
And Samuel Johnson At The
Mitre Tavern
Nineteenth-century colored engraving

SAMUEL JOHNSON

1709–1784

Many readers know Samuel Johnson only through the biography written by his contemporary and ardent admirer, James Boswell. That is unfortunate, because the Samuel Johnson who is revealed through his own writings is a man with much to say on a variety of subjects—a man who, despite the excellence of Boswell's portrait, is best read firsthand. During his own lifetime, Johnson was widely recognized as the most influential literary figure of his day as well as a brilliant and witty conversationalist. Indeed, the second half of the eighteenth century is often called the Age of Johnson.

Johnson's success was hard won. The son of a bookseller in Lichfield, a small town north of Birmingham, he grew up in poverty. He described himself as a "poor diseased infant." A series of childhood illnesses left him physically weak and facially disfigured. A brilliant child who read *Hamlet* at the age of eight, Johnson feared that insanity would deprive him of his single advantage, his intellect. He entered Pembroke College, Oxford, in 1728 but was forced to leave after fourteen months because of a lack of funds. For six years thereafter, until deciding to pursue a literary career in earnest, he was a Lichfield bookseller and schoolmaster, reading widely and occasionally working on translations. At the age of twenty-six, he married a widow much older than he, to whom he remained devoted until her death.

In 1737 he moved to London. Despite critical praise for his early writing, he failed to gain a large audience. It was Johnson's *Dictionary of the English Language,* published in 1755, that earned him a permanent place in English letters. For the next two years, he wrote "The Idler," a series of articles for a weekly newspaper, and completed one of his best-loved works, *Rasselas,* a moral romance.

Johnson was awarded an annual pension of 300 pounds in 1762, which made him something of a man of leisure. The next year he and twenty-three-year-old James Boswell met for the first time in the back parlor of Tom Davis's bookshop. It was a fateful meeting, one that led, after many further meetings, to Boswell's *The Life of Johnson,* a book generally regarded as the finest biography in English.

In 1765 Johnson published an acclaimed edition of Shakespeare. His last important work, *The Lives of the Poets,* appeared in ten volumes between 1779 and 1781. It is a group of fifty-two critical biographies that cover about 200 years of English literary history. Late in life Johnson received honorary degrees from Oxford and from Trinity College, Dublin—thus the "Dr." that often precedes his name. He is buried in Westminster Abbey.

GUIDE FOR INTERPRETING

Letter to Lord Chesterfield; *from* The Preface to A Dictionary of the English Language; *from* A Dictionary of the English Language

Writers' Techniques

Diction and Style. In written communication, *diction* means word choice. A careful writer chooses words that are clear, correct, and effective. The distinctive way in which those words are combined in phrases, sentences, and paragraphs is called *style*. Diction and style change over the years, just as fashion changes. Writing tends to be more casual today than it was 200 years ago, although formal situations still require formal diction and style. The intended audience for a piece of writing helps to determine appropriate diction and style.

Commentary

According to contemporary reports, Johnson was enthralled by words, especially their histories. No doubt this led to his keen interest in diction and style. The following story sheds light on the process of compiling a dictionary—as well as on Samuel Johnson's character.

The story has it that an anonymous source once sent Johnson a letter containing his derivation of "curmudgeon," an ill-tempered person. The unknown contributor claimed that the word came from the French *coeur méchant;* literally, "heart wicked," or wicked heart. This wild guess so pleased Johnson that he used it in his *Dictionary,* giving due credit to the "unknown correspondent."

The matter came up again twenty years later, when Dr. John Ash, compiling his own dictionary, came across the entry in Johnson's *Dictionary*. He, too, found it interesting and decided to use it. Unlike Johnson, however, Ash wanted to claim full credit for discovering the word's history, so he wrote that *curmudgeon* was created from *coeur,* meaning "unknown," and *méchant,* meaning "correspondent." Do you think it is necessary to give credit for a word's history? Can anyone "own" a word?

Focus

In your local newspaper, find a letter to the editor with which you disagree. Jot down your points of disagreement. Then write the opening paragraph of a response. Try to match your diction and style to that of the published letter you have chosen.

Letter to Lord Chesterfield

Samuel Johnson

Shortly after the completion of the Dictionary, *Lord Chesterfield published two articles praising it. He had earlier ignored Johnson's appeals for financial assistance for the writing of the* Dictionary.

To the Right Honorable
the Earl of Chesterfield

February 7, 1755

My Lord:

I have been lately informed by the proprietor of the *World*[1] that two papers in which my *Dictionary* is recommended to the public were written by your Lordship. To be so distinguished is an honor which, being very little accustomed to favors from the great, I know not well how to receive, or in what terms to acknowledge.

When upon some slight encouragement I first visited your Lordship, I was overpowered like the rest of mankind by the enchantment of your address,[2] and could not forbear to wish that I might boast myself *"Le vainqueur du vainqueur de la terre"*;[3] that I might obtain that regard for which I saw the world contending, but I found my attendance so little encouraged that neither pride nor modesty would suffer me to continue it. When I had once addressed your Lordship in public, I had exhausted all the art of pleasing which a retired and uncourtly scholar can possess. I had done all that I could; and no man is well pleased to have his all neglected, be it ever so little.

Seven years, my Lord, have now passed since I waited in your outward rooms or was repulsed from your door, during which time I have been pushing on my work through difficulties of which it is useless to complain and have brought it at last to the verge of publication without one act of assistance, one word of encouragement, or one smile of favor. Such treatment I did not expect, for I never had a patron before.

The shepherd in Virgil grew at last acquainted with love, and found him a native of the rocks.[4] Is not a patron, my Lord, one who looks with unconcern on a man struggling for life in the water and when he has reached ground encumbers him with help. The notice which you have been pleased to take of my labors, had it been early, had been kind; but it has been delayed till I am indifferent and cannot enjoy it, till I am solitary and cannot impart it, till I am known and do not want[5] it.

1. **the *World*:** A newspaper in which Lord Chesterfield had praised Johnson's *Dictionary.*
2. **address:** Conversation.
3. *Le vainqueur du vainqueur de la terre* (lə van kər′ dyoo van kər′ də lä ter′): French for "the conqueror of the conqueror of the earth."

4. **The shepherd . . . rocks:** In Virgil's *Eclogue*, a shepherd complains that love must have been born among jagged rocks.
5. **want:** Need.

I hope it is no very cynical asperity not to confess obligation where no benefit has been received, or to be unwilling that the public should consider me as owing that to a patron which Providence has enabled me to do for myself.

Having carried on my work thus far with so little obligation to any favorer of learning, I shall not be disappointed though I should conclude it, if less be possible, with less; for I have been long wakened from that dream of hope, in which I once boasted myself with so much exultation, my Lord,

> Your Lordship's most humble,
> most obedient servant,
> Samuel Johnson

RESPONDING TO THE SELECTION

Your Response

1. If you had been in Samuel Johnson's place, what kind of a letter would you have written to Lord Chesterfield?

Recalling

2. (a) How did Johnson learn of Lord Chesterfield's articles in the *World?* (b) Why does he feel the need to respond?
3. How much time has passed since Johnson first tried to get financial assistance from Lord Chesterfield for work on the dictionary?
4. What does Johnson say will not cause him any disappointment at this point?

Interpreting

5. How does the definition of a patron in the fourth paragraph apply to Johnson's experience with Lord Chesterfield?
6. From Johnson's remarks in the next to last paragraph, what misinformation do you think Chesterfield may have conveyed in his *World* articles concerning his relationship with Johnson?

Applying

7. Suppose Lord Chesterfield had assisted Johnson throughout the development of his diction-

ary. How do you think Johnson would then have responded to the articles in the *World?*

ANALYZING LITERATURE

Diction and Style

Diction in writing is word choice. **Style** is the overall effect of a writer's choice and arrangement of words. In fact, Lord Chesterfield once called style "the dress of thought." Diction and style are influenced by purpose, audience, and the period in which the writing is done. In his "Letter to Lord Chesterfield," Samuel Johnson intends his diction and style to deliver an unmistakable message.

1. (a) What is the purpose of the letter? (b) What is its audience? (c) How does Johnson feel about the audience?
2. What are ten words that you consider to be especially well chosen by Johnson for the point he wants to make and the way in which he wants to make it?
3. What are three stylistic devices that Johnson uses effectively? Give one example of each from the letter. (Among the possibilities are parallelism, understatement, overstatement, and quotation.)

from The Preface to A Dictionary of the English Language

Samuel Johnson

It is the fate of those who toil at the lower employments of life, to be rather driven by the fear of evil, than attracted by the prospect of good; to be exposed to censure, without hope of praise; to be disgraced by miscarriage, or punished for neglect, where success would have been without applause, and diligence without reward.

Among these unhappy mortals is the writer of dictionaries; whom mankind have considered, not as the pupil, but the slave of science, the pioneer of literature, doomed only to remove rubbish and clear obstructions from the paths through which learning and genius press forward to conquest and glory, without bestowing a smile on the humble drudge that facilitates their progress. Every other author may aspire to praise; the lexicographer can only hope to escape reproach, and even this negative recompense has been yet granted to very few.

I have, notwithstanding this discouragement, attempted a dictionary of the English language, which, while it was employed in the cultivation of every species of literature, has itself been hitherto neglected; suffered to spread under the direction of chance, into wild exuberance; resigned to the tyranny of time and fashion: and exposed to the corruptions of ignorance and caprices of innovation.

When I took the first survey of my undertaking, I found our speech copious without order and energetic without rule: wherever I turned my view, there was perplexity to be disentangled and confusion to be regulated; choice was to be made out of boundless variety, without any established principle of selection; adulterations were to be detected, without a settled test of purity; and modes of expression to be rejected or received, without the suffrages of any writers of classical reputation or acknowledged authority.

Having therefore no assistance but from general grammar, I applied myself to the perusal of our writers; and noting whatever might be of use to ascertain or illustrate any word or phrase, accumulated in time the materials of a dictionary, which, by degrees, I reduced to method, establishing to myself, in the progress of the work, such rules as experience and analogy suggested to me; experience, which practice and observation were continually increasing; and analogy, which, though in some other words obscure, was evident in others . . .

In hope of giving longevity to that which its own nature forbids to be immortal, I have devoted this book, the labor of years, to the honor of my country, that we may no longer yield the palm of philology, without a contest to the nations of the continent. The chief glory of every people arises from its authors. Whether I shall add anything by my own writings to the reputation of English literature, must be left to time. Much of my life has been lost under the pressures of disease; much has been trifled away; and much has always been spent in provision for the day that was passing over me; but I shall not think my employment useless or ignoble, if by my assistance foreign nations and distant ages gain access to the propagators of knowledge, and understand the teachers of truth; if my labors afford light to the repositories of science, and add celebrity to Bacon, to Hooker, to Milton, and to Boyle.[1]

When I am animated by this wish, I look with pleasure on my book, however defective, and deliver it to the world with the spirit of a man that has endeavored well. That it will immediately become popular, I have not promised to myself. A few wild blunders, and risible absurdities, from which no work of such multiplicity was ever free, may for a time furnish folly with laughter, and harden ignorance into contempt; but useful diligence will at last prevail, and there never can be wanting some who distinguish desert; who will consider that no dictionary of a living tongue ever can be perfect, since, while it is hastening to publication, some words are budding, and some falling away; that a whole life cannot be spent upon syntax and etymology, and that even a whole life would not be sufficient; that he, whose design includes whatever language can express, must often speak of what he does not understand; that a writer will sometimes be hurried by eagerness to the end, and sometimes faint with weariness under a task which Scaliger[2] compares to the labors of the anvil and the mine; that what is obvious is not always known, and what is known is not always present; that sudden fits of inadvertency will surprise vigilance, slight avocations[3] will seduce attention, and casual eclipses of the mind will darken learning; and that the writer shall often in vain trace his memory at the moment of need, for that which yesterday he knew with intuitive readiness, and which will come uncalled into his thoughts tomorrow.

In this work, when it shall be found that much is omitted, let it not be forgotten that much likewise is performed; and though no book was ever spared out of tenderness to the author, and the world is little solicitous to know whence proceed the faults of that which it condemns; yet it may gratify curiosity to inform it, that the *English Dictionary* was written with little assistance of the learned, and without any patronage of the great; not in the soft obscurities of retirement, or under the shelter of academic bowers, but amidst inconvenience and distraction, in sickness and in sorrow. It may repress the triumph of malignant criticism to observe that if our language is not here fully displayed, I have only failed in an attempt which no human powers have hitherto completed. If the lexicons of ancient tongues, now immutably fixed and comprised in a few volumes, be yet, after the toil of successive ages, inadequate and delusive; if the aggregated knowledge and cooperating diligence of the Italian academicians did not secure them from the censure of Beni;[4] if the embodied critics of France, when fifty years had been spent upon their work, were obliged to change its economy[5] and give their second edition another form, I may surely be contented without the praise of perfection, which, if I could obtain, in this gloom of solitude, what would it avail me? I have protracted my work till most of those whom I wished to please have sunk into the grave,[6] and success and miscarriage are empty sounds: I therefore dismiss it with frigid tranquility, having little to fear or hope from censure or from praise.

1. Bacon . . . Boyle: Writers quoted by Johnson in the *Dictionary.*
2. Scaliger: Joseph Justus Scaliger (1540–1609), a scholar who suggested that criminals should be condemned to writing dictionaries.
3. avocation: Something that calls one away or distracts one from something.

4. Beni: Paolo Beni severely criticized the first Italian dictionary.
5. economy: Organization.
6. sunk . . . grave: Johnson's wife had died three years earlier.

RESPONDING TO THE SELECTION

Your Response

1. Do you agree that "The chief glory of every people arises from its authors?" Why or why not?

Recalling

2. (a) Among what class of workers does Johnson place writers of dictionaries? (b) What is the lexicographer's "negative recompense"?
3. (a) When Johnson "took the first survey," what did he find English speech to be lacking? (b) What gave him his only assistance?
4. To whom or what does Johnson say he has "devoted this book"?
5. Why, according to the preface, can "no dictionary of a living tongue ever be perfect"?

Interpreting

6. (a) What is Johnson's reason for having undertaken the task of writing a dictionary of English? (b) What can you conclude about prior dictionary-making in England?
7. How did Johnson collect the words for his dictionary?
8. Johnson seems to have mixed feelings about his efforts. (a) Do you think he is hopeful or pessimistic (or perhaps both) about the fate of his dictionary? Explain. (b) How have his efforts held up against the test of time?

Applying

9. What opinion do you think Johnson would have of the unabridged English dictionaries of today?
10. How have computers changed the role of dictionary makers?

THINKING AND WRITING

Comparing and Contrasting Styles

A **writer's style** is the distinctive way in which he or she uses language. No two writers have exactly the same style, although you may notice obvious similarities, especially among writers of the same era. Think about other writers' works that you have read in this book. Which writer has a style the most like—or, if you prefer, the least like—that of Samuel Johnson? To answer the question, you will need to consider diction, sentence structure, tone, and point of view. Once you have made your choice, write a short essay in which you compare and contrast the style of Johnson with that of the other writer you have chosen. Take notes before you start your first draft. Be specific as to the similarities and differences between the two styles you are comparing. When you revise for your final draft, make sure that your observations about style are accurate and that your quoted excerpts are correct.

LEARNING OPTIONS

1. **Language.** Become a lexicographer like Johnson and update a dictionary. Write your own entries for words that are not yet included in a standard dictionary, like contemporary slang words and technological terms. In writing your entries, keep your style consistent.
2. **Multicultural Activity.** Johnson wanted at first to guard English from changes. American English, however, has acquired many new words from the great variety of cultures represented in the United States. With a small group of classmates, research and create a list of words that are derived from several cultural traditions found in this country. Share your compilation with the class.

from A Dictionary of the English Language

Samuel Johnson

athle′tick. Strong of body; vigorous; lusty; robust.

> Science distinguishes a man of honor from one of those *athletick* brutes, whom underservedly we call heroes. Dryden.

bang. A blow; a thump; a stroke: a low word.

> I am a bachelor. That's to say, they are fools that marry; you'll bear me a *bang* for that. Shakespeare, *Julius Caesar.*

to ba′rbecue. A term used in the West Indies for dressing a hog whole; which, being split to the backbone, is laid flat upon a large gridiron, raised about two foot above a charcoal fire, with which it is surrounded.

> Oldfield, with more than harpy throat endu'd,
> Cries, send me, gods, a whole hog *barbecu'd.* Pope.

bu′ffleheaded. A man with a large head, like a buffalo; dull; stupid; foolish.

cream. The unctuous or oily part of milk, which, when it is cold, floats on the top, and is changed by the agitation of the churn into butter; the flower of milk.

electri′city. A property in some bodies, whereby, when rubbed so as to grow warm, they draw little bits of paper, or such like substances, to them. Quincy.

> Such was the account given a few years ago of electricity; but the industry of the present age, first excited by the experiments of Gray, has discovered in electricity a multitude of philosophical wonders. Bodies electrified by a sphere of glass, turned nimbly round, not only emit flame, but may be fitted with such a quantity of the electrical vapor as, if discharged at once upon a human body, would endanger life. The force of this vapor has hitherto appeared instantaneous, persons at both ends of a long chain seeming to be struck at once. The philosophers are now endeavoring to intercept the strokes of lightning.

to fu′rnace. To throw out as sparks from a furnace. A bad word.

> He *furnaces*
> The thick sighs from him. Shakespeare's *Cymbeline.*

gang. A number herding together; a troop; a company; a tribe; a herd. It is seldom used but in contempt or abhorrence.

ha′tchet-face. An ugly face; such, I suppose, as might be hewn out of a block by a hatchet.

An ape his own dear image will embrace;
An ugly beau adores a *hatchet-face.*
Dryden.

lifegua'rd. The guard of a king's person.

mo'dern. In Shakespeare, vulgar; mean; common.

We have our philosophical persons to make *modern* and familiar things supernatural and causeless. Shakespeare.

pa'tron. One who countenances, supports or protects. Commonly a wretch who supports with insolence, and is paid with flattery.

pi'ckle. Condition; state. A word of contempt and ridicule.

How cam'st though in this *pickle?*
Shakespeare.

plu'mper. Something worn in the mouth to swell out the cheeks.

She dex'trously her *plumpers* draws,
That serve to fill her hollow jaws. Swift's *Miscellanies.*

shill-I-shall-I. A corrupt reduplication of *shall I?* The question of a man hesitating. To stand *shill-I-shall-I,* is to continue hesitating and procrastinating.

I am somewhat dainty in making a resolution, because when I make it, I keep it; I don't stand *shill-I-shall-I* then; if I say't, I'll do't. Congreve's *Way of the World.*

to sneeze. To emit wind audibly by the nose.

wi'llow. A tree worn by forlorn lovers.

to wipe. To cheat; to defraud.

The next bordering lords commonly encroach one upon another, as one is stronger, or lie still in wait to *wipe* them out of their lands. Spenser, *On Ireland.*

you'ngster, you'nker. A young person. In contempt.

youth. The part of life succeeding to childhood and adolescence; the time from fourteen to twenty-eight.

Your Response

1. Do you find Johnson's definitions more useful or less useful than those in modern dictionaries? Explain.

Recalling

2. What is Johnson's definition of (a) *lifeguard* and (b) *modern?*
3. According to Johnson, what is (a) a "tree worn by forlorn lovers"? (b) a person "from fourteen to twenty-eight"?

Interpreting

4. How does Johnson indicate that a word is a verb?
5. Why do you think the word *electricity* receives such a long definition?
6. Given what you know of Johnson's life, how do you account for his comment about *patron:* "a wretch who supports with insolence, and is paid with flattery"?
7. In a modern dictionary, how is the entry for *shill-I-shall-I* spelled?

Applying

8. Dictionaries are generally objective works. Johnson's dictionary, however, is filled with opinions and value judgments. What are three conspicuous examples of the kind of wording that would not appear in a modern dictionary?

CRITICAL THINKING AND READING

Making Inferences About Tone

Tone, the manner in which a writer communicates, shows the writer's attitude toward his or her subject. It often displays traces of the writer's personality or set of values. When tone seems to be completely straightforward, as in a newspaper report, a reader will tend to accept the writer's message at face value. If tone appears to be ironic or sarcastic, as in a satirical essay, a reader will be on guard for less obvious meanings. Tone can usually be described by one or two adjectives. Review Johnson's definitions of the following words. Then, in a brief paragraph, describe Johnson's tone in each definition.

1. bang   4. hatchet-face
2. cream   5. youngster
3. to furnace

THINKING AND WRITING

Writing Johnsonian Dictionary Entries

Take a look once again at the entries from Johnson's *Dictionary.* Pay close attention to exactly how they are written. Then search through a standard modern dictionary and find at least five words that might be imaginatively redefined through Johnson's eyes. Finally, write Johnsonian definitions for these words. Follow his style in every way possible, including markings for pronunciation, diction, and candor.

LEARNING OPTION

Language. Dictionary entries today are quite different from those in Johnson's *Dictionary.* Choose any three words in his dictionary and look them up in a modern dictionary. Write the complete entries from the modern dictionary. Then describe the ways in which today's dictionary entries differ from Johnson's.

JAMES BOSWELL

1740–1795

Not until the twentieth century did James Boswell rise from the fringes of literary history to take his place as perhaps the greatest biographer in English literature. Best known for his biography of Samuel Johnson, Boswell wrote with vigor, training his eye on both the picturesque and the grotesque.

Born into an aristocratic family in Edinburgh, Scotland, Boswell was educated at the University of Glasgow, the University of Edinburgh, and the University of Utrecht. Although he received his degree in law and was admitted to the bar in both Scotland and England, Boswell's true passion was literature. His father, a prominent judge, was angered by what he saw as his son's "shallow" values. The extremely sensitive young Boswell interpreted this dissatisfaction as rejection, which led in turn to feelings of inferiority. In an effort to overcome his low self-esteem and at the same time find a suitable father figure, Boswell became a celebrity chaser, seeking out the acquaintance of the great men and women of his day. To his credit, many of them became his lifelong friends.

Among these was the writer Samuel Johnson, whom Boswell met while visiting London in 1763. After his acceptance into the prestigious Literary Club, Boswell devoted thirty years to compiling detailed records of Johnson's activities and conversations. From these assorted bits and pieces he distilled his famous work, *The Life of Samuel Johnson,* a precise and wonderfully intimate portrait of the colorful poet. "The great art of biography," Boswell wrote, "is to keep the person whose life we are giving always in the reader's view." This he does by depicting Johnson variously as "a rhinoceros, in a kind of good humoured growl," and as "blowing out his breath like a whale" following an argument.

In addition to his portrait of Johnson, Boswell wrote numerous personal journals. *An Account of Corsica* (1768) is a sympathetic report of his meeting with the Corsican patriot Paoli and of Corsica's struggle for independence. *The Journal of a Tour in the Hebrides with Samuel Johnson, L.L.D* (1785), published after Johnson's death, tells of the trip he made with the sage to Scotland.

During his lifetime Boswell's popularity was stifled by the biting criticism leveled at his work by the poet Thomas Gray, who caustically noted that "any fool may write a valuable book by chance, if he will only tell what he heard and saw. . . ." It is only since the 1920's, when a batch of Boswell's private papers were discovered in Malahide Castle, that the reading public has had any real awareness of this often rowdy, often vain young gentleman who gave the world its closest look at Samuel Johnson.

GUIDE FOR INTERPRETING

from The Life of Samuel Johnson

Literary Forms

Biography. A biography is an account of someone's life by another person, usually written, though sometimes communicated orally. Effective biography will present the subject's life accurately and thoroughly. A good biography, in other words, paints a complete portrait, giving as much space to the subject's flaws and limitations as to his or her most admirable traits. An important milestone in the writing of biography was James Boswell's *The Life of Samuel Johnson*. Boswell displayed an impressive grasp of Johnson's character by presenting countless particular details rather than a distant and generalized view of the man. The art of the biography has continued into the twentieth century with such monumental works as Carl Sandburg's saga on the life of Abraham Lincoln, which spans several volumes.

Commentary

Boswell claimed that his biography of Johnson would be the most complete life of a person ever penned, but in a curious way he was proved wrong: The one he wrote about himself is far more complete. When his eighteen volumes of journals were published after his death, he became, according to critic Joseph Wood Krutch, "perhaps the best self-documented man in all history."

Boswell began jotting down occasional notes in 1758. By 1762 he was writing in his journal regularly, a practice he continued until about thirteen months before he died. He published only a few excerpts from his journals during his life. As he did not intend the bulk of the material for public eyes, the journals are free and open expressions of his feelings and clearly reveal his decision to write the truth about himself.

Since he had no intention of publishing his journals, why did he spend so much time on them? As he wrote, "Know thyself, for surely this knowledge is of all the most important." And what better way for a person to gain self-awareness than by "attending to the feelings of his heart and to his external actions. . . . I have therefore determined to keep a daily journal in which I shall set down my various conduct, which will be not only useful but very agreeable."

What do Boswell's accounts of Johnson reveal about himself?

Focus

Imagine that you were able to interview a person whom you greatly admire. The person in question may be an athlete, film star, author, or the like. Prepare a list of questions that you think would reveal the individual behind the public mask.

from The Life of Samuel Johnson

James Boswell

Boswell Meets Johnson

1763

This is to me a memorable year; for in it I had the happiness to obtain the acquaintance of that extraordinary man whose memoirs I am now writing; an acquaintance which I shall ever esteem as one of the most fortunate circumstances in my life. Though then but two-and-twenty, I had for several years read his works with delight and instruction, and had the highest reverence for their author, which had grown up in my fancy into a kind of mysterious veneration, by figuring to myself a state of solemn elevated abstraction, in which I supposed him to live in the immense metropolis of London. . . .

Mr. Thomas Davies[1] the actor, who then kept a bookseller's shop in Russel Street, Covent Garden, told me that Johnson was very much his friend, and came frequently to his house, where he more than once invited me to meet him; but by some unlucky accident or other he was prevented from coming to us.

At last, on Monday the 16th day of May, when I was sitting in Mr. Davies's back parlor, after having drunk tea with him and Mrs. Davies, Johnson unexpectedly came into the shop; and Mr. Davies having perceived him through the glass door in the room in which we were sitting, advancing towards us—he announced his aweful[2] approach to me, somewhat in the manner of an actor in the part of Horatio, when he addresses Hamlet on the appearance of his father's ghost, "Look, my Lord, it comes,"[3] I found that I had a very perfect idea of Johnson's figure, from the portrait of him painted by Sir Joshua Reynolds[4] soon after he had published his *Dictionary,* in the attitude of sitting in his easy chair in deep meditation, which was the first picture his friend did for him, which Sir Joshua very kindly presented to me, and from which an engraving has been made for this work. Mr. Davies mentioned my name, and respectfully introduced me to him. I was much agitated; and recollecting his prejudice against the Scotch, of which I had heard much, I said to Davies, "Don't tell where I come from." "From Scotland," cried Davies roguishly. "Mr. Johnson," said I, "I do indeed come from Scotland, but I cannot help it." I am willing to flatter myself that I meant this as light pleasantry to sooth and conciliate him, and not as an humiliating abasement at the expense of my country. But however that might be, this speech was somewhat

1. **Thomas Davies:** An English bookseller and unsuccessful actor (1712–1785).

2. **aweful:** Awe-inspiring.
3. **Horatio " . . . it comes":** From Shakespeare's *Hamlet* (Act I, Scene iv).
4. **Sir Joshua Reynolds:** A celebrated portrait painter at the time (1723–1792).

unlucky; for with that quickness of wit for which he was so remarkable, he seized the expression "come from Scotland," which I used in the sense of being of that country; and, as if I had said that I had come away from it, or left, retorted, "That, Sir, I find, is what a very great many of your countrymen cannot help." This stroke stunned me a good deal; and when we had sat down, I felt myself not a little embarrassed, and apprehensive of what might come next. He then addressed himself to Davies: "What do you think of Garrick?[5] He has refused me an order for the play for Miss Williams, because he knows the house will be full, and that an order would be worth three shillings." Eager to take any opening to get into conversation with him, I ventured to say, "O, Sir, I cannot think Mr. Garrick would grudge such a trifle to you." "Sir," said he, with a stern look, "I have known David Garrick longer than you have done: and I know no right you have to talk to me on the subject." Perhaps I deserved this check; for it was rather presumptuous in me, an entire stranger, to express any doubt of the justice of his animadversion upon his old acquaintance and pupil. I now felt myself much mortified, and began to think that the hope which I had long indulged of obtaining his acquaintance was blasted. And, in truth, had not my ardor been uncommonly strong, and my resolution uncommonly persevering, so rough a reception might have deterred me forever from making any further attempts. Fortunately, however, I remained upon the field not wholly discomfited; and was soon rewarded by hearing some of his conversation, of which I preserved the following short minute,[6] without marking the questions and observations by which it was produced.

"People," he remarked, "may be taken in once, who imagine that an author is greater in private life than other men. Uncommon parts require uncommon opportunities for their exertion."

"In barbarous society, superiority of parts is of real consequence. Great strength or great wisdom is of much value to an individual. But in more polished times there are people to do everything for money; and then there are a number of other superiorities, such as those of birth and fortune, and rank, that dissipate men's attention, and leave no extraordinary share of respect for personal and intellectual superiority. This is wisely ordered by Providence, to preserve some equality among mankind."

"Sir, this book (*The Elements of Criticism*,[7] which he had taken up) is a pretty essay, and deserves to be held in some estimation, though much of it is chimerical."

Speaking of one[8] who with more than ordinary boldness attacked public measures and the royal family, he said, "I think he is safe from the law, but he is an abusive scoundrel; and instead of applying to my Lord Chief Justice to punish him, I would send half a dozen footmen and have him well ducked."[9]

"The notion of liberty amuses the people of England, and helps to keep off the *taedium vitae*.[10] When a butcher tells you that his heart bleeds for his country, he has, in fact, no uneasy feeling."

"Sheridan[11] will not succeed at Bath with his oratory. Ridicule has gone down before him, and, I doubt,[12] Derrick[13] is his enemy."

---

5. Garrick: David Garrick (1717–1779), a famous actor who had been educated by Johnson. Garrick was also one of the managing partners of the Drury Lane Theater in London.
6. minute: Note.

7. *Elements of Criticism:* One of the works of Scottish philosophical writer Henry Home (1696–1782).
8. one: John Wilkes (1727–1797), an English political agitator.
9. ducked: Tied to a chair at the end of a plank and plunged into water.
10. *taedium vitae* (tī'dē əm vē' tī): Boredom.
11. Sheridan: Thomas Sheridan (1719–1788), an Irish actor and author. At the time, Sheridan was reading lectures at the Oratory at Bath.
12. doubt: Fear.
13. Derrick: The Master of Ceremonies of the Oratory at Bath.

"Derrick may do very well, as long as he can outrun his character; but the moment his character gets up with him, it is all over."

It is, however, but just to record, that some years afterwards, when I reminded him of this sarcasm, he said, "Well, but Derrick has now got a character that he need not run away from."

I was highly pleased with the extraordinary vigor of his conversation, and regretted that I was drawn away from it by an engagement at another place. I had, for a part of the evening, been left alone with him, and had ventured to make an observation now and then, which he received very civilly; so that I was satisfied that though there was a roughness in his manner, there was no ill nature in his disposition. Davies followed me to the door, and when I complained to him a little of the hard blows which the great man had given me he kindly took upon him to console me by saying, "Don't be uneasy. I can see he likes you very well."

Johnson's Character

The character of Samuel Johnson has, I trust, been so developed in the course of this work, that they who have honored it with a perusal, may be considered as well acquainted with him. As, however, it may be expected that I should collect into one view the capital and distinguishing features of this extraordinary man, I shall endeavor to acquit myself of that part of my biographical undertaking, however difficult it may be to do that which many of my readers will do better for themselves.

His figure was large and well formed, and his countenance of the cast of an ancient statue; yet his appearance was rendered strange and somewhat uncouth by convulsive cramps, by the scars of that distemper[14] which it was once imagined the royal touch could cure,[15] and by a slovenly mode of dress. He had the use only of one eye; yet so much does mind govern and even supply the deficiency of organs, that his visual perceptions, as far as they extended, were uncommonly quick and accurate. So morbid was his temperament, that he never knew the natural joy of a free and vigorous use of his limbs: when he walked, it was like the struggling gait of one in fetters; when he rode, he had no command or direction of his horse, but was carried as if in a balloon. That with his constitution and habits of life he should have lived seventy-five years, is a proof that an inherent *vivida vis*[16] is a powerful preservative of the human frame.

Man is, in general, made up of contradictory qualities; and these will ever show themselves in strange succession, where a consistency in appearance at least, if not in reality, has not been attained by long habits of philosophical discipline. In proportion to the native vigor of the mind, the contradictory qualities will be the more prominent, and more difficult to be adjusted; and, therefore, we are not to wonder that Johnson exhibited an eminent example of this remark which I have made upon human nature. At different times, he seemed a different man, in some respects; not, however, in any great or essential article, upon which he had fully employed his mind, and settled certain principles of duty, but only in his manners and in the display of argument and fancy in his talk. He was prone to superstition, but not to credulity. Though his imagination might incline him to a belief of the marvelous and the mysterious, his vigorous reason examined the evidence with jealousy.[17] He was a sincere and zealous Christian, of high Church of England and monarchical princi-

---

14. distemper *n.*: Scrofula, a type of tuberculosis that causes swelling and scarring of the neck.

15. royal touch . . . cure: It was at one time believed that the touch of an English monarch had the power to heal. As a child Johnson was taken to Queene Anne to receive her touch in the hope that it would cure him.
16. *vivida vis*: Lively force.
17. jealousy: Suspicion.

ples, which he would not tamely suffer to be questioned; and had, perhaps, at an early period, narrowed his mind somewhat too much, both as to religion and politics. His being impressed with the danger of extreme latitude in either, though he was of a very independent spirit, occasioned his appearing somewhat unfavorable to the prevalence of that noble freedom of sentiment which is the best possession of man. Nor can it be denied, that he had many prejudices; which, however, frequently suggested many of his pointed sayings that rather show a playfulness of fancy than any settled malignity. He was steady and inflexible in maintaining the obligations of religion and morality; both from a regard for the order of society, and from a veneration for the Great Source of all order; correct, nay, stern in his taste; hard to please, and easily offended; impetuous and irritable in his temper, but of a most humane and benevolent heart, which showed itself not only in a most liberal charity, as far as his circumstances would allow, but in a thousand instances of active benevolence. He was afflicted with a bodily disease, which made him often restless and fretful; and with a constitutional melancholy, the clouds of which darkened the brightness of his fancy, and gave a gloomy cast to his whole course of thinking: we, therefore, ought not to wonder at his sallies of impatience and passion at any time; especially when provoked by obtrusive ignorance, or presuming petulance; and allowance must be made for his uttering hasty and satirical sallies even against his best friends. And, surely, when it is considered, that, "amidst sickness and sorrow," he exerted his faculties in so many works for the benefit of mankind, and particularly that he achieved the great and admirable Dictionary of our language, we must be astonished at his resolution. The solemn text, "of him to whom much is given, much will be required," seems to have been ever present to his mind, in a rigorous sense, and to have made him dissatisfied with his labors and

acts of goodness, however comparatively great; so that the unavoidable consciousness of his superiority was, in that respect, a cause of disquiet. He suffered so much from this, and from the gloom which perpetually haunted him and made solitude frightful, that it may be said of him, "If in this life only he had hope, he was of all men most miserable."[18] He loved praise, when it was brought to him; but was too proud to seek for it. He was somewhat susceptible of flattery. As he was general and unconfined in his studies, he cannot be considered as master of any one particular science; but he had accumulated a vast and various collection of learning and knowledge, which was so arranged in his mind, as to be ever in readiness to be brought forth. But his superiority over other learned men consisted chiefly in what may be called the art of thinking, the art of using his mind; a certain continual power of seizing the useful substance of all that he knew and exhibiting it in a clear and forcible manner; so that knowledge, which we often see to be no better than lumber[19] in men of dull understanding, was, in him, true, evident, and actual wisdom. His moral precepts are practical; for they are drawn from an intimate acquaintance with human nature. His maxims carry conviction; for they are founded on the basis of common sense, and a very attentive and minute survey of real life. His mind was so full of imagery, that he might have been perpetually a poet; yet it is remarkable, that, however rich his prose is in this respect, his poetical pieces, in general, have not much of that splendor, but are rather distinguished by strong sentiment and acute observation, conveyed in harmonious and energetic verse, particularly in heroic couplets. Though usually grave, and even aweful, in his deportment, he possessed uncommon and peculiar powers of wit and humor; he frequently indulged himself in colloquial pleasantry; and the hearti-

---

18. **"If . . . miserable":** From I Corinthians 15:19.
19. **lumber:** Rubbish.

est merriment was often enjoyed in his company; with this great advantage, that as it was entirely free from any poisonous tincture of vice or impiety, it was salutary to those who shared in it. He had accustomed himself to such accuracy in his common conversation, that he at all times expressed his thoughts with great force, and an elegant choice of language, the effect of which was aided by his having a loud voice, and a slow deliberate utterance. In him were united a most logical head with a most fertile imagination, which gave him an extraordinary advantage in arguing: for he could reason close or wide, as he saw best for the moment. Exulting in his intellectual strength and dexterity, he could, when he pleased, be the greatest sophist[20] that ever contended in the lists of declamation; and, from a spirit of contradiction and a delight in showing his powers, he would often maintain the wrong side with equal warmth and ingenuity; so that, when there was an audience, his real opinions could seldom be gathered from his talk; though when he was in company with a single friend, he would discuss a subject with genuine fairness: but he was too conscientious to make error permanent and pernicious, by deliberately writing it; and, in all his numerous works, he earnestly inculcated what appeared to him to be the truth; his piety being constant, and the ruling principle of all his conduct.

Such was Samuel Johnson, a man whose talents, acquirements, and virtues, were so extraordinary, that the more his character is considered the more he will be regarded by the present age, and by posterity, with admiration and reverence.

---

20. sophist (säf′ ist) *n.*: One who makes misleading arguments.

MULTICULTURAL CONNECTION

Dictionaries and Academies

Samuel Johnson, the subject of Boswell's biography, fostered the correct use of English by writing one of the first English dictionaries. In countries other than England, however, the task of preserving language usually was given to an academy. The word *academy* is derived from "the olive grove of Academe," a wooded, brook-filled area where the ancient Greek philosopher Plato discussed ideas. Today the word is used to describe any institution in which learning and study are encouraged.

Academies in different countries. It was only after Plato's academy that academies were established to consolidate and purify the language of a nation. Most of these academies set out clear rules of usage. One of the earliest and most famous of these institutions, the Accademia della Crusca, was founded during the Renaissance to preserve and purify the Italian language.

In 1635, Cardinal Richelieu established the Académie Française to ensure correct usage of the French language. Similar academies were launched in Spain, Sweden, Switzerland, and the Netherlands. Today there are also academies for Arabic and Hebrew.

None of these academies, however, has been able to prevent the changing of a language. Most modern dictionaries and grammar handbooks, therefore, are less concerned with dictating standards than with recording the everyday changes that languages undergo.

Exploring

How many slang words can you find in a dictionary? What does your research suggest about the way language changes?

from *The Life of Samuel Johnson* 527

RESPONDING TO THE SELECTION

Your Response

1. What is your impression of Johnson after reading Boswell's account? Would you be interested in talking with Johnson if he were alive today? Why or why not?

Recalling

2. What aspects of Johnson's appearance prompt Boswell to describe him as "strange and somewhat uncouth"?

3. What, according to the selection, was Johnson's position (a) on superstition? (b) on religion? (c) on praise? (d) on flattery?

Interpreting

4. What details of Johnson's personality in this excerpt explain (a) his sarcastic remark about Scotland in "Boswell Meets Johnson"? (b) his desire to obtain a free theater ticket for a friend? (c) his harsh reply to Boswell's comment on Garrick?

5. What do you learn about Boswell himself from this passage? Support your comments with evidence.

Applying

6. (a) Which of the observations presented in this excerpt do you think generally apply to most people? (b) Do you think the inclusion of these details detracts from the integrity of Boswell's biography? Explain your answer.

7. (a) What similarities do you detect between the lifestyles and habits of celebrities of the eighteenth century and those of our own age? (b) What differences do you detect?

ANALYZING LITERATURE

Understanding Biography

A **biography** is a history of a person told or written by others. A good biography meets several criteria. It presents (1) the subject in an im-

partial light; (2) a complete and unified picture of the subject; (3) the subject against the backdrop of the times in which he or she lived. Based on the excerpt from Boswell's *The Life of Samuel Johnson*, state how well you think the work meets these criteria. In making your assessment, consider the following questions.

1. Can Boswell's statement that he "was much agitated" upon meeting Johnson be taken as an admission that he was not in a frame of mind to report facts impartially? Why?

2. On page 524, Boswell notes that he preserved Johnson's observations "without marking the questions and observations" that led up to them. Does this suggest a lack of completeness? Why?

CRITICAL THINKING AND READING

Recognizing Subjective Information

Subjective information is information colored by a person's own attitudes and feelings. *Objective* information is information that preserves some widely held truth. The statement "I like to eat chicken" is a piece of subjective information. The statement "Chicken is a source of protein" is a piece of objective information. Biography, if it is interesting, will usually contain a mixture of subjective and objective statements.

Bearing in mind what you read about Boswell in the biographical sketch of him on page 520, decide which of the details in this excerpt you think are subjective. Explain your answer.

THINKING AND WRITING

Writing From Johnson's Point of View

Write an account of the meeting described in this excerpt from Samuel Johnson's point of view. Before beginning, review Boswell's quotations of Johnson in order to help you form an impression of the older man's prose style and general attitude toward life. Feel free to add original details that may have escaped Boswell's attention.

Pre-Romantic Poetry

HAYMAKERS, 1785
George Stubbs

THOMAS GRAY

1716–1771

Although Thomas Gray produced precious little poetry during his lifetime, his scant output was more a result of his perfectionism than it was of any lack of ideas. Gray was a scholar, with interests ranging from literature to art to science and beyond. Had he lived in an era more compatible with the romantic yearnings of his soul, he might, as the poet Matthew Arnold suggested, have been capable of far greater things.

Gray was born in the Cornhill section of London. He suffered from convulsions, a condition that forced his mother on at least one occasion to open a vein in his head to relieve pressure on the brain. He was educated at Eton and Cambridge and, after completing his studies, traveled through Europe with his friend Horace Walpole.

At the end of three years, Gray returned to England and lived for a time with his mother and sister in the village of Stoke Poges. It was in this sleepy hamlet during the summer of 1742 that he wrote his first important poems—"On the Spring," "On a Distant Prospect of Eton College," and "Hymn to Adversity." It was also around this time that Gray penned his most famous poetic work, "Elegy Written in a Country Churchyard." A copy of the elegy that he sent to Walpole accidentally fell into the hands of a dishonest editor. Ultimately it was retrieved, though only after a great struggle, which adds a touch of irony to Gray's having refused to accept payment for the poem when at last it was published.

After reaching the age of thirty, Gray lived an increasingly quiet country life, becoming something of a hermit. A confirmed bachelor, he busied himself with books and experimented with new poetic forms, while conducting private studies in classical literature at Cambridge. His work of this period, which includes the odes "The Bard" (1757) and "The Descent of Odin" (1761), reflects his love of Celtic and Norse mythology and his interest in history and language. In 1771, while planning a visit to a friend in Switzerland, the poet suffered a violent attack of gout and died on July 30. Seven years after his death, a monument honoring him was erected in Westminster Abbey.

Although Gray was a less than energetic poet, the small body of work that he left behind is notable for its juxtaposition of established forms and novel sentiments. His "Elegy Written in a Country Churchyard," in particular, skillfully combines the neoclassical style of his own century with the Romantic ideals of the next.

GUIDE FOR INTERPRETING

Elegy Written in a Country Churchyard

Literary Forms

Elegy. An elegy is a lyric poem or musical composition that laments a death. The form, which dates back to ancient Greece and Rome, flourished during the European Renaissance, which spanned the fourteenth through the sixteenth centuries. Although an elegy usually mourns the death of an individual, it may also address the ravages of time or may function as a meditation on the nature of loss. The elegy, while conforming to no rigid structural guidelines, often opens with an expression of grief and moves gradually toward a philosophical acceptance of the loss. Thomas Gray's "Elegy Written in a Country Churchyard," inspired by the death of the poet's close friend Richard West, marks one of three high points of the elegiac form in English literature, the others being Milton's "Lycidas" and Tennyson's *In Memoriam, A.H.H.*

Focus

Gray's elegy ends with an epitaph, a poetic inscription intended to appear on a gravestone. Many epitaphs mention a property or trait of the deceased for which he or she might best be remembered. Write an epitaph for yourself or for a friend. Focus, using as few words as possible, on the individual's most memorable quality.

Primary Source

Whether Gray wrote his own epitaph has not been recorded, but several other writers of the time did leave behind the poems they wanted inscribed on their gravestones. Alexander Pope, for example, left the following lines for his gravestone:

> Under this marble, or under the sill,
> Or under this turf, or e'en what they will;
> Whatever an heir, or a friend in his stead,
> Or any good creature shall lay o'er my head;
> Lies he who ne'er car'd, and still cares not a pin,
> What they said, or may say of the mortal within.
> But who living and dying, serene still and free,
> Trusts in God, that as well as he was, he shall be.

Several years later, Coleridge penned this epitaph for himself:

> Here sleeps at length poor Col., and without screaming;
> Who died as he lived, a-dreaming:
> Shot dead, while sleeping, by the gout within—
> All alone and unknown, at Edinbro' in an inn.

As you read, look for the differences between the epitaph that ends Gray's elegy and the ones Pope and Coleridge wrote for themselves.

Elegy Written in a Country Churchyard

Thomas Gray

The curfew tolls the knell of parting day,
　　The lowing herd winds slowly o'er the lea,[1]
The plowman homeward plods his weary way,
　　And leaves the world to darkness and to me.

5　Now fades the glimmering landscape on the sight,
　　And all the air a solemn stillness holds,
Save where the beetle wheels his droning flight,
　　And drowsy tinklings lull the distant folds;

Save that from yonder ivy-mantled tower,
10　　The moping owl does to the moon complain
Of such as, wandering near her secret bower,
　　Molest her ancient solitary reign.

Beneath those rugged elms, that yew tree's shade,
　　Where heaves the turf in many a moldering heap,
15　Each in his narrow cell forever laid,
　　The rude[2] forefathers of the hamlet sleep.

The breezy call of incense-breathing morn,
　　The swallow twittering from the straw-built shed,
The cock's shrill clarion, or the echoing horn,[3]
20　　No more shall rouse them from their lowly bed.

For them no more the blazing hearth shall burn,
　　Or busy housewife ply her evening care;
No children run to lisp their sire's return,
　　Or climb his knees the envied kiss to share.

---

1. lea: Meadow.
2. rude: Uneducated.
3. horn: The hunter's horn.

25 Oft did the harvest to their sickle yield,
       Their furrow oft the stubborn glebe[4] has broke;
     How jocund did they drive their team afield!
       How bowed the woods beneath their sturdy stroke!

     Let not Ambition mock their useful toil,
30   Their homely joys, and destiny obscure;
     Nor Grandeur hear with a disdainful smile
       The short and simple annals of the poor.

     The boast of heraldry,[5] the pomp of power,
       And all that beauty, all that wealth e'er gave,
35   Awaits alike the inevitable hour.
       The paths of glory lead but to the grave.

---

4. glebe: Soil.
5. heraldry: Noble descent.

Nor you, ye proud, impute to these the fault,
    If memory o'er their tomb no trophies[6] raise,
Where through the long-drawn aisle and fretted vault[7]
40   The pealing anthem swells the note of praise.

Can storied urn,[8] or animated[9] bust,
    Back to its mansion call the fleeting breath?
Can honor's voice provoke[10] the silent dust,
    Or Flattery soothe the dull cold ear of Death?

45 Perhaps in this neglected spot is laid
    Some heart once pregnant with celestial fire;
Hands, that the rod of empire might have swayed,
    Or waked to ecstasy the living lyre.

But Knowledge to their eyes her ample page
50   Rich with the spoils of time did ne'er unroll;
Chill Penury repressed their noble rage,
    And froze the genial current of the soul.

Full many a gem of purest ray serene
    The dark unfathomed caves of ocean bear:
55 Full many a flower is born to blush unseen,
    And waste its sweetness on the desert air.

Some village Hampden,[11] that, with dauntless breast,
    The little tyrant of his fields withstood,
Some mute inglorious Milton[12] here may rest,
60   Some Cromwell[13] guiltless of his country's blood.

The applause of listening senates to command,
    The threats of pain and ruin to despise,
To scatter plenty o'er a smiling land,
    And read their history in a nation's eyes,

65 Their lot forbade: nor circumscribed alone
    Their growing virtues, but their crimes confined
Forbade to wade through slaughter to a throne,
    And shut the gates of mercy on mankind,

---

6. trophies: Symbolic figures or pictures depicting the achievements of the dead man.
7. fretted vault: A church ceiling decorated with intersecting lines.
8. storied urn: A funeral urn with an epitaph inscribed on it.
9. animated: Lifelike.
10. provoke: Call forth.
11. Hampden: John Hampden (1594–1643), an English statesman who defied King Charles I by resisting the king's efforts to revive the obsolete tax of ship-money without the authority of Parliament.
12. Milton: English poet, John Milton (1608–1674).
13. Cromwell: Oliver Cromwell (1599–1658), English revolutionary leader and Lord Protector of the Commonwealth from 1653 to 1658.

The struggling pangs of conscious truth to hide,
70   To quench the blushes of ingenuous shame,
Or heap the shrine of Luxury and Pride
      With incense kindled at the Muse's flame.

Far from the madding[14] crowd's ignoble strife,
      Their sober wishes never learned to stray;
75 Along the cool sequestered vale of life
      They kept the noiseless tenor of their way.

Yet even these bones from insult to protect
      Some frail memorial still erected nigh,
With uncouth rhymes and shapeless sculpture decked,[15]
80   Implores the passing tribute of a sigh.

Their name, their years, spelt by the unlettered Muse,[16]
      The place of fame and elegy supply:
And many a holy text around she strews,
      That teach the rustic moralist to die.

85 For who, to dumb Forgetfulness a prey,
      This pleasing anxious being e'er resigned,
Left the warm precincts of the cheerful day,
      Nor cast one longing lingering look behind?

On some fond breast the parting soul relies,
90   Some pious drops[17] the closing eye requires;
Even from the tomb the voice of Nature cries,
      Even in our ashes live their wonted fires.

For thee,[18] who, mindful of the unhonored dead,
      Dost in these lines their artless tale relate;
95 If chance, by lonely contemplation led,
      Some kindred spirit shall enquire thy fate,

Haply[19] some hoary-headed[20] swain may say,
      "Oft have we seen him at the peep of dawn
Brushing with hasty steps the dews away,
100   To meet the sun upon the upland lawn.

---

14. madding: Frenzied.
15. Some . . . decked: Contrasts with "the storied urn[s] or animated bust[s]" (line 41) inside the church.
16. the unlettered Muse: The uneducated gravestone carver.
17. drops: Tears.
18. thee: Gray himself.
19. haply: Perhaps.
20. hoary-headed: White-haired.

"There at the foot of yonder nodding beech,
    That wreathes its old fantastic roots so high,
His listless length at noontide would he stretch,
    And pore upon the brook that babbles by.

105 "Hard by yon wood, now smiling as in scorn,
    Muttering his wayward fancies he would rove;
Now drooping, woeful wan, like one forlorn,
    Or crazed with care, or crossed in hopeless love.

"One morn I missed him on the customed hill,
110   Along the heath, and near his favorite tree;
Another came; nor yet beside the rill,[21]
    Nor up the lawn, nor at the wood was he;

"The next, with dirges due in sad array
    Slow through the churchway path we saw him borne.
115 Approach and read (for thou canst read) the lay
    Graved on the stone beneath yon aged thorn."[22]

The Epitaph

Here rests his head upon the lap of Earth
    A youth, to Fortune and to Fame unknown.
Fair Science[23] *frowned not on his humble birth,*
120   *And melancholy marked him for her own.*

Large was his bounty, and his soul sincere,
    Heaven did a recompense as largely send:
He gave to misery (all he had) a tear,
    He gained from Heaven ('twas all he wished) a friend.

125 *No farther seek his merits to disclose,*
    Or draw his frailties from their dread abode
(There they alike in trembling hope repose),
    The bosom of his Father and his God.

---

21. rill: Brook.
22. thorn: Hawthorn tree.
23. Science: Learning.

RESPONDING TO THE SELECTION

Your Response

1. What thoughts and feelings does Gray's elegy evoke in you?

Recalling

2. The first four stanzas establish the setting of the poem. (a) Where is the speaker? (b) What time of day is it?
3. According to lines 21–25, what pleasure will these "rude forefathers" no longer partake of?
4. In lines 57–60, what sorts of lives does the speaker speculate these people might have led under other circumstances?
5. To whom is "The Epitaph" in the last three stanzas dedicated?

Interpreting

6. What do you think is meant by (a) "the inevitable hour" in line 35? (b) by "its mansion" in line 42?
7. How would you summarize the sentiment expressed (a) in lines 53–56? (b) in lines 77–92?

Applying

8. (a) Tell who or what the poet is elegizing. (b) State whether you share his sense of loss, giving reasons for your answer.

ANALYZING LITERATURE

Understanding an Elegy

An **elegy** is a lyric poem that expresses mourning, usually over the death of an individual, though an elegy can also lament the toll that time's passage takes on youth or beauty. Typically the elegy begins solemnly, with the poet's expression of sadness over his or her loss, and ends with an insight that enables the poet to cope with this loss.

1. (a) Whom does the poet grieve in "Elegy Written in a Country Churchyard"? (b) What do these people seem to represent to the poet? (c) What words express the poet's sadness?
2. (a) Does the poet come to accept his loss by the end of the poem? Explain your answer.

(b) What insight helps him to reach this acceptance? (c) What ideas or thoughts bridge his grief and his acceptance?

CRITICAL THINKING AND READING

Evaluating Inverted Sentences

In English the most common sentence structure is subject-verb-object. That is, the doer of the action is usually named first, the word specifying the action appears second, and the recipient of the action comes last. In poetry the parts of the sentence are sometimes **inverted,** or reversed, to emphasize a particular idea. In line 90, for example, the poet places the object, "some pious drops," before both the subject and verb of the sentence, to focus the reader's attention on the idea of tears. Locate the following lines and identify the order of the sentence parts. Then tell what idea is being stressed.

1. line 5   3. lines 49–50
2. lines 13–16   4. lines 81–82

THINKING AND WRITING

Writing an Elegy

With the epitaph you created for the Focus activity on page 531 as a starting point, write an elegy. Use as many of the features of Gray's elegy as you can, including inverted sentence structure and vivid verbs. Remember to begin your elegy with an expression of your grief and to end it with a statement of acceptance.

LEARNING OPTION

Community Connections. Visit an old cemetery in or near your community and write down some of the epitaphs that you find. What different varieties can you find? What patterns do you see among them? What concerns and values do they express? What do the epitaphs tell you about the historical period during which they were composed? Report your findings to the class.

ROBERT BURNS

1759–1796

No other name is more synonymous with the title "The voice of Scotland" than that of the poet Robert Burns. A farmer and a farmer's son, Burns was born at Alloway, in Ayrshire, and spent his early years in the two-room clay cottage his father had built. Although poverty prevented Burns from receiving a formal education, with his father's encouragement he read widely, studying the Bible, Shakespeare, and Alexander Pope on his own. His mother, though herself illiterate, instilled in him a love of Scottish folk songs, legends, and proverbs.

In 1786 Burns published his first collection of poems through a small local press. Although the collection, which included "To a Mouse," was successful, Burns only came to the attention of the public at large the following year when a fuller collection, *Poems: Chiefly in Scottish,* was published at Edinburgh. He was invited to the Scottish capital, where he was swept into the social scene, if only as something of a rustic curiosity. He left Edinburgh in 1788 to explore the English border region and the Highlands.

Later that year he married Jean Armour, his sweetheart of many years, and returned to the farm to work the land. The soil proved unproductive, however, and so to supplement his income he took a position with the Excise Service—Scotland's department of taxation. All the while he continued to refine his poetic style, turning out some of his finest verses. At the outbreak of the French Revolution, he became an outspoken supporter of the republican cause, a move that threatened his job and alienated many of his friends. His spirits low and his health taxed by a weak heart he had had since childhood, Burns contracted a fever from which he never recovered. Thousands of people from all social levels followed his coffin to the grave, and he was acclaimed the national poet of Scotland.

Burns's numerous adventures produced many lyrics that figure among the most natural and spontaneous ever produced in the English language. His poems, written for the most part in dialect, are characterized by innocence, honesty, and simplicity. First and last a people's poet, Burns crafted poetic "melodies" that speak to and speak for "the sons and daughters of labor and poverty." Though some of the poet's work had its origins in folk tunes, "it is not," as James Douglas wrote, "easy to tell where the vernacular ends and the personal magic begins."

GUIDE FOR INTERPRETING

To a Mouse; To a Louse;
Afton Water; John Anderson, My Jo

Writers' Techniques

Dialect. Dialect is the language, and particularly the speech habits, of a particular social class, region, or group. A dialect may vary from the standard form of a language in grammar, in pronunciation, and in the use of certain expressions. In literature it can serve to establish character, tone, and setting. The use of dialect by a writer or poet can also add to the immediacy and familiarity of a piece of literature.

In the eighteenth century, the belief was widespread among writers that only formal diction was acceptable in poetry. Rules were thus developed concerning the subjects and styles that were thought to be appropriate for poetry. Common life and colloquial language were almost always excluded from the poet's domain. Robert Burns rebelled against these rules, by both his use of Scottish dialect and his celebration of the rural and working life. Like so many poets of that age who ushered in the Romanticism of the next generation, Burns strived to capture in words the language and experiences of the human heart.

Focus

Write an account titled "A Day in the Life of a _____," filling in the blank with one of the following: Dog, Cat, Bird, Squirrel, Goldfish, or Gerbil. Try to get inside the mind of the subject of your narrative, imagining the triumphs, defeats, fears, and hopes your creature experiences on a typical day.

Primary Source

Like many writers, Burns kept a Commonplace Book, a place to record scraps of lyrics, topics for poetry, and various thoughts and ideas on numerous different topics. A number of his entries reveal that he had long considered using dialect and adapting legendary Scotch songs in his poetry. In one entry, he remarked:

> There is a degree of wild irregularity in many of the compositions & Fragments which are daily sung to them by my compeers, the common people—a certain happy arrangement of old Scotch syllables, & yet, very frequently, nothing, not even like rhyme, or sameness of jingle at the ends of the lines. —This has made me sometimes imagine that perhaps, it might be possible for a Scotch Poet, with a nice, judicious ear, to set compositions to many of our favorite airs, particularly the class of them mentioned above, independent of rhyme altogether.—

To a Mouse

On Turning Her up in Her Nest with the Plow, November, 1785

Robert Burns

Wee, sleekit,[1] cow'rin', tim'rous beastie,
O, what a panic's in thy breastie!
Thou need na start awa sae hasty,
    Wi' bickering brattle![2]
5 I wad be laith[3] to rin an' chase thee
    Wi' murd'ring pattle![4]

---

1. sleekit: Sleek.
2. Wi' . . . brattle: In sudden flight.
3. wad be laith: Would be loath.
4. pattle: Paddle for cleaning a plow.

I'm truly sorry man's dominion
Has broken Nature's social union,
An' justifies that ill opinion,
10   Which makes thee startle,
At me, thy poor, earth-born companion,
        An' fellow-mortal!

I doubt na, whyles,[5] but thou may thieve;
What then? poor beastie, thou maun[6] live!
15   A daimen icker in a thrave[7]
        'S a sma' request:
I'll get a blessin' wi' the lave,[8]
        And never miss't!

Thy wee bit housie, too, in ruin!
20   Its silly wa's[9] the win's are strewin'!
An' naething, now, to big[10] a new ane,
        O' foggage[11] green!
An' bleak December's winds ensuin',
        Baith snell[12] an keen!

25   Thou saw the fields laid bare and waste,
An' weary winter comin' fast,
An' cozie here, beneath the blast,
        Thou thought to dwell,
Till crash! the cruel coulter[13] past
30   Out through thy cell.

That wee bit heap o' leaves an' stibble,
Has cost thee mony a weary nibble!
Now thou's turned out, for a' thy trouble,
        But[14] house or hald,[15]
35   To thole[16] the winter's sleety dribble,
        An' cranreuch[17] cauld!

---

5. whyles: At times.
6. maun: Must.
7. A . . . thrave: An occasional ear of grain in a bundle.
8. lave: Rest.
9. silly wa's: Feeble walls.
10. big: Build.
11. foggage: Rough grass.
12. snell: Sharp.
13. coulter: Plow blade.
14. But: Without.
15. hald: Property.
16. thole: Withstand.
17. cranreuch (krən' rəkh): Frost.

But, Mousie, thou art no thy lane,[18]
In proving foresight may be vain:
The best laid schemes o' mice an' men
40   Gang aft a-gley,[19]
An' lea'e us nought but grief an' pain,
      For promised joy.

Still thou art blest, compared wi' me!
The present only toucheth thee:
45 But, och! I backward cast my e'e
      On prospects drear!
An' forward, though I canna see,
      I guess an' fear!

_____

18. no thy lane: Not alone.
19. Gang aft a-gley: Go often awry.

■ RESPONDING TO THE SELECTION

Your Response

1. How would you have reacted to the plight of the mouse?

Recalling

2. What is the setting of the poem?
3. For what reason does the speaker apologize to the mouse?
4. Why does the speaker say that, compared with him, the mouse is blessed?

Interpreting

5. To what "social union" do you think the speaker is referring in line 7?
6. What does the sentiment in lines 13–14 suggest about the speaker's own moral code?
7. (a) What famous line in the poem carries the poem's theme? (b) How would you state this theme in your own words?

Applying

8. What value do you place on foresight? Explain your answer.

■ ANALYZING LITERATURE

Recognizing Dialect

Dialect is the speech habits and patterns of a specific group, class, or region. A dialect possesses its own unique grammar, pronunciation, and vocabulary. One of the first poets to write using the Scottish dialect of English, Robert Burns placed himself in direct opposition to the poetic standards of the eighteenth century.

1. (a) What does the use of dialect in this poem suggest about the speaker's social station? (b) How does it help carry across the poem's theme?
2. Like the standard language, dialects of a language follow rules. Find at least two examples in the poem of each of the following pronunciation rules for Scottish English. (a) Final consonants are dropped. (b) The letter _o_ is replaced by either _ae_ or _a._
3. How would the effect of this poem have been different if it had been written in standard English?

To a Louse

On Seeing One on a
Lady's Bonnet at Church

Robert Burns

Ha! whare ye gaun, ye crowlin' ferlie![1]
Your impudence protects you sairly:[2]
I canna say but ye strunt[3] rarely,
     Owre gauze and lace;
5 Though faith! I fear ye dine but sparely
     On sic a place.

Ye ugly, creepin', blastit wonner,[4]
Detested, shunned by saunt an' sinner,
How dare ye set your fit[5] upon her,
10   Sae fine a lady?
Gae somewhere else, and seek your dinner
     On some poor body.

Swith![6] in some beggar's haffet[7] squattle;[8]
There ye may creep, and sprawl, and sprattle[9]
15 Wi' ither kindred, jumping cattle,
     In shoals and nations;
Whare horn nor bane[10] ne'er dare unsettle
     Your thick plantations.

Now haud[11] ye there, ye're out o' sight,
20 Below the fatt'rels,[12] snug an' tight;
Na, faith ye yet![13] ye'll no be right
     Till ye've got on it,
The vera tapmost, tow'ring height
     O' Miss's bonnet.

---

1. **crowlin' ferlie:** Crawling wonder.
2. **sairly:** Sorely.
3. **strunt:** Strut.
4. **blastit wonner:** Blasted wonder.
5. **fit:** Foot.
6. **swith:** Swift.
7. **haffet:** Locks.
8. **squattle:** Sprawl.
9. **sprattle:** struggle.
10. **horn nor bane:** Comb nor poison.
11. **haud:** Hold.
12. **fatt'rels:** Ribbon ends.
13. **Na faith ye yet!:** Confound you!

25 My sooth! right bauld ye set your nose out,
As plump and gray as onie grozet;[14]
O for some rank, mercurial rozet,[15]
    Or fell,[16] red smeddum,[17]
I'd gie you sic a hearty dose o't,
30   Wad dress your droddum![18]

I wad na been surprised to spy
You on an auld wife's flannen toy;[19]
Or aiblins some bit duddie boy,[20]
    On's wyliecoat;[21]
35 But Miss's fine Lunardi![22] fie,
    How daur ye do't?

O, Jenny, dinna toss your head,
An' set your beauties a' abread![23]
Ye little ken what cursèd speed
40   The blastie's[24] makin'!
Thae[25] winks and finger-ends, I dread,
    Are notice takin'!

O wad some Pow'r the giftie gie us
To see oursels as ithers see us!
45 It wad frae monie a blunder free us
    And foolish notion:
What airs in dress an' gait wad lea'e us,
    And ev'n devotion!

---

14. onie grozet (grŏz' it): Any gooseberry.
15. rozet (rŏz' it): Rosin.
16. fell: Sharp.
17. smeddum: Powder.
18. Wad . . . droddum: Would put an end to you.
19. flannen toy: Flannel cap.
20. Or . . . boy: Or perhaps on some little ragged boy.
21. wyliecoat (wī' lē kōt'): Undershirt.
22. Lunardi: A balloon-shaped bonnet, named for Vincenzo Lunardi, a balloonist of the late 1700's.
23. abread: Abroad.
24. blastie's: Creature's.
25. Thae: Those.

RESPONDING TO THE SELECTION

Your Response

1. Do you think a louse is a suitable subject for a poem? Why or why not?

Recalling

2. (a) What is the louse doing? (b) What does the speaker command it to do instead?
3. What does the speaker say he would like to do in lines 27–30?
4. (a) Whom does the speaker address in the seventh stanza? (b) What does he warn her against?

Interpreting

5. (a) What conclusions can you draw about Jenny's character? (b) What evidence supports these assumptions?
6. What is the poet's tone—that is, his attitude toward his subject?
7. Like "To a Mouse," this poem contains a famous line that suggests the poem's theme. (a) What is that line? (b) What is the poem's theme?

Applying

8. William Hazlitt wrote, "Life is the art of being well deceived." How do you think Burns would respond to this statement? Explain your answer.

CRITICAL THINKING AND READING

Recognizing Satire

Satire is writing in which humor and wit are used to expose folly and flaws of humans or institutions. Popular since ancient Greek and Roman times, satire has long been an effective tool of both writers and reformers. In order to recognize the target of the poet's satire, reread the brief biography of Robert Burns on page 538. Based on information you find there and on the poem itself, answer the following questions about "To a Louse."

1. What do you imagine to be the social class (a) of the speaker? Why? (b) of Jenny? Why?

2. (a) What is the louse's "crime"? What does the speaker have in common with those he seems to feel the louse belongs to? (b) What is ironic about this?

THINKING AND WRITING

Comparing and Contrasting Two Poems

"To a Mouse" and "To a Louse" are often considered to be companion poems. Indeed, both poems address creatures of nature, and both are written in the Scottish dialect. Apart from these obvious similarities, consider other traits the poems share, as well as features that set the two apart. Consider in particular the theme of each poem and the attitude of the poet toward society. Discuss your findings with your classmates. Then write an essay comparing and contrasting the two poems. When you revise, make sure you have presented both similarities and differences. Proofread your essay and prepare a final draft.

LEARNING OPTIONS

1. **Writing.** Choose several stanzas of "To a Mouse" or "To a Louse" and rewrite Burns's Scottish dialect as standard modern English. You may have to change the meter and rhyme to some extent, but try to stay as close as possible to Burns's original. Share your version orally with the class. Be prepared to discuss the problems you encountered in translating.

2. **Speaking and Listening.** Practice reading "To a Louse" or "To a Mouse" aloud. Even without trying to reproduce a Scottish accent, what adjustments must you make when reading the dialect words? When you are comfortable enough with the poem, read it aloud to the class. Discuss the results with your classmates. How does the dialect add to the appeal of the poems? What would they lose without it?

Afton[1] Water

Robert Burns

Flow gently, sweet Afton, among thy green braes,[2]
Flow gently, I'll sing thee a song in thy praise;
My Mary's asleep by thy murmuring stream,
Flow gently, sweet Afton, disturb not her dream.

5   Thou stock-dove whose echo resounds through the glen,
Ye wild whistling blackbirds in yon thorny den,
Thou green-crested lapwing, thy screaming forbear,
I charge you, disturb not my slumbering fair.

How lofty, sweet Afton, thy neighboring hills,
10 Far marked with the courses of clear, winding rills;
There daily I wander as noon rises high,
My flocks and my Mary's sweet cot[3] in my eye.

---

1. Afton: The Afton is a river in Ayrshire, a former county in Southwestern Scotland.
2. braes (brāz): Slopes.
3. cot: Cottage.

THE RIVER DEE NEAR EATON HALL
Richard Wilson
The Barber Institute of Fine Arts
The University of Birmingham

How pleasant thy banks and green valleys below,
Where wild in the woodlands the primroses blow;
15   There oft as mild evening weeps over the lea,[4]
The sweet-scented birk[5] shades my Mary and me.

Thy crystal stream, Afton, how lovely it glides,
And winds by the cot where my Mary resides;
How wanton thy waters her snowy feet lave,
20   As gathering sweet flowerets she stems thy clear wave.

Flow gently, sweet Afton, among thy green braes,
Flow gently, sweet river, the theme of my lays;
My Mary's asleep by thy murmuring stream,
Flow gently, sweet Afton, disturb not her dream.

----

4. lea: Meadow.
5. birk: Birch.

RESPONDING TO THE SELECTION

Your Response
1. What moods and thoughts do slow-moving rivers evoke in you? How do they compare with the feelings conveyed in this poem?

Recalling
2. (a) Why does the speaker ask the Afton to "flow gently"? (b) What three other things does he command to be silent?
3. What is the speaker's occupation?

Interpreting
4. (a) What is the poem's mood—the feeling it conveys to the reader? (b) What words and phrases help create this mood?
5. (a) What assumptions can you make about Mary based on the poem? (b) about the speaker's feelings toward her?

6. Do you think the author, in composing these lines, had any purpose in mind other than to entertain? Explain your answer.

Applying
7. What songs or lullabies are you familiar with that carry the same message as this poem?

LEARNING OPTION

Cross-curricular Connection. Recordings of Scottish music can be found in most larger libraries. Find a recording of traditional Scottish music, including, if possible, the song "Flow Gently, Sweet Afton" or other songs with lyrics by Robert Burns. Play the recordings in class and discuss whether the music conveys qualities you would have expected, based on Burns's poems.

John Anderson, My Jo[1]

Robert Burns

John Anderson, my jo, John,
    When we were first acquent,
Your locks were like the raven,
    Your bonnie[2] brow was brent;[3]
5 But now your brow is beld,[4] John,
    Your locks are like the snow;
But blessings on your frosty pow,[5]
    John Anderson, my jo.

John Anderson, my jo, John,
10   We clamb[6] the hill thegither;
And monie[7] a canty[8] day, John,
    We've had wi' ane anither:
Now we maun[9] totter down, John,
    And hand in hand we'll go,
15 And sleep thegither at the foot,
    John Anderson, my Jo.

---

1. jo: Joy.
2. bonnie: Pretty.
3. brent: Unwrinkled.
4. beld: Bald.
5. pow: Head.
6. clamb: Climbed.
7. monie: Many.
8. canty: Cheerful.
9. maun: Must.

RESPONDING TO THE SELECTION

Your Response

1. Do you consider "John Anderson, My Jo" to be a sad poem or a happy one? Explain.

Recalling

2. (a) How does the speaker say John Anderson looked when she and he first met? (b) How does he look now?
3. What does the speaker say she and John Anderson will do now?

Interpreting

4. What do you suppose to be the relationship between the speaker and John Anderson? Explain your assumption.
5. (a) How would you paraphrase what the speaker is saying in the first four lines of the second stanza? (b) In the last four lines?

Applying

6. It has been noted that "John Anderson, My Jo" reveals Robert Burns's great talent for writing romantic poetry. Explain why you agree or disagree with this observation.

THINKING AND WRITING

Writing About Dialect

Three of the four poems you have read by Robert Burns are written in dialect. In an essay, explain how you believe the impact of these poems would have been different if the poet had written them in standard English. Before writing, consider the following questions. What factors do you think influenced Burns's decision to use dialect? What qualities of tone are communicated through the use of dialect? Of theme? What aspects of the message in "Afton Water" may have prompted the poet to write in standard English?

MULTICULTURAL CONNECTION

Dialects in Various Cultures

In his poem "John Anderson, My Jo," Robert Burns wrote in a Scottish dialect that differed greatly from the dialect of people living in nearby England. Unlike different languages, dialects can usually be understood by those who speak a different dialect but share a common language. Different dialects of the same language, however, may show differences in grammar as well as in vocabulary and pronunciation.

Dialect or language? The boundaries between languages and dialects are often hard to distinguish. Because speakers of Norwegian, Swedish, and Danish can understand one another, these languages are considered by some linguists to be dialects of a single, common language. In China, the eight major varieties of Chinese are considered dialects even though they differ among each other as much as French differs from Spanish. Among Native Americans, dialects and even some languages are spoken by fewer than fifty people.

Dialects have often been the first steps toward the creation of new languages. For example, when the Romans conquered Spain in the second century B.C., the soldiers who were stationed there spoke a dialect known as Vulgar Latin. This dialect eventually developed into the Romance languages: French, Spanish, Italian, Portuguese, and Romanian.

Increase in dialects. For centuries, the number of dialects steadily increased, largely because people stayed in one place and there was no great need to communicate with the outside world.

Today, thanks to television, tourism, and the fact that many people move from one part of their country to another, dialects may be slowly dying out. Will the world ever be a place in which everyone speaks only one language in only one way?

Exploring

Find out more about a dialect that is spoken in your region. Report on your findings.

WILLIAM BLAKE

1757–1827

When William Blake was four years old, he screamed because he saw God at his window. At age eight, while walking in the fields, he saw a tree filled with angels. To outside observers, Blake's "spells" might have seemed a cause for grave concern. In the home of his parents—themselves followers of the mystical teachings of Emanuel Swedenborg—the boy's "gift of vision" was something to be revered and nurtured. At least partly as a result of the family's way of life, the world was given a painter and a poet whose contributions are as rare as they are brilliant.

Blake was born in London, where his father ran a hosiery shop. He was never sent to school but instead, after expressing a desire to become a painter, was apprenticed to an engraver. Ultimately self-taught, he found his way into art and literature.

Between the ages of twelve and twenty, Blake wrote a series of poems, *Poetical Sketches,* that followed the tradition of English lyric poetry yet brought a new innocence to his subject matter. When he was thirty-two, he published his *Songs of Innocence,* which he had composed when he was younger, and which explored his favorite subject—the destiny of the human spirit. Instead of printing the collection, he developed a unique process whereby the words and illustrations were etched on metal plates with varnish, then painted in by hand. Because the process was time consuming, few books could be produced, and so to support himself, Blake hired himself out to other authors as an illustrator and sold what he could of his own works for one pound apiece. He also continued to write and in 1794 brought out a companion to *Songs of Innocence,* titled *Songs of Experience*.

In *Songs of Innocence,* Blake had suggested that by recapturing the imagination and wonderment of childhood, we could achieve the goal of self-awareness. The poems thus present views of the world as filtered through the eyes and mind of a child. In *Songs of Experience,* he insisted that a return to innocence was not, at least by itself, sufficient for us to attain an awareness of our true identity—that we must also recognize and attempt to understand the evils around us. Thus, Blake's credo was that there must be a union of opposites, a fusion of innocence and experience.

Unrecognized by his peers and living only slightly above poverty level, Blake spent his seventy years in constant creative activity. Only later, many years after his death, was his work understood. His poetry operates on two levels, one of them symbolic, the other literal. Both levels, however, address a single purpose—the renewal of the human spirit.

GUIDE FOR INTERPRETING

The Lamb; The Tiger; The Human Abstract; Infant Sorrow; A Poison Tree

Writers' Techniques

Symbolism. Symbolism is the use of a person, an object, a place, or an idea that represents itself and something beyond itself at the same time. Two well-known examples of symbolism are the use of the Stars and Stripes to represent the United States and the use of a skull and crossbones to represent something poisonous. While symbolism occurs in all types of literature, poetry, by virtue of its purity as an art form, is an especially natural vehicle for the presentation of ideas in symbolic form. Symbolism also permits the poet to introduce, in relatively little space, concepts and ideas that would ordinarily require more extensive treatment. In "The Tiger" William Blake uses the jungle cat to symbolize the savage and untamed forces in the world.

Focus

Imagine that suddenly you are four or five years old again. Look around at the people and objects in your presence, and describe what you see. Use words that you believe would be appropriate to a small child, and remember that much of what you take for granted now would seem new and wonderful to a younger you.

Primary Source

To realize Blake's importance in the history of engraving, it is important to know that engraving on metal had been abandoned since the sixteenth century. It was replaced by the easier method of etching, which did not involve as much labor and training.

Much attention has been focused on Blake's mastery of this difficult art form. The following excerpt is from a famous description of how Blake discovered his process of engraving.

> Blake, after deeply perplexing himself as to the mode of accomplishing the publication of his illustrated songs, without their being subject to the expense of letter-press, his brother Robert stood before him in one of his visionary imaginations, and so decidedly directed him in the way in which he thought he ought to proceed, that he immediately followed his advice, by writing his poetry, and drawing his marginal subjects of embellishments in outline upon the copper-plate with an impervious liquid, and then eating the plain parts or lights away with *aqua fortis* considerably below them, so that the outlines were left as a stereotype.

The Lamb

William Blake

Little Lamb, who made thee?
Dost thou know who made thee?
Gave thee life, and bid thee feed,
By the stream and o'er the mead;
5 Gave thee clothing of delight,
Softest clothing, woolly, bright;
Gave thee such a tender voice,
Making all the vales rejoice?
Little Lamb, who made thee?
10 Dost thou know who made thee?

Little Lamb, I'll tell thee,
Little Lamb, I'll tell thee.
He is called by thy name,
For He calls Himself a Lamb.
15 He is meek, and He is mild;
He became a little child.
I a child, and thou a lamb,
We are callèd by His name.
Little Lamb, God bless thee!
20 Little Lamb, God bless thee!

From a manuscript of "The Lamb," by William Blake
Lessing J. Rosenwald Collection, Library of Congress,
Washington, D.C.

RESPONDING TO THE SELECTION

Your Response

1. Is your response to a lamb similar to Blake's response? Why or why not?

Recalling

2. (a) What questions does the speaker ask in the first stanza? (b) What answer does he give in the second?
3. How does the speaker identify himself in the second stanza?

Interpreting

4. Blake uses repetition to create a mood, or overall feeling, in this poem. (a) What words does he repeat? (b) What feeling is created?
5. (a) How would you characterize the creator imagined in this poem? (b) Find at least three words that support your opinion.

Applying

6. Assume that you were asked to illustrate this poem. (a) What kinds of images would you use to represent the words? (b) What style of drawing might you use?

ANALYZING LITERATURE

A **symbol** is a thing, idea, person, or place that stands for more than just itself. For example, an old, bent man with a scythe symbolizes the end of the year. In poetry, symbolism enhances meaning. In "The Lamb" Blake offers two separate but related symbolic representations of the lamb.

1. What two things does the lamb symbolize? What about a lamb suggests its use as a symbol? What is the origin of the symbolic interpretation of the lamb in the second stanza?
2. Restate "The Lamb" in purely literal language. (a) What is the poet's message? (b) Is that message altered by restating the poem in literal terms? Explain.

The Tiger

William Blake

Tiger! Tiger! burning bright
In the forests of the night,
What immortal hand or eye
Could frame thy fearful symmetry?

5 In what distant deeps or skies
Burnt the fire of thine eyes?
On what wings dare he aspire?
What the hand dare seize the fire?

And what shoulder, and what art,
10 Could twist the sinews of thy heart?
And when thy heart began to beat,
What dread hand? and what dread feet?

What the hammer? what the chain?
In what furnace was thy brain?
15 What the anvil? what dread grasp
Dare its deadly terrors clasp?

When the stars threw down their spears,
And watered heaven with their tears,
Did he smile his work to see?
20 Did he who made the Lamb make thee?

Tiger! Tiger! burning bright
In the forests of the night,
What immortal hand or eye
Dare frame thy fearful symmetry?

RESPONDING TO THE SELECTION

Your Response

1. Do you agree with Blake's choice of the tiger to symbolize the awesome forces of nature? Why or why not? If not, what animal would you choose?

Recalling

2. What question is raised (a) in the first stanza? (b) in the second stanza? (c) in the fifth stanza?

Interpreting

3. (a) What properties of the tiger are suggested by the images mentioned in the fourth stanza? (b) What emotional impact is created by those images?
4. (a) What do you suppose to be the answer to the central question of the poem? (b) Is it the same answer as that given in "The Lamb"? Explain.

Applying

5. "The Lamb" was included in *Songs of Innocence;* "The Tiger" appeared in *Songs of Experience.* What does the use of the tiger as a symbol of experience suggest about Blake's view of that world?

LEARNING OPTION

Art. Blake's illustration for "The Tiger" (see page 555) shows a tiger looking much less fierce than the animal described in the poem. Make a drawing or painting of Blake's tiger that you think effectively illustrates its "fearful symmetry" and "deadly terrors." Display your artwork in the classroom.

ONE WRITER'S PROCESS

William Blake and "The Tiger"

PREWRITING

A Writer's Visions Blake's visions were apparently internal; he imagined them, and he never claimed to "see" things outside himself. He saw nothing surprising or spectacular about his visions—he simply thought it was the most obvious way to receive poetic inspiration.

He urged young poets to use visionary power whenever possible. This suggests that he felt that visions were available to anyone open to the idea.

Writing From Dictation Blake's visions were apparently exact, to the extent that he could draw the faces of famous people who would appear to him. Sometimes the visions appeared not as faces, but as voices. When they spoke to him, he wrote down the words, calling it dictation.

Whenever Blake stopped having his visions, he would feel completely unable to work until they returned.

DRAFTING

Making Choices Although Blake described himself as simply a vehicle through which the voices spoke, there is plenty of evidence that he did not write the words exactly as he heard them. In a letter, he says, ". . . I therefore have produced a variety in every line, both in cadences & number of syllables. Every word and every letter is studied and put into its fit place; the terrific numbers are reserved for the terrific parts, the mild & gentle for the mild & gentle parts, and the prosaic for inferior parts; all are necessary to each other."

Signs of Change In the poems written in his notebook, there is evidence of much hesitation, with many deletions and changes in line order. Look at the following first draft of "The Tiger." (Blake used the spelling *tyger.*) The words in parentheses are deleted on the manuscript; Blake crossed them out as he wrote, so these are not really revisions, but rather fast changes he made while writing the first draft:

The Tyger

Tyger, Tyger, burning bright
In the forests of the night,
What immortal hand or eye
(Could) (Dare) frame thy fearful symmetry?

(In what) (Burnt in) distant deeps or skies
(Burnt the) (The cruel) fire of thine eyes?
On what wings dare he aspire?
What the hand dare seize the fire?

And what should & what art
Could twist the sinews of thy heart?
And when thy heart began to beat
What dread hand and what dread feet
(Could fetch it from the furnace deep
And in thy horrid ribs dare steep
In the well of sanguine woe?
In what clay & in what mould
Were thy eyes of fury roll'd?)

(What) Where the hammer? (What) Where
    the chain?
In what furnace was thy brain?
What the anvil? What (the arm) (arm)
    (grasp) (clasp) dread grasp?

Tyger, Tyger burning bright
In the forests of the night,
What immortal hand & eye
Dare (form) frame thy fearful symmetry?

And (did he laugh) dare he (smile) (laugh)
    his work to see?

(What the (shoulder) ancle? what the
  knee?)
(Did) Dare he who made the lamb make
  thee?
When the stars threw down their spears
And water'd heaven with their tears?

If you look at "The Tiger" on page 553, you will see which of the deleted words Blake chose to keep. Notice that the entire fourth stanza has been deleted, and the last, or seventh, stanza has changed places with the sixth.

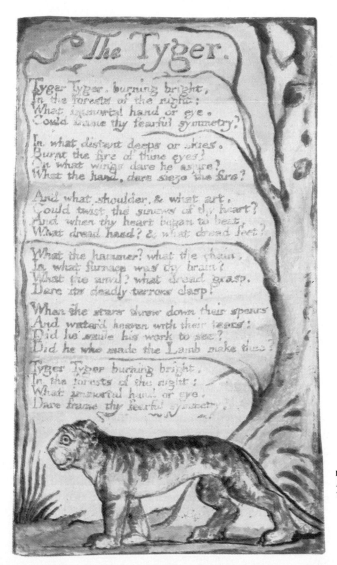

FROM A MANUSCRIPT OF "THE TIGER"
by William Blake
The Metropolitan Museum of Art

Inspiration Versus Editing When asked about the discrepancy between his claim of "dictation" and the heavily edited first drafts he produced, Blake wrote in a letter: "When I am commanded by the Spirits, then I write, and the moment I have written, I see the words fly about the room in all directions— It is then published—The Spirits can read and my MS: is of no further use . . ." Perhaps the reference to the flying words is Blake's poetic way of describing his editing process.

PUBLISHING

In 1876, nearly fifty years after Blake's death, a book titled *Works by William Blake* was published. The title page reads "Reproduced in Facsimile From the Original Editions. One hundred copies printed For private circulation." A publisher's name is not given. For the first time, the complete versions of "Songs of Innocence and Experience," including their illustrations, were published and made available along with Blake's other works.

THINKING ABOUT THE PROCESS

1. Do you agree with Blake that visions are available to everyone?
2. **Writing.** Choose a poem you have written and experiment with different revisions. Try transposing two of the stanzas, or try substituting different words for some you had initially chosen. How does your revision compare with the original poem?

The Human Abstract

William Blake

Pity would be no more,
If we did not make somebody Poor;
And Mercy no more could be,
If all were as happy as we;

5 And mutual fear brings peace,
Till the selfish loves increase;
Then Cruelty knits a snare,
And spreads his baits with care.

He sits down with holy fears,
10 And waters the ground with tears;
Then Humility takes its root
Underneath his foot.

Soon spreads the dismal shade
Of Mystery over his head;
15 And the Caterpillar and Fly
Feed on the Mystery.

And it bears the fruit of Deceit,
Ruddy and sweet to eat;
And the Raven his nest has made
20 In its thickest shade.

The Gods of the earth and sea,
Sought through Nature to find this Tree,
But their search was all in vain:
There grows one in the Human Brain.

RESPONDING TO THE SELECTION

Your Response

1. Do you think Blake has created an effective means of expressing his view of human nature in this poem? Why or why not?

Recalling

2. (a) What, according to the first stanza, would happen if no one in the world were poor? (b) If everyone were happy?
3. A tree is described in the third and following stanzas. Where is this tree said to grow?

Interpreting

4. In the fifth stanza, Blake writes of "the fruit of Deceit." (a) What do you think this phrase is intended to symbolize? (b) What other symbols are present in the poem? (c) How do they expand the poem's meaning?

Applying

5. (a) What does the title suggest about the poet's outlook? (b) Do you agree with the view he presents here? Explain your answer.

LEARNING OPTION

Writing. An abstract is a brief summary of the essential nature or content of something. Blake's vision of humanity may not match yours. Create your own "human abstract." Think about how you would express your understanding of the human condition in a manner both succinct and memorable. You may choose to write a poem, or you may write a prose abstract. Then share your abstract with your classmates.

Infant Sorrow

William Blake

My mother groaned, my father wept,
Into the dangerous world I leapt;
Helpless, naked, piping loud,
Like a fiend hid in a cloud.

5   Struggling in my father's hands,
Striving against my swaddling bands,
Bound and weary, I thought best
To sulk upon my mother's breast.

RESPONDING TO THE SELECTION

Your Response

1. Do you think Blake's picture of infancy in this poem is truthful? Why or why not?

Recalling

2. (a) How does the speaker describe each of his parents in the opening stanza? (b) The world?
3. What event has just occurred?

Interpreting

4. How would you describe this poem's tone—the feelings it awakens in the reader? What words contribute to these feelings?
5. (a) In what sense do you think the speaker is "bound," as he describes himself in line 7? (b) Where do you suppose he would prefer to be?

Applying

6. In which of the two volumes, *Songs of Innocence* or *Songs of Experience,* do you think this poem was included? Explain your assumption.

LEARNING OPTION

Writing. Write a brief poem on the subject of infancy. Your poem may have formal meter and rhyme or be written in free verse. What thoughts, feelings, memories, and activities do you associate with infancy? Like Blake, you might want to write your poem from the point of view of a newborn infant. What are your first experiences in the world? What do you remember? What are your fears and desires?

A Poison Tree

William Blake

I was angry with my friend:
I told my wrath, my wrath did end.
I was angry with my foe:
I told it not, my wrath did grow.

5   And I watered it in fears,
Night and morning with my tears;
And I sunnèd it with smiles,
And with soft deceitful wiles.

And it grew both day and night,
10   Till it bore an apple bright.
And my foe beheld it shine,
And he knew that it was mine,

And into my garden stole
When the night had veiled the pole;[1]
15   In the morning glad I see
My foe outstretched beneath the tree.

---

1. **pole:** Sky.

From a manuscript of "A Poison Tree," by William Blake
Lessing J. Rosenwald Collection, Library of Congress,
Washington, D. C.

RESPONDING TO THE SELECTION

Your Response

1. When do you think it is appropriate to express anger? How should it be expressed?

Recalling

2. (a) What does the speaker say occurred when he revealed his anger? (b) When he did not?
3. What "grows" out of the speaker's anger?

Interpreting

4. What sort of person do you find the speaker of this poem to be? What evidence can you find in support of your view?
5. (a) What symbols are used in the poem? (b) How effective do you find them to be?

Applying

6. (a) In what other famous piece of literature does an apple appear as a symbol? (b) What relationship can you detect between its symbolic value there and here?
7. (a) Of which other poem by Blake printed here is "A Poison Tree" most reminiscent in theme, structure, and symbolism? (b) Which do you think states its message more clearly? Give your reasons.

THINKING AND WRITING

Writing About Symbolism

Blake wrote to communicate his deeply mystical belief that coming of age forces a child to leave "Eden and struggle with a world that has lost its Paradise." For Blake, the uniting of innocence and experience carries with it an awareness of the inseparability of good and evil. His poems make extensive use of symbolism to convey that notion. List the symbols used by Blake in the six poems to represent these opposing forces of good and evil. Then in an essay discuss how these symbols clarify and add dimension to the notion underlying the poems. When you revise, make sure you have included adequate examples. Proofread your essay and prepare a final draft.

Primary Source

Why do people come to respect each other? It is intriguing to speculate on the interactions of great contemporaries and to wonder why this one or that one could not plainly see the merits of the other—which seem so clear to us from a distance of two centuries! An article that appeared in *The Examiner* in 1809, for example, described Blake as "an unfortunate lunatic whose personal inoffensiveness secures him from confinement." His now-famous *Descriptive Catalogue* was blasted as "the wild effusions of a distempered brain." At least one well-regarded peer did recognize Blake's talent, however.

In a letter dated May 24, writer Charles Lamb described Blake as "a most extraordinary man. . . . [His] wild designs accompany a splendid folio edition of the Night Thoughts. . . . He paints in water colors marvelous strange pictures, visions of his brain, which he asserts that he has seen. They have great merit. He has *seen* the Old Welsh bards on Snowdon . . . and has painted them from memory (I have seen his paintings). . . . His Pictures—one in particular, the Canterbury Pilgrims (far above Stothard's)—have great merit, but hard, dry, yet with grace. He has written a Catalogue of them, with a most spirited criticism on Chaucer, but mystical and full of Vision. . . . There is one [song] to a tiger, which I have heard recited . . . which is glorious, but alas! I have not the book; for the man is flown, whither I know not. . . . But I must look on his as one of the most extraordinary persons of the age."

The Restoration and the Eighteenth Century 1660–1798

A CALL FOR ORDER

The spirit of adventure, independence, and individualism that had characterized the sixteenth and early seventeenth centuries gave way in the eighteenth century to a desire for order, regularity, and certainty in all aspects of life. "How barbarously we yet write and speak," exclaimed John Dryden, uttering a commonly held view. Different versions of English were still used in different regions, including, for example, the Scots dialect Robert Burns immortalized. As with society itself, English had simply gotten out of hand! From 1660 to the end of the eighteenth century, one of the most important concerns facing the literary establishment was the reform of English.

LATIN PROVIDES A MODEL

Many looked back to Latin, the language of mathematics and theology, for a model of regular grammar, spelling, and style. Dryden, for example, confessed that at times he had to translate an idea into Latin in order to decide on the correct way to express it in English! It seemed to some that English, in its current wild state, could not last. Latin, on the other hand, had prevailed because it had a definite set of rules.

"A PROPOSAL FOR CORRECTING, IMPROVING, AND ASCERTAINING THE ENGLISH TONGUE"

Jonathan Swift was a particularly strong voice in the call for language reform. For example, he objected to words being shortened. While many of these words—such as *rep* for "reputation" and *incog* for "incognito"—have passed out of use, we have retained *mob* for "mobile," as well as inventing scores of new ones, such as *taxi, bus,* and *phone.* He equally detested the shortening of verbs, calling such words as *rebuk'd* and *disturb'd* "the disgrace of our language." He also proposed an end to slang terms, condemning "all the modern terms of art, *sham, banter, mob, bubble, bully, cutting, shuffling,* and *palming.*"

His 1712 call for the establishment of an English Academy—"A Proposal for Correcting, Improving, and Ascertaining the English Tongue"—was echoed in many quarters. Some gathered support from Italian and French models of language improvement. The Italians, for example, had specifically commissioned an Academy to order their language. In France Cardinal Richelieu had founded the Académie Française to purify French. Their task was "to labor with all possible care and diligence to give definite rules to our language, and to render it pure, eloquent and capable of treating the arts and sciences."

Nonetheless, the idea of an English Academy never gathered enough support to become a reality. Writer Daniel Defoe, for example, lent his voice to those opposing the idea, for he felt that if an official Academy was established to dictate correct grammar, "it would be as criminal to coin words as money."

THE QUESTION OF GRAMMAR AND SPELLING

But more and more educated people seriously examined English. They began with grammar, but to their dismay, they discovered that English had no grammar. Latin had rules; English had none. Even the notion that there should be a right way of spelling was foreign to many letter writers and printers, as the uneven spelling of their books and papers shows. Swift had this to say about the turmoil of English spelling:

> Another Cause . . . which hath contributed not a little to the maiming of our Language, is a foolish Opinion, advanced of late Years, that we ought to spell exactly as we speak; which besides the obvious Inconvenience of utterly destroying our Etymology, would be a thing we should never see an End of. Not only the several Towns and Countries of England have a different way of Pronouncing, but even here in London, they clip their Words after one Manner about the Court, another in the City, and a third in the Suburbs. . . .

The practice of spelling as you spoke had produced such monstrosities as "sartinly" (certainly), "gine" (join), and "byled" (boiled). Things had gotten even more confusing when writers had changed words based on mistaken derivations, so that *iland* became "island," *sissors*, "scissors." The time had come for a standardized source book.

SAMUEL JOHNSON'S *DICTIONARY*

While there had been other dictionaries, none approached the scope of Johnson's *Dictionary.* Johnson and his six assistants worked nine years, filling eighty large notebooks with the practical definitions of more than 40,000 words. His resulting two-volume work is a landmark that stood unrivalled for more than a century. In Boswell's words the *Dictionary* "conferred stability on the language of his country."

As the century drew to a close, English became increasingly refined and standardized as the language of power and learning.

Allegory of the Royal Society by Hollar

YOUR WRITING PROCESS

WRITING A NARRATIVE

"Persons attempting to find a motive in this narrative will be prosecuted; persons attempting to find a moral in it will be banished; persons attempting to find a plot in it will be shot. BY ORDER OF THE AUTHOR."

Mark Twain

Everyone loves a good story, and several of the selections in this unit fit that description: Pepys's diary, Defoe's journal, and "The Rape of the Lock." What makes a good story? Some ingredients are vivid details, believable characters, and dramatic action. Imagine that you have been asked to write a story for your school paper. How could you make your narrative both entertaining and informative?

> **Focus**
>
> **Assignment:** Write a narrative of an important event.
> **Purpose:** To entertain and inform.
> **Audience:** Readers of your school newspaper.

Prewriting

1. What's been happening? Brainstorm with a partner to come up with a list of possible topics. Think about community service, sports, academics, drama, music, art, awards, faculty or staff news, or special one-time projects.

2. Be a reporter. Once you have chosen a subject, interview some of the people involved to get their perspectives and insights. Prepare questions beforehand, and use a tape recorder or take careful notes. Be on the lookout for direct quotations that can add variety and life to your article.

3. Use a timeline. Whenever you write a narrative, a timeline can be used as an organizational tool. For example, this student made a timeline to summarize an eventful basketball season.

Student Model

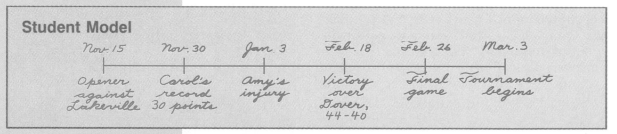

Nov. 15	Nov. 30	Jan. 3	Feb. 18	Feb. 26	Mar. 3
Opener against Lakeville	Carol's record 30 points	Amy's injury	Victory over Dover, 44–40	Final game	Tournament begins

4. With a partner, read and observe. Look at three or four news articles in your school newspaper and make observations abut style, organization, content, point of view, and level of formality. What do the articles seem to have in common? What makes each unique?

Drafting

1. Is the chronology clear? Make sure that you clearly indicate the passage of time in your narrative. Specific references are helpful, such as, *on Friday night* or *at 5:00.* Also, transitional words and phrases—such as *subsequently, meanwhile,* or *an hour later*—can indicate time relationships.

2. Include dialogue or quotations. Good stories make readers feel as if they are there, right in the middle of the action. Direct quotations will help to convey that sense of immediacy.

3. Try to incorporate sensory appeal. A good narrative also includes vivid descriptions. To make your descriptions come to life, use specific images in your draft and try to appeal to the five senses.

> ### Student Model
> In the final seconds of the last game of the season, the gym vibrated with stomping, clapping and chanting— "You can do it, Marauders!" The red digits on the scoreboard read 46-46 as the five girls huddled around their coach.

Revising and Editing

1. Show, don't tell. This rule is especially essential to narrative writing. Don't just make claims; provide your readers with concrete, specific details and word images that speak for themselves.

> ### Student Model
> The girls' basketball team ~~had their best season ever.~~ *ended the season with a 13-0 record and 663 points, stats that no other Marauder team ever approached.*

2. Be on your guard for clichés. If a phrase sounds too familiar, replace it. For example, instead of "As the ball arched, it was so quiet you could hear a pin drop," you might write, "As the ball arched, it was so quiet that I heard my neighbors breathing."

3. Four eyes are better than two. It's impossible for most writers to proofread their own work with complete accuracy. Trade narratives with a peer and proofread for each other. Read final copies more than once for grammar, usage, mechanics, and spelling.

VIEW IN HAMPSHIRE
Patrick Nasmyth

THE ROMANTIC AGE
1798–1832

One impulse from a vernal wood
  May teach you more of man,
Of moral evil and of good,
  Than all the sages can.

Sweet is the lore which Nature brings;
  Our meddling intellect
Misshapes the beauteous forms of things—
  We murder to dissect.

Enough of Science and of Art;
  Close up those barren leaves;
Come forth, and bring with you a heart
  That watches and receives.

from "The Tables Turned"
William Wordsworth

The preceding stanzas from "The Tables Turned," written in 1798, capture some of the main sentiments of a new age in British literature, an age in which writers "turned the tables" on eighteenth century thinking, insisting that the world be viewed through the heart, not the mind. During this period, which was named the Romantic Age by historians during the late 1800's, nearly all the attitudes and tendencies of eighteenth-century classicism and rationalism were redefined or changed dramatically. To understand how these changes occurred, it is necessary to examine not only the impact of events in Britain, but also the effects of the social and political upheaval that began taking place in other parts of the world.

Revolution and Reaction

Toward the end of the eighteenth century, two revolutions occurred outside England that indirectly threatened the stability of the British political and social systems. During the 1770's, the American colonies revolted against British rule, eventually winning their independence and forming a government based on the principles of freedom and equality. While the American Revolution divided British public opinion and aroused some awareness of the need for reform, its impact on British society was not nearly as great as that of the French Revolution, which demonstrated that it was possible for a long-standing government to be successfully challenged on its own soil.

The French Revolution began on July 14, 1789, when a group of French citizens stormed the Bastille, a Paris prison for political prisoners. In the weeks that followed, the revolutionaries placed limits on the powers of King Louis XVI, established a new government, and approved a document called the Declaration of the Rights of Man, affirming the principles of "liberty, equality, and fraternity." France became a constitutional monarchy.

Opposing Views

From the start, the revolution evoked strong reactions from both liberals and conservatives throughout the rest of Europe. In England, the ruling class felt threatened by the implications of the events in France, while most intellectuals, including several of the most important and influential writers of the Romantic Age, enthusiastically supported the revolution and the democratic ideals on which it was grounded. One ardent supporter of the revolution was Charles James Fox, leader of the Whig party, who declared, "How much the greatest event it is that ever happened in the world! and how much the best!" Poet William Wordsworth also spoke out in support of the revolution, and philosopher and novelist William Godwin (1756–1836) reacted to the revolution by writing *An Enquiry Concerning Political Justice* (1793), in which he predicted that British society would evolve peacefully into a nation characterized by freedom and equality. In contrast, Whig political thinker Edmund Burke (1729–1797), who had sympathized with the American Revolution, condemned the events in France. In *Reflections on the Revolution in France* (1790), he argued that the French, unlike the Americans, were attacking the very fabric of their society with complete disregard for their roots and ancestry. Burke warned that the revolution was bound to grow violent and mourned that "the age of chivalry is gone . . . and the glory of Europe is extinguished forever."

The Reign of Terror

Burke's views did not win wide acceptance in Britain until his dire predictions began coming true. As royalists, moderates, and radicals jockeyed for power, the French Revolution became more and more chaotic. In 1792, France declared war on Austria, touching off an invasion by Austrian and Prussian troops, whose leader proclaimed the intention of restoring the French king to full authority. Fuming with patriotic indignation, a radical group called the Jacobins gained control of the French legislative assembly, abolished the monarchy, and declared the nation a republic. Mobs attacked and killed many prisoners—including former aristocrats and priests—and soon French refugees began pouring into England with tales of these bloody "September massacres." Within weeks the revolutionaries had tried and convicted Louis XVI on a charge of treason. When Louis XVI went to the guillotine early in 1793, a revolutionary leader, Georges Danton, exclaimed: "The kings of Europe would challenge us. We throw them the head of a king!"

Following the execution, revolutionary violence reached its peak, as the Jacobins, under the leadership of Maximilien Robespierre, began what is called the Reign of Terror. Before the terror ended in the summer of 1794, revolutionary authorities had imprisoned thousands of royalists, moderates, and even radicals, sending some 17,000 of them—including Danton and finally Robespierre himself—to the guillotine.

British Reaction

The September massacres and the Reign of Terror were so shocking that even Britons who had sympathized with the French Revolution now turned against it. Conservative Britons, already hostile to the Revolution, demanded a crackdown on reformers within Britain, whom they denounced as dangerous Jacobins. Adding to British alarm was the success of France's new "citizen army," which expelled the Austrian and Prussian invaders and then set out to "liberate" other European nations from despotic rule. British leaders did not want France or any other nation to win dominance on the European continent. In 1793, France took the initiative by declaring war on Britain. Thus began a series of wars that would drag on for twenty-two years, creating fear and rigidity within Britain and effectively squelching during that time all hope of reform within British society.

The Tory government led by William Pitt (the Younger) began the reaction by outlawing all talk of parliamentary reform outside the halls of Parliament, banning public meetings, and suspending certain basic rights. Later, Pitt's government crushed a rebellion in Ireland. Liberal-minded Britons had no political outlet for their hopes and dreams. Many turned to literature and art as a way to find in the pristine world of romanticized nature the source of beauty and truth.

The Napoleonic Wars

Britain's battles against France took a new turn after 1799, when a military leader named Napoleon Bonaparte came to power in Paris. Napoleon had grandiose plans for French military expansion, and he was an able leader. After a brief break in French-British hostilities in 1802–1803, war resumed in earnest. Napoleon, who had declared himself emperor of France, planned an invasion of Britain, but had to abandon the plan after a British fleet under Lord Nelson defeated the French fleet at the Battle of Trafalgar, off Spain, in 1805. Napoleon's armies fought well against Britain's European allies, however, and by 1807 they controlled almost all of Europe as far east as the borders of Russia. Britain ruled the ocean, but Napoleon ruled Europe.

In 1812, Napoleon finally overextended himself by invading Russia. There his armies suffered a series of bloody defeats. At the same time, Napoleon was experiencing reverses in the west. His forces were defeated in the Peninsular War (1808–1814) in Portugal and Spain and, in 1814, British and allied armies closed in on him and forced him to abandon his crown. Napoleon was not finished, however. Exiled to the Mediterranean island of Elba, he plotted a return, and in 1815 he managed to escape to France, assemble an army, and resume rule for a period known as the Hundred Days. Napoleon's attempt to regain his former glory

NAPOLEON (THE CAMPAIGN IN FRANCE, 1814)
J.L.E. Meissonier

The Romantic Age (A.D. 1798– A.D. 1832)

Rosetta
Stone

Napoleon

Jane
Austen

| 1800 | 1806 | 1812 |

BRITISH EVENTS

- **William Wordsworth** and **Samuel Taylor Coleridge** publish *Lyrical Ballads.*
- Wolfe Tone Rebellion in Ireland.
  - Act of Union creates United Kingdom of Great Britain and Ireland.
  - Union Jack becomes official flag.
    - J.M.W. Turner's *Calais Pier* exhibited in London.
      - Henry Shrapnel invents exploding shell.
        - Battle of Trafalgar.

- Thomas Moore writes *Irish Melodies.*

- King George III declared permanently insane.
  - **Byron** publishes *Childe Harold's Pilgrimage.*
    - Jane Austen publishes *Pride and Prejudice.*
      - George Stephenson constructs first successful steam locomotive.
      - Walter Scott publishes *Waverley.*

WORLD EVENTS

- France: Napoleon becomes head of revolutionary government.
- Egypt: Rosetta Stone, key to deciphering hieroglyphics, discovered.
  - Italy: Volta builds first electric battery.
  - Spain: Goya paints *The Two Majas.*
    - Haiti: Toussaint L'Ouverture leads rebellion against French rule.
      - United States: Louisiana Territory purchased from France.
      - Germany: French occupy Hanover.
        - Germany: Beethoven composes *Symphony No. 3.*
        - France: Napoleon crowns himself emperor.
          - Eastern Europe: Napoleon defeats allies at Austerlitz.

- United States: Fulton's steamboat navigates Hudson River.
  - Italy: Excavation of Pompeii begins.
  - Germany: Goethe publishes *Faust,* Part I.
    - United States: Washington Irving writes "Rip Van Winkle."
      - South America: Simón Bolívar leads rebellions against Spanish rule.

- Russia: Napoleon loses hundreds of thousands of troops in retreat from Moscow.
- United States: War with Britain declared.
  - Mexico: Independence declared.
  - France: Napoleon abdicates and is exiled to Elba.
  - France: Napoleon returns for "Hundred Days."
  - Belgium: Napoleon defeated at Waterloo.
    - United States: William Cullen Bryant publishes "Thanatopsis."

Robert Fulton's Steamboat

John Keats

London in the 1820's

1818

1824

1830

- John MacAdam constructs roads of crushed stone.
  - **William Hazlitt** writes *Characters of Shakespeare's Plays*.
    - **Mary Wollstonecraft Shelley** publishes *Frankenstein, or the Modern Prometheus*.
      - Peterloo Massacre in Manchester.
      - **Percy Bysshe Shelley** publishes "Ode to the West Wind."
        - **John Keats** publishes "Ode on a Grecian Urn."
          - *Manchester Guardian* begins publication.
          - John Constable paints *The Grove*.

- First labor unions permitted.
  - Horse-drawn buses begin operating in London.
  - John Nash completes rebuilding of Buckingham Palace.
    - System for purifying London water installed.

- Liverpool-Manchester railway opens.
  - Michael Faraday demonstrates electromagnetic induction.
    - First Reform Act extends voting rights.
  - Catholic Emancipation Act passed.
  - Robert Peel establishes Metropolitan Police in London.

- First steamship crosses Atlantic.
  - Greece: War with Turkey begins.
  - Germany: Heinrich Heine publishes *Poems*.
    - Russia: Aleksandr Pushkin publishes *Eugene Onegin*.
      - United States: Monroe Doctrine closes Americas to further European colonization.

- Russia: Bolshoi Ballet established.
  - Germany: Mendelssohn composes *Overture to A Midsummer Night's Dream*.
  - United States: James Fenimore Cooper publishes *The Last of the Mohicans*.
    - France: Alexandre Dumas publishes *The Three Musketeers*.

- France: Stendhal publishes *The Red and the Black*.
  - United States: Edgar Allan Poe publishes *Poems*.
  - France: Victor Hugo publishes *The Hunchback of Notre Dame*.

ended on the battlefield at Waterloo, Belgium, in 1815, when the Duke of Wellington, British hero of the Peninsular War, led an allied army to a decisive victory.

All over Britain, people celebrated the end of the Napoleonic Wars with bonfires and other festivities. Royalists hailed the restoration of monarchical authority throughout Europe, while radicals mourned the failure of the revolutionary ideals of liberty and equality.

Coping With Society's Problems

Throughout the long wars with France, Britain's government kept a tight lid on domestic dissent. It ignored the problems caused by the Industrial Revolution—including the overcrowding of factory towns, the unpleasant and unsafe working conditions in the factories, and the long working hours and low pay experienced by the workers—and the problems only got worse.

Rumblings Among the People

Britain's government claimed to be following a hands-off policy, but in fact it sided openly with employers against workers, even helping to crush the workers' attempts to form unions. Meanwhile, the working class grew steadily larger and more restless. In the factory towns of northern England, workers protested the loss of jobs to new machinery in the violent Luddite Riots (1811–1813). In Manchester, mounted soldiers charged a peaceful mass meeting of cotton workers and killed several of them in what came to be known as the Peterloo Massacre (1819). To many, it seemed that British society was splitting into two angry camps—the working classes, who demanded reform, and the ruling classes, who resisted fiercely.

Beginnings of Reform

During this time, Britain had a series of weak and ineffective royal heads. George III, long subject to bouts of insanity, went irretrievably mad in 1811. His eldest son, the scandal-plagued and

unpopular George, Prince of Wales, ruled as Regent from 1811 to 1820—a period known as the Regency. Then the old king died and the Regent became George IV. When he died in 1830, his brother took over as William IV—an old and weak but amiable king, who ruled until 1837.

The weakness of these kings helped to enhance the power of the prime ministers—in theory named by the king, but in practice chosen by the strongest party in Parliament. The Tory leaders who held power during and immediately after the Napoleonic Wars rejected all suggestions of reform. A new generation of Tories emerged in the 1820's, however, and a trickle of reforms began. A law was passed in 1824 permitting Britain's first labor unions to organize, and in 1829 the Catholic Emancipation Act restored economic and religious freedoms to Roman Catholics.

The trickle grew into a stream of reforms following a Whig victory in the election of 1830. The Reform Bill of 1832 brought sweeping changes to British political life. By extending voting rights to the small but important middle class (males only), this law threatened the traditional dominance of land-owning aristocrats in Parliament. Moreover, in 1833 Parliament passed the first law governing factory safety. That same year, it also abolished slavery.

The Beginnings of Romanticism

Writers of the Romantic Age reacted strongly to the events of their time. They felt stirrings of excitement or repulsion as they contemplated the French Revolution. They saw the dramatic changes being wrought by the Industrial Revolution and longed for the simplicity and purity of the past. They sensed the rumblings of discontent and desperation that could not be silenced, even by the repressive measures of the war years. Those who had applauded the French Revolution, envisioning a new age of democracy and equality in Britain, were left in a state of bitter disappointment. They turned their attention to literary endeavors, creating a Romantic style that offered a new perspective on the world—a perspective that focused on nature and "the common people."

New Literary Concerns

Just as the French revolutionaries had at first discarded the customs and procedures that had traditionally governed French society, the Romantic writers abandoned many of the dominant attitudes and principles of eighteenth-century literature. New literary concerns emerged, many of which had been shaped either by the French revolutionary spirit or by the effects of the Industrial Revolution. The Romantic writers' interest in the trials and dreams of common people and their desire for radical change developed out of the democratic idealism that characterized the early part of the French Revolution, while their deep attachment to nature was a response to the consequences of industrialization. These and other characteristics of Romantic literature represent a distinct departure from the concerns associated with eighteenth-century classicism and rationalism. Because of this dichotomy, the prevailing ideas and attitudes of Romanticism are most easily grasped when viewed in contrast to those of the eighteenth century. The following chart identifies some of the contrasting tendencies.

It is customary to set the beginning of Britain's Romantic Age in 1798, the year in which William Wordsworth and Samuel Taylor Cole-

	Classicism and Rationalism	Romanticism
Sources of Inspiration	scientific observation of the outer world; logic	examination of inner feelings, emotions; imagination
	classical Greek and Roman literature	the literature of the Middle Ages
Attitudes and Interests	pragmatic	idealistic
	interested in science, technology	interested in the mysterious and supernatural
	concerned with general, universal experiences	concerned with the particular
	believed in following standards and traditions	sought to develop new forms of expression
	felt optimistic about the present	romanticized the past
	emphasized moderation and self-restraint	tended toward excess and spontaneity
	appreciated elegance, refinement	appreciated folk traditions
Social Concerns	valued stability and harmony	desired radical change
	favored a social hierarchy	favored democracy
	interested in maintaining the aristocracy	concerned with common people
	concerned with society as a whole	concerned with the individual
	believed that nature should be controlled by humans	felt that nature should be untamed

ridge published the *Lyrical Ballads,* establishing the Romantic principles that would dominate British literature for several decades. However, the ideas of Romanticism arose on continental Europe well before the turn of the century. Even in Britain a handful of poets—most notably Thomas Gray, Robert Burns, and William Blake—had displayed some of the characteristics of Romantic thinking before *Lyrical Ballads* was published.

Jean-Jacques Rousseau

Though he died before the start of the Romantic Age, Swiss-born writer Jean-Jacques Rousseau (1712–1778), a leading philosopher of eighteenth-century France, planted one of the seeds from which Romanticism grew. Rousseau saw society as a force of evil that infringed on personal liberty and human happiness. "Man is born free," he wrote, "and everywhere he is in chains." He reasoned that humanity should revert to its natural state, abandoning its stifling social institutions and outworn philosophies and listening instead to nature, instinct, and intuition.

Rousseau prepared the way for political revolution. The Americans who declared their independence in 1776 quoted Rousseau often, and the French revolutionaries of 1789 quoted him even more frequently. Rousseau also prepared the way for a new artistic movement, Romanticism. During the latter part of the eighteenth century, in the German-speaking areas of Europe, which were not yet a unified nation and often suffered from the repressive policies of powerful Prussia and Austria, a group of nationalistically minded writers began incorporating Rousseau's ideas into major works of poetry, drama, and fiction.

Johann Wolfgang von Goethe

The most influential of this group was Johann Wolfgang von Goethe (1749–1832). In search of inspiration, Goethe turned to the German literature of the Middle Ages, early vernacular works filled with myth and superstition, adventure and passion, not unlike the Anglo-Saxon *Beowulf.* In these works Goethe found not only a source of pride for a new generation of German writers but also a primitive simplicity much in keeping with Rousseau's ideas and values. A fascination with medieval times—the same Middle Ages that "enlightened" thinkers had despised—soon became characteristic of the emerging artistic movement. In fact, the movement would later be named the Romantic Age because of its interest in medieval *romances*—imaginary tales of adventure written in one of the Roman dialects, the early forms of languages derived from Latin.

The Romantic Age in British Poetry

Romanticism was a movement that affected not only literature but all the arts. In music, it produced such brilliant European composers as Germany's Ludwig van Beethoven (1770–1827) and Austria's Franz Schubert (1797–1828), but no one of comparable stature in Britain. In painting, it influenced the intensely personal and warmly spontaneous rural landscapes of Britain's John Constable (1776–1837) and J.M.W. Turner (1775–1851). However, it is for literature, and especially for poetry, that Britain's Romantic Age is most famous.

Wordsworth and Coleridge: A Break With the Past

When William Wordsworth (1770–1850) asked his friend Samuel Taylor Coleridge (1772–1834) to collaborate with him in the publication of *Lyrical Ballads,* he was well aware that their collection of poetry would make a distinct break with the past. To underscore that break, Wordsworth included in the second (1800) and third (1802) editions of *Lyrical Ballads* a preface explaining the new poetic principles he and Coleridge had employed. That preface defined poetry as "the spontaneous overflow of powerful feelings" and explained that poetry "takes its origin from emotion recollected in tranquility." An emphasis on the emotions, then, was central to the

CALAIS PIER: AN ENGLISH PACKET ARRIVING
J.M.W. Turner

new Romantic poetry the two men were creating.

Equally important was subject matter. According to the preface, poetry should deal with "incidents and situations from common life" over which the poet throws "a certain coloring of imagination, whereby ordinary things should be presented . . . in an unusual way." Wordsworth's poems gave "the charm of novelty to things of every day," as Coleridge later said. Coleridge, on the other hand, provided the "coloring of imagination," creating imaginative settings and mysterious sequences of events.

Finally, Wordsworth's preface spoke about incorporating human passions with "the beautiful and permanent forms of nature." An emphasis on nature would become another important characteristic of British Romantic verse, and Wordsworth would frequently be described as a "nature poet."

The Romantic view of nature was quite different from that of most eighteenth-century litera-ture. Nature was not a force to be tamed and analyzed scientifically; rather, it was a wild, free force that could inspire poets to instinctive spiritual understanding. In "The Tables Turned," Wordsworth advised readers to

Come forth into the light of things,
Let Nature be your Teacher.

In idealizing unspoiled nature, Wordsworth and the other Romantics were not merely abandoning the philosophies of classicism and rationalism; they were condemning the Industrial Revolution and its encroachment on the English countryside.

Lyrical Ballads met a cool reception at first, but with time it came to be regarded as the cornerstone of Britain's Romantic Age. Also with time, Wordsworth and Coleridge became respected members of Britain's literary establishment. Their literary ideas began to seem less radical than they once had, and their political thinking—deeply marked by events in France—grew more conservative.

The Second Generation of Romantic Poets

Wordsworth and Coleridge blazed the way for a new generation of British Romantic poets—the so-called "second generation" of poets, which included Byron, Shelley, and Keats. Coming of age during the Napoleonic era and the Regency, these younger poets rebelled even more strongly than Wordsworth and Coleridge against the British conservatism of the time. All three died abroad after tragically short lives, and their viewpoints were those of disillusioned outsiders.

George Gordon, Lord Byron (1788–1824), did not begin life as an outsider. On the contrary, he was part of the British aristocracy—a member of the House of Lords, an intimate of high-born men and women. Although critics responded unfavorably to his early poetry, Byron persisted and finally achieved success when he published *Childe Harold's Pilgrimage* (1812). Handsome, egotistical, and aloof, Byron became the darling of elegant society—but not for long. Shocked by Byron's radical politics and scandalous love affairs, London hostesses began to shun him, and Byron left Britain in 1816, never to return. He died of a fever while fighting with Greek revolutionaries in their struggle to win independence from Turkey.

SKETCH FOR HADLEIGH CASTLE, c. 1828–29
John Constable

Because they had abandoned their democratic ideals, Byron wrote scornfully about Wordsworth and Coleridge. However, much of his work reflects their Romantic style. His long narrative poems often feature brooding, passionate, rebellious figures. Such "Byronic" heroes and heroines became a common feature of the literature of the Romantic Age. On the other hand, some of Byron's work—such as his poem *Don Juan* (1819–1824)—owes more to eighteenth-century mock epics than it does to Wordsworth and Coleridge.

Byron's friend Percy Bysshe Shelley (1792–1822) was also well-born and politically radical—more consistently radical, in fact, than Byron. In poems such as "Song to the Men of England" (1819), Shelley urged England's lower classes to rebel.

Like Byron, Shelley was shunned for his radical ideas; he left Britain for good in 1818. Unlike Byron, however, Shelley did not attain fame in his own lifetime. Yet he is now remembered for the fervor he brought to lyric poetry in such intensely personal and emotional verses as "To a Skylark" (1821).

John Keats (1795–1821), the third great figure in the second generation of Romantic poets, was also a master of lyrical poetry. Unlike Byron and Shelley, Keats was born outside elegant society, the son of a London stable keeper. Keats trained to be a doctor, then abandoned his medical career to pursue his passion for poetry. He produced many of his greatest poems in a burst of creativity during the first nine months of 1819—works like *The Fall of Hyperion* and "Ode on a Grecian Urn." Unfortunately, however, Keats was already struggling against tuberculosis. Hoping to recuperate in a warmer climate, he traveled to Italy, where he died at the age of twenty-five. By his own request, his epitaph reads: "Here lies one whose name was writ in water."

The Romantic Age in British Prose

Poetry was the dominant literary form during the Romantic Age, but not the only one. Many significant prose works also appeared, mainly in the form of essays and novels. This was a dry period for drama; only two theaters were licensed to produce plays, and they tended to feature popular spectacles rather than serious plays. However, Shelley and other poets did write closet dramas, verse works intended to be read rather than produced on the stage.

The Romantic Essayists

British readers of the Romantic Age could find brilliant literary criticism and topical essays in a variety of new periodicals. The earliest of these periodicals reflected the conservative and neoclassical ideals of an earlier age; they roundly condemned the Romantic poets and their work. In time, however, periodicals that were more sympathetic to the Romantics came into being. One such publication, *The London Magazine,* although it appeared only from 1820 to 1829, attracted major contributions from the three greatest essayists of the era: Charles Lamb (1775–1834), William Hazlitt (1778–1830), and Thomas De Quincey (1785–1859). Lamb, in particular, transformed the informal essay of the eighteenth century into a more personal, more introspective Romantic composition.

The Romantic Novelists

Unlike the Romantic poets, the novelists of the Romantic Age did not make a sharp break with the past. In fact, the three main types of Romantic novels—the Gothic novel, the novel of manners, and the historical romance—all represented elaborations on earlier forms.

The Gothic novel first appeared in the middle of the eighteenth century. It featured a number of standard ingredients, including brave heroes and heroines, threatening scoundrels, vast eerie castles, and ghosts. The Romantic fascination with mystery and the supernatural made such novels quite popular during the Romantic Age. One of the most successful was *Frankenstein, or the Modern Prometheus* (1818), written by Shelley's wife, Mary Wollstonecraft Shelley (1797–1851).

SIR WALTER SCOTT/ABBOTSFORD FAMILY, 1804
Sir David Wilkie

The Romantic novel of manners carried on in the tradition of earlier writers by turning a satirical eye on British customs. The most highly regarded writer of novels of manners was Jane Austen (1775–1817), whose works include *Sense and Sensibility* (1811) and *Pride and Prejudice* (1813). Her incisive portrayals of character are more reflective of the classical sensibility of the eighteenth century than the Romantic notions of the new age.

Historical romances—imaginative works of fiction built around a real person or historical event—had appeared long before the Romantic Age, but they attained their peak of popularity in the work of Sir Walter Scott (1771–1832). Passionately devoted to his native Scotland, Scott wrote about the days of knights and chivalry. Although he expressed a Scottish nationalism not unlike the nationalism of Germany's Romantic writers, Scott remained popular with England's ruling class, who apparently did not view his tales of a bygone age as a threat to the status quo.

The close of Britain's Romantic Age is usually set in 1832, the year of the passage of the First Reform Bill. However, the ideas of Romanticism remained a strong influence on many writers from following generations. In fact, even today we can detect elements of Romanticism in many major works of contemporary fiction and poetry as well as in TV dramas, movies, and popular songs.

BRITISH VOICES

Bliss was it on that dawn to be alive . . .
France standing on the top of golden hours
And human nature seemed born again.
  William Wordsworth, *The Prelude*

 But yet I know, where'er I go.
That there hath past away a glory from the earth . . .
 nothing can bring back the hour
Of splendor in the grass, of glory in the flower.
  William Wordsworth, "Ode: Intimations of Immortality from
    Recollections of Early Childhood"

Poetry is not the proper antithesis to prose, but to science.
  Samuel Taylor Coleridge, *Definitions of Poetry*

One half the world cannot understand the pleasures of the
other.
  Jane Austen, *Emma*

It is a truth universally acknowledged that a man in
possession of a good fortune must be in want of a wife.
  Jane Austen, *Pride and Prejudice*

Clear writers, like fountains, do not seem so deep as
they are.
  Charles Lamb, *Imaginary Conversation*

I love not man the less, but Nature more.
  George Gordon, Lord Byron, *Childe Harold's Pilgrimage*

If Winter comes, can Spring be far behind?
  Percy Bysshe Shelley, "Ode to the West Wind"

The poetry of earth is never dead.
  John Keats, "Sonnet: On the Grasshopper and the Cricket"

"Beauty is truth, truth beauty"—that is all
Ye know on earth, and all ye need to know.
  John Keats, "Ode on a Grecian Urn"

READING CRITICALLY

The Literature of 1798–1832

When you read literature, it is important to place it in its historical context. Doing so will help you to see how it reflects the dominant ideas of its time and appreciate the techniques the writer used in conveying these ideas.

HISTORICAL CONTEXT During the years from 1798 to 1832, English life was dramatically influenced by the aftereffects of the French Revolution and the realities of industrialization. While many English intellectuals supported the democratic ideals upon which the French Revolution was grounded, the English ruling class took measures to ensure that a similar revolution could not occur in England. At the same time, the industrial revolution was having a profound social and economic impact on the nation. English cities grew rapidly and became the nation's economic centers. Factory workers labored long hours for extremely low wages, and young children often had to work to help support their families. It became increasingly clear that new government policies were needed to accommodate these changes. Yet few political changes occurred until 1832, when the First Reform Bill was passed.

LITERARY MOVEMENTS Toward the end of the eighteenth century, an artistic movement which came to be known as Romanticism developed as a reaction against the dominant ideas and standards of Rationalism. Unlike the Rationalists, who stressed logic and reason, Romantic writers emphasized emotions and the imagination. They also possessed a strong belief in democracy, an interest in mystery and the supernatural, a belief in excess and spontaneity, a concern for common people, and a love of nature.

WRITERS' TECHNIQUES The Romantic period was an age in which poetry flourished. Using the language of common people, the Romantic poets wrote lyric poems that generally focused on ordinary situations and ordinary people. Although poetry was the major form of literary expression during the period, a number of significant novels and essays were also produced. Like Romantic poetry, these works reflect the dominant ideas and attitudes of the age.

WILLIAM WORDSWORTH

1770–1850

William Wordsworth is among the small group of writers and poets who truly deserve the title "pioneer." His name is almost synonymous with the movement known as Romanticism. Wordsworth demonstrated that poetry was a free—a *living*—form of artistic expression, a view that contrasted sharply with that held by the generation writing before him. Whereas the Neoclassicists, as these earlier poets were called, insisted that poetry address a narrow range of topics and be rigidly structured, Wordsworth's poems were written for the common people—and in a common language.

Born in the beautiful Lake District of England, Wordsworth loved to roam the hills and sit and meditate by the streams. He was well suited to country living and in later years found nature to be the source of his poetic inspiration and internal peace. Though his parents died when he was young—his mother when he was eight, his father when he was thirteen—Wordsworth's education was seen to, and in 1787 he entered Cambridge. After graduation he traveled through Europe, spending considerable time in France. There he became caught up in the popular side of the French Revolution, with its emphasis on the rights of the individual. He also found time to fall in love with a young woman named Annette Vallon.

Wordworth's involvement in the revolution and his affair with Annette ended abruptly, however, when England declared war on France in 1793 and he was forced to return to his homeland. A year later the revolution was halted altogether with the execution of its leader, Robespierre. Wordsworth, seeing his ideals dashed, lapsed into a deep depression. Two people who came to his spiritual rescue were his sister Dorothy and his good friend Samuel Taylor Coleridge.

With Coleridge, Wordsworth composed *Lyrical Ballads* (1798), a collection of poems that reflected his "revolutionary" approach to poetry. In the preface to the collection, Wordsworth put forth his view that poetry should deal with common people and ordinary experiences—that its style and form should reflect "a spontaneous overflow of emotion." Though the book was not received favorably at first, it eventually gained recognition as a major poetic work and is seen today as one of the most influential works on poetic theory ever written in the English language.

GUIDE FOR INTERPRETING

Lines Composed a Few Miles Above Tintern Abbey; My Heart Leaps Up When I Behold

Writers' Techniques

Romanticism. Romanticism was a literary movement in Europe in the late eighteenth century. It grew out of a negative reaction to the rigid, formal guidelines and forced subject matter that typified the poetry and art of the previous age. Whereas rationalism and a reliance on scientific doctrine were highly valued by the earlier Neoclassicists, Romanticists believed in the virtues of the imagination and fantasy. The Romantic writer was not only permitted, but encouraged, to give vent to his or her emotions—to write spontaneously, from the heart. Love of nature, and an idealization of rural life were basic to Romantic poetry. Many of these aspects of the Romantic credo figure in the poems of William Wordsworth. Subjectivity in particular is clearly visible in his "Lines Composed a Few Miles Above Tintern Abbey."

Focus

Think about a place you have been that made a vivid impression on you. You might choose a place you visited on vacation or one where you lived. Close your eyes and try to visualize this locale, concentrating on details. Then write about it, describing everything you "see."

Primary Source

To offset the cost of a hike to the Valley of Stones, Wordsworth and Coleridge planned to collaborate on a ballad for publication in *The New Monthly Magazine*. They began to compose "The Ancient Mariner" as they walked but soon realized that their styles were too different. Instead, they decided to collaborate on a book of poems. Twenty years later, in 1817, Coleridge described the division of labor:

> The thought suggested itself (to which of us I do not recollect) that a series of poems might be composed of two sorts. In the one, the incidents and agents were to be, in part at least, supernatural. . . . For the second class, subjects were to be chosen from ordinary life; the characters and incidents were to be such as will be found in every village and vicinity. . . .

Lines Composed a Few Miles Above Tintern Abbey

William Wordsworth

This poem was written in 1798 during Wordsworth's second visit to the valley of the River Wye and the ruins of Tintern Abbey, once a great medieval church, in Wales. Wordsworth had passed through the region alone five years earlier; this time he brought his sister with him to share the experience. Of this visit and the poem it inspired, Wordsworth wrote, "No poem of mine was composed under circumstances more pleasant for one to remember than this."

Five years have past; five summers, with the length
Of five long winters! and again I hear
These waters, rolling from their mountain springs
With a soft inland murmur. Once again
5 Do I behold these steep and lofty cliffs,
That on a wild secluded scene impress
Thoughts of more deep seclusion; and connect
The landscape with the quiet of the sky.
The day is come when I again repose
10 Here, under this dark sycamore, and view
These plots of cottage ground, these orchard tufts,
Which at this season, with their unripe fruits,
Are clad in one green hue, and lose themselves
'Mid groves and copses. Once again I see
15 These hedgerows, hardly hedgerows, little lines
Of sportive wood run wild: these pastoral farms,
Green to the very door; and wreaths of smoke
Sent up, in silence, from among the trees!
With some uncertain notice, as might seem
20 Of vagrant dwellers in the houseless woods,
Or of some hermit's cave, where by his fire
The hermit sits alone.

            These beauteous forms,
Through a long absence, have not been to me
As is a landscape to a blind man's eye:
25 But oft, in lonely rooms, and 'mid the din
Of towns and cities, I have owed to them

TINTERN ABBEY
J. M. W. Turner
British Museum

Lines Composed a Few Miles Above Tintern Abbey 581

In hours of weariness, sensations sweet,
Felt in the blood, and felt along the heart;
And passing even into my purer mind,
30   With tranquil restoration—feelings too
Of unremembered pleasure: such, perhaps,
As have no slight or trivial influence
On that best portion of a good man's life.
His little, nameless, unremembered, acts
35   Of kindness and of love. Nor less, I trust,
To them I may have owed another gift,
Of aspect more sublime; that blessed mood,
In which the burthen[1] of the mystery,
In which the heavy and the weary weight
40   Of all this unintelligible world,
Is lightened—that serene and blessed mood,
In which the affections gently lead us on—
Until, the breath of this corporeal frame[2]
And even the motion of our human blood
45   Almost suspended, we are laid asleep
In body, and become a living soul;
While with an eye made quiet by the power
Of harmony, and the deep power of joy,
We see into the life of things.

                               If this
50   Be but a vain belief, yet, oh! how oft—
In darkness and amid the many shapes
Of joyless daylight; when the fretful stir
Unprofitable, and the fever of the world,
Have hung upon the beatings of my heart—
55   How oft, in spirit, have I turned to thee,
O sylvan[3] Wye! thou wanderer through the woods,
How often has my spirit turned to thee!

      And now, with gleams of half-extinguished thought,
With many recognitions dim and faint,
60   And somewhat of a sad perplexity,
The picture of the mind revives again;
While here I stand, not only with the sense
Of present pleasure, but with pleasing thoughts
That in this moment there is life and food
65   For future years. And so I dare to hope,
Though changed, no doubt, from what I was when first
I came among these hills; when like a roe[4]

---

1. burthen: Burden.
2. corporeal (kôr pôr′ ē əl) **frame:** Body.
3. sylvan (sil′ vən): Wooded.
4. roe: A type of deer.

I bounded o'er the mountains, by the sides
Of the deep rivers, and the lonely streams,
70   Wherever nature led: more like a man
Flying from something that he dreads, than one
Who sought the thing he loved. For nature then
(The coarser pleasures of my boyish days,
And their glad animal movements all gone by)
75   To me was all in all—I cannot paint
What then I was. The sounding cataract
Haunted me like a passion; the tall rock,
The mountain, and the deep and gloomy wood,
Their colors and their forms, were then to me
80   An appetite; a feeling and a love,
That had no need of a remoter charm,
By thought supplied, nor any interest
Unborrowed from the eye. That time is past,
And all its aching joys are now no more,
85   And all its dizzy raptures. Not for this
Faint[5] I, nor mourn nor murmur; other gifts
Have followed; for such loss, I would believe,
Abundant recompense. For I have learned
To look on nature, not as in the hour
90   Of thoughtless youth; but hearing oftentimes
The still, sad music of humanity,
Nor harsh nor grating, though of ample power
To chasten and subdue. And I have felt
A presence that disturbs me with the joy
95   Of elevated thoughts; a sense sublime
Of something far more deeply interfused,
Whose dwelling is the light of setting suns,
And the round ocean and the living air,
And the blue sky, and in the mind of man;
100   A motion and a spirit, that impels
All thinking things, all objects of all thought,
And rolls through all things. Therefore am I still
A lover of the meadows and the woods
And mountains; and of all that we behold
105   From this green earth; of all the mighty world
Of eye, and ear—both what they half create,
And what perceive; well pleased to recognize
In nature and the language of the sense,
The anchor of my purest thoughts, the nurse,
110   The guide, the guardian of my heart, and soul
Of all my moral being.

                    Nor perchance.
If I were not thus taught, should I the more

_____
5. faint: Lose heart.

Suffer[6] my genial spirits[7] to decay;
For thou art with me here upon the banks
115   Of this fair river; thou my dearest Friend,[8]
My dear, dear Friend, and in thy voice I catch
The language of my former heart, and read
My former pleasures in the shooting lights
Of thy wild eyes. Oh! yet a little while
120   May I behold in thee what I was once,
My dear, dear Sister! and this prayer I make,
Knowing that Nature never did betray
The heart that loved her; 'tis her privilege,
Through all the years of this our life, to lead
125   From joy to joy; for she can so inform
The mind that is within us, so impress
With quietness and beauty, and so feed
With lofty thoughts, that neither evil tongues,
Rash judgments, nor the sneers of selfish men,
130   Nor greetings where no kindness is, nor all
The dreary intercourse of daily life,
Shall e'er prevail against us, or disturb
Our cheerful faith, that all which we behold
Is full of blessings. Therefore let the moon
135   Shine on thee in thy solitary walk;
And let the misty mountain winds be free
To blow against thee: and, in after years,
When these wild ecstasies shall be matured
Into a sober pleasure; when thy mind
140   Shall be a mansion for all lovely forms,
Thy memory be as a dwelling place
For all sweet sounds and harmonies; oh! then,
If solitude, or fear, or pain, or grief,
Should be thy portion, with what healing thoughts
145   Of tender joy wilt thou remember me,
And these my exhortations! Nor, perchance—
If I should be where I no more can hear
Thy voice, nor catch from thy wild eyes these gleams
Of past existence—wilt thou then forget
150   That on the banks of this delightful stream
We stood together; and that I, so long
A worshipper of Nature, hither came
Unwearied in that service: rather say
With warmer love—oh! with far deeper zeal
155   Of holier love. Nor wilt thou then forget,
That after many wanderings, many years

---

6. suffer: Allow.
7. genial spirits: Creative powers.
8. Friend: His sister Dorothy.

Of absence, these steep woods and lofty cliffs,
And this green pastoral landscape, were to me
More dear, both for themselves and for thy sake!

RESPONDING TO THE SELECTION

Your Response

1. Have you ever returned to a special place after a long absence? What was your reaction?

Recalling

2. In "Lines Composed a Few Miles Above Tintern Abbey," how have the poet's memories of his first visit to the Wye valley altered him?
3. (a) Apart from his pleasure at the moment, what does the poet hope to gain from his second visit to the valley? (b) What does he hope his sister will gain?

Interpreting

4. (a) At what time of year does the poet make his second visit to the area near Tintern Abbey? (b) Find evidence in the poem that supports your answer.
5. In line 35 of the poem, the poet mentions "another gift" that his contact with this rural scene has bestowed upon him. Briefly describe this gift.

Applying

6. Do you think it was Wordsworth's wish that everyone attempt to share his experience with and attitudes toward nature? Do you think he believed everyone was capable? Explain.

ANALYZING LITERATURE

Understanding Romanticism

Romanticism stressed the importance of emotion and imagination as tools of the artist. To Wordsworth, one of the movement's foremost practitioners, Romanticism also meant a return to nature and an escape from the contamination of modern civilization. Wordsworth urged the poet to explore his or her innermost feelings—to become attuned to the stirrings of the soul. For this reason, much of Romantic art and poetry has a spiritual, at times almost mystical, quality.

Look again at "Lines Composed a Few Miles Above Tintern Abbey," and as you read be on the lookout for the words *soul, heart,* and *spirit.* Paraphrase (state in your own words) each of the poet's thoughts that contains one or more of these words. Explain how each thought relates to the ideals of the Romantic movement.

CRITICAL THINKING AND READING

Comparing and Contrasting Experiences

A careful reading of "Tintern Abbey" reveals that even as a young man Wordsworth was a sensitive and perceptive person. And yet the poem details certain differences between his first and second trips to the Wye valley. Skim the poem for details and then describe:

1. the differences in the poet's behavior.
2. the differences and similarities in his thoughts and attitudes.

THINKING AND WRITING

Writing About Romanticism

The twentieth-century American writer Thomas Wolfe defined the true Romantic feeling as "not the desire to escape life, but to prevent life from escaping you." Freewrite, exploring the meaning of this quotation. Then write an essay explaining how "Tintern Abbey" typifies the true Romantic feeling as defined by Wolfe. When you revise, make sure you have supported your opinion with details from the poem.

My Heart Leaps Up When I Behold

William Wordsworth

My heart leaps up when I behold
    A rainbow in the sky:
So was it when my life began;
So is it now I am a man;
So be it when I shall grow old,
    Or let me die!
The child is father of the Man;
And I could wish my days to be
Bound each to each by natural piety.[1]

---

1. natural piety: Devotion to nature.

LANDSCAPE WITH RAINBOW
Joseph Wright of Derby
Derby Art Gallery

Your Response

1. Does a rainbow make you feel the kind of excitement the poet feels? Why or why not?

Recalling

2. What is the poet's hope in the poem "My Heart Leaps Up When I Behold"?

Interpreting

3. What general statement might the poet have used in place of the first two lines?

4. What do you think the poet means when he speaks of "natural piety"?

Applying

5. (a) What interest of yours would you like to share with other people? (b) How best might you communicate this to them?

■ CRITICAL THINKING AND READING

Interpreting a Paradox

A **paradox** is a statement that makes sense in spite of an apparent contradiction. "Youth is wasted on the young," for example, is paradoxical. However, it makes perfect sense when we consider that the experience of age can help us better appreciate our youth.

1. "The child is Father of the Man" is one of the most famous paradoxes in literature. Explain how this seeming contradiction can be true.

2. Explain what belief of the Romantic movement this paradox illustrates.

■ THINKING AND WRITING

Writing a Nature Poem

Write a short poem about the joy you find in some aspect of nature. The poem need not rhyme but should describe the source of your pleasure and tell how this aspect of nature makes you feel.

When you revise, make sure you have used sensory details to make your description of nature vivid. Have you chosen words that carry the appropriate connotations?

MULTICULTURAL CONNECTION

The Rainbow as a Symbol

As Wordsworth's poem indicates, to many in the Western world rainbows symbolize hope, promise, or a dream fulfilled. Other cultures see the rainbow in a variety of ways.

In Scandinavian myth, the rainbow is called "Bifrost" and serves as a bridge that dead heroes cross to reach paradise, or Valhalla. The rainbow is also a heavenly bridge to native Hawaiians, and the Catawba people of North America describe it as a pathway for the souls of the dead.

In other cultures, the rainbow is viewed as a heavenly weapon. The legends of the Altai Tatars of Central Asia describe it as the bow of the Sky Warrior, who uses lightning as his arrow.

The image of the rainbow as a huge snake appears in the myths of Native Americans and in the legends of West Africans. In aboriginal Australia, a rainbow snake is considered to be the Great Father and creator.

Not all cultures see the rainbow as a positive symbol. In parts of Malaya, where the rainbow touches the ground is considered unhealthy. According to another Malayan belief, a partial rainbow sighted over water means impending death for a prince. The folklore of the Arawak people of South America also views rainbows as a sign of bad luck, especially if they are sighted over land.

Exploring and Sharing

Do you know any proverbs or sayings that express a cultural point of view about rainbows? Share them with the class.

GUIDE FOR INTERPRETING

The World Is Too Much with Us; It Is a Beauteous Evening, Calm and Free; The Solitary Reaper

Literary Forms

The Sonnet. A sonnet is a fourteen-line poem in which each line contains five strong beats and five weak beats. Although most sonnets follow one of two general rhyme schemes—the Shakespearean (or English) and the Petrarchan (or Italian)—many poets adapt the rhyme to fit their own needs.

The sonnet occupies a particular place of distinction among the poems of Wordsworth. Though a champion of freedom and spontaneity in poetry, Wordsworth nevertheless recognized the importance of order and discipline. The sonnet, as a relatively short and decisive poetic statement, was the logical vehicle for treating such subjects as the human condition and the importance of nature to the human spirit. "Scarcely one of my poems," Wordsworth wrote, "does not aim to direct attention to some moral sentiment." His purpose, as he saw it, was "to console the afflicted" and "to add sunshine to daylight by making the happy happier." These and related goals could best be served, he felt, through the sonnet.

Writers' Techniques

Diction. In writing, *diction* refers to an author's choice of words. Choosing the most appropriate words to express meaning effectively is an important part of any writer's job, but it is particularly essential to the poet's art. A poet carefully selects words to create nuance and mood. When composing a poem, he or she will decide whether the words should be formal or informal, abstract or concrete, plain or ornate.

Wordsworth effected something of a revolution in poetic diction. As subjects for his poems, he said, he wanted "to choose incidents and situations from common life," and while he hoped to reveal in these everyday occurrences something unusual and exciting, he strove to write in language "really used by men," not in what was then perceived as "poetic" diction.

Focus

Think of a topic that holds importance for you. The topic could range from such social issues as finding shelter for the homeless of our country to such personal ones as the love between a pet and a person. Write down specific details of your topic that might be featured in a poem.

The World Is Too Much with Us

William Wordsworth

The world is too much with us; late and soon,
Getting and spending, we lay waste our powers:
Little we see in Nature that is ours;
We have given our hearts away, a sordid boon![1]
5   This sea that bares her bosom to the moon;
The winds that will be howling at all hours,
And are upgathered now like sleeping flowers;
For this, for everything, we are out of tune;
It moves us not.—Great God! I'd rather be
10 A Pagan suckled in a creed outworn;
So might I, standing on this pleasant lea,[2]
Have glimpses that would make me less forlorn;
Have sight of Proteus[3] rising from the sea;
Or hear old Triton[4] blow his wreathèd horn.

---

1. boon: Favor.
2. lea: Meadow.
3. Proteus (prō′ tyo͞os): In Greek mythology, a sea god who could change his appearance at will.
4. Triton: In Greek mythology, a sea god with the head and upper body of a man and the tail of a fish.

RESPONDING TO THE SELECTION

Your Response

1. When are you likely to feel that "the world is too much with us"? Explain.

Recalling

2. In "The World Is Too Much with Us," what does the poet say "we" have given away?

Interpreting

3. Explain what the poet means by the words *world* and *Nature.*

4. (a) Why would the poet rather be "A Pagan suckled in a creed outworn"? (b How would even a "creed outworn" be preferable to the materialistic faith Wordsworth observed?

Applying

5. In 1955 in the United States, Erich Fromm wrote, "We live in a world of things, and our only connection with them is that we know how to manipulate or to consume them." How do you think Wordsworth would respond to this contemporary viewpoint?

It Is a Beauteous Evening, Calm and Free

William Wordsworth

It is a beauteous evening, calm and free,
The holy time is quiet as a Nun
Breathless with adoration; the broad sun
Is sinking down in its tranquility;
5   The gentleness of heaven broods o'er the Sea:
Listen! the mighty Being is awake,
And doth with his eternal motion make
A sound like thunder—everlastingly.
Dear Child! dear Girl! that walkest with me here,
10   If thou appear untouched by solemn thought,
Thy nature is not therefore less divine:
Thou liest in Abraham's bosom[1] all the year;
And worship'st at the Temple's inner shrine,
God being with thee when we know it not.

---

1. Abraham's bosom: Heaven (Luke 16:22).

RESPONDING TO THE SELECTION

Your Response

1. Do you think "solemn thought" is necessary for achieving a deep understanding of life? Explain.

Recalling

2. Describe the setting of "It Is a Beauteous Evening, Calm and Free."
3. Who is the poet's companion?

Interpreting

4. What do you think is meant by "eternal motion" and "thunder"?
5. How does the poet's response to the scene differ from that of the child?
6. How would you summarize the poet's advice (a) to the child? (b) to the reader?

Applying

7. What differences in the last six lines of the poem might you expect if they were addressed to another adult? Explain.

CORNFIELD BY MOONLIGHT
Samuel Palmer
British Museum

ANALYZING LITERATURE

Recognizing a Sonnet

A **sonnet** is a poem of fourteen lines, each with five strong and five weak beats. Sonnets are generally classified as one of two main types, Shakespearean or Petrarchan, on the basis of rhyme scheme and stanza division. The Shakespearean sonnet is divided into three *quatrains* (or stanzas of four lines) and a closing *couplet* (pair of lines). Its rhyme scheme is most often *abab cdcd efef gg*. The Petrarchan sonnet, by contrast, is composed of a group of eight lines (called an *octet*), followed by a group of six (the *sestet*). The rhyme scheme is usually *abbaabba cdecde,* though variations exist in the sestet.

1. Which kind of sonnet is "It Is a Beauteous Evening, Calm and Free"?
2. What is its rhyme scheme?
3. (a) What is the subject matter of the first eight lines? (b) What is the subject matter of the last six lines? (c) Explain how the parts complement each other.

The Solitary Reaper

William Wordsworth

*This poem was inspired by a passage
from Thomas Willkinson's* Tour of
Scotland *(1824): "Passed a female who
was reaping alone; she sung in Erse
(Scottish Gaelic) as she bended over her
sickle; the sweetest human voice I ever
heard: her strains were tenderly melancholy,
and felt delicious long after they were
heard no more."*

Behold her, single in the field,
Yon solitary Highland lass!
Reaping and singing by herself;
Stop here, or gently pass!
5 Alone she cuts and binds the grain,
And sings a melancholy strain;
O listen! for the vale profound
Is overflowing with the sound.

No nightingale did ever chaunt
10 More welcome notes to weary bands
Of travelers in some shady haunt,
Among Arabian sands;
A voice so thrilling ne'er was heard
In springtime from the cuckoo-bird,
15 Breaking the silence of the seas
Among the farthest Hebrides.

Will no one tell me what she sings?—
Perhaps the plaintive numbers flow
For old, unhappy, far-off things,
20 And battles long ago;
Or is it some more humble lay,
Familiar matter of today?
Some natural sorrow, loss, or pain,
That has been, and may be again?

25 Whate'er the theme, the maiden sang
As if her song could have no ending;
I saw her singing at her work,
And o'er the sickle bending;
I listened, motionless and still;
30 And, as I mounted up the hill,
The music in my heart I bore,
Long after it was heard no more.

RESPONDING TO THE SELECTION

Your Response
1. Has an ordinary scene or event ever taken on special significance for you? Explain.

Recalling
2. What is the "solitary Highland lass" doing when the speaker sees her?
3. What possible subjects of the woman's song does the speaker imagine?
4. What does the speaker bear in his heart as he continues his walk?

Interpreting
5. What do the comparisons in the second stanza suggest about the woman's song?
6. What does the final stanza reveal about the impact of the experience on the speaker?

Applying
7. In what ways does the type of life portrayed in the poem contrast with the type of life you would imagine the nineteenth-century factory workers must have led?

ANALYZING LITERATURE

Appreciating a Writer's Diction
Diction refers to choice of words—a writer uses language that is appropriate for his or her subject.
1. In this poem Wordsworth uses simple, direct language. Why is this type of language appropriate?
2. Why would the poem be less effective if it were written in elegant, ornate language?

CRITICAL THINKING AND READING

Understanding Sound Devices
In "The Solitary Reaper," Wordsworth uses a number of sound devices to give the poem a musical quality. For example, he uses *alliteration*—the repetition of similar sounds, usually consonants, at the beginnings of words and accented syllables—in line 9, repeating the *n* sound: "*N*o *n*ightingale did ever chaunt." Wordsworth also uses *assonance,* or the repetition of similar vowel sounds. Notice the repetition of the *i* sound in line 1: "Behold her, s*i*ngle *i*n the field."
1. Find two more examples of alliteration.
2. Find two more examples of assonance.
3. How does the poem's musical quality reflect its meaning?

THINKING AND WRITING

Writing a Poem
Write a poem in which the Highland lass describes the experience that Wordsworth's speaker observes. Use your imagination to develop her character. When writing your poem, make sure it conveys the character you have developed. Reveal the subject of her song and present her impressions of the speaker of Wordsworth's poem. When you revise, make sure you have used concrete images, or word pictures.

SAMUEL TAYLOR COLERIDGE

1772–1834

Samuel Taylor Coleridge's life presents the classic case of the gifted writer whose genius was hampered by lifelong problems, among them self-doubt and poor health. Coleridge was born in Ottery St. Mary on the Devon coast of England, the last of fourteen children, only four of whom survived. Spoiled by his father, Coleridge withdrew into a world of books and fantasy. At age nine, after his father died, Coleridge was sent to school in London. There the boy excelled and developed an ability to hold an audience spellbound when speaking on such matters as philosophy.

In 1791 Coleridge entered Cambridge University on a scholarship, but left before he graduated. He discussed plans with several other thinkers of the age to start a colony in America whose members would live on a high intellectual plane. It was agreed that each member would have a wife. Though the plans for the community fell through, Coleridge's marriage plans did not, and in 1795 he married Sara Fricker.

With his wife, Coleridge moved in 1797 to Somerset, where he developed a close friendship with William Wordsworth, an important poet of the period. In 1798 the two turned out *Lyrical Ballads,* a joint collection of their work. The four poems that make up Coleridge's contribution to the volume deal with matters of the spiritual world and include his masterpiece, "The Rime of the Ancient Mariner." Though a first public response to this collection of poems was lukewarm, the book slowly gained critical attention, ultimately causing a revolution in poetic style and thought, firmly establishing the movement known as Romanticism.

As Coleridge's fame grew, his marriage, his health, and his friendship with Wordsworth all gradually failed. He suffered increasingly from asthma and rheumatism, and he began to rely heavily on painkillers, which dulled his creative powers. Still, Coleridge managed to produce a good deal of work in the years left him. He worked variously as a journalist, as a lecturer on Shakespeare and Milton, as an essayist, and as a playwright, earning a tidy sum of money in 1813 with his tragedy *Remorse*. Despite his personal hardships, Coleridge continued to make himself available to visitors, which proved to have a great impact on the young crop of Romanticists writing at that time.

Perhaps Coleridge's greatest legacy is the insight he affords his reader on the role of imagination in literature. His belief that literature is a magical blend of thought and emotion is at the very heart of his greatest works, in which the unreal is often made to seem real.

GUIDE FOR INTERPRETING

The Rime of the Ancient Mariner

Sound Devices. The relationship between poetry and music has often been noted. Just as music achieves its effect through rhythms and harmonies, so poetry achieves its effect through sound devices and techniques that enhance the meter and rhyme of a poem.

Chief among the sound devices available to the poet is *alliteration,* the repetition of a consonant sound at the beginning of words or of accented syllables that occur close together. Notice, for example, the repeated *f* sound in these lines from "The Rime of the Ancient Mariner": "The *f*air breeze blew, the white *f*oam *f*lew,/ The *f*urrow *f*ollowed *f*ree. . . . "

Consonance, a device related to alliteration, is the repetition of a consonant sound at the end of words or of accented syllables. Consider another line from Coleridge, this one capitalizing on the *v* sound: "When the i*v*y tod is hea*v*y with snow. . . ."

In the sound device known as *assonance,* it is a vowel sound that is repeated in nearby words or syllables. In the following passage, the long *a* sound is so treated: "The western w*a*ve was all afl*a*me./ The d*a*y was well-nigh done!"

Internal rhyme, a fourth sound device, features rhyming words within the space of a single line. As an example, note the following line: "With heavy *thump,* a lifeless *lump.* . . ."

Coleridge once opened an essay by asking his readers to "sit down to a book . . . as a well-behaved visitor does to a banquet." But he knew that good readers need more than manners. To make his point, he discussed what he saw as the four kinds of readers:

1. Sponges, who absorb all they read and return it nearly in the same state, only a little dirtied.
2. Sand-glasses, who retain nothing and are content to get through a book for the sake of getting through the time.
3. Strain-bags, who retain merely the dregs of what they read.
4. Mogul diamonds, equally rare and valuable, who profit from what they read and enable others to profit by it also.

What type of reader are you?

Imagine a contest: A friend has dreamed of a skeleton ship manned by spectral figures. You and a group of friends must each flesh out the dream. The best narrative will win the contest. Write your tale of this skeleton ship.

The Rime of the Ancient Mariner

Samuel Taylor Coleridge

"The Rime of the Ancient Mariner," based on a dream of Coleridge's friend, John Cruikshank, was originally planned as a collaboration between Coleridge and Wordsworth. Eventually Wordsworth dropped out of the project, but not before making a number of valuable suggestions, including the shooting of the albatross and the navigation of the ship by the dead men. Several years after the poem was first published in Lyrical Ballads *(1798), Coleridge added the prose explanations in the margins to aid the reader in understanding the poem's meaning.*

Argument

How a Ship having passed the Line[1] was driven by storms to the cold Country towards the South Pole: and how from thence she made her course to the tropical Latitude of the Great Pacific Ocean; and of the strange things that befell: and in what manner the Ancyent Marinere came back to his own Country.

Part I

An ancient Mariner meeteth three Gallants bidden to a wedding feast and detaineth one.

It is an ancient Mariner,
And he stoppeth one of three.
"By thy long gray beard and glittering eye,
Now wherefore stopp'st thou me?

"The Bridegroom's doors are opened wide,   5
And I am next of kin;
The guests are met, the feast is set:
May'st hear the merry din."

---

1. Line: Equator.

The Wedding Guest is
spellbound by the eye of
the old seafaring man
and constrained to hear
his tale.

He holds him with his skinny hand,
"There was a ship," quoth he.   10
"Hold off! unhand me, graybeard loon!"
Eftsoons[2] his hand dropped he.

He holds him with his glittering eye—
The Wedding Guest stood still,
And listens like a three years' child: 15
The Mariner hath his will.

The Wedding Guest sat on a stone:
He cannot choose but hear;
And thus spake on that ancient man,
The bright-eyed Mariner.   20

"The ship was cheered, the harbor cleared,
Merrily did we drop

The Mariner tells how the
ship sailed southward
with a good wind and fair
weather till it reached the
Line.

Below the kirk,[3] below the hill,
Below the lighthouse top.

"The Sun came up upon the left,   25
Out of the sea came he!
And he shone bright, and on the right
Went down into the sea.

"Higher and higher every day,
Till over the mast at noon[4]—"   30
The Wedding Guest here beat his breast,
For he heard the loud bassoon.

The Wedding Guest hear-
eth the bridal music; but
the Mariner continueth
his tale.

The bride hath paced into the hall.
Red as a rose is she;
Nodding their heads before her goes   35
The merry minstrelsy.

The Wedding Guest he beat his breast,
Yet he cannot choose but hear;
And thus spake on that ancient man
The bright-eyed Mariner.   40

The ship driven by a
storm toward the South
Pole.

"And now the Storm blast came, and he
Was tyrannous and strong:
He struck with his o'ertaking wings,
And chased us south along.

---

2. eftsoons: Immediately.
3. kirk: Church.
4. over . . . noon: The ship has reached the equator.

"With sloping masts and dipping prow,   45
As who pursued with yell and blow
Still treads the shadow of his foe,
And forward bends his head,
The ship drove fast, loud roared the blast,
And southward aye[5] we fled.   50

"And now there came both mist and snow.
And it grew wondrous cold;
And ice, mast-high, came floating by,
As green as emerald.

"And through the drifts the snowy clifts[6]   55
Did send a dismal sheen;
Nor shapes of men nor beasts we ken[7]—
The ice was all between.

"The ice was here, the ice was there,
The ice was all around;   60
It cracked and growled, and roared and howled,
Like noises in a swound![8]

"At length did cross an Albatross,
Thorough[9] the fog it came;
As if it had been a Christian soul,   65
We hailed it in God's name.

"It ate the food it ne'er had eat,[10]
And round and round it flew.
The ice did split with a thunder-fit;
The helmsman steered us through!   70

"And a good south wind sprung up behind;
The Albatross did follow,
And every day, for food or play,
Came to the mariner's hollo!

"In mist or cloud, on mast or shroud,[11]   75
It perched for vespers[12] nine;
Whiles all the night, through fog-smoke white,
Glimmered the white Moonshine."

---

5. aye: Ever.
6. clifts: Icebergs.
7. ken: knew.
8. swound: swoon.
9. thorough: Through.
10. eat (et): Old form of *eaten*.
11. shroud *n.*: Ropes stretching from the ship's side to the masthead.
12. vespers: Evenings.

ENGRAVING BY GUSTAVE DORÉ FOR THE RIME OF THE ANCIENT MARINER
by Samuel Taylor Coleridge

The ancient Mariner in-
hospitably killeth the
pious bird of good omen.

"God save thee, ancient Mariner!
From the fiends, that plague thee thus!—   80
Why look'st thou so?"[13] "With my crossbow
I shot the Albatross."

Part II

"The Sun now rose upon the right:[14]
Out of the sea came he,
Still hid in mist, and on the left   85
Went down into the sea.

"And the good south wind still blew behind,
But no sweet bird did follow.
Nor any day for food or play
Came to the mariners' hollo!   90

His shipmates cry out
against the ancient Mari-
ner for killing the bird of
good luck.

"And I had done a hellish thing,
And it would work 'em woe:
For all averred, I had killed the bird
That made the breeze to blow.
Ah wretch! said they, the bird to slay,   95
That made the breeze to blow!

But when the fog cleared
off, they justify the same,
and thus make them-
selves accomplices in the
crime.

"Nor dim nor red, like God's own head,
The glorious Sun uprist;[15]
Then all averred, I had killed the bird
That brought the fog and mist.   100
'Twas right, said they, such birds to slay,
That bring the fog and mist.

The fair breeze continues;
the ship enters the Pacific
Ocean, and sails north-
ward, even till it reaches
the Line.

"The fair breeze blew, the white foam flew,
The furrow[16] followed free;
We were the first that ever burst   105
Into that silent sea.

The ship hath been sud-
denly becalmed.

"Down dropped the breeze, the sails dropped
            down,
'Twas sad as sad could be;
And we did speak only to break
The silence of the sea!   110

---

13. **God . . . so:** Spoken by the Wedding Guest.
14. **The Sun . . . right:** The ship is now headed north.
15. **uprist:** Arose.
16. **furrow:** Ship's wake.

ENGRAVING BY GUSTAVE DORÉ FOR THE RIME OF THE ANCIENT MARINER
by Samuel Taylor Coleridge

ENGRAVING BY GUSTAVE DORÉ FOR THE RIME OF THE ANCIENT MARINER
by Samuel Taylor Coleridge

"All in a hot and copper sky,
The bloody Sun, at noon,
Right up above the mast did stand,
No bigger than the Moon.

"Day after day, day after day,   115
We stuck, nor breath nor motion;
As idle as a painted ship
Upon a painted ocean.

And the Albatross begins
to be avenged.

"Water, water, everywhere,
And all the boards did shrink;   120
Water, water, everywhere,
Nor any drop to drink.

"The very deep did rot: O Christ!
That ever this should be!
Yea, slimy things did crawl with legs   125
Upon the slimy sea.

"About, about, in reel and rout[17]
The death fires[18] danced at night;
The water, like a witch's oils,
Burned green, and blue and white.   130

A Spirit had followed
them; one of the invisible
inhabitants of this planet,
neither departed souls
nor angels. They are very
numerous, and there is
no climate or element
without one or more.

"And some in dreams assurèd were
Of the Spirit that plagued us so;
Nine fathom deep he had followed us
From the land of mist and snow.

"And every tongue, through utter drought,   135
Was withered at the root;
We could not speak, no more than if
We had been choked with soot.

The shipmates, in their
sore distress, would fain
throw the whole guilt on
the ancient Mariner: in
sign whereof they hang
the dead sea bird round
his neck.

"Ah! well a-day! what evil looks
Had I from old and young!   140
Instead of the cross, the Albatross
About my neck was hung.

---

17. rout: Disorderly crowd.
18. death fires: St. Elmo's fire, a visible electrical discharge from a ship's mast, believed by sailors to be an omen of disaster.

Part III

"There passed a weary time. Each throat
Was parched, and glazed each eye.
A weary time! a weary time!   145
How glazed each weary eye,
When looking westward, I beheld
A somethling in the sky.

"At first it seemed a little speck,
And then it seemed a mist;   150
It moved and moved, and took at last
A certain shape, I wist.¹⁹

"A speck, a mist, a shape, I wist!
And still it neared and neared:
As if it dodged a water sprite,   155
It plunged and tacked and veered.

"With throats unslaked, with black lips baked,
We could nor laugh nor wail;
Through utter drought all dumb we stood!
I bit my arm, I sucked the blood,   160
And cried, A sail! a sail!

"With throats unslaked, with black lips
    baked,
Agape they heard me call:

Gramercy!²⁰ they for joy did grin,
And all at once their breath drew in,   165
As they were drinking all.

"See! see! (I cried) she tacks no more!
Hither to work us weal;²¹
Without a breeze, without a tide,
She steadies with upright keel!   170

"The western wave was all aflame.
The day was well nigh done!
Almost upon the western wave
Rested the broad bright Sun;
When that strange shape drove suddenly   175
Betwixt us and the Sun.

---

19. wist: Knew.
20. Gramercy (grə mur' sē): Great thanks.
21. work us weal: Assist us.

*It seemeth him but the
skeleton of a ship.*

"And straight the Sun was flecked with bars,
(Heaven's Mother send us grace!)
As if through a dungeon grate he peered
With broad and burning face.   180

*And its ribs are seen as
bars on the face of the
setting Sun. The Specter
Woman and her Death-
mate, and no other on
board the skeleton ship.*

"Alas! (thought I, and my heart beat loud)
How fast she nears and nears!
Are those *her* sails that glance in the Sun,
Like restless gossameres?[22]

"Are those *her* ribs through which the
   Sun   185
Did peer, as through a grate?
And is that Woman all her crew?
Is that a Death? and are there two?
Is Death that woman's mate?

Like vessel, like crew!

*Death and Life-in-Death
have diced for the ship's
crew, and she (the latter)
winneth the ancient Mari-
ner.*

"*Her* lips, were red, *her* looks were free,   190
Her locks were yellow as gold;
Her skin was as white as leprosy,
The Nightmare Life-in-Death was she,
Who thicks man's blood with cold.

"The naked hulk alongside came,   195
And the twain were casting dice;
'The game is done! I've won! I've won!'
Quoth she, and whistles thrice.

*No twilight within the
courts of the Sun.*

"The Sun's rim dips; the stars rush out:
At one stride comes the dark;   200
With far-heard whisper, o'er the sea,
Off shot the specter bark.

At the rising of the Moon,

"We listened and looked sideways up!
Fear at my heart, as at a cup,
My lifeblood seemed to sip!   205
The stars were dim, and thick the night,
The steersman's face by his lamp gleamed
   white;
From the sails the dew did drip—
Till clomb[23] above the eastern bar
The hornèd[24] Moon, with one bright star   210
Within the nether tip.

---

22. gossameres: Floating cobwebs.
23. clomb: Climbed.
24. hornèd: Crescent.

"One after one, by the star-dogged Moon,[25]
Too quick for groan or sigh,
Each turned his face with a ghastly pang,
And cursed me with his eye.   215

*His shipmates drop down
dead.*

"Four times fifty living men,
(And I heard nor sigh nor groan)
With heavy thump, a lifeless lump,
They dropped down one by one.

*But Life-in-Death begins
her work on the ancient
Mariner.*

"The souls did from their bodies fly—   220
They fled to bliss or woe!
And every soul, it passed me by,
Like the whizz of my crossbow!"

Part IV

*The Wedding Guest fear-
eth that a Spirit is talking
to him;*

"I fear thee, ancient Mariner!
I fear thy skinny hand!   225
And thou art long, and lank, and brown,
As is the ribbed sea sand.

"I fear thee and thy glittering eye,
And thy skinny hand, so brown."

*But the ancient Mariner
assureth him of his bodily
life, and proceedeth to relate his horrible penance.*

"Fear not, fear not, thou Wedding Guest!   230
This body dropped not down.

"Alone, alone, all, all alone,
Alone on a wide wide sea!
And never a saint took pity on
My soul in agony.   235

*He despiseth the crea-
tures of the calm,*

"The many men, so beautiful!
And they all dead did lie:
And a thousand thousand slimy things
Lived on; and so did I.

*And envieth that they
should live, and so many
lie dead.*

"I looked upon the rotting sea,   240
And drew my eyes away;
I looked upon the rotting deck,
And there the dead men lay.

"I looked to heaven, and tried to pray;
But or[26] ever a prayer had gushed,   245
A wicked whisper came, and made
My heart as dry as dust.

---

25. star-dogged Moon: An omen of impending evil to sailors.
26. or: Before.

"I closed my lids, and kept them close,
And the balls like pulses beat;
For the sky and the sea and the sea and the
  sky   250
Lay like a load on my weary eye,
And the dead were at my feet.

But the curse liveth for
him in the eye of the
dead men.

"The cold sweat melted from their limbs,
Nor rot nor reek did they;
The look with which they looked on me   255
Had never passed away.

"An orphan's curse would drag to hell
A spirit from on high;
But oh! more horrible than that
Is the curse in a dead man's eye!   260
Seven days, seven nights, I saw that curse,
And yet I could not die.

In his loneliness and fix-
edness he yearneth to-
wards the journeying
Moon, and the stars that
still sojourn, yet still
move onward; and every-
where the blue sky be-
longs to them, and is
their appointed rest, and
their native country and
their own natural homes,
which they enter unan-
nounced, as lords that
are certainly expected
and yet there is a silent
joy at their arrival.
By the light of the Moon
he beholdeth God's crea-
tures of the great calm.

"The moving Moon went up the sky,
And nowhere did abide:
Softly she was going up,   265
And a star or two beside—

"Her beams bemocked the sultry main,[27]
Like April hoarfrost spread;
But where the ship's huge shadow lay,
The charmèd water burned alway   270
A still and awful red.

"Beyond the shadow of the ship,
I watched the water snakes:
They moved in tracks of shining white,
And when they reared, the elfish light   275
Fell off in hoary flakes.

"Within the shadow of the ship
I watched their rich attire:
Blue, glossy green, and velvet black,
They coiled and swam; and every track   280
Was a flash of golden fire.

Their beauty and their
happiness.

"O happy living things! no tongue
Their beauty might declare:
A spring of love gushed from my heart,
And I blessed them unaware;   285
Sure my kind saint took pity on me,
And I blessed them unaware.

He blesseth them in his
heart.

---

27. main: Open sea.

The spell begins to break.

"The selfsame moment I could pray;
And from my neck so free
The Albatross fell off, and sank   290
Like lead into the sea.

Part V

"Oh sleep! it is a gentle thing,
Beloved from pole to pole!
To Mary Queen the praise be given!
She sent the gentle sleep from Heaven,   295
That slid into my soul.

*By grace of the holy
Mother, the ancient Mari-
ner is refreshed with rain.*

"The silly[28] buckets on the deck.
That had so long remained,
I dreamed that they were filled with dew;
And when I awoke, it rained.   300

"My lips were wet, my throat was cold,
My garments all were dank;
Sure I had drunken in my dreams,
And still my body drank.

"I moved, and could not feel my limbs: 305
I was so light—almost
I thought that I had died in sleep,
And was a blessèd ghost.

*He heareth sounds and
seeth strange sights and
commotions in the sky
and the element.*

"And soon I heard a roaring wind:
It did not come anear;   310
But with its sound it shook the sails,
That were so thin and sere.[29]

"The upper air burst into life!
And a hundred fire flags sheen,[30]
To and fro they were hurried about!   315
And to and fro, and in and out,
The wan stars danced between.

"And the coming wind did roar more loud,
And the sails did sigh like sedge;[31]
And the rain poured down from one black
    cloud;   320
The Moon was at its edge.

---

28. silly: Empty.
29. sere: Dried up.
30. fire flags sheen: The aurora australis, or southern lights, shone.
31. sedge *n.*: A rushlike plant that grows in wet soil.

ENGRAVING BY GUSTAVE DORÉ FOR THE RIME OF THE ANCIENT MARINER
by Samuel Taylor Coleridge

"The thick black cloud was cleft, and still
The Moon was at its side:
Like waters shot from some high crag,
The lightning fell with never a jag,   325
A river steep and wide.

The bodies of the ship's crew are inspired[32] and the ship moves on;

"The loud wind never reached the ship,
Yet now the ship moved on!
Beneath the lightning and the Moon
The dead men gave a groan.   330

"They groaned, they stirred, they all uprose,
Nor spake, nor moved their eyes;
It had been strange, even in a dream,
To have seen those dead men rise.

"The helmsman steered, the ship moved
   on: 335
Yet never a breeze up-blew;
The mariners all 'gan work the ropes,
Where they were wont[33] to do;
They raised their limbs like lifeless tools—
We were a ghastly crew.   340

"The body of my brother's son
Stood by me, knee to knee;
The body and I pulled at one rope,
But he said nought to me.

"I fear thee, ancient Mariner!"   345
"Be calm, thou Wedding Guest!
'Twas not those souls that fled in pain,
Which to their corses[34] came again,
But a troop of spirits blessed:

But not by the souls of the men, nor by demons of earth or middle air, but by a blessed troop of angelic spirits, sent down by the invocation of the guardian saint.

"For when it dawned—they dropped their
   arms,   350
And clustered round the mast;
Sweet sounds rose slowly through their
   mouths,
And from their bodies passed.

---

32. inspired: Inspirited.
33. wont: Accustomed.
34. corses: Corpses.

"Around, around, flew each sweet sound,
Then darted to the Sun;   355
Slowly the sounds came back again,
Now mixed, now one by one.

"Sometimes a-dropping from the sky
I heard the skylark sing;
Sometimes all little birds that are,   360
How they seemed to fill the sea and air
With their sweet jargoning![35]

"And now 'twas like all instruments,
Now like a lonely flute;
And now it is an angel's song,   365
That makes the heavens be mute.

"It ceased; yet still the sails made on
A pleasant noise till noon,
A noise like of a hidden brook
In the leafy month of June,   370
That to the sleeping woods all night
Singeth a quiet tune.

"Till noon we quietly sailed on,
Yet never a breeze did breathe;
Slowly and smoothly went the ship,   375
Moved onward from beneath.

The lonesome Spirit from the South Pole carries on the ship as far as the Line, in obedience to the angelic troop, but still requireth vengeance.

"Under the keel nine fathom deep,
From the land of mist and snow,
The spirit slid; and it was he
That made the ship to go.   380
The sails at noon left off their tune,
And the ship stood still also.

"The Sun, right up above the mast,
Had fixed her to the ocean:
But in a minute she 'gan stir,   385
With a short uneasy motion—
Backwards and forwards half her length
With a short uneasy motion.

"Then like a pawing horse let go,
She made a sudden bound: 390
It flung the blood into my head,
And I fell down in a swound.

---

35. jargoning: Singing.

The Polar Spirit's fellow demons, the invisible inhabitants of the element, take part in his wrong; and two of them relate, one to the other, that penance long and heavy for the ancient Mariner hath been accorded to the Polar Spirit, who returneth southward.

"How long in that same fit I lay,
I have not to declare;
But ere my living life returned,   395
I heard and in my soul discerned
Two voices in the air.

"'Is it he?' quoth one, 'Is this the man?
By him who died on cross,
With his cruel bow he laid full low   400
The harmless Albatross.

"'The spirit who bideth by himself
In the land of mist and snow,
He loved the bird that loved the man
Who shot him with his bow.'   405

"The other was a softer voice,
As soft as honeydew:
Quoth he, 'The man hath penance done,
And penance more will do.'

Part VI

FIRST VOICE

"'But tell me, tell me! speak again,   410
Thy soft response renewing—
What makes that ship drive on so fast?
What is the ocean doing?'

SECOND VOICE

"'Still as a slave before his lord,
The ocean hath no blast;   415
His great bright eye most silently
Up to the Moon is cast—

"'If he may know which way to go;
For she guides him smooth or grim.
See, brother, see! how graciously   420
She looketh down on him.'

FIRST VOICE

"'But why drives on that ship so fast,
Without or wave or wind?'

The Mariner hath been cast into a trance; for the angelic power causeth the vessel to drive northward faster than human life could endure.

"'The air is cut away before,
And closes from behind.   425

"'Fly, brother, fly! more high, more high!
Or we shall be belated;
For slow and slow that ship will go,
When the Mariner's trance is abated.'

The super-natural motion   "I woke, and we were sailing on   430
is retarded; the Mariner   As in a gentle weather;
awakes, and his penance   'Twas night, calm night, the moon was high;
begins anew.   The dead men stood together.

"All stood together on the deck,
For a charnel dungeon[36] litter;   435
All fixed on me their stony eyes,
That in the Moon did glitter.

"The pang, the curse, with which they died,
Had never passed away;
I could not draw my eyes from theirs,   440
Nor turn them up to pray.

The curse is finally expi-   "And now this spell was snapped; once more
ated.   I viewed the ocean green,
And looked far forth, yet little saw
Of what had else been seen—   445

"Like one, that on a lonesome road
Doth walk in fear and dread,
And having once turned round walks on,
And turns no more his head;
Because he knows, a frightful fiend   450
Doth close behind him tread.

"But soon there breathed a wind on me,
Nor sound nor motion made:
Its path was not upon the sea,
In ripple or in shade.   455

"It raised my hair, it fanned my cheek
Like a meadow-gale of spring—
It mingled strangely with my fears,
Yet it felt like a welcoming.

---

36. charnel dungeon: Vault where corpses or bones are deposited.

"Swiftly, swiftly flew the ship,   460
Yet she sailed softly too:
Sweetly, sweetly blew the breeze—
On me alone it blew.

"Oh! dream of joy! is this indeed
The lighthouse top I see?   465
Is this the hill? is this the kirk?
Is this mine own countree?

"We drifted o'er the harbor bar,
And I with sobs did pray—
O let me be awake, my God!   470
Or let me sleep alway.

"The harbor bay was clear as glass,
So smoothly it was strewn!³⁷
And on the bay the moonlight lay,
And the shadow of the Moon.   475

"The rock shone bright, the kirk no less,
That stands above the rock;
The moonlight steeped in silentness
The steady weathercock.

"And the bay was white with silent light,   480
Till rising from the same,
Full many shapes, that shadows were,
In crimson colors came.

"A little distance from the prow
Those crimson shadows were;   485
I turned my eyes upon the deck—
Oh, Christ! what saw I there!

"Each corse lay flat, lifeless and flat,
And, by the holy rood!³⁸
A man all light, a seraph³⁹ man,   490
On every corse there stood.

"This seraph band, each waved his hand:
It was a heavenly sight!
They stood as signals to the land,
Each one a lovely light;   495

---

37. strewn: spread.
38. rood: Cross.
39. seraph: Angel.

"This seraph band, each waved his hand,
No voice did they impart—
No voice; but oh! the silence sank
Like music on my heart.

"But soon I heard the dash of oars,   500
I heard the Pilot's cheer;
My head was turned perforce away
And I saw a boat appear.

"The Pilot and the Pilot's boy,
I heard them coming fast: 505
Dear Lord in Heaven! it was a joy
The dead men could not blast.

"I saw a third—I heard his voice:
It is the Hermit good!
He singeth loud his godly hymns   510
That he makes in the wood.
He'll shrieve[40] my soul, he'll wash away
The Albatross's blood.

Part VII

The Hermit of the Wood.

"This Hermit good lives in that wood
Which slopes down to the sea.   515
How loudly his sweet voice he rears!
He loves to talk with mariners
That come from a far countree.

"He kneels at morn, and noon, and eve—
He hath a cushion plump: 520
It is the moss that wholly hides
The rotted old oak-stump.

"The skiff boat neared; I heard them talk.
'Why, this is strange, I trow![41]
Where are those lights so many and fair,   525
That signal made but now?'

Approacheth the ship with wonder.

" 'Strange, by my faith!' the Hermit said—
'And they answered not our cheer!
The planks looked warped! and see those
    sails,
How thin they are and sere!   530
I never saw aught like to them,
Unless perchance it were

40. shrieve (shrēv): Absolve from sin.
41. trow: Believe.

"'Brown skeletons of leaves that lag
My forest brook along;
When the ivy tod[42] is heavy with snow,   535
And the owlet whoops to the wolf below,
That eats the she-wolf's young.'

"'Dear Lord! it hath a fiendish look'
(The Pilot made reply)
'I am a-feared'—'Push on, push on!'   540
Said the Hermit cheerily.

"The boat came closer to the ship,
But I nor spake nor stirred;
The boat came close beneath the ship,
And straight[43] a sound was heard.   545

"Under the water it rumbled on,
Still louder and more dread;
It reached the ship, it split the bay;
The ship went down like lead.

"Stunned by that loud and dreadful sound,   550
Which sky and ocean smote,
Like one that hath been seven days drowned
My body lay afloat;
But swift as dreams, myself I found
Within the Pilot's boat.   555

"Upon the whirl, where sank the ship,
The boat spun round and round;
And all was still, save that the hill
Was telling of the sound.

"I moved my lips—the Pilot shrieked   560
And fell down in a fit;
The holy Hermit raised his eyes,
And prayed where he did sit.

"I took the oars; the Pilot's boy,
Who now doth crazy go,   565
Laughed loud and long, and all the while
His eyes went to and fro.
'Ha! ha!' quoth he, 'full plain I see,
The Devil knows how to row.'

The ship suddenly sink-eth.

The ancient Mariner is saved in the Pilot's boat.

---

42. tod: Bush.
43. straight: Immediately.

"And now, all in my own countree,   570
I stood on the firm land!
The Hermit stepped forth from the boat,
And scarcely he could stand.

"'O shrieve me, shrieve me, holy man!'
The Hermit crossed his brow.[44]   575
'Say, quick,' quoth he, 'I bid thee say—
What manner of man art thou?'

"Forthwith this frame of mine was wrenched
With a woeful agony,
Which forced me to begin my tale;   580
And then it left me free.

"Since then, at an uncertain hour,
That agony returns;
And till my ghastly tale is told,
This heart within me burns.   585

"I pass, like night, from land to land;
I have strange power of speech;
That moment that his face I see,
I know the man that must hear me:
To him my tale I teach.   590

"What loud uproar bursts from that door!
The wedding guests are there;
But in the garden bower the bride
And bridemaids singing are;
And hark the little vesper bell,   595
Which biddeth me to prayer!

"O Wedding Guest! this soul hath been
Alone on a wide wide sea:
So lonely 'twas, that God himself
Scarce seemed there to be.   600

"O sweeter than the marriage feast,
'Tis sweeter far to me,
To walk together to the kirk
With a goodly company!—

---

44. crossed his brow: Made the sign of the cross on his forehead.

"To walk together to the kirk,   605
And all together pray,
While each to his great Father bends,
Old men, and babes, and loving friends
And youths and maidens gay!

"Farewell, farewell! but this I tell   610
To thee, thou Wedding Guest!
He prayeth well, who loveth well
Both man and bird and beast.

"He prayeth best, who loveth best
All things both great and small;   615
For the dear God who loveth us,
He made and loveth all."

The Mariner, whose eye is bright,
Whose beard with age is hoar,
Is gone; and now the Wedding Guest   620
Turned from the bridegroom's door.

He went like one that hath been stunned
And is of sense forlorn;
A sadder and a wiser man,
He rose the morrow morn.   625

RESPONDING TO THE SELECTION

Your Response

1. What is your reaction to the fantastic and supernatural elements in this poem? Explain.

Recalling

2. (a) What "hellish thing" does the Mariner do? (b) How do the other sailors at first react to this deed? (c) What changes their minds?
3. (a) Who is the crew of the strange ship that appears in Part III? (b) What happens to the Mariner's shipmates soon after the appearance of this ship?
4. (a) What changes take place in the Mariner in Part IV? (b) What burden is he freed of as a result of these changes?

5. (a) According to the margin notes in Part V, what force causes the ship to move? (b) Who serves as the crew of the ship on this leg of its journey? (c) What force takes control of the ship at the equator?
6. What does the Mariner hope the Hermit will do for him?
7. What is the Mariner's lifelong penance?

Interpreting

8. What do you think the Albatross symbolizes, or stands for? Find evidence to support your answer.
9. In what ways might the journey of the Mariner be seen as spiritual as well as actual?
10. Some of the events Coleridge describes are real and some are supernatural. Why do you think he includes both kinds in this poem?

Applying

11. Reread lines 614–617. How might this advice be useful for today's world?
12. What do we mean when we say that some past action stays with a person "like an albatross around his or her neck"?

ANALYZING LITERATURE

Understanding Sound Devices

Alliteration, consonance, assonance, and internal rhyme are four sound devices used to enhance the meaning and create the mood of a poem. *Alliteration* is the repetition of a first consonant sound in words or in accented syllables ("the owlet *wh*oops to the *w*olf"). *Consonance* is the repetition of a final consonant sound in words or in accented syllables ("thy ski*nn*y ha*nd*, so brow*n*"). *Assonance* is the repetition of a vowel sound ("the Sun's r*i*m d*i*ps"). *Internal rhyme* is a rhyme within a line ("on the *bay* the moonlight *lay*").

Identify the sound device or devices in each of the following liens from "The Rime of the Ancient Mariner."

1. lines 7–8
2. lines 31–32
3. lines 121–122
4. lines 236–237
5. lines 452–453
6. lines 478–479

CRITICAL THINKING AND READING

Analyzing the Effects of Sound Devices

Sound devices in poetry please the ear and also reinforce meaning and create moods. In lines 41–44, for example, the repetition of the *s* sound, through both alliteration and consonance, enables us almost to hear the hissing of the sea foam as the ship is tossed about.

1. Reread lines 331–340. Identify the sound devices used and explain how they add to the eerie mood of the scene.

2. Reread lines 472–483. State the feeling you think Coleridge was trying to establish in his reader. Tell whether, in your opinion, his use of sound devices helps, and give your reasons.

THINKING AND WRITING

Responding to a Statement

Coleridge wrote that successful poetry is poetry that will arouse "the sympathy of the reader by a faithful adherence to the truth of nature" while, at the same time, "giving the interest of novelty by the modifying colors of imagination." In an essay, argue whether or not you feel Coleridge met these standards in "The Rime of the Ancient Mariner." Begin by defining *sympathy* and *interest* as you believe he has used the words here. Support your claims by quoting passages from the poem. When you revise make sure you have included details from the poem to support your judgment. Proofread your essay and prepare a final draft.

LEARNING OPTIONS

1. **Performance.** With one or two classmates, choose an excerpt from "The Rime of the Ancient Mariner" that you find compelling and that can be given as a dramatic reading. Assign "parts" and rehearse your reading, making sure that your interpretation evokes the atmosphere and action in the poem. Perform your reading in class.

2. **Art.** Create a poster-sized collage that illustrates the Ancient Mariner's journey. Devise ways to represent the major events in the "Rime" either realistically or symbolically. Present your collage in class and be prepared to point out the events in chronological order.

GUIDE FOR INTERPRETING

Kubla Khan

Literary Movements

Romanticism. Romanticism was a literary and artistic movement that began in Europe toward the end of the eighteenth century. A rebellion against the cold rationalism and strict adherence to form that typified the earlier Neoclassical movement, Romanticism stressed imagination and subjectivity as key literary virtues. The Romantic writer was free to express his or her personal views in a spontaneous and nonlogical fashion. The goal of the Romantic poets was to bring people to an awareness of their "oneness" with all other living things. It was in the spirit of this movement and its goal that Coleridge gave his poem "Kubla Khan" the subtitle "A Vision in a Dream." The word *vision* here reminds us that the Romantic poets were fond of mysticism and fantasy—the stuff of visions. The word *dream* calls to mind a freedom from the rules and logical order of the day-to-day world—traits that were at the very heart of Romanticism.

Focus

Recall as best you can a dream you had in which you made a trip to a strange place. Write a vivid description. Use as many details of sight, sound, touch, taste, and smell as you can.

Primary Source

From his memories of childhood, it is apparent that Romanticism exerted a tug at Coleridge's nature from the very start. He was especially taken with mystery and fantasy:

> My father's sister kept an *every-thing* shop at Crediton," he recalled, "and there I read through all the gilt-covered little books that could be had at that time, and likewise all the uncovered tales of *Tom Hickathrift, Jack the Giant-Killer,* etc. and . . . I used to lie by the wall, and mope—and my spirits used to come upon me suddenly, and in a flood—and then I was accustomed to run up and down the church-yard, and act over all I had been reading on the docks, the nettles, and the rank-grass. At six years old . . . I found the Arabian Nights entertainments—one tale of which . . . made so deep an impression on me (I had read it in the evening while my mother was mending stockings) that I was haunted by specters whenever I was in the dark—and I distinctly remember the anxious and fearful eagerness with which I used to watch the window in which the books lay—and whenever the sun lay upon them, I would seize it, carry it by the wall, and bask, and read. My father found out the effect which these books had produced—and burnt them. So I became a dreamer. . . .

Kubla Khan

Samuel Taylor Coleridge

This poem was inspired by a passage about Kubla Khan (kōō′ ble kän′), the founder of the Mongol dynasty in China in the thirteenth century, in Samuel Purchas's Purchas His Pilgrimage *(1613): "Here the Khan Kubla commanded a palace to be built, and a stately garden thereunto. And thus ten miles of fertile ground were inclosed with a wall." Coleridge claims to have fallen asleep while reading this passage due to the effects of medication he was taking for an illness at the time (1797). Three hours later, he awoke from a dream, finding his mind was filled with two to three hundred lines of poetry, which were an elaboration of the description he had read immediately before drifting off to sleep. Coleridge immediately began to write down the lines that filled his head, but when he was interrupted by a visitor, he forgot the lines that he had not yet transcribed. As a result, he was unable to complete the poem.*

In Xanadu[1] did Kubla Khan
A stately pleasure dome decree:
Where Alph,[2] the sacred river, ran
Through caverns measureless to man
5   Down to a sunless sea.
So twice five miles of fertile ground
With walls and towers were girdled round;
And there were gardens bright with sinuous rills,[3]
Where blossomed many an incense-bearing tree;
10 And here were forests ancient as the hills,
Enfolding sunny spots of greenery.

But oh! that deep romantic chasm which slanted
Down the green hill athwart[4] a cedarn cover![5]
A savage place! as holy and enchanted
15 As e'er beneath a waning moon was haunted
By woman wailing for her demon lover!
And from this chasm, with ceaseless turmoil seething,
As if this earth in fast thick pants were breathing.

---

1. Xanadu (zan′ ə dōō): An indefinite area in China.
2. Alph: Probably derived from the Greek river Alpheus, the waters of which, it was believed in Greek mythology, joined with a stream to form a fountain in Sicily.
3. rills: Brooks.
4. athwart: Across.
5. cedarn cover: Covering of cedar trees.

A mighty fountain momently was forced;
20   Amid whose swift half-intermitted burst
Huge fragments vaulted like rebounding hail,
Or chaffy grain beneath the thresher's flail;
And 'mid these dancing rocks at once and ever
It flung up momently the sacred river.
25   Five miles meandering with a mazy motion
Through wood and dale the sacred river ran,
Then reached the caverns measureless to man,
And sank in tumult to a lifeless ocean:
And 'mid this tumult Kubla heard from far
30   Ancestral voices prophesying war!
        The shadow of the dome of pleasure
        Floated midway on the waves;
        Where was heard the mingled measure
        From the fountain and the caves.
35   It was a miracle of rare device.[6]
A sunny pleasure dome with caves of ice!

        A damsel with a dulcimer[7]
        In a vision once I saw:
        It was an Abyssinian[8] maid,
40   And on her dulcimer she played,
        Singing of Mount Abora.[9]
        Could I revive within me
        Her symphony and song,
        To such a deep delight 'twould win me,
45   That with music loud and long,
I would build that dome in air,
That sunny dome! those caves of ice!
And all who heard should see them there,
And all should cry, Beware! Beware!
50   His flashing eyes, his floating hair!
Weave a circle round him thrice,
And close your eyes with holy dread,
For he on honeydew hath fed,
And drunk the milk of Paradise.

---

6. device: Design.
7. dulcimer: (dul′ sə mər) *n.*: A musical instrument with metal
strings which produce sounds when struck by two small hammers.
8. Abyssinian (ab ə sin′ ē ən): Ethiopian.
9. Mount Abora: Probably Mount Amara in Abyssinia.

KUBLAI KHAN
Chinese Silk Album Leaf, Yuan Dynasty

RESPONDING TO THE SELECTION

Your Response

1. Coleridge never finished this poem. Does it seem incomplete to you? Explain.

Recalling

2. What was the size of the palatial estate that Kubla Khan ordered built?
3. What did Kubla Khan hear in the noise made by the river emptying into the ocean?
4. (a) According to the last stanza, what did the speaker once see in a vision? (b) What part of that vision does the speaker wish he could revive?

Interpreting

5. Using your own words, explain what the speaker says would happen to him and "all who heard" if he were able to revive his vision.
6. What statement do you think Coleridge is making here about the power of imagination?
7. (a) Find one example each of Coleridge's use of alliteration and assonance. (b) Explain how each example enhances the meaning or mood of the words.
8. (a) Do you feel that Coleridge's imagination and "music" combine to make his vision seem real to the reader? (b) Support your answer with quotations from the poem.

Applying

9. Do you think people should be governed more by their emotions or their reason? Do you think there should be a balance between the two? Explain your answer.

GEORGE GORDON, LORD BYRON

1788–1824

In his life as well as in his work, George Gordon, Lord Byron, typified the Romanticist's zest for life. As much a public figure as a literary genius, Byron lived life "in the fast lane"—a point that was looked on with disapproval by his contemporaries.

It is significant to note that Byron was born in London to a father whose good looks—which his son inherited—made him irresistible to women. The father, John Byron, died when his son was three. When the young Byron was ten, the death of a great-uncle brought him the title of Baron, along with an estate at Newstead. Here the boy and his mother went to live until, at seventeen, Byron left home to attend Trinity College at Cambridge. At college Byron made many friends, played many sports, and spent much money. He also published his first book of poems, *Hours of Idleness* (1807), which received harsh criticism from the *Edinburgh Review*. He was hurt but not crushed by this attack on his work, and two years later he came out with *English Bards and Scotch Reviewers,* a poem poking fun at the magazine.

Byron then journeyed to the Near East, and spent the next two years traveling. When he returned home, he brought with him two sections of a book-length poem titled *Childe Harold's Pilgrimage* which depicted a young hero not unlike himself—moody, reckless, sensitive, and adventuresome. The work was received with great enthusiasm, and Byron became a very popular figure in important English circles. So great was his popularity, in fact, that his next published work, *The Corsair,* sold 10,000 copies in one day.

During this period Byron saw a great many women. In 1815 he married Anne Isabella Milbanke, with whom he had a daughter. The couple seemed mismatched from the start and, after about a year, separated. Hurt by nasty gossip, Byron left England, never to return. It was in Italy that he began work on his most ambitious opus, *Don Juan* (pronounced "jōō′ən"), a mock epic of the Romantic hero.

It was also at this point that tragedy struck, and then struck again—first with the death of his daughter, later with that of his friend, the poet Shelley. In 1823 Bryon joined a group of revolutionaries seeking to free Greece from Turkish rule. Before the revolt got underway, however, Byron died of rheumatic fever, at the age of thirty-six.

Although Byron openly spurned the works of other Romantic poets, including Wordsworth and Coleridge, his independence was a hallmark of the Romantic movement.

GUIDE FOR INTERPRETING

She Walks in Beauty;
So We'll Go No More A-Roving;
Apostrophe to the Ocean

Writers' Techniques

Figurative Language. Figurative language is the name given to a class of literary conventions that purposely distort language to make ideas more interesting and memorable. Unlike literal language, it is not to be taken at face value. When a poet writes, for instance, of trees "standing by the side of the road like sentinels," he or she is attempting to get the reader to picture trees that are very upright, much like soldiers.

Focus

Develop a list of about twenty adjectives and descriptive phrases, such as *blue, filled with holes, slippery,* and so on. Randomly choose three entries from your list and write them at the top of a sheet of paper. Then try to think of two objects that share the three traits. Write a sentence that compares one of the objects to the other. Try this with at least four pairs of objects.

Primary Source

Lady Caroline Lamb, wildly in love with Byron, confided in her diary that he was "Mad, bad, and dangerous to know." Whether or not we completely believe her, we cannot deny that Byron had an astonishing effect on those he met. Critic Gilbert Highet has an intriguing theory to explain Byron's remarkable personality.

Highet claims that Byron was "not naturally a slender, elegant, athletic, grave young man at all. Naturally, he was a plump, pleasant, pot-bellied person, and he spent tremendous, almost unremitting efforts on keeping down his natural fat. He was about five feet eight. When he was nineteen years old, he weighed 202 pounds. . . . He resolved to get it off, and keep it off. He did so by painful exercises and the most Spartan regime of dieting, which may well have wrecked his liver. He took exercise wearing seven waistcoats and a heavy topcoat; then he took hot baths; he ate hardly anything. By the time he was twenty, he had got down to 147 pounds. . . . He was starving.

"He was a thin man, and inside him was a fat man roaring to be set free. . . . Byron had several vultures with their beaks buried deep into his vitals; but the one which he felt most constantly, if not most painfully, was that haggard-eyed, sharp-clawed, tireless monster, a starvation diet."

She Walks in Beauty

George Gordon, Lord Byron

This poem, written to be set to music, was inspired by Byron's first meeting with Lady Wilmot Horton, his cousin by marriage, who wore a black mourning gown with spangles.

She walks in beauty, like the night
    Of cloudless climes and starry skies;
And all that's best of dark and bright
    Meet in her aspect and her eyes:
5 Thus mellowed to that tender light
    Which heaven to gaudy day denies.

One shade the more, one ray the less,
    Had half impaired the nameless grace
Which waves in every raven tress,
10   Or softly lightens o'er her face;
Where thoughts serenely sweet express
    How pure, how dear their dwelling place.

And on that cheek, and o'er that brow,
    So soft, so calm, yet eloquent,
15 The smiles that win, the tints that glow,
    But tell of days in goodness spent,
A mind at peace with all below,
    A heart whose love is innocent!

■ RESPONDING TO THE SELECTION

Your Response

1. Do you think the speaker idealizes the subject of this poem? Explain.

Recalling

2. In "She Walks in Beauty," to what does the speaker of the poem compare the lady's beauty?

Interpreting

3. What do you think is the meaning of "that tender light" in line 5?

4. What does the speaker believe the woman's appearance reveals about her character?

Applying

5. For Byron, why was nature a compelling concept with which to compare a lady's beauty?

So We'll Go No More A-Roving

George Gordon, Lord Byron

This poem was included in a letter to Thomas Moore, written from Venice on February 28, 1817. Carnival season had just passed and Byron, at the age of twenty-nine, found himself in a prolonged period of reflection. The poem is based on the refrain of the Scottish song, "The Jolly Beggar."

So we'll go no more a-roving
    So late into the night,
Though the heart be still as loving,
    And the moon be still as bright.

5 For the sword outwears its sheath,
    And the soul wears out the breast,
And the heart must pause to breathe,
    And Love itself have rest.

Though the night was made for loving,
10   And the day returns too soon,
Yet we'll go no more a-roving
    By the light of the moon.

▌R ESPONDING TO THE SELECTION

Your Response

1. Have you ever experienced the mood described in this poem? What prompted it for you? Did it last?

Recalling

2. What does the speaker say that "Love itself" must have?

Interpreting

3. (a) What do you think is meant by the line "And the soul wears out the breast"? (b) Why must the heart "pause to breathe"?
4. (a) Why will the speaker "go no more a-roving"? (b) How might you summarize the speaker's message in one sentence?

Applying

5. Which properties of the Romantic spirit are evident in this poem?

from Childe Harold's Pilgrimage
Apostrophe to the Ocean

George Gordon, Lord Byron

There is a pleasure in the pathless woods,
There is a rapture on the lonely shore,
There is society, where none intrudes,
By the deep sea, and music in its roar;
5   I love not man the less, but nature more,
From these our interviews, in which I steal
From all I may be, or have been before,
To mingle with the universe, and feel
What I can ne'er express, yet cannot all conceal.

10   Roll on, thou deep and dark blue ocean—roll!
Ten thousand fleets sweep over thee in vain;
Man marks the earth with ruin—his control
Stops with the shore; upon the watery plain
The wrecks are all thy deed, nor doth remain
15   A shadow of man's ravage, save[1] his own,
When, for a moment, like a drop of rain,
He sinks into thy depths with bubbling groan,
Without a grave, unknelled, uncoffined, and unknown.

His steps are not upon thy paths—thy fields
20   Are not a spoil for him—thou dost arise
And shake him from thee; the vile strength he wields
For earth's destruction thou dost all despise,
Spurning him from thy bosom to the skies,
And send'st him, shivering in thy playful spray
25   And howling, to his gods, where haply[2] lies
His petty hope in some near port or bay,
And dashest him again to earth—there let him lay.[3]

---

1. save: Except.
2. haply: Perhaps.
3. lay: A note on Byron's proof suggests that he intentionally made
this grammatical error for the sake of the rhyme.

SHIPWRECK
J.C.C. Dahl
Munich Neue Pinakothek/Kavaler

The armaments which thunderstrike the walls
Of rock-built cities, bidding nations quake,
30   And monarchs tremble in their capitals,
The oak leviathans,[4] whose huge ribs make
Their clay creator[5] the vain title take
Of lord of thee, and arbiter of war—
These are thy toys, and, as the snowy flake,
35   They melt into thy yeast of waves, which mar
Alike the Armada's[6] pride or spoils of Trafalgar.[7]

Thy shores are empires, changed in all save thee—
Assyria, Greece, Rome, Carthage, what are they?
Thy waters washed them power while they were free,
40   And many a tyrant since; their shores obey

4. leviathans (lə vī′ ə thənz): Monstrous sea creatures, described in
the Old Testament. Here the word means giant ships.
5. clay creator: Human beings.
6. Armada's: Refers to the Spanish Armada, defeated by the English
in 1588.
7. Trafalgar: The battle in 1805 during which the French and
Spanish fleets were defeated by the British fleet led by Lord Nelson.

The stranger, slave, or savage; their decay
Has dried up realms to deserts—not so thou,
Unchangeable, save to thy wild waves' play.
Time writes no wrinkle on thine azure brow:
45 Such as creation's dawn beheld, thou rollest now.

Thou glorious mirror, where the Almighty's form
Glasses[8] itself in tempests; in all time,
Calm or convulsed—in breeze, or gale, or storm,
Icing the pole, or in the torrid clime
50 Dark-heaving—boundless, endless, and sublime;
The image of eternity, the throne
Of the Invisible; even from out thy slime
The monsters of the deep are made; each zone
Obeys thee; thou goest forth, dread, fathomless, alone.

55 And I have loved thee, ocean! and my joy
Of youthful sports was on thy breast to be
Borne, like thy bubbles, onward; from a boy
I wantoned with thy breakers—they to me
Were a delight; and if the freshening sea
60 Made them a terror—'twas a pleasing fear,
For I was as it were a child of thee,
And trusted to thy billows far and near,
And laid my hand upon thy mane—as I do here.

---

8. glasses: Mirrors.

Primary Source

How do poets evaluate their own works? How did Byron feel about his much-celebrated *Childe Harold's Pilgrimage*? In a letter to his printer, Byron offered his opinion.

Dear Sir,

I enclose a sheet for correction, if you ever get to another edition. You will observe the blunder in printing makes it appear as if the Château was over St. Gingo, instead of being on the opposite shore of the Lake, over Clarens. So, separate the paragraphs, otherwise my topography will be seen as inaccurate as your typography on this occasion.

The other day I wrote to convey my proposition with regard to the 4th and concluding canto [of *Childe Harold's Pilgrimage*]. I have gone over and extended it to one hundred and fifty stanzas. . . . I look upon Childe Harold as my best; and as I begun, I think of concluding with it. But I make no resolutions on that head, as I broke my former intention with regard to "The Corsair." However, I fear that I shall never do better; and yet, not being thirty years of age, for some moons to come, one ought to be progressive as far as Intellect goes for many a good year. But I have had a devilish deal of wear and tear of mind and body in my time, besides having published too often and much already.

RESPONDING TO THE SELECTION

Your Response

1. What aspect of nature evokes the strongest response in you? Why?

Recalling

2. How does the speaker of the poem say the ocean makes him feel?
3. How does he say the ocean treats such things as warships and sea monsters?
4. What childhood memories of the ocean does the speaker have?

Interpreting

5. In line 10 the speaker describes the movement of ships over the ocean as "in vain." What might he mean by this?
6. What property of the ocean does the speaker admire in the fifth stanza?
7. What double meaning might the speaker have intended in his reference to the ocean as a glorious mirror in line 46?

Applying

8. Do you believe it is still true today that humans' control of the planet "stops with the shore," as Byron puts it in "Apostrophe to the Ocean"? Explain.

ANALYZING LITERATURE

Understanding Figurative Language

Figurative language is language that links, in one way or another, things or ideas that are generally unrelated. Also known as figures of speech, figurative language is actually a category heading for a number of literary devices. *Simile,* among the best known of these, is a comparison using a word such as *like* or *as.* The line "the sheen of their spears was like stars on the sea" contains a simile.

Metaphor, often thought of as a companion to the simile, compares two objects without making use of a linking word. The line "The moon was a ghostly galleon tossed upon cloudy seas" contains a metaphor.

A third device, *personification,* gives human characteristics to nonhuman objects. The line "The moon peeked out from behind a cloud" contains an example of personification.

Identify the type of figurative language in each quotation, and express in your own words what it adds to the poem.

1. "She walks in beauty, like the night . . ." (p. 690)
2. ". . . the heart must pause to breathe . . ." (p. 691)
3. ". . . like a drop of rain,/He sinks into thy depths . . ." (p. 692)
4. "These are thy toys, and, as the snowy flake,/They melt into the yeast of waves . . ." (p. 693)
5. "Thou glorious mirror, where the Almighty's form/Glasses itself . . ." (p. 694)

THINKING AND WRITING

Evaluating a Poem

When you read a review of a film or book in a newspaper, you are reading an evaluation. Write an evaluation of one of the three poems by Byron. First, jot down ideas about this poem. Then, write your first draft. Mention such things as language, style, and subject matter, and conclude with your personal reactions to the piece, giving conclusive reasons for why you feel as you do. When you revise, make sure that your arguments are sound. Proofread your essay and prepare a final draft.

LEARNING OPTION

Cross-curricular Connection. The ocean has inspired artists and composers as well as writers. Investigate visual representations or musical evocations of the ocean. Look for a painting that reflects your image of the sea, or find a symphonic "tone-poem" that re-creates the sounds and sensations at the shore. Try not to limit your explorations to art and music from Europe. Bring the print or recording to class and explain your interest in it. Provide some background on the artist or composer and answer any questions.

GUIDE FOR INTERPRETING

from Don Juan

Literary Forms

Mock Epic. A mock epic is a long poem that mocks, or pokes fun at, a trivial subject by treating it in the grand style of epic poetry. The epic poem, which finds its loftiest expression in such timeless works as the *Iliad,* the *Odyssey,* and *Paradise Lost,* is defined not only by its style but also by certain regular features. The poem usually begins, for example, with an *invocation,* or request for inspiration and guidance from a muse or deity, and it is usually divided into long sections called *cantos,* or books. In addition, the epic generally contains lengthy speeches by heroes and includes descriptions of battles fought by noble warriors. In a mock epic, however, a combination of a lofty style and a common subject leads to humorous results. When, for example, the romantic adventures of a beautiful young man are narrated in a grand fashion, as is the case in *Don Juan,* the resulting product is hilarious.

Focus

Think of an ordinary activity such as walking a dog or going to the supermarket for groceries. Then, think of several adjectives that might be used—or *misused*—to describe this activity in a heroic manner. Finally, write a "mini-mock-epic" that paints a lofty picture of this routine task.

Commentary

Despite a great enthusiasm for reading, public taste became increasingly conservative during the Romantic Age. Groups such as the Society for the Suppression of Vice were remarkably effective in controlling public taste. The fear of prosecution made many booksellers unwilling to print works that were either risqué or immoral. Byron's publisher, for example, was reluctant to print the first two cantos of *Don Juan* because he feared he might be prosecuted. When *Don Juan* did appear, the vice society took no action against it, although many reviewers denounced it as indecent and immoral. The *Eclectic Review,* for example, warned that Byron wrote poetry "such as no brother could read aloud to his sister, no husband to his wife—poetry in which the deliberate purpose of the author is to corrupt by inflaming the mind." One woman was horrified when a clergyman told her he had bought an edition of Byron's poems, though he "boasted that he had burned *Don Juan.*"

What do you see in this excerpt from *Don Juan* that might have inflamed readers in Byron's day?

from **Don Juan**

George Gordon, Lord Byron

Though it is unfinished, Don Juan *is generally regarded as Byron's finest work. A mock epic described by Shelley as "something wholly new and relative to the age," it satirizes the political and social problems of Byron's time.*

Traditionally Don Juan, the poem's hero, had been portrayed as a wicked and immoral character driven solely by his obsession with beautiful women. In Byron's work Don Juan is depicted as an innocent young man whose physical beauty, charm, and spirit prove to be extremely alluring to ladies. As a result, he finds himself in many difficult situations.

Many people feel that Don Juan *would not be a great poem without the periodic pauses in the story during which the speaker drifts away from the subject. In these digressions the speaker comments on the issues of the time and on life in general. In this excerpt the speaker sets aside the adventures of his hero to reflect on old age and death.*

But now at thirty years my hair is gray
    (I wonder what it will be like at forty?
I thought of a peruke[1] the other day)—
    My heart is not much greener; and, in short, I
5 Have squandered my whole summer while 'twas May,
    And feel no more the spirit to retort; I
Have spent my life, both interest and principal,
And deem not, what I deemed, my soul invincible.

No more—no more—Oh! never more on me
10   The freshness of the heart can fall like dew,
Which out of all the lovely things we see
    Extracts emotions beautiful and new,
Hived in our bosoms like the bag o' the bee:
    Think'st thou the honey with those objects grew?
15 Alas! 'twas not in them, but in thy power
To double even the sweetness of a flower.

No more—no more—Oh! never more, my heart,
    Canst thou be my sole world, my universe!

---

1. peruke (pə ro͞ok'): Wig.

Once all in all, but now a thing apart,
20   Thou canst not be my blessing or my curse:
The illusion's gone forever, and thou art
      Insensible, I trust, but none the worse,
And in thy stead I've got a deal of judgment,
Though heaven knows how it ever found a lodgment.

25   My days of love are over; me no more
      The charms of maid, wife, and still less of widow
Can make the fool of which they made before—
      In short, I must not lead the life I did do;
The credulous hope of mutual minds is o'er,
30   The copious use of claret is forbid too,
So for a good old-gentlemanly vice,
I think I must take up with avarice.

Ambition was my idol, which was broken
      Before the shrines of Sorrow and of Pleasure;
35   And the two last have left me many a token
      O'er which reflection may be made at leisure:
Now, like Friar Bacon's brazen head, I've spoken,
      "Time is, Time was, Time's past,"[2] a chymic[3] treasure
Is glittering youth, which I have spent betimes—
40   My heart in passion, and my head on rhymes.

What is the end of fame? 'tis but to fill
      A certain portion of uncertain paper:
Some liken it to climbing up a hill,
      Whose summit, like all hills, is lost in vapor;
45   For this men write, speak, preach, and heroes kill,
      And bards burn what they call their "midnight taper,"
To have, when the original is dust,
A name, a wretched picture, and worse bust.

What are the hopes of man? Old Egypt's King
50   Cheops erected the first pyramid
And largest, thinking it was just the thing
      To keep his memory whole, and mummy hid:
But somebody or other rummaging
      Burglariously broke his coffin's lid:
55   Let not a monument give you or me hopes,
Since not a pinch of dust remains of Cheops.

---

2. Friar Bacon . . . Time's past": In Robert Greene's comedy *Friar Bacon and Friar Burgandy* (1594), these words are spoken by a bronze bust, made by Friar Bacon.
3. chymic (kim' ik): Alchemic; counterfeit.

But I, being fond of true philosophy,
     Say very often to myself, "Alas!
All things that have been born were born to die,
60   And flesh (which Death mows down to hay) is grass;
You've passed your youth not so unpleasantly,
     And if you had it o'er again—'twould pass—
So thank your stars that matters are no worse,
And read your Bible, sir, and mind your purse."

65 But for the present, gentle reader! and
     Still gentler purchaser! the bard—that's I—
Must, with permission, shake you by the hand,
     And so your humble servant, and good-bye!
We meet again, if we should understand
70   Each other; and if not, I shall not try
Your patience further than by this short sample—
'Twere well if others followed my example.

"Go, little book, from this my solitude!
     I cast thee on the waters—go thy ways!
75 And if, as I believe, thy vein be good,
     The world will find thee after many days."[4]
When Southey's read, and Wordsworth understood,
     I can't help putting in my claim to praise—
The four first rhymes are Southey's, every line:
80 For God's sake, reader! take them not for mine!

---

4. "Go . . . days": The lines are from the last stanza of Robert Southey's (1774–1843) *Epilogue to the Lay of the Laureate.*

![R]ESPONDING TO THE SELECTION

Your Response
1. Do you share the speaker's attitude toward ambition? Why or why not?

Recalling
2. (a) What, according to lines 17 and 18, does the speaker say has been his "sole world" and "universe" up until now? (b) According to the fourth stanza, with what "old-gentlemanly vice" will he replace it?

Interpreting
3. In the fifth stanza, the speaker notes that "glittering youth" is a "chymic," or counterfeit, "treasure." What do you think he means by this?
4. Summarize in your own words the point the speaker is making in his mention of Cheops.

Applying
5. What do you think is meant by the remark "flesh . . . is grass" in line 60?

![T]HINKING AND WRITING

Writing About the Byronic Hero
Byron saw himself as melancholy, sensitive, rebellious, fearless, moody, and adventurous. These traits characterize the "Byronic hero." Choose a fictional character that comes close to fitting this description. In an essay, explain in what ways this character is, and is not, a Byronic hero. When you revise, be sure you have supported your main idea.

PERCY BYSSHE SHELLEY

1792–1822

When he died in a boating accident at age thirty, Percy Bysshe Shelley was eulogized by his friend Byron as "without exception the best and least selfish man I ever knew." This seems strange praise indeed, considering it was directed at a man whose disenchantment with the world was at least as great as his appreciation of its beauties. At once modest and intense, Shelley was a poet of rare gift. He was also a self-appointed reformer who believed that humankind was capable of attaining a more nearly perfect society.

Shelley was born in Sussex and raised on a fine country estate where he spent a quiet childhood. He was sent to excellent schools—first Eton, a prestigious boarding school, and later Oxford—but was never able to settle into the routine of a student. Instead, he preferred to wander the countryside or perform private scientific experiments. At Oxford Shelley became friends with a young man named Thomas Jefferson Hogg, whose political views were as strong as his own. The friendship further fueled Shelley's rebellious nature, and with Hogg's support he wrote a pamphlet titled *The Necessity of Atheism.* Both were expelled.

The incident led to trouble between Shelley and his father, and instead of going home, Shelley headed for London. There he met sixteen-year-old Harriet Westbrook, who played on his sympathy for the underdog by describing her miserable situation at home and at school. The two married and went to Ireland, where Shelley tried unsuccessfully to "deliver the Irish people from tyranny."

In 1813 he completed his first important poem, "Queen Mab," a philosophical work that explored some of the ideas he had read in Godwin's *Political Justice.* Shelley's view—that government and institutions should be reshaped to better conform to the will of the people—was evident in much of his poetry, even in his nature poems.

Shelley's marriage, meanwhile, was in trouble. Harriet felt she could not keep up with her husband, whose political ideals, in any case, she had come to question. Shelley was unhappy too. After divorcing Harriet in 1814, he married Mary Wollstonecraft Godwin.

Shelley spent the last four years of his life in Italy, where he became close friends with Byron. Here Shelley wrote some of his best poetry, including "Ode to the West Wind" and *Prometheus Unbound,* the second of these a long poem predicting that someday humanity would be free of tyranny.

Shelley has been called the perfect poet of the Romantic era. One need only consider his emotional response to life and his belief in personal freedom to appreciate how fitting that title is.

GUIDE FOR INTERPRETING

Ozymandias; Ode to the West Wind; To a Skylark; To—; A Dirge

Literary Forms

The Ode. Poetic structure is the framework or blueprint on which a poem is built. The structure takes into account the number of stanzas, the rhyme scheme, and the rhythmic patterns to be used.

An **ode** is a lyrical poem that pays homage to a person, a quality, or a thing. The first odes were written by the Greek poet Pindar (552?–443? B.C.) and the Latin poet Horace (65–8 B.C.) The Pindaric ode, which is the more-often imitated of the two types, consists mainly of three-line stanzas called *triads*. Shelley's "Ode to the West Wind" is a Pindaric ode.

Focus

Think of several individuals, objects, and qualities that you hold in high regard. To get yourself started, you might think of people in your community who have such character traits as honesty and reliability. Write each at the top of a sheet of paper and under it jot down some of your thoughts.

Commentary

The following story is told about Shelley's death. On July 8, 1822, Shelley and Edward Williams boarded their small boat to return to their summer home on the Gulf of Spezia, but their friend E. J. Trelawny was denied port clearance. As Trelawny stood sullenly on the dock watching his friends sail off, a sailor pointed to the water and said, "Look at the smoke on the water; the devil is brewing mischief." Oppressed by the heat, Trelawny dozed off. When he awoke around dinnertime, a fierce storm had blown in. Although Trelawny anxiously scanned every dot on the horizon, he could see no sign of Shelley's small boat. Three days passed in terrible anxiety as he spoke with the crews of all returning boats.

On the morning of the third day, Trelawny rode to Pisa, where he summoned Byron and dispatched a number of searchers. A waterkeg and some bottles from Shelley's boat had washed up on the sand. More than a week later, the two bodies were found on the shore. Although the bodies were badly mutilated, Trelawny recognized his friend by the volume of Sophocles in one pocket and a copy of Keats's poems in the other. He also identified Williams's body. Shortly thereafter he arranged to have both bodies cremated. Despite the fierce blaze, the poet's heart did not burn. Trelawny snatched it out of the fire, badly burning his hand. He gave the relic to Mary Shelley. He took the remains to a Protestant cemetery near Rome, where they were buried. When Trelawny died in 1881, his ashes were buried in a tomb beside that of his friend.

Ozymandias[1]

Percy Bysshe Shelley

I met a traveler from an antique land
Who said: Two vast and trunkless legs of stone
Stand in the desert. Near them, on the sand,
Half sunk, a shattered visage lies, whose frown,
5 And wrinkled lip, and sneer of cold command,
Tell that its sculptor well those passions read
Which yet survive, stamped on these lifeless things,
The hand that mocked them and the heart that fed:
And on the pedestal these words appear:
10 "My name is Ozymandias, king of kings:
Look on my works, ye Mighty, and despair!"
Nothing beside remains. Round the decay
Of that colossal wreck, boundless and bare,
The lone and level sands stretch far away.

---

1. Ozymandias (ōz ĭ män′ dē əs): The Greek name for Ramses.
Ramses II, the king referred to in the poem, was a pharaoh who ruled
Egypt during the thirteenth century B.C. and built many great palaces
and statues. One statue was inscribed with the words: "I am
Ozymandias, king of kings, if anyone wishes to know what I am and
where I lie, let him surpass me in some of my exploits."

RESPONDING TO THE SELECTION

Your Response
1. Do you think that the message of this poem is pertinent to today's world? Explain.

Recalling
2. (a) Whom has the speaker met? (b) What sight does this person describe?

Interpreting
3. Think of the words on the pedestal. (a) Why is it ironic that the statue has crumbled? (b) Why is it ironic that it is surrounded by desert?
4. What is the theme of this poem?

Applying
5. (a) What is your definition of *power*? (b) What is your definition of *pride*? (c) In what way do the two complement each other?

ANALYZING LITERATURE

Understanding Poetic Structure
The poetic structure of a poem is the plan on which it is built. Poetic structure includes such elements as rhyme, rhythm, and number of stanzas. Analyze the poetic structure of "Ozymandias." State whether or not you feel this structure enhances the poem's message. When you revise, make sure you have provided adequate support for your main idea.

THE COLOSSI OF MEMNON

Ode to the West Wind

Percy Bysshe Shelley

Shelley composed this poem in the woods near Florence, Italy. He described the day of its composition as one "when that tempestuous wind, whose temperature is at once mild and animating, was collecting the vapors which pour down the autumnal rains."

I

O wild West Wind, thou breath of Autumn's being,
Thou, from whose unseen presence the leaves dead
Are driven, like ghosts from an enchanter fleeing,

Yellow, and black, and pale, and hectic red,
5 Pestilence-stricken multitudes: O thou,
Who chariotest to their dark and wintry bed

The wingèd seeds, where they lie cold and low,
Each like a corpse within its grave, until
Thine azure sister of the Spring[1] shall blow

10 Her clarion[2] o'er the dreaming earth, and fill
(Driving sweet buds like flocks to feed in air)
With loving hues and odors plain and hill:

Wild Spirit, which art moving everywhere;
Destroyer and preserver; hear, oh, hear!

II

15 Thou on whose stream, 'mid the steep sky's commotion,
Loose clouds like earth's decaying leaves are shed,
Shook from the tangled boughs of Heaven and Ocean,

Angels[3] of rain and lightning: there are spread
On the blue surface of thine aery surge,
20 Like the bright hair uplifted from the head

---

1. sister of Spring: The south wind.
2. clarion: *n.*: A trumpet producing clear, sharp, shrill tones.
3. angels: Messengers.

Of some fierce Maenad,[4] even from the dim verge
Of the horizon to the zenith's height,
The locks of the approaching storm. Thou dirge

Of the dying year, to which this closing night
25 Will be the dome of a vast sepulcher,
Vaulted with all thy congregated might

Of vapors, from whose solid atmosphere
Black rain, and fire, and hail will burst: oh, hear!

III

Thou who didst waken from his summer dreams
30 The blue Mediterranean, where he lay,
Lulled by the coil of his crystalline streams,

---

4. Maenad (mē′ nad): A priestess of Bacchus, the Greek and Roman
god of wine and revelry.

Beside a pumice[5] aisle in Baiae's bay,[6]
And saw in sleep old palaces and towers
Quivering within the wave's intenser day,

35 All overgrown with azure moss and flowers
So sweet, the sense faints picturing them! Thou
For whose path the Atlantic's level powers

Cleave themselves into chasms, while far below
The sea-blooms and the oozy woods which wear
40 The sapless foliage of the ocean, know

Thy voice, and suddenly grow gray with fear,
And tremble and despoil themselves: oh, hear!

IV

If I were a dead leaf thou mightest bear;
If I were a swift cloud to fly with thee;
45 A wave to pant beneath thy power, and share

The impulse of thy strength, only less free
Than thou, O uncontrollable! If even
I were as in my boyhood, and could be

The comrade of thy wanderings over Heaven,
50 As then, when to outstrip thy skyey speed
Scarce seemed a vision; I would ne'er have striven

As thus with thee in prayer in my sore need.
Oh, lift me as a wave, a leaf, a cloud!
I fall upon the thorns of life! I bleed!

55 A heavy weight of hours has chained and bowed
One too like thee: tameless, and swift, and proud.

V

Make me thy lyre,[7] even as the forest is:
What if my leaves are falling like its own!
The tumult of thy mighty harmonies

---

5. pumice (pum′ is) *n.*: Volcanic rock.
6. Baiae's (bā′ yēz) **bay:** An ancient Roman resort near Naples.
7. lyre: Aeolian (ē o′ lē ən) lute, or wind harp, a stringed instrument
which produces musical sounds when the wind passes over it.

60　Will take from both a deep, autumnal tone,
　　Sweet though in sadness. Be thou, Spirit fierce,
　　My spirit! Be thou me, impetuous one!

　　Drive my dead thought over the universe
　　Like withered leaves to quicken a new birth!
65　And, by the incantation of this verse,

　　Scatter, as from an extinguished hearth
　　Ashes and sparks, my words among mankind!
　　Be through my lips to unawakened earth

　　The trumpet of a prophecy! O Wind,
70　If Winter comes, can Spring be far behind?

▚ RESPONDING TO THE SELECTION

Your Response
1. What aspect of nature would you choose to express the ideas of renewal and freedom? Explain.

Recalling
2. According to the poem, with what season is the west wind associated?
3. (a) What does the wind do to dead leaves? (b) What does it do to the ocean?
4. What does the speaker ask of the wind in section V of the poem?

Interpreting
5. In what sense is the wind a "destroyer and preserver"?
6. (a) How, according to section IV, has the speaker changed? (b) What caused this change?
7. Whose "new birth" (line 65) do you think the speaker wishes to bring about?
8. (a) Interpret the last line of this poem. (b) How

does this famous last line tie the poem together?

Applying
9. In what way is the message in this poem related to Shelley's lifelong mission?

▚ ANALYZING LITERATURE

Understanding the Ode
An **ode** is a poem that honors an individual, a thing, or a trait. The form dates back to classical times, when odes were written to be sung at festivals or in plays. Many features of the classical ode are found in "Ode to the West Wind." Find evidence of each of the following properties in Shelley's poem.
1. Direct form of address to the individual, trait, or thing being honored
2. An almost fearful reverence for the thing or person being honored
3. Dignified and lofty language and examples

To a Skylark

Percy Bysshe Shelley

Hail to thee, blithe spirit!
　　Bird thou never wert,
That from heaven, or near it,
　　Pourest thy full heart
5　In profuse strains of unpremeditated art.

　　Higher still and higher,
　　From the earth thou springest
Like a cloud of fire;
　　The blue deep thou wingest,
10　And singing still dost soar, and soaring ever singest.

　　In the golden lightning
　　Of the sunken sun,
O'er which clouds are brightening,
　　Thou dost float and run;
15　Like an unbodied joy whose race is just begun.

　　The pale purple even[1]
　　Melts around thy flight;
Like a star of heaven,
　　In the broad daylight
20　Thou art unseen, but yet I hear thy shrill delight,

　　Keen as are the arrows
　　Of that silver sphere,[2]
Whose intense lamp narrows
　　In the white dawn clear,
25　Until we hardly see—we feel that it is there.

　　All the earth and air
　　With thy voice is loud,
As, when night is bare,
　　From one lonely cloud
30　The moon rains out her beams, and Heaven is overflowed.

---

1. even: Evening.
2. silver sphere: The morning star.

What thou art we know not;
   What is most like thee?
From rainbow clouds there flow not
   Drops so bright to see,
35 As from thy presence showers a rain of melody.

   Like a poet hidden
     In the light of thought,
   Singing hymns unbidden,
     Till the world is wrought
40 To sympathy with hopes and fears it heeded not:

   Like a highborn maiden
     In a palace tower,
   Soothing her love-laden
     Soul in secret hour
45 With music sweet as love, which overflows her bower:

   Like a glowworm golden
     In a dell of dew,
   Scattering unbeholden
     Its aerial hue
50 Among the flowers and grass, which screen it from the
     view!

Like a rose embowered
   In its own green leaves,
By warm winds deflowered,[3]
   Till the scent it gives
55   Makes faint with too much sweet those heavy-wingèd
      thieves.[4]

Sound of vernal showers
   On the twinkling grass,
Rain-awakened flowers,
   All that ever was
60   Joyous, and clear, and fresh, thy music doth surpass:

Teach us, sprite or bird,
   What sweet thoughts are thine:
I have never heard
   Praise of love or wine
65   That panted forth a flood of rapture so divine.

Chorus Hymeneal,[5]
   Or triumphal chant,
Matched with thine would be all
   But an empty vaunt,
70   A thing wherein we feel there is some hidden want.

What objects are the fountains[6]
   Of thy happy strain?
What fields, or waves, or mountains?
   What shapes of sky or plain?
75   What love of thine own kind? what ignorance of pain?

With thy clear keen joyance
   Languor cannot be;
Shadow of annoyance
   Never came near thee;
80   Thou lovest—but ne'er knew love's sad satiety.

Waking or asleep,
   Thou of death must deem[7]
Things more true and deep
   Than we mortals dream,
85   Or how could thy notes flow in such a crystal stream?

---

3. deflowered: Fully open.
4. thieves: The "warm winds."
5. Chorus Hymeneal (hī′ mə nē′ əl): Marriage song, named after
Hymen, the Greek god of marriage.
6. fountains: Sources, inspiration.
7. deem: Know.

We look before and after,
    And pine for what is not;
Our sincerest laughter
    With some pain is fraught;
90   Our sweetest songs are those that tell of saddest thought.

Yet if[8] we could scorn
    Hate, and pride, and fear;
If we were things born
    Not to shed a tear,
95   I know not how thy joy we ever should come near.

Better than all measures
    Of delightful sound,
Better than all treasures
    That in books are found,
100   Thy skill to poet were,[9] thou scorner of the ground!

Teach me half the gladness
    That thy brain must know,
Such harmonious madness
    From my lips would flow,
105   The world should listen then, as I am listening now.

---

8. if: Even if.
9. were: Would be.

RESPONDING TO THE SELECTION

Your Response

1. Are you more optimistic than Shelley that the kind of pure joy he describes is possible for human beings? Why or why not?

Recalling

2. At what time of day does the "blithe spirit" fly?
3. (a) To what four things does the speaker compare the bird in lines 36–55? (b) In what ways does he say the bird is like these things?

Interpreting

4. Why does the poet say of the bird, "Bird thou never wert"?

5. What do you suppose the speaker means in line 80 by "love's sad satiety"?
6. (a) How is the poet's song different from the bird's song? (b) Why can the bird's song "flow in such a crystal stream"?
7. (a) What does the speaker ask the skylark to teach him? (b) What effect does he think this would have on the world? (c) Why does he feel this way?

Applying

8. The twentieth-century poet W. H. Auden wrote, "A verbal art like poetry is reflective; it stops to think. Music is immediate; it goes on to become." Discuss the meaning of this quotation.

To ———

Percy Bysshe Shelley

Music, when soft voices die,
Vibrates in the memory—
Odors, when sweet violets sicken,
Live within the sense they quicken.

5 Rose leaves, when the rose is dead,
Are heaped for the belovèd's bed;
And so thy thoughts,[1] when thou art gone,
Love itself shall slumber on.

---

1. thy thoughts: Thoughts of thee.

RESPONDING TO THE SELECTION

Your Response

1. Do you think the speaker argues his point convincingly? Why or why not?

Recalling

2. What does the speaker of the poem say will happen to "thy thoughts, when thou art gone"?

Interpreting

3. Explain how music, odors, and roses will live on.
4. What idea about love is the speaker communicating?

Applying

5. Would this idea come across differently if it were presented in simple prose rather than as a poem? Explain.

CRITICAL THINKING AND READING

Recognizing an Author's Style

Style is an author's selection and arrangement of words to express ideas. Just as no two personalities are identical, no two writing styles are identical. Sentence length, variation in sentence patterns, and word usage are among the features that define a writer's style. Carefully reread "To ———" and any other poem of your choice by Shelley, noting stylistic similarities in the areas mentioned above. Briefly describe this style, and tell whether or not you like it and why. When you revise, make sure you have included details from the poems to support your thesis.

THINKING AND WRITING

Writing an Ode

Select one of the objects, people, or qualities about which you jotted down some thoughts in the Focus activity. Examine the observations you made and decide whether you want to change, add, or remove any of them. Then write an ode to that person, quality, or thing. When you revise, make sure you have created a vivid description.

A Dirge

Percy Bysshe Shelley

Rough wind, that moanest loud
    Grief too sad for song;
Wild wind, when sullen cloud
    Knells all the night long;
5 Sad storm, whose tears are vain,
Bare woods, whose branches strain,
Deep caves and dreary main,—
    Wail, for the world's wrong!

RESPONDING TO THE SELECTION

Your Response

1. Has your reaction to "the world's wrong" ever been similar to the speaker's? Explain.

Recalling

2. What does the speaker of the poem ask the wind, a storm, and bare branches to do?

Interpreting

3. What do you think the speaker means by "the world's wrong"?
4. What effect is created by calling upon the natural elements to bemoan the world's wrong? How does this device help portray the poet's sense of moral indignation?

Applying

5. If Shelley were living in the contemporary world, what aspects of life might he bemoan?

THINKING AND WRITING

Comparing and Contrasting Nature Views

Select a poem by one of the other Romantic poets you have read so far, and compare that poet's view of nature with Shelley's. Start by jotting down notes about each poem. Use quotes from each of the poems to illustrate similarities and differences. When you revise, make sure you have presented your information in logical order.

LEARNING OPTION

Cross-curricular Connection. "Dirge" reveals a glimpse of Shelley's lifelong concern for social reform. Investigate Shelley's activities as a political idealist during the Romantic era. What were some of the social and political problems prevalent during his lifetime? How were they similar to or different from the kinds of problems we face today? How did Shelley use his writing to publicize his beliefs? Share your findings with the class.

JOHN KEATS

1795–1821

Despite his early death and the fact that the most important of his works were composed in the space of two years, John Keats remains one of the major influences on English poetry. Known as a pure artist, Keats saw the appreciation of beauty as an end in itself and made the pursuit of beauty the goal of his poetry. As Keats himself so eloquently put it, "Beauty is truth, truth beauty."

Born in London of working-class parents, Keats was unusually handsome and active as a child. He developed a reputation for fighting, not so much out of rowdiness as from a readiness to take sides in a worthy cause. It was not until he became a close friend of his schoolmaster's son, Charles Cowden Clarke, that Keats developed an interest in poetry and became an avid reader.

In 1815 Keats began the study of medicine at a London hospital. By this time he had already begun writing poetry, and though his studies earned him a pharmacist's license, he ultimately abandoned medicine for a career as a poet. His first major effort, *Endymion,* published in the spring of 1818, was severely attacked by the journals of the day. Part of the reason for the harsh criticism was Keats's association with Leigh Hunt, a radical poet, but much of it had to do with the verse itself. Far from being crushed by the assault, Keats began the second of his long poems, *Hyperion,* which was never completed.

The end of the year found Keats mourning the loss of his brother Tom to tuberculosis. It also found the poet deliriously happy over his engagement to Fanny Brawne, a lively eighteen-year-old who was a light in Keats's life. The following year, 1819, Keats turned out his finest work, including "The Eve of St. Agnes," "The Eve of St. Mark," and his famous odes. This might have been only the beginning, but Keats's health took a turn for the worse. He moved to Italy, which promised a warmer climate, but to no avail. After a long battle with tuberculosis, the disease that had claimed his brother, he died at age twenty-five.

Though Keats and Shelley knew each other, their visions of what the poet should be could not have been more different. Keats did not share Shelley's rebellious spirit, nor did he feel that poetry was the proper vehicle for political statements. Rather, Keats sought to refine his idea of beauty, and in so doing, he refined ours. His extraordinary sensitivity enabled him to see beauty in the most ordinary of circumstances, while his mastery of verse enabled him to unveil that beauty to the world.

On First Looking into Chapman's Homer; Bright Star, Would I Were Steadfast as Thou Art; When I Have Fears That I May Cease to Be

Literary Forms

The Sonnet. The sonnet is a poem of fourteen lines arranged according to a specific rhyme scheme, with five strong beats and five weak beats per line. In each of the two basic types of sonnet, Petrarchan and Shakespearean, one portion of the poem is used to present a problem or ask a question, and another portion resolves it. Despite the demands of its form, the successful sonnet is one that flows smoothly, creates powerful impressions, and delivers an important message without sounding forced. These features are hallmarks of the sonnets written by Keats.

Focus

Think about a book you have read or a film or work of art you have seen that in some way has changed your life. Consider the particular features of the work that affected you. Then freewrite, comparing this experience to other moving experiences people have.

Primary Source

We now know that ill health, aggravated by severe financial and family problems, was the true cause of Keats's premature death. However, for many years his early death was blamed on the effects of two vicious articles published in leading literary journals of his day.

Both attacks were anonymous. One article assaulted Keats as a member of fellow author Leigh Hunt's radical literary circle in London. The other piece ripped into his poem *Endymion*. Although Keats himself had the common sense to see that the attacks were brought about by political and social snobbery, many of his contemporaries supported the myth that the attack caused his death. One in particular was Lord Byron, who penned the following epitaph:

> John Keats, who was really killed off by one critique
> Just as he really promised something great,
> If not intelligible, without Greek
> Contrived to talk about the gods of late
> Much as they might have been supposed to speak.
> Poor fellow! His was an untoward fate;
> 'Tis strange the mind, that very fiery particle,
> Should let itself be snuffed out by an article.

On First Looking into Chapman's Homer

John Keats

*When Keats was twenty-one, his former teacher,
Charles Cowden Clarke, introduced him to a translation of
Homer by Elizabethan poet George Chapman. The two men
spent the evening reading this book, and early the next
morning Keats presented this sonnet to Clarke.*

Much have I traveled in the realms of gold,
    And many goodly states and kingdoms seen;
    Round many western islands have I been
Which bards in fealty to Apollo[1] hold.
5 Oft of one wide expanse had I been told
    That deep-browed Homer ruled as his demesne;[2]
    Yet did I never breathe its pure serene[3]
Till I heard Chapman speak out loud and bold:
Then felt I like some watcher of the skies
10   When a new planet swims into his ken;
Or like stout Cortez[4] when with eagle eyes
    He stared at the Pacific—and all his men
Looked at each other with a wild surmise—
    Silent, upon a peak in Darien.[5]

---

1. Apollo: In Greek and Roman mythology, the god of music, poetry,
and medicine.
2. demesne (di mān'): Realm.
3. serene: Clear air.
4. Cortez: Here, Keats was mistaken. The Pacific was discovered in
1513 by Balboa, not Cortez.
5. Darien (der' ē ən): The Isthmus of Panama.

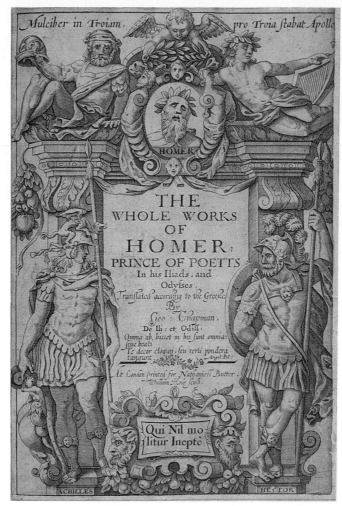

FRONTISPIECE, HOMER'S ILIAD AND ODYSSEY, 1612
William Hole
The British Library

Your Response

1. How do you feel when you've made a great new discovery? Is your reaction similar to the speaker's? Explain.

Recalling

2. What does the speaker of the poem claim he missed before reading Chapman?

Interpreting

3. Dante Gabriel Rossetti, a poet of the nineteenth century, wrote that "A Sonnet is a coin; its face reveals/The soul—its converse, to what Power 'tis due." (a) How would you describe Keats's "soul," as it is revealed in "On First Looking into Chapman's Homer"? (b) What is the "power" to which that soul owes its due?

Applying

4. Do you think books can change people's lives? Explain your answer.

Bright Star, Would I Were Steadfast as Thou Art

John Keats

Bright star, would I were steadfast as thou art—
    Not in lone splendor hung aloft the night
And watching, with eternal lids apart,
    Like nature's patient, sleepless Eremite,[1]
5 The moving waters at their priestlike task
    Of pure ablution round earth's human shores,
Or gazing on the new soft-fallen mask
    Of snow upon the mountains and the moors—
No—yet still steadfast, still unchangeable,
10   Pillowed upon my fair love's ripening breast,
To feel forever its soft fall and swell,
    Awake forever in a sweet unrest,
Still, still to hear her tender-taken breath,
And so live ever—or else swoon to death.

---

1. Eremite (ĕr′ ə mīt′): Hermit.

RESPONDING TO THE SELECTION

Your Response

1. Can you identify with Keats's desire to live forever? Why or why not?

Recalling

2. What two things does the speaker say the star watches from its position in the sky?

Interpreting

3. (a) In what ways does the speaker wish to be like the star? (b) In what ways does he wish to be different?

4. What do you think is meant by "sweet unrest" in line 12?

5. In a Petrarchan, or Italian, sonnet, the first eight lines pose a question or problem, whereas the last six lines offer a solution or comment on or extend the issue. (a) What question or problem is presented in the octave, or first eight lines? (b) What response is given in the sestet, or next six lines? (c) What word signals this response?

Applying

6. Based on this poem, describe Keats's attitudes toward nature and emotion. Explain how these attitudes are typical of the Romantic movement.

When I Have Fears That I May Cease to Be

John Keats

When I have fears that I may cease to be
    Before my pen has gleaned my teeming brain,
Before high-piled books, in charactery,[1]
    Hold like rich garners[2] the full ripened grain;
5 When I behold, upon the night's starred face,
    Huge cloudy symbols of a high romance,
And think that I may never live to trace
    Their shadows, with the magic hand of chance;[3]
And when I feel, fair creature of an hour,
10   That I shall never look upon thee more,
Never have relish in the fairy power
    Of unreflecting love—then on the shore
Of the wide world I stand alone, and think
Till love and fame to nothingness do sink.

---

1. **charactery:** Written or printed letters of the alphabet.
2. **garners:** Storehouses for grain.
3. **chance:** Inspiration.

JOHN KEATS, 1821
Joseph Severn
By Courtesy of the National Portrait Gallery, London

RESPONDING TO THE SELECTION

Your Response

1. What methods have you developed to put your worries in perspective? Explain.

Recalling

2. What does the speaker say he fears missing (a) in lines 1–8? (b) in lines 9–12?

Interpreting

3. What do you think is meant by "cloudy symbols of a high romance" in line 6?
4. How does the speaker resolve his fears?

Applying

5. What does this poem suggest about Keats's views on death? Do you feel these views were held by the other Romantic poets you have read? Why or why not?

THINKING AND WRITING

Comparing and Contrasting Sonnets

Choose one of the sonnets by William Wordsworth (pages 589–590). On a sheet of paper, take notes on how this sonnet is similar to and different from the sonnets of Keats in form, subject matter, word usage, and theme. In an essay of one page or more, write about your findings. When you revise, make sure you have included details from the poems as support.

GUIDE FOR INTERPRETING

Ode to a Nightingale; Ode on a Grecian Urn; To Autumn

Writers' Techniques

Imagery. Imagery is language that helps a reader form a mental picture of an object or idea by appealing to one or more of the five senses. Taken by itself, the word *bread,* for example, is little more than just that—a word. When, however, the word is part of the image "warm loaf of freshly baked bread," our sense of sight and especially our sense of smell are both called into play. In his odes, Keats used imagery with a degree of skill that few poets before or since have achieved.

Commentary

It's not easy to describe the writing process. We all have different methods of writing, depending on our audience, topic, and purpose as well as on our personalities and moods. Sometimes we need a great deal of time to gather and arrange our thoughts; at other times we can write with feverish haste, inspired perhaps by a vivid image or idea. At times, too, we may want to recount our creative experiences somewhat differently from how they actually occurred. Perhaps we want to make the story more impressive or try to conform to prevailing ideas of creativity.

After Keats's friend Charles Brown found some scraps of paper containing the poet's ode to the nightingale, he began a search for more of Keats's work. With Keats's help, Brown found other short poems, which otherwise might have vanished. "From that day on he gave me permission to copy any verses he might write," Brown recounts. "He cared so little for them himself when once, as it appeared to me, his imagination was released from their influence, that it required a friend at hand to preserve them."

We have no reason to doubt Brown's account, yet perhaps his version is colored by the Romantic notion of creativity. What do you see in Brown's account and Keats's poetry that supports the Romantic idea that poetry is "the spontaneous overflow of powerful feelings"? What other Romantic ideas do you find here?

Focus

Picture a setting in nature with which you are very familiar—a park, a wooded area, or the like. On a sheet of paper, jot down as many physical features of the scene as you can. You might, for instance, mention trees, grass, rocks, and sky. Lastly, think up an image for each feature that would enable a reader to develop a strong mental picture of it.

Ode to a Nightingale

John Keats

Keats composed the following ode in 1819, while living in Hampstead with his friend Charles Brown. Brown wrote the following description about how the ode was composed: "In the spring of 1819 a nightingale had built her nest near my house. Keats felt a tranquil and continued joy in her song; and one morning he took his chair from the breakfast table to the grass plot under the plum tree, where he sat for two or three hours. When he came into the house, I perceived he had some scraps of paper in his hand, and these he was quietly thrusting behind the books. On inquiry, I found those scraps, four or five in number, contained his poetic feeling on the song of our nightingale."

I

My heart aches, and a drowsy numbness pains
    My sense, as though of hemlock[1] I had drunk,
Or emptied some dull opiate to the drains
    One minute past, and Lethe-wards[2] had sunk:
5 'Tis not through envy of thy happy lot,
    But being too happy in thine happiness,—
      That thou, light-winged Dryad[3] of the trees,
        In some melodious plot
    Of beechen green, and shadows numberless,
10   Singest of summer in full-throated ease.

II

O, for a draft[4] of vintage! that hath been
    Cooled a long age in the deep-delved earth,
Tasting of Flora[5] and the country green,
    Dance, and Provençal[6] song, and sunburnt mirth!

---

1. hemlock: A poisonous herb.
2. Lethe-wards: Toward Lethe, the river of forgetfulness in Hades, the underworld, in classical mythology.
3. Dryad (drī′ əd): In classical mythology, a wood nymph.
4. draft: Drink.
5. Flora: In classical mythology, the goddess of flowers, or the flowers themselves.
6. Provençal (prō′ vən säl′): Pertaining to Provence, a region in southern France, renowned in the late Middle Ages for its troubadours, who composed and sang love songs.

SMALL BIRD ON A FLOWERING PLUM BRANCH
Attributed to Ma Lin
The Gotoh Museum

15   O for a beaker full of the warm South,
        Full of the true, the blushful Hippocrene,[7]
           With beaded bubbles winking at the brim,
           And purple-stained mouth;
        That I might drink, and leave the world unseen,
20   And with thee fade away into the forest dim:

---

7. Hippocrene (hĭp′ ə krēn′): In classical mythology, the fountain of the Muses on Mt. Helicon. From this fountain flowed the waters of inspiration.

III

Fade far away, dissolve, and quite forget
    What thou among the leaves hast never known,
The weariness, the fever, and the fret
    Here, where men sit and hear each other groan;
25 Where palsy shakes a few, sad, last gray hairs,
    Where youth grows pale, and specter-thin, and dies;[8]
      Where but to think is to be full of sorrow
        And leaden-eyed despairs,
      Where Beauty cannot keep her lustrous eyes,
30   Or new Love pine at them beyond tomorrow.

IV

Away! away! for I will fly to thee,
    Not charioted by Bacchus[9] and his pards,
But on the viewless[10] wings of Poesy,[11]
    Though the dull brain perplexes and retards:
35 Already with thee! tender is the night,
    And haply[12] the Queen-Moon is on her throne,
      Clustered around by all her starry Fays;[13]
        But here there is no light,
    Save what from heaven is with the breezes blown
40   Through verdurous[14] glooms and winding mossy
        ways.

V

I cannot see what flowers are at my feet,
    Nor what soft incense hangs upon the boughs,
But, in embalmed[15] darkness, guess each sweet
    Wherewith the seasonable month endows
45 The grass, the thicket, and the fruit-tree wild;
    White hawthorn, and the pastoral eglantine;[16]
      Fast fading violets covered up in leaves;
        And mid-May's eldest child,
    The coming musk-rose, full of dewy wine,
50   The murmurous haunt of flies on summer eves.

---

8. youth . . . dies: Keats is referring to his brother, Tom, who had died from tuberculosis the previous winter.
9. Bacchus (băk′ əs): In classical mythology, the god of wine, who was often represented in a chariot drawn by leopards ("pards").
10. viewless: Invisible.
11. Poesy: Poetic fancy.
12. haply: Perhaps.
13. Fays: Fairies.
14. verdurous: Green-foliaged.
15. embalmed: Perfumed.
16. eglantine (eg′ lən tīn′): Sweetbrier or honeysuckle.

VI

Darkling[17] I listen; and, for many a time
 I have been half in love with easeful Death,
Called him soft names in many a mused[18] rhyme,
 To take into the air my quiet breath;
55 Now more than ever seems it rich to die,
 To cease upon the midnight with no pain,
  While thou art pouring forth thy soul abroad
   In such an ecstasy!
 Still wouldst thou sing, and I have ears in vain—
60   To thy high requiem become a sod.

VII

Thou wast not born for death, immortal Bird!
 No hungry generations tread thee down;
The voice I hear this passing night was heard
 In ancient days by emperor and clown:
65 Perhaps the selfsame song that found a path
 Through the sad heart of Ruth,[19] when, sick for home,
  She stood in tears amid the alien corn;
   The same that ofttimes hath
 Charmed magic casements, opening on the foam
70   Of perilous seas, in fairylands forlorn.

VIII

Forlorn! the very word is like a bell
 To toll me back from thee to my sole self!
Adieu! the fancy cannot cheat so well
 As she is famed[20] to do, deceiving elf.
75 Adieu! adieu! thy plaintive anthem[21] fades
 Past the near meadows, over the still stream,
  Up the hillside; and now 'tis buried deep
   In the next valley-glades:
 Was it a vision, or a waking dream?
80   Fled is that music:—Do I wake or sleep?

---

17. darkling: In the dark.
18. mused: Meditated.
19. Ruth: In the Bible (Ruth 2:1–23), a widow who left her home and went to Judah to work in the corn (wheat) fields.
20. famed: Reported.
21. anthem: Hymn.

Your Response

1. Have you ever experienced a mood similar to the speaker's while you were in natural surroundings? Explain.

Recalling

2. What is the speaker's mood in stanza I?
3. (a) What wish does the speaker express at the end of stanza II and at the beginning of stanza III? (b) According to stanza IV, how will he accomplish this wish?
4. What effect does "forlorn" have on the speaker in stanza VIII?

Interpreting

5. (a) What is the "draught of vintage" the speaker craves in stanza II? (b) What would it help him to escape?
6. (a) What differences between the speaker's world and the bird's are described in stanza IV? (b) What is meant in line 38 by "here there is no light"?
7. (a) What does the speaker find tempting in stanza VI? (b) What changes his mind in stanza VII?

Applying

8. The poem ends with a question. What is its relevance, both to the poem and to the spirit of the Romantic movement?
9. Twentieth-century American novelist F. Scott Fitzgerald took the title of one of his novels from line 35: "Already with thee! Tender is the night." (a) In what way can the night be tender? (b) Why are the words "tender is the night" especially appropriate for one who has been "half in love with easeful Death"?

Using Imagery

Imagery is language that appeals to the senses, and, by so doing, creates a vivid picture in the reader's mind. The phrase "blustery, wind-swept day" provides the reader with a strong impression that the simple phrase "cold day" does not. Such is the impact of imagery. Find an everyday equivalent for each of the following images from "Ode to a Nightingale." Then state which of Keats's words are central to his image.

1. "With beaded bubbles winking at the brim,/ And purple-stained mouth;" (lines 17–18)
2. "Where palsy shakes a few, sad, last gray hairs,/Where youth grows pale, and specter-thin, and dies;" (lines 25–26)
3. "The coming musk-rose, full of dewy wine,/The murmurous haunt of flies on summer eves." (lines 49–50)

1. **Art.** In "Ode to a Nightingale," Keats uses words to describe a state of being between the real world and the ideal realm of the spirit. Use a medium of your choice to express visually this state of being. You might work with the image of Keats listening to the nightingale, or you may develop your own images to illustrate this state. Display your artwork in class.
2. **Cross-curricular Connection.** Find out more about nightingales. What do they look and sound like? What is their natural habitat? Are there more than one kind? Are they endangered? You can easily find a photograph or drawing of a nightingale, and you can probably find a recording of its song. Bring these to class and present your findings orally.

Ode on a Grecian Urn

John Keats

I

Thou still unravished bride of quietness,
    Thou foster child of silence and slow time,
Sylvan[1] historian, who canst thus express
    A flowery tale more sweetly than our rhyme:
5   What leaf-fringed legend haunts about thy shape
        Of deities or mortals, or of both,
          In Tempe[2] or the dales of Arcady?[3]
      What men or gods are these? What maidens loath?[4]
What mad pursuit? What struggle to escape?
10   What pipes and timbrels?[5] What wild ecstasy?

II

Heard melodies are sweet, but those unheard
    Are sweeter; therefore, ye soft pipes, play on;
Not to the sensual[6] ear, but, more endeared,
    Pipe to the spirit ditties of no tone:
15 Fair youth, beneath the trees, thou canst not leave
    Thy song, nor ever can those trees be bare;
      Bold Lover, never, never canst thou kiss,
Though winning near the goal—yet, do not grieve;
    She cannot fade, though thou hast not thy bliss,
20   Forever wilt thou love, and she be fair!

III

Ah, happy, happy boughs! that cannot shed
    Your leaves, nor ever bid the Spring adieu;
And, happy melodist, unwearied,
    Forever piping songs forever new;

---

1. sylvan: Rustic, representing the woods or forest.
2. Tempe (tem′ pē): A beautiful valley in Greece that has become a symbol of supreme rural beauty.
3. Arcady (är′ kə dē): A region in Greece that has come to represent supreme pastoral contentment.
4. loath: Unwilling.
5. timbrels: Tambourines.
6. sensual: Involving the physical sense of hearing.

25   More happy love! more happy, happy love!
          Forever warm and still to be enjoyed,
              Forever panting, and forever young;
      All breathing human passion far above,
          That leaves a heart high-sorrowful and cloyed,
30   A burning forehead, and a parching tongue.

                              IV
      Who are these coming to the sacrifice?
          To what green altar, O mysterious priest,
      Lead'st thou that heifer lowing at the skies,
          And all her silken flanks with garlands dressed?
35   What little town by river or seashore,
          Or mountain-built with peaceful citadel,
              Is emptied of this folk, this pious morn?
      And, little town, thy streets forevermore
          Will silent be; and not a soul to tell
40   Why thou art desolate, can e'er return.

**COLUMN KRATER (CALLED THE "ORCHARD VASE"),
SIDE A: WOMEN GATHERING APPLES**
The Metropolitan Museum of Art

O Attic[7] shape! Fair attitude! with brede[8]
 Of marble men and maidens overwrought,[9]
With forest branches and the trodden weed;
 Thou, silent form, dost tease us out of thought
45 As doth eternity: Cold[10] Pastoral!
 When old age shall this generation waste,
  Thou shalt remain, in midst of other woe
Than ours, a friend to man, to whom thou say'st,
 "Beauty is truth, truth beauty,"—that is all
50   Ye know on earth, and all ye need to know.

---

7. Attic: Attica was the region of Greece in which Athens was located;
a region characterized by grace and simplicity.
8. brede: An interwoven pattern.
9. overwrought: All over.
10. cold: Unchanging.

▌R ESPONDING TO THE S ELECTION

Your Response
1. For Keats, great art embodies the ideals of unchanging beauty, love, truth, and eternity. What human values does art convey to you?

Recalling
2. As the speaker studies the scene on a Grecian urn, it takes hold of his imagination. (a) Whom does the speaker address in stanza II of the poem? (b) Whom does he address in stanza III?
3. What ritual is described in the first four lines of stanza IV?

Interpreting
4. (a) In what way is the urn a "Sylvan historian"? (b) How can it tell its "flowery tale more sweetly than our rhyme"?

5. (a) Interpret lines 11–12. "Heard melodies are sweet, but those unheard/Are sweeter . . ." (b) What do these lines indicate about the power of the imagination?
6. (a) Why might the lover in stanza II grieve? (b) Why does the speaker advise him not to grieve?
7. (a) What is the "Cold Pastoral" mentioned in line 45? (b) With what does the speaker contrast it?

Applying
8. (a) Explain the meaning of the last two lines of the poem. (b) In what ways might this ending also have been appropriate to "Ode to a Nightingale"?
9. In *Endymion,* John Keats wrote, "A thing of beauty is a joy forever;/Its loveliness increases; it will never/Pass into nothingness." Compare and contrast the idea of beauty expressed in these lines with that expressed in lines 49–50 of "Ode on a Grecian Urn."

To Autumn

John Keats

I

Season of mists and mellow fruitfulness,
    Close bosom-friend of the maturing sun;
Conspiring with him how to load and bless
    With fruit the vines that round the thatch-eves run;
5 To bend with apples the mossed cottage-trees,
    And fill all fruit with ripeness to the core;
      To swell the gourd, and plump the hazel shells
    With a sweet kernel; to set budding more,
And still more, later flowers for the bees,
10 Until they think warm days will never cease,
      For Summer has o'er-brimmed their clammy cells.

II

Who hath not seen thee oft amid thy store?
    Sometimes whoever seeks abroad may find
Thee sitting careless on a granary floor,
15   Thy hair soft-lifted by the winnowing[1] wind;
Or on a half-reaped furrow sound asleep,
    Drowsed with the fume of poppies, while thy hook[2]
      Spares the next swath and all its twined flowers:
And sometimes like a gleaner thou dost keep
20   Steady thy laden head across a brook;
    Or by a cider-press, with patient look,
      Thou watchest the last oozings hours by hours.

III

Where are the songs of Spring? Ay, where are they?
    Think not of them, thou hast thy music too—
25 While barred clouds bloom the soft-dying day,
    And touch the stubble-plains with rosy hue;
Then in a wailful choir the small gnats mourn
    Among the river sallows,[3] borne aloft
      Or sinking as the light wind lives or dies;

---

1. winnowing: Fanning; winnowing is a process in which the chaff is fanned from the grain.
2. hook: Scythe.
3. sallows: Willow trees.

30   And full-grown lambs loud bleat from hilly bourn;[4]
        Hedge-crickets sing; and now with treble soft
        The red-breast whistles from a garden croft;[5]
        And gathering swallows twitter in the skies.

---

4. bourn: Region.
5. croft: An enclosed plot of farm land.

HARVEST FIELD WITH GLEANERS, MAYWOOD, HEREFORDSHIRE
George Robert Lewis
The Tate Gallery, London

Your Response

1. Which of the images that Keats uses to describe autumn best evokes the season for you? Explain.

Recalling

2. (a) In stanza I of the poem, what is the season described as "doing"? (b) With whom is the season "conspiring"?
3. What are some of the songs of autumn?

Interpreting

4. In what way can autumn be described as a "close bosom-friend of the maturing sun"?
5. (a) What activities frequently associated with the season are described in the second stanza? (b) What impression of autumn is created by mentioning these activities?
6. Why do you think the speaker mentions "the songs of Spring" in stanza III?

Applying

7. What do you suppose was Keats's attitude toward winter? Explain your answer in terms of the three odes you have just read.

Comparing and Contrasting Odes

Choose one of the odes written by Shelley. Reread it, noting such features as word choice, stanza structure, and overall message. In a one-page composition, discuss the ways in which the three odes by Keats are similar to and different from Shelley's. Include mention of whose work you like better and state your reasons.

1. **Speaking and Listening.** In "To Autumn" Keats mentions "the songs of Spring." In fact, many of the images he uses in the poem suggest music. Find a recording of a piece of music that you feel would be an appropriate accompaniment for "To Autumn." Try reading the poem aloud as the music plays. Bring the recording to class and read the poem as you practiced it.
2. **Writing.** Write an ode to your favorite season. You may choose to write a poem, as Keats did, or you may use prose to describe the sensations you associate with the season and to express your feelings and insights.

ONE WRITER'S PROCESS

John Keats and "To Autumn"

Composing in a Fever John Keats believed that in writing poetry, inspiration was crucial. In fact, he argued that if poetry "comes not as naturally as the Leaves to a tree it had better not come at all." Yet by the time he wrote the ode "To Autumn," his last great poem, he said that he was feeling "quieter in my pulse, improved in my digestion; exerting myself against vexing speculations—scarcely content to write the best verses for the fever they leave behind. I want to compose without this fever." Keats, of course, suffered from an illness far more disturbing than the fever of inspiration—tuberculosis—and he succumbed to this disease not long after writing "To Autumn."

Counting on Inspiration Keats's reliance on inspiration was described by a friend, Richard Woodhouse: "He has repeatedly said in conversation that he never sits down to write unless he is full of ideas, and then thoughts come about him in troops as though soliciting to be accepted and he selects." If this statement is true, Keats was indeed fortunate to have such a rich choice of poetic ideas.

PREWRITING

The Stimulus for "To Autumn" This particular poem was inspired by a visit in 1819 to the town of Winchester. There, Keats took a walk alone in the stubble-fields— fields that had been burned down following the harvest. Keats first mentioned writing the poem in a letter to Richard Woodhouse: "How beautiful the season is now—How fine the air. A temperate sharpness about it. Really, without joking, chaste weather—Dian skies—I never lik'd stubble fields so much as now—Aye better than the chilly green of the spring. Somehow a stubble plain looks warm—this struck me so much in my sunday's [sic] walk that I composed upon it."

DRAFTING

A Handwritten Manuscript A manuscript of "To Autumn" in Keats's handwriting constitutes a record of his writing process. The appearance of the draft, with its helter-skelter deletions, suggests that Keats did compose the poem in a state of inspiration.

The excerpt on the facing page is a printed version of the manuscript, showing the changes that Keats made to stanza 2 (the errors in spelling are Keats's). As you review these changes, note the words and lines that Keats crossed out.

REVISING

Impatience With Revisions Is it probable that Keats made these changes while drafting instead of returning later to the manuscript to revise it? Keats's friend Woodhouse reported that the poet told him, "My judgment . . . is as active while I am actually writing as my imagination. In fact all my faculties are strongly excited and in their full play—and shall I afterwards, when my imagination is idle, and the heat in which I wrote has gone off, sit down coldly to criticize when in possession of only one faculty what I have written when almost inspired . . ."

oft amid thy stores?
Who hath not seen thee? ~~for thy haunts are many~~
abroad
Sometimes whoeever seeks ~~for thee~~ may find
Thee sitting careless on a granary floorr
Thy hair soft lifted by the winnowing wind
~~husky~~
~~While bright the Sun slants through the barn;~~
~~orr on a half reap'd furrow sound asleep~~
~~Or sound asleep in a half reaped field~~
~~Dose'd with read poppies; while thy reaping hook~~
~~Spares form Some slumbrous~~
~~minutes while warm slumpers creep~~
Or on a half reap'd furrow sound asleep
Dos'd with the fume of poppies, while thy hook
Spares the next swath and all its twined flouers
~~Spares for some slumbrous minutes the next swath;~~
And sometimes like a gleans thost dost keep
Steady thy laden head across the brook;
Or by a Cyder-press with patent look
Thou watchest the last oozing hours by hours

Astonishment at His Own Work Wood-house continued, "He has said that he has often not been aware of the beauty of some thought or expression until after he had composed and written it down—It has then struck him with astonishment and seemed rather the production of another person than his own. He has wondered how he came to hit upon it . . . It seemed to him to come by chance or magic—to be as it were something given to him."

PUBLISHING

Problems With the Critics Although Keats published poetry during his lifetime, he was aware that the critics were not well-disposed toward much of his work.

For nineteen years following his death, none of his poems were reprinted in England. Upper-class and middle-class critics continued to look down on this poet from the lower classes. In 1835 his publisher John Taylor wrote, "I should like to print a complete Edition of Keats's Poems . . . but the world cares nothing for him—I fear that even 250 copies would not sell."

It was not until the second half of the nineteenth century that Keats's work became famous.

THINKING ABOUT THE PROCESS

1. What are the advantages and disadvantages of revising a poem only during the drafting stage and not rewriting it later? Explain.
2. **Writing.** Review the printed version of Keats's draft of "To Autumn" (stanza 2). Then choose a line Keats crossed out and compare and contrast it to the line he replaced it with. In a brief paragraph, explain which version you think is better and why.

MARY SHELLEY

1797–1851

Even the most serious and dedicated of writers have their lighter moments. It is interesting to note that had it not been for such a moment involving two of English literature's most gifted writers, one of the most celebrated Gothic novels of all time might never have been written. The novel in question, *Frankenstein,* was penned by neither of the aforementioned greats—the poets Percy Bysshe Shelley and Lord Byron—but by the wife of the former, Mary Shelley.

Born in London, Mary Wollstonecraft Godwin was the daughter of William Godwin, a political thinker and writer given to radical ideas. One of her father's books, *Political Justice,* managed to attract the attention of the young and equally radically minded Percy Shelley, who became one of Godwin's disciples. Mary Godwin in turn became a great admirer of the young poet, and the two of them eloped to France when she was seventeen.

Mary Shelley's first piece of writing, *History of a Six Weeks' Tour* (1817), was a collaborative effort with her husband. Her first solo work—the novel with which her name is most often associated today—grew out of idle conversation between Byron and another friend during a visit to the Shelleys' home on Lake Geneva in 1816. As a result of the conversation, the four friends decided they would each attempt to write a ghost story. Though the results of the contest were largely unremarkable, Mary Shelley's horrific tale of the creation of a monster so impressed the gathering that her husband later urged her to develop it into a full-length novel. Thus was born *Frankenstein* (1818), and the creature that has thrilled countless readers and fueled the imaginations of generations of filmmakers.

After *Frankenstein,* Mary Shelley produced five more novels: *Valperga* (1823) and *The Fortunes of Perkin Warbeck* (1830), which are historical works; the autobiographical *Lodore* (1835); *Falkner* (1837), a complicated mystery tale; and *The Last Man* (1826).

If *Frankenstein* is, as scholars have noted, structurally weak, it is nevertheless a "good read." More important from a historical perspective, the novel was the first in a long line of works to explore the potential dangers of technology that falls into the wrong hands.

GUIDE FOR INTERPRETING

Introduction to *Frankenstein*

Gothic Tradition. The Gothic novel was a late eighteenth-century revival of the tale of terror, which has its roots in antiquity. Gothic fiction, or Gothicism, is formally defined by two elements—the historical and the "wonderful," or supernatural. One of the earliest and best-known Gothic novels was Horace Walpole's *The Castle of Otranto* (1765), a hair-raising account of a castle terrorized by a giant. Within the pages of Walpole's thriller, paintings and statues come to life for the first time in fiction. The next important contributor to the "renaissance of wonder" was Clara Reeve, a critic whose *The Old English Baron* (1777) was, in her own humble opinion, an improvement on Walpole's haunted-castle story. The Gothic tradition was refined considerably in the hands of Matthew Gregory Lewis, who, at the age of twenty, published *The Monk* (1796), a cleverly conceived and simply told tale of a Spanish friar who enters into a contract with the devil. The first novel to depict its horrors in graphic terms, *The Monk* paved the way for Mary Shelley's *Frankenstein* (1818), whose main character breathes life into one of the best-known and most terrifying monsters of all times.

Mary Shelley's mother, Mary Wollstonecraft, was as radical a thinker as her father, William Godwin. Her 1792 book, *A Vindication of the Rights of Woman,* was the first great work devoted to equality for women.

For centuries, she said, women had willingly served men. To escape from slavery, women must cultivate their minds, find new occupations, and refuse to accept an inferior role. Equality for women could help all people fulfill their potential, she wrote.

If her book had appeared earlier, it might merely have provoked amusement, but it fell upon a frightened world. Educators vetoed the freedom for which Wollstonecraft pleaded. Female writers urged that women accept their subordinate position and use their "feminine wiles"—acting delicate and helpless, for example—to get their way with men.

Wollstonecraft died eleven days after Mary's birth, but her ideas permeate her daughter's work. Where in the "Introduction to *Frankenstein*" do you see the influence of her writing and beliefs?

Give some thought to ideas that might be incorporated into a tale of terror. Well-used but always-dependable possibilities include graveyards at night, dark winding staircases, and ghosts. Sketch a rough outline for a story that contains some of these ideas.

Introduction to *Frankenstein*

Mary Wollstonecraft Shelley

In this introduction to the third edition of Frankenstein, *published in 1831, Mary Shelley recalls the circumstances that led her to write the novel during the summer of 1816.*

The Publishers of the Standard Novels, in selecting *Frankenstein* for one of their series, expressed a wish that I should furnish them with some account of the origin of the story. I am the more willing to comply, because I shall thus give a general answer to the question, so very frequently asked me: "How I, then a young girl, came to think of, and to dilate upon, so very hideous an idea?" It is true that I am very averse to bringing myself forward in print; but as my account will only appear as an appendage to a former production, and as it will be confined to such topics as have connection with my authorship alone, I can scarcely accuse myself of a personal intrusion. . . .

In the summer of 1816, we[1] visited Switzerland, and became the neighbors of Lord Byron. At first we spent our pleasant hours on the lake or wandering on its shores; and Lord Byron, who was writing the third canto of *Childe Harold,* was the only one among us who put his thoughts upon paper. These, as he brought them successively to us, clothed in all the light and harmony of poetry, seemed to stamp as divine the glories of heaven and earth, whose influences we partook with him.

But it proved a wet, ungenial summer, and incessant rain often confined us for days to the house. Some volumes of ghost stories, translated from the German into French,[2] fell into our hands. There was "The History of the Inconstant Lover,"[3] who, when he thought to clasp the bride to whom he had pledged his vows, found himself in the arms of the pale ghost of her whom he had deserted. There was the tale of the sinful founder of his race,[4] whose miserable doom it was to bestow the kiss of death on all the younger sons of his fated house, just when they reached the age of promise. His gigantic, shadowy form, clothed like the ghost in Hamlet, in complete armor but with the beaver[5] up, was seen at midnight, by the moon's fitful beams, to advance slowly along the gloomy avenue. The shape was lost beneath the shadow of the castle walls; but soon a gate swung back, a step was heard, the door of the chamber opened, and he advanced to the couch of the blooming youths, cradled in healthy sleep. Eternal sorrow sat upon his face as he bent down and kissed the foreheads of the boys, who from that hour withered like flowers snap-

---

1. we: Mary Shelley, her husband Percy Bysshe Shelley, and their two children.

2. volumes . . . French: *Fantasmagoriana,* or *Collected Stories of Apparitions of Specters, Ghosts, Phantoms, Etc.,* published anonymously in 1812.
3. "The History . . . Lover": The true name of the story is "The Dead Fiancée."
4. the tale . . . race: "Family Portraits."
5. beaver: The hinged piece of armor that covers the face.

A VIEW OF CHAMONIX AND MT. BLANC
Julius Schnon von Carolsfeld
Austrian Gallery, Vienna

ped upon the stalk. I have not seen these stories since then, but their incidents are as fresh in my mind as if I had read them yesterday.

"We will each write a ghost story," said Lord Byron; and his proposition was acceded to. There were four of us.[6] The noble author began a tale, a fragment of which he printed at the end of his poem of Mazeppa. Shelley, more apt to embody ideas and sentiments in the radiance of brilliant imagery, and in the music of the most melodious verse that adorns our language, than to invent the machinery of a story, commenced one founded on the experiences of his early life. Poor Polidori had some terrible idea about a skull-headed lady, who was so punished for peeping through a keyhole —what to see I forget—something very shocking and wrong of course; but when she

was reduced to a worse condition than the renowned Tom of Coventry,[7] he did not know what to do with her, and was obliged to despatch her to the tomb of the Capulets,[8] the only place for which she was fitted. The illustrious poets also, annoyed by the platitude of prose, speedily relinquished their uncongenial task.

I busied myself *to think of a story*— a story to rival those which had excited us to this task. One which would speak to the mysterious fears of our nature and awaken thrilling horror—one to make the reader dread to look round, to curdle the blood, and quicken the beatings of the heart. If I did not accomplish these things, my ghost story would be unworthy of its name. I thought and pondered—vainly. I felt that blank in-

---

6. four of us: Byron, the two Shelleys, and John William Polidori, Byron's physician.

7. Tom of Coventry: "Peeping Tom" who, according to legend, was struck blind for looking at Lady Godiva as she rode naked through Coventry.
8. tomb of the Capulets: Where Romeo and Juliet died.

capability of invention which is the greatest misery of authorship, when dull Nothing replies to our anxious invocations. *Have you thought of a story?* I was asked each morning, and each morning I was forced to reply with a mortifying negative. . . .

Many and long were the conversations between Lord Byron and Shelley, to which I was a devout but nearly silent listener. During one of these, various philosophical doctrines were discussed, and among others the nature of the principle of life and whether there was any probability of its ever being discovered and communicated. They talked of the experiments of Dr. Darwin[9] (I speak not of what the Doctor really did or said that he did, but, as more to my purpose, of what was then spoken of as having been done by him), who preserved a piece of vermicelli in a glass case till by some extraordinary means it began to move with voluntary motion. Not thus, after all, would life be given. Perhaps a corpse would be reanimated: galvanism[10] had given token of such things. Perhaps the component parts of a creature might be manufactured, brought together, and endued with vital warmth.

Night waned upon this talk, and even the witching hour had gone by, before we retired to rest. When I placed my head on my pillow, I did not sleep, nor could I be said to think. My imagination, unbidden, possessed and guided me, gifting the successive images that arose in my mind with a vividness far beyond the usual bounds of reverie. I saw—with shut eyes but acute mental vision—I saw the pale student of unhallowed arts kneeling beside the thing he had put together. I saw the hideous phantasm of a man stretched out, and then, on the working of some powerful engine, show signs of life and stir with an uneasy, half vital motion. Frightful must it be, for supremely frightful would be the effect of any human endeavor to mock the stupendous mechanism of the Creator of the world. His success would terrify the artist; he would rush away from his odious handiwork, horror-stricken. He would hope that, left to itself, the slight spark of life which he had communicated would fade; that this thing, which had received such imperfect animation, would subside into dead matter; and he might sleep in the belief that the silence of the grave would quench forever the transient existence of the hideous corpse which he had looked upon as the cradle of life. He sleeps; but he is awakened; he opens his eyes; behold the horrid thing stands at his bedside, opening his curtains, and looking on him with yellow, watery, but speculative eyes.

I opened mine in terror. The idea so possessed my mind, that a thrill of fear ran through me, and I wished to exchange the ghastly image of my fancy for the realities around. I see them still: the very room, the dark parquet,[11] the closed shutters, with the moonlight struggling through, and the sense I had that the glassy lake and white high Alps were beyond. I could not so easily get rid of my hideous phantom: still it haunted me. I must try to think of something else. I recurred to my ghost story—my tiresome unlucky ghost story! O! if I could only contrive one which would frighten my reader as I myself had been frightened that night!

Swift as light and as cheering was the idea that broke in upon me. "I have found it! What terrified me will terrify others, and I need only describe the specter which had haunted my midnight pillow." On the morrow I announced that I had *thought of a story*. I began that day with the words, *It was on a dreary night of November*, making only a transcript of the grim terrors of my waking dream.

At first I thought but of a few pages—of

9. Dr. Darwin: Erasmus Darwin (1731–1802), physician, natural scientist, and poet.
10. galvanism: The use of electric current to induce twitching in dead muscles.

11. parquet (pär kā′): Flooring made of wooden pieces arranged in a pattern.

a short tale—but Shelley urged me to develop the idea at greater length. I certainly did not owe the suggestion of one incident, nor scarcely of one train of feeling, to my husband, and yet but for his incitement, it would never have taken the form in which it was presented to the world. From this declaration I must except the preface. As far as I can recollect, it was entirely written by him.

And now, once again, I bid my hideous progeny go forth and prosper. I have an affection for it, for it was the offspring of happy days, when death and grief were but words, which found no true echo in my heart. Its several pages speak of many a walk, many a drive, and many a conversation, when I was not alone; and my companion was one who, in this world, I shall never see more. But this is for myself: my readers have nothing to do with these associations.

RESPONDING TO THE SELECTION

Your Response
1. Why do you think horror stories appeal to readers?

Recalling
2. What question does the author say people frequently ask her?
3. (a) What forced the author, her husband, and their friends to stay indoors? (b) What did they do to pass the time?
4. What was Byron's proposition?
5. (a) What provided the author with inspiration for her story? (b) What "vision" came to the author after she retired for the night?

Interpreting
6. What do the goals the author sets for herself in writing her ghost story suggest about her as a person?
7. Based on her description of her vision, what seems to be the author's attitude toward work of the sort carried out by Dr. Darwin?

Applying
8. Many areas of scientific investigation carry both potential benefits and potential dangers for humankind. (a) What such areas in our own age can you name? (b) Which areas do you believe human beings should never have become involved in? Give reasons for your answer.

ANALYZING LITERATURE

Recognizing Gothic Tradition
The Gothic tradition of the horror story began in the eighteenth century. In *The Spirit of the Public Journals,* a 1797 pamphlet, a "recipe" for the Gothic novel is given. Among the "ingredients" listed are: an old castle; a long gallery with secret doors; three freshly murdered bodies; assorted skeletons; and "noises, whispers, and groans." In *Frankenstein,* Mary Shelley endeavored to improve on that formula.
1. Based on your reading of her introduction, what most likely is the theme of *Frankenstein?*
2. Based on the French translations of ghost stories Shelley mentions, what other "ingredients" might be added to the above list?

THINKING AND WRITING

Writing in the Gothic Tradition
Review the ideas and outline you developed for the assignment under Focus on page 671. Then write an original story or episode that follows the Gothic tradition. You may add as many of the elements mentioned as you wish. If you can, build a theme into your horror story. When you revise, make sure you have told your tale in chronological order.

Goethe's *Faust*

The play opens in a narrow, high-vaulted Gothic room. Faust, a deeply learned scholar, speaks restlessly from his armchair by the desk:

> I have pursued, alas, philosophy,
> Jurisprudence, and medicine,
> And, help me God, theology,
> With fervent zeal through thick and
>   thin.
> And here, poor fool, I stand once
>   more,
> No wiser than I was before.

His life is dull, dusty, and empty; he has neither fame and fortune nor contentment. In despair he tries a less legitimate road to knowledge and satisfaction:

> So I resorted to Magic's art,
> To see if by spirit mouth and might
> Many a secret might come to light;
> So I need toil no longer so,
> Propounding what I do not know.

Mephistopheles, the Devil, appears from the mist. Faust gladly signs a pact with him—in blood!—exchanging his soul for knowledge, "all treasures of the human mind." The Devil promises Faust that

> I shall be at your service by this
>   bond
> Without relief or respite here on
>   earth;

but makes the scholar swear

> And if or when we meet again
>   beyond,
> You are to give me equal worth.

With this, a great change comes over the life of the learned doctor. He tastes experience through a great many wondrous adventures but does not find the happiness he is seeking until the very last act. And this is what Goethe is asking: What is happiness? Is it living within your abilities? Or is it daring to be more than human? Faust—and the audience—learn the answer as the curtain drops.

A LIFETIME OF WORK

The legend of Doctor Faustus, the famous magician who sells his soul to the devil in return for knowledge of mystical secrets, is a thrilling horror story with a moral. It was first published in 1587, and different versions were sold year after year at country fairs. In Christopher Marlowe's hands, the legend became a play for the Elizabethan stage. The theme was taken up by troupes of traveling puppeteers and soon became a favorite around the country.

Young Goethe, familiar with the Faust legend through the early books and the puppet shows, sensed that the wild tale would allow him to explore the exciting new aspirations of the human soul. In the early 1770's, he began to jot down the first scenes for a projected Faust play. When he moved to Weimar in the autumn of 1775—where he would settle for the rest of his life—he brought these sketches with him. He worked on the manuscript on and off for more than a decade. Fearing that he would never complete it, he issued an unfinished version in 1790. Encouraged by his friend Schiller, he finally published *Faust, Part One* in 1808. Meanwhile he had begun work on the second part, very different from the first in time, place, and style. Although he released portions of *Part Two* during his life, he worked on the manuscript right up until his death. The complete play was published in 1832, more than sixty years after he had first begun it. The lifetime of work yielded the masterpiece of Germany's finest poet.

FAUST AND ROMANTICISM

Although Romanticism didn't cause a political upheaval in Germany, it did spark the imagination of German writers. Like their English and French counterparts, young German writers began to rebel against the restraints of Neoclassicism.

The Romantic movement exploded on the German scene during the *Sturm und Drang* (storm and stress) movement of the 1770's. As the name suggests, the era saw the rise of highly emotional writing. Goethe, as with many writers of the time, was inspired by the movement to explore the new values of imagination and emotion.

To previous generations Faust was a symbol of humanity gone astray, and his story was taken as a warning. To the Romantics, in contrast, Faust represented human freedom from authority. Whether his decision would lead to salvation or not, his courage in venturing into the world of the forbidden makes him heroic. As he struggles between the real and the ideal, we see Goethe's deep love of humanity.

Goethe's *Faust* is the greatest and most famous version of the Faust legend, the one upon which all subsequent retellings are based. Fascinating, provocative, and compelling, *Faust* probes deeply into the human soul in its search for answers to the timeless quest for the meaning of human existence.

FAUST: HENRY IRVING AS MEPHISTOPHELES
Theatre Museum

THE CHANGING ENGLISH LANGUAGE

The Romantic Age 1798–1832

BRITANNIA RULES THE WAVES

During the Romantic Age, Britannia ruled the waves and English ruled much of the land. Great Britain's smashing conquests in the course of the Napoleonic Wars in the beginning of the century—culminating in Nelson's famous victory at Trafalgar in 1805—had left her in a position of undisputed naval supremacy. This, in turn, gave her control over most of the world's commerce. As English ships traveled throughout the world, they left the language of the mother country in their wake.

New inventions and improvements affected the spread of English within the mother country as well. The establishment of the first affordable newspaper in 1816 and the creation of inexpensive postage in 1840 served to more closely unite the different parts of England and spread the influence of standard speech. Improved means of travel and communication brought about by the railroad, the steamboat, and the telegraph also served to unify the country and blanket the language across the land.

COLONIES ASSERT THEMSELVES

Not everyone accepted the dominance of British English quite so placidly, however. As England's larger colonies became increasingly independent, their citizens felt entitled to speak English in their fashion. Feisty Americans, for example, flushed with the acquisition of great tracts of land, asserted their right to speak American English, complete with such Native-American words as *caribou, hickory, moccasin, moose, opossum, raccoon, skunk, squaw, toboggan, tomahawk, totem,* and *wigwam.*

American English was also marked by borrowings from other peoples. From the Mexicans we took *chili, chocolate, tomato;* from Cuba and the West Indies came *barbecue, canoe,* and *hurricane.*

NEW PLACES, NEW VOCABULARY

The most obvious results of English expansion can be seen in growth of the vocabulary. The acquisition of new lands meant new experiences, new products, and new occupations to name. From India, English acquired such varied and important words as *bandanna, bangle, Bengal, Brahman, bungalow, calico, cashmere, china, chintz, coolie, cot, curry, dinghy, juggernaut, jungle, jute, loot, mandarin, nirvana, pariah, polo, punch* (beverage), *rajah, rupee, thug, toddy, tom-tom,* and *verandah.* From even farther East, the language welcomed terms that have today become commonplace: *gingham, indigo,* and *mango.* One of the most interesting new words was *seersucker,* an Indian corruption of a Persian expression meaning "milk and sugar" that came to be linked to a thin, striped cotton fabric. Many words entered English from Africa as well, either directly or from contact with Dutch and Portuguese traders. These include *banana, Boer, boorish, chimpanzee, gorilla, gumbo, voodoo,* and *zebra.* Although Australia has not given us many words, two have become extremely common: *boomerang* and *kangaroo.*

GRAMMAR REFORMS TAKE SHAPE

The language reforms begun in the Restoration and eighteenth century continued into the Romantic era. There was an especially strong movement to reorganize grammar, now that spelling improvements were well underway. Those seeking to mend grammar wanted to create rules, settle disputed points, and isolate errors to improve the language. As one writer commented in the preface to his grammar book:

> It is not the Language, but the Practice that is at fault. The Truth is, Grammar is very much neglected among us; and it is not the difficulty of the Language, but on the contrast the simplicity and the facility of it, that occasions this neglect. Were the Language less easy and simple, we should find ourselves under a necessity of studying it with more care and attention.

Many of the grammar rules we follow were first established during this period. The distinction between "lie" and "lay" was set out in the late eighteenth century; the preference for "different from" (rather than "different than") and the condemnation of "between you and I" and "it is me," in the early nineteenth. "Between" came to be used for groups of two; "among" came to be used for groups of three or more. It was decided that the comparative rather than the superlative should be used when only two things are involved ("the bigger," not "biggest," of two). Finally, we can note that the double negative was abolished in the late eighteenth century. One grammarian stated the rule that now binds us: "Two Negatives in English destroy one another, or are equivalent to an Affirmative." Here, as elsewhere, grammar reformers were setting down what was apparently a frequent but not absolute tendency in the written language.

Although the rules many seem arbitrary and annoying, the results were noteworthy. English was no longer a language without rules. We now had guidelines to help us integrate the new words acquired through exploration and conquest.

Like people in the colonies, Scottish and Irish writers asserted their national identity. Sir Walter Scott is credited with reviving interest in the Scots tongue.

SIR WALTER SCOTT
Sir Edwin Landseer
National Portrait Gallery, London

YOUR WRITING PROCESS

WRITING A REFLECTIVE ESSAY

"Let Nature be your teacher."

William Wordsworth

Many readers consider William Wordsworth to be the greatest of the Romantic poets. Imagine that the editors of a journal dedicated to the study of Wordsworth are sponsoring a contest with a $100 prize for high school students. The editors want to publish essays that testify to Wordsworth's continued relevance in the modern world.

> **Focus**
>
> **Assignment:** Write a reflective essay about William Wordsworth.
> **Purpose:** To show his relevance in the modern world.
> **Audience:** Readers of a Wordsworth journal.

Prewriting

1. What are the issues? In pairs, small groups, or as an entire class, brainstorm to develop a list of what you consider the most important issues facing us today. Think about civics, technology, religion, education, economics, ethics, and the environment. Which ones would have concerned Wordsworth? Why?

2. Reread and note relevant information. You will find useful information in the introduction to this unit and in the biographical material on page 578. From the poems themselves, you can deduce Wordsworth's concerns, beliefs, and prejudices. Read between the lines and draw connections to today's world.

3. What if Wordsworth were alive today? Imagine that Wordsworth could visit your town. What would amuse him? What would outrage him? What would be familiar? What would frighten him? Do some freewriting to imagine the scene. This should help you to find ideas and images to use in your essay.

Drafting

1. Be reflective. A reflective essay is a thoughtful, personal consideration of a subject. Its organization can be informal, following the paths of your own ideas.

2. Be lively. Remember that *thoughtful* is not a synonym for *dull*. Use quotations from Wordsworth's poems to make your points.

> **Student Model**
>
> Wordsworth writes that the natural world "moves us not," but he never could have imagined how indifferent to the environment humans could become. "We are out of tune," he says of nineteenth-century Britons, but today I shout, "We can't even hear the song!"

Revising and Editing

1. Have you met the requirements? Review your essay and see whether or not it satisfies the rules of the contest. Does it explain how Wordsworth is relevant to the modern world?

2. Check your facts. If you have made a claim without supporting it with evidence, do some research as you revise. For example, if you have written, "Many endangered species have become extinct because human beings didn't care," find out which species have become extinct and when this happened.

3. Keep it parallel. Parallel clauses or phrases can add style and formality to your writing. Experiment with parallel constructions; be careful to keep even single, sequential words in parallel structure.

> **Student Model**
>
> Wordsworth admires majestic rainbows, silent sunrises, calm evenings, and the pastoral countrysides of England.

4. Economize. As always, look for ways to economize with language by finding vivid, specific nouns to replace pale, overly modified ones. Find punchy active verbs to replace weaker ones. Remove "I think" in any form. If you are not sure if a word is necessary, it probably isn't.

5. Read and listen. When you are satisfied with your revision, have a peer editor read your essay aloud as you sit and listen. Stop him or her if you hear something that you are not happy with. Discuss ways to make it more vivid, succinct, or emphatic. Then, read your partner's essay aloud and discuss its strengths and weaknesses.

Writer's Hint

Don't use the word *there*. It may look harmless, but it seldom adds anything but filler to a good sentence. For example, instead of writing, "There was something wrong," just write "Something was wrong." The second sentence is more effective.

Options for Publishing

- Hold a "Wordsworth Appreciation Day" in which students read aloud several of his poems along with several of these essays.
- Create an anthology of the Wordsworth essays and make it available to the class.

Reviewing Your Writing Process

1. Did reviewing Wordsworth's biography help you draft the essay? Why or why not?

2. Did your opinion of Wordsworth's poetry change as you wrote this essay? Explain.

QUEEN VICTORIA'S VISIT TO CHERBOURG
Jules Achille Noel
Royal Academy, London

THE VICTORIAN AGE
(1833–1901)

The year's at the spring
And the day's at the morn;
Morning's at seven;
The hillside's dew-pearled;
The lark's on the wing;
The snail's on the thorn;
God's in his heaven—
All's right with the world!
    From "Pippa Passes"
    Robert Browning

Queen Victoria reigned for sixty-four years, from 1837 to 1901—the longest reign of any British monarch. With occasional exceptions, those were years of prosperity for Britain. Robert Browning's lines on the preceding page echo the ringing optimism and self-assurance that marked the Victorian Age. The Victorians recognized that, in fact, all was not really "right with the world," and they worked hard to make improvements. Yet they firmly believed that theirs was the best nation in the best era history had yet produced.

Living in the Victorian Age

Britain's booming economy and rapid expansion encouraged great optimism. Profiting from its early industrial revolution, Britain became the world leader in manufacturing. Factories dotted the land. Factory towns grew into large cities. Banks, retail shops, and other businesses expanded. These changes in turn spurred the growth of two important classes—an industrial working class and a modern middle class, able to live a better life because of the low cost and large variety of mass-produced factory goods.

As its industry and commerce prospered, Britain expanded its merchant fleet and its powerful navy. Economic and military power helped Britain to acquire new colonies in far-flung parts of the globe. Victorians could quite literally boast that "the sun never sets on the British empire."

Yet, for all its self-satisfaction, the Victorian Age was also a time of social concern. Victorian writers exposed a dark underside of the industrial age—brutal factory conditions and stinking slums that bred poverty and disease. Goaded by reformers and radicals of many sorts, Victorian leaders took steps to expand democracy and better the lot of the poor. By the time Victoria died in 1901, Britain had shed some of its complacency and was grappling with the social and economic problems industrialization had caused.

Victoria and Albert

Victoria became queen at the age of eighteen. She impressed the members of Parliament with her grace and self-assurance, but she could also be very stubborn. In 1840, she insisted on marrying a first cousin, a minor German princeling named Albert

LONDON'S CRYSTAL PALACE
(detail)
The British Museum

of Saxe-Coburg-Gotha. Many Britons disliked the marriage: What if Prince Albert filled the queen's head with "European" notions of absolute rule? As it turned out, Albert understood the limited powers of British royalty. His wisdom and impartial advice did much to soften the personality of the queen. (It was she who reigned; Albert was not king but *prince consort* — the monarch's husband.)

Victoria and Albert produced a large family and restored to the monarchy a sense of decorum sadly lacking since the madness of George III and the scandalous behavior of his sons. The twentieth century would tend to look back on Victoria as prim to the point of prudishness. However, we must remember that her restrained behavior came in reaction to those earlier royal excesses.

When Albert died of typhoid fever in 1861, Victoria went into deep mourning. For a time she was almost a recluse, leaving day-to-day government in the hands of her prime ministers. Victoria's limited involvement in political affairs helped to turn Britain into the modern constitutional monarchy it is today, in which the duties of the sovereign are largely ceremonial.

Victorian Politics

The prime ministers who govern Britain serve at the sufferance of Parliament, and can be dismissed at any time by a vote of no confidence. Such a system produces a more rapid turnover of leadership than does our own presidential system.

The years of Victoria's reign brought a change in the policies and even the names of the two parties that had dominated eighteenth-century politics. The Whig party formerly had championed Britain's commercial dominance and colonial empire. Gradually, the Whigs adopted new attitudes and became known as the Liberal party. Liberals often attacked colonial expansion and, under the leadership of William Gladstone, pressed for reforms at home and in Ireland. Meanwhile, the Tory party began to abandon its old stance of isolationism in foreign affairs and stubborn resistance to social change. The Tories (or Conservatives, as they came to be called) now supported imperialism — the expansion of empire. Under leaders like Benjamin Disraeli, the Conservatives also supported electoral reform. It was Disraeli who helped push through the Second Reform Bill of 1867, doubling the electorate by granting voting rights to tenant farmers and to better-paid male workers.

The Liberals and Conservatives alternated in power. Each party had its die-hard followers, but each had to compete for the same middle-of-the-road "swing" voters. As a result, Victorian politics emphasized compromise and slow reform.

Domestic Problems and Reforms

Two key issues — trade policy and electoral reform — dominated domestic politics during the first half of the Victorian era. Trade debate centered on the Corn Laws, which had long slapped high tariffs on "corn" (grain). This discouraged food imports and helped British landlords and farmers. However, it also tended to keep food prices high, which angered consumers and the poorer classes. At stake was not just money but life itself, as became evident in 1845, when a failure of Ireland's potato crop caused a massive famine in which as many as one million Irish people died.

Seeking to increase the supply of food, Parliament repealed the Corn Laws in 1846. Over the following decade, Parliament changed other trade laws, putting an end to the policy of protectionism (restriction of imports to protect domestic producers). Instead, Britain now adopted a policy of free trade (allowing imports and exports with few or no restrictions). The new policy reflected the interests of rising British industries, which prospered by importing raw materials and exporting finished goods. Times had changed, and Britain was fast becoming an industrial rather than an agricultural nation.

Many Britons thought that the second issue — electoral reform — had been settled in 1832, when the Reform Law gave the vote to middle-class males. They were wrong; working-class people wanted further reform. In 1838, a group of radicals drew up a "People's Charter" demanding, among other things, universal suffrage for males. This so-called Chartist movement fizzled out after a decade or so, but new demands for electoral

The Victorian Age (A.D. 1833–A.D. 1901)

Charles
Dickens

Queen Victoria

Richard Wagner

| 1830 | 1845 | 1860 |

BRITISH EVENTS

- Slavery abolished in British empire.
  - Victoria becomes queen.
  - **Charles Dickens** writes *Oliver Twist*.
  - Thomas Carlyle writes *The French Revolution*.
    - Michael Faraday experiments with electric currents.
      - **William Wordsworth** becomes poet laureate.
        - George Williams founds YMCA.

- Irish Potato Famine begins.
  - Factory Act passed.
  - Charlotte Brontë publishes *Jane Eyre*.
  - Emily Brontë publishes *Wuthering Heights*.
    - Women begin attending University of London.
      - Britain enters Crimean War.
  - Charles Darwin publishes *On the Origin of Species*.

- Florence Nightingale founds school for nurses.
  - Construction of London Underground begins.
    - **Robert Browning** publishes *The Ring and the Book*.
    - London Fire Department established.
    - Lewis Carroll publishes *Alice's Adventures in Wonderland*.
      - Debtors' prisons abolished.

WORLD EVENTS

- United States: Ralph Waldo Emerson publishes *Nature*.
  - South Pacific: New Zealand becomes a British colony.
    - Asia: Hong Kong becomes a British colony.
    - France: Honoré de Balzac publishes *The Human Comedy*.
      - United States: Samuel F. B. Morse patents telegraph.

- France: Revolution establishes new republic under Louis Napoleon.
  - France: Life insurance introduced.
    - Australia: Gold discovered in New South Wales.
      - Eastern Europe: Crimean War begins.
      - Japan: Trade with West reopened.
    - United States: Henry David Thoreau publishes *Walden*.
      - India: Sepoy Mutiny against British.

- United States: Civil War begins.
  - Russia: Leo Tolstoy publishes *War and Peace*.
  - Austria: Gregor Mendel proposes laws of heredity.
    - Europe: Seven Weeks' War leads to unification of modern Germany.
      - Egypt: Suez Canal completed.
        - France: Jules Verne publishes *Around the World in Eighty Days*.

Alice's
Adventures
in Wonderland

Suez Canal

Boxer Rebellion

1875   1890   1905

- Salvation Army established.
  - Joseph Swan installs first electric lighting.
    - Robert Louis Stevenson publishes *Treasure Island*.
      - First edition of *Oxford English Dictionary* published.
        - English Lawn Tennis Association founded at Wimbledon.
          - Jack the Ripper stalks London's East End.

- **Thomas Hardy** publishes *Tess of the d'Urbervilles*.
  - **Rudyard Kipling** publishes *Barrack-room Ballads*.
    - Oscar Wilde publishes *The Importance of Being Earnest*.
      - **A. E. Housman** publishes *A Shropshire Lad*.
        - Queen Victoria dies.

- United States: Alexander Graham Bell patents telephone.
  - United States: Thomas Edison patents phonograph.
    - South Africa: Zulu War against British.
      - Russia: Feodor Dostoevsky publishes *The Brothers Karamazov*.
        - Egypt: Britain invades and conquers nation.
          - United States: Mark Twain publishes *The Adventures of Huckleberry Finn*.

- Asia: Sino-Japanese War begins.
  - Greece: First modern Olympics held.
    - China: Boxer Rebellion against foreign influence.
    - France: Marie and Pierre Curie discover radium.
      - Russia: Anton Chekhov publishes *Uncle Vanya*.

DUDLEY STREET, SEVEN DIALS, LONDON, 1872
Gustave Doré

change led to the Second Reform Bill of 1867 and to almost complete male suffrage in 1885.

The urge for reform also affected many other areas. Women, although still not eligible to vote, began to attend universities. Parliament passed laws to reduce the working day for women and children, to establish a system of free grammar schools, and to legalize trade unions. It voted to improve public sanitation and to regulate factories and housing. Still, such measures did not go far enough to suit everyone, and agitation continued for further reform.

One of the most important issues left unresolved in the Victorian Age was the future of Ireland, where widespread poverty had bred bitter opposition to British control. In the 1880's and 1890's, the Liberal leader William Gladstone supported Irish demands for home rule (self-government). However, a hard-line faction of Liberals joined Conservatives to block action on Gladstone's proposals.

Empire and Foreign Policy

Britain was not alone in its drive to form a world empire in the Victorian Age. Other European powers were grabbing colonies too. British diplomats tried to protect and expand the British empire while promoting a balance of power within Europe.

The Imperialist Urge

Victorian Britons who supported a policy of imperialism could cite a long list of arguments: Colonies would provide raw materials and markets for British industry. They would offer a home for British settlers. Britain had no choice; if it didn't seize a territory, one of its European rivals would do so. Perhaps the clinching argument was the writer Rudyard Kipling's notion of "the white man's burden." Victorians tended to believe that Western civilization—commonly perceived as white, Christian, and progressive—was superior to all other cultures. This attitude led many Victorians to look condescendingly on non-Westerners as people in need of assistance. What could be more noble than to help those "natives" by offering them the protection of the British empire? While such an argument seems faintly ridiculous by today's lights, many Victorians sincerely believed it.

Britain's empire had two sorts of land—"settled" territories, where whites made up a large part of the population, and outright colonies, in which few whites lived. During the Victorian Age, Britain granted considerable self-government to "settled" territories such as Canada, Australia, and New Zealand. On the other hand, it exercised strict rule over places such as Hong Kong (acquired from China in 1842). After a rebellion in 1857 by sepoys (Indian troops under British command), Britain shouldered aside the British East India Company and took direct control of India. Victoria would thus add "Empress of India" to her formal titles.

The Crimean War

The Victorian years were generally peaceful. Britain fought only one major European war—the Crimean War (1853–1856), so called because it took place on the Crimean peninsula in southern Russia. Britain, France, and Turkey teamed up to thwart Russian expansion, but the battles were largely inconclusive. Today we remember the war mainly for the brave but disastrous charge of Britain's Light Brigade. This was commemorated in a famous poem by Alfred, Lord Tennyson, including these lines:

> Theirs not to make reply,
> Theirs not to reason why,
> Theirs but to do and die.

Britain as a World Power

In the last three decades of Victoria's rule, Britain reached new heights of wealth and power. It gained control of the new Suez Canal in Egypt. It acquired Cyprus, an island in the eastern Mediterranean. It joined other European powers in a scramble to carve up Africa, acquiring such territories as Kenya, Uganda, Nigeria, and Rhodesia (Zimbabwe). Also, Britain expanded its control over what is now South Africa, defeating Dutch settlers there in the Boer War of 1899–1902.

Even in those years of expansion, however, Britons could not help worrying about the future. Other nations, especially the United States and Germany, were rapidly building up industry and competing with Britain in world markets. How long could Britain maintain its economic superiority? How would economic changes affect the balance of power? For how long would Britain's navy "rule the waves"? By the end of Victoria's reign in 1901, British leaders had many disturbing questions to ponder.

Victorian Thought

Victorian thinkers often disagreed on the crucial issues of their times, but they shared a deep confidence in humanity's ability to better itself. "Man is not the creature of circumstances," said Benjamin Disraeli. "Circumstances are the creatures of man." This spirit of optimism prevailed up to the closing years of the Victorian era.

Responses to Industrialization

The changes brought about by the Industrial Revolution stirred conflicting feelings among Victorian thinkers. On the one hand, they admired the material benefits industrialization had brought. On the other, they deplored the brutality of factory life and of industrial slums.

We can divide into three groups the political and economic theories Victorians employed for dealing with the changed conditions of the industrial age:

Theories

- **Laissez-faire theory.** This theory holds that government should avoid meddling in the affairs of business—should "let it be" (the sense of the French term). When allowed full freedom, the theory goes, industry will use the most efficient techniques and reach the highest possible level of prosperity.
- **Reformist liberalism.** Those who held this theory believed that rapid change brings problems that *laissez-faire* policies cannot solve. They argued that government intervention and regulation were sometimes necessary to protect the rights of the weak against the strong.
- **Socialism.** Some thinkers and activists favored a more far-reaching policy, ending private ownership of major industries and substituting public ownership. Supporters of socialism also called for sweeping government measures to promote equality and help the poor.

Religion and Science

At the same time they were debating the political problems posed by industrialization, the Victorians were grappling with the religious and philosophical implications of modern life. A religious movement called evangelicalism influenced many Victorians. The movement linked strict personal morality with a strong commitment to social reform, leading to the founding of such institutions as the Young Men's Christian Association (YMCA) and the Salvation Army. The Liberal leader William Gladstone was among those inspired by evangelicalism to devote his life to public service and social reform. The Oxford Movement expressed a second strain of religious thought, seeking a return to more traditional church ritual.

Other Victorians turned to science for answers. The theory of evolution proposed by Charles Darwin (1809–1882) in *On the Origin of Species* (1859) stirred bitter controversy. Some Victorian thinkers saw Darwin's theory as a direct challenge to Biblical truth and traditional religious faith. Some accepted both Darwin's theory and religion, striving to reconcile scientific and religious insights.

Darwin believed that a process called natural selection guides evolution. By this process, some organisms survive (because they can adapt to changing conditions) and some die out (because they cannot adapt). A social scientist named Herbert Spencer (1820–1903) applied Darwin's idea —which Spencer called "the survival of the fittest"—to social life. In Spencer's harsh philosophy, called Social Darwinism, the "fittest" humans achieve social and economic success, while the "unfit" fail. Neither government nor private charities should attempt to interfere with this "natural" process, said the Social Darwinists—applying *laissez-faire* theory to social as well as economic life.

Victorian Literature

The ideas of the Victorian Age—political and moral, scientific and religious—helped to shape the works you will read in this unit. Indeed, they helped to define the Victorians themselves. Education was spreading in the Victorian Age, and as literacy increased, so did the impact of the written word. Probably at no other time before or since did books enjoy such enormous popularity and influence.

Romanticism, Realism, and Naturalism

The Romantic movement continued to influence writers of the Victorian Age, but new styles of writing came into vogue. Romanticism had begun as a radical departure from literary practice; now it was part of mainstream culture, safe but slightly stale. A new generation of writers, coming of age in a time of rapid technological change, began to examine the social effects of that change. The heroes of the new generation's literature would be ordinary people facing the day-to-day problems of life. Life would be presented as it is, rather than as it might be. We call this new literary movement realism, because it sought to portray human life realistically, as it is actually lived, without sugar coating.

Romantic thinking had lent itself to poetic language, and we study the Romantic Age chiefly for its poetry. Realism, on the other hand, focused on more down-to-earth or prosaic events especially suited to prose. The shift in style helped to make the Victorian Age the great age of the British novel.

By focusing on ordinary people, realist literature reflected the nineteenth-century trend to democracy and appealed to a growing middle-class audience. Realist writing often dealt with family relationships, religion and morality, social change, and social reform—topics of special interest to middle-class readers.

New ideas in science also made their mark on Victorian literature. A movement known as naturalism—an outgrowth of realism—sought to apply the techniques of scientific observation to writing about life in the industrial age. Naturalists crammed their novels with details—the sour smells of poverty, the harsh sounds of factory life—often with the aim of promoting social reform. Naturalist writers directly contradicted the romantic view of nature as kindly and benevolent. To naturalists, the idea that nature mirrored human feelings was false—a "pathetic fallacy." Instead, naturalist writers portrayed nature as harsh and indifferent to the human suffering it often caused.

It would be a mistake to assume that Victorian writers abandoned romanticism altogether. Some writers blended romanticism with realism or naturalism; others sought to revive romanticism as the radical force it once had been. Two Victorian literary movements deserve special mention here. One is a group of painters and poets known as the

Pre-Raphaelite Brotherhood. Formed about 1848, this short-lived group sought to ignore the ugliness of industrial life by portraying nature with the fidelity found in medieval Italian art before the Renaissance painter Raphael (1483–1520). The leading Pre-Raphaelite was Dante Gabriel Rossetti (1828–1882), who excelled both as a painter and as a poet. The second group, known as the aesthetic movement, appeared toward the end of the Victorian Age. Aesthetes like the writer Oscar Wilde (1854–1900) turned away from the everyday world and sought to create "art for art's sake"—works whose sole reason for being was their perfection or beauty.

Victorian Poetry

The Victorian Age produced a large and diverse body of poetry. The Romantic style predominated at first, but Realism and Naturalism gained force as time went on.

The most popular poet of the era, however, was a Romantic—Alfred, Lord Tennyson (1809–1892). Influenced by earlier Romantic poets, especially Walter Scott, Tennyson wrote many long narrative poems on ancient and medieval themes like the King Arthur legend. His verse displays a keen sense of the music of language, and some of his more sentimental lyrics reappeared in popular songs. Yet Tennyson also revealed a deeper, more thoughtful side in such powerful poems as "Ulysses" (1842) and *In Memoriam, A.H.H.* (1850). Tennyson became poet laureate after Wordsworth died in 1850.

Robert Browning (1812–1889) produced a body of poetry as diverse as Tennyson's, although in his lifetime he never achieved equal public acclaim. Many of Browning's poems display Romantic attitudes. Others, however, show the influence of Realism in seeking to portray individuals with un-Romantic authenticity. Critics have especially admired Browning's use of the dramatic monologue—a long speech by an imaginary character—to expose pretense and reveal a character's inner self. In 1846, Browning plunged into one of literature's most famous romances when he eloped with the poet Elizabeth Barrett, whose father had forbidden the marriage. At the time, Elizabeth was

CARICATURE OF ALFRED, LORD TENNYSON, 1871
Carlo Pellegrini

a more famous poet than Robert. History has since reversed that verdict, but Elizabeth Barrett Browning (1806–1861) is still remembered for the beautiful love poems she wrote her husband.

A number of other Victorian poets also worked in the Romantic vein. You have already read of the Pre-Raphaelites, who include Dante Gabriel Rossetti; his sister, Christina Rossetti (1830–1894); and George Meredith (1828–1909). Another poet with a romantic style was Emily Brontë (1818–1848), who often described characters and settings from the imaginative world of her own childhood.

Matthew Arnold (1822–1888) was probably the first Victorian poet to focus on "the bewildering confusion" of the industrial age. Many of Arnold's poems deal with alienation: separation from nature, isolation from other human beings. In his most famous poem, "Dover Beach" (1867), he breaks with poetic tradition and employs free verse—poetry with no fixed rhythm—to portray the confusion and loss of faith of his times. Arnold was a forerunner of the more pessimistic Naturalist writers.

Late Victorian Naturalism found its strongest voice in Thomas Hardy (1840–1928), whose poetry, like his prose, focuses on workers and farmers overwhelmed by the forces of nature and society. Life's disappointments were also a frequent subject of A. E. Housman (1859–1936), whose quiet lyrics speak of personal loss and rural change.

Rudyard Kipling (1865–1936), who wrote fiction and children's stories as well as poetry, gained great popularity in the 1890's. Kipling created action-packed narrative poems such as "Gunga Din" (1892) and many short lyric poems that became popular songs. He employs the dialect of working-class soldiers in Realist poems such as "Tommy" (1892):

> For it's Tommy this, an' Tommy that,
>   an' "Chuck 'im out, the brute!"
> But it's "Savior of 'is Country" when
>   the guns begin to shoot.

One final Victorian poet, Gerard Manley Hopkins (1844–1889), remained unpublished during his own century but would later inspire twentieth-century poets. Hopkins, a Catholic priest, wrote deeply religious verse influenced by the earlier romantic poets and the philosopher Duns Scotus. He was also an innovative craftsman, introducing a rhythmic pattern called sprung rhythm that abandoned traditional metric feet.

Victorian Drama

Compared to poetry, drama in the Victorian Age seemed pale and uninspired. Playhouses were few in number and hemmed in by government restrictions. Only toward the end of the century did the theater begin to show some sparkle, with serious dramas like Sir Arthur Wing Pinero's *The Second Mrs. Tanqueray* (1893) and satirical ones like Oscar Wilde's *The Importance of Being Earnest* (1895).

BAYSWATER OMNIBUS
G. W. Joy
Museum of London

Victorian Fiction

If one form of literature can be seen as quintessentially Victorian, it is the novel. Members of the new middle class were avid readers, and they loved novels—especially novels that reflected the main social issues of the day. Responding to the demand, weekly and monthly magazines published novels chapter by chapter, in serial form. Curious readers had to keep buying the magazine to learn what happened next. Most of the best novelists of the day wrote, at one time or another, for the magazines.

Romanticism heavily influenced early Victorian novels, especially those written by three sisters —Emily Brontë (1818–1848), Charlotte Brontë (1816–1855), and the lesser-known Anne Brontë (1820–1849). Emily's classic *Wuthering Heights* (1847) tells the poetic tale of the doomed passions of Catherine Earnshaw and of Heathcliff, one of English fiction's outstanding Byronic heroes. Charlotte's famous *Jane Eyre* (1847) recounts the adventures of a governess who falls in love with her mysterious employer, Mr. Rochester. Nevertheless, both works also contain elements of the new Realism—as in *Jane Eyre*'s vivid portrait of the heroine's harsh childhood.

The Realistic elements of *Jane Eyre* probably owe much to the influence of Charles Dickens (1812–1870), who surpassed all other Victorian novelists in popularity. Dickens never forgot his impoverished childhood, filling his novels with poignant details that dramatized the problems of a grimy industrial England. Although Dickens treated social problems realistically and became an outspoken voice for social reform, he tempered his criticism with humor. Many of his characters are comic caricatures in which a particular human foible or vice is exaggerated. Dickens also showed a sentimental side, providing happy endings for many of his plucky heroes and heroines.

Other Victorian Realists were less sentimental in their portraits of people and society. George Meredith, already mentioned as a Romantic poet, produced careful psychological studies of characters and their motives in novels such as *The Egoist* (1879). Mary Ann Evans, writing under the pen name George Eliot (1819–1880), examined moral issues and personal relationships in novels such as *Adam Bede* (1859). Also choosing Realistic themes were William Makepeace Thackeray (1811–1863), Anthony Trollope (1815–1882), Elizabeth Gaskell (1810–1865), and Samuel Butler (1835–1902).

As the century drew to a close, British novelists leaned more and more to Naturalism. Thomas Hardy was the most highly regarded of late Victorian Naturalists. Hardy set his fiction in western England, which he called by its old Saxon name, Wessex. His pessimistic novels often portray rural characters who have been disappointed in life and love.

Such downbeat themes did not attract the enthusiastic reception for Naturalist novels that earlier Realist novels had won. Late Victorian readers tended to prefer the action-packed adventure stories of writers like Robert Louis Stevenson (1850–1894) and Rudyard Kipling or the Sherlock Holmes mysteries of Sir Arthur Conan Doyle (1859–1930).

Nonfiction Prose

Novels, of course, were only one of the many types of prose available to Victorian readers. British writers poured out a steady stream of histories, biographies, essays, and criticism.

Greatest of the historians were Thomas Carlyle (1795–1881) and Thomas Babington Macaulay (1800–1859). Carlyle also wrote historical biographies. Perhaps the outstanding literary biography of the era was Elizabeth Gaskell's *Life of Charlotte Brontë* (1857), still a primary source of information on the Brontë family.

All the great Victorian thinkers produced influential prose works. Matthew Arnold, for example, made a sharp attack on the British class system in *Culture and Anarchy* (1869), his most famous work of social criticism. Other influential works included *Modern Painters* (1843) by John Ruskin (1819–1900), *On Liberty* (1859) by John Stuart Mill (1806–1873), *The Idea of a University Defined* (1873) by John Henry Newman (1801–1890), and *Studies in the History of the Renaissance* (1873) by Walter Pater (1839–1894).

All in all, the Victorian Age produced a diverse body of literature—entertaining, scholarly, humorous, profound. Because the era is so close to our own times—and because in it we see the beginnings of our own problems, many of them still unresolved—Victorian literature has a special relevance to readers in the twentieth century. In addition, the Victorian writers were brilliant storytellers, and we read their works not only for literary appreciation and historical understanding but for pure reading pleasure.

HYDE PARK NEAR GROSVENOR GATE, 1842 (detail)
Thomas Shotter Boys
Guildhall Art Gallery

Man is a tool-making animal.
Thomas Carlyle, *Sartor Resartus*

Youth is a blunder; manhood a struggle; old age a regret.
Benjamin Disraeli, *Coningsby*

If thou must love me, let it be for naught
Except for love's sake only.
Elizabeth Barrett Browning, *Sonnets from the Portuguese*

The only purpose for which power can be rightfully
exercised over any member of a civilized community, against
his will, is to prevent harm to others.
John Stuart Mill, *On Liberty*

You cannot fight against the future. Time is on our side.
William E. Gladstone in a speech on the Second Reform Bill

It's them as take advantage
that get advantage i'
this world.
George Eliot, *Adam Bede*

'Tis better to have loved and lost
Than never to have loved at all.
Alfred, Lord Tennyson, *In Memoriam, A.H.H.*

A man's reach should exceed his grasp,
Or what's a heaven for?
Robert Browning, "Andrea del Sarto"

He had used the word in its Pickwickian sense.
Charles Dickens, *The Pickwick Papers*

READING CRITICALLY

The Literature of 1832–1901

When you read literature it is important to place it in its historical context. Doing so will help you to see how the writer was influenced by the dominant ideas and attitudes of the time and how the work fits into a particular literary movement.

HISTORICAL CONTEXT The Victorian Age was a period marked by industrial and scientific advances, social progress, political stability, and economic prosperity. When the period began, England was the world's wealthiest and most powerful nation, and the British Empire spanned the globe. As the age progressed, the nation continued to flourish, as industrial growth and development strengthened its economy and the empire reached its peak. With the expansion of industry, the middle class became a dominant force in British society, and their belief in hard work and strict morality came to represent the age. The middle class also possessed a sense of social responsibility that helped to bring about reforms that gradually improved the living and working conditions of the lower classes.

LITERARY MOVEMENTS The dominant attitudes and beliefs of the Victorian period are reflected in the literature of the time. Whereas some writers embodied the Victorian ideals, others reacted against them. Many Victorian works conveyed the optimism and conservatism that characterized the age. Other works explored the problems that arose from industrialization and confronted the materialism, hypocrisy, and social pretense that accompanied the nation's prosperity. Because of the contrasting approaches of writers of the time, Victorian literature is extremely varied and diverse.

WRITERS' TECHNIQUES The English novel came of age during the Victorian period. Often published in serial form, Victorian novels are generally characterized by their episodic plots and their realistic portrayal of nineteenth-century life. In poetry, writers displayed a wide array of voices and styles. However, Victorian poets were generally more detached and objective than their predecessors from the Romantic Age.

ALFRED, LORD TENNYSON

1809–1892

When Alfred Tennyson was named baron by Queen Victoria in 1883, he was doubly honored—first by the title *Lord,* second by being the first English writer so titled. The honor seemed fitting for one whom most Victorians regarded as the poetic voice of their age. His commitment to responsible action and his belief in the inherent goodness of people were just two of many traits that made Tennyson the object of his contemporaries' admiration and affection. Yet, beyond these qualities was the man himself, forever struggling to overcome shyness and self-doubt, his mind keenly attuned to the problems of his century. Tennyson's best poems reflect both the inner and outer being, expressing through a clear and richly haunting music those certainties that sustain the human spirit.

Tennyson was born in the rural town of Somersby in Lincolnshire, the fourth of twelve children. His father, a rector, had a large library and personally supervised his son's early education. In 1827 Tennyson entered Trinity College, Cambridge, where he became close friends with Arthur Henry Hallam, the son of a noted historian and a great fan of Tennyson's early efforts at poetry. In 1830, with Hallam's encouragement, Tennyson published *Poems, Chiefly Lyrical,* which he followed up two years later with the simply titled *Poems.* When Hallam died suddenly in Vienna in 1833, the loss left a void in Tennyson's life that nearly destroyed him.

Grief, however, was ultimately to be the inspiration behind some of the poet's greatest work. Relatively soon after Hallam's death, Tennyson began work on a collection of memorial poems dedicated to his friend. When the lengthy tribute, titled *In Memoriam, A.H.H.,* finally appeared in 1850, the queen's husband, Prince Albert, was so impressed that he encouraged her to appoint Tennyson next Poet Laureate of England. For the next forty years, Tennyson continued to publish regularly. Among his most celebrated works was *Idylls of the King,* a series of poems based on the legend of King Arthur, which began appearing in 1859 and was completed in 1885.

Modern scholars are in general agreement that there is much of lasting value in Tennyson's works. Certainly there is no denying what the twentieth-century poet and critic T. S. Eliot has called the "abundance, variety, and complete competence" in Tennyson's poetry. Nor can one ignore the number of quotable lines Tennyson has added to the English language, among them " 'Tis better to have loved and lost, than never to have loved at all." These aspects of his verse and others have earned Tennyson yet another honor—that of being one of the best-known poets of all time.

GUIDE FOR INTERPRETING

The Lady of Shalott; Tears, Idle Tears

Writers' Techniques

Meter and Stanza Structure. Meter is the regular pattern of stressed and unstressed syllables in poetry. Stanza structure is a term that takes into account the meter, rhyme scheme, line length, and number of lines in each stanza of a poem. Through the structure of the stanza, the poet establishes unity, of both form and thought, within a poem.

For "The Lady of Shalott," a poem inspired by Arthurian legend, Tennyson appropriately chose a meter and stanza structure that recalled medieval romances—tales in verse that described the deeds of knights and ladies. The stanzaic structure of these romances, known as a *tail-rhyme stanza,* was traditionally six lines long and composed of two pairs of rhyming lines, each followed by a short third line, or "tail." The rhyming lines, moreover, customarily contained four stressed syllables, or beats, whereas the tail contained three. Tennyson altered this traditional pattern somewhat in "The Lady of Shalott," and in so doing, lent his poem a magical, almost dreamlike quality.

Commentary

"Modern fame is nothing," Tennyson remarked to a friend. "I'd rather have an acre of land. I shall go down, down! I'm up now. Action and reaction."

At the time of Tennyson's death, he was indeed immensely popular. But shortly thereafter, just as he had predicted, a reaction against his work set in, and as with a pebble thrown into a pond, rippled ever wider. It became fashionable in the 1920's and 1930's to belittle his work; critic Harold Nicholson, for example, called him "a morbid and unhappy mystic" who "should be read carelessly or not at all."

By the 1940's, however, the ripples had ceased to expand, and critic Arthur J. Carr could write, "At some crucial points Tennyson is a modern poet, and there are compelling reasons why we should try to comprehend him."

Do you think such a swing in opinion is inevitable? Why do you think that Tennyson's poetry might appeal to us today?

Focus

Imagine that the only view of the world you had was a reflection of it, as through a mirror. Freewrite, describing the sensations you would miss in not experiencing life firsthand, and tell how this would make you feel.

The Lady of Shalott

Alfred, Lord Tennyson

Part I

On either side the river lie
Long fields of barley and of rye,
That clothe the wold[1] and meet the sky;
And through the field the road runs by
5   To many-towered Camelot,[2]
And up and down the people go,
Gazing where the lilies blow[3]
Round an island there below,
        The island of Shalott.

10   Willows whiten, aspens quiver,
Little breezes dusk and shiver
Through the wave that runs forever
By the island in the river
        Flowing down to Camelot.
15   Four gray walls, and four gray towers,
Overlook a space of flowers,
And the silent isle imbowers
        The Lady of Shalott.

By the margin, willow-veiled.
20   Slide the heavy barges trailed
By slow horses; and unhailed
The shallop[4] flitteth silken-sailed
        Skimming down to Camelot:
But who hath seen her wave her hand?
25   Or at the casement seen her stand?
Or is she known in all the land,
        The Lady of Shalott?

Only reapers, reaping early
In among the bearded barley,
30   Hear a song that echoes cheerly,

---

1. wold: Rolling plains.
2. Camelot: A legendary English town where King Arthur had his court and Round Table.
3. blow: Bloom.
4. shallop: A light open boat.

From the river winding clearly,
    Down to towered Camelot:
And by the moon the reaper weary,
Piling sheaves in uplands airy,
35   Listening, whispers, "'Tis the fairy
    Lady of Shalott."

Part II

There she weaves by night and day
A magic web with colors gay.
She has heard a whisper say,
40   A curse is on her if she stay
    To look down to Camelot.
She knows not what the curse may be,
And so she weaveth steadily,
And little other care hath she,
45   The Lady of Shalott.

THE LADY OF SHALOTT
John Waterhouse
The Tate Gallery, London

And moving through a mirror[5] clear
That hangs before her all the year,
Shadows of the world appear.
There she sees the highway near
50   Winding down to Camelot:
There the river eddy whirls,
And there the surly village churls,
And the red cloaks of market girls,
        Pass onward from Shalott.

55 Sometimes a troop of damsels glad,
An abbot on an ambling pad,[6]
Sometimes a curly shepherd lad,
Or long-haired page in crimson clad,
        Goes by to towered Camelot;
60 And sometimes through the mirror blue
The knights come riding two and two:
She hath no loyal knight and true,
        The Lady of Shalott.

But in her web she still delights
65 To weave the mirror's magic sights,
For often through the silent nights
A funeral, with plumes and lights
        And music, went to Camelot:
Or when the moon was overhead,
70 Came two young lovers lately wed;
"I am half sick of shadows," said
        The Lady of Shalott.

Part III

A bow-shot from her bower eaves,
He rode between the barley sheaves,
75 The sun came dazzling through the leaves,
And flamed upon the brazen greaves[7]
        Of bold Sir Lancelot.
A red-cross knight[8] forever kneeled
To a lady in his shield,
80 That sparkled on the yellow field,
        Beside remote Shalott.

---

5. mirror: Weavers placed mirrors in front of their looms, so that they could view the progress of their work.
6. pad: An easy-paced horse.
7. greaves: Armor that protects the legs below the kneecaps.
8. red-cross knight: Refers to the Redcrosse Knight from *The Faerie Queene* by Edmund Spenser. In Spenser's work, the knight represents St. George, the patron saint of England, in addition to being a symbol of holiness.

The gemmy[9] bridle glittered free,
Like to some branch of stars we see
Hung in the golden Galaxy.[10]
85   The bridle bells rang merrily
          As he rode down to Camelot:
And from his blazoned baldric[11] slung
A mighty silver bugle hung,
And as he rode his armor rung,
90   Beside remote Shalott.

All in the blue unclouded weather
Thick-jeweled shone the saddle leather,
The helmet and the helmet feather
Burned like one burning flame together,
95   As he rode down to Camelot.
As often through the purple night,
Below the starry clusters bright,
Some bearded meteor, trailing light,
              Moves over still Shalott.

100   His broad clear brow in sunlight glowed;
On burnish'd hooves his war horse trode;
From underneath his helmet flowed
His coal-black curls as on he rode,
          As he rode down to Camelot.
105   From the bank and from the river
He flashed into the crystal mirror,
"Tirra lirra," by the river
          Sang Sir Lancelot.

She left the web, she left the loom,
110   She made three paces through the room,
She saw the waterlily bloom,
She saw the helmet and the plume,
          She looked down to Camelot.
Out flew the web and floated wide;
115   The mirror cracked from side to side;
"The curse is come upon me," cried
          The Lady of Shalott.

Part IV

In the stormy east wind straining,
The pale yellow woods were waning,

---

9. gemmy: Jeweled.
10. Galaxy: The Milky Way.
11. blazoned baldric: A decorated sash worn diagonally across the
chest.

120　The broad stream in his banks complaining,
　　Heavily the low sky raining
　　　　Over towered Camelot;
　　Down she came and found a boat
　　Beneath a willow left afloat,
125　And round about the prow she wrote
　　　　The Lady of Shalott.

　　And down the river's dim expanse
　　Like some bold seër in a trance,
　　Seeing all his own mischance—
130　With a glassy countenance
　　　　Did she look to Camelot.
　　And at the closing of the day
　　She loosed the chain, and down she lay;
　　The broad stream bore her far away,
135　　　The Lady of Shalott.

　　Lying, robed in snowy white
　　That loosely flew to left and right—
　　The leaves upon her falling light—
　　Through the noises of the night
140　　　She floated down to Camelot:
　　And as the boathead wound along
　　The willowy hills and fields among,
　　They heard her singing her last song,
　　　　The Lady of Shalott.

145　Heard a carol, mournful, holy,
　　Chanted loudly, chanted lowly,
　　Till her blood was frozen slowly,
　　And her eyes were darkened wholly,
　　　　Turned to towered Camelot.
150　For ere she reached upon the tide
　　The first house by the waterside,
　　Singing in her song she died,
　　　　The Lady of Shalott.

　　Under tower and balcony,
155　By garden wall and gallery,
　　A gleaming shape she floated by,
　　Dead-pale between the houses high,
　　　　Silent into Camelot.
　　Out upon the wharfs they came,
160　Knight and burgher, lord and dame,
　　And round the prow they read her name,
　　　　The Lady of Shalott.

Who is this? and what is here?
And in the lighted palace near
165 Died the sound of royal cheer;
And they crossed themselves for fear,
All the knights at Camelot:
But Lancelot mused a little space;
He said, "She has a lovely face;
170 God in his mercy lend her grace,
The Lady of Shalott."

RESPONDING TO THE SELECTION

Your Response

1. Do you think the Lady makes the right decision in leaving the tower and sailing for Camelot? Explain.

Recalling

2. What does the Lady spend all of her time doing, and why?
3. Where does she glimpse "shadows of the world"?
4. (a) What action does the Lady take when she sees Sir Lancelot in the mirror? (b) What happens to her as a result?

Interpreting

5. In line 42 the speaker says the Lady "knows not what the curse may be." Explain the curse in your own words.
6. Critics have seen this poem as a commentary on the plight of the artist. In light of this interpretation, what is meant by the Lady's complaint in lines 71–72?
7. (a) Why do you think the author devotes so much space to his description of Sir Lancelot? (b) How does it relate to the Lady's action and to the overall meaning of the poem?

Applying

8. Why do you find the legend of King Arthur an especially effective—or especially poor—vehicle for the author's commentary on art and the artist in "The Lady of Shalott"?

ANALYZING LITERATURE

Recognizing Meter and Stanza Structure

Meter is a pattern of stressed and unstressed syllables that creates a predictable rhythm in a poem. Meter is expressed in units called *feet,* each consisting of one stressed syllable and one or more unstressed syllables. Meter is but one ingredient in a poem's **stanza structure,** which also takes into account such matters as variation in line length, overall number of lines, and rhyme scheme. In "The Lady of Shalott," Tennyson adapted—or altered to suit his needs—an ancient stanza form that had the following structure: six lines per stanza; four feet in lines 1, 2, 4, and 5; three feet in lines 3 and 6; and the rhyme scheme *aabccb.*

Examine several stanzas of "The Lady of Shalott." Note the ways in which the stanza structure differs from the above. Tell how the changes add to the poem's chantlike effect.

CRITICAL THINKING AND READING

Understanding the Author's Purpose

It has been suggested that Tennyson's purpose in writing "The Lady of Shalott" was to show how the past reflects the problems of the present.

1. Which events or statements in the poem point to a possible problem?
2. What is the nature of that problem?
3. What specific instances of this problem are evident in modern society?

from The Princess

Alfred, Lord Tennyson

The Princess (1847) is a long narrative poem that contains a number of songs. Some of these songs, including the one that follows, are considered to be among the finest of Tennyson's lyrics.

Tears, Idle Tears

Tears, idle tears, I know not what they mean,
Tears from the depth of some divine despair
Rise in the heart, and gather to the eyes,
In looking on the happy autumn fields,
5 And thinking of the days that are no more.

Fresh as the first beam glittering on a sail,
That brings our friends up from the underworld,
Sad as the last which reddens over one
That sinks with all we love below the verge;
10 So sad, so fresh, the days that are no more.

Ah, sad and strange as in dark summer dawns
The earliest pipe of half-awakened birds
To dying ears, when unto dying eyes
The casement slowly grows a glimmering square;
15 So sad, so strange, the days that are no more.

Dear as remembered kisses after death,
And sweet as those by hopeless fancy feigned
On lips that are for others; deep as love,
Deep as first love, and wild with all regret;
20 O Death in Life, the days that are no more.

RESPONDING TO THE SELECTION

Your Response

1. What is your attitude toward the past? How does it compare with the speaker's feelings in this poem?

Recalling

2. According to the first stanza, what causes the tears to rise?
3. In what three ways does the speaker describe "the days that are no more"?

Interpreting

4. Why are the tears described as "idle"?
5. What do you think is meant in line 2 by "some divine despair"?
6. What comment is Tennyson making about our ability to remember things past?
7. A refrain is a repeated line or phrase in a poem or song. Identify the refrain in this poem, and explain how you think it was intended to make the reader feel.

Applying

8. (a) Why do you think people feel nostalgia for "days that are no more"? (b) In what way is nostalgia bittersweet?

THINKING AND WRITING

Describing the Poet's Style

A poet's **style** is the way in which he or she strings together words and ideas to communicate a particular image or message. In "Tears, Idle Tears," Tennyson's style grows out of his abundant use of repetition and his juxtaposition of positive and negative impressions (such as "sad" and "fresh" in the second stanza). Write an essay explaining how Tennyson's style relates to his theme. Begin by stating the theme of the poem. Use quotations freely to illustrate the points you make. When you revise, make sure you have quoted exactly and punctuated your quotations accurately.

LEARNING OPTIONS

1. **Writing.** Imagine you are working on a screenplay for a movie entitled *The Princess* that is set in the Middle Ages. Write a plot summary delineating a series of events that move the heroine to sing "Tears, Idle Tears."
2. **Art.** In "Tears, Idle Tears" some striking images are used to good advantage. Following are some examples: "happy autumn fields" (line 4), "beam glittering on a sail" (line 6), and "dark summer dawns" (line 11). Choose one of these images and either draw or find pictures to represent what you see in your mind.
3. **Cross-curricular Connection.** Along with other songs from *The Princess,* "Tears, Idle Tears" has been set to music and sung. Find and listen to a recording of these selections. Do you think the music enhances the poem? If not, how do you think the music should sound? Play the recording for the class and ask for responses from your classmates.
4. **Performance.** Write your own musical setting for "Tears, Idle Tears." Think about the mood the poem conveys and create music to express that mood. You might want to decide whether the verses should be set to the same refrain or if each verse should reflect a different musical idea. When you are finished composing, perform, or have a friend perform, your piece in class.

GUIDE FOR INTERPRETING

from In Memoriam, A. H. H.; The Lotos-Eaters; Ulysses; Crossing the Bar

Literary Forms

Elegy. An elegy is any poem that mourns the passing of an individual. Elegies are an ancient form and, since the Renaissance, have been an enduring tradition among English poets. Tennyson's *In Memoriam, A.H.H.* is widely acknowledged as one of the finest elegies ever written. The poem not only laments the death of Tennyson's closest friend, Arthur Henry Hallam, but also provides a "chronicle" of the poet/speaker's emotions as he moves gradually away from sheer grief and doubt toward understanding, acceptance, and faith.

Dramatic Monologue. A dramatic monologue is a poem in which a single speaker reveals his or her personality in an address to a silent listener or listeners. The entire dramatic situation—the setting, the conflict, and the main characters—is disclosed through the speaker's words alone. In Tennyson's "Ulysses" we have a vivid example of this poetic form that was so popular during the Victorian Age.

Writers' Techniques

Symbol. A symbol is a person, place, object, or action that represents an abstract idea. For example, a parent might be a symbol of authority, and a spring flower might be a symbol of rebirth. Poets often use symbols to give images deeper significance. In "The Lady of Shalott," Tennyson uses the web and mirror as symbols for, respectively, art and the artist's tendency to experience life secondhand. In "Crossing the Bar," he uses symbols to describe a universal human experience.

Focus

The sudden death of a friend or relative, especially a young one, can stir up a wide range of emotions in the survivors, including despair, anger, and doubt. Describe what in particular might lead to these feelings after such a loss. Then read the excerpt from *In Memoriam, A.H.H.* to see how Tennyson felt about his friend's death.

Primary Source

Critics have written enthusiastically about *In Memoriam, A.H.H.* Paul F. Baum, for instance, finds the elegy form well matched both to its subject and to Tennyson's genius. "*In Memoriam*," he writes, "is not only a monument to Arthur Hallam and a record of Tennyson's personal suffering at Hallam's early death, it is also 'the way of the soul' . . . his representation of everyman's pain when confronted with death, the struggle with doubt, and the triumphant assertion of God's love."

from In Memoriam, A. H. H.

Alfred, Lord Tennyson

In Memoriam, A.H.H. is an elegiac poem that conveys Tennyson's feelings and reflections about the death of his close friend Arthur Hallam, a talented young man who died suddenly at the age of twenty-two. Though Milton's Lycidas and Shelley's Adonais also lamented the deaths of promising young men, the structure of Tennyson's poem is quite different from these earlier elegies. In Memoriam, A.H.H. is made up of 131 seemingly self-sustaining lyrics that were composed over a period of seventeen years, as the poet struggled to come to terms with the feelings of doubt and despair that stemmed from his friend's early death.

1

I held it truth, with him who sings
    To one clear harp in divers tones,
    That men may rise on stepping stones
Of their dead selves to higher things.

5   But who shall so forecast the years
    And find in loss a gain to match?
    Or reach a hand through time to catch
The far-off interest of tears?

Let Love clasp Grief lest both be drowned,
10   Let darkness keep her raven gloss.
    Ah, sweeter to be drunk with loss,
To dance with death, to beat the ground,

Than that the victor Hours should scorn
    The long result of love, and boast,
15   "Behold the man that loved and lost,
But all he was is overworn."

7

Dark house, by which once more I stand
    Here in the long unlovely street,
    Doors, where my heart was used to beat
20   So quickly, waiting for a hand,

NOCTURNE IN GREY AND GOLD: CHELSEA SNOW, 1876
James McNeill Whistler
The Fogg Art Museum, Cambridge, Mass.

A hand that can be clasped no more—
    Behold me, for I cannot sleep,
    And like a guilty thing I creep
At earliest morning to the door.

25 He is not here; but far away
    The noise of life begins again,
    And ghastly through the drizzling rain
On the bald street breaks the blank day.

82

I wage not any feud with Death
30   For changes wrought on form and face;
    No lower life that earth's embrace
May breed with him, can fright my faith.

Eternal process moving on,
    From state to state the spirit walks;
35   And these are but the shattered stalks,
Or ruined chrysalis of one.

Nor blame I Death, because he bare
    The use of virtue out of earth;
    I know transplanted human worth
40 Will bloom to profit, otherwhere.

For this alone on Death I wreak
    The wrath that garners in my heart;
    He put our lives so far apart
We cannot hear each other speak.

130

45 Thy voice is on the rolling air;
    I hear thee where the waters run;
    Thou standest in the rising sun,
And in the setting thou art fair.

What art thou then? I cannot guess;
50   But though I seem in star and flower
    To feel thee some diffusive power,
I do not therefore love thee less.

My love involves the love before;
    My love is vaster passion now;
55   Though mixed with God and Nature thou,
I seem to love thee more and more.

Far off thou art, but ever nigh;
    I have thee still, and I rejoice;
    I prosper, circled with thy voice;
60 I shall not lose thee though I die.

RESPONDING TO THE SELECTION

Your Response

1. Do you agree with the speaker that love can deepen in spite of loss or death? Why or why not?

Recalling

2. In Part 1, what truth does the speaker say he once held but now doubts?
3. Where is the speaker standing in Part 7?
4. For what one thing, in Part 82, does the speaker "wreak the wrath" in his heart on death?
5. In Part 130, what does the speaker say has happened to his love for his friend?

Interpreting

6. (a) According to the excerpts, what part of his friend does the poet finally accept is lost forever? (b) What part does he come to recognize will live forever?
7. Explain the paradox in line 57: "Far off thou art, but ever nigh."
8. Compare the first two excerpts with the last two. How have the poet's emotions changed?

Applying

9. (a) If you had to console someone who had lost a loved one, what advice might you give to help that person cope? (b) How close would your ideas be to those implied in the last excerpt of *In Memoriam, A.H.H.*?
10. The English novelist Samuel Butler has written, "To die completely, a person must not only forget but be forgotten, and he who is not forgotten is not dead." (a) Discuss the meaning of this quotation. (b) How does it relate to *In Memoriam, A.H.H.*?

ANALYZING LITERATURE

Understanding an Elegy

An **elegy** is a poem or song that laments a death, usually recent. *In Memoriam, A.H.H.,* is an especially strong elegy since, as Tennyson himself put it, the poem is "rather the cry of the whole human race than mine. In the poem altogether private grief swells out into thought of, and hope for, the whole world."

1. Which details in the four excerpts seem particularly "private"?
2. Which seem to apply to "the whole human race"?
3. What hope for future generations is implied in the final excerpt?

CRITICAL THINKING AND READING

Making Inferences About the Subject

In *In Memoriam, A.H.H.,* Tennyson never actually describes his friend directly but rather drops clues to the man's personality. The reader must thus **infer,** or piece together from these clues, a picture of the man. What personality traits can you infer from the following?

1. Tennyson's reminiscence in Part 7 of his friend's hand clasp.
2. His comparing of his friend's remains to a "ruined crysalis."
3. His sensing in Part 130 of his friend's "diffusive power" in a star and flower.

LEARNING OPTIONS

1. **Writing.** Imagine finding a diary entry in which Tennyson records his reflections on the friendship he mourns in *In Memoriam, A.H.H.* What might such an entry say? Would the diary reveal a different perspective on the friend than the poem does? Write your own version of this diary entry in which the significance of the relationship is examined.
2. **Community Connections.** Each Memorial Day we remember national heroes and others who have died in the defense of our nation. Many organizations sponsor parades and other activities to remind us of the sacrifices of men and women in the past. Visit a local historical society, veterans organization, or library to find information on Memorial Day observances in your community. Then share your findings in a brief oral presentation to the class.

The Lotos-Eaters

Alfred, Lord Tennyson

In Homer's epic poem, the Odyssey, *the Greek veterans of the Trojan War come upon the land of the Lotos-Eaters while on their long voyage home. Upon consuming the lotos's honeyed fruit, they are tempted to discontinue their journey. The men forget about going home and want instead to stay in the land of the Lotos-Eaters forever.*

In his poem "The Lotos-Eaters," Tennyson expands upon Homer's brief account of the men's stay in this strange land. He delves deeper, exploring the men's desire for rest and the feeling of guilt that grow out of that desire.

"Courage!" he[1] said, and pointed toward the land,
"This mounting wave will roll us shoreward soon."
In the afternoon they came unto a land
In which it seemed always afternoon.
5   All round the coast the languid air did swoon,
Breathing like one that hath a weary dream.
Full-faced above the valley stood the moon;
And like a downward smoke, the slender stream
Along the cliff to fall and pause and fall did seem.

10   A land of streams! some, like a downward smoke,
Slow-dropping veils of thinnest lawn[2] did go;
And some through wavering lights and shadows broke,
Rolling a slumbrous sheet of foam below.
They saw the gleaming river seaward flow
15   From the inner land: far off, three mountaintops,
Three silent pinnacles of aged snow,
Stood sunset-flushed; and, dewed with showery drops,
Up clomb the shadowy pine above the woven copse.

The charmed sunset lingered low adown
20   In the red West: through mountain clefts the dale
Was seen far inland, and the yellow down[3]
Bordered with palm, and many a winding vale
And meadow, set with slender galingale;[4]
A land where all things always seemed the same!

---

1. he: Odysseus (ō dis' ē əs) (or Ulysses), the hero of the *Odyssey*.
2. lawn *n.*: A fine, thin linen.
3. down *n.*: An expanse of open, high, grassy land.
4. galingale *n.*: A plant similar in appearance to tall grass.

25 And round about the keel with faces pale,
Dark faces pale against that rosy flame,
The mild-eyed melancholy Lotos-eaters came.

Branches they bore of that enchanted stem,
Laden with flower and fruit, whereof they gave
30 To each, but whoso did receive of them,
And taste, to him, the gushing of the wave
Far far away did seem to mourn and rave
On alien shores; and if his fellow spake,
His voice was thin, as voices from the grave;
35 And deep asleep he seemed, yet all awake,
And music in his ears his beating heart did make.

They sat them down upon the yellow sand,
Between the sun and moon upon the shore;
And sweet it was to dream of Fatherland,
40 Of child, and wife, and slave; but evermore
Most weary seemed the sea, weary the oar,
Weary the wandering fields of barren foam.
Then someone said, "We will return no more";
And all at once they sang, "Our island home[5]
45 Is far beyond the wave; we will no longer roam."

Choric Song[6]

I

There is sweet music here that softer falls
Than petals from blown roses on the grass,
Or night dews on still waters between walls
Of shadowy granite, in a gleaming pass;
50 Music that gentler on the spirit lies,
Than tired eyelids upon tired eyes;
Music that brings sweet sleep down from the blissful skies.
Here are cool mosses deep.
And through the moss the ivies creep,
And in the stream the long-leaved flowers weep,
55 And from the craggy ledge the poppy hangs in sleep.

II

Why are we weighed upon with heaviness
And utterly consumed with sharp distress,
While all things else have rest from weariness?
All things have rest: why should we toil alone,
60 We only toil, who are the first of things,

---

5. **home:** Ithaca, an island off the coast of Greece.
6. **Choric Song:** Sung by the Greek travelers in chorus.

And make perpetual moan,
Still from one sorrow to another thrown;
Nor ever fold our wings,
And cease from wanderings,
65   Nor steep our brows in slumber's holy balm;
Nor harken what the inner spirit sings,
"There is no joy but calm!"
Why should we only toil, the roof and crown of things?[7]

III

Lo! in the middle of the wood,
70   The folded leaf is wooed from out the bud
With winds upon the branch, and there
Grows green and broad, and takes no care,
Sun-steeped at noon, and in the moon
Nightly dew-fed; and turning yellow
75   Falls, and floats adown the air.
Lo! sweetened with the summer light,
The full-juiced apple, waxing over-mellow,
Drops in a silent autumn night.
All its allotted length of days,
80   The flower ripens in its place,
Ripens and fades, and falls, and hath no toil,
Fast-rooted in the fruitful soil.

IV

Hateful is the dark-blue sky,
Vaulted o'er the dark-blue sea.
85   Death is the end of life; ah, why
Should life all labor be?
Let us alone. Time driveth onward fast,
And in a little while our lips are dumb.
Let us alone. What is it that will last?
90   All things are taken from us, and become
Portions and parcels of the dreadful Past.
Let us alone. What pleasure can we have
To war with evil? Is there any peace
In ever climbing up the climbing wave?
95   All things have rest, and ripen toward the grave
In silence; ripen, fall and cease:
Give us long rest or death, dark death, or dreamful ease.[8]

---

7. Why . . . things?: This line echoes the following passage from
Edmund Spenser's *Faerie Queene*: "Why then dost thou, O man, that
of them all/Art Lord, and eke of nature Soveraine/willfully . . . waste
thy joyous hours in needless pain . . . ?"

8. All . . . ease: This passage echoes the following lines in Spenser's
Faerie Queene: "Sleep after toyle, port after stormie seas/Ease after
war, death after life does greatly please."

V

How sweet it were, hearing the downward stream,
With half-shut eyes ever to seem
100 Falling asleep in a half dream!
To dream and dream, like yonder amber light,
Which will not leave the myrrh[9] bush on the height;
To hear each other's whispered speech;
Eating the Lotos day by day,
105 To watch the crisping[10] ripples on the beach,
And tender curving lines of creamy spray;
To lend our hearts and spirits wholly
To the influence of mild-minded melancholy;
To muse and brood and live again in memory,
110 With those old faces of our infancy
Heaped over with a mound of grass,
Two handfuls of white dust, shut in an urn of brass!

VI

Dear is the memory of our wedded lives,
And dear the last embraces of our wives
115 And their warm tears; but all hath suffered change;
For surely now our household hearths are cold,
Our sons inherit us, our looks are strange,
And we should come like ghosts to trouble joy.
Or else the island princes[11] over-bold
120 Have eat our substance, and the minstrel sings
Before them of the ten years' war in Troy,
And our great deeds, as half-forgotten things.
Is there confusion in the little isle?
Let what is broken so remain.
125 The Gods are hard to reconcile;
'Tis hard to settle order once again.
There *is* confusion worse than death,
Trouble on trouble, pain on pain,
Long labor unto aged breath,
130 Sore task to hearts worn out by many wars
And eyes grown dim with gazing on the pilot stars.

---

9. myrrh (mŭr) *n.*: A plant that produces a fragrant gum resin used in making incense and perfume.
10. crisping *adj.*: Curling.
11. princes: Suitors who were courting Ulysses' wife, Penelope.

VII

But, propped on beds of amaranth[12] and moly,[13]
How sweet (while warm airs lull us, blowing lowly)
With half-dropped eyelid still,
135   Beneath a heaven dark and holy,
To watch the long bright river drawing slowly
His waters from the purple hill—
To hear the dewy echoes calling
From cave to cave through the thick-twined vine—
140   To watch the emerald-colored water falling
Through many a woven acanthus[14] wreath divine!
Only to hear and see the far-off sparkling brine,
Only to hear were sweet, stretched out beneath the pine.

---

12. amaranth (am′ ə ranth′) *n.*: An imaginary flower that never fades or dies.
13. moly (mō′ lē) *n.*: In classical mythology, an herb of magic powers. In the Odyssey, Ulysses uses moly to protect himself from the incantation of Circe (sər′ sē), an enchantress who turned men into swine.
14. acanthus (ə kan′ thəs) *n.*: A thistlelike plant.

ULYSSES MOURNING FOR HOME
Carved Gem of Light Brown Sardonyx
Roman 3rd to 2nd Century B.C.
Staatliche Museen zu Berlin

The Lotos-Eaters   715

The Lotos blooms below the barren peak,
145 The Lotos blows by every winding creek;
All day the wind breathes low with mellower tone;
Through every hollow cave and alley lone
Round and round the spicy downs the yellow Lotos dust is
    blown.
We have had enough of action, and of motion we,
150 Rolled to starboard, rolled to larboard, when the surge was
    seething free,
Where the wallowing monster spouted his foam fountains
    in the sea.
Let us swear an oath, and keep it with an equal mind,
In the hollow Lotos land to live and lie reclined
On the hills like Gods together, careless of mankind.
155 For they lie beside their nectar, and the bolts[15] are hurled
Far below them in the valleys, and the clouds are lightly
    curled
Round their golden houses, girdled with the gleaming
    world;
Where they smile in secret, looking over wasted lands,
Blight and famine, plague and earthquake, roaring deeps
    and fiery sands,
160 Clanging fights, and flaming towns, and sinking ships, and
    praying hands.
But they smile, they find a music centered in a doleful song.
Steaming up, a lamentation and an ancient tale of wrong,
Like a tale of little meaning though the words are strong;
Chanted from an ill-used race of men that cleave the soil,
165 Sow the seed, and reap the harvest with enduring toil,
Storing yearly little dues of wheat, and wine and oil;
Till they perish and they suffer—some, 'tis
    whispered—down in hell
Suffer endless anguish, others in Elysian valleys[16] dwell,
Resting weary limbs at last on beds of asphodel.[17]
170 Surely, surely, slumber is more sweet than toil, the shore
Than labor in the deep mid-ocean, wind and wave and oar;
Oh rest ye, brother mariners, we will not wander more.

---

15. bolts: Thunderbolts.
16. Elysian (i lizh′ ən) **valleys:** In Greek mythology, heroes went to
Elysia after death.
17. asphodel (as′ fə del′): A plant with yellow or white lilylike
flowers.

RESPONDING TO THE SELECTION

Your Response

1. If you were one of the sailors in the land of the Lotos-Eaters, how would you respond to life there? Explain.

Recalling

2. What strange property of the land is mentioned in lines 4 and 24 of the poem?
3. (a) How do the men describe this new land in the poem's Choric Song? (b) How do they describe the lives they had led up till now? (c) Why do they want to remain?

Interpreting

4. (a) What do the men find so appealing about the land of the Lotos-Eaters? (b) What nagging concerns haunt them in spite of the effect of the lotos plants?
5. (a) What differences exist between the odd-numbered and even-numbered stanzas of the Choric Song? (b) What do these differences suggest about the decision the men have made?

Applying

6. To what extent do you think Tennyson is "prescribing" the sailors' decision in "The Lotos-Eaters" as a solution to problems of life in his time? Explain your answer.

CRITICAL THINKING AND READING

Recognizing Allusions

An **allusion** is a reference to a person, place, statement, or event in another work of art or cultural work. Writers use allusions to help the reader grasp a greater truth. Suppose that Tennyson had written "The Lotos-Eaters" without any of its allusions to classical mythology.

1. What general truth might be missed?
2. How would the poem be diminished?
3. What qualities might be more evident?

LEARNING OPTIONS

1. **Art.** "The Lotos-Eaters" describes a fanciful world that lures the Greek veterans from their goal of returning home. Many books have described ideal worlds, full of happiness and pleasure. List all the things you would include in an ideal world. Then create one or more illustrations of this imaginary place.
2. **Speaking and Listening.** Imagine that you are Odysseus addressing his crew in the land of the Lotos-Eaters. What would you say? Write a speech in which you express being torn between reaching home and the pleasures of the present. Deliver your speech in class.

MULTICULTURAL CONNECTION

The Symbolism of the Lotus

A sacred flower. In Tennyson's "The Lotos-Eaters," the honeyed taste of the lotus flower enchants Odysseus' shipmates and puts them in a state of dreamy forgetfulness. As a symbol of fertility, fruitfulness, and cosmic abundance, the lotus has found a privileged place in religions as diverse as Buddhism, Taoism, and Hinduism. In Egypt, the lotus, or white water lily, grows on the banks of the Nile River and is designated the national emblem. In China, incense is burned to the spirit of the lotus to ward off evil.

In Hindu mythology and literature, the lotus is the main standard of beauty.

Contentment and forgetfulness. The lotus has also had more down-to-earth uses. In ancient times, wine made from the fruit of the lotus was believed to bring about contentment and a pleasant forgetfulness. In its water-lily form, the lotus appears in Hindu temples and carvings, decorates Egyptian columns, and serves as the basis for both the Assyrian sacred tree design and the ornamental capitals of Phoenician columns.

Exploring

Investigate other flowers with symbolic meanings. How do different cultures respond to these flowers? Share your findings in class.

Ulysses

Alfred, Lord Tennyson

*In this poem Tennyson extends the story of Ulysses (yōo lis'
ēz), the hero of the Odyssey, beyond the narrative in Homer's
epic. Here we learn that he has grown restless in the years
since returning to his home in Ithaca. Although he had been
away for twenty long years—ten fighting in the Trojan War
and another ten making the long and adventure-filled voyage back—Ulysses finds that he is contemplating making
another, final journey.*

It little profits that an idle king,
By this still hearth, among these barren crags,
Matched with an aged wife, I mete and dole[1]
Unequal[2] laws unto a savage race,
5 That hoard, and sleep, and feed, and know not me.
I cannot rest from travel; I will drink
Life to the lees.[3] All times I have enjoyed
Greatly, have suffered greatly, both with those
That loved me, and alone; on shore, and when
10 Through scudding drifts the rainy Hyades[4]
Vexed the dim sea. I am become a name;
For always roaming with a hungry heart
Much have I seen and known—cities of men
And manners, climates, councils, governments,
15 Myself not least, but honored of them all—
And drunk delight of battle with my peers,
Far on the ringing plains of windy Troy.
I am a part of all that I have met;
Yet all experience is an arch wherethrough
20 Gleams that untraveled world, whose margin fades
Forever and forever when I move.
How dull it is to pause, to make an end,
To rust unburnished, not to shine in use!

---

1. mete and dole: Measure and give out.
2. unequal: Unfair.
3. lees: Sediment.
4. Hyades (hī' ə dez): A group of stars whose rising
was assumed to be followed by rain.

ULYSSES
Jean-Auguste-Dominique Ingres
National Gallery of Art, Washington

As though to breathe were life. Life piled on life
25   Were all too little, and of one to me
Little remains; but every hour is saved
From that eternal silence, something more,
A bringer of new things; and vile it were
For some three suns to store and hoard myself,
30   And this gray spirit yearning in desire
To follow knowledge like a sinking star,
Beyond the utmost bound of human thought.

This is my son, mine own Telemachus,
To whom I leave the scepter and the isle[5]
35 Well-loved of me, discerning to fulfill
This labor, by slow prudence to make mild
A rugged people, and through soft degrees
Subdue them to the useful and the good.
Most blameless is he, centered in the sphere
40 Of common duties, decent not to fail
In offices of tenderness, and pay
Meet[6] adoration to my household gods,
When I am gone. He works his work, I mine.
　　　There lies the port; the vessel puffs her sail;
45 There gloom the dark broad seas. My mariners,
Souls that have toiled and wrought, and thought with
　　me—
That ever with a frolic welcome took
The thunder and the sunshine, and opposed
Free hearts, free foreheads—you and I are old;
50 Old age hath yet his honor and his toil;
Death closes all; but something ere the end,
Some work of noble note, may yet be done,
Not unbecoming men that strove with Gods.
The lights begin to twinkle from the rocks;
55 The long day wanes; the slow moon climbs; the deep
Moans round with many voices. Come, my friends,
'Tis not too late to seek a newer world.
Push off, and sitting well in order smite
The sounding furrows; for my purpose holds
60 To sail beyond the sunset, and the baths
Of all the western stars, until I die.
It may be that the gulfs will wash us down;
It may be we shall touch the Happy Isles,[7]
And see the great Achilles,[8] whom we knew.
65 Though much is taken, much abides; and though
We are not now that strength which in old days
Moved earth and heaven, that which we are, we are—
One equal temper of heroic hearts,
Made weak by time and fate, but strong in will
70 To strive, to seek, to find, and not to yield.

---

5. isle: Ithaca, an island off the coast of Greece.
6. meet: Appropriate.
7. Happy Isles: Elysium, or the Islands of the Blessed; in classical mythology, the place where heroes went after death.
8. Achilles (ə' kil' ēz): The Greek hero of the Trojan War.

RESPONDING TO THE SELECTION

Your Response

1. Ulysses' attitude is that it is never "too late to seek a newer world." Do you agree? Why or why not?

Recalling

2. (a) How does Ulysses describe his current situation? (b) What past experiences does he describe?
3. What work is Ulysses leaving to Telemachus?
4. According to lines 58–61, what is Ulysses' purpose?
5. What comments does Ulysses make about his present condition in the final six lines?

Interpreting

6. How does Ulysses' current situation contrast with his previous experiences?
7. (a) What is Ulysses' attitude toward his experiences and accomplishments? (b) What are his feelings about aging? (c) What is his attitude toward life in general?
8. How is Telemachus different from his father?
9. What is the poem's theme?

Applying

10. Do you think that most people share Ulysses' feelings about aging? Why or why not?

ANALYZING LITERATURE

Understanding Dramatic Monologues

A **dramatic monologue** is a poem in which one character speaks to one or more silent listeners at a critical point in the speaker's life. The speaker's comments reveal the circumstances and offer insights into his or her personality. For example, in Tennyson's poem Ulysses reveals his attitudes concerning old age and death.

1. Why is the occasion of this poem a critical point in Ulysses' life?
2. What do Ulysses' comments reveal about the way in which he views his purpose in life?

3. What are the dominant traits of Ulysses' personality?

CRITICAL THINKING AND READING

Understanding a Character's Motivation

In portraying any type of character, a writer must provide a motivation, or a stated or implied reason for the character's behavior, to make the character's actions believable. The motivation is the cause for the action. The ensuing action is the effect, or result. Tennyson makes it clear that Ulysses' desire to make a final voyage is partly the result of his disenchantment with his current situation.

1. Name one other motivation for Ulysses' desire to make a final voyage.
2. How is this motivation conveyed in the poem?

THINKING AND WRITING

Writing a Continuation of the Poem

Write a dramatic monologue in which Ulysses describes the final voyage that he contemplates in Tennyson's poem. Brainstorm about the details and outcome of the journey. Arrange the events in chronological order. Then write your poem, using formal, dignified language similar to the language Tennyson uses in "Ulysses." When you revise, make sure you have used concrete details in describing the voyage. After you have finished revising, proofread your poem and share it with your classmates.

LEARNING OPTION

Community Connections. Interview an older person in your community or family who has had a particularly adventurous life and has traveled to other countries. Based on your reading of Tennyson's poem, ask questions to help you understand how that person feels about his or her past adventures as well as about possible further travel. Share your interview with the class.

Crossing the Bar

Alfred, Lord Tennyson

Tennyson requested that this poem, written three years before his death, be printed at the end of all editions of his poetry.

Sunset and evening star,
    And one clear call for me!
And may there be no moaning of the bar,[1]
    When I put out to sea,

5   But such a tide as moving seems asleep,
    Too full for sound and foam,
When that[2] which drew from out the boundless deep
    Turns again home.

Twilight and evening bell,
10   And after that the dark!
And may there be no sadness of farewell,
    When I embark;

For though from out our bourne[3] of Time and Place
    The flood may bear me far,
15   I hope to see my Pilot face to face
    When I have crossed the bar.

---

1. bar: Sandbar.
2. that: The soul.
3. bourne: Boundary.

THE ANGRY SEA
James McNeill Whistler
Freer Gallery of Art, Smithsonian Institution

RESPONDING TO THE SELECTION

Your Response

1. How do you respond when you are faced with an unfamiliar experience? Explain.

Recalling

2. What does the speaker of the poem request in lines 3–4 and again in lines 11–12?

Interpreting

3. What do you think is actually meant by the phrase "crossing the bar"?
4. Who do you think the "Pilot" is?

Applying

5. Which excerpt from *In Memoriam* do you think is most in keeping with the attitude Tennyson expresses in "Crossing the Bar"? Explain why you feel as you do.

ANALYZING LITERATURE

Recognizing Symbols

A **symbol** is a thing, person, place, or idea whose meaning transcends, or goes beyond, its usual literal definition. When the reader of "Crossing the Bar" recognizes that the sea journey described in the poem is in actuality the passage into death, the symbolic meaning of many of the ideas and images becomes obvious. State the meaning symbolized by each of the following:

1. moaning of the bar.
2. putting out to sea.
3. twilight.
4. the dark.
5. the flood bearing one far.

CRITICAL THINKING AND READING

Comparing Attitudes

Writers may write about the same subject but take very different positions. Read each of the following statements about death. Explain which one you feel comes closest to the attitude Tennyson expresses in "Crossing the Bar."

1. Oliver Wendell Holmes: "Death tugs at my ear and says: 'Live, I am coming.'"
2. John Dryden: "To die is landing on some distant shore."
3. Genesis 3:19: "Dust thou art, and unto dust shalt thou return."
4. Ralph Waldo Emerson: "Our fear of death is like our fear that summer will be short, but when we will have had our swing of pleasure, our fill of fruit, and our swelter of heat, we say we have had our day."
5. William Hazlitt: "Our repugnance to death increases in proportion to our consciousness of having lived in vain."

THINKING AND WRITING

Writing About Symbols

In "Crossing the Bar" Tennyson uses a series of interrelated symbols to deliver his thoughts on the issues of serenity at life's end and faith in an afterlife. He might, of course, have selected a different set of symbols to express these thoughts. Choose a symbolic vehicle other than a boat trip that could stand for the journey at life's end. Some possibilities are a walk up a hill or the writing of the last chapter of a book. Make notes on the various details that might be used in such a symbolic representation. Then express Tennyson's ideas in either a poem or brief story that uses this set of symbols.

LEARNING OPTION

Speaking and Listening. "Crossing the Bar" might serve as an epitaph for Tennyson. An epitaph is a short, pithy saying that functions as an important reminder of a person and is usually written on the person's tombstone. For example, Martin Luther King, Jr.'s epitaph is "Free at Last, Free at Last, Thank God Almighty, I'm Free at Last." Find some other famous epitaphs and share them with the class.

ROBERT BROWNING

1812–1889

In Victorian England, clubs to promote the works of the masters of English literature were fairly common. In 1881, a group of amateur scholars banded together to found one such club, the Browning Society. What made this literary club unique was that the poet it paid tribute to was *living.* Yet if honor in this form came unusually early to Robert Browning, then fame came unusually late, for it was not until nearly a half century after the publication of his first book that the public came to recognize his genius.

Robert Browning was born in London and spent the first twenty-eight years of his life there. Like Tennyson, he was educated mainly at home, spending much of his time during his early years in his father's large library. There he immersed himself in art, history, literature, philosophy, religion, music, medicine, and zoology. At twenty-one Browning published his first book, *Pauline,* a highly personal record of his religious skepticism, no doubt influenced by the writings of Shelley. Discouraged by the book's poor critical reception, Browning tried his hand next at something less personal, publishing *Paracelsus,* a long dramatic poem, in 1835. Failing again to please the critics, he turned to drama and two years later produced *Strafford,* a play that closed after five performances.

Despite his inability to establish himself in the public eye as a writer to be reckoned with, Browning was shaping the distinctive dramatic voice that would ensure his eventual fame. In *Dramatic Lyrics* (1842), *Dramatic Romances and Lyrics* (1845), and *Men and Women* (1855) he reveals a rich and varied talent in both the short lyrical poem and the dramatic monologue.

In 1846 he married Elizabeth Barrett, a poet whose fame greatly exceeded his own. They established a home in Florence, Italy, a setting that figures in many of Browning's works. The marriage was an extremely happy one, and when his wife died in 1861, Browning, unable to face constant reminders of her in Florence, returned to London. There he soon became a popular figure, especially among university students, who were attracted to his next book, *Dramatis Personae* (1864). This was followed by his masterpiece, *The Ring and the Book* (1868), which was hailed as the most "profound spiritual treasure that England had produced since the days of Shakespeare." Based on an actual seventeenth-century Italian murder trial, this long poem comprises ten dramatic monologues.

Browning's dramatic monologues have greatly influenced many twentieth-century poets. Today he is admired not only for these complex psychological portraits, but also for his masterly blending of natural speech rhythms with strict poetic forms.

GUIDE FOR INTERPRETING

My Last Duchess; Home-Thoughts, from Abroad; Love Among the Ruins

Literary Forms

Dramatic Monologue. A dramatic monologue is a poem with a single speaker that is much like a speech in a play. Unlike a play, however, in which each speech is preceded by the name of its speaker, the dramatic monologue contains no such label. Rather, the identity of the speaker is revealed through his or her words. In "My Last Duchess," we learn, strictly through the speaker's conversation with an unnamed companion, the setting of the poem and—more important—the inner conflict that prompts the character's speech.

Focus

Write a brief fictional account of *your* life in the Oval Office titled "I, The President." Focus not on affairs of state but on the day-to-day routine in your household—your relationship with your family and friends, the stress that your job places on those relationships, and so on. Be sure to answer, somewhere in your account, the question "How has power changed me?"

Primary Source

In contemporary life we often live by the dictum that less is more. Alfred, Lord Tennyson once told Robert Browning that "if he got rid of two-thirds, the remaining third would be much finer." Tennyson then expanded on his comments as follows:

> "It is necessary to respect the limits," he explained. "An artist is one who recognizes bounds to his work as a necessity, and does not overflow illimitably [boundlessly] to all extent about a matter. I soon found that if I meant to make any mark at all, it must be done by shortness, for all the men before me had been so diffuse, and all the big things had been done. To get workmanship as nearly perfect as possible is the best chance for going down the stream of time. A small vessel on fine lines is likely to float further than a great raft."

Do you agree with Tennyson's definition of an artist? What do you think he meant by the "big things," "a small vessel on fine lines," and "a great raft"? Would Browning's poems be better if he had followed Tennyson's advice?

My Last Duchess

Robert Browning

This poem, set in the sixteenth century in a castle in northern Italy, is based on events from the life of the Duke of Ferrara, an Italian nobleman, whose first wife died after only three years of marriage. Following his wife's death, the Duke began making arrangements to remarry. In Browning's poem, the Duke is showing a painting of his first wife to an agent who represents the father of the woman he hopes to marry.

That's my last Duchess painted on the wall,
Looking as if she were alive. I call
That piece a wonder, now: Frà Pandolf's[1] hands
Worked busily a day, and there she stands.
5   Will 't please you sit and look at her? I said
"Frà Pandolf" by design, for never read
Strangers like you that pictured countenance,
The depth and passion of its earnest glance,
But to myself they turned (since none puts by
10   The curtain I have drawn for you, but I)
And seemed as they would ask me, if they durst,[2]
How such a glance came there; so, not the first
Are you to turn and ask thus. Sir, 'twas not
Her husband's presence only, called that spot
15   Of joy into the Duchess' cheek: perhaps
Frà Pandolf chanced to say "Her mantle laps
Over my lady's wrist too much," or "Paint
Must never hope to reproduce the faint
Half-flush that dies along her throat"; such stuff
20   Was courtesy, she thought, and cause enough
For calling up that spot of joy. She had
A heart—how shall I say?—too soon made glad,
Too easily impressed; she liked whate'er
She looked on, and her looks went everywhere.
25   Sir, 'twas all one! My favor at her breast,
The dropping of the daylight in the West,
The bough of cherries some officious fool
Broke in the orchard for her, the white mule
She rode with round the terrace—all and each

---

1. Frà Pandolf's: The work of Brother Pandolf, an imaginary painter.
2. durst: Dared.

ANTEA
Parmigianino
Museo Nazionale di Capodimonte, Naples

30   Would draw from her alike the approving speech,
        Or blush, at least. She thanked men—good! but thanked
        Somehow—I know not how—as if she ranked
        My gift of a nine-hundred-years-old name
        With anybody's gift. Who'd stoop to blame
35   This sort of trifling? Even had you skill
        In speech—(which I have not)—to make your will
        Quite clear to such an one, and say, "Just this
        Or that in you disgusts me; here you miss,
        Or there exceed the mark"—and if she let
40   Herself be lessoned so, nor plainly set
        Her wits to yours, forsooth,[3] and made excuse,
        —E'en then would be some stooping; and I choose
        Never to stoop. Oh sir, she smiled, no doubt,
        Whene'er I passed her; but who passed without
45   Much the same smile? This grew; I gave commands;
        Then all smiles stopped together. There she stands
        As if alive. Will 't please you rise? We'll meet
        The company below, then. I repeat,
        The Count your master's known munificence
50   Is ample warrant that no one just pretense
        Of mine for dowry will be disallowed;
        Though his fair daughter's self, as I avowed
        At starting, is my object. Nay, we'll go
        Together down, sir! Notice Neptune,[4] though,
55   Taming a sea horse, thought a rarity,
        Which Claus of Innsbruck[5] cast in bronze for me!

---

3. forsooth: In truth.
4. Neptune: In Roman mythology, the god of the sea.
5. Claus of Innsbruck: An imaginary Austrian sculptor.

RESPONDING TO THE SELECTION

Your Response
1. What questions would you ask the Duke if you were his companion?

Recalling
2. (a) Where are the speaker and his companion? (b) What are they looking at?
3. What was the Duke's "gift" to his wife?

Interpreting
4. (a) What question are we to understand the speaker's companion to have asked? (b) What is the speaker's reply?
5. (a) What aspects of the Duke's personality are revealed by his keeping the painting behind a curtain? (b) What aspects are revealed by his being the only one allowed to draw the curtain?

6. (a) What has happened to the "last" Duchess? (b) Where in the poem is this revealed?
7. (a) How would you state the sentiment expressed in lines 21–22? (b) What examples does the speaker give as an illustration of this trait? (c) What feelings did it stir up in him?

Applying

8. The eighteenth-century English statesman and writer Edmund Burke has written, "The greater the power, the more dangerous the abuse." What are your reactions to this statement?

ANALYZING LITERATURE

Dramatic Monologue

A **dramatic monologue** is a poem that reveals a character's personality through what he or she says in a dramatic situation. In most dramatic monologues, the character addresses another character who is merely a silent listener. By drawing conclusions based on the character's words, the reader can piece together the poem's setting, the situation that prompts the character to speak, and the character's motives and actions.

1. Imagine that this dramatic monologue is part of a play or movie that you are directing. Describe the setting and the situation that prompts the Duke's speech.
2. What tone of voice do you think the Duke uses? Explain your answer.
3. What motives do you suppose the Duke has for showing the Count's agent the portrait of his dead wife?
4. The Count's agent never speaks. How do you imagine he acts when he learns of the Duke's displeasure with his wife?
5. (a) What makes this kind of poem an especially strong vehicle for conveying information about a character? (b) Would you see the Duke differently if Browning had written "My Last Duchess" as a short story?

CRITICAL THINKING AND READING

Making Inferences About the Speaker

An **inference** is a conclusion arrived at through known facts or evidence. In "My Last Duchess," Browning never directly describes the Duke's personality. Rather, he relies upon the reader to make inferences, from selected information, about the sort of man the Duke is. Find evidence in the poem that the Duke is: (1) jealous, (2) overly proud, (3) determined to have things his way, (4) preoccupied with possessions, (5) a stern boss.

THINKING AND WRITING

Writing a Dramatic Monologue

Assume for the moment that the Duke has presented an accurate description of his last Duchess. List as many of her personality traits as you can. Then write an original dramatic monologue in which the Duchess reveals her impressions of her husband. In planning your monologue, consider the setting you want to convey and the occasion that prompts the speech. When you revise, make sure you have created a consistent picture of the Duchess.

LEARNING OPTIONS

1. **Art.** Create your own portrait of the Duchess. Use details from the poem, as well as your imagination, to help you express her personality and capture her relationship with the Duke in a visual image.
2. **Writing.** Imagine you are a police detective who suspects that the Duke had a hand in the Duchess's demise. Write a memorandum to your supervisor in which you provide details about your investigations, conclusions based on this evidence, and recommendations about how to proceed. In your report, use references from the poem to identify clues that strengthen your case.

IN EARLY SPRING
John William Inchbold
Ashmolean Museum, Oxford

Home-Thoughts, from Abroad

Robert Browning

Oh, to be in England
Now that April's there,
And whoever wakes in England
Sees, some morning, unaware,

5   That the lowest boughs and the brushwood sheaf
Round the elm-tree bole are in tiny leaf,
While the chaffinch[1] sings on the orchard bough
In England—now!

And after April, when May follows,
10   And the whitethroat[2] builds, and all the swallows!
Hark, where my blossomed pear tree in the hedge
Leans to the field and scatters on the clover
Blossoms and dewdrops—at the bent spray's edge—
That's the wise thrush; he sings each song twice over..

15   Lest you should think he never could recapture
The first fine careless rapture!
And though the fields look rough with hoary dew,
All will be gay when noontide wakes anew
The buttercups, the little children's dower
20   —Far brighter than this gaudy melon flower![3]

---

1. chaffinch (chaf′ finch′) *n.*: A small European songbird.
2. whitethroat *n.*: Bird having white around the throat.
3. melon flower: The large, yellow flower of melon plants, native to a warm climate.

RESPONDING TO THE SELECTION

Your Response

1. How does your response to the arrival of spring compare with the speaker's?

Recalling

2. List four birds and six plants that the speaker says "whoever wakes in England" sees.

Interpreting

3. (a) Where do you suppose the speaker of the poem is? (b) What details provide clues?

4. How do you think the speaker is using the phrase "the little children's dower" in line 19?

5. Browning wrote this poem in England, following a trip to Italy. Why do you think he chose to write the poem as though he were far away at the time?

Applying

6. Think of a time when you were homesick, or try to imagine what it would be like. What details of home do you think would come to mind?

Love Among the Ruins

Robert Browning

This poem presents the contrast between past and present through the eyes of a shepherd, eager to return to his waiting wife. The ruins that the shepherd and his wife live among may be the remains of ancient Babylon or Nineveh or one of the Etruscan cities of Italy.

Where the quiet-colored end of evening smiles,
     Miles and miles
On the solitary pastures where our sheep
     Halt asleep
5 Tinkle homeward through the twilight, stray or stop
     As they crop—
Was the site once of a city great and gay
     (So they say),
Of our country's very capital, its prince
10   Ages since
Held his court in, gathered councils, wielding far
     Peace or war.

Now—the country does not even boast a tree,
     As you see,
15 To distinguish slopes of verdure, certain rills
     From the hills
Intersect and give a name to (else they run
     Into one),
Where the domed and daring palace shot its spires
20   Up like fires
O'er the hundred-gated circuit of a wall
     Bounding all,
Made of marble, men might march on nor be pressed,
     Twelve abreast.

25 And such plenty and perfection, see, of grass
     Never was!
Such a carpet as, this summertime, o'erspreads
     And embeds
Every vestige of the city, guessed alone,[1]
30   Stock or stone—

---

1. guessed alone: Because the site of the city is now covered with grass, one can only guess where it was.

Where a multitude of men breathed joy and woe
    Long ago;
Lust of glory pricked their hearts up, dread of shame
    Struck them tame;
35 And that glory and that shame alike, the gold
    Bought and sold.

Now—the single little turret that remains
    On the plains,
By the caper[2] overrooted, by the gourd
40   Overscored,
While the patching houseleek's[3] head of blossom winks
    Through the chinks—
Marks the basement whence a tower in ancient time
    Sprang sublime,
45 And a burning ring, all round, the chariots traced
    As they raced,
And the monarch and his minions and his dames
    Viewed the games.

---

2. caper *n.*: A prickly, trailing Mediterranean bush.
3. houseleek *n.*: A plant with yellow, pink, or red flowers and
compact rosettes of thick, fleshy leaves.

50 And I know, while thus the quiet-colored eve
        Smiles to leave
To their folding, all our many-tinkling fleece
        In such peace,
And the slopes and rills, in undistinguished gray
        Melt away—
55 That a girl with eager eyes and yellow hair
        Waits me there
In the turret whence the charioteers caught soul
        For the goal,
When the king looked, where she looks now, breathless,
    dumb
60   Till I come.

But he looked upon the city, every side,
        Far and wide,
All the mountains topped with temples, all the glades'
        Colonnades,[4]
65 All the causeys,[5] bridges, aqueducts—and then,
        All the men!
When I do come, she will speak not, she will stand,
        Either hand
On my shoulder, give her eyes the first embrace
70   Of my face,
Ere we rush, ere we extinguish sight and speech
        Each on each.

In one year they sent a million fighters forth
        South and North,
75 And they built their gods a brazen pillar[6] high
        As the sky,
Yet reserved a thousand chariots in full force—
        Gold, of course.
Oh heart! oh blood that freezes, blood that burns!
80   Earth's returns
For whole centuries of folly, noise and sin!
        Shut them in,
With their triumphs and their glories and the rest!
        Love is best.

---

4. Colonnades (käl′ ə nādz′) *n.*: Series of columns set at regular
intervals; here, groups of trees surrounding an open area.
5. causeys *n.*: Causeways or raised roads.
6. brazen pillar: Built from the brass of captured chariots.

Your Response

1. The speaker concludes by suggesting that love in the present is worth more than all the glories and triumphs of history. Do you agree? Why or why not?

Recalling

2. (a) What does the speaker say once stood where sheep pastures now stand? (b) What single trace remains?
3. What does the speaker say awaits him on the pastures at twilight?

Interpreting

4. What do you suppose is the identity of the speaker?
5. (a) How would you summarize the speaker's comments on the civilization mentioned in lines 33–36? (b) How would you describe his feelings toward this civilization?
6. (a) What do you think is the purpose of the speaker's noting in line 67 that his companion "will not speak" when he arrives? (b) What might he expect his companion to say?
7. (a) What do you think is the meaning of the speaker's lament in lines 81–82? (b) To what "folly" might he be referring?
8. Explain why "Love Among the Ruins" is or is not an appropriate title for the poem.

Applying

9. Reread "Ozymandias" by Shelley, on page 638. (a) What similarities do you see between the messages in the two poems? (b) What differences do you see in the conclusions reached by the two poets?

CRITICAL THINKING AND READING

Interpreting Tone

Tone is the author's attitude toward his or her subject or audience. A work may have a tone that is lighthearted or serious, ironic or sincere, or any of numerous other possibilities. Just as a person's tone of voice can affect the way a remark is interpreted by others, so the tone of a literary work affects how the reader perceives the author's purpose.

1. How would you describe the tone of the speaker of "Love Among the Ruins" (a) with respect to the ruined splendor? (b) with respect to the civilization? (c) with respect to his companion?
2. Consider what other tone Browning might have used to make the point he makes here. Would another tone strengthen or weaken the poem's impact? Explain your answer.

THINKING AND WRITING

Comparing and Contrasting Two Places

Think about how your town or city might have appeared one hundred years ago. Write a description of the "two faces" of your city. Begin by listing ways in which the locale has undoubtedly changed and ways in which it has probably remained the same over the century. In writing your description, use vivid details so that your audience will be able to picture both the old city and the new one.

LEARNING OPTIONS

1. **Art.** Imagine that "Love Among the Ruins" is part of a scene in a play and that you are the set designer. What might the set look like? Create a model set that reflects the details in the poem. Use photographs of ruins in Italy, Greece, or the Middle East to help you with historical accuracy.
2. **Cross-curricular Connection.** Old cities in Europe and Asia often lie buried beneath modern cities, coming to light only when archaeologists dig. Find out as much as you can about one such city that has been excavated in recent times. Bring photographs and diagrams to class and provide a brief account of the city's historical importance.

GUIDE FOR INTERPRETING

Sonnet 43

Elizabeth Barrett Browning (1806–1861) was one of the best-known poets of her time. The oldest of twelve children in an upper middle-class family, she received no formal education, but a zest for knowledge enabled her to learn eight languages on her own. She began writing poetry as a child, and by the time she reached adulthood she had published four immensely popular volumes of verse.

Though a longtime illness made her something of a recluse, Barrett was able to meet many of the leading writers of the day. In 1845 she began to receive letters from the poet Robert Browning, who, after five months of correspondence, paid her a visit. They fell in love, and when her stern father refused to allow her to spend the winter of 1846 in Italy as her doctors had advised her to, she and Browning eloped there.

In 1849 their son was born, whom they nicknamed Pen. A year later Mrs. Browning revised and published *Sonnets from the Portuguese,* a sequence of forty-four love poems written to her husband. *Aurora Leigh* (1857), a love story written in blank verse, was completed during the second of two trips she made back to London.

Literary Forms

The Sonnet. A sonnet is a lyric poem that has fourteen lines and a fixed rhyme scheme. Of the two most common forms of sonnet, the Italian and English, the Italian is the older, dating back to the thirteenth century. The form, also known as the Petrarchan sonnet, was named for Francesco Petrarch (1304–1374), who wrote more than three hundred sonnets to a woman named Laura. The Italian sonnet has two parts—the *octave,* consisting of eight lines, which asks a question or raises a problem; and the *sestet,* consisting of six lines, which answers the question or resolves the problem. Though the rhyme scheme of the *sestet* varies, the *octave* always has the rhyme scheme *abbaabba.*

Despite occasional lapses in popularity, the sonnet has been the form of choice for many poets throughout the ages. In the nineteenth century, Elizabeth Barrett Browning helped to revive the *sonnet cycle,* a series of sonnets loosely connected by a common subject or theme. Her cycles characteristically treat the subject of love.

Focus

Write the word *love* at the top of a sheet of paper. Then write ten complete sentences that explore your thoughts and feelings on the subject. Avoid mentioning the names of specific individuals. When you have finished writing, review your work and decide which of your impressions might be unique to you and could, therefore, be expanded into a poem or series of personal reflections.

Sonnet 43

Elizabeth Barrett Browning

How do I love thee? Let me count the ways.
I love thee to the depth and breadth and height
My soul can reach, when feeling out of sight
For the ends of Being and ideal Grace.
5 I love thee to the level of every day's
Most quiet need, by sun and candlelight.
I love thee freely, as men strive for Right;
I love thee purely, as they turn from Praise.
I love thee with the passion put to use
10 In my old griefs, and with my childhood's faith.
I love thee with a love I seemed to lose
With my lost saints—I love thee with the breath,
Smiles, tears, of all my life!   and, if God choose,
I shall but love thee better after death.

RESPONDING TO THE SELECTION

Your Response

1. How effective do you think the speaker is in describing her love? Does the poem seem realistic to you? Explain.

Recalling

2. (a) What question does the speaker ask?
   (b) How many answers does she give?

Interpreting

3. (a) What do you think the speaker means in lines 9–10 by "with the passion put to use/In my old griefs"? (b) By "with a love I seemed to lose/With my lost saints" in lines 11–12?
4. What effect is created by the repetition of the words "I love thee" throughout the poem?

Applying

5. Consult the list of ten sentences you wrote for the Focus assignment on page 736. What thoughts and feelings of your own might you add to those expressed by Elizabeth Barrett Browning in this poem?

ANALYZING LITERATURE

Understanding a Sonnet

A **sonnet** is a fourteen-line lyric poem with a fixed pattern of rhyme. The Italian sonnet has two parts. The first part, the octave, poses a question or presents a problem in eight lines. The second part, the sestet, answers that question or problem in six lines.

1. What line in the octave (first eight lines) ends with an irregular rhyming word? How might this irregularity be explained?
2. What is the rhyme scheme of the sestet?
3. Based on what you have learned about the Italian sonnet, tell in what critical way Sonnet 43 violates the rules. How does this deviation help the poem to deliver its message?

CHARLES DICKENS

1812–1870

No writer since Shakespeare has occupied as important a place in popular culture as Charles Dickens. From his own time on, his works, with their unforgettable characters, have held special appeal for both scholars and the public at large, and have been dramatized time and again in plays and films.

Dickens was born in Portsmouth on England's southern coast. Except for a few happy years at Chatham, east of London, his childhood was darkened by his father's wavering economic status. After years of eluding creditors, his father was finally sent to debtor's prison. Dickens, in the meantime, was sent to a "prison" of his own—a factory in which he worked long hours pasting labels. These experiences and other ills of the newly industrialized society figure prominently in his novels.

After becoming a law clerk at the age of fifteen, Dickens taught himself shorthand and became a court reporter. At twenty-one, while reporting on the Parliamentary debates, he began applying his keen powers of observation to humorous literary sketches of everyday life in London. A collection of these, *Sketches by Boz* (1835–1836), earned him a small following, which he built up considerably with his first novel, *The Pickwick Papers,* published in 1837.

Next came such favorites as *Oliver Twist* (1837), *Nicholas Nickleby* (1839), and, after a trip to America where his fame had already spread, *A Christmas Carol* (1843). In these early novels, which paint a sweeping satiric picture of Victorian England, Dickens displayed both a passion for social reform and a unique ability to combine humor with horror—themes and techniques that became the hallmark of all his fiction. He also developed his lifelong practice of writing for serial publications. Paid by the word, he wove elaborate plots with vast numbers of characters.

A turn toward more serious planning and characterization of greater psychological depth are evident in *Dombey and Son* (1848) and *David Copperfield* (1850), which also contain social criticism that is more direct and less optimistic. In the later novels, Dickens blended these elements most successfully, and the results were his masterpieces: *Bleak House* (1853), *Hard Times* (1854), and *Great Expectations* (1861). "The Signalman" was published in 1866 in a collection that included several other railway stories.

Dickens never gave up journalism as a second outlet for his social conscience. In later life the work load imposed by his many writing responsibilities, coupled with his exhausting public-reading tours, took its toll on his health. In 1870, while at work on a novel, *The Mystery of Edwin Drood,* he died of a stroke.

GUIDE FOR INTERPRETING

The Signalman

Writers' Techniques

Plot in a Ghost Story. Plot deals with the events that make up a story or novel. Plot can be structured in a straight *chronological* progression, from the earliest event to the latest, or it can jump backward and forward in time. In either case, plot generally builds on some *conflict,* or struggle between characters or forces, until it reaches a *climax,* or height of tension. The portion of the story from this point to the end, during which all remaining problems are solved, is called the *resolution.*

In a ghost story, the plot is built around *supernatural* elements—events beyond the normal order of things. The conflict is often between these supernatural forces and the human beings whose world they have invaded. At times, however, the conflict takes the form of a difference of opinion between two characters as to the explanation of certain mysterious events. In "The Signalman," for example, the first-person narrator attempts to explain away in rational terms the "ghost" that is plaguing a railroad employee.

Focus

Prepare the groundwork for an original ghost story. Consider the story's setting and characters by asking yourself questions such as the following: Is the story to take place in the present? What form will the ghost take? Who will be the person haunted by the ghost, and what will be the ghost's purpose? Jot down your answers to these and related questions.

Primary Source

Ghost stories are a special—and particularly enjoyable—type of fantastic literature. Alberto Manguel describes fantastic literature in the following manner:

> . . . fantastic literature deals with what can be best defined as the impossible seeping into the possible, what Wallace Stevens calls "black water breaking into reality." Fantastic literature never really explains everything. Like the ghost train at the fair, it takes us through the darkness of a real world, from terror to laughable terror, diving into walls that swing away at the very last minute, racing under eerie nothings that touch us with cobweb fingers, suddenly slowing down and lengthening that last encounter (with what? with what?), using our expectancy of horror more effectively than horror itself.

The Signalman

Charles Dickens

"Halloa! Below there!"

When he heard a voice thus calling to him, he was standing at the door of his box, with a flag in his hand, furled round its short pole. One would have thought, considering the nature of the ground, that he could not have doubted from what quarter the voice came; but instead of looking up to where I stood on the top of the steep cutting nearly over his head, he turned himself about, and looked down the Line. There was something remarkable in his manner of doing so, though I could not have said for my life what. But I know it was remarkable enough to attract my notice, even though his figure was foreshortened and shadowed, down in the deep trench, and mine was high above him, so steeped in the glow of an angry sunset, that I had shaded my eyes with my hand before I saw him at all.

"Halloa! Below!"

From looking down the Line, he turned himself about again, and, raising his eyes, saw my figure high above him.

"Is there any path by which I can come down and speak to you?"

He looked up at me without replying, and I looked down at him without pressing him too soon with a repetition of my idle question. Just then there came a vague vibration in the earth and air, quickly changing into a violent pulsation, and an oncoming rush that caused me to start back, as though it had force to draw me down. When such vapor as rose to my height from this rapid train had passed me and was skimming away over the landscape, I looked down again, and saw him refurling the flag he had shown while the train went by.

I repeated my inquiry. After a pause, during which he seemed to regard me with fixed attention, he motioned with his rolled-up flag towards a point on my level, some two or three hundred yards distant. I called down to him, "All right!" and made for that point. There, by dint of looking closely about me, I found a rough zigzag descending path notched out, which I followed.

The cutting was extremely deep, and unusually precipitate. It was made through a clammy stone, that became oozier and wetter as I went down. For these reasons, I found the way long enough to give me time to recall a singular air of reluctance or compulsion with which he had pointed out the path.

When I came down low enough upon the zigzag descent to see him again, I saw that he was standing between the rails on the way by which the train had lately passed, in an attitude as if he were waiting for me to appear. He had his left hand at his chin, and that left elbow rested on his right hand, crossed over his breast. His attitude was one of such expectation and watchfulness, that I stopped a moment, wondering at it.

I resumed my downward way, and stepping out upon the level of the railroad, and drawing nearer to him, saw that he was a dark sallow man, with a dark beard and rather heavy eyebrows. His post was in as solitary and dismal a place as ever I saw. On either side, a dripping-wet wall of jagged stone, excluding all view but a strip of sky; the perspective one way only a crooked prolongation of this great dungeon; the shorter perspective in the other direction terminating in a gloomy red light, and the gloomier entrance to a black tunnel, in whose massive architecture there was a barbarous, depressing, and forbidding air. So little sunlight ever found its way to this spot, that it had an earthy, deadly smell; and so much cold wind rushed through it, that it struck chill to me, as if I had left the natural world.

Before he stirred, I was near enough to him to have touched him. Not even then removing his eyes from mine, he stepped back one step, and lifted his hand.

This was a lonesome post to occupy (I said), and it had riveted my attention when I looked down from up yonder. A visitor was a rarity, I should suppose; not an unwelcome rarity, I hoped? In me, he merely saw a man who had been shut up within narrow limits all his life, and who, being at last set free, had a newly awakened interest in these great works. To such purpose I spoke to him; but I am far from sure of the terms I used; for, besides that I am not happy in opening any conversation, there was something in the man that daunted me.

He directed a most curious look towards the red light near the tunnel's mouth, and looked all about it, as if something were missing from it, and then looked at me.

That light was part of his charge? Was it not?

He answered in a low voice, "Don't you know it is?"

The monstrous thought came into my mind, as I perused the fixed eyes and the saturnine face, that this was a spirit, not a man. I have speculated since, whether there may have been infection in his mind.

In my turn, I stepped back. But in making the action, I detected in his eyes some latent fear of me. This put the monstrous thought to flight.

"You look at me," I said, forcing a smile, "as if you had a dread of me."

"I was doubtful," he returned, "whether I had seen you before."

"Where?"

He pointed to the red light he had looked at.

"There?" I said.

Intently watchful of me, he replied (but without sound), "Yes."

"My good fellow, what should I do there? However, be that as it may, I never was there, you may swear."

"I think I may," he rejoined. "Yes, I am sure I may."

His manner cleared, like my own. He replied to my remarks with readiness, and in well-chosen words. Had he much to do there? Yes; that was to say, he had enough responsibility to bear; but exactness and watchfulness were what was required of him, and of actual work—manual labor—he had next to none. To change that signal, to trim those lights, and to turn this iron handle now and then, was all he had to do under that head. Regarding those many long and lonely hours of which I seemed to make so much, he could only say that the routine of his life had shaped itself into that form, and he had grown used to it. He had taught himself a language down here—if only to know it by sight, and to have formed his own crude ideas of its pronunciation, could be called learning it. He had also worked at fractions and decimals, and tried a little algebra; but he was, and had been as a boy, a poor hand at figures. Was it necessary for him when on duty always to remain in that channel of damp air, and could he never rise into the sunshine from between those high stone walls? Why, that depended upon times and circumstances. Under some conditions there would be less upon the Line than under others, and the same held good as to certain hours of the day and night. In bright weather, he did choose occasions for getting a little above these lower shadows; but, being at all times liable to be called by his electric bell, and at such times listening for it with redoubled anxiety, the relief was less than I would suppose.

He took me into his box, where there was a fire, a desk for an official book in which he had to make certain entries, a telegraphic instrument with its dial, face, and needles, and the little bell of which he had spoken. On my trusting that he would excuse the

TWO TUNNELS, 1975
Guy Worsdell

remark that he had been well educated, and (I hoped I might say without offense) perhaps educated above that station, he observed that instances of slight incongruity in such wise would rarely be found wanting among large bodies of men; that he had heard it was so in workhouses, in the police force, even in that last desperate resource, the army; and that he knew it was so, more or less, in any great railway staff. He had been, when young (if I could believe it, sitting in that hut—he scarcely could), a student of natural philosophy, and had attended lectures; but he had run wild, misused his opportunities, gone down, and never risen again. He

had no complaint to offer about that. He had made his bed, and he lay upon it. It was far too late to make another.

All that I have here condensed, he said in a quiet manner, with his grave dark regards divided between me and the fire. He threw in the word, "Sir," from time to time, and especially when he referred to his youth, as though to request me to understand that he claimed to be nothing but what I found him. He was several times interrupted by the little bell, and had to read off messages, and send replies. Once he had to stand without the door, and display a flag as a train passed, and make some verbal communication to the driver. In the discharge of his duties, I observed him to be remarkably exact and vigilant, breaking off his discourse at a syllable, and remaining silent until what he had to do was done.

In a word, I should have set this man down as one of the safest of men to be employed in that capacity, but for the circumstance that while he was speaking to me he twice broke off with a fallen color, turned his face towards the little bell when it did NOT ring, opened the door of the hut (which was kept shut to exclude the unhealthy damp), and looked out towards the red light near the mouth of the tunnel. On both of those occasions, he came back to the fire with the inexplicable air upon him which I had remarked, without being able to define, when we were so far asunder.

Said I, when I rose to leave him, "You almost make me think that I have met with a contented man."

(I am afraid I must acknowledge that I said it to lead him on.)

"I believe I used to be so," he rejoined, in the low voice in which he had first spoken; "but I am troubled, sir, I am troubled."

He would have recalled the words if he could. He had said them, however, and I took them up quickly.

"With what? What is your trouble?"

"It is very difficult to impart, sir. It is very, very difficult to speak of. If ever you make me another visit, I will try to tell you."

"But I expressly intend to make you another visit. Say, when shall it be?"

"I go off early in the morning, and I shall be on again at ten tomorrow night, sir."

"I will come at eleven."

He thanked me, and went out at the door with me. "I'll show my white light, sir," he said, in his peculiar low voice, "till you have found the way up. When you have found it, don't call out! And when you are at the top, don't call out!"

His manner seemed to make the place strike colder to me, but I said no more than, "Very well."

"And when you come down tomorrow night, don't call out! Let me ask you a parting question. What made you cry, 'Halloa! Below there!' tonight?"

"Heaven knows," said I. "I cried something to that effect—"

"Not to that effect, sir. Those were the very words. I know them well."

"Admit those were the very words. I said them, no doubt, because I saw you below."

"For no other reason?"

"What other reason could I possibly have?"

"You had no feeling that they were conveyed to you in any supernatural way?"

"No."

He wished me good night, and held up his light. I walked by the side of the down Line of rails (with a very disagreeable sensation of a train coming behind me) until I found the path. It was easier to mount than to descend, and I got back to my inn without any adventure.

Punctual to my appointment, I placed my foot on the first notch of the zigzag next night, as the distant clocks were striking eleven. He was waiting for me at the bottom, with his white light on. "I have not called out," I said, when we came close together; "may I speak now?" "By all means, sir." "Good night, then, and here's my hand." "Good night, sir, and here's mine." With that we walked side by side to his box, entered it, closed the door, and sat down by the fire.

"I have made up my mind, sir," he began, bending forward as soon as we were seated, and speaking in a tone but a little above a whisper, "that you shall not have to ask me twice what troubles me. I took you for someone else yesterday evening. That troubles me."

"That mistake?"

"No. That someone else."

"Who is it?"

"I don't know."

"Like me?"

"I don't know. I never saw the face. The

left arm is across the face, and the right arm is waved—violently waved. This way."

I followed his action with my eyes, and it was the action of an arm gesticulating, with the utmost passion and vehemence, "For God's sake, clear the way!"

"One moonlight night," said the man, "I was sitting here, when I heard a voice cry, 'Halloa! Below there!' I started up, looked from that door, and saw this Someone else standing by the red light near the tunnel, waving as I just now showed you. The voice seemed hoarse with shouting, and it cried, 'Look out! Look out!' And then again, 'Halloa! Below there! Look out!' I caught up my lamp, turned it on red, and ran towards the figure, calling, 'What's wrong? What has happened? Where?' It stood just outside the blackness of the tunnel. I advanced so close upon it that I wondered at its keeping the sleeve across its eyes. I ran right up at it, and had my hand stretched out to pull the sleeve away, when it was gone."

"Into the tunnel," said I.

"No. I ran on into the tunnel, five hundred yards. I stopped, and held my lamp above my head, and saw the figures of the measured distance, and saw the wet stains stealing down the walls and trickling through the arch. I ran out again faster than I had run in (for I had a mortal abhorrence of the place upon me), and I looked all round the red light with my own red light, and I went up the iron ladder to the gallery top of it, and I came down again, and ran back here. I telegraphed both ways, 'An alarm has been given. Is anything wrong?' The answer came back, both ways, 'All well.'"

Resisting the slow touch of a frozen finger tracing out my spine, I showed him how that this figure must be a deception of his sense of sight; and how that figures, originating in disease of the delicate nerves that minister to the functions of the eye, were known to have often troubled patients, some of whom had become conscious of the nature of their affliction, and had even proved it by experiments upon themselves. "As to

an imaginary cry," said I, "do but listen for a moment to the wind in this unnatural valley while we speak so low, and to the wild harp it makes of the telegraph wires!"

That was all very well, he returned, after we had sat listening for a while, and he ought to know something of the wind and the wires—he who so often passed long winter nights there, alone and watching. But he would beg to remark that he had not finished.

I asked his pardon, and he slowly added these words, touching my arm:

"Within six hours after the Appearance, the memorable accident on this Line happened, and within ten hours the dead and wounded were brought along through the tunnel over the spot where the figure had stood."

A disagreeable shudder crept over me, but I did my best against it. It was not to be denied, I rejoined, that this was a remarkable coincidence, calculated deeply to impress his mind. But it was unquestionable that remarkable coincidences did continually occur, and they must be taken into account in dealing with such a subject. Though to be sure I must admit, I added (for I thought I saw that he was going to bring the objection to bear upon me), men of common sense did not allow much for coincidences in making the ordinary calculations of life.

He again begged to remark that he had not finished.

I again begged his pardon for being betrayed into interruptions.

"This," he said, again laying his hand upon my arm, and glancing over his shoulder with hollow eyes, "was just a year ago. Six or seven months passed, and I had recovered from the surprise and shock, when one morning, as the day was breaking, I, standing at the door, looked towards the red light, and saw the specter again." He stopped, with a fixed look at me.

"Did it cry out?"

"No. It was silent."

"Did it wave its arm?"

"No. It leaned against the shaft of the light, with both hands before the face. Like this."

Once more I followed his action with my eyes. It was an action of mourning. I have seen such an attitude in stone figures on tombs.

"Did you go up to it?"

"I came in and sat down, partly to collect my thoughts, partly because it had turned me faint. When I went to the door again, daylight was above me, and the ghost was gone."

"But nothing followed? Nothing came of this?"

He touched me on the arm with his forefinger twice or thrice, giving a ghastly nod each time:

"That very day, as a train came out of the tunnel, I noticed, at a carriage window on my side, what looked like a confusion of hands and heads, and something waved. I saw it just in time to signal the driver, Stop! He shut off, and put his brake on, but the train drifted past here a hundred and fifty yards or more. I ran after it, and, as I went along, heard terrible screams and cries. A beautiful young lady had died instantaneously in one of the compartments, and was brought in here, and laid on this floor between us."

Involuntarily I pushed my chair back, as I looked from the boards at which he pointed to himself.

"True, sir. True. Precisely as it happened, so I tell it you."

I could think of nothing to say, to any purpose, and my mouth was very dry. The wind and the wires took up the story with a long lamenting wail.

He resumed. "Now, sir, mark this, and judge how my mind is troubled. The specter came back a week ago. Ever since, it has been there, now and again, by fits and starts."

"At the light?"

"At the Danger light."

"What does it seem to do?"

He repeated, if possible with increased passion and vehemence, that former gesticulation of, "For God's sake, clear the way!"

Then he went on. "I have no peace or rest for it. It calls to me, for many minutes together, in an agonized manner, 'Below there! Look out! Look out!' It stands waving to me. It rings my little bell——"

I caught at that. "Did it ring your bell yesterday evening when I was here, and you went to the door?"

"Twice."

"Why, see," said I, "how your imagination misleads you. My eyes were on the bell, and my ears were open to the bell, and if I am a living man, it did NOT ring at those times. No, nor at any other time, except when it was rung in the natural course of physical things by the station communicating with you."

He shook his head. "I have never made a mistake as to that yet, sir. I have never confused the specter's ring with the man's. The ghost's ring is a strange vibration in the bell that it derives from nothing else, and I have not asserted that the bell stirs to the eye. I don't wonder that you failed to hear it. But *I* heard it."

"And did the specter seem to be there, when you looked out?"

"It WAS there."

"Both times?"

He repeated firmly: "Both times."

"Will you come to the door with me, and look for it now?"

He bit his under lip as though he were somewhat unwilling, but arose. I opened the door, and stood on the step, while he stood in the doorway. There was the Danger light. There was the dismal mouth of the tunnel. There were the high, wet stone walls of the cutting. There were the stars above them.

"Do you see it?" I asked him, taking particular note of his face. His eyes were prominent and strained, but not very much more so, perhaps, than my own had been when I had directed them earnestly towards the same spot.

"No," he answered. "It is not there."

"Agreed," said I.

We went in again, shut the door, and resumed our seats. I was thinking how best to improve this advantage, if it might be called one, when he took up the conversation in such a matter-of-course way, so assuming that there could be no serious question of fact between us, that I felt myself placed in the weakest of positions.

"By this time you will fully understand, sir," he said, "that what troubles me so dreadfully is the question, What does the specter mean?"

I was not sure, I told him, that I did fully understand.

"What is its warning against?" he said, ruminating, with his eyes on the fire, and only by times turning them on me. "What is the danger? Where is the danger? There is danger overhanging somewhere on the Line. Some dreadful calamity will happen. It is not to be doubted this third time, after what has gone before. But surely this is a cruel haunting of *me*. What can *I* do?"

He pulled out his handkerchief, and wiped the drops from his heated forehead.

"If I telegraph Danger, on either side of me, or on both, I can give no reason for it," he went on, wiping the palms of his hands. "I should get into trouble, and do no good. They would think I was mad. This is the way it would work: Message: "Danger! Take care!" Answer: "What Danger? Where?" Message: "Don't know. But for God's sake, take care!" They would displace me. What else could they do?"

His pain of mind was most pitiable to see. It was the mental torture of a conscientious man, oppressed beyond endurance by an unintelligible responsibility involving life.

"When it first stood under the Danger light," he went on, putting his dark hair back from his head, and drawing his hands outward across and across his temples in an extremity of feverish distress, "why not tell me where that accident was to happen—if it must happen? Why not tell me how it could be averted—if it could have been averted? When on its second coming it hid its face, why not tell me, instead, "She is going to die. Let them keep her at home"? If it came, on those two occasions, only to show me that its warnings were true, and so to prepare me for the third, why not warn me plainly now? And I, Lord help me! A mere poor signalman on this solitary station! Why not go to somebody with credit to be believed, and power to act?"

When I saw him in this state, I saw that for the poor man's sake, as well as for the public safety, what I had to do for the time was to compose his mind. Therefore, setting aside all question of reality or unreality between us, I represented to him that whoever thoroughly discharged his duty must do well, and that at least it was his comfort that he understood his duty, though he did not understand these confounding Appearances. In this effort I succeeded far better than in the attempt to reason him out of his conviction. He became calm; the occupations incidental to his post as the night advanced began to make larger demands on his attention: and I left him at two in the morning. I had offered to stay through the night, but he would not hear of it.

That I more than once looked back at the red light as I ascended the pathway, that I did not like the red light, and that I should have slept but poorly if my bed had been under it, I see no reason to conceal. Nor did I like the two sequences of the accident and the dead girl. I see no reason to conceal that either.

But what ran most in my thoughts was the consideration how ought I to act, having become the recipient of this disclosure? I had proved the man to be intelligent, vigilant, painstaking, and exact; but how long might he remain so, in his state of mind? Though in a subordinate position, still he held a most important trust, and would I (for

RED VIRGINIA CREEPER
Edvard Munch

instance) like to stake my own life on the chances of his continuing to execute it with precision?

Unable to overcome a feeling that there would be something treacherous in my communicating what he had told me to his superiors in the Company, without first being plain with himself and proposing a middle course to him, I ultimately resolved to offer to accompany him (otherwise keeping his secret for the present) to the wisest medical practitioner we could hear of in those parts, and to take his opinion. A change in his time of duty would come round next night, he had apprised me, and he would be off an hour or two after sunrise, and on again soon after sunset. I had appointed to return accordingly.

Next evening was a lovely evening, and I walked out early to enjoy it. The sun was not yet quite down when I traversed the field-path near the top of the deep cutting. I would extend my walk for an hour, I said to myself, half an hour on and half an hour back, and it would then be time to go to my signal-man's box.

Before pursuing my stroll, I stepped to the brink, and mechanically looked down, from the point from which I had first seen him. I cannot describe the thrill that seized upon me, when, close at the mouth of the tunnel, I saw the appearance of a man, with his left sleeve across his eyes, passionately waving his right arm.

The nameless horror that oppressed me passed in a moment, for in a moment I saw that this appearance of a man was a man indeed, and that there was a little group of other men, standing at a short distance, to whom he seemed to be rehearsing the gesture he made. The Danger light was not yet lighted. Against its shaft, a little low hut, entirely new to me, had been made of some wooden supports and tarpaulin. It looked no bigger than a bed.

With an irresistible sense that something was wrong—with a flashing self-reproachful fear that fatal mischief had come of my leaving the man there, and causing no one to be sent to overlook or correct what he did—I descended the notched path with all the speed I could make.

"What is the matter?" I asked the men.

"Signalman killed this morning, sir."

"Not the man belonging to that box?"

"Yes, sir."

"Not the man I know?"

"You will recognize him, sir, if you knew him," said the man who spoke for the others, solemnly uncovering his own head, and raising an end of the tarpaulin, "for his face is quite composed."

"O, how did this happen, how did this happen?" I asked, turning from one to another as the hut closed in again.

"He was cut down by an engine, sir. No man in England knew his work better. But somehow he was not clear of the outer rail. It was just at broad day. He had struck the light, and had the lamp in his hand. As the engine came out of the tunnel, his back was towards her, and she cut him down. That man drove her, and was showing how it happened. Show the gentleman, Tom."

The man, who wore a rough dark dress, stepped back to his former place at the mouth of the tunnel.

"Coming round the curve in the tunnel, sir," he said, "I saw him at the end, like as if I saw him down a perspective-glass. There was no time to check speed, and I knew him to be very careful. As he didn't seem to take heed of the whistle, I shut it off when we were running down upon him, and called to him as loud as I could call."

"What did you say?"

"I said, 'Below there! Look out! Look out! For God's sake, clear the way!'"

I started.

"Ah! it was a dreadful time, sir. I never left off calling to him. I put this arm before my eyes not to see, and I waved this arm to the last; but it was no use."

Without prolonging the narrative to dwell on any one of its curious circumstances more than on any other, I may, in closing it, point out the coincidence that the warning of the Engine Driver included, not only the words which the unfortunate Signalman had repeated to me as haunting him, but also the words which I myself—not he—had attached and that only in my own mind, to the gesticulation he had imitated.

Your Response

1. How would you explain the apparition in this story?

Recalling

2. (a) How does the signalman behave during his first meeting with the narrator? (b) What explanation for this behavior is given in the second meeting?
3. (a) What tragedy follows the specter's first appearance? (b) Its second appearance? (c) How has it been warning the signalman lately?
4. What happens to the signalman?

Interpreting

5. Do you think the narrator is totally convinced of his own explanations of the events on the railroad line? Explain.
6. (a) What do you think is the narrator's view of the supernatural? (b) What evidence are you given that the events he narrates have changed his views?

Applying

7. In light of his description of the signalman's job, how does this story serve Dickens's goal of promoting social change in England?

ANALYZING LITERATURE

Following the Plot in a Ghost Story

The **plot** is the series of events in a story or novel that answers the question "What happens?" Plot usually involves a *conflict,* or clash between characters or opposing forces, that builds to a high point called the *climax.* In a ghost story, the plot revolves around supernatural—or otherworldly—elements.

1. What supernatural elements are featured in "The Signalman"? How do these elements tie in directly to the story's plot?
2. The story features several different conflicts.

Identify:
a. The conflict between the narrator and the signalman.
b. The signalman's inner conflict.
c. The narrator's inner conflict.

CRITICAL THINKING AND READING

Separating Details

Like any good ghost story, "The Signalman" is filled with details that lend themselves to both realistic and supernatural interpretation. What the signalman identifies as the specter's cry, the narrator "writes off" as the sound of the wind whistling through the telegraph wires. Yet not all details in the story can be explained away so simply. Identify the realistic and supernatural significance of each of the following details.

1. The ringing of the bell.
2. The words "For God's sake, clear the way!"
3. A figure with its left sleeve across its face and its right arm waving frantically.

THINKING AND WRITING

Writing a Ghost Story

Using the notes you developed earlier, write an original ghost story. Before you proceed, map out your story's plot. Ask: What will happen in the story, and in what order will I report the events? What is the conflict, and whom does it involve? How will the conflict be resolved? When you have answered these questions, you may begin your first draft.

LEARNING OPTION

Community Connections. Are there tales of supernatural events, mysterious places, or other unexplained phenomena in your community? Investigate such stories by visiting your local historical society or doing research at the library. See if you can explain the mystery using clues that you gather. Then share your findings with the class.

ONE WRITER'S PROCESS

Charles Dickens

A Parliamentary Reporter In Charles Dickens's novel *David Copperfield,* the young protagonist observes, "I had heard that many men distinguished in various pursuits had begun life by reporting the debates in Parliament." This passage is a joking reference to Dickens's own early experience as a political reporter.

In 1833, when he began to publish his literary writing, Dickens had been a reporter on the *Mirror of Parliament* for at least two years. His experience in this demanding profession was to shape both his literary aims and his writing habits. Early in his literary career, he wrote in a letter to Catherine Hogarth that the daily excitement of a reporter's life was a necessary condition for his creative work: "I never can write with effect—especially in the serious way—until I have got my steam up, or in other words until I have become so excited with my subject that I cannot leave off!"

An Appetite for Reform In addition, Dickens had developed an appetite for reform by observing the parliamentary process, and his sympathy for the downtrodden contributed greatly to his urge to tell a story. The desire to shame society into treating the poor with respect and generosity was a motivating force that drove him to write about social issues.

His early training as a reporter also provided Dickens with a standard for accuracy that he maintained throughout his literary career. He researched some of his novels painstakingly. In 1838, for instance, he took a trip to the industrial Midlands, because he thought it important to describe accurately the poverty of this region in his developing novel, *Nicholas Nickleby.*

PREWRITING

Planning Out a Chapter As a reporter, Dickens had learned how to write rapidly. Nevertheless, he spent time planning his novels as he went along. For example, the following is a printed version of Dickens's handwritten outline for a chapter of his novel *Little Dorritt:*

A Plea in The Marshalsea.

Ever downward, always downward

Clennam Ill

Little Dorrit's return, and her offer.

Arthur's refusal of Little

Scene between her and Arthur   star

D s offer

Close with John Chivery stealing

in at night, to bring

her "undying love" to him

DRAFTING

The Greatest Patience Dickens wrote in a letter to the English writer Wilkie Collins in 1852 of "the conceited idiots who suppose that volumes are to be tossed off like pancakes, and that any writing can be done without the utmost application, the greatest patience, and the steadiest energy of which the writer is capable." Dickens was a man who worked intensely at his craft.

Dickens at Work Dickens's ability to concentrate was so great that he could write while surrounded by chatting people. Here is one account of Dickens at work, recalled by Henry Burnett: "One night in Doughty

Street, Mrs. Charles Dickens, my wife and myself were sitting round the fire cozily enjoying a chat, when Dickens, for some purpose, came suddenly into the room. 'What, you here!' he exclaimed; 'I'll bring down my work.' It was his monthly portion of *Oliver Twist* for Bentley's. In a few minutes he returned, manuscript in hand, and while he was pleasantly discoursing he employed himself in carrying to a corner of the room a little table, at which he seated himself and recommenced his writing. We, at his bidding, went on talking our 'little nothings,'—he, every now and then (the feather of his pen still moving rapidly from side to side), put in a cheerful interlude. It was interesting to watch, upon the sly, the mind and the muscles working (or, if you please, playing), in company, as new thoughts were being dropped upon the paper. And to note the working brow, the set of the mouth, with the tongue tightly pressed against the closed lips, as was his habit."

REVISING

Discipline and Deadlines During his formative years as a writer, Dickens wrote to strict deadlines. Many of his novels appeared piece by piece, or serialized, in magazines, and the demands of magazine publishing left little time for revision. Yet Dickens remained the most careful of writers, crafting his sentences precisely. He paid strict attention to the smallest details of structure and style. Dickens took special care to make the names of his characters memorable, humorous, and fitting. For instance, the following is a typed version of some of his handwritten notes concerning the novel *Martin Chuzzlewit:*

chevy ~~Slyme~~ Slyme Esquire.—~~M͏ͬ Flick~~

~~M͏ͬ Sweetletee.~~

Young Martin Chuzzlewit.

In many of Dickens's novels, such as *Nicholas Nickleby,* it was the serialization itself that contributed to the timeliness of the subject matter. Periodicals may have relied on Dickens to fill their columns, but Dickens also benefited from this arrangement. He was able to use the journalistic style he had cultivated to flesh out his narratives with contemporary issues.

PUBLISHING

Dickens's first published sketch was "A Dinner at Poplar Walk." It appeared in 1833 in a magazine, as did so much of his subsequent work. An issue of the *Spectator* magazine in 1838 commented on the effect the serialization of his works had on Dickens's popularity: "Had the Pickwick [*Pickwick Papers*] been first published in a volume, it is questionable whether its circulation would have reached one-fifth of its actual extent, or whether the work would have been read through by the multitude." The popular craze for Dickens's serialization of *Pickwick Papers* was unlike anything that had happened before. It made him literally world-famous at the age of twenty-five.

As George Bernard Shaw said of him, "He is, by the pure force of genius, one of the greatest writers of the world. . . . There is no 'greatest book' of Dickens; all his books form one great life-work: a Bible in fact . . . all are magnificent."

THINKING ABOUT THE PROCESS

1. How would your writing process be affected if you were to write in installments for a monthly magazine? Would it impair your imagination, or would it give you extra motivation and inspiration? Explain.
2. **Writing** Write a story in three episodes. Give yourself several deadlines to meet, and try to stick to them. Develop the plot and characters so that readers, upon reaching the end of one installment, will want to read the next.

MATTHEW ARNOLD

1822–1888

Of all the great Victorian poets, Matthew Arnold strikes many twentieth-century readers as the most modern. The persistent theme of his poems—people's isolation and alienation from nature and from one another—has been echoed by many writers and thinkers of our own age. His pessimistic outlook—that "there is everything to be endured, nothing to be done"—also coincides with the view of many today that we are a generation of lost souls.

Matthew Arnold was born in Laleham, Middlesex, and educated at Rugby School, where his father, a believer in the good of social change, was headmaster. After entering Oxford in 1841, Arnold startled his contemporaries by dressing and behaving like an aristocratic dandy. Yet behind this Byronic mask was developing the serious and sensitive social conscience that was to guide Arnold's career as a public servant, poet, and literary critic.

In 1851 Arnold accepted the post of Inspector of Schools, which he held until two years before his death. In this job he traveled through England and the Continent, and published reports that did much to improve public education in Great Britain. All the while, he remained a poet at heart, though his first two books, published in 1849 and 1852, met with little success.

His fortunes changed in 1853 with the publication of *Poems,* which included a long preface that established Arnold as a writer of clear critical prose as well as of quality poetry. With *New Poems* (1867), which contained his celebrated "Dover Beach," Arnold felt that he had expressed everything he had to say in poetry. From that point on, he focused his creative energies on literary criticism.

The melancholy outlook of his poems, Arnold himself noted, was unrelieved by hope. Nevertheless, it was his belief that the role of literature was to "inspirit and rejoice the reader: that it shall convey a charm and infuse delight." In such critical works as *Culture and Anarchy* (1869), Arnold argued also that literature should train us to open our minds to what is true and valuable in life. For Arnold, then, literature's truth and cultural value lay in its ability to enlarge and develop humanity's "moral and social passion for doing good." Even his critical examinations of the classics and of Dante and Shakespeare were in part attempts to help readers of his day find permanent values in an industrialized society that Arnold viewed as increasingly materialistic and self-serving.

Despite his own opinions about the shortcomings of his poetic vision, Arnold's "dark" poems are a mirror of his critical beliefs: They charm and delight audiences while pointing out enduring truths.

GUIDE FOR INTERPRETING

To Marguerite—Continued;
Dover Beach

Writers' Techniques

Imagery and Mood. Imagery is language that appeals to one or more of the senses. Poets rely on imagery to help establish *mood,* the overall feeling that a poem conveys. For example, if a poet wishes to create a mood of frustration, he or she may rely on imagery associated with a summer traffic jam—the sight of countless cars gleaming in the sunshine, the sound of motors humming, the feel of the heat rising from the pavement, the smell and perhaps even the taste of exhaust fumes. The same imagery, however, can be used to convey a mood of excitement and energy when the focus of the poem becomes a raceway, where roaring cars zoom past cheering spectators.

Figurative Language. Figurative language is the name applied to a group of literary devices that use words and phrases in an unorthodox way to create interesting effects. Figurative language is not to be taken literally. Among the many figures of speech used by poets are *apostrophe,* in which the poet directly addresses an absent person or some object or idea, and *personification,* the assigning of human qualities to nonhuman things. Both of these devices are used by Matthew Arnold in "Dover Beach."

Commentary

Critics assume that Arnold wrote "Dover Beach" with his wife in mind. The lines ". . . the world, which seems/To lie before us like a land of dreams,/So various, so beautiful, so new," and the image of Dover Beach in the moonlight perhaps represent the stop that the poet and his wife made at Dover on their wedding journey in June of 1851. The wild beauty of the famed "white cliffs of Dover" continues to attract scores of people yearly.

The Straits of Dover, about twenty-one miles across, connect the English Channel and the Atlantic Ocean with the North Sea. It is a strikingly beautiful spot, for both the French and English shores are lined by high chalk cliffs. The outcropping of the stark white cliffs is the result of the swift erosion of the soft chalk. The lashing of the waves, wind, and rain and the seeping of groundwater combine to create striking shore-front sculpture.

Why do you think Arnold picked Dover Beach as the setting for his poem? How does the imagery help create the poem's mood?

Focus

Imagine yourself on a beach, watching the ebb and flow of the ocean. Freewrite, exploring the thoughts that spring to mind.

To Marguerite—Continued

Matthew Arnold

Yes! in the sea of life enisled,[1]
With echoing straits between us thrown,
Dotting the shoreless watery wild,
We mortal millions live *alone.*
5   The islands feel the enclasping flow,
And then their endless bounds they know.

But when the moon their hollows lights,
And they are swept by balms of spring,
And in their glens, on starry nights,
10   The nightingales divinely sing;
And lovely notes, from shore to shore,
Across the sounds and channels pour—

Oh! then a longing like despair
Is to their farthest caverns sent;
15   For surely once, they feel, we were
Parts of a single continent!
Now round us spreads the watery plain—
Oh might our marges meet again!

Who ordered, that their longing's fire
20   Should be, as soon as kindled, cooled?
Who renders vain their deep desire?
A God, a God their severance ruled!
And bade betwixt their shores to be
The unplumbed, salt, estranging sea.

----

1. enisled (in īld′) *adj.*: Isolated, as if placed on an island.

RESPONDING TO THE SELECTION

Your Response

1. Besides the actions of a "God," what else might explain the condition of isolation that the speaker describes in the poem?

Recalling

2. Where and how, according to lines 1–4, do "we mortal millions live"?
3. (a) According to lines 7–14, what sights and sounds seem to trigger "a longing like despair"? (b) What true cause for this longing is explained in lines 15–18?
4. According to the last stanza, who ordered that this longing's "fire" be "cooled"?

Interpreting

5. To what or whom do you think Arnold is comparing the islands?
6. What human condition is Arnold lamenting in this poem?
7. (a) Who do you suppose the "God" mentioned in line 22 might be? (b) What evidence do you have that this is not a good god?

Applying

8. John Donne wrote, "No man is an island entire of itself; every man is a piece of the continent, a part of the main." Arnold's "Yes!" at the beginning of this poem seems to be a flat contradiction of Donne's view. Which poet's view do you agree with more? Why?

ANALYZING LITERATURE

Creating Imagery and Mood

An **image** is a word or phrase that appeals to one or more of the five senses. Poets string together images to create a particular **mood,** or overall feeling in the poem. In "To Marguerite—Continued," the dominant imagery is intended to help the reader form a mental picture of islands in a vast ocean. Arnold contrasts this imagery, however, with images of springtime in the second stanza.

1. What mood does Arnold establish with the island imagery in the first stanza? How do the sounds of the words themselves contribute to this mood?
2. What mood is suggested by the springtime images in the second stanza? How does the third stanza destroy this mood? How does this intentional undermining of a positive mood fit the theme of the poem?

THINKING AND WRITING

Writing About Imagery and Mood

The image of an island is an almost perfect vehicle for suggesting a mood of loneliness and, in the case of Arnold's poem, for a commentary on human isolation. Consider other images Arnold might have chosen that would have created a similar mood and been equally well suited to his theme. Make notes on one such image and on the senses to which it would appeal. Then write a brief poem or prose narrative that conveys the message of "To Marguerite—Continued." When you revise, make sure you have used as many descriptive words as you can to enhance the vividness of your imagery and to sharpen the piece's mood.

LEARNING OPTIONS

1. **Speaking and Listening.** How might Marguerite, to whom this poem is addressed, have responded to the speaker's sentiments? Write a brief poem that expresses her reactions to his view of life. Recite your poem in class.
2. **Writing.** Imagine you are stranded on a remote, unpopulated island and have survived for many years without communicating with the world. One day you discover a corked bottle. Write a message in which you express the view of life you have developed during your solitary existence.

Dover Beach

Matthew Arnold

The sea is calm tonight.
The tide is full, the moon lies fair
Upon the straits:[1] on the French coast the light
Gleams and is gone; the cliffs of England stand,
5 Glimmering and vast, out in the tranquil bay.
Come to the window, sweet is the night air!
Only, from the long line of spray

Where the sea meets the moon-blanched land,
Listen! you hear the grating roar
10 Of pebbles which the waves draw back, and fling,
At their return, up the high strand,[2]
Begin, and cease, and then again begin,
With tremulous cadence slow, and bring
The eternal note of sadness in.

15 Sophocles[3] long ago
Heard it on the Aegaean,[4] and it brought
Into his mind the turbid ebb and flow
Of human misery; we
Find also in the sound a thought,
20 Hearing it by this distant northern sea.

The Sea of Faith
Was once, too, at the full, and round earth's shore
Lay like the folds of a bright girdle furled.
But now I only hear
25 Its melancholy, long, withdrawing roar,
Retreating, to the breath
Of the night wind, down the vast edges drear
And naked shingles[5] of the world.

---

1. straits: Straits of Dover, between England and France.
2. strand: Shore.
3. Sophocles (säf′ ə klēz′): A Greek tragic dramatist (496?–406 B.C.)
4. Aegaean (ē jē′ ən): The arm of the Mediterranean Sea between Greece and Turkey.
5. shingles n.: Beaches covered with large, coarse, waterworn gravel.

Ah, love, let us be true

30 To one another! for the world, which seems
To lie before us like a land of dreams,
So various, so beautiful, so new,
Hath really neither joy, nor love, nor light,
Nor certitude, nor peace, nor help for pain;

35 And we are here as on a darkling[6] plain
Swept with confused alarms of struggle and flight,
Where ignorant armies clash by night.

---

6. darkling *adj.*: In the dark.

RESPONDING TO THE SELECTION

Your Response

1. Do you agree with the speaker's view of the world? Why or why not?

Recalling

2. (a) According to the first stanza, what does the speaker see and hear from his window? (b) What does the "tremulous cadence" of the pebbles against the beach "bring in"? (c) Who else does the speaker say "long ago" heard this same sound?

3. What sad reality does the speaker describe for his companion in lines 30–34?

Interpreting

4. A symbol is a thing, person, or place that stands for something beyond itself. (a) What might the "cliffs of England" symbolize in line 4? (b) The "naked shingles of the world" in line 28? (c) "Night" in line 37?

5. (a) What effect do you think Arnold aimed to achieve by varying the length of lines and using an irregular rhyme scheme? (b) How do these poetic devices relate to the theme?

6. (a) How is the battle image in the last three lines a fitting conclusion to this poem? (b) How would you state the message of these lines in your own words?

Applying

7. (a) To what extent does Arnold's plea to "be true to one another" in lines 29–30 provide a satisfactory solution to the "ebb and flow of human misery" he sees in the world? (b) Where does this solution break down?

8. (a) State the similarities in theme and imagery you find between this poem and "To Marguerite—Continued" on page 754. (b) State the differences.

THINKING AND WRITING

Writing About a Victorian Poet

From what you know of Victorian society and of Arnold's career, which attitudes of the Victorian Age do you think his poems reflect? Consider, among other things, the effects that industrialization and science had on nineteenth-century England—both positive and negative. Comment on the effects of such forces in an essay that establishes Arnold's place as a poet of his time. When you revise, make sure you have mentioned mood and theme in your treatment of the topic.

THOMAS HARDY

1840–1928

Both a novelist and a poet, Thomas Hardy is sometimes called "the last of the great Victorians." Like Matthew Arnold, Hardy had a pessimistic view of the world. In his novels he depicted people struggling for survival in an indifferent natural universe and an uncaring human society. Unlike Arnold, who sought to improve society, Hardy remained merely an observer and chronicler of the ills of his century; if he offered comfort, it was expressed in a hope that the future would at least be different, if not any better.

Thomas Hardy was born in Dorset, the region in southwest England on which he based his fictional setting of Wessex. It is an area noted for its agriculture and, perhaps more important, for its ruins, which date from Roman and Anglo-Saxon times. After leaving school at the age of fifteen, Hardy was trained as an architect. He developed a strong interest in fiction and poetry, however, and eventually decided to focus his energy on writing. His first novel, *Desperate Remedies,* was published anonymously in 1871, and the following year he achieved success with the publication of *Under the Greenwood Tree.*

In *Far From the Madding Crowd* (1874), *The Return of the Native* (1878), *The Mayor of Casterbridge* (1886), *Tess of the d'Urbervilles* (1891), and his masterpiece, *Jude the Obscure* (1895), Hardy created characters whose destinies are shaped by forces beyond their control. Many suffer the plight of the underdog, victims of a callous society. They live in a haunting landscape that is both ancient and modern, starkly beautiful yet indifferent to the tragic lives of its inhabitants. Some of his works, including "The Three Strangers," also contain an element of mystery, resulting in part from the distinctive setting.

The bleakness of his fiction was disturbing to readers, and the response to *Jude the Obscure,* in particular, was so hostile that Hardy abandoned fiction and focused his energies on writing poetry. He earned immense public acclaim with *The Dynasts,* an epic verse drama about the Napoleonic Wars. With each book of verse he produced over the next two decades, his reputation as a man of letters grew.

Hardy's poetry marks a transition from the Victorian Age to the Modernist movement of the twentieth century. In his use of strict meters and stanza structure, Hardy was unmistakably Victorian, but his "nonpoetic" language and odd rhymes, coupled with a fatalistic outlook, were both source and inspiration for numerous twentieth-century writers.

GUIDE FOR INTERPRETING

The Three Strangers

Writers' Techniques

Setting and Mood. Setting is the time and place in which the events in a story occur. This information is sometimes vital to a story's *mood,* or the feelings it conveys. If, for example, the story is set in a crowded, bustling city, the mood might be tense and hectic. If, on the other hand, the story is set on a lush tropical island, the mood would probably be calm and tranquil.

Focus

Imagine that a stranger appeared at the front door of your home one evening. Letting your imagination run free, describe this person's appearance, as well as yours and your family's initial reaction to him or her. Finally, state the reason for the stranger's visit.

Primary Source

One afternoon, Robert Graves, his wife, and T. E. Lawrence found themselves near Hardy's home in Dorchester. Since they had met Hardy not long before, when he had traveled to Oxford to receive an honorary degree from the university, they decided to visit him.

Graves, himself a well-known poet, novelist, and critic, wrote a record of their conversation. It clearly shows the influence of setting and mood on Hardy's word choice and writing style.

> He said that he regarded professional critics as parasites no less noxious than autograph-hunters, and wished the world rid of them. He also wished that he had not listened to them when he was a young man; on their advice he had cut out dialect-words from his early poems, though they had no exact synonyms to fit the context. And still the critics were plaguing him. One of them recently complained of a poem of his where he had written "his shape *smalled* in the distance." Now what in the world else could he have written? Hardy then laughed a little and said that once or twice recently he had looked up a word in the dictionary for fear of being again accused of coining, and had found it there right enough—only to read on and find that the sole authority quoted was himself in a half-forgotten novel! He talked of early literary influences, and said that he had none at all, for he did not come of literary stock. Then he corrected himself and said that a friend, a fellow-apprentice in the architect's office where he had worked as a young man, used to lend him books.

How do you think the language of "The Three Strangers" might have differed if Hardy had used another setting and mood?

The Three Strangers

Thomas Hardy

Among the few features of agricultural England which retain an appearance but little modified by the lapse of centuries, may be reckoned the long, grassy and furzy downs, coombs,[1] or ewe-leases, as they are called according to their kind, that fill a large area of certain counties in the south and southwest. If any mark of human occupation is met with hereon, it usually takes the form of the solitary cottage of some shepherd.

Fifty years ago such a lonely cottage stood on such a down, and may possibly be standing there now. In spite of its loneliness, however, the spot, by actual measurement, was not three miles from a county town. Yet that affected it little. Three miles of irregular upland, during the long inimical seasons, with their sleets, snows, rains, and mists, afford withdrawing space enough to isolate a Timon[2] or a Nebuchadnezzar;[3] much less, in fair weather, to please that less repellent tribe, the poets, philosophers, artists, and others who "conceive and meditate of pleasant things."

Some old earthen camp or barrow,[4] some clump of trees, at least some starved fragment of ancient hedge is usually taken advantage of in the erection of these forlorn dwellings. But, in the present case, such a kind of shelter had been disregarded. Higher Crowstairs, as the house was called, stood quite detached and undefended. The only reason for its precise situation seemed to be the crossing of two footpaths at right angles hard by, which may have crossed there and thus for a good five hundred years. Hence the house was exposed to the elements on all sides. But, though the wind up here blew unmistakably when it did blow, and the rain hit hard whenever it fell, the various weathers of the winter season were not quite so formidable on the down as they were imagined to be by dwellers on low ground. The raw rimes[5] were not so pernicious as in the hollows, and the frosts were scarcely so severe. When the shepherd and his family who tenanted the house were pitied for their sufferings from the exposure, they said that upon the whole they were less inconvenienced by "wuzzes and flames" (hoarses and phlegms) than when they had lived by the stream of a snug neighboring valley.

The night of March 28, 182– was precisely one of the nights that were wont to call forth these expressions of commiseration. The level rainstorm smote walls, slopes, and hedges like the clothyard shafts of Senlac and Crecy.[6] Such sheep and outdoor animals as had no shelter stood with their buttocks to the winds; while the tails of little birds trying to roost on some scraggy thorn were blown inside out like umbrellas. The gable-end of the cottage was stained with wet, and the eavesdroppings flapped against the wall. Yet never was commiseration for the shepherd more misplaced. For that cheerful rustic was entertaining a large

---

1. coombs (ko͞oms) *n*.: Deep, narrow valleys.
2. Timon (tī'mən): A fifth-century Greek hermit who lived in a cave.
3. Nebuchadnezzar (neb' yə kəd nez' ər): A Babylonian king who isolated himself in the fields after becoming insane.
4. barrow *n*.: A heap of earth or rocks marking a grave.

5. rimes (rīmz) *n*.: White frost.
6. clothyard . . . Crecy (krā sē'): Yard-long arrows used in battles fought in England (at Senlac) and France (at Crecy).

party in glorification of the christening of his second girl.

The guests had arrived before the rain began to fall, and they were all now assembled in the chief or living room of the dwelling. A glance into the apartment at eight o'clock on this eventful evening would have resulted in the opinion that it was as cozy and comfortable a nook as could be wished for in boisterous weather. The calling of its inhabitant was proclaimed by a number of highly polished sheep crooks without stems that were hung ornamentally over the fireplace, the curl of each shining crook varying from the antiquated type engraved in the patriarchal pictures of old family Bibles to the most approved fashion of the last local sheep fair. The room was lighted by half a dozen candles, having wicks only a trifle smaller than the grease which enveloped them, in candlesticks that were never used but at high days, holy days, and family feasts. The lights were scattered about the room, two of them standing on the chimney piece. This position of candles was in itself significant. Candles on the chimney piece always meant a party.

On the hearth, in front of a backbrand to give substance, blazed a fire of thorns, that crackled "like the laughter of the fool."

Nineteen persons were gathered here. Of these, five women, wearing gowns of various bright hues, sat in chairs along the wall; girls shy and not shy filled the window bench; four men, including Charley Jake the hedge carpenter, Elijah New the parish clerk, and John Pitcher, a neighboring dairyman, the shepherd's father-in-law, lolled in the settle; a young man and maid, who were blushing over tentative *pourparlers*[7] on a life companionship, sat beneath the corner cupboard; and an elderly engaged man of fifty or upward moved restlessly about from spots where his betrothed was not to the spot where she was. Enjoyment was pretty general, and so much the more

prevailed in being unhampered by conventional restrictions. Absolute confidence in each other's good opinion begat perfect ease, while the finishing stroke of manner, amounting to a truly princely serenity, was lent to the majority by the absence of any expression or trait denoting that they wished to get on in the world, enlarge their minds, or do any eclipsing thing whatever —which nowadays so generally nips the bloom and *bonhomie*[8] of all except the two extremes of the social scale.

Shepherd Fennel had married well, his wife being a dairyman's daughter from a vale at a distance, who brought fifty guineas in her pocket—and kept them there, till they should be required for ministering to the needs of a coming family. This frugal woman had been somewhat exercised as to the character that should be given to the gathering. A sit-still party had its advantages; but an undisturbed position of ease in chairs and settles was apt to lead on the men to such an unconscionable deal of toping[9] that they would sometimes fairly drink the house dry. A dancing party was the alternative; but this, while avoiding the foregoing objection on the score of good drink, had a counterbalancing disadvantage in the matter of good victuals, the ravenous appetites engendered by the exercise causing immense havoc in the buttery. Shepherdess Fennel fell back upon the intermediate plan of mingling short dances with short periods of talk and singing, so as to hinder any ungovernable rage in either. But this scheme was entirely confined to her own gentle mind: the shepherd himself was in the mood to exhibit the most reckless phases of hospitality.

The fiddler was a boy of those parts, about twelve years of age, who had a wonderful dexterity in jigs and reels, though his fingers were so small and short as to necessitate a constant shifting for the high notes, from which he scrambled back to the first

---

7. pourparlers (po͞or′ pär lä′): Informal discussions (French).

8. bonhomie (bän′ ə mē′): Good nature (French).
9. toping: Drinking.

SUMMER, AFTERNOON AFTER A SHOWER
John Constable
The Tate Gallery, London

position with sounds not of unmixed purity of tone. At seven the shrill tweedle-dee of this youngster had begun, accompanied by a booming ground bass from Elijah New, the parish clerk, who had thoughtfully brought with him his favorite musical instrument, the serpent.[10] Dancing was instantaneous, Mrs. Fennel privately enjoining the players on no account to let the dance exceed the length of a quarter of an hour.

But Elijah and the boy in the excitement of their position quite forgot the injunction. Moreover, Oliver Giles, a man of seventeen, one of the dancers, who was enamored of his partner, a fair girl of thirty-three rolling years, had recklessly handed a new crown-piece to the musicians, as a bribe to keep going as long as they had muscle and wind. Mrs. Fennel seeing the steam begin to generate on the countenances of her guests, crossed over and touched the fiddler's elbow and put her hand on the serpent's mouth. But they took no notice, and fearing she might lose her character of genial hostess if she were to interfere too markedly, she retired and sat down helpless. And so the dance whizzed on with cumulative fury, the performers moving in their planet-like courses, direct and retrograde,[11] from apogee to perigee,[12] till the hand of the well-kicked clock at the bottom of the room had traveled over the circumference of an hour.

While these cheerful events were in course of enactment within Fennel's pastoral dwelling an incident having considerable bearing on the party had occurred in the gloomy night without. Mrs. Fennel's concern about the growing fierceness of the dance corresponded in point of time with the ascent of a human figure to the solitary hill of Higher Crowstairs from the direction of the distant town. This personage strode on through the rain without a pause, following the little-worn path which, further on in its course, skirted the shepherd's cottage.

It was nearly the time of full moon, and on this account, though the sky was lined with a uniform sheet of dripping cloud, ordi-

---

10. serpent *n.*: An obsolete, coiled bass wind instrument.

11. direct and retrograde: Orbital directions.
12. from apogee to perigee: From the points in orbit farthest from and nearest to the earth.

nary objects out of doors were readily visible. The sad wan light revealed the lonely pedestrian to be a man of supple frame; his gait suggested that he had somewhat passed the period of perfect and instinctive agility, though not so far as to be otherwise than rapid of motion when occasion required. At a rough guess, he might have been about forty years of age. He appeared tall, but a recruiting sergeant, or other person accustomed to the judging of men's heights by the eye, would have discerned that this was chiefly owing to his gauntness, and that he was not more than five-feet-eight or nine.

Notwithstanding the regularity of his tread there was caution in it, as in that of one who mentally feels his way; and despite the fact that it was not a black coat nor a dark garment of any sort that he wore, there was something about him which suggested that he naturally belonged to the black-coated tribes[13] of men. His clothes were of fustian,[14] and his boots hobnailed, yet in his progress he showed not the mud-accustomed bearing of hobnailed and fustianed peasantry.

By the time that he had arrived abreast of the shepherd's premises the rain came down, or rather came along, with yet more determined violence. The outskirts of the little settlement partially broke the force of wind and rain, and this induced him to stand still. The most salient of the shepherd's domestic erections was an empty sty at the forward corner of his hedgeless garden, for in these latitudes the principle of masking the homelier features of your establishment by a conventional frontage was unknown. The traveler's eye was attracted to this small building by the pallid shine of the wet slates that covered it. He turned aside, and, finding it empty, stood under the pent roof for shelter.

While he stood the boom of the serpent within the adjacent house, and the lesser strains of the fiddler, reached the spot as an accompaniment to the surging hiss of the flying rain on the sod, its louder beating on the cabbage leaves of the garden, on the straw hackles of eight or ten beehives just discernible by the path, and its dripping from the eaves into a row of buckets and pans that had been placed under the walls of the cottage. For at Higher Crowstairs, as at all such elevated domiciles, the grand difficulty of housekeeping was an insufficiency of water; and a casual rainfall was utilized by turning out, as catchers, every utensil that the house contained. Some queer stories might be told of the contrivances for economy in suds and dishwaters that are absolutely necessitated in upland habitations during the droughts of summer. But at this season there were no such exigencies; a mere acceptance of what the skies bestowed was sufficient for an abundant store.

At last the notes of the serpent ceased and the house was silent. This cessation of activity aroused the solitary pedestrian from the reverie into which he had lapsed, and, emerging from the shed, with an apparently new intention, he walked up the path to the house door. Arrived here, his first act was to kneel down on a large stone beside the row of vessels, and to drink a copious draft from one of them. Having quenched his thirst he rose and lifted his hand to knock, but paused with his eye upon the panel. Since the dark surface of the wood revealed absolutely nothing, it was evident that he must be mentally looking through the door, as if he wished to measure thereby all the possibilities that a house of this sort might include, and how they might bear upon the question of his entry.

In his indecision he turned and surveyed the scene around. Not a soul was anywhere visible. The garden path stretched downward from his feet, gleaming like the track of a snail; the roof of the little well (mostly dry), the well cover, the top rail of the garden gate, were varnished with the same dull liquid glaze; while, far away in the vale, a faint whiteness of more than usual extent showed that the rivers were high in the meads. Beyond all this winked a few bleared lamplights through the beating drops —lights that denoted the situation of the county town from which he had appeared to come. The absence of all notes of life in that direction seemed to clinch his intentions, and he knocked at the door.

Within, a desultory chat had taken the place of movement and musical sound. The hedge carpenter was suggesting a song to the company, which nobody just then was inclined to undertake, so that the knock afforded a not unwelcome diversion.

"Walk in!" said the shepherd promptly.

The latch clicked upward, and out of the night our pedestrian appeared upon the doormat. The shepherd arose, snuffed two of the nearest candles, and turned to look at him.

Their light disclosed that the stranger was dark in complexion and not unprepossessing as to feature. His hat, which for a moment he did not remove, hung low over his eyes, without concealing that they were large, open, and determined, moving with a flash rather than a glance around the room. He seemed pleased with his survey, and, baring his shaggy head, said, in a rich deep voice, "The rain is so heavy, friends, that I ask leave to come in and rest awhile."

"To be sure, stranger," said the shepherd. "And faith, you've been lucky in choosing your time, for we are having a bit of a fling for a glad cause—though, to be sure, a man could hardly wish that glad cause to happen more than once a year."

"Nor less," spoke up a woman. "For 'tis best to get your family over and done with, as soon as you can, so as to be all the earlier out of the fag o't."[15]

"And what may be this glad cause?" asked the stranger.

"A birth and christening," said the shepherd.

The stranger hoped his host might not be made unhappy either by too many or too few of such episodes, and being invited by a gesture to a pull at the mug, he readily acquiesced. His manner, which, before entering, had been so dubious, was now altogether that of a careless and candid man.

"Late to be traipsing athwart this coomb —hey?" said the engaged man of fifty.

"Late it is, master, as you say.—I'll take a seat in the chimney corner, if you have nothing to urge against it, ma'am; for I am a little moist on the side that was next the rain."

Mrs. Shepherd Fennel assented, and made room for the self-invited comer, who, having got completely inside the chimney corner, stretched out his legs and his arms with the expansiveness of a person quite at home.

"Yes, I am rather cracked in the vamp,"[16] he said freely, seeing that the eyes of the shepherd's wife fell upon his boots, "and I am not well fitted either. I have had some rough times lately, and have been forced to pick up what I can get in the way of wearing, but I must find a suit better fit for working days when I reach home."

"One of hereabouts?" she inquired.

"Not quite that—farther up the country."

"I thought so. And so be I; and by your tongue you come from my neighborhood."

"But you would hardly have heard of me," he said quickly. "My time would be long before yours, ma'am, you see."

This testimony to the youthfulness of his hostess had the effect of stopping her cross-examination.

"There is only one thing more wanted to make me happy," continued the newcomer. "And that is a little baccy,[17] which I am sorry to say I am out of."

"I'll fill your pipe," said the shepherd.

"I must ask you to lend me a pipe likewise."

"A smoker, and no pipe about 'ee?"

---

15. fag o't: Fatigue of it.

16. vamp *n*.: The part of a shoe or boot covering the instep.
17. baccy: Tobacco.

"I have dropped it somewhere on the road."

The shepherd filled and handed him a new clay pipe, saying, as he did so, "Hand me your baccy box—I'll fill that too, now I am about it."

The man went through the movement of searching his pockets.

"Lost that too?" said his entertainer, with some surprise.

"I am afraid so," said the man with some confusion. "Give it to me in a screw of paper." Lighting his pipe at the candle with a suction that drew the whole flame into the bowl, he resettled himself in the corner and bent his looks upon the faint steam from his damp legs, as if he wished to say no more.

Meanwhile the general body of guests had been taking little notice of this visitor by reason of an absorbing discussion in which they were engaged with the band about a tune for the next dance. The matter

being settled, they were about to stand up when an interruption came in the shape of another knock at the door.

At sound of the same the man in the chimney corner took up the poker and began stirring the brands as if doing it thoroughly were the one aim of his existence; and a second time the shepherd said, "Walk in!" In a moment another man stood upon the straw-woven doormat. He too was a stranger.

This individual was one of a type radically different from the first. There was more of the commonplace in his manner, and a certain jovial cosmopolitanism sat upon his features. He was several years older than the first arrival, his hair being slightly frosted, his eyebrows bristly, and his whiskers cut back from his cheeks. His face was rather full and flabby, and yet it was not altogether a face without power. A few grog blossoms marked the neighborhood of his nose. He flung back his long drab greatcoat, revealing that beneath it he wore a suit of cinder-gray shade throughout, large heavy seals, of some metal or other that would take a polish, dangling from his fob as his only personal ornament. Shaking the water drops from his low-crowned glazed hat, he said, "I must ask for a few minutes' shelter, comrades, or I shall be wetted to my skin before I get to Casterbridge."

"Make yourself at home, master," said the shepherd, perhaps a trifle less heartily than on the first occasion. Not that Fennel had the least tinge of niggardliness in his composition; but the room was far from large, spare chairs were not numerous, and damp companions were not altogether desirable at close quarters for the women and girls in their bright-colored gowns.

However, the second comer, after taking off his greatcoat, and hanging his hat on a nail in one of the ceiling beams as if he had been specially invited to put it there, advanced and sat down on the table. This had been pushed so closely into the chimney corner, to give all available room to the dancers, that its inner edge grazed the elbow of the man who had ensconced himself by the fire; and thus the two strangers were brought into close companionship. They nodded to each other by way of breaking the ice of unacquaintance, and the first stranger handed his neighbor the family mug—a huge vessel of brown ware, having its upper edge worn away like a threshold by the rub of whole generations of thirsty lips that had gone the way of all flesh, and bearing the following inscription burnt upon its rotund side in yellow letters:

THERE IS NO FUN
UNTiLL i CUM

The other man, nothing loth,[18] raised the mug to his lips, and drank on, and on, and on—till a curious blueness overspread the countenance of the shepherd's wife, who had regarded with no little surprise the first stranger's free offer to the second of what did not belong to him to dispense.

"I knew it!" said the toper to the shepherd with much satisfaction. "When I walked up your garden before coming in, and saw the hives all of a row, I said to myself, 'Where there's bees there's honey, and where there's honey there's mead.' But mead of such a truly comfortable sort as this I really didn't expect to meet in my older days." He took yet another pull at the mug, till it assumed an ominous elevation.

"Glad you enjoy it!" said the shepherd warmly.

"It is goodish mead," assented Mrs. Fennel, with an absence of enthusiasm which seemed to say that it was possible to buy praise for one's cellar at too heavy a price. "It is trouble enough to make—and really I hardly think we shall make any more. For honey sells well, and we ourselves can make shift with a drop o' small mead and metheglin[19] for common use from the comb-washings."

"O, but you'll never have the heart!" reproachfully cried the stranger in cinder gray, after taking up the mug a third time and setting it down empty. "I love mead, when 'tis old like this, as I love to go to church o' Sundays, or to relieve the needy any day of the week."

"Ha, ha, ha!" said the man in the chimney corner, who, in spite of the taciturnity induced by the pipe of tobacco, could not or would not refrain from this slight testimony to his comrade's humor.

Now the old mead of those days, brewed of the purest first-year or maiden honey, four pounds to the gallon—with its due complement of white of eggs, cinnamon, ginger, cloves, mace, rosemary, yeast, and processes of working, bottling, and cellaring —tasted remarkably strong; but it did not taste so strong as it actually was. Hence,

---

18. nothing loth: Not reluctant.

19. small mead and metheglin: Weaker types of mead.

presently, the stranger in cinder gray at the table, moved by its creeping influence, unbuttoned his waistcoat, threw himself back in his chair, spread his legs, and made his presence felt in various ways.

"Well, well, as I say," he resumed, "I am going to Casterbridge, and to Casterbridge I must go. I should have been almost there by this time; but the rain drove me into your dwelling, and I'm not sorry for it."

"You don't live in Casterbridge?" said the shepherd.

"Not as yet; though I shortly mean to move there."

"Going to set up in trade, perhaps?"

"No, no," said the shepherd's wife. "It is easy to see that the gentleman is rich, and don't want to work at anything."

The cinder-gray stranger paused, as if to consider whether he would accept that definition of himself. He presently rejected it by answering, "Rich is not quite the word for me, dame. I do work, and I must work. And even if I only get to Casterbridge by midnight I must begin work there at eight tomorrow morning. Yes, het or wet, blow or snow, famine or sword, my day's work tomorrow must be done."

"Poor man! Then, in spite o' seeming, you be worse off than we?" replied the shepherd's wife.

"'Tis the nature of my trade, men and maidens. 'Tis the nature of my trade more than my poverty. . . . But really and truly I must up and off, or I shan't get a lodging in the town." However, the speaker did not move, and directly added, "There's time for one more draft of friendship before I go; and I'd perform it at once if the mug were not dry."

"Here's a mug o' small," said Mrs. Fennel. "Small, we call it, though to be sure 'tis only the first wash o' the combs."

"No," said the stranger disdainfully. "I won't spoil your first kindness by partaking o' your second."

"Certainly not," broke in Fennel. "We don't increase and multiply every day, and I'll fill the mug again." He went away to the dark place under the stairs where the barrel stood. The shepherdess followed him.

"Why should you do this?" she said reproachfully, as soon as they were alone. "He's emptied it once, though it held enough for ten people; and now he's not contented wi' the small, but must needs call for more o' the strong! And a stranger unbeknown to any of us. For my part, I don't like the look o' the man at all."

"But he's in the house, my honey; and 'tis a wet night, and a christening. Daze it, what's a cup of mead more or less? There'll be plenty more next bee-burning."

"Very well—this time, then," she answered, looking wistfully at the barrel. "But what is the man's calling, and where is he one of, that he should come in and join us like this?"

"I don't know. I'll ask him again."

The catastrophe of having the mug drained dry at one pull by the stranger in cinder gray was effectually guarded against this time by Mrs. Fennel. She poured out his allowance in a small cup, keeping the large one at a discreet distance from him. When he had tossed off his portion, the shepherd renewed his inquiry about the stranger's occupation.

The latter did not immediately reply, and the man in the chimney corner, with sudden demonstrativeness, said, "Anybody may know my trade—I'm a wheelwright."

"A very good trade for these parts," said the shepherd.

"And anybody may know mine—if they've the sense to find it out," said the stranger in cinder gray.

"You may generally tell what a man is by his claws," observed the hedge carpenter, looking at his own hands. "My fingers be as full of thorns as an old pincushion is of pins."

The hands of the man in the chimney corner instinctively sought the shade, and he gazed into the fire as he resumed his pipe. The man at the table took up the hedge carpenter's remark, and added smartly, "True; but the oddity of my trade is that, instead of setting a mark upon me, it sets a mark upon my customers."

No observation being offered by anybody in elucidation of this enigma the shepherd's wife once more called for a song. The same obstacles presented themselves as at the former time—one had no voice, another had forgotten the first verse. The stranger at the table, whose soul had now risen to a good working temperature, relieved the difficulty by exclaiming that, to start the company, he would sing himself. Thrusting one thumb into the armhole of his waistcoat, he waved the other hand in the air, and, with an extemporizing gaze at the shining sheep crooks above the mantelpiece, began:

> "O my trade it is the rarest one,
> Simple shepherds all—
> My trade is a sight to see;
> For my customers I tie, and
>   take them up on high,
> And waft 'em to a far countree!"

The room was silent when he had finished the verse—with one exception, that of the man in the chimney corner, who, at the singer's word, "Chorus!" joined him in a deep bass voice of musical relish—

> "And waft 'em to a far countree!"

Oliver Giles, John Pitcher the dairyman, the parish clerk, the engaged man of fifty, the row of young women against the wall, seemed lost in thought not of the gayest kind. The shepherd looked meditatively on the ground, the shepherdess gazed keenly at the singer, and with some suspicion; she was doubting whether this stranger were merely singing an old song from recollection, or was composing one there and then for the occasion. All were as perplexed at the obscure revelation as the guests at Belshazzar's Feast,[20] except the man in the chimney

corner, who quietly said, "Second verse, stranger," and smoked on.

The singer thoroughly moistened himself from his lips inwards, and went on with the next stanza as requested:

> "My tools are but common ones,
> Simple shepherds all—
> My tools are no sight to see:
> A little hempen string, and a post
>   whereon to swing,
> Are implements enough for me!"

Shepherd Fennel glanced round. There was no longer any doubt that the stranger was answering his question rhythmically. The guests one and all started back with suppressed exclamations. The young woman engaged to the man of fifty fainted halfway, and would have proceeded, but finding him wanting in alacrity for catching her she sat down trembling.

"Oh, he's the—!" whispered the people in the background, mentioning the name of an ominous public officer. "He's come to do it! 'Tis to be at Casterbridge jail tomorrow—the man for sheep-stealing—the poor clockmaker we heard of, who used to live away at Shottsford and had no work to do—Timothy Summers, whose family were a-starving, and so he went out of Shottsford by the high road, and took a sheep in open daylight, defying the farmer and the farmer's wife and the farmer's lad, and every man jack among 'em. He" (and they nodded towards the stranger of the deadly trade) "is come from up the country to do it because there's not enough to do in his own county town, and he's got the place here now our own county man's dead; he's going to live in the same cottage under the prison wall."

The stranger in cinder gray took no notice of this whispered string of observations, but again wetted his lips. Seeing that his friend in the chimney corner was the only one who reciprocated his joviality in any way, he held out his cup towards that appreciative comrade, who also held out his own. They clinked together, the eyes of the rest of

---

20. as the . . . Belshazzar's (bel shaz'ərz) **Feast:** In the Old Testament, writing appeared on the wall during a feast held by the king of Babylon warning him of defeat (Ezekiel 5:1).

the room hanging upon the singer's actions. He parted his lips for the third verse; but at that moment another knock was audible upon the door. This time the knock was faint and hesitating.

The company seemed scared; the shepherd looked with consternation towards the entrance, and it was with some effort that he resisted his alarmed wife's deprecatory glance, and uttered for the third time the welcoming words, "Walk in!"

The door was gently opened, and another man stood upon the mat. He, like those who had preceded him, was a stranger. This time it was a short, small personage, of fair complexion, and dressed in a decent suit of dark clothes.

"Can you tell me the way to—?" he began; when, gazing round the room to observe the nature of the company amongst whom he had fallen, his eyes lighted on the stranger in cinder gray. It was just at the instant when the latter, who had thrown his mind into his song with such a will that he scarcely heeded the interruption, silenced all whispers and inquiries by bursting into his third verse:

"Tomorrow is my working day,
Simple shepherds all—
Tomorrow is a working day for me:
For the farmer's sheep is slain,
  and the lad who did it ta'en,
And on his soul may God ha' merc-y!"

The stranger in the chimney corner, waving cups with the singer so heartily that his mead splashed over on the hearth, repeated in his bass voice as before:—

"And on his soul may God ha' merc-y!"

All this time the third stranger had been standing in the doorway. Finding now that he did not come forward or go on speaking, the guests particularly regarded him. They noticed to their surprise that he stood before them the picture of abject terror—his knees trembling, his hand shaking so violently

that the door latch by which he supported himself rattled audibly; his white lips were parted, and his eyes fixed on the merry officer of justice in the middle of the room. A moment more and he had turned, closed the door, and fled.

"What a man can it be?" said the shepherd.

The rest, between the awfulness of their late discovery and the odd conduct of this third visitor, looked as if they knew not what to think, and said nothing. Instinctively they withdrew farther and farther from the grim gentleman in their midst, whom some of them seemed to take for the Prince of Darkness himself, till they formed a remote circle, an empty space of floor being left between them and him—. . . *circulus, cujus centrum diabolus.*[21] The room was so silent—though there were more than twenty people in it—that nothing could be heard but the patter of the rain against the window shutters, accompanied by the occasional hiss of a stray drop that fell down the chimney into the fire, and the steady puffing of the man in the corner, who had now resumed his pipe of long clay.

The stillness was unexpectedly broken. The distant sound of a gun reverberated through the air—apparently from the direction of the county town.

"Be jiggered!" cried the stranger who had sung the song, jumping up.

"What does that mean?" asked several.

"A prisoner escaped from the jail—that's what it means."

All listened. The sound was repeated, and none of them spoke but the man in the chimney corner, who said quietly, "I've often been told that in this county they fire a gun at such times; but I never heard it till now."

"I wonder if it is *my* man?" murmured the personage in cinder gray.

"Surely it is!" said the shepherd invol-

---

21. circulus . . . diabolus: A circle with the devil at its center.

untarily. "And surely we've zeed him! That little man who looked in at the door by now, and quivered like a leaf when he zeed ye and heard your song!"

"His teeth chattered, and the breath went out of his body," said the dairyman.

"And his heart seemed to sink within him like a stone," said Oliver Giles.

"And he bolted as if he'd been shot at," said the hedge carpenter.

"True—his teeth chattered, and his heart seemed to sink; and he bolted as if he'd been shot at," slowly summed up the man in the chimney corner.

"I didn't notice it," remarked the hangman.

"We were all a-wondering what made him run off in such a fright," faltered one of the women against the wall, "and now 'tis explained!"

The firing of the alarm gun went on at intervals, low and sullenly, and their suspicions became a certainty. The sinister gentleman in cinder gray roused himself. "Is there a constable here?" he asked, in thick tones. "If so, let him step forward."

The engaged man of fifty stepped quavering out from the wall, his betrothed beginning to sob on the back of the chair.

"You are a sworn constable?"

"I be, sir."

"Then pursue the criminal at once, with assistance, and bring him back here. He can't have gone far."

"I will, sir, I will—when I've got my staff. I'll go home and get it, and come sharp here, and start in a body."

"Staff!—never mind your staff; the man'll be gone!"

"But I can't do nothing without my staff —can I, William, and John, and Charles Jake? No; for there's the king's royal crown a painted on en in yaller and gold, and the lion and the unicorn, so as when I raise en up and hit my prisoner, 'tis made a lawful blow thereby. I wouldn't 'tempt to take up a man without my staff—no, not I. If I hadn't the law to gie me courage, why, instead o' my taking up him he might take up me!"

"Now, I'm a king's man myself, and can give you authority enough for this," said the formidable officer in gray. "Now then, all of ye, be ready. Have ye any lanterns?"

"Yes—have ye any lanterns?—I demand it!" said the constable.

"And the rest of you able-bodied—"

"Able-bodied men—yes—the rest of ye!" said the constable.

"Have you some good stout staves and pitchforks—"

"Staves and pitchforks—in the name o' the law! And take 'em in yer hands and go in quest, and do as we in authority tell ye!"

Thus aroused, the men prepared to give chase. The evidence was, indeed, though circumstantial, so convincing, that but little argument was needed to show the shepherd's guests that after what they had seen it would look very much like connivance if they did not instantly pursue the unhappy third stranger, who could not as yet have gone more than a few hundred yards over such uneven country.

A shepherd is always well provided with lanterns; and, lighting these hastily, and with hurdle staves in their hands, they poured out of the door, taking a direction along the crest of the hill, away from the town, the rain having fortunately a little abated.

Disturbed by the noise, or possibly by unpleasant dreams of her baptism, the child who had been christened began to cry heartbrokenly in the room overhead. These notes of grief came down through the chinks of the floor to the ears of the women below, who jumped up one by one, and seemed glad of the excuse to ascend and comfort the baby, for the incidents of the last half-hour greatly oppressed them. Thus in the space of two or three minutes the room on the ground floor was deserted quite.

But it was not for long. Hardly had the sound of footsteps died away when a man returned round the corner of the house from the direction the pursuers had taken. Peeping in at the door, and seeing nobody there, he entered leisurely. It was the stranger of the chimney corner, who had gone out with the rest. The motive of his return was shown by his helping himself to a cut piece of skimmer cake that lay on a ledge beside where he had sat, and which he had apparently forgotten to take with him. He also poured out half a cup more mead from the quantity that remained, ravenously eating and drinking these as he stood. He had not finished when another figure came in just as quietly—his friend in cinder gray.

"O—you here?" said the latter, smiling. "I thought you had gone to help in the capture." And this speaker also revealed the object of his return by looking solicitously round for the fascinating mug of old mead.

"And I thought you had gone," said the other, continuing his skimmer cake with some effort.

"Well, on second thoughts, I felt there were enough without me," said the first confidentially, "and such a night as it is, too. Besides, 'tis the business o' the government to take care of its criminals—not mine."

"True; so it is. And I felt as you did, that there were enough without me."

"I don't want to break my limbs running over the humps and hollows of this wild country."

"Nor I neither, between you and me."

"These shepherd people are used to it —simple-minded souls, you know, stirred up to anything in a moment. They'll have him ready for me before the morning, and no trouble to me at all."

"They'll have him, and we shall have saved ourselves all labor in the matter."

"True, true. Well, my way is to Caster-bridge; and 'tis as much as my legs will do to take me that far. Going the same way?"

"No, I am sorry to say! I have to get home over there" (he nodded indefinitely to the right), "and I feel as you do, that it is quite enough for my legs to do before bedtime."

The other had by this time finished the mead in the mug, after which, shaking hands heartily at the door, and wishing each other well, they went their several ways.

In the meantime the company of pursuers had reached the end of the hog's-back elevation which dominated this part of the down. They had decided on no particular plan of action; and, finding that the man of the baleful trade was no longer in their company, they seemed quite unable to form any such plan now. They descended in all directions down the hill, and straightway several of the party fell into the snare set by Nature for all misguided midnight ramblers over this part of the cretaceous formation. The 'lanchets,' or flint slopes, which belted the escarpment at intervals of a dozen yards, took the less cautious ones unawares, and losing their footing on the rubbly steep they slid sharply downwards, the lanterns rolling from their hands to the bottom, and there lying on their sides till the horn was scorched through.

When they had again gathered themselves together the shepherd, as the man who knew the country best, took the lead, and guided them round these treacherous inclines. The lanterns, which seemed rather to dazzle their eyes and warn the fugitive than to assist them in the exploration, were extinguished, due silence was observed; and in this more rational order they plunged into the vale. It was a grassy, briery, moist defile, affording some shelter to any person who had sought it; but the party perambulated it in vain, and ascended on the other side. Here they wandered apart, and after an interval closed together again to report progress. At the second time of closing in they found themselves near a lonely ash, the single tree on this part of the coomb, probably sown there by a passing bird some fifty years before. And here, standing a little to one side of the trunk, as motionless as the trunk itself, appeared the man they were in quest of, his outline being well defined against the sky beyond. The band noiselessly drew up and faced him.

"Your money or your life!" said the constable sternly to the still figure.

"No, no," whispered John Pitcher. "'Tisn't our side ought to say that. That's the doctrine of vagabonds like him, and we be on the side of the law."

"Well, well," replied the constable impatiently; "I must say something, mustn't I? and if you had all the weight o' this undertaking upon your mind, perhaps you'd say the wrong thing too! Prisoner at the bar, surrender, in the name of the Father—the Crown, I mane!"

The man under the tree seemed now to notice them for the first time, and, giving them no opportunity whatever for exhibiting their courage, he strolled slowly towards them. He was, indeed, the little man, the third stranger; but his trepidation had in a great measure gone.

"Well, travelers," he said, "did I hear ye speak to me?"

"You did; you've got to come and be our prisoner at once!" said the constable. "We arrest 'ee on the charge of not biding in Casterbridge jail in a decent proper manner to be hung tomorrow morning. Neighbors, do your duty, and seize the culpet!"

On hearing the charge the man seemed enlightened, and, saying not another word, resigned himself with preternatural civility to the search party, who, with their staves in their hands, surrounded him on all sides, and marched him back towards the shepherd's cottage.

It was eleven o'clock by the time they arrived. The light shining from the open door, a sound of men's voices within, proclaimed to them as they approached the house that some new events had arisen in their absence. On entering they discovered the shepherd's living room to be invaded by two officers from Casterbridge jail, and a well-known magistrate who lived at the nearest county seat, intelligence of the escape having become generally circulated.

"Gentlemen," said the constable, "I have brought back your man—not without risk and danger; but everyone must do his duty! He is inside this circle of able-bodied persons, who have lent me useful aid, considering their ignorance of Crown work. Men, bring forward your prisoner!" And the third stranger was led to the light.

"Who is this?" said one of the officials.

"The man," said the constable.

"Certainly not," said the turnkey; and the first corroborated his statement.

"But how can it be otherwise?" asked the constable. "Or why was he so terrified at sight o' the singing instrument of the law who sat there?" Here he related the strange behavior of the third stranger on entering the house during the hangman's song.

"Can't understand it," said the officer coolly. "All I know is that it is not the condemned man. He's quite a different character from this one; a gauntish fellow, with dark hair and eyes, rather good-looking, and with a musical bass voice that if you heard it once you'd never mistake as long as you lived."

"Why, souls—'twas the man in the chimney corner!"

"Hey—what?" said the magistrate, coming forward after inquiring particulars from the shepherd in the background. "Haven't you got the man after all?"

"Well, sir," said the constable, "he's the man we were in search of, that's true; and yet he's not the man we were in search of. For the man we were in search of was not the man we wanted, sir, if you understand my everyday way; for 'twas the man in the chimney corner!"

"A pretty kettle of fish altogether!" said the magistrate. "You had better start for the other man at once."

The prisoner now spoke for the first time. The mention of the man in the chimney corner seemed to have moved him as nothing else could do. "Sir," he said, stepping forward to the magistrate, "take no more trouble about me. The time is come when I may as well speak. I have done nothing; my crime is that the condemned man is my brother. Early this afternoon I left home at Shottsford to tramp it all the way to Casterbridge jail to bid him farewell. I was benighted, and called here to rest and ask the way. When I opened the door I saw before me the very man, my brother, that I thought to see in the condemned cell at Casterbridge. He was in this chimney corner; and jammed close to him, so that he could not have got out if he had tried, was the executioner who'd come to take his life, singing a song about it and not knowing that it was his victim who was close by, joining in to save appearances. My brother threw a glance of agony at me, and I knew he meant, 'Don't reveal what you see; my life depends on it.' I was so terror-struck that I could hardly stand, and, not knowing what I did, I turned and hurried away."

The narrator's manner and tone had the stamp of truth, and his story made a great impression on all around. "And do you know where your brother is at the present time?" asked the magistrate.

"I do not. I have never seen him since I closed this door."

"I can testify to that, for we've been between ye ever since," said the constable.

"Where does he think to fly to? What is his occupation?"

"He's a watch-and-clock-maker, sir."

"'A said 'a was a wheelwright—a wicked rogue," said the constable.

"The wheels of clocks and watches he meant, no doubt," said Shepherd Fennel. "I thought his hands were palish for's trade."

"Well, it appears to me that nothing can be gained by retaining this poor man in custody," said the magistrate; "your business lies with the other, unquestionably."

And so the little man was released offhand; but he looked nothing the less sad on that account, it being beyond the power of magistrate or constable to raze out the written troubles in his brain, for they concerned another whom he regarded with more solicitude than himself. When this was done, and the man had gone his way, the night was found to be so far advanced that it was deemed useless to renew the search before the next morning.

Next day, accordingly, the quest for the clever sheep stealer became general and keen, to all appearance at least. But the intended punishment was cruelly disproportioned to the transgression, and the sympathy of a great many country folk in that district was strongly on the side of the fugitive. Moreover, his marvelous coolness and daring in hob-and-nobbing with the hangman, under the unprecedented circumstances of the shepherd's party, won their admiration. So that it may be questioned if all those who ostensibly made themselves so busy in exploring woods and fields and lanes were quite so thorough when it came to the private examination of their own lofts and outhouses. Stories were afloat of a mysterious figure being occasionally seen in some old overgrown trackway or other, remote from turnpike roads; but when a search was instituted in any of these suspected quarters nobody was found. Thus the days and weeks passed without tidings.

In brief, the bass-voiced man of the chimney corner was never recaptured. Some said that he went across the sea, others that he did not, but buried himself in the depths of a populous city. At any rate, the gentleman in cinder gray never did his morning's work at Casterbridge, nor met anywhere at all, for business purposes, the genial comrade with whom he had passed an hour of relaxation in the lonely house on the slope of the coomb.

The grass has long been green on the graves of Shepherd Fennel and his frugal wife; the guests who made up the christening party have mainly followed their entertainers to the tomb; the baby in whose honor they all had met is a matron in the sere and yellow leaf. But the arrival of the three strangers at the shepherd's that night, and the details connected therewith, is a story as well known as ever in the country about Higher Crowstairs.

RESPONDING TO THE SELECTION

Your Response

1. What were your feelings toward the sheep stealer? Explain.

Recalling

2. (a) Where and when does the story take place? (b) What event is being celebrated?
3. Describe the appearance of (a) the first stranger. (b) the second stranger.
4. (a) Whom does Shepherd Fennel assume the third stranger to be? (b) Why?

Interpreting

5. What do the speech habits of the Fennels and their guests reveal about them?
6. (a) At what point did you guess the identity of the first stranger? (b) The second? (c) The third? (d) What clues did you use?

Applying

7. What does this story suggest about its author's respect for institutions such as the law in nineteenth-century England? Explain.

ANALYZING LITERATURE

Setting and Mood

The **setting** of a story is when and where the action occurs. In addition to such "factual" details as place names and historical references, setting includes time of day, season, weather conditions, and so on. Aspects of setting help determine a story's **mood**—the emotion it conveys. Read the following details of setting from "The Three Strangers." Identify the mood suggested by each detail and by all of them together. Explain why each detail creates the mood it does.

1. Fifty years ago such a lonely cottage stood.
2. The level rainstorm smote walls, slopes, and hedges . . . ; the tails of little birds trying to roost on some scraggy thorn were blown inside out like umbrellas. The gable-end of the cottage was stained wet.
3. The room was lighted by half a dozen candles. . . . On the hearth . . . blazed a fire of thorns that crackled.

CRITICAL THINKING AND READING

Inferring the Author's Attitude

In "The Three Strangers," fate plays an important—and sometimes fickle—role. Had fate not decreed a rainstorm, the sheep stealer might never have come face-to-face with his executioner. And it is the same fateful rainstorm that enables the guilty man to escape capture by his pursuers. From these and other events in the story, attempt to **infer,** or arrive at an understanding of, Hardy's attitude toward the role of fate. Ask yourself: Does he seem to feel that fate governs our lives? To what extent does he believe that we can and should alter fate by exercising our own free will?

THINKING AND WRITING

Describing a Place

Choose a place that you know well—perhaps the neighborhood you live in or a city that you have visited often. On a sheet of paper, jot down as many details of the place as you can think of. Try to include features that make the location unique, or at least easy to visualize. Then convert your notes into a description that would enable a stranger to picture it with little difficulty. Be prepared to share your description with the class.

LEARNING OPTION

Speaking and Listening. Hardy has several of the characters in "The Three Strangers" speak in a Dorset dialect. His evocation of this dialect includes words you may not be familiar with (such as *athwart*) as well as spellings that approximate the sound of the characters' speech. With one or more classmates, choose a passage from the story that contains dialogue written in dialect. Assign roles and practice reading the passage. Use a dictionary to find meanings of unusual words, and make sure you know what standard words the oddly spelled words represent. Then use your Dorset "accents" to read the passage to the class.

MASTERS OF THE VICTORIAN NOVEL

The Victorian Novel

From the sprawling canvas of Dickens's London to the compelling atmosphere of Emily Brontë's wild moors, the Victorian novel has made a lasting impression on literature and readers. Most of the novels written during this era are concerned with manners, morals, and money. Frequently the plot centers around the struggles of a main character to find self-knowledge—in love or marriage, through family or neighbors, or within the working world. Sometimes the quest for self has spiritual overtones, as in the later novels of Thomas Hardy, although the major Victorian novelists were more concerned with people's relationships to society than to religion.

The novels were frequently published in inexpensive monthly installments. To hold their readers' interest, the writers built a minor climax into each installment. This led to a loose, episodic treatment with an intricate plot, numerous characters, and much repetition to jog the reader's memory. Modern novelist Henry James called Victorian novels "large loose baggy monsters," but readers delighted in the suspenseful form.

Giants of the Victorian Novel

In such novels as *Ivanhoe* (1819), Sir Walter Scott, the first major historical novelist, created vivid portraits of Scotland, England, and the Continent from medieval times to the eighteenth century. William Makepeace Thackeray's foray into the historical novel, *Henry Esmond* (1852), was very successful, but *Vanity Fair* (1847) remains his masterpiece. Because of its skillful narration and vivid characterization, this satire immediately established his reputation as one of the major literary figures of the time. Many heroines were modeled on the main character, Becky Sharp. Charlotte Brontë's fictionalized autobiography of a young orphan, *Jane Eyre* (1847), sparked a series of novels on governesses, which became a popular genre through which to explore women's role in society. Her sister Emily's unique tale of love, revenge, and redemption, *Wuthering Heights,* comments on the tensions of nineteenth-century life in a different fashion. The most popular writer of the age, Charles Dickens, combined vivid storytelling, humor, pathos, and irony with sharp social criticism and acute observations of people and places, both real and imagined. His fame was based on an astonishing stream of novels, including *Nicholas Nickleby* (1838–1839), *Bleak House* (1852–1853), and *Great Expectations* (1861).

"The art of novels," wrote Thackeray, "*is* to represent nature: to convey as strongly as possible the sentiment of reality." The continued appeal of Victorian novels comes in large part from their realistic portrayal of Victorian life.

GUIDE FOR INTERPRETING

The Darkling Thrush; The Man He Killed; "Ah, Are You Digging on My Grave?"

Writers' Technique

Simile and Metaphor. A simile is a figure of speech that compares two unlike things, using *like* or *as.* In "Love Among the Ruins," Robert Browning uses a simile to compare the towers on a castle to flames: ". . . the doomed and daring palace shot its spires/Up *like* fires. . . ." A metaphor is a figure of speech that compares two unlike things directly, without the use of an intervening word. Matthew Arnold bases his poem "To Marguerite—Continued" on a central metaphor— "the sea of life." Poets use similes and metaphors to broaden the meanings of their images by making surprising connections between generally unrelated things and ideas.

Irony. Irony arises from the disparity between expectation and reality in a poem or story. In *situational* irony the outcome of an event or situation is different from what the author has led the reader to predict. By using situational irony in "'Ah, Are You Digging on My Grave?'" Hardy communicates an especially strong message to the reader.

Focus

Write an account of an occasion when something relatively unimportant managed to change your mood entirely. Consider possibilities such as a beautiful flower growing through a crack in the pavement of a city sidewalk. Give details of how you felt before and after the mood-changing experience.

Primary Source

Although Hardy had written many poems in his late twenties, his first book of poetry was not published until he was fifty-eight years old. In the thirty years remaining to him, he published nearly one thousand poems. Why would a highly successful novelist abandon prose for poetry? We know that writing novels caused him great stress, and the uproar over *Jude the Obscure* sickened him. But there was more to it. Looking back in 1918, he wrote: "A sense of the truth of poetry, of its supreme place in literature, had awakened itself in me. At the risk of ruining all my worldly prospects I dabbled in it. . . . was forced out of it. . . . It came back upon me. . . . All was of the nature of being led by a mood, without foresight, or regard to whither it led."

The Darkling[1] Thrush

Thomas Hardy

I leant upon a coppice gate[2]
    When Frost was specter-gray,
And Winter's dregs made desolate
    The weakening eye of day.
5 The tangled bine-stems[3] scored the sky
    Like strings of broken lyres,
And all mankind that haunted nigh
    Had sought their household fires.

The land's sharp features seemed to be
10   The Century's corpse[4] outleant,
His crypt the cloudy canopy,
    The wind his death-lament.
The ancient pulse of germ[5] and birth
    Was shrunken hard and dry,
15 And every spirit upon earth
    Seemed fervorless as I.

At once a voice arose among
    The bleak twigs overhead
In a full-hearted evensong
20   Of joy illimited;
An aged thrush, frail, gaunt, and small,
    In blast-beruffled plume,
Had chosen thus to fling his soul
    Upon the growing gloom.

25 So little cause for carolings
    Of such ecstatic sound
Was written on terrestrial things
    Afar or nigh around,
That I could think there trembled through
30   His happy good-night air
Some blessed Hope, whereof he knew
    And I was unaware.

---

1. darkling *adj.*: In the dark.
2. coppice (kop′ is) **gate:** Gate leading to a thicket, or small wood.
3. bine-stems: Twining stems.
4. Century's corpse: This poem was written on December 31, 1900,
the last day of the nineteenth century.
5. germ: Seed or bud.

RESPONDING TO THE SELECTION

Your Response

1. With what feeling does this poem leave you? Explain.

Recalling

2. In what season of the year and at what time of day is the poem set?
3. What do the "land's sharp features" suggest to the speaker?
4. (a) What does the speaker suddenly hear in the third stanza? (b) What does the speaker think about as a result of this experience?

Interpreting

5. (a) What mood does the poet establish in the first two stanzas? (b) What images contribute to this mood? (c) With what does the poet contrast these images in the last two stanzas?
6. (a) Why do you think the poet characterizes the thrush as he does in lines 21–22? (b) What might the thrush symbolize?

Applying

7. Depressed people react in different ways to others who display "joy illimited." The poem describes one possible reaction. What are some other possibilities?
8. Reread "To a Skylark" by Shelley on pages 644–646. (a) What similarities are evident in the speaker's response to the thrush in this poem? (b) What differences do you detect?

ANALYZING LITERATURE

Using Simile and Metaphor

A **simile** is a figure of speech that compares basically dissimilar things, using such connective words as *like* or *as.* Consider the following simile from Tennyson's "The Lotos-Eaters," which makes use of the connective word *than:* "There is sweet music here that softer falls/Than petals from blown roses on the grass. . . ." A **metaphor** also compares basically dissimilar things but without the use of a connective word. When, again in "The Lotos-Eaters," Tennyson refers to the ocean as "fields of barren foam," he is speaking in metaphorical terms. Similes and metaphors are used by poets to heighten the meanings of their images.

1. Identify the following italicized images from "The Darkling Thrush" as either a simile or a metaphor. Tell what two things are being compared in each case.
   a. Winter's dregs made desolate/The *weakening eye of day.* (Lines 3–4)
   b. The tangled bine-stems *scored the sky/Like strings of broken lyres. . . .* (Lines 5–6)
2. To what are the land's sharp features compared in lines 9–11? Explain why this metaphor is especially appropriate for the time and place in which the poem is set.

LEARNING OPTION

Speaking and Listening. Hardy's novels and many of his poems are set in "Wessex," his fictional name for the Dorset countryside that he loved. Using reference books, biographies of Hardy, histories of the Victorian Age, and Hardy's own works, prepare an oral report on some aspect of Hardy's Wessex. You might consider one of the following topics:
   a. the geography of Wessex (Dorset).
   b. the history of the region (prehistoric, Roman, Anglo-Saxon).
   c. Wessex life in Victorian times.
   d. Wessex as depicted in Hardy's works.

The Man He Killed

Thomas Hardy

"Had he and I but met
By some old ancient inn,
We should have sat us down to wet
Right many a nipperkin![1]

5   "But ranged as infantry,
And staring face to face,
I shot at him as he at me,
And killed him in his place.

"I shot him dead because—
10 Because he was my foe,
Just so: my foe of course he was;
That's clear enough; although

"He thought he'd 'list,[2] perhaps,
Off-hand like—just as I—
15 Was out of work—had sold his traps—
No other reason why.

"Yes; quaint and curious war is!
You shoot a fellow down
You'd treat if met where any bar is,
20 Or help to half-a-crown."[3]

---

1. nipperkin *n.*: A small glass for beer or wine.
2. 'list: Enlist.
3. half-a-crown: A British coin.

![R]ESPONDING TO THE SELECTION

Your Response

1. How does your attitude toward war compare with the one expressed in the poem?

Recalling

2. What similarities between himself and the other man does the speaker note in lines 13–16?

Interpreting

3. (a) What do you think is the significance of the quotation marks in each stanza? (b) Who do you suppose the speaker is? (c) To whom do you think the poem is addressed?
4. Why do you think the speaker hesitates at the end of line 9?
5. In what way is war "quaint and curious," as the speaker notes in line 17?
6. Do you think Hardy is writing about a specific war or about war in general? Explain your answer.

Applying

7. Why is it easier for an enemy to be faceless than to have a face?

"Ah, Are You Digging on My Grave?"

Thomas Hardy

"Ah, are you digging on my grave
    My loved one?—planting rue?"
—"No: yesterday he went to wed
One of the brightest wealth has bred.
5 'It cannot hurt her now,' he said,
    'That I should not be true.'"

"Then who is digging on my grave?
    My nearest dearest kin?"
—"Ah, no: they sit and think, 'What use!
10 What good will planting flowers produce?
No tendance of her mound can loose
    Her spirit from Death's gin.'"[1]

"But some one digs upon my grave?
    My enemy?—prodding sly?"
15 —"Nay: when she heard you had passed the Gate
That shuts on all flesh soon or late,
She thought you no more worth her hate,
    And cares not where you lie."

"Then, who is digging on my grave?
20   Say—since I have not guessed!"
—"O it is I, my mistress dear,
Your little dog, who still lives near,
And much I hope my movements here
    Have not disturbed your rest?"

25   "Ah, yes! *You* dig upon my grave . . .
    Why flashed it not on me
That one true heart was left behind!
What feeling do we ever find
To equal among human kind
30   A dog's fidelity!"

---

1. gin *n.*: Trap.

"Mistress, I dug upon your grave
   To bury a bone, in case
I should be hungry near this spot
When passing on my daily trot.
35   I am sorry, but I quite forgot
   It was your resting-place."

RESPONDING TO THE SELECTION

Your Response

1. Do you feel sorry for the speaker in this poem? Why or why not?

Recalling

2. (a) In the first stanza, who does the dead woman suspect is digging on her grave? (b) In the second stanza? (c) In the third stanza?
3. (a) Who in fact is doing the digging? (b) How does the woman react? (c) What reason does the digger give for disturbing the grave?

Interpreting

4. (a) At what point do you begin to suspect the identity of the voice responding to the woman's questions? (b) What effect does Hardy achieve by withholding this information?
5. (a) What mood does Hardy create by having a dead person speak? (b) How does this mood change once the digger is identified?
6. What point about human vanity and self-esteem is Hardy making in this poem?

Applying

7. (a) Of "The Darkling Thrush," "The Man He Killed," and this poem, which strikes you as the most pessimistic? (b) The least pessimistic? (c) Why?

ANALYZING LITERATURE

Understanding Irony

Irony is a purposeful contrast between expectation and reality. In "Ah, Are You Digging on My Grave?" Hardy uses situational irony. That is, he leads the reader to expect one kind of outcome but instead delivers another.

1. What is ironic about the voice in the last four lines of each of the first three stanzas?
2. What emotions does the dead woman express when she learns the identity of the digger? How do the digger's final words ironically alter the woman's emotional expectations?
3. Irony is often related to tone—the author's attitude toward the subject or audience. Explain how the irony in this poem is related to Hardy's pessimistic and unsentimental tone.

THINKING AND WRITING

Writing a Response to a Poem

In "'Ah, Are You Digging on My Grave?'" Hardy delivers pessimistic pronouncements on two different but related topics—human self-worth and human apathy. Consider your reaction to Hardy's views on these subjects by asking yourself questions such as the following: To what extent are Hardy's attitudes typical only of the era in which he lived? To what degree are tributes to the dead really tributes to the living? How thoroughly do we know the feelings others have toward us? How well do we understand our own feelings toward others? In an essay, sum up your response to the views Hardy presents. When you revise, make sure you have provided adequate support for your opinion.

GERARD MANLEY HOPKINS

1844–1889

Though Gerard Manley Hopkins saw none of his work published during his lifetime, he was, ironically, the most innovative poet of the Victorian Age. Born in Essex, just outside London, Hopkins was the oldest of nine children in a well-educated and prosperous family. While still in grammar school, Hopkins began writing poetry, a practice that he maintained throughout his years at Oxford, where he also studied the classics.

It was during his third year at Oxford that Hopkins decided to become a Catholic, much to the dismay of his parents, who were devout Anglicans. Upon being accepted into the Society of Jesus in 1868, he symbolically burned his early poems, resolving "to write no more." Though he remained true to his word for the next seven years, Hopkins continued to keep detailed notebooks—as he had done ever since childhood—that recorded his fascination with words and his love of nature.

In 1874, as part of his preparation for the priesthood, Hopkins went to St. Bueno's College in Wales to study theology. There he learned to speak Welsh. He also began again to write poetry, though of a sort that was different not only from his earlier verse but from anything ever before attempted in English. Encouraged by a Jesuit superior, Hopkins wrote a long poem about a tragic shipwreck in which five nuns had drowned. "The Wreck of the Deutschland," apart from the great emotional power packed into it, was the first poem in which Hopkins used what he called "sprung rhythm." This is a system of versification in which accented syllables are grouped in emphatic patterns somewhat like those of Anglo-Saxon alliterative verse. The resulting meter is quite different from conventional English meter, in which accented and unaccented syllables alternate in regular patterns.

In 1877, the year he was ordained a priest, Hopkins wrote some of his finest and best-known poems, including "God's Grandeur" and "Pied Beauty." Like most of Hopkins's poems, the goal of these was to reveal and glorify the individual essence—or "inscape," as he called it—of everything in nature.

Hopkins served as a parish priest and missionary preacher among the poor in London, Liverpool, and Glasgow. Despite his total dedication to his calling, long hours and a tendency toward perfectionism left him depressed and in poor health. He died of typhoid fever one month before his forty-fifth birthday.

God's Grandeur; Pied Beauty; Spring and Fall

Writers' Techniques

Rhythm and Rhyme. Rhythm is the pattern of stressed and unstressed syllables in a line of poetry. Every poem has rhythm, but not every poem has *meter,* a regular, predictable rhythmic pattern made up of units called *feet.* Each foot consists of one stressed syllable and a fixed number of unstressed syllables. In the 1870's Gerard Manley Hopkins created a new kind of rhythm that resembled natural speech. In *sprung* rhythm, as Hopkins termed his creation, the number of unstressed syllables varies from foot to foot. Precisely which syllables receive stress, moreover, is not accidental but carefully planned to help convey meaning and emotion. Finally, sprung rhythm calls for the innovative use of language, for the combining of existing words, the extending of word meanings, the invention of new words, and the elimination of words that do not add to the desired effect.

Rhyme is the repetition of the same or similar sounds in two or more words. When rhyme occurs at the ends of lines in a poem it is called *end* rhyme. When rhyme occurs within a single line it is called *internal* rhyme. Again breaking with tradition, Hopkins used both types of rhyme, as well as *approximate* rhyme, or rhyme that relates words similar in function or meaning.

Focus

Write the name of a prized possession, much-loved pastime, or favorite season at the top of a sheet of paper. Write whatever words and phrases come to mind. Read over what you have written. Note phrases and words whose *sounds* seem to relate to your topic.

Primary Source

In his work among the poor, Hopkins no doubt encountered scenes such as this one described by a fellow worker:

> I attended a family of thirteen—twelve of whom had typhus fever, without a bed in the *cellar,* without straw or timber shavings—frequent substitutes. They lay on the floor, and so crowded that I could scarcely pass between them . . . there is only one supply of water for all its inhabitants and it occupies a good deal of time to procure it and carry it back to the different rooms, where it soon becomes covered with black scum . . . One woman informed me that her husband lay dead, and that she could not obtain water without the greatest difficulty to wash his "rags" . . . the deaths . . . were for that year 36, or 1 death to 14.6 persons.

God's Grandeur

Gerard Manley Hopkins

The world is charged with the grandeur of God.
    It will flame out, like shining from shook foil;[1]
    It gathers to a greatness, like the ooze of oil
Crushed.[2] Why do men then now not reck his rod?[3]
Generations have trod, have trod, have trod;
    And all is seared with trade; bleared, smeared with toil;
    And wears man's smudge and shares man's smell: the
        soil
Is bare now, nor can foot feel, being shod.

And for all this, nature is never spent;
10   There lives the dearest freshness deep down things;
And though the last lights off the black West went
    Oh, morning, at the brown brink eastward, springs—
Because the Holy Ghost over the bent
    World broods with warm breast and with ah! bright
        wings.

---

1. foil *n.*: Tinsel.
2. crushed: Squeezed from olives.
3. reck his rod: Heed God's authority.

RESPONDING TO THE SELECTION

Your Response

1. Do you think that the speaker presents an accurate view of humanity's relationship with nature? Do you agree that "nature is never spent"? Explain.

Recalling

2. (a) According to lines 5–8, what has humankind done to God's grandeur? (b) According to line 9, what difference has man's behavior made? Explain.

3. (a) What is the Holy Ghost compared to in the last two lines? (b) What verb describes what it does? (c) What two adjectives describe it?

Interpreting

4. What kind of emotional response do you suppose Hopkins hoped to awaken in the reader in lines 1–4? Do you think he succeeds?

5. What do you think is the meaning of the question raised in line 4?

BIRD'S NEST
Ros. W. Jenkins
Warrington Museum and Art Gallery

6. (a) What effect do you think the poet hoped to achieve by the repetition in line 5? (b) By the alliteration, or consonant repetition, of *sm* in lines 6–7?

7. "God's Grandeur" is a sonnet, a poetic form with very specific rhyme requirements. Note, for instance, the number of words rhyming with *God* and *foil* in the first eight lines. (a) Why do you suppose Hopkins chose so rigid a poetic form for this poem? In what way does the form reinforce his message? (b) What effect do you think Hopkins wanted to achieve by the sounds of the words *ooze, oil,* and *crushed* in lines 3 and 4? By the repetition of *d* sounds in line 10? Of *b* sounds in the last two lines?

Applying

8. (a) Although Hopkins notes many abuses in this poem, do you think his overall outlook is optimistic or pessimistic? Explain. (b) How would you define the difference between an optimist and a pessimist?

Pied Beauty

Gerard Manley Hopkins

Glory be to God for dappled things—
    For skies of couple-color as a brinded[1] cow;
      For rose-moles all in stipple[2] upon trout that swim;
Fresh-firecoal chestnut-falls;[3] finches' wings;
     5   Landscape plotted and pieced—fold, fallow, and plow;
      And áll trádes, their gear and tackle and trim.

All things counter,[4] original, spare, strange;
    Whatever is fickle, freckled (who knows how?)
      With swift, slow; sweet, sour; adazzle, dim;
 10 He fathers-forth whose beauty is past change:
      Praise him.

---

1. brinded *adj.*: Having a gray or tawny coat streaked with a darker color.
2. stipple *n.*: Dots or small spots.
3. fresh-firecoal chestnut-falls: Roasted chestnuts.
4. counter: Contrary.

RESPONDING TO THE SELECTION

Your Response

1. What aspects of Hopkins's use of language do you think are most effective in this poem?

Recalling

2. What five "dappled things" does the speaker name in the first five lines?
3. What does the speaker ask the reader to do in line 11?

Interpreting

4. (a) What do you think is the meaning of "couple-color" in line 2? (b) Why do you think Hopkins chose this phrase, rather than a more conventional way of expressing the thought?
5. What difference can you see between the "dappled things" of the first stanza and the sorts of things hinted at in the second?
6. What significance do you attach to the words in parentheses in line 8?

7. What do you think is meant by the phrase "whose beauty is past change" in line 10?

Applying

8. Compare "Pied Beauty" with "God's Grandeur." (a) In what ways are the two poems similar? (b) How are they different in their outlook on the world as altered by humans? (c) How might Hopkins have explained this paradox, or apparent contradiction?

LEARNING OPTION

Art. "Pied Beauty" is filled with striking visual images. Create a piece of art that captures the images in the poem. To suggest the poem's theme of variety in nature, you might wish to make a collage using photographs from magazines or a mobile that expresses the many facets of the natural world.

Spring and Fall
To a Young Child

Gerard Manley Hopkins

A MOTHER AND CHILD ON THE ISLE OF WIGHT
James Collinson
Yale Center for British Art

Márgarét, áre you gríeving
Over Goldengrove unleaving?
Leáves, líke the things of man, you
With your fresh thoughts care for, can you?
5 Áh! ás the heart grows older
It will come to such sights colder
By and by, nor spare a sigh
Though worlds of wanwood[1] leafmeal[2] lie;
And yet you wíll weep and know why.
10 Now no matter, child, the name:
Sórrow's spríngs áre the same.
Nor mouth had, no nor mind, expressed
What heart heard of, ghost[3] guessed:
15 It ís the blight man was born for,
It is Margaret you mourn for.

---

1. wanwood (wän' wŏŏd): Pale wood.
2. leafmeal: Ground-up decomposed leaves.
3. ghost: Spirit.

RESPONDING TO THE SELECTION

Your Response

1. Do you agree with the speaker that the heart grows colder as a person ages? Why or why not?

Recalling

2. According to the speaker, in what way will Margaret change as she grows older?

Interpreting

3. What do you think is meant by "fresh thoughts" in line 4? By "worlds of wanwood leafmeal" in line 8?
4. What is the theme?

Applying

5. (a) What is the relevance of the title "Spring and Fall"? (b) What might "spring" stand for? (c) What second meaning of "fall" might be relevant to the speaker's advice to the child?

THINKING AND WRITING

Writing Margaret's Reply

Imagine that you are Margaret. Try to put yourself in the position of a child who has just suffered a grave disappointment over something an adult would find trivial. Now write a response to the adult speaker of "Spring and Fall" that gives the child's view of the world. Your response may take the form of either a poem or prose piece.

A. E. HOUSMAN

1859–1936

A leading classical scholar of his age, Alfred Edward Housman devoted his life to teaching and translating the great Latin poets. Yet, most modern readers who know Housman know him as the author of three slender volumes of poetry that are as romantic and melancholy as any ever written.

Housman was born in Worcestershire, the oldest of seven children in a middle-class family. His childhood came to an end when his mother died, following a long illness, on his twelfth birthday. Money became a problem for the family, but Housman, a bright and resourceful young man, won a scholarship to Oxford, where he studied classical literature and philosophy. Though he was a brilliant student, his intolerance of imperfections in himself or others left him with few friends.

While at Oxford, Housman fell secretly in love with a person who was interested only in his friendship. His despair over this relationship, combined with his unhappy teen years, seems to have darkened the rest of Housman's life and to have given his poetry its bitter undertones.

Upon leaving Oxford, Housman went to work in the Patent Office. Determined to prove himself in the classics, he studied Greek and Latin at night and wrote scholarly articles for academic journals. In 1892 his hard-earned reputation as an expert in his field led to his appointment as professor of Latin at University College in London.

Though Housman spent the balance of his life engaged in scholarly pursuits, he found time to write poetry. His first and most famous collection of verse, *A Shropshire Lad* (1896), has as its fictitious narrator a homesick farm boy living in the city. In simple, precise language and brisk, regular rhythms, Housman focuses on the grim realities and fleeting joys of life. Housman paid for the first publication of *A Shropshire Lad* out of his own pocket, but it soon became highly popular. More than twenty-five years later, *Last Poems* (1922) was an instant best-seller. After Housman's death, his brother Laurence edited and published *More Poems* (1936).

In a famous lecture that he delivered in 1933, Housman, who worked at projecting a public image as an emotionless intellectual, stated that the goal of poetry is to "transfuse emotion," not to transmit thought. A well-written poem, he maintained, should make as physical an impact on the reader as a shiver down the spine or a punch in the stomach. It is because of this impact in much of his own work that the best of A. E. Housman's poems have been marked for immortality.

To an Athlete Dying Young; Loveliest of Trees; When I Was One-and-Twenty

Writers' Techniques

Theme. The theme in a literary work is the insight into life that it communicates to the reader. One of several recurring themes in Housman's verse is the bittersweet notion that youth is beautiful but that, like beauty itself, it passes too quickly. Even in those upbeat instances when Housman is describing happiness and glory, the reader senses an undercurrent of doom and a concern with the courage and endurance that will be required to face it. The charming, easy rhymes in his poems contrast sharply with his melancholy themes, which reflect both the pessimism of the late Victorian Age and the sadness in his own life.

Commentary

Housman led a life of harsh self-discipline and solitary habits: By the age of twenty-seven, he had fully embraced the monklike seclusion that would characterize the rest of his life. Although a thorough teacher, he was distant and humorless. Much respected for his keen intelligence and devotion to his duties, neither his students nor colleagues were comfortable with him, and he had few close friends. By the time he was in his mid-forties, A Shropshire Lad had become a best-seller. But despite his fame and affluence, he still spent his evenings working on his studies or reading detective stories, especially those of Conan Doyle, which were then very popular. His scholarly excellence was rewarded in 1911 when he was made Kennedy Professor of Latin at Cambridge University and a Fellow at Trinity College. He soon established the same reputation in his new positions as he had in his old: meticulous with his work, sour and surly with people. His rooms at Trinity were as grim as the man: The only decoration was a large tortoise shell; there was not even a comfortable chair. He refused the many honors and awards he was offered, including the royal Order of Merit; he would be condescended to by no one, not even the king. How do you see the man in his work?

Focus

Reflect on a topic to which you have a strong response—both positive and negative. Possibilities include the promise of the future mixed with its uncertainties or bittersweet memories of a favorite afterschool gathering spot that no longer exists. Freewrite, using vivid details to capture the happy and sad aspects of your topic.

To an Athlete Dying Young

A. E. Housman

The time you won your town the race
We chaired you through the marketplace;
Man and boy stood cheering by,
And home we brought you shoulder-high.

5   Today, the road all runners come,
Shoulder-high we bring you home,
And set you at your threshold down,
Townsman of a stiller town.

Smart lad, to slip betimes away
10 From fields where glory does not stay
And early though the laurel[1] grows
It withers quicker than the rose.

Eyes the shady night has shut
Cannot see the record cut,
15 And silence sounds no worse than cheers
After earth has stopped the ears:

Now you will not swell the rout
Of lads that wore their honors out,
Runners whom renown outran
20 And the name died before the man.

So set, before its echoes fade,
The fleet foot on the sill of shade.
And hold to the low lintel up
The still-defended challenge cup.

25 And round that early-laureled head
Will flock to gaze the strengthless dead,
And find unwithered on its curls
The garland briefer than a girl's.

---

1. laurel: A symbol of victory.

Your Response

1. If you were the young athlete and could listen from beyond the grave, how would you respond to the speaker of the poem?

Recalling

2. (a) In what sport did the athlete excel? (b) What did the townspeople do to show their admiration for the athlete following the contest mentioned in the first stanza?
3. (a) Where is the athlete "today"? (b) What does the speaker say the athlete will not have to be concerned about "now"?

Interpreting

4. (a) What visual image presented in the first stanza is repeated in the second stanza? (b) How is the meaning of the image different in the second stanza? (c) How does this difference affect the mood?
5. (a) How would you summarize the speaker's comments in lines 9–20? (b) What is meant by "the name died before the man"?
6. (a) In what way is the challenge cup mentioned in line 24 "still-defended"? (b) What double meaning might the poet have intended for the word "still"?

Applying

7. Tell whether you agree or disagree with the speaker in this poem. Give reasons for your answer.
8. What advice would you give an athlete who is concerned about growing old and losing his or her "glory"?

ANALYZING LITERATURE

Finding the Theme

The **theme** in a poem is its insight into life. A poem's theme should not be confused with its subject, which can usually be described in a single word, such as "love" or "war." Rather, the theme reflects the author's thoughts on that subject—for instance, "love is blind," "love is a battlefield." Since poets seldom state the theme directly, the reader must *inter,* or figure out, the theme from the events and descriptions in the poem. One effective way of doing this is by constructing a series of meaningful questions that take into account the facts of the poem, as well as such features as its setting, tone, and mood. Answer the following questions to "To an Athlete Dying Young." Then state the poem's theme.

1. (a) Who is the "main character" in the poem? (b) What is the character's main accomplishment?
2. (a) What has happened to this character that is the occasion for this poem? (b) What details in the second stanza alert you to this happening? (c) What is the speaker's tone—that is, what seems to be his true feelings toward this happening?
3. (a) What does the speaker assume in lines 9–20 might have happened to the main character in later years? (b) On what evidence does the speaker most likely base this assumption?
4. (a) What generalization might be made about the relationship between accomplishment and praise? (b) To what other areas of life might this generalization apply?
5. What is the speaker's attitude toward life and death?
6. What is the theme of the poem?

LEARNING OPTION

Cross-curricular Connection. Find information about a major sports figure—Len Bias, for example—or another celebrity who has died young or needed to retire because of illness. Use the newspaper file at the library to learn the public response to the event. Notice the difference in tone between information given in the sports pages and stories included in the news section. Present your findings to the class.

Loveliest of Trees

A. E. Housman

Loveliest of trees, the cherry now
Is hung with bloom along the bough,
And stands about the woodland ride
Wearing white for Eastertide.

5   Now, of my threescore years and ten,
Twenty will not come again,
And take from seventy springs a score,
It only leaves me fifty more.

And since to look at things in bloom
10   Fifty springs are little room,
About the woodlands I will go
To see the cherry hung with snow.

RESPONDING TO THE SELECTION

Your Response

1. Do you think a human lifetime is too brief? How do you respond to the transitory nature of life?

Recalling

2. (a) During what season of the year is the poem set? (b) How can you tell?
3. What is the speaker of the poem doing?
4. (a) How old is the speaker? (b) To what age does he expect to live?

Interpreting

5. What realization does the speaker come to in the second stanza?
6. In the third stanza the speaker makes a resolution for himself. Do you think this resolution has to do only with trees? Explain.

Applying

7. (a) What is the theme of the poem? (b) Judging from this theme, what would you guess is the speaker/poet's attitude toward an afterlife?

LEARNING OPTION

Writing. Find a blade of grass, a leaf, a flower, or some other living plant. Bring it indoors and observe the changes it goes through. What thoughts and feelings does the process evoke in you? Write a brief poem that expresses your point of view. You might wish to indicate your age, as the speaker does in "Loveliest of Trees." Recite your poem to the class.

When I Was One-and-Twenty

A. E. Housman

When I was one-and-twenty
    I heard a wise man say,
"Give crowns and pounds and guineas[1]
    But not your heart away;
5 Give pearls away and rubies
    But keep your fancy free."
But I was one-and-twenty,
    No use to talk to me.

When I was one-and-twenty
10   I heard him say again,
"The heart out of the bosom
    Was never given in vain;
'Tis paid with sighs a plenty
    And sold for endless rue."
15 And I am two-and-twenty,
    And oh, 'tis true, 'tis true.

---

1. crowns . . . guineas: Denominations of money.

RESPONDING TO THE SELECTION

Your Response

1. Do you think the wise man gives the speaker good advice? Why or why not?

Recalling

2. (a) What does the speaker say he "heard a wise man say" when he was "one-and-twenty?" (b) What, according to lines 7–8, was the speaker's reaction to this advice?
3. What is the speaker's comment in the last line on the wise man's second piece of advice?

Interpreting

4. With what is the speaker equating the age of one-and-twenty? Explain your answer.
5. (a) What is significant about the fact that the speaker has twice received advice? (b) How is this relevant in light of the poem's theme?
6. What do you suppose happened to the speaker that changed his mind?

Applying

7. What event in Housman's life may have prompted the writing of this poem?

LEARNING OPTION

Writing. Imagine the speaker of this poem is writing to a newspaper advice columnist for help. How might the speaker describe his concerns in such a letter? What kind of assistance might he ask for? What advice would the columnist give? Write a brief letter from each point of view.

BIOGRAPHIES

Dante Gabriel Rossetti (1828–1882)

A successful painter as well as a poet, Dante Gabriel Rossetti grew up in a bilingual household under the watchful eyes of parents who were devoted to literature and the arts. At twenty Rossetti founded the Pre-Raphaelite Brotherhood, and his poems are often filled with the colorful pictorial detail so admired by this group. He published *The House of Life,* a cycle of sonnets reflecting various aspects of love, in 1870. In his later poems Rossetti also anticipated the pessimism of many modern writers.

George Meredith (1828–1909)

Meredith was born in the coastal city of Portsmouth. When his first volume of verse, *Poems* (1851), failed to sell, he turned to fiction but, again, enjoyed little success. It was not until the publication of *The Egoist* in 1879 that Meredith received the public recognition he had been seeking. Though Meredith is known primarily as a novelist, he always thought of himself first and foremost as a poet. Indeed, his best poems evoke the power of nature and the joy of humanity's relationship to it.

Christina Rossetti (1830–1894)

The younger sister of the poet Dante Gabriel Rossetti, Christina Rossetti is considered by some critics to be the greatest woman poet in all of English literature. In 1871 Rossetti fell victim to a disease that disfigured her and left her an invalid. In spite of this, she continued to write, turning out in the space of her lifetime five collections of verse, a book of poems for children, a book of prayers, and a book of religious meditations. Her simple, lyrical poems exhibit a grace and precision that are rare.

Rudyard Kipling (1865–1936)

Rudyard Kipling was equally skillful as a poet and as a writer of prose. Born in Bombay, India, to English parents, Kipling was placed, when he was five, in a foster home in England. Kipling returned to India in 1882 to work as a journalist. During the next seven years, he published a number of witty poems and stories, and by the time he visited London in 1890, he was a celebrity. Kipling wrote several books that have since become children's classics: *The Jungle Books* (1895), *Captains Courageous* (1897), and *Kim* (1901).

GUIDE FOR INTERPRETING

Silent Noon; Lucifer in Starlight; A Birthday; Recessional

Imagery. Imagery is language, often in the form of poetic details, that appeals to one or more of the five senses. Poets use imagery to communicate experience vividly, to make you see, feel, hear, smell, and taste the ideas they present to you in words. Since imagery is often visual, images are often thought of as "word pictures." The Pre-Raphaelite poets included images in their poems of details that would ordinarily go unnoticed, such as shadows on a wall or the scraping sound of chairs pushed across a floor. The poems of Dante Gabriel Rossetti, George Meredith, and Christina Rossetti show influences of the Pre-Raphaelite movement. The sense-related details and elaborate word pictures in their verse provide a sharp contrast to the more stately images of Kipling's "Recessional."

The Victorian tendency toward self-congratulation was especially evident at the Great Exhibition of 1851, the first international public display of commercial products. The exhibition was hugely successful: Queen Victoria, for example, visited it forty-four times that summer. Addressing a dinner at the exhibition, Albert, the Prince Consort, voiced the nation's optimism when he said:

> Nobody who has paid any attention to the peculiar features of our present era will doubt for a moment that we are living at a period of the most wonderful transition which tends rapidly to accomplish that Great End, to which, indeed, all history points—the realization of the unity of mankind . . .
>
> The distances which separated the different nations and parts of the globe are rapidly vanishing before the achievements of modern invention . . . thought is communicated with the rapidity, and even by the power of lightning. On the other hand, the great principle of the division of labor—which may be called the moving power of civilization, is being extended to all branches of science, industry and art.

How might the tone and content of Albert's speech move Kipling to write a poem such as "Recessional"?

Try to recall an experience you had that created vivid sense impressions, such as weathering a violent storm, or attempting to sleep on a blisteringly hot night without the aid of a fan or air conditioner. Freewrite about your experience.

Silent Noon

Dante Gabriel Rossetti

Your hands lie open in the long fresh grass—
    The finger-points look through like rosy blooms:
    Your eyes smile peace. The pasture gleams and glooms
'Neath billowing skies that scatter and amass.
5 All round our nest, far as the eye can pass,
    Are golden kingcup fields with silver edge
    Where the cow-parsley skirts the hawthorn hedge.
'Tis visible silence, still as the hourglass.

    Deep in the sun-searched growths the dragonfly
10 Hangs like a blue thread loosened from the sky—
    So this winged hour is dropped to us from above.
Oh! clasp we to our hearts, for deathless dower,
This close-companioned inarticulate hour
    When twofold silence was the song of love.

"WEY" CHINTZ
William Morris

▮ RESPONDING TO THE SELECTION

Your Response

1. Do you think silence can convey love as strongly as words can? Explain.

Recalling

2. (a) Where are the speaker and his companion? (b) What time of day is it? (c) What time of year? (d) How can you tell?

Interpreting

3. Is it possible for silence to be "visible," as the speaker states in line 8? Explain.
4. Explain the paradox in the last line.

Applying

5. Under what circumstances does silence have an effect opposite to the one described? What details might the poet have used to "paint" an impression of that kind of silence?

Lucifer in Starlight

George Meredith

On a starred night Prince Lucifer uprose.
Tired of his dark dominion swung the fiend
Above the rolling ball in cloud part screened,
Where sinners hugged their specter of repose.
5 Poor prey to his hot fit of pride were those.
And now upon his western wing he leaned,
Now his huge bulk o'er Afric's sands careened,
Now the black planet shadowed Arctic snows.
Soaring through wider zones that pricked his scars
10 With memory of the old revolt from Awe,
He reached a middle height, and at the stars,
Which are the brain of heaven, he looked, and sank.
Around the ancient track marched, rank on rank,
The army of unalterable law.

RESPONDING TO THE SELECTION

Your Response

1. Do you think good always triumphs over evil? Explain.

Recalling

2. (a) Why does Prince Lucifer rise up? (b) Where does he go?
3. (a) What does he look at when he reaches "the middle height"? (b) What is his reaction to what he sees?

Interpreting

4. What do you understand "the rolling ball in cloud part screened" in line 3 to signify?
5. (a) Who or what makes up "the army of unalterable law"? (b) What situation is unalterable?
6. "Lucifer in Starlight" is a sonnet. (a) What question or problem is raised in the octet? (b) What answer or resolution is provided in the sestet?

7. In Milton's *Paradise Lost,* Satan (also known as Lucifer) is an angel who has fallen from grace and has thus been cast out of Heaven. How might this allusion explain Lucifer's feelings and "mission" in "Lucifer in Starlight"? What might be the meaning of "old revolt from Awe" in line 10?
8. In classical mythology, Lucifer (which means "lightbearer") was the morning star—that is, the planet Venus at dawn. Thus the rising of Prince Lucifer also refers to the appearance of Venus on the horizon. How does knowing this enhance your appreciation of the poem?

Applying

9. Meredith may have come upon the idea for this poem while gazing up at a nighttime sky. What thoughts come to you when you gaze up at the stars? What themes might the vastness of the sky suggest?

A Birthday

Christina Rossetti

My heart is like a singing bird
    Whose nest is in a watered shoot:
My heart is like an apple tree
    Whose boughs are bent with thickset fruit;
5 My heart is like a rainbow shell
    That paddles in a halcyon sea;
My heart is gladder than all these
    Because my love is come to me.

Raise me a dais of silk and down;
10   Hang it with vair[1] and purple dyes;
Carve it in doves and pomegranates,
    And peacocks with a hundred eyes;
Work it in gold and silver grapes,
    In leaves and silver fleurs-de-lys;[2]
15 Because the birthday of my life
    Is come, my love is come to me.

---

1. vair *n.*: Squirrel fur.
2. fleurs-de-lys (flʉr′ də lēz′) *n*: Emblems resembling lilies or irises.

RESPONDING TO THE SELECTION

Your Response

1. What images would you use to help express a moment of great joy?

Recalling

2. (a) To what three things does the speaker compare her heart in the first stanza? (b) Why does she feel as she does?
3. (a) What does the speaker ask for in the second stanza? (b) What has arrived?

Interpreting

4. (a) What feeling does the poem convey? (b) Find three images that evoke that feeling.

5. The poet makes abundant use of repetition, especially in the first stanza. How does this affect the mood of the poem?
6. What possible meanings might you attach to the phrase "the birthday of my life"?

Applying

7. The second stanza of "A Birthday" has been called a "fully Pre-Raphaelite word-picture." Using what you have learned about the Pre-Raphaelite movement along with evidence from the poem, explain why you think this is so.

Recessional[1]

Rudyard Kipling

In 1897 a national celebration called the "Diamond Jubilee" was held in honor of the sixtieth anniversary of Queen Victoria's reign. The occasion prompted a great deal of boasting about the strength and greatness of the empire. Kipling responded to the celebration by writing this poem, reminding the people of England that the British empire might not last forever.

God of our fathers, known of old—
 Lord of our far-flung battle-line—
Beneath whose awful Hand we hold
 Dominion over palm and pine—
5 Lord God of Hosts, be with us yet,
Lest we forget—lest we forget!

The tumult and the shouting dies—
 The Captains and the Kings depart—
Still stands Thine ancient Sacrifice,
10 An humble and a contrite heart.[2]
Lord God of Hosts, be with us yet,
Lest we forget—lest we forget!

Far-called, our navies melt away—
 On dune and headland sinks the fire[3]—
15 Lo, all our pomp of yesterday
 Is one with Nineveh[4] and Tyre![5]
Judge of the Nations, spare us yet,
Lest we forget—lest we forget!

---

1. recessional *n.*: A hymn sung at the end of a religious service.
2. An . . . heart: An allusion to the Bible (Psalms 51:17): "The sacrifices of God are a broken spirit: a broken and contrite heart, O God, thou wilt not despise."
3. On . . . fire: Bonfires were lit on high ground all over Britain as part of the opening ceremonies of the Jubilee celebration.
4. Nineveh (nin' ə və): The ancient capital of the Assyrian Empire, the ruins of which were discovered buried in desert sands in the 1850's.
5. Tyre (tīr): Once a great port and the center of ancient Phoenician culture, now a small town in Lebanon.

THE TRIUMPHS OF THE BRITISH ARMY AND NAVY, 1897
Lithograph

If, drunk with sight of power, we loose
20   Wild tongues that have not Thee in awe—
Such boasting as the Gentiles use
        Or lesser breeds without the Law[6]—
Lord God of Hosts, be with us yet,
Lest we forget—lest we forget!

25   For heathen heart that puts her trust
        In reeking tube[7] and iron shard[8]—
All valiant dust that builds on dust,
        And guarding calls not Thee to guard—
For frantic boast and foolish word,
30   Thy mercy on Thy People, Lord!

---

6. Such boasting . . . Law: An allusion to the Bible (Romans 2:14):
"For when the Gentiles, which have not the law, do by nature things
contained in the law, these, having not the law, are a law unto
themselves."
7. tube: The barrel of a gun.
8. shard: Fragment of a bombshell.

RESPONDING TO THE SELECTION

Your Response

1. Do you think this poem has relevance to contemporary American society? Explain.

Recalling

2. (a) To whom is this poem addressed? (b) To whom is Kipling really speaking?
3. What does the speaker suggest, in lines 15–16, happens to "our pomp of yesterday?"
4. What does the speaker beg for in the last line?

Interpreting

5. What qualities and actions does the poem condemn? Support your answer.
6. What is the poem's theme?

Applying

7. What differences do you detect in the images used by Kipling in "Recessional" and those used by George Meredith in "Lucifer in Starlight"? Which poet's imagery do you find more effective? Explain.

THINKING AND WRITING

Writing About Historical Context

Kipling's "Recessional" may be seen as a rejection of some of the values of the England in which he lived. Supplement what you have learned about Victorian England by consulting an encyclopedia or other historical reference. Note, in addition to the economic, political, and religious climates of the period, specific events that may have shaped the thoughts of the citizenry. Weigh all possible influences on Kipling when he composed this poem in 1897 and discard those that are irrelevant. Then write an explanatory paper in which you identify "Recessional" as a product of its period. Refer to specific lines of the poem to strengthen your thesis. When you revise, make sure your essay is organized in a logical order.

Changing Views of Women

SEVENTEENTH-CENTURY VIEWS

Times were tough for women in seventeenth-century England. Although womanhood was idealized in the courtly love poetry of the day, the more common view held that women were conniving and inconstant. A popular writer expressed the general attitude against women in 1615:

> Eagles eat not men till they are
> dead but women devour them alive,
> for a woman will pick thy pocket
> and empty thy purse, laugh in thy
> face and cut thy throat, they are
> ungrateful, perjured, full of fraud,
> flouting and deceit, unconstant,
> waspish, toyish, light, sullen,
> proud, discourteous, and cruel.

Things were hardly better across the ocean. Although women in New England enjoyed relative equality battling side-by-side with their men to survive in a hostile land, there were limits to their rights. Mental, not physical, strength was at issue here, for women's minds were thought too frail to absorb excessive learning. Puritan culture reinforced the power of the father as the head of the family, and the penalty for trespassing the accepted order was dire indeed. Governor John Winthrop reported the following sad case in his diary entry for April 13, 1645:

> Mr. Hopkins, the governor of
> Hartford upon Connecticut, came to
> Boston, and brought his wife with
> him who was fallen into a sad
> infirmity, the loss of her
> understanding and reason, which
> had been growing upon her divers
> years, by occasion of her giving
> herself wholly to reading and

writing, and had written many books. Her husband, being very loving and tender with her, was loath to grieve her; but he saw his error, when it was too late. For if she had attended her household affairs, and such things as belong to women, and not gone out of her way and calling to meddle in such things as are proper for men, whose minds are stronger, etc., she had kept her wits, and might have improved them usefully and honorably in the place God had sent her.

RESTORATION VIEWS

Society's view of women had not changed drastically by the Restoration and early eighteenth century, although growing urbanization paved the way for the entrance of women into areas previously closed to them. After Charles II granted licenses to theaters, women dramatists such as Aphra Behn began publishing their own plays. With the end of the patronage system for the support of authors, women freely entered the ranks of novelists, wisely realizing that writing was one of the few careers open to them. Despite these inroads, women were still scorned. Many agreed with Alexander Pope's famous judgment—"Most women have no character at all." By the nineteenth century, satire gave way to sentiment, and views of women changed.

VICTORIAN VIEWS

Women in Victorian England were considered incapable of governing themselves. A wife separated from her husband for whatever reason had no right to see her children. Married women could not own property; Charlotte Brontë was astonished to learn upon her marriage in 1854 that the copyrights of her novels and any royalties paid had passed from her hands to her husband's.

But the Victorian Age saw the start of women's emancipation. The first important step came in 1857, when the Divorce Act moved matrimonial cases from the religious to a nonreligious court. A woman could divorce her husband if he had been unfaithful and cruel, but divorce still carried a sizable social stigma. The greatest change came in 1881 with the Married Women's Property Act, granting women rights to their own possessions.

Despite these strides, many men—as well as women—still felt that women were best suited for hearth and home. A woman writing in 1837 stressed:

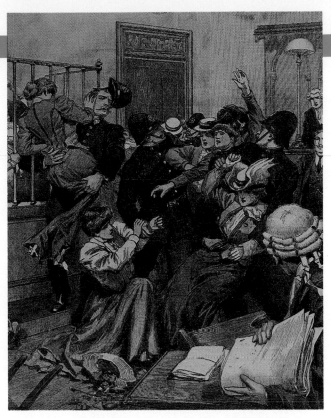

SUFFRAGETTES EXPELLED AFTER DEMONSTRATING AT WESTMINSTER
A. Beltrame

"In everything that women attempt, they should show their consciousness of dependence. There is something so unpleasant in female self-sufficiency. . . . Their sex should ever teach them to be subordinate; and they should remember that, by them, influence is to be obtained, not by assumption, but by a delicate appeal to affection or principle. Women, in this respect, are something like children: the more they show their need of support, the more engaging they are."

Curiously, these rules held only for affluent women, who were thought too delicate for anything but the mildest pastimes. Their delicate nerves had to be cared for as carefully as their bodies. Although remarkably productive, Elizabeth Barrett Browning, for example, spent six years in bed following her brother's death.

Someone had to pick up the slack— hence, a different view of working-class women. They were thought to be healthy and strong, although in truth they suffered far more from contagious diseases and complications from childbirth than their wealthy counterparts. A visitor to a cotton mill in 1897 reported on working conditions, "The place was full of women, young, all of them, some large with child, and obliged to stand twelve hours each day. . . . The heat was excessive in some of the rooms; the stink pestiferous, and in all an atmosphere of cotton flue. I nearly fainted."

By the twentieth century, the position of women and views toward them had changed dramatically, as men and women made strides toward equalizing all areas of life.

THE CHANGING ENGLISH LANGUAGE

The Victorian Age 1833–1901

LANGUAGE CONTINUES TO GROW

The swift progress in every field of intellectual activity in the Victorian period was marked by a corresponding increase in new words. Great advances in industry, science, and modes of living all added new words to the vocabulary. The explosive number of words contributed by science is especially dramatic. Because of the new field of electricity, for example, words like *dynamo, alternating current,* and *arc light* entered the language about 1870.

Although some new words are technical terms used only by specialists, the vast numbers of new scientific words contributed

to English during the Victorian age have since passed into general use. We now have names for medical conditions such as *anemia, appendicitis, bronchitis,* and *diphtheria,* to mention just a few.

Bacteriology and *immunology* were also coined during this age. Although the study of bacteria began with Dutch naturalist van Leeuwenhoek in 1683, the science of bacteriology was not firmly established until the nineteenth century. In 1860 Louis Pasteur established that bacteria come only from other similar organisms; in 1880 scientists began discovering immunity against specific bacteria. The bacteria for typhoid fever was isolated in 1880; tetanus, 1885; tuberculosis, 1890; and plague, 1894.

Thanks to Victorian scientists, we run *clinics* to help the ill, can *vaccinate* against many diseases, and use *anesthesia* to relieve pain. British chemist Sir Humphry Davy discovered the gas nitrous oxide about 1800; it was first used by an American dentist, Horace Wells, in 1844. In 1847 British physician Sir James Simpson found chloroform to be an effective anesthesia.

We have efficient remedies such as *iodine* and *aspirin,* too. Although a crude aspirin compound found in the bark of the willow tree was used by the ancient Greeks and American Indians, it is bitter and irritates the stomach. German chemist Felix Hoffman first synthesized a purer form of aspirin in 1893 in response to the urging of his father, who suffered painfully from rheumatism.

And the movies! William Talbot in England and Louis Daguerre in France perfected the first practical photographic process in 1839; by 1861 American inventor Coleman Sellers had patented the Kinematoscope, the

DISRAELI AND QUEEN VICTORIA (cartoon)
John Tenniel

"NEW CROWNS FOR OLD ONES!"
(ALADDIN ADAPTED.)

first *moving picture.* Thomas Edison patented a refined version in 1891; by 1895 coin-operated machines projecting fifty feet of film appeared in London, Berlin, and Paris. Edison's assistant produced a rudimentary talking picture in 1889, and the term *cinema* was coined.

ENGLISH BECOMES FORMAL

Despite the onslaught of new terms, the Victorians were extremely cautious about their language. Language was formal, polite—and a sure sign of social class. *Etiquette for the Ladies: Eighty Maxims on Dress, Manners and Accomplishments,* published in 1837, includes these guidelines on language:

> It is not only absurd, it is in bad taste, for people of inadequate means to ape the manners of the great. . . . Scarcely anything is so repulsive in a lady, so utterly plebeian, as speaking in a loud, harsh voice. . . . In speaking to her husband, a lady may address him by his Christian name. In speaking of him to others, it is more proper to style him Mr —. To degrade him to a mere initial, to call him *Mr. A.* or *Mr. B.*, is worse than vulgar, it is heathenish.

Not everyone was pleased by the stuffy formality English had acquired under Victoria's reign. Noted Victorian humorist Edward Lear, writing in 1844, remarked, "The uniform apathetic tone assumed by lofty society irks me *dreadfully*: nothing I long for half so much as to giggle heartily and to hop on one leg down the great gallery—but I dare not."

DIALECTS

Language was strictly conventional among the upper classes—and those who aspired to join their "betters"—but such was not the case among the common folk, as this excerpt from the Cockney Song "Wot Cher! O, Knocked 'em in the Old Kent Road" shows:

> Last week down our alley came a toff,
> Nice old geezer with a nasty cough,
> Sees my Missus, takes 'is topper off
>   In a very gentlemanly way!
>
> 'Ma'am,' says 'e, 'I'ave some news to tell,
> Your rich Uncle Tom of Camberwell
> Popped off recent, which it ain't a sell,
>   Leaving' you 'is little Donkey Shay.'
> 'Wot cher!' all the neighbors cried,
>   'Who're yer going' to meet, Bill?
>   Have yer bought the street, Bill?'
> Laugh! I thought I should 'ave died,
> Knocked 'em in the Old Kent Road!

A story is told that Tennyson stood looking at his grand home just after its completion, turned to his friend, and said, "You will live longer than I shall. That house will last five hundred years." His friend answered, "I think the English language will last longer."

By all indications, his friend was right.

YOUR WRITING PROCESS

WRITING A PERSUASIVE MEMO

> "Poetry is simply the most beautiful, impressive, and widely effective mode of saying things."
>
> **Matthew Arnold**

Imagine that your yearbook staff has asked you to choose a passage of poetry to accompany your portrait. The passage should reflect your beliefs, philosophy, hopes, or understanding of the world. Imagine, too, that the editors have asked you to explain your choice in a memo and that excerpts from your memo will be published along with the poem.

Focus

Assignment: Write a persuasive memo explaining why you have chosen a passage from a poem.

Purpose: To show how a piece of literature mirrors your own beliefs or feelings.

Audience: Editors of the school yearbook.

Prewriting

1. Skim and reflect. Look back through all the poems in this unit to recall those that had a special meaning for you. Which ones made you feel strong emotions? Which ones reminded you of an experience or idea that you have had?

2. Look at specific passages. You will be choosing a short passage. Jot down two or three possibilities on separate sheets of paper and freewrite about each.

3. Freewrite about the passages. Use questions such as these to inspire your freewriting: What experience does this passage bring to mind? What are the most important words in this passage? How would I paraphrase these lines?

4. Talk with another writer. Read the passage you have chosen to another writer. Together, discuss its possible meanings. Take notes as you talk and listen. Then, listen to the passage your partner has chosen.

Drafting

1. Write in the first-person voice. Refer to yourself as *I* and don't be afraid to express yourself *about* yourself. Stay close to your own emotions and opinions as you write. This piece of writing is as much about *you* as it is about a particular poem.

2. Be specific. Don't settle for vague generalities. "These lines reminded me of how much I like to play music" might be a good start, but you can push yourself to be more specific and personal.

Student Model

Tennyson refers to "Music that gentler on the spirit lies,/Than tired eyelids upon tired eyes." If I've missed the bus, bombed a math test or found the 7:00 News especially depressing, playing the saxophone at the end of the day will soothe my aching spirit even more than sleep.

3. Stay close to your purpose. In this kind of highly personal writing, it's easy to ramble and wander. Don't let yourself get too far afield. Stick close to your purpose: to show why this passage is relevant to you.

Revising and Editing

1. Prune your prose. Unnecessary words and phrases will weaken your argument. A good peer editor can help you spot words and phrases that pad your prose. For example, you can probably eliminate all sentences beginning with "I think."

Student Model

~~I think~~ Tennyson ^*seems to*^ ~~wants~~ us to relax ~~a little more, to~~ ^*and*^ ~~rest a little more, to~~ enjoy life a little more, ~~and~~ I agree ~~with him. I think~~ we work too hard and ~~we~~ place too much emphasis on ~~work.~~ ^*achievement.*^ ~~In my opinion,~~ ^*Perhaps*^ we should work two days a week and ~~relax~~ ^*meditate*^ for five ~~days a week.~~

2. Sentence combining. Experiment with different combinations of clauses and phrases. Use a variety of constructions: coordination, subordination, appositives, adverb clauses, participial phrases, and infinitives.

3. Proofread your memo. The editors of the yearbook will be more likely to accept your arguments if your memo is free of errors in grammar and punctuation. Also, make sure that you include a brief heading indicating whom you are addressing, your name, the subject, and the date.

Grammar Tip

Be on the lookout for forms of the verb *to be*. They often signal a weak sentence that can be combined with another. For example, note how the following sentences can be combined.
First draft: Several birds were on the wire. Some of them were small. Some of them were large.
Revision: Several birds, small and large, perched on the wire.

Options for Publishing

• Create a class yearbook that includes the poetry passages and excerpts from the memos. You might also add photographs of each student.
• Send the passage you have chosen and your memo to the editors of your school's yearbook.

Reviewing Your Writing Process

1. Did you find it difficult to explain why this passage of poetry is meaningful to you? Why or why not?
2. Which tip helped you the most as you drafted your explanation? Explain.

BIG BEN, 1905–1906
André Derain

THE TWENTIETH CENTURY

1901–Present

We are living at one of the great turning points of history. . . .
Yesterday, we split the atom. We assaulted that colossal citadel
of power, the tiny unit of the substance of the universe. And
because of this, the great dream and the great nightmare of
centuries of human thought have taken flesh and walk beside
us all, day and night.

from "The Small Personal Voice"
Doris Lessing

The twentieth century dawned bright with promise. Science and technology were helping to make life easier and the world more comprehensible. *Progress* was the word on everyone's lips. In Great Britain complacency about the future marked the years prior to 1914. The British Empire stood at the height of its power and influence. What could possibly go wrong? Plenty, as it turned out. While steady advances in communications and transportation drew the world closer together, the scourge of modern war—William Butler Yeats's "blood-dimmed tide"—wrenched it apart. The First World War (1914–1918) ended with more than 8 million people dead. The Second World War (1939–1945) killed some 45 million more. A long "cold war" followed (1945–1990) in which two superpowers, the United States, a democracy, and the Soviet Union, a totalitarian state, threatened each other (and the survival of the planet) with nuclear weapons of awesome destructiveness.

A STAR SHELL, c. 1916
Christopher Richard Wynne Nevinson
The Tate Gallery, London

Yet the twentieth century, despite its wars and dictatorships, bred a spirit of innovation. While British military and political power declined after the Second World War, Great Britain's literary and artistic life remained vibrant. Poets and novelists, as always, mirrored the times. Disillusionment, though widespread, was accompanied by vigorous inventiveness. "Make it new," exhorted American poet Ezra Pound (1885–1972), the London representative of Chicago's *Poetry* magazine, and Pound's advice became the rallying cry of writers throughout the English-speaking world.

The Edwardian Age

When Queen Victoria died in 1901, her eldest son, Edward, succeeded her on the throne. Although King Edward VII died in 1910, the years from 1901 to 1914 are commonly called the Edwardian Age.

The rigid class distinctions and moral certainties of Victorian times lingered on into the Edwardian Age. The word *Edwardian* itself is still used to signify fashionable elegance. Such elegance had its price, of course. At the beginning of the century, one Briton in every six worked as a servant.

Rapid changes in the early twentieth century doomed genteel Edwardianism. Electricity, the "silent servant," made the jobs of many servants obsolete. Telephones and automobiles revolutionized communications and travel. Women marched for the right to vote. A new Labor party demanded greater benefits for the working class. In Ireland and in Britain's colonies, nationalists agitated for home rule or independence. By the time King George V came to the British throne in 1910, the nineteenth-century way of life was fading into memory.

The First World War and Its Consequences

Long-standing tensions among the nations of Europe brought about a series of interlocking alliances and an ominous arms race. The merest spark could, and did, ignite a war. The deadly spark came on June 28, 1914, with the assassination of Austria-Hungary's Archduke Francis Ferdinand. When Germany invaded neutral Belgium, Great Britain joined with France to assist Belgium and stem the aggression.

The people of Great Britain went to war in a lighthearted and confident spirit, expecting "good sport" and an easy victory. Soon, however, they recoiled in horror from the grim, relentless slaughter occurring across the Channel in France. Clouds of poison gas, massive artillery barrages, staccato machine-gun fire, and the terrible futility of trench warfare shattered many illusions, decimated a generation, and shredded the very fabric of British society.

As if the fighting in France were not enough, wartime troubles for the British also erupted in Ireland. The Easter Rebellion of 1916 pitted Irish nationalists against their British rulers. The rebellion failed, and its leaders were executed, but many saw the fallen rebels as martyrs, which led to a great upsurge in Irish nationalism and further violence. Guerilla warfare drew harsh reprisals from British troops. In 1921 Britain capitulated, granting independence to twenty-six counties of the Irish Free State (now the Republic of Ireland) but retaining control over the six mainly Protestant counties in the province of Ulster (Northern Ireland). Terrorism and armed clashes continue to this day over the future of Northern Ireland.

In 1917, in the midst of war, revolution broke out in Russia, resulting in the overthrow of the czar and the establishment of the world's first communist state, the Soviet Union. By the time the Armistice was signed on November 11, 1918, other empires and monarchies had also been swept away, including imperial Germany and the Austro-Hungarian monarchy. An uneasy peace, its harsh terms spelled out in the Treaty of Versailles, followed the four-year conflict, a conflict that, because no one dared imagine a second more destructive global war, was naively called the Great War.

Between the Wars

Exhausted by war, the nations of Europe struggled to recover and rebuild. Economic hard

OVER THE TOP (AT MARCOING, DECEMBER 1917)
John Nash

times hampered the efforts, and the rise of dictatorships boded ill for the future. In Britain, labor unrest kept industry in turmoil. Although Britain's overseas empire remained intact, stirrings of discontent began to trouble the tranquillity of colonies like India and Burma. Angry voices increasingly questioned the right of European powers to rule distant lands.

Unrest led to cynicism and despair. People spoke of the disillusioned youth of postwar Europe as a "lost generation." Some young people masked their lack of purpose by the pursuit of pleasure—fast cars, wild jazz, giddy fads. Avant-garde young women called "flappers" bobbed their hair and wore daringly short dresses.

Not all was disenchantment or frivolity, of course. British women won the right to vote in 1918. A needed international naval treaty was signed in 1921. Still, most of the political news between the wars was disturbing. Destitute and jobless Europeans pinned their hopes on political extremes. In Russia the exhausted populace embraced communism. In Italy and Germany, people turned to fascism. Each of these nihilistic *-isms* spawned dictators: Lenin and Stalin in Russia, Mussolini in Italy, and Hitler in Germany.

The rise of Adolf Hitler loomed as the darkest cloud on the horizon. Hitler—aggressive, antisemitic, harboring grandiose plans for a "Thousand-year Reich"—remilitarized the Rhineland, annexed Austria, and demanded and was

The Twentieth Century
(A.D. 1901 to Present)

Winston Churchill

Battle Scene From World War I

Mandolin and Guitar

1900   **1920**   **1940**

BRITISH EVENTS

- Edward VII becomes king.
  - Joseph Conrad publishes *Heart of Darkness*.
    - **George Bernard Shaw** publishes *Pygmalion*.
      - **D. H. Lawrence** publishes *Sons and Lovers*.
        - Britain enters World War I.

- Irish Free State formed.
  - **T. S. Eliot** publishes *The Waste Land*.
    - **W. B. Yeats** writes "Sailing to Byzantium."
      - **W. H. Auden** publishes *Poems*.
        - First BBC television broadcast.
          - Britain enters World War II.

- Winston Churchill becomes prime minister.
  - **George Orwell** publishes *Animal Farm*.
    - Irish Free State becomes Republic of Ireland.
      - Elizabeth II becomes queen.
        - William Golding publishes *Lord of the Flies*.

WORLD EVENTS

- Germany: Thomas Mann publishes *Buddenbrooks*.
  - Asia: Russo-Japanese War begins.
    - Germany: Albert Einstein proposes theory of relativity.
      - Austria: Sigmund Freud publishes *Introduction to Psychoanalysis*.
        - Russia: Czar overthrown; Bolsheviks seize power.

- India: Mohandas Gandhi leads nonviolent protests.
  - France: **James Joyce** publishes *Ulysses*.
    - Austria: Franz Kafka publishes *The Trial*.
      - United States: Charles Lindbergh flies solo to Paris.
        - Spain: Civil War begins.
          - Europe: Hitler invades Poland; World War II begins.

- United States: United States enters World War II after Japanese bomb Pearl Harbor.
  - Japan: Atomic bombs dropped on Hiroshima and Nagasaki; World War II ends.
    - France: Albert Camus publishes *The Plague*.
      - Mideast: Palestine partitioned; nation of Israel established.
        - United States: Martin Luther King, Jr., leads black boycott of buses in Montgomery, Alabama.
          - Russia: *Sputnik I*, first spaceship, launched.

World
War II
Ends

Mohandas
Gandhi

Direct Rule Imposed
on Northern Ireland

Margaret Thatcher

1960   **1980**   **Present**

- **Doris Lessing** publishes
  The Golden Notebook.

  - Britain imposes direct
    rule on Northern Ireland.

    - North Sea Oil
      production begins.

      - John Fowles publishes
        Daniel Martin.

        - Margaret Thatcher
          becomes prime minister.

- **V. S. Naipaul** publishes
  A Bend in the River.

  - Hillsborough Agreement gives
    Republic of Ireland voice in
    governing Northern Ireland.

    - **Nadine Gordimer** wins Nobel
      Prize for Literature.

      - Great Britain participates in
        Persian Gulf War.

- United States: President John F.
  Kennedy assassinated.

  - India: Indira Gandhi becomes
    prime minister.

    - Colombia: Gabriel García
      Márquez publishes *One
      Hundred Years of Solitude.*

      - United States: *Apollo 11* lands
        on moon.

        - Iran: Ayatollah Khomeini
          overthrows shah.

- United States: Ronald Reagan
  elected president.

  - Ethiopia's warfare and drought
    result in great famine.

    - Germany: Berlin Wall torn
      down; reunification of East
      and West Germany followed.

      - Eastern Europe: Soviet
        Union dissolved.

      - Middle East: Iraq defeated
        by United Nations forces in
        Persian Gulf War.

INDUSTRIAL LANDSCAPE
(detail)
L. S. Lowry
The Tate Gallery, London

given territory from Czechoslovakia. Only when his armed forces invaded Poland on September 1, 1939, did the appeasement stop. Peace had lasted less than a generation when the nations of Europe once again went to war.

The Second World War

The Second World War was even more destructive than the First World War. Hitler's "final solution" to "the Jewish problem" brought death to 6 million Jews. The German invasion of Russia in 1941 killed soldiers and civilians by the millions. Fighting raged from Europe to North Africa, from the mountains of Burma and China to the Hawaiian Islands. Massive bombing raids turned the cities of London, Dresden, and Tokyo into infernos. Finally, in early August of 1945, American atomic bombs blasted two Japanese cities, Hiroshima and Nagasaki, into cinder and ash, bringing the war to an abrupt end. The war's death toll by then had mounted to at least four times that of the First World War—not counting the

millions who died in German concentration camps.

The darkest days for Britain came in 1940, when France had fallen and Britain alone bore the brunt of German air attacks. Inspired by Prime Minister Winston Churchill, and joined in 1941 by two powerful allies, the United States and the Soviet Union, Britain fought on to victory.

The Aftermath of War

The Second World War shook British society to its very core. Victory had come at a high price, ending Britain's long age of imperial glory and forcing Britons in the first few postwar months to subsist on meager food rations amid the ruins of bombed-out cities. To the surprise of many, British voters rejected the wartime coalition government of Winston Churchill and voted in a Labor government committed to nationalizing major industries, improving social services, and transforming the class-bound nation into a modern welfare state.

It was once said that the sun never set on the British Empire. After the Second World War, that claim lost its luster. In Asia and Africa, nationalist leaders challenged colonial rule and demanded freedom for their people—by negotiation if possible, by force if necessary.

The British response was mixed. Sometimes diplomats sought to ensure an orderly transfer of power. Sometimes troops struggled to put down rebellions. On the Indian subcontinent, Britain tried to avoid conflict between Muslims and Hindus by splitting off Pakistan (mainly Muslim) from India (mainly Hindu). Partition and independence came in 1947. Bloody fighting followed almost immediately.

In the Middle East, Britain's efforts to mediate the bitter Arab-Jewish feud over Palestine failed, and British troops withdrew. The United Nations voted to partition Palestine and make Israel an independent state. Israel's birth in 1948 touched off the first of many Arab-Israeli wars.

The dismantling of empire went no more smoothly in Africa. Ethnic, racial, and border conflicts led to bloodshed in many newly independent African nations, including Kenya, Uganda, and Zimbabwe, as well as others emerging from colonial rule.

On the Continent, British power declined sharply after the war. The wartime alliance that linked Britain and the United States with the Soviet Union quickly dissolved. In its place appeared an "iron curtain"—Churchill's term—that divided Eastern Europe (dependent or "satellite" nations dominated by the Soviet Union) from Western Europe (democratic republics, including Great Britain, influenced by the United States). A "cold war" between East and West, which would last until the dismantling of the Berlin Wall in 1989, became the metaphor for international policy.

Recovery and Contemporary Problems

By the 1960's Britons had put many of their troubles behind them, and the nation was once again a center of cultural excitement. The dazzling popularity of the Beatles made British rock music

KING'S COOKHAM RISE, 1947
Stanley Spencer
The Metropolitan Museum of Art

famous worldwide. The "mod" fashions of London's Carnaby Street exerted great influence on men's and women's clothing styles.

Of course, rock bands and boutiques could not support the nation's whole economy. Certain basic industries—textiles, steelmaking, shipbuilding—that had been vital to Britain since the Industrial Revolution were no longer competing successfully. Many of Britain's aging factories were forced to close their gates.

Economic troubles were not the only postwar shocks facing the British people. British society was changing rapidly. Among the changes were these:

- *Large-scale immigration.* Indians, Africans, West Indians, and others poured in from Britain's former colonies, and Britain was transformed into a multiracial "melting-pot" society.
- *Greater equality.* The barriers that had long divided Britons by social class began to break down. Changes in the system of education opened new opportunities to working-class people.
- *New roles for women.* Although Britain had been ruled by several remarkable queens throughout its history, women had held few other leadership positions. In 1979, however, the Conservative party gained a majority in Parliament and named Margaret Thatcher as the nation's first female prime minister. More and more women were rising to prominence in science, business, education, and the arts.

MARGARET THATCHER, 1983

Prime Minister Thatcher prescribed a stiff dose of free enterprise as the cure for Britain's troubles. For much of the 1980's, this prescription served a portion of the population, but many other Britons were excluded from the prosperity. In the late 1980's, the economy took a downturn, and Thatcher, the only three-term prime minister of the twentieth century, began losing popularity. She resigned her office in 1990, to be replaced by her own handpicked Conservative party successor, John Major. In 1992 Major defied the pre-election odds (which favored the Labor party) to retain his post as Britain's prime minister.

Many problems remain as Britain seeks to adapt to a much-changed world. Her participation in the European Economic Community—a trading bloc of some 300 million people—should be a boon but is yet to be fully defined. Violence continues in Northern Ireland (Ulster), with some glimmers of hope, such as the 1985 agreement giving the Republic of Ireland a consultative role in Ulster's affairs; but no fully satisfactory end is in sight. The economy, weakened by the decline of its industrial base, must find a way to compete on the Continent (and elsewhere) with the powerful economies of Germany and France.

Tradition has always been strong in Great Britain. The ancient rites of monarchy still play a central role in the British consciousness, inspiring awe and reverence in many citizens. As in previous times of trial, Britons seem to have turned to the past as a source of pride and comfort while simultaneously moving forward into the swirl and bustle of contemporary life.

Literature of the Twentieth Century

British writing from 1900 to 1945 does not fit neatly into categories or movements. The period can be divided into three broad stages, however. In the first stage, from the turn of the century to the start of the First World War, writers used the techniques of realism and naturalism to examine the social problems caused by rapid change. In the second stage, from the First World War to the start of the Great Depression, writers produced their most radical and experimental works—especially in the early years of postwar disillusionment. In the third stage, from the Great Depression through the Second World War, writers were caught up in the maelstrom of economic hard times, the rise of fascism, and the horrors of total war.

Cutting across these three stages was the Irish Literary Revival, spurred by an explosion of nationalism in Ireland. The Revival, which is also called the Irish Literary Renaissance or Celtic Renaissance, began in late Victorian times. It sought to revive the dying Gaelic language, to explore early Celtic history and literature, and to express the Irish spirit.

After the Second World War, British literature displayed great diversity, both in subject matter and in style. Faced with an ever-shrinking world, some writers turned outward, addressing such global concerns as the destruction of the environment and the threat of nuclear war. Other writers turned inward, exploring personal relationships and the trials of urban and suburban life. Many recent works have examined Britain's proud past or her new role as a secondary world power. With the decline of empire has come a blossoming of post-colonial literature. Writers in Ireland and in many former British colonies have taken a searching look at the legacy of empire.

Modernism and the International Artistic Community

Modernism has been perhaps the most important artistic movement of the twentieth century. In the early years of the century, more than ever before, writers, painters, composers, and architects left their own countries to pursue their careers abroad—sometimes as refugees from war, sometimes by choice. Cultural centers like London, Paris, New York, and Berlin became centers of a truly international artistic community.

Creativity in this new community of writers and artists led to controversy. How many ways were there to innovate, after all? Were all the new ways valid? Why did modern writers like D. H. Lawrence and George Orwell focus so much attention on human weakness and social problems? What did the odd shapes and figures in the paintings of Pablo Picasso and Georges Braque really mean? Could people actually live and work in the glass-and-steel structures of the Bauhaus school of architecture?

Although the specific movements that composed what we now call Modernism were often short-lived, they had a number of characteristics in common. First, each movement sought to be new and different, to experiment with new forms, to innovate, to startle, even to shock. In these lines from "L'Art 1910," the American poet Ezra Pound (1885–1972) describes a Modernist painting:

> Green arsenic smeared on an egg-white
> cloth,
> Crushed strawberries! Come, let us
> feast our eyes.

Pound's poem illustrates some of the principles of Imagism, a significant movement in the early 1900's. Imagism uses striking words and phrases—*images* that can be perceived by the senses—to communicate its message. It employs *precise language* and *everyday speech,* not the arty "poetic" diction used in some late nineteenth-century works. It uses *free verse* instead of the standard meter, rhyme, and stanza form of most

EZRA POUND, 1938–39
Wyndham Lewis

earlier poetry. Finally, it *suggests* its message rather than stating it directly.

The following features are characteristic of much Modernist literature.

- *Use of images as symbols.* In part, this approach stemmed from the influence of nineteenth-century French symbolists such as Charles Baudelaire (1821–1867) and Stéphane Mallarmé (1842–1898). These writers produced intensely personal poetry, using imaginative symbols to evoke emotions in readers' minds.

- *Presentation of human experiences in fragments.* Readers or viewers had to piece together these fragments for themselves, as in Picasso's cubist paintings. The dadaists, who came after the cubists, saw the world as a meaningless jumble. A dadaist might simply cut out words, dump them in a hat, and remove them randomly to form a "poem."

- *Use of previously taboo subjects.* Often this meant taking up subjects previously considered too trivial or unpleasant for the visual arts or literature. Sometimes it meant using the techniques of realism (focusing on the details of everyday life) or naturalism (examining social and economic problems of the working class).

- *Attention to new psychological insights.* The work of pioneering psychologists—Austria's Sigmund Freud, Switzerland's Carl Jung, and America's William James—greatly influenced writers of the twentieth century. Based on the psychological insight that the human mind leaps from thought to thought in a series of associations, the stream-of-consciousness technique was used by some writers to attempt to duplicate the inner workings of their characters' minds.

Twentieth-Century Achievements in Poetry

The stages of Modernism are clearly evident in twentieth-century poetry, sometimes even within the evolving styles of individual poets. The poetry of William Butler Yeats (1865–1939), a leading light of the Irish Literary Revival, offers an example. Yeats's early poems, with their traditional rhyme and verse patterns, blend a romantic love of nature with an interest in the myths of Celtic antiquity. His later poems adopt the direct, more colloquial diction of the Modernists and explore troubling questions of modern life.

Despite the rise of unromantic Modernism, a romantic strain remains evident in British poetry of the early twentieth century. Even the brutally realistic poems spawned by the First World War sometimes reflect romantic longings—to flee

STUDLAND BEACH (detail)
Vanessa Bell
The Tate Gallery, London

battle for the peace and beauty of the English countryside, for example. A few first-rate British poets died in the Great War, including Rupert Brooke (1887–1915) and Wilfred Owen (1893–1918). Two other notable wartime poets, Siegfried Sassoon (1886–1967) and Robert Graves (1895–1985), continued writing long after hostilities ended.

Many of the poets who survived the war went on to express the attitudes of the "lost generation" in the Modernist poetry of the 1920's. One important influence on these poets was Gerard Manley Hopkins (1844–1889), an innovative Victorian writer whose verse appeared posthumously in 1918. Hopkins's use of what he called "sprung rhythm"—the variation of unstressed syllables from foot to foot—helped to prepare the way for Modernist experiments with new verse forms. Other influences were the works of John Donne and the other metaphysical poets of the seventeenth century, which were highly philosophical and in which paradoxes were often coined.

Preeminent among the Modernist poets of the 1920's was T. S. Eliot (1888–1965), whose poem "The Love Song of J. Alfred Prufrock" is a dramatic monologue, offering the fragmentary interior thoughts of the speaker's stream of consciousness. Eliot's long poem *The Waste Land* (1922) stands as a monument to the bitterness and despair of the "lost generation."

In the 1930's and 1940's, poets showed an increasing concern with political and social issues. W. H. Auden (1907–1973), Louis MacNeice (1907–1963), Stephen Spender (born 1909), and Henry Reed (1914–1986) did not abandon subtle symbolism and imagery, but they sometimes made direct statements of social protest as well. Consider these lines from Auden's famous poem "September 1, 1939," commenting on the outbreak of the Second World War:

> I sit in one of the dives
> On Fifty-second Street
> Uncertain and afraid
> As the clever hopes expire
> Of a low dishonest decade. . . .

Still, Romanticism did not die out completely, even in the later years of the modern period. Indeed, it flared into wild brilliance in the poetry of Dylan Thomas (1914–1953), a Welsh poet who achieved great popularity in his brief lifetime.

During the 1950's and 1960's, a number of outstanding British poets associated themselves with what is called simply the Movement. These poets rejected the romantic style of poets such as Dylan Thomas, preferring instead to capture everyday experiences in the language of common people, as Thomas Hardy had done in his native English style. Philip Larkin (1922–1985), one of the finest poets in the Movement, brought to his well-crafted verse a background as a music critic. Two other poets who were active in the Movement are Donald Davie (born 1922) and Thom Gunn (born 1929). Both have taught at universities in the United States.

Well-known British poets are quite likely to give readings before live audiences. Colorful festivals keep alive the Anglo-Saxon and Celtic traditions of oral poetry recitation. Poets have even recited their verse for rush-hour commuters at London's Waterloo Station. One of the first contemporary poets to stress oral performance was Stevie Smith, born Florence Margaret Smith (1902–1971). Influenced by simple folk lyrics and early church music, Smith often recited her verse on radio and television in the singsong manner of traditional English bards.

One of the noteworthy British poets of recent years, Ted Hughes (born 1930), was named Britain's poet laureate in 1984. Hughes, once married to the tragically fated American poet Sylvia Plath, writes frequently of the beauty and violence of nature. His best-known volumes include *The Hawk in the Rain* (1957) and *Crow* (1970). Nature is a common subject, too, in the work of Irish poet Seamus Heaney (born 1939), though his poetry also explores the terror and hope of Ireland's stormy history. Another Irish poet of note is Eavan Boland (born 1944), whose subjects range from Irish legends to the concerns of women in today's Dublin.

Two remarkable poets have appeared from former British colonies in the West Indies: James Berry (born 1925) and Nobel Prize winner Derek Walcott (born 1930). Berry, a native of Jamaica, writes and recites poetry that is deeply rooted in Afro-Caribbean culture. Walcott, born on the island of St. Lucia, sometimes deals in his writing with the legacy of European imperialism in the Caribbean. Walcott is an accomplished playwright as well as a poet.

Twentieth-Century Achievements in Drama

A single major playwright dominates late Victorian, Edwardian, and early modern drama. He is Irish-born George Bernard Shaw (1856–1950). Even before the turn of the century, Shaw was delving into the problems of a changing society. His plays, many of them still popular today, blend realism with witty satire, evoking laughter while prodding theatergoers to think about social issues such as class prejudice, the role of women, education, poverty, and war.

In the depression years of the 1930's, Noel Coward (1899–1973) won attention with a series of smartly sophisticated dramas and musicals. In 1935 the poet T. S. Eliot revived verse drama with his *Murder in the Cathedral,* a play about Saint Thomas Becket, an archbishop of twelfth-century England.

The Irish Literary Revival led to the founding in 1904 of an Irish national theater, the Abbey Theatre of Dublin, which produced some of the modern period's finest plays. John Millington Synge (1871–1909) vividly captures Irish rural life in plays like *The Playboy of the Western World* (1907), whereas Sean O'Casey (1880–1964), focusing on urban themes, depicts the life of the poor in violence-torn Dublin in tragicomedies like *The Shadow of a Gunman* (1923).

Britain has continued to enjoy prominence in the world of drama throughout the second half of the twentieth century. In New York City, the theater capital of America, the most successful new plays on Broadway are often British imports, such as *Cats* and *Aspects of Love.* British television, too, has produced a string of noteworthy original dramas and many fine adaptations of classic novels and plays, particularly on *Masterpiece Theatre.*

Contemporary British dramatists often use the techniques of realism. One such playwright is Shelagh Delaney (born 1939), who specializes in slice-of-life dramas such as *A Taste of Honey*

THE ARTIST'S GARDEN AT
DURBINS, c. 1915
Roger Fry
Yale Center for British Art,
Paul Mellon Fund

(1958). Her works are acutely realistic in depicting the lives of ordinary people. In the 1950's and 1960's, a group of dramatists known as Britain's "angry young men" likewise used realistic techniques in plays attacking the injustices of Britain's class system. Typical of their work is John Osborne's *Look Back in Anger* (1956), which depicts a working-class youth rebelling against the establishment.

A second strain of contemporary British drama is represented by the so-called theater of the absurd. Plays in this style often feature dialogue and actions that seem disconnected and senseless —as if to say that life itself is a pointless series of misfortunes. Dublin-born Samuel Beckett (1906– 1989), author of *Waiting for Godot* (1952), is foremost among the playwrights who use this approach. The early plays of Harold Pinter (born 1930) also show the influence of the theater of the absurd.

A third type of British play is the historical drama, which presents people, events, and attitudes from times past. One such play is *A Man for All Seasons* (1960) by Robert Bolt (born 1924), which tells the story of Thomas More, the sixteenth-century scholar and Catholic martyr. In powerful, almost Shakespearean language, the play captures the grandeur of that era. Yet Bolt creates a narrator called the Common Man, through whose eyes More's life unfolds—a strikingly modern touch. Tom Stoppard (born 1937) uses a similar device in *Rosencrantz and Guildenstern Are Dead* (1964).

Twentieth-Century Achievements in Prose

Twentieth-century fiction does not fit into neat, clear categories. It swings between Romanticism and realism, between lighthearted fantasy and cynical disillusionment. Sometimes it probes the human mind, dwelling on the thoughts and yearnings of isolated individuals. Sometimes it sweeps across the vastness of history, pondering both human achievement and human anguish.

The Edwardian Age produced a number of brilliant writers of realist and naturalist fiction. Joseph Conrad, one of the pioneers of psychological realism, examines the individual's struggle with nature in tales of the sea such as *Lord Jim* (1900) and portrays colonialism in the brooding short novel *Heart of Darkness* (1902). The Polishborn Conrad, who settled in London after learning English as a sailor on a British merchant ship, wrote two other acclaimed short novels, *Youth* (1902) and *Typhoon* (1903), and helped to popularize the short novel, or novella, in English.

The class system and the plight of the industrial worker emerged as key themes in the novels and short stories of D. H. Lawrence (1885–1930). Lawrence wrote naturalistically, but he had a Romantic abhorrence for the spread of factories across the rural landscape. His savage hatred of conventional British manners and morals gives bite to novels like *Sons and Lovers* (1913) and the notorious *Lady Chatterley's Lover* (1928).

Perhaps the greatest pioneer of Modernist fiction was the Irish writer James Joyce (1882–1941). Joyce revolutionized the form and structure of both the short story and the novel. In *Dubliners* (1914), he presents a group of realistic short tales about working-class life in Dublin, trying to have each story achieve what he called an epiphany—a flash of awareness in which all the story elements come together to illuminate the story's meaning. Joyce labored for years on his brilliant novel *Ulysses* (1922), using a great variety of techniques—including stream of consciousness—and symbols to pair an ancient Greek myth with a tale of twentieth-century Dublin.

Another novelist famous for her stream-of-consciousness writing is Virginia Woolf (1882–1941). A distinguished member of a group of Modernists known as the Bloomsbury set, named for the London neighborhood in which they congregated, Woolf is best known for her novels *Mrs. Dalloway* (1925) and *To the Lighthouse* (1927). E. M. Forster, who knew several in the Bloomsbury set, details the tragic clash of British and Indian cultures in his most celebrated novel, *A Passage to India* (1924).

One writer of this period who is famous chiefly for her short stories is New Zealand-born Katherine Mansfield (1888–1923). Mansfield's most notable collection, *The Garden Party and Other Stories,* was published the year before her death.

As political and social issues gained increasing attention in the 1930's and 1940's, a new group of novelists emerged. Aldous Huxley (1894–1963) put biting satire into his futuristic novel *Brave New World* (1932), showing the misuse of science in despotic states. George Orwell (1903–1950) ridicules communism in his modern fable *Animal Farm* (1945) and paints a frightening picture of a totalitarian future in the novel *1984* (1949). Other noteworthy British fiction writers of the era include Evelyn Waugh (1903–1966), Nancy Mitford (1904–1973), C. P. Snow (1905–1980), and the Irish writer Elizabeth Bowen (1899–1973).

One novelist whose career began before the Second World War and continued into contemporary times is Graham Greene (1904–1991). Greene divided his time between serious novels, such as *The Power and the Glory* (1940), and what he called "entertainments," like *Our Man in Havana* (1958). Another popular writer was P. G. Wodehouse (1881–1975), whose series of humorous novels about the dimwitted Bertie Wooster and his clever butler, Jeeves, commenced in 1924 and continued to appear until 1971.

Among more recent British novelists are William Golding (born 1911), Anthony Burgess (born 1917), Kingsley Amis (born 1922), John Fowles (born 1926), and Alan Sillitoe (born 1928). Golding's *Lord of the Flies* (1954) tells of a group of British schoolboys who revert to savage behavior after being stranded on a tropical island. Golding, who also wrote *The Spire,* won the Nobel Prize for Literature in 1983. Burgess, like Orwell before him, imagines a brutal future in his novel *A Clockwork Orange* (1962). Amis displays a comic touch in such novels as *Lucky Jim* (1954) and *Stanley and the Women* (1984). Fowles often experiments with form, as in *The Collector* (1963), which tells the same story from two different characters' points of view. Sillitoe earned acclaim for his first novel, *Saturday Night and Sunday Morning* (1958), but is perhaps best known as a short-story writer.

In literature as in other aspects of British life, women have been highly visible and productive in the latter half of the twentieth century. Irish-born Iris Murdoch (born 1919) is known for her intricate novels exploring human relationships, among them *The Message to the Planet* (1990). Doris Lessing (born 1919) grew up in Rhodesia (now Zimbabwe) and gained fame for a series of novels set in Africa, including the autobiographical

Martha Quest (1952) and *The Four-Gated City* (1969). Another important woman writer is Nadine Gordimer (born 1923), who writes novels and short stories that examine the moral and political dilemmas of racially divided South Africa, where she lives. Gordimer, whose novels include *The Soft Voice of the Serpent* (1952) and *A Guest of Honor* (1970), won the Nobel Prize for Literature in 1991. Still another woman writer of note is Margaret Drabble (born 1939). Her well-received novels include *A Summer Bird-Cage* (1963) and *The Realms of Gold* (1975).

Many writers of nonfiction have also gained recognition in the twentieth century. Bertrand Russell (1872–1970), a philosopher, mathematician, and political activist, wrote *The Principles of Mathematics,* one of his major works, in 1903. Lawrence Durrell (1912–1990), a novelist and poet, has won consistent praise for his travel writing and humorous sketches. Antonia Fraser (born 1932), wife of the playwright Harold Pinter, is a widely read popular historian. Finally, many British poets, novelists, and short-story writers have earned enhanced reputations as able literary critics.

In recent years a number of talented writers from what used to be the far-flung British Empire have added to the richness of English literature.

Among these are Frank Sargeson (1903–1982) of New Zealand; Patrick White (1912–1990), the Nobel Prize winner from Australia; Wilson Harris (born 1921) of Guyana; Chinua Achebe (born 1930) and Nobel Prize winner Wole Soyinka (born 1934), both of Nigeria; and Mordecai Richler (born 1931) of Canada. A writer from the island of Trinidad, V. S. Naipaul (born 1932), has achieved success with both fiction and nonfiction. His award-winning novel *In a Free State* (1971) is one of his finest works.

How do these ex-colonials feel about the nation that for so long controlled the fate of their homelands? Not surprisingly, their views differ. Most deplore the repression and economic exploitation of colonialism. Yet some of these writers would surely agree with Derek Walcott's observation: "My generation of West Indian writers has felt such a powerful elation at having the privilege of writing about places and people for the first time and, simultaneously, having behind them the tradition of knowing how well it can be done—by a Defoe, a Dickens, a Richardson."

These ex-colonial writers are busy making classics for a new age. Borrowing a famous line from Shakespeare's *The Tempest,* we can say that they are transforming English literature "into something rich and strange."

BRITISH VOICES

Quotations by Prominent Figures of the Period

And what rough beast, its hour come round at last,
Slouches towards Bethlehem to be born?
William Butler Yeats, "The Second Coming"

Nothing could have been more obvious to the peoples of the
early twentieth century than the rapidity with which war
was becoming impossible. And as certainly they did not see
it. They did not see it until the atomic bombs burst in their
fumbling hands.
H. G. Wells, *The World Set Free*

I have nothing to offer but blood, toil, tears, and sweat. . . .
Winston Churchill in his first speech as Prime Minister

Ireland is the old sow that eats her farrow.
James Joyce, *A Portrait of the Artist as a Young Man*

Women have served all these centuries as looking glasses
possessing the magic and delicious power of reflecting the
figure of man at twice its natural size.
Virginia Woolf, *A Room of One's Own*

Why does my Muse only speak when she is unhappy?
She does not, I only listen when I am unhappy.
Stevie (Florence Margaret) Smith, "My Muse"

Columbus' huckstering breath
Blew inland through North America

Killing the last of the mammoths.
Ted Hughes, "Fourth of July," from *Lupercal*

Life should be a humane
undertaking. I know. I
undertook it. Yet have found
that in every move
I prevent someone
from stepping where I step.
Thom Gunn, "Positives"

Eternity is a terrible thought. I mean, where's it going
to end?
Tom Stoppard, *Rosencrantz and Guildenstern Are Dead*

READING CRITICALLY

The Literature of 1901 to the Present

When you read literature, it is important to place it in its historical context. Doing so will help you to see how it was shaped by the events and attitudes of the time.

HISTORICAL CONTEXT The twentieth century has been one of the most turbulent and traumatic times in British history. The country has suffered through two tragic world wars and experienced a severe economic depression. During the Modern Age, these startling events caused the English people to lose much of the optimism and self-assurance that had characterized the Victorian Age. Instead, they felt a sense of uncertainty, disjointedness, and disillusionment. In the aftermath of World War II, the British people struggled to rebuild their nation. During this period, many British colonies were granted their independence, and the British Empire was gradually transformed into the British Commonwealth. Despite the resulting decline in economic and political status, the government has sought in recent years to ensure adequate health care, housing, education, and pensions for the entire British population.

LITERARY MOVEMENTS In the early years of the century, major figures in the new literary movement called Modernism rejected previous literary traditions and sought to capture the essence of modern life in both the form and content of their work. They delved into the minds of their characters, and they also reflected the disjointedness of modern life by shunning the use of exposition, resolution, transition, and explanation found in traditional works. Recent British literature is extremely diverse in content. Contemporary writers focus on people's inner thoughts and feelings, but they also explore the changes and problems evident in post-colonial British society.

WRITERS' TECHNIQUES During the Modern Age, writers experimented with free verse, shifting points of view, and the stream-of-consciousness technique. At the same time, they often relied upon such traditional devices as symbols and allusions to convey the themes of their works. Contemporary British writers still use some of the unconventional forms that came into use during the Modern Age, but they are comfortable drawing upon the traditions of many eras. In addition, writers from former British colonies have drawn upon the literary legacy of their various cultures to inform their current work.

Prose

GARDENS IN THE POUND, COOKHAM, 1936
Stanley Spencer
Leeds City Art Galleries

JOSEPH CONRAD

1857–1924

To become one of the most distinguished novelists of one's age would be accomplishment enough for most writers. To do so in a language other than one's native tongue, as Joseph Conrad did, is an achievement almost without parallel.

Born in Poland to a scholarly father, Josef Teodor Konrad Nalecz Korzeniowski was orphaned at the age of eleven. He fled his Russian-occupied homeland to France and then England when he was sixteen, and spent the next dozen years as an apprentice seaman. The voyages that he made to exotic corners of the globe—Asia, Africa, and South America—were later put to use as the vivid settings for much of his fiction. In 1886 he became a ship's captain and an English citizen.

It was not until he was thirty-eight that Conrad published his first novel, *Almayer's Folly*. That year, 1895, also marked his marriage and his retirement from the sea. In the next few years, Conrad so far overcame the difficulties of writing in an adopted tongue (English was actually his third language; Polish and Russian were his first and second) that he became one of the masters of Modernist prose. In 1897 he published his first important novel, *The Nigger of the Narcissus,* and within the next seven years produced three masterpieces: *Lord Jim* (1900); *Youth,* a collection of shorter pieces that includes his well-known "Heart of Darkness" (1902); and the ambitious *Nostromo* (1904).

After a brief collaboration with novelist Ford Maddox Ford, Conrad published two novels about revolutionaries, *The Secret Agent* (1907) and *Under Western Eyes* (1911). Remaining active to the end of his life, he was at work on *Suspense,* an ambitious historical novel in the classic tradition, when he died in 1924.

Conrad often used the tradition of the sea yarn to create what, on the surface, were thrilling adventure tales. His serious thematic concerns, however, are readily apparent. Almost invariably the notion of "voyage" in a Conrad novel translates to a voyage of self-discovery. The menacing jungles and vast oceans that confront his characters become metaphors for the hidden depths of the self; the requirement for loyalty among crew members of a ship, often unmet, symbolizes the frailty of human relationships in a world filled with deception, corruption, and betrayal.

If Conrad's themes were Modernist, his technical treatments of those themes were even more so. Often, and memorably, as in "The Lagoon," he shifts the point of view from which the story is told.

GUIDE FOR INTERPRETING

The Lagoon

Writers' Techniques

A Story Within a Story. The device of having a fictional character tell a story, thereby creating a story within a story, is not new. Nearly two thousand years ago, the Roman writer Apuleius (ap yōō lē′ əs) composed a novel in which various characters tell stories. The Spanish author Cervantes (sʉr vän′ tās) also used fictional narrators in *Don Quixote.* Joseph Conrad used the story within a story to excellent advantage in works like *Lord Jim,* "Heart of Darkness," and "The Lagoon." For Conrad, this device aided in evoking the many-sidedness of experience. By using one or more fictional narrators, he could suggest various perspectives on the same theme or plot. In "The Lagoon," for instance, the narrative describing the approach to Arsat's isolated house gives added meaning to the story Arsat tells. Similarly, the reaction of "the white man" to that story prompts us to think more deeply about it.

Commentary

"The Lagoon" is one of Conrad's most admired tales. Although it was only the fourth story he published, it nonetheless shows many elements that would become characteristic of his later work: exotic setting, intriguing ending, and unique narrative style. "The Lagoon" has the distinction of being the first tale in which Conrad borrowed from himself. When his editors requested a piece more characteristic of his exotic style, Conrad tried to reproduce the tangled landscape of his Malayan novels, complete with "forests rivers—stars—wind sunrise." Perhaps part of the story's enduring appeal stems from its eerie atmosphere, for "The Lagoon" is more of a mood piece than any of his other tales. Conrad was fond of the story himself: In 1897, thanking an acquaintance for a note of praise, he called it his favorite short story, written to please himself. Although the context of the letter and other information from his life suggest that his remark may have been voiced more out of politeness than genuine conviction, it nonetheless suggests that the mysterious tale exerted a hold even over its author.

Focus

Try to recall, or invent, an occasion when a friend took you into his or her confidence and shared a problem with you. In a paragraph, describe the emotions you experienced as you listened to your friend. Note in particular whether you were sympathetic to your friend's dilemma, whether you were able to offer any useful advice, and whether there were implications of the problem that applied to yourself and others.

The Lagoon

Joseph Conrad

The white man, leaning with both arms over the roof of the little house in the stern of the boat, said to the steersman—

"We will pass the night in Arsat's clearing. It is late."

The Malay[1] only grunted, and went on looking fixedly at the river. The white man rested his chin on his crossed arms and gazed at the wake of the boat. At the end of the straight avenue of forests cut by the intense glitter of the river, the sun appeared unclouded and dazzling, poised low over the water that shone smoothly like a band of metal. The forests, somber and dull, stood motionless and silent on each side of the broad stream. At the foot of big, towering trees, trunkless nipa palms rose from the mud of the bank, in bunches of leaves enormous and heavy, that hung unstirring over the brown swirl of eddies. In the stillness of the air every tree, every leaf, every bough, every tendril of creeper and every petal of minute blossoms seemed to have been bewitched into an immobility perfect and final. Nothing moved on the river but the eight paddles that rose flashing regularly, dipped together with a single splash; while the steersman swept right and left with a periodic and sudden flourish of his blade describing a glinting semicircle above his head. The churned-up water frothed alongside with a confused murmur. And the

white man's canoe, advancing up stream in the short-lived disturbance of its own making, seemed to enter the portals of a land from which the very memory of motion had forever departed.

The white man, turning his back upon the setting sun, looked along the empty and broad expanse of the sea-reach. For the last three miles of its course the wandering, hesitating river, as if enticed irresistibly by the freedom of an open horizon, flows straight into the sea, flows straight to the east—to the east that harbors both light and darkness. Astern of the boat the repeated call of some bird, a cry discordant and feeble, skipped along over the smooth water and lost itself, before it could reach the other shore, in the breathless silence of the world.

The steersman dug his paddle into the stream, and held hard with stiffened arms, his body thrown forward. The water gurgled aloud; and suddenly the long straight reach seemed to pivot on its center, the forests swung in a semicircle, and the slanting beams of sunset touched the broadside of the canoe with a fiery glow, throwing the slender and distorted shadows of its crew upon the streaked glitter of the river. The white man turned to look ahead. The course of the boat had been altered at right-angles to the stream, and the carved dragonhead of its prow was pointing now at a gap in the fringing bushes of the bank. It glided through, brushing the overhanging twigs, and disappeared from the river like some

---

1. Malay (mã′ lã): A native of the Malay peninsula in Southeast Asia.

slim and amphibious creature leaving the water for its lair in the forests.

The narrow creek was like a ditch: tortuous, fabulously deep; filled with gloom under the thin strip of pure and shining blue of the heaven. Immense trees soared up, invisible behind the festooned draperies of creepers. Here and there, near the glistening blackness of the water, a twisted root of some tall tree showed amongst the tracery of small ferns, black and dull, writhing and motionless, like an arrested snake. The short words of the paddlers reverberated loudly between the thick and somber walls of vegetation. Darkness oozed out from between the trees, through the tangled maze of the creepers, from behind the great fantastic and unstirring leaves; the darkness, mysterious and invincible; the darkness scented and poisonous of impenetrable forests.

The men poled in the shoaling[2] water. The creek broadened, opening out into a wide sweep of a stagnant lagoon. The forests receded from the marshy bank, leaving a level strip of bright green, reedy grass to frame the reflected blueness of the sky. A fleecy pink cloud drifted high above, trailing the delicate coloring of its image under the floating leaves and the silvery blossoms of the lotus. A little house, perched on high piles, appeared black in the distance. Near it, two tall nibong palms, that seemed to have come out of the forests in the background, leaned slightly over the ragged roof, with a suggestion of sad tenderness and care in the droop of their leafy and soaring heads.

---

2. shoaling: Shallow.

The steersman, pointing with his paddle, said, "Arsat is there. I see his canoe fast between the piles."

The polers ran along the sides of the boat glancing over their shoulders at the end of the day's journey. They would have preferred to spend the night somewhere else than on this lagoon of weird aspect and ghostly reputation. Moreover, they disliked Arsat, first as a stranger, and also because he who repairs a ruined house, and dwells in it, proclaims that he is not afraid to live amongst the spirits that haunt the places abandoned by mankind. Such a man can disturb the course of fate by glances or words; while his familiar ghosts are not easy to propitiate by casual wayfarers upon whom they long to wreak the malice of their human master. White men care not for such things, being unbelievers and in league with the Father of Evil, who leads them unharmed through the invisible dangers of this world. To the warnings of the righteous they oppose an offensive pretense of disbelief. What is there to be done?

So they thought, throwing their weight on the end of their long poles. The big canoe glided on swiftly, noiselessly, and smoothly, toward Arsat's clearing, till, in a great rattling of poles thrown down, and the loud murmurs of "Allah[3] be praised!" it came with a gentle knock against the crooked piles below the house.

The boatmen with uplifted faces shouted discordantly, "Arsat! O Arsat!" Nobody came. The white man began to climb the rude ladder giving access to the bamboo platform before the house. The juragan[4] of the boat said sulkily, "We will cook in the sampan,[5] and sleep on the water."

"Pass my blankets and the basket," said the white man curtly.

He knelt on the edge of the platform to receive the bundle. Then the boat shoved off, and the white man, standing up, confronted Arsat, who had come out through the low door of his hut. He was a man young, powerful, with a broad chest and muscular arms. He had nothing on but his sarong.[6] His head was bare. His big, soft eyes stared eagerly at the white man, but his voice and demeanor were composed as he asked, without any words of greeting—

"Have you medicine, Tuan?"[7]

"No," said the visitor in a startled tone. "No. Why? Is there sickness in the house?"

"Enter and see," replied Arsat, in the same calm manner, and turning short round, passed again through the small doorway. The white man, dropping his bundles, followed.

In the dim light of the dwelling he made out on a couch of bamboos a woman stretched on her back under a broad sheet of red cotton cloth. She lay still, as if dead; but her big eyes, wide open, glittered in the gloom, staring upward at the slender rafters, motionless and unseeing. She was in a high fever, and evidently unconscious. Her cheeks were sunk slightly, her lips were partly open, and on the young face there was the ominous and fixed expression—the absorbed, contemplating expression of the unconscious who are going to die. The two men stood looking down at her in silence.

"Has she been long ill?" asked the traveler.

"I have not slept for five nights," answered the Malay, in a deliberate tone. "At first she heard voices calling her from the water and struggled against me who held her. But since the sun of today rose she hears nothing—she hears not me. She sees nothing. She sees not me—me!"

He remained silent for a minute, then asked softly—

---

3. Allah (al′ ə): The Muslim name for God.
4. juragan (jōō rä′ gän): Captain or master.
5. sampan: A small flat-bottomed boat with a cabin formed by mats.

---

6. sarong: A long, brightly colored strip of cloth worn like a skirt.
7. Tuan (twan): Malayan for "sir."

"Tuan, will she die?"

"I fear so," said the white man sorrowfully. He had known Arsat years ago, in a far country in times of trouble and danger, when no friendship is to be despised. And since his Malay friend had come unexpectedly to dwell in the hut on the lagoon with a strange woman, he had slept many times there, in his journeys up and down the river. He liked the man who knew how to keep faith in council and how to fight without fear by the side of his white friend. He liked him—not so much perhaps as a man likes his favorite dog—but still he liked him well enough to help and ask no questions, to think sometimes vaguely and hazily in the midst of his own pursuits, about the lonely man and the long-haired woman with audacious face and triumphant eyes, who lived together hidden by the forests—alone and feared.

The white man came out of the hut in time to see the enormous conflagration of sunset put out by the swift and stealthy shadows that, rising like a black and impalpable vapor above the treetops, spread over the heaven, extinguishing the crimson glow of floating clouds and the red brilliance of departing daylight. In a few moments all the stars came out above the intense blackness of the earth, and the great lagoon gleaming suddenly with reflected lights resembled an oval patch of night sky flung down into the hopeless and abysmal night of the wilderness. The white man had some supper out of the basket, then collecting a few sticks that lay about the platform, made up a small fire, not for warmth, but for the sake of the smoke, which would keep off the mosquitos. He wrapped himself in his blankets and sat with his back against the reed wall of the house, smoking thoughtfully.

Arsat came through the doorway with noiseless steps and squatted down by the fire. The white man moved his outstretched legs a little.

"She breathes," said Arsat in a low voice, anticipating the expected question.
"She breathes and burns as if with a great fire. She speaks not; she hears not—and burns!"

He paused for a moment, then asked in a quiet, incurious tone—

"Tuan . . . will she die?"

The white man moved his shoulders uneasily, and muttered in a hesitating manner—

"If such is her fate."

"No, Tuan," said Arsat calmly. "If such is my fate. I hear, I see, I wait. I remember . . . Tuan, do you remember the old days? Do you remember my brother?"

"Yes," said the white man. The Malay rose suddenly and went in. The other, sitting still outside, could hear the voice in the hut. Arsat said: "Hear me! Speak!" His words were succeeded by a complete silence. "O Diamelen!" he cried suddenly. After that cry there was a deep sigh. Arsat came out and sank down again in his old place.

They sat in silence before the fire. There was no sound within the house, there was no sound near them; but far away on the lagoon they could hear the voices of the boatmen ringing fitful and distinct on the calm water. The fire in the bows of the sampan shone faintly in the distance with a hazy red glow. Then it died out. The voices ceased. The land and the water slept invisible, unstirring and mute. It was as though there had been nothing left in the world but the glitter of stars streaming, ceaseless and vain, through the black stillness of the night.

The white man gazed straight before him into the darkness with wide-open eyes. The fear and fascination, the inspiration and the wonder of death—of death near, unavoidable, and unseen, soothed the unrest of his race and stirred the most indistinct, the most intimate of his thoughts. The ever-ready suspicion of evil, the gnawing suspicion that lurks in our hearts, flowed out into the stillness round him—into the stillness profound and dumb, and made it appear untrustworthy and infamous, like the placid and impenetrable mask of an unjustifiable violence. In that fleeting and powerful disturbance of his being the earth enfolded in the starlight peace became a shadowy country of inhuman strife, a battlefield of phantoms terrible and charming, august or ignoble, struggling ardently for the possession of our helpless hearts. An unquiet and mysterious country of inextinguishable desires and fears.

A plaintive murmur rose in the night; a murmur saddening and startling, as if the great solitudes of surrounding woods had tried to whisper into his ear the wisdom of their immense and lofty indifference. Sounds hesitating and vague floated in the air round him, shaped themselves slowly into words; and at last flowed on gently in a murmuring stream of soft and monotonous sentences. He stirred like a man waking up and changed his position slightly. Arsat, motionless and shadowy, sitting with bowed head under the stars, was speaking in a low and dreamy tone—

". . . for where can we lay down the heaviness of our trouble but in a friend's heart? A man must speak of war and of love. You, Tuan, know what war is, and you have seen me in time of danger seek death as other men seek life! A writing may be lost; a lie may be written; but what the eye has seen is truth and remains in the mind!"

"I remember," said the white man quietly. Arsat went on with mournful composure—

"Therefore I shall speak to you of love. Speak in the night. Speak before both night and love are gone—and the eye of day looks upon my sorrow and my shame; upon my blackened face; upon my burnt-up heart."

A sigh, short and faint, marked an almost imperceptible pause, and then his words flowed on, without a stir, without a gesture.

"After the time of trouble and war was over and you went away from my country in the pursuit of your desires, which we, men of the islands, cannot understand, I and my brother became again, as we had been before, the sword bearers of the Ruler. You know we were men of family, belonging to a ruling race, and more fit than any to carry on our right shoulder the emblem of power. And in the time of prosperity Si Dendring showed us favor, as we, in time of sorrow, had showed to him the faithfulness of our courage. It was a time of peace. A time of deer hunts and cock fights; of idle talks and foolish squabbles between men whose bellies are full and weapons are rusty. But the sower watched the young rice shoots grow up without fear, and the traders came and went, departed lean and returned fat into the river of peace. They brought news too. Brought lies and truth mixed together, so that no man knew when to rejoice and when to be sorry. We heard from them about you also. They had seen you here and had seen you there. And I was glad to hear, for I remembered the stirring times, and I always remembered you, Tuan, till the time came when my eyes could see nothing in the past, because they had looked upon the one who is dying there—in the house."

He stopped to exclaim in an intense whisper, "O Mara bahia! O Calamity!" then went on speaking a little louder.

"There's no worse enemy and no better friend than a brother, Tuan, for one brother knows another, and in perfect knowledge is strength for good or evil. I loved my brother. I went to him and told him that I could see nothing but one face, hear nothing but one voice. He told me: 'Open your heart so that she can see what is in it—and wait. Patience is wisdom. Inchi Midah may die or our Ruler may throw off his fear of a woman!' . . . I waited! . . . You remember the lady with the veiled face, Tuan, and the fear of our Ruler before her cunning and temper. And if she wanted her servant, what could I do? But I fed the hunger of my heart on short glances and stealthy words. I loitered on the path to the bath houses in the daytime, and when the sun had fallen behind the forest I crept along the jasmine hedges of the women's courtyard. Unseeing, we spoke to one another through the scent of flowers, through the veil of leaves, through the blades of long grass that stood still before our lips; so great was our prudence, so faint was the murmur of our great longing. The time passed swiftly . . . and there were whispers amongst women—and our enemies watched—my brother was gloomy, and I began to think of killing and of a fierce death. . . . We are of a people who take what they want—like you whites. There is a time when a man should forget loyalty and respect. Might and authority are given to rulers, but to all men is given love and strength and courage. My brother said, 'You shall take her from their midst. We are two who are like one.' And I answered, 'Let it be soon, for I find no warmth in sunlight that does not shine upon her.' Our time came when the Ruler and all the great people went to the mouth of the river to fish by torchlight. There were hundreds of boats, and on the white sand, between the water and the forests, dwellings of leaves were built for the households of the Rajahs.[8] The smoke of cooking fires was like a blue mist of the evening, and many voices rang in it joyfully. While they were making the boats ready to beat up the fish, my brother came to me and said, 'Tonight!' I looked to my weapons, and when the time came our canoe took its place in the circle of boats carrying the torches. The lights blazed on the water, but behind the boats there was darkness. When the shouting began and the excitement made them like mad we dropped out. The water swallowed our fire, and we floated back to the shore that was dark with only here and there the glimmer of embers. We could hear the talk of slave girls amongst the sheds. Then we found a place deserted and silent. We waited there. She came. She came running along the shore, rapid and leaving no trace, like a leaf driven by the wind into the sea. My brother said gloomily, 'Go and take

_____
8. Rajahs (ra′ jəz): Malayan chiefs.

her; carry her into our boat.' I lifted her in my arms. She panted. Her heart was beating against my breast. I said, 'I take you from those people. You came to the cry of my heart, but my arms take you into my boat against the will of the great!' 'It is right,' said my brother. 'We are men who take what we want and can hold it against many. We should have taken her in daylight.' I said, 'Let us be off'; for since she was in my boat I began to think of our Ruler's many men. 'Yes. Let us be off,' said my brother. 'We are cast out and this boat is our country now —and the sea is our refuge.' He lingered with his foot on the shore, and I entreated him to hasten, for I remembered the strokes of her heart against my breast and thought that two men cannot withstand a hundred. We left, paddling downstream close to the bank; and as we passed by the creek where they were fishing, the great shouting had ceased, but the murmur of voices was loud like the humming of insects flying at noonday. The boats floated, clustered together, in the red light of torches, under a black roof of smoke; and men talked of their sport. Men that boasted, and praised, and jeered—men that would have been our friends in the morning, but on that night were already our enemies. We paddled swiftly past. We had no more friends in the country of our birth. She sat in the middle of the canoe with covered face; silent as she is now; unseeing as she is now—and I had no regret at what I was leaving because I could hear her breathing close to me—as I can hear her now.''

He paused, listened with his ear turned to the doorway, then shook his head and went on.

''My brother wanted to shout the cry of challenge—one cry only—to let the people know we were freeborn robbers who trusted our arms and the great sea. And again I begged him in the name of our love to be silent. Could I not hear her breathing close to me? I knew the pursuit would come quick enough. My brother loved me. He dipped his paddle without a splash. He only said,

'There is half a man in you now—the other half is in that woman. I can wait. When you are a whole man again, you will come back with me here to shout defiance. We are sons of the same mother.' I made no answer. All my strength and all my spirit were in my hands that held the paddle—for I longed to be with her in a safe place beyond the reach of men's anger and of women's spite. My love was so great, that I thought it could guide me to a country where death was unknown, if I could only escape from Inchi Midah's fury and from our Ruler's sword. We paddled with haste, breathing through our teeth. The blades bit deep into the smooth water. We passed out of the river; we flew in clear channels amongst the shallows. We skirted the black coast; we skirted the sand beaches where the sea speaks in whispers to the land; and the gleam of white sand flashed back past our boat, so swiftly she ran upon the water. We spoke not. Only once I said, 'Sleep, Diamelen, for soon you may want all your strength.' I heard the sweetness of her voice, but I never turned my head. The sun rose and still we went on. Water fell from my face like rain from a cloud. We flew in the light and heat. I never looked back, but I knew that my brother's eyes, behind me, were looking steadily ahead, for the boat went as straight as a bushman's dart, when it leaves the end of the sumpitan.[9] There was no better paddler, no better steersman than my brother. Many times, together, we had won races in that canoe. But we never had put out our strength as we did then—then, when for the last time we paddled together! There was no braver or stronger man in our country than my brother. I could not spare the strength to turn my head and look at him, but every moment I heard the hiss of his breath getting louder behind me. Still he did not speak. The sun was high. The heat clung to my back like a flame of fire. My ribs

were ready to burst, but I could no longer get enough air into my chest. And then I felt I must cry out with my last breath. 'Let us rest!' . . . 'Good!' he answered; and his voice was firm. He was strong. He was brave. He knew not fear and no fatigue . . . My brother!''

A murmur powerful and gentle, a murmur vast and faint; the murmur of trembling leaves, of stirring boughs, ran through the tangled depths of the forests, ran over the starry smoothness of the lagoon, and the water between the piles lapped the slimy timber once with a sudden splash. A breath of warm air touched the two men's faces and passed on with a mournful sound—a breath loud and short like an uneasy sigh of the dreaming earth.

Arsat went on in an even, low voice:

''We ran our canoe on the white beach of a little bay close to a long tongue of land that seemed to bar our road; a long wooded cape going far into the sea. My brother knew that place. Beyond the cape a river has its entrance, and through the jungle of that land there is a narrow path. We made a fire and cooked rice. Then we lay down to sleep on the soft sand in the shade of our canoe, while she watched. No sooner had I closed my eyes than I heard her cry of alarm. We leaped up. The sun was halfway down the sky already, and coming in sight in the opening of the bay we saw a prau[10] manned by many paddlers. We knew it at once; it was one of our Rajah's praus. They were watching the shore, and saw us. They beat the gong, and turned the head of the prau into the bay. I felt my heart become weak within my breast. Diamelen sat on the sand and covered her face. There was no escape by sea. My brother laughed. He had the gun you had given him, Tuan, before you went away, but there was only a handful of powder. He spoke to me quickly: 'Run with her along the path. I shall keep them back, for they have

---

9. sumpitan (sump′ ə tăn): A Malayan blowgun which discharges poisonous darts.

10. prau (prou) *n.*: A swift Malayan boat with a large sail.

no firearms, and landing in the face of a man with a gun is certain death for some. Run with her. On the other side of that wood there is a fisherman's house—and a canoe. When I have fired all the shots I will follow. I am a great runner, and before they can come up we shall be gone. I will hold out as long as I can, for she is but a woman—that can neither run nor fight, but she has your heart in her weak hands.' He dropped behind the canoe. The prau was coming. She and I ran, and as we rushed along the path I heard shots. My brother fired—once—twice—and the booming of the gong ceased. There was silence behind us. That neck of land is narrow. Before I heard my brother fire the third shot I saw the shelving shore, and I saw the water again: the mouth of a broad river. We crossed a grassy glade. We ran down to the water. I saw a low hut above the black mud, and a small canoe hauled up. I heard another shot behind me. I thought, 'That is his last charge.' We rushed down to the canoe; a man came running from the hut, but I leaped on him, and we rolled together in the mud. Then I got up, and he lay still at my feet. I don't know whether I had killed him or not. I and Diamelen pushed the canoe afloat. I heard yells behind me, and I saw my brother run across the glade. Many men were bounding after him. I took her in my arms and threw her into the boat, then leaped in myself. When I looked back I saw that my brother had fallen. He fell and was up again, but the men were closing round him. He shouted, 'I am coming!' The men were close to him. I looked. Many men. Then I looked at her. Tuan, I pushed the canoe! I pushed it into deep water. She was kneeling forward looking at me, and I said, 'Take your paddle,' while I struck the water with mine. Tuan, I heard him cry. I heard him cry my name twice; and I heard voices shouting, 'Kill! Strike!' I never turned back. I heard him calling my name again with a great shriek, as when life is going out together with the voice—and I never turned my head. My own

name! . . . My brother! Three times he called—but I was not afraid of life. Was she not there in that canoe? And could I not with her find a country where death is forgotten—where death is unknown!''

The white man sat up. Arsat rose and stood, an indistinct and silent figure above the dying embers of the fire. Over the lagoon a mist drifting and low had crept, erasing slowly the glittering images of the stars. And now a great expanse of white vapor covered the land; it flowed cold and gray in the darkness, eddied in noiseless whirls round the tree-trunks and about the platform of the house, which seemed to float upon a restless and impalpable illusion of a sea. Only far away the tops of the trees stood outlined on the twinkle of heaven, like a somber and forbidding shore—a coast deceptive, pitiless and black.

Arsat's voice vibrated loudly in the profound peace.

"I had her there! I had her! To get her I would have faced all mankind. But I had her—and—''

His words went out ringing into the empty distances. He paused, and seemed to listen to them dying away very far—beyond help and beyond recall. Then he said quietly—

"Tuan, I loved my brother.''

A breath of wind made him shiver. High above his head, high above the silent sea of mist the drooping leaves of the palms rattled together with a mournful and expiring sound. The white man stretched his legs. His chin rested on his chest, and he murmured sadly without lifting his head—

"We all love our brothers.''

Arsat burst out with an intense whispering violence—

"What did I care who died? I wanted peace in my own heart.''

He seemed to hear a stir in the house—listened—then stepped in noiselessly. The white man stood up. A breeze was coming in fitful puffs. The stars shone paler as if they had retreated into the frozen depths of immense space. After a chill gust of wind there were a few seconds of perfect calm and absolute silence. Then from behind the black and wavy line of the forests a column of golden light shot up into the heavens and spread over the semicircle of the eastern horizon. The sun had risen. The mist lifted, broke into drifting patches, vanished into thin flying wreaths; and the unveiled lagoon lay, polished and black, in the heavy shadows at the foot of the wall of trees. A white eagle rose over it with a slanting and ponderous flight, reached the clear sunshine and appeared dazzlingly brilliant for a moment, then soaring higher, became a dark and motionless speck before it vanished into the blue as if it had left the earth forever. The white man, standing gazing upward before the doorway, heard in the hut a confused and broken murmur of distracted words ending with a loud groan. Suddenly Arsat stumbled out with outstretched hands, shivered, and stood still for some time with fixed eyes. Then he said—

"She burns no more."

Before his face the sun showed its edge above the treetops, rising steadily. The breeze freshened; a great brilliance burst upon the lagoon, sparkled on the rippling water. The forests came out of the clear shadows of the morning, became distinct, as if they had rushed nearer—to stop short in a great stir of leaves, of nodding boughs, of swaying branches. In the merciless sunshine the whisper of unconscious life grew louder, speaking in an incomprehensible voice round the dumb darkness of that human sorrow. Arsat's eyes wandered slowly, then stared at the rising sun.

"I can see nothing," he said half aloud to himself.

"There is nothing," said the white man, moving to the edge of the platform and waving his hand to his boat. A shout came faintly over the lagoon and the sampan began to glide toward the abode of the friend of ghosts.

"If you want to come with me, I will wait all the morning," said the white man, looking away upon the water.

"No, Tuan," said Arsat softly. "I shall not eat or sleep in this house, but I must first see my road. Now I can see nothing—see nothing! There is no light and no peace in the world; but there is death—death for many. We were sons of the same mother —and I left him in the midst of enemies; but I am going back now."

He drew a long breath and went on in a dreamy tone:

"In a little while I shall see clear enough to strike—to strike. But she has died, and . . . now . . . darkness."

He flung his arms wide open, let them fall along his body, then stood still with unmoved face and stony eyes, staring at the sun. The white man got down into his canoe. The polers ran smartly along the sides of the boat, looking over their shoulders at the beginning of a weary journey. High in the stern, his head muffled up in white rags, the juragan sat moody, letting his paddle trail in the water. The white man, leaning with both arms over the grass roof of the little cabin, looked back at the shining ripple of the boat's wake. Before the sampan passed out of the lagoon into the creek he lifted his eyes. Arsat had not moved. He stood lonely in the searching sunshine; and he looked beyond the great light of a cloudless day into the darkness of a world of illusions.

RESPONDING TO THE SELECTION

Your Response

1. Do you think "The Lagoon" effectively dramatizes the idea that life is a "world of illusions"? Explain.

Recalling

2. Why do the members of the white man's crew want nothing to do with Arsat?
3. What happened to Arsat's brother?
4. At the end of the story, what does Arsat say he will do?

Interpreting

5. Compare and contrast the white man and Arsat.
6. What events in the story are paralleled by the "conflagration of sunset" (page 831) and the rattling of the palm trees (page 835)?
7. When, following Diamelen's death, Arsat says, "I can see nothing," the white man replies, "There is nothing" (page 836). (a) What do you think is meant by this remark? (b) How might it relate to the final line of the story?

Applying

8. (a) What might have been Conrad's purpose in not naming the white man in this story? (b) How does his decision reinforce the theme?

ANALYZING LITERATURE

Understanding a Story Within a Story

A story within a story is a tale told by a character in a fictional narrative. Conrad uses this device in "The Lagoon" to enhance the meaning of Arsat's tale. The outer narrative provides a framework for Arsat's story. It allows us to see him through the eyes of the polers and the white man. By contrast, Arsat's narration gives us his own view of the events that led to his isolated life.

1. What specific information would you lack if the entire story had been narrated by Arsat?
2. Why do you think Conrad chose to have Arsat narrate his own story?
3. How does the use of a story within a story contribute to the theme of "The Lagoon"?

CRITICAL THINKING AND READING

Making Inferences About a Moral Code

When, for the second time in the story, Arsat says, "I loved my brother" (page 835), the white man observes that "We all love our brothers." Though the remark might be taken at face value, the theme of the story suggests that its author is stating a larger truth about the "brotherhood" of all human beings and about the rules by which we should, but perhaps do not always, conduct our lives. Tell, based on Arsat's narrative, what you believe to be Conrad's views on the following moral issues:

1. The division of a society into classes.
2. The crossing of class lines in such a society.
3. The defiance of law in any society.
4. The degree to which we should feel free to pursue a goal.

THINKING AND WRITING

Responding to Theme

A lagoon is a pool of brackish water separated from the sea by sandbars and reefs. Knowing this, write an essay explaining the relevance of the story's title to its theme. Begin by stating the theme. Then develop your essay around the following questions. In Conrad's view, what does the lagoon represent? What is represented by the sea beyond? What does a voyage to and from the lagoon represent? Feel free to add and answer questions of your own that you feel clarify the relationship between theme and title.

LEARNING OPTION

Performance. Arrange a theatrical reading of "The Lagoon" in class. After assigning the parts of the narrator, the white man, and Arsat (you may wish to have several readers do the longer parts), consider what sound effects you will need and how they might be achieved. The sound of the men in pursuit might be undertaken by the class as a whole. When you have finished planning and rehearsing, perform your reading.

ONE WRITER'S PROCESS

Joseph Conrad and "The Lagoon"

Writing About Obsessions Writers sometimes find that writing can be one way to free themselves of an obsession: The idea finds its way onto paper and begins an independent life of its own.

Joseph Conrad was a man obsessed with certain themes and ideas, which he explored over and over again in his work. "The Lagoon" deals with several of the themes. As in so many of his stories, the European narrator remains nameless, as if to symbolize "Everyman." He moves through a dreamlike and exotic jungle landscape. He encounters a native who tells him a tale of passion and betrayal. Conrad has said that this story was conceived in the same mood which produced *Almayer's Folly* and *An Outcast of the Islands.* Writers often explore the same ideas and themes through many separate works before they move on to something new.

English as a Second (or Third) Language In 1874, Conrad left his native Poland for Marseilles, a seaport in France, to learn seamanship. It was his first experience away from Poland and Russia, and he had to learn French quickly to survive. It is this early experience with the French language, which he learned before English, that influenced the structure of his sentences when he started writing in English.

In "The Lagoon," Conrad's use of adjectives frequently follows the French pattern rather than the English—the adjectives are often positioned *after* the noun instead of before it: The sun . . . *unclouded and dazzling;* forests *somber and dull;* leaves *enormous and heavy;* immobility *perfect and final;* a cry *discordant and feeble.*

This variation demonstrates that authors who write in languages other than their own bring valuable perspective to their work. Students learning English as a second language should read Conrad for an idea of what it is possible to achieve.

DRAFTING

Writer's Block In 1898, the same year *Tales of Unrest* was published, Conrad wrote to a friend about his writing process: "I *never mean* to be slow. The stuff comes out at its own rate. I am always ready to put it down; nothing would induce me to lay down my pen if I *feel* a sentence—or even a word ready to my hand. The trouble is that too often—alas!—I've to wait for the sentence—for the word."

He continues, "What wonder then that during the long blank hours the doubt creeps into the mind and I ask myself whether I am fitted for that work. The worst is that while I am thus powerless to produce my imagination is extremely active: whole paragraphs, whole pages, whole chapters pass through my mind. Everything is there: descriptions, dialogue, reflexion—everything—everything but the belief, the conviction, the only thing needed to make me put pen to paper. . . . The effort I put out should give birth to Masterpieces as big as Mountains—and it brings forth a ridiculous Mouse now and then."

It is inspiring to note that although Conrad suffered from writer's block, he managed to finish many novels and stories. About Conrad's difficulty in writing, the English novelist Ford Maddox Ford, his collaborator, said, "The fact is that I could make Conrad write at periods when his despair and fatigue were such that in no other way would it have been possible to him. . . . If Conrad became too tired to go on I could complete a paragraph or episode in his own words—though they might have been words of a week, a month, or several years before." This was an extremely rare and generous kind of collaboration: one novelist helping another to complete his work.

REVISING

Collaboration Conrad's situation was unusual in that he had a partner throughout much of his career who helped him revise his work. Together, Conrad and Ford published three books: *Romance, The Inheritors,* and *The Nature of a Crime.* Ford has said, "I believe that in the millions of phrases that we must have written or pored over together we never once disagreed over the words a sentence contained once it was given its final form." Ford worked on most of Conrad's other books as well, either correcting the proofs, discussing the plots or incidents, writing passages from Conrad's dictation—or actually writing in passages of his own. In effect, Ford was helping Conrad to revise his work by reading the passages with him and analyzing what needed to be changed. He did this mostly when Conrad was too ill to write himself.

PUBLISHING

Writing for Print "Of the five stories in this volume (*Tales of Unrest*) 'The Lagoon,' the last in order, is the earliest in date," said Conrad. "It is the first short story I ever wrote and marks, in a manner of speaking, the end of my first phase, with its special subject. . . ."

The story was first published in the *Cornhill Magazine;* this was Conrad's first appearance in a literary magazine. The story was later mocked in an article written by Max Beerbohm, a contemporary critic and satirist, in a volume of parodies entitled *A Christmas Garland.* Beerbohm took issue with Conrad's exploration of guilt and morality in a tropical setting as being far-fetched and unrealistic. Far from being upset by this, Conrad said, "I was immensely gratified. I began to believe in my public existence. I have much to thank 'The Lagoon' for." Criticism is something all writers have to deal with eventually. Conrad's response was to feel flattered!

THINKING ABOUT THE PROCESS

1. Have you ever suffered from writer's block? Explain.
2. **Writing** Try writing with a collaborator, as Conrad did. Invent an imaginary landscape, then write a few descriptive paragraphs about it. Divide the work in the way that seems best. For instance, you can write alternate paragraphs, or one of you can write the first draft and the other can revise it. After you have finished, discuss with other pairs of students the experience of collaborating.

E. M. FORSTER

1879–1970

To understand who E. M. Forster was, it is perhaps best to start with what he was not. He was staunchly opposed to imperialism, to capitalism, to ecclesiasticism, and to just about any other *ism* except for humanism. Forster's ideal, in short, was a civilization in which the rights of the individual are held above those of any collective or organization. It is precisely this message that serves as the theme in most of his novels.

Having lost his father at the age of one, Edward Morgan Forster was raised by his mother and a wealthy aunt. It was the latter's money that made it possible for him to attend the finest schools, beginning with Tonbridge School in Kent, which Forster later attacked as typifying what he called the "materialism of the English school system." In 1897 he entered King's College at Cambridge, which he considered his "spiritual home." After receiving his degree, he traveled to Greece and then lived for some time in Italy.

While abroad, he penned his first three novels. *Where Angels Fear to Tread* (1905) and *A Room with a View* (1908), set in Italy, examine the conflict between culture and falseness on the one hand, and passion and truth on the other. *The Longest Journey* (1907) recalls Forster's days at his beloved Cambridge, where he returned in 1910 to complete work on an advanced degree. It was in this same year that Forster published *Howards End,* a carefully drawn portrait of pre-war society in England.

In 1912 Forster had visited India. After serving in the International Red Cross during World War I, he returned there in 1921. His experiences and observations provided the inspiration for his most celebrated work, *A Passage to India* (1924). The novel, which treats the difficulties that arise in attempting to establish personal relationships, also delivers a prophetic glimpse of England's relations with India.

Dabbling in criticism and in shorter fiction as well, Forster turned out *Aspects of the Novel* in 1927 and *The Eternal Moment,* a collection of short stories, the following year. He also produced several collections of essays, including *Abinger Harvest* (1936) and *Two Cheers for Democracy* (1951). In 1969 he was named to the Order of Merit.

Although some critics have suggested that Forster's novels deal ultimately with the age-old struggle between good and evil, his themes are more complicated than that. Invariably, his villains value possessions over people and appearances over realities. And invariably, as in "The Helping Hand," those villains are made, in the end, to pay for their shallowness.

GUIDE FOR INTERPRETING

The Helping Hand

Writers' Techniques

Characterization. Characterization Is the technique whereby a writer makes known the personality of the characters in a work of fiction. Characterization can be accomplished in one of two ways—directly or indirectly. In direct characterization the writer comments openly on the character's personality, using descriptive phrases and adjectives to convey impressions straight to the reader. In indirect characterization the writer permits the reader to make up his or her own mind as to what kind of person the character is. To enable the reader to do this, the writer provides information in the form of one or more of the following: (1) the character's words, including speech patterns; (2) the character's actions; (3) the character's appearance; (4) the character's thoughts and feelings; and (5) the views of that character held by other characters in the story. Because it mimics the process we use in life to form impressions and opinions of the people we meet, indirect characterization has the effect of making the characters in a story seem real and lifelike.

Focus

Write a rough draft of a short poem or story titled "The Borrower." You may, if you wish, base it on a real-life occurrence, but avoid using the real names of individuals. The poem or story should tell about an individual who borrows habitually and never returns the items borrowed. Include descriptions of the personalities of both the borrower and the lender.

Primary Source

Forster's work is unified by a concern with shared humanity and the importance of personal relationships, as the title "The Helping Hand" suggests. The epigraph of his 1910 novel *Howards End*—"Only connect!"—introduces this theme, picked up later when one of the characters cries, "Only connect the prose and the passion, and both will be exalted, and human love will soon be at its height." But Forster's experience had taught him that this is far more easily said than done. *A Passage to India,* his last novel, represents the climax of this theme in his fiction. Some have seen the haunting image at the novel's end as representing the impossibility of forging true connections between people and cultures. The Englishman Fielding, debating the role of the British in India, asks the Indian Aziz, "Why can't we be friends now?" The novel ends with the narrator's answer: "But the horses didn't want it—they swerved apart; the earth didn't want it, sending up rocks through which riders must pass single file. . . ."

Do you think people can ever truly "connect" with each other?

The Helping Hand

E. M. Forster

When Lady Anstey's book on Giovanni da Empoli[1] was published, Mr. Henderson found in it much that needed forgiveness. His friend did not write as charmingly as she talked: a horrid slime of culture oozed over her style, her criticisms were affected, her enthusiasms abominable. This he could have forgiven; but how could he forgive the subject matter? The dear lady had appropriated, without acknowledgement, facts and theories for which he, and he alone, was responsible. He had studied Giovanni da Empoli for years, and the premature fruit of his labors now lay upon the breakfast table —a little apple-green book, four shillings net, being one of Messrs. Angerstein's series of Pocket Painters.

Mrs. Henderson, a devoted wife, was turning over the leaves with a smile upon her face, for she was pleased that the words of Lady Anstey had been printed on such heavy paper. She knew nothing of the shameful plagiarism, her interest in art being sympathetic rather than intelligent: she was always glad when her friends and her husband got on in it, just as she was glad when her son got on at school.

"What a long list of books she has read to write it!" she observed. "Did you know she could read German? And when did she go to Italy? Wasn't Empoli[2] the place you made us go to—the dirty hotel where we had to hunt the chickens out of the bedroom window?"

"Yes," replied Mr. Henderson, remembering with anguish the nights at Empoli which he had spent and Lady Anstey had not.

"Why did we go there? I've forgotten."

"I had things to look up in the archives." He held up the newspaper as a screen.

"I think you look up too much. Here's Lady Anstey who a little time back knew no more about Italian art than I do, and yet look! I wish you'd write a little book like this. I'm sure you could do it."

"I haven't the knack of putting things brightly." He never said all he thought about the Pocket Painters and similar editions, believing that anything which induces people to look at pictures has its value.

"Yes: I dare say it's all superficial and wrong."

He answered with some animation, "What makes you think so?"

"Because I mistrust new theories—not that I should have known there was a theory. But she says there is one in the preface."

"Giovanni da Empoli," said Mr. Henderson eagerly, "is one of the great puzzles of the Quattrocento.[3] It is highly probable from internal and external evidence that many pictures attributed to other painters should be given to him."

---

1. Giovanni (jō vän′ ē) **da Empoli** (em′ pō lē): A fictional painter.
2. Empoli: Town in central Italy.

3. Quattrocento (kwät′ trō chen′ tō): The fifteenth century.

"Cut your bread and butter, dear, do not bite it," said Mrs. Henderson to their son.

"If we take one of the Pieros[4] in the National Gallery, the portrait in the Poldi-Pezzoli at Milan, the so-called Baldovinetti[5] at Naples, and the *cassoni* attributed to Pesellino,[6] we notice in all a certain—"

"'Empoli is a quaint old town not untinged with the modern spirit,'" interrupted their son, who was reading out of Lady Anstey's book in the nasal twang that is considered humorous by the young. "'Here in 1409'—then a long note saying why not in 1429—"

---

4. **Pieros** (pye′ rōz): Paintings by Italian painter Piero della Francesca (1410 or 1420–1492).
5. **Baldovinetti** (bäl′ dō vē net′ tē): Painting by Florentine painter Alessio Baldovinetti (1425–1499).
6. **Pesellino** (pes ə lē′ nō): Francesco Pesellino, an Italian Renaissance painter (1422–1457).

"Exactly," said his father.

"'—in 1409 young Giovanni was born, here, when not on his travels, he lived, and here he died in 1473. Our painter never married. Of his six children four—'"

"Don't read at meals, dear," said his mother, taking the book. "This is a great surprise to me and a great pleasure. I never thought Lady Anstey had it in her."

No more she had. The book was the work of Mr. Henderson. He had no one to blame but himself. Lady Anstey had said, "I want to write a book about Giovanni da Empoli: tell me everything you know," and he had told her, cautiously at first in barren statements, then, as he grew warm, infusing the facts with life, till at last the whole theory stood up before her delighted eyes. "Tell it me again," she said, for she was not quick at following, and he had told it her again and she had made notes of it, and he had placed his own notes at her disposal.

THE NEWSPAPER
Edouard Vuillard
The Phillips Collection

He reminded himself that facts are universal property, and it is no matter who gives them to the world. But ideas—should there not be some copyright in ideas? He had only meant to stimulate Lady Anstey, not to equip her. However, she had Virgil[7] on her side, and Molière[8] and Shakespeare, and all the ancient Greeks who had taken everything and said nothing to anybody, and splendid fellows they were.

She was perfectly open when they next met, greeting him with "And here is someone else to whom I owe more than I can say." For her book was a success, and Messrs. Angerstein had asked her to do one on Botticelli.[9]

"I'm so glad he's been of use," said Mrs. Henderson, imagining herself to be engaged in conventional civilities. "I never knew he had studied the man." For Mr. Henderson had decided to bear his burden in silence, and neither to his wife nor to anyone else did he give one hint of his mortification. He had in him something of the saint, and knew it would be wrong as well as undignified to repine.

"And now tell me all about Botticelli," said Lady Anstey. But Mr. Henderson told very little about Botticelli. He regarded Lady Anstey with frozen admiration, almost with terror, as a being devoid of conscience and consciousness. They continued great friends, but he saw her as seldom as possible.

Her book, in spite of its popular form, made a considerable impression in artistic circles, and she was soon drawn into the congenial and lucrative atmosphere of controversy. In a fortunate hour Sir William Magnus disagreed with her, and a duel ensued, conducted with courtesy on his side and spirit on hers. Wisely refraining from venturing into new fields, she contented herself with repeating the statements she had made in her book. Mrs. Henderson, who always followed anything personal, was able to write her a hearty letter of congratulation on her victory.

Mr. Henderson did not write. The triumph of his theory gave him no pleasure, for it had triumphed in a mangled form. Lady Anstey had wielded it fairly well, but she had missed all the subtleties, she had spoiled the purity of its outline. Yet she had not spoiled it enough to justify his publishing it anew, under his own name.

He suffered a good deal, though he trained himself to laugh at the irony of the situation. He would like to have found someone to laugh with, but all his friends were embroiled on one side or the other, and he could not trust them to keep silent. As for his wife, she did not believe in irony. Meanwhile the book ran through several editions, and there was a rumor that the powers that be in the National Gallery were troubled, and meditated changing the label on the Piero della Francesca.

By the time Professor Rinaldi came to England, Mr. Henderson was tired of laughing and needed sympathy. Rinaldi, whom Mrs. Henderson called the Italian, was a man of great learning and artistic insight, who had become so disgusted with controversies over beauty that he had left Rome and retired to the curatorship of a small provincial gallery. There he lived, or as others said rotted, studying continually because he could not help it, but avowing his intention of never publishing again.

Here was a man to whom Mr. Henderson could speak freely. They were old friends, and he determined to pay him a visit in London.

"Do," said Mrs. Henderson, "and I will finish off the spring cleaning."

Mr. Henderson left on the Thursday, and Mrs. Henderson turned out the dining room. On Friday she did the drawing room. On Saturday she began at her husband's study, and came across a pasteboard box labeled Giovanni da Empoli.

---

7. Virgil: Classical Roman poet (70–19 B.C.).

8. Molière (mōl yer′): French dramatist (1622–1673).

9. Botticelli (bät′ ə chel′ ē): Italian Renaissance painter (1445?–1510).

Recognizing the name, she opened it and read on the top sheet inside: "Reasons for believing G. to be born in 1409." A strange impulse moved her, and she went for Lady Anstey's book. It gave identical reasons.

Then in one moment the loving wife became a student of art. All Saturday she sat with the book and the papers before her, and discovered that they coincided, not here and there but everywhere. The last paper in the box was a letter from Lady Anstey saying "Many thanks for loan of notes, which have been most acceptable."

All Sunday she thought over the revelation, all Monday and all Tuesday she acted on it. Mr. Henderson returned on the Wednesday.

He was looking more cheerful than she had seen him for weeks. "The world is ruled by irony," he observed, and smiled, as if he found the rule easy to bear.

"And how is the Italian?" she asked, rather ill at ease.

"As fine as ever. 'A little less imagination in archaeology and a little more in art' was his advice to Sir William yesterday."

The word "art" gave her an opening, and she exclaimed, "Yes indeed! Yes indeed! Yes indeed!"

"Why this enthusiasm?"

"You dear thing!" she cried, embracing him; "you're too good to be alive!"

"What have I done?" he asked, looking grave.

"I've found you out—that you wrote Lady Anstey's book—that she took all your facts and ideas and never said a word. And all these months you've let her talk and become famous and make money. I do admire and love you for it—but do be glad I'm different!"

"What have you been doing?" he said sternly.

"Nothing rude—don't be cross. I only let it out in the course of conversation, or put it in a letter if I was writing one."

"And to whom have you written?"

"Oh, not to Lady Anstey: to Lady Magnus about the vacuum cleaner, and one or two more. And yesterday I met the editor of the *Dudley* and he was horrified. Don't be angry—no, I don't mind if you are angry; it's simple justice I want; she shall *not* pick your brains and no one know; you *shall* have the credit for your own theory."

"Unfortunate," said Mr. Henderson. "Professor Rinaldi has just proved to me that the theory in question is wrong, that the facts are wrong, that the book is wrong, that I am wrong. Unfortunate."

![R]ESPONDING TO THE SELECTION

Your Response

1. Do you agree with Mr. Henderson's statement that "the world is ruled by irony"? Explain.

Recalling

2. (a) How does Mr. Henderson feel when Lady Anstey's book appears? Why? (b) How does his wife feel? Why?
3. (a) What do Lady Anstey's publishers ask her to do following the success of her book? (b) What does she, in turn, ask of Mr. Henderson?
4. (a) What does Mrs. Henderson come across during her cleaning? (b) What does she do as a result of this discovery? (c) What is her husband's response to her actions?

Interpreting

5. What is ironic about Lady Anstey's having that title?
6. Why do you suppose Mr. Henderson decides to "bear his burden in silence?"
7. (a) What does Mrs. Henderson's behavior at the breakfast table reveal about her? (b) What

does Lady Anstey's request for information on Botticelli reveal about her?
8. Do you find the title of the story appropriate? Why or why not?

Applying

9. (a) How did you feel at the end of the story? (b) How would you have behaved if you had been Mr. Henderson?

![A]NALYZING LITERATURE

Understanding Characterization

Characterization is the method a writer uses to reveal the personalities of characters in a story. In direct characterization the writer tells us directly what sort of person the character is. In indirect characterization the writer allows us to arrive at our own judgments based on what the character says, does, thinks, and looks like, as well as on how the character is regarded by other characters in the story. In "The Helping Hand," Forster uses a mixture of the two types of characterization. Identify the following characterizations as direct or indirect. For each example of indirect characterization, find the quoted words in the story. Then tell what trait each of the indirect characterizations reveals and to which character each refers.

1. Mrs. Henderson, a devoted wife, was turning over the leaves with a smile . . . (page 842)
2. "I think you look up too much. . . ." (page 842)
3. He held up the newspaper as a screen. (page 842)
4. "I haven't the knack of putting things brightly." (page 842)
5. . . . he had told her, cautiously at first . . . , then, as he grew warm, infusing the facts with life. . . . (page 843)
6. Wisely refraining from venturing into new fields, she contented herself with repeating the statements she had made in her book. (page 844)
7. "Nothing rude—don't be cross. I only let it out in the course of a conversation, or put it in a letter if I was writing one." (page 846)
8. "Unfortunate," said Mr. Henderson. "Professor Rinaldi has just proved to me that the theory in question is wrong, that the facts are wrong, that the book is wrong, that I am wrong. Unfortunate." (page 846)

CRITICAL THINKING AND READING

Making Inferences About Character

When a writer uses indirect characterization, the reader must **infer,** or piece together from presented facts, a profile of the character. Read the following profiles of the three main characters in the story. State which of the traits you think are applicable and which are not, backing up your opinions with evidence from the story.

Mr. Henderson: defensive, overly cautious, meek, given to rationalization

Mrs. Henderson: simplistic, shallow, dishonest, a good friend
Lady Anstey: intelligent, poised, treacherous, self-centered

THINKING AND WRITING

Writing About a Character

Choose one of the undeveloped characters in the story—the Hendersons' son, Sir William Magnus, or Professor Rinaldi—and, expanding on the little information provided, create a personality for that character. You may describe the person's appearance and likes and dislikes, but focus the main part of your description on what the person is like. To begin, ask yourself in what ways this person is different from and similar to the other characters in the story. Then write the first draft of your character sketch. Strive for originality. When you revise, make sure you have fleshed out your character with vivid details. Proofread your sketch and prepare a final draft.

LEARNING OPTIONS

1. **Performance.** Imagine the conversation that Mr. Henderson, Lady Anstey, and the editor of the *Dudley* might have after the conclusion of the story. With two other classmates, create a dialogue among these three characters, keeping in mind the personality traits that Forster develops in the story. Perform your dialogue for the class.
2. **Cross-curricular Connection.** Recently, a number of E. M. Forster's novels have been adapted for film. These include *A Passage to India, A Room with a View, Where Angels Fear to Tread,* and *Howards End.* View one of these films and report on it to the class.

VIRGINIA WOOLF

1882–1941

One can scarcely think of twentieth-century trends in fiction without thinking of "stream of consciousness," the technique whereby a character's innermost thoughts, emotions, and memories are woven together into a complex psychological fabric. And one can scarcely think of stream of consciousness without thinking of Virginia Woolf, the brilliant literary pioneer whose novels and short stories helped introduce this technique to the world.

Ironically for a writer who would become one of the leading lights of Modernism, Virginia Woolf was born into a family of prim and proper Victorians. Her father, Leslie Stephen, who served as the first editor of the renowned *Dictionary of National Biography,* saw to it that his daughter grew up surrounded by books, and at the age of twenty-three Virginia began contributing reviews to the Literary Supplement of *The Times of London.* In 1912 she married Leonard Woolf, an author and social reformer, with whom she founded the Hogarth Press. Their house in the Bloomsbury section of London became an informal meeting place for some of the more important thinkers of the era, attracting such figures as the writers E. M. Forster and Lytton Strachey, the art critic Roger Fry, and the economist John Maynard Keynes.

Woolf's first two novels, *The Voyage Out* (1915) and *Night and Day* (1919) were more or less conventional works. Her third was anything but. *Jacob's Room* (1922), which shattered the conventions of modern fiction, tells the story of a young man's life entirely through an examination of his room and its cluttered contents. Although we never actually meet the title character, we come to know a great deal about him through an artful arrangement of photographs.

In the years between the wars, Woolf continued to refine her fluid, inward-looking style with three more stream-of-consciousness novels—*Mrs. Dalloway* (1925), *To the Lighthouse* (1927), and *The Waves* (1931)—and with four slightly less experimental ones. In her more revolutionary works, she virtually abolished the traditional concept of plot, preferring instead to concentrate on what she called "an ordinary mind on an ordinary day."

For much of her adult life, Woolf suffered episodes of serious depression brought on by poor health and a consuming hatred of war. In 1941, two years after the outbreak of World War II, she took her own life. Today Woolf is recognized, along with James Joyce, whose life span almost exactly paralleled her own, as being among the most influential shapers of contemporary modern fiction.

The Lady in the Looking Glass

Writers' Techniques

Stream of Consciousness. Stream of consciousness is a narrative technique that relies on a character's feelings, memories, and thoughts, and the intermingling of the three, to tell a story. Pioneered in the early 1920's by Virginia Woolf, James Joyce, and the American novelist William Faulkner, stream of consciousness is an attempt to tune in directly to the workings of the character's mind—to capture the random flow of insights and thoughts much as they would naturally occur, moment by moment.

The stream-of-consciousness narrative dispenses with such conventions of traditional fiction as chronological ordering of events and the use of formal transitions. The responsibility for organizing the fragments into a meaningful whole often falls to the reader, who thus becomes more actively involved in the work than is the case with fiction of a more conventional design. The reader must piece together—from memories, unconnected thoughts, and glimpses of the subconscious mind—a meaningful whole. Though its demands on the reader are great, use of the technique often results in an intensely revealing, psychologically complete portrait of a human being.

Focus

Make a list of the contents of a person's room, using your own room at home, the room of someone you know, or an imaginary one. Beside each item, jot down some notes about its origin, its physical appearance, and its significance to the occupant.

Primary Source

Woolf's most famous explanation of her stream-of-consciousness technique appears in her essay "Modern Fiction." Focusing on an "ordinary mind on an ordinary day," Woolf notes: "The mind receives a myriad of impressions—trivial, fantastic, evanescent, or engraved with the sharpness of steel. From all sides they come, an incessant shower of innumerable atoms; and as they fall, as they shape themselves into the life of Monday or Tuesday, the accent falls differently from of old; the moment of importance came not here but there; so that, if a writer were a free man and not a slave, if he could write what he chose, not what he must, if he could base his work upon his own feeling and not upon convention, there would be no plot, no comedy, no tragedy, no love interest or catastrophe in the accepted style, and perhaps not a button sewn on as the Bond Street tailors would have it. . . . Life is a luminous halo, a semi-transparent envelope surrounding us from the beginning of consciousness to the end."

The Lady in the Looking Glass

A Reflection

Virginia Woolf

People should not leave looking glasses hanging in their rooms any more than they should leave open checkbooks or letters confessing some hideous crime. One could not help looking, that summer afternoon, in the long glass that hung outside in the hall. Chance had so arranged it. From the depths of the sofa in the drawing room one could see reflected in the Italian glass not only the marble-topped table opposite, but a stretch of the garden beyond. One could see a long grass path leading between banks of tall flowers until, slicing off an angle, the gold rim cut it off.

The house was empty, and one felt, since one was the only person in the drawing room, like one of those naturalists who, covered with grass and leaves, lie watching the shyest animals—badgers, otters, kingfishers—moving about freely, themselves unseen. The room that afternoon was full of such shy creatures, lights and shadows, curtains blowing, petals falling—things that never happen, so it seems, if someone is looking. The quiet old country room with its rugs and stone chimney pieces, its sunken bookcases and red and gold lacquer cabinets, was full of such nocturnal creatures. They came pirouetting across the floor, stepping delicately with high-lifted feet and spread tails and pecking allusive beaks as if

they had been cranes or flocks of elegant flamingoes whose pink was faded, or peacocks whose trains were veiled with silver. And there were obscure flushes and darkening too, as if a cuttlefish had suddenly suffused the air with purple; and the room had its passions and rages and envies and sorrows coming over it and clouding it, like a human being. Nothing stayed the same for two seconds together.

But, outside, the looking glass reflected the hall table, the sunflowers, the garden path so accurately and so fixedly that they seemed held there in their reality unescapably. It was a strange contrast—all changing here, all stillness there. One could not help looking from one to the other. Meanwhile, since all the doors and windows were open in the heat, there was a perpetual sighing and ceasing sound, the voice of the transient and the perishing, it seemed, coming and going like human breath, while in the looking glass things had ceased to breathe and lay still in the trance of immortality.

Half an hour ago the mistress of the house, Isabella Tyson, had gone down the grass path in her thin summer dress, carrying a basket, and had vanished, sliced off by the gilt rim of the looking glass. She had gone presumably into the lower garden to pick flowers; or as it seemed more natural to

The Lady in the Looking Glass: A Reflection   851

suppose, to pick something light and fantastic and leafy and trailing, traveler's-joy, or one of those elegant sprays of convolvulus that twine round ugly walls and burst here and there into white and violet blossoms. She suggested the fantastic and the tremulous convolvulus rather than the upright aster, the starched zinnia, or her own burning roses alight like lamps on the straight posts of their rose trees. The comparison showed how very little, after all these years, one knew about her; for it is impossible that any woman of flesh and blood of fifty-five or sixty should be really a wreath or a tendril. Such comparisons are worse than idle and superficial—they are cruel even, for they come like the convolvulus itself trembling between one's eyes and the truth. There must be truth; there must be a wall. Yet it was strange that after knowing her all these years one could not say what the truth about Isabella was; one still made up phrases like this about convolvulus and traveler's joy. As for facts, it was a fact that she was a spinster; that she was rich; that she had bought this house and collected with her own hands—often in the most obscure corners of the world and at great risk from poisonous stings and Oriental diseases—the rugs, the chairs, the cabinets which now lived their nocturnal life before one's eyes. Sometimes it seemed as if they knew more about her than we, who sat on them, wrote at them, and trod on them so carefully, were allowed to know. In each of these cabinets were many little drawers, and each almost certainly held letters, tied with bows of ribbon, sprinkled with sticks of lavender or rose leaves. For it was another fact—if facts were what one wanted—that Isabella had known many people, had had many friends; and thus if one had the audacity to open a drawer and read her letters, one would find the traces of many agitations, of appointments to meet, of upbraidings for not having met, long letters of intimacy and affection, violent letters of jealousy and reproach, terrible final words of parting—for all those interviews and assignations had led to nothing —that is, she had never married, and yet, judging from the masklike indifference of her face, she had gone through twenty times more of passion and experience than those whose loves are trumpeted forth for all the world to hear. Under the stress of thinking about Isabella, her room became more shadowy and symbolic; the corners seemed darker, the legs of chairs and tables more spindly and hieroglyphic.

Suddenly these reflections were ended violently and yet without a sound. A large black form loomed into the looking glass; blotted out everything, strewed the table with a packet of marble tablets veined with pink and gray, and was gone. But the picture was entirely altered. For the moment it was unrecognizable and irrational and entirely out of focus. One could not relate these tablets to any human purpose. And then by degrees some logical process set to work on them and began ordering and arranging them and bringing them into the fold of common experience. One realized at last that they were merely letters. The man had brought the post.

There they lay on the marble-topped table, all dripping with light and color at first and crude and unabsorbed. And then it was strange to see how they were drawn in and arranged and composed and made part of the picture and granted that stillness and immortality which the looking glass conferred. They lay there invested with a new reality and significance and with a greater heaviness, too, as if it would have needed a chisel to dislodge them from the table. And, whether it was fancy or not, they seemed to have become not merely a handful of casual letters but to be tablets graven with eternal truth—if one could read them, one would know everything there was to be known about Isabella, yes, and about life, too. The pages inside those marble-looking envelopes must be cut deep and scored thick with meaning. Isabella would come in, and take them, one by one, very slowly, and open them, and read them carefully word by word, and then with a profound sigh of comprehension, as if she had seen to the bottom of everything, she would tear the envelopes to little bits and tie the letters together and lock the cabinet drawer in her determination to conceal what she did not wish to be known.

The thought served as a challenge. Isabella did not wish to be known—but she should no longer escape. It was absurd, it was monstrous. If she concealed so much and knew so much one must prize her open with the first tool that came to hand—the imagination. One must fix one's mind upon her at that very moment. One must fasten her down there. One must refuse to be put off any longer with sayings and doings such as the moment brought forth—with dinners and visits and polite conversations. One must put oneself in her shoes. If one took the phrase literally, it was easy to see the shoes in which she stood, down in the lower garden, at this moment. They were very narrow and long and fashionable —they were made of the softest and most flexible leather. Like everything she wore, they were exquisite. And she would be standing under the high hedge in the lower part of the garden, raising the scissors that were tied to her waist to cut some dead flower, some overgrown branch. The sun would beat down on her face, into her eyes; but no, at the critical moment a veil of cloud covered the sun, making the expression of her eyes doubtful—was it mocking or tender, brilliant or dull? One could only see the indeterminate outline of her rather faded, fine face looking at the sky. She was thinking, perhaps, that she must order a new net for the strawberries; that she must send flowers to Johnson's widow; that it was time she drove over to see the Hippesleys in their new house. Those were the things she talked about at dinner certainly. But one was tired of the things that she talked about at dinner. It was her profounder state of being that one wanted to catch and turn to

words, the state that is to the mind what breathing is to the body, what one calls happiness or unhappiness. At the mention of those words it became obvious, surely, that she must be happy. She was rich; she was distinguished; she had many friends; she traveled—she bought rugs in Turkey and blue pots in Persia. Avenues of pleasure radiated this way and that from where she stood with her scissors raised to cut the trembling branches while the lacy clouds veiled her face.

Here with a quick movement of her scissors she snipped the spray of traveler's joy and it fell to the ground. As it fell, surely some light came in too, surely one could penetrate a little farther into her being. Her mind then was filled with tenderness and regret. . . . To cut an overgrown branch saddened her because it had once lived, and life was dear to her. Yes, and at the same time the fall of the branch would suggest to her how she must die herself and all the futility and evanescence of things. And then again quickly catching this thought up, with her instant good sense, she thought life had treated her well; even if fall she must, it was to lie on the earth and molder sweetly into the roots of violets. So she stood thinking. Without making any thought precise—for she was one of those reticent people whose minds hold their thoughts enmeshed in clouds of silence—she was filled with thoughts. Her mind was like her room, in which lights advanced and retreated, came pirouetting and stepping delicately, spread their tails, pecked their way; and then her whole being was suffused, like the room again, with a cloud of some profound knowledge, some unspoken regret, and then she was full of locked drawers, stuffed with letters, like her cabinets. To talk of "prizing her open" as if she were an oyster, to use any but the finest and subtlest and most pliable tools upon her was impious and absurd. One must imagine— here was she in the looking glass. It made one start.

She was so far off at first that one could not see her clearly. She came lingering and pausing, here straightening a rose, there lifting a pink to smell it, but she never stopped; and all the time she became larger and larger in the looking glass, more and more completely the person into whose mind one had been trying to penetrate. One verified her by degrees—fitted the qualities one had discovered into this visible body. There were her gray-green dress, and her long shoes, her basket, and something sparkling at her throat. She came so gradually that she did not seem to derange the pattern in the glass, but only to bring in some new element which gently moved and altered the other objects as if asking them, courteously, to make room for her. And the letters and the table and the grass walk and the sunflowers which had been waiting in the looking glass separated and opened out so that she might be received among them. At last there she was, in the hall. She stopped dead. She stood by the table. She stood perfectly still. At once the looking glass began to pour over her a light that seemed to fix her; that seemed like some acid to bite off the unessential and superficial and to leave only the truth. It was an enthralling spectacle. Everything dropped from her—clouds, dress, basket, diamond—all that one had called the creeper and convolvulus. Here was the hard wall beneath. Here was the woman herself. She stood naked in that pitiless light. And there was nothing. Isabella was perfectly empty. She had no thoughts. She had no friends. She cared for nobody. As for her letters, they were all bills. Look, as she stood there, old and angular, veined and lined, with her high nose and her wrinkled neck, she did not even trouble to open them.

People should not leave looking glasses hanging in their rooms.

RESPONDING TO THE SELECTION

Your Response

1. Do you think that knowledge about someone's true nature can be firmly "fastened down"? Explain.

Recalling

2. (a) What has Isabella Tyson gone to do? (b) What arrives while she is out?
3. What do the letters turn out to be?

Interpreting

4. Who do you think is the narrator of the story? Explain your answer.
5. (a) Based on the information provided, how would you describe Isabella? (b) How would you summarize what the narrator wishes to "prize" from her?
6. The last sentence of the story repeats the first sentence. What is the effect of this repetition, if you consider it together with the story's title and subtitle?
7. What, in your view, is the theme of the story?

Applying

8. Have you ever sought to know what made another person, perhaps a celebrity, "tick" and been disappointed by what you discovered? Give details of your experience and discuss the general truth it suggests.

ANALYZING LITERATURE

Recognizing Stream of Consciousness

Stream of consciousness is a literary technique that attempts to reproduce a character's thought processes as they might naturally occur. Often fragmented and seemingly unconnected, the thoughts, emotions, and memories that make up a stream-of-consciousness narrative paint a telling, if somewhat challenging, portrait of the character.

Reread carefully the paragraph of the story that begins, "Here with a quick movement of her scissors . . ." (page 853). Then answer the following questions.

1. If one traces her thought patterns from the cutting of the flower through the mention of the "locked drawers" of her mind, how many stages of thought can Isabella be seen to go through? What details of her personality are revealed in this paragraph?
2. What comment on her own technique of stream of consciousness does the author seem to be making in this paragraph?
3. What conclusion about Isabella does the narrator draw from this imaginative examination of Isabella's thoughts?

CRITICAL THINKING AND READING

Evaluating an Author's Purpose

Usually, behind a work of literature is a **purpose,** or intention, that was uppermost in the author's mind when he or she sat down to write. The purpose of some stories is to impart an understanding about people or life in general, while the purpose of others is merely to entertain. For Virginia Woolf, one ever-present purpose in her writing was to get beyond what she termed "the tyranny of plot"—that is, the requirement of "stylizing" a character's words and actions in accordance with the rules of traditional storytelling.

Give a short synopsis, or summary, of the "plot" implied in "The Lady in the Looking Glass." Then find evidence of the following aspects of Woolf's stream-of-consciousness technique, and tell how they helped her achieve her purpose:

1. The use of random details to develop a character.
2. The repetition of details of setting.
3. The repetition of specific images, words, and phrases.

THINKING AND WRITING

Using Stream of Consciousness

Use the list of possessions you developed earlier to tell a story about the occupant of the room. Use a stream-of-consciousness approach, modeling your story on Woolf's. Before you begin to write, map out what happens to the main character, using the time and manner in which the various objects were acquired as a guideline. When you revise, make sure you capture the intermingling of conscious thought and memory. Be prepared to share your story with your class.

Commentary

In her fiction Virginia Woolf tried to find a way to convey the interplay of thought, emotion, and insight that lies below the surface of reality. In this attempt she boldly experimented with radical ways of telling her stories. Stream of consciousness, new structure, and innovative experiments with time were the result. She was influential in her own day for her brilliant personality as well as for her work; however, her reputation has fallen somewhat in the postwar years. The violence of World War II made her subtleties of technique seem mild and old-fashioned. The revolution in technique she furthered is taken for granted where it has not been eclipsed by the political and social concerns of more recent works. Yet one critic believes that in the final analysis ''she did supremely well what no one else has attempted to do. She mapped the world of the mind . . . under certain precise conditions of character and environment.''

D. H. LAWRENCE

1885–1930

D. H. Lawrence occupies a unique position among the leading Modernist writers of the generation that came of age before the outbreak of the First World War. The originality of his literary achievements was partly clouded by the explosive controversy attached to his name during his lifetime and for some years after. As with Shelley and Byron before him, the controversy that swirled around Lawrence touched on several points, not the least of which were his unorthodox opinions on politics, society, and morality.

David Herbert Lawrence was born near Nottingham in the English Midlands, the son of a miner. His childhood was marked by poverty, illness, constant bickering between his parents, and his mother's driving ambition to make something of her son. After attending local schools, the young Lawrence spent several years as a teacher before turning to writing as a livelihood.

As a writer, Lawrence was deeply influenced by the pioneering psychological theories of Sigmund Freud and by the philosophy of Friedrich Nietzsche. He restlessly searched their writings, seeking confirmation of the underlying moral rightness of his strongest convictions—that the industrial social order was unjust, that open expression of sexuality was healthy, and that human beings could find true fulfillment only by living in harmony with nature.

In 1913, shortly before eloping to Germany with a woman several years older than himself, Lawrence published his first major novel, *Sons and Lovers*—a thinly disguised autobiographical account of his childhood and adolescent years. During World War I he returned with his wife to England, where he published his next major work, *The Rainbow* (1915). His frank treatment of sexuality in the book caused it to be declared obscene.

At the end of the war, the Lawrences left England for extended travels in Italy, Ceylon, Australia, Mexico, and the United States. Lawrence used many of these locales in his fiction: *Kangaroo* (1923), for example, is set in Australia, and *The Plumed Serpent* (1926) is steeped in the mythology of ancient Mexico. It was during his prolonged absence from England that Lawrence found a publisher for one of his greatest novels, *Women in Love* (1921). Ill from tuberculosis, Lawrence completed his last novel, *Lady Chatterley's Lover* (1928), while living in Italy.

In the half century since his death, society's views on Lawrence's writings have changed profoundly. Today his fiction is almost universally admired for its vivid settings, fine craftsmanship, and psychological insight.

GUIDE FOR INTERPRETING

The Rocking-Horse Winner

Writers' Techniques

Omniscient Narration. Omniscient narration means an all-knowing third-person point of view. Unlike the first-person narrator, who doubles as a character, the third-person narrator is strictly an observer who reports the events of the story from an outside perspective. Because of this remote vantage point, the third-person narrator is said to be omniscient, or all-knowing—privileged with the ability to see into the minds of the characters and to know what fate holds in store for them. While such a narrator is bound by literary convention to remain neutral—is prohibited, that is, from meddling in the affairs of the characters—the particular style of the narration often adds another, and sometimes colorful, dimension to the story. In "The Rocking-Horse Winner," for example, D. H. Lawrence adopts a third-person narrative style reminiscent of that used in fairy tales—a choice that is especially well suited to the curious proceedings in the story.

Commentary

"The Rocking-Horse Winner," like much of Lawrence's work, has sparked a staggering outpouring of critical commentary. Nevertheless, the story's richness still leaves room for inquiry. In an article entitled "A Rocking-Horse: The Symbol, the Pattern, the Way to Live," critic W. D. Snodgrass scrutinizes the various meanings the rocking horse might have in the story. In one of his most insightful points, Snodgrass examines the names of the horses upon which Paul, his uncle Oscar, and Bassett the gardener gamble. Snodgrass notes that Paul's first winner, Singhalese, and his last, Malabar, have names that refer to former British colonial regions in India. He sees in a third name, Mirza, the suggestion of still another colony, Mirzapur. Did Lawrence deliberately select the names of former British colonies to make a point in his story? Snodgrass would have us think so. He notes that for years these colonies were winners for the British Empire. Like any colonial power or large corporation, the British tried to control peoples and materials with which they had little direct contact. He sees a clear parallel between the fate of the British Empire and Paul's fate. As you read the story, decide whether you agree with Snodgrass's conclusion.

Focus

Think about people who believe in such things as superstitions, fortune-telling, and the like. List the qualities that these people have in common. Then attempt to develop a profile of someone who believes in what many others regard as coincidence or chance.

The Rocking-Horse Winner

D. H. Lawrence

There was a woman who was beautiful, who started with all the advantages, yet she had no luck. She married for love, and the love turned to dust. She had bonny children, yet she felt they had been thrust upon her, and she could not love them. They looked at her coldly, as if they were finding fault with her. And hurriedly she felt she must cover up some fault in herself. Yet what it was that she must cover up she never knew. Nevertheless, when her children were present, she always felt the center of her heart go hard. This troubled her, and in her manner she was all the more gentle and anxious for her children, as if she loved them very much. Only she herself knew that at the center of her heart was a hard little place that could not feel love, no, not for anybody. Everybody else said of her: "She is such a good mother. She adores her children." Only she herself, and her children themselves, knew it was not so. They read it in each other's eyes.

There were a boy and two little girls. They lived in a pleasant house, with a garden, and they had discreet servants, and felt themselves superior to anyone in the neighborhood.

Although they lived in style, they felt always an anxiety in the house. There was never enough money. The mother had a small income, and the father had a small income, but not nearly enough for the social position which they had to keep up. The father went into town to some office. But though he had good prospects, these pros-

pects never materialized. There was always the grinding sense of the shortage of money, though the style was always kept up.

At last the mother said, "I will see if *I* can't make something." But she did not know where to begin. She racked her brains, and tried this thing and the other, but could not find anything successful. The failure made deep lines come into her face. Her children were growing up, they would have to go to school. There must be more money, there must be more money. The father, who was always very handsome and expensive in his tastes, seemed as if he never *would* be able to do anything worth doing. And the mother, who had a great belief in herself, did not succeed any better, and her tastes were just as expensive.

And so the house came to be haunted by the unspoken phrase: *There must be more money! There must be more money!* The children could hear it all the time, though nobody said it aloud. They heard it at Christmas, when the expensive and splendid toys filled the nursery. Behind the shining modern rocking horse, behind the smart doll's house, a voice would start whispering: "There *must* be more money! There *must* be more money!" And the children would stop playing, to listen for a moment. They would look into each other's eyes to see if they had all heard. And each one saw in the eyes of the other two that they too had heard. "There *must* be more money! There *must* be more money!"

It came whispering from the springs of

the still-swaying rocking horse, and even the horse, bending his wooden, champing head, heard it. The big doll, sitting so pink and smirking in her new pram,[1] could hear it quite plainly, and seemed to be smirking all the more self-consciously because of it. The foolish puppy, too, that took the place of the teddy bear, he was looking so extraordinarily foolish for no other reason but that he heard the secret whisper all over the house: "There *must* be more money."

Yet nobody ever said it aloud. The whisper was everywhere, and therefore no one spoke it. Just as no one ever says: "We are breathing!" in spite of the fact that breath is coming and going all the time.

"Mother!" said the boy Paul one day. "Why don't we keep a car of our own? Why do we always use uncle's, or else a taxi?"

"Because we're the poor members of the family," said the mother.

"But why *are* we, mother?"

"Well—I suppose," she said slowly and bitterly, "it's because your father has no luck."

The boy was silent for some time.

"Is luck money, mother?" he asked, rather timidly.

"No, Paul! Not quite. It's what causes you to have money."

"Oh!" said Paul vaguely. "I thought when Uncle Oscar said *filthy lucker,* it meant money."

"*Filthy lucre* does mean money," said the mother. "But it's lucre, not luck."

"Oh!" said the boy. "Then what *is* luck, mother?"

"It's what causes you to have money. If you're lucky you have money. That's why it's better to be born lucky than rich. If you're rich, you may lose your money. But if you're lucky, you will always get more money."

"Oh! Will you! And is father not lucky?"

"Very unlucky, I should say," she said bitterly.

---

1. **pram:** Baby carriage.

The boy watched her with unsure eyes.

"Why?" he asked.

"I don't know. Nobody ever knows why one person is lucky and another unlucky."

"Don't they? Nobody at all? Does *nobody* know?"

"Perhaps God! But He never tells."

"He ought to, then. And aren't you lucky either, mother?"

"I can't be, if I married an unlucky husband."

"But by yourself, aren't you?"

"I used to think I was, before I married. Now I think I am very unlucky indeed."

"Why?"

"Well—never mind! Perhaps I'm not really," she said.

The child looked at her, to see if she meant it. But he saw, by the lines of her mouth, that she was only trying to hide something from him.

"Well, anyhow," he said stoutly, "I'm a lucky person."

"Why?" said his mother, with a sudden laugh.

He stared at her. He didn't even know why he had said it.

"God told me," he asserted, brazening it out.

"I hope He did, dear!" she said, again with a laugh, but rather bitter.

"He did, mother!"

"Excellent!" said the mother, using one of her husband's exclamations.

The boy saw she did not believe him; or rather, that she paid no attention to his assertion. This angered him somewhere, and made him want to compel her attention.

He went off by himself, vaguely, in a childish way, seeking for the clue to "luck." Absorbed, taking no heed of other people, he went about with a sort of stealth, seeking inwardly for luck. He wanted luck, he wanted it, he wanted it. When the two girls were playing dolls, in the nursery, he would sit on his big rocking horse, charging madly into space, with a frenzy that made the little girls peer at him uneasily. Wildly the horse careered, the waving dark hair of the boy tossed, his eyes had a strange glare in them. The little girls dared not speak to him.

When he had ridden to the end of his mad little journey, he climbed down and stood in front of his rocking horse, staring fixedly into its lowered face. Its red mouth was slightly open, its big eye was wide and glassy bright.

"Now!" he would silently command the snorting steed. "Now take me to where there is luck! Now take me!"

And he would slash the horse on the neck with the little whip he had asked Uncle Oscar for. He *knew* the horse could take him to where there was luck, if only he forced it. So he would mount again, and start on his furious ride, hoping at last to get there. He knew he could get there.

"You'll break your horse, Paul!" said the nurse.

"He's always riding like that! I wish he'd leave off!" said his elder sister Joan.

But he only glared down on them in silence. Nurse gave him up. She could make nothing of him. Anyhow he was growing beyond her.

One day his mother and his Uncle Oscar came in when he was on one of his furious rides. He did not speak to them.

"Hallo! you young jockey! Riding a winner?" said his uncle.

"Aren't you growing too big for a rocking horse? You're not a very little boy any longer, you know," said his mother.

But Paul only gave a blue glare from his big, rather close-set eyes. He would speak to nobody when he was in full tilt. His mother watched him with an anxious expression on her face.

At last he suddenly stopped forcing his horse into the mechanical gallop, and slid down.

"Well, I got there!" he announced fiercely, his blue eyes still flaring, and his sturdy long legs straddling apart.

"Where did you get to?" asked his mother.

"Where I wanted to go to," he flared back at her.

"That's right, son!" said Uncle Oscar. "Don't you stop till you get there. What's the horse's name?"

"He doesn't have a name," said the boy.

"Gets on without all right?" asked the uncle.

"Well, he has different names. He was called Sansovino last week."

"Sansovino, eh? Won the Ascot.[2] How did you know his name?"

"He always talks about horse races with Bassett," said Joan.

The uncle was delighted to find that his small nephew was posted with all the racing news. Bassett, the young gardener who had been wounded in the left foot in the war, and had got his present job through Oscar Cresswell, whose batman[3] he had been, was a perfect blade of the "turf."[4] He lived in the racing events, and the small boy lived with him.

Oscar Cresswell got it all from Bassett.

"Master Paul comes and asks me, so I can't do more than tell him, sir," said Bassett, his face terribly serious, as if he were speaking of religious matters.

"And does he ever put anything on a horse he fancies?"

"Well—I don't want to give him away—he's a young sport, a fine sport, sir. Would you mind asking him yourself? He sort of takes a pleasure in it, and perhaps he'd feel I was giving him away, sir, if you don't mind."

Bassett was serious as a church.

The uncle went back to his nephew, and took him off for a ride in the car.

"Say, Paul, old man, do you ever put anything on a horse?" the uncle asked.

The boy watched the handsome man closely.

"Why, do you think I oughtn't to?" he parried.

---

2. Ascot: A major English horse race.
3. batman: A British military officer's orderly.
4. blade ... "turf": Horse-racing fan.

"Not a bit of it! I thought perhaps you might give me a tip for the Lincoln."[5]

The car sped on into the country, going down to Uncle Oscar's place in Hampshire.

"Honor bright?" said the nephew.

"Honor bright, son!" said the uncle.

"Well, then, Daffodil."

"Daffodil! I doubt it, sonny. What about Mirza?"

"I only know the winner," said the boy. "That's Daffodil!"

"Daffodil, eh?"

There was a pause. Daffodil was an obscure horse comparatively.

"Uncle!"

"Yes, son?"

"You won't let it go any further, will you? I promised Bassett."

"Bassett be hanged, old man! What's he got to do with it?"

"We're partners! We've been partners from the first! Uncle, he lent me my first five shillings, which I lost. I promised him, honor bright, it was only between me and him: only you gave me that ten-shilling note I started winning with, so I thought you were lucky. You won't let it go any further, will you?"

The boy gazed at his uncle from those big, hot, blue eyes, set rather close together. The uncle stirred and laughed uneasily.

"Right you are, son! I'll keep your tip private. Daffodil, eh! How much are you putting on him?"

"All except twenty pounds," said the boy. "I keep that in reserve."

The uncle thought it a good joke.

"You keep twenty pounds in reserve, do you, you young romancer? What are you betting, then?"

"I'm betting three hundred," said the boy gravely. "But it's between you and me, Uncle Oscar! Honor bright?"

The uncle burst into a roar of laughter.

"It's between you and me all right, you young Nat Gould,"[6] he said, laughing. "But where's your three hundred?"

"Bassett keeps it for me. We're partners."

"You are, are you! And what is Bassett putting on Daffodil?"

"He won't go quite as high as I do, I expect. Perhaps he'll go a hundred and fifty."

"What, pennies?" laughed the uncle.

"Pounds," said the child, with a surprised look at his uncle. "Bassett keeps a bigger reserve than I do."

Between wonder and amusement, Uncle Oscar was silent. He pursued the matter no further, but he determined to take his nephew with him to the Lincoln races.

"Now, son," he said, "I'm putting twenty on Mirza, and I'll put five for you on any horse you fancy. What's your pick?"

"Daffodil, uncle!"

"No, not the fiver on Daffodil!"

"I should if it was my own fiver," said the child.

"Good! Good! Right you are! A fiver for me and a fiver for you on Daffodil."

The child had never been to a race meeting before, and his eyes were blue fire. He pursed his mouth tight, and watched. A Frenchman just in front had put his money on Lancelot. Wild with excitement, he flayed his arms up and down, yelling *Lancelot! Lancelot!* in his French accent.

Daffodil came in first, Lancelot second, Mirza third. The child, flushed and with eyes blazing, was curiously serene. His uncle brought him five five-pound notes: four to one.

"What am I to do with these?" he cried, waving them before the boy's eyes.

"I suppose we'll talk to Bassett," said the boy. "I expect I have fifteen hundred now; and twenty in reserve; and this twenty."

---

5. Lincoln: A major English horse race.

6. Nat Gould: A famous English sportswriter and authority on horse racing.

His uncle studied him for some moments.

"Look here, son!" he said. "You're not serious about Bassett and that fifteen hundred, are you?"

"Yes, I am. But it's between you and me, uncle! Honor bright!"

"Honor bright all right, son! But I must talk to Bassett."

"If you'd like to be a partner, uncle, with Bassett and me, we could all be partners. Only you'd have to promise, honor bright, uncle, not to let it go beyond us three. Bassett and I are lucky, and you must be lucky, because it was your ten shillings I started winning with. . . ."

Uncle Oscar took both Bassett and Paul into Richmond Park for an afternoon, and there they talked.

"It's like this, you see, sir," Bassett said. "Master Paul would get me talking about racing events, spinning yarns, you know, sir. And he was always keen on knowing if I'd made or if I'd lost. It's about a year since, now, that I put five shillings on Blush of Dawn for him—and we lost. Then the luck turned, with that ten shillings he had from you, that we put on Singhalese. And since that time, it's been pretty steady, all things considering. What do you say, Master Paul?"

"We're all right when we're *sure*," said Paul. "It's when we're not quite sure that we go down."

"Oh, but we're careful then," said Bassett.

"But when are you *sure?*" smiled Uncle Oscar.

"It's Master Paul, sir," said Bassett, in a secret, religious voice. "It's as if he had it from heaven. Like Daffodil now, for the Lincoln. That was as sure as eggs."

"Did you put anything on Daffodil?" asked Oscar Cresswell.

"Yes, sir. I made my bit."

"And my nephew?"

Bassett was obstinately silent, looking at Paul.

"I made twelve hundred, didn't I,

Bassett? I told uncle I was putting three hundred on Daffodil."

"That's right," said Bassett, nodding.

"But where's the money?" asked the uncle.

"I keep it safe locked up, sir. Master Paul, he can have it any minute he likes to ask for it."

"What, fifteen hundred pounds?"

"And twenty! And *forty,* that is, with the twenty he made on the course."

"It's amazing!" said the uncle.

"If Master Paul offers you to be partners, sir, I would, if I were you; if you'll excuse me," said Bassett.

Oscar Cresswell thought about it.

"I'll see the money," he said.

They drove home again, and sure enough, Bassett came round to the garden house with fifteen hundred pounds in notes. The twenty pounds reserve was left with Joe Glee, in the Turf Commission deposit.

"You see, it's all right, uncle, when I'm *sure!* Then we go strong, for all we're worth. Don't we, Bassett?"

"We do that, Master Paul."

"And when are you sure?" said the uncle, laughing.

"Oh, well, sometimes I'm *absolutely* sure, like about Daffodil," said the boy, "and sometimes I have an idea; and sometimes I haven't even an idea, have I, Bassett? Then we're careful, because we mostly go down."

"You do, do you! And when you're sure, like about Daffodil, what makes you sure, sonny?"

"Oh, well, I don't know," said the boy uneasily. "I'm sure, you know, uncle; that's all."

"It's as if he had it from heaven, sir," Bassett reiterated.

"I should say so!" said the uncle.

But he became a partner. And when the Leger was coming on, Paul was "sure" about Lively Spark, which was a quite inconsiderable horse. The boy insisted on putting a thousand on the horse, Bassett went for five hundred, and Oscar Cresswell two hundred. Lively Spark came in first, and the betting had been ten to one against him. Paul had made ten thousand.

"You see," he said. "I was absolutely sure of him."

Even Oscar Cresswell had cleared two thousand.

"Look here, son," he said, "this sort of thing makes me nervous."

"It needn't, uncle! Perhaps I shan't be sure again for a long time."

"But what are you going to do with your money?" asked the uncle.

"Of course," said the boy, "I started it for mother. She said she had no luck, because father is unlucky, so I thought if *I* was lucky, it might stop whispering."

"What might stop whispering?"

"Our house! I *hate* our house for whispering."

"What does it whisper?"

"Why—why"—the boy fidgeted—"why, I don't know! But it's always short of money, you know, uncle."

"I know it, son, I know it."

"You know people send mother writs, don't you, uncle?"

"I'm afraid I do," said the uncle.

"And then the house whispers like people laughing at you behind your back. It's awful, that is! I thought if I was lucky . . ."

"You might stop it," added the uncle.

The boy watched him with big blue eyes, that had an uncanny cold fire in them, and he said never a word.

"Well then!" said the uncle. "What are we doing?"

"I shouldn't like mother to know I was lucky," said the boy.

"Why not, son?"

"She'd stop me."

"I don't think she would."

"Oh!"—and the boy writhed in an odd way— "I *don't* want her to know, uncle."

"All right, son! We'll manage it without her knowing."

They managed it very easily. Paul, at the other's suggestion, handed over five thousand pounds to his uncle, who deposited it with the family lawyer, who was then to inform Paul's mother that a relative had put five thousand pounds into his hands, which sum was to be paid out a thousand pounds at a time, on the mother's birthday, for the next five years.

"So she'll have a birthday present of a thousand pounds for five successive years," said Uncle Oscar. "I hope it won't make it all the harder for her later."

Paul's mother had her birthday in November. The house had been "whispering" worse than ever lately, and even in spite of his luck, Paul could not bear up against it. He was very anxious to see the effect of the birthday letter, telling his mother about the thousand pounds.

When there were no visitors, Paul now took his meals with his parents, as he was beyond the nursery control. His mother went into town nearly every day. She had discovered that she had an odd knack of sketching furs and dress materials, so she worked secretly in the studio of a friend who was the chief "artist" for the leading drapers. She drew the figures of ladies in furs and ladies in silk and sequins for the newspaper advertisements. This young woman artist earned several thousand pounds a year, but Paul's mother only made several hundreds, and she was again dissatisfied. She so wanted to be first in something, and she did not succeed, even in making sketches for drapery advertisements.

She was down to breakfast on the morning of her birthday. Paul watched her face as she read her letters. He knew the lawyer's letter. As his mother read it, her face hardened and became more expressionless. Then a cold, determined look came on her mouth. She hid the letter under the pile of others, and said not a word about it.

"Didn't you have anything nice in the post for your birthday, mother?" said Paul.

"Quite moderately nice," she said, her voice cold and absent.

She went away to town without saying more.

But in the afternoon Uncle Oscar appeared. He said Paul's mother had had a long interview with the lawyer, asking if the whole five thousand could not be advanced at once, as she was in debt.

"What do you think, uncle?" said the boy.

"I leave it to you, son."

"Oh, let her have it, then! We can get some more with the other," said the boy.

"A bird in the hand is worth two in the bush, laddie!" said Uncle Oscar.

"But I'm sure to *know* for the Grand National; or the Lincolnshire; or else the Derby.[7] I'm sure to know for *one* of them," said Paul.

So Uncle Oscar signed the agreement, and Paul's mother touched the whole five thousand. Then something very curious happened. The voices in the house suddenly went mad, like a chorus of frogs on a spring evening. There were certain new furnishings, and Paul had a tutor. He was *really* going to Eton,[8] his father's school, in the following autumn. There were flowers in the winter, and a blossoming of the luxury Paul's mother had been used to. And yet the voices in the house, behind the sprays of mimosa and almond blossom, and from under the piles of iridescent cushions, simply trilled and screamed in a sort of ecstasy: "There *must* be more money! Oh-h-h! There *must* be more money! Oh, now, now-w! now-w-w—there *must* be more money!—more than ever! More than ever!"

It frightened Paul terribly. He studied away at his Latin and Greek with his tutors. But his intense hours were spent with Bassett. The Grand National had gone by: he had not "known," and had lost a hundred pounds. Summer was at hand. He was in agony for the Lincoln. But even for the Lincoln he didn't "know," and he lost fifty pounds. He became wild-eyed and strange, as if something were going to explode in him.

"Let it alone, son! Don't you bother about it!" urged Uncle Oscar. But it was as if the boy couldn't really hear what his uncle was saying.

"I've got to know for the Derby! I've *got* to know for the Derby!" the child reiterated, his big blue eyes blazing with a sort of madness.

His mother noticed how overwrought he was.

"You'd better go to the seaside. Wouldn't you like to go now to the seaside, instead of waiting? I think you'd better," she said, looking down at him anxiously, her heart curiously heavy because of him.

But the child lifted his uncanny blue eyes.

"I couldn't possibly go before the Derby, mother!" he said. "I couldn't possibly!"

"Why not?" she said, her voice becoming heavy when she was opposed. "Why not? You can still go from the seaside to see the Derby with your Uncle Oscar, if that's what you wish. No need for you to wait here. Besides, I think you care too much about these races. It's a bad sign. My family has been a gambling family, and you won't know till you grow up how much damage it has done. But it has done damage. I shall have to send Bassett away, and ask Uncle Oscar not to talk racing to you, unless you promise to be reasonable about it; go away to the seaside and forget it. You're all nerves!"

"I'll do what you like, mother, so long as you don't send me away till after the Derby," the boy said.

"Send you away from where? Just from this house?"

"Yes," he said, gazing at her.

"Why, you curious child, what makes you care about this house so much, suddenly? I never knew you loved it!"

He gazed at her without speaking. He had a secret within a secret, something he had not divulged, even to Bassett or to his Uncle Oscar.

---

7. Grand National . . . Derby: Major English horse races.

8. Eton: A prestigious private school in England.

But his mother, after standing undecided and a little bit sullen for some moments, said:

"Very well, then! Don't go to the seaside till after the Derby, if you don't wish it. But promise me you won't let your nerves go to pieces! Promise you won't think so much about horse racing and *events,* as you call them!"

"Oh, no!" said the boy, casually. "I won't think much about them, mother. You needn't worry. I wouldn't worry, mother, if I were you."

"If you were me and I were you," said his mother, "I wonder what we *should* do!"

"But you know you needn't worry, mother, don't you?" the boy repeated.

"I should be awfully glad to know it," she said wearily.

"Oh, well, you *can,* you know. I mean you *ought* to know you needn't worry!" he insisted.

"Ought I? Then I'll see about it," she said.

Paul's secret of secrets was his wooden horse, that which had no name. Since he was emancipated from a nurse and a nursery governess, he had had his rocking horse removed to his own bedroom at the top of the house.

"Surely you're too big for a rocking horse!" his mother had remonstrated.

"Well, you see, mother, till I can have a *real* horse, I like to have *some* sort of animal about," had been his quaint answer.

"Do you feel he keeps you company?" she laughed.

"Oh, yes! He's very good, he always keeps me company, when I'm there," said Paul.

So the horse, rather shabby, stood in an arrested prance in the boy's bedroom.

The Derby was drawing near, and the boy grew more and more tense. He hardly heard what was spoken to him, he was very frail, and his eyes were really uncanny. His mother had sudden strange seizures of uneasiness about him. Sometimes, for half an hour, she would feel a sudden anxiety about him that was almost anguish. She wanted to rush to him at once, and know he was safe.

Two nights before the Derby, she was at a big party in town, when one of her rushes of anxiety about her boy, her firstborn, gripped her heart till she could hardly speak. She fought with the feeling, might and main, for she believed in common sense. But it was too strong. She had to leave the dance and go downstairs to telephone to the country. The children's nursery governess was terribly surprised and startled at being rung up in the night.

"Are the children all right, Miss Wilmot?"

"Oh yes, they are quite all right."

"Master Paul? Is he all right?"

"He went to bed as right as a trivet.[9] Shall I run up and look at him?"

"No!" said Paul's mother reluctantly. "No! Don't trouble. It's all right. Don't sit up. We shall be home fairly soon." She did not want her son's privacy intruded upon.

"Very good," said the governess.

It was about one o'clock when Paul's mother and father drove up to their house. All was still. Paul's mother went to her room and slipped off her white fur cloak. She had told her maid not to wait up for her. She heard her husband downstairs, mixing a whisky-and-soda.

And then, because of the strange anxiety at her heart, she stole upstairs to her son's room. Noiselessly she went along the upper corridor. Was there a faint noise? What was it?

She stood, with arrested muscles, outside his door, listening. There was a strange, heavy, and yet not loud noise. Her heart stood still. It was a soundless noise, yet rushing and powerful. Something huge, in violent, hushed motion. What was it? What in God's name was it? She ought to know. She felt that she *knew* the noise. She knew what it was.

---

9. right as a trivet: Perfectly right.

Yet she could not place it. She couldn't say what it was. And on and on it went, like a madness.

Softly, frozen with anxiety and fear, she turned the door handle.

The room was dark. Yet in the space near the window, she heard and saw something plunging to and fro. She gazed in fear and amazement.

Then suddenly she switched on the light, and saw her son, in his green pajamas, madly surging on his rocking horse. The blaze of light suddenly lit him up, as he urged the wooden horse, and lit her up, as she stood, blond, in her dress of pale green and crystal, in the doorway.

"Paul!" she cried. "Whatever are you doing?"

"It's Malabar!" he screamed, in a powerful, strange voice. "It's Malabar!"

His eyes blazed at her for one strange and senseless second, as he ceased urging his wooden horse. Then he fell with a crash to the ground, and she, all her tormented motherhood flooding upon her, rushed to gather him up.

But he was unconscious, and unconscious he remained, with some brain fever. He talked and tossed, and his mother sat stonily by his side.

"Malabar! It's Malabar! Bassett, Bassett, I *know* it's Malabar!"

So the child cried, trying to get up and urge the rocking horse that gave him his inspiration.

"What does he mean by Malabar?" asked the heart-frozen mother.

"I don't know," said the father, stonily.

"What does he mean by Malabar?" she asked her brother Oscar.

"It's one of the horses running for the Derby," was the answer.

And, in spite of himself, Oscar Cresswell spoke to Bassett, and himself put a thousand on Malabar: at fourteen to one.

The third day of the illness was critical: they were watching for a change. The boy, with his rather long, curly hair, was tossing ceaselessly on the pillow. He neither slept nor regained consciousness, and his eyes were like blue stones. His mother sat, feeling her heart had gone, turned actually into a stone.

In the evening, Oscar Cresswell did not come, but Bassett sent a message, saying could he come up for one moment, just one moment? Paul's mother was very angry at the intrusion, but on second thoughts she agreed. The boy was the same. Perhaps Bassett might bring him to consciousness.

The gardener, a shortish fellow with a little brown moustache and sharp little brown eyes, tiptoed into the room, touched his imaginary cap to Paul's mother, and stole to the bedside, staring with glittering, smallish eyes at the tossing, dying child.

"Master Paul!" he whispered. "Master Paul! Malabar came in first all right, a clean win. I did as you told me. You've made over seventy thousand pounds, you have; you've got over eighty thousand. Malabar came in all right, Master Paul."

"Malabar! Malabar! Did I say Malabar, mother? Did I say Malabar? Do you think I'm lucky, mother? I knew Malabar, didn't I? Over eighty thousand pounds! I call that lucky, don't you, mother? Over eighty thousand pounds! I knew, didn't I know I knew? Malabar came in all right. If I ride my horse till I'm sure, then I tell you, Bassett, you can go as high as you like. Did you go for all you were worth, Bassett?"

"I went a thousand on it, Master Paul."

"I never told you, mother, that if I can ride my horse, and *get there*, then I'm absolutely sure—oh, absolutely! Mother, did I ever tell you? I *am* lucky!"

"No, you never did," said the mother.

But the boy died in the night.

And even as he lay dead, his mother heard her brother's voice saying to her: "My God, Hester, you're eighty-odd thousand to the good, and a poor devil of a son to the bad. But, poor devil, poor devil, he's best gone out of a life where he rides his rocking horse to find a winner."

Your Response

1. What is your impression of Paul's relationship with his mother? Explain.

Recalling

2. Why is the family in the story always short of money?
3. How does Paul try to change the family's luck?
4. (a) What birthday present does Paul give his mother? (b) What is her reaction to it?
5. What does Paul's mother discover upon returning from the big party?

Interpreting

6. What comment does Lawrence seem to be making about the concerns of Paul's parents?
7. On page 859 Paul's mother describes her husband as unlucky. (a) What do you think she means by this? (b) What does the remark reveal about her as a person?
8. What comment about life do you think the author is suggesting in Uncle Oscar's statement on Paul's death at the story's close?
9. Identify Lawrence's theme in this story.

Applying

10. Tell to what extent the problems Lawrence addresses are problems primarily of this century.

■ A NALYZING LITERATURE

Understanding Omniscient Narration

Omniscient narration is narration by a third-person speaker who, knowing all, is able to "read" the characters' minds and see into their futures. In "The Rocking-Horse Winner," D. H. Lawrence uses a narrative style of the sort ordinarily found in fairy tales. The opening line of the story, for example, has some of the ring of the familiar "Once upon a time" beginning.

1. Identify at least two other features of the story that give it the flavor of a fairy tale. Describe what you feel these features add to the impact of the ending.
2. (a) How different might your overall impression of the story be if Lawrence had used the mother as the narrator? (b) If he had used Uncle Oscar?

■ T HINKING AND WRITING

Retelling From a Different Point of View

Imagine that Paul, and not an omniscient narrator, were telling the story. Try to imagine, based on examples Lawrence provides of the child's language, what words Paul might use to express events. More important, try to envision what takes place inside Paul's mind when he is astride his horse and galloping toward another "victory." Then retell a portion of the story from Paul's point of view. You may wish to concentrate on the section that immediately precedes Paul's lapse into unconsciousness. When you revise, make sure you have maintained a consistent point of view. Have you included information Paul would not know? Does your narrator sound like Paul? Proofread your story and prepare a final draft. Read it aloud to your classmates.

■ L EARNING OPTION

Speaking and Listening. Throughout history people have sought ways to predict the future. Some of these methods include using astrology, reading palms, reading tarot cards, interpreting dreams, and observing the flight patterns of birds. Have any of these procedures been successful? Investigate one of these, or another method of prediction, and share your findings orally with the class.

KATHERINE MANSFIELD

1888–1923

Katherine Mansfield was born Kathleen Mansfield Beauchamp in Wellington, New Zealand. At the age of fifteen, she traveled to London, where she studied for three years at Queens College. In London she became acquainted with a number of important literary figures, including Virginia Woolf. Mansfield's first collection of stories, *In a German Pension,* was published in 1911 and showed the influence of the Russian writer Anton Chekhov. In 1918 Virginia Woolf and her husband, Leonard Woolf, published Mansfield's next collection, *Prelude.* This volume, along with *Bliss* (1920), firmly established Mansfield's reputation as an important short-story writer. Some of her finest stories were included in *The Garden Party and Other Stories* (1922), in which she successfully combined her angry and sentimental impulses in portraits of impoverished single women.

Her writing brought her into contact with John Middleton Murry, who published a story and some poems of hers in his literary magazine, *Rhythm.* The two eventually married and became publishing partners. They lived a nomadic and at times penniless life, moving back and forth between continental Europe and London. During this period they became friends with D. H. Lawrence and his wife, Frieda, and for a time the two couples lived as neighbors in Cornwall. Mansfield and Murry later became the models for two central characters in Lawrence's novel *Women in Love.* Increasingly ill with tuberculosis, Mansfield spent the last few years of her life in and out of clinics and hospitals, searching for health in the French Riviera and the Swiss Alps, before the disease finally claimed her in 1923.

Critics credit Mansfield with having greatly refined the art of the short story. Her works have often been compared to those of James Joyce and Anton Chekhov, both of whom she greatly admired. In contrast to the traditional short story, which emphasizes vivid events unfolding in chronological order, Mansfield's stories focus on the disclosure of interior states of being and heightened moments of awareness. Although little may happen outwardly, conversations in her stories reveal complex moods and hidden conflicts. Murry found "a kind of *purity*" in her work. "It is as though the glass through which she looked upon life were crystal clear," he said.

When called upon to describe her motivation as a writer, Katherine Mansfield replied that she wrote out of both a sense of joy and a sense of doom. Indeed, her short stories—which alternately express cynicism toward the corruption of modern English society and recall fond memories of childhood happiness—reflect this dual outlook.

GUIDE FOR INTERPRETING

A Dill Pickle

Writers' Techniques

Dialogue. Dialogue in a literary work consists of the conversations that characters have. Through the use of dialogue, writers are able to convey important aspects of the characters' personalities and motivations. Besides being a tool for characterization, dialogue can help move the plot along, develop the theme, and establish the setting, tone, and mood in a piece of literature. In "A Dill Pickle," Katherine Mansfield develops portraits, almost entirely through dialogue, of two characters and their world of longing, regret, and emotional ambivalence.

Focus

Have you ever been reminded of a special time that is long gone? What made it special? What about it would you like to repeat? Write about the thoughts and feelings associated with this remembrance.

Primary Source

Katherine Mansfield could be a harsh critic of her friends' literary works as well as of their personalities. In the following account, Mansfield provides a behind-the-scenes look at her volatile friends D. H. Lawrence and his wife, Frieda: "He simply raves, roars, beats the table, abuses everybody. But that's not such great matter. What makes these attacks insupportable is the feeling one has at the back of one's mind that he is completely out of control. Swallowed up in acute insane irritation. . . . They are both too tough for me to enjoy playing with. . . . I cannot discuss blood affinity to beasts for instance if I have to keep ducking to avoid the flat irons and the saucepans." Mansfield's attitude toward Lawrence also extended to his books. Writing to her husband, John Middleton Murry, about Lawrence's novel *The Lost Girl,* Mansfield concluded: "Lawrence denies his humanity. He denies the powers of the Imagination. He denies Life—I mean *human* life. His hero and heroine are non-human. They are animals on the prowl. They do not feel: they scarcely speak. There is not one memorable *word.* They submit to the physical response and for the rest go veiled—blind—*faceless—mindless*. This is a doctrine of mindlessness."

A Dill Pickle

Katherine Mansfield

And then, after six years, she saw him again. He was seated at one of those little bamboo tables decorated with a Japanese vase of paper daffodils. There was a tall plate of fruit in front of him, and very carefully, in a way she recognized immediately as his "special" way, he was peeling an orange.

He must have felt that shock of recognition in her for he looked up and met her eyes. Incredible! He didn't know her! She smiled; he frowned. She came toward him. He closed his eyes an instant, but opening them his face lit up as though he had struck a match in a dark room. He laid down the orange and pushed back his chair, and she took her little warm hand out of her muff and gave it to him.

"Vera!" he exclaimed. "How strange. Really, for a moment I didn't know you. Won't you sit down? You've had lunch? Won't you have some coffee?"

She hesitated, but of course she meant to.

"Yes, I'd like some coffee." And she sat down opposite him.

"You've changed. You've changed very much," he said, staring at her with that eager, lighted look. "You look so well. I've never seen you look so well before."

"Really?" She raised her veil and unbuttoned her high fur collar. "I don't feel very well. I can't bear this weather, you know."

"Ah, no. You hate the cold. . . ."

"Loathe it." She shuddered. "And the worst of it is that the older one grows . . . "

He interrupted her. "Excuse me," and tapped on the table for the waitress. "Please bring some coffee and cream." To her: "You are sure you won't eat anything? Some fruit, perhaps. The fruit here is very good."

"No, thanks. Nothing."

"Then that's settled." And smiling just a hint too broadly he took up the orange again. "You were saying—the older one grows—"

"The colder," she laughed. But she was thinking how well she remembered that trick of his—the trick of interrupting her—and of how it used to exasperate her six years ago. She used to feel then as though he, quite suddenly, in the middle of what she was saying, put his hand over her lips, turned from her, attended to something different, and then took his hand away, and with just the same slightly too broad smile, gave her his attention again. . . . Now we are ready. That is settled.

"The colder!" He echoed her words, laughing too. "Ah, ah. You still say the same things. And there is another thing about you that is not changed at all—your beautiful voice—your beautiful way of speaking." Now he was very grave; he leaned toward her, and she smelled the warm, stinging scent of the orange peel. "You have only to say one word and I would know your voice among all other voices. I don't know what it is—I've often wondered—that makes your voice such a—haunting memory. . . . Do you remember that first afternoon we spent together at Kew Gardens? You were so surprised because I did not know the names of any flowers. I am still just as ignorant for all your telling me. But whenever it is very fine and warm, and I see some bright colors— it's awfully strange—I hear your voice saying: 'Geranium, marigold and verbena.' And I feel those three words are all I recall of some forgotten, heavenly language. . . . You remember that afternoon?"

"Oh, yes, very well." She drew a long,

WHITE CUP AND SAUCER, NO. 1016
Fantin-Latour
Fitzwilliam Museum, Cambridge

soft breath, as though the paper daffodils between them were almost too sweet to bear. Yet, what had remained in her mind of that particular afternoon was an absurd scene over the tea table. A great many people taking tea in a Chinese pagoda, and he behaving like a maniac about the wasps— waving them away, flapping at them with his straw hat, serious and infuriated out of all proportion to the occasion. How delighted the sniggering tea drinkers had been. And how she had suffered.

But now, as he spoke, that memory faded. His was the truer. Yes, it had been a wonderful afternoon, full of geranium and marigold and verbena, and—warm sunshine. Her thoughts lingered over the last two words as though she sang them.

In the warmth, as it were, another memory unfolded. She saw herself sitting on a lawn. He lay beside her, and suddenly, after a long silence, he rolled over and put his head in her lap.

"I wish," he said, in a low, troubled voice, "I wish that I had taken poison and were about to die—here now!"

At that moment a little girl in a white dress, holding a long, dripping water lily, dodged from behind a bush, stared at them, and dodged back again. But he did not see. She leaned over him.

"Ah, why do you say that? I could not say that."

But he gave a kind of soft moan, and taking her hand he held it to his cheek.

"Because I know I am going to love you too much—far too much. And I shall suffer so terribly, Vera, because you never, never will love me."

He was certainly far better looking now than he had been then. He had lost all that dreamy vagueness and indecision. Now he had the air of a man who has found his place in life, and fills it with a confidence and an assurance which was, to say the least, impressive. He must have made money, too.

His clothes were admirable, and at that moment he pulled a Russian cigarette case out of his pocket.

"Won't you smoke?"

"Yes, I will." She hovered over them. "They look very good."

"I think they are. I get them made for me by a little man in St. James's Street. I don't smoke very much. I'm not like you—but when I do, they must be delicious, very fresh cigarettes. Smoking isn't a habit with me; it's a luxury—like perfume. Are you still so fond of perfumes? Ah, when I was in Russia . . ."

She broke in: "You've really been to Russia?"

"Oh, yes. I was there for over a year. Have you forgotten how we used to talk of going there?"

"No, I've not forgotten."

He gave a strange half laugh and leaned back in his chair. "Isn't it curious. I have really carried out all those journeys that we planned. Yes, I have been to all those places that we talked of, and stayed in them long enough to—as you used to say, 'air oneself' in them. In fact, I have spent the last three years of my life traveling all the time. Spain, Corsica, Siberia, Russia, Egypt. The only country left is China, and I mean to go there, too, when the war is over."

As he spoke, so lightly, tapping the end of his cigarette against the ashtray, she felt the strange beast that had slumbered so long within her bosom stir, stretch itself, yawn, prick up its ears, and suddenly bound to its feet, and fix its longing, hungry stare upon those faraway places. But all she said was, smiling gently: "How I envy you."

He accepted that. "It has been," he said, "very wonderful—especially Russia. Russia was all that we had imagined, and far, far more. I even spent some days on a river boat on the Volga. Do you remember that boatman's song that you used to play?"

"Yes." It began to play in her mind as she spoke.

"Do you ever play it now?"

"No, I've no piano."

He was amazed at that. "But what has become of your beautiful piano?"

She made a little grimace. "Sold. Ages ago."

"But you were so fond of music," he wondered.

"I've no time for it now," said she.

He let it go at that. "That river life," he went on, "is something quite special. After a day or two you cannot realize that you have ever known another. And it is not necessary to know the language—the life of the boat creates a bond between you and the people that's more than sufficient. You eat with them, pass the day with them, and in the evening there is that endless singing."

She shivered, hearing the boatman's song break out again loud and tragic, and seeing the boat floating on the darkening river with melancholy trees on either side. . . . "Yes, I should like that," said she, stroking her muff.

"You'd like almost everything about Russian life," he said warmly. "It's so informal, so impulsive, so free without question. And then the peasants are so splendid. They are such human beings—yes, that is it. Even the man who drives your carriage has—has some real part in what is happening. I remember the evening a party of us, two friends of mine and the wife of one of them, went for a picnic by the Black Sea. We took supper and champagne and ate and drank on the grass. And while we were eating the coachman came up. 'Have a dill pickle,' he said. He wanted to share with us. That seemed to me so right, so—you know what I mean?"

And she seemed at that moment to be sitting on the grass beside the mysteriously Black Sea, black as velvet and rippling against the banks in silent, velvet waves. She saw the carriage drawn up to one side of the road, and the little group on the grass, their faces and hands white in the moonlight. She saw the pale dress of the woman outspread and her folded parasol, lying on the grass like a huge pearl crochet hook. Apart from them, with his supper in a cloth on his knees, sat the coachman. "Have a dill pickle," said he, and although she was not certain what a dill pickle was, she saw the greenish glass jar with a red chili like a parrot's beak glimmering through. She sucked in her cheeks; the dill pickle was terribly sour. . . .

"Yes, I know perfectly what you mean," she said.

In the pause that followed they looked at each other. In the past when they had looked at each other like that they had felt such a boundless understanding between them that their souls had, as it were, put their arms round each other and dropped into the same sea, content to be drowned, like mournful lovers. But now, the surprising thing was that it was he who held back. He who said:

"What a marvelous listener you are. When you look at me with those wild eyes I feel that I could tell you things that I would never breathe to another human being."

Was there just a hint of mockery in his voice or was it her fancy? She could not be sure.

"Before I met you," he said, "I had never spoken of myself to anybody. How well I remember one night, the night that I brought you the little Christmas tree, telling you all about my childhood. And of how I was so miserable that I ran away and lived under a cart in our yard for two days without being discovered. And you listened, and your eyes shone, and I felt that you had even made the little Christmas tree listen too, as in a fairy story."

But of that evening she had remembered a little pot of caviar. It had cost seven and sixpence. He could not get over it. Think of it—a tiny jar like that costing seven and sixpence. While she ate it he watched her, delighted and shocked.

"No, really, that is eating money. You could not get seven shillings into a little pot that size. Only think of the profit they must make. . . ." And he had begun some immensely complicated calculations. . . . But now good-bye to the caviar. The Christmas tree was on the table, and the little boy lay under the cart with his head pillowed on the yard dog.

"The dog was called Bosun," she cried delightedly.

But he did not follow. "Which dog? Had you a dog? I don't remember a dog at all."

"No, no. I mean the yard dog when you were a little boy." He laughed and snapped the cigarette case to.

"Was he? Do you know I had forgotten that. It seems such ages ago. I cannot believe that it is only six years. After I had recognized you today—I had to take such a leap—I had to take a leap over my whole life to get back to that time. I was such a kid then." He drummed on the table. "I've often thought how I must have bored you. And now I understand so perfectly why you wrote to me as you did—although at the time that letter nearly finished my life. I found it again the other day, and I couldn't help laughing as I read it. It was so clever—such a true picture of me." He glanced up. "You're not going?"

She had buttoned her collar again and drawn down her veil.

"Yes, I am afraid I must," she said, and managed a smile. Now she knew that he had been mocking.

"Ah, no, please," he pleaded. "Don't go just for a moment," and he caught up one of her gloves from the table and clutched at it as if that would hold her. "I see so few people to talk to nowadays, that I have turned into a sort of barbarian," he said. "Have I said something to hurt you?"

"Not a bit," she lied. But as she watched him draw her glove through his fingers, gently, gently, her anger really did die down, and besides, at the moment he looked more like himself of six years ago. . . .

"What I really wanted then," he said softly, "was to be a sort of carpet—to make myself into a sort of carpet for you to walk on

SUN, WIND, AND RAIN
David Cox
The City Museum and Art Gallery, Birmingham

so that you need not be hurt by the sharp stones and the mud that you hated so. It was nothing more positive than that—nothing more selfish. Only I did desire, eventually, to turn into a magic carpet and carry you away to all those lands you longed to see."

As he spoke she lifted her head as though she drank something; the strange beast in her bosom began to purr. . . .

"I felt that you were more lonely than anybody else in the world," he went on, "and yet, perhaps, that you were the only person in the world who was really, truly alive. Born out of your time," he murmured, stroking the glove, "fated."

What had she done! How had she dared to throw away her happiness like this. This was the only man who had ever understood her. Was it too late? Could it be too late? *She* was that glove that he held in his fingers. . . .

"And then the fact that you had no friends and never had made friends with people. How I understood that, for neither had I. Is it just the same now?"

"Yes," she breathed. "Just the same. I am as alone as ever."

"So am I," he laughed gently, "just the same."

Suddenly with a quick gesture he handed her back the glove and scraped his chair on the floor. "But what seemed to me so mysterious then is perfectly plain to me now. And to you, too, of course. . . . It simply was that we were such egoists, so self-engrossed, so wrapped up in ourselves that we hadn't a corner in our hearts for anybody else. Do you know," he cried, naive and hearty, and dreadfully like another side of that old self again, "I began studying a Mind System when I was in Russia, and I found that we were not peculiar at all. It's quite a well known form of . . ."

She had gone. He sat there, thunderstruck, astounded beyond words. . . . And then he asked the waitress for his bill.

"But the cream has not been touched," he said. "Please do not charge me for it."

RESPONDING TO THE SELECTION

Your Response

1. Which of the two principal characters do you like better, Vera or her friend? Explain.
2. Do you think that Vera makes the right decision in leaving at the end of the story? Why or why not?
3. Does the story leave you feeling sad that the two are still not able to connect with each other? Why or why not?

Recalling

4. (a) How does Vera's friend react when he first sees her? (b) How does this make Vera feel?
5. (a) What does the man remember about the first afternoon they spent together? (b) What does Vera remember?
6. Where has the man been for the past six years?
7. (a) What does Vera begin to feel toward the end of the story, as her friend explains their mutual loneliness? (b) What changes her mind?

Interpreting

8. (a) What difference between Vera and her friend is revealed in the first two paragraphs of the story? (b) What difference is revealed through their attitudes toward the pot of caviar?
9. Vera decides that her friend's recollections of the afternoon at Kew Gardens are "truer" than hers. What does this reveal about her?
10. What action do you think is symbolized by Vera's unbuttoning and buttoning her collar?
11. Do you think Vera's and the man's behavior reveal the truth of his statement about their being egoists? Support your answer with details from the story.
12. (a) What do you think is the significance of the story's title? (b) Do you think the title is an appropriate one? Explain.

Applying

13. The man claims that Vera and he were so wrapped up in themselves that they didn't have room in their hearts for anyone else. What qualities do you think are necessary for a person to be open to love?

ANALYZING LITERATURE

Understanding Dialogue

Dialogue is conversation that takes place between two or more characters in a literary work. One key purpose of dialogue is to present information about the characters in a direct and interesting manner. Knowing precisely when to let a character speak for himself or herself through dialogue and when to speak *for* that character requires great skill on the part of a writer.

Locate the following passages from the story, and read the paragraphs that precede and follow each. In each case, explain what effect you feel the author achieves through dialogue that would be lost in direct narration.

1. "Loathe it." She shuddered. "And the worst of it is that the older one grows . . ." (page 870)
2. "The colder!" He echoed her words, laughing too. "Ah, ah. You still say the same things." (page 870)
3. "And while we were eating, the coachman came up. 'Have a dill pickle,' he said. He wanted to share with us. That seemed to me so right, so—you know what I mean?" (page 872)
4. "What a marvelous listener you are . . ." (page 873)

CRITICAL THINKING AND READING

Making Inferences Based on Dialogue

It has been said that language is "a window on the mind." If we accept this observation as true, then we can use dialogue to learn a great deal about the workings of a character's mind. Notice, for instance, Vera's tendency to speak in very short, almost clipped, sentences—a habit that might lead us to infer that she is a guarded, cautious person, which, in fact, the narrator assures us she is. Her friend, too, reveals much about his thoughts, feelings, and ideas through his dialogue, though in this instance we receive no additional clues from the narrator.

What impression do you form of the narrator from what he says? Find lines of dialogue to support your answer.

THINKING AND WRITING

Writing a Dialogue

Think about what Vera's first conversation with her friend six years previously might have been like. What clues to the eventual outcome of their relationship may have been present in what they said to each other? Use evidence in the story to develop a dialogue reproducing this conversation. As you ·write, make sure that what the characters say is consistent with the way they are depicted in "A Dill Pickle." You might share your dialogue with a classmate and compare your versions of the conversation.

LEARNING OPTION

Art. "A Dill Pickle" is set in England in the years preceding World War I. Working alone or with one or two classmates, review the story to find clues about the physical appearance of Vera and her friend. What were they wearing? What was the fabric like? Investigate styles of clothing, hair, and cosmetics that were popular during the period. Find as many drawings or photographs that you can. Then draw or paint the characters in an illustration for the story. You may want to pay particular attention to details like Vera's gloves, her coat, and her veil.

JAMES JOYCE

1882–1941

Although James Joyce left Ireland early in his career and associated with the radical literary experimentalists on the Continent, he never lost the respect for tradition that he had learned from his Jesuit teachers. All of his works are set in his native Dublin, and all have firm roots in the literature of the past. If Joyce's innovativeness in the areas of plot, character, and language are undeniable, so then is the notion that part of his greatness was his ability to reinterpret and transform familiar literary forms.

James Joyce was born and educated in Dublin. Choosing, much to the disappointment of his family and teachers, not to enter the priesthood, he briefly considered careers in medicine and singing. His true calling, however, was as a writer, and in 1907 he published *Chamber Music,* a collection of poems. At the time of the book's publication, Joyce was living in Trieste, Italy, where he remained until the outbreak of the First World War.

The year he relocated to Zurich, 1914, also marks the appearance of his landmark volume of short stories, *Dubliners.* This collection of deceptively simple tales focuses on people who, on the surface, are quite ordinary but whose minds are filled with raging psychological and emotional conflicts. Each of the main characters in *Dubliners* experiences in some way a growth of self-awareness that leads to a climactic peak in the story.

This process is developed still more fully in *A Portrait of the Artist as a Young Man,* a fictionalized account of Joyce's own life from infancy through age twenty. Like Joyce, Stephen Dedalus, the novel's main character, finds himself in conflict with his family, the Roman Catholic Church, and the nationalistic fervor of his countrymen. The book also reveals a heightened awareness of the power of language and a deeper immersion into the mind of the character. Both these traits are carried forward into *Ulysses* (1922), whose ultimate banning in England and the United States made Joyce famous, if not wealthy. This novel, which roughly parallels Homer's *Odyssey,* presents a single day in the life of three Dubliners. The world Joyce depicts, while as solidly three-dimensional as any conjured up by nineteenth-century realists, is nevertheless one in which language can be seen to provide keys to the exploration of truth.

Joyce's last novel, *Finnegan's Wake* (1939), was in many ways the most challenging. Written in what one scholar terms "a dream language of Joyce's own invention," this highly experimental work presents its author's view of human existence as moving through various cycles.

GUIDE FOR INTERPRETING

Araby

Writers' Techniques

Epiphany. Epiphany (i pif′ ə nē) is a profound mental or spiritual revelation experienced by the hero of a literary work. The term is derived from Greek mythology, where it was used to describe the occasion when a god or goddess, wearing a disguise or concealed in a cloud, would suddenly reveal his or her true divine identity to a mortal. In modern fiction epiphany generally occurs in stories that operate on a mental, or "cerebral," level, rather than on a purely physical level. In such stories the major events are so constructed as to lead up to this dawning, or sudden awareness of an important truth, on the part of a character. What the character *thinks* under circumstances of this sort is more important than what he or she *does*. In his collection of stories *Dubliners,* James Joyce frequently depicts characters who experience epiphany.

Focus

Logan Pearsall Smith wrote, "All mirrors are magical mirrors; never can we see our faces in them." Freewrite, exploring the meaning of the quotation and your reactions to it.

Primary Source

The reactions people have to others may shed light on their own character. What was Joyce's reaction to William Butler Yeats, an older and more established writer? By 1905, when he was forty years old, Yeats was a famous man in Ireland: A greatly admired poet and playwright, he was also a leader in both the Irish Literary Revival and the Irish National Movement. In 1905 James Joyce was only twenty-three. In contrast to Yeats, he had yet to publish anything; his first work, a collection of poems called *Chamber Music,* was still two years off. One would think, then, that Joyce would be very much in awe of Yeats's accomplishments in light of his own youth and inexperience. Just the opposite was true, as revealed in the famous story his friend Oliver St. John Gogarty recounts: "We both lived on the north side of the city, and we were going up Rutland Square, I think it was a horse-drawn tram in those days. I happened to mention that thing that the newspapers were full of—that it was Yeats's fortieth birthday and that Lady Gregory had collected from his friends forty pounds with which she bought a Kelmscott edition of Chaucer by William Morris. Everybody knew that it was Yeats's birthday. But when I made an epiphany, so to speak, and told Joyce this, at the first tram stop he got out. Yeats was lodging in the Cavendish Hotel, in Rutland Square, and he solemnly walked in and knocked at Yeats's door. When Yeats opened the door of the sitting-room he said, 'What age are you, sir?' and Yeats said, 'I'm 40.'—'You are too old for me to help. I bid you goodbye.' And Yeats was greatly impressed at the impertinence of the thing."

ST. PATRICK'S CLOSE
Walter Osborne
National Gallery of Ireland

Araby

James Joyce

North Richmond Street, being blind,[1] was a quiet street except at the hour when the Christian Brothers' School set the boys free. An uninhabited house of two stories stood at the blind end, detached from its neighbors in a square ground. The other houses of the street, conscious of decent lives within them, gazed at one another with brown imperturbable faces.

The former tenant of our house, a priest, had died in the back drawing room. Air, musty from having been long enclosed, hung in all the rooms, and the waste room behind the kitchen was littered with old useless papers. Among these I found a few paper-covered books, the pages of which were curled and damp: *The Abbot,* by Walter Scott, *The Devout Communicant* and *The Memoirs of Vidocq.*[2] I liked the last best because its leaves were yellow. The wild garden behind the house contained a central apple tree and a few straggling bushes under one of which I found the late tenant's rusty bicycle pump. He had been a very charitable priest; in his will he had left all his money to institutions and the furniture of his house to his sister.

When the short days of winter came dusk fell before we had well eaten our dinners. When we met in the street the houses had grown somber. The space of sky above us was the color of ever-changing violet and toward it the lamps of the street lifted their feeble lanterns. The cold air stung us and we played till our bodies glowed. Our shouts echoed in the silent street. The career of our play brought us through the dark muddy lanes behind the houses where we ran the gantlet of the rough tribes from the cottages, to the back doors of the dark dripping gardens where odors arose from the ashpits, to the dark odorous stables where a coachman smoothed and combed the horse or shook music from the buckled harness. When we returned to the street, light from the kitchen windows had filled the areas. If my uncle was seen turning the corner we hid in the shadow until we had seen him safely housed. Or if Mangan's sister came out on the doorstep to call her brother in to his tea we watched her from our shadow peer up and down the street. We waited to see whether she would remain or go in and, if she remained, we left our shadow and walked up to Mangan's steps resignedly. She was waiting for us, her figure defined by the light from the half-opened door. Her brother always teased her before he obeyed and I stood by the railings looking at her. Her dress swung as she moved her body and the soft rope of her hair tossed from side to side.

Every morning I lay on the floor in the front parlor watching her door. The blind was pulled down to within an inch of the sash so that I could not be seen. When she came out on the doorstep my heart leaped. I

---

1. blind: Dead end.
2. The Abbot . . . Vidocq: A historical tale, a religious manual, and the remembrances of a French adventurer, respectively.

ran to the hall, seized my books and followed her. I kept her brown figure always in my eye and, when we came near the point at which our ways diverged, I quickened my pace and passed her. This happened morning after morning. I had never spoken to her, except for a few casual words, and yet her name was like a summons to all my foolish blood.

Her image accompanied me even in places the most hostile to romance. On Saturday evenings when my aunt went marketing I had to go to carry some of the parcels. We walked through the flaring streets, jostled by drunken men and bargaining women, amid the curses of laborers, the shrill litanies of shopboys who stood on guard by the barrels of pigs' cheeks, the nasal chanting of street singers, who sang a *come-all-you* about O'Donovan Rossa,[3] or a ballad about the troubles in our native land. These noises converged in a single sensation of life for me: I imagined that I bore my chalice safely through a throng of foes. Her name sprang to my lips at moments in strange prayers and praises which I myself did not understand. My eyes were often full of tears (I could not tell why) and at times a flood from my heart seemed to pour itself out into my bosom. I thought little of the future. I did not know whether I would ever speak to her or not or, if I spoke to her, how I could tell her of my confused adoration. But my body was like a harp and her words and gestures were like fingers running upon the wires.

One evening I went into the back drawing-room in which the priest had died. It was a dark rainy evening and there was no sound in the house. Through one of the broken panes I heard the rain impinge upon the earth, the fine incessant needles of water playing in the sodden beds. Some distant lamp or lighted window gleamed below me. I was thankful that I could see so little. All my senses seemed to desire to veil themselves and, feeling that I was about to slip from them, I pressed the palms of my hands together until they trembled, murmuring: *"O love! O love!"* many times.

At last she spoke to me. When she addressed the first words to me I was so confused that I did not know what to answer. She asked me was I going to *Araby*. I forget whether I answered yes or no. It would be a splendid bazaar, she said; she would love to go.

"And why can't you?" I asked.

While she spoke she turned a silver bracelet round and round her wrist. She could not go, she said, because there would be a retreat[4] that week in her convent.[5] Her brother and two other boys were fighting for their caps and I was alone at the railings. She held one of the spikes, bowing her head towards me. The light from the lamp opposite our door caught the white curve of her neck, lit up her hair that rested there and, falling, lit up the hand upon the railing. It fell over one side of her dress and caught the white border of a petticoat, just visible as she stood at ease.

"It's well for you," she said.

"If I go," I said, "I will bring you something."

What innumerable follies laid waste my waking and sleeping thoughts after that evening! I wished to annihilate the tedious intervening days. I chafed against the work of school. At night in my bedroom and by day in the classroom her image came between me and the page I strove to read. The syllables of the word *Araby* were called to me through the silence in which my soul luxuriated and cast an Eastern enchantment over me. I asked for leave to go to the bazaar on Saturday night. My aunt was surprised and hoped it was not some Freemason[6] affair. I answered few questions in

---

3. come-all-you ... Rossa: The opening of a ballad about an Irish hero.

4. retreat *n.*: A period of retirement or seclusion for prayer, religious study, and meditation.
5. convent *n.*: A school run by an order of nuns.
6. Freemason: The Free and Accepted Masons, an international secret society.

class. I watched my master's face pass from amiability to sternness; he hoped I was not beginning to idle. I could not call my wandering thoughts together. I had hardly any patience with the serious work of life which, now that it stood between me and my desire, seemed to me child's play, ugly monotonous child's play.

On Saturday morning I reminded my uncle that I wished to go to the bazaar in the evening. He was fussing at the hallstand, looking for the hat brush, and answered me curtly:

"Yes, boy, I know."

As he was in the hall I could not go into the front parlor and lie at the window. I left the house in bad humor and walked slowly toward the school. The air was pitilessly raw and already my heart misgave me.

When I came home to dinner my uncle had not yet been home. Still it was early. I sat staring at the clock for some time and, when its ticking began to irritate me, I left the room. I mounted the staircase and gained the upper part of the house. The high cold empty gloomy rooms liberated me and I went from room to room singing. From the front window I saw my companions playing below in the street. Their cries reached me weakened and indistinct and, leaning my forehead against the cool glass, I looked over at the dark house where she lived. I may have stood there for an hour, seeing nothing but the brown-clad figure cast by my imagination, touched discreetly by the lamplight at the curved neck, at the hand upon the railings and at the border below the dress.

When I came downstairs again I found Mrs. Mercer sitting at the fire. She was an old garrulous woman, a pawnbroker's widow, who collected used stamps for some pious purpose. I had to endure the gossip of the tea table. The meal was prolonged beyond an hour and still my uncle did not come. Mrs. Mercer stood up to go: she was sorry she couldn't wait any longer, but it was after eight o'clock and she did not like to be out late, as the night air was bad for her. When she had gone I began to walk up and down the room, clenching my fists. My aunt said:

"I'm afraid you may put off your bazaar for this night of Our Lord."

At nine o'clock I heard my uncle's latchkey in the hall door. I heard him talking to himself and heard the hallstand rocking when it had received the weight of his overcoat. I could interpret these signs. When he was midway through his dinner I asked him to give me the money to go to the bazaar. He had forgotten.

"The people are in bed and after their first sleep now," he said.

I did not smile. My aunt said to him energetically:

"Can't you give him the money and let him go? You've kept him late enough as it is."

My uncle said he was very sorry he had forgotten. He said he believed in the old saying: *All work and no play makes Jack a dull boy.* He asked me where I was going and, when I had told him a second time he asked me did I know *The Arab's Farewell to His Steed.*[7] When I left the kitchen he was about to recite the opening lines of the piece to my aunt.

I held a florin[8] tightly in my hand as I strode down Buckingham Street toward the station. The sight of the streets thronged with buyers and glaring with gas recalled to me the purpose of my journey. I took my seat in a third-class carriage of a deserted train. After an intolerable delay the train moved out of the station slowly. It crept onward among ruinous houses and over the twinkling river. At Westland Row Station a crowd of people pressed to the carriage doors; but the porters moved them back, saying that it was a special train for the bazaar. I remained alone in the bare car-

---

7. The Arab's . . . His Steed: A popular nineteenth-century poem.
8. florin n.: A former two-shilling coin.

riage. In a few minutes the train drew up beside an improvised wooden platform. I passed out onto the road and saw by the lighted dial of a clock that it was ten minutes to ten. In front of me was a large building which displayed the magical name.

I could not find any sixpenny entrance and, fearing that the bazaar would be closed, I passed in quickly through a turnstile, handing a shilling to a weary-looking man. I found myself in a big hall girdled at half its height by a gallery. Nearly all the stalls were closed and the greater part of the hall was in darkness. I recognized a silence like that which pervades a church after a service. I walked into the center of the bazaar timidly. A few people were gathered about the stalls which were still open. Before a curtain, over which the words *Café Chantant*[9] were written in colored lamps, two men were counting money on a salver.[10] I listened to the fall of the coins.

Remembering with difficulty why I had come I went over to one of the stalls and examined porcelain vases and flowered tea sets. At the door of the stall a young lady was talking and laughing with two young gentlemen. I remarked their English accents and listened vaguely to their conversation.

---

9. Café Chantant: A café with musical entertainment.
10. salver *n.*: A tray usually used for the presentation of letters or visiting cards.

"O, I never said such a thing!"
"O, but you did!"
"O, but I didn't!"
"Didn't she say that?"
"Yes. I heard her."
"O, there's a . . .fib!"

Observing me the young lady came over and asked me did I wish to buy anything. The tone of her voice was not encouraging; she seemed to have spoken to me out of a sense of duty. I looked humbly at the great jars that stood like Eastern guards at either side of the dark entrance to the stall and murmured:

"No, thank you."

The young lady changed the position of one of the vases and went back to the two young men. They began to talk of the same subject. Once or twice the young lady glanced at me over her shoulder.

I lingered before her stall, though I knew my stay was useless, to make my interest in her wares seem the more real. Then I turned away slowly and walked down the middle of the bazaar. I allowed the two pennies to fall against the sixpence in my pocket. I heard a voice call from one end of the gallery that the light was out. The upper part of the hall was now completely dark.

Gazing up into the darkness I saw myself as a creature driven and derided by vanity; and my eyes burned with anguish and anger.

▌RESPONDING TO THE SELECTION

Your Response

1. Have you ever been frustrated when a friend or family member failed to keep his or her word about plans you had made? How did you feel?
2. As the narrator does, do you ever agree to do something and later regret it? Explain.

Recalling

3. (a) Why is going to the bazaar so important to the narrator? (b) Why is he late getting there? (c) What does he buy?
4. How does the narrator feel at the end of the story?

Interpreting

5. How would you describe the mood, or feeling, established in the opening paragraphs?

6. What might have been the author's reason for not giving Mangan's sister a name?
7. What makes the narrator feel as he does at the end of the story?
8. (a) Why do you think the author chose "Araby" as a name for the bazaar? (b) As a title for the story? (c) How does it relate to the narrator's experiences?

Applying

9. (a) Look up the meanings of the word *vanity*. Which meaning is intended in the last paragraph of this story? (b) Do you agree with the narrator that he is a "creature driven and derided by vanity"? Support your answer. (c) Do you think vanity is or is not necessary to some degree for survival in today's world? Explain your answer.

ANALYZING LITERATURE

Understanding Epiphany

Epiphany is the sudden recognition of an important truth by a character in a work of fiction. Tracing back to Greek mythology where it referred to the sudden disclosure to one character of a deity's identity, epiphany in contemporary fiction is the unmasking of a truth that was present all along in a character's mind. In the short stories of James Joyce, this truth usually relates to the essential nature of something commonplace—a person, situation, or object—that the character now sees in a new light.

1. Where in "Araby" does the epiphany occur?
2. What does the hero suddenly realize?
3. What suddenly causes him to feel this way?

CRITICAL THINKING AND READING

Analyzing Joyce's Attitude

It is important to keep in mind that, as with many stories told from the first-person point of view, the narrator of "Araby" is not the author. Yet as with any such story, the author expresses his attitude toward the character of the narrator through the character's words, thoughts, and actions. Read the following quotes from "Araby." Tell what they reveal, as a whole, about Joyce's attitude toward his narrator's romantic goals.

1. "Every morning I lay on the floor in the front parlor watching her door." (page 881)
2. "Her image accompanied me even in places the most hostile to romance." (page 882)
3. "Her name sprang to my lips at moments in strange prayers. . . ." (page 882)
4. "'If I go,' I said, 'I will bring you something.'" (page 882)

THINKING AND WRITING

Writing an Extended Conversation

Choose an episode from the story involving the narrator and Mangan's sister—perhaps when he passes her going to school or when they talk about the bazaar. Imagine an extended conversation between them, giving particular emphasis to what they might say and the way in which they would most likely say it. Write down this bit of dialogue, permitting yourself ample time to revise any sections that do not ring true.

LEARNING OPTIONS

1. **Art.** Make a poster for the *Araby* bazaar. Reread the story to find details about the bazaar that you may want to use in your design. Consider what information should appear on your poster and what images might best advertise the bazaar. You might also want to investigate how posters from the turn of the century looked and try to imitate that style.

2. **Writing.** Working with one or two classmates, write a brief stage adaptation of "Araby." Use the dialogue from the story as the backbone of your script. Write additional dialogue (or use any additional dialogue written in the Thinking and Writing activity) and include stage directions to indicate action. If possible, cast the play and perform it in class.

ELIZABETH BOWEN

1899–1973

The fiction of Elizabeth Bowen is distinguished by the author's subtle observation of landscape, by her innovative and believable use of the supernatural, and by her haunting portrayal of England during one of the darkest eras of that country's history—the years between 1939 and 1945.

Bowen was born in Dublin and raised in County Cork, Ireland. She published her first novel, *The Hotel,* in 1927. During the 1930's she perfected her craft and in 1938, on the eve of the Second World War, completed one of her best-known works, *The Death of the Heart.* This novel traces the intertwining loves and fortunes of a group of sophisticated but vulnerable Londoners in the 1930's.

During the war Bowen observed England's hardships keenly and with compassion. The brutal realities of the conflict—air raids, blackouts, and espionage—were incorporated into some of her best short stories. Typically, she played on the heightening of emotions and perceptions in wartime to probe the inner workings of her characters' minds. Shortly after the end of the war Bowen published another novel, *The Heat of the Day* (1949), which was received with much acclaim. Set in wartime London, the work movingly juxtaposes a tragic love affair with the larger national dilemma of a country's fight for its survival.

After the war, Bowen widened her literary activities to include literary criticism and book reviews for such journals as the *Tatler,* as well as scripts for the British Broadcasting Corporation. She was honored by her own country in 1948, when she received a prestigious award, the C.B.E. (Commander, Order of the British Empire). During the 1950's she spent a great deal of time in the United States, writing and lecturing.

After the death of her husband in 1952, Bowen returned to Ireland to live. Although her earlier work was influenced by the psychological realism of Henry James, her later novels—*A World of Love* (1955), *The Little Girls* (1964), and *Eva Trout* (1969)—exhibit a more symbolic, more poetic style. Bowen never fully adopted the stream-of-consciousness technique practiced by her contemporaries Virginia Woolf and James Joyce. Yet readers may easily sense more than a trace of this technique in Bowen's novels and stories—such is her sensitivity to fine shades of emotion and her eye for small but important detail.

Bowen defined the novel as the "non-poetic statement of poetic truth," and in her straightforward, deceptively simple writing style and exploration of complex human relationships, she achieved this literary integrity and verisimilitude.

GUIDE FOR INTERPRETING

The Demon Lover

Historical Context

War and the Ghost Story. Despite the number of times humans have waged warfare on one another throughout history, war has never, happily, become a natural state of affairs for the species. The unnaturalness of a civilization in wartime is especially evident off the battlefield, in the streets of a city. Here the horrors that attend war—loss of life, destruction of property, suffering, fear, and despair—seem ever so much like the work of a band of demonic spirits. The Second World War, in particular, struck individuals living in the war-ravaged cities of Europe as akin to a nightmare. Warning sirens and blackouts were a part of everyday life; whole communities were sometimes evacuated against the danger of an enemy attack, leaving street after street of deserted buildings. These "ghost towns" within metropolises like London impressed some writers as ideal backdrops for stories that deal in events of the supernatural, or ghost stories. One such writer was Elizabeth Bowen, who sought in "The Demon Lover" to pit the horrifying landscape of the battlefield against the still more horrifying landscape closer to home.

Commentary

"The Demon Lover" is, in part, a subtle reworking of an English ballad of the same name. In the ballad a faithless, fickle woman betrays her absent lover and marries another man. When the lover returns years later—now supposedly very wealthy—the woman is quick to abandon her husband and children to run off with him. Too late, she discovers that the lover is, in fact, not at all what she imagined. On a superficial level, Bowen's story resembles the ballad, and one critic, Douglas A. Hughes, has remarked that the author even relies on the poem to suggest how the story's main character, Mrs. Drover, views herself. But Bowen's genius in this story lies partly in the way she refashions the ballad's basic plot and terrifying atmosphere to suggest important things about the effect of war's devastation on the human psyche. In a recent study of Elizabeth Bowen, critic Allan E. Austin wrote that "'The Demon Lover' is a ghost story that builds up and then culminates like an Alfred Hitchcock movie."

Focus

Imagine that a mysterious letter or other piece of mail is delivered to your home. In a brief narrative, describe the specific contents of the letter, as well as your and your family's reaction to it. Conclude your account with an explanation of how the mystery was resolved.

The Demon Lover

Elizabeth Bowen

Toward the end of her day in London Mrs. Drover went round to her shut-up house to look for several things she wanted to take away. Some belonged to herself, some to her family, who were by now used to their country life. It was late August; it had been a steamy, showery day: at the moment the trees down the pavement glittered in an escape of humid yellow afternoon sun. Against the next batch of clouds, already piling up ink-dark, broken chimneys and parapets stood out. In her once familiar street, as in any unused channel, an unfamiliar queerness had silted up; a cat wove itself in and out of railings, but no human eye watched Mrs. Drover's return. Shifting some parcels under her arm, she slowly forced round her latchkey in an unwilling lock, then gave the door, which had warped, a push with her knee. Dead air came out to meet her as she went in.

The staircase window having been boarded up, no light came down into the hall. But one door, she could just see, stood ajar, so she went quickly through into the room and unshuttered the big window in there. Now the prosaic woman, looking about her, was more perplexed than she knew by everything that she saw, by traces of her long former habit of life—the yellow smoke stain up the white marble mantelpiece, the ring left by a vase on the top of the escritoire;[1] the bruise in the wallpaper where, on the door being thrown open widely, the china handle had always hit the wall. The piano, having gone away to be stored, had left what looked like claw marks on its part of the parquet.[2] Though not much dust had seeped in, each object wore a film of another kind; and, the only ventilation being the chimney, the whole drawing room smelled of the cold hearth. Mrs. Drover put down her parcels on the escritoire and left the room to proceed upstairs; the things she wanted were in a bedroom chest.

She had been anxious to see how the house was—the part-time caretaker she shared with some neighbors was away this week on his holiday, known to be not yet back. At the best of times he did not look in often, and she was never sure that she trusted him. There were some cracks in the structure, left by the last bombing, on which she was anxious to keep an eye. Not that one could do anything—

A shaft of refracted daylight now lay across the hall. She stopped dead and stared at the hall table—on this lay a letter addressed to her.

She thought first—then the caretaker *must* be back. All the same, who, seeing the house shuttered, would have dropped a letter in at the box? It was not a circular, it was not a bill. And the post office redirected, to the address in the country, everything for her that came through the post. The care-

---

1. **escritoire** (es′ krə twär′) *n.*: A writing desk or table.

2. **parquet** (pär kā′) *n.*: A flooring of inlaid woodwork in geometric forms.

taker (even if he *were* back) did not know she was due in London today—her call here had been planned to be a surprise—so his negligence in the manner of this letter, leaving it to wait in the dusk and the dust, annoyed her. Annoyed, she picked up the letter, which bore no stamp. But it cannot be important, or they would know . . . She took the letter rapidly upstairs with her, without a stop to look at the writing till she reached what had been her bedroom, where she let in light. The room looked over the garden and other gardens: the sun had gone in; as the clouds sharpened and lowered, the trees and rank lawns seemed already to smoke with dark. Her reluctance to look again at the letter came from the fact that she felt intruded upon—and by someone contemptuous of her ways. However, in the tenseness preceding the fall of rain she read it: it was a few lines.

DEAR KATHLEEN,

You will not have forgotten that today is our anniversary, and the day we said. The years have gone by at once slowly and fast. In view of the fact that nothing has changed, I shall rely upon you to keep your promise. I was sorry to see you leave London, but was satisfied that you would be back in time. You may expect me, therefore, at the hour arranged.

Until then . . . K.

Mrs. Drover looked for the date: it was today's. She dropped the letter onto the bedsprings, then picked it up to see the writing again—her lips, beneath the remains of lipstick, beginning to go white. She felt so much the change in her own face that

HOLY BUSH HILL, HAMPSTEAD, 1921
Ethelbert White

she went to the mirror, polished a clear patch in it and looked at once urgently and stealthily in. She was confronted by a woman of forty-four, with eyes starting out under a hatbrim that had been rather carelessly pulled down. She had not put on any more powder since she left the shop where she ate her solitary tea. The pearls her husband had given her on their marriage hung loose round her now rather thinner throat, slipping into the V of the pink wool jumper her sister knitted last autumn as they sat round the fire. Mrs. Drover's most normal expression was one of controlled worry, but of assent. Since the birth of the third of her little boys, attended by a quite serious illness, she had had an intermittent muscular flicker to the left of her mouth, but in spite of this she could always sustain a manner that was at once energetic and calm.

Turning from her own face as precipitately as she had gone to meet it, she went to the chest where the things were, unlocked it, threw up the lid and knelt to search. But as rain began to come crashing down she could not keep from looking over her shoulder at the stripped bed on which the letter lay. Behind the blanket of rain the clock of the church that still stood struck six— with rapidly heightening apprehension she counted each of the slow strokes. "The hour arranged . . . My God," she said, "*What hour? How should I . . . ?* After twenty-five years. . . ."

The young girl talking to the soldier in the garden had not ever completely seen his face. It was dark; they were saying goodbye under a tree. Now and then—for it felt, from not seeing him at this intense moment, as though she had never seen him at all—she verified his presence for these few moments longer by putting out a hand, which he each time pressed, without very much kindness, and painfully, on to one of the breast buttons of his uniform. That cut of the button on the palm of her hand was, principally,

what she was to carry away. This was so near the end of a leave from France that she could only wish him already gone. It was August 1916. Being not kissed, being drawn away from and looked at intimidated Kathleen till she imagined spectral glitters in the place of his eyes. Turning away and looking back up the lawn she saw, through branches of trees, the drawing-room window alight; she caught a breath for the moment when she could go running back there into the safe arms of her mother and sister, and cry: "What shall I do, what shall I do? He has gone."

Hearing her catch her breath, her fiancé said, without feeling: "Cold?"

"You're going away such a long way."

"Not so far as you think."

"I don't understand?"

"You don't have to," he said. "You will. You know what we said."

"But that was—suppose you—I mean, suppose."

"I shall be with you," he said, "sooner or later. You won't forget that. You need do nothing but wait."

Only a little more than a minute later she was free to run up the silent lawn. Looking in through the window at her mother and sister, who did not for the moment perceive her, she already felt that unnatural promise drive down between her and the rest of all humankind. No other way of having given herself could have made her feel so apart, lost and foresworn. She could not have plighted a more sinister troth.

Kathleen behaved well when, some months later, her fiancé was reported missing, presumed killed. Her family not only supported her but were able to praise her courage without stint because they could not regret, as a husband for her, the man they knew almost nothing about. They hoped she would, in a year or two, console herself—and had it been only a question of consolation things might have gone much straighter ahead. But her trouble, behind just a little grief, was a complete dislocation from everything. She did not reject other lovers, for these failed to appear: for years she failed to attract men—and with the approach of her thirties she became natural enough to share her family's anxiousness on this score. She began to put herself out, to wonder; and at thirty-two she was very greatly relieved to find herself being courted by William Drover. She married him, and the two of them settled down in this quiet, arboreal part of Kensington; in this house the years piled up, her children were born and they all lived till they were driven out by the bombs of the next war. Her movements as Mrs. Drover were circumscribed, and she dismissed any idea that they were still watched.

As things were—dead or living the letter writer sent her only a threat. Unable, for some minutes, to go on kneeling with her back exposed to the empty room, Mrs. Drover rose from the chest to sit on an upright chair whose back was firmly against the wall. The desuetude of her former bedroom, her married London home's whole air of being a cracked cup from which memory, with its reassuring power, had either evaporated or leaked away, made a crisis—and at just this crisis the letter writer had, knowledgeably, struck. The hollowness of the house this evening canceled years on years of voices, habits and steps. Through the shut windows she only heard rain fall on the roofs around. To rally herself, she said she was in a mood—and, for two or three seconds shutting her eyes, told herself that she had imagined the letter. But she opened them—there it lay on the bed.

On the supernatural side of the letter's entrance she was not permitting her mind to dwell. Who, in London, knew she meant to call at the house today? Evidently, however, this had been known. The caretaker, *had* he come back, had had no cause to expect her: he would have taken the letter in his pocket, to forward it, at his own time, through the post. There was no other sign that the caretaker had been in—but, if not?

OX HOUSE, SHAFTESBURY, 1932
John R. Biggs

Letters dropped in at doors of deserted houses do not fly or walk to tables in halls. They do not sit on the dust of empty tables with the air of certainty that they will be found. There is needed some human hand—but nobody but the caretaker had a key. Under circumstances she did not care to consider, a house can be entered without a key. It was possible that she was not alone now. She might be being waited for, downstairs. Waited for—until when? Until "the hour arranged." At least that was not six o'clock; six has struck.

She rose from the chair and went over and locked the door.

The thing was, to get out. To fly? No, not that: she had to catch her train. As a woman whose utter dependability was the keystone of her family life she was not willing to return to the country, to her husband, her little boys and her sister, without the objects she had come up to fetch. Resuming work at the chest she set about making up a number of parcels in a rapid, fumbling-decisive way. These, with her shopping parcels, would be too much to carry; these meant a taxi—at the thought of the taxi her heart went up and her normal breathing resumed. I will ring up the taxi now; the taxi cannot come too soon; I shall hear the taxi out there running its engine, till I walk calmly down to it through the hall. I'll ring up—But no: the telephone is cut off . . . She tugged at a knot she had tied wrong.

The idea of flight . . . He was never kind to me, not really. I don't remember him kind at all. Mother said he never considered me. He was set on me, that was what it was —not love. Not love, not meaning a person well. What did he do, to make me promise like that? I can't remember—But she found that she could.

She remembered with such dreadful acuteness that the twenty-five years since then dissolved like smoke and she instinctively looked for the weal left by the button on the palm of her hand. She remembered not only all that he said and did but the complete suspension of *her* existence during that August week. I was not myself —they all told me so at the time. She remembered—but with one white burning blank as where acid has dropped on a photograph: *under no conditions* could she remember his face.

So wherever he may be waiting, I shall not know him. You have no time to run from a face you do not expect.

The thing was to get to the taxi before any clock struck what could be the hour. She would slip down the street and round the side of the square to where the square gave on the main road. She would return in the taxi, safe, to her own door, and bring the solid driver into the house with her to pick up the parcels from room to room. The idea of the taxi driver made her decisive, bold; she unlocked her door, went to the top of the staircase and listened down.

She heard nothing—but while she was hearing nothing the *passé*[3] air of the staircase was disturbed by a draft that traveled up to her face. It emanated from the basement: down there a door or window was being opened by someone who chose this moment to leave the house.

The rain had stopped; the pavements steamily shone as Mrs. Drover let herself out by inches from her own front door into the empty street. The unoccupied houses opposite continued to meet her look with their damaged stare. Making toward the thoroughfare and the taxi, she tried not to keep looking behind. Indeed, the silence was so intense—one of those creeks of London silence exaggerated this summer by the damage of war—that no tread could have gained on hers unheard. Where her street debouched on the square where people went on living, she grew conscious of, and checked, her unnatural pace. Across the open end of the square two buses impassively passed each other; women, a perambulator,[4] cyclists, a man wheeling a barrow signalized, once again, the ordinary flow of life. At the square's most populous corner should be—and was—the short taxi rank. This evening, only one taxi—but this, although it presented its blank rump, appeared already to be alertly waiting for her. Indeed, without looking round the driver started his engine as she panted up from behind and put her hand on the door. As she did so, the clock struck seven. The taxi faced the main road. To make the trip back to her house it would have to turn—she had settled back on the seat and the taxi *had* turned before she, surprised by its knowing movement, recollected that she had not "said where." She leaned forward to scratch

***

3. **passé** (pa sā') *adj.*: Stale.
4. **perambulator:** A baby carriage.

at the glass panel that divided the driver's head from her own.

The driver braked to what was almost a stop, turned round and slid the glass panel back. The jolt of this flung Mrs. Drover forward till her face was almost into the glass. Through the aperture driver and passenger, not six inches between them, remained for an eternity eye to eye. Mrs. Drover's mouth hung open for some seconds before she could issue her first scream. After that she continued to scream freely and to beat with her gloved hands on the glass all round as the taxi, accelerating without mercy, made off with her into the hinterland of deserted streets.

RESPONDING TO THE SELECTION

Your Response

1. Do you feel sympathetic toward Mrs. Drover in her situation? Why or why not?

Recalling

2. (a) Who has written the letter Mrs. Drover discovers? (b) Why is she so upset by it?
3. (a) How does Mrs. Drover plan to escape from the house? (b) Does she succeed in her plan? Explain.

Interpreting

4. In the first paragraph the narrator remarks that "no human eye watched Mrs. Drover's return" to her house. In what way is this remark ironic?
5. (a) What words does the author use to describe Mrs. Drover's reaction to the letter? (b) What feelings do you think the author hoped this description would prompt in the reader?
6. One of the strengths of this short story is its ambiguity. Provide both a supernatural and a rational explanation for (a) the letter, and (b) the cab driver's knowing in which direction to take his passenger before she has spoken.
7. Why do you think the author devotes so much space to Mrs. Drover's thought processes following the flashback?
8. What do you think is Mrs. Drover's ultimate fate? Explain the basis for your answer.

Applying

9. The story seems to be suggesting that one of the most damaging effects of war is the psychological vulnerability it produces in human beings. Do you agree? Defend your opinion.

ANALYZING LITERATURE

Considering War and the Ghost Story

The devastation that was war-torn London— shells of bombed-out dwellings facing empty streets, periods of blackout, the roar of airplane engines in the sky—provides a choice setting for a story involving the presence of a ghostlike figure. In fact, for the people who lived during that era, the specter was very real, lurking in every darkened doorway and known variously by the names of fear, desperation, and grief. Consider the following war-related details in "The Demon Lover," and explain how each in its own turn adds to the terror Mrs. Drover feels.

1. The empty house in which the Drovers had lived
2. The break in the routine of mail delivery
3. The prospect of never knowing the fate of a loved one reported "missing in action"
4. The blocks of deserted streets in an evacuated neighborhood

GRAHAM GREENE

1904–1991

The search for a source of inner peace, launched earlier in the century by such poets as William Butler Yeats and T. S. Eliot, continues in the novels and short stories of Graham Greene. A religious convert like Eliot, Greene wrote—like Eliot—of pain, fear, despair, and alienation. His conclusion, which again mirrors the poet's, was that the ultimate key to salvation is a belief in God.

Greene was born in the town of Berkhamsted in Hertfordshire and educated at Berkhamsted School, where his father was headmaster. Though his grades were good enough to earn him admission to Oxford, he disliked school, describing it later as his "first impression of hell."

Much of Greene's early working life was spent as a journalist and travel writer. His training in these areas helped him develop the powers of keen observation, sensitivity to atmosphere, and simplicity of language that have become hallmarks of his fictional style. His journey to Mexico in 1938 provided the setting for his best-known novel, *The Power and the Glory* (1940). His trips to Africa resulted in travelogues as well as two novels, *The Heart of the Matter* (1948) and *A Burnt-Out Case* (1961).

Greene was also an author of books for children, an essayist, and an editor, and he enjoyed considerable success writing films and adapting his own stories for the screen. His cinematic work is tied to yet another outlet for his creativity, which Greene called his "entertainments." These are adventure stories and spy thrillers, often dealing with the secret service and with pursuit. Among these are *Our Man in Havana* (1958) and *The Human Factor* (1978).

Greene's more serious work focuses more on the psychology of human character than on plot. Many of his protagonists are people without roots or beliefs—people in pain. They come across as real and believable individuals in whom good and evil, weakness and strength are intermingled. Though the characters in a Greene story often provide the reader with little reason for finding them likable, they almost always excite the reader's curiosity and pity—and, almost always, their author treats them with compassion.

The settings for Greene's fiction are usually hot, decaying, and poorly governed places, like the border town in "Across the Bridge." These parched, crumbling landscapes, presented to us in vivid detail, represent the distressed condition of a key character's troubled soul.

GUIDE FOR INTERPRETING

Across the Bridge

Writers' Techniques

Theme and Point of View. Theme is the central idea of a work of literature. The theme of a work should not be confused with its subject, which can often be summed up in a single word or phrase, such as "love of money." Rather, the theme is a commentary on the subject and is presented in the form of a statement; for example, "The love of money is the root of all evil." Of the many fiction elements that bear on a work's theme, one of the most critical is point of view, or the vantage point from which the events of the story are related. By choosing a first-person point of view—telling the story from the vantage point of "I" or "we"—an author creates an illusion of immediacy, which adds emphasis to certain themes. The theme suggested by the events described in "Across the Bridge," for example, comes home to the reader with special force partly because those events are related by a firsthand observer of them.

Commentary

Graham Greene was among the most private of writers and always discouraged speculation about his personality. His autobiographical writings discuss his publications, not his personal life, as if the man was created by his work and not the other way around. Although he shared a number of characteristics with other writers of his generation—he came from the English professional classes, his father was the headmaster of a private school, and he was aware of World War I but was too young to fight in it—his playful sense of humor set him apart. He was an active practical joker all of his life, a trait reflected in his writing. A surprising number of the characters in his works are named Greene, as well as Henry, the name he was christened. The tragic hero in *The Heart of the Matter* is named Henry Scobie; the narrator in *Travels with My Aunt* is Henry Pulling. *Yes and No* has a character named Henry Privet (a privet is an evergreen shrub). Greene frequently mentioned the color green in his work. Can you find the reference to green in "Across the Bridge"?

Focus

After obtaining the person's permission, observe a friend or family member for an entire day, or perhaps over the course of a weekend. Keep a detailed journal on where this person goes and what he or she does. Note any patterns of behavior in which the person engages, as well as any strange moves he or she might make.

Across the Bridge

Graham Greene

"They say he's worth a million," Lucia said. He sat there in the little hot damp Mexican square, a dog at his feet, with an air of immense and forlorn patience. The dog attracted your attention at once; for it was very nearly an English setter, only something had gone wrong with the tail and the feathering. Palms wilted over his head, it was all shade and stuffiness round the bandstand, radios talked loudly in Spanish from the little wooden sheds where they changed your pesos into dollars at a loss. I could tell he didn't understand a word from the way he read his newspaper—as I did myself picking out the words which were like English ones. "He's been here a month," Lucia said. "They turned him out of Guatemala and Honduras."

You couldn't keep any secrets for five hours in this border town. Lucia had only been twenty-four hours in the place, but she knew all about Mr. Joseph Calloway. The only reason I didn't know about him (and I'd been in the place two weeks) was because I couldn't talk the language any more than Mr. Calloway could. There wasn't another soul in the place who didn't know the story —the whole story of the Halling Investment Trust and the proceedings for extradition. Any man doing dusty business in any of the wooden booths in the town is better fitted by long observation to tell Mr. Calloway's tale than I am, except that I was in—literally —at the finish. They all watched the drama proceed with immense interest, sympathy and respect. For, after all, he had a million.

Every once in a while through the long steamy day, a boy came and cleaned Mr. Calloway's shoes: he hadn't the right words to resist them—they pretended not to know his English. He must have had his shoes cleaned the day Lucia and I watched him at least half a dozen times. At midday he took a stroll across the square to the Antonio Bar and had a bottle of beer, the setter sticking to heel as if they were out for a country walk in England (he had, you may remember, one of the biggest estates in Norfolk). After his bottle of beer, he would walk down between the money changers' huts to the Rio Grande[1] and look across the bridge into the United States: people came and went constantly in cars. Then back to the square till lunchtime. He was staying in the best hotel, but you don't get good hotels in this border town: nobody stays in them more than a night. The good hotels were on the other side of the bridge: you could see their electric signs twenty stories high from the little square at night, like lighthouses marking the United States.

You may ask what I'd been doing in so drab a spot for a fortnight. There was no interest in the place for anyone; it was just damp and dust and poverty, a kind of shabby replica of the town across the river: both had squares in the same spots; both had the same number of cinemas. One was cleaner than the other, that was all, and more ex-

---

1. Rio Grande (rē' ō grand'): River that flows between Mexico and Texas.

pensive, much more expensive. I'd stayed across there a couple of nights waiting for a man a tourist bureau said was driving down from Detroit to Yucatan and would sell a place in his car for some fantastically small figure—twenty dollars, I think it was. I don't know if he existed or was invented by the optimistic half-caste in the agency; anyway, he never turned up and so I waited, not much caring, on the cheap side of the river. It didn't much matter; I was living. One day I meant to give up the man from Detroit and go home or go south, but it was easier not to decide anything in a hurry. Lucia was just waiting for a car going the other way, but she didn't have to wait so long. We waited together and watched Mr. Calloway waiting —for God knows what.

I don't know how to treat this story—it was a tragedy for Mr. Calloway, it was poetic retribution, I suppose, in the eyes of the shareholders he'd ruined with his bogus transactions, and to Lucia and me, at this stage, it was pure comedy—except when he kicked the dog. I'm not a sentimentalist about dogs, I prefer people to be cruel to animals rather than to human beings, but I couldn't help being revolted at the way he'd kick that animal—with a hint of cold-blooded venom, not in anger but as if he were getting even for some trick it had played him a long while ago. That generally happened when he returned from the bridge: it was the only sign of anything resembling emotion he showed. Otherwise he looked a small, set, gentle creature with

silver hair and a silver moustache, and gold-rimmed glasses, and one gold tooth like a flaw in character.

Lucia hadn't been accurate when she said he'd been turned out of Guatemala and Honduras; he'd left voluntarily when the extradition proceedings seemed likely to go through and moved north. Mexico is still not a very centralized state, and it is possible to get round governors as you can't get round cabinet ministers or judges. And so he waited there on the border for the next move. That earlier part of the story is, I suppose, dramatic, but I didn't watch it and I can't invent what I haven't seen—the long waiting in anterooms, the bribes taken and refused, the growing fear of arrest, and then the flight—in gold-rimmed glasses —covering his tracks as well as he could, but this wasn't finance and he was an amateur at escape. And so he'd washed up here, under my eyes and Lucia's eyes, sitting all day under the bandstand, nothing to read but a Mexican paper, nothing to do but look across the river at the United States, quite unaware, I suppose, that everyone knew everything about him, once a day kicking his dog. Perhaps in its semi-setter way it reminded him too much of the Norfolk estate —though that, too, I suppose, was the reason he kept it.

And the next act again was pure comedy. I hesitate to think what this man worth a million was costing his country as they edged him out from this land and that. Perhaps somebody was getting tired of the business, and careless; anyway, they sent across two detectives, with an old photograph. He'd grown his silvery moustache since that had been taken, and he'd aged a lot, and they couldn't catch sight of him. They hadn't been across the bridge two hours when everybody knew that there were two foreign detectives in town looking for Mr. Calloway—everybody knew, that is to say, except Mr. Calloway, who couldn't talk Spanish. There were plenty of people who could have told him in English, but they didn't. It wasn't cruelty, it was a sort of awe and respect: like a bull, he was on show, sitting there mournfully in the plaza with his dog, a magnificent spectacle for which we all had ringside seats.

I ran into one of the policemen in the Bar Antonio. He was disgusted; he had had some idea that when he crossed the bridge life was going to be different, so much more color and sun, and—I suspect—love, and all he found were wide mud streets where the nocturnal rain lay in pools, and mangy dogs, smells and cockroaches in his bedroom, and the nearest to love, the open door of the Academia Comercial, where pretty mestizo[2] girls sat all the morning learning to typewrite. Tip-tap-tip-tap-tip—perhaps they had a dream, too—jobs on the other side of the bridge, where life was going to be so much more luxurious, refined and amusing.

We got into conversation; he seemed surprised that I knew who they both were and what they wanted. He said: "We've got information this man Calloway's in town."

"He's knocking around somewhere," I said.

"Could you point him out?"

"Oh, I don't know him by sight," I said.

He drank his beer and thought a while. "I'll go out and sit in the plaza. He's sure to pass sometime."

I finished my beer and went quickly off and found Lucia. I said, "Hurry, we're going to see an arrest." We didn't care a thing about Mr. Calloway, he was just an elderly man who kicked his dog and swindled the poor, and who deserved anything he got. So we made for the plaza; we knew Calloway would be there, but it had never occurred to either of us that the detectives wouldn't recognize him. There was quite a surge of people round the place; all the fruit-sellers and bootblacks in town seemed to have arrived together; we had to force our way through, and there in the little green stuffy

---

2. mestizo (mes tē′ zō) *adj.*: Of Spanish and Indian parentage.

center of the place, sitting on adjoining seats, were the two plainclothesmen and Mr. Calloway. I've never known the place so silent; everybody was on tiptoe, and the plainclothesmen were staring at the crowd looking for Mr. Calloway, and Mr. Calloway sat on his usual seat staring out over the money-changing booths at the United States.

"It can't go on. It just can't," Lucia said. But it did. It got more fantastic still. Somebody ought to write a play about it. We sat as close as we dared. We were afraid all the time we were going to laugh. The semi-setter scratched for fleas and Mr. Calloway watched the U.S.A. The two detectives watched the crowd, and the crowd watched the show with solemn satisfaction. Then one of the detectives got up and went over to Mr. Calloway. That's the end, I thought. But it wasn't, it was the beginning. For some reason they had eliminated him from their list of suspects. I shall never know why. The man said:

"You speak English?"

"I *am* English," Mr. Calloway said.

Even that didn't tear it, and the strangest thing of all was the way Mr. Calloway came alive. I don't think anybody had spoken to him like that for weeks. The Mexicans were too respectful—he was a man with a million—and it had never occurred to Lucia and me to treat him casually like a human being; even in our eyes he had been magnified by the colossal theft and the worldwide pursuit.

He said: "This is rather a dreadful place, don't you think?"

"It is," the policeman said.

"I can't think what brings anybody across the bridge."

"Duty," the policeman said gloomily. "I suppose you are passing through."

"Yes," Mr. Calloway said.

"I'd have expected over here there'd have been—you know what I mean—life. You read things about Mexico."

"Oh, life," Mr. Calloway said. He spoke firmly and precisely, as if to a committee of shareholders. "That begins on the other side."

"You don't appreciate your own country until you leave it."

"That's very true," Mr. Calloway said. "Very true."

At first it was difficult not to laugh, and then after a while there didn't seem to be much to laugh at; an old man imagining all the fine things going on beyond the international bridge. I think he thought of the town opposite as a combination of London and Norfolk—theaters and cocktail bars, a little shooting and a walk round the field at evening with the dog—that miserable imitation of a setter—poking the ditches. He'd never been across, he couldn't know that it was just the same thing over again—even the same layout; only the streets were paved and the hotels had ten more stories, and life was more expensive, and everything was a little bit cleaner. There wasn't anything Mr. Calloway would have called living—no galleries, no bookshops, just *Film Fun* and the local paper, and *Click* and *Focus* and the tabloids.

"Well," said Mr. Calloway, "I think I'll take a stroll before lunch. You need an appetite to swallow the food here. I generally go down and look at the bridge about now. Care to come, too?"

The detective shook his head. "No," he said, "I'm on duty. I'm looking for a fellow." And that, of course, gave *him* away. As far as Mr. Calloway could understand, there was only one "fellow" in the world anyone was looking for—his brain had eliminated friends who were seeking their friends, husbands who might be waiting for their wives, all objectives of any search but just the one. The power of elimination was what had made him a financier—he could forget the people behind the shares.

That was the last we saw of him for a while. We didn't see him going into the Botica Paris to get his aspirin, or walking back from the bridge with his dog. He simply disappeared, and when he disappeared, people began to talk, and the detectives heard the talk. They looked silly enough, and they got busy after the very man they'd been sitting next to in the garden. Then they, too, disappeared. They, as well as Mr. Calloway, had gone to the state capital to see the Governor and the Chief of Police, and it must have been an amusing sight there, too, as they bumped into Mr. Calloway and sat with him in the waiting rooms. I suspect Mr. Calloway was generally shown in first, for everyone knew he was worth a million. Only in Europe is it possible for a man to be a criminal as well as a rich man.

Anyway, after about a week the whole pack of them returned by the same train. Mr. Calloway traveled Pullman,[3] and the two policemen traveled in the day coach. It was evident that they hadn't got their extradition order.

Lucia had left by that time. The car came and went across the bridge. I stood in Mexico and watched her get out at the United States Customs. She wasn't anything in particular but she looked beautiful at a distance as she gave me a wave out of the United States and got back into the car. And I suddenly felt sympathy for Mr. Calloway, as if there were something over there which you couldn't find here, and turning round I saw him back on his old beat, with the dog at his heels.

I said "Good afternoon," as if it had been all along our habit to greet each other. He looked tired and ill and dusty, and I felt sorry for him—to think of the kind of victory he'd been winning, with so much expenditure of cash and care—the prize this dirty and dreary town, the booths of the money changers, the awful little beauty parlors with their wicker chairs and sofas looking like the reception rooms of brothels, that hot and stuffy garden by the bandstand.

He replied gloomily, "Good morning,"

and the dog started to sniff at some ordure and he turned and kicked it with fury, with depression, with despair.

And at that moment a taxi with the two policemen in it passed us on its way to the bridge. They must have seen that kick; perhaps they were cleverer than I had given them credit for, perhaps they were just sentimental about animals, and thought they'd do a good deed, and the rest happened by accident. But the fact remains—those two pillars of the law set about the stealing of Mr. Calloway's dog.

He watched them go by. Then he said, "Why don't you go across?"

"It's cheaper here," I said.

"I mean just for an evening. Have a meal at that place we can see at night in the sky. Go to the theater."

"There isn't a chance."

He said angrily, sucking his gold tooth, "Well, anyway, get away from here." He stared down the hill and up the other side. He couldn't see that that street climbing up from the bridge, contained only the same money-changers' booths as this one.

I said, "Why don't *you* go?"

He said evasively. "Oh—business."

I said, "It's only a question of money. You don't *have* to pass by the bridge."

He said with faint interest, "I don't talk Spanish."

"There isn't a soul here," I said, "who doesn't talk English."

He looked at me with surprise. "Is that so?" he said. "Is that so?"

It's as I have said; he'd never tried to talk to anyone, and they respected him too much to talk to him—he was worth a million. I don't know whether I'm glad or sorry that I told him that. If I hadn't he might be there now, sitting by the bandstand having his shoes cleaned—alive and suffering.

Three days later his dog disappeared. I found him looking for it, calling it softly and shamefacedly between the palms of the garden. He looked embarrassed. He said in a low angry voice, "I *hate* that dog. The beastly mongrel," and called "Rover, Rover" in a voice which didn't carry five yards. He said, "I bred setters once. I'd have shot a dog like that." It reminded him, I *was* right, of Norfolk, and he lived in the memory, and he hated it for its imperfection. He was a man without a family and without friends, and his only enemy was that dog. You couldn't call the law an enemy; you have to be intimate with an enemy.

Late that afternoon someone told him they'd seen the dog walking across the bridge. It wasn't true, of course, but we didn't know that then—they'd paid a Mexican five pesos to smuggle it across. So all that afternoon and the next Mr. Calloway sat in the garden having his shoes cleaned over and over again, and thinking how a dog could just walk across like that, and a human being, an immortal soul, was bound here in the awful routine of the little walk and the unspeakable meals and the aspirin at the botica. That dog was seeing things he couldn't see—that hateful dog. It made him mad—I think literally mad. You must remember the man had been going on for months. He had a million and he was living on two pounds a week, with nothing to spend his money on. He sat there and brooded on the hideous injustice of it. I think he'd have crossed over one day in any case, but the dog was the last straw.

Next day when he wasn't to be seen, I guessed he'd gone across and I went too. The American town is as small as the Mexican. I knew I couldn't miss him if he was there, and I was still curious. A little sorry for him, but not much.

I caught sight of him first in the only drugstore, having a Coca-Cola, and then once outside a cinema looking at the posters; he had dressed with extreme neatness, as if for a party, but there was no party. On my third time round, I came on the detectives—they were having Coca-Colas in the drugstore, and they must have missed Mr. Calloway by inches. I went in and sat down at the bar.

"Hello," I said, "you still about." I suddenly felt anxious for Mr. Calloway, I didn't want them to meet.

One of them said, "Where's Calloway?"

"Oh," I said, "he's hanging on."

"But not his dog," he said, and laughed. The other looked a little shocked, he didn't like anyone to *talk* cynically about a dog. Then they got up—they had a car outside.

"Have another?" I said.

"No thanks. We've got to keep moving."

The man bent close and confided to me: "Calloway's on this side."

"No!" I said.

"And his dog."

"He's looking for it," the other said.

"I'm damned if he is," I said, and again one of them looked a little shocked, as if I'd insulted the dog.

I don't think Mr. Calloway was looking for his dog, but his dog certainly found him. There was a sudden hilarious yapping from the car and out plunged the semi-setter and gamboled furiously down the street. One of the detectives—the sentimental one—was into the car before we got to the door and was off after the dog. Near the bottom of the long road to the bridge was Mr. Calloway—I do believe he'd come down to look at the Mexican side when he found there was nothing but the drugstore and the cinemas and the paper shops on the American. He saw the dog coming and yelled at it to go home—"home, home, home," as if they were in Norfolk—it took no notice at all, pelting towards him. Then he saw the police car coming, and ran. After that, everything happened too quickly, but I think the order of events was this—the dog started across the road right in front of the car, and Mr. Calloway yelled, at the dog or the car, I don't know which. Anyway, the detective swerved—he said later, weakly, at the inquiry, that he couldn't run over a dog, and down went Mr. Calloway, in a mess of broken glass and gold rims and silver hair, and blood. The dog was on to him before any of us could reach him, licking and whimpering and licking. I saw Mr. Calloway put up his hand, and down it went across the dog's neck and the whimper rose to a stupid bark of triumph, but Mr. Calloway was dead—shock and a weak heart.

"Poor old geezer," the detective said, "I bet he really loved that dog," and it's true that the attitude in which he lay looked more like a caress than a blow. I thought it was meant to be a blow, but the detective may have been right. It all seemed to me a little too touching to be true as the old crook lay there with his arm over the dog's neck, dead with his million between the money-changers' huts, but it's as well to be humble in the face of human nature. He had come across the river for something, and it may, after all, have been the dog he was looking for. It sat there, baying its stupid and mongrel triumph across his body, like a piece of sentimental statuary. The nearest he could get to the fields, the ditches, the horizon of his home. It was comic and it was pitiable; but it wasn't less comic because the man was dead. Death doesn't change comedy to tragedy, and if that last gesture was one of affection, I suppose it was only one more indication of a human being's capacity for self-deception, our baseless optimism that is so much more appalling than our despair.

![] RESPONDING TO THE SELECTION

Your Response

1. What was your attitude toward Mr. Calloway? Where you sympathetic to his predicament? Explain.

Recalling

2. (a) Where does the story take place? (b) What is Mr. Calloway's reason for being there? (c) What is the narrator's reason?
3. (a) Who is Mr. Calloway's constant "companion"? (b) How does he treat this companion?
4. Why don't the two detectives arrest Mr. Calloway at first?
5. (a) What finally brings Mr. Calloway across the bridge? (b) What happens to him?

Interpreting

6. What effect does the repetition of the sentence "He was worth a million" have on you?

7. What trait of Mr. Calloway's personality is revealed by his not knowing that the inhabitants of the town speak English?
8. Both Mr. Calloway and the detectives are disappointed by what they find on the "other side" of the bridge. (a) What proverb does this call to mind? (b) How does this disappointment reflect the story's theme?
9. Consider the role of justice in the story. (a) In what ways is justice served by Mr. Calloway's death? (b) In what way is Mr. Calloway "saved"?

Applying

10. At the end of the story, the narrator says, ". . . I suppose it was only one more indication of a human being's capacity for self-deception, our baseless optimism that is so much more appalling than our despair." Explain your reactions to this statement.

ANALYZING LITERATURE

Understanding Theme and Point of View

Theme is the insight into life revealed in a literary work. Often misidentified with a story's subject, the theme is a statement about the subject. **Point of view**—the angle from which the story is told—can affect the reader's grasp of the theme. When a story is told by a first-person narrator, the reader is made to feel almost a part of the events. This in turn brings the theme, or "moral," into sharp focus. Consider the theme of "Across the Bridge." Evaluate the impact that the following facts of narration have on the reader's awareness of the theme.

1. The narrator, in the fourth paragraph, gives us his firsthand impressions of the town on the American side.
2. The description of Mr. Calloway's relationship with the dog comes from one who is, by his own admission, not a lover of dogs.
3. The narrator begins to feel sympathy toward Mr. Calloway.

CRITICAL THINKING AND READING

Understanding Comedy and Tragedy

On page 897 of the story, the narrator states, "I don't know how to treat this story—it was a tragedy for Mr. Calloway . . . [while to] me, at this stage, it was pure comedy. . . ." Again, at the end, after Mr. Calloway has died, he observes, "It was comic and it was pitiable; but it wasn't less comic because the man was dead. Death doesn't change comedy to tragedy. . . ."

1. In what sense might the death of Mr. Calloway have struck the narrator as comical?
2. Do you agree that death doesn't change comedy to tragedy? Why or why not?
3. The ancient Greeks defined comedy as a play in which the main character triumphs over opposing forces. According to this definition, would you consider "Across the Bridge" more comedy than tragedy, or vice versa? Explain your answer.

THINKING AND WRITING

Analyzing the Effects of Point of View

Choose another story that you read in this book, and identify its theme and its narrative point of view. In an essay, explain how the point of view affects the theme. Structure your essay on the following questions: Would the impact of the theme have been different had the author used a first-person (or third-person) narrator? What details of narration helped make the theme apparent? What facets of the narrator's character were relevant to the theme? Make sure your essay opens with a clear thesis statement. When you revise, make sure you have provided adequate support for your thesis. Proofread your essay and prepare a final draft.

LEARNING OPTIONS

1. **Writing.** Imagine that "Across the Bridge" is being made into a television movie and you are the casting director. What actors would you choose to play the roles in the story? Write a list of your choices. Include brief explanations to convince the director to follow your recommendations.
2. **Multicultural Activity.** Greene's story is set in the border region between Mexico and the United States. Find photographs of border towns that depict what the setting of "Across the Bridge" might look like. Also investigate life along the border. What kinds of people live there? What do they do? Display the pictures in class and discuss your findings.

GEORGE ORWELL

1903–1950

Although George Orwell's popular fame is most directly linked to his two novels of political satire, *Animal Farm* and *1984,* many discerning readers insist that his genius is most readily apparent in his essays and nonfiction. Orwell's prose style, precise yet informal, contributed to making his essays some of the most eloquent short works of the twentieth century.

George Orwell was the pen name chosen by Eric Blair, born in colonial Bengal, an eastern region of India. Schooled in England at Eton, Orwell returned to the East—like H. H. Munro (Saki)—to serve in the Imperial Police in Burma. His experiences in that post, which span the years 1922 to 1927, form the basis of his first novel, *Burmese Days* (1934). Disillusioned by his country's policy in the Orient, Orwell left military service to pursue jobs in journalism, publishing, and bookselling in England and France. This period of his life was marked by struggles with poverty, as he recalls in his autobiographical *Down and Out in Paris and London* (1933).

During the 1930's Orwell became deeply involved in social and international causes. *The Road to Wigan Pier* (1937) movingly chronicles the miseries of the English working class during the later phases of the Depression. The Spanish Civil War (1936–1939) found Orwell firmly committed to the Republican cause. Deploring what he saw as the totalitarianism of the Nationalist victors of the conflict, Orwell paid tribute to the victims in *Homage to Catalonia* (1938).

During World War II, Orwell served as literary editor of the *Tribune* from 1943 to 1945 and also contributed political columns to a number of newspapers and journals. In 1945 he published *Animal Farm,* a savage fable that indirectly denounces the evils of both Fascism and Communism. Suffering acutely from the tuberculosis that would ultimately end his life, he completed *1984* (1948), a grim vision of a future in which all language and thought would be manipulated to serve totalitarian ends.

Orwell's passionate concern for the preservation of political freedom was allied with his efforts to save the English language from "double speak," jargon, and bureaucratic vagueness. In "Politics and the English Language," he dramatically demonstrates how language can be used subtly to conceal political corruption, thereby blinding members of a society to the necessity of moral choice. Although 1984 has come and gone without the fulfillment of Orwell's grim prophecies, his lifelong commitment to political freedom and to the integrity of language remain as relevant today as ever.

GUIDE FOR INTERPRETING

Shooting an Elephant

Tone. Tone is the attitude the writer of a literary work takes toward his or her subject, his or her audience, or a character. Just as a speaker's tone of voice can affect the way in which a remark is taken, so the tone of a literary work will help shape the reader's response to it. Tone in a piece of literature is conveyed through the particular words the writer chooses, as well as through details of description. For example, a writer who adopts a lighthearted and carefree tone toward the subject of sunshine might refer to the "kiss of warm rays," while the same writer, in approaching the subject with a bitter tone, might make reference to the sun's "cruel, harsh glare." In his essay "Shooting an Elephant," George Orwell's diction, or word choice, clearly reveals his attitude toward the task that has fallen to him as a military police officer in Burma, as well as toward the people to whom he must account for his actions.

Considerable family sacrifice and reduced tuition enabled Orwell's parents to send their only son to a fashionable preparatory school on the south coast of England while they remained in India. But the boy was intimidated by the wealth and position of the others at school: "I had no money, I was weak, I was ugly, I was unpopular, I had a chronic cough, I smelt," he later wrote. Despite his later academic success—at age thirteen he was awarded not one but two scholarships to England's most prestigious private high schools—he never lost his ability to identify with society's downtrodden. As he remarked: "The conviction, that it was not possible for me to be a success went deep enough to influence my actions till far into adult life." Out of the desire for personal escape rather than from any political conviction, he took a position with the Indian Imperial Police in Burma rather than continuing his education at Cambridge University, as expected. His ability to see life through the eyes of the underdog forms the basis of "Shooting an Elephant" and partly explains why the essay was ranked as a classic in his own lifetime. The essay reflects Orwell's own early humiliations and frustrations as a poor boy among wealthier classmates, recalled now in the difficult and hurtful official relationships between the British and Burmese.

What is power? Freewrite about the meaning of the word, exploring its effects on both the person who exerts power and the people on whom power is brought to bear.

Shooting an Elephant

George Orwell

In Moulmein, in lower Burma, I was hated by large numbers of people—the only time in my life that I have been important enough for this to happen to me. I was subdivisional police officer of the town, and in an aimless, petty kind of way anti-European feeling was very bitter. No one had the guts to raise a riot, but if a European woman went through the bazaars alone somebody would probably spit betel juice over her dress. As a police officer I was an obvious target and was baited whenever it seemed safe to do so. When a nimble Burman tripped me up on the football field and the referee (another Burman) looked the other way, the crowd yelled with hideous laughter. This happened more than once. In the end the sneering yellow faces of young men that met me everywhere, the insults hooted after me when I was at a safe distance, got badly on my nerves. The young Buddhist priests were the worst of all. There were several thousands of them in the town and none of them seemed to have anything to do except stand on street corners and jeer at Europeans.

All this was perplexing and upsetting. For at that time I had already made up my mind that imperialism was an evil thing and the sooner I chucked up my job and got out of it the better. Theoretically—and secretly, of course—I was all for the Burmese and all against their oppressors, the British. As for the job I was doing, I hated it more bitterly than I can perhaps make clear. In a job like that you see the dirty work of Empire at close quarters. The wretched prisoners huddling in the stinking cages of the lockups, the gray, cowed faces of the long-term convicts, the scarred buttocks of the men who had been flogged with bamboos—all these oppressed me with an intolerable sense of guilt. But I could get nothing into perspective. I was young and ill educated and I had had to think out my problems in the utter silence that is imposed on every Englishman in the East. I did not even know that the British Empire is dying, still less did I know that it is a great deal better than the younger empires that are going to supplant it. All I knew was that I was stuck between my hatred of the empire I served and my rage against the evil-spirited little beasts who tried to make my job impossible. With one part of my mind I thought of the British Raj[1] as an unbreakable tyranny, as something clamped down, *in saecula saeculorum,*[2] upon the will of prostrate peoples; with another part I thought that the greatest joy in the world would be to drive a bayonet into a Buddhist priest's guts. Feelings like these are the normal byproducts of imperialism; ask any Anglo-Indian official, if you can catch him off duty.

One day something happened which in a roundabout way was enlightening. It was a tiny incident in itself, but it gave me a better glimpse than I had had before of the real

---

1. **Raj** (räj): Rule.
2. *in saecula saeculorum* (sē′ k o͞o lə sē′ k o͞o lôr′ əm): Forever and ever.

nature of imperialism—the real motives for which despotic governments act. Early one morning the subinspector at a police station the other end of the town rang me up on the phone and said that an elephant was ravaging the bazaar. Would I please come and do something about it? I did not know what I could do, but I wanted to see what was happening and I got onto a pony and started out. I took my rifle, an old .44 Winchester and much too small to kill an elephant, but I thought the noise might be useful *in terrorem*.[3] Various Burmans stopped me on the way and told me about the elephant's doings. It was not, of course, a wild elephant, but a tame one which had gone "must."[4] It had been chained up, as tame elephants always are when their attack of "must" is due, but on the previous night it had broken its chain and escaped. Its mahout,[5] the only person who could manage it when it was in that state, had set out in pursuit, but had taken the wrong direction and was now twelve hours' journey away, and in the morning the elephant had suddenly reappeared in the town. The Burmese population had no weapons and were quite helpless against it. It had already destroyed somebody's bamboo hut, killed a cow and raided some fruit stalls and devoured the stock; also it had met the municipal rubbish van and, when the driver jumped out and took to his heels, had turned the van over and inflicted violences upon it.

The Burmese subinspector and some Indian constables were waiting for me in the quarter where the elephant had been seen. It was a very poor quarter, a labyrinth of squalid bamboo huts, thatched with palm leaf, winding all over a steep hillside. I remember that it was a cloudy, stuffy morning at the beginning of the rains. We began questioning the people as to where the elephant had gone and, as usual, failed to get

any definite information. That is invariably the case in the East; a story always sounds clear enough at a distance, but the nearer you get to the scene of events the vaguer it becomes. Some of the people said that the elephant had gone in one direction, some said that he had gone in another, some professed not even to have heard of any elephant. I had almost made up my mind that the whole story was a pack of lies, when we heard yells a little distance away. There was a loud, scandalized cry of "Go away, child! Go away this instant!" and an old woman with a switch in her hand came round the corner of a hut, violently shooing away a crowd of naked children. Some more women followed, clicking their tongues and exclaiming; evidently there was something that the children ought not to have seen. I rounded the hut and saw a man's dead body sprawling in the mud. He was an Indian, a black Dravidian[6] coolie,[7] almost naked, and he could not have been dead many minutes.

---

3. *in terrorem*: For terror.
4. must: Into a dangerous, frenzied state.
5. mahout (mə hoot′): An elephant keeper and rider.

6. Dravidian (drə vid′ ē ən): Belonging to the race of people inhabiting southern India.
7. coolie: Laborer.

The people said that the elephant had come suddenly upon him round the corner of the hut, caught him with its trunk, put its foot on his back and ground him into the earth. This was the rainy season and the ground was soft, and his face had scored a trench a foot deep and a couple of yards long. He was lying on his belly with arms crucified and head sharply twisted to one side. His face was coated with mud, the eyes wide open, the teeth bared and grinning with an expression of unendurable agony. (Never tell me, by the way, that the dead look peaceful. Most of the corpses I have seen looked devilish.) The friction of the great beast's foot had stripped the skin from his back as neatly as one skins a rabbit. As soon as I saw the dead man I sent an orderly to a friend's house nearby to borrow an elephant rifle. I had already sent back the pony, not wanting it to go mad with fright and throw me if it smelled the elephant.

The orderly came back in a few minutes with a rifle and five cartridges, and meanwhile some Burmans had arrived and told us that the elephant was in the paddy fields[8] below, only a few hundred yards away. As I started forward practically the whole population of the quarter flocked out of the houses and followed me. They had seen the rifle and were all shouting excitedly that I was going to shoot the elephant. They had not shown much interest in the elephant when he was merely ravaging their homes, but it was different now that he was going to be shot. It was a bit of fun to them, as it would be to an English crowd; besides they wanted the meat. It made me vaguely uneasy. I had no intention of shooting the elephant—I had merely sent for the rifle to defend myself if necessary—and it is always unnerving to have a crowd following you. I marched down the hill, looking and feeling a fool, with the rifle over my shoulder and an ever-growing army of people jostling at my heels. At the bottom, when you got away from the huts, there was a metaled road[9] and beyond that a miry waste of paddy fields a thousand yards across, not yet plowed but soggy from the first rains and dotted with coarse grass. The elephant was standing eight yards from the road, his left side toward us. He took not the slightest notice of the crowd's approach. He was tearing up bunches of grass, beating them against his knees to clean them, and stuffing them into his mouth.

I had halted on the road. As soon as I saw the elephant I knew with perfect certainty that I ought not to shoot him. It is a serious matter to shoot a working elephant—it is comparable to destroying a huge and costly piece of machinery—and obviously one ought not to do it if it can possibly be avoided. And at that distance, peacefully eating, the elephant looked no more dangerous than a cow. I thought then and I think now that his attack of "must" was already passing off; in which case he would merely wander harmlessly about until the mahout came back and caught him. Moreover, I did not in the least want to shoot him. I decided that I would watch him for a little while to make sure that he did not turn savage again, and then go home.

But at that moment I glanced round at the crowd that had followed me. It was an immense crowd, two thousand at the least and growing every minute. It blocked the road for a long distance on either side. I looked at the sea of yellow faces above the garish clothes—faces all happy and excited over this bit of fun, all certain that the elephant was going to be shot. They were watching me as they would watch a conjurer about to perform a trick. They did not like me, but with the magical rifle in my hands I was momentarily worth watching. And suddenly I realized that I should have to shoot the elephant after all. The people expected it of me and I had got to do it; I could feel their two thousand wills pressing me forward,

---

8. paddy fields: Rice fields.

9. metaled road: A road in which the pavement is reinforced with metal strips.

irresistibly. And it was at this moment, as I stood there with the rifle in my hands, that I first grasped the hollowness, the futility of the white man's dominion in the East. Here was I, the white man with his gun, standing in front of the unarmed native crowd —seemingly the leading actor of the piece; but in reality I was only an absurd puppet pushed to and fro by the will of those yellow faces behind. I perceived in this moment that when the white man turns tyrant it is his own freedom that he destroys. He becomes a sort of hollow, posing dummy, the conventionalized figure of a sahib.[10] For it is the condition of his rule that he shall spend his life in trying to impress the "natives," and so in every crisis he has got to do what the "natives" expect of him. He wears a mask, and his face grows to fit it. I had got to shoot the elephant. I had committed myself to doing it when I sent for the rifle. A sahib has got to act like a sahib; he has got to appear resolute, to know his own mind and do definite things. To come all that way, rifle in hand, with two thousand people marching at my heels, and then to trail feebly away, having done nothing—no, that was impossible. The crowd would laugh at me. And my whole life, every white man's life in the East, was one long struggle not to be laughed at.

But I did not want to shoot the elephant. I watched him beating his bunch of grass against his knees with that preoccupied grandmotherly air that elephants have. It seemed to me that it would be murder to shoot him. At that age I was not squeamish about killing animals, but I had never shot an elephant and never wanted to. (Somehow it always seems worse to kill a *large* animal.) Besides, there was the beast's owner to be considered. Alive, the elephant was worth at least a hundred pounds, dead, he would only be worth the value of his tusks, five pounds, possibly. But I had got to act quickly. I turned to some experienced-looking Burmans who had been there when we arrived, and asked them how the elephant had been behaving. They all said the same thing: he took no notice of you if you left him alone, but he might charge if you went too close to him.

It was perfectly clear to me what I ought to do. I ought to walk up to within, say, twenty-five yards of the elephant and test his behavior. If he charged, I could shoot; if he took no notice of me, it would be safe to leave him until the mahout came back. But also I knew that I was going to do no such thing. I was a poor shot with a rifle and the ground was soft mud into which one would sink at every step. If the elephant charged and I missed him, I should have about as much chance as a toad under a steam-roller. But even then I was not thinking particularly of my own skin, only of the watchful yellow faces behind. For at that moment, with the crowd watching me, I was not afraid in the ordinary sense, as I would have been if I had been alone. A white man mustn't be frightened in front of "natives"; and so, in general, he isn't frightened. The sole thought in my mind was that if anything went wrong those two thousand Burmans would see me pursued, caught, trampled on, and reduced to a grinning corpse like that Indian up the hill. And if that happened it was quite probable that some of them would laugh. That would never do. There was only one alternative. I shoved the cartridges into the magazine and lay down on the road to get a better aim.

The crowd grew very still, and a deep, low, happy sigh, as of people who see the theater curtain go up at last, breathed from innumerable throats. They were going to have their bit of fun, after all. The rifle was a beautiful German thing with cross-hair sights. I did not then know that in shooting an elephant one would shoot to cut an imaginary bar running from ear hole to ear hole. I ought, therefore, as the elephant was sideways on, to have aimed straight at his ear-

---

10. sahib (sä′ ib): Indian word for European gentleman.

hole; actually I aimed several inches in front of this, thinking the brain would be further forward.

When I pulled the trigger I did not hear the bang or feel the kick—one never does when a shot goes home—but I heard the devilish roar of glee that went up from the crowd. In that instant, in too short a time, one would have thought, even for the bullet to get there, a mysterious, terrible change had come over the elephant. He neither stirred nor fell, but every line of his body had altered. He looked suddenly stricken, shrunken, immensely old, as though the frightful impact of the bullet had paralyzed him without knocking him down. At last, after what seemed a long time—it might have been five seconds, I dare say—he sagged flabbily to his knees. His mouth slobbered. An enormous senility seemed to have settled upon him. One could have imagined him thousands of years old. I fired again into the same spot. At the second shot he did not collapse but climbed with desperate slowness to his feet and stood weakly upright, with legs sagging and head drooping. I fired a third time. That was the shot that did for him. You could see the agony of it jolt his whole body and knock the last remnant of strength from his legs. But in falling he seemed for a moment to rise, for as his hind legs collapsed beneath him he seemed to tower upward like a huge rock toppling, his trunk reaching skyward like a tree. He trumpeted, for the first and only time. And then down he came, his belly toward me, with a crash that seemed to shake the ground even where I lay.

I got up. The Burmans were already racing past me across the mud. It was obvious that the elephant would never rise again, but he was not dead. He was breathing very rhythmically with long rattling gasps, his great mound of a side painfully rising and falling. His mouth was wide open—I could see far down into caverns of pale pink throat. I waited a long time for him to die, but his breathing did not weaken. Finally I fired my two remaining shots into the spot where I thought his heart must be. The thick blood welled out of him like red velvet, but still he did not die. His body did not even jerk when the shots hit him, the tortured breathing continued without a pause. He was dying, very slowly and in great agony, but in some world remote from me where not even a bullet could damage him further. I felt that I had got to put an end to that dreadful noise. It seemed dreadful to see the great beast lying there, powerless to move and yet powerless to die, and not even to be able to finish him. I sent back for my small rifle and poured shot after shot into his heart and down his throat. They seemed to make no impression. The tortured gasps continued as steadily as the ticking of a clock.

In the end I could not stand it any longer and went away. I heard later that it took him half an hour to die. Burmans were bringing dahs[11] and baskets even before I left, and I was told they had stripped his body almost to the bones by the afternoon.

Afterward, of course, there were endless discussions about the shooting of the elephant. The owner was furious, but he was only an Indian and could do nothing. Besides, legally I had done the right thing, for a mad elephant has to be killed, like a mad dog, if its owner fails to control it. Among the Europeans opinion was divided. The older men said I was right, the younger men said it was a shame to shoot an elephant for killing a coolie, because an elephant was worth more than any Coringhee[12] coolie. And afterward I was very glad that the coolie had been killed; it put me legally in the right and it gave me a sufficient pretext for shooting the elephant. I often wondered whether any of the others grasped that I had done it solely to avoid looking a fool.

---

11. **dahs** (däz): Knives.
12. **Coringhee** (cor in' gē): Southern Indian.

Your Response

1. If you were in the narrator's position, would you give up your job? Why or why not?

Recalling

2. (a) Why was the narrator hated in Burma? (b) Why were his reactions to this hatred mixed?
3. What grisly sight does the narrator encounter when he arrives in the quarter where the elephant has been seen?
4. (a) What reasons does the narrator give for not wanting to shoot the elephant? (b) Why does he shoot it in spite of these reasons?

Interpreting

5. How would you summarize the sentiments the narrator expresses in the first two paragraphs?
6. What do you think the narrator means when he states at the beginning of the third paragraph that this incident was "enlightening" in "a round-about way"?
7. What do you think was the narrator's reason for providing his lengthy and detailed description of the elephant's death?
8. (a) What evidence is there in this essay that the narrator was divided in his sympathies? (b) How might the narrator's complex feelings be related to the essay's theme?

Applying

9. In the act of shooting the elephant, the narrator recognizes "the futility of the white man's dominion in the East." Why is colonial rule ultimately problematic?

ANALYZING LITERATURE

Identifying Tone

Tone is a writer's attitude toward his or her subject, audience, or a character. In a literary work, tone is communicated through details and the author's choice of words. As a recollection of an incident from a period of George Orwell's life that was "perplexing and upsetting," "Shooting an Elephant" sums up the author's attitude toward several separate but related subjects. In your own words, identify the author's tone toward each of the following subjects, and locate specific words and passages that support your assumption.

1. The Burmans
2. The British Empire
3. Killing and death

CRITICAL THINKING AND READING

Understanding Stereotypes

A **stereotype** is a generalization about a whole group of people that does not apply to all individuals in the group. The acceptance and use of stereotypes are forms of prejudice. In "Shooting an Elephant," Orwell explains that he was disliked by Burmans not because of any specific limitation of his own character but because he was European. The Burmans, thus, had a preconceived notion, or stereotype, of the European. What do you think is Orwell's reaction to stereotypes? Explain your answer.

THINKING AND WRITING

Supporting an Opinion

In an opinion paper, argue your belief that Orwell was justified, or not justified, in shooting the elephant. Your essay should not only support your own position but should pinpoint and refute arguments that might be raised by the opposition. Draw, if you can, from outside sources to drive home your point. When you revise, make sure you have provided adequate support for your opinion.

LEARNING OPTION

Multicultural Activity. Investigate the effects of the British colonial presence in Asia. Why did Britain colonize the territories in the first place? What effects, both positive and negative, did the British Raj have on the indigenous populations? What influences have the Asian cultures, such as that of India and Burma, had on British culture? What are relations like currently between the now independent Asian nations and Britain? Present your findings to the class in an oral report.

WILLIAM TREVOR

1928–

Having lived in both Ireland and England, William Trevor writes about people from both countries, ordinary individuals whose lives are often tragic and lonely, shaped—and sometimes crushed—by historical events that are beyond their control. "I don't really have any heroes or heroines," he has said. "I don't seem to go in for them. I think I am interested in people who are not necessarily the victims of other people, but simply the victims of circumstances. . . . I'm very interested in the sadness of fate, the things that just happen to people."

Trevor was born in County Cork, Ireland, but he moved to England after embarking upon his writing career. His stories and novels explore a wide variety of subjects and themes. Displaying a deep understanding of human nature, Trevor often portrays the pointless misunderstandings that often develop between individuals or groups of people. Perhaps Trevor's clear insights come from his unusual education. The son of a bank manager, he was enrolled at various times in thirteen different schools. For long periods, however, he was left simply to roam the countryside, occasionally being tutored by neighboring farmers or clergymen. Interestingly, he was able to complete his education formally, graduating from Trinity College in Dublin in 1950.

Previously a history and art teacher, a sculptor, and an advertising copywriter, Trevor turned to fiction writing, he says, to express a humanity he could not find in the visual arts. He uses his art background, however, to help describe the craft of writing: "A short story is like an impressionist painting. You cut down everything enormously and you get the effects from one big splash or explosion. You have to cut to the very edge. What excites me is to go as far as I can."

Trevor has written many novels, collections of short stories, and plays. His first novel, *A Standard of Behavior,* was published in 1958. His collections of stories include *The Day We Got Drunk on Cake, and Other Stories* (1967); *Angels at the Ritz, and Other Stories* (1975); and *Family Sins* (1989). Trevor's stories have been compared to those of Anton Chekhov, Muriel Spark, and James Joyce. One critic likened Joyce and Trevor in this way: "Both Trevor and the early Joyce are geniuses at presenting a seemingly ordinary life as it is, socially, psychologically, morally, and then revealing the force of these conditions in the threatened individual's moment of resistance to them. This is the deeper realism: accurate observation turning into moral vision."

GUIDE FOR INTERPRETING

The Distant Past

Characterization. Characterization is the act of creating and developing a character in a literary work. The amount of detail and depth of analysis that a writer uses to reveal a character's personality depends on whether the writer wants the character to be round or flat. A round character is complex, well developed, and possesses a variety of traits. Round characters are usually dynamic—they change during the course of the story. In "The Distant Past," for example, the lives of the main characters change dramatically, largely as a result of the sweeping historical events that led to Ireland's independence from England. In contrast, flat characters are simple, usually exhibiting a single quality, and are static—they do not change. Writers often include both flat and round characters in their stories. They do so to convey a sense of stability and predictability, as well as to mirror the progression of events and the development of human personalities.

One of the characters created by James Joyce asserts that "history is a nightmare" from which he is trying to awaken. Jot down some of the ideas that this statement conjures in your mind.

William Trevor's short fiction is part of a long history of Irish storytelling, as the author points out in the following account: "When the novel, in the nineteenth century, broke upon the English public, England was right for it. In a stable, leisurely society there was time both to write novels and to read them. Ireland at that time was a country of considerable disaffection, with two religions, one of them repressed, two languages, one of them repressed. It was not a place with the kind of wealth or ease to be found in what I always think of as the great big mahogany establishment which England was in the nineteenth century. Ireland was the opposite of that, a rough-and-ready place.

I think the communication of the past simply continued, that very rapid communication of people telling stories, not taking time—nor even possessing the education sometimes—to scribble them down. That used to be the case in England also, but it kept going in Ireland, and when this antique story form was turned inside out by Chekhov in Russia and Elizabeth Bowen in Ireland, Ireland still had a healthy storytelling tradition. The short story thrives in countries which aren't quite settled."

The Distant Past

William Trevor

In the town and beyond it they were regarded as harmlessly peculiar. Odd, people said, and in time this reference took on a burnish of affection.

They had always been thin, silent with one another, and similar in appearance: a brother and sister who shared a family face. It was a bony countenance, with pale blue eyes and a sharp, well-shaped nose and high cheekbones. Their father had had it too, but unlike them their father had been an irresponsible and careless man, with red flecks in his cheeks that they didn't have at all. The Middletons of Carraveagh the family had once been known as, but now the brother and sister were just the Middletons, for Carraveagh didn't count any more, except to them.

They owned four Herefords,[1] a number of hens, and the house itself, three miles outside the town. It was a large house, built in the reign of George II,[2] a monument that reflected in its glory and later decay the fortunes of a family. As the brother and sister aged, its roof increasingly ceased to afford protection, rust ate at its gutters, grass thrived in two thick channels all along its avenue. Their father had mortgaged his inherited estate, so local rumor claimed, in order to keep a Catholic Dublin woman in brandy and jewels. When he died, in 1924, his two children discovered that they possessed only a dozen acres. It was locally said also that this adversity hardened their will and that because of it they came to love the remains of Carraveagh more than they could ever have loved a husband or a wife. They blamed for their ill-fortune the Catholic Dublin woman whom they'd never met and they blamed as well the new national regime, contriving in their eccentric way to relate the two. In the days of the union jack[3] such women would have known their place —wasn't it all part and parcel?

Twice a week, on Fridays and Sundays, the Middletons journeyed into the town, first of all in a trap[4] and later in a Ford Anglia car. In the shops and elsewhere they made, quite gently, no secret of their continuing loyalty to the past. They attended on Sundays St. Patrick's Protestant Church, a place that matched their mood, for prayers were still said there for the King whose sovereignty their country had denied. The revolutionary regime would not last, they quietly informed the Reverend Packham—what sense was there in green-painted pillar boxes[5] and a language that nobody understood?

On Fridays, when they took seven or eight dozen eggs to the town, they dressed in pressed tweeds and were accompanied over the years by a series of red setters, the breed there had always been at Carraveagh. They sold the eggs in Keogh's grocery and then had a drink with Mrs. Keogh in the part of her shop that was devoted to the consumption of refreshment. They enjoyed the occasion, for they liked Mrs. Keogh and were liked by her in return. Afterwards they

---

1. **Herefords** n.: A breed of cattle.
2. **reign of George II:** 1727–1760.
3. **union jack:** The British flag; the symbol of British rule.
4. **trap** n.: A two-wheeled horse-drawn carriage.
5. **pillar boxes:** Mail collection boxes.

shopped, chatting to the shopkeepers about whatever news there was, and then they went to Healy's Hotel for a few more drinks before driving home.

. . . In spite of their loyalty to the past, they built up convivial relationships with the people of the town. Fat Driscoll, who kept the butcher's shop, used even to joke about the past when he stood with them in Healy's Hotel or stood behind his own counter cutting their slender chops or thinly slicing their liver. "Will you ever forget it, Mr. Middleton? I'd ha' run like a rabbit if you'd lifted a finger at me." Fat Driscoll would laugh then, rocking back on his heels with a glass of stout in his hand or banging their meat on to his weighing-scales. Mr. Middleton would smile. "There was alarm in your eyes, Mr. Driscoll," Miss Middleton would murmur, smiling also at the memory of the distant occasion.

Fat Driscoll, with a farmer called Maguire and another called Breen, had stood in the hall of Carraveagh, each of them in charge of a shotgun. The Middletons, children then, had been locked with their mother and father and an aunt into an upstairs room. Nothing else had happened: the expected British soldiers had not, after all, arrived and the men in the hall had eventually relaxed their vigil. "A massacre they wanted," the Middletons' father said after they'd gone. . . . "Bloody ruffians."

The Second World War took place. Two Germans, a man and his wife called Winkelmann who ran a glove factory in the town, were suspected by the Middletons of being spies for the Third Reich.[6] People laughed, for they knew the Winkelmanns well and could lend no credence to the Middletons' latest fantasy—typical of them, they explained to the Winkelmanns, who had been worried. Soon after the War the Reverend Packham died and was replaced by the Reverend Bradshaw, a younger man who laughed also and regarded the Middletons as

___
6. Third Reich (rīk): The German government under the Nazis (1933–1945).

an anachronism. They protested when prayers were no longer said for the Royal Family in St. Patrick's, but the Reverend Bradshaw considered that their protests were as absurd as the prayers themselves had been. Why pray for the monarchy of a neighboring island when their own island had its chosen President now? The Middletons didn't reply to that argument. In the Reverend Bradshaw's presence they rose to their feet when the BBC played "God Save the King," and on the day of the coronation of Queen Elizabeth II they drove into the town with a small union jack propped up in the back window of their Ford Anglia. "Bedad, you're a holy terror, Mr. Middleton!" Fat Driscoll laughingly exclaimed, noticing the flag as he lifted a tray of pork steaks from his display shelf. The Middletons smiled. It was a great day for the Commonwealth of Nations, they replied, a remark which further amused Fat Driscoll and which he later repeated in Phelan's public house. "Her Britannic Majesty," guffawed his friend Mr. Breen.

Situated in a valley that was noted for its beauty and with convenient access to rich rivers and bogs over which gamebirds flew, the town benefited from post-war tourism. Healy's Hotel changed its title and became, overnight, the New Ormonde. Shopkeepers had their shopfronts painted and Mr. Healy organized an annual Salmon Festival. Even Canon Kelly, who had at first commented severely on the habits of the tourists, and in particular on the summertime dress of the women, was in the end obliged to confess that the morals of his flock remained unaffected. "God and good sense," he proclaimed, meaning God and his own teaching. In time he even derived pride from the fact that people with other values came briefly to the town and that the values esteemed by his parishioners were in no way diminished. . . .

From the windows of their convent the Loretto nuns observed the long, sleek cars with G.B. plates; English and American accents drifted on the breeze to them. Mothers cleaned up their children and sent them to the Golf Club to seek employment as caddies. Sweet shops sold holiday mementoes. The brown, soda and currant breads of Murphy-Flood's bakery were declared to be delicious. Mr. Healy doubled the number of local girls who served as waitresses in his dining room, and in the winter of 1961 he had the builders in again, working on an extension for which the Munster and Leinster Bank had lent him twenty-two thousand pounds.

But as the town increased its prosperity Carraveagh continued its decline. The Middletons were in their middle sixties now and were reconciled to a life that became more uncomfortable with every passing year. Together they roved the vast lofts of their house, placing old paint tins and flowerpot saucers beneath the drips from the roof. At night they sat over their thin chops in a dining room that had once been gracious and which in a way was gracious still, except for the faded appearance of furniture that was dry from lack of polish and of a wallpaper that time had rendered colorless. In the hall their father gazed down at them, framed in ebony and gilt, in the uniform of the Irish Guards. He had conversed with Queen Victoria, and even in their middle sixties they could still hear him saying that God and Empire and Queen formed a trinity unique in any worthy soldier's heart. In the hall hung the family crest, and on ancient Irish linen the Cross of St. George.[7]

The dog that accompanied the Middletons now was called Turloch, an animal whose death they dreaded for they felt they couldn't manage the antics of another pup. Turloch, being thirteen, moved slowly and was blind and a little deaf. He was a reminder to them of their own advancing years and of the effort it had become to tend the Herefords and collect the weekly eggs. More and more they looked forward to Fridays, to the warm companionship of Mrs. Keogh and Mr. Healy's chatter in the hotel. They stayed longer now with Mrs. Keogh and in the hotel, and idled longer in the shops, and

drove home more slowly. Dimly, but with no less loyalty, they still recalled the distant past and were listened to without ill-feeling when they spoke of it and of Carraveagh as it had been, and of the Queen whose company their careless father had known.

The visitors who came to the town heard about the Middletons and were impressed. It was a pleasant wonder, more than one of them remarked, that old wounds could heal so completely, that the Middletons continued in their loyalty to the past and that, in spite of it, they were respected in the town. When Miss Middleton had been ill with a form of pneumonia in 1958 Canon Kelly had driven out to Carraveagh twice a week with pullets and young ducks that his housekeeper had dressed. "An upright couple," was the Canon's public opinion of the Middletons, and he had been known to add that eccentric views would hurt you less than malice. "We can disagree without guns in this town," Mr. Healy pronounced in his cocktail room, and his visitors usually replied that as far as they could see that was the result of living in a Christian country. That the Middletons bought their meat from a man who had once locked them into an upstairs room and had then waited to shoot soldiers in their hall was a fact that amazed the seasonal visitors. You lived and learned, they remarked to Mr. Healy.

The Middletons, privately, often considered that they led a strange life. Alone in their two beds at night they now and again wondered why they hadn't just sold Carraveagh forty-eight years ago when their father had died—why had the tie been so strong and why had they in perversity encouraged it? They didn't fully know, nor did they attempt to discuss the matter in any way. Instinctively they had remained at Carraveagh, instinctively feeling that it would have been cowardly to go. Yet often it seemed to them now to be no more than a game they played, this worship of the distant past. And at other times it seemed as real and as important as the remaining acres of land, and the house itself.

---

7. St. George: The patron saint of England.

"Isn't that shocking?" Mr. Healy said one day in 1967. "Did you hear about that, Mr. Middleton, blowing up them post offices in Belfast?"

Mr. Healy, red-faced and short-haired, spoke casually in his Cocktail Room, making midday conversation. He had commented in much the same way at breakfast-time, looking up from the *Irish Independent*. Everyone in the town had said it too: that the blowing up of sub-post offices in Belfast was a shocking matter.

"A bad business," Fat Driscoll remarked, wrapping the Middletons' meat. "We don't want that old stuff all over again."

"We didn't want it in the first place," Miss Middleton reminded him. He laughed, and she laughed, and so did her brother. Yes, it was a game, she thought—how could any of it be as real or as important as the afflictions and problems of the old butcher himself, his rheumatism and his reluctance to retire? Did her brother, she wondered, privately think so too?

"Come on, old Turloch," he said, stroking the flank of the red setter with the point of his shoe, and she reflected that you could never tell what he was thinking. Certainly it wasn't the kind of thing you wanted to talk about.

"I've put him in a bit of mince," Fat Driscoll said, which was something he often did these days, pretending the mince would otherwise be thrown away. There'd been a red setter about the place that night when he waited in the hall for the soldiers; Breen and Maguire had pushed it down into a cellar, frightened of it.

"There's a heart of gold in you, Mr. Driscoll," Miss Middleton murmured, nodding and smiling at him. He was the same age as she was, sixty-six—he should have shut up shop years ago. He would have, he'd once told them, if there'd been a son to leave the business to. As it was, he'd have to sell it and when it came to the point he found it hard to make the necessary arrangements. "Like us and Carraveagh," she'd said, even

though on the face of it it didn't seem the same at all.

Every evening they sat in the big old kitchen, hearing the news. It was only in Belfast and Derry, the wireless said; outside Belfast and Derry you wouldn't know anything was happening at all. On Fridays they listened to the talk in Mrs. Keogh's bar and in the hotel. "Well, thank God it has nothing to do with the South," Mr. Healy said often, usually repeating the statement.

The first British soldiers landed in the North of Ireland, and soon people didn't so often say that outside Belfast and Derry you wouldn't know anything was happening. There were incidents in Fermanagh and Armagh, in border villages and towns. One Prime Minister resigned and then another one. The troops were unpopular, the newspapers said; internment became part of the machinery of government. In the town, in St. Patrick's Protestant Church and in the Church of the Holy Assumption, prayers for peace were offered, but no peace came.

"We're hit, Mr. Middleton," Mr. Healy said one Friday morning. "If there's a dozen visitors this summer it'll be God's own stroke of luck for us."

"Luck?"

"Sure, who wants to come to a country with all that malarkey in it?"

"But it's only in the North."

"Tell that to your tourists, Mr. Middleton."

The town's prosperity ebbed. The border was more than sixty miles away, but over that distance had spread some wisps of the fog of war. As anger rose in the town at the loss of fortune so there rose also the kind of talk there had been in the distant past. There was talk of atrocities and counteratrocities, and of guns and gelignite[8] and the rights of people. There was bitterness suddenly in Mrs. Keogh's bar because of the lack of trade, and in the empty hotel there was bitterness also.

---

8. gelignite *n*.: An explosive.

On Fridays, only sometimes at first, there was a silence when the Middletons appeared. It was as though, going back nearly twenty years, people remembered the union jack in the window of their car and saw it now in a different light. It wasn't something to laugh at any more, nor were certain words that the Middletons had gently spoken, nor were they themselves just an old, peculiar couple. Slowly the change crept about, all around them in the town, until Fat Driscoll didn't wish it to be remembered that he had ever given them mince for their dog. He had stood with a gun in the enemy's house, waiting for soldiers so that soldiers might be killed—it was better that people should remember that.

One day Canon Kelly looked the other way when he saw the Middleton's car coming and they noticed this movement of his head, although he hadn't wished them to. And on another day Mrs. O'Brien, who had always been keen to talk to them in the hotel, didn't reply when they addressed her.

The Middletons naturally didn't discuss these rebuffs but they each of them privately knew that there was no conversation they could have at this time with the people of the town. The stand they had taken and kept to for so many years no longer seemed ridiculous in the town. Had they driven with a union jack now they would, astoundingly, have been shot.

"It will never cease." He spoke disconsolately one night, standing by the dresser where the wireless was.

She washed the dishes they'd eaten from, and the cutlery. "Not in our time," she said.

"It is worse than before."

"Yes, it is worse than before."

They took from the walls of the hall the portrait of their father in the uniform of the Irish Guards because it seemed wrong to them that at this time it should hang there. They took down also the crest of their family and the Cross of St. George, and from a vase on the drawing-room mantelpiece they removed the small union jack that had been there since the coronation of Queen Elizabeth II. They did not remove these articles in fear but in mourning for the *modus vivendi*[9] that had existed for so long between them and the people of the town. They had given their custom to a butcher who had planned to shoot down soldiers in their hall and he, in turn, had given them mince for their dog. For fifty years they had experienced, after suspicion had seeped away, a tolerance that never again in the years that were left to them would they know.

One November night their dog died and he said to her after he had buried it that they must not be depressed by all that was happening. They would die themselves and the house would become a ruin because there was no one to inherit it, and the distant past would be set to rest. But she disagreed: the *modus vivendi* had been easy for them, she pointed out, because they hadn't really minded the dwindling of their fortunes while the town prospered. It had given them a life, and a kind of dignity: you could take a pride out of living in peace.

He did not say anything and then, because of the emotion that both of them felt over the death of their dog, he said in a rushing way that they could no longer at their age hope to make a living out of the remains of Carraveagh. They must sell the hens and the four Herefords. As he spoke, he watched her nodding, agreeing with the sense of it. Now and again, he thought, he would drive slowly into the town, to buy groceries and meat with the money they had saved, and to face the silence that would sourly thicken as their own two deaths came closer and death increased in another part of their island. She felt him thinking that and she knew that he was right. Because of the distant past they would die friendless. It was worse than being murdered in their beds.

---

9. modus vivendi (vi ven′ dī): Manner of getting along.

RESPONDING TO THE SELECTION

Your Response

1. To what degree do you think the Middletons are responsible for their own fate? Explain.

Recalling

2. Whom do the Middletons blame for the decay of their estate?
3. What event do Fat Driscoll and the Middletons recall when they visit Driscoll's butcher shop?
4. (a) What do the Middletons do on the day of Queen Elizabeth II's coronation? (b) How do the townspeople respond to this action?
5. Why does the town prosper in the years after World War II?
6. (a) What type of relationship do the Middletons have with the townspeople? (b) How does the relationship change after the town's prosperity fades?

Interpreting

7. How does the decline of the Middletons' fortunes parallel the decline of the British Empire?
8. What is ironic, or surprising, about the fact that throughout most of the story the townspeople respected the Middletons?
9. What does the change in the townspeople's attitude toward the Middletons reveal about human nature?

Applying

10. Why do you think that many Irish people feel a sense of resentment toward the British?

ANALYZING LITERATURE

Understanding Characterization

A variety of different types of characters are used in literary works. When a character is well developed and possesses a variety of traits, he or she is referred to as a round character. A character who embodies a single trait, ideal, or quality is referred to as a flat character. Static characters are characters who do not change during the course of a literary work. Dynamic characters are characters who do change. For example, they may change by responding to events that occur in the historical context of the story: Real history may intervene in the characters' lives and shape them in unexpected ways.

1. Are the Middletons flat characters or round characters? Support your answer.
2. Are the Middletons static characters or dynamic characters? Support your answer.
3. Are the townspeople static characters or dynamic characters? Support your answer.

CRITICAL THINKING AND READING

Understanding a Character's Motivation

In portraying any type of character, a writer must provide a **motivation,** a stated or implied reason for the character's behavior, to make the character's actions believable. For example, in "The Distant Past" it is clear that the Middletons' actions on the day of Queen Elizabeth II's coronation are motivated by their loyalty to Great Britain.

1. What motivates the townspeople to change their behavior toward the Middletons?
2. How does Trevor reveal this motivation?

THINKING AND WRITING

Writing a Diaglogue

Write a dialogue in which the Middletons discuss the decline in their fortunes and the change in the townspeople's attitude toward them. Reread the story, trying to put yourself in the Middletons' place. Then write your dialogue, having the Middletons discuss the reasons for and feelings about their present situation. When you finish writing, revise your dialogue and share it with your classmates.

DORIS LESSING

1919–

Doris Lessing is one of the most powerful of contemporary authors. Her novels and short stories explore the evils of racism, the role of women in modern life, the importance of intuition, and the limits of idealism in solving the problems facing society. Her books, profound and highly personal, confront a host of post-World War II issues, supplying almost a history of the times, with special emphasis on Africa and feminism.

The focus on Africa in Doris Lessing's work is not surprising. Born in Persia of British parents, she grew up on a three-thousand-acre farm in Southern Rhodesia (now Zimbabwe), where her parents raised maize with the help of native labor. She remained in Africa through two unsuccessful marriages, living principally in the Rhodesian capital of Salisbury, until she was thirty.

Explaining how her career began, Lessing said: "I've always been a writer . . . but not until I was quite old—twenty-six or -seven—did I realize that I'd better . . . get down to business. I was working in a lawyer's office at the time, and I remember walking in and saying to my boss, 'I'm giving up my job because I'm going to write a novel.' He very properly laughed, and I indignantly walked home and wrote *The Grass Is Singing.*"

She moved to London in 1949 and published her first novel, *The Grass Is Singing,* the next year, having brought the manuscript with her from Rhodesia. Her African experiences provided the material for this deeply moving, highly acclaimed work. In an interview in 1962, Lessing commented, "I feel the best thing that ever happened to me was that I was brought up out of England. I took for granted kinds of experiences that would be impossible to a middle-class girl here."

The Golden Notebook, published in 1962, is her most renowned and technically sophisticated work. It represents a junction between the two main paths her fiction has taken—her realistic, sometimes reportorial early style, and her visionary, at times apocalyptic, "inner space fiction" that came later. The dominant theme in *The Golden Notebook* is that of the free woman who struggles for individuality and equality despite her social and psychological conditioning.

A self-described "architect of the soul," Lessing is one of the most serious and intelligent of today's writers. Hers is a uniquely twentieth-century odyssey. Writing in what she calls a "straight, broad, direct" manner, she has produced a remarkable body of novels and short stories, works that are distinguished not only for their breadth of subject matter but also for their breadth of vision.

GUIDE FOR INTERPRETING

A Mild Attack of Locusts

Writers' Techniques

Conflict. One of the ingredients of an effective story or play is conflict, the struggle between a main character and another person or force. Often the conflict involves two main characters—protagonist and antagonist—as in many of Shakespeare's tragedies. Sometimes the conflict is between a main character and society as a whole, or between a main character and nature. These conflicts are external. An external conflict is one between a main character and another person or between a character and an outside force. There may also be internal conflict, or psychological conflict. Internal conflict occurs within the mind of a main character. Many plots contain both external and internal conflicts. Fictional conflicts, like real-life conflicts, are often complex, and you may occasionally find them puzzling to sort out.

Focus

Human beings are often pitted against nature in both real life and in fiction. For example, a family may struggle against a fast-flowing river, or fire fighters may battle a forest fire. Make a list of natural forces against which human beings must battle—and win—to survive.

Primary Source

Lessing describes life on an isolated South African farm..

> Our neighbors were four, five, seven miles off. . . . The seasons were bad, prices bad, crops failed. This was the sort of thing that made it impossible for him [her father] ever to "get off the farm," which, he agreed with my mother, was what he most wanted to do. . . . But it was my mother who suffered. After a period of neurotic illness, which was a protest against her situation, she became brave and resourceful. But she never saw that her husband was not living in a real world, that he had made a captive of her common sense. We were always about to "get off the farm." A miracle would do it—a sweepstake, a goldmine, a legacy. And then? What a question! We would go to England where life would be normal with people coming in for musical evenings and nice supper parties at the Trocadero after a show. Poor woman, for the twenty years we were on the farm, she waited for when life would begin for her and for her children, for she never understood that what was a calamity for her was for them a blessing.

> As you read "A Mild Attack of Locusts," see how Margaret's conflicts parallel those Lessing's mother faced.

A Mild Attack of Locusts

Doris Lessing

The rains that year were good; they were coming nicely just as the crops needed them —or so Margaret gathered when the men said they were not too bad. She never had an opinion of her own on matters like the weather, because even to know about what seems a simple thing like the weather needs experience. Which Margaret had not got. The men were Richard her husband, and old Stephen, Richard's father, a farmer from way back; and these two might argue for hours whether the rains were ruinous or just ordinarily exasperating. Margaret had been on the farm three years. She still did not understand how they did not go bankrupt altogether, when the men never had a good word for the weather, or the soil, or the Government. But she was getting to learn the language. Farmers' language. And they neither went bankrupt nor got very rich. They jogged along doing comfortably.

Their crop was maize.[1] Their farm was three thousand acres on the ridges that rise up toward the Zambesi escarpment[2]—high, dry windswept country, cold and dusty in winter, but now, in the wet season, steamy with the heat rising in wet soft waves off miles of green foliage. Beautiful it was, with the sky blue and brilliant halls of air, and the bright green folds and hollows of country beneath, and the mountains lying sharp and bare twenty miles off across the rivers.

The sky made her eyes ache; she was not used to it. One does not look so much at the sky in the city she came from. So that evening when Richard said: "The Government is sending out warnings that locusts are expected, coming down from the breeding grounds up North," her instinct was to look about her at the trees. Insects —swarms of them—horrible! But Richard and the old man had raised their eyes and were looking up over the mountain. "We haven't had locusts in seven years," they said. "They go in cycles, locusts do." And then: "There goes our crop for this season!"

But they went on with the work of the farm just as usual until one day they were coming up the road to the homestead for the midday break, when old Stephen stopped, raised his finger and pointed: "Look, look, there they are!"

Out ran Margaret to join them, looking at the hills. Out came the servants from the kitchen. They all stood and gazed. Over the rocky levels of the mountain was a streak of rust-colored air. Locusts. There they came.

At once Richard shouted at the cookboy. Old Stephen yelled at the houseboy. The cookboy ran to beat the old plowshare[3] hanging from a tree branch, which was used to summon the laborers at moments of crisis. The houseboy ran off to the store to collect tin cans, any old bit of metal. The farm was ringing with the clamor of the gong; and they could see the laborers come

---

1. **maize** (māz) n.: Corn.
2. **Zambesi** (zam bē' zē) **escarpment:** Steep cliffs along the Zambesi River in southern Africa.

3. **plowshare** n.: The cutting blade of a plow.

pouring out of the compound, pointing at the hills and shouting excitedly. Soon they had all come up to the house, and Richard and old Stephen were giving them orders —Hurry, hurry, hurry.

And off they ran again, the two white men with them, and in a few minutes Margaret could see the smoke of fires rising from all around the farmlands. Piles of wood and grass had been prepared there. There were seven patches of bared soil, yellow and ox-blood color and pink, where the new mealies[4] were just showing, making a film of bright green; and around each drifted up thick clouds of smoke. They were throwing wet leaves on to the fires now, to make it acrid and black. Margaret was watching the hills. Now there was a long, low cloud advancing, rust-color still, swelling forward and out as she looked. The telephone was ringing. Neighbors—quick, quick, there come the locusts. Old Smith had had his crop eaten to the ground. Quick, get your fires started. For of course, while every farmer hoped the locusts would overlook his farm and go on to the next, it was only fair to warn each other; one must play fair. Everywhere, fifty miles over the countryside, the smoke was rising from myriads of fires. Margaret answered the telephone calls, and between calls she stood watching the locusts. The air was darkening. A strange darkness, for the sun was blazing—it was like the darkness of a veldt fire, when the air gets thick with smoke. The sunlight comes down distorted, a thick, hot orange. Oppressive it was, too, with the heaviness of a storm. The locusts were coming fast. Now half the sky was darkened. Behind the reddish veils in front, which were the advance guards of the swarm, the main swarm showed in dense black cloud, reaching almost to the sun itself.

Margaret was wondering what she could do to help. She did not know. Then up came

---

4. **mealies** *n.*: Ears of corn.

old Stephen from the lands. "We're finished, Margaret, finished! Those beggars can eat every leaf and blade off the farm in half an hour! And it is only early afternoon—if we can make enough smoke, make enough noise till the sun goes down, they'll settle somewhere else perhaps. . . ." And then: "Get the kettle going. It's thirsty work, this."

So Margaret went to the kitchen, and stoked up the fire, and boiled the water. Now, on the tin roof of the kitchen she could hear the thuds and bangs of falling locusts, or a scratching slither as one skidded down. Here were the first of them. From down on the lands came the beating and banging and clanging of a hundred gasoline cans and bits of metal. Stephen impatiently waited while one gasoline can was filled with tea, hot, sweet and orange-colored, and the other with water. In the meantime, he told Margaret about how twenty years back he was eaten out, made bankrupt, by the locust armies. And then, still talking, he hoisted up the gasoline cans, one in each hand, by the wood pieces set cornerwise across each, and jogged off down to the road to the thirsty laborers. By now the locusts were falling like hail on to the roof of the kitchen. It sounded like a heavy storm. Margaret looked out and saw the air dark with a criss-cross of the insects, and she set her teeth and ran out into it—what the men could do, she could. Overhead the air was thick, locusts everywhere. The locusts were flopping against her, and she brushed them off, heavy red-brown creatures, looking at her with their beady old-men's eyes while they clung with hard, serrated legs. She held her breath with disgust and ran through into the house. There it was even more like being in a heavy storm. The iron roof was reverberating, and the clamor of iron from the lands was like thunder. Looking out, all the trees were queer and still, clotted with insects, their boughs weighed to the ground. The earth seemed to be moving, locusts crawling everywhere, she could not see the lands at

all, so thick was the swarm. Towards the mountains it was like looking into driving rain—even as she watched, the sun was blotted out with a fresh onrush of them. It was a half-night, a perverted blackness. Then came a sharp crack from the bush—a branch had snapped off. Then another. A tree down the slope leaned over and settled heavily to the ground. Through the hail of insects a man came running. More tea, more water was needed. She supplied them. She kept the fires stoked and filled cans with liquid, and then it was four in the afternoon, and the locusts had been pouring across overhead for a couple of hours. Up came old Stephen again, crunching locusts underfoot with every step, locusts clinging all over him; he was cursing and swearing, banging with his old hat at the air. At the doorway he stopped briefly, hastily pulling at the clinging insects and throwing them off, then he plunged into the locust-free living-room.

"All the crops finished. Nothing left," he said.

But the gongs were still beating, the men still shouting, and Margaret asked: "Why do you go on with it, then?"

"The main swarm isn't settling. They are heavy with eggs. They are looking for a place to settle and lay. If we can stop the main body settling on our farm, that's everything. If they get a chance to lay their eggs, we are going to have everything eaten flat with hoppers[5] later on." He picked a stray locust off his shirt and split it down with his thumbnail—it was clotted inside with eggs. "Imagine that multiplied by millions. You ever seen a hopper swarm on the march? Well, you're lucky."

Margaret thought an adult swarm was bad enough. Outside now the light on the earth was a pale, thin yellow, clotted with moving shadows; the clouds of moving insects thickened and lightened like driving rain. Old Stephen said, "They've got the wind behind them, that's something."

"Is it very bad?" asked Margaret fearfully, and the old man said emphatically: "We're finished. This swarm may pass over, but once they've started, they'll be coming down from the North now one after another. And then there are the hoppers—it might go on for two or three years."

Margaret sat down helplessly, and thought: Well, if it's the end, it's the end. What now? We'll all three have to go back to town. . . . But at this, she took a quick look at Stephen, the old man who had farmed forty years in this country, been bankrupt twice, and she knew nothing would make him go and become a clerk in the city. Yet her heart ached for him, he looked so tired, the worry lines deep from nose to mouth. Poor old man. . . . He had lifted up a locust that had got itself somehow into his pocket, holding it in the air by one leg. "You've got the strength of a steel-spring in those legs of yours," he was telling the locust, good-humoredly. Then, although he had been fighting locusts, squashing locusts, yelling at locusts, sweeping them in great mounds into the fires to burn for the last three hours, nevertheless he took this one to the door and carefully threw it out to join its fellows, as if

---

5. hoppers *n.*: Baby locusts.

he would rather not harm a hair of its head. This comforted Margaret; all at once she felt irrationally cheered. She remembered it was not the first time in the last three years the man had announced their final and irremediable ruin.

"Get me a drink, lass," he then said, and she set the bottle of whisky by him.

In the meantime, out in the pelting storm of insects, her husband was banging the gong, feeding the fires with leaves, the insects clinging to him all over—she shuddered. "How can you bear to let them touch you?" she asked. He looked at her, disapproving. She felt suitably humble—just as she had when he had first taken a good look at her city self, hair waved and golden, nails red and pointed. Now she was a proper farmer's wife, in sensible shoes and a solid skirt. She might even get to letting locusts settle on her—in time.

Having tossed back a whisky or two, old Stephen went back into the battle, wading now through glistening brown waves of locusts.

Five o'clock. The sun would set in an hour. Then the swarm would settle. It was as thick overhead as ever. The trees were ragged mounds of glistening brown.

Margaret began to cry. It was all so hopeless—if it wasn't a bad season, it was locusts; if it wasn't locusts, it was army worm[6] or veldt fires. Always something. The rustling of the locust armies was like a big forest in the storm; their settling on the roof was like the beating of the rain; the ground was invisible in a sleek, brown, surging tide—it was like being drowned in locusts, submerged by the loathsome brown flood. It seemed as if the roof might sink in under the weight of them, as if the door might give in under their pressure and these rooms fill with them—and it was getting so dark . . . she looked up. The air was thinner; gaps of blue showed in the dark, moving clouds. The

---

6. army worm: Larva of certain moths that travel in large groups, ruining crops.

blue spaces were cold and thin—the sun must be setting. Through the fog of insects she saw figures approaching. First old Stephen, marching bravely along, then her husband, drawn and haggard with weariness. Behind them the servants. All were crawling all over with insects. The sound of the gongs had stopped. She could hear nothing but the ceaseless rustle of a myriad wings.

The two men slapped off the insects and came in.

"Well," said Richard, kissing her on the cheek, "the main swarm has gone over."

"For the Lord's sake," said Margaret angrily, still half-crying, "what's here is bad enough, isn't it?" For although the evening air was no longer black and thick, but a clear blue, with a pattern of insects whizzing this way and that across it, everything else—trees, buildings, bushes, earth, was gone under the moving brown masses.

"If it doesn't rain in the night and keep them here—if it doesn't rain and weight them down with water, they'll be off in the morning at sunrise."

"We're bound to have some hoppers. But not the main swarm—that's something."

Margaret roused herself, wiped her eyes, pretended she had not been crying, and fetched them some supper, for the servants were too exhausted to move. She sent them down to the compound to rest.

She served the supper and sat listening. There is not one maize plant left, she heard. Not one. The men would get the planters out the moment the locusts had gone. They must start all over again.

But what's the use of that, Margaret wondered, if the whole farm was going to be crawling with hoppers? But she listened while they discussed the new government pamphlet that said how to defeat the hoppers. You must have men out all the time, moving over the farm to watch for movement in the grass. When you find a patch of hoppers, small lively black things, like crickets, then you dig trenches around the patch or spray them with poison from pumps supplied by the Government. The Government wanted them to cooperate in a world plan for eliminating this plague forever. You should attack locusts at the source. Hoppers, in short. The men were talking as if they were planning a war, and Margaret listened, amazed.

In the night it was quiet; no sign of the settled armies outside, except sometimes a branch snapped, or a tree could be heard crashing down.

Margaret slept badly in the bed beside Richard, who was sleeping like the dead, exhausted with the afternoon's fight. In the morning she woke to yellow sunshine lying across the bed—clear sunshine, with an occasional blotch of shadow moving over it. She went to the window. Old Stephen was ahead of her. There he stood outside, gazing down over the bush. And she gazed, astounded—and entranced, much against her will. For it looked as if every tree, every bush, all the earth, were lit with pale flames. The locusts were fanning their wings to free them of the night dews. There was a shimmer of red-tinged gold light everywhere.

She went out to join the old man, stepping carefully among the insects. They stood and watched. Overhead the sky was blue, blue and clear.

"Pretty," said old Stephen, with satisfaction.

Well, thought Margaret, we may be ruined, we may be bankrupt, but not everyone has seen an army of locusts fanning their wings at dawn.

Over the slopes, in the distance, a faint red smear showed in the sky, thickened and spread. "There they go," said old Stephen. "There goes the main army, off south."

And now from the trees, from the earth all round them, the locusts were taking wing. They were like small aircraft, maneuvering for the take-off, trying their wings to see if they were dry enough. Off they went. A reddish-brown steam was rising off the miles of bush, off the lands, the earth. Again the sunlight darkened.

And as the clotted branches lifted, the weight on them lightening, there was nothing but the black spines of branches, trees. No green left, nothing. All morning they watched, the three of them, as the brown crust thinned and broke and dissolved, flying up to mass with the main army, now a brownish-red smear in the southern sky. The lands which had been filmed with green, the new tender mealie plants, were stark and bare. All the trees stripped. A devastated landscape. No green, no green anywhere.

By midday the reddish cloud had gone. Only an occasional locust flopped down. On the ground were the corpses and the wounded. The African laborers were sweeping these up with branches and collecting them in tins.

"Ever eaten sun-dried locust?" asked old Stephen. "That time twenty years ago, when I went broke, I lived on mealie meal and dried locusts for three months. They aren't bad at all—rather like smoked fish, if you come to think of it."

But Margaret preferred not even to think of it.

After the midday meal the men went off to the lands. Everything was to be replanted. With a bit of luck another swarm would not come traveling down just this way. But they hoped it would rain very soon, to spring some new grass, because the cattle would die otherwise—there was not a blade of grass left on the farm. As for Margaret, she was trying to get used to the idea of three or four years of locusts. Locusts were going to be like bad weather, from now on, always imminent. She felt like a survivor after war—if this devastated and mangled countryside was not ruin, well, what then was ruin?

But the men ate their supper with good appetites.

"It could have been worse," was what they said. "It could be much worse."

RESPONDING TO THE SELECTION

Your Response

1. What feelings does the description of the locusts crashing against the roofs, covering the ground, and landing on people evoke in you?

Recalling

2. What are the farmers' two main defenses against the locusts?
3. Why do the farmers want to prevent the main swarm of locusts from settling?
4. What three problems besides locusts do the farmers sometimes have to face?
5. (a) How much damage do the locusts do to the farm? (b) When morning comes, what do the locusts do?

Interpreting

6. What is Margaret's attitude toward the locust attack?
7. Why does old Stephen fight on even after saying they are finished?
8. Why do you think Margaret is comforted when Stephen releases the locust that was in his pocket?
9. In what sense is the locust attack "mild," as the title of the story calls it?

Applying

10. People react differently when faced with what seems to be a hopeless situation. (a) How does this story make that point? (b) What have you seen in your own experience that proves it?

ANALYZING LITERATURE

Recognizing Conflict

In a work of fiction, the opposition between a character and another force is the story's conflict. This conflict may be external—as between the farmers and the invading locusts in "A Mild Attack of Locusts"—or it may be internal—as in Margaret's love for her husband as opposed to her despair for his future as a farmer on the veldt.

1. There are a number of conflicts in "A Mild Attack of Locusts." One of them concerns Margaret's struggle to define herself as a farmer's wife. What evidence is there in the story that she does not regard herself as entirely satisfied with her role in life?
2. The immediate external conflict in the story is the locust attack. But there is a long-term conflict as well, one that is unresolved by the farmers' minor victory in keeping the main swarm from settling. (a) What is the long-term, unresolved external conflict? (b) How successful do you think Richard, Stephen, and Margaret will be in resolving it?

THINKING AND WRITING

Writing About a Paradox

A **paradox** is a statement or circumstance that at first seems untrue or self-contradictory but upon reflection proves to be true in some sense. In "A Mild Attack of Locusts," Margaret, after a day of feeling revulsion for the locusts, is entranced the next morning as they fan their wings, making "a shimmer of red-tinged gold light everywhere." Her feelings are paradoxical. Write a composition in which you explain the paradox of how something so destructive and even loathsome can also be beautiful. When revising your first draft, make sure you have supported your ideas with specific details.

LEARNING OPTION

Cross-curricular Connection. The locust is a fascinating insect with an unusual life cycle. Learn as much as you can about locusts: the various types, ways in which they reproduce, their development from larvae to adult moths, and why they appear only periodically. You might use local newspaper archives to try to determine if and when a locust attack has ever occurred in your area and what its effects were. Then investigate modern methods of controlling locusts and the ecological consequences of using such methods. Share your findings in a brief oral report to the class.

NADINE GORDIMER

1923–

The fiction of Nadine Gordimer has been shaped by her life in South Africa and by her firm opposition to the government's policy of apartheid. Initially honored for her short fiction, she says that in time she found the short story "too delicate for what I have to say." In recent years her novels, some of them banned in South Africa, have gained an international reputation.

Nadine Gordimer was born in Springs, South Africa, a small town near Johannesburg. Her mother took her out of a local private school when she was eleven, and from then until she was sixteen she "read tremendously," wrote much fiction, and published her first adult short story, "Come Again Tomorrow," when she was fifteen. She studied for a year at the University of Witwatersrand, continuing to write short stories. *The Soft Voice of the Serpent* (1952) was the first collection of her stories to be published in the United States.

Following the critical success of that book, Gordimer's stories began appearing in *The New Yorker,* the *Atlantic, Harper's,* and other well-known periodicals. In her stories she often describes the enforced entrapment of whites who have inherited political and economic power in South Africa's closed society. Frequently she builds a personal tale around a fleeting but sharply focused moment of insight.

In her short stories, and later in her novels—including the critically acclaimed *A Guest of Honor* (1970), *The Conservationist* (1974), and *Burger's Daughter* (1979)—she displays an ability to write from the perspectives of Anglo, black, and Afrikaner and to delineate a variety of economic and social settings. She writes as a compassionate observer of the human condition. In lyric tones, yet without sentimentality, she pictures the South African scene with awareness and humanity, stressing the themes of understanding, adjustment, and forgiveness.

Until she was thirty, Nadine Gordimer had never been outside South Africa. Since then she has traveled widely and lectured in a number of universities, including Princeton, Columbia, and the University of Michigan. In recent years she has won many literary awards, including the Nobel Prize in 1991.

Since 1954 Gordimer has been married to Reinhold Cassier, the director of the Johannesburg branch of Sotheby Parke Bernet. She has two children, one by a previous marriage. Called "a luminous symbol of at least one white person's understanding of the black man's burden," there can be little doubt that she is one of the leading African novelists writing in English.

GUIDE FOR INTERPRETING

The Train from Rhodesia

Writers' Techniques

Theme. Theme is the insight into life revealed by a work of literature. In fiction the writer's central idea becomes the theme of the
work. Often the theme can be stated in a single sentence, such as
"A small mistake in judgment can have serious consequences."
Sometimes it demands a more detailed description. A work of fiction may have one theme or several. In developing a theme, the
writer introduces *conflict,* typically a problem or problems that must
be solved by the protagonist, or main character.

When the protagonist has to choose between two or more undesirable alternatives, he or she faces a *dilemma*. In familiar terms
a dilemma is a choice between the frying pan and the fire; in mythological terms, between Scylla and Charybdis. A dilemma involves a
difficult choice between actions or values, and any choice that the
character makes may have unfortunate results.

Commentary

An author's entire literary output is frequently characterized by one
overriding theme that ties together all the individual works. The works
rarely state the same theme in the same way. Rather, readers can
see one general concern expressed differently in each poem, story,
novel, or essay. This theme can be drawn from the writer's personal
situation or combined with some political, social, or moral concern
of the day. On the surface, it would not seem possible that Nadine
Gordimer's work would show one dominant theme, since she writes
about such a wide range of people and places. Indeed, one critic
has remarked that "the image of the bazaar comes to mind when
one thinks of Miss Gordimer's variety and resourcefulness." For
example, many of her stories concern wealthy, sophisticated, and
frequently bored urban and suburban people in Johannesburg, South
Africa. Other tales deal with people on the lowest economic rung ek-
ing out a bare living under wretched conditions. Many of her best
tales, such as "The Train from Rhodesia," intermingle these two
worlds to more fully illuminate the situation in contemporary South
Africa. But critic Robert F. Haugh has identified a tension between
"what might be" and "what is" in a majority of her work. How do you
see this theme in "The Train from Rhodesia"?

Focus

According to an African proverb, "The earth is a beehive; we all enter by the same door but live in different cells." Freewrite, exploring
the meaning of this proverb.

The Train from Rhodesia[1]

Nadine Gordimer

The train came out of the red horizon and bore down toward them over the single straight track.

The stationmaster came out of his little brick station with its pointed chalet roof, feeling the creases in his serge uniform in his legs as well. A stir of preparedness rippled through the squatting native vendors waiting in the dust; the face of a carved wooden animal, eternally surprised, stuck out of a sack. The stationmaster's barefoot children wandered over. From the gray mud huts with the untidy heads that stood within a decorated mud wall, chickens, and dogs with their skin stretched like parchment over their bones, followed the piccanins[2] down to the track. The flushed and perspiring west cast a reflection, faint, without heat, upon the station, upon the tin shed marked "Goods," upon the walled kraal,[3] upon the gray tin house of the stationmaster and upon the sand, that lapped all around, from sky to sky, cast little rhythmical cups of shadow, so that the sand became the sea, and closed over the children's black feet softly and without imprint.

The stationmaster's wife sat behind the mesh of her veranda. Above her head the hunk of a sheep's carcass moved slightly, dangling in a current of air.

They waited.

The train called out, along the sky; but there was no answer; and the cry hung on: I'm coming . . . I'm coming . . .

The engine flared out now, big, whisking a dwindling body behind it; the track flared out to let it in.

Creaking, jerking, jostling, gasping, the train filled the station.

Here, let me see that one—the young woman curved her body further out of the corridor window. Missus? smiled the old boy, looking at the creatures he held in his hand. From a piece of string on his gray finger hung a tiny woven basket; he lifted it, questioning. No, no, she urged, leaning down toward him, across the height of the train, toward the man in the piece of old rug; that one, that one, her hand commanded. It was a lion, carved out of soft dry wood that looked like spongecake; heraldic, black and white, with impressionistic detail burnt in. The old man held it up to her still smiling, not from the heart, but at the customer. Between its Vandyke[4] teeth, in the mouth opened in an endless roar too terrible to be heard, it had a black tongue. Look, said the young husband, if you don't mind! And round the neck of the thing, a piece of fur (rat? rabbit? meerkat?); a real mane, majestic, telling you somehow that the artist had delight in the lion.

---

1. **Rhodesia** (rō de′ zhə): Former name of Zimbabwe (zim bä′ bwe), a country in southern Africa.
2. **piccanins** *n.*: Native children.
3. **kraal** (kräl) *n.*: A fenced-in enclosure for cattle or sheep.

---

4. **Vandyke** (van dīk′) *adj.*: Tapering to a point, like a Vandyke beard.

All up and down the length of the train in the dust the artists sprang, walking bent, like performing animals, the better to exhibit the fantasy held toward the faces on the train. Buck, startled and stiff, staring with round black and white eyes. More lions, standing erect, grappling with strange, thin, elongated warriors who clutched spears and showed no fear in their slits of eyes. How much, they asked from the train, how much?

Give me penny, said the little ones with nothing to sell. The dogs went and sat, quite still, under the dining car, where the train breathed out the smell of meat cooking with onion.

A man passed beneath the arch of reaching arms meeting gray-black and white in the exchange of money for the staring wooden eyes, the stiff wooden legs sticking up in the air; went along under the voices and the bargaining, interrogating the wheels. Past the dogs; glancing up at the dining car where he could stare at the faces, behind glass, drinking beer, two by two, on either side of a uniform railway vase with its pale dead flower. Right to the end, to the guard's van, where the stationmaster's children had just collected their mother's two loaves of bread; to the engine itself, where the stationmaster and the driver stood talking against the steaming complaint of the resting beast.

The man called out to them, something loud and joking. They turned to laugh, in a twirl of steam. The two children careered over the sand, clutching the bread, and burst through the iron gate and up the path through the garden in which nothing grew.

Passengers drew themselves in at the corridor windows and turned into compartments to fetch money, to call someone to look. Those sitting inside looked up: suddenly different, caged faces, boxed in, cut off, after the contact of outside. There was an orange a piccanin would like. . . . What about that chocolate? It wasn't very nice. . . .

A young girl had collected a handful of the hard kind, that no one liked, out of the chocolate box, and was throwing them to the dogs, over at the dining car. But the hens darted in, and swallowed the chocolates, incredibly quick and accurate, before they had even dropped in the dust, and the dogs, a little bewildered, looked up with their brown eyes, not expecting anything.

—No, leave it, said the girl, don't take it. . . .

Too expensive, too much, she shook her head and raised her voice to the old boy, giving up the lion. He held it up where she had handed it to him. No, she said, shaking her head. Three-and-six?[5] insisted her husband, loudly. Yes baas! laughed the boy. *Three-and-six?*—the young man was incredulous. Oh leave it—she said. The young man stopped. Don't you want it? he said, keeping his face closed to the boy. No, never mind, she said, leave it. The old native kept his head on one side, looking at them sideways, holding the lion. Three-and-six, he murmured, as old people repeat things to themselves.

The young woman drew her head in. She went into the coupé[6] and sat down. Out of the window, on the other side, there was nothing; sand and bush; a thorn tree. Back through the open doorway, past the figure of her husband in the corridor, there was the station, the voices, wooden animals waving, running feet. Her eye followed the funny little valance of scrolled wood that outlined the chalet roof of the station; she thought of the lion and smiled. That bit of fur round the neck. But the wooden buck, the hippos, the elephants, the baskets that already bulked out of their brown paper under the seat and on the luggage rack! How will they look at home? Where will you put them? What will they mean away from the places you found

---

5. three-and-six: Three shillings and sixpence.
6. coupé (kōō pā′) *n.*: A half-compartment at the end, with seats on only one side.

them? Away from the unreality of the last few weeks? The man outside. But he is not part of the unreality; he is for good now. Odd . . . somewhere there was an idea that he, that living with him, was part of the holiday, the strange places.

Outside, a bell rang. The stationmaster was leaning against the end of the train, green flag rolled in readiness. A few men who had got down to stretch their legs sprang on to the train, clinging to the observation platforms, or perhaps merely standing on the iron step, holding the rail; but on the train, safe from the one dusty platform, the one tin house, the empty sand.

There was a grunt. The train jerked. Through the glass the beer drinkers looked out, as if they could not see beyond it. Behind the flyscreen, the stationmaster's wife sat facing back at them beneath the darkening hunk of meat.

There was a shout. The flag drooped out. Joints not yet coordinated, the segmented body of the train heaved and bumped back against itself. It began to move; slowly the scrolled chalet moved past it, the yells of the natives, running alongside, jetted up into the air, fell back at different levels. Staring wooden faces waved drunkenly, there, then gone, questioning for the last time at the windows. Here, one-and-six baas!—As one automatically opens a hand to catch a thrown ball, a man fumbled wildly down his pocket, brought up the shilling and sixpence and threw them out; the old native, gasping, his skinny toes splaying the sand, flung the lion.

The piccanins were waving, the dogs stood, tails uncertain, watching the train go: past the mud huts, where a woman turned to look, up from the smoke of the fire, her hand pausing on her hip.

The stationmaster went slowly in under the chalet.

The old native stood, breath blowing out the skin between his ribs, feet tense, balanced in the sand, smiling and shaking his head. In his opened palm, held in the attitude of receiving, was the retrieved shilling and sixpence.

The blind end of the train was being pulled helplessly out of the station.

The young man swung in from the corridor, breathless. He was shaking his head with laughter and triumph. Here! he said. And waggled the lion at her. One-and-six!

What? she said.

He laughed. I was arguing with him for fun, bargaining—when the train had pulled out already, he came tearing after. . . . One-and-six baas! So there's your lion.

She was holding it away from her, the head with the open jaws, the pointed teeth, the black tongue, the wonderful ruff of fur facing her. She was looking at it with an expression of not seeing, of seeing something different. Her face was drawn up, wryly, like the face of a discomforted child. Her mouth lifted nervously at the corner. Very slowly, cautious, she lifted her finger and touched the mane, where it was joined to the wood.

But how could you, she said. He was shocked by the dismay of her face.

Good heavens, he said, what's the matter?

If you wanted the thing, she said, her voice rising and breaking with the shrill impotence of anger, why didn't you buy it in the first place? If you wanted it, why didn't you pay for it? Why didn't you take it decently, when he offered it? Why did you have to wait for him to run after the train with it, and give him one-and-six? One-and-six!

She was pushing it at him, trying to force him to take it. He stood astonished, his hands hanging at his sides.

But you wanted it! You liked it so much?

—It's a beautiful piece of work, she said fiercely, as if to protect it from him.

You liked it so much! You said yourself it was too expensive—

Oh *you*—she said, hopeless and furious. *You*. . . . She threw the lion onto the seat.

He stood looking at her.

She sat down again in the corner and, her face slumped in her hand, stared out of the window. Everything was turning around inside her. One-and-six. One-and-six. One-and-six for the wood and the carving and the sinews of the legs and the switch of the tail. The mouth open like that and the teeth. The black tongue, rolling, like a wave. The mane round the neck. To give one-and-six for that. The heat of shame mounted through her legs and body and sounded in her ears like the sound of sand pouring. Pouring, pouring. She sat there, sick. A weariness, a tastelessness, the discovery of a void made her hands slacken their grip, atrophy emptily, as if the hour was not worth their grasp. She was feeling like this again. She had thought it was something to do with singleness, with being alone and belonging too much to oneself.

She sat there not wanting to move or speak, or to look at anything, even; so that the mood should be associated with nothing, no object, word or sight that might recur and so recall the feeling again. . . . Smuts blew in grittily, settled on her hands. Her back remained at exactly the same angle, turned against the young man sitting with his hands drooping between his sprawled legs, and the lion, fallen on its side in the corner.

The train had cast the station like a skin. It called out to the sky, I'm coming, I'm coming; and again, there was no answer.

RESPONDING TO THE **S**ELECTION

Your Response

1. How do you view the bargaining custom described in the story? Do you think it is an example of exploitation? Explain.

Recalling

2. At the beginning of the story, what are three details that show the isolation of the small-town railway station?

3. (a) How much money does the vendor want for the carved lion? (b) How much does he finally accept?

4. (a) What have the young couple already bought on their holiday? (b) After the "unreality" of the vacation, what does the wife realize "is for good now"?

5. (a) At the end of the story, how is the young woman sitting in her seat? (b) Where is the lion?

Interpreting

6. Why is the arrival of the train important to the people in the town?

7. Why do you think the young woman wants the carved lion?

8. (a) Why is the young woman angry when her husband bargains for and obtains the lion at a low price? (b) What does she mean to imply when she says, "If you wanted the thing . . . why didn't you pay for it"?

9. This story is highly symbolic. (a) What may the train symbolize? (b) The station?

Applying

10. At the end of the story, the young wife feels isolated and alone. Her husband is confused by her unexpected reactions. (a) What has happened in this apparently trivial incident to make her feel shame, sickness, weariness, and emptiness? (b) How would you advise her husband to try to reassure her?

ANALYZING LITERATURE

Understanding Theme

Theme is the central idea in a literary work. *Conflict,* which occurs as the theme is developed, may present one or more *dilemmas.* A dilemma is a situation in which the main character, or protagonist, has to choose between undesirable alternatives. A short-story writer will not necessarily resolve all dilemmas, but may leave them for the reader to ponder. With a partner or in a small group, discuss two of the dilemmas—apart from isolation in marriage—that the young woman in "The Train from Rhodesia" appears to be facing. For example:

1. The dilemma of belonging to the well-to-do white minority in an impoverished black nation.
2. The dilemma of trying to make connections with other people in a setting that makes it hard to do so.

CRITICAL THINKING AND READING

Understanding Cultural Attitudes

The scene at the railway station that is described in "The Train from Rhodesia" is probably unfamiliar to you. The custom of white train passengers bargaining with native artisans for the purchase of their hand-carved wares reflects circumstances in southern Africa at the time the fictional incident occurs. Both the passengers on the train and the local people at the station accept the custom as normal. They see nothing to object to, although to an outside observer it might suggest inequality, racism, and exploitation.

Describe the scene at a subway, bus station, train station, or airport in your community or nearby. Your viewpoint should be that of a total stranger to your community—a visitor from another country, perhaps. Point out any behavior, habits, or activities that appear unusual to you as an outsider.

THINKING AND WRITING

Writing About Theme

The events in "The Train from Rhodesia" work together to reveal an insight into life. Identify the major theme in "The Train from Rhodesia." Write it in one carefully considered sentence. Then choose another short story in this book that has a similar theme. Write this theme, too, in a single sentence. Then write an essay in which you explain the similarities and differences between the two stories. Be specific. Give examples to support your main points. In revising the first draft, pay close attention to word choice. Have you chosen the right word in each place where an exact word is important—not merely a word that comes close? Careful word choice is one distinguishing mark of a good writer. Proofread your essay and share it with your classmates.

LEARNING OPTIONS

1. **Multicultural Activity.** Find a book or recording of folk tales that come from the southern part of Africa. Try to locate folk tales that reflect the special character of the people in this part of the world. Then give a reading of the folk tales or play the recording in class.
2. **Art.** What might the carved lion in this story look like? Locate an art book that shows examples of African sculpture and bring it to class. You may wish to create your own sculpture or carving that echoes an African style.
3. **Cross-curricular Connection.** Significant changes have occurred in Rhodesia, now Zimbabwe, since the time described in Gordimer's story. Using sources such as the *New York Times Index* and others suggested by a librarian, find out about the important changes in this African nation during the last forty years. Share your findings with the class.

ALAN SILLITOE

1928–

When Alan Sillitoe's first novel, *Saturday Night and Sunday Morning,* was published in 1958, one critic commented, "For the first time, English working-class life is treated . . . as a normal aspect of the human condition and as normal subject matter for a writer." Most of Sillitoe's heroes are rebellious members of the laboring class, "simple men caught in the cog-wheels of society."

Alan Sillitoe, the son of a tannery worker, was born and raised in Nottingham, an industrial city northwest of London. He left school at fourteen and worked in a bicycle plant and a plywood mill. From 1946 to 1949, he served in the Royal Air Force as a radio operator in Malaya.

He began to write while in Malaya, scrapping the manuscripts of nine complete novels before publishing and achieving immediate success with *Saturday Night and Sunday Morning*.

Sillitoe had been called one of the last of Britain's "angry young men," a group of writers in the 1950's and 1960's whose protagonists defy what they regard as outmoded political traditions and social norms. Like the other authors in this group, Sillitoe explores the theme of rebellion. Unlike them, he keeps his heroes firmly rooted in the working class, seeking self-discovery through a shared opposition to much of organized society.

His first collection of short stories, *The Loneliness of the Long-Distance Runner,* appeared in 1959. This collection, like his first novel, won immediate acclaim. The title story tells of a young juvenile delinquent who refuses to repent of the crimes that have landed him in an English reform school.

Sillitoe has also written poems and plays. Although his later work extends the range of his protagonists' rebellion, he remains primarily a chronicler of the English working classes. His restless energy has produced a body of work that is sometimes compared with that of D. H. Lawrence, another writer from Nottingham.

As with Lawrence, being poor left a permanent impression on Sillitoe's writing. Most of his work revolves around those scratching out a living on the lowest rungs of society's ladder. His understanding of poverty's effects is shown in this excerpt from his essay on the subject: "The very poor are too busy surviving to want to get on. To get on is something often dinned into them, handed down by the culture beneath which they exist. They are unable to take advantage of it, for to reach next week with clothes on your back, food still on the table, and enough life in your brain to face another week is the most they can do."

GUIDE FOR INTERPRETING

The Fiddle

Writers' Techniques

Setting. The setting in a work of fiction is the place and time in which the action occurs. In some stories the setting is of great importance; in others it is not. A writer presents setting in various ways. A playwright can use costumes and stage scenery to help establish the place and time of the events. A novelist or short-story writer, on the other hand, has to do it all with words. The most direct way is through extended description, although this tends to slow down the action. Many contemporary writers prefer to establish the setting by interspersing description with ongoing narration. If the setting is vital to the theme and action of the story, the writer is likely to give it prominence, often through detailed and memorable description.

Focus

Every time and every place provides a setting. As you read this assignment, you are in a setting of your own. You may be in a classroom. You may be in a living room or a bedroom or a kitchen. Think of some words and ideas that you associate with your present setting. Jot them down. Then write ten descriptive sentences that show the main features of your immediate environment.

Primary Source

From 1953 to 1958, Sillitoe and his wife lived as inexpensively as possible in Majorca, while he tried to get his work published. He supplemented his small service pension by translating and teaching; his wife worked for a travel agency. Sillitoe sent several of his poems to Robert Graves, who was already famous. Graves, too, was living in Majorca, in a home he had built from the royalties from *I, Claudius*. At Graves's invitation, Sillitoe visited him one Sunday, arriving on a borrowed bicycle. Graves autographed a copy of his book while they talked of England and the problems that writers face. Sillitoe recorded this exchange:

> "Some of your poems are good," he said, still looking at me as if waiting for some sort of recognition. "At least you end them well. So many people get off to a good start, then fizzle out half way through" . . . I said I found his remarks about my poetry encouraging, but that so far none had been published. "That doesn't matter," he replied. "As long as you keep on writing them." This wasn't the sort of truth I wanted to hear: "I'd like to see them in print." "That's no problem if you keep writing."

Graves was right; soon after, Sillitoe published his first book and has published steadily ever since.

The Fiddle

Alan Sillitoe

On the banks of the sinewy River Leen, where it flowed through Radford, stood a group of cottages called Harrison's Row. There must have been six to eight of them, all in a ruinous condition, but lived in nevertheless.

They had been put up for stockingers[1] during the Industrial Revolution a hundred years before, so that by now the usual small red English housebricks had become weatherstained and, in some places, almost black.

Harrison's Row had a character all of its own, both because of its situation, and the people who lived there. Each house had a space of pebbly soil rising in front, and a strip of richer garden sloping away from the kitchen door down to the diminutive River Leen at the back. The front gardens had almost merged into one piece of common ground, while those behind had in most cases retained their separate plots.

As for the name of the isolated row of cottages, nobody knew who Harrison had been, and no one was ever curious about it. Neither did they know where the Leen came from, though some had a general idea as to where it finished up.

A rent man walked down cobblestoned Leen Place every week to collect what money he could. This wasn't much, even at the best of times which, in the "thirties," were not too good—though no one in their conversation was able to hark back to times when they had been any better.

From the slight rise on which the houses stood, the back doors and windows looked across the stream into green fields, out towards the towers and pinnacles of Wollaton Hall in one direction, and the woods of Aspley Manor in the other.

After a warm summer without much rain the children were able to wade to the fields on the other side. Sometimes they could almost paddle. But after a three-day downpour when the air was still heavy with undropped water, and colored a menacing gun-metal blue, it was best not to go anywhere near the river, for one false slip and you would get sucked in, and be dragged by the powerful current along to the Trent some miles away. In that case there was no telling where you'd end up. The water seemed to flow into the River Amazon[2] itself, indicated by the fact that Frankie Buller swore blind how one day he had seen a crocodile snapping left and right downstream with a newborn baby in its mouth. You had to be careful—and that was a fact. During the persistent rain of one autumn water came up over the gardens and almost in at the back doors.

Harrison's Row was a cut-off place in that not many people knew about it unless they were familiar with the district. You went to it along St. Peter's Street, and down

---

1. **stockingers** *n.*: Stocking weavers.

2. **River Amazon:** The largest, most powerful river in South America.

HILLSIDE IN WALES (detail)
L.S. Lowry
The Tate Gallery, London

Leen Place. But it was delightful for the kids who lived there because out of the back gardens they could go straight into the stream of the Leen. In summer an old tin hip bath would come from one of the houses. Using it for a boat, and stripped to their white skins, the children were happy while sun and weather lasted.

The youths and older kids would eschew this fun and set out in a gang, going far beyond, to a bend of the canal near Wollaton Pit where the water was warm—almost hot —due to some outlet from the mine itself. This place was known as "'otties," and they'd stay all day with a bottle of lemonade and a piece of bread, coming back late in the evening looking pink and tired as if out of a prolonged dipping in the ritual bath. But a swim in 'otties was only for the older ones, because a boy of four had once been drowned there.

Harrison's Row was the last of Nottingham where it met the countryside. Its houses were at the very edge of the city, in the days before those numerous housing estates had been built beyond. The line of dwellings called Harrison's Row made a sort of outpost bastion before the country began.

Yet the houses in the city didn't immediately start behind, due to gardens and a piece of wasteground, which gave to Harrison's Row a feeling of isolation. It stood somewhat on its own, as if the city intended one day to leapfrog over it and obliterate the country beyond.

On the other hand, any foreign army attacking from the west, over the green fields that glistened in front, would first have to flatten Harrison's Row before getting into the innumerable streets of houses behind.

Across the Leen, horses were sometimes to be seen in the fields and, in other fields beyond, the noise of combine harvesters could be heard at work in the summer. Children living there, and adults as well, had the advantage of both town and country. On a fine evening late in August one of the unemployed husbands might be seen looking across at the noise of some machinery working in a field, his cap on but wearing no shirt, as if wondering why he was here and not over there, and why in fact he had ever left those same fields in times gone by to be forced into this bit of a suburb where he now had neither work nor purpose in life. He was not bitter, and not much puzzled perhaps, yet he couldn't help being envious of those still out there in the sunshine.

In my visions of leaving Nottingham for good—and they were frequent in those days—I never reckoned on doing so by the high road or railway. Instead I saw myself wading or swimming the Leen from Harrison's Row, and setting off west once I was on the other side.

A tale remembered with a laugh at that time told about how young Ted Griffin, who had just started work, saw two policemen one day walking down Leen Place towards Harrison's Row. Convinced they had come to arrest him for meter-breaking, he ran through the house and garden, went over the fence, jumped into the Leen—happily not much swollen—waded across to the field, then four-legged it over the railway, and made his way to Robins Wood a mile or so beyond. A perfect escape route. He stayed two days in hiding, and then crept home at night, famished and soaked, only to find that the police had not come for him, but to question Blonk next door, who was suspected of poaching. When they did get Ted Griffin he was pulled out of bed one morning even before he'd had time to open his eyes and think about a spectacular escape across the Leen.

Jeff Bignal was a young unmarried man of twenty-four. His father had been killed in the Great War,[3] and he lived with his mother at Number Six Harrison's Row, and worked down nearby Radford Pit. He was short in height, and plump, his white skin scarred back and front with livid blue patches where he had been knocked with coal at the mine face. When he went out on Saturday night he brilliantined his hair.

After tea in summer while it was still light and warm he would sit in his back garden playing the fiddle, and when he did everybody else came out to listen. Or they opened the doors and windows so that the sound of his music drifted in, while the woman stayed at the sink or wash-copper,

---

3. Great War: World War I.

or the man at his odd jobs. Anyone with a wireless would turn it down or off.

Even tall dark sallow-faced elderly Mrs. Deaffy (a kid sneaked into her kitchen one day and thieved her last penny-packet of cocoa and she went crying to tell Mrs. Atkin who, when her youngest came in, hit him so hard with her elbow that one of his teeth shot out and the blood washed away most of the cocoa-stains around his mouth)—old Mrs. Deaffy stood by her back door as if she weren't stone deaf any more and could follow each note of Jeffrey Bignal's exquisite violin. She smiled at seeing everyone occupied, fixed or entranced, and therefore no torment to herself, which was music enough to her whether she could hear it or not.

And Blonk, in the secretive dimness of the kitchen, went on mending his poaching nets before setting out with Arthur Bede next door on that night's expedition to Gunthorpe by the banks of the Trent, where the green escarpment between there and Kneeton was riddled with warrens and where, so it was said, if you stood sufficiently still the rabbits ran over your feet, and it was only necessary to make a quick grab to get one.

Jeff sat on a chair, oblivious to everybody, fed up with his day's work at the pit and only wanting to lose himself in his own music. The kids stopped splashing and shouting in the water, because if they didn't they might get hauled in and clouted with just the right amount of viciousness to suit the crime and the occasion. It had happened before, though Jeff had always been too far off to notice.

His face was long, yet generally cheerful—contrary to what one would expect—a smile settling on it whenever he met and passed anybody on the street, or on his way to the group of shared lavatories at the end of the Row. But his face was almost down and lost to the world as he sat on his chair and brought forth his first sweet notes of a summer's evening.

It was said that a neighbor in the last place they had lived had taught him to play like that. Others maintained it was an uncle who had shown him how. But nobody knew for sure because when someone asked directly he said that if he had any gift at all it must have come from God above. It was known that on some Sundays of the year, if the sun was out, he went to the Methodist chapel on St. Peter's Street.

He could play anything from "Greensleeves" to "Mademoiselle from Armentières." He could do a beautiful heart-pulling version of Handel's *Largo*, and throw in bits from *The Messiah* as well. He would go from one piece to another with no rhyme or reason, from ridiculousness to sublimity, with almost shocking abruptness, but as the hour or so went by it all appeared easy and natural, part of a long piece coming from Jeff Bignal's fiddle while the ball of the sun went down behind his back.

To a child it seemed as if the songs lived in the hard collier's muscle at the top of his energetic arm, and that they queued one by one to get out. Once free, they rushed along his flesh from which the shirtsleeves had been rolled up, and split into his fingertips, where they were played out with ease into the warm evening air.

The grass in the fields across the stream was livid and lush, almost blue, and a piebald horse stood with bent head, eating oats out of a large old pram whose wheels had long since gone. The breeze wafted across from places farther out, from Robins Wood and the Cherry Orchard, Wollaton Roughs and Bramcote Hills and even, on a day that was not too hot, from the tops of the Pennines in Derbyshire.

Jeff played for himself, for the breeze against his arm, for the soft hiss of the flowing Leen at the end of the garden, and maybe also for the horse in the field, which took no notice of anything and which, having grown tired of its oats in the pram, bent its head over the actual grass and began to roam in search of succulent pastures.

In the middle of the winter Jeff's fiddling was forgotten. He went into the coal mine before it was light, and came up only after it had got dark. Walking down Leen Place, he complained to Blonk that it was hard on a man not to see daylight for weeks at a time.

"That's why I wain't go anywhere near the bleddy pit," Blonk said vehemently, though he had worked there from time to time, and would do so again when harried by his wife and children. "You'd do better to come out on a bit o' poaching with me and Arthur," he suggested.

It was virtually true that Jeff saw no daylight, because even on Sunday he stayed in bed most of the day, and if it happened to be dull there was little enough sky to be seen through his front bedroom window, which looked away from the Leen and up the hill.

The upshot of his complaint was that he would do anything to change such a situation. A man was less than an animal for putting up with it.

"I'd do anything," he repeated to his mother over his tea in the single room downstairs.

"But what, though?" she asked. "What can you do, Jeff?"

"Well, how do I know?" he almost snapped at her. "But I'll do summat,[4] you can be sure of that."

He didn't do anything till the weather got better and life turned a bit sweeter. Maybe this improvement finally got him going, because it's hard to help yourself towards better things when you're too far down in the dumps.

On a fine blowy day with both sun and cloud in the sky Jeff went out in the morning, walking up Leen Place with his fiddle under his arm. The case had been wiped and polished.

In the afternoon he came back without it.

"Where's your fiddle?" Ma Jones asked.

He put an awkward smile on to his pale face, and told her: "I sold it."

---

4. summat: Something.

"Well I never! How much for?"

He was too shocked at her brazen question not to tell the truth: "Four quid."

"That ain't much."

"It'll be enough," he said roughly.

"Enough for what, Jeff?"

He didn't say, but the fact that he had sold his fiddle for four quid rattled up and down the line of cottages till everybody knew of it. Others swore he'd got ten pounds for it, because something that made such music must be worth more than a paltry four, and in any case Jeff would never say how much he'd really got for it, for fear that someone would go in and rob him.

They wondered why he'd done it, but had to wait for the answer, as one usually does. But there was nothing secretive about Jeff Bignal, and if he'd sold his music for a mess of pottage he saw no point in not letting them know why. They'd find out sooner or later, anyway.

All he'd had to do was make up his mind, and he'd done that lying on his side at the pit face while ripping coal out with his pick and shovel. Decisions made like that can't be undone, he knew. He'd brooded on it all winter, till the fact of having settled it seemed to have altered the permanent expression of his face, and given it a new look which caused people to wonder whether he would ever be able to play the fiddle again anyway—at least with his old spirit and dash.

With the four quid he paid the first week's rent on a butcher's shop on Denman Street, and bought a knife, a chopper, and a bit of sharpening stone, as well as a wooden block. Maybe he had a quid or two more knocking around, though if he had it couldn't have been much, but with four quid and a slice of bluff he got enough credit from a wholesaler at the meat market downtown to stock his shop with mutton and beef, and in a couple of days he was in trade. The people of Harrison's Row were amazed at how easy it was, though nobody had ever thought of doing it themselves.

Like a serious young man of business Mr. Bignal—as he was now known —parted his hair down the middle, so that he didn't look so young any more, but everyone agreed that it was better than being at Radford Pit. They'd seen how he had got fed up with selling the sweat of his brow.

No one could say that he prospered, but they couldn't deny that he made a living. And he didn't have to suffer the fact of not seeing daylight for almost the whole of the winter.

Six months after opening the shop he got married. The reception was held at the chapel on St. Peter's Street, which seemed to be a sort of halfway house between Harrison's Row on the banks of the Leen and the butcher's shop on Denman Street farther up.

Everybody from Harrison's Row was invited for a drink and something to eat; but he knew them too well to let any have either chops or chitterlings (or even black puddings) on tick[5] when they came into his shop.

The people of Harrison's Row missed the sound of his fiddle on long summer evenings, though the children could splash and shout with their tin bathtub undisturbed, floundering through shallows and scrambling up to grass on the other bank, and wondering what place they'd reach if they walked without stopping till it got dark.

Two years later the Second World War began, and not long afterwards meat as well as nearly everything else was put on the ration. Apart from which, Jeff was only twenty-six, so got called up into the army. He never had much chance to make a proper start in life, though people said that he came out all right in the end.

The houses of Harrison's Row were condemned as unfit to live in, and a bus depot stands on the site.

---

5. tick: Credit.

The packed mass of houses on the hill behind—forty years after Jeff Bignal sold his violin—is also vanishing, and high-rise hencoops (as the people call them) are put in their place. The demolition crew knock down ten houses a day—though the foreman told me there was still work for another two years.

Some of the houses would easily have lasted a few more decades, for the bricks were perfect, but as the foreman went on:

"You can't let them stand in the way of progress"—whatever that means.

The people have known each other for generations but, when they are moved to their new estates and blocks of flats,[6] they will know each other for generations more, because as I listen to them talking, they speak a language which, in spite of everything and everyone, never alters.

_____

6. flats: Apartments.

RESPONDING TO THE SELECTION

Your Response

1. What do you think of Jeff's decision to sell his fiddle? How happy do you think Jeff's butcher shop made him? Explain.

Recalling

2. (a) What is the time, or era, of the events in this story? (b) In what city is Harrison's Row? (c) In what section of the city is the mine in which Jeff Bignal works?
3. (a) Where do the younger children swim? (b) Why do they not swim there after a heavy rain? (c) Where do the older children swim?
4. (a) What does Jeff finally do with his fiddle? (b) Why does he do this?

Interpreting

5. Why is the River Leen important to the people of Harrison's Row?
6. Why is the fiddle important to Jeff Bignal?
7. (a) How does Jeff rebel against his situation in life? (b) How does Blonk rebel?
8. Why won't Jeff extend credit to the people from Harrison's Row?
9. (a) What do you think the fiddle symbolizes? (b) How does this symbol help reveal the story's theme?

Applying

10. How does the area in which you live affect your values, goals, and outlook on life? Explain.

ANALYZING LITERATURE

Understanding Setting

Setting is the time and place in which the events in a literary work occur. In "The Fiddle" Alan Sillitoe describes the physical setting of Harrison's Row and the activities that formerly went on there. The entire first section of the story establishes the setting. You learn a great deal about Harrison's Row before you learn anything at all about the protagonist, Jeff Bignal. The setting helps to define the people in the story.

1. The narrator is deeply interested in the history and geography of Harrison's Row. Nevertheless, he says that "no one knew who Harrison had been, and no one was ever curious about it. Neither did they know where the Leen came from, though some had a general idea as to where it finished up." How do those details about the setting help to characterize the people who live in Harrison's Row?
2. The brief last section of the story returns to the setting. How do you think the narrator feels about a bus depot standing on the site of Harrison's Row and the construction of "high-rise hencoops"? Explain.
3. Slang is highly informal language that is appropriate among friends or in casual situations. (a) Find three examples of slang in "The Fiddle." (b) How does the use of slang add local color to the story?

MARGARET DRABBLE

1939–

If Margaret Drabble had not become a novelist, she might have become a famous actress. While at Cambridge University, she concentrated on the theater and at one point played opposite the noted actor Derek Jacobi. Upon graduation she joined the Royal Shakespeare Company, understudying Vanessa Redgrave as Imogen in *Cymbeline*. She then left the theater, began writing fiction, and succeeded so well in her new career that a critic in 1980 observed, "She is becoming the novelist people will turn to a hundred years from now to find out how things were. . . ."

Born in Sheffield, Drabble came from a cultured and well-educated family. Her father was a circuit judge and her mother an English teacher. "A fiery child with a hyperactive mind," according to her mother, Margaret attended a Quaker boarding school prior to Cambridge. After college she abandoned the theater for motherhood. While she was pregnant with the first of her three children, she began to write fiction. Her first novel, *A Summer Bird-Cage,* was published in 1962. Over the years she has continued to write novels that have gained both critical and popular success. Among her best-known works are *The Millstone* (1965), *The Waterfall* (1969), *The Realms of Gold* (1975), and *The Middle Ground* (1980). Most of Drabble's protagonists are, like their creator, well-educated professional women: scholars, poets, journalists.

Sociable, composed, and levelheaded, Drabble is in great demand for interviews and personal appearances. In the fall of 1980, she received a great honor when the Queen Mother dubbed her a Commander of the British Empire. Although she possesses enormous creative energy, Drabble does not regard herself as remarkable, but—in keeping with her themes—"ordinary" and fortunate. She is a clear and perceptive writer whose dry humor and penetrating technical skill have become the hallmarks of her style. Her work has steadily flowered; many critics and readers believe that in its maturity it will achieve greatness.

Drabble, on commenting on her own work, declares that she is firmly committed to the realistic tradition of the nineteenth century. Although sometimes called a "women's novelist," she disavows feminism as a theme, believing that equal rights and opportunity for women are part of a larger whole. She maintains that her fundamental concerns are "privilege, justice, and salvation." Working in the literary tradition of Jane Austen, Charlotte Brontë, and George Eliot, she creates brilliantly realized characters who reflect the dilemmas of women in the modern world, women who are trying to integrate the demands of family life and a career.

GUIDE FOR INTERPRETING

A Voyage to Cythera

Writers' Techniques

Flat and Round Characters. In literature a flat character, sometimes called a stereotype or stock character, is a one-dimensional human being. For example, in "Araby" James Joyce does not portray Mangan's sister in depth. She is treated more as a symbol of the narrator's romantic aspirations than as a real person. She is a flat character who does not change in the course of the story and who contributes to the plot in a predictable way.

The fictional opposite of a flat character is a round character. A round character is a fully developed portrait that readers can accept as resembling an actual person. The writer may provide a detailed description of the character. More important, the writer will reveal the character's motivations, emotions, and inner conflicts. Round characters may be complex, unpredictable, and inconsistent, just like real people. In narrative fiction they are generally *dynamic*—that is, they change or grow in some way during the story. (Flat characters are *static*—they do not change or grow.) An example of a round character in a short story is Margaret in Doris Lessing's "A Mild Attack of Locusts."

Focus

An epigraph is a quotation at the beginning of a book, chapter, or story. Read the epigraph to Margaret Drabble's story carefully. Then brainstorm for several minutes on the associations and emotions suggested by this fragment of Rilke's poetry. Jot down your impressions of what the epigraph (and the story's title) may suggest about the narrative to follow.

Primary Source

Margaret Drabble's comments in *A Woman Writer* relate closely to the dilemma that Helen, the main character in "A Voyage to Cythera," faces. Drabble thinks that the large amount of fiction written by women recently shows that "a lot of women worry about the same things at the same time, and turned to fiction to express their anxieties—not only because . . . they still had nowhere else to turn, but also because fiction is ideally suited to such themes. . . . Many people read novels in order to find patterns or images for a possible future—to know how to behave, what to hope to be like. We do not want to resemble the women of the past, but where is our future. . . . We live in an uncharted world, as far as manners and morals are concerned, we are having to make up our own morality as we go. Our subject matter is enormous, there are whole new patterns to create."

A Voyage to Cythera[1]

Margaret Drabble

Beloved, lost to begin with, never greeted,
I do not know what tones most please you.
No more when the future's wave
hangs poised is it you I try to discern there.
All the greatest images in me,
far-off experienced landscape,
towers and towns and bridges and
unsuspected turns of the way,
and the power of those lands
once intertwined with the life of the gods:
mount up within me to mean you,
who forever elude.

Oh, you are the garden. . . .
—Rainer Maria Rilke[2]

There are some people who cannot get onto a train without imagining that they are about to voyage into the significant unknown; as though the notion of movement were inseparably connected with the notion of discovery, as though each displacement of the body were a displacement of the soul. Helen was so much this way, and with so little lasting justification, that she was continually surprising herself by the intensity of her expectation; she could get excited by the prospect of any journey longer than 30 miles, and the thought of travel to the Conti-

nent was enough to reduce her to a state of feverish anticipation. The mere mention of the names of certain places would make her tremble, and she was addicted to railway stations, air terminals, ports, motorways, travel brochures, and all other points and emblems of departure. A phrase in a novel could make her feel weak with desire, and when once at the Gare de l'Est[3] in Paris she saw a train with Budapest written on it, she felt her skin tighten and her hair stand on end. Her most erotic dreams were not of men but of places; she would dream of piazzas and marble fountains, of mountains and terraces with great lumps of baroque statuary, of great buildings abandoned in green fields, and she would wake from these dreams cold with the sweat of fading passion. There was a certain angle of road that never failed to affect her, whenever she approached it: a rising angle, with a bare empty curve breasting infinity, the blue-sky space of infinity. She always felt that the sea might lie beyond such rising nothingness, and sometimes it was the sea, but more often it was the Caledonian[4] Market or a row of Hampstead houses; though whatever it was was somehow irrelevant, for it was that tense moment of expectation before revelation that she so much cherished.

Once she talked of this preoccupation of hers to a much-traveled old man, and he said that she felt this way because whenever

---

1. Cythera (si t hir′ ə): A Greek island, near which the Greek goddess of love, Aphrodite, was supposed to have arisen full-grown from the sea.
2. Rainer Maria Rilke: A German poet (1875–1926). The lines are from an untitled poem by Rilke.

3. Gare de l'Est (gär də lest): A Paris train station.
4. Caledonian: Scottish.

she went to a new place she hoped to fall in love. He had been the same, he said; restless, expectant; and she knew that he was telling the truth, for his life illustrated his explanation. "When I was young," he said, "I thought there was a woman waiting for me in every railway compartment, on every airplane, in every hotel. How can one not think this? One thinks the plane will crash, and that one will die, and that one must die in the arms of the woman in the next seat. Isn't that so?"

And she had, in a way, thought that it was so, though the truth was that she herself would never fall in love in any of these temporary places, for she could not speak to strangers. Though that in itself proved nothing, for she supposed that nevertheless she might one day do so, and that it might be for this one moment of sudden communication that she so persistently sought. People spoke to her, from time to time, but always the wrong people, always the motherly and the fatherly men and the dull irrepressible youths. Her own kind did not speak to her, nor she to them. She traveled once overnight from Milan, alone in a compartment with a girl who was reading the same book she herself was reading; a book both of them might have been proud to acknowledge and not a word did they exchange. Another time, in a crowded train from Edinburgh, she sat opposite a woman who started to weep as the train left the station; she wept silently and effortlessly for hours, great tears rolling down her white cheeks into the neck of her emerald-green sweater, and at York Helen offered her a cigarette, and she declined it, and ceased weeping. On another occasion a man kissed her in a corridor as they drew into Oxford; she liked him, he was a lovely man, but he was drunk and she turned away her face and turned up the collar of her coat.

And yet despite these wasted opportunities she continued to expect. Truly, she thought to herself, as she got into the London train at Reading Station late one cold night, truly, it is a proof of madness that the prospect of this journey should not appall. It is cold, the train is half an hour late, I am hungry; this is the kind of situation about which I hear my friends most tirelessly and tiresomely complain. And yet I am looking forward to it. I shall sit here in the dark and the cold, with nothing to watch but the reflection of my own face in the cold pane, and I shall not care. As soon as the train moves, I shall sit back, and feel it move with me, and feel that I am moving, although I know quite well that all I am doing is going back home again to an empty flat.[5] There will be rain and steam on the glass of this window by my face, and I shall look at it, and that will be all. What a hardened case I am, that such dull mileage should recall those other landscapes, those snowy precipices, those sunny plains, those fields of corn, those gritty swaying breakfasts in the pale light of transient Switzerland or angel-watched Marseilles. I am a child, I like to rock and dream, I dream as if I were in a cradle.

And she shut her eyes, waiting for the whistle and the metallic connections of machinery; so with her eyes shut she did not see the man come into the compartment, and could never know for certain whether he had seen her, whether he had joined her because he had wanted to join her. All she knew was that when she opened her eyes, aware of the intrusion, aware of the draft from the opened door, he was already there, putting his overcoat up on the rack, arranging his books and papers on the seat next to him, settling himself in the empty compartment as far away from her as he could, on the corridor side, diagonally opposite, where she could not fail to watch him. She turned her fur collar up defensively against her face, and arranged her legs more tidily together, and opened her book upon her knee, disclaiming all threat of human contact, coldly repelling any acknowledgment of her

_____

5. **flat** *n.*: Apartment.

presence, and all the time she watched him discreetly through her half-shut eyes. Because the truth was that not since she was 17, more years ago than she cared to think, had she sat on a train so near to such a man. When she was 17 she had sat in a compartment with an actor, on the late night train to Brighton, and he had talked to her all the way, and amused her by imitating Laurence Olivier[6] for her and other famous men whom she did not recognize and when they had parted on the station he had kissed her soft and girlish and impressionable cheek, and murmured, ''Bless you, bless you,'' as though he had a right to bless. She had subsequently followed his unremarkable career, catching sight of his name in the *Radio Times*, admiring him once on the television, glimpsing him as he passed on the cinema screen; she felt quietly possessive about him, quietly amused by her sense of intimacy with one who must so long ago have forgotten her, and who would hardly now recognize her from what she then had been. Sometimes she wondered idly whether her preoccupation with journeys might not date from this experience; but chronologically this was not so, for her preoccupation had long preceded it. She had been this way since childhood, when she had shrunk and trembled at the sight of the huge pistons, when she had stopped her ears in delighted terror as she heard the roar of the approaching seaside train.

This man, this night, did not look as though he wished to amuse her with imitations of Laurence Olivier. He looked preoccupied. In fact, the more she watched him, the more she realized that he was almost grotesquely preoccupied. He was restless; he could not sit still: he kept picking up one book from his pile, then another, then turning over the pages of his *New Statesman*, then staring out into the corridor and onto the dark platform. At first she thought that he might be waiting for someone to come, half-expecting somebody to join him, but she decided that this was not so, for she could perceive no augmenting of his anxiety as the time drew on, no sudden start when the loudspeaker apologized for the delay and said that the train would leave in two minutes; nor did his nervousness seem to be directed toward the door and the platform, as it would have been had he been waiting. She recalled that she herself had once developed a dreadful pain in the neck from sitting with her neck to the window through which she knew that she might glimpse the first sign of a long-awaited arrival. But this man's nervousness was as it were diffused, rather than directed; it attached itself to nothing and to everything. She could not take her eyes off him, and not only because of the nakedness of his condition, which in another might have appeared merely ludicrous; indeed, embarrassment would have turned away her eyes, had it not been for the extreme elegance of his gestures, and the lovely angles into which each struggle against immobility brought him. There was the way he had of clutching his eyebrows with one wide-spanned long nicotine-fingered hand that filled her with an intense delight; the hand covered the eyes, bringing to him no doubt an illusion of concealment, but she could see beneath it the anxious movement of the lips, trembling with some expression that she could not catch, with speech or smiling or perhaps with a sigh. And as he made this gesture, each time, he tossed his head slightly backward, and then again forward, so that his long hair fell tenderly over his fingers. It was the color that she had always liked, but she had never before seen it adorning such vexed, haggard, and experienced features: for it was a dark gold, the color of health and innocence. It was a dark golden yellow, and it was streaked with gray. It was soft hair, and it fell gently.

---

6. Laurence Olivier: A famous British actor (1907–1989).

When the train moved off, he flung himself back into his corner, and shut his eyes, with an appearance of resolution, as though his own restlessness had finally begun to irritate him: as though he had decided to sit still. Helen looked out of the window by her face, into the lights and darkness of the disappearing town. In one piece of glass she could see the reflection of his face, and she watched it, quite confidently aware that he would not be able to keep his eyes shut, and after a few minutes he was leaning forward in his seat once more, his elbows on his knees, staring at the ground. Then, even as she watched, she saw a thought strike him: she saw the conception of the idea, she saw him reach into his pocket and take out a pack of cigarettes and a box of matches, and abstract a cigarette, and light it, all with the dreamy movements of a habitual smoker, and yet with a kind of surprise, for the truth was, as she could so clearly see, that he had even in his abstraction forgotten the possibility of such a trivial solace. As he drew on the cigarette she could see his relief, his gratitude toward his own recollection. The smoke consoled him, and she could feel in her the nature of the consolation: for she herself, when tormented by love, had found comfort in the repetition of small and necessary acts, in washing cups and emptying bins and fastening her stockings and remembering that it was time to have a meal. It seemed clear to her that it was love that was tormenting him: she knew those painful symptoms of disease.

And indeed, ten minutes later, when the ash of his last activity lay scattered all over the floor and all over his trousers, he stood up and got a packet of letters out of his overcoat pocket, and began to read them. He could not more clearly have indicated his malady if he had turned to her and told her what was in his mind. She watched the reflection of his face as he read, ashamed now to watch him directly, though she knew that he could not know that she so keenly watched him, that she was so expert in the intimate language of his state. She felt that she could tell everything from the way he handled those letters: he was still rapt in the first five minutes of love, that brief and indefinite breathless pause before familiarity, affection, disillusion, rot, decay. The number of letters in his hands supported her divination, as well as the quality of his attention; there were five of them, only five, and the paper of them was new, although they were crumbling wearily at the folds from overuse. She felt such pangs, in his presence, of she knew not what: of envy, of regret, of desire. At his age, with those graying strands and those profound wrinkles, he must surely know the folly of his obsession, and the inevitable tragic close before him; and she found such a willful confrontation of pain almost unbearably moving. She herself, enduring daily the painful death of such an attitude, the chilly destination of such deliberately romantic embarkations, could hardly prevent the tears from rising to her eyes; and in fact, they rose, warm in the cold skin of her lids, making her nose prick and her eyes ache, yet warm, coming from within her, and chilling only at the touch of the outside air. Absurd, she said to herself, absurd: absurd to weep. His image turned into a blur, and it was like the image of time itself, human, lovely, perishing, intent.

When he had read and reread his letters, he stood up again, and got a pen out of his coat pocket, and tore a piece of paper off a block of typing paper, and started to write. He wrote slowly, after the first three words, hesitantly, as though what he was saying was of no interest, as though all the interest lay in the way of saying it. She wondered what he was, who he was, what his woman was, and jealously whether she were worth such care. He took a quarter of an hour to write his letter, and when he had finished it he had covered only half a page. She wondered whether he would have an envelope,

SHUNTERS 1965
James Dolby

and saw that he had; it was a brown business envelope. He folded his letter up and put it in the envelope, and then sealed it up. She waited for him to write the address, but he did not write the address: he sat there looking down at the small brown oblong, and as he looked at it she became in some indefinable way aware that he had become aware of her own presence, that he was at last considering her, in some significant way. Later, she wondered how this shadowy and delicate intimation could ever have reached her—for reach her it did, and she was one of those who believe that no intimations are too delicate to exist—and she concluded that it could only have been a sudden stillness on his part, a sudden fading of restlessness, as he returned from whatever other place he had been in to contemplate her in her proximity. She felt his attention: she endured it, for five minutes at least, before he spoke.

She was pretending to read when he spoke to her. He said to her, "I wonder, I wonder if you would do something for me?" and she looked up and met his eyes, and found that he was smiling at her with a most peculiar mixture of diffidence and vanity: he was truly nervous at the prospect of speaking to her, and those five silent minutes were a measure of his nervousness, and yet at the same time he had taken the measure of her curiosity and helpless attraction: she knew that he knew that she would like to be addressed. And his tone enchanted her, for it was her own tone: a tone of cool, anxious, irresistible appeal. She knew that he too did not speak often to strangers.

"It depends what it is," she said, smiling back at him with his own smile.

"It's a very simple thing," he said, "not at all incriminating. Or at least, not for you."

"It would be, then, for you?" she said.

"Of course it would," he said. "That's why I'm making the effort of asking you to do it."

"What is it?" she said.

"I wondered if you would address this envelope for me," he said.

"Well, yes," she said. "I don't see any harm in that. I'd do that for you."

"I thought you would do it," he said. "If I hadn't thought that you would, I wouldn't have asked you. I wouldn't have liked it if you had said no."

"I might ask you what it was about me that made you think I would say yes," she said, "but such a question might embarrass you."

"Oh," he said, "oh, no," rising to his feet and crossing to her with the envelope, "oh, no, I don't mind answering, it was because of that book you're reading, and the kind of shoes you're wearing, and the way your hair is. I liked that book when I read it."

And then he sat down by her, and handed her the envelope, and said, "Look, I'll write it down for you and you can copy it. It's hard to hear when people dictate things, isn't it?"

And he wrote the name and address on another piece of his block of paper. He wrote:

Mrs. H. Smithson,
24 Victoria Place,
London N.W.1.

And Helen dutifully copied it out, on the brown envelope, then handed it back to him.

"I hope," she said, "that my handwriting is sufficiently unlike yours."

"I was thinking," he said, "that after all it's rather similar. But dissimilar enough."

Then he said no more, but he remained sitting by her. She would in a way have preferred him to move, because where he now was she could not really see him, either overtly or covertly. And she had nothing to say to him: for she could hardly have said, I was right about you, I guessed right. He said nothing to her, for a while: he got a wallet from his pocket, and took out a sheet of fourpenny stamps, and tore one off, licked it, and stuck it on. She liked watching his hands, and the way they moved. Then, still holding the letter, he said to her, "Where do you live?"

She must have recoiled slightly from the question, because immediately he followed it up with, "Only, I was meaning, from the point of view of postmarks."

"Oh," she said. "I see. Yes. I live in S.W.7. You want me to post it, do you?"

"Would you mind posting it?" he asked.

"No. I would post it for you," she said.

"You take my point very quickly," he said, then, with some difficulty, looking downward and away from her, hardly able to bring himself to thank her more formally.

"I've had to make such points before myself," she said.

"I thought, somehow, that you would not mind about such things," he said.

"You wouldn't have asked me if you'd thought I minded. Tell me, do you really trust me to remember to post it?"

"Of course I do," he said. "One wouldn't not post a stranger's letter."

And this was so exactly the truth that it silenced her, and they said no more to each other until the train drew into Paddington: and as they walked together off the platform, he said, "Thank you, and good-bye."

And she said, "Good-bye," and she carried the letter in her hand all the way home, and dropped it into the letterbox on her block. Then she went down the basement steps to her dark flat, and she knew that the name and the address, written there in her own writing, so strangely, were imprinted upon her memory forever.

And indeed, over the next month, she sometimes fancied that she thought of little else. She knew that this was not the truth, that it was merely a fancy, because of course she did think of other things: of her job, of her friends, of her mother, of what to buy for supper, of whether she wanted to go to the cinema on Wednesday night. But she did not think of these other things in the mad, romantic, obsessive way that she thought of Mrs. H. Smithson, and the nameless man, and the whole curious, affecting incident: in a sense she resented the incident, because it did so much to vindicate her own crazy expectancy, her foolish faith in revelation. She knew, in her better, saner self, that such faith was foolish, and she suspected that such partial hints of its validity were a delusion, a temptation, and that if she heeded them she would be disabled forever, and disqualified from real life, as Odysseus would have been by the Sirens.[7] And yet at the same time she knew, in her other self, that it was that man she was thinking about, however unreasonably. She looked for him as she walked along the streets of London, and she could not convince herself that it was not for him that she was looking.

---

7. Odysseus . . . Sirens: In Homer's *Odyssey*, Odysseus, the hero, plugs his ears so that he will not be tempted by the singing of the sirens, sea nymphs whose enchanting songs lured sailors to their deaths on rocky coastlines.

She speculated about the identity and appearance of Mrs. Smithson, and supplied her endlessly with Christian names, until she remembered that the H. might well have stood for her husband's name, not hers. She speculated about the deceived husband. Although most of her own friends were married and had children, she still found it hard to acknowledge that Mrs. Smithson might well be a woman of her own generation, for the prefix *Mrs.* invariably supplied her with a material image, the image of her own mother: and she would realize from time to time, with a start, that the women that she thought of as mothers were in fact grandmothers, and that the young girls she saw pushing prams on Saturday mornings and quarreling with vigorous toddlers on buses were not in fact elder sisters but mothers, Mrs. Smithson, Mrs. Smithson. She could not give form to Mrs. Smithson.

It was in the week before Christmas that she decided to go and have a look at Mrs. Smithson. The idea occurred to her at lunchtime one day, in the middle of a lunchtime business Christmas party. She stood there, drinking too much and not getting enough to eat, defeated as ever by the problems of buffet technique, and as she listened to a very nice man whom she had known and liked for several years describe to her the felicities of his new central heating, she suddenly decided to go and look at Mrs. Smithson. After all, she said to herself, what could be more harmless, what more undetectable? All I need to do is to knock on her door and ask, say, for Alice. And then I would know. I don't know what I would know, but I would know it. And she smiled at the man, and allowed her glass to be once more filled, and then told him politely all about some other friends of hers whose central heating had entirely ruined all their antique furniture, and split all the antique paneling of their rather priceless house. And as she talked, she was already in her heart on her way to Mrs. Smithson's, already surrendering to the lure of that fraught, romantic, painful world, which seemed to call her, to call her continually from the endurable sorrows of daily existence to some possible other country of the passions, a country where she felt she would recognize, though strange to it, the scenery and landmarks. She thought often of this place, as of some place perpetually existing, and yet concealed: and she could describe it to herself only in terms of myth or allegory, unsatisfactory terms, she felt, and perniciously implanted in her by her classical education. It was a place other than the real world, or what she felt to be the real world, and it was both more beautiful and more valid, though valid in itself only: and it could be entered not at will, but intermittently, by accident, and yet always with some sense of temptation and surrender. Some people, she could see, passed most of their lives in its confines, and governed by its laws only, like that old man, himself a poet, who had first defined for her the nature of her expectations. There were enough of such people in the world to keep alive before her the possibility of a permanent, irreversible entry through those mysteriously inscribed and classic gates: a poet, a drunken Frenchman, a girl she had known who said one day: "I will go to Baghdad," and went. They crossed her path, these people, or their names came to her, garlanded with wreaths of that unfamiliar foliage: Yves was seen in Marseilles carrying a lobster, Esther was seen in a bookshop in New York wearing a fur coat and with diamonds in her hair, Esther was in Marrakesh, living in one room with an Arab. Yves had gone to Ireland and started a lobster farm. Oh, messages from a foreign country, oh, disquieting glimpses of brightness. Helen gulped down the remains of her fourth glass of wine, and looked at her watch, which said that it was five past three; and said to the central-heating man that she must go.

She walked to Victoria Place, pausing dazed at traffic lights, stumbling at each irregularity of the pavement, running her hand idly along grimy railings. It was cold, but she could not feel the cold: her face was burning. She knew her way because she had looked Victoria Place up a month ago, the day after she had posted the letter, in her *A to Z Guide to London:* she remembered the moment when she had done so, because she had pretended to herself that she was doing no such thing, and her mind had not known what her hands and eyes were doing. But her mind now remembered what it had then refused to acknowledge, and she took herself there as though entranced, the trance persisting long after the effects of walking had dispelled the effects of so much drink on so empty a stomach. I must be mad, she said to herself more than once: I must be mad. And at the very end of the journey she began, very slightly, to lose her nerve: she thought that she would not dare to knock upon the door, she thought that perhaps after all only insignificant disaffection could await her, that she could do no more than dispel what had already in its own way been perfection.

But there was no need to knock at the door. Victoria Place, when she reached it, was a short main street of tall terraced houses, either newly recovered or so smart that they had never lapsed: the number 24 was brightly illuminated, shining brightly forth into the gathering darkness. She walked slowly toward it, realizing that she would be able to see whatever there was to see without knocking: realizing that fate had connived with her curiosity by providing a bus stop directly outside the house, so that she could stand there and wait without fear of detection. She took her place at the bus stop, and stood there for a moment before she gathered her courage to turn around, and then she turned. The lights were on in the two lower floors, and she could see straight into the basement, a room

which most closely resembled in shape the one where she herself lived. The room seemed at first sight to be full of people, and there was so much activity that it took some time to sort them out. There were two women, and four children; no, five children, for there was a baby sitting in a corner on a blue rug. The larger children were putting up a Christmas tree, and one of the women was laying the table for tea, while the other, her back to the window, one elbow on the mantelpiece, appeared to be reading aloud a passage from a book. It was a large, bright room, with a green carpet, and white walls, and red painted wooden furniture; even the table was painted red. A children's room. It shone, it glittered. A mobile of golden fishes hung from the ceiling, and the carpet was strewn with colored glass and tinsel decorations for the tree. The plates on the table were blue and white, and the silver knives caught the light; on the mantelpiece stood two many-faceted cut glasses and an open bottle of wine. Two of the children had fair hair, and the other three were dark: and the woman laying the table had red hair, a huge coil of dark red hair from which whole heavy locks escaped, dragging down the back of her neck, falling against her face at each movement, and she moved endlessly, restlessly, vigorously, taking buns out of a bag, slicing bread, pouring black currant juice into beakers, turning to listen to the other woman, and suddenly laughing, throwing back her head with a kind of violence and laughing: and the other woman at the mantelpiece laughed too, her thin shoulders shaking, and the children, irritated by their mother's laughter, flung themselves at her, clinging angrily onto her knees, shouting, until the red-haired woman tried to silence them with slices of bread and butter, which were rejected and flung around the floor: so she followed them up with the iced buns, tossing them round and yet talking, all the time talking, to the other woman and not to the children, intent upon some point, some anecdote too precious to lose, and the children chewed at the buns while she scooped up the torn pieces of bread and bestowed them all, with a smile of such lovely passing affection, upon the baby, a smile so tender and amused and solicitous that Helen, overseeing it, felt her heart stand still.

And as she stood there, out there in the cold, and watched, she felt herself stiffen slowly into the breathlessness of attention: because it seemed to her that she had been given, freely, a vision of something so beautiful that its relevance could not be measured. The hints and arrows that had led her here took on the mysterious significance of fate itself: she felt that everything was joined and drawn together, that all things were part of some pattern of which she caught by sheer chance a sudden hopeful sense: and that those two women, and their children, and the man on the train, and the bright and radiant uncurtained room, an island in the surrounding darkness, were symbols to her of things too vague to name, of happiness, of hope, of brightness, warmth, and celebration. She gazed into that room, where emotion lay, like water unimaginably profound. The red-haired woman was kneeling now, on the green carpet, rubbing with a corner of the tea towel at a buttery mark on the carpet, and at the same time looking up and listening, with an expression upon her face in which vexation with the children, carelessness of her own vexation, and a kind of soft rapt delight in the other woman's company were inextricably confused; and the other woman had turned slightly, so that Helen from the window could see her face, and she was twisting in her hands a length of red-and-silver tinsel, idly pulling shreds from it as she spoke. And Helen thought of all the other dark cold rooms of London and the world, of loneliness, of the blue chilly flickerings of television sets, of sad children, silenced mothers, and unmarried girls and she wondered if so much delight were truly gathered up and concentrated into one place, or whether these windows were not windows through which she viewed the real huge spacious anterior lovely world. And it seemed possible to see them so, because she did not know that house, nor those women, nor their names, nor the name of the man who had led her there: the poetry of inspiration being to a certain extent, as she knew, the poetry of ignorance, and the connections between symbols a destructive folly to draw. She did not even know which of these women was Mrs. Smithson, whom she had come to see, for if one woman had laid the table, the other cleared it, equally at home. She knew nothing, and could therefore believe everything, drawing faith from such a vision, as she had drawn faith from unfamiliar cities: drawing faith from the passionate vision of intimacy, where intimacy itself failed her; as Wordsworth turned from his life to his keener recollections,[8] and Yeats to lions and towers and hawks.[9]

By the time that one of the children was sent to draw the curtains, she was stiff and white with cold. She turned away, as the child, a small girl with straight dark hair and a face suddenly grave with the weight of her task, began to struggle with the heavy floor-length hangings, shutting inch by inch away from her the colored angles of refracted light, the Christmas tree, the airy fishes, the verdant green, the small angelic innocent faces, the shining spheres of glass, and those two young worn women: and as she turned she felt the first snowflakes of the year settle softly on her skin, and looking up, she saw the dim blue sky full of snow.

---

8. Wordsworth . . . recollections: British poet William Wordsworth (1770–1850) delved into memories of his youth in his poetry, recollecting the emotion of childhood in the tranquility of adulthood.
9. Yeats . . . hawks: British poet William Butler Yeats (1865–1939) developed his own mythology.

She glanced back, to see if the child had seen it, but the curtains were already drawn, and she saw nothing but her own image, pale in the glass. So she started to walk down the street, away from the house, away from the bus stop, but before she had taken ten steps a car drew up, just by her side, a slow yard from her, and there was the man from the train, sitting there and looking at her. She paused, and he opened the door, and sitting there still he said to her, "I don't know what to say to you, you look so fragile that a word might hurt you." And she smiled at him, a slow dazed smile, knowing that as he for her, so she for him was some mysterious apparition, some faintly gleaming memorable image: and she turned away, and walked down the street away from him into the snowy darkness, and he got out of his car and went into the house.

She walked carefully, because her ankles were so brittle from the cold that she feared that if she stumbled, they would snap.

RESPONDING TO THE SELECTION

Your Response

1. What is your opinion of Helen? What would you say to her if you met her?

Recalling

2. (a) As the story opens, what is Helen's attitude toward journeys? (b) According to "a much-traveled old man," why does she feel this way?
3. What conclusion does Helen reach about the man on the train from Reading to London?
4. (a) At Victoria Place, what does Helen observe? (b) Who arrives as she walks away?

Interpreting

5. Why do you think Helen is so obsessed with catching a glimpse of Mrs. Smithson?
6. In the last scene, what meaning does the "vision" that Helen sees have for her?
7. (a) The title of this story is an allusion. The reader must know that Cythera is a Greek island where Aphrodite, goddess of love, arose from the sea. How are the implications of the story's title fulfilled unexpectedly at the end? (b) How do the title and the theme relate?

Applying

8. What do you think the chances are that Helen will ever fall in love with a specific man?

CRITICAL THINKING AND READING

Identifying Kinds of Evidence

Direct evidence is straightforward factual information that leads to an obvious conclusion. When the narrator says that the man on the train "took out a sheet of fourpenny stamps, and tore one off, licked it, and stuck it on" the envelope, you have direct evidence of an intent to mail the letter. **Indirect evidence** requires more interpretation. When the narrator says, "there was no need to knock at the door" of the house on Victoria Place, you can infer that Helen is relieved to avoid meeting Mrs. Smithson. The evidence is indirect because you have to use other information about Helen to reach that conclusion.

1. Identify the kind of evidence—direct or indirect—in each inference: (a) that Helen had been to France; (b) that Helen liked the man who kissed her on a train to Oxford; (c) that Helen received an excellent education; (d) that Helen was bored by the man at the party.
2. (a) What kind of evidence does Helen use to support her conclusion about the unnamed man? (b) How accurately has she interpreted the evidence?

THINKING AND WRITING

Writing About Characterization

Fictional characters—flat or round—must be believable. They may act in unexpected ways, but they should not act out of character. Helen is a complex but consistent character. Write an essay discussing three of Helen's encounters with other people. Explain how in each she acts true to the personality Drabble has given her. First, choose three encounters. As you write your first draft, show Helen's consistent behavior in each encounter. Revise your draft, making sure to supply clear connections.

V. S. NAIPAUL

1932–

Few writers are better suited than V. S. Naipaul to examine post-colonial culture in countries that once belonged to the British Empire. Naipaul, whose family came from India, was born in Trinidad, then a part of the British West Indies. There he grew up in the Hindu culture and went to British schools. These experiences, combined with living in England as a young man and traveling all over the world since, make up what Naipaul calls his "many-sided background."

In his book of autobiographical writings, *Finding the Center: Two Narratives* (1984), Naipaul recounts how his grandfather came to Trinidad as an indentured laborer. While life for such Asian-Indian immigrants was certainly better than it was for the Africans enslaved in the West Indies two hundred years previously, the terms of indenture were not always strictly adhered to, and members of the Indian community faced many frustrations. The next generation fared somewhat better; Naipaul's father became a popular journalist with the main Trinidadian newspaper.

Naipaul was an excellent writer even as a student, and he won a scholarship to Oxford University. While in his final year there, he learned that his father had died. His family wanted him to return to Trinidad, but Naipaul decided to remain in Britain. He soon found work writing about the West Indies for BBC Radio in London. Far from home, he began to write stories that drew on his memories of Trinidad. Those early stories were eventually collected in *Miguel Street* (1959).

In 1961, Naipaul published *A House for Mr. Biswas,* a novel about a forlorn journalist, a protagonist who resembles the author's own father. Since then, in many other novels and books of journalism, Naipaul has frequently written about people living on the margins of the modern world, people who have to struggle against rootlessness and overwhelming change. For his novel *In a Free State* (1971) Naipaul won the prestigious Booker Prize, a British award similar to the Pulitzer Prize in the United States.

Naipaul lives in Wiltshire, in southern England, but he still travels a great deal to do research for his books. In his most recent book, *India: A Million Mutinies Now* (1990), Naipaul describes a long visit to the country of his ancestors, a nation that has spent fifty years on the brink of civil war.

B. Wordsworth

**Writers'
Techniques**

First-Person Narration. Narration is the act of describing a series of events—a story. The story told may be a true one, as in history or biography, or a fictional one, as in novels and short stories.

The speaker who tells the story, the narrator, may be someone who is involved in the events or someone who merely observes them. A narrator who participates—at least in part—in the events described is called a first-person narrator. He or she is identified by the first-person pronoun *I*. A narrator who stands outside the events described is called a third-person narrator and uses the pronouns *he, she,* or *they.*

First-person narration gets our attention because it puts us in the presence of a particular human voice. It is important, however, not to identify the narrator's voice with that of the author. The narrator serves merely as a persona, or mask, through which the author tells the story. Being a fictional creation as well, the narrator does not necessarily reflect the author's own experiences, attitudes, or beliefs.

Focus

Why do some people affect us so much more than others? Is it because of something in themselves, or because we meet them at a crucial point in our lives? In this story, the character B. Wordsworth makes a strong impact on the narrator. Think about people who have had a strong influence on your life. Choose one to write about. Describe the circumstances under which the person affected you and the details of his or her impact on you. Then consider how your life might be different had you never known this person.

Primary Source

In "B. Wordsworth," V. S. Naipaul used a first-person narrator to recreate for us an environment he knew well in his own childhood—Trinidad in the 1940's. It was fitting that the narrator be a child. In *Finding the Center: Two Narratives*, Naipaul says the following about a different story that has the same narrator:

> The story developed a first-person narrator. And for the sake of speed, to avoid complications, . . . this narrator could not be myself. My narrator lived alone with his mother in a house on the street. He had no father; he had no other family. So, very simply, all the crowd of my mother's extended family, as cumbersome in real life as it would have been to a writer, was abolished; and, again out of my wish to simplify, I had a narrator more in tune with the life of the street than I had been.

B. Wordsworth

V. S. Naipaul

Three beggars called punctually every day at the hospitable houses in Miguel Street. At about ten an Indian came in his dhoti[1] and white jacket, and we poured a tin of rice into the sack he carried on his back. At twelve an old woman smoking a clay pipe came and she got a cent. At two a blind man led by a boy called for his penny.

Sometimes we had a rogue. One day a man called and said he was hungry. We gave him a meal. He asked for a cigarette and wouldn't go until we had lit it for him. That man never came again.

The strangest caller came one afternoon at about four o'clock. I had come back from school and was in my home-clothes. The man said to me, "Sonny, may I come inside your yard?"

He was a small man and he was tidily dressed. He wore a hat, a white shirt and black trousers.

I asked, "What do you want?"

He said, "I want to watch your bees."

We had four small gru-gru palm trees[2] and they were full of uninvited bees.

I ran up the steps and shouted, "Ma, it have a man outside here. He say he want to watch the bees."

My mother came out, looked at the man and asked in an unfriendly way, "What you want?"

The man said, "I want to watch your bees."

His English was so good, it didn't sound natural, and I could see my mother was worried.

She said to me, "Stay here and watch him while he watch the bees."

The man said, "Thank you, Madam. You have done a good deed today."

He spoke very slowly and very correctly as though every word was costing him money.

We watched the bees, this man and I, for about an hour, squatting near the palm trees.

The man said, "I like watching bees. Sonny, do you like watching bees?"

I said, "I ain't have the time."

He shook his head sadly. He said, "That's what I do, I just watch. I can watch ants for days. Have you ever watched ants? And scorpions, and centipedes, and congorees[3]—have you watched those?"

I shook my head.

I said, "What you does do, mister?"

He got up and said, "I am a poet."

I said, "A good poet?"

He said, "The greatest in the world."

"What your name, mister?"

"B. Wordsworth."

"B for Bill?"

---

1. dhoti (dō′ tē): Traditional loincloth worn by Hindu men.

2. gru-gru (gro͞o′-gro͞o′) **palm trees:** West Indian palms that yield edible nuts.

3. congorees (kăŋ gər ēz): Conger or congo eels; large, scaleless eels found in the warm waters of the West Indies.

MAN FROM THE VILLAGE
Carlton Murrell
Courtesy of the Artist

"Black. Black Wordsworth. White Wordsworth[4] was my brother. We share one heart. I can watch a small flower like the morning glory and cry."

I said, "Why you does cry?"

---

4. White Wordsworth: The English Romantic poet, William Wordsworth (1770–1850).

"Why, boy? Why? You will know when you grow up. You're a poet, too, you know. And when you're a poet you can cry for everything."

I couldn't laugh.

He said, "You like your mother?"

"When she not beating me."

He pulled out a printed sheet from his hip-pocket and said, "On this paper is the greatest poem about mothers and I'm going to sell it to you at a bargain price. For four cents."

I went inside and I said, "Ma, you want to buy a poetry for four cents?"

My mother said, "Tell that blasted man to haul his tail away from my yard, you hear."

I said to B. Wordsworth, "My mother say she ain't have four cents."

B. Wordsworth said, "It is the poet's tragedy."

And he put the paper back in his pocket. He didn't seem to mind.

I said, "Is a funny way to go round selling poetry like that. Only calypsonians[5] do that sort of thing. A lot of people does buy?"

He said, "No one has yet bought a single copy."

"But why you does keep on going round, then?"

He said, "In this way I watch many things, and I always hope to meet poets."

I said, "You really think I is a poet?"

"You're as good as me," he said.

And when B. Wordsworth left, I prayed I would see him again.

About a week later, coming back from school one afternoon, I met him at the corner of Miguel Street.

He said, "I have been waiting for you for a long time."

I said, "You sell any poetry yet?"

He shook his head.

He said, "In my yard I have the best mango tree in Port-of-Spain.[6] And now the mangoes are ripe and red and very sweet and juicy. I have waited here for you to tell you this and to invite you to come and eat some of my mangoes."

He lived in Alberto Street in a one-roomed hut placed right in the center of the lot. The yard seemed all green. There was the big mango tree. There was a coconut tree and there was a plum tree. The place looked wild, as though it wasn't in the city at all. You couldn't see all the big concrete houses in the street.

He was right. The mangoes were sweet and juicy. I ate about six, and the yellow mango juice ran down my arms to my elbows and down my mouth to my chin and my shirt was stained.

My mother said when I got home, "Where you was? You think you is a man now and could go all over the place? Go cut a whip for me."

She beat me rather badly, and I ran out of the house swearing that I would never come back. I went to B. Wordsworth's house. I was so angry, my nose was bleeding.

B. Wordsworth said, "Stop crying, and we will go for a walk."

I stopped crying, but I was breathing short. We went for a walk. We walked down St. Clair Avenue to the Savannah and we walked to the race-course.

B. Wordsworth said, "Now, let us lie on the grass and look up at the sky, and I want you to think how far those stars are from us."

I did as he told me, and I saw what he meant. I felt like nothing, and at the same time I had never felt so big and great in all my life. I forgot all my anger and all my tears and all the blows.

When I said I was better, he began telling me the names of the stars, and I particularly remembered the constellation of Orion the Hunter,[7] though I don't really know why. I can spot Orion even today, but I have forgotten the rest.

---

5. calypsonians (kə lip sō′ nē ənz): Those who sing calypso songs, the characteristic satirical street ballads of Trinidad.

6. Port-of-Spain: Seaport capital of Trinidad and Tobago.

---

7. constellation of Orion (ō rī′ ən) **the Hunter:** The group of stars named after a mythological giant who was killed accidentally by the goddess of hunting, Diana.

Then a light was flashed into our faces, and we saw a policeman. We got up from the grass.

The policeman said, "What you doing here?"

B. Wordsworth said, "I have been asking myself the same question for forty years."

We became friends, B. Wordsworth and I. He told me, "You must never tell anybody about me and about the mango tree and the coconut tree and the plum tree. You must keep that a secret. If you tell anybody, I will know, because I am a poet."

I gave him my word and I kept it.

I liked his little room. It had no more furniture than George's front room,[8] but it looked cleaner and healthier. But it also looked lonely.

One day I asked him, "Mister Wordsworth, why you does keep all this bush in your yard? Ain't it does make the place damp?"

He said, "Listen, and I will tell you a story. Once upon a time a boy and girl met each other and they fell in love. They loved each other so much they got married. They were both poets. He loved words. She loved grass and flowers and trees. They lived happily in a single room, and then one day, the girl poet said to the boy poet, 'We are going to have another poet in the family.' But this poet was never born, because the girl died, and the young poet died with her, inside her. And the girl's husband was very sad, and he said he would never touch a thing in the girl's garden. And so the garden remained, and grew high and wild."

I looked at B. Wordsworth, and as he told me this lovely story, he seemed to grow older. I understood his story.

We went for long walks together. We went to the Botanical Gardens and the Rock Gardens. We climbed Chancellor Hill in the late afternoon and watched the darkness fall on Port-of-Spain, and watched the lights go on in the city and on the ships in the harbor.

He did everything as though he were doing it for the first time in his life. He did everything as though he were doing some church rite.

He would say to me, "Now, how about having some ice cream?"

And when I said, yes, he would grow very serious and say, "Now, which café shall we patronize?" As though it were a very important thing. He would think for some time about it, and finally say, "I think I will go and negotiate the purchase with that shop."

The world became a most exciting place.

One day, when I was in his yard, he said to me, "I have a great secret which I am now going to tell you."

I said, "It really secret?"

"At the moment, yes."

I looked at him, and he looked at me. He said, "This is just between you and me, remember. I am writing a poem."

"Oh." I was disappointed.

He said, "But this is a different sort of poem. This is the greatest poem in the world."

I whistled.

He said, "I have been working on it for more than five years now. I will finish it in about twenty-two years from now, that is, if I keep on writing at the present rate."

"You does write a lot, then?"

He said, "Not any more. I just write one line a month. But I make sure it is a good line."

I asked, "What was last month's good line?"

He looked up at the sky, and said, *"The past is deep."*

I said, "It is a beautiful line."

B. Wordsworth said, "I hope to distill the experiences of a whole month into that single line of poetry. So, in twenty-two years, I

---

8. George's front room: George is a character in one of the companion stories in Naipaul's book, *Miguel Street*.

THE RED HOUSE
Carlton Murrell
Courtesy of the Artist

shall have written a poem that will sing to all humanity."

I was filled with wonder.

Our walks continued. We walked along the sea-wall at Docksite one day, and I said, "Mr. Wordsworth, if I drop this pin in the water, you think it will float?"

He said, "This is a strange world. Drop your pin, and let us see what will happen."

The pin sank.

I said, "How is the poem this month?"

But he never told me any other line. He merely said, "Oh, it comes, you know. It comes."

Or we would sit on the sea-wall and watch the liners come into the harbor.

But of the greatest poem in the world I heard no more.

I felt he was growing older.

"How you does live, Mr. Wordsworth?" I asked him one day.

He said, "You mean how I get money?"

When I nodded, he laughed in a crooked way.

He said, "I sing calypsoes in the calypso season."

"And that last you the rest of the year?"

"It is enough."

"But you will be the richest man in the world when you write the greatest poem?"

He didn't reply.

One day when I went to see him in his little house, I found him lying on his little bed. He looked so old and so weak, that I found myself wanting to cry.

He said, "The poem is not going well."

He wasn't looking at me. He was looking through the window at the coconut tree, and he was speaking as though I wasn't there. He said, "When I was twenty I felt the power within myself." Then, almost in front of my eyes, I could see his face growing older and more tired. He said, "But that—that was a long time ago."

And then—I felt it so keenly, it was as though I had been slapped by my mother. I could see it clearly on his face. It was there for everyone to see. Death on the shrinking face.

He looked at me, and saw my tears and sat up.

He said, "Come." I went and sat on his knees.

He looked into my eyes, and he said, "Oh, you can see it, too. I always knew you had the poet's eye."

He didn't even look sad, and that made me burst out crying loudly.

He pulled me to his thin chest, and said, "Do you want me to tell you a funny story?" and he smiled encouragingly at me.

But I couldn't reply.

He said, "When I have finished this story, I want you to promise that you will go away and never come back to see me. Do you promise?"

I nodded.

He said, "Good. Well, listen. That story I told you about the boy poet and the girl poet, do you remember that? That wasn't true. It was something I just made up. All this talk about poetry and the greatest poem in the world, that wasn't true, either. Isn't that the funniest thing you have heard?"

But his voice broke.

I left the house, and ran home crying, like a poet, for everything I saw.

I walked along Alberto Street a year later, but I could find no sign of the poet's house. It hadn't vanished, just like that. It had been pulled down, and a big, two-storied building had taken its place. The mango tree and the plum tree and the coconut tree had all been cut down, and there was brick and concrete everywhere.

It was just as though B. Wordsworth had never existed.

RESPONDING TO THE SELECTION

Your Response

1. Looking at the stars with B. Wordsworth, the boy says, "I felt like nothing, and at the same time I had never felt so big and great in all my life." Have you ever felt like that? Explain.

Recalling

2. What reason does B. Wordsworth give for wanting to come into the boy's yard?
3. What promise does B. Wordsworth ask the boy to make at their last meeting?

Interpreting

4. What does the opening description of the daily visitors to the narrator's house tell you about the city in which the story is set?
5. B. Wordsworth says that he always hopes to meet "poets" and that the boy is a "poet." How do you think he would define that term?
6. The narrator says that B. Wordsworth "did everything as though he was doing it for the first time." What does he mean by that?

Applying

7. Eccentric people, like B. Wordsworth, sometimes have different or deeper insights concerning the world around them. Why do you think this is the case?

ANALYZING LITERATURE

First-Person Narration

As you read a story, you know that the events did not happen, but you accept them as if they did. Samuel Taylor Coleridge called this "a willing suspension of disbelief." When the first-person narrator of "B. Wordsworth" says that three beggars "called punctually every day" at his home, we believe him because he presents himself as an eyewitness. However, we know nothing more than the narrator knows. When B. Wordsworth tells the narrator that he earns a living as a singer, neither we nor the boy know whether this is true.

1. How would the story be different if it were told from B. Wordsworth's point of view?
2. Identify two elements in the story about which

you would like to know more than this narrator can convey.

3. Do you think the story would be as effective if it were narrated from a third-person point of view, so that you knew all the characters' thoughts? Why or why not?

CRITICAL THINKING AND READING

Appreciating Dialect

Various forms of English appear in "B. Wordsworth." First, we encounter the narrator's English, precise and literate. Next is B. Wordsworth's speech, which is slightly affected. Finally, we hear the boy's Trinidadian English which, because of its local idiosyncrasies, is most easily identified as a **dialect.** Naipaul's clever juxtapositioning of these three enhances our enjoyment of the story.

1. The narrator says that B. Wordsworth's English "was so good, it didn't sound natural." Why is that statement humorous?
2. What evidence can you find in the story that B. Wordsworth's use of language is part of his appeal for the narrator?

THINKING AND WRITING

Writing a First-Person Narrative

Write a story using a first-person narrator. You may use a series of events that you actually experienced, but choose a narrator who is different from you. For example, your narrator might be of a different gender or age from you or might have come from a background different from yours. Remember not to include details that your narrator cannot know, like another character's thoughts.

LEARNING OPTION

Cross-curricular Connection. Investigate the history of the British presence in the West Indies, from earliest explorations through colonization and independence. Prepare an oral presentation for the class providing background on the multiracial nature of the West Indies and the factors contributing to the present political and economic status of Trinidad in particular.

Drama

SET DESIGN OF COVENT GARDEN FOR PYGMALION
Donald Oenslager
Harvard Theatre Collection

GEORGE BERNARD SHAW

1856–1950

During his ninety-four years, George Bernard Shaw was a novelist, a critic on many subjects, a champion of all sorts of reform, and, finally, a playwright. Original, witty, and opinionated, he often managed to offend people when he was not busy charming them.

Born in Ireland to a family with musical talent but little money, Shaw saw to his own education. At the age of twenty, he arrived in London, where he remained for the rest of his life. After trying, and essentially failing, as a writer of fiction, he turned to reviewing—first books, then paintings, and finally music.

Shaw was a restless man, however, with boundless tastes and interests. In 1883 he joined the Fabian Society, an organization whose aim was the peaceful reform of social, economic, and political systems. His personal ambition, as he put it, was "to force the public to reconsider its morals," and toward this end he invested every ounce of his energies. In the process he established himself as a debater and public speaker of some stature.

The enjoyment he derived from crafting lines for his public addresses, coupled with his earlier enthusiasm for writing criticism, naturally led him in the direction of drama criticism. From there it was a short jump to playwriting itself. Shaw's first play, *Widower's Houses* (1891), was a rather heavy-handed and ironical exposure of the slum landlord practices and municipal graft that were common ills of the day. His next effort, *Mrs. Warren's Profession* (1894), ran into trouble with official censorship due to its serious treatment of prostitution and the inequities of industrialism. In the same year, *Arms and the Man* enjoyed a limited success.

If people would not attend productions of his plays, Shaw reasoned, they might at least read them. In 1898 he published his first collection, *Plays Pleasant and Unpleasant,* adding the prefaces and epilogues that came to be his trademark.

Shaw's plays, forty-seven in all, continued to challenge the "spiritual sleep" of England's "middle-class morality." When *Pygmalion* was completed in 1913, it was produced in German in Vienna, as a means of avoiding the usual bad press. Its success there led it to London, where, in April of 1914, it opened to immediate acclaim. Like his professor of phonetics, Henry Higgins, Shaw believed in the power of language to break down class barriers. In his will he left a sizable bequest to furthering a system of phonetic spelling. In the interests of spelling simplification, he left out the apostrophe in some contractions, as in this text.

GUIDE FOR INTERPRETING

Preface to Pygmalion; Pygmalion, Act I

Historical Context

The Play. Historical context refers both to the backdrop of historical events against which a work is set and to attitudes and events of the time during which the author lived. The first of these two aspects relates to such matters as when and where the work takes place, whether the author has used real places and people, and the degree to which the events have been fictionalized. The second aspect of historical context—the relevance of "current events" and attitudes of the author's day—takes into account any social conditions and values that may have impacted on the subject matter of the work or its execution.

Focus

To demonstrate the irregularities of English spelling, George Bernard Shaw once suggested that the word *fish* be written *ghoti*. (The *gh*, he explained, was to be pronounced as it is in *rough,* the *o* as in *women,* and the *ti* as in *station*.) Play with English spellings until you have devised three or four "outrageous" words of your own. Show these to your classmates on paper, and see if anyone can read them correctly.

Primary Source

More than any of Shaw's other plays, *Pygmalion* shows how seemingly minor events simmered in his mind, emerging years later transformed in his work. According to Shaw, the play's opening scene was suggested by the following incident:

> Some time ago, happening to be caught in a pelting shower in St. Martin's Lane on a gloomy evening, I took refuge in the entry to a narrow court, where I was presently joined by three men of prosaic appearance, apparently respectable artisans. To my surprise, instead of beginning to talk about horses, they began to talk about music— . . . illustrating their conversation by singing passages in which certain pet singers of theirs had come out wonderfully. This led to a discussion as to whether they could remember some work which had been an old favorite of theirs. Finally, one of them pulled out a pitch pipe; the three sang a chord; and away they went, *sotto voce,* but very prettily, into a three-part song, raising their voices a little when they found that the passersby were too preoccupied by the deluge to notice them. They were wholly untroubled by a consciousness of the distinguished critic lurking in the shadow a few feet off, greatly pleased with the performance but withal sufficiently master of his business not to be surprised at this survival.

Preface to Pygmalion

Bernard Shaw

A Professor of Phonetics

The English have no respect for their language, and will not teach their children to speak it. They cannot spell it because they have nothing to spell it with but an old foreign alphabet of which only the consonants—and not all of them—have any agreed speech value. Consequently no man can teach himself what it should sound like from reading it; and it is impossible for an Englishman to open his mouth without making some other Englishman despise him. Most European languages are now accessible in black and white to foreigners: English and French are not thus accessible even to Englishmen and Frenchmen. The reformer we need most today is an energetic phonetic enthusiast: that is why I have made such a one the hero of a popular play.

There have been heroes of that kind crying in the wilderness for many years past. When I became interested in the subject towards the end of the eighteen-seventies, the illustrious Alexander Melville Bell, the inventor of Visible Speech, had emigrated to Canada, where his son invented the telephone; but Alexander J. Ellis[1] was still a London Patriarch, with an impressive head always covered by a velvet skull cap, for which he would apologize to public meetings in a very courtly manner. He and Tito Pagliardini, another phonetic veteran, were men whom it was impossible to dislike.

Henry Sweet,[2] then a young man, lacked their sweetness of character: he was about as conciliatory to conventional mortals as Ibsen[3] or Samuel Butler.[4] His great ability as a phonetician (he was, I think the best of them all at his job) would have entitled him to high official recognition, and perhaps enabled him to popularize his subject, but for his Satanic contempt for all academic dignitaries and persons in general who thought more of Greek than of phonetics. Once, in the days when the Imperial Institute rose in South Kensington, and Joseph Chamberlain[5] was booming the Empire, I induced the editor of a leading monthly review to commission an article from Sweet on the imperial importance of his subject. When it arrived, it contained nothing but a savagely derisive attack on a professor of language and literature whose chair Sweet regarded as proper to a phonetic expert only. The article, being libellous, had to be returned as impossible; and I had to renounce my dream of dragging its author into the limelight. When I met him afterwards, for the first time for many years, I found to my astonishment that he, who had been a quite tolerably presentable young man, had actually managed by sheer scorn to alter his personal appearance until he had become a sort of

---

1. **Alexander J. Ellis:** English phonetician and mathematician (1814–1890).

2. **Henry Sweet:** English phonetician (1845–1912).
3. **Ibsen:** Norwegian playwright Henrik Ibsen (1828–1906).
4. **Samuel Butler:** English novelist (1835–1902).
5. **Joseph Chamberlain:** British statesman (1836–1914).

walking repudiation of Oxford and all its traditions. It must have been largely in his own despite that he was squeezed into something called a Readership[6] of phonetics there. The future of phonetics rests probably with his pupils, who all swore by him; but nothing could bring the man himself into any sort of compliance with the university to which he nevertheless clung by divine right in an intensely Oxonian[7] way. I daresay his papers, if he has left any, include some satires that may be published without too destructive results fifty years hence. He was, I believe, not in the least an ill-natured man: very much the opposite, I should say; but he would not suffer fools gladly; and to him all scholars who were not rabid phoneticians were fools.

Those who knew him will recognize in my third act the allusion to the Current Shorthand in which he used to write postcards. It may be acquired from a four and sixpenny manual published by the Clarendon Press. The postcards which Mrs Higgins describes are such as I have received from Sweet. I would decipher a sound which a cockney would represent by *zerr*, and a Frenchman by *seu*, and then write demanding with some heat what on earth it meant. Sweet, with boundless contempt for my stupidity, would reply that it not only meant but obviously was the word Result, as no other word containing that sound, and capable of making sense with the context, existed in any language spoken on earth. That less expert mortals should require fuller indications was beyond Sweet's patience. Therefore, though the whole point of his Current Shorthand is that it can express every sound in the language perfectly, vowels as well as consonants, and that your hand has to make no stroke except the easy and current ones with which you write m, n, and u, l, p, and q, scribbling them at whatev-

er angle comes easiest to you, his unfortunate determination to make this remarkable and quite legible script serve also as a shorthand reduced it in his own practice to the most inscrutable of cryptograms. His true objective was the provision of a full, accurate, legible script for our language; but he was led past that by his contempt for the popular Pitman system of shorthand, which he called the Pitfall system. The triumph of Pitman was a triumph of business organization: there was a weekly paper to persuade you to learn Pitman: there were cheap textbooks and exercise books and transcripts of speeches for you to copy, and schools where experienced teachers coached you up to the necessary proficiency. Sweet could not organize his market in that fashion. He might as well have been the Sybil[8] who tore up the leaves of prophecy that nobody would attend to. The four and sixpenny manual, mostly in his lithographed handwriting, that was never vulgarly advertized, may perhaps some day be taken up by a syndicate and pushed upon the public as The Times[9] pushed the Encyclopoedia Britannica; but until then it will certainly not prevail against Pitman. I have bought three copies of it during my lifetime; and I am informed by the publishers that its cloistered existence is still a steady and healthy one. I actually learned the system two several times; and yet the shorthand in which I am writing these lines is Pitman's. And the reason is, that my secretary cannot transcribe Sweet, having been perforce taught in the schools of Pitman. In America I could use the commercially organized Gregg shorthand, which has taken a hint from Sweet by making its letters writable (current, Sweet would have called them) instead of having to be geometrically drawn like Pitman's; but all these systems, including

---

6. Readership *n.*: A position as a lecturer or instructor.
7. Oxonian *adj.*: Pertaining to Oxford University.

8. Sybil: One of the women consulted as prophetesses by the ancient Greeks or Romans.
9. The Times: The *London Times*, a British newspaper.

Sweet's, are spoilt by making them available for verbatim reporting, in which complete and exact spelling and word division are impossible. A complete and exact phonetic script is neither practicable nor necessary for ordinary use; but if we enlarge our alphabet to the Russian size, and make our spelling as phonetic as Spanish, the advance will be prodigious.

Pygmalion Higgins is not a portrait of Sweet, to whom the adventure of Eliza Doolittle would have been impossible; still, as will be seen, there are touches of Sweet in the play. With Higgins's physique and temperament Sweet might have set the Thames on fire. As it was, he impressed himself professionally on Europe to an extent that made his comparative personal obscurity, and the failure of Oxford to do justice to his eminence, a puzzle to foreign specialists in his subject. I do not blame Oxford, because I think Oxford is quite right in demanding a certain social amenity from its nurslings (heavens knows it is not exorbitant in its requirement!); for although I well know how hard it is for a man of genius with a seriously underrated subject to maintain serene and kindly relations with the men who underrate it, and who keep all the best places for less important subjects which they profess without originality and sometimes without much capacity for them, still, if he overwhelms them with wrath and disdain, he cannot expect them to heap honors on him.

Of the later generations of phoneticians I know little. Among them towered Robert Bridges, to whom perhaps Higgins may owe his Miltonic sympathies, though here again I must disclaim all portraiture. But if the play makes the public aware that there are such people as phoneticians, and that they are among the most important people in England at present, it will serve its turn.

I wish to boast that Pygmalion has been an extremely successful play, both on stage and screen, all over Europe and North America as well as at home. It is so intensely and deliberately didactic, and its subject is esteemed so dry, that I delight in throwing it at the heads of the wiseacres who repeat the parrot cry that art should never be didactic. It goes to prove my contention that great art can never be anything else.

Finally, and for the encouragement of people troubled with accents that cut them off from all high employment, I may add that the change wrought by Professor Higgins in the flower-girl is neither impossible nor uncommon. The modern concierge's daughter who fulfills her ambition by playing the Queen of Spain in Ruy Blas[10] at the Théâtre Français is only one of many thousands of men and women who have sloughed off their native dialects and acquired a new tongue. Our West End shop assistants and domestic servants are bilingual. But the thing has to be done scientifically, or the last state of the aspirant may be worse than the first. An honest slum dialect is more tolerable than the attempts of phonetically untaught persons to imitate the plutocracy. Ambitious flower-girls who read this play must not imagine that they can pass themselves off as fine ladies by untutored imitation. They must learn their alphabet over again, and different, from a phonetic expert. Imitation will only make them ridiculous.

---

10. Ruy Blas (r$\overline{oo}$ ē′ bläs′): A play by French writer Victor Hugo (1802–1885).

NOTE FOR TECHNICIANS. A complete representation of the play as printed in this edition is technically possible only on the cinema screen or on stages furnished with exceptionally elaborate machinery. For ordinary theatrical use the scenes separated by rows of asterisks are to be omitted.

In the dialogue an e upside down indicates the indefinite vowel, sometimes called obscure or neutral, for which, though it is one of the commonest sounds in English speech, our wretched alphabet has no letter.

Pygmalion

CHARACTERS

Henry Higgins
Colonel Pickering
Freddy Eynsford Hill
Alfred Doolittle
Bystanders

Eliza Doolittle
Mrs Eynsford Hill
Miss Eynsford Hill
Mrs Higgins
Mrs Pearce
Parlormaid

Taximen
Count Nepommuck
Host
Hostess
Footmen
Constables

ACT I

London at 11.15 P.M. *Torrents of heavy summer rain. Cab whistles blowing frantically in all directions. Pedestrians running for shelter into the portico of St Paul's church (not Wren's cathedral but Inigo Jones's church in Covent Garden vegetable market), among them a lady and her daughter in evening dress. All are peering out gloomily at the rain, except one man with his back turned to the rest, wholly preoccupied with a notebook in which he is writing.*

The church clock strikes the first quarter.[1]

THE DAUGHTER [*in the space between the central pillars, close to the one on her left*] I'm getting chilled to the bone. What can Freddy be doing all this time? He's been gone twenty minutes.

THE MOTHER [*on her daughter's right*] Not so long. But he ought to have got us a cab by this.

A BYSTANDER [*on the lady's right*] He wont get no cab not until half-past eleven, missus, when they come back after dropping their theatre fares.

THE MOTHER. But we must have a cab. We cant stand here until half-past eleven. It's too bad.

THE BYSTANDER. Well, it ain't my fault, missus.

THE DAUGHTER. If Freddy had a bit of gumption, he would have got one at the theatre door.

THE MOTHER. What could he have done, poor boy?

THE DAUGHTER. Other people got cabs. Why couldn't he?

FREDDY *rushes in out of the rain from the Southampton Street side, and comes between them closing a dripping umbrella.*

He is a young man of twenty, in evening dress, very wet round the ankles.

THE DAUGHTER. Well, havnt you got a cab?

FREDDY. Theres not one to be had for love or money.

THE MOTHER. Oh, Freddy, there must be one. You cant have tried.

THE DAUGHTER. It's too tiresome. Do you expect us to go and get one ourselves?

FREDDY. I tell you theyre all engaged. The rain was so sudden: nobody was prepared; and everybody had to take a cab. Ive been to Charing Cross one way and nearly to Ludgate Circus the other; and they were all engaged.

THE MOTHER. Did you try Trafalgar Square?

FREDDY. There wasn't one at Trafalgar Square.

THE DAUGHTER. Did you try?

FREDDY. I tried as far as Charing Cross Station. Did you expect me to walk to Hammersmith?

THE DAUGHTER. You havnt tried at all.

THE MOTHER. You really are very helpless, Freddy. Go again; and dont come back until you have found a cab.

FREDDY. I shall simply get soaked for nothing.

THE DAUGHTER. And what about us? Are we to stay here all night in this draught,[2] with next to nothing on? You selfish pig—

FREDDY. Oh, very well: I'll go, I'll go. [*He opens his umbrella and dashes off Strandwards, but comes into collision with a flower girl who is hurrying in for shelter, knocking her basket out of her hands. A blinding flash of lightning, followed instantly by a rattling peal of thunder, orchestrates the incident*].

THE FLOWER GIRL. Nah then, Freddy: look wh' y' gowin, deah.

---

1. first quarter: Fifteen minutes past the hour.

2. draught (draft): Draft.

FREDDY. Sorry [*he rushes off*].

THE FLOWER GIRL [*picking up her scattered flowers and replacing them in the basket*] Theres menners f' yer! Tə-oo banches o voylets trod into the mad. [*She sits down on the plinth[3] of the column sorting her flowers, on the lady's right. She is not at all a romantic figure. She is perhaps eighteen, perhaps twenty, hardly older. She wears a little sailor hat of black straw that has long been exposed to the dust and soot of London and has seldom if ever been brushed. Her hair needs washing rather badly: its mousy color can hardly be natural. She wears a shoddy black coat that reaches nearly to her knees and is shaped to her waist. She has a brown skirt with a coarse apron. Her boots are much the worse for wear. She is no doubt as clean as she can afford to be; but compared to the ladies she is very dirty. Her features are no worse than theirs; but their condition leaves something to be desired; and she needs the services of a dentist*].

THE MOTHER. How do you know that my son's name is Freddy, pray?

THE FLOWER GIRL. Ow, eez yə-ooa, san, is e? Wal, fewd dan y' də-ooty bawmz a mather should, eed now bettern to spawl a pore gel's flahrzn than ran away athaht pyin. Will ye-oo py me f'them? [*Here, with apologies, this desperate attempt to represent her dialect without a phonetic alphabet must be abandoned as unintelligible outside London*].

THE DAUGHTER. Do nothing of the sort, mother. The idea!

THE MOTHER. Please allow me, Clara. Have you any pennies?

THE DAUGHTER. No. Ive nothing smaller than sixpence.

THE FLOWER GIRL [*hopefully*] I can give you change for a tanner,[4] kind lady.

---

3. **plinth:** The block at the base of a column.
4. **tanner:** Slang for a sixpence.

THE MOTHER [*to* CLARA] Give it to me. [CLARA *parts reluctantly*]. Now [*to the* GIRL] This is for your flowers.

THE FLOWER GIRL. Thank you kindly, lady.

THE DAUGHTER. Make her give you the change. These things are only a penny a bunch.

THE MOTHER. Do hold your tongue, Clara. [*To the* GIRL] You can keep the change.

THE FLOWER GIRL. Oh, thank you, lady.

THE MOTHER. Now tell me how you know that young gentleman's name.

THE FLOWER GIRL. I didnt.

THE MOTHER. I heard you call him by it. Dont try to deceive me.

THE FLOWER GIRL [*protesting*] Who's trying to deceive you? I called him Freddy or Charlie same as you might yourself if you was talking to a stranger and wished to be pleasant.

THE DAUGHTER. Sixpence thrown away! Really, mamma, you might have spared Freddy that. [*She retreats in disgust behind the pillar*].

An elderly gentleman of the amiable military type rushes into the shelter, and closes a dripping umbrella. He is in the same plight as FREDDY, *very wet above the ankles. He is in evening dress, with a light overcoat. He takes the place left vacant by* THE DAUGHTER.

THE GENTLEMAN. Phew!

THE MOTHER. [*to the* GENTLEMAN] Oh, sir, is there any sign of its stopping?

THE GENTLEMAN. I'm afraid not. It started worse than ever about two minutes ago [*he goes to the plinth beside the* FLOWER GIRL; *puts up his foot on it; and stoops to turn down his trouser ends*].

THE MOTHER. Oh dear! [*She retires sadly and joins her daughter*].

THE FLOWER GIRL [taking advantage of the military gentleman's proximity to establish friendly relations with him] If it's worse, it's a sign it's nearly over. So cheer up, Captain; and buy a flower off a poor girl.

THE GENTLEMAN. I'm sorry. I havnt any change.

THE FLOWER GIRL. I can give you change, Captain.

THE GENTLEMAN. For a sovereign? Ive nothing less.

THE FLOWER GIRL. Garn! Oh do buy a flower off me, Captain. I can change half-a-crown. Take this for tuppence.

THE GENTLEMAN. Now dont be troublesome: theres a good girl. [Trying his pockets] I really havnt any change—Stop: heres three hapence, if thats any use to you [he retreats to the other pillar].

THE FLOWER GIRL [disappointed, but thinking three half-pence better than nothing] Thank you, sir.

THE BYSTANDER [to the GIRL] You be careful: give him a flower for it. Theres a bloke here behind taking down every blessed word youre saying. [All turn to the man who is taking notes].

THE FLOWER GIRL [springing up terrified] I aint done nothing wrong by speaking to the gentleman. Ive a right to sell flowers if I keep off the kerb. [Hysterically] I'm a respectable girl: so help me, I never spoke to him except to ask him to buy a flower off me.

General hubbub, mostly sympathetic to the FLOWER GIRL, but deprecating her excessive sensibility. Cries of Dont start hollerin. Who's hurting you? Nobody's going to touch you. Whats the good of fussing? Steady on. Easy, easy, etc., come from the elderly staid spectators, who pat her comfortingly. Less patient ones bid her shut her head, or ask her roughly what is wrong with her. A remoter group, not knowing what the matter is, crowd in and increase the noise with question and answer: What's the row? What-she do? Where is he? A tec[5] taking her down. What! him? Yes: him over there: Took money off the gentleman, etc.

THE FLOWER GIRL [breaking through them to the GENTLEMAN, crying wildly] Oh, sir, dont let him charge me. You dunno what it means to me. Theyll take away my character and drive me on the streets for speaking to gentlemen. They—

THE NOTE TAKER [coming forward on her right, the rest crowding after him] There! there! there! there! who's hurting you, you silly girl? What do you take me for?

THE BYSTANDER. It's aw rawt: e's a genleman: look at his bə-oots. [Explaining to the NOTE TAKER] She thought you was a copper's nark, sir.

THE NOTE TAKER [with quick interest] Whats a copper's nark?

THE BYSTANDER [inapt at definition] It's a—well, it's a copper's nark, as you might say. What else would you call it? A sort of informer.

THE FLOWER GIRL [still hysterical] I take my Bible oath I never said a word—

THE NOTE TAKER [overbearing but good-humored] Oh, shut up, shut up. Do I look like a policeman?

THE FLOWER GIRL [far from reassured] Then what did you take down my words for? How do I know whether you took me down right? You just shew me what youve wrote about me. [The NOTE TAKER opens his book and holds it steadily under her nose, though the pressure of the mob trying to read it over his shoulders would upset a weaker man]. Whats that? That aint proper writing. I cant read that.

THE NOTE TAKER. I can. [Reads, reproducing her pronunciation exactly] "Cheer ap, Keptin; n' baw ya flahr orf a pore gel."

5. tec: A slang abbreviation for detective.

THE FLOWER GIRL [*much distressed*] It's because I called him Captain. I meant no harm. [*To the* GENTLEMAN] Oh, sir, dont let him lay a charge agen me for a word like that. You—

THE GENTLEMAN. Charge! I make no charge. [*To the* NOTE TAKER] Really, sir, if you are a detective, you need not begin protecting me against molestation by young women until I ask you. Anybody could see that the girl meant no harm.

THE BYSTANDERS GENERALLY [*demonstrating against police espionage*] Course they could. What business is it of yours? You mind your own affairs. He wants promotion, he does. Taking down people's words! Girl never said a word to him. What harm if she did? Nice thing a girl cant shelter from the rain without being insulted, etc., etc., etc. [*She is conducted by the more sympathetic demonstrators back to her plinth, where she resumes her seat and struggles with her emotion*].

THE BYSTANDER. He aint a tec. He's a blooming busybody: thats what he is. I tell you, look at his bə-oots.

THE NOTE TAKER [*turning on him genially*] And how are all your people down at Selsey?

THE BYSTANDER [*suspiciously*] Who told you my people come from Selsey?

THE NOTE TAKER. Never you mind. They did. [*To the* GIRL] How do you come to be up so far east? You were born in Lisson Grove.

THE FLOWER GIRL [*appalled*] Oh, what harm is there in my leaving Lisson Grove? It wasnt fit for a pig to live in; and I had to pay four-and-six a week. [*In tears*] Oh, boo—hoo—oo—

THE NOTE TAKER. Live where you like; but stop that noise.

THE GENTLEMAN [*to the* GIRL] Come, come! he cant touch you: you have a right to live where you please.

A SARCASTIC BYSTANDER [*thrusting himself between the* NOTE TAKER *and the* GENTLEMAN] Park Lane, for instance. I'd like to go into the Housing Question with you, I would.

THE FLOWER GIRL [*subsiding into a brooding melancholy over her basket, and talking very low-spiritedly to herself*] I'm a good girl, I am.

THE SARCASTIC BYSTANDER [*not attending to her*] Do you know where I come from?

THE NOTE TAKER [*promptly*] Hoxton.

Titterings. Popular interest in the NOTE TAKER*'s performance increases.*

THE SARCASTIC ONE [*amazed*] Well, who said I didnt? Bly me! you know everything, you do.

THE FLOWER GIRL [*still nursing her sense of injury*] Aint no call to meddle with me, he aint.

THE BYSTANDER [*to her*] Of course he aint. Dont you stand it from him. [*To the* NOTE TAKER] See here: what call have you to know about people what never offered to meddle with you?

THE FLOWER GIRL. Let him say what he likes. I dont want to have no truck with him.

THE BYSTANDER. You take us for dirt under your feet, dont you? Catch you taking liberties with a gentleman!

THE SARCASTIC BYSTANDER. Yes: tell him where he come from if you want to go fortune-telling.

THE NOTE TAKER. Cheltenham, Harrow, Cambridge, and India.

THE GENTLEMAN. Quite right.

Great laughter. Reaction in the NOTE TAKER*'s favor. Exclamations of* He knows all about it. Told him proper. Hear him tell the toff[6] where he come from? *etc.*

---

6. toff: English slang for a fashionable person.

THE GENTLEMAN. May I ask, sir, do you do this for your living at a music hall?

THE NOTE TAKER. I've thought of that. Perhaps I shall some day.

The rain has stopped; and the persons on the outside of the crowd begin to drop off.

THE FLOWER GIRL [*resenting the reaction*] He's no gentleman, he aint, to interfere with a poor girl.

THE DAUGHTER [*out of patience, pushing her way rudely to the front and displacing the* GENTLEMAN, *who politely retires to the other side of the pillar*] What on earth is Freddy doing? I shall get pneumownia if I stay in this draught any longer.

THE NOTE TAKER [*to himself, hastily making a note of her pronunciation of "monia"*] Earlscourt.

THE DAUGHTER [*violently*] Will you please keep your impertinent remarks to yourself.

THE NOTE TAKER. Did I say that out loud? I didn't mean to. I beg your pardon. Your mother's Epsom, unmistakeably.

THE MOTHER [*advancing between the* DAUGHTER *and the* NOTE TAKER] How very curious! I was brought up in Largelady Park, near Epsom.

THE NOTE TAKER [*uproariously amused*] Ha! ha! What a devil of a name! Excuse me. [*To the* DAUGHTER] You want a cab, do you?

THE DAUGHTER. Dont dare speak to me.

THE MOTHER. Oh please, please, Clara. [*Her daughter repudiates her with an angry shrug and retires haughtily*] We should be so grateful to you, sir, if you found us a cab. [*The* NOTE TAKER *produces a whistle*] Oh, thank you. [*She joins her daughter*].
The NOTE TAKER *blows a piercing blast.*

THE SARCASTIC BYSTANDER. There! I knowed he was a plainclothes copper.

THE BYSTANDER. That aint a police whistle: thats a sporting whistle.

THE FLOWER GIRL [*still preoccupied with her wounded feelings*] He's no right to take away my character. My character is the same to me as any lady's.

THE NOTE TAKER. I dont know whether youve noticed it; but the rain stopped about two minutes ago.

THE BYSTANDER. So it has. Why didn't you say so before? and us losing our time listening to your silliness! [*He walks off towards the Strand*].

THE SARCASTIC BYSTANDER. I can tell where you come from. You come from Anwell. Go back there.

THE NOTE TAKER [*helpfully*] Hanwell.

THE SARCASTIC BYSTANDER [*affecting great distinction of speech*] Thenk you, teacher. Haw haw! So long [*he touches his hat with mock respect and strolls off*].

THE FLOWER GIRL. Frightening people like that! How would he like it himself?

THE MOTHER. It's quite fine now, Clara. We can walk to a motor bus. Come. [*She gathers her skirts above her ankles and hurries off towards the Strand*].

THE DAUGHTER. But the cab—[*her mother is out of hearing*]. Oh, how tiresome! [*She follows angrily*].

All the rest have gone except the NOTE TAKER, *the* GENTLEMAN, *and the* FLOWER GIRL, *who sits arranging her basket, and still pitying herself in murmurs.*

THE FLOWER GIRL. Poor girl! Hard enough for her to live without being worrited and chivied.[7]

THE GENTLEMAN [*returning to his former place on the* NOTE TAKER*'s left*] How do you do it, if I may ask?

THE NOTE TAKER. Simple phonetics. The science of speech. Thats my profession: also

_____

7. worrited and chivied: Worried and tormented.

my hobby. Happy is the man who can make a living by his hobby! You can spot an Irishman or a Yorkshireman by his brogue. *I* can place any man within six miles. I can place him within two miles in London. Sometimes within two streets.

THE FLOWER GIRL. Ought to be ashamed of himself, unmanly coward.

THE GENTLEMAN. But is there a living in that?

THE NOTE TAKER. Oh yes. Quite a fat one. This is an age of upstarts. Men begin in Kentish Town with £80 a year, and end in Park Lane with a hundred thousand. They want to drop Kentish Town; but they give themselves away every time they open their mouths. Now I can teach them—

THE FLOWER GIRL. Let him mind his own business and leave a poor girl—

THE NOTE TAKER [*explosively*] Woman: cease this detestable boohooing instantly; or else seek the shelter of some other place of worship.

THE FLOWER GIRL [*with feeble defiance*] Ive a right to be here if I like, same as you.

THE NOTE TAKER. A woman who utters such depressing and disgusting sounds has no right to be anywhere—no right to live. Remember that you are a human being with a soul and the divine gift of articulate speech: that your native language is the language of Shakespear and Milton and The Bible; and dont sit there crooning like a bilious pigeon.

THE FLOWER GIRL [*quite overwhelmed, looking up at him in mingled wonder and deprecation without daring to raise her head*] Ah-ah-ah-ow-ow-ow-oo!

THE NOTE TAKER [*whipping out his book*] Heavens! what a sound! [*He writes; then holds out the book and reads, reproducing her vowels exactly*] Ah-ah-ah-ow-ow-ow-oo!

THE FLOWER GIRL [*tickled by the performance, and laughing in spite of herself*] Garn!

THE NOTE TAKER. You see this creature with her kerbstone English: the English that will keep her in the gutter to the end of her days. Well, sir, in three months I could pass that girl off as a duchess at an ambassador's garden party. I could even get her a place as lady's maid or shop assistant, which requires better English.

THE FLOWER GIRL. What's that you say?

THE NOTE TAKER. Yes, you squashed cabbage leaf, you disgrace to the noble architecture of these columns, you incarnate insult to the English language: I could pass you off as the Queen of Sheba. [*To the* GENTLEMAN] Can you believe that?

THE GENTLEMAN. Of course I can. I am myself a student of Indian dialects; and—

THE NOTE TAKER [*eagerly*] Are you? Do you know Colonel Pickering, the author of Spoken Sanscrit?

THE GENTLEMAN. I am Colonel Pickering. Who are you?

THE NOTE TAKER. Henry Higgins, author of Higgins's Universal Alphabet.

PICKERING [*with enthusiasm*] I came from India to meet you.

HIGGINS. I was going to India to meet you.

PICKERING. Where do you live?

HIGGINS. 27A Wimpole Street. Come and see me tomorrow.

PICKERING. I'm at the Carlton. Come with me now and lets have a jaw over some supper.

HIGGINS. Right you are.

THE FLOWER GIRL [*to* PICKERING, *as he passes her*] Buy a flower, kind gentleman. I'm short for my lodging.

PICKERING. I really havnt any change. I'm sorry [*he goes away*].

HIGGINS [*shocked at the* GIRL's *mendacity*] Liar. You said you could change half-a-crown.

THE FLOWER GIRL [*rising in desperation*] You ought to be stuffed with nails, you ought. [*Flinging the basket at his feet*] Take the whole blooming basket for sixpence.

The church clock strikes the second quarter.

HIGGINS [*hearing in it the voice of God, rebuking him for his Pharisaic*[8] *want of charity to the poor girl*] A reminder. [*He raises his hat solemnly; then throws a handful of money into the basket and follows* PICKERING].

THE FLOWER GIRL [*picking up a half-crown*] Ah-ow-ooh! [*Picking up a couple of florins*] Aaah-ow-ooh! [*Picking up several coins*] Aaaaah-ow-ooh! [*Picking up a half-sovereign*] Aaaaaaaaaaaah-ow-ooh!!!

FREDDY [*springing out of a taxicab*] Got one at last. Hello! [*To the* GIRL] Where are the two ladies that were here?

THE FLOWER GIRL. They walked to the bus when the rain stopped.

FREDDY. And left me with a cab on my hands! Damnation!

THE FLOWER GIRL [*with grandeur*] Never mind, young man. I'm going home in a taxi. [*She sails off to the cab. The driver puts his hand behind him and holds the door firmly shut against her. Quite understanding his mistrust, she shews him her handful of money*]. A taxi fare aint no object to me, Charlie. [*He grins and opens the door*]. Here. What about the basket?

THE TAXIMAN. Give it here. Tuppence extra.

LIZA. No: I dont want nobody to see it. [*She crushes it into the cab and gets in, continuing the conversation through the window*] Good-bye, Freddy.

FREDDY [*dazedly raising his hat*] Goodbye.

TAXIMAN. Where to?

---

8. **Pharisaic** (far′ ə sā′ ik) *adj.*: Referring to the Pharisees, an ancient Jewish party or fellowship that carefully observed the written law; hypocritically self-righteous.

LIZA. Bucknam Pellis [Buckingham Palace].

TAXIMAN. What d'ye mean—Bucknam Pellis?

LIZA. Dont you know where it is? In the Green Park, where the King lives. Goodbye, Freddy. Dont let me keep you standing there. Goodbye.

FREDDY. Goodbye [*He goes*].

TAXIMAN. Here? Whats this about Bucknam Pellis? What business have you at Bucknam Pellis?

LIZA. Of course I havnt none. But I wasn't going to let him know that. You drive me home.

TAXIMAN. And wheres home?

LIZA. Angel Court, Drury Lane, next Meiklejohn's oil shop.

TAXIMAN. That sounds more like it, Judy. [*He drives off*].

*   *   *   *   *   *

Let us follow the taxi to the entrance to Angel Court, a narrow little archway between two shops, one of them Meiklejohn's oil shop. When it stops there, Eliza gets out, dragging her basket with her.

LIZA. How much?

TAXIMAN [*indicating the taximeter*] Cant you read? A shilling.

LIZA. A shilling for two minutes!!

TAXIMAN. Two minutes or ten: it's all the same.

LIZA. Well, I dont call it right.

TAXIMAN. Ever been in a taxi before?

LIZA [*with dignity*] Hundreds and thousands of times, young man.

TAXIMAN [*laughing at her*] Good for you, Judy. Keep the shilling, darling, with best love from all at home. Good luck! [*He drives off*].

LIZA [*humiliated*] Impidence!

She picks up the basket and trudges up the alley with it to her lodging: a small room with very old wall paper hanging loose in the damp places. A broken pane in the window is mended with paper. A portrait of a popular actor and a fashion plate of ladies' dresses, all wildly beyond poor ELIZA*'s means, both torn from newspapers, are pinned up on the wall. A birdcage hangs in the window; but its tenant died long ago: it remains as a memorial only.*

These are the only visible luxuries: the rest is the irreducible minimum of poverty's needs: a wretched bed heaped with all sorts of coverings that have any warmth in them, a draped packing case with a basin and jug on it and a little looking glass over it, a chair and table, the refuse of some suburban kitchen, and an American alarum clock on the shelf above the unused fireplace: the whole lighted with a gas lamp with a penny in the slot meter. Rent: four shillings a week.

Here Eliza, chronically weary, but too excited to go to bed, sits, counting her new riches and dreaming and planning what to do with them, until the gas goes out, when she enjoys for the first time the sensation of being able to put in another penny without grudging it. This prodigal mood does not extinguish her gnawing sense of the need for economy sufficiently to prevent her from calculating that she can dream and plan in bed more cheaply and warmly than sitting up without a fire. So she takes off her shawl and skirt and adds them to the miscellaneous bedclothes. Then she kicks off her shoes and gets into bed without any further change.

RESPONDING TO THE SELECTION

Your Response

1. How important do you think speech patterns such as pronunciation, vocabulary, and grammar are in a person's life? Explain.

Recalling

2. What kind of reformer does Shaw claim, in the Preface, that "we need most today"?
3. (a) What is the point of Current Shorthand? (b) Why does Shaw find it superior to previous systems?
4. (a) Where and when does the play open? (b) What are the mother and daughter doing?
5. How does The Note Taker amaze the crowd?
6. What feat does The Note Taker say he could accomplish in three months?

Interpreting

7. Based on Shaw's description of Henry Sweet in the Preface, what traits might you say the two men shared?

8. (a) What effect does Shaw achieve by spelling out words according to the speaker's pronunciation? (b) by identifying characters by labels at first?

Applying

9. In the seventh century, Ali ibn-abi-Talib, who was fourth caliph of the Muslims, wrote, "A man is hid under his tongue." Explain the meaning of this quotation.

ANALYZING LITERATURE

Understanding Historical Context

Historical context refers both to a play's historical validity (if it depicts events at a time other than that at which it was written) and to events and attitudes of the author's day that may have been influential. *Pygmalion* provides us with a glimpse of English city life shortly after the turn of the century. Tell what the following details from Act I reveal about that lifestyle, and describe any differences you might expect today in your own city.

1. Freddy's searching for a cab while his mother and sister remain sheltered.
2. The crowd's suspicions about The Note Taker.
3. The verbal exchanges (a) between The Note Taker and The Flower Girl. (b) between The Flower Girl and the Taximan.

CRITICAL THINKING AND READING

Generalizing About People

The Note Taker in Act I bases his assumptions about the speech habits of Eliza and the others on well-founded **generalizations,** or observations that apply to classes of people. While such observations, when based on scientific principles as they are here, can be valid, generalizing as a rule is a dangerous practice. Tell what generalizations underlie the following, and judge their validity.

1. Shaw's remarking in the Preface that "it is impossible for an Englishman to open his mouth without making some other Englishman despise him."
2. Eliza's assuming that Higgins is a "tec."
3. The crowd's sizing up Pickering as a "toff."
4. The Taximan's holding the door shut against Eliza when she first approaches.

THINKING AND WRITING

Writing About Historical Context

Reread Shaw's Preface to the play. Then write a short essay evaluating the Preface's contribution to the play's historical context. Begin by asking yourself the following questions. How relevant are Shaw's attitudes about language to the events of Act I? How important is the background information on Henry Sweet? On systems of shorthand? When you revise, make sure you have provided details from the Preface and from Act I to support your thesis. Proofread your essay and prepare a final draft.

LEARNING OPTIONS

1. **Speaking and Listening.** Locate a recording of *Pygmalion* or *My Fair Lady,* the musical that is based on the play, and listen to it in class. Discuss the ways in which the characters' speech patterns compare with the ways you imagined they would sound.
2. **Language.** A dialect is a collection of speech habits that typifies a particular social class or region. A dialect may vary from the standard form of a language in pronunciation, in grammar, and in the use of certain expressions. Whatever its defining features may be, every dialect is *systematic*—or governed by rules. The cockney accent used by Eliza is used to this day by some inhabitants of London's East End. With two or three classmates read aloud examples of Eliza's speech. After "translating" them into standard English, develop as many rules of pronunciation and grammar as you can for the cockney dialect.

GUIDE FOR INTERPRETING

Pygmalion, Act II

Writers' Techniques

Character Development. Character development is the fleshing out of a character in a work of fiction through confrontations with other characters or forces. Depending upon the extent to which a character changes as a result of these confrontations, he or she is said to be either static or dynamic. A *static* character is one who remains relatively unchanged by events. A *dynamic* character, by contrast, is one who changes considerably, sometimes shedding altogether character traits that he or she possessed earlier in the work. In Shakespeare's *The Taming of the Shrew,* for example, the character Kate begins as a feisty, hot-tempered individual but, through the course of the play, is transformed into a mellow, even-tempered person.

Commentary

Shaw's own character, like the ones he created, was developed through encounters with different forces. These forces must have been powerful, for at twenty-four Shaw did not seem destined for greatness. He was considered a total failure, ignored by his mother, despised by his sister, passed over by relatives and family friends. St. John Ervine describes him as "tall, over six feet in height, and pale with the pallor of people with red hair, although his was not notably red. . . . It was worn flat on his head, divided in the middle, and was matched on his chin by a thin, scrubby beard which was slow in its growth. . . . His eyes were his most notable feature, far more notable than the long, slightly twisted nose which seemed at first sight to prevail over the whole face, or the tightly-drawn lips or the large projecting ears. The eyebrows . . . revealed already the strange dissimilarity between the two sides of his face. . . . One side was genial, almost benign and full of fun and laughter; the other side had a brooding look that was to become almost tormented in his old age. . . . He wears the features of a sober young man, over-earnest, perhaps about the state of the world and eager to deliver messages, though unable yet to find an audience which will listen for more than a minute or two; but he shows in his laughing eye as well as in the eye that is somber, and in the resolute lips, that he will one day make the casual and disinterested passers-by stand and look and listen."

Focus

What motivates people to change? Why do people decide to alter the way they look, behave, or even speak? Freewrite, exploring your thoughts on these questions.

ACT II

Next day at 11 A.M. HIGGINS'S *laboratory in Wimpole Street. It is a room on the first floor, looking on the street, and was meant for the drawing room. The double doors are in the middle of the back wall; and persons entering find in the corner to their right two tall file cabinets at right angles to one another against the walls. In this corner stands a flat writing-table, on which are a phonograph, a laryngoscope,[1] a row of tiny organ pipes with a bellows, a set of lamp chimneys for singing flames with burners attached to a gas plug in the wall by an indiarubber tube, several tuning-forks of different sizes, a life-size image of half a human head, shewing in section the vocal organs, and a box containing a supply of wax cylinders for the phonograph.*

Further down the room, on the same side, is a fireplace, with a comfortable leather-covered easy-chair at the side of the hearth nearest the door, and a coal-scuttle. There is a clock on the mantlepiece. Between the fireplace and the phonograph table is a stand for newspapers.

On the other side of the central door, to the left of the visitor, is a cabinet of shallow drawers. On it is a telephone and the telephone directory. The corner beyond, and most of the side wall, is occupied by a grand piano, with the keyboard at the end furthest from the door, and a bench for the players extending the full length of the keyboard. On the piano is a dessert dish heaped with fruit and sweets, mostly chocolates.

The middle of the room is clear. Besides the easy-chair, the piano bench, and two chairs at the phonograph table, there is one stray chair. It stands near the fireplace. On the walls, engravings: mostly Piranesis[2] and mezzotint[3] portraits. No paintings.

---

1. laryngoscope (lə riŋ′ gō skōp′) *n*.: An instrument for examining the throat.
2. Piranesis (pēr′ ə nā′ zēz): Works of Italian artist Giambattista Piranesi (1720–1778).
3. mezzotint: An engraving made from a copper or steel plate.

PICKERING *is seated at the table, putting down some cards and a tuning-fork which he has been using.* HIGGINS *is standing up near him, closing two or three file drawers which are hanging out. He appears in the morning light as a robust, vital, appetizing sort of man of forty or thereabouts, dressed in a professional-looking black frock-coat with a white linen collar and black silk tie. He is of energetic, scientific type, heartily, even violently interested in everything that can be studied as a scientific subject, and careless about himself and other people, including their feelings. He is, in fact, but for his years and size, rather like a very impetuous baby "taking notice" eagerly and loudly, and requiring almost as much watching to keep him out of unintended mischief. His manner varies from genial bullying when he is in a good humor to stormy petulance when anything goes wrong; but he is so entirely frank and void of malice that he remains likeable even in his least reasonable moments.*

HIGGINS [*as he shuts the last drawer*] Well, I think thats the whole show.

PICKERING. It's really amazing. I havnt taken half of it in, you know.

HIGGINS. Would you like to go over any of it again?

PICKERING [*rising and coming to the fireplace, where he plants himself with his back to the fire*] No, thank you: not now. I'm quite done up for this morning.

HIGGINS [*following him, and standing beside him on his left*] Tired of listening to sounds?

PICKERING. Yes. It's a fearful strain. I rather fancied myself because I can pronounce twenty-four distinct vowel sounds; but your hundred and thirty beat me. I cant hear a bit of difference between most of them.

HIGGINS [*chuckling, and going over to the piano to eat sweets*] Oh, that comes with practice. You hear no difference at first; but you keep on listening, and presently you find theyre all as different as A from B. [MRS PEARCE *looks in; she is* HIGGINS's *housekeeper*]. Whats the matter?

MRS PEARCE [*hesitating, evidently perplexed*] A young woman asks to see you, sir.

HIGGINS. A young woman! What does she want?

MRS PEARCE. Well, sir, she says youll be glad to see her when you know what she's come about. She's quite a common girl, sir. Very common indeed. I should have sent her away, only I thought perhaps you wanted her to talk into your machines. I hope Ive not done wrong; but really you see such queer people sometimes—youll excuse me, I'm sure, sir—

HIGGINS. Oh, thats all right, Mrs Pearce. Has she an interesting accent?

MRS PEARCE. Oh, something dreadful, sir, really. I dont know how you can take an interest in it.

HIGGINS [*to* PICKERING] Lets have her up. Shew her up, Mrs Pearce [*he rushes across to his working table and picks out a cylinder to use on the phonograph*].

MRS PEARCE [*only half resigned to it*] Very well, sir. It's for you to say. [*She goes downstairs*].

HIGGINS. This is rather a bit of luck. I'll shew you how I make records. We'll set her talking; and I'll take it down first in Bell's Visible Speech; then in broad Romic; and then we'll get her on the phonograph so that you can turn her on as often as you like with the written transcript before you.

MRS PEARCE [*returning*] This is the young woman, sir.

The FLOWER GIRL *enters in state. She has a hat with three ostrich feathers, orange, sky-blue, and red. She has a nearly clean apron, and the shoddy coat has been tidied a little. The pathos of this deplorable figure, with its innocent vanity and consequential air, touches* PICKERING, *who has already straightened himself in the presence of* MRS PEARCE. *But as to* HIGGINS, *the only distinction he makes between men and women is that when he is neither bullying nor exclaiming to the heavens against some feather-weight cross,*[4] *he coaxes women as a child coaxes its nurse when it wants to get anything out of her.*

HIGGINS [*brusquely, recognizing her with unconcealed disappointment, and at once, babylike, making an intolerable grievance of it*] Why, this is the girl I jotted down last night. She's no use: I've got all the records I want of the Lisson Grove lingo; and I'm not going to waste another cylinder on it. [*To the* GIRL] Be off with you: I dont want you.

THE FLOWER GIRL. Dont you be so saucy. You aint heard what I come for yet. [*To* MRS PEARCE, *who is waiting at the door for further instructions*] Did you tell him I come in a taxi?

MRS PEARCE. Nonsense, girl! What do you think a gentleman like Mr Higgins cares what you came in?

THE FLOWER GIRL. Oh, we are proud! He aint above giving lessons, not him: I heard him say so. Well, I aint come here to ask for any compliment; and if my money's not good enough I can go elsewhere.

HIGGINS. Good enough for what?

THE FLOWER GIRL. Good enough for yə-oo. Now you know, dont you? I've come to have lessons, I am. And to pay for em tə-oo: make no mistake.

HIGGINS [*stupent*[5]] Well!!! [*Recovering his breath with a gasp*] What do you expect me to say to you?

THE FLOWER GIRL. Well, if you was a gentleman, you might ask me to sit down, I think. Dont I tell you I'm bringing you business?

---

4. **feather-weight cross:** A very minor inconvenience.
5. **stupent:** Astonished.

HIGGINS. Pickering: shall we ask this baggage to sit down, or shall we throw her out of the window?

THE FLOWER GIRL [*running away in terror to the piano, where she turns at bay*] Ah-ah-oh-ow-ow-ow-oo! [*Wounded and whimpering*] I wont be called a baggage when Ive offered to pay like any lady.

Motionless, the two men stare at her from the other side of the room, amazed.

PICKERING [*gently*] But what is it you want?

THE FLOWER GIRL. I want to be a lady in a flower shop stead of sellin at the corner of Tottenham Court Road. But they wont take me unless I can talk more genteel. He said he could teach me. Well, here I am ready to pay him—not asking any favor—and he treats me zif I was dirt.

MRS PEARCE. How can you be such a foolish ignorant girl as to think you could afford to pay Mr Higgins?

THE FLOWER GIRL. Why shouldnt I? I know what lessons cost as well as you do; and I'm ready to pay.

HIGGINS. How much?

THE FLOWER GIRL [*coming back to him, triumphant*] Now youre talking! I thought youd come off it when you saw a chance of getting back a bit of what you chucked at me last night. [*Confidentially*] Youd had a drop in,[6] hadn't you?

HIGGINS [*peremptorily*] Sit down.

THE FLOWER GIRL. Oh, if youre going to make a compliment of it—

HIGGINS [*thundering at her*] Sit down.

MRS PEARCE [*severely*] Sit down, girl. Do as youre told.

THE FLOWER GIRL. Ah-ah-ah-ow-ow-oo! [*She stands, half rebellious, half bewildered*].

---

6. **had a drop in:** Been drinking.

PICKERING [*very courteous*] Wont you sit down? [*He places the stray chair near the hearthrug between himself and* HIGGINS].

LIZA [*coyly*] Dont mind if I do. [*She sits down.* PICKERING *returns to the hearthrug*].

HIGGINS. Whats your name?

THE FLOWER GIRL. Liza Doolittle.

HIGGINS [*declaiming gravely*]
    Eliza, Elizabeth, Betsy and Bess,
    They went to the woods to get a bird's nes':

PICKERING. They found a nest with four eggs in it:

HIGGINS. They took one apiece, and left three in it.
They laugh heartily at their own fun.
LIZA. Oh, dont be silly.

MRS PEARCE [*placing herself behind* ELIZA's *chair*] You mustnt speak to the gentleman like that.

LIZA. Well, why wont he speak sensible to me?

HIGGINS. Come back to business. How much do you propose to pay me for the lessons?

LIZA. Oh, I know whats right. A lady friend of mine gets French lessons for eighteenpence an hour from a real French gentleman. Well, you wouldnt have the face to ask me the same for teaching me my own language as you would for French; so I wont give more than a shilling. Take it or leave it.

HIGGINS [*walking up and down the room, rattling his keys and his cash in his pockets*] You know, Pickering, if you consider a shilling, not as a simple shilling, but as a percentage of this girl's income, it works out as fully equivalent to sixty or seventy guineas from a millionaire.

PICKERING. How so?

HIGGINS. Figure it out. A millionaire has about £150 a day. She earns about half-a-crown.

LIZA [haughtily] Who told you I only—

HIGGINS [continuing] She offers me two-fifths of her day's income for a lesson. Two-fifths of a millionaire's income for a day would be somewhere about £60. It's handsome. By George, it's enormous! it's the biggest offer I ever had.

LIZA [rising, terrified] Sixty pounds! What are you talking? I never offered you sixty pounds. Where would I get—

HIGGINS. Hold your tongue.

LIZA [weeping] But I aint got sixty pounds. Oh—

MRS PEARCE. Dont cry, you silly girl. Sit down. Nobody is going to touch your money.

HIGGINS. Somebody is going to touch you, with a broomstick, if you dont stop snivelling. Sit down.

LIZA [obeying slowly] Ah-ah-ah-ow-oo-o! One would think you was my father.

HIGGINS. If I decide to teach you, I'll be worse than two fathers to you. Here [he offers her his silk handkerchief]!

LIZA. Whats this for?

HIGGINS. To wipe your eyes. To wipe any part of your face that feels moist. Remember: thats your handkerchief; and thats your sleeve. Dont mistake the one for the other if you wish to become a lady in a shop.
LIZA, utterly bewildered, stares helplessly at him.

MRS PEARCE. It's no use talking to her like that, Mr Higgins: she doesnt understand you. Besides, youre quite wrong: she doesnt do it that way at all [she takes the handkerchief].

LIZA [snatching it] Here! You give me that handkerchief. He gev it to me, not to you.

PICKERING [laughing] He did. I think it must be regarded as her property, Mrs Pearce.

MRS PEARCE [resigning herself] Serve you right, Mr Higgins.

PICKERING. Higgins: I'm interested. What about the ambassador's garden party? I'll say youre the greatest teacher alive if you make that good. I'll bet you all the expenses of the experiment you cant do it. And I'll pay for the lessons.

LIZA. Oh, you are real good. Thank you, Captain.

HIGGINS [tempted, looking at her] It's almost irresistible. She's so deliciously low—so horribly dirty—

LIZA [protesting extremely] Ah-ah-ah-ah-ow-ow-oo-oo!!! I aint dirty: I washed my face and hands afore I come, I did.

PICKERING. Youre certainly not going to turn her head with flattery, Higgins.

MRS PEARCE [uneasy] Oh, dont say that, sir: theres more ways than one of turning a girl's head; and nobody can do it better than Mr Higgins, though he may not always mean it. I do hope, sir, you wont encourage him to do anything foolish.

HIGGINS [becoming excited as the idea grows on him] What is life but a series of inspired follies? The difficulty is to find them to do. Never lose a chance: it doesnt come every day. I shall make a duchess of this draggle-tailed guttersnipe.

LIZA [strongly deprecating this view of her] Ah-ah-ah-ow-ow-oo!

HIGGINS [carried away] Yes: in six months —in three if she has a good ear and a quick tongue—I'll take her anywhere and pass her off as anything. We'll start today: now! this moment! Take her away and clean her, Mrs Pearce. Monkey Brand,[7] if it wont come off any other way. Is there a good fire in the kitchen?

MRS PEARCE [protesting] Yes; but—

HIGGINS [storming on] Take all her clothes off and burn them. Ring up Whitely or some-

---

7. **Monkey Brand:** A strong cleaning agent.

body for new ones. Wrap her up in brown paper til they come.

LIZA. Youre no gentleman, youre not, to talk of such things. I'm a good girl, I am; and I know what the like of you are, I do.

HIGGINS. We want none of your Lisson Grove prudery here, young woman. Youve got to learn to behave like a duchess. Take her away, Mrs Pearce. If she gives you any trouble, wallop her.

LIZA [*springing up and running between* PICKERING *and* MRS PEARCE *for protection*] No! I'll call the police, I will.

MRS PEARCE. But Ive no place to put her.

HIGGINS. Put her in the dustbin.

LIZA. Ah-ah-ah-ow-ow-oo!

PICKERING. O come, Higgins! be reasonable.

MRS PEARCE [*resolutely*] You must be reasonable, Mr Higgins: really you must. You cant walk over everybody like this.

HIGGINS, *thus scolded, subsides. The hurricane is succeeded by a zephyr of amiable surprise.*

HIGGINS [*with professional exquisiteness of modulation*] I walk over everybody! My dear Mrs Pearce, my dear Pickering, I never had the slightest intention of walking over anyone. All I propose is that we should be kind to this poor girl. We must help her to prepare and fit herself for her new station in life. If I did not express myself clearly it was because I did not wish to hurt her delicacy, or yours.

LIZA, *reassured, steals back to her chair.*

MRS PEARCE [*to* PICKERING] Well, did you ever hear anything like that, sir?

PICKERING [*laughing heartily*] Never, Mrs Pearce: never.

HIGGINS [*patiently*] Whats the matter?

MRS PEARCE. Well, the matter is, sir, that you cant take a girl up like that as if you were

picking up a pebble on the beach.

HIGGINS. Why not?

MRS PEARCE. Why not! But you dont know anything about her. What about her parents? She may be married.

LIZA. Garn!

HIGGINS. There! As the girl very properly says, Garn! Married indeed! Dont you know that a woman of that class looks a worn out drudge of fifty a year after she's married?

LIZA. Whood marry me?

HIGGINS [*suddenly resorting to the most thrillingly beautiful low tones in his best elocutionary style*] By George, Eliza, the streets will be strewn with the bodies of men shooting themselves for your sake before Ive done with you.

MRS PEARCE. Nonsense, sir. You mustnt talk like that to her.

LIZA [*rising and squaring herself determinedly*] I'm going away. He's off his chump, he is. I dont want no balmies teaching me.

HIGGINS [*wounded in his tenderest point by her insensibility to his elocution*] Oh, indeed! I'm mad, am I? Very well, Mrs Pearce: you neednt order the new clothes for her. Throw her out.

LIZA [*whimpering*] Nah-ow. You got no right to touch me.

MRS PEARCE. You see now what comes of being saucy. [*Indicating the door*] This way, please.

LIZA [*almost in tears*] I didnt want no clothes. I wouldnt have taken them [*she throws away the handkerchief*]. I can buy my own clothes.

HIGGINS [*deftly retrieving the handkerchief and intercepting her on her reluctant way to the door*] Youre an ungrateful wicked girl. This is my return for offering to take you out of the gutter and dress you beautifully and make a lady of you.

MRS PEARCE. Stop, Mr Higgins. I wont allow it. It's you that are wicked. Go home to your parents, girl; and tell them to take better care of you.

LIZA. I aint got no parents. They told me I was big enough to earn my own living and turned me out.

MRS PEARCE. Wheres your mother?

LIZA. I aint got no mother. Her that turned me out was my sixth stepmother. But I done without them. And I'm a good girl, I am.

HIGGINS. Very well, then, what on earth is all this fuss about? The girl doesnt belong to anybody—is no use to anybody but me. [*He goes to* MRS PEARCE *and begins coaxing*]. You can adopt her, Mrs Pearce: I'm sure a daughter would be a great amusement to you. Now don't make any more fuss. Take her downstairs; and—

MRS PEARCE. But whats to become of her? Is she to be paid anything? Do be sensible, sir.

HIGGINS. Oh, pay her whatever is necessary: put it down in the housekeeping book. [*Impatiently*] What on earth will she want with money? She'll have her food and her clothes. She'll only drink if you give her money.

LIZA [*turning on him*] Oh you are a brute. It's a lie: nobody ever saw the sign of liquor on me. [*To* PICKERING] Oh, sir: youre a gentleman: dont let him speak to me like that.

PICKERING [*in good-humored remonstrance*] Does it occur to you, Higgins, that the girl has some feelings?

HIGGINS [*looking critically at her*] Oh no, I dont think so. Not any feelings that we need bother about. [*Cheerily*] Have you, Eliza?

LIZA. I got my feelings same as anyone else.

HIGGINS [*to* PICKERING, *reflectively*] You see the difficulty?

PICKERING. Eh? What difficulty?

HIGGINS. To get her to talk grammar. The mere pronunciation is easy enough.

LIZA. I dont want to talk grammar. I want to talk like a lady in a flower-shop.

MRS PEARCE. Will you please keep to the point, Mr Higgins. I want to know on what terms the girl is to be here. Is she to have any wages? And what is to become of her when youve finished your teaching? You must look ahead a little.

HIGGINS [*impatiently*] Whats to become of her if I leave her in the gutter? Tell me that, Mrs Pearce.

MRS PEARCE. Thats her own business, not yours, Mr Higgins.

HIGGINS. Well, when Ive done with her, we can throw her back into the gutter; and then it will be her own business again; so thats all right.

LIZA. Oh, youve no feeling heart in you: you dont care for nothing but yourself. [*She rises and takes the floor resolutely*]. Here! Ive had enough of this. I'm going [*making for the door*]. You ought to be ashamed of yourself, you ought.

HIGGINS [*snatching a chocolate cream from the piano, his eyes suddenly beginning to twinkle with mischief*] Have some chocolates, Eliza.

LIZA [*halting, tempted*] How do I know what might be in them? Ive heard of girls being drugged by the like of you.

HIGGINS *whips out his penknife; cuts a chocolate in two; puts one half into his mouth and bolts it; and offers her the other half.*

HIGGINS. Pledge of good faith, Eliza. I eat one half: you eat the other. [LIZA *opens her mouth to retort: he pops the half chocolate into it*]. You shall have boxes of them, barrels of them, every day. You shall live on them. Eh?

LIZA [*who has disposed of the chocolate after being nearly choked by it*] I wouldnt have ate it, only I'm too ladylike to take it out of my mouth.

HIGGINS. Listen, Eliza. I think you said you came in a taxi.

LIZA. Well, what if I did? Ive as good a right to take a taxi as anyone else.

HIGGINS. You have, Eliza; and in future you shall have as many taxis as you want. You shall go up and down and round the town in a taxi every day. Think of that, Eliza.

MRS PEARCE. Mr Higgins: youre tempting the girl. It's not right. She should think of the future.

HIGGINS. At her age! Nonsense! Time enough to think of the future when you havnt any future to think of. No, Eliza: do as this lady does: think of other people's futures; but never think of your own. Think of chocolates, and taxis, and gold, and diamonds.

LIZA. No: I dont want no gold and no diamonds. I'm a good girl, I am. [*She sits down again, with an attempt at dignity*].

HIGGINS. You shall remain so, Eliza, under the care of Mrs Pearce. And you shall marry an officer in the Guards, with a beautiful moustache: the son of a marquis, who will disinherit him for marrying you, but will relent when he sees your beauty and goodness—

PICKERING. Excuse me, Higgins; but I really must interfere. Mrs Pearce is quite right. If this girl is to put herself in your hands for six months for an experiment in teaching, she must understand thoroughly what she's doing.

HIGGINS. How can she? She's incapable of understanding anything. Besides, do any of

us understand what we are doing? If we did, would we ever do it?

PICKERING. Very clever, Higgins; but not to the present point. [*To* ELIZA] Miss Doolittle—

LIZA [*overwhelmed*] Ah-ah-ow-oo!

HIGGINS. There! Thats all youll get out of Eliza. Ah-ah-ow-oo! No use explaining. As a military man you ought to know that. Give her her orders: thats enough for her. Eliza: you are to live here for the next six months, learning how to speak beautifully, like a lady in a florist's shop. If youre good and do whatever youre told, you shall sleep in a proper bedroom, and have lots to eat, and money to buy chocolates and take rides in taxis. If youre naughty and idle you will sleep in the back kitchen among the black beetles, and be walloped by Mrs Pearce with a broomstick. At the end of six months you shall go to Buckingham Palace in a carriage, beautifully dressed. If the King finds out youre not a lady, you will be taken by the police to the Tower of London, where your head will be cut off as a warning to other presumptuous flower girls. If you are not found out, you shall have a present of seven-and-sixpence to start life with as a lady in a shop. If you refuse this offer you will be a most ungrateful wicked girl; and the angels will weep for you. [*To* PICKERING] Now are you satisfied, Pickering? [*To* MRS PEARCE] Can I put it more plainly and fairly, Mrs Pearce?

MRS PEARCE [*patiently*] I think youd better let me speak to the girl properly in private. I dont know that I can take charge of her or consent to the arrangement at all. Of course I know you dont mean her any harm; but when you get what you call interested in people's accents, you never think or care what may happen to them or you. Come with me, Eliza.

HIGGINS. Thats all right. Thank you, Mrs Pearce. Bundle her off to the bath-room.

LIZA [*rising reluctantly and suspiciously*] Youre a great bully, you are. I wont stay here if I dont like. I wont let nobody wallop me. I never asked to go to Bucknam Palace, I didnt. I was never in trouble with the police, not me. I'm a good girl—

MRS PEARCE. Dont answer back, girl. You dont understand the gentleman. Come with me. [*She leads the way to the door, and holds it open for* ELIZA].

LIZA [*as she goes out*] Well, what I say is right. I wont go near the King, not if I'm going to have my head cut off. If I'd known what I was letting myself in for, I wouldnt have come here. I always been a good girl; and I never offered to say a word to him; and I dont owe him nothing; and I dont care; and I wont be put upon; and I have my feelings the same as anyone else—

MRS PEARCE *shuts the door; and* ELIZA*'s plaints are no longer audible.*

★　　★　　★　　★　　★　　★

Eliza is taken upstairs to the third floor greatly to her surprise; for she expected to be taken down to the scullery.[8] There Mrs Pearce opens a door and takes her into a spare bedroom.

MRS PEARCE. I will have to put you here. This will be your bedroom.

LIZA. O-h, I couldn't sleep here, missus. It's too good for the likes of me. I should be afraid to touch anything. I aint a duchess yet, you know.

MRS PEARCE. You have got to make yourself as clean as the room: then you wont be afraid of it. And you must call me Mrs Pearce, not missus. [*She throws open the door of the dressingroom, now modernized as a bathroom*].

LIZA. Gawd! whats this? Is this where you wash clothes? Funny sort of copper[9] I call it.

---

8. scullery *n.*: A room adjoining the kitchen, where pots and pans are cleaned and stored.
9. copper *n.*: A large metal container or boiler used for washing clothes.

MRS PEARCE. It is not a copper. This is where we wash ourselves, Eliza, and where I am going to wash you.

LIZA. You expect me to get into that and wet myself all over! Not me. I should catch my death. I knew a woman did it every Saturday night; and she died of it.

MRS PEARCE. Mr Higgins has the gentlemen's bathroom downstairs; and he has a bath every morning, in cold water.

LIZA. Ugh! He's made of iron, that man.

MRS PEARCE. If you are to sit with him and the Colonel and be taught you will have to do the same. They wont like the smell of you if you don't. But you can have the water as hot as you like. There are two taps: hot and cold.

LIZA [weeping] I couldnt. I dursnt. Its not natural: it would kill me. I've never had a bath in my life: not what youd call a proper one.

MRS PEARCE. Well, dont you want to be clean and sweet and decent, like a lady? You know you cant be a nice girl inside if youre a dirty slut outside.

LIZA. Boohoo!!!!

MRS PEARCE. Now stop crying and go back into your room and take off all your clothes. Then wrap yourself in this [Taking down a gown from its peg and handing it to her] and come back to me. I will get the bath ready.

LIZA [all tears] I cant. I wont. I'm not used to it. Ive never took off all my clothes before. It's not right: it's not decent.

MRS PEARCE. Nonsense, child. Dont you take off all your clothes every night when you go to bed?

LIZA [amazed] No. Why should I? I should catch my death. Of course I take off my skirt.

MRS PEARCE. Do you mean that you sleep in the underclothes you wear in the daytime?

LIZA. What else have I to sleep in?

MRS PEARCE. You will never do that again as long as you live here. I will get you a proper nightdress.

LIZA. Do you mean change into cold things and lie awake shivering half the night? You want to kill me, you do.

MRS PEARCE. I want to change you from a frowzy slut to a clean respectable girl fit to sit with the gentlemen in the study. Are you going to trust me and do what I tell you or be thrown out and sent back to your flower basket?

LIZA. But you dont know what the cold is to me. You dont know how I dread it.

MRS PEARCE. Your bed won't be cold here: I will put a hot water bottle in it. [Pushing her into the bedroom] Off with you and undress.

LIZA. Oh, if only I'd known what a dreadful thing it is to be clean I'd never have come. I didnt know when I was well off. I—[MRS PEARCE pushes her through the door, but leaves it partly open lest her prisoner should take to flight].

MRS PEARCE puts on a pair of white rubber sleeves, and fills the bath, mixing hot and cold, and testing the result with the bath thermometer. She perfumes it with a handful of bath salts and adds a palmful of mustard. She then takes a formidable looking long handled scrubbing brush and soaps it profusely with a ball of scented soap.

ELIZA comes back with nothing on but the bath gown huddled tightly round her, a piteous spectacle of abject terror.

MRS PEARCE. Now come along. Take that thing off.

LIZA. Oh I couldnt, Mrs Pearce: I reely couldnt. I never done such a thing.

MRS PEARCE. Nonsense. Here: step in and tell me whether its hot enough for you.

LIZA. Ah-oo! Ah-oo! It's too hot.

MRS PEARCE [*deftly snatching the gown away and throwing* ELIZA *down on her back*]. It wont hurt you. [*She sets to work with the scrubbing brush*].

ELIZA*'s screams are heartrending.*

*　　*　　*　　*　　*　　*

Meanwhile the Colonel has been having it out with Higgins about Eliza. Pickering has come from the hearth to the chair and seated himself astride of it with his arms on the back to cross-examine him.

PICKERING. Excuse the straight question, Higgins. Are you a man of good character where women are concerned?

HIGGINS [*moodily*] Have you ever met a man of good character where women are concerned?

PICKERING. Yes: very frequently.

HIGGINS [*dogmatically, lifting himself on his hands to the level of the piano, and sitting on it with a bounce*] Well, I havnt. I find that the moment I let a woman make friends with me, she becomes jealous, exacting, suspicious, and a damned nuisance. I find that the moment I let myself make friends with a woman, I become selfish and tyrannical. Women upset everything. When you let them into your life, you find that the woman is driving at one thing and youre driving at another.

PICKERING. At what, for example?

HIGGINS [*coming off the piano restlessly*] Oh, Lord knows! I suppose the woman wants to live her own life; and the man wants to live his; and each tries to drag the other on to the wrong track. One wants to go north and the other south; and the result is that both have to go east, though they both hate the east wind. [*He sits down on the bench at the keyboard*]. So here I am, a confirmed old bachelor, and likely to remain so.

PICKERING [*rising and standing over him gravely*] Come, Higgins! You know what I mean. If I'm to be in this business I shall feel responsible for that girl. I hope it's understood that no advantage is to be taken of her position.

HIGGINS. What! That thing! Sacred, I assure you. [*Rising to explain*] You see, she'll be a pupil; and teaching would be impossible unless pupils were sacred. Ive taught scores of American millionairesses how to speak English: the best looking women in the world. I'm seasoned. They might as well be blocks of wood. *I* might as well be a block of wood. It's—

MRS PEARCE *opens the door. She has* ELIZA*'s hat in her hand.* PICKERING *retires to the easy-chair at the hearth and sits down.*

HIGGINS [*eagerly*] Well, Mrs Pearce is it all right?

MRS PEARCE [*at the door*] I just wish to trouble you with a word, if I may, Mr. Higgins.

HIGGINS. Yes, certainly. Come in. [*She comes forward*]. Dont burn that, Mrs Pearce. I'll keep it as a curiosity. [*He takes the hat*].

MRS PEARCE. Handle it carefully, sir, please. I had to promise her not to burn it; but I had better put it in the oven for a while.

HIGGINS [*putting it down hastily on the piano*] Oh! thank you. Well, what have you to say to me?

PICKERING. Am I in the way?

MRS PEARCE. Not in the least, sir. Mr Higgins: will you please be very particular what you say before the girl?

HIGGINS [*sternly*] Of course. I'm always particular about what I say. Why do you say this to me?

MRS PEARCE [*unmoved*] No, sir: youre not at all particular when youve mislaid anything or when you get a little impatient. Now it doesnt matter before me: I'm used to it. But you really must not swear before the girl.

HIGGINS [*indignantly*] I swear! [*Most emphatically*] I never swear. I detest the habit. What the devil do you mean?

MRS PEARCE [*stolidly*] Thats what I mean, sir. You swear a great deal too much. I dont mind your damning and blasting, and what the devil and where the devil and who the devil—

HIGGINS. Mrs Pearce: this language from your lips! Really!

MRS PEARCE [*not to be put off*]—but there is a certain word I must ask you not to use. The girl used it herself when she began to enjoy the bath. It begins with the same letter as bath. She knows no better: she learnt it at her mother's knee. But she must not hear it from your lips.

HIGGINS [*loftily*] I cannot charge myself with having ever uttered it, Mrs Pearce. [*She looks at him steadfastly. He adds, hiding an uneasy conscience with a judicial air*] Except perhaps in a moment of extreme and justifiable excitement.

MRS PEARCE. Only this morning, sir, you applied it to your boots, to the butter, and to the brown bread.

HIGGINS. Oh, that! Mere alliteration, Mrs Pearce, natural to a poet.

MRS PEARCE. Well, sir, whatever you choose to call it, I beg you not to let the girl hear you repeat it.

HIGGINS. Oh, very well, very well. Is that all?

MRS PEARCE. No, sir. We shall have to be very particular with this girl as to personal cleanliness.

HIGGINS. Certainly. Quite right. Most important.

MRS PEARCE. I mean not to be slovenly about her dress or untidy in leaving things about.

HIGGINS [*going to her solemnly*] Just so. I intended to call your attention to that. [*He passes on to* PICKERING, *who is enjoying the conversation immensely*]. It is these little things that matter, Pickering. Take care of the pence and the pounds will take care of themselves is as true of personal habits as of money. [*He comes to anchor on the hearth-rug, with the air of a man in an unassailable position*].

MRS PEARCE. Yes, sir. Then might I ask you not to come down to breakfast in your dressing-gown, or at any rate not to use it as a napkin to the extent you do, sir. And if you would be so good as not to eat everything off the same plate, and to remember not to put the porridge saucepan out of your hand on the clean tablecloth, it would be a better example to the girl. You know you nearly choked yourself with a fishbone in a jam only last week.

HIGGINS [*routed from the hearthrug and drifting back to the piano*] I may do these things sometimes in absence of mind; but surely I dont do them habitually. [*Angrily*] By the way: my dressing-gown smells most damnably of benzine.

MRS PEARCE. No doubt it does, Mr Higgins. But if you will wipe your fingers—

HIGGINS [*yelling*] Oh very well, very well: I'll wipe them in my hair in future.

MRS PEARCE. I hope youre not offended, Mr Higgins.

HIGGINS [*shocked at finding himself thought capable of an unamiable sentiment*] Not at all, not at all. Youre quite right, Mrs Pearce: I shall be particularly careful before the girl. Is that all?

MRS PEARCE. No, sir. Might she use some of those Japanese dresses you brought from abroad? I really cant put her back into her old things.

HIGGINS. Certainly. Anything you like. Is that all?

MRS PEARCE. Thank you, sir. Thats all. [*She goes out*].

HIGGINS. You know, Pickering, that woman has the most extraordinary ideas about me. Here I am, a shy, diffident sort of man. I've never been able to feel really grown-up and tremendous, like other chaps. And yet she's firmly persuaded that I'm an arbitrary overbearing bossing kind of person. I cant account for it.

MRS PEARCE *returns.*

MRS PEARCE. If you please, sir, the trouble's beginning already. Theres a dustman[10] downstairs, Alfred Doolittle, wants to see you. He says you have his daughter here.

PICKERING [*rising*] Phew! I say!

HIGGINS [*promptly*] Send the blackguard[11] up.

MRS PEARCE. Oh, very well, sir. [*She goes out*].

PICKERING. He may not be a blackguard, Higgins.

HIGGINS. Nonsense. Of course he's a blackguard.

PICKERING. Whether he is or not, I'm afraid we shall have some trouble with him.

HIGGINS [*confidently*] Oh no: I think not. If theres any trouble he shall have it with me, not I with him. And we are sure to get something interesting out of him.

PICKERING. About the girl?

HIGGINS. No. I mean his dialect.

PICKERING. Oh!

MRS PEARCE [*at the door*] Doolittle, sir. [*She admits* DOOLITTLE *and retires*].

ALFRED *is an elderly but vigorous dustman, clad in the costume of his profession, including a hat with a back brim covering his neck and shoulders. He has well marked and rather interesting features, and seems equally free from fear and conscience. He has a remarkably expressive voice, the result of a habit of giving vent to his feelings without reserve. His present pose is that of wounded honor and stern resolution.*

---

10. **dustman** *n.*: A garbage collector.
11. **blackguard** (blag' ərd) *n.*: Scoundrel.

DOOLITTLE [*at the door, uncertain which of the two gentlemen is his man*] Professor Iggins?

HIGGINS. Here. Good morning. Sit down.

DOOLITTLE. Morning, Governor. [*He sits down magisterially*]. I come about a very serious matter, Governor.

HIGGINS [*to* PICKERING] Brought up in Hounslow. Mother Welsh, I should think. [DOOLITTLE *opens his mouth, amazed.* HIGGINS *continues*] What do you want, Doolittle?

DOOLITTLE [*menacingly*] I want my daughter: thats what I want. See?

HIGGINS. Of course you do. Youre her father, arnt you? You dont suppose anyone else wants her, do you? I'm glad to see you have some spark of family feeling left. She's upstairs. Take her away at once.

DOOLITTLE [*rising, fearfully taken aback*] What!

HIGGINS. Take her away. Do you suppose I'm going to keep your daughter for you?

DOOLITTLE [*remonstrating*] Now, now, look here, Governor. Is it reasonable? Is it fairity to take advantage of a man like this? The girl belongs to me. You got her. Where do I come in? [*He sits down again*].

HIGGINS. Your daughter had the audacity to come to my house and ask me to teach her how to speak properly so that she could get a place in a flower-shop. This gentleman and my housekeeper have been here all the time. [*Bullying him*] How dare you come here and attempt to blackmail me? You sent her here on purpose.

DOOLITTLE [*protesting*] No, Governor.

HIGGINS. You must have. How else could you possibly know that she is here?

DOOLITTLE. Don't take a man up like that, Governor.

HIGGINS. The police shall take you up. This is a plant—a plot to extort money by threats. I

shall telephone for the police [*he goes reso-lutely to the telephone and opens the directory*]

DOOLITTLE. Have I asked you for a brass farthing? I leave it to the gentleman here: have I said a word about money?

HIGGINS [*throwing the book aside and marching down on* DOOLITTLE *with a poser*] What else did you come for?

DOOLITTLE [*sweetly*] Well, what would a man come for? Be human, Governor.

HIGGINS [*disarmed*] Alfred: did you put her up to it?

DOOLITTLE. So help me, Governor. I never did. I take my Bible oath I aint seen the girl these two months past.

HIGGINS. Then how did you know she was here?

DOOLITTLE [*"most musical, most melancholy"*] I'll tell you, Governor, if youll only let me get a word in. I'm willing to tell you. I'm wanting to tell you. I'm waiting to tell you.

HIGGINS. Pickering: this chap has a certain natural gift of rhetoric. Observe the rhythm of his native woodnotes wild. "I'm willing to tell you: I'm wanting to tell you: I'm waiting to tell you." Sentimental rhetoric! thats the Welsh strain in him. It also accounts for his mendacity and dishonesty.

PICKERING. Oh, please, Higgins: I'm west country myself. [*To* DOOLITTLE] How did you know the girl was here if you didnt send her?

DOOLITTLE. It was like this, Governor. The girl took a boy in the taxi to give him a jaunt. Son of her landlady, he is. He hung about on the chance of her giving him another ride home. Well, she sent him back for her luggage when she heard you was willing for her to stop here. I met the boy at the corner of Long Acre and Endell Street.

HIGGINS. Public house. Yes?

DOOLITTLE. The poor man's club, Governor: why shouldnt I?

PICKERING. Do let him tell his story, Higgins.

DOOLITTLE. He told me what was up. And I ask you, what was my feelings and my duty as a father? I says to the boy, "You bring me the luggage," I says—

PICKERING. Why didnt you go for it yourself?

DOOLITTLE. Landlady wouldnt have trusted me with it, Governor. She's that kind of woman: you know. I had to give the boy a penny afore he trusted me with it, the little swine. I brought it to her just to oblige you like, and make myself agreeable. Thats all.

HIGGINS. How much luggage?

DOOLITTLE. Musical instrument, Governor. A few pictures, a trifle of jewelry, and a bird-cage. She said she didn't want no clothes. What was I to think from that, Governor? I ask you as a parent what was I to think?

HIGGINS. So you came to rescue her from worse than death, eh?

DOOLITTLE [*appreciatively: relieved at being so well understood*] Just so, Governor. That's right.

PICKERING. But why did you bring her luggage if you intended to take her away?

DOOLITTLE. Have I said a word about taking her away? Have I now?

HIGGINS [*determinedly*] Youre going to take her away, double quick. [*He crosses to the hearth and rings the bell*].

DOOLITTLE [*rising*] No, Governor. Dont say that. I'm not the man to stand in my girl's light. Heres a career opening for her, as you might say; and—

MRS PEARCE *opens the door and awaits orders.*

HIGGINS. Mrs Pearce: this is Eliza's father. He has come to take her away. Give her to him. [*He goes back to the piano, with an air of* *washing his hands of the whole affair*].

DOOLITTLE. No. This is a misunderstanding. Listen here—

MRS PEARCE. He cant take her away. Mr Higgins: how can he? You told me to burn her clothes.

DOOLITTLE. Thats right. I cant carry the girl through the streets like a blooming monkey, can I? I put it to you.

HIGGINS. You have put it to me that you want your daughter. Take your daughter. If she has no clothes go out and buy her some.

DOOLITTLE [*desperate*] Wheres the clothes she come in? Did I burn them or did your missus here?

MRS PEARCE. I am the housekeeper, if you please. I have sent for some clothes for your girl. When they come you can take her away. You can wait in the kitchen. This way, please.

DOOLITTLE, *much troubled, accompanies her to the door; then hesitates; finally turns confidentially to* HIGGINS.

DOOLITTLE. Listen here, Governor. You and me is men of the world, aint we?

HIGGINS. Oh! Men of the world, are we? Youd better go, Mrs Pearce.

MRS PEARCE. I think so, indeed, sir. [*She goes, with dignity*].

PICKERING. The floor is yours, Mr Doolittle.

DOOLITTLE [*to* PICKERING] I thank you, Governor. [*To* HIGGINS, *who takes refuge on the piano bench, a little overwhelmed by the proximity of his visitor; for* DOOLITTLE *has a professional flavour of dust about him*]. Well, the truth is, I've taken a sort of fancy to you, Governor; and if you want the girl, I'm not so set on having her back home again but what I might be open to an arrangement. Regarded in the light of a young woman, she's a fine handsome girl. As a daughter she's not worth her keep; and so I tell you straight. All I ask is my rights as a father; and youre the last man alive to expect me to let her go for nothing; for I can see youre one of the straight sort, Governor. Well, whats a five-pound note to you? and whats Eliza to me? [*He turns to his chair and sits down judicially*].

PICKERING. I think you ought to know, Doolittle, that Mr Higgins's intentions are entirely honorable.

DOOLITTLE. Course they are, Governor. If I thought they wasnt, I'd ask fifty.

HIGGINS [*revolted*] Do you mean to say that you would sell your daughter for £50?

DOOLITTLE. Not in a general way I would; but to oblige a gentleman like you I'd do a good deal, I do assure you.

PICKERING. Have you no morals, man?

DOOLITTLE [*unabashed*] Cant afford them, Governor. Neither could you if you was as poor as me. Not that I mean any harm, you know. But if Liza is going to have a bit out of this, why not me too?

HIGGINS [*troubled*] I dont know what to do, Pickering. There can be no question that as a matter of morals it's a positive crime to give this chap a farthing. And yet I feel a sort of rough justice in his claim.

DOOLITTLE. Thats it, Governor. Thats all I say. A father's heart, as it were.

PICKERING. Well, I know the feeling; but really it seems hardly right—

DOOLITTLE. Dont say that, Governor. Dont look at it that way. What am I, Governors both? I ask you, what am I? I'm one of the undeserving poor: thats what I am. Think of what that means to a man. It means that he's up agen middle class morality all the time. If theres anything going, and I put in for a bit of it, it's always the same story: "Youre undeserving; so you cant have it." But my needs is as great as the most deserving widows' that ever got money out of six different charities in one week for the death of the same husband. I dont need less than a deserving man: I need more. I dont eat less hearty than him; and I drink a lot more. I want a bit of amusement, cause I'm a thinking man. I want cheerfulness and a song and a band when I feel low. Well, they charge me just the same for everything as they charge the deserving. What is middle class morality? Just an excuse for never giving me anything. Therefore, I ask you, as two gentlemen, not to play that game on me. I'm playing straight with you. I aint pretending to be deserving. I'm undeserving; and I mean to go on being undeserving. I like it; and thats the truth. Will you take advantage of a man's nature to do him out of the price of his own daughter what he's brought up and fed and clothed by the sweat of his brow until she's growed big enough to be interesting to you two gentlemen? Is five pounds unreasonable? I put it to you; and I leave it to you.

HIGGINS [*rising, and going over to* PICKERING] Pickering: if we were to take this man in hand for three months, he could choose between a seat in the Cabinet and a popular pulpit in Wales.

PICKERING. What do you say to that, Doolittle?

DOOLITTLE. Not me, Governor, thank you kindly. Ive heard all the preachers and all the prime ministers—for I'm a thinking man and game for politics or religion or social reform same as all the other amusements—and I tell you it's a dog's life any way you look at it. Undeserving poverty is my line. Taking one station in society with another, it's—it's—well, it's the only one that has any ginger in it, to my taste.

HIGGINS. I suppose we must give him a fiver.

PICKERING. He'll make a bad use of it, I'm afraid.

DOOLITTLE. Not me, Governor, so help me I wont. Dont you be afraid that I'll save it and spare it and live idle on it. There wont be a penny of it left by Monday: I'll have to go to work same as if I'd never had it. It wont pauperize me, you bet. Just one good spree for myself and the missus, giving pleasure to ourselves and employment to others, and satisfaction to you to think it's not been throwed away. You couldn't spend it better.

HIGGINS [*taking out his pocket book and coming between* DOOLITTLE *and the piano*] This is irresistible. Lets give him ten. [*He offers two notes to the* DUSTMAN]

DOOLITTLE. No, Governor. She wouldnt have the heart to spend ten; and perhaps I shouldnt neither. Ten pounds is a lot of money: it makes a man feel prudent like; and then good-bye to happiness. You give me what I ask you, Governor: not a penny more, and not a penny less.

PICKERING. Why dont you marry that missus of yours? I rather draw the line at encouraging that sort of immorality.

DOOLITTLE. Tell her so, Governor: tell her so. I'm willing. It's me that suffers by it. Ive no hold on her. I got to be agreeable to her. I got to give her presents. I got to buy her clothes something sinful. I'm a slave to that woman, Governor, just because I'm not her lawful husband. And she knows it too. Catch her marrying me! Take my advice, Governor: marry Eliza while she's young and dont know no better. If you dont youll be sorry for it after. If you do, she'll be sorry for it after; but better her than you, because youre a man, and she's only a woman and dont know how to be happy anyhow.

HIGGINS. Pickering: if we listen to this man another minute, we shall have no convictions left. [*To* DOOLITTLE] Five pounds I think you said.

DOOLITTLE. Thank you kindly, Governor.

HIGGINS. Youre sure you wont take ten?

DOOLITTLE. Not now. Another time, Governor.

HIGGINS [*handing him a five-pound note*] Here you are.

DOOLITTLE. Thank you, Governor. Good morning. [*He hurries to the door, anxious to get away with his booty. When he opens it he is confronted with a dainty and exquisitely clean young Japanese lady in a simple blue cotton kimono printed cunningly with small white jasmine blossoms.* MRS PEARCE *is with her. He gets out of her way deferentially and apologizes*]. Beg pardon, miss.

THE JAPANESE LADY. Garn! Dont you know your own daughter?

DOOLITTLE	*exclaiming*	Bly me! it's Eliza!
HIGGINS	*simul-*	Whats that? This!
PICKERING	*taneously*	By Jove!

LIZA. Dont I look silly?

HIGGINS. Silly?

MRS PEARCE [*at the door*] Now, Mr Higgins, please dont say anything to make the girl conceited about herself.

HIGGINS [*conscientiously*] Oh! Quite right, Mrs Pearce. [*To* ELIZA] Yes: damned silly.

MRS PEARCE. Please, sir.

HIGGINS [*correcting himself*] I mean extremely silly.

LIZA. I should look all right with my hat on. [*She takes up her hat; puts it on; and walks across the room to the fireplace with a fashionable air*].

HIGGINS. A new fashion, by George! And it ought to look horrible!

DOOLITTLE [*with fatherly pride*] Well, I never thought she'd clean up as good looking as that, Governor. She's a credit to me, aint she?

LIZA. I tell you, it's easy to clean up here. Hot and cold water on tap, just as much as you like, there is. Woolly towels, there is; and a towel horse[12] so hot, it burns your fingers. Soft brushes to scrub yourself, and a wooden bowl of soap smelling like primroses. Now I know why ladies is so clean. Washing's a treat for them. Wish they could see what it is for the like of me!

HIGGINS. I'm glad the bathroom met with your approval.

LIZA. It didnt: not all of it; and I dont care who hears me say it. Mrs Pearce knows.

HIGGINS. What was wrong, Mrs Pearce?

MRS PEARCE [*blandly*] Oh, nothing, sir. It doesnt matter.

LIZA. I had a good mind to break it. I didnt know which way to look. But I hung a towel over it, I did.

HIGGINS. Over what?

MRS PEARCE. Over the looking-glass, sir.

HIGGINS. Doolittle: you have brought your daughter up too strictly.

DOOLITTLE. Me! I never brought her up at all, except to give her a lick of a strap now and again. Dont put it on me, Governor. She aint accustomed to it, you see: thats all. But she'll soon pick up your free-and-easy ways.

LIZA. I'm a good girl, I am; and I wont pick up no free-and-easy ways.

HIGGINS. Eliza: if you say again that youre a good girl, your father shall take you home.

LIZA. Not him. You dont know my father. All he come here for was to touch you for some money to get drunk on.

DOOLITTLE. Well, what else would I want money for? To put into the plate in church, I suppose. [*She puts out her tongue at him. He is so incensed by this that* PICKERING *presently finds it necessary to step between*

---

12. towel horse: Towel rack; in this case the rack is heated to dry the towels.

them]. Dont you give me none of your lip; and dont let me hear you giving this gentleman any of it neither, or youll hear from me about it. See?

HIGGINS. Have you any further advice to give her before you go, Doolittle? Your blessing, for instance.

DOOLITTLE. No, Governor: I aint such a mug as to put up my children to all I know myself. Hard enough to hold them in without that. If you want Eliza's mind improved, Governor, you do it yourself with a strap. So long, gentlemen. [*He turns to go*].

HIGGINS [*impressively*] Stop. Youll come regularly to see your daughter. It's your duty, you know. My brother is a clergyman; and he could help you in your talks with her.

DOOLITTLE [*evasively*] Certainly, I'll come, Governor. Not just this week, because I have a job at a distance. But later on you may depend on me. Afternoon, gentlemen. Afternoon, maam. [*He touches his hat to* MRS PEARCE, *who disdains the salutation and goes out. He winks at* HIGGINS, *thinking him probably a fellow-sufferer from* MRS PEARCE's *difficult disposition, and follows her*].

LIZA. Dont you believe the old liar. He'd as soon you set a bulldog on him as a clergyman. You wont see him again in a hurry.

HIGGINS. I dont want to, Eliza. Do you?

LIZA. Not me. I dont want never to see him again, I dont. He's a disgrace to me, he is, collecting dust,[13] instead of working at his trade.

PICKERING. What is his trade, Eliza?

LIZA. Talking money out of other people's pockets into his own. His proper trade's a navvy;[14] and he works at it sometimes too —for exercise—and earns good money at it. Aint you going to call me Miss Doolittle any more?

PICKERING. I beg your pardon, Miss Doolittle. It was a slip of the tongue.

LIZA. Oh, I dont mind; only it sounded so genteel. I should just like to take a taxi to the corner of Tottenham Court Road and get out there and tell it to wait for me, just to put the girls in their place a bit. I wouldnt speak to them, you know.

PICKERING. Better wait til we get you something really fashionable.

HIGGINS. Besides, you shouldnt cut your old friends now that you have risen in the world. Thats what we call snobbery.

LIZA. You dont call the like of them my friends now, I should hope. Theyve took it out of me often enough with their ridicule when they had the chance; and now I mean to get a bit of my own back. But if I'm to have fashionable clothes, I'll wait. I should like to have some. Mrs Pearce says youre going to give me some to wear in bed at night different to what I wear in the daytime; but it do seem a waste of money when you could get something to shew. Besides, I never could fancy changing into cold things on a winter night.

---

13. **collecting dust:** Picking up garbage.
14. **navvy** (nav' ē) n.: An unskilled laborer.

MRS PEARCE [coming back] Now, Eliza. The new things have come for you to try on.

LIZA. Ah-ow-oo-ooh! [She rushes out].

MRS PEARCE [following her] Oh, dont rush about like that, girl. [She shuts the door behind her].

HIGGINS. Pickering: we have taken on a stiff job.

PICKERING [with conviction] Higgins: we have.

    ★   ★   ★   ★   ★   ★

There seems to be some curiosity as to what Higgins's lessons to Eliza were like. Well, here is a sample: the first one.

Picture Eliza, in her new clothes, and feeling her inside put out of step by a lunch, dinner, and breakfast of a kind to which it is unaccustomed, seated with Higgins and the Colonel in the study, feeling like a hospital out-patient at a first encounter with the doctors.

Higgins, constitutionally unable to sit still, discomposes her still more by striding restlessly about. But for the reassuring presence and quietude of her friend the Colonel she would run for her life, even back to Drury Lane.

HIGGINS. Say your alphabet.

LIZA. I know my alphabet. Do you think I know nothing? I dont need to be taught like a child.

HIGGINS [thundering] Say your alphabet.

PICKERING. Say it, Miss Doolittle. You will understand presently. Do what he tells you; and let him teach you in his own way.

LIZA. Oh well, if you put it like that—Ahyee, bəyee, cəyee, dəyee—

HIGGINS [with the roar of a wounded lion] Stop. Listen to this, Pickering. This is what we pay for as elementary education. This unfortunate animal has been locked up for nine years in school at our expense to teach her to speak and read the language of

Shakespear and Milton. And the result is Ahyee, Bə-yee, Cə-yee, Dəyee. [*To* ELIZA] Say A, B, C, D.

LIZA [*almost in tears*] But I'm sayin it. Ahyee, Bəyee, Cəyee—

HIGGINS. Stop. Say a cup of tea.

LIZA. A cappətə-ee.

HIGGINS. Put your tongue forward until it squeezes against the top of your lower teeth. Now say cup.

LIZA. C-c-c—I cant. C-Cup.

PICKERING. Good. Splendid, Miss Doolittle.

HIGGINS. By Jupiter, she's done it the first shot. Pickering: we shall make a duchess of her. [*To* ELIZA] Now do you think you could possibly say tea? Not tə-yee, mind: if you ever say bə-yee cə-yee də-yee again you shall be dragged round the room three times by the hair of your head. [*Fortissimo*] T, T, T, T.

LIZA [*weeping*] I cant hear no difference cep that it sounds more genteel-like when you say it.

HIGGINS. Well, if you can hear the difference, what the devil are you crying for? Pickering: give her a chocolate.

PICKERING. No, no. Never mind crying a little, Miss Doolittle: you are doing very well; and the lessons wont hurt. I promise you I wont let him drag you round the room by your hair.

HIGGINS. Be off with you to Mrs Pearce and tell her about it. Think about it. Try to do it by yourself: and keep your tongue well forward in your mouth instead of trying to roll it up and swallow it. Another lesson at half-past four this afternoon. Away with you.

ELIZA, *still sobbing, rushes from the room.*

And that is the sort of ordeal Eliza has to go through for months before we meet her again on her first appearance in London society of the professional class.

RESPONDING TO THE SELECTION

Your Response
1. Do you think Higgins will be successful in transforming Eliza into a "lady"? Why or why not?

Recalling
2. (a) Why has Eliza come to see Higgins? (b) With what does she offer to pay him?
3. What are the terms of the bet that Pickering proposes?
4. (a) What are Mrs. Pearce's concerns in regard to the arrangement? (b) What are Pickering's?
5. (a) What is the purpose of Alfred Doolittle's visit? (b) How does Higgins respond to his demands?

Interpreting
6. What differences between Higgins and Pickering are pointed out in Act II?
7. (a) What is revealed about the role of women of this era? (b) About middle-class and lower-class ideals?

Applying
8. (a) How does Higgins's treatment of Eliza strike you? (b) Do you think this was Shaw's intention? Explain.

ANALYZING LITERATURE

Understanding Character Development
Character development is the technique of showing change and growth in characters by their

reactions to other characters and unfolding events. A static character is essentially unaltered by involvements of plot, whereas a dynamic character is affected, sometimes radically. In order to observe changes in a character, we must have a clear idea of what qualities that character possesses in the first place.

Using at least five adjectives or descriptive phrases, profile each of the five characters appearing in Act II. Then tell which of the characters is static and which is dynamic, giving your reasons for your classifications.

CRITICAL THINKING AND READING

Making Inferences About Characters

Occasionally, in a literary work, we receive conflicting reports on a character's ambitions, motives, and thoughts. This is because, as in real life, a character's self-image often differs drastically from the image other characters have of her or him. It is the responsibility of the alert reader to consider all information and then to **infer,** or conclude from the evidence, what the character is really like. Tell what impression the speaker of each of the following lines hopes to convey, and what impression he or she succeeds in conveying.

1. THE FLOWER GIRL. Did you tell him I come in a taxi? (page 984)
2. HIGGINS. *I* walk over everybody! My dear Mrs. Pearce, my dear Pickering, I never had the slightest intention of walking over anyone. (page 987)
3. DOOLITTLE. I come about a very serious matter, Governor. (page 994)

THINKING AND WRITING

Comparing and Contrasting Characters

Using information you have accumulated about the characters thus far, write an essay that explores similarities and differences between any two of the characters in Act II. First, select the characters and jot down notes about them. Then, write your first draft, remembering to pay attention to underlying motives and stage directions in arriving at an understanding of each character. When you revise, make sure your essay is ordered logically and that you have supported your thesis with details from the play. Proofread your essay and prepare a final draft.

LEARNING OPTIONS

1. **Performance.** Dialogue consists of lines that represent the actual speech or conversations of the characters in a literary work. In a play, dialogue is everything. Ideally, dialogue should give the impression of actual conversation, not separate speeches. Shaw orchestrated his dialogue like music, varying tempo and intonation to emphasize the ideas and attitudes being expressed. With a group of classmates choose sections of Act II, assign roles, and stage an in-class reading. To make the dialogue as natural and lifelike as possible, consider what you know about each character, including his or her speech habits.

2. **Speaking and Listening.** Find one or more versions of the Greek myth of Pygmalion. Who was he? What work of art did he create? What goddess granted him a favor? After you have become familiar with the story, practice telling it in your own words. You should remember to include important plot details, and you may want to embellish the descriptions of the characters. Recite your version of the Pygmalion myth for the class. Discuss the elements of the myth that are apparent in the portion of Shaw's play you have read.

GUIDE FOR INTERPRETING

Pygmalion, Act III

Writers' Techniques

Satire. Satire is a technique that combines humor with criticism to expose flaws and shortcomings in institutions or human beings. Shaw, as an advocate of reform, saw in this brand of "serious comedy" an effective tool. "After all," he wrote, "the salvation of the world depends on the men who will not take evil good-humoredly, and whose laughter destroys the fool instead of encouraging him." The targets, methods, and styles of satire are many and varied. Unfair or outdated laws, pointless rules and regulations, prejudices and mindless conventions, illogical political policies, fads and styles—all have been held up to ridicule in poems, novels, essays, and plays. Today satire flourishes in such diverse media as film, television, cartoons, comic strips, and comedy acts, not to mention, of course, literature. Novels such as George Orwell's *1984,* Evelyn Waugh's *The Loved One,* and Joseph Heller's *Catch-22* satirize many aspects of twentieth-century life.

Focus

Brainstorm in small groups to come up with a list of styles and habits that you find especially laughable. Attempt to pinpoint the features of your subject that seem silly, unreasonable, or unfair.

Primary Source

One of the literary weapons that Shaw used in *Pygmalion* to right society's wrongs was satire. In his criticism as well, he pointed out society's faults through whatever means might be effective—and he never hesitated to voice his opinion. Answering complaints that his criticism was full of personal feeling, he said,

> It is the capacity for making good or bad art a personal matter that makes a man a critic. When people do less than their best, and do that less at once badly and self-complacently, I hate them, loathe them, detest them, long to tear them limb from limb. . . . In the same way, really fine artists inspire me with the warmest personal regard, which I gratify in writing my notices without the smallest reference to . . . justice, impartiality, and the rest of the ideals. When my critical mood is at its height, personal feeling is not the word: it is passion: the passion for artistic perfection—for the noblest beauty of sound, sight, and action—that rages in me. Let all young artists look to it, and pay no heed to the idiots who declare that criticism should be free from personal feeling. The true critic, I repeat, is the man who becomes your personal enemy on the sole provocation of a bad performance and will only be appeased by a good performance.

ACT III

It is MRS HIGGINS'*s at-home day.*[1] *Nobody has yet arrived. Her drawing room, in a flat on Chelsea Embankment, has three windows looking on the river; and the ceiling is not so lofty as it would be in an older house of the same pretension. The windows are open, giving access to a balcony with flowers in pots. If you stand with your face to the windows, you have the fireplace on your left and the door in the right-hand wall close to the corner nearest the windows.*

MRS HIGGINS *was brought up on Morris*[2] *and Burne Jones;*[3] *and her room, which is very unlike her son's room in Wimpole Street, is not crowded with furniture and little tables and nicknacks. In the middle of the room there is a big ottoman; and this, with the carpet, the Morris wall-papers, and the Morris chintz window curtains and brocade covers of the ottoman and its cushions, supply all the ornament, and are much too handsome to be hidden by odds and ends of useless things. A few good oil-paintings from the exhibitions in the Grosvenor Gallery thirty years ago (the Burne Jones, not the Whistler*[4] *side of them) are on the walls. The only landscape is a Cecil Lawson*[5] *on the scale of a Rubens.*[6] *There is a portrait of* MRS HIGGINS *as she was when she defied the fashion in her youth in one of the beautiful Rossettian*[7] *costumes which, when caricatured by people who did not understand, led to the absurdities of popular estheticism in the eighteen-seventies.*

In the corner diagonally opposite the door MRS HIGGINS, *now over sixty and long past taking the trouble to dress out of the fashion, sits writing at an elegantly simple writing-table with a bell button within reach of her hand. There is a Chippendale chair further back in the room between her and the window nearest her side. At the other side of the room, further forward, is an Elizabethan chair roughly carved in the taste of Inigo Jones.*[8] *On the same side a piano in a decorated case. The corner between the fireplace and the window is occupied by a divan cushioned in Morris chintz.*

It is between four and five in the afternoon.

The door is opened violently; and HIGGINS *enters with his hat on.*

MRS HIGGINS [*dismayed*] Henry! [*Scolding him*] What are you doing here today? It is my at-home day: you promised not to come. [*As he bends to kiss her, she takes his hat off, and presents it to him*].

HIGGINS. Oh bother! [*He throws the hat down on the table*].

MRS HIGGINS. Go home at once.

HIGGINS [*kissing her*] I know, mother. I came on purpose.

MRS HIGGINS. But you mustnt. I'm serious, Henry. You offend all my friends: they stop coming whenever they meet you.

HIGGINS. Nonsense! I know I have no small talk; but people dont mind. [*He sits on the settee*].

MRS HIGGINS. Oh! dont they? Small talk indeed! What about your large talk? Really, dear, you mustnt stay.

---

1. at-home day: The day of the week when a lady regularly receives visitors.
2. Morris: William Morris (1834–1896), English poet, artist, and craftsman.
3. Burne Jones: Sir Edward Corley Burne-Jones (1833–1898), English painter and designer.
4. Whistler: James Abbott McNeill Whistler (1834–1903), an American painter who lived in England.
5. Cecil Lawson: Cecil Gordon Lawson (1851–1882), English landscape painter.
6. Rubens: Peter Paul Rubens (1577–1640), a Flemish painter famous for his large paintings.
7. Rossettian: Referring to Dante Gabriel Rossetti (1828–1882), English poet and painter.

8. Inigo Jones: English architect and stage designer (1573–1652).

HIGGINS. I must. Ive a job for you. A phonetic job.

MRS HIGGINS. No use, dear. I'm sorry; but I cant get round your vowels; and though I like to get pretty postcards in your patent shorthand, I always have to read the copies in ordinary writing you so thoughtfully send me.

HIGGINS. Well, this isn't a phonetic job.

MRS HIGGINS. You said it was.

HIGGINS. Not your part of it. Ive picked up a girl.

MRS HIGGINS. Does that mean that some girl has picked you up?

HIGGINS. Not at all. I dont mean a love affair.

MRS HIGGINS. What a pity!

HIGGINS. Why?

MRS HIGGINS. Well, you never fall in love with anyone under forty-five. When will you discover that there are some rather nice-looking young women about?

HIGGINS. Oh, I cant be bothered with young women. My idea of a lovable woman is somebody as like you as possible. I shall never get into the way of seriously liking young women: some habits lie too deep to be changed. [*Rising abruptly and walking about, jingling his money and his keys in his trouser pockets*] Besides, theyre all idiots.

MRS HIGGINS. Do you know what you would do if you really loved me, Henry?

HIGGINS. Oh bother! What? Marry, I suppose.

MRS HIGGINS. No. Stop fidgeting and take your hands out of your pockets. [*With a gesture of despair, he obeys and sits down again*]. Thats a good boy. Now tell me about the girl.

HIGGINS. She's coming to see you.

MRS HIGGINS. I dont remember asking her.

HIGGINS. You didn't. *I* asked her. If youd known her you wouldnt have asked her.

MRS HIGGINS. Indeed! Why?

HIGGINS. Well, it's like this. She's a common flower girl. I picked her off the kerbstone.

MRS HIGGINS. And invited her to my at-home!

HIGGINS [*rising and coming to her to coax her*] Oh, thatll be all right. Ive taught her to speak properly; and she has strict orders as to her behavior. She's to keep to two subjects: the weather and everybody's health —Fine day and How do you do, you know —and not to let herself go on things in general. That will be safe.

MRS HIGGINS. Safe! To talk about our health! about our insides! perhaps about our outsides! How could you be so silly, Henry?

HIGGINS [*impatiently*] Well, she must talk about something. [*He controls himself and sits down again*]. Oh, she'll be all right: dont you fuss. Pickering is in it with me. Ive a sort of bet on that I'll pass her off as a duchess in six months. I started on her some months ago; and she's getting on like a house on fire. I shall win my bet. She has a quick ear; and she's easier to teach than my middle-class pupils because she's had to learn a complete new language. She talks English almost as you talk French.

MRS HIGGINS. Thats satisfactory, at all events.

HIGGINS. Well, it is and it isnt.

MRS HIGGINS. What does that mean?

HIGGINS. You see, Ive got her pronunciation all right; but you have to consider not only how a girl pronounces, but what she pronounces; and that's where—

They are interrupted by the PARLORMAID, *announcing guests.*

THE PARLORMAID. Mrs and Miss Eynsford Hill. [*She withdraws*].

HIGGINS. Oh Lord! [*He rises; snatches his hat from the table; and makes for the door; but before he reaches it his mother introduces him*].

Mrs and Miss Eynsford Hill are the mother and daughter who sheltered from the rain in Covent Garden. The mother is well bred, quiet, and has the habitual anxiety of straitened means. The daughter has acquired a gay air of being very much at home in society: the bravado of genteel poverty.

MRS EYNSFORD HILL [*to* MRS HIGGINS] How do you do? [*They shake hands*].

MISS EYNSFORD HILL. How d'you do? [*She shakes*].

MRS HIGGINS [*introducing*] My son Henry.

MRS EYNSFORD HILL. Your celebrated son! I have so longed to meet you, Professor Higgins.

HIGGINS [*glumly, making no movement in her direction*] Delighted. [*He backs against the piano and bows brusquely*].

MISS EYNSFORD HILL [*going to him with confident familiarity*] How do you do?

HIGGINS [*staring at her*] Ive seen you before somewhere. I havnt the ghost of a notion where; but Ive heard your voice. [*Drearily*] It doesnt matter. Youd better sit down.

MRS HIGGINS. I'm sorry to say that my celebrated son has no manners. You mustnt mind him.

MISS EYNSFORD HILL [*gaily*] I dont. [*She sits in the Elizabethan chair*].

MRS EYNSFORD HILL [*a little bewildered*] Not at all. [*She sits on the ottoman between her daughter and* MRS HIGGINS, *who has turned her chair away from the writing-table*].

HIGGINS. Oh, have I been rude? I didnt mean to be.

He goes to the central window, through which, with his back to the company, he contemplates the river and the flowers in Battersea Park on the opposite bank as if they were a frozen desert.

The PARLORMAID *returns, ushering in* PICKERING.

THE PARLORMAID. Colonel Pickering. [*She withdraws*].

PICKERING. How do you do, Mrs Higgins?

MRS HIGGINS. So glad youve come. Do you know Mrs Eynsford Hill—Miss Eynsford Hill? [*Exchange of bows. The* COLONEL *brings the Chippendale chair a little forward between* MRS HILL *and* MRS HIGGINS, *and sits down*].

PICKERING. Has Henry told you what weve come for?

HIGGINS. [*over his shoulder*] We were interrupted: damn it!

MRS HIGGINS. Oh, Henry, Henry, really!

MRS EYNSFORD HILL [*half rising*] Are we in the way?

MRS HIGGINS [*rising and making her sit down again*] No, no. You couldnt have come more fortunately: we want you to meet a friend of ours.

HIGGINS [*turning hopefully*] Yes, by George! We want two or three people. You'll do as well as anybody else.

The PARLORMAID *returns, ushering* FREDDY.

THE PARLORMAID. Mr Eynsford Hill.

HIGGINS [*almost audibly, past endurance*] God of Heaven! another of them.

FREDDY [*shaking hands with* MRS HIGGINS] Ahdedo?

MRS HIGGINS. Very good of you to come. [*Introducing*] Colonel Pickering.

FREDDY [*bowing*] Ahdedo?

MRS HIGGINS. I don't think you know my son, Professor Higgins.

FREDDY [*going to* HIGGINS] Ahdedo?

HIGGINS [*looking at him much as if he were a pickpocket*] I'll take my oath Ive met you before somewhere. Where was it?

FREDDY. I dont think so.

HIGGINS [*resignedly*] It dont matter, anyhow. Sit down.

He shakes FREDDY'*s hand, and almost slings him on to the ottoman with his face to the window; then comes round to the other side of it.*

HIGGINS. Well, here we are, anyhow! [*He sits down on the ottoman next* MRS EYNSFORD HILL, *on her left*] And now, what the devil are we going to talk about until Eliza comes?

MRS HIGGINS. Henry: you are the life and soul of the Royal Society's soirées;[9] but really youre rather trying on more commonplace occasions.

HIGGINS. Am I? Very sorry. [*Beaming suddenly*] I suppose I am, you know. [*Uproariously*] Ha, ha!

MISS EYNSFORD HILL [*who considers* HIGGINS *quite eligible matrimonially*] I sympathize. *I* havnt any small talk. If people would only be frank and say what they really think!

HIGGINS [*relapsing into gloom*] Lord forbid!

MRS EYNSFORD HILL [*taking up her daughter's cue*] But why?

HIGGINS. What they think they ought to think is bad enough, Lord knows; but what they really think would break up the whole show. Do you suppose it would be really agreeable if I were to come out now with what *I* really think?

MISS EYNSFORD HILL [*gaily*] Is it so very cynical?

HIGGINS. Cynical! Who the dickens said it was cynical? I mean it wouldnt be decent.

MRS EYNSFORD HILL [*seriously*] Oh! I'm sure you dont mean that, Mr Higgins.

HIGGINS. You see, we're all savages, more or less. We're supposed to be civilized and cultured—to know all about poetry and philosophy and art and science, and so on; but how many of us know even the meanings of these names? [*To* MISS HILL] What do you know of poetry? [*To* MRS HILL] What do you know of science? [*Indicating* FREDDY] What does he know of art or science or anything else? What the devil do you imagine I know of philosophy?

MRS HIGGINS [*warningly*] Or of manners, Henry?

THE PARLORMAID [*opening the door*] Miss Doolittle. [*She withdraws*].

HIGGINS [*rising hastily and running to* MRS HIGGINS] Here she is, mother. [*He stands on tiptoe and makes signs over his mother's head to* ELIZA *to indicate to her which lady is her hostess*].

ELIZA, *who is exquisitely dressed, produces an impression of such remarkable distinction and beauty as she enters that they all rise, quite fluttered. Guided by* HIGGINS'*s signals, she comes to* MRS HIGGINS *with studied grace.*

LIZA [*speaking with pedantic correctness of pronunciation and great beauty of tone*] How do you do, Mrs Higgins? [*She gasps slightly in making sure of the H in Higgins, but is quite successful*]. Mr Higgins told me I might come.

MRS HIGGINS [*cordially*] Quite right: I'm very glad indeed to see you.

PICKERING. How do you do, Miss Doolittle?

LIZA [*shaking hands with him*] Colonel Pickering, is it not?

MRS EYNSFORD HILL. I feel sure we have met before, Miss Doolittle. I remember your eyes.

LIZA. How do you do? [*She sits down on the ottoman gracefully in the place just left vacant by* HIGGINS].

MRS EYNSFORD HILL [*introducing*] My daughter Clara.

---

9. soirées (swä räz') *n.*: Parties held in the evening.

LIZA. How do you do?

CLARA [impulsively] How do you do? [She sits down on the ottoman beside ELIZA, devouring her with her eyes].

FREDDY [coming to their side of the ottoman] Ive certainly had the pleasure.

MRS EYNSFORD HILL [introducing] My son Freddy.

LIZA. How do you do?

FREDDY bows and sits down in the Elizabethan chair, infatuated.

HIGGINS [suddenly] By George, yes: it all comes back to me! [They stare at him]. Covent Garden! [Lamentably] What a damned thing!

MRS HIGGINS. Henry, please! [He is about to sit on the edge of the table] Dont sit on my writing-table: youll break it.

HIGGINS [sulkily] Sorry.

He goes to the divan, stumbling into the fender and over the fire-irons on his way; extricating himself with muttered imprecations; and finishing his disastrous journey by throwing himself so impatiently on the divan that he almost breaks it. MRS HIGGINS looks at him, but controls herself and says nothing.

A long and painful pause ensues.

MRS HIGGINS [at last, conversationally] Will it rain, do you think?

LIZA. The shallow depression in the west of these islands is likely to move slowly in an easterly direction. There are no indications of any great change in the barometrical situation.

FREDDY. Ha! ha! how awfully funny!

LIZA. What is wrong with that, young man? I bet I got it right.

FREDDY. Killing!

MRS EYNSFORD HILL. I'm sure I hope it wont turn cold. Theres so much influenza about. It runs right through our whole family regularly every spring.

LIZA [darkly] My aunt died of influenza: so they said.

MRS EYNSFORD HILL [clicks her tongue sympathetically]!!!

LIZA [in the same tragic tone] But it's my belief they done the old woman in.

MRS HIGGINS [puzzled] Done her in?

LIZA. Y-e-e-e-es, Lord love you! Why should she die of influenza? She come through diphtheria right enough the year before. I saw her with my own eyes. Fairly blue with it, she was. They all thought she was dead; but my father he kept ladling gin down her throat til she came to so sudden that she bit the bowl off the spoon.

MRS EYNSFORD HILL [startled] Dear me!

LIZA [piling up the indictment] What call would a woman with that strength in her have to die of influenza? What become of her new straw hat that should have come to me? Somebody pinched it; and what I say is, them as pinched it done her in.

MRS EYNSFORD HILL. What does doing her in mean?

HIGGINS [hastily] Oh, thats the new small talk. To do a person in means to kill them.

MRS EYNSFORD HILL [to ELIZA, horrified] You surely dont believe that your aunt was killed?

LIZA. Do I not! Them she lived with would have killed her for a hat-pin, let alone a hat.

MRS EYNSFORD HILL. But it cant have been right for your father to pour spirits down her throat like that. It might have killed her.

LIZA. Not her. Gin was mother's milk to her. Besides, he'd poured so much down his own throat that he knew the good of it.

MRS EYNSFORD HILL. Do you mean that he drank?

LIZA. Drank! My word! Something chronic.

MRS EYNSFORD HILL. How dreadful for you!

LIZA. Not a bit. It never did him no harm what I could see. But then he did not keep it up regular. [*Cheerfully*] On the burst, as you might say, from time to time. And always more agreeable when he had a drop in. When he was out of work, my mother used to give him fourpence and tell him to go out and not come back until he'd drunk himself cheerful and loving-like. Theres lots of women has to make their husbands drunk to make them fit to live with. [*Now quite at her ease*] You see, it's like this. If a man has a bit of conscience, it always takes him when he's sober; and then it makes him low-spirited. A drop of booze just takes that off and makes him happy. [*To* FREDDY, *who is in convulsions of suppressed laughter*] Here! what are you sniggering at?

FREDDY. The new small talk. You do it so awfully well.

LIZA. If I was doing it proper, what was you laughing at? [*To* HIGGINS] Have I said anything I oughtnt?

MRS HIGGINS [*interposing*] Not at all, Miss Doolittle.

LIZA. Well, thats a mercy, anyhow. [*Expansively*] What I always say is—

HIGGINS [*rising and looking at his watch*] Ahem!

LIZA [*looking round at him; taking the hint; and rising*] Well: I must go. [*They all rise.* FREDDY *goes to the door*]. So pleased to have met you. Goodbye. [*She shakes hands with* MRS HIGGINS].

MRS HIGGINS. Goodbye.

LIZA. Goodbye, Colonel Pickering.

PICKERING. Goodbye, Miss Doolittle. [*They shake hands*].

LIZA [*nodding to the others*] Goodbye, all.

FREDDY [*opening the door for her*] Are you walking across the Park, Miss Doolittle? If so——

LIZA [*with perfectly elegant diction*] Walk! Not bloody likely. [*Sensation*]. I am going in a taxi. [*She goes out*].

PICKERING *gasps and sits down.* FREDDY *goes out on the balcony to catch another glimpse of* ELIZA.

MRS EYNSFORD HILL [*suffering from shock*] Well, I really cant get used to the new ways.

CLARA [*throwing herself discontentedly into the Elizabethan chair*] Oh, it's all right, mamma, quite right. People will think we never go anywhere or see anybody if you are so old-fashioned.

MRS EYNSFORD HILL. I daresay I am very old-fashioned; but I do hope you wont begin using that expression, Clara. I have got accustomed to hear you talking about men as rotters, and calling everything filthy and beastly; though I do think it horrible and unladylike. But this last is really too much. Dont you think so, Colonel Pickering?

PICKERING. Dont ask me. Ive been away in India for several years; and manners have changed so much that I sometimes dont know whether I'm at a respectable dinner-table or in a ship's forecastle.

CLARA. It's all a matter of habit. Theres no right or wrong in it. Nobody means anything by it. And it's so quaint, and gives such a smart emphasis to things that are not in themselves very witty. I find the new small talk delightful and quite innocent.

MRS EYNSFORD HILL [*rising*] Well, after that, I think it's time for us to go.

PICKERING *and* HIGGINS *rise*.

CLARA [*rising*] Oh yes: we have three at-homes to go to still. Goodbye, Mrs Higgins. Goodbye, Colonel Pickering. Goodbye, Professor Higgins.

HIGGINS [*coming grimly at her from the divan, and accompanying her to the door*] Goodbye. Be sure you try on that small talk at the three at-homes. Dont be nervous about it. Pitch it in strong.

CLARA [*all smiles*] I will. Goodbye. Such nonsense, all this early Victorian prudery!

HIGGINS [*tempting her*] Such damned nonsense!

CLARA. Such bloody nonsense!

MRS EYNSFORD HILL [*convulsively*] Clara!

CLARA. Ha! Ha! [*She goes out radiant, conscious of being thoroughly up to date, and is heard descending the stairs in a stream of silvery laughter*].

FREDDY [*to the heavens at large*] Well, I ask you— [*He gives it up, and comes to* MRS HIGGINS]. Goodbye.

MRS HIGGINS [*shaking hands*] Goodbye. Would you like to meet Miss Doolittle again?

FREDDY [*eagerly*] Yes, I should, most awfully.

MRS HIGGINS. Well, you know my days.

FREDDY. Yes. Thanks awfully. Goodbye. [*He goes out*].

MRS EYNSFORD HILL. Goodbye, Mr Higgins.

HIGGINS. Goodbye. Goodbye.

MRS EYNSFORD HILL [*to* PICKERING] It's no use. I shall never be able to bring myself to use that word.

PICKERING. Dont. It's not compulsory, you know. Youll get on quite well without it.

MRS EYNSFORD HILL. Only, Clara is so down on me if I am not positively reeking with the latest slang. Goodbye.

PICKERING. Goodbye [*They shake hands*].

MRS EYNSFORD HILL. [*to* MRS HIGGINS] You mustnt mind Clara. [PICKERING, *catching from her lowered tone that this is not meant for him to hear, discreetly joins* HIGGINS *at the window*]. We're so poor! and she gets so few parties, poor child! She doesn't quite know. [MRS HIGGINS, *seeing that her eyes are moist, takes her hand sympathetically and goes with her to the door*]. But the boy is nice. Dont you think so?

MRS HIGGINS. Oh, quite nice. I shall always be delighted to see him.

MRS EYNSFORD HILL. Thank you, dear. Goodbye. [*She goes out*].

HIGGINS [*eagerly*] Well? Is Eliza presentable [*he swoops on his mother and drags her to the ottoman, where she sits down in* ELIZA'*s place with her son on her left*]?

PICKERING *returns to his chair on her right.*

MRS HIGGINS. You silly boy, of course she's not presentable. She's a triumph of your art and of her dressmaker's; but if you suppose for a moment that she doesn't give herself away in every sentence she utters, you must be perfectly cracked about her.

PICKERING. But dont you think something might be done? I mean something to eliminate the sanguinary[10] element from her conversation.

MRS HIGGINS. Not as long as she is in Henry's hands.

HIGGINS [*aggrieved*] Do you mean that my language is improper?

MRS HIGGINS. No, dearest: it would be quite proper—say on a canal barge; but it would not be proper for her at a garden party.

HIGGINS [*deeply injured*] Well I must say—

PICKERING [*interrupting him*] Come, Higgins: you must learn to know yourself. I havnt heard such language as yours since we used to review the volunteers in Hyde Park twenty years ago.

HIGGINS [*sulkily*] Oh, well, if you say so, I suppose I dont always talk like a bishop.

---

10. sanguinary (saŋ′ gwi ner′ ē) *adj.*: Bloody.

MRS HIGGINS [*quieting* HENRY *with a touch*] Colonel Pickering: will you tell me what is the exact state of things in Wimpole Street?

PICKERING [*cheerfully: as if this completely changed the subject*] Well, I have come to live there with Henry. We work together at my Indian Dialects; and we think it more convenient—

MRS HIGGINS. Quite so. I know all about that: it's an excellent arrangement. But where does this girl live?

HIGGINS. With us, of course. Where should she live?

MRS HIGGINS. But on what terms? Is she a servant? If not, what is she?

PICKERING [*slowly*] I think I know what you mean, Mrs Higgins.

HIGGINS. Well, dash me if *I* do! Ive had to work at the girl every day for months to get her to her present pitch. Besides, she's useful. She knows where my things are, and remembers my appointments and so forth.

MRS HIGGINS. How does your housekeeper get on with her?

HIGGINS. Mrs Pearce? Oh, she's jolly glad to get so much taken off her hands; for before Eliza came, she used to have to find things and remind me of my appointments. But she's got some silly bee in her bonnet about Eliza. She keeps saying "You dont think, sir": doesn't she, Pick?

PICKERING. Yes: thats the formula. "You dont think, sir." Thats the end of every conversation about Eliza.

HIGGINS. As if I ever stop thinking about the girl and her confounded vowels and consonants. I'm worn out, thinking about her, and watching her lips and her teeth and her tongue, not to mention her soul, which is the quaintest of the lot.

MRS HIGGINS. You certainly are a pretty pair of babies, playing with your live doll.

HIGGINS. Playing! The hardest job I ever tackled: make no mistake about that, mother. But you have no idea how frightfully interesting it is to take a human being and change her into a quite different human being by creating a new speech for her. It's filling up the deepest gulf that separates class from class and soul from soul.

PICKERING [*drawing his chair closer to* MRS HIGGINS *and bending over to her eagerly*] Yes: it's enormously interesting. I assure you, Mrs Higgins, we take Eliza very seriously. Every week—every day almost—there is some new change. [*Closer again*] We keep records of every stage—dozens of gramophone disks and photographs—

HIGGINS [*assailing her at the other ear*] Yes, by George: it's the most absorbing experiment I ever tackled. She regularly fills our lives up: doesn't she, Pick?

PICKERING. We're always talking Eliza.

HIGGINS. Teaching Eliza.

PICKERING. Dressing Eliza.

MRS HIGGINS. What!

HIGGINS. Inventing new Elizas.

	(speaking together)	
HIGGINS.		You know, she has the most extraordinary quickness of ear:
PICKERING.		I assure you, my dear Mrs Higgins, that girl
HIGGINS.		just like a parrot. Ive tried her with every
PICKERING.		is a genius. She can play the piano quite beautifully.
HIGGINS.		possible sort of sound that a human being can make—
PICKERING.		We have taken her to classical concerts and to music
HIGGINS.		Continental dialects, African dialects, Hottentot

PICKERING. (speaking together) halls; and it's all the same to her: she plays everything

HIGGINS. clicks, things it took me years to get hold of; and

PICKERING. she hears right off when she comes home, whether it's

HIGGINS. she picks them up like a shot, right away, as if she had

PICKERING. Beethoven and Brahms or Lehar, and Lionel Monckton;

HIGGINS. / PICKERING. been at it all her life. though six months ago, she'd never as much as touched a piano—

MRS HIGGINS [putting her fingers in her ears, as they are by this time shouting one another down with an intolerable noise] Sh-sh-sh—sh! [They stop].

PICKERING. I beg your pardon. [He draws his chair back apologetically].

HIGGINS. Sorry. When Pickering starts shouting nobody can get a word in edgeways.

MRS HIGGINS. Be quiet, Henry. Colonel Pickering: dont you realize that when Eliza walked in Wimpole Street, something walked in with her?

PICKERING. Her father did. But Henry soon got rid of him.

MRS HIGGINS. It would have been more to the point if her mother had. But as her mother didnt something else did.

PICKERING. But what?

MRS HIGGINS. (unconsciously dating herself by the word) A problem.

PICKERING. Oh, I see. The problem of how to pass her off as a lady.

HIGGINS. I'll solve that problem. Ive half solved it already.

MRS HIGGINS. No, you two infinitely stupid male creatures: the problem of what is to be done with her afterwards.

HIGGINS. I dont see anything in that. She can go her own way, with all the advantages I have given her.

MRS HIGGINS. The advantages of that poor woman who was here just now! The manners and habits that disqualify a fine lady from earning her own living without giving her a fine lady's income! Is that what you mean?

PICKERING. [Indulgently, being rather bored] Oh, that will be all right, Mrs Higgins. [He rises to go].

HIGGINS. [Rising also] We'll find her some light employment.

PICKERING. She's happy enough. Dont you worry about her. Goodbye. [He shakes hands as if he were consoling a frightened child, and makes for the door].

HIGGINS. Anyhow, theres no good bothering now. The thing's done. Goodbye, mother. [He kisses her, and follows PICKERING].

PICKERING [turning for a final consolation] There are plenty of openings. We'll do whats right. Goodbye.

HIGGINS [to Pickering as they go out together] Lets take her to the Shakespear exhibition at Earls Court.

PICKERING. Yes: lets. Her remarks will be delicious.

HIGGINS. She'll mimic all the people for us when we get home.

PICKERING. Ripping. [Both are heard laughing as they go downstairs].

MRS HIGGINS [rises with an impatient bounce, and returns to her work at the writing-table. She sweeps a litter of disarranged papers out of the way; snatches a *sheet of paper from her stationery case; and tries resolutely to write. At the third time she gives it up; flings down her pen; grips the table angrily and exclaims*] Oh, men! men!! men!!!

*   *   *   *   *   *

Clearly Eliza will not pass as a duchess yet; and Higgins's bet remains unwon. But the six months are not yet exhausted and just in time Eliza does actually pass as a princess. For a glimpse of how she did it imagine an Embassy in London one summer evening after dark. The hall door has an awning and a carpet across the sidewalk to the kerb, because a grand reception is in progress. A small crowd is lined up to see the guests arrive.

A Rolls-Royce car drives up. Pickering in evening dress, with medals and orders, alights, and hands out Eliza, in opera cloak, evening dress, diamonds, fan, flowers and all accessories. Higgins follows. The car drives off; and the three go up the steps and into the house, the door opening for them as they approach.

Inside the house they find themselves in a spacious hall from which the grand staircase rises. On the left are the arrangements for the gentlemen's cloaks. The male guests are depositing their hats and wraps there.

On the right is a door leading to the ladies' cloakroom. Ladies are going in cloaked and coming out in splendor. Pickering whispers to Eliza and points out the ladies' room. She goes into it. Higgins and Pickering take off their overcoats and take tickets for them from the attendant.

One of the guests, occupied in the same way, has his back turned. Having taken his ticket, he turns round and reveals himself as an important looking young man with an astonishingly hairy face. He has an enormous moustache, flowing out into luxuriant whiskers. Waves of hair cluster on his brow. His hair is cropped closely at the back, and glows with oil. Otherwise he is very smart. He wears several worthless orders. He is evidently a foreigner, guessable as a whis-

kered Pandour[11] from Hungary; but in spite of the ferocity of his moustache he is amiable and genially voluble.

Recognizing Higgins, he flings his arms wide apart and approaches him enthusiastically.

WHISKERS. Maestro, maestro. [*He embraces* HIGGINS *and kisses him on both cheeks*]. You remember me?

HIGGINS. No I dont. Who the devil are you?

WHISKERS. I am your pupil: your first pupil, your best and greatest pupil. I am little Nepommuck, the marvellous boy. I have made your name famous throughout Europe. You teach me phonetic. You cannot forget ME.

HIGGINS. Why dont you shave?

NEPOMMUCK. I have not your imposing appearrance, your chin, your brow. Nobody notice me when I shave. Now I am famous: they call me Hairy Faced Dick.

HIGGINS. And what are you doing here among all these swells?

NEPOMMUCK. I am interpreter. I speak 32 languages. I am indispensable at these international parties. You are great cockney specialist: you place a man anywhere in London the moment he open his mouth. I place any man in Europe.

A FOOTMAN *hurries down the grand staircase and comes to* NEPOMMUCK.

FOOTMAN. You are wanted upstairs. Her Excellency cannot understand the Greek gentleman.

NEPOMMUCK. Thank you, yes, immediately.

The FOOTMAN *goes and is lost in the crowd.*

NEPOMMUCK [*to* HIGGINS] This Greek diplomatist pretends he cannot speak nor understand English. He cannot deceive me. He is the son of a Clerkenwell watchmaker. He

---

11. Pandour: A bodyguard or servant of Hungarian nobles.

speaks English so villainously that he dare not utter a word of it without betraying his origin. I help him to pretend; but I make him pay through the nose. I make them all pay. Ha ha! [*He hurries upstairs*].

PICKERING. Is this fellow really an expert? Can he find out Eliza and blackmail her?

HIGGINS. We shall see. If he finds her out I lose my bet.

ELIZA *comes from the cloakroom and joins them.*

PICKERING. Well, Eliza, now for it. Are you ready?

LIZA. Are you nervous, Colonel?

PICKERING. Frightfully. I feel exactly as I felt before my first battle. It's the first time that frightens.

LIZA. It is not the first time for me, Colonel. I have done this fifty times—hundreds of times—in my little piggery in Angel Court in my day-dreams. I am in a dream now. Promise me not to let Professor Higgins wake me; for if he does I shall forget everything and talk as I used to in Drury Lane.

PICKERING. Not a word, Higgins. [*To* ELIZA] Now, ready?

LIZA. Ready.

PICKERING. Go.

They mount the stairs, HIGGINS *last.* PICKERING *whispers to the* FOOTMAN *on the first landing.*

FIRST LANDING FOOTMAN. Miss Doolittle, Colonel Pickering, Professor Higgins.

SECOND LANDING FOOTMAN. Miss Doolittle, Colonel Pickering, Professor Higgins.

At the top of the staircase the AMBASSADOR *and his* WIFE, *with* NEPOMMUCK *at her elbow, are receiving.*

HOSTESS [*taking* ELIZA'*s hand*] How d'ye do?

HOST [*same play*] How d'ye do? How d'ye do, Pickering?

LIZA [*with a beautiful gravity that awes her hostess*] How do you do? [*She passes on to the drawingroom*].

HOSTESS. Is that your adopted daughter, Colonel Pickering? She will make a sensation.

PICKERING. Most kind of you to invite her for me. [*He passes on*].

HOSTESS [*to* NEPOMMUCK] Find out all about her.

NEPOMMUCK [*bowing*] Excellency—[*he goes into the crowd*].

HOST. How d'ye do, Higgins? You have a rival here tonight. He introduced himself as your pupil. Is he any good?

HIGGINS. He can learn a language in a fortnight—knows dozens of them. A sure mark of a fool. As a phonetician, no good whatever.

HOSTESS. How d'ye do, Professor?

HIGGINS. How do you do? Fearful bore for you this sort of thing. Forgive my part in it. [*He passes on*].

In the drawing room and its suite of salons the reception is in full swing. Eliza passes through. She is so intent on her ordeal that she walks like a somnambulist in a desert instead of a débutante in a fashionable crowd. They stop talking to look at her, admiring her dress, her jewels, and her strangely attractive self. Some of the younger ones at the back stand on their chairs to see.

The Host and Hostess come in from the staircase and mingle with their guests. Higgins, gloomy and contemptuous of the whole business, comes into the group where they are chatting.

HOSTESS. Ah, here is Professor Higgins: he will tell us. Tell us all about the wonderful young lady, Professor.

HIGGINS [*almost morosely*] What wonderful young lady?

HOSTESS. You know very well. They tell me there has been nothing like her in London since people stood on their chairs to look at

Mrs Langtry.[12]

NEPOMMUCK *joins the group, full of news.*

HOSTESS. Ah, here you are at last, Nepommuck. Have you found out all about the Doolittle lady?

NEPOMMUCK. I have found out all about her. She is a fraud.

HOSTESS. A fraud! Oh no.

NEPOMMUCK. YES, yes. She cannot deceive me. Her name cannot be Doolittle.

HIGGINS. Why?

NEPOMMUCK. Because Doolittle is an English name. And she is not English.

HOSTESS. Oh, nonsense! She speaks English perfectly.

NEPOMMUCK. Too perfectly. Can you shew me any English woman who speaks English as it should be spoken? Only foreigners who have been taught to speak it speak it well.

HOSTESS. Certainly she terrified me by the way she said How d'ye do. I had a schoolmistress who talked like that; and I was mortally afraid of her. But if she is not English what is she?

NEPOMMUCK. Hungarian.

ALL THE REST. Hungarian!

NEPOMMUCK. Hungarian. And of royal blood. I am Hungarian. My blood is royal.

HIGGINS. Did you speak to her in Hungarian?

NEPOMMUCK. I did. She was very clever. She said "Please speak to me in English: I do not understand French." French! She pretend not to know the difference between Hungarian and French. Impossible: she knows both.

HIGGINS. And the blood royal? How did you find that out?

NEPOMMUCK. Instinct, maestro, instinct. Only the Magyar races can produce that air of the divine right, those resolute eyes. She is a princess.

HOST. What do you say, Professor?

HIGGINS. I say an ordinary London girl out of the gutter and taught to speak by an expert. I place her in Drury Lane.

NEPOMMUCK. Ha ha ha! Oh, maestro, maestro, you are mad on the subject of cockney dialects. The London gutter is the whole world for you.

HIGGINS [*to the* HOSTESS] What does your Excellency say?

HOSTESS. Oh, of course I agree with Nepommuck. She must be a princess at least.

HOST. Not necessarily legitimate, of course. Morganatic[13] perhaps. But that is undoubtedly her class.

HIGGINS. I stick to my opinion.

HOSTESS. Oh, you are incorrigible.
The group breaks up, leaving HIGGINS *isolated.* PICKERING *joins him.*

PICKERING. Where is Eliza? We must keep an eye on her.

ELIZA *joins them.*

LIZA. I don't think I can bear much more. The people all stare so at me. An old lady has just told me that I speak exactly like Queen Victoria. I am sorry if I have lost your bet. I have done my best; but nothing can make me the same as these people.

PICKERING. You have not lost it, my dear. You have won it ten times over.

HIGGINS. Let us get out of this. I have had enough of chattering to these fools.

PICKERING. Eliza is tired; and I am hungry. Let us clear out and have supper somewhere.

---

12. Mrs. Langtry: Lily Langtry (1852–1929), a beautiful English actress.

13. Morganatic (môr′ gə nat′ ik) *adj.*: Referring to a form of marriage in which a person of royalty or nobility marries a spouse of inferior social status. While such a marriage is considered valid, children produced by it do not inherit titles.

Your Response

1. After reading Act III, what is your opinion of Henry Higgins? Explain.

Recalling

2. How does Higgins explain Eliza's language to the Eynsford Hills?
3. Who does Nepommuck declare Eliza to be?
4. Explain the outcome of Pickering's bet with Higgins.

Interpreting

5. (a) What humor arises out of Higgins's telling Eliza to limit her conversation to two topics? (b) Out of Nepommuck's "investigation" of Eliza?
6. At the end of the embassy ball, Eliza comments that "nothing can make me the same as these people." (a) What do you suppose to be her state of mind as she utters this comment? Why? (b) What is Shaw suggesting about Eliza through this comment?

Applying

7. What parallels to an "at-home day," if any, can you find in modern American social customs? Explain the similarities and point out any differences.

ANALYZING LITERATURE

Using Satire

Satire is a technique that unites comedy and criticism to ridicule an offensive behavior or institution. The targets of satire, since its origins in ancient Greek and Roman drama, have included unjust or overly harsh laws, mindless social customs, and shallow trends. In Act III of *Pygmalion,* Shaw aims his satiric arrows at several customs and foibles of his day that continue to exist in our own. These include:

1. the need (of some) to make small talk.
2. proper social etiquette.
3. the effort to pass oneself off as someone one is not.

Locate and describe the places in Act III where Shaw pokes fun at each of these human failings.

CRITICAL THINKING AND READING

Comparing and Contrasting Attitudes

In Act III of *Pygmalion,* the characters express a variety of attitudes on a number of topics. Compare and contrast the following characters' views on the topics mentioned, and tell how you believe each of the characters came by those views.

1. Good manners: Higgins, Mrs. Higgins
2. Love: Higgins, Mrs. Higgins, Freddy
3. Slang: Mrs. Eynsford Hill, her daughter
4. The fate of Eliza: Mrs. Higgins, Higgins, Pickering
5. Formal dress affairs: Eliza, Higgins, Pickering

THINKING AND WRITING

Evaluating the Effectiveness of Satire

Satire is a difficult form of comedy to write. A well-conceived satire will neither be so light as to lack punch nor so biting as to lack humor. In a short essay, explain whether or not you find the humor and criticism of Shaw's satire in Act III well balanced. To get yourself started, answer questions such as the following. What is funny and why? What is being criticized? How clear are Shaw's intentions? When you revise, make sure you have included examples from Act III to support your thesis.

LEARNING OPTION

Language. Slang is language that is used and understood by members of a particular group of people or culture. Unlike standard language, which changes very slowly over long periods of time, slang terms come into and go out of fashion very quickly. Some of the slang terms used by the characters in Act III include "done her in" (page 1011), "somebody pinched it" (page 1011), "on the burst" (page 1012), and "he had a drop in" (page 1012). With a group of classmates, come up with a list of slang terms you used a year or more ago. Then make another list of slang terms you currently use. Compare the two to see how quickly slang goes out of style.

GUIDE FOR INTERPRETING

Pygmalion, Act IV

Crisis. Crisis is a high point of emotion or action that occurs near the end of a work of fiction. Also known as *climax,* the crisis is one key point in the carefully arranged sequence of elements in a story known as *plot*. Historically the plot contains five such elements, the first of which, the *exposition,* is a playbill of sorts. The exposition tells us who the characters are and what sort of *conflict,* or struggle, they face. Often this conflict is between the characters themselves, although at times an outside force like nature or society is involved. In any event, *complications* arise in one form or another, causing the action or emotional intensity to build. Once the crisis has been reached, the work begins to wind down. In this final stage, known as the *resolution* or *denouement,* all problems are solved and any loose ends are tied up. This pattern of elements has been abandoned in whole or in part by a number of modern writers. Shaw, in an effort to create a more lifelike drama, deviated somewhat from this formula, especially in his comedies.

Imagine you are sitting in a theater watching this play. The curtain has come down on Act III. During intermission you turn to the person sitting next to you and discuss the play. Create a conversation in which both of you provide ideas on what will happen next.

Shaw broke away from the traditional arrangement of plot elements in a drama. He explained his reasoning this way:

> You will understand that my plays are not constructed plays: they grow naturally. If you "construct" a play: that is, if you plan your play beforehand, and then carry out your plan, you will find yourself in the position of a person putting together a jig-saw puzzle . . . which, to a spectator, is unbearably dull. The scenes must be born alive. If they are not new to you as you write, and sometimes quite contrary to the expectations with which you have begun them, they are dead wood. A live play constructs itself with a subtlety, and often with a mechanical ingenuity, that often deludes critics into holding the author up as the most crafty of artificers when he has never, in writing his play, known what one of his characters would say until another gave the clue. . . . Now what the drama can do, and what it actually does, is to take this unmeaning, haphazard show of life . . . and arrange it in such a way as to make you think very much more deeply about it than you ever dreamed of thinking about actual incidents that came to your knowledge.

ACT IV

The Wimpole Street laboratory. Midnight. Nobody in the room. The clock on the mantelpiece strikes twelve. The fire is not alight: it is a summer night.

    Presently HIGGINS *and* PICKERING *are heard on the stairs.*

HIGGINS [*calling down to* PICKERING] I say, Pick: lock up, will you? I shant be going out again.

PICKERING. Right. Can Mrs Pearce go to bed? We dont want anything more, do we?

HIGGINS. Lord, no!

ELIZA *opens the door and is seen on the lighted landing in all the finery in which she has just won* HIGGINS*'s bet for him. She comes to the hearth, and switches on the electric lights there. She is tired: her pallor contrasts strongly with her dark eyes and hair; and her expression is almost tragic. She takes off her cloak; puts her fan and gloves on the piano: and sits down on the bench, brooding and silent.* HIGGINS, *in evening dress, with overcoat and hat, comes in, carrying a smoking jacket which he has picked up downstairs. He takes off the hat and overcoat; throws them carelessly on the newspaper stand; disposes of his coat in the same way; puts on the smoking jacket; and throws himself wearily into the easy-chair at the hearth.* PICKERING, *similarly attired, comes in. He also takes off his hat and overcoat, and is about to throw them on* HIGGINS*'s when he hesitates.*

PICKERING. I say: Mrs Pearce will row if we leave these things lying about in the drawing room.

HIGGINS. Oh, chuck them over the bannisters into the hall. She'll find them there in the morning and put them away all right. She'll think we were drunk.

PICKERING. We are, slightly. Are there any letters?

HIGGINS. I didnt look. [PICKERING *takes the overcoats and hats and goes downstairs.* HIGGINS *begins half singing half yawning an air from* La Fanciulla Dcl Golden West.[1] *Suddenly he stops and exclaims*] I wonder where the devil my slippers are!

ELIZA *looks at him darkly; then rises suddenly and leaves the room.*

    HIGGINS *yawns again, and resumes his song.*

    PICKERING *returns, with the contents of the letter-box in his hand.*

---

    1. La Fanciulla (fan ᴄho͞o′ la) **del Golden West:** *The Girl of the Golden West,* an opera by Italian composer Giacomo Puccini (1858–1924).

PICKERING. Only circulars, and this coroneted billet-doux[2] for you. [*He throws the circulars into the fender, and posts himself on the hearthrug, with his back to the grate*].

HIGGINS [*glancing at the billet-doux*] Money-lender. [*He throws the letter after the circulars*].

ELIZA *returns with a pair of large down-at-heel slippers. She places them on the carpet before* HIGGINS, *and sits as before without a word.*

HIGGINS [*yawning again*] Oh Lord! What an evening! What a crew! What a silly tomfoolery! [*He raises his shoe to unlace it, and catches sight of the slippers. He stops unlacing and looks at them as if they had appeared there of their own accord*]. Oh! theyre there, are they?

PICKERING [*stretching himself*]. Well, I feel a bit tired. It's been a long day. The garden party, a dinner party, and the reception! Rather too much of a good thing. But youve won your bet, Higgins. Eliza did the trick, and something to spare, eh?

HIGGINS [*fervently*] Thank God it's over!

ELIZA *flinches violently; but they take no notice of her; and she recovers herself and sits stonily as before.*

PICKERING. Were you nervous at the garden party? *I* was. Eliza didnt seem a bit nervous.

HIGGINS. Oh, she wasnt nervous. I knew she'd be all right. No: it's the strain of putting the job through all these months that has told on me. It was interesting enough at first, while we were at the phonetics; but after that I got deadly sick of it. If I hadnt backed myself to do it I should have chucked the whole thing up two months ago. It was a silly notion: the whole thing has been a bore.

PICKERING. Oh come! the garden party was

---

2. **billet-doux** (bil' ā dōō'): Love letter.

frightfully exciting. My heart began beating like anything.

HIGGINS. Yes, for the first three minutes. But when I saw we were going to win hands down, I felt like a bear in a cage, hanging about doing nothing. The dinner was worse: sitting gorging there for over an hour, with nobody but a damned fool of a fashionable woman to talk to! I tell you, Pickering, never again for me. No more artificial duchesses. The whole thing has been simple purgatory.

PICKERING. Youve never been broken in properly to the social routine. [*Strolling over to the piano*] I rather enjoy dipping into it occasionally myself: it makes me feel young again. Anyhow, it was a great success: an immense success. I was quite frightened once or twice because Eliza was doing it so well. You see, lots of the real people cant do it at all: theyre such fools that they think style comes by nature to people in their position; and so they never learn. Theres always something professional about doing a thing superlatively well.

HIGGINS. Yes: thats what drives me mad: the silly people dont know their own silly business. [*Rising*] However, it's over and done with; and now I can go to bed at last without dreading tomorrow.

ELIZA'*s beauty becomes murderous.*

PICKERING. I think I shall turn in too. Still, it's been a great occasion: a triumph for you. Goodnight. [*He goes*].

HIGGINS [*following him*] Goodnight. [*Over his shoulder, at the door*] Put out the lights, Eliza; and tell Mrs Pearce not to make coffee for me in the morning: I'll take tea. [*He goes out*].

ELIZA *tries to control herself and feel indifferent as she rises and walks across to the hearth to switch off the lights. By the time she gets there she is on the point of screaming. She sits down in* HIGGINS'*s chair and holds on hard to the arms. Finally she gives way and flings herself furiously on the floor, raging.*

HIGGINS [*in despairing wrath outside*] What the devil have I done with my slippers? [*He appears at the door*].

LIZA [*snatching up the slippers, and hurling them at him one after the other with all her force*] There are your slippers. And there. Take your slippers; and may you never have a day's luck with them!

HIGGINS [*astounded*] What on earth—! [*He comes to her*]. Whats the matter? Get up. [*He pulls her up*] Anything wrong?

LIZA [*(breathless*] Nothing wrong—with you. Ive won your bet for you, havnt I? Thats enough for you. *I* dont matter, I suppose.

HIGGINS. You won my bet! You! Presumptuous insect! *I* won it. What did you throw those slippers at me for?

LIZA. Because I wanted to smash your face. I'd like to kill you, you selfish brute. Why didnt you leave me where you picked me out of—in the gutter? You thank God it's all over, and that now you can throw me back again there, do you? [*She crisps her fingers*[3] *frantically*].

HIGGINS [*looking at her in cool wonder*] The creature is nervous, after all.

LIZA [*gives a suffocated scream of fury, and instinctively darts her nails at his face*]!!

HIGGINS [*catching her wrists*] Ah! would you? Claws in, you cat. How dare you shew your temper to me? Sit down and be quiet. [*He throws her roughly into the easy-chair*].

LIZA [*crushed by superior strength and weight*] Whats to become of me? Whats to become of me?

HIGGINS. How the devil do I know whats to become of you? What does it matter what becomes of you?

LIZA. You dont care. I know you dont care. You wouldnt care if I was dead. I'm nothing

---

3. **crisps her fingers:** Clenches her fingers into fists.

to you—not so much as them slippers.

HIGGINS [*thundering*] Those slippers.

LIZA [*with bitter submission*]. Those slippers. I didnt think it made any difference now.

A pause. ELIZA *hopeless and crushed.* HIGGINS *a little uneasy.*

HIGGINS [*in his loftiest manner*] Why have you begun going on like this? May I ask whether you complain of your treatment here?

LIZA. No.

HIGGINS. Has anybody behaved badly to you? Colonel Pickering? Mrs Pearce? Any of the servants?

LIZA. No.

HIGGINS. I presume you dont pretend that *I* have treated you badly?

LIZA. No.

HIGGINS. I am glad to hear it. [*He moderates his tone*]. Perhaps youre tired after the strain of the day. Will you have a glass of champagne? [*He moves towards the door*].

LIZA. No. [*Recollecting her manners*] Thank you.

HIGGINS [*good-humored again*] This has been coming on you for some days. I suppose it was natural for you to be anxious about the garden party. But thats all over now. [*He pats her kindly on the shoulder. She writhes*]. Theres nothing more to worry about.

LIZA. No. Nothing more for you to worry about. [*She suddenly rises and gets away from him by going to the piano bench, where she sits and hides her face*]. Oh God! I wish I was dead.

HIGGINS [*staring after her in sincere surprise*] Why? In heaven's name, why? [*Reasonably, going to her*] Listen to me, Eliza. All this irritation is purely subjective.

LIZA. I dont understand. I'm too ignorant.

HIGGINS. It's only imagination. Low spirits and nothing else. Nobody's hurting you. Nothing's wrong. You go to bed like a good girl and sleep it off. Have a little cry and say your prayers: that will make you comfortable.

LIZA. I heard your prayers. "Thank God it's all over!"

HIGGINS [*impatiently*] Well, dont you thank God it's all over? Now you are free and can do what you like.

LIZA [*pulling herself together in desperation*] What am I fit for? What have you left me fit for? Where am I to go? What am I to do? Whats to become of me?

HIGGINS [*enlightened, but not at all impressed*] Oh, thats whats worrying you, is it? [*He thrusts his hands into his pockets, and walks about in his usual manner, rattling the contents of his pockets, as if condescending to a trivial subject out of pure kindness*]. I shouldnt bother about it if I were you. I should imagine you wont have much difficulty in settling yourself somewhere or other, though I hadnt quite realized that you were going away. [*She looks quickly at him: he does not look at her, but examines the dessert stand on the piano and decides that he will eat an apple*]. You might marry, you know. [*He bites a large piece out of the apple and munches it noisily*]. You see, Eliza, all men are not confirmed old bachelors like me and the Colonel. Most men are the marrying sort [poor devils!]; and youre not bad-looking: it's quite a pleasure to look at you sometimes—not now, of course, because youre crying and looking as ugly as the very devil; but when youre all right and quite yourself, youre what I should call attractive. That is, to the people in the marrying line, you understand. You go to bed and have a good nice rest; and then get up and look at yourself in the glass; and you wont feel so cheap.

ELIZA *again looks at him, speechless, and does not stir.*

The look is quite lost on him: he eats his apple with a dreamy expression of happiness, as it is quite a good one.

HIGGINS [*a genial afterthought occurring to him*] I daresay my mother could find some chap or other who would do very well.

LIZA. We were above that at the corner of Tottenham Court Road.

HIGGINS [*waking up*] What do you mean?

LIZA. I sold flowers. I didnt sell myself. Now youve made a lady of me I'm not fit to sell anything else. I wish youd left me where you found me.

HIGGINS [slinging the core of the apple decisively into the grate] Tosh, Eliza. Dont you insult human relations by dragging all this cant about buying and selling into it. You neednt marry the fellow if you dont like him.

LIZA. What else am I to do?

HIGGINS. Oh, lots of things. What about your old idea of a florist's shop? Pickering could set you up in one: he has lots of money. [Chuckling] He'll have to pay for all those togs you have been wearing today; and that, with the hire of the jewellery, will make a big hole in two hundred pounds. Why, six months ago you would have thought it the millennium to have a flower shop of your own. Come! youll be all right. I must clear off to bed: I'm devilish sleepy. By the way, I came down for something: I forgot what it was.

LIZA. Your slippers.

HIGGINS. Oh yes, of course. You shied them at me. [He picks them up, and is going out when she rises and speaks to him].

LIZA. Before you go, sir—

HIGGINS [dropping the slippers in his surprise at her calling him Sir] Eh?

LIZA. Do my clothes belong to me or to Colonel Pickering?

HIGGINS [coming back into the room as if her question were the very climax of unreason] What the devil use would they be to Pickering?

LIZA. He might want them for the next girl you pick up to experiment on.

HIGGINS [shocked and hurt] Is that the way you feel towards us?

LIZA. I dont want to hear anything more about that. All I want to know is whether anything belongs to me. My own clothes were burnt.

HIGGINS. But what does it matter? Why need you start bothering about that in the middle of the night?

LIZA. I want to know what I may take away with me. I dont want to be accused of stealing.

HIGGINS [now deeply wounded] Stealing! You shouldnt have said that, Eliza. That shews a want of feeling.

LIZA. I'm sorry. I'm only a common ignorant girl; and in my station I have to be careful. There cant be any feelings between the like of you and the like of me. Please will you tell me what belongs to me and what doesnt?

HIGGINS [very sulky] You may take the whole damned houseful if you like. Except the jewels. Theyre hired. Will that satisfy you? [He turns on his heel and is about to go in extreme dudgeon].

LIZA [drinking in his emotion like nectar, and nagging him to provoke a further supply] Stop, please. [She takes off her jewels]. Will you take these to your room and keep them safe? I don't want to run the risk of their being missing.

HIGGINS [furious] Hand them over. [She puts them into his hands]. If these belonged to me instead of to the jeweller, I'd ram them down your ungrateful throat. [He perfunctorily thrusts them into his pockets, unconsciously decorating himself with the protruding ends of the chains].

LIZA [taking a ring off]. This ring isnt the jeweller's: it's the one you bought me in Brighton. I dont want it now. [HIGGINS dashes the ring violently into the fireplace, and turns on her so threateningly that she crouches over the piano with her hands over her face, and exclaims] Dont you hit me.

HIGGINS. Hit you! You infamous creature, how dare you accuse me of such a thing? It is you who have hit me. You have wounded me to the heart.

LIZA [thrilling with hidden joy] I'm glad. Ive got a little of my own back, anyhow.

HIGGINS [*with dignity, in his finest professional style*] You have caused me to lose my temper: a thing that has hardly ever happened to me before. I prefer to say nothing more tonight. I am going to bed.

LIZA [*pertly*] Youd better leave a note for Mrs Pearce about the coffee; for she wont be told by me.

HIGGINS [*formally*] Damn Mrs Pearce; and damn the coffee; and damn you; and [*wildly*] damn my own folly in having lavished my hard-earned knowledge and the treasure of my regard and intimacy on a heartless guttersnipe. [*He goes out with impressive decorum, and spoils it by slamming the door savagely*].

ELIZA *goes down on her knees on the hearthrug to look for the ring. When she finds it she considers for a moment what to do with it. Finally she flings it down on the dessert stand and goes upstairs in a tearing rage.*

★   ★   ★   ★   ★   ★

The furniture of Eliza's room has been increased by a big wardrobe and a sumptuous dressing-table. She comes in and switches on the electric light. She goes to the wardrobe; opens it; and pulls out a walking dress, a hat, and a pair of shoes, which she throws on the bed. She takes off her evening dress and shoes; then takes a padded hanger from the wardrobe; adjusts it carefully in the evening dress; and hangs it in the wardrobe, which she shuts with a slam. She puts on her walking shoes, her walking dress, and hat. She takes her wrist watch from the dressing-table and fastens it on. She pulls on her gloves; takes her vanity bag; and looks into it to see that her purse is there before hanging it on her wrist. She makes for the door. Every movement expresses her furious resolution.

She takes a last look at herself in the glass.

She suddenly puts out her tongue at herself; then leaves the room, switching off the electric light at the door.

Meanwhile, in the street outside, Freddy Eynsford Hill, lovelorn, is gazing up at the second floor, in which one of the windows is still lighted.

The light goes out.

FREDDY. Goodnight, darling, darling, darling.

ELIZA *comes out, giving the door a considerable bang behind her.*

LIZA. Whatever are you doing here?

FREDDY. Nothing. I spend most of my nights here. It's the only place where I'm happy. Dont laugh at me, Miss Doolittle.

LIZA. Dont you call me Miss Doolittle, do you hear? Liza's good enough for me. [*She breaks down and grabs him by the shoulders*] Freddy: you dont think I'm a heartless guttersnipe, do you?

FREDDY. Oh no, no, darling: how can you imagine such a thing? You are the loveliest, dearest—

He loses all self-control and smothers her with kisses. She, hungry for comfort, responds. They stand there in one another's arms.

An elderly police constable arrives.

CONSTABLE [*scandalized*] Now then! Now then!! Now then!!!

They release one another hastily.

FREDDY. Sorry, constable. Weve only just become engaged.

They run away.

The constable shakes his head, reflecting on his own courtship and on the vanity of human hopes. He moves off in the opposite direction with slow professional steps.

The flight of the lovers takes them to Cavendish Square. There they halt to consider their next move.

LIZA [*out of breath*] He didnt half give me a fright, that copper. But you answered him proper.

FREDDY. I hope I havnt taken you out of your way. Where were you going?

LIZA. To the river.

FREDDY. What for?

LIZA. To make a hole in it.

FREDDY [horrified] Eliza, darling. What do you mean? What's the matter?

LIZA. Never mind. It doesnt matter now. There's nobody in the world now but you and me, is there?

FREDDY. Not a soul.

They indulge in another embrace, and are again surprised by a much younger constable.

SECOND CONSTABLE. Now then, you two! What's this? Where do you think you are? Move along here, double quick.

FREDDY. As you say, sir, double quick.

They run away again, and are in Hanover Square before they stop for another conference.

FREDDY. I had no idea the police were so devilishly prudish.

LIZA. It's their business to hunt girls off the street.

FREDDY. We must go somewhere. We cant wander about the streets all night.

LIZA. Cant we? I think it'd be lovely to wander about for ever.

FREDDY. Oh, darling.

They embrace again, oblivious of the arrival of a crawling taxi. It stops.

TAXIMAN. Can I drive you and the lady anywhere, sir?

They start asunder.

LIZA. Oh, Freddy, a taxi. The very thing.

FREDDY. But, damn it, I've no money.

LIZA. I have plenty. The Colonel thinks you should never go out without ten pounds in your pocket. Listen. We'll drive about all night; and in the morning I'll call on old Mrs Higgins and ask her what I ought to do. I'll tell you all about it in the cab. And the police wont touch us there.

FREDDY. Righto! Ripping. [*To the* TAXIMAN] Wimbledon Common. [*They drive off*].

RESPONDING TO THE SELECTION

Your Response

1. What do you think Higgins should do at this point? Explain.

Recalling

2. (a) How are Higgins and Pickering feeling as the act opens? (b) How does Eliza feel?

3. What does Higgins suggest when Eliza asks what will become of her?

4. (a) What does Eliza do after Higgins goes to bed? (b) Whom does she run into?

Interpreting

5. (a) What two characters earlier in the play anticipated the concern Eliza expresses here? (b) What was Higgins's response to them?

6. (a) In what ways does Higgins act differently from how he behaved earlier in the play? (b) In what ways is his behavior predictable? (c) What does his behavior reveal about him?

Applying

7. What aspects of being a woman of this era compound Eliza's problems?

ANALYZING LITERATURE

Explaining Crisis

The **crisis** in a work of fiction is the turning point—that moment when the conflict presented earlier in the work comes to a head. Also referred to as the *climax,* this high point, which occurs close to the end of the work, is followed by a resolution of all problems. The crisis in Act IV of *Pygmalion* is quite obviously the outgrowth of a conflict between Higgins and Eliza.

1. What is the nature of that conflict; that is, what has each of the two characters been trying to achieve from the start?
2. What problems mentioned (or raised) in Act IV remain to be resolved? How do you think they will be resolved? Explain why you feel as you do.

CRITICAL THINKING AND READING

Understanding Cause and Effect

Events, both in real life and in fiction, seldom happen in a vacuum. More commonly put, "one thing leads to another." Your ride to school does not show up and, therefore, you are late to your first-period class. Because of your lateness, you miss getting down an important assignment due the following day, and so on. An event that leads to a particular result is called a **cause.** The result of the cause is called an **effect.** Most works of fiction are chains of causes and effects.

For each of the following events, supply one cause and one effect.

1. Eliza pays Professor Higgins a visit.
2. Pickering proposes a bet with Higgins.
3. Higgins appears at his mother's "at-home."
4. Eliza throws Higgins's slippers at him.

THINKING AND WRITING

Writing a Letter of Advice

What do you think about the engagement of Eliza and Freddy? Is she making the right choice? Does she have other options? List any suggestions you would offer Eliza. Then write a letter to her offering advice. When you revise your letter, make sure your advice is practical. Have you presented it in a persuasive manner? Proofread your letter and prepare a final draft.

LEARNING OPTIONS

1. **Art.** Create a model set for one or more of the scenes in the play. Make sure that your model reflects physical details mentioned in the stage directions and dialogue. If you wish, include costumed figures that represent the characters. Display your model in class.
2. **Writing.** Imagine you write an etiquette column for your school newspaper in which you discuss appropriate behavior for various situations. Summarize the rules for attending a semiformal party for high school students. Topics might include clothing, conversation, manners, and choosing dance partners. Your column may be either practical or satirical. Have your classmates give you their reactions to your rules of conduct.

GUIDE FOR INTERPRETING

Pygmalion, Act V

The Complete Play. A play consists of many elements. The first of these is *plot,* the sequence of events. Will the plot be structured chronologically, moving ever forward in time? Or will it contain flashbacks? Next comes *setting,* the when and where of the play. How will time and location be conveyed to the audience? Through speakers' words? Through stage sets? Another element is *characters,* the people in the action. How many characters will be round, that is, complex and true-to-life? How many will be flat, one-dimensional figures included purely to advance the plot? Then comes *tone,* the playwright's attitude toward his or her subject or audience. Will the tone be lighthearted? Serious? A mixture? There is the issue of *symbols*—people, places, and events that stand for something beyond themselves. Last but not least is *theme,* the central idea of the play. What central idea or insight into life does the play communicate to the audience?

How will the play end? Based on the first four acts, draft your own ending. What will become of Eliza? Of Higgins? Of Freddy? Compare your hunches with those of your classmates.

Much of *Pygmalion* was radically different from what theatergoers were accustomed to seeing. In "An Aside" in *To Myself and My Friends,* Shaw explained the radical changes he introduced into modern English theater. He began:

> In a generation which knew nothing of any sort of acting but drawing-room acting, and which considered a speech of more than twenty words impossibly long, I went back to the classical style and write long rhetorical speeches like operatic solos, regarding my plays as musical performances precisely as Shakespeare did. As a producer I went back to the forgotten heroic stage business and the exciting or impressive declamation I had learnt from oldtimers like Risotori, Salvini, and Barry Sullivan. Yet so novel was my post-Marx post-Ibsen outlook on life that nobody suspected that my methods were as old as the stage itself. They would have seemed the merest routine to Kemble or Mrs. Siddons; but to the Victorian leading ladies they seemed to be un-leadingladylike barnstorming. . . . I was continually struggling with the conscientious efforts of our players to underdo their parts lest they should be considered stagey. . . . It took a European war to cure them of wanting to be ladies and gentlemen first and actresses and actors later.

ACT V

MRS HIGGINS'*s drawing room. She is at her writing-table as before. The* PARLORMAID *comes in.*

THE PARLORMAID [*at the door*] Mr Henry, maam, is downstairs with Colonel Pickering.

MRS HIGGINS. Well, shew them up.

THE PARLORMAID. Theyre using the telephone, maam. Telephoning to the police, I think.

MRS HIGGINS. What!

THE PARLORMAID [*coming further in and lowering her voice*] Mr Henry is in a state, maam. I thought I'd better tell you.

MRS HIGGINS. If you had told me that Mr Henry was not in a state it would have been more surprising. Tell them to come up when theyve finished with the police. I suppose he's lost something.

THE PARLORMAID. Yes, maam [*going*].

MRS HIGGINS. Go upstairs and tell Miss Doolittle that Mr Henry and the Colonel are here. Ask her not to come down til I send for her.

THE PARLORMAID. Yes, maam.

HIGGINS *bursts in. He is, as the* PARLORMAID *has said, in a state.*

HIGGINS. Look here, mother: heres a confounded thing!

MRS HIGGINS. Yes, dear. Good morning. [*He checks his impatience and kisses her, whilst the* PARLORMAID *goes out*]. What is it?

HIGGINS. Eliza's bolted.

MRS HIGGINS [*calmly continuing her writing*] You must have frightened her.

HIGGINS. Frightened her! nonsense! She was left last night, as usual, to turn out the lights and all that; and instead of going to bed she changed her clothes and went right off: her bed wasnt slept in. She came in a cab for her things before seven this morning; and that fool Mrs Pearce let her have them without telling me a word about it. What am I to do?

MRS HIGGINS. Do without, I'm afraid, Henry. The girl has a perfect right to leave if she chooses.

HIGGINS [*wandering distractedly across the room*] But I cant find anything. I dont know what appointments Ive got. I'm—[PICKERING *comes in.* MRS HIGGINS *puts down her pen and turns away from the writing-table*].

PICKERING [*shaking hands*] Good morning, Mrs Higgins. Has Henry told you? [*He sits down on the ottoman*].

HIGGINS. What does that ass of an inspector say? Have you offered a reward?

MRS HIGGINS [*rising in indignant amazement*] You dont mean to say you have set the police after Eliza.

HIGGINS. Of course. What are the police for? What else could we do? [*He sits in the Elizabethan chair*].

PICKERING. The inspector made a lot of difficulties. I really think he suspected us of some improper purpose.

MRS HIGGINS. Well, of course, he did. What right have you to go to the police and give the girl's name as if she were a thief, or a lost umbrella, or something? Really! [*She sits down again, deeply vexed*].

HIGGINS. But we want to find her.

PICKERING. We cant let her go like this, you know, Mrs Higgins. What were we to do?

MRS HIGGINS. You have no more sense, either of you, than two children. Why—

The PARLORMAID *comes in and breaks off the conversation.*

THE PARLORMAID. Mr Henry: a gentleman wants to see you very particular. He's been sent on from Wimpole Street.

HIGGINS. Oh, bother! I cant see anyone now. Who is it?

THE PARLORMAID. A Mr Doolittle, sir.

PICKERING. Doolittle! Do you mean the dustman?

THE PARLORMAID. Dustman! Oh no, sir: a gentleman.

HIGGINS [springing up excitedly] By George, Pick, it's some relative of hers that she's gone to. Somebody we know nothing about. [To the PARLORMAID] Send him up, quick.

THE PARLORMAID. Yes, sir. [She goes].

HIGGINS [eagerly, going to his mother] Genteel relatives! now we shall hear something. [He sits down in the Chippendale chair].

MRS HIGGINS. Do you know any of her people?

PICKERING. Only her father: the fellow we told you about.

THE PARLORMAID [announcing] Mr Doolittle. [She withdraws].

DOOLITTLE enters. He is resplendently dressed as for a fashionable wedding, and might, in fact, be the bridegroom. A flower in his buttonhole, a dazzling silk hat, and patent leather shoes complete the effect. He is too concerned with the business he has come on to notice MRS HIGGINS. He walks straight to HIGGINS, and accosts him with vehement reproach.

DOOLITTLE [indicating his own person] See here! Do you see this? You done this.

HIGGINS. Done what, man?

DOOLITTLE. This, I tell you. Look at it. Look at this hat. Look at this coat.

PICKERING. Has Eliza been buying you clothes?

DOOLITTLE. Eliza! not she. Why would she buy me clothes?

MRS HIGGINS. Good morning, Mr Doolittle. Wont you sit down?

DOOLITTLE [taken aback as he becomes conscious that he has forgotten his hostess]

Asking your pardon, maam. [He approaches her and shakes her proffered hand]. Thank you. [He sits down on the ottoman, on PICKERING's right]. I am that full of what has happened to me that I cant think of anything else.

HIGGINS. What the dickens has happened to you?

DOOLITTLE. I shouldn't mind if it had only happened to me: anything might happen to anybody and nobody to blame but Providence, as you might say. But this is something that you done to me: yes, you, Enry Iggins.

HIGGINS. Have you found Eliza?

DOOLITTLE. Have you lost her?

HIGGINS. Yes.

DOOLITTLE. You have all the luck, you have. I aint found her; but she'll find me quick enough now after what you done to me.

MRS HIGGINS. But what has my son done to you, Mr Doolittle?

DOOLITTLE. Done to me! Ruined me. Destroyed my happiness. Tied me up and delivered me into the hands of middle class morality.

HIGGINS [rising intolerantly and standing over DOOLITTLE] Youre raving. Youre drunk. Youre mad. I gave you five pounds. After that I had two conversations with you, at half-a-crown an hour. Ive never seen you since.

DOOLITTLE. Oh! Drunk am I? Mad am I? Tell me this. Did you or did you not write a letter to an old blighter in America that was giving five millions to found Moral Reform Societies all over the world, and that wanted you to invent a universal language for him?

HIGGINS. What! Ezra D. Wannafeller! He's dead. [He sits down again carelessly].

DOOLITTLE. Yes: he's dead; and I'm done for. Now did you or did you not write a letter to him to say that the most original moralist at

present in England, to the best of your knowledge, was Alfred Doolittle, a common dustman?

HIGGINS. Oh, after your first visit I remember making some silly joke of the kind.

DOOLITTLE. Ah! You may well call it a silly joke. It put the lid on me right enough. Just give him the chance he wanted to shew that Americans is not like us: that they reckonize and respect merit in every class of life, however humble. Them words is in his blooming will, in which, Henry Higgins, thanks to your silly joking, he leaves me a share in his Predigested Cheese Trust worth [three] thousand a year on condition that I lecture for his Wannafeller Moral Reform World League as often as they ask me up to six times a year.

HIGGINS. The devil he does! Whew! [*Brightening suddenly*] What a lark!

PICKERING. A safe thing for you, Doolittle. They wont ask you twice.

DOOLITTLE. It aint the lecturing I mind. I'll lecture them blue in the face, I will, and not turn a hair. It's making a gentleman of me that I object to. Who asked him to make a gentleman of me? I was happy. I was free. I touched pretty nigh everybody for money when I wanted it, same as I touched you, Enry Iggins. Now I am worrited; tied neck and heels; and everybody touches me for money. It's a fine thing for you, says my solicitor.[1] Is it? says I. You mean it's a good

---

1. solicitor *n.*: A member of the legal profession who is not allowed to plead cases in superior court.

thing for you, I says. When I was a poor man and had a solicitor once when they found a pram[2] in the dust cart, he got me off, and got shut of me and got me shut of him as quick as he could. Same with the doctors: used to shove me out of the hospital before I could hardly stand on my legs, and nothing to pay. Now they finds out that I'm not a healthy man and cant live unless they looks after me twice a day. In the house I'm not let do a hand's turn for myself: somebody else must do it and touch me for it. A year ago I hadnt a relative in the world except two or three that wouldn't speak to me. Now Ive fifty, and not a decent week's wages among the lot of them. I have to live for others and not for myself: that middle class morality. You talk of losing Eliza. Dont you be anxious: I bet she's on my doorstep by this: she that could support herself easy by selling flowers if I wasnt respectable. And the next one to touch me will be you, Enry Iggins. I'll have to learn to speak middle class language from you, instead of speaking proper English. Thats where youll come in; and I daresay thats what you done it for.

MRS HIGGINS. But, my dear Mr Doolittle, you need not suffer all this if you are really in earnest. Nobody can force you to accept this bequest. You can repudiate it. Isnt that so, Colonel Pickering?

PICKERING. I believe so.

DOOLITTLE [*softening his manner in deference to her sex*] Thats the tragedy of it, maam. It's easy to say chuck it; but I havnt the nerve. Which of us has? We're all intimidated. Intimidated, maam: thats what we are. What is there for me if I chuck it but the workhouse in my old age? I have to dye my hair already to keep my job as a dustman. If I was one of the deserving poor, and had put by a bit, I could chuck it; but then why should I, acause the deserving poor might as well be millionaires for all the happiness they ever has. They dont know what happi-

ness is. But I, as one of the undeserving poor, have nothing between me and the pauper's uniform but this here blasted three thousand a year that shoves me into the middle class. (Excuse the expression, maam; youd use it yourself if you had my provocation). Theyve got you every way you turn: it's a choice between the Skilly of the workhouse and the Char Bydis[3] of the middle class; and I havnt the nerve for the workhouse. Intimidated: thats what I am. Broke. Bought up. Happier men than me will call for my dust, and touch me for their tip; and I'll look on helpless, and envy them. And thats what your son has brought me to. [*He is overcome by emotion*].

MRS HIGGINS. Well, I'm very glad youre not going to do anything foolish, Mr Doolittle. For this solves the problem of Eliza's future. You can provide for her now.

DOOLITTLE [*with melancholy resignation*] Yes, maam: I'm expected to provide for everyone now, out of [three] thousand a year.

HIGGINS [*jumping up*] Nonsense! he cant provide for her. He shant provide for her. She doesnt belong to him. I paid him five pounds for her. Doolittle: either youre an honest man or a rogue.

DOOLITTLE [*tolerantly*] A little of both, Henry, like the rest of us: a little of both.

HIGGINS. Well, you took that money for the girl; and you have no right to take her as well.

MRS HIGGINS. Henry: dont be absurd. If you want to know where Eliza is, she is upstairs.

HIGGINS [*amazed*] Upstairs!!! Then I shall

---

2. pram *n.*: Baby carriage.

3. Skilly . . . Char Bydis: Doolittle means Scylla (sil′ ə) and Charybdis (kə rib′ dis), a dangerous rock and whirlpool on either side of the narrow passage between Italy and Sicily. Scylla and Charybdis, personified by the ancient Greeks as two monsters, have come to stand for any two dangers neither of which can be evaded without risking the other.

jolly soon fetch her downstairs. [*He makes resolutely for the door*].

MRS HIGGINS [*rising and following him*] Be quiet, Henry. Sit down.

HIGGINS. I—

MRS HIGGINS. Sit down, dear; and listen to me.

HIGGINS. Oh very well, very well, very well. [*He throws himself ungraciously on the ottoman, with his face towards the windows*]. But I think you might have told us this half an hour ago.

MRS HIGGINS. Eliza came to me this morning. She told me of the brutal way you two treated her.

HIGGINS [*bounding up again*] What!

PICKERING [*rising also*] My dear Mrs Higgins, she's been telling you stories. We didnt treat her brutally. We hardly said a word to her; and we parted on particularly good terms. [*Turning on* Higgins] Higgins: did you bully her after I went to bed?

HIGGINS. Just the other way about. She threw my slippers in my face. She behaved in the most outrageous way. I never gave her the slightest provocation. The slippers came bang into my face the moment I entered the room—before I had uttered a word. And used perfectly awful language.

PICKERING [*astonished*] But why? What did we do to her?

MRS HIGGINS. I think I know pretty well what you did. The girl is naturally rather affectionate, I think. Isnt she, Mr Doolittle?

DOOLITTLE. Very tender-hearted, maam. Takes after me.

MRS HIGGINS. Just so. She had become attached to you both. She worked very hard for you, Henry. I don't think you quite realize what anything in the nature of brain work means to a girl of her class. Well, it seems that when the great day of trial came, and she did this wonderful thing for you without making a single mistake, you two sat there and never said a word to her, but talked together of how glad you were that it was all over and how you had been bored with the whole thing. And then you were surprised because she threw your slippers at you! *I* should have thrown the fire-irons at you.

HIGGINS. We said nothing except that we were tired and wanted to go to bed. Did we, Pick?

PICKERING [*shrugging his shoulders*] That was all.

MRS HIGGINS [*ironically*] Quite sure?

PICKERING. Absolutely. Really, that was all.

MRS HIGGINS. You didnt thank her, or pet her, or admire her, or tell her how splendid she'd been.

HIGGINS [*impatiently*] But she knew all about that. We didnt make speeches to her, if thats what you mean.

PICKERING [*conscience stricken*] Perhaps we were a little inconsiderate. Is she very angry?

MRS HIGGINS [*returning to her place at the writing-table*] Well, I'm afraid she wont go back to Wimpole Street, especially now that Mr Doolittle is able to keep up the position you have thrust on her; but she says she is quite willing to meet you on friendly terms and to let bygones be bygones.

HIGGINS [*furious*] Is she, by George? Ho!

MRS HIGGINS. If you promise to behave yourself, Henry, I'll ask her to come down. If not, go home; for you have taken up quite enough of my time.

HIGGINS. Oh, all right. Very well. Pick: you behave yourself. Let us put on our best Sunday manners for this creature that we picked out of the mud. [*He flings himself sulkily into the Elizabethan chair*].

DOOLITTLE [*remonstrating*] Now, now, Enry Iggins! Have some consideration for my feelings as a middle class man.

MRS HIGGINS. Remember your promise, Henry. [*She presses the bell-button on the writing-table*]. Mr Doolittle: will you be so good as to step out on the balcony for a moment. I dont want Eliza to have the shock of your news until she has made it up with these two gentlemen. Would you mind?

DOOLITTLE. As you wish, lady. Anything to help Henry to keep her off my hands. [*He disappears through the window*].

The PARLORMAID *answers the bell.* PICKERING *sits down in* DOOLITTLE*'s place.*

MRS HIGGINS. Ask Miss Doolittle to come down, please.

THE PARLORMAID. Yes, maam. [*She goes out*].

MRS HIGGINS. Now, Henry: be good.

HIGGINS. I am behaving myself perfectly.

PICKERING. He is doing his best, Mrs Higgins.

A pause. HIGGINS *throws back his head; stretches out his legs; and begins to whistle.*

MRS HIGGINS. Henry, dearest, you dont look at all nice in that attitude.

HIGGINS [*pulling himself together*] I was not trying to look nice, mother.

MRS HIGGINS. It doesnt matter, dear. I only wanted to make you speak.

HIGGINS. Why?

MRS HIGGINS. Because you cant speak and whistle at the same time.

HIGGINS *groans. Another very trying pause.*

HIGGINS [*springing up, out of patience*] Where the devil is that girl? Are we to wait here all day?

ELIZA *enters, sunny, self-possessed, and giving a staggeringly convincing exhibition of ease of manner. She carries a little work-basket, and is very much at home.* PICKERING *is too much taken aback to rise.*

LIZA. How do you do, Professor Higgins? Are you quite well?

HIGGINS [*choking*] Am I— [*He can say no more*].

LIZA. But of course you are: you are never ill. So glad to see you again, Colonel Pickering. [*He rises hastily; and they shake hands*]. Quite chilly this morning, isn't it? [*She sits down on his left. He sits beside her*].

HIGGINS. Dont you dare try this game on me. I taught it to you; and it doesnt take me in. Get up and come home; and dont be a fool.

ELIZA *takes a piece of needlework from her basket, and begins to stitch at it, without taking the least notice of this outburst.*

MRS HIGGINS. Very nicely put, indeed, Henry. No woman could resist such an invitation.

HIGGINS. You let her alone, mother. Let her speak for herself. You will jolly soon see whether she has an idea that I havnt put into her head or a word that I havnt put into her mouth. I tell you I have created this thing out of the squashed cabbage leaves of Covent Garden; and now she pretends to play the fine lady with me.

MRS HIGGINS [*placidly*] Yes, dear; but youll sit down, wont you?

HIGGINS *sits down again, savagely.*

LIZA [*to* PICKERING, *taking no apparent notice of* HIGGINS, *and working away deftly*] Will you drop me altogether now that the experiment is over, Colonel Pickering?

PICKERING. Oh dont. You mustnt think of it as an experiment. It shocks me, somehow.

LIZA. Oh, I'm only a squashed cabbage leaf—

PICKERING [*impulsively*] No.

LIZA [*continuing quietly*]—but I owe so much to you that I should be very unhappy if you forgot me.

PICKERING. It's very kind of you to say so, Miss Doolittle.

LIZA. It's not because you paid for my dresses. I know you are generous to everybody with money. But it was from you that I learnt really nice manners; and that is what makes one a lady, isnt it? You see it was so very difficult for me with the example of Professor Higgins always before me. I was brought up to be just like him, unable to control myself, and using bad language on the slightest provocation. And I should never have known that ladies and gentlemen didnt behave like that if you hadnt been there.

HIGGINS. Well!!

PICKERING. Oh, thats only his way, you know. He doesnt mean it.

LIZA. Oh, *I* didnt mean it either, when I was a flower girl. It was only my way. But you see I did it; and thats what makes the difference after all.

PICKERING. No doubt. Still, he taught you to speak; and I couldn't have done that, you know.

LIZA [*trivially*] Of course: that is his profession.

HIGGINS. Damnation!

LIZA [*continuing*] It was just like learning to dance in the fashionable way: there was nothing more than that in it. But do you know what began my real education?

PICKERING. What?

LIZA [*stopping her work for a moment*] Your calling me Miss Doolittle that day when I first came to Wimpole Street. That was the beginning of self-respect for me. [*She resumes her stitching*] And there were a hundred little things you never noticed, because they came naturally to you. Things about standing up and taking off your hat and opening doors—

PICKERING. Oh, that was nothing.

LIZA. Yes: things that shewed you thought and felt about me as if I were something better than a scullery-maid; though of course I know you would have been just the same to a scullery-maid if she had been let into the drawing room. You never took off your boots in the dining room when I was there.

PICKERING. You mustnt mind that. Higgins takes off his boots all over the place.

LIZA. I know. I am not blaming him. It is his way, isn't it? But it made such a difference to me that you didnt do it. You see, really and truly, apart from the things anyone can pick up (the dressing and the proper way of speaking, and so on), the difference between a lady and a flower girl is not how she behaves, but how she's treated. I shall always be a flower girl to Professor Higgins, because he always treats me as a flower girl, and always will; but I know I can be a lady to you, because you always treat me as a lady, and always will.

MRS HIGGINS. Please dont grind your teeth, Henry.

PICKERING. Well, this is really very nice of you, Miss Doolittle.

LIZA. I should like you to call me Eliza, now, if you would.

PICKERING. Thank you. Eliza, of course.

LIZA. And I should like Professor Higgins to call me Miss Doolittle.

HIGGINS. I'll see you damned first.

MRS HIGGINS. Henry! Henry!

PICKERING [*laughing*] Why dont you slang back at him? Dont stand it. It would do him a lot of good.

LIZA. I cant. I could have done it once; but now I cant go back to it. You told me, you know, that when a child is brought to a foreign country, it picks up the language in a few weeks, and forgets its own. Well, I am a child in your country. I have forgotten my own language, and can speak nothing but yours. Thats the real break-off with the

corner of Tottenham Court Road. Leaving Wimpole Street finishes it.

PICKERING [*much alarmed*] Oh! but youre coming back to Wimpole Street, arnt you? Youll forgive Higgins?

HIGGINS [*rising*] Forgive! Will she, by George! Let her go. Let her find out how she can get on without us. She will relapse into the gutter in three weeks without me at her elbow.

DOOLITTLE *appears at the centre window. With a look of dignified reproach at* HIGGINS, *he comes slowly and silently to his daughter, who, with her back to the window, is unconscious of his approach.*

PICKERING. He's incorrigible, Eliza. You wont relapse, will you?

LIZA. No: not now. Never again. I have learnt my lesson. I dont believe I could utter one of the old sounds if I tried. [DOOLITTLE *touches her on the left shoulder. She drops her work, losing her self-possession utterly at the spectacle of her father's splendor*] A-a-a-a-ah-ow-ooh!

HIGGINS [*With a crow of triumph*] Aha! Just so. A-a-a-a-ahowooh! A-a-a-a-ahowooh! A-a-a-a-ahowooh! Victory! Victory! [*He throws himself on the divan, folding his arms, and spraddling arrogantly*].

DOOLITTLE. Can you blame the girl? Dont look at me like that, Eliza. It aint my fault. Ive come into some money.

LIZA. You must have touched a millionaire this time, dad.

DOOLITTLE. I have. But I'm dressed something special today. I'm going to St George's, Hanover Square. Your stepmother is going to marry me.

LIZA [*angrily*] Youre going to let yourself down to marry that low common woman!

PICKERING [*quietly*] He ought to, Eliza. [*To* DOOLITTLE] Why has she changed her mind?

DOOLITTLE [*sadly*] Intimidated, Governor. Intimidated. Middle class morality claims its victim. Wont you put on your hat, Liza, and come and see me turned off?

LIZA. If the Colonel says I must, I—I'll [*almost sobbing*] I'll demean myself. And get insulted for my pains, like enough.

DOOLITTLE. Dont be afraid: she never comes to words with anyone now, poor woman! respectability has broke all the spirit out of her.

PICKERING [*squeezing* ELIZA's *elbow gently*] Be kind to them, Eliza. Make the best of it.

LIZA [*forcing a little smile for him through her vexation*] Oh well, just to shew theres no ill feeling. I'll be back in a moment. [*She goes out*].

DOOLITTLE [*sitting down beside* PICKERING] I feel uncommon nervous about the ceremony, Colonel. I wish youd come and see me through it.

PICKERING. But youve been through it before, man. You were married to Eliza's mother.

DOOLITTLE. Who told you that, Colonel?

PICKERING. Well, nobody told me. But I concluded—naturally——

DOOLITTLE. No: that aint the natural way, Colonel: it's only the middle class way. My way was always the undeserving way. But dont say nothing to Eliza. She dont know: I always had a delicacy about telling her.

PICKERING. Quite right. We'll leave it so, if you dont mind.

DOOLITTLE. And youll come to the church, Colonel, and put me through straight?

PICKERING. With pleasure. As far as a bachelor can.

MRS HIGGINS. May I come, Mr Doolittle? I should be very sorry to miss your wedding.

DOOLITTLE. I should indeed be honored by your condescension, maam; and my poor old woman would take it as a tremenjous compliment. She's been very low, thinking of the happy days that are no more.

MRS HIGGINS [*rising*] I'll order the carriage and get ready. [*The men rise, except* HIGGINS]. I shant be more than fifteen minutes. [*As she goes to the door* ELIZA *comes in, hatted and buttoning her gloves*]. I'm going to the church to see your father married, Eliza. You had better come in the brougham[4] with me. Colonel Pickering can go on with the bridegroom.

MRS HIGGINS *goes out.* ELIZA *comes to the middle of the room between the centre window and the ottoman.* PICKERING *joins her.*

DOOLITTLE. Bridegroom. What a word! It makes a man realize his position, somehow. [*He takes up his hat and goes towards the door*].

PICKERING. Before I go, Eliza, do forgive Higgins and come back to us.

LIZA. I dont think dad would allow me. Would you, dad?

DOOLITTLE [*sad but magnanimous*] They played you off very cunning, Eliza, them two sportsmen. If it had been only one of them, you could have nailed him. But you see, there was two; and one of them chaperoned the other, as you might say. [*To* PICKERING] It was artful of you, Colonel; but I bear no malice: I should have done the same myself. I been the victim of one woman after another all my life, and I dont grudge you two getting the better of Liza. I shant interfere. It's time for us to go, Colonel. So long, Henry. See you in St George's, Eliza. [*He goes out*].

PICKERING. [*coaxing*] Do stay with us, Eliza. [*He follows Doolittle*].

ELIZA *goes out on the balcony to avoid being alone with* HIGGINS. *He rises and joins her there. She immediately comes back into the room and makes for the door; but he*

goes along the balcony and gets his back to the door before she reaches it.

HIGGINS. Well, Eliza, you've had a bit of your own back, as you call it. Have you had enough? and are you going to be reasonable? Or do you want any more?

LIZA. You want me back only to pick up your slippers and put up with your tempers and fetch and carry for you.

HIGGINS. I havnt said I wanted you back at all.

LIZA. Oh, indeed. Then what are we talking about?

HIGGINS. About you, not about me. If you come back I shall treat you just as I have always treated you. I cant change my nature; and I dont intend to change my manners. My manners are exactly the same as Colonel Pickering's.

LIZA. That's not true. He treats a flower girl as if she was a duchess.

HIGGINS. And I treat a duchess as if she was a flower girl.

LIZA. I see [*She turns away composedly, and sits on the ottoman, facing the window*]. The same to everybody.

HIGGINS. Just so.

LIZA. Like father.

HIGGINS [*grinning, a little taken down*] Without accepting the comparison at all points, Eliza, it's quite true that your father is not a snob, and that he will be quite at home in any station of life to which his eccentric destiny may call him. [*Seriously*] The great secret, Eliza, is not having bad manners or good manners or any other particular sort of manners, but having the same manner for all human souls: in short, behaving as if you were in Heaven, where there are no third-class carriages, and one soul is as good as another.

LIZA. Amen. You are a born preacher.

---

4. brougham (bro͞om) *n.*: A type of carriage.

HIGGINS [irritated] The question is not whether I treat you rudely, but whether you ever heard me treat anyone else better.

LIZA [with sudden sincerity] I dont care how you treat me. I dont mind you swearing at me. I shouldnt mind a black eye: Ive had one before this. But [standing up and facing him] I wont be passed over.

HIGGINS. Then get out of my way; for I wont stop for you. You talk about me as if I were a motor bus.

LIZA. So you are a motor bus: all bounce and go, and no consideration for anyone. But I can do without you: dont think I cant.

HIGGINS. I know you can. I told you you could.

LIZA [wounded, getting away from him to the other side of the ottoman with her face to the hearth] I know you did, you brute. You wanted to get rid of me.

HIGGINS. Liar.

LIZA. Thank you. [She sits down with dignity]

HIGGINS. You never asked yourself, I suppose, whether I could do without you.

LIZA . [earnestly] Don't you try to get round me. You'll have to do without me.

HIGGINS [arrogant] I can do without anybody. I have my own soul: my own spark of divine fire. But [with sudden humility] I shall miss you, Eliza. [He sits down near her on the ottoman] I have learnt something from your idiotic notions: I confess that humbly and gratefully. And I have grown accustomed to your voice and appearance. I like them, rather.

LIZA. Well, you have both of them on your gramophone and in your book of photographs. When you feel lonely without me, you can turn the machine on. It's got no feelings to hurt.

HIGGINS. I cant turn your soul on. Leave me those feelings; and you can take away the voice and the face. They are not you.

LIZA. Oh, you are a devil. You can twist the heart in a girl as easy as some could twist her arms to hurt her. Mrs Pearce warned me. Time and again she has wanted to leave you; and you always got round her at the last minute. And you dont care a bit for her. And you dont care a bit for me.

HIGGINS. I care for life, for humanity; and you are a part of it that has come my way and been built into my house. What more can you or anyone ask?

LIZA. I wont care for anybody that doesnt care for me.

HIGGINS. Commercial principles, Eliza. Like [reproducing her Covent Garden pronunciation with professional exactness] s'yollin voylets [selling violets], isnt it?

LIZA. Dont sneer at me. It's mean to sneer at me.

HIGGINS. I have never sneered in my life. Sneering doesnt become either the human face or the human soul. I am expressing my righteous contempt for Commercialism. I dont and wont trade in affection. You call me a brute because you couldnt buy a claim on me by fetching my slippers and finding my spectacles. You were a fool: I think a woman fetching a man's slippers is a disgusting sight: did I ever fetch your slippers? I think a good deal more of you for throwing them in my face. No use slaving for me and then saying you want to be cared for: who cares for a slave? If you come back, come back for the sake of good fellowship; for youll get nothing else. Youve had a thousand times as much out of me as I have out of you; and if you dare to set up your little dog's tricks of fetching and carrying slippers against my creation of a Duchess Eliza, I'll slam the door in your silly face.

LIZA. What did you do it for if you didnt care for me?

HIGGINS [heartily] Why, because it was my job.

LIZA. You never thought of the trouble it would make for me.

HIGGINS. Would the world ever have been made if its maker had been afraid of making trouble? Making life means making trouble. Theres only one way of escaping trouble; and thats killing things. Cowards, you notice, are always shrieking to have troublesome people killed.

LIZA. I'm no preacher: I dont notice things like that. I notice that you dont notice me.

HIGGINS [*jumping up and walking about intolerantly*] Eliza: youre an idiot. I waste the treasures of my Miltonic mind by spreading them before you. Once for all, understand that I go my way and do my work without caring twopence what happens to either of us. I am not intimidated, like your father and your stepmother. So you can come back or go to the devil: which you please.

LIZA. What am I to come back for?

HIGGINS [*bouncing up on his knees on the ottoman and leaning over it to her*] For the fun of it. Thats why I took you on.

LIZA [*with averted face*] And you may throw me out tomorrow if I dont do everything you want me to?

HIGGINS. Yes; and you may walk out tomorrow if I dont do everything you want me to.

LIZA. And live with my stepmother?

HIGGINS. Yes, or sell flowers.

LIZA. Oh, if I only could go back to my flower basket! I should be independent of both you and father and all the world! Why did you take my independence from me? Why did I give it up? I'm a slave now, for all my fine clothes.

HIGGINS. Not a bit. I'll adopt you as my daughter and settle money on you if you like. Or would you rather marry Pickering?

LIZA [*looking fiercely round at him*] I wouldnt marry you if you asked me; and youre nearer my age than what he is.

HIGGINS [*gently*] Than he is: not "than what he is."

LIZA [*losing her temper and rising*] I'll talk as I like. Youre not my teacher now.

HIGGINS [*reflectively*] I dont suppose Pickering would, though. He's as confirmed an old bachelor as I am.

LIZA. Thats not what I want; and dont you think it. I've always had chaps enough wanting me that way. Freddy Hill writes to me twice and three times a day, sheets and sheets.

HIGGINS [*disagreeably surprised*] Damn his impudence! [*He recoils and finds himself sitting on his heels*].

LIZA. He has a right to if he likes, poor lad. And he does love me.

HIGGINS [*getting off the ottoman*] You have no right to encourage him.

LIZA. Every girl has a right to be loved.

HIGGINS. What! By fools like that?

LIZA. Freddy's not a fool. And if he's weak and poor and wants me, may be he'd make me happier than my betters that bully me and dont want me.

HIGGINS. Can he make anything of you? Thats the point.

LIZA. Perhaps I could make something of him. But I never thought of us making anything of one another; and you never think of anything else. I only want to be natural.

HIGGINS. In short, you want me to be as infatuated about you as Freddy? Is that it?

LIZA. No I dont. Thats not the sort of feeling I want from you. And dont you be too sure of yourself or of me. I could have been a bad girl if I'd liked. Ive seen more of some things than you, for all your learning. Girls like me can drag gentlemen down to make love to them easy enough. And they wish each other dead the next minute.

HIGGINS. Of course they do. Then what in thunder are we quarrelling about?

LIZA [*much troubled*] I want a little kindness. I know I'm a common ignorant girl, and you a book-learned gentleman; but I'm not dirt under your feet. What I done [*correcting herself*] what I did was not for the dresses and the taxis: I did it because we were pleasant together and I come—came—to care for you; not to want you to make love to me, and not forgetting the difference between us, but more friendly like.

HIGGINS. Well, of course. Thats just how I feel. And how Pickering feels. Eliza: youre a fool.

LIZA. Thats not a proper answer to give me [*she sinks on the chair at the writing-table in tears*].

HIGGINS. It's all youll get until you stop being a common idiot. If youre going to be a lady, youll have to give up feeling neglected if the men you know dont spend half their time snivelling over you and the other half giving you black eyes. If you cant stand the coldness of my sort of life, and the strain of it, go back to the gutter. Work til youre more a brute than a human being; and then cuddle and squabble and drink til you fall asleep. Oh, it's a fine life, the life of the gutter. It's real: it's warm: it's violent: you can feel it through the thickest skin: you can taste it and smell it without any training or any work. Not like Science and Literature and Classical Music and Philosophy and Art. You find me cold, unfeeling, selfish, dont you? Very well: be off with you to the sort of people you like. Marry some sentimental hog or other with lots of money, and a thick pair of lips to kiss you with and a thick pair of boots to kick you with. If you cant appreciate what youve got, youd better get what you can appreciate.

LIZA. [*Desperate*] Oh, you are a cruel tyrant. I cant talk to you: you turn everything against me: I'm always in the wrong. But you know very well all the time that youre nothing but a bully. You know I cant go back to the gutter, as you call it, and that I have no real friends in the world but you and the Colonel. You know well I couldnt bear to live with a low common man after you two; and it's wicked and cruel of you to insult me by pretending I could. You think I must go back to Wimpole Street because I have nowhere else to go but father's. But dont you be too sure that you have me under your feet to be trampled on and talked down. I'll marry Freddy, I will, as soon as I'm able to support him.

HIGGINS [*thunderstruck*] Freddy!!! that young fool! That poor devil who couldnt get a job as an errand boy even if he had the guts to try for it! Woman: do you not understand that I have made you a consort for a king?

LIZA. Freddy loves me: that makes him king enough for me. I dont want him to work: he wasnt brought up to it as I was. I'll go and be a teacher.

HIGGINS. Whatll you teach, in heaven's name?

LIZA. What you taught me. I'll teach phonetics.

HIGGINS. Ha! ha! ha!

LIZA. I'll offer myself as an assistant to that hairyfaced Hungarian.

HIGGINS [*rising in a fury*] What! That imposter! that humbug! that toadying ingoramus! Teach him my methods! my discoveries! You take one step in his direction and I'll wring your neck. [*He lays hands on her*]. Do you hear?

LIZA [*defiantly non-resistant*] Wring away. What do I care? I knew youd strike me some day. [*He lets her go, stamping with rage at having forgotten himself, and recoils so hastily that he stumbles back into his seat on the ottoman*]. Aha! Now I know how to deal with you. What a fool I was not to think of it before! You cant take away the knowledge you gave me. You said I had a finer ear than you. And I can be civil and kind to people, which is more than you can. Aha!

[*Purposely dropping her aitches to annoy him*] Thats done you, Enry Iggins, it az. Now I dont care that [*snapping her fingers*] for your bullying and your big talk. I'll advertize it in the papers that your duchess is only a flower girl that you taught, and that she'll teach anybody to be a duchess just the same in six months for a thousand guineas. Oh, when I think of myself crawling under your feet and being trampled on and called names, when all the time I had only to lift up my finger to be as good as you, I could just kick myself.

HIGGINS [*wondering at her*] You damned impudent slut, you! But it's better than snivelling; better than fetching slippers and finding spectacles, isnt it? [*Rising*] By George, Eliza. I said I'd make a woman of you; and I have. I like you like this.

LIZA. Yes: you turn round and make up to me now that I'm not afraid of you, and can do without you.

HIGGINS. Of course I do, you little fool. Five minutes ago you were like a millstone round my neck. Now youre a tower of strength: a consort battleship. You and I and Pickering will be three old bachelors instead of only two men and a silly girl.

MRS HIGGINS *returns, dressed for the wedding.* ELIZA *instantly becomes cool and elegant.*

MRS HIGGINS. The carriage is waiting, Eliza. Are you ready?

LIZA. Quite. Is the Professor coming?

MRS HIGGINS. Certainly not. He cant behave himself in church. He makes remarks out loud all the time on the clergyman's pronunciation.

LIZA. Then I shall not see you again, Professor. Goodbye. [*She goes to the door*].

MRS HIGGINS [*coming to* HIGGINS] Goodbye, dear.

HIGGINS. Goodbye, mother. [*He is about to

kiss her, when he recollects something*]. Oh, by the way, Eliza, order a ham and a Stilton cheese, will you? And buy me a pair of reindeer gloves, number eights, and a tie to match that new suit of mine. You can choose the color. [*His cheerful, careless, vigorous voice shews that he is incorrigible*].

LIZA [*disdainfully*] Number eights are too small for you if you want them lined with lamb's wool. You have three new ties that you have forgotten in the drawer of your washstand. Colonel Pickering prefers double Gloucester to Stilton; and you dont notice the difference. I telephoned Mrs Pearce this morning not to forget the ham. What you are to do without me I cannot imagine. [*She sweeps out*].

MRS HIGGINS. I'm afraid youve spoilt that girl, Henry. I should be uneasy about you and her if she were less fond of Colonel Pickering.

HIGGINS. Pickering! Nonsense: she's going to marry Freddy. Ha ha! Freddy! Freddy!! Ha ha ha ha ha!!!!! [*He roars with laughter as the play ends*].

Epilogue

The rest of the story need not be shewn in action, and indeed, would hardly need telling if our imaginations were not so enfeebled by their lazy dependence on the ready-mades and reach-me-downs of the ragshop in which Romance keeps its stock of "happy endings" to misfit all stories. Now, the history of Eliza Doolittle, though called a romance because the transfiguration it records seems exceedingly improbable, is common enough. Such transfigurations have been achieved by hundreds of resolutely ambitious young women since Nell Gwynne[1] set them the example by playing queens and fascinating kings in the theatre in which she began by selling oranges. Nevertheless, people in all directions have assumed, for no other reason than that she became the heroine of a romance, that she must have married the hero of it. This is unbearable, not only because her little drama, if acted on such a thoughtless assumption, must be spoiled, but because the true sequel is patent to anyone with a sense of human nature in general, and of feminine instinct in particular.

Eliza, in telling Higgins she would not marry him if he asked her, was not coquetting: she was announcing a well-considered decision. When a bachelor interests, and dominates, and teaches, and becomes important to a spinster, as Higgins with Eliza, she always, if she has character enough to be capable of it, considers very seriously indeed whether she will play for becoming that bachelor's wife, especially if he is so little interested in marriage that a determined and devoted woman might capture him if she set herself resolutely to do it. Her decision will depend a good deal on whether she is really free to choose; and that, again, will depend on her age and income. If she is at the end of her youth, and has no security for her livelihood, she will marry him because she must marry anybody who will provide for her. But at Eliza's age a good-looking girl does not feel that pressure: she feels free to pick and choose. She is therefore guided by her instinct in the matter. Eliza's instinct tells her not to marry Higgins. It does not tell her to give him up. It is not in the slightest doubt as to his remaining one of the strongest personal interests in her life. It would be very sorely strained if there was another woman likely to supplant her with him. But as she feels sure of him on that last point, she has no doubt at all as to her course, and would not have any, even if the difference of twenty years in age, which seems so great to youth, did not exist between them.

As our own instincts are not appealed to by her conclusion, let us see whether we

1. **Nell Gwynne:** Eleanor Gwynne (1650–1687), an English actress and favorite of Charles II.

cannot discover some reason in it. When Higgins excused his indifference to young women on the ground that they had an irresistible rival in his mother, he gave the clue to his inveterate old-bachelordom. The case is uncommon only to the extent that remarkable mothers are uncommon. If an imaginative boy has a sufficiently rich mother who has intelligence, personal grace, dignity of character without harshness, and a cultivated sense of the best art of her time to enable her to make her house beautiful, she sets a standard for him against which very few women can struggle, besides effecting for him a disengagement of his affections, his sense of beauty, and his idealism from his specifically sexual impulses. This makes him a standing puzzle to the huge number of uncultivated people who have been brought up in tasteless homes by commonplace or disagreeable parents, and to whom, consequently, literature, painting, sculpture, music, and affectionate personal relations come as modes of sex if they come at all. The word passion means nothing else to them; and that Higgins could have a passion for phonetics and idealize his mother instead of Eliza, would seem to them absurd and unnatural. Nevertheless, when we look round and see that hardly anyone is too ugly or disagreeable to find a wife or a husband if he or she wants one, whilst many old maids and bachelors are above the average in quality and culture, we cannot help suspecting that the disentanglement of sex from the associations with which it is so commonly confused, a disentanglement which persons of genius achieve by sheer intellectual analysis, is sometimes produced or aided by parental fascination.

Now, though Eliza was incapable of thus explaining to herself Higgins's formidable powers of resistance to the charm that prostrated Freddy at the first glance, she was instinctively aware that she could never obtain a complete grip of him, or come between him and his mother (the first necessity of the married woman). To put it shortly, she knew that for some mysterious reason he had not the makings of a married man in him, according to her conception of a husband as one to whom she would be his nearest and fondest and warmest interest. Even had there been no mother-rival, she would still have refused to accept an interest in herself that was secondary to philosophic interests. Had Mrs Higgins died, there would still have been Milton and the Universal Alphabet. Landor's[2] remark that to those who have the greatest power of loving, love is a secondary affair, would not have recommended Landor to Eliza. Put that along with her resentment of Higgins's domineering superiority, and her mistrust of his coaxing cleverness in getting round her and evading her wrath when he had gone too far with his impetuous bullying, and you will see that Eliza's instinct had good grounds for warning her not to marry her Pygmalion.

And now, whom did Eliza marry? For if Higgins was a predestinate old bachelor, she was most certainly not a predestinate old maid. Well, that can be told very shortly to those who have not guessed it from the indications she has herself given them.

Almost immediately after Eliza is stung into proclaiming her considered determination not to marry Higgins, she mentions the fact that young Mr Frederick Eynsford Hill is pouring out his love for her daily through the post. Now Freddy is young, practically twenty years younger than Higgins: he is a gentleman [or, as Eliza would qualify him, a toff], and speaks like one. He is nicely dressed, is treated by the Colonel as an equal, loves her unaffectedly, and is not her master, nor ever likely to dominate her in spite of his advantage of social standing. Eliza has no use for the foolish romantic tradition that all women love to be mastered, if not actually bullied and beaten. "When

---

2. Landor's: Referring to Walter Savage Landor (1775–1864), an English writer.

you go to women" says Nietzsche[3] "take your whip with you." Sensible despots have never confined that precaution to women: they have taken their whips with them when they have dealt with men, and been slavishly idealized by the men over whom they have flourished the whip much more than by women. No doubt there are slavish women as well as slavish men; and women, like men, admire those that are stronger than themselves. But to admire a strong person and to live under that strong person's thumb are two different things. The weak may not be admired and hero-worshipped; but they are by no means disliked or shunned; and they never seem to have the least difficulty in marrying people who are too good for them. They may fail in emergencies; but life is not one long emergency: it is mostly a string of situations for which no exceptional strength is needed, and with which even rather weak people can cope if they have a stronger partner to help them out. Accordingly, it is a truth everywhere in evidence that strong people, masculine or feminine, not only do not

---

3. Nietzsche (nē' chə): German philosopher Friedrich Wilhelm Nietzsche (1844–1900).

marry stronger people, but do not shew any preference for them in selecting their friends. When a lion meets another with a louder roar "the first lion thinks the last a bore." The man or woman who feels strong enough for two, seeks for every other quality in a partner than strength.

The converse is also true. Weak people want to marry strong people who do not frighten them too much; and this often leads them to make the mistake we describe metaphorically as "biting off more than they can chew." They want too much for too little; and when the bargain is unreasonable beyond all bearing, the union becomes impossible: it ends in the weaker party being either discarded or borne as a cross, which is worse. People who are not only weak, but silly or obtuse as well, are often in these difficulties.

This being the state of human affairs, what is Eliza fairly sure to do when she is placed between Freddy and Higgins? Will she look forward to a lifetime of fetching Higgins's slippers or to a lifetime of Freddy fetching hers? There can be no doubt about the answer. Unless Freddy is biologically repulsive to her, and Higgins biologically attractive to a degree that overwhelms all her other instincts, she will, if she marries either of them, marry Freddy.

And that is just what Eliza did.

Complications ensued; but they were economic, not romantic. Freddy had no money and no occupation. His mother's jointure,[4] a last relic of the opulence of Largelady Park, had enabled her to struggle along in Earlscourt with an air of gentility, but not to procure any serious secondary education for her children, much less give the boy a profession. A clerkship at thirty shillings a week was beneath Freddy's dignity, and extremely distasteful to him besides. His prospects consisted of a hope that if he kept up appearances somebody would do something for him. The something appeared vaguely to his imagination as a private secretaryship or a sinecure[5] of some sort. To his mother it perhaps appeared as a marriage to some lady of means who could not resist her boy's niceness. Fancy her feelings when he married a flower girl who had become disclassed under extraordinary circumstances which were now notorious!

It is true that Eliza's situation did not seem wholly ineligible. Her father, though formerly a dustman, and now fantastically disclassed, had become extremely popular in the smartest society by a social talent which triumphed over every prejudice and every disadvantage. Rejected by the middle class, which he loathed, he had shot up at once into the highest circles by his wit, his dustmanship (which he carried like a banner), and his Nietzschean transcendence of good and evil. At intimate ducal dinners he sat on the right hand of the Duchess; and in country houses he smoked in the pantry and was made much of by the butler when he was not feeding in the dining room and being consulted by cabinet ministers. But he found it almost as hard to do all this on [three] thousand a year as Mrs Eynsford Hill to live in Earlscourt on an income so pitiably smaller that I have not the heart to disclose its exact figure. He absolutely refused to add the last straw to his burden by contributing to Eliza's support.

Thus Freddy and Eliza, now Mr and Mrs Eynsford Hill, would have spent a penniless honeymoon but for a wedding present of £500 from the Colonel to Eliza. It lasted a long time because Freddy did not know how to spend money, never having had any to spend, and Eliza, socially trained by a pair of old bachelors, wore her clothes as long as they held together and looked pretty, without the least regard to their being many months out of fashion. Still, £500 will not

---

4. jointure n.: Widow's inheritance.

5. sinecure (sĭ′ nə kyoor′) n.: Any office or position that brings advantage but involves little or no work.

last two young people for ever; and they both knew, and Eliza felt as well, that they must shift for themselves in the end. She could quarter herself on Wimpole Street because it had come to be her home; but she was quite aware that she ought not to quarter Freddy there, and that it would not be good for his character if she did.

Not that the Wimpole Street bachelors objected. When she consulted them, Higgins declined to be bothered about her housing problem when that solution was so simple. Eliza's desire to have Freddy in the house with her seemed of no more importance than if she had wanted an extra piece of bedroom furniture. Pleas as to Freddy's character, and the moral obligation on him to earn his own living, were lost on Higgins. He denied that Freddy had any character, and declared that if he tried to do any useful work some competent person would have the trouble of undoing it: a procedure involving a net loss to the community, and great unhappiness to Freddy himself, who was obviously intended by Nature for such light work as amusing Eliza, which, Higgins declared, was a much more useful and honorable occupation than working in the city. When Eliza referred again to her project of teaching phonetics, Higgins abated not a jot of his violent opposition to it. He said she was not within ten years of being qualified to meddle with his pet subject; and as it was evident that the Colonel agreed with him, she felt she could not go against them in this grave matter, and that she had no right, without Higgins's consent, to exploit the knowledge he had given her; for his knowledge seemed to her as much his private property as his watch: Eliza was no communist. Besides, she was superstitiously devoted to them both, more entirely and frankly after her marriage than before it.

It was the Colonel who finally solved the problem, which had cost him much perplexed cogitation. He one day asked Eliza, rather shyly, whether she had quite given up her notion of keeping a flower shop. She replied that she had thought of it, but had put it out of her head, because the Colonel had said, that day at Mrs Higgins's, that it would never do. The Colonel confessed that when he said that, he had not quite recovered from the dazzling impression of the day before. They broke the matter to Higgins that evening. The sole comment vouchsafed by him very nearly led to a serious quarrel with Eliza. It was to the effect that she would have in Freddy an ideal errand boy.

Freddy himself was next sounded on the subject. He said he had been thinking of a shop himself; though it had presented itself to his pennilessness as a small place in which Eliza should sell tobacco at one counter whilst he sold newspapers at the opposite one. But he agreed that it would be extraordinarily jolly to go early every morning with Eliza to Covent Garden and buy flowers on the scene of their first meeting: a sentiment which earned him many kisses from his wife. He added that he had always been afraid to propose anything of the sort, because Clara would make an awful row about a step that must damage her matrimonial chances, and his mother could not be expected to like it after clinging for so many years to that step of the social ladder on which retail trade is impossible.

This difficulty was removed by an event highly unexpected by Freddy's mother. Clara, in the course of her incursions into those artistic circles which were the highest within her reach, discovered that her conversational qualifications were expected to include a grounding in the novels of Mr H. G. Wells.[6] She borrowed them in various directions so energetically that she swallowed them all within two months. The result was a conversion of a kind quite common today. A modern Acts of the Apostles would fill fifty whole Bibles if anyone were capable of writing it.

Poor Clara, who appeared to Higgins and

---

6. H. G. Wells: Herbert George Wells (1866–1946), English novelist and historian.

his mother as a disagreeable and ridiculous person, and to her own mother as in some inexplicable way a social failure, had never seen herself in either light; for, though to some extent ridiculed and mimicked in West Kensington like everybody else there, she was accepted as a rational and normal—or shall we say inevitable?—sort of human being. At worst they called her The Pusher; but to them no more than to herself had it ever occurred that she was pushing the air, and pushing it in a wrong direction. Still, she was not happy. She was growing desperate. Her one asset, the fact that her mother was what the Epsom greengrocer called a carriage lady, had no exchange value, apparently. It had prevented her from getting educated, because the only education she could have afforded was education with the Earlscourt greengrocer's daughter. It had led her to seek the society of her mother's class; and that class simply would not have her, because she was much poorer than the greengrocer, and, far from being able to afford a maid, could not afford even a housemaid, and had to scrape along at home with an illiberally treated general servant. Under such circumstances nothing could give her an air of being a genuine product of Largelady Park. And yet its tradition made her regard a marriage with anyone within her reach as an unbearable humiliation. Commercial people and professional people in a small way were odious to her. She ran after painters and novelists; but she did not charm them; and her bold attempts to pick up and practise artistic and literary talk irritated them. She was, in short, an utter failure, an ignorant, incompetent, pretentious, unwelcome, penniless, useless little snob; and though she did not admit these disqualifications (for nobody ever faces unpleasant truths of this kind until the possibility of a way out dawns on them) she felt their effects too keenly to be satisfied with her position.

Clara had a startling eyeopener when,
on being suddenly wakened to enthusiasm by a girl of her own age who dazzled her and produced in her a gushing desire to take her for a model, and gain her friendship, she discovered that this exquisite apparition had graduated from the gutter in a few months time. It shook her so violently, that when Mr H. G. Wells lifted her on the point of his puissant[7] pen, and placed her at the angle of view from which the life she was leading and the society to which she clung appeared in its true relation to real human needs and worthy social structure, he effected a conversion and a conviction of sin comparable to the most sensational feats of General Booth[8] or Gypsy Smith.[9] Clara's snobbery went bang. Life suddenly began to move with her. Without knowing how or why, she began to make friends and enemies. Some of the acquaintances to whom she had been a tedious or indifferent or ridiculous affliction, dropped her: others became cordial. To her amazement she found that some "quite nice" people were saturated with Wells, and that this accessibility to ideas was the secret of their niceness. People she had thought deeply religious, and had tried to conciliate on that tack with disastrous results, suddenly took an interest in her, and revealed a hostility to conventional religion which she had never conceived possible except among the most desperate characters. They made her read Galsworthy; and Galsworthy exposed the vanity of Largelady Park and finished her. It exasperated her to think that the dungeon in which she had languished for so many unhappy years had been unlocked all the time, and that the impulses she had so carefully struggled with and stifled for the sake of keeping well with society, were pre-

---

7. **puissant** (py$\overline{oo}$′ i sənt) *adj.*: Powerful.
8. **General Booth:** William Booth (1829–1912), the founder of the Salvation Army.
9. **Gypsy Smith:** Gipsy Rodney Smith (1860–1947), an English evangelist.

cisely those by which alone she could have come into any sort of sincere human contact. In the radiance of these discoveries, and the tumult of their reaction, she made a fool of herself as freely and conspicuously as when she so rashly adopted Eliza's expletive in Mrs Higgins's drawing room; for the new-born Wellsian had to find her bearings almost as ridiculously as a baby; but nobody hates a baby for its ineptitudes, or thinks the worse of it for trying to eat the matches; and Clara lost no friends by her follies. They laughed at her to her face this time; and she had to defend herself and fight it out as best she could.

When Freddy paid a visit to Earlscourt (which he never did when he could possibly help it) to make the desolating announcement that he and his Eliza were thinking of blackening the Largelady scutcheon[10] by opening a shop, he found the little household already convulsed by a prior announcement from Clara that she also was going to work in an old furniture shop in Dover Street, which had been started by a fellow Wellsian. This appointment Clara owed, after all, to her old social accomplishment of Push. She had made up her mind that, cost what it might, she would see Mr Wells in the flesh; and she had achieved her end at a garden party. She had better luck than so rash an enterprise deserved. Mr Wells came up to her expectations. Age had not withered him, nor could custom stale his infinite variety in half an hour. His pleasant neatness and compactness, his small hands and feet, his teeming ready brain, his unaffected accessibility, and a certain fine apprehensiveness which stamped him as susceptible from his topmost hair to his tipmost toe, proved irresistible. Clara talked of nothing else for weeks and weeks afterwards. And as she happened to talk to the lady of the furniture shop, and that lady also desir-

ed above all things to know Mr Wells and sell pretty things to him, she offered Clara a job on the chance of achieving that end through her.

And so it came about that Eliza's luck held, and the expected opposition to the flower shop melted away. The shop is in the arcade of a railway station not very far from the Victoria and Albert Museum; and if you live in that neighbourhood you may go there any day and buy a buttonhole from Eliza.

Now here is a last opportunity for romance. Would you not like to be assured that the shop was an immense success, thanks to Eliza's charms and her early business experience in Covent Garden? Alas! the truth is the truth: the shop did not pay for a long time, simply because Eliza and her Freddy did not know how to keep it. True, Eliza had not to begin at the very beginning: she knew the names and prices of the cheaper flowers; and her elation was unbounded when she found that Freddy, like all youths educated at cheap, pretentious, and thoroughly inefficient schools, knew a little Latin. It was very little, but enough to make him appear to her a Porson or Bentley,[11] and to put him at his ease with botanical nomenclature. Unfortunately he knew nothing else; and Eliza, though she could count money up to eighteen shillings or so, and had acquired a certain familiarity with the language of Milton from her struggles to qualify herself for winning Higgins's bet, could not write out a bill without utterly disgracing the establishment. Freddy's power of stating in Latin that Balbus built a wall and that Gaul was divided into three parts[12] did not carry with it the slightest knowledge of accounts or business: Colonel

<hr>

10. **scutcheon** (skuch′ ən) *n.*: Coat of arms.

11. **Porson, Bentley:** Richard Porson (1759–1808) and Richard Bentley (1662–1742), English classical scholars.
12. **Balbus . . . parts:** Referring to elementary Latin exercises.

Pickering had to explain to him what a cheque book and a bank account meant. And the pair were by no means easily teachable. Freddy backed up Eliza in her obstinate refusal to believe that they could save money by engaging a bookkeeper with some knowledge of the business. How, they argued, could you possible save money by going to extra expense when you already could not make both ends meet? But the Colonel, after making the ends meet over and over again, at last gently insisted; and Eliza, humbled to the dust by having to beg from him so often, and stung by the uproarious derision of Higgins, to whom the notion of Freddy succeeding at anything was a joke that never palled, grasped the fact that business, like phonetics, has to be learned.

On the piteous spectacle of the pair spending their evenings in shorthand schools and polytechnic classes, learning bookkeeping and typewriting with incipient junior clerks, male and female, from the elementary schools, let me not dwell. There were even classes at the London School of Economics, and a humble personal appeal to the director of that institution to recommend a course bearing on the flower busi-

ness. He, being a humorist, explained to them the method of the celebrated Dickensian essay on Chinese Metaphysics by the gentleman who read an article on China and an article on Metaphysics and combined the information. He suggested that they should combine the London School with Kew Gardens. Eliza, to whom the procedure of the Dickensian gentleman seemed perfectly correct (as in fact it was) and not in the least funny (which was only her ignorance), took the advice with entire gravity. But the effort that cost her the deepest humiliation was a request to Higgins, whose pet artistic fancy, next to Milton's verse, was calligraphy, and who himself wrote a most beautiful Italian hand, that he would teach her to write. He declared that she was congenitally incapable of forming a single letter worthy of the least of Milton's words; but she persisted; and again he suddenly threw himself into the task of teaching her with a combination of stormy intensity, concentrated patience, and occasional bursts of interesting disquisition on the beauty and nobility, the august mission and destiny, of human handwriting. Eliza ended by acquiring an extremely uncommercial script which was a positive extension of her personal beauty, and spending three times as much on stationery as anyone else because certain qualities and shapes on paper became indispensable to her. She could not even address an envelope in the usual way because it made the margins all wrong.

Their commercial schooldays were a period of disgrace and despair for the young couple. They seemed to be learning nothing about flower shops. At last they gave it up as hopeless, and shook the dust of the shorthand schools, and the polytechnics, and the London School of Economics from their feet for ever. Besides, the business was in some mysterious way beginning to take care of itself. They had somehow forgotten their objections to employing other people. They came to the conclusion that their own way was the best, and that they had really a remarkable talent for business. The Colonel, who had been compelled for some years to keep a sufficient sum on current account at his bankers to make up their deficits, found that the provision was unnecessary: the young people were prospering. It is true that there was not quite fair play between them and their competitors in trade. Their week-ends in the country cost them nothing, and saved them the price of their Sunday dinners; for the motor car was the Colonel's; and he and Higgins paid the hotel bills. Mr F. Hill, florist and greengrocer (they soon discovered that there was money in asparagus; and asparagus led to other vegetables), had an air which stamped the business as classy; and in private life he was still Frederick Eynsford Hill, Esquire. Not that there was any swank[13.] about him: nobody but Eliza knew that he had been christened Frederick Chaloner. Eliza herself swanked like anything.

That is all. That is how it has turned out. It is astonishing how much Eliza still manages to meddle in the housekeeping at Wimpole Street in spite of the shop and her own family. And it is notable that though she never nags her husband, and frankly loves the Colonel as if she were his favorite daughter, she has never got out of the habit of nagging Higgins that was established on the fatal night when she won his bet for him. She snaps his head off on the faintest provocation, or on none. He no longer dares to tease her by assuming an abysmal inferiority of Freddy's mind to his own. He storms and bullies and derides; but she stands up to him so ruthlessly that the Colonel has to ask her from time to time to be kinder to Higgins; and it is the only request of his that brings a mulish expression into her face. Nothing but some emergency or calamity great enough to break down all likes and dislikes, and throw them both back on their common humanity—and may they be spared any such trial!—will ever alter this. She knows that Higgins does not need her,

just as her father did not need her. The very scrupulousness with which he told her that day that he had become used to having her there, and dependent on her for all sorts of little services, and that he should miss her if she went away (it would never have occurred to Freddy or the Colonel to say anything of the sort) deepens her inner certainty that she is "no more to him than them slippers"; yet she has a sense, too, that his indifference is deeper than the infatuation of commoner souls. She is immensely interested in him. She has even secret mischievous moments in which she wishes she could get him alone, on a desert island, away from all ties and with nobody else in the world to consider, and just drag him off his pedestal and see him making love like any common man. We all have private imaginations of that sort. But when it comes to business, to the life that she really leads as distinguished from the life of dreams and fancies, she likes Freddy and she likes the Colonel; and she does not like Higgins and Mr Doolittle. Galatea never does quite like Pygmalion:[14] his relation to her is too godlike to be altogether agreeable.

---

13. swank *n.*: Ostentatious behavior.

14. Galatea (gal'ə tē'ə) **. . . Pygmalion:** Pygmalion was a mythological king of Cyprus who carved a statue of a woman so beautiful that he fell in love with her. The king prayed to the gods to bring the statue, Galatea, to life, and his prayers were answered by Aphrodite, the goddess of love.

RESPONDING TO THE SELECTION

Your Response

1. Do you think Higgins has damaged or improved Eliza's life with the "trouble" he has caused her? Explain.

Recalling

2. (a) What has happened to Alfred Doolittle? (b) How has this change affected his life?
3. Why is Eliza grateful to Pickering?
4. (a) In their conversation together, what does Eliza tell Higgins she wants from him? (b) What does he want from her?
5. (a) What, according to the Epilogue, becomes of Eliza? (b) Of Clara Eynsford Hill?

Interpreting

6. Explain what the changes in Alfred Doolittle suggest is Shaw's attitude toward "middle-class morality."
7. Do you think the outcome of Higgins's last discussion with Eliza was inevitable? Why or why not?

Applying

8. The Epilogue describes developments in Eliza's life after the action of the play. Would you have preferred to see these developments played out? Explain your reasons.

ANALYZING LITERATURE

Understanding the Complete Play

The paradoxical saying that "the whole is greater than the sum of its parts" is true of works of art. A play is a weaving-together of many elements, among them the plot (or story line), the setting (time and place of the action), the characters (roles), the tone (playwright's attitude toward the subject or audience), the symbols (representative values attached to events, people, or things), and the theme (main idea). When these separate elements come together, a "chemical reaction" results. Create a checklist similar to the following for *Pygmalion*.

plot	setting	character	tone	symbol	theme

Write a brief description for each of the play's elements, entering "NA" when the element is not applicable. Then discuss how the various elements interact in Shaw's play. (Consider, for example, how setting affects theme.)

CRITICAL THINKING AND READING

Summarizing a Play

When a newspaper or magazine critic writes a review of a play, he or she includes a **summary,** or brief description of the action. A good summary captures a sense of the play as a whole, focusing not only on what is said and done but on such details as setting. The amount of information that a summary provides depends, of course, on its overall length. List the details you find important to include in a one-page summary of *Pygmalion*. Decide how you would handle such matters as Shaw's Preface and Epilogue.

THINKING AND WRITING

Writing About the Title

At the end of the Epilogue, Shaw mentions Pygmalion and Galatea, who are figures from Greek mythology. The sculptor Pygmalion created a statue of a beautiful woman. After he fell in love with his creation, the goddess Aphrodite brought her to life. Write an essay discussing the effectiveness of the title Shaw chose for his play. Proceed by addressing the following questions: How godlike do you think Eliza finds Higgins? To what extent has Higgins "created" a new person? Might Higgins's feelings toward Eliza at any point in the play be fairly described as love? How much impact will the title have on a person who views, rather than reads, the play and who is, therefore, unfamiliar with the Epilogue? When you revise, make sure you have included adequate support for your theses.

Pygmalion Becomes *My Fair Lady*

It was the undisputed smash musical of 1956. From the moment the first hints drifted north from Philadelphia—where the musical was having its tryout run—tickets were eagerly snatched up. By March 15, when the show officially opened in New York City, only a few tickets were still available. By March 16 tickets were sold out for months ahead. Critics raved: "One of the best musicals of the century!" Writer James Thurber proclaimed it to be "the finest union of comedy and music" in his experience. Its male lead made the cover of the July 23 issue of *Time* magazine. Although it was one of those rare musicals that did not have a title song—it took its name from an old poem about London Bridge falling down—within weeks an astonishing number of its songs were famous. People were humming "The Rain in Spain," "I Could Have Danced All Night," and "Get Me to the Church on Time." By 1962, when it completed its run of 2,717 performances, its 1912 period costumes had even influenced American fashion. What play had taken America by such storm? Why, *My Fair Lady*, of course!

LERNER AND LOEWE

What could account for the play's outrageous success and impact on American culture? Obviously much of its success was due to Lerner and Loewe, the brilliant duo responsible for such classic hits as *Brigadoon* (1947) and *Camelot* (1960). Except for the play's girl-gets-boy ending that Shaw would not have tolerated, Lerner had the sense not to tamper with a good thing—almost all of *My Fair Lady* comes directly from Shaw's *Pygmalion*.

Recall that Shaw declared in the Epilogue to *Pygmalion* that to assume that the heroine of a romance "must have married the hero of it" is "unbearable." But perhaps in his adaptation Lerner was only doing what so many had wanted to do before him. Take, for instance, the case of the first actor to play Henry Higgins, Beerbohm Tree. Handpicked by Shaw for the role, the actor nonetheless chose to ignore Shaw's directions and play the role his own way. Accounts have it that Shaw was absolutely livid with Tree who, when the curtain fell in the last act, threw a flower to Eliza—indicating his affections for her and holding out the hope that they would indeed be united. Aside from the ending, Lerner was much more respectful of Shaw's writing and made almost no changes in the original.

In at least one spot, Lerner changed a scene's location, though the plot remains the same. In *Pygmalion* Henry Higgins first

presents Eliza to society at his mother's house. In *My Fair Lady* her presentation is at the Ascot races, where there are many more chances for Eliza to slip back into her Tottenham Court Road lingo. He has also eliminated or added minor characters to point up situations. In the main, however, he has faithfully followed Shaw's lead. Stage directions are, for the most part, word for word from Shaw. As the critic for *Time* magazine remarked, "At bottom, *My Fair Lady* is nothing more than George Bernard Shaw's play *Pygmalion* with music added."

A GLITTERING CAST

Credit is also due to the glittering cast. Theatergoers and fellow actors alike were stunned by Harrison's brilliant performance as Henry Higgins. Famed actor Charles Laughton rushed backstage to offer his congratulations to his friend Harrison: "In all my theater experience," he raved, "I've only seen a handful of performances to match Rex's. He makes every man in the audience laugh at himself, and every woman laugh at the man beside her." Interestingly, Harrison had met Shaw in person in the course of performing in Shaw's play *Major Barbara* in 1934. *My Fair Lady* marked the debut of twenty-year-old English actress Julie Andrews, who was described as playing the role of the flower-girl Eliza with "heart-lifting simplicity."

THE MOVIE VERSION

If possible, the 1964 movie version was as splendid as the stage play. Studio head Jack Warner originally wanted Cary Grant or Rock Hudson to play Higgins and James Cagney to be Doolittle. Cary Grant refused Warner's offer by saying that if the studio mogul chose anyone but Rex Harrison for the role of Higgins he would not even bother to see the film. Without a bankable leading man, Warner was worried: After all, he had put up more than five million for the rights to the musical, set aside nearly twenty million for production costs, and promised the authors and producers of the stage show almost fifty percent of the net. As it turned out, his fears were groundless. The screen version proved a stunning hit, earning Oscars for Best Picture, Best Actor, Best Director, Best Color Cinematography, Best Costume Design, Best Musical Score, Best Sound, and Best Art Direction. The only major award it did not win was Best Actress. In one of life's little twists of fate, Julie Andrews won Best Actress that year for her role in Mary Poppins—and Audrey Hepburn did not even receive a nomination as Eliza Doolittle.

In the long run, however, we must go back to Shaw and present our laurels to him, for without him there would be no *Pygmalion;* and without *Pygmalion* there would be no *My Fair Lady.*

Poetry

HOUSES OF PARLIAMENT, 1903
Claude Monet

WILLIAM BUTLER YEATS

1865–1939

Winner of the Nobel Prize for Literature in 1923, William Butler Yeats (yāts) is generally regarded as one of the finest poets of this century. Born near Dublin, Ireland, Yeats was educated there and in London, but his heart lay to the west, in County Sligo, Ireland, where he spent childhood vacations with his grandparents. In the shadow of Sligo's barren mountains, he became immersed in the mythology and legends of Ireland.

After three years of studying painting in Dublin, Yeats moved to London to pursue a literary career. He became friends with the poet Arthur Symons, who awakened his interest in the symbolic poetry of William Blake and the French Symbolists. Yeats's early poetry shows the Symbolist influence as well as that of the Pre-Raphaelites, a group who believed that art needs a moral center which they felt it had lost nearly three centuries earlier. Symbolism, Pre-Raphaelism, and Irish myth combined in Yeats's first important collection, *The Wanderings of Oisin,* published in 1889.

Yeats led the Irish Literary Revival, helping to establish the Irish Literary Society in London in 1892 and the Irish National Literary Society in Dublin. He was also active in the Irish National Movement, whose members sought Ireland's independence from England. In this, he was spurred by his unrequited love for the beautiful actress and revolutionary, Maud Gonne. To his sorrow—after many refusals of his proposals—she chose a soldier, and Yeats, years later, married another woman.

Near the end of the century, Yeats joined with his friend Lady Augusta Gregory in founding the Irish National Theatre Society. He turned his attention to writing plays, among them *The Shadowy Waters* (1900) and *Deirdre* (1907). When he returned to poetry, it was with a new voice, subtler but more powerful than the one he had used before that time. The poems in *The Tower,* published in 1928, show Yeats at the height of his abilities.

In 1922 Yeats was appointed a senator of the new Irish Free State, and on his seventieth birthday he was hailed by his nation as the greatest living Irishman. He continued to write poems until a day or two before his death at Roquebrune, France. One of his last poems contains his famous epitaph: Cast a cold eye / On life, on death. / Horseman, pass by!

When You Are Old; The Lake Isle of Innisfree; The Wild Swans at Coole; An Irish Airman Foresees His Death

Writers' Techniques

Speaker and Lyric Voice. A lyric poem expresses personal thoughts and feelings on a specific subject. Among the most common subjects are love, death, nature, and war. Sometimes the speaker in a lyric poem—the one whose voice comes through—is, or appears to be, the poet. In Milton's "When I Consider How My Light Is Spent," for example, the speaker seems clearly to be the poet. In Christopher Marlowe's "The Passionate Shepherd to His Love," on the other hand, the speaker is almost certainly not the poet. In many lyric poems, such as William Blake's "The Tiger," you cannot tell for sure whether the speaker is or is not the poet.

Focus

Think of a subject about which you have strong feelings, either positive or negative, such as education, friendship, or marriage. Jot down some brief notes that express your feelings on the subject. Then think of a fictional character based either on your reading or your imagination. Write at least three sentences, or three lines of poetry, in which the fictional character expresses your feelings on the subject you have chosen.

Primary Source

Sean O'Faolain tried to explain the extraordinary influence William Butler Yeats exerted on all phases of Irish life. Elected a member of the Irish Academy of Letters founded the year before by Yeats and Shaw, O'Faolain worked with Yeats on several projects as Yeats's remarkable career drew to its close. "He had been our inspiration and our justification in the sense that all the rest of us younger men and women could not, between us, represent literature with anything like his achievement and authority in the eyes of the public. When he retired to Rapallo to die, and most of his generation had passed away or gone into exile one by one . . . there was nothing to do but wait until Time, if it ever did, created new reputations of equal authority. Time did not and could not. It was not a matter alone of literary achievement. Had, for example, Joyce returned to live in Dublin his presence would have made no difference. For the source of Yeats's authority, like the source of his poetry, was the extraordinary union in his nature of a powerful imagination, the will to enforce it, and a persistent dramatic self-image of himself as a seer and leader. . . . It was the blend that at once bestowed greatness on him and condemned him to loneliness. . . . It was his need of his nature, as poet and man, to live a foot off the ground, a foot or two, or more, away from common life."

When You Are Old

William Butler Yeats

When you are old and gray and full of sleep,
And nodding by the fire, take down this book,
And slowly read, and dream of the soft look
Your eyes had once, and of their shadows deep;

5 How many loved your moments of glad grace,
And loved your beauty with love false or true,
But one man loved the pilgrim soul in you,
And loved the sorrows of your changing face;

And bending down beside the glowing bars,
10 Murmur, a little sadly, how Love fled
And paced upon the mountains overhead
And hid his face amid a crowd of stars.

RESPONDING TO THE SELECTION

Your Response

1. What do you think it is like to feel "old and gray and full of sleep" (line 1)?

Recalling

2. What does the speaker ask the person being addressed to do?

Interpreting

3. Who do you think the "one man" in the second stanza is?
4. What does the phrase "pilgrim soul" suggest about the person being addressed?
5. Why is the word *Love* capitalized in line 10?

Applying

6. When love is not reciprocated, it may be withdrawn, as it apparently was in this poem. Under what circumstances do you think it is right to withdraw love that is not being returned?

ANALYZING LITERATURE

Understanding Speaker and Lyric Voice

The speaker in a lyric poem may or may not be the poet. Sometimes the identity of the speaker is obvious, but often it is hard to be sure. Knowing about the poet's life, while not essential to your enjoyment of a poem, may provide clues to the identity of the speaker.

1. Look back at the biography of Yeats. What event in his life might have prompted him to write this poem?
2. In line 2 the speaker advises the person being addressed to "take down this book." In what way might that advice furnish a clue to the identity of the speaker?

The Lake Isle of Innisfree

William Butler Yeats

I will arise and go now, and go to Innisfree,
And a small cabin build there, of clay and wattles[1] made:
Nine bean-rows will I have there, a hive for the honeybee,
And live alone in the bee-loud glade.

5 And I shall have some peace there, for peace comes
      dropping slow,
Dropping from the veils of the morning to where the cricket
      sings;
There midnight's all a glimmer, and noon a purple glow,
And evening full of the linnet's wings.[2]

I will arise and go now, for always night and day
10 I hear lake water lapping with low sounds by the shore;
While I stand on the roadway, or on the pavements gray,
I hear it in the deep heart's core.

OLD HOUSE (IVY COTTAGE),
SHOREHAM, 1831–32
Samuel Palmer
Ashmolean Museum, Oxford

---

1. wattles *n.*: Stakes interwoven with twigs or branches.
2. linnet's wings: The wings of a European singing bird.

RESPONDING TO THE SELECTION

Your Response
1. When do you feel like you would like to get away to a beautiful, peaceful place? Explain.

Recalling
2. (a) What does the speaker want most to find at Innisfree? (b) How will each of the four times of day he mentions contribute to his goal?

Interpreting
3. Why do you think Innisfree, as the speaker describes it, has so much more appeal for him than where he is now?

4. (a) Do you think the speaker is expressing a wish or a genuine intent to go to Innisfree? (b) What evidence in the poem is there to support your answer?
5. What techniques or devices in the poem help to create a vivid picture of Innisfree?

Applying
6. Popular music sometimes deals with the theme of leaving one place and going to a more desirable place. What song or songs can you think of that have that theme?

The Wild Swans at Coole

William Butler Yeats

The trees are in their autumn beauty,
The woodland paths are dry,
Under the October twilight the water
Mirrors a still sky;
5 Upon the brimming water among
    the stones
Are nine-and-fifty swans.

The nineteenth autumn has come
    upon me
Since I first made my count;
I saw, before I had well finished,
10 All suddenly mount
And scatter wheeling in great broken
    rings
Upon their clamorous wings.

I have looked upon those brilliant
    creatures,
And now my heart is sore.
15 All's changed since I, hearing at twilight,
The first time on this shore,
The bell-beat of their wings above
    my head,
Trod with a lighter tread.

Unwearied still, lover by lover,
20 They paddle in the cold
Companionable streams or climb the air;
Their hearts have not grown old;
Passion or conquest, wander where
    they will,
Attend upon them still.

25 But now they drift on the still water,
Mysterious, beautiful;
Among what rushes will they build,
By what lake's edge or pool
Delight men's eyes when I awake
    some day
30 To find they have flown away?

RESPONDING TO THE SELECTION

Your Response

1. In what ways do beautiful, wild animals remind you, as the swans remind the speaker, of the mysteries of human life?

Recalling

2. (a) What was the speaker's reaction when he first heard "the bell-beat of their wings"? (b) Why is his reaction different now?

Interpreting

3. For what thematic purpose does the speaker emphasize the setting in the first two stanzas?
4. What might the swans symbolize to the speaker?

Applying

5. Why does great beauty sometimes arouse a sense of sadness and loss?

CRITICAL THINKING AND READING

Evaluating the Use of Imagery

Imagery in literature is created when the writer's words, singly or in combination, produce a picture in the reader's mind. Images may appeal to any of the five senses—sometimes to several at once. The phrase "a crisp, shiny, sweet apple" appeals to hearing, sight, *and* taste. If imagery is to work effectively, readers must know the key words and their meanings. For example, a reader who has never heard the word *clamorous* will not appreciate the imagery of "clamorous wings." Locate the following images from "The Wild Swans of Coole" and identify the sense or senses to which each appeals.

1. . . . the water/Mirrors a still sky
2. And scatter wheeling in great broken rings/ Upon their clamorous wings
3. The bell-beat of their wings
4. They paddle in the cold/Companionable streams

LEARNING OPTION

Multicultural Activity. Give a presentation about the depiction of swans in various cultures. Consider songs and fairy tales as well as fiction and poetry. Visual representations might include architectural decorations and book illustrations.

An Irish Airman Foresees His Death

William Butler Yeats

Major Robert Gregory, a young Irish artist who was the son of Yeats's friend Lady Augusta Gregory, was killed during World War I while flying over Italy as a member of England's Royal Flying Corps. Gregory's death inspired Yeats to write this poem.

I know that I shall meet my fate
Somewhere among the clouds above;
Those that I fight I do not hate,
Those that I guard I do not love;[1]
5 My country is Kiltartan[2] Cross,
My countrymen Kiltartan's poor,
No likely end could bring them loss
Or leave them happier than before.
Nor law, nor duty bade me fight,
10 Nor public men, nor cheering crowds,
A lonely impulse of delight
Drove to this tumult in the clouds;
I balanced all, brought all to mind,
The years to come seemed waste of breath,
15 A waste of breath the years behind
In balance with this life, this death.

---

1. Those . . . love: Because Ireland was under English rule during World War I, many Irish fought as members of the English forces during the war. However, because of their desire for independence many of the Irish felt a great deal of resentment toward the English.
2. Kiltartan: A village near Lady Gregory's estate.

RESPONDING TO THE SELECTION

Your Response
1. Do you agree that the speaker's life is a "waste of breath," as he sees it to be?

Recalling
2. (a) How does he feel about those he is fighting against? (b) Why is he fighting them?
3. How does he view (a) his past? (b) his future?

Interpreting
4. The airman does not love those he guards—the English. (a) Do you think his lack of love extends to those he calls his countrymen—Kiltartan's poor? (b) What lines in the poem support your answer?
5. (a) To what extent does the airman seem worried about his fate? (b) How would you describe the airman's character?

Applying
6. Suppose the airman were to survive the war. What do you think he might do with the rest of his life? Explain your answer.

THINKING AND WRITING

Writing About the Use of a Speaker
In writing "An Irish Airman Foresees His Death," Yeats had in mind Major Robert Gregory, the son of Yeats's close friend Lady Augusta Gregory. A volunteer in England's Royal Flying Corps, Major Gregory was killed during World War I while flying over Italy. Think about why Yeats may have chosen to write his poem with Major Gregory as the first-person speaker. Write a brief essay in which you explain why the poem, as written, allows Yeats to express his thoughts about the frailty of life, the futility of war, and the problems of Ireland more powerfully than a third-person point of view would have permitted. When you revise, make sure you have included details from the poem to support your opinion.

An Irish Airman Foresees His Death   1065

GUIDE FOR INTERPRETING

The Second Coming; After Long Silence; Sailing to Byzantium

Writers' Techniques

Symbols. In its broadest, most basic sense, a symbol is something that stands for something else. The word *horse* is a symbol for an actual, recognizable animal. In our culture an olive branch is a symbol for peace. A symbol in literature is a word, person, object, or action that stands for something beyond itself. For example, the white whale in Herman Melville's *Moby-Dick* is often said to stand for evil. In the art and literature of the late nineteenth century, symbolism took on special significance. A group of French artists and poets, reacting against realism, promoted the use of symbols to achieve intensity and complexity in their work, a technique that sometimes approached mysticism. Yeats, an adherent of this type of symbolism in his early poetry, abandoned it later. However, in the last decade of his life, he created an elaborate symbolic system of his own, a system that is largely a curiosity for modern readers. His later poems abound in symbols, but Yeats remains first and foremost a poet, not a system-maker or a philosopher. In his best poems, the symbols do not require mastery of his system, but only the practiced eye of a careful reader.

Focus

If you wished to picture Canada symbolically, you might draw a maple leaf; for Great Britain you might draw a lion, and for New York City, an apple. Countries, states, cities, companies, high schools, professional athletic teams—all sometimes develop symbols for easy and perhaps emotional identification. Think about such symbols. Jot down a number of them, identifying what each one symbolizes.

Primary Source

It's tempting to think that famous writers are free from the doubts that the rest of us sometimes feel. That Eliot and Yeats both received great praise in their day does not mean that they were immune to a touch of professional jealousy. Writer Richard Ellmann noted their long incompatibility in this encounter:

> "Among their various mild collisions none was more defined than the dinner at Wellesley College when Yeats, seated next to Eliot but oblivious of him, conversed with the guest on the other side until late in the meal. Then he turned and said, 'My friend here and I have been discussing the defects of T. S. Eliot's poetry. What do you think of that poetry?'
>
> "Eliot held up his place card to excuse himself from the jury."

The Second Coming

William Butler Yeats

"The Second Coming" was inspired by Yeats's belief that history occurs in two-thousand-year cycles, with one civilization passing through stages of development, growth, and decay, before crumbling and giving way to a new civilization that stands in direct opposition to the preceding civilization. The birth of Christ had brought about the end of one civilization and the birth of another, and Yeats believed that the society of the early twentieth century was in a state of decay that would lead to a similar sort of rebirth.

Turning and turning in the widening gyre
The falcon cannot hear the falconer;
Things fall apart; the center cannot hold;
Mere anarchy is loosed upon the world,
5 The blood-dimmed tide is loosed, and everywhere
The ceremony of innocence is drowned;
The best lack all conviction, while the worst
Are full of passionate intensity.[1]

Surely some revelation is at hand;
10 Surely the Second Coming is at hand.
The Second Coming! Hardly are those words out
When a vast image out of *Spiritus Mundi*[2]
Troubles my sight: somewhere in sands of the desert
A shape with lion body and the head of a man,[3]
15 A gaze blank and pitiless as the sun,
Is moving its slow thighs, while all about it
Reel shadows of the indignant desert birds.
The darkness drops again; but now I know
That twenty centuries[4] of stony sleep
20 Were vexed to nightmare by a rocking cradle,[5]
And what rough beast, its hour come round at last,
Slouches towards Bethlehem to be born?

---

1. Mere . . . intensity (lines 4-8): Refers to the Russian Revolution of 1917.
2. Spiritus Mundi (spir′i təs moon′dē): The Universal Spirit or soul, the Universal Subconscious in which the memories of the entire human race are forever preserved.
3. A . . . man: A sphinx.
4. twenty centuries: The historical cycle preceding the birth of Christ.
5. rocking cradle: The cradle of Jesus Christ.

RESPONDING TO THE SELECTION

Your Response

1. Do you agree that in the modern world "things fall apart; the center cannot hold"? Explain.

Recalling

2. Why does the falcon not return to the falconer, as it ordinarily would in falconry (the hunting of game with falcons)?
3. In the first stanza, what is happening to government and innocence?
4. What does the speaker believe is at hand?
5. (a) What has begun to stir in the desert? (b) How long has it been dormant?
6. What does the speaker say is about to be born?

Interpreting

7. How does Yeats use the unhearing falcon as a symbol of what is happening in the world?
8. What is the imagery in lines 5–6?
9. When did the previous "twenty centuries of stony sleep" occur (that is, before the twentieth century)?
10. (a) What would you expect to appear at the Second Coming? (b) How does that differ from what the speaker suggests will appear?

Applying

11. What historical forces do you think prompt people, including poets, to predict vast upheavals, new civilizations, and even the end of the world?

ANALYZING LITERATURE

Understanding Symbols

A literary **symbol** is a word, person, object, or action that stands for something beyond itself.

In "The Second Coming," for instance, the falcon flying in ever-widening circles is more than just a trained hunting bird that has lost its way. It represents something—it symbolizes something. A symbol always requires interpretation. To interpret the falcon, it would help you to know Yeats's theories about "gyres," or cycles, which were a part of his symbolic system, although such knowledge is not really essential to an understanding of the poem.

1. Yeats does not merely talk about twenty centuries of silence. He symbolizes them. (a) What symbol does he use? (b) Why do you think he presents it through a description of its features rather than by naming it outright?
2. (a) What symbolism, if any, do you find in line 6: "The ceremony of innocence is drowned"? (b) What might the "indignant desert birds" in line 17 represent?
3. (a) What symbol does Yeats use to represent the coming era? (b) What characteristics do you associate with this symbol?

LEARNING OPTIONS

1. **Art.** The speaker of the poem is troubled by "a vast image" of the Second Coming. Create your own illustration of this cataclysmic event, based on the details included in the poem. Have your artwork reflect the ominous mood expressed in the poem. Display your work in class.
2. **Writing.** How might the world end and a new world be born? Think about the ways in which the world as we know it could be dramatically and permanently transformed. Write a brief narrative that describes the cause and some of the effects of this apocalypse. Your description can be either realistic or imaginary.

After Long Silence

William Butler Yeats

Speech after long silence; it is right,
All other lovers being estranged or dead,
Unfriendly lamplight hid under its shade,
The curtains drawn upon unfriendly night,
5   That we descant and yet again descant
Upon the supreme theme of Art and Song:
Bodily decrepitude is wisdom; young
We loved each other and were ignorant.

RESPONDING TO THE SELECTION

Your Response
1. Do you agree with the speaker's idea that wisdom comes only with age and "physical decrepitude"? Explain.

Recalling
2. What does the speaker say should follow long silence?
3. The speaker describes two things as unfriendly. What are they?
4. What is the "supreme theme" that should be talked about after long silence?
5. Why does the speaker believe the old have more reason than the young to "descant and yet again descant"?

Interpreting
6. (a) What relationship exists between the people who are being urged to speak? (b) How can you tell?
7. What do you suppose was taking place during the period of long silence?
8. The speaker seems to have mixed feelings about old age. How would you describe his feelings?

Applying
9. How fully do you accept the idea that the young cannot talk meaningfully about "Art and Song"? Explain.

THINKING AND WRITING

Writing a Poem About Silence
"After Long Silence" treats the idea of silence symbolically. Silence, according to Yeats, is the time when human beings have little of intellectual importance to communicate to one another. That is one interpretation of silence, but only one. Choose another approach to the subject of silence. Think about it. Write some notes. Then write a poem that expresses your own view of silence. Remember that a poem requires at least as much revision as an essay does.

LEARNING OPTION

Speaking and Listening. With a partner, create a dialogue between Youth and Age on the themes of love and creativity, or any other subject you choose. Your dialogue may have any tone you wish, but make sure that both speakers are allowed to make strong claims for their points of view. Present your dialogue in class.

Sailing to Byzantium[1]

W. B. Yeats

I

That is no country for old men. The young
In one another's arms, birds in the trees
—Those dying generations—at their song,
The salmon-falls, the mackerel-crowded seas,
5 Fish, flesh, or fowl, commend all summer long
Whatever is begotten, born, and dies.
Caught in that sensual music all neglect
Monuments of unaging intellect.

II

An aged man is but a paltry thing,
10 A tattered coat upon a stick, unless
Soul clap its hands and sing, and louder sing
For every tatter in its mortal dress,
Nor is there singing school but studying
Monuments of its own magnificence;
15 And therefore I have sailed the seas and come
To the holy city of Byzantium.

III

O sages standing in God's holy fire
As in the gold mosaic of a wall,[2]
Come from the holy fire, perne in a gyre,[3]
20 And be the singing-masters of my soul.
Consume my heart away; sick with desire
And fastened to a dying animal
It knows not what it is; and gather me
Into the artifice of eternity.

---

1. Byzantium (bi zan' shē əm): The ancient capital of the Eastern
Roman (or Byzantine) Empire and the seat of the Greek Orthodox
Church; today, Istanbul, Turkey. For Yeats, it symbolized the sensual
and artistic world as opposed to the natural and biological world.
2. sages . . . wall: Wise old men and saints portrayed in gold mosaic
on the walls of Byzantine churches.
3. perne . . . gyre: Spin in a spiraling motion.

IV

25 Once out of nature I shall never take
My bodily form from any natural thing,
But such a form as Grecian goldsmiths make
Of hammered gold and gold enameling
To keep a drowsy Emperor awake;
30 Or set upon a golden bough to sing⁴
To lords and ladies of Byzantium
Of what is past, or passing, or to come.

---

4. To . . . sing: Yeats wrote, "I have read somewhere that in the Emperor's palace at Byzantium was a tree made of gold and silver, and artificial birds that sang."

⬛ Responding to the Selection

Your Response

1. Do you think it is possible to escape the effects of time? Explain.

Recalling

2. (a) What do the people of the country referred to in the first stanza "commend"? (B) What do they neglect?
3. How is "an aged man" described in lines 9–10?
4. What does the speaker do in lines 15–16?
5. What does the speaker ask of the sages in the third stanza?
6. What bodily form does the speaker wish to take when he is "out of nature"?

Interpreting

7. How does Byzantium contrast with the country described in the first two stanzas?
8. (a) What do the desires that the speaker expresses in stanzas 3 and 4 reveal about his attitude toward aging and death? (b) How does he hope to immortalize himself?
9. What does this poem suggest about the motives of artists and the purpose of art?

Applying

10. Do you think that most people hope to immortalize themselves in some way? Why or why not?

⬛ Learning Options

1. **Performance.** What might Yeats's golden bird sing about while sitting in its artificial tree at the Emperor's palace? Make up the lyrics to a song it might chant to the citizens of Byzantium. If you play an instrument, you may want to compose music to accompany your lyrics. Perform your song in class.
2. **Art.** Find examples of Byzantine art, such as mosaics, in an art or world history book. Display the illustrations in class. If you wish, create your own mosaic in a Byzantine style.

BIOGRAPHIES

Siegfried Sassoon (1886–1967)

Born into a wealthy family in Brenchley, Kent, Siegfried Sassoon published a number of pastoral poems and parodies while still in his early twenties. When war broke out in 1914, Sassoon joined the army and showed such reckless courage in battle that he earned the nickname Mad Jack along with a medal for gallantry. By the time he was wounded in April 1917, however, his attitude toward war had changed. He began to write what he called "trench poems," the starkly realistic and agonized verses on which his reputation rests. When Sassoon returned to the front in 1918, a British sentry shot him by mistake, and Sassoon spent the rest of the war in a hospital. Although he wrote for almost fifty years after the Armistice, Sassoon produced little to match his searing wartime verses.

Rupert Brooke (1887–1915)

Having begun writing poetry as a child, Rupert Brooke established himself as a serious poet before World War I. When war broke out in 1914, he joined the Royal Naval Division. After participating in the disastrous expedition to Antwerp, he was ordered to the Dardanelles, where the British hoped to strike a blow against the Turks. He contracted blood poisoning on the way and died in a French military hospital in Greece. Brooke's war sonnets, traditional and idealistic, were among the last from the soldier-poets of World War I that expressed an unalloyed patriotism. Brooke saw little of the trench warfare that so affected the vision of Sassoon, Owen, and other poets who served in the army.

Wilfred Owen (1893–1918)

As a young boy, Wilfred Owen read constantly, and he was disappointed when later he failed to win a scholarship to London University. He joined the army in 1915 and became a conscientious and sympathetic officer. Wounded three times in 1917, Owen was sent home to recuperate from a nervous collapse. In late summer of 1918, he returned to the front and won a medal for outstanding bravery. A week before the Armistice that ended the war, Owen was killed in battle. Though Owen's pre-war poetry reflected his admiration for the Romantic poet John Keats, the war changed his writing completely. Like Sassoon, he was horrified by the suffering endured by the ordinary soldier. About his poetry he wrote, "Above all I am not concerned with poetry. My subject is war, and the pity of war. The poetry is in the pity."

GUIDE FOR INTERPRETING

Wirers; The Soldier; Anthem for Doomed Youth

Historical Context

World War I Poets. Sometimes a historical event creates such an impact that poets feel compelled to comment on, and perhaps to explain, what happened. World War I was such an event. After a few indecisive early battles, the war became one of attrition as opposing forces entrenched themselves on opposite sides of a front line extending 400 miles from the North Sea to neutral Switzerland. On one side, filthy, muddy, and smelly trenches housed British, French, and Belgian troops. Just a short distance away were the relatively clean, efficient, and sometimes even comfortable trenches of the Germans. Artillery fire took a huge toll. An estimated 7,000 British soldiers and officers were killed or wounded every day.

The war's unprecedented devastation and slaughter inspired millions of words—patriotic, indignant, disillusioned, depending on who wrote them. Rupert Brooke's "The Soldier" reflects the buoyantly patriotic mood of the British public at the outbreak of the war. As the war dragged on, however, the troops, all too aware of the horrors of the trenches and the growing number of casualties, found little to cheer about. Soldier-poets Siegfried Sassoon and Wilfred Owen both regarded their poems as truthful reports to the home front. Sassoon sought to shock the British public with the realities of war, whereas Owen wanted to arouse compassion for the common soldier fallen in battle.

Focus

What images does the word *soldier* conjure up for you? Where do your images come from: movies, television, the stories of people you know? Write down some of your thoughts about soldiers.

Primary Source

It was in a war hospital in Edinburgh that Siegfried Sassoon befriended fellow patient and poet Wilfred Owen. When Owen returned to battle, it was to Sassoon that he confided his most gruesome war experiences. In one letter he wrote: "The boy by my side, shot through the head, lay on top of me, soaking my shoulder, for half an hour." After Owen was killed in battle, Sassoon collected and edited Owen's poems for publication. He later wrote about Owen's poetry: ". . . he seldom brought his poems to their final form without considerable re-casting and revision. There was a slowness and sobriety in his method, which was, I think, nondramatic and elegiac rather than leapingly lyrical. I do not doubt that, had he lived longer, he would have produced poems of sustained grandeur and ample design."

Wirers[1]

Siegfried Sassoon

"Pass it along, the wiring party's going out"—
And yawning sentries mumble, "Wirers going out."
Unraveling; twisting; hammering stakes with muffled thud,
They toil with stealthy haste and anger in their blood.

5   The Boche[2] sends up a flare. Black forms stand rigid there,
Stock-still like posts; then darkness, and the clumsy ghosts
Stride hither and thither, whispering, tripped by clutching
   snare
Of snags and tangles.
         Ghastly dawn with vaporous coasts
10 Gleams desolate along the sky, night's misery ended.

Young Hughes was badly hit; I heard him carried away,
Moaning at every lurch; no doubt he'll die today.
But *we* can say the front-line wire's been safely mended.

---

1. wirers: Soldiers who were responsible for repairing the
barbed-wire fences that protected the trenches in World War I.
2. Boche (bôsh): German soldier.

RESPONDING TO THE SELECTION

Your Response

1. How does this poem affect your response to
war? Explain.

Recalling

2. What are the wirers getting ready to do at the
beginning of the poem?
3. What happens when an enemy flare lights the
scene?
4. What does the speaker say will probably be
the fate of the soldier named Hughes?

Interpreting

5. How do you think the wirers feel about the job
they have to do?
6. (a) What is the speaker's attitude toward what
has happened to young Hughes? (b) How do
you explain that attitude?

Applying

7. (a) What kinds of nonmilitary jobs may lead to
a routine acceptance of the daily presence of
danger? (b) What is the difference between
those jobs and a soldier's job?

ANALYZING LITERATURE

Understanding Historical Context

Siegfried Sassoon and other World War I poets often wrote their poems at the front lines. Even if you knew no history at all, their vivid and shocking images would make the horrors of war quite real. However, you should have some knowledge of trench warfare during World War I and therefore have clues to the historical context of "Wirers."

1. What details in the poem identify its historical context as World War I and not another war?
2. Toward whom do the wirers have "anger in their blood?" How do you know?
3. Who is the "we" of the last line? How does the line accentuate Sassoon's purpose in writing poetry from the front?

LEARNING OPTIONS

1. **Cross-curricular Connection.** Find out more about trench warfare during World War I and prepare a brief oral report for your class. Choose one of the following aspects to report on: types of weapons, the role of planes, the role of the United States, or how the war was won. If possible, provide a map showing the location of the trenches.
2. **Speaking and Listening.** Every war produces its own literature. Locate poetry that has been written about the Vietnam War. Choose one poem to read aloud to the class. Give some background about the author and briefly compare the tone of the poem you read to the tone of "Wirers."

The Soldier

Rupert Brooke

WAR POSTER

If I should die, think only this of me:
    That there's some corner of a foreign field
That is forever England. There shall be
    In that rich earth a richer dust concealed;
5 A dust whom England bore, shaped, made aware,
    Gave, once, her flowers to love, her ways to roam,
A body of England's, breathing English air,
    Washed by the rivers, blest by suns of home.

And think, this heart, all evil shed away,
10   A pulse in the eternal mind, no less
      Gives somewhere back the thoughts by England
        given;
Her sights and sounds; dreams happy as her day;
    And laughter, learnt of friends; and gentleness,
      In hearts at peace, under an English heaven.

RESPONDING TO THE SELECTION

Your Response
1. What is your response to the speaker's patriotism? Explain.

Recalling
2. How does the speaker ask his readers to remember him if he should die?
3. What are three things that England gave to the speaker?

Interpreting
4. (a) How does the speaker feel toward England? (b) How idealistic, or realistic, do you think his recollections are?
5. What is the "richer dust" that will be found in a foreign field?
6. The speaker says his heart will become a "pulse in the eternal mind." In your own words, what does he mean?

Applying
7. How would you define patriotism?

THINKING AND WRITING

Writing About Patriotism
    A number of young British poets died in World War I. One of them, Charles Sorley, said of Rupert Brooke's patriotism, "He has clothed his attitude in fine words; but he has taken the sentimental attitude." Write an essay responding to this remark. First, explain what you think Sorley means. Then, based on your reading of "The Soldier," tell whether you agree or disagree. Be sure to back your assertions with specific evidence from the poem.

Anthem for Doomed Youth

Wilfred Owen

What passing-bells for these who die as cattle?
Only the monstrous anger of the guns.
Only the stuttering rifles' rapid rattle
Can patter out their hasty orisons.[1]
5 No mockeries for them from prayers or bells,
Nor any voice of mourning save the choirs—
The shrill, demented choirs of wailing shells;
And bugles calling for them from sad shires.[2]

What candles may be held to speed them all?
10 Not in the hands of boys, but in their eyes
Shall shine the holy glimmers of good-byes.
The pallor of girls' brows shall be their pall;
Their flowers the tenderness of patient minds,
And each slow dusk a drawing-down of blinds.

---

1. orisons (ô′ ri zənz) n: Prayers.
2. shires (shīrz) n: Any of the counties of England.

RESPONDING TO THE SELECTION

Your Response

1. How does the speaker's response to the tragedy of war compare to your own? Explain.

Recalling

2. What are the only voices heard mourning the dying soldiers?
3. Where do the "holy glimmers of good-byes" shine?

Interpreting

4. What does the poet suggest by comparing the soldiers to cattle?
5. Why would prayers and bells be mockeries?
6. Who are the girls with pallid brows?
7. "Anthem for Doomed Youth" is a sonnet. In what way does the sestet answer or comment on the octave?

Applying

8. Could the theme of this poem apply to other wars besides World War I? Explain.

CRITICAL THINKING AND READING

Understanding Contrast

An anthem is a religious choral song, and in "Anthem for Doomed Youth" Wilfred Owen develops his theme by contrasting the sacred rites normally performed for the dead with the reality of what happens to those who die in battle.

1. For each item below, identify the substitute that the dead soldiers receive on the battlefield.

passing-bells	orisons	choirs
candles	pall	flowers
drawn blinds		

2. What ironic statement is the poet making when he contrasts the reality of death in battle with the customary funeral rituals?

T. S. ELIOT

1888–1965

Thomas Stearns Eliot is one of the dominant figures in twentieth-century English literature. A poet, playwright, critic, thinker, and cultural pioneer who changed the consciousness of an entire generation of writers, he emerged in the 1920's as the acknowledged leader of what is now called the Modernist movement. Eliot's work is often difficult to understand, drawing as it does upon myth, history, religion, allusion, and symbol. His poems and plays raise fundamental questions about human aspirations and the nature of civilized society.

Eliot has ties to both the United States and Great Britain. Born in St. Louis, Missouri, he was educated at Smith and Milton academies, Harvard University, the Sorbonne, and Oxford. The outbreak of World War I found Eliot in England, where he remained throughout most of his adult life, eventually acquiring British citizenship. In 1915 he married the sensitive, witty, but highly neurotic Vivian Haigh-Wood. While writing poetry and critical reviews, Eliot taught school, worked for the banking firm of Lloyd's, and in 1925 took an editorial position with the publishing company that became Faber and Faber.

His earliest work, owing to its unconventional style, was greeted with less than universal acclaim, although the poet Ezra Pound was a vocal supporter from the beginning. Pound saw, as many did not, that Eliot spoke in an authentic new voice and offered an original, if bleak, vision. From *Prufrock and Other Observations* (1917) through *The Waste Land* (1922) and "The Hollow Men" (1925), Eliot pictured the disturbed, fragmented western world wrought by World War I and its aftermath. Then, gradually, came renewed hope through religion, his faith leading him to join the Church of England in 1927. "Journey of the Magi" (1927) and "Ash Wednesday" (1930) mark the new religious phase of his life and writing, capped by his poetic masterpiece, *Four Quartets,* published in 1943 during the dark days of World War II.

As he grew older, Eliot turned his attention increasingly to poetic drama and criticism. Although *Murder in the Cathedral* (1935) and *The Cocktail Party* (1950) are often performed, none of his plays have gained the widespread critical admiration accorded his poetry. As a literary critic, Eliot's influence on his contemporaries was profound. His *Notes Towards the Definition of Culture,* one of many noteworthy critical works, appeared in 1948, the same year in which he received the Nobel Prize for Literature. In 1967, on the second anniversary of Eliot's death, a memorial was unveiled in Poet's Corner, Westminster Abbey.

GUIDE FOR INTERPRETING

Preludes; Journey of the Magi

Writers' Techniques

Synecdoche. Synecdoche (si nĕk′ də kē) is a figure of speech in which a part stands for the whole, an individual for a class, a material for the thing—or the reverse of any of these. For example, in the sentence, "Give us this day our daily bread," the word *bread* (part) stands for *food* (whole). In the sentence "The thief knew that a loud noise would bring the law," the word *law* (whole) stands for *police officer* (part). As a poetic device, synecdoche can sometimes make thought-provoking connections that startle and enlighten the reader.

Mood. Mood is the dominant emotion created by a piece of writing. If the mood of a poem is serious and reflective, the reader, upon finishing it, will in all likelihood be somber and pensive. If, on the other hand, the mood of a poem is light and whimsical, the reader, upon completing it, should be in high spirits and perhaps smiling. Mood must not be confused with either theme or subject matter. For instance, "The Cremation of Sam McGee," a ballad by Robert Service, deals with the death and cremation of a man in the Yukon, but the mood of the ballad is anything but melancholy.

Focus

Look through a newspaper or magazine for examples of synecdoche. When you have collected ten or more examples, write a brief analysis of the device. In your analysis indicate (a) which kind of synecdoche occurs most often, and (b) why you think the device came into such common use in English.

Primary Source

Eliot's distinctive style and theme lend themselves very easily to parody; fortunately, he had a sense of humor where such imitations were concerned. "Most parodies of one's own work strike one as very poor," Mr. Eliot writes, "but there is one which deserves the success it has had, Henry Reed's 'Chard Whitlow.'" Judge for yourself from the following excerpt:

Chard Whitlow

(Mr. Eliot's Sunday Evening Postscript)
AS WE GET OLDER we do not get any younger.
Seasons return, and today I am fifty-five,
And this time last year I was fifty-four,
And this time next year I shall be sixty-two.
And I cannot say I should like (to speak for myself)
To see my time over again—if you can call it time:
Fidgeting uneasily under a draughty stair,
Or counting sleepless nights in the crowded tube . . .

Preludes

T. S. Eliot

BOLTON, 1938 (detail)
William Coldstream
The National Gallery of Canada, Ottawa

I

The winter evening settles down
With smell of steaks[1] in passageways.
Six o'clock.
The burnt-out ends of smoky days.
5   And now a gusty shower wraps
The grimy scraps
Of withered leaves about your feet
And newspapers from vacant lots;
The showers beat
10 On broken blinds and chimney-pots,
And at the corner of the street
A lonely cab-horse steams and stamps.
And then the lighting of the lamps.

II

The morning comes to consciousness
15 Of faint stale smells of beer
From the sawdust-trampled street
With all its muddy feet that press
To early coffee-stands.
With the other masquerades
20 That time resumes,
One thinks of all the hands
That are raising dingy shades
In a thousand furnished rooms.

III

You tossed a blanket from the bed,
25 You lay upon your back, and waited;
You dozed, and watched the night revealing
The thousand sordid images
Of which your soul was constituted;
They flickered against the ceiling.

---

1. steaks: In 1910, when this poem was composed,
steaks were inexpensive and were commonly eaten by
members of the lower class.

30 And when all the world came back
    And the light crept up between the shutters
    And you heard the sparrows in the gutters,
    You had such a vision of the street
    As the street hardly understands;
35 Sitting along the bed's edge, where
    You curled the papers from your hair,
    Or clasped the yellow soles of feet
    In the palms of both soiled hands.

IV

    His soul stretched tight across the skies
40 That fade behind a city block,
    Or trampled by insistent feet
    At four and five and six o'clock;
    And short square fingers stuffing pipes,
    And evening newspapers, and eyes
45 Assured of certain certainties,
    The conscience of a blackened street
    Impatient to assume the world.

        I am moved by fancies that are curled
    Around these images, and cling:
50 The notion of some infinitely gentle
    Infinitely suffering thing.

    Wipe your hands across your mouth, and laugh;
    The worlds revolve like ancient women
    Gathering fuel in vacant lots.

Your Response

1. What do you think is the "infinitely gentle infinitely suffering thing" the speaker mentions in lines 50–51? Explain.

Recalling

2. In Prelude I what is (a) the time of year? (b) the time of day?
3. In Prelude II what is taking place "in a thousand furnished rooms"?
4. What did "you" hear in Prelude III "when all the world came back"?
5. What are the "ancient women" in the simile doing in Prelude IV?

Interpreting

6. (a) To what social class do the people in "Preludes" belong? (b) How can you tell?
7. The symbol of cycles, or cyclic progression, says one critic, "is almost Mr. Eliot's trademark." What cycle do you find in "Preludes"?
8. A musical prelude can introduce a longer work or can stand alone. Each of Eliot's four preludes stands alone, but they all project a similar mood. How would you describe that mood?

Applying

9. "Preludes," written in 1910–1911, reflects Eliot's views before the renewal of his religious faith. How might this poem be different if Eliot had written it twenty years later?

ANALYZING LITERATURE

Using Synecdoche

Synecdoche is a figure of speech in which a part stands for the whole ("Five thousand tongues applauded") or the whole for one of its parts ("Wall Street believes that . . ."). In literature, a synecdoche can enable readers to see an idea or an object in a new light. Sometimes, especially in Eliot's poetry, a synecdoche functions as a symbol. In Prelude II Eliot pictures the crowds of people that hurry to get their morning coffee before going to work. Rather than making such a prosaic statement, however, he uses the synecdoche "muddy feet" (line 17), providing the reader with a more visual and revealing image of the faceless morning bustle in a large city. For each of the following lines from "Preludes," (a) identify the synecdoche; (b) tell what the key word stands for; and (c) comment on how it adds to the mood of the poem.

1. The morning comes to consciousness (line 14)
2. One thinks of all the hands (line 21)
3. . . . all the world came back (line 30)
4. You had such a vision of the street/As the street hardly understands (lines 33–34)
5. . . . and eyes/Assured of certain certainties (lines 44–45)

THINKING AND WRITING

Writing a Poem Using Synecdoche

Choose a theme that interests you and write an original poem on it. You may choose any rhyme scheme and any metric pattern you like, and the poem may be of any reasonable length. Think carefully about how you can work two synecdoches into your poem—one using the part for the whole, the other using the whole for the part. Write the poem, using the synecdoches. Even with good planning, you will find that thoughtful revision is essential to a well-written poem.

LEARNING OPTION

Cross-curricular Connection. Like much of Eliot's early poetry, "Preludes" implies disenchantment with the twentieth century and reflects a bleak outlook on life. In this respect his poetry has much in common with the music composed in the early twentieth century. Investigate modern composers and their music, finding pieces of music that express a similar disillusionment and seem to complement Eliot's poem. If possible, obtain a tape or tapes to bring to class for listening and discussion.

Journey of the Magi

T. S. Eliot

In this poem, the speaker, one of the three wise men who traveled to Bethlehem to pay homage to the baby Jesus, reflects upon the meaning of his journey.

"A cold coming we had of it,
Just the worst time of the year
For a journey, and such a long journey:
The ways deep and the weather sharp,
5   The very dead of winter."[1]
And the camels galled, sore-footed, refractory,
Lying down in the melting snow.
There were times we regretted
The summer palaces on slopes, the terraces,
10   And the silken girls bringing sherbet.
Then the camel men cursing and grumbling
And running away, and wanting their liquor and women,
And the night-fires going out, and the lack of shelters,
And the cities hostile and the towns unfriendly
15   And the villages dirty and charging high prices:
A hard time we had of it.
At the end we preferred to travel all night,
Sleeping in snatches,
With the voices singing in our ears, saying
20   That this was all folly.

Then at dawn we came down to a temperate valley,
Wet, below the snow line, smelling of vegetation;
With a running stream and a water-mill beating the
   darkness,
And three trees on the low sky,
25   And an old white horse galloped away in the meadow.
Then we came to a tavern with vine-leaves over the lintel,
Six hands at an open door dicing for pieces of silver,
And feet kicking the empty wine-skins.

---

1. "A . . . winter.": Adapted from a part of a sermon delivered by 17th-century Bishop Lancelot Andrews: "A cold coming they had of it at this time of year, just the worst time of the year to take a journey, and specially a long journey in. The ways deep, the weather sharp, the days short, the sun farthest off . . . the very dead of winter."

But there was no information, and so we continued
30 And arrived at evening, not a moment too soon
Finding the place; it was (you may say) satisfactory.

All this was a long time ago, I remember,
And I would do it again, but set down
This set down
35 This: were we led all that way for
Birth or Death? There was a Birth, certainly,
We had evidence and no doubt. I had seen birth and death,
But had thought they were different; this Birth was
Hard and bitter agony for us, like Death, our death.
40 We returned to our places, these Kingdoms,
But no longer at ease here, in the old dispensation,
With an alien people clutching their gods.
I should be glad of another death.

RESPONDING TO THE SELECTION

Your Response
1. Have you ever had an experience that felt like both a death and a birth to you? Explain.

Recalling
2. What kind of weather do the speaker and his companions have on their journey?
3. What are three other problems they encounter?
4. How have circumstances changed for the speaker and his companions when they return home?

Interpreting
5. Why do others, and perhaps the wise men themselves, think that "this was all folly"?
6. Why do you think the speaker uses understatement, including the parenthetical "you may say," in line 31?
7. In lines 33–35 the speaker says, and then repeats, the words "set down this." What do you think is the purpose of the repetition?
8. The last line of the poem is ambiguous; there is no single, agreed-upon meaning for it. What do you think it means?

Applying
9. In "Journey of the Magi" Eliot retells the story of the wise men traveling to Bethlehem to visit the newborn Jesus. He adds something of his own to the story. What other biblical stories do you know that Eliot might have treated in a similar way?

ANALYZING LITERATURE

Conveying a Mood
The main feeling or atmosphere a piece of writing conveys is its **mood.** Mood is independent of content and theme, since the same story can be presented in various moods. Indeed, Eliot's "Journey of the Magi" has a different mood from the biblical story on which it is based. Read the original story (Matthew 2:1–12).
1. How does the mood of Eliot's poem differ from the mood of the biblical story?
2. "Journey of the Magi" was published in 1927. How is the ending of the poem consistent with Eliot's views following his renewal of religious faith in the late 1920's?

Analyzing Eliot's Use of Ambiguity

Although Eliot's poetry was viewed by his contemporaries as a break from tradition, Eliot maintained, as do critics today, that it is steeped in tradition. The continuing challenge of his poems lies in their many layers of meaning and their seeming lack of connectedness. This intentional complexity grows out of Eliot's deep learning, his conscious use of the literature of the past, and his belief that serious themes demand the "logic of the imagination."

Ambiguity means "having the potential for being understood in two or more ways." Once, when a magazine editor wished to find out movie actor Cary Grant's age, he sent Grant's agent a telegram: "How old Cary Grant?" The telegraphic response came back: "Old Cary Grant fine." Poets often use ambiguity intentionally and quite seriously, as Eliot does in the last line of "Journey of the Magi." If your class has discussed question 8, you already have some idea of the different possible interpretations of that line. If not, think about them now. There are at least three reasonable and entirely different interpretations. Jot them down—and any others you can think of—before beginning to write. Then write a brief analytical essay in which you state these interpretations and comment on them. Indicate which one or ones you think Eliot intended. Give your reasons. Before handing in the final draft of your paper, read it over carefully for logic. Refer to the poem, making sure that what you say is defensible in the context of what Eliot has written.

MULTICULTURAL CONNECTION

The Magi in Different Cultures

T. S. Eliot's poem, "Journey of the Magi," is a dramatic monologue spoken by one of the three magi who visited the baby Jesus twelve days after his birth. The commemoration of this visit, known as Epiphany, or Twelfth Night, is an important part of Christmas celebrations in Europe and Latin America. The word *epiphany* comes from the ancient Greek language and means "an apparition of a divine being." In many countries, January 6th is a day of feasts, bright lights, religious services, and gift-giving. In fact, children in many countries receive their presents on Epiphany instead of on Christmas Day itself.

Who were the magi? The word *magi* means "wise men" and was used to describe kings who were well-versed in astronomy. The magi mentioned in the Bible were apparently a diverse group. Traditionally, Balthasar has been depicted as dark-skinned and is thought to have come from Ethiopia. Melchior often appears with red hair and is supposed to have come from India. Gaspar, usually portrayed with blue eyes, is believed to have made the journey from Greece.

Magi in other countries. Many cultures hold Three Kings' celebrations that rival the attention paid to Santa Claus. In Cataluña, in eastern Spain, children spend the day banging on drums and blowing tin whistles to make sure that the gift-bearing kings don't pass their town over. Throughout the Spanish-speaking world, *El Día de los Reyes*, "The Day of the Kings," is celebrated with a parade in which the stand-ins for the three kings ride camels through the streets. In the United States, such a parade can be seen in New York City's Hispanic communities.

Exploring and Sharing

Can you think of someone who has taken a trip for religious reasons? Look up the word *pilgrimage* in the encyclopedia and share your findings with the class.

GUIDE FOR INTERPRETING

The Hollow Men

Tone. A speaker uses a certain tone in communicating a message to his or her audience. A writer does much the same thing, but a writer—lacking pitch, stress, and other features of spoken language—must rely on the choice of details, words, and syntax to convey tone. In poetry, tone reveals a great deal about the writer's attitude toward the subject. In fact, identifying the tone of a poem is vital to a full understanding of the poem's meaning.

Find a short letter to the editor in your local newspaper that is written in a tone that is easy to recognize and describe. Ordinarily you can describe tone with a single word—*outraged,* perhaps, or *reasonable,* or *amused*. Then rewrite the letter in an entirely different tone. If the tone is outraged, make it sweet and pleasant. If the tone is amused, make it bitter and angry.

The tone of "The Hollow Men" makes T. S. Eliot seem very stern and removed from the concerns and cares of daily life. His wide learning and brilliant publications—combined with his deep religious faith—made him seem even more unapproachable and intimidating. But Dylan Thomas's friend Roy Campbell recalls an encounter with Eliot (whom they had nicknamed the Archbishop) that shows a very different side to his character.

> Dylan Thomas had failed his medical test for the army, and he and Caitlin [Thomas's wife] were broke. My three pounds a week did not carry far: so one day Dylan and I decided to go on a borrowing raid. "But you must stay outside, Roy," he said. "We'll never raise a penny if they see you with me, except in the case of so-and-so and so-and-so." Dylan proposed to make a vast tour . . . of all the newly rich poets in their new offices in the Central Office of Information and the Ministry of Information. . . . But we raised no cash. Dylan said that it had been the same in every office where he had been without me. We stood outside the M.O.I. scratching our heads. "What about His Grace?" I asked, "He lives around there." "You mean the Archbishop?" gasped Dylan, "I wouldn't dare."—"Come on, you'll see. He's not only a saint in his poems, he's a bloody saint in his life too." We went to see Eliot, and the great man helped us so lavishly that it lasted till by some curious coincidence we both got our first considerable radio jobs, almost simultaneously, and were able to pay Eliot back. (Dylan never forgot his kindness. Neither do I.)

The Hollow Men

T. S. Eliot

Mistah Kurtz[1]*—he dead.*

A penny for the Old Guy[2]

I

We are the hollow men
We are the stuffed men
Leaning together
Headpiece filled with straw. Alas!
5   Our dried voices, when
We whisper together
Are quiet and meaningless
As wind in dry grass
Or rats' feet over broken glass
10 In our dry cellar

Shape without form, shade without color,
Paralyzed force, gesture without motion;

Those who have crossed
With direct eyes, to death's other Kingdom[3]
15 Remember us—if at all—not as lost
Violent souls, but only
As the hollow men
The stuffed men.

---

1. Mistah Kurtz: A character in Joseph Conrad's *Heart of Darkness* who travels to Africa hoping to improve the lives of the natives, but finds that, instead, he falls prey to his own worst instincts. Horrified by what he had become, Kurtz dies in the jungle.

2. A . . . Guy: A traditional cry used by children on Guy Fawkes Day. Guy Fawkes (1570–1606) was executed for participating in a plot to blow up the king and both Houses of Parliament in 1605. Each year on November 5, children beg for pennies to buy firecrackers which they use to destroy stuffed dummies representing Fawkes.

3. Those . . . Kingdom: An allusion to Dante's *Paradiso*, in which those "with direct eyes" are blessed by God in Heaven.

II

Eyes I dare not meet in dreams
20 In death's dream kingdom
These do not appear:
There, the eyes are
Sunlight on a broken column
There, is a tree swinging
25 And voices are
In the wind's singing
More distant and more solemn
Than a fading star.

Let me be no nearer
30 In death's dream kingdom
Let me also wear
Such deliberate disguises
Rat's coat, crowskin, crossed staves
In a field[4]
35 Behaving as the wind behaves
No nearer—

Not that final meeting
In the twilight kingdom

III

This is the dead land
40 This is cactus land
Here the stone images
Are raised, here they receive
The supplication of a dead man's hand
Under the twinkle of a fading star.

45 Is it like this
In death's other kingdom
Waking alone
At the hour when we are
Trembling with tenderness
50 Lips that would kiss
Form prayers to broken stone.

---

4. crossed . . . field: Scarecrows.

IV

The eyes are not here
There are no eyes here
In this valley of dying stars
55 In this hollow valley
This broken jaw of our lost kingdoms

In this last of meeting places
We grope together
And avoid speech
60 Gathered on this beach of the tumid river[5]

Sightless, unless
The eyes reappear
As the perpetual star[6]
Multifoliate rose[7]
65 Of death's twilight kingdom
The hope only
Of empty men.

V

Here we go round the prickly pear
Prickly pear prickly pear
70 *Here we go round the prickly pear*
At five o'clock in the morning.[8]

Between the idea
And the reality
Between the motion
75 And the act[9]
Falls the Shadow

For Thine is the Kingdom[10]

---

5. river: From Dante's *Inferno*, the river Archeron, the river which
the dead cross over as they pass into Hell.
6. star: A traditional symbol for Christ.
7. Multifoliate rose: In Dante's *Paradiso*, Paradise was described as
a "multifoliate rose," or a rose with many leaves. Also, the rose is a
traditional symbol for the Virgin Mary.
8. Here . . . morning: Adaptation of a common nursery rhyme. A
prickly pear is a cactus.
9. Between . . . act: A reference to *Julius Caesar*, Act II, Scene i,
63–65: "Between the acting of a dreadful thing/And the first motion,
all the interim is/Like a phantasma or hideous dream."
10. For . . . Kingdom: From the ending of the Lord's Prayer.

Between the conception
And the creation
80 Between the emotion
And the response
Falls the Shadow

Life is very long[11]

Between the desire
85 And the spasm
Between the potency
And the existence
Between the essence
And the descent
90 Falls the Shadow

For Thine is the Kingdom

For Thine is
Life is
For Thine is the

95 *This is the way the world ends*
This is the way the world ends
This is the way the world ends
Not with a bang but a whimper.

---

11. Life . . . long: Quotation from Joseph Conrad's *An Outcast of the Islands.*

RESPONDING TO THE SELECTION

Your Response

1. What do you think would add meaning to the lives of the hollow men in the poem? Explain.

Recalling

2. In "death's dream kingdom" what disguise will the speaker wear?
3. What do the hollow men do in the "hollow valley . . . this last of meeting places"?
4. What is it that forever falls between idea and achievement, preventing the hollow men from accomplishing anything?
5. According to the speaker, how does the world end?

Interpreting

6. Although Kurtz was a "hollow sham" and Guy Fawkes was a traitor, the speaker suggests that they were superior to the hollow men. Why were they superior?
7. What aspects of modern life might the "stone images" in part III represent?
8. Both part III and part V suggest a particular kind of landscape in which the hollow men exist. What kind of landscape is it?
9. What do you think "the Shadow" is in part V?

Applying

10. In "The Hollow Men," published in 1925, Eliot presents a bleak picture of his generation. To what extent, if at all, do you think his implied criticism applies to the people of today?

ANALYZING LITERATURE

Conveying Tone

The **tone** of a poem reveals the writer's attitude toward the subject or theme. Tone is conveyed through details and images—hollow men stuffed with straw, a cactus land, a twilight kingdom. It is also carried by words and their connotations—*hollow, meaningless, fading, death, shadow, whimper.* Syntax, the way in which words are put together, plays a part, too—"Shape without form, shade without color" (parallelism); "The hope only/Of empty men" (ambiguity). How would you describe the tone of "The Hollow Men"? (One adjective can usually describe tone, but since Eliot's poem is more complex than most, you may find it necessary to go into greater detail.)

CRITICAL THINKING AND READING

Interpreting Allusions

An **allusion** in literature is a brief, often indirect, reference to a person, a place, an event, or another literary work. "The Hollow Men" is a poem rich in allusions. Choose any three of the following allusions from "The Hollow Men." Explain each one. Tell how the allusion adds meaning to the poem by introducing, as a kind of literary shorthand, a number of associations through the use of only a few words. Try to go somewhat beyond the footnote text.

1. *Mistah Kurtz—he dead.*
2. Those who have crossed/With direct eyes, to death's other Kingdom
3. As the perpetual star/Multifoliate rose
4. Between the motion/And the act
5. *For Thine is the Kingdom*

THINKING AND WRITING

Writing About Tone

Write an essay in which you analyze the tone of T. S. Eliot's poetry. Describe the tone of each of the three Eliot poems in this unit and explain how the tone adds to the meaning of each one. Use quotations from the poems to illustrate and support your points. Follow the three basic steps in the writing process. In prewriting, take notes and make a rough outline. Then write your first draft, using appropriate quotations. In revising, make any major changes that are needed—structural, logical, organizational—as well as checking your grammar and usage. Finally, make any needed proofreading corrections.

ROBERT GRAVES

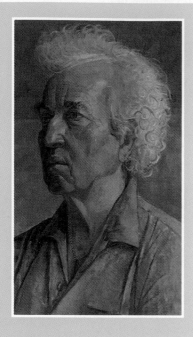

1895–1985

Robert Graves wrote successfully in almost every literary form, but he is perhaps most widely known as the author of the best-selling novel *I, Claudius* (1934), which was made into an outstanding BBC television series a few years ago. Graves achieved his first fame in 1929 with a classic memoir of World War I, *Good-bye to All That.* Despite his prose efforts, however, Graves's true calling was poetry, as he has said. Ever since his first two volumes appeared in 1916, he has been recognized as a major British poet.

The son of a prominent poet, Robert Graves grew up in a London household with an extensive private library, which provided much of his early education. World War I began while he was attending the Charterhouse School and producing his earliest poems. Graves enlisted in the Royal Welsh Fusiliers, the outfit to which Siegfried Sassoon belonged. Fighting in the trenches, he was severely wounded and falsely reported dead. He later suffered shell shock and received a medical discharge. Graves, like Sassoon, lost all illusions about the glory of war, as shown by his two wartime poetry collections, *Over the Brazier* (1916) and *Fairies and Fusiliers* (1917).

Graves studied at Oxford, received his degree, and in 1927 took a teaching position at the Royal Egyptian University in Cairo. For a number of years, he collaborated with the American poet Laura Riding on many writing and publishing projects. In 1929 he and Riding settled in Majorca, an island off the coast of Spain, where he remained except for intervals during the Spanish Civil War, World War II, and a teaching stint at Oxford in the 1960's.

A respected scholar and critic, Graves aroused controversy in 1948 with the publication of *The White Goddess,* a critical study of the origin, value, and history of poetry, whose main thesis—the dominance of a mythic female Muse—is impressively argued but widely questioned. Its influence on Graves's poetry, however, has been substantial and beneficial. His poems, a blend of traditional and modern, sometimes exhibit a deceptive simplicity. According to the American poet Richard Wilbur, they "have the air of being spontaneous answers to actual experience."

Graves refused to seek praise, for fame, he felt, would make him hostage to public opinion. To him, a poet who writes for others has forsaken his honor, which "consists in his not forming ties that can impair critical independence, or prevent him from telling the whole truth about anything, or force him to do anything out of character." Yet, in his independence, Graves achieved immortality.

GUIDE FOR INTERPRETING

One Hard Look; She Tells Her Love While Half Asleep

Historical Context

Reaction to Modernism. The Modernist movement, which flourished in the years following World War I, was characterized by the works of writers, artists, and musicians who sought new forms and new subjects to reflect the alienation they felt as a result of the war. The Modernists demanded a recognition that the old ways of expressing meaning were no longer valid.

Not all writers, however, embraced Modernism. Although Robert Graves wrote throughout the Modern period, he rejected the styles developed by the Modernists. Graves had begun his career among the ranks of the Georgian poets, who wrote pastoral, lyrical, realistic poems, but his subsequent break with them did not signal a move in the direction of other ex-Georgians like D. H. Lawrence. He did not find imagism useful, nor did the various techniques employed by James Joyce, Ezra Pound, or T. S. Eliot influence him. Instead, Graves's poetry developed in its own distinctive way.

For a while Graves participated in the Metaphysical revival, but he did not like to be associated with a "school" of poetry. Myth figured prominently in his work at times, but he was not a follower *per se* of Yeats. In the end Graves was praised for the distance he maintained from Modernism. By the 1950's his work was greatly admired by younger writers for its native English formalism. Manifest in his poems are craftsmanship, clarity, and realism, qualities present in Modernist works as well but which Graves had achieved in reaction to Modernist tenets.

Focus

Write for five minutes about an everyday object. What about it could be seen as extraordinary? Note any insights about the object.

Primary Source

In his World War I memoir *Goodbye to All That,* Graves recalls an exchange with Siegfried Sassoon.

> . . . I was getting my first book of poems, *Over the Brazier,* ready for the press; I had one or two drafts . . . and showed them to Siegfried. He frowned and said that war should not be written about in such a realistic way. In return, he showed me some of his own poems. One of them began:
>
>> Return to greet me, colors that were my joy,
>> Not in the woeful crimson of men slain . . .
>
> Siegfried had not yet been in the trenches. I told him, in my old-soldier manner, that he would soon change his style.

One Hard Look

Robert Graves

Small gnats that fly
In hot July
And lodge in sleeping ears,
Can rouse therein
5   A trumpet's din
With Day of Judgment fears.

Small mice at night
Can wake more fright
Than lions at midday;
10   A straw will crack
The camel's back—
There is no easier way.

One smile relieves
A heart that grieves
15   Though deadly sad it be,
And one hard look
Can close the book
That lovers love to see.

RESPONDING TO THE SELECTION

Your Response

1. How effective do you think the rhythm and rhyme in this poem are? Explain.

Recalling

2. What does the buzz of a gnat sound like in the ear of a sleeper?
3. What can one hard look do?

Interpreting

4. What is the common characteristic of gnats, mice, and straw that contributes to the meaning of the poem?
5. What main observation does the poem make?

Applying

6. (a) Do you agree with Graves's observation? (b) What experience have you had that supports or casts doubt on what he says?

She Tells Her Love While Half Asleep

Robert Graves

She tells her love while half asleep,
   In the dark hours,
      With half-words whispered low:
As Earth stirs in her winter sleep
5   And puts out grass and flowers
      Despite the snow,
      Despite the falling snow.

RESPONDING TO THE SELECTION

Your Response

1. Do you ever have notable thoughts, feelings, memories, or insights in the state between sleeping and waking? Explain.

Recalling

2. What is the time of day in the poem?
3. "Despite the falling snow," what does the Earth do?

Interpreting

4. To what in nature are the "half-words whispered low" compared?
5. What might falling snow represent metaphorically in the relationship between the speaker and the one who "tells her love"?

Applying

6. The flowers of spring are probably the most widely used symbol of rebirth. Why do you think this is so?

ANALYZING LITERATURE

Understanding Historical Context

It is important to remember that although Modernism was the prevailing movement during the period after World War I, not all writers subscribed to its ideologies and styles. Graves, for one, did not abandon rhyme and recognizable meters in favor of free verse. Nor did he treat the subjects of his poems in a fragmented, disjointed way. Much of Graves's work can be seen as a reaction against Modernism, a reaction that was championed by other writers later in the twentieth century.

1. How do these two poems by Graves differ in form from those of T. S. Eliot?
2. (a) What are the rhyme schemes of the poems? (b) What meter does each have?
3. (a) What is the subject matter of "One Hard Look"? (b) Of "She Tells Her Love While Half Asleep"? (c) How is each different from subjects generally treated by the Modernists?

LEARNING OPTION

Writing. Think about what the woman in this poem might say "while half asleep." Imagine whom she is speaking to and how her drowsiness might affect what she says. Write a brief monologue for her.

W. H. AUDEN

1907–1977

Much as T. S. Eliot became established as the poetic voice of the 1920's, so W. H. Auden emerged as the voice of the 1930's. Born in York, England, Auden moved to the United States at the age of thirty-two and took out citizenship papers, reversing the odyssey of Eliot, who was born in St. Louis, Missouri, and became a British subject. The youthful Auden was greatly influenced by Eliot's *The Waste Land,* but in later life both men replaced their anger and despair with a staunch Christian faith. Versatility, wit, and dazzling technique characterize Auden's poetry.

Wystan Hugh Auden, the son of a doctor, was interested in science as a child and planned to become an engineer. He received his education at St. Edmund's School and Gresham's School, and later attended Oxford University. His first appearance in print was in *Oxford Poetry,* a series of annual collections of verse by the university's undergraduates. The volumes in which his poems appear—1926, 1927, and 1928—also contain poems by Stephen Spender, C. Day-Lewis, and Louis MacNeice, all of whom became important poets.

Auden's first published collection, entitled simply *Poems,* appeared in 1930. These poems, innovative and eloquent, struck many readers of the day as strange, even impenetrable. His second volume, *On This Island,* published in 1937, is more down-to-earth and generated greater enthusiasm. He was awarded the King's Poetry Medal that year. In 1939 Auden left England for the United States, where he taught in a number of universities while continuing to write. He became an American citizen in 1946, and his poetry collection, *The Age of Anxiety,* won a Pulitzer Prize in 1948. In 1956, having been elected Professor of Poetry at Oxford University, he returned to England, where he remained through 1961.

Auden was a more prolific poet than Eliot, and his output is remarkable for its variety, originality, and craftsmanship. He wrote equally well in the idiom of the street or in the archaic measures of *Beowulf,* in the sing-song manner of a traditional ballad or in the formal cadences of an elegy. He has been called "the most provocative as well as the most unpredictable poet of his generation." With Yeats and Eliot, he shares honors as the most significant British poet of the first half of the twentieth century.

GUIDE FOR INTERPRETING

In Memory of W. B. Yeats;
Musée des Beaux Arts

Writers' Techniques

Elegy and Figurative Language. An elegy is a poem of mourning for the dead. The great Greek and Latin elegies, forerunners of elegies in English, were written in distichs. A *distich* is a pair of rhyming lines considered a unit. The third part of W. H. Auden's "In Memory of W. B. Yeats" is composed of distichs, or couplets, similar to those in a classical elegy. Elegies sum up, often in heroic terms, the lifetime accomplishments of an individual, or, as in Gray's "Elegy Written in a Country Churchyard," a group of people. Elegies frequently make use of figurative language; that is, language rich in figures of speech such as simile, metaphor, and personification. An elegy may also contain literary devices such as paradox and allusion.

Commentary

One of Auden's friends has remarked that Auden thought of himself as "a giant personal enterprise—Auden, Auden, Auden, and Company." The remark is fitting, for it suggests that a poet's personality is multi-faceted, bounded by contrast and intricacy. Early poems such as "Musée des Beaux Arts" (1938) and "In Memory of W. B. Yeats" (1939) are deeply serious explorations of the nature and function of poetry and the artist's special role in society. Later poems, in contrast, are lighter in tone. They often use surprising, comic touches to probe the place of art in the world and eternity. Auden's discussion of the role of art and the artist in *Secondary Worlds,* a series of lectures he delivered in 1967, serves to reaffirm what he created thirty years earlier in "Musée des Beaux Arts," and "In Memory of W. B. Yeats," as well as in much of his later work. "To believe in the value of art," he wrote, "is to believe that it is possible to make an object, be it an epic or a two-line epigram, which will remain permanently on hand in the world." This function of art, Auden emphasizes, is the opposite of much of the work of the world, which is to make things designed to be obsolete. To Auden, then, a work of art can give us the moral and intellectual nourishment we need to survive. What role do you think art serves in today's world?

Focus

Think of a person, living or dead, whom you greatly admire. This person can be either someone you know (or knew) firsthand or someone famous. Write a few memorial lines for the person, using a figure of speech in each of the lines. Try to use at least one simile, one metaphor, and one personification.

In Memory of W. B. Yeats

W. H. Auden

1

He disappeared in the dead of winter:
The brooks were frozen, the airports almost deserted,
And snow disfigured the public statues;
The mercury sank in the mouth of the dying day.
5 O all the instruments agree
The day of his death was a dark cold day.

Far from his illness
The wolves ran on through the evergreen forests,
The peasant river was untempted by fashionable quays;[1]
10 By mourning tongues
The death of the poet was kept from his poems.

But for him it was his last afternoon as himself,
An afternoon of nurses and rumors;
The provinces of his body revolted,
15 The squares of his mind were empty,
Silence invaded the suburbs,
The current of his feeling failed: he became his admirers.

Now he is scattered among a hundred cities
And wholly given over to unfamiliar affections;
20 To find his happiness in another kind of wood
And be punished by another code of conscience.
The words of a dead man
Are modified in the guts of the living.

But in the importance and noise of tomorrow
25 When the brokers are roaring like beasts on the floor of the
    Bourse,[2]
And the poor have the sufferings to which they are fairly
    accustomed,

---

1. quays (kēz): Wharfs with facilities for loading or unloading ships.
2. Bourse (bŏŏrs): The Paris Stock Exchange.

And each in the cell of himself is almost convinced of his
    freedom;
A few thousand will think of this day
As one thinks of a day when one did something slightly
    unusual.

30   O all the instruments agree
The day of his death was a dark cold day.

2

You were silly like us: your gift survived it all;
The parish of rich women, physical decay,
Yourself; mad Ireland hurt you into poetry.
35   Now Ireland has her madness and her weather still,
For poetry makes nothing happen: it survives
In the valley of its saying where executives
Would never want to tamper; it flows south
From ranches of isolation and the busy griefs,
40   Raw towns that we believe and die in; it survives,
A way of happening, a mouth.

3

Earth, receive an honored guest;
William Yeats is laid to rest:
Let the Irish vessel lie
45   Emptied of its poetry.

Time that is intolerant
Of the brave and innocent,
And indifferent in a week
To a beautiful physique,

50   Worships language and forgives
Everyone by whom it lives;
Pardons cowardice, conceit
Lays its honors at their feet.

Time with this strange excuse
55   Pardoned Kipling and his views,[3]

---

3. Kipling . . . views: English writer Rudyard Kipling (1865–1936)
was a supporter of imperialism.

And will pardon Paul Claudel,[4]
Pardons him for writing well.

In the nightmare of the dark
All the dogs of Europe bark,
60 And the living nations wait,
Each sequestered in its hate;

Intellectual disgrace
Stares from every human face,
And the seas of pity lie
65 Locked and frozen in each eye.

Follow, poet, follow right
To the bottom of the night,
With your unconstraining voice
Still persuade us to rejoice;

70 With the farming of a verse
Make a vineyard of the curse,
Sing of human unsuccess
In a rapture of distress;

In the deserts of the heart
75 Let the healing fountain start,
In the prison of his days
Teach the free man how to praise.

---

4. pardon Paul Claudel (klō del′): French poet, dramatist, and
diplomat. Paul Claudel (1868–1955) had antidemocratic political
views, which Yeats at times shared.

RESPONDING TO THE SELECTION

Your Response

1. The speaker hopes that poetry will teach people "how to praise." What do you think the main role of literature is?

Recalling

2. What two things were present on Yeats's last afternoon "as himself"?
3. What was it that "hurt" Yeats into writing poetry?

4. According to the third section of the poem, to whom is time (a) intolerant? (b) indifferent?
5. What does the speaker ask the poet to teach free men?

Interpreting

6. Twice in the first section, the speaker uses the words "all the instruments agree." What instruments might he mean (a) in a literal sense? (b) in a metaphorical sense?
7. What do you think the poet means by stating in line 18 that Yeats is now "scattered among a hundred cities"?

8. Whom is the speaker addressing in (a) the second section? (b) the third section?
9. (a) How favorably or unfavorably does the speaker view the situation in Europe? (b) How does he think the poet should react to it? Find evidence to support your answer.

Applying

10. This poem is an elegy to William Butler Yeats. Yet, in a sense, it could be addressed to any poet, for Auden sets down the responsibilities and rewards he thinks belong to the poet. What are these responsibilities and rewards?

ANALYZING LITERATURE

Understanding Elegy

An **elegy** is a poem that pays tribute to a person (or, less commonly, more than one person) who has died. Throughout history elegies have been written to immortalize people who, at least in the eyes of the poet, have achieved greatness. Most elegies contain imaginative comparisons—figures of speech such as simile, metaphor, and personification. W. H. Auden uses all three of these kinds of figurative language in "In Memory of W. B. Yeats." Write the line or lines of the poem in which each of the following occurs.

1. Personification in which a day coming to an end is said to display a facial feature.
2. Personification of a body of water as being susceptible to temptation.
3. Metaphor that compares body and mind to geographic areas.
4. Simile in which certain professional people are compared to wild animals.
5. Simile that compares thinking about the death of a great man with thinking about doing something unusual.
6. Personification in which something inanimate and abstract has the power to worship and pardon.

7. Metaphor that relates something bad to a place where grapes are grown.

CRITICAL THINKING AND READING

Understanding the Legacy of an Artist

"In Memory of W. B. Yeats" is a poet's tribute not to a lost friend but to a fellow poet. Auden never knew Yeats personally, but he knew of him by reading his poetry. Most poets, as you might suppose, read poetry as well as write it. They are aware of the classics and the trends. Poetry—indeed, all literature—is part of an ever-expanding archive, one in which, as in the National Archives, "the past is prologue." Auden, in his elegy, is responding to the loss he believes the world should feel at the death of a great artist. Yet he is also aware, as the poem makes clear, that while Yeats himself is gone, the poetry of Yeats lives on.

1. What does Auden mean in line 11, "The death of the poet was kept from his poems"?
2. In the third section of the poem, what evidence is there that Auden is mourning the passing of an artist more than the passing of Yeats the man?

THINKING AND WRITING

Writing About a Paradox

In line 36 Auden observes that "poetry makes nothing happen." But in the next section of the poem, he beseeches the poet (any poet) to use his or her gift to lead the human race out of the darkness of hatred. How, you may ask, is it possible for a poet to accomplish this monumental task if "poetry makes nothing happen"? In an essay, explain this apparent contradiction—this paradox—by drawing upon other insights from the poem. When you revise, make sure your essay is well organized and that you have provided adequate support for your thesis.

Musée des Beaux Arts[1]

W. H. Auden

About suffering they were never wrong,
The Old Masters: how well they understood
Its human position; how it takes place
While someone else is eating or opening a window or just
    walking dully along;
5 How, when the aged are reverently, passionately waiting
For the miraculous birth, there always must be
Children who did not specially want it to happen, skating
On a pond at the edge of the wood:
They never forgot
10 That even the dreadful martyrdom must run its course
Anyhow in a corner, some untidy spot
Where the dogs go on with their doggy life and the
    torturer's horse
Scratches its innocent behind on a tree.

In Brueghel's *Icarus*,[2] for instance: how everything turns
    away
15 Quite leisurely from the disaster; the ploughman may
Have heard the splash, the forsaken cry,
But for him it was not an important failure; the sun shone
As it had to on the white legs disappearing into the green
Water; and the expensive delicate ship that must have seen
20 Something amazing, a boy falling out of the sky,
Had somewhere to get to and sailed calmly on.

---

1. Musée des Beaux Arts: The Museum of Fine Arts in Brussels,
Belgium.
2. Brueghel's (broo′ gəlz) *Icarus* (ik′ ə rəs): *The Fall of Icarus*, a
painting by Flemish painter Pieter Brueghel (1522?–1599).

THE FALL OF ICARUS
Pieter Brueghel
Musées Royaux des Beaux-Arts de Belgique

RESPONDING TO THE SELECTION

Your Response

1. In the poem life goes on in the presence of a disaster. Do you think Auden is expressing a pessimistic or optimistic outlook? Explain.

Recalling

2. (a) What do the Old Masters show "someone else" doing while suffering occurs? (b) According to the speaker, what do the Old Masters understand about martyrdom?

3. (a) How does the ploughman react to the disaster in the Brueghel painting *Icarus*? (b) How does the ship respond?

Interpreting

4. What do you think Auden intends the activities in line 4 to represent?

5. What is your understanding of the "miraculous birth" the aged are awaiting?

6. Icarus is a figure in Greek mythology who flies with artificial wings. He flies too close to the sun, the wax of his wings melts, and he falls into the sea and drowns. (a) What does Brueghel mean to imply by calling his painting *Icarus* but showing only Icarus's disappearing legs in the corner of the picture? (b) How closely does Auden's poem adhere to the same theme?

Applying

7. The poem describes an age-old irony. (a) In your own words, what is this irony? (b) What are some examples of it that exist today?

LOUIS MACNEICE

1907–1963

Four members of the "Auden group" at Oxford went on to achieve an honored place in English literature: Auden himself, C. Day Lewis, Stephen Spender, and Louis MacNeice. Of these, MacNeice was generally regarded as the junior member, not because of age but rather because he lacked the artistic certainty and political commitments of the others. A lyric and reflective poet of distinction, he was always modest about the aims of poetry, doubting that poetry could truly change the world. MacNeice's reputation has risen steadily over the years, and today many consider him second only to Auden among the poets of his generation.

MacNeice, the son of a Protestant clergyman, was born in Belfast, Northern Ireland. Surrounded by books as a child, he began to write poetry at the age of seven. By the time he went to Merton College, Oxford, he was familiar with the works of T. S. Eliot and other modern poets. MacNeice's first collection of poems, *Blind Fireworks,* appeared in 1929, while he was still an undergraduate. *Poems,* the collection that established his reputation, came out six years later.

A teacher during the 1930's, MacNeice lectured in Classics at the University of Birmingham from 1930 to 1936 and in Greek at Bedford College for Women from 1936 to 1940. As a writer, he tried his hand at various genres, including drama, but his lasting achievements are in poetry. One of his notable books from the late 1930's, *Letters from Iceland* (1937), co-authored by W. H. Auden, is an unusual travel book in which the poetry outweighs the prose.

In 1941 MacNeice joined the British Broadcasting Corporation as a feature writer and producer. Among his radio credits are two powerful BBC plays, *Christopher Columbus* (1944) and *The Dark Tower* (1947). He wrote *The Poetry of W. B. Yeats* (1941), a critical summary of that author's work, and produced a number of excellent translations, including Aeschylus' *Agamemnon* and Goethe's *Faust.* MacNeice died in London in 1963 while he was working on his autobiography.

MacNeice's poetry, usually dealing with contemporary life, is restrained and precise, with overtones of melancholy. It is the poetry of a man who, as the poet Edwin Muir put it, "is never swept off his feet."

The Sunlight on the Garden; Sunday Morning

Writers' Techniques

Scansion. Scansion is the analysis of lines of poetry according to their patterns of rhythm. The key to scansion is meter. Meter is a recurring pattern of stressed and unstressed syllables in poetry. Meter is to poetry approximately what beat is to music. In scansion, stressed syllables are marked with a /; unstressed syllables are marked with a ∪. Each group of syllables makes up a foot. Feet are marked off with a |. In scansion, do not expect to find perfectly regular patterns repeated over and over. After you have identified a metrical foot, look for and expect to find irregularities or breaks from the pattern.

Focus

Choose four lines from any poem that appears earlier in this book. First, mark all the syllables in the lines as either stressed or unstressed. To do this, say the lines aloud. Next, find the pattern of stress that predominates. There are four common patterns:

1. Unstressed/stressed (iambic)
2. Stressed/unstressed (trochaic)
3. Stressed/unstressed/unstressed (dactylic)
4. Unstressed/unstressed/stressed (anapaestic)

Finally, put in the vertical bars that show the end of one foot and the beginning of another. Notice that a vertical bar may divide a word rather than going between two words, as in the line below from a poem by William Wordsworth.

```
∪   /  ∪ /  ∪  /  ∪ /  ∪   /
With sac|rifice|before|the ris|ing morn
```

Primary Source

MacNeice's 1938 book *Modern Poetry* is primarily a defense of modern verse, especially the work of Auden, Spender, Day-Lewis, and MacNeice himself. It also offers an intriguing glimpse into MacNeice's own poetic theories. Mainly, he tried to bridge the gap between the poet and the ordinary person. He felt that the poet should communicate and, to best accomplish this goal, be "a blend of the entertainer and the critic or informer." In fact, the poet is a great deal like MacNeice himself: "I would have a poet able-bodied, fond of talking, a reader of newspapers, capable of pity and laughter, informed in economics, appreciative of women, involved in personal relationships, actively interested in politics, susceptible to physical impressions."

The Sunlight on the Garden

Louis MacNeice

The sunlight on the garden
Hardens and grows cold,
We cannot cage the minute
Within its nets of gold,
5 When all is told
We cannot beg for pardon.

Our freedom as free lances
Advances towards its end;
The earth compels, upon it
10 Sonnets and birds descend;
And soon, my friend,
We shall have no time for dances.

The sky was good for flying
Defying the church bells
15 And every evil iron
Siren and what it tells:
The earth compels,
We are dying, Egypt, dying[1]

And not expecting pardon,
20 Hardened in heart anew,
But glad to have sat under
Thunder and rain with you,
And grateful too
For sunlight on the garden.

---

1. We . . . dying: An allusion to a line
spoken by Antony to Cleopatra after he
has been mortally wounded in Shakespeare's
Antony and Cleopatra: "I am dying, Egypt,
dying."

OLD THATCHED SUMMER HOUSE
Lilian Stannard
Christopher Wood Gallery, London

Your Response

1. Under what circumstances are you apt to think about the quick passage of time?

Recalling

2. What does the speaker say we shall soon have no time for?
3. What two things does the speaker say he is happy to have experienced?

Interpreting

4. In line 6 and again in line 19 the speaker uses the word *pardon.* From what do you think he is implying there is no pardon?
5. There is an apparent reference to wartime in this poem. What is it?
6. What or whom do you think is dying in this poem—the speaker, a generation, a nation, or something or someone else? Explain your answer.

Applying

7. Death is a familiar theme in poetry. (a) What other poem have you read that conveys an attitude similar to the one expressed here? (b) How does that poem differ from MacNeice's?

A NALYZING LITERATURE

Understanding Scansion

Most poems contain regular rhythmic patterns of stressed and unstressed syllables. The identification of these patterns is called **scansion,** and the act of reading a poem to identify its patterns is called **scanning.**

1. On a sheet of paper, copy "The Sunlight on the Garden." Scan the poem, analyzing it for unstressed and stressed syllables and for feet. Your analysis will show both the recurring patterns and any deviations from them.
2. The poem has an unusual rhyme scheme. Look carefully at the rhyming words MacNeice uses. What makes his rhyme scheme different from that in most poems?

Sunday Morning

Louis MacNeice

Down the road someone is practicing scales,
The notes like little fishes vanish with a wink of tails,
Man's heart expands to tinker with his car
For this is Sunday morning, Fate's great bazaar;
5 Regard these means as ends, concentrate on this Now,
And you may grow to music or drive beyond Hindhead[1]
   anyhow,
Take corners on two wheels until you go so fast
That you can clutch a fringe or two of the windy past,
That you can abstract this day and make it to the week of
   time
10 A small eternity, a sonnet self-contained in rhyme.

But listen, up the road, something gulps, the church spire
Opens its eight bells out, skulls' mouths which will not tire
To tell how there is no music or movement which secures
Escape from the weekday time. Which deadens and
   endures.

---

1. Hindhead: A district in the county of Surrey, England.

SUNDAY MORNING
Jamelle Kalil, Student,
Erie, Pennsylvania
Courtesy of the Artist

Your Response

1. Do you agree that there is no "escape from the weekday time"? Explain.

Recalling

2. What are two Sunday morning activities the speaker mentions?
3. What will "skulls' mouths" never tire of telling?

Interpreting

4. Why do you think the speaker refers to Sunday morning as "Fate's great bazaar"?
5. The last four lines contrast rather sadly with the first ten. What is the point of the contrast?

Applying

6. "The Sunlight on the Garden" and "Sunday Morning" express a similar futile wish. In your own words, what is that wish?

THINKING AND WRITING

Writing About Rhyme and Rhythm

Modern poets differ in their use of rhyme and rhythm. In "Sunday Morning," MacNeice uses a basic *aabb* rhyme scheme. Scan the poem to determine its metric pattern. Then, in a brief essay, explain what effects the rhyme and rhythm of the poem have on your appreciation of it. Also, try to answer these broader questions: (a) Do you generally prefer rhyming poems to free verse? (b) What effect, if any, does rhyme have on meaning? (c) Do you think subject matter helps to determine the appropriate rhyme and rhythm for a poem?

Before you start to write, make at least a sketchy outline of the main points you will cover. Your first draft may follow this outline closely or may deviate from it as necessary. When you revise the paper for your final draft, pay special attention to organization. Make sure that your points appear in logical and persuasive order.

MULTICULTURAL CONNECTION

Sunday in Different Cultures

For Louis MacNeice, Sunday is a day of rest and worship. Although this is generally true in the Christian world, the English word refers to the day's pagan beginnings. Early Teutonic peoples, believing the sun was sacred, gave the day its name, meaning "day of the sun."

In several European countries the name for this day is derived from the Latin *dies dominica,* meaning "the Lord's day." In Spanish it is *domingo;* in French, *dimanche;* and in Italian, *domenica.*

Sunday as a day of rest. The first Christians worked on Sunday just as they did every day. Times were hard and they couldn't afford the luxury of taking a day off. By about A.D. 300, however, both church and state officially recognized Sunday as a day of rest throughout Europe.

Sunday in America. In the American colonies, Sunday was strictly observed by the Puritan settlers. All physical labor and games and amusements were strictly forbidden.

Sunday in other countries. In Israel, Sunday is the first day of the workweek. Israelis celebrate Saturday, their seventh day, as the Sabbath. In other countries, such as Hungary and Turkey, Sunday is the traditional marketing day. In fact, the words for Sunday in Hungarian and Turkish mean "market day."

For Class Discussion

Discuss with classmates how you spend your Sundays. If there are students from other countries in the class, they may have different ways of spending their Sundays.

Stephen Spender (1909–   )

No poet of the 1930's has provided posterity with a more detailed and honest picture of the era between the wars than has Stephen Spender. Much of his early poetry deals with the world of the Thirties, that "low dishonest decade" that saw the world lurch from depression to fascism to war. Yet Spender, never a pessimist in the manner of T. S. Eliot, celebrates technology at the same time he confronts the problems of industrial civilization.

The son of a political journalist, Spender was born in London and educated at University College, Oxford, where he met and fell under the spell of W. H. Auden. In 1928, while at Oxford, he hand-printed a limited edition of Auden's *Poems*. Spender contributed his own early poems to *Oxford Poetry*. He lived in Germany in the early 1930's and published his first important book, *Poems,* in 1933, the year Hitler became chancellor of the Third Reich.

Spender, a political activist, traveled to Spain to promote antifascist propaganda during the Spanish Civil War. From 1939 to 1941, he coedited the literary magazine *Horizon* and later coedited the political, cultural, and literary review *Encounter*. In his autobiography *World Within World* (1951), Spender is candid and perceptive about people, politics, and himself, as he explores and attempts to integrate his lyrical and idealistic vision with the realities of society.

Henry Reed (1914–1986)

Although Henry Reed is well-known in England for his many radio plays, his reputation as a poet rests mainly on one slim volume, *A Map of Verona,* published in 1946. In fact, it rests principally on thirty lines in that collection—"Naming of Parts," which is a satirical section of a longer poem, "Lessons of War." Reed's few poems, always precise and assured, vary widely in subject matter, mood, and theme. So do his highly regarded radio plays, among which are an adaptation of *Moby-Dick,* the partly autobiographical *Return to Naples,* and a dramatic prose poem, *The Streets of Pompeii.*

Henry Reed was born in Birmingham, England, and educated at King Edward VI School and the University of Birmingham. After graduation he worked for several years on a biography of Thomas Hardy, then taught school for a year before being drafted into the army in 1941. He received a transfer to the Foreign Office, where he worked in Naval Intelligence. Most of Reed's career since the end of World War II has involved radio drama for the British Broadcasting Corporation (BBC), with some time out for translating and for teaching at the University of Washington in Seattle. His poetic output, though limited, is of high quality.

GUIDE FOR INTERPRETING

What I Expected; Naming of Parts

Speaker. The speaker in a poem is the poem's narrator. Narration can occur either in the first person *(I, we)* or in the third person *(he, she, it, they)*. Often a first-person speaker is a persona created by the poet. Consider, for instance, the first-person speakers who are already dead, as, for example, in Edgar Lee Masters's *Spoon River Anthology*. Even if the speaker is presented as being alive, he or she may not be the poet. In Robert Browning's "My Last Duchess," for example, no one would mistake the speaker (the cruel Duke of Ferrara) for the likable Browning. Sometimes a poet uses a first-person speaker to lend immediacy to the poem's content.

Satire. Satire is writing in which wit and humor are used to attack human follies, stupidities, and abuses. It can be directed at a single person or at an entire society. Satire can be written in any genre—novels, short stories, poems, or plays. Always a mixture of humor and criticism, it is intended to persuade the reader, without the use of formal argument, to accept the author's viewpoint. Among the most famous satires in English are Jonathan Swift's *Gulliver's Travels* and George Orwell's *Animal Farm*.

Henry Reed and Louis MacNeice led an astonishing array of brilliant talent onto the airwaves in the twenty years following World War II. With such poets as Dylan Thomas, Sylvia Plath, Ted Hughes, and Stevie Smith, Reed and MacNeice created a series of masterpieces for the British Broadcasting System. Office hours were largely ignored, and a generation of talent was nurtured in the BBC studios and two adjacent pubs. Reed was closely involved with the exceptional groups of writers, composers, actors, and technical staff that essentially constituted a permanent company. Consequently he wrote many of his radio scripts with particular players in mind, and their individual ability often sparked his imagination. *The Complete Lessons of War,* for example, broadcast in 1960, was written with actor Frank Duncan in the role of the drill sergeant; Reed spoke the descriptive passages himself.

Choose an event in history that happened long before you were born. Possibilities include the signing of the Declaration of Independence, the defense of the Alamo, and the assassination of Abraham Lincoln. Put yourself in the place of a participant in the event. Jot down notes in the first person, just as if you had observed what happened. Include as many details as you can that, prior to your account, were unknown to the general public.

What I Expected

Stephen Spender

What I expected, was
Thunder, fighting,
Long struggles with men
And climbing.
5   After continual straining
I should grow strong;
Then the rocks would shake
And I rest long.

What I had not foreseen
10 Was the gradual day
Weakening the will
Leaking the brightness away,
The lack of good to touch,
The fading of body and soul
15 Smoke before wind,
Corrupt, unsubstantial.

The wearing of Time,
And the watching of cripples pass
With limbs shaped like questions
20 In their odd twist,
The pulverous grief
Melting the bones with pity,
The sick falling from earth—
These, I could not foresee.

25 Expecting always
Some brightness to hold in trust
Some final innocence
Exempt from dust,
That, hanging solid,
30 Would dangle through all
Like the created poem,
Or the faceted crystal.

RESPONDING TO THE SELECTION

Your Response

1. How do you react when your expectations go unfulfilled? Explain.

Recalling

2. What are four things the speaker says he expected?
3. What are six things he had not foreseen?
4. Besides "Some brightness to hold in trust," what was the speaker always expecting?

Interpreting

5. (a) What do you think is the setting of this poem? (b) What lines in the poem support your answer?
6. In line 12 and again in line 26, the speaker mentions "brightness." What do you think this brightness represents?
7. In line 22 the speaker mentions the melting of bones. To whose bones is he referring?

Applying

8. The speaker seems to have been deeply disappointed when reality did not match his expectations. In the eighteenth century, the poet Alexander Pope wrote, "Blessed is he who expects nothing, for he shall never be disappointed." How do you think the speaker would react to this statement? Support your answer.

ANALYZING LITERATURE

Determining the Speaker

The **speaker** in a poem is the individual who does the telling, the narrator. Speakers fall into two main categories, (1) first person (I, we), in which the speaker is in essence a character in the poem; and (2) third person (he, she, it, they), in which the speaker is an outsider. Sometimes a first-person speaker is the poet, but more often he or she is not. Rather, the speaker is assuming a particular role to create a desired effect. When determining whether a first-person speaker is the poet, it may help you to know something of the poet's life. For instance, you know that Rupert Brooke and the soldier-speaker in "The Soldier" might be one and the same. On the other hand, if you know that Stephen Spender was not a front-line soldier in World War II, you would know he could not have written a first-person battlefield scene except through an assumed identity.

1. Identify the kind of speaker in Stephen Spender's "What I Expected."
2. In view of the subject matter of the poem, why is Spender's choice of speaker a logical one?
3. The speaker and the poet are not one and the same in "What I Expected." How do you know?

THINKING AND WRITING

Comparing and Contrasting Two Poems

Reread Louis MacNeice's "The Sunlight on the Garden," noting in particular the references to flying and to sirens in the third stanza. Some critics have called this a war poem, pointing to "flying" as a reference to fighter planes and to the "evil iron siren" as an air-raid siren. Assuming that this interpretation is correct, write an essay in which you compare and contrast MacNeice's "The Sunlight on the Garden" with Spender's "What I Expected." Concentrate not only on the subject matter of the two poems, but also on their structure—speakers, metric patterns, line lengths, and rhyme schemes. Begin by taking notes on both poems. When you write your first draft, quote lines from the poems where appropriate. In revising, be sure you have made your comparisons and contrasts clear.

LEARNING OPTION

Speaking and Listening. Does age always bring with it "the fading of body and soul"? Imagine yourself as an older person looking back on life. Write a brief monologue entitled "What I Expected," in which you describe dreams that did or did not come true. Read your monologue aloud in class.

Naming of Parts

Henry Reed

Today we have naming of parts. Yesterday,
We had daily cleaning. And tomorrow morning,
We shall have what to do after firing. But today,
Today we have naming of parts. Japonica[1]
5 Glistens like coral in all of the neighboring gardens,
  And today we have naming of parts.

This is the lower sling swivel. And this
Is the upper sling swivel, whose use you will see,
When you are given your slings. And this is the piling
 swivel,
10 Which in your case you have not got. The branches
Hold in the gardens their silent, eloquent gestures,
  Which in our case we have not got.

This is the safety-catch, which is always released
With an easy flick of the thumb. And please do not let me
15 See anyone using his finger. You can do it quite easy
If you have any strength in your thumb. The blossoms
Are fragile and motionless, never letting anyone see
  Any of them using their finger.

And this you can see is the bolt. The purpose of this
20 Is to open the breech, as you see. We can slide it
Rapidly backwards and forwards: we call this
Easing the spring. And rapidly backwards and forwards
The early bees are assaulting and fumbling the flowers:
  They call it easing the Spring.

25 They call it easing the Spring: it is perfectly easy
If you have any strength in your thumb; like the bolt,
And the breech, and the cocking-piece, and the point of
 balance,
Which in our case we have not got; and the almond-blossom
Silent in all of the gardens and the bees going backwards
 and forwards,
30 For today we have naming of parts.

---

1. japonica (jə pän′ i kə): A spiny plant with pink or red flowers.

RESPONDING TO THE SELECTION

Your Response

1. What do you hear in the speaker's tone? Sarcasm? Bewilderment? Resignation? Something else? Explain.

Recalling

2. (a) What does the speaker say the members of his group ("we") had yesterday? (b) What will they have tomorrow?
3. What part of the rifle does the speaker not have?
4. What is the purpose of the bolt?
5. What is silent in the gardens?

Interpreting

6. (a) Who are the members of the group identified as "we" in the poem? (b) Why are they having "naming of parts"?
7. (a) In the fourth stanza, what are the two meanings of "easing the Spring"? (b) In the fifth stanza, what are two possible meanings of "the point of balance"?

Applying

8. Suppose you were the instructor giving the "naming of parts" lesson, and you became aware of what is on the mind of the speaker (or second voice). (a) How would you react? (b) How would you rate the chances of the recruit becoming a good soldier?

ANALYZING LITERATURE

Using Satire

Satire is writing that shows the folly or evil of something through the use of wit and humor. In "Naming of Parts," the poet is not directly attacking war or the military despite the sharp contrast he draws between instruction in rifle parts and the wonders of spring.

1. What specifically is Reed satirizing in the poem?
2. How does he use the repetition of words and phrases to make his point? Give at least two examples.

CRITICAL THINKING AND READING

Comparing and Contrasting Speakers

There may be two speakers in this poem, one the instructor-speaker, the other the trainee-speaker. Or there may be only one speaker who first parrots the dull, mechanical words of the instructor, then gives his own personal thoughts on the attractions of nature in springtime. Whichever way you interpret Reed's method (two different speakers or two opposing voices within the same speaker), the satiric message is the same.

1. (a) Which lines, or parts of lines, in each stanza are the instructor's words or mechanical repetitions of them? (b) Which express the personal feelings of the trainee?
2. Which stanza deviates from this pattern?
3. Describe the similarities and differences between the language of the two voices (or speakers).

THINKING AND WRITING

Writing About Satire

A number of newspaper and magazine columnists write satire. Erma Bombeck's satiric columns on domestic life and Art Buchwald's on politics, among others, have been reprinted in many books. Find a modern satirical column, either original or reprinted, and write an essay analyzing it. Before you start to write, read the column carefully, making a list of devices the writer uses—exaggeration, understatement, analogy, figurative language, and so on. Jot down an example of each device. When you begin to write, first identify the author, topic, and source of the column you are analyzing. Then write the first draft of your essay. Stick to the point; avoid clever but irrelevant comments. When you revise, pay special attention to unity. Every sentence in your essay should relate to the main point you want to make.

DYLAN THOMAS

1914–1953

When Dylan Thomas burst upon the literary scene in 1933, he was barely twenty years old. His poems, romantic, effusive, and melodic, spoke to readers then, as now, in a voice that could be mistaken for no one else's. Despite some critical bewilderment at first, Thomas gained remarkable popularity in his lifetime, probably greater than that of any poet since Byron. The rich, glowing magic of his language propels the reader onward in spite of its often complex imagery, visionary landscapes, and puzzling ambiguities. Stephen Spender called Thomas "a linguistic genius." The critic Louis Untermeyer says that his lines "leap and shout and all but leave the printed page. . . ."

Dylan Thomas was born in Swansea, an industrial city on the southern coast of Wales. His father was a schoolteacher, and young Dylan, surrounded by his father's books, seems to have spent his childhood training to be a poet. He attended Swansea Grammar School until 1931, after which he worked intermittently as a newspaper reporter, radio broadcaster, and film scriptwriter. In 1941 he published a collection of stories abut his childhood and youth, *Portrait of the Artist as a Young Dog*. He recorded a number of his poems, as well as his "play for voices," *Under Milk Wood,* which premiered in May 1953 at the Fogg Theater of Harvard University, with Thomas reading all the parts.

Thomas did his best work while living in Wales, far from the temptations of London and New York. At work he was a meticulous craftsman, shy when sober, exercising strict formal control over what on paper seems so spontaneous. But in London, and on his four speaking tours to the United States, he was a different man, flamboyant, childish, hard-drinking, dissolute, an "outlaw defiant." His marriage to the Irish beauty Caitlin Macnamara was stormy but enduring. She was at his side when he died of the effects of alcoholism at St. Vincent's Hospital in New York City.

Poetry, to Thomas, was "the rhythmic, inevitably narrative, movement from an overclothed blindness to a naked vision." That vision is almost always free of the political themes and overtones found in the works of such contemporaries as Auden and Spender. On Thomas's place in literary history, the verdict is mixed. The poet Conrad Aiken sums him up as a "language-lover and language-juggler." The critic David Daiches says that "he was growing in poetic stature to the last" but, more important, "he wrote some poems that the world will not willingly let die."

GUIDE FOR INTERPRETING

The Force That Through the Green Fuse Drives the Flower; Fern Hill; Do Not Go Gentle into That Good Night

Writers' Techniques

Parallelism. Parallelism is the matching or contrasting of two or more ideas through the use of similar phrasing. Sometimes parallelism can produce almost a list or catalog, as in Ecclesiastes 3:4: "A time to weep, and a time to laugh; a time to mourn, and a time to dance." Another well-known example of this kind of parallelism, also featuring contrasts, is the beginning of Charles Dickens's *A Tale of Two Cities:* "It was the best of times; it was the worst of times. . . ." In poetry, parallelism can appear within a single line, as in Coleridge's "Without a breeze, without a tide." Or it can be within a stanza, as in Shelley's "The seed ye sow, another reaps/The wealth ye find, another keeps." It can be from stanza to stanza, as in Byron's "And there lay the steed with his nostril all wide" [stanza four]; "And there lay the rider distorted and pale" [stanza five].

Villanelle. A villanelle is a nineteen-line poem with specific and rather complicated requirements. The first fifteen lines are arranged in three-line stanzas. The first and third lines of the opening stanza are repeated alternately as the closing line of each of the remaining three-line stanzas. They then appear together as a concluding couplet. Only two rhymes are permitted throughout the poem, the rhyme scheme being this: *aba aba aba aba aba abaa.* The villanelle originated in fifteenth-century France, where its aim was to lend a surface simplicity to pastoral poems. Following its revival in the nineteenth century, the villanelle has been used for a broad range of subjects.

Commentary

What image do you get when you think of a poet? According to critic David Daiches, Dylan Thomas was "the most poetical poet of our time. He talked and dressed and behaved like a poet; he was reckless, flamboyant, irreverent, innocent. . . . His verse, too, had a romantic wildness about it that even a reader who could make nothing of it recognized as 'poetic.'"

Focus

Describe a chain of events in your life, beginning each link of the chain with the words, "If it were not for . . ." You might write, for example, "If it were not for my family moving to this city two years ago, I would not have attended this school. If it were not for my attending this school, I would not have met my best friend. If it were not for having met by best friend . . ." and so on. See how far you can take your chain by the end of one page.

The Force That Through the Green Fuse Drives the Flower

Dylan Thomas

The force that through the green fuse drives the flower
Drives my green age; that blasts the roots of trees
Is my destroyer.
And I am dumb to tell[1] the crooked rose
5   My youth is bent by the same wintry fever.

The force that drives the water through the rocks
Drives my red blood; that dries the mouthing streams
Turns mine to wax.
And I am dumb to mouth unto my veins
10   How at the mountain spring the same mouth sucks.

The hand that whirls the water in the pool
Stirs the quicksand; that ropes the blowing wind
Hauls my shroud sail.
And I am dumb to tell the hanging man
15   How of my clay is made the hangman's lime.[2]

The lips of time leech to the fountain head;
Love drips and gathers, but the fallen blood
Shall calm her sores.
And I am dumb to tell a weather's wind
20   How time has ticked a heaven round the stars.

And I am dumb to tell the lover's tomb
How at my sheet goes the same crooked worm.

---

1. dumb to tell: Unable to tell.
2. hangman's lime: Quicklime used to bury those who had been hanged.

RESPONDING TO THE SELECTION

Your Response

1. How does your attitude toward the forces of nature compare with that of the speaker in this poem?

Recalling

2. (a) What does the speaker say he is unable to tell the hangman? (b) What is he unable to tell the lover's tomb?

Interpreting

3. What do you think the speaker means by the phrase (a) "green fuse"? (b) "green age"?
4. What force do you think the speaker has in mind in the first two stanzas?
5. The force brings about two very different outcomes. In general terms what are they?

Applying

6. To what extent would you describe this poem as one about faith? Explain.

ANALYZING LITERATURE

Using Parallelism

Parallelism, which is a form of repetition, matches or contrasts ideas through the use of similar phrasing or grammatical structures. In "The Force That Through the Green Fuse Drives the Flower," Dylan Thomas uses a complex, interlocking parallelism within stanzas:

> The force   that   drives the green fuse
> drives the flower
> Drives my green age
> that   blasts the roots of trees

He also uses parallelism from stanza to stanza.

1. In what way are the second lines of the first three stanzas parallel?
2. In what way are the fourth lines of the first four stanzas parallel?
3. What parallel element exists in the last lines of the last four stanzas?

Primary Source

Like Joyce, Yeats, and Hopkins, Thomas was in love with words. According to critic William York Tindall, "words were Thomas's matter, his tool, and his refuge; but so great his delight in them and in what Rimbaud [a French symbolist poet] called their 'alchemy' that, as Thomas complains, they sometimes got between him and the object. Sometimes they became the object." People are often bothered by the ambiguity of Thomas's language, but he celebrated the different meanings that words held and the ways in which they could be manipulated to suggest layers of meaning. He fiddled with the sound and shape of words to create his poetic images. In an often-quoted letter, he remarks, "A poem by myself needs a host of images, because its center is a host of images. I make one image . . . let it breed another, let that image contradict the first, make of the third image bred out of the two together, a fourth contradictory image, and let them all, within my formal imposed limits, conflict." Once in New York, not long before he died, he was talking to a friend about writing. "When I experience anything," he said, "I experience it as a thing and a word at the same time, both equally amazing." Writing the "Ballad of the Long Legged Bait," he said, had been like carrying a huge armful of words to a table he thought was upstairs, and wondering if he could reach it in time, or if it would still be there.

Fern Hill

Dylan Thomas

Now as I was young and easy under the apple boughs
About the lilting house and happy as the grass was green,
    The night above the dingle starry,
      Time let me hail and climb
5   Golden in the heydays of his eyes,
And honored among wagons I was prince of the apple
   towns
And once below a time I lordly had the trees and leaves
      Trail with daisies and barley
    Down the rivers of the windfall light.

10 And as I was green and carefree, famous among the barns
About the happy yard and singing as the farm was home,
    In the sun that is young once only,
      Time let me play and be
    Golden in the mercy of his means,
15 And green and golden I was huntsman and herdsman, the
   calves
Sang to my horn, the foxes on the hills barked clear and
   cold,
      And the sabbath rang slowly
    In the pebbles of the holy streams.

All the sun long it was running, it was lovely, the hay
20 Fields high as the house, the tunes from the chimneys, it
   was air
    And playing, lovely and watery
      And fire green as grass.
    And nightly under the simple stars
As I rode to sleep the owls were bearing the farm away,
25 All the moon long I heard, blessed among stables, the
   nightjars[1]
    Flying with the ricks,[2] and the horses
      Flashing into the dark.

And then to awake, and the farm, like a wanderer white
With the dew, come back, the cock on his shoulder; it was
   all

---

1. nightjars *n.*: Common nocturnal birds, named for the whirring
sound which the male makes.
2. ricks *n.*: Haystacks.

THE MAGIC APPLE TREE, c. 1830
Samuel Palmer
Fitzwilliam Museum, Cambridge

30 Shining, it was Adam and maiden,
         The sky gathered again
     And the sun grew round that very day.
So it must have been after the birth of the simple light
In the first, spinning place, the spellbound horses walking
     warm
35   Out of the whinnying green stable
         On to the fields of praise.

And honored among foxes and pheasants by the gay house
Under the new made clouds and happy as the heart was
     long,
         In the sun born over and over,
40   I ran my heedless ways,
         My wishes raced through the house-high hay
And nothing I cared, at my sky blue trades, that time allows
In all his tuneful turning so few and such morning songs
         Before the children green and golden
45   Follow him out of grace,

Nothing I cared, in the lamb white days, that time would
     take me
Up to the swallow thronged loft by the shadow of my hand,
         In the moon that is always rising,
             Nor that riding to sleep
50   I should hear him fly with the high fields
And wake to the farm forever fled from the childless land.
Oh as I was young and easy in the mercy of his means,
     Time held me green and dying
Though I sang in my chains like the sea.

RESPONDING TO THE SELECTION

Your Response

1. Why do you think the spontaneous joys of childhood often do not survive into adulthood?

Recalling

2. What two colors does the speaker use repeatedly to describe himself as a youth?
3. What does the speaker say happened each night as he "rode to sleep"?
4. In the last stanza, where does the speaker suggest that time has taken him?

Interpreting

5. (a) How would you describe the speaker's feelings about his childhood? (b) What are some of the words and phrases that convey this feeling?
6. What do you think is meant in lines 33–34 by "the birth of the simple light/In the first, spinning place"?
7. The mood in the last stanza changes from that in the preceding stanzas. (a) What is the change? (b) What are two lines or phrases earlier in the poem that foreshadow this change?
8. Line 53, "Time held me green and dying," expresses the basic idea of the poem. In your own words, tell what the line means.

Applying

9. Passing from the innocence of childhood to the reality and responsibility of adulthood is the subject of many rituals, proverbs, and literary works. What are a few of these?

CRITICAL THINKING AND READING

Interpreting Connotative Meaning

The **connotation** of a word is the meaning the word has beyond its dictionary definition. For example, *lilting,* in line 2, means "metrical, rhythmic," but, beyond that meaning—or *denotation*—the word has favorable connotations of melodic singing and cheerfulness. By contrast, the word *eurhythmic* has a denotation similar to that of *lilting,* but its connotations, if not actually unfavor-

able, are rather stuffy and academic. Poets take great care with the connotations of the words they use. Dylan Thomas is said to have been unhappy with the word *heedless* in line 40, but could not find a word he considered more appropriate for his meaning.

Find the following words and phrases in "Fern Hill." Explain what connotations you believe the poet intends:

1. apple towns (line 6); 2. sun (line 18); 3. moon (line 25); 4. sky blue trades (line 42); 5. lamb white (line 46); 6. swallow thronged loft (line 47); 7. in my chains (line 54); 8. like the sea (line 54).

THINKING AND WRITING

Writing a Poem About Childhood

The farm in "Fern Hill" belonged to Ann Jones, Dylan Thomas's aunt. As a child, Thomas spent many vacations and holidays there. As an adult, he remembered it as a happy world, an innocent Eden forever lost. Write a poem about the place where you spent some or all of your childhood. You may have pleasant recollections, like Thomas, or ones that are less pleasant. Write in whatever poetic form you wish. Include as many images as you can to help a reader visualize both the setting and your experiences. Remember that a poem requires prewriting and revision just as other forms of composition do.

LEARNING OPTION

Art. Choose one of the many vibrant and unusual images that Thomas creates in "Fern Hill." Some examples include "apple boughs about the lilting house" (lines 1–2), "pebbles of the holy streams" (line 18), "fire green as grass" (line 22), "owls were bearing the farm away" (line 24), "horses flashing into the dark" (lines 26–27), "wanderer white with the dew" (lines 28–29), "house-high hay" (line 41), "lamb white days" (line 46), and "swallow thronged loft by the shadow of my hand" (line 47). Illustrate the image in whatever medium you prefer, capturing the fanciful feelings that Thomas's words evoke.

Do Not Go Gentle into That Good Night

Dylan Thomas

Do not go gentle into that good night,
Old age should burn and rave at close of day;
Rage, rage against the dying of the light.

Though wise men at their end know dark is right,
5 Because their words had forked no lightning they
Do not go gentle into that good night.

Good men, the last wave by, crying how bright
Their frail deeds might have danced in a green bay,
Rage, rage against the dying of the light.

10 Wild men who caught and sang the sun in flight,
And learn, too late, they grieved it on its way,
Do not go gentle into that good night.

Grave men, near death, who see with blinding sight
Blind eyes could blaze like meteors and be gay,
15 Rage, rage against the dying of the light.

And you, my father, there on the sad height,
Curse, bless, me now with your fierce tears, I pray.
Do not go gentle into that good night.
Rage, rage against the dying of the light.

┃RESPONDING TO THE SELECTION

Your Response

1. Given the inevitability of death, what do you think might be gained from raging "against the dying of the light"? Explain.

Recalling

2. Starting with the second stanza of this villanelle, what four kinds of men does the speaker describe as they go "into that good night"?

Interpreting

3. (a) In this poem, what does *night* seem to represent? (b) What does *light* represent?
4. Considering the speaker's advice to "rage" against the "dying of the light," why do you think he regards night as "good"?
5. What double meaning does the word *grave* have in line 13?
6. How would you paraphrase the speaker's advice in the final couplet?

KNOCKALLA HILLS, DONEGAL
Dan O'Neill
Ulster Museum, Belfast

Applying

7. Do you think "Do Not Go Gentle into That Good Night" might have been a better poem if Thomas had chosen to work with a less restrictive poetic form than the villanelle? Explain your reasoning.

LEARNING OPTION

Writing. Write a response to "Do Not Go Gentle into That Good Night" from the point of view of a person who is near death. You may write your response in prose or in poetry; you might even write your own villanelle. How might someone who is facing the "close of day" react to what the speaker says? Would he or she identify with being "wise," "good," "wild," or "grave"? What insights might such a person have that the speaker in Thomas's poem does not? Share your response with the class by reading it aloud.

BIOGRAPHIES

Philip Larkin (1922–1985)

Writing in a poetic form that approximates conversation, Philip Larkin raised familiar experiences to the level of art. His poems are often wry, self-critical, and understated. Larkin was born in Coventry, England. Not happy at school and dominated at home by a father who held him accountable to rigid standards of achievement, Larkin developed in his childhood the sense of detachment that would become central to much of his verse. After graduating from St. John's College, Oxford, Larkin began writing as a novelist and columnist. His poetry, the source of his international fame, displays a clear-eyed honesty that captures moments of startling truth.

Stevie Smith (1902–1971)

One critic calls Stevie Smith's poetry "a forest of themes and attitudes." Indeed, the work of this poet is difficult to categorize because of its variations in tone, form, and perspective. Born Florence Margaret Smith in Hull, Yorkshire, Smith moved with her mother and sister to an unfashionable London suburb when she was three. Because of her mother's ill health, she was raised primarily by her beloved Auntie Lion, with whom she continued to live in her adult life. Smith worked for many years for a magazine, but she frequently gave poetry readings on radio and television. Ultimately, she published three novels and more than ten collections of poetry.

Ted Hughes (1930–   )

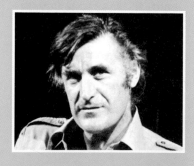

A major contemporary poet, Ted Hughes has been widely praised for his portrayal of nature in all its fierceness and cruelty. His fascination with nature can be traced to his childhood in the Calder Valley in Yorkshire, which was full of animals of all kinds. Hughes studied archaeology and anthropology and worked a variety of jobs before he and his friends published a poetry magazine in 1956. With his wife, poet and novelist Sylvia Plath, he taught briefly in the United States. Since the mid-1960's, Hughes has produced a number of major collections of poetry. His work continues to show his masterful ability to link the universal force of nature and the human condition.

GUIDE FOR INTERPRETING

Days; The Explosion; Not Waving but Drowning; Pretty; Hawk Roosting; The Horses

Writers' Techniques

Tone and Voice. In conversation, the way a person chooses and says words suggests his or her attitude. In poetry, the poet's attitude toward a subject is called **tone.** The tone of a poem might be solemn, playful, cynical, angry, or have some other quality. It reflects the poet's attitude or mood and puts the reader in the same kind of mood. Tone is created by the ideas in the poem as well as by verbal elements such as meter, sentence structure, diction, and imagery.

When you read a poem, you "hear" a voice. It is the speaker's voice—with its pauses, stresses, and even pitch—that you experience. In poetry, then, **voice** is an aspect of tone that refers to the idiom, rhythm, and intonation used by the speaker. An important part of the poet's craft lies in his or her ability to create a personality with the voice in a poem so that alert readers can perceive the feelings behind the speaker's voice.

Personification. Personification is a figure of speech in which a thing, a quality, or an idea is given human attributes. For example, when Edmund Spenser writes that envy "rode upon a ravenous wolf," he is using personification. Sometimes personification is extended well beyond a phrase or sentence and involves point of view. Events are observed through the eyes and mind of a nonhuman narrator or speaker. A familiar example of such extended personification is Jack London's *The Call of the Wild,* in which the story is told from the viewpoint of Buck, a dog. Like simile, metaphor, and other figures of speech, personification presents ideas in fresh, original ways.

Focus

Freewrite quickly for a few minutes. Use your own natural voice and grammar. Then read over what you have written. What adjectives would you use to describe your written voice?

Primary Source

In *Larkin at Sixty,* Anthony Thwaite records a conversation between Philip Larkin and fellow writer Kingsley Amis. When asked, "What chance of the Nobel [Prize]?" Larkin replied, "I thought they might be keeping it warm for a chap like me—you know, a chap who never *writes* anything or *does* anything or *says* anything. But now I find they've just given it to a . . . [fellow] who never *writes* anything or *does* anything or *says* anything. No, that's gone." About the Poet Laureateship of Great Britain, Larkin mused, "I dream about that sometimes . . . *and wake up screaming.* Nah, with any luck they'll pass me over."

Days

Philip Larkin

What are days for?
Days are where we live.
They come, they wake us
Time and time over.
5 They are to be happy in;
Where can we live but days?

Ah, solving that question
Brings the priest and the doctor
In their long coats
10 Running over the fields.

RESPONDING TO THE SELECTION

Your Response

1. Do you think that "the priest and the doctor" are qualified to solve the speaker's questions about days? Why or why not?

Recalling

2. In your own words, what is the speaker's answer to the first question in the poem?

Interpreting

3. Why does the answer to the second question bring the priest and the doctor running?

Applying

4. What would be different about the thought in this poem if Larkin had substituted "life" for "days"?

ANALYZING LITERATURE

Understanding Tone

Tone is the attitude that a writer takes toward his or her subject, characters, or audience. In a poem tone is conveyed to a great extent by word choice.

1. How would you describe the tone of "Days"?
2. How does the interjection "Ah" at the beginning of line 7 affect the tone of the poem?
3. How would the tone of the poem be different if lines 7–10 did not exist?

LEARNING OPTION

Writing. Write a dialogue between the priest and the doctor, giving their respective insights on the meaning of days. As you draft your dialogue, think about how the philosophies of these two figures might differ. About what might they agree? Ask a classmate to give you suggestions for revising your dialogue. Make sure the point of view of each speaker is clearly expressed.

The Explosion

Philip Larkin

On the day of the explosion
Shadows pointed towards the pithead:
In the sun the slagheap slept.

Down the lane came men in pitboots
5   Coughing oath-edged talk and pipe-smoke,
Shouldering off the freshened silence.

One chased after rabbits; lost them;
Came back with a nest of lark's eggs;
Showed them; lodged them in the grasses.

<pre>
 10   So they passed in beards and moleskins,
      Fathers, brothers, nicknames, laughter,
      Through the tall gates standing open.

      At noon, there came a tremor; cows
      Stopped chewing for a second; sun,
 15   Scarfed as in a heat-haze, dimmed.

      The dead go on before us, they
      Are sitting in God's house in comfort,
      We shall see them face to face—

      Plain as lettering in the chapels
 20   It was said, and for a second
      Wives saw men of the explosion

      Larger than in life they managed—
      Gold as on a coin, or walking
      Somehow from the sun towards them,

 25   One showing the eggs unbroken.
</pre>

RESPONDING TO THE SELECTION

Your Response

1. How does Larkin's treatment of time affect your reaction to the events described in the poem? Explain.

Recalling

2. Where do the events in the poem occur?
3. What immediate effect does the explosion have on life above ground?
4. (a) What do the widows of the miners see "for a second" at the funeral services? (b) What else in the poem lasts "for a second"?

Interpreting

5. How does the first stanza foreshadow events in the poem?
6. In your own words, explain line 5.
7. (a) What is the mood of the men going to work? (b) What details show this mood?

8. Why are lines 16–18 printed in italics?
9. What is the symbolic meaning of the eggs?
10. How would you describe the tone of "The Explosion"?

Applying

11. What relationship is there between the theme of "Days" and the theme of "The Explosion"?

LEARNING OPTION

Cross-curricular Connection. Find out about coal mining in England. How long has coal been mined there? Where are the major mining districts? What political battles have been fought as a result of conflicts between the miners and the companies that own the mines? Consult recent newspapers and periodicals to investigate political and economic developments in the British coal-mining industry. Share your findings with the class.

Not Waving but Drowning

Stevie Smith

Nobody heard him, the dead man,
But still he lay moaning:
I was much further out than you thought
And not waving but drowning.

5 Poor chap, he always loved larking
And now he's dead
It must have been too cold for him his heart gave way,
They said.

Oh, no no no, it was too cold always
10 (Still the dead one lay moaning)
I was much too far out all my life
And not waving but drowning.

RESPONDING TO THE SELECTION

Your Response

1. What experiences have you had that left you feeling "too far out"? Explain.

Recalling

2. Five lines in the poem are spoken by the dead man. Which lines are they?
3. (a) How did the spectators interpret the dead man's waving? (b) What led them to make this interpretation?

Interpreting

4. What does "it" represent in line 9, "Oh, no no no, it was too cold always"?
5. In what sense was the dead man "too far out" all his life?
6. In line 4 the phrase "not waving but drowning" seems to be the literal truth. In line 12 the same phrase has a metaphorical meaning. What is its metaphorical meaning?

Applying

7. What kinds of distress signals in ordinary life might be interpreted as "waving"?

ANALYZING LITERATURE

Understanding Voice

"Not Waving but Drowning" appears to be simple, but the appearance is deceptive. Three speakers can be identified in it: a narrator, a spectator (or spectators), and the dead man. The narrator's voice (lines 1, 2, and 10) is matter-of-fact and neutral, if a bit puzzled. The narrator's double use of "moaning" adds to your understanding of the dead man's distress.

1. Study lines 5–7. What adjective or adjectives do you think accurately describe the voice of the spectators? Explain.
2. What adjective or adjectives describe the voice of the dead man? Explain.

Pretty

Stevie Smith

Why is the word pretty so underrated?
In November the leaf is pretty when it falls
The stream grows deep in the woods after rain
And in the pretty pool the pike stalks

5   He stalks his prey, and this is pretty too,
The prey escapes with an underwater flash
But not for long, the great fish has him now
The pike is a fish who always has his prey

And this is pretty. The water rat is pretty
10 His paws are not webbed, he cannot shut his nostrils
As the otter can and the beaver, he is torn between
The land and water. Not "torn," he does not mind.

The owl hunts in the evening and it is pretty
The lake water below him rustles with ice
15 There is frost coming from the ground, in the air mist
All this is pretty, it could not be prettier.

Yes, it could always be prettier, the eye abashes
It is becoming an eye that cannot see enough,
Out of the wood the eye climbs. This is prettier
20 A field in the evening, tilting up.

The field tilts to the sky. Though it is late
The sky is lighter than the hill field
All this looks easy but really it is extraordinary
Well, it is extraordinary to be so pretty.

25 And it is careless, and that is always pretty
This field, this owl, this pike, this pool are careless,
As Nature is always careless and indifferent
Who sees, who steps, means nothing, and this is pretty.

So a person can come along like a thief—pretty!—
30 Stealing a look, pinching the sound and feel,
Lick the icicle broken from the bank
And still say nothing at all, only cry pretty.

Cry pretty, pretty, pretty and you'll be able
Very soon not even to cry pretty
35 And so be delivered entirely from humanity
This is prettiest of all, it is very pretty.

Your Response

1. Do you think the word *pretty* is "underrated"? What uses for it do you think are appropriate? Explain.

Recalling

2. In the first four stanzas, what are seven things that the speaker says are pretty?
3. Why does the speaker feel the need to see beyond the wood?
4. What is "prettiest of all"?

Interpreting

5. The speaker does not define "pretty" directly but through examples. What is the speaker's implied definition?
6. How does the speaker feel about the fact that nature is "careless and indifferent"?
7. (a) What do you think the speaker means by "being delivered entirely from humanity"? (b) Why might the speaker regard that as pretty?

Applying

8. What aspect of nature—other than its pretti-ness—can serve as a useful example for human beings? Explain.

THINKING AND WRITING

Evaluating a Poem

Write an essay evaluating either of Stevie Smith's poems. Begin by deciding which poem you prefer, or which poem you believe will allow you to express the most convincing opinion. Write a thesis sentence that states your opinion clearly. Use lines from the poem in writing your first draft.

When you revise, make a special effort to see that the quoted lines fit smoothly and effectively into what you have written. Your final draft should be as error-free as you can make it. Prepare this draft and share it with your classmates. Compare your reaction to the poem with theirs.

LEARNING OPTIONS

1. **Speaking and Listening.** Give a reading of "Pretty" in class. To prepare, review the poem carefully, discovering as much about its tone and the changes in the speaker's attitude as you can. What clues in the syntax and diction of the poem can you find to help you determine how it should be read? Also pay attention to the punctuation so that you know when to pause at the end of a line and when not to pause. Then think about ways you can use your voice to express the changes in the speaker's mood from beginning to end. Practice your reading, perhaps taping it so you can monitor the effect of your interpretation. Finally, read "Pretty" to the class. Ask your classmates to respond to your interpretation and to state whether they "heard" the poem the same way when they read it silently.

2. **Art.** The poem moves from visual image to visual image, a progression that you can re-produce by arranging drawings, paintings, or photographs in a linear fashion. First, review "Pretty" to identify the images you want to high-light (between five and ten). Then, find works of art, or create your own, to illustrate each of these images. As you search for or make the illustrations, take into consideration the the-matic shift that occurs toward the end. How will your illustrations reflect this shift? Display your visual representation of the poem in class.

Hawk Roosting

Ted Hughes

I sit in the top of the wood, my eyes closed.
Inaction, no falsifying dream
Between my hooked head and hooked feet:
Or in sleep rehearse perfect kills and eat.

5   The convenience of the high trees!
The air's buoyancy and the sun's ray
Are of advantage to me;
And the earth's face upward for my inspection.

My feet are locked upon the rough bark.
10 It took the whole of Creation
To produce my foot, my each feather:
Now I hold Creation in my foot

Or fly up, and revolve it all slowly—
I kill where I please because it is all mine.
15 There is no sophistry in my body:
My manners are tearing off heads—

The allotment of death.
For the one path of my flight is direct
Through the bones of the living.
20 No arguments assert my right:

The sun is behind me.
Nothing has changed since I began.
My eye has permitted no change.
I am going to keep things like this.

RESPONDING TO THE SELECTION

Your Response

1. What is your reaction to the seeming arrogance in the hawk's attitude? Explain.

Recalling

2. (a) Who is the speaker in the poem? (b) Where is the speaker sitting?
3. What are three advantages that allow the speaker to "kill where I please"?

Interpreting

4. What does stanza 3 suggest about the physical makeup and abilities of the speaker?
5. In lines 14–16, how does the speaker refute the "falsifying dream" that nature is invariably pleasant and nonviolent?
6. (a) What do you think the speaker means by "Nothing has changed since I began"? (b) How might you interpret this in another way?
7. (a) What does the poet's (not the speaker's) view of nature seem to be? (b) How do you feel about that view?

Applying

8. Nature can be violent. What in your own experience shows this to be true? What moods can you identify in nature? Provide examples that reveal these moods.

ANALYZING LITERATURE

Using Personification

Giving human attributes to a thing, a quality, or an idea is called **personification.** In "Hawk Roosting," Ted Hughes uses the technique to present his ideas about nature in an unusual and striking way.

1. Personification requires giving human attributes to something nonhuman. How is the hawk personified in Hughes's poem?
2. Why do you think Hughes has the hawk speak for itself in the poem rather than having a human speaker interpret what the hawk might be thinking?

THINKING AND WRITING

Using Personification in a Poem

Choose a bird very unlike the hawk. For example, you might choose a sparrow or a lark. Freewrite, exploring what this animal might see as it looks at the world. Then write a poem in which you personify this creature. Your poem can be short or long, rhymed or unrhymed. Have the bird speak, telling what it sees. When you revise, make sure you have given your bird human characteristics.

Commentary

In view of the striking personifications of nature's creatures and often merciless view of the world in Hughes's poetry, it is especially surprising that he is a prolific and important writer of children's books. His books for children include six books of poetry, two of fiction, and one of plays, though several of his children's plays for radio have never been collected. In addition, he has written an introduction to poetry for young readers. Originally published in England under the title *Poetry in the Making*, the American edition is called *Poetry Is.*

In part, his dedication to children's literature arises from his belief that "every new child is nature's chance to correct culture's error." To Hughes, children have the ability to reclaim the world's goodness. Their innocence and wonder can defeat evil and darkness. How does he express this idea in the following stanza?

In the little girl's angel gaze
Crow lost every feather
In the little boy's wondering eyes
Crow's bones splintered

The Horses

Ted Hughes

I climbed through woods in the hour-before-dawn dark.
Evil air, a frost-making stillness,

Not a leaf, not a bird—
A world cast in frost. I came out above the wood

5   Where my breath left tortuous statues in the iron light.
But the valleys were draining the darkness

Till the moorline—blackening dregs of the brightening
   gray—
Halved the sky ahead. And I saw the horses:

Huge in the dense gray—ten together—
10   Megalith-still. They breathed, making no move,

With draped manes and tilted hind-hooves,
Making no sound.

I passed: not one snorted or jerked its head.
Gray silent fragments

15   Of a gray silent world.

I listened in emptiness on the moor-ridge.
The curlew's[1] tear turned its edge on the silence.

Slowly detail leafed from the darkness. Then the sun
Orange, red, red erupted

20   Silently, and splitting to its core tore and flung cloud,
Shook the gulf open, showed blue,

And the big planets hanging—
I turned

Stumbling in the fever of a dream, down towards
25   The dark woods, from the kindling tops.

---

1. **curlew** (kʉr′ lo͞o) *n.*: A large, brownish wading bird with long legs.

And came to the horses.

There, still they stood,
But now steaming and glistening under the flow of light,

Their draped stone manes, their tilted hind-hooves
30 Stirring under a thaw while all around them

The frost showed its fires. But still they made no sound.
Not one snorted or stamped,

Their hung heads patient as the horizons,
High over valleys, in the red leveling rays—

35 In din of the crowded streets, going among the years, the
    faces,
May I still meet my memory in so lonely a place

Between the streams and the red clouds, hearing curlews,
Hearing the horizons endure.

RESPONDING TO THE SELECTION

Your Response

1. Think of a place you would like to remember later, in "the crowded streets, going among the years." (a) What kind of place is it? (b) Why would you like to remember it?

Recalling

2. How are the horses different in the second sighting than in the first?
3. What wish does the speaker make in the last four lines of the poem?

Interpreting

4. (a) In your own words, what does "detail leafed from the darkness" in line 18 mean? (b) What does "the sun/Orange, red, red erupted" in lines 19 and 20 mean?
5. (a) What is the figure of speech in line 33? (b) How do you explain the comparison?
6. The view of nature is different in "The Horses" from that in "Hawk Roosting." What is the basic difference?

Applying

7. What are some of the reasons people may have for cherishing memories of solitary experiences?

THINKING AND WRITING

Comparing Poems

Reread William Wordsworth's "Lines Composed a Few Miles Above Tintern Abbey." Then write an essay in which you compare Wordsworth's view of nature with that of Ted Hughes in "The Horses." Make notes before you begin to write. Jot down a few specific lines from each poem to support your comparison. In writing your first draft, be willing to speculate on the reasons for the differences between the poems. When you revise your first draft, check to be sure that your statements are supported by evidence from the poems.

BIOGRAPHIES

Seamus Heaney (1939–   )

Born in County Derry, Northern Ireland, Seamus Heaney has devoted much of his poetry to the life, history, and conflict of his homeland. He is a gifted traditionalist whom the American poet Robert Lowell has called "the most important Irish poet since Yeats." The eldest of nine children, Heaney spent a happy childhood on the farm that had been in his family for generations. He has said that his deep regard for tradition and the past grew from his early experiences in the rich, boggy land of his ancestors. He first published as an undergraduate at Queen's University in Belfast. Long having struggled with the role of the artist in political situations, Heaney left Northern Ireland in 1972 and moved into a cottage on an estate in County Wicklow. His departure was termed by some an artistic necessity; by others, a betrayal.

Despite his fame, Heaney is known to be modest and unaffected. A friend recalls that when he met Heaney "fresh from a reading at Harvard and dressed for dinner at the Princeton Club, he still managed to convey the easy intimacy of a gathering around a peat fire."

Eavan Boland (1944–   )

Born in Dublin to a mother who was a painter and a father who was a diplomat, Eavan Boland spent many of her early years away from Ireland. When her father was ambassador to Great Britain in the 1950's, Boland recalls experiencing anti-Irish hostility and feeling "a great sense of isolation." Returning in 1959 to her native land to attend a convent school near Dublin, Boland found "the contact with Ireland again after a childhood away a great imaginative release."

After graduating from the convent school, Boland worked as a housekeeper in a Dublin hotel and with her own earnings published a pamphlet, *23 Poems,* which she now describes as "truly frightful." She later attended Trinity College in Dublin and, after graduating, became a junior lecturer. Boland found that academic life interfered with poetry writing, however, and she resigned. Since 1967, she has published several collections of poetry, including *The War Horse, In Her Own Image,* and *Night Feed.*

Boland is married to a novelist and has two daughters. Though many of her poems treat motherhood and domestic life, Eavan Boland shuns the label "woman poet." "What needs to be done," she asserts, "is to work one's way carefully . . . to the essence of the statement which is bound to be human."

GUIDE FOR INTERPRETING

Follower; Shore Woman; The Achill Woman; Outside History

Contemporary Irish Poets. In a country often preoccupied with the political question of Northern Ireland, contemporary Irish poets have deliberately rejected the nationalist position that Ireland is one monolithic culture and have instead, like their literary predecessor William Butler Yeats, embraced the variety of Irish experience. At the same time (and also like Yeats), they have incorporated Irish history, including its literary history, into their work.

Seamus Heaney finds a connection between history and contemporary events in the Irish bogs—the wet, spongy, richly vegetated land of Ireland's central plain. Because the area was relatively untouched until recently, astonishingly well-preserved bodies, clothing, food, and artifacts have been unearthed there. Thus Heaney finds in the bogs echoes of an ancient Ireland. In his famous "bog poems" he links the battles of long-gone Vikings, whose remains are found in the bogs, to the struggles of the present-day Irish.

Both Heaney and Boland find a connection with Irish history in the people who still live and work close to the land. Heaney's "Shore Woman" and "Follower" celebrate the lives of people who are deeply connected to the landscape around them, as does Boland's "The Achill Woman." Thus, while rejecting easy solutions to the problems of contemporary Ireland, Irish poets look to that history for their inspiration and for welcome perspective on the present.

Focus

Write about someone you know who makes you feel connected to your history, to your roots. What shared history do you have with the person? What have you learned from her or him?

Primary Source

For all of his preoccupation with Irish history, Seamus Heaney is well aware that a poet's first subject must be himself—his thoughts, feelings, and perceptions. In an interview in the late 1970's, he talked about a new direction for his poetry.

> ". . . [F]or me now it's just the usual middle-age coasting toward extinction, but trying to define the self. I'm not interested in my poetry canvassing public events deliberately any more. I would like to write poems of myself at this age. Poems, so far, have been fueled by a world that is gone or a world that is too much with us—public events. Just through accident and all the things we've been talking about, I've ended up with myself, and I have to start there, you know."

He could well be speaking for any contemporary Irish poet.

Follower

Seamus Heaney

My father worked with a horse plow,
His shoulders globed like a full sail strung
Between the shafts and the furrow.
The horses strained at his clicking tongue.

5 An expert. He would set the wing
And fit the bright steel-pointed sock.
The sod rolled over without breaking.
At the headrig, with a single pluck

Of reins, the sweating team turned round
10 And back into the land. His eye
Narrowed and angled at the ground,
Mapping the furrow exactly.

I stumbled in his hobnailed wake,
Fell sometimes on the polished sod;
15 Sometimes he rode me on his back
Dipping and rising to his plod.

I wanted to grow up and plow,
To close one eye, stiffen my arm.
All I ever did was follow
20 In his broad shadow round the farm.

I was a nuisance, tripping, falling,
Yapping always. But today
It is my father who keeps stumbling
Behind me, and will not go away.

Your Response

1. Have you ever felt about an adult the way the speaker felt about his father? Explain.

Recalling

2. How does the speaker show that his father was an expert at plowing?
3. As the boy accompanied his father, what did he want to do?
4. (a) What three verbs does the speaker use to describe his actions as he followed his father? (b) What parallel verb does he use in speaking of his father today?

Interpreting

5. (a) What do you think is the approximate age of the speaker in the plowing scene he describes? (b) How can you tell?
6. Why do you think the boy wanted to close one eye and stiffen his arm?
7. The speaker says: "All I ever did was follow/In his broad shadow. . . ." What double meaning do those words suggest?
8. What is the tone of this poem? Find evidence to support your answer.

Applying

9. (a) What does this poem suggest about the changing roles of parents and children? (b) Do you think most young people are prepared for these changing roles? Explain your answer.

ANALYZING LITERATURE

Understanding Historical Context

To poets, history is more than just an account of past events. For them, history can also be found in the landscape where the events were played out and in the people who still inhabit that landscape. In "Follower" Seamus Heaney affirms his connection with Irish soil by evoking his relationship with his father.

1. How does the father's occupation connect the speaker with Irish history?
2. What does the speaker mean when he says that his father "will not go away"?

CRITICAL THINKING AND READING

Understanding Figurative Language

Figurative language is language that is not meant to be interpreted literally. When Heaney writes that his father's shoulders "globed like a full sail," he does not mean that they became an actual sphere or that they were as large as a ship's wind-filled sail. Yet the points of resemblance give you a clear, striking picture of his father walking behind the plow.

1. "Mapping the furrow" (line 12) is an example of figurative language. (a) Why? (b) How would you express the idea literally? (c) What does the figurative language add to the thought?
2. The line about "my father . . . stumbling" (line 23) is figurative. (a) Why? (b) How would you express the idea literally?

LEARNING OPTIONS

1. **Writing.** Imagine that the speaker's father recalls the same situation described in the poem—plowing while his young son toddles behind him. Write a monologue in which the speaker's father tells what he remembers about plowing with his child. You might have him comment on his present relationship with his son.
2. **Cross-curricular Connection.** Find out more about farming in contemporary Ireland. What are the main crops? What percentage of the people are farmers? What is the average size of an Irish farm? Does Ireland export or import food? Present your findings in an illustrated chart.

Shore Woman

Seamus Heaney

Man to the hills, woman to the shore.
                    Gaelic proverb

I have crossed the dunes with their whistling bent
Where dry loose sand was riddling round the air
And I'm walking the firm margin. White pocks
Of cockle, blanched roofs of clam and oyster
5 Hoard the moonlight, woven and unwoven
Off the bay. At the far rocks
A pale sud comes and goes.

Under boards the mackerel slapped to death
Yet still we took them in at every cast,
10 Stiff flails of cold convulsed with their first breath.
My line plumbed certainly the undertow,
Loaded against me once I went to draw
And flashed and fattened up towards the light.
He was all business in the stern. I called
15 "This is so easy that it's hardly right,"
But he unhooked and coped with frantic fish
Without speaking. Then suddenly it lulled,
We'd crossed where they were running, the line rose
Like a let-down and I was conscious
20 How far we'd drifted out beyond the head.
"Count them up at your end," was all he said
Before I saw the porpoises' thick backs
Cartwheeling like the flywheels[1] of the tide,
Soapy and shining. To have seen a hill
25 Splitting the water could not have numbed me more
Than the close irruption of that school,
Tight viscous muscle, hooped from tail to snout,
Each one revealed complete as it bowled out
And under.
30   They will attack a boat.
I knew it and I asked him to put in
But he would not, declared it was a yarn
My people had been fooled by far too long
And he would prove it now and settle it.

---

1. flywheels *n.*: Heavy wheels for regulating the speed and uniformity
of motion of a machine.

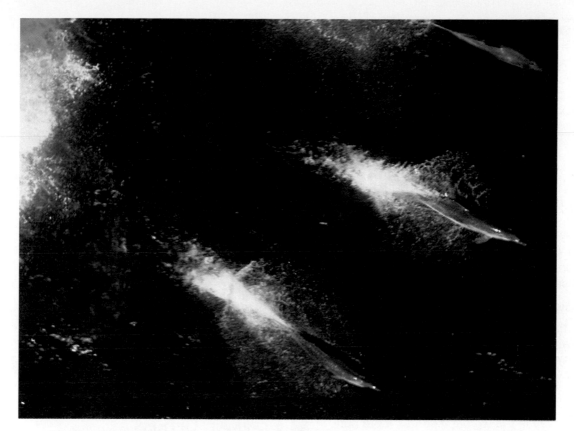

35   Maybe he shrank when those sloped oily backs
      Propelled towards us: I lay and screamed
      Under splashed brine in an open rocking boat
      Feeling each dunt and slither through the timber,
      Sick at their huge pleasures in the water.

40   I sometimes walk this strand for thanksgiving
      Or maybe it's to get away from him
      Skittering his spit across the stove. Here
      Is the taste of safety, the shelving sand
      Harbors no worse than razorshell[2] or crab—
45   Though my father recalls carcasses of whales
      Collapsed and gasping, right up to the dunes.
      But tonight such moving sinewed dreams lie out
      In darker fathoms, far beyond the head.
      Astray upon a debris of scrubbed shells
50   Between parched dunes and salivating wave,
      I have rights on this fallow avenue,
      A membrane between moonlight and my shadow.

---

2. razorshell *n.*: The shell of razor clams, burrowing clams with
elongated, narrow shells that resemble a straight razor.

RESPONDING TO THE SELECTION

Your Response

1. Do you feel more sympathetic toward the speaker or toward the man in the boat with her? Explain.

Recalling

2. Where is the speaker in the first and the last stanzas?
3. (a) What were the speaker and the man doing in the open boat? (b) How successful were they?
4. (a) Why was the speaker frightened at the sight of the porpoises? (b) What was the man's reaction? (c) Who was right about the porpoises—the speaker or the man?

Interpreting

5. What basic difference is there between the speaker and the man in the encounter with the porpoises? Explain your answer.
6. (a) How close does the relationship between speaker and the man appear to be when the two are at sea? (b) How close is it on land?
7. In what way is the woman seen as more connected to history than the man is?

Applying

8. Faced with the possibility of danger, do you think it is better to be cautious or to face the danger boldly? Explain.

CRITICAL THINKING AND READING

Recognizing Sound and Meaning

Poets use a number of devices to create the kinds of sounds that complement the meaning of their words. Rhyme, rhythm, repetition, harsh or soft consonants and vowels, and onomatopoeia all help to produce the desired effects.

1. What is one example of onomatopoeia in the first stanza?

2. What are three examples of repetition of sound in the second stanza?
3. Sound is used very effectively in line 42. What devices make this line work so well?

THINKING AND WRITING

Analyzing the Use of Sound in a Poem

Write an essay in which you analyze the devices for creating sound in "Shore Woman." To appreciate the sound in the poem, read it aloud at least once before you begin. Jot down notes about the sound devices. What impression do they create? Then write your first draft. Remember that when you write an analysis of this kind, you have to do more than just point out the devices. You also have to explain what they add to the poem's meaning. When you revise, make sure you have provided details from the poem to support your analysis.

LEARNING OPTIONS

1. **Cross-curricular Connection.** Find out more about porpoises. Where do they live? What do they eat? Does the poem portray their behavior accurately? Why or why not? How do they relate to people? What dangers do they face from human activities? Share your findings with the class.
2. **Multicultural Activity.** "Shore Woman" takes its title from the Gaelic proverb that serves as its epigraph. What do you think this proverb means? Find out more about Gaelic proverbs and folk wisdom. Locate other examples in anthologies of Gaelic literature or histories of Celtic peoples. Providing appropriate background and analysis, share three or four of them with the class.

The Achill[1] Woman

Eavan Boland

She came up the hill carrying water.
She wore a half-buttoned, wool cardigan,
a tea-towel round her waist.

She pushed the hair out of her eyes with
5   her free hand and put the bucket down.

The zinc-music of the handle on the rim
tuned the evening. An Easter moon rose.
In the next-door field a stream was
a fluid sunset; and then, stars.

10   I remember the cold rosiness of her hands.
She bent down and blew on them like broth.
And round her waist, on a white background,
in coarse, woven letters, the words "glass cloth."

And she was nearly finished for the day.
15   And I was all talk, raw from college—
weekending at a friend's cottage
with one suitcase and the set text
of the Court poets of the Silver Age.[2]

We stayed putting down time until
20   the evening turned cold without warning.
She said goodnight and started down the hill.

The grass changed from lavender to black.
The trees turned back to cold outlines.
You could taste frost

25   but nothing now can change the way I went
indoors, chilled by the wind

THE POTATO DIGGERS, 1912
Paul Henry
National Gallery of Ireland

---

1. Achill (a′ kəl): Mountainous island off the west
coast of Ireland.
2. Court . . . Age: Poets who are considered inferior
to their predecessor, Chaucer, and their successor,
Shakespeare, and who relied on the patronage of
nobility.

and made a fire
and took down my book
and opened it and failed to comprehend

30   the harmonies of servitude,
the grace music gives to flattery
and language borrows from ambition—

and how I fell asleep
oblivious to

35   the planets clouding over in the skies,
the slow decline of the spring moon,
the songs crying out their ironies.

RESPONDING TO THE SELECTION

Your Response

1. Which of the two women is more appealing to you? Why?

Recalling

2. What time of day and what time of year does the poem describe?
3. What does the speaker do after leaving the hill?

Interpreting

4. Why does the woman carrying water come up the hill?
5. What contrast does the speaker imply between herself and the woman she meets on the hill?
6. Why do you think the speaker describes herself as "raw from college"?
7. What effect does meeting the woman on the hill have on the speaker?

Applying

8. "The Achill Woman" portrays an encounter between two people with very different ways of life—the academic and the working class. Do you think people from very different backgrounds can have meaningful relationships? Explain your answer.

CRITICAL THINKING AND READING

Understanding the Use of Detail

Vivid specific details make a scene come alive, whether the scene is described in a poem, essay, short story, or novel. Details that appeal to several of the five senses involve the reader in the description on more than one level.

1. Find one detail that suggests the economic status of the woman on the hill.
2. Find two details that appeal to senses other than sight.
3. The speaker mentions that she was studying the court poets of the Silver Age. How would the meaning of the poem be different if she had been studying Shakespeare, Chaucer, or some other major poet?

THINKING AND WRITING

Using Details in Writing

Write a poem, essay, or short story in which you describe a chance encounter with someone whom you find interesting. Make your writing come alive for readers by using vivid details. List all of the details you want to include. Try to appeal to several senses. Ask a classmate to read your draft and to suggest where more details might help the reader feel a part of the scene. When you revise, make sure the details are clearly developed.

Outside History

Eavan Boland

There are outsiders, always. These stars—
these iron inklings of an Irish January,
whose light happened

thousands of years before
5 our pain did: they are, they have always
     been
outside history.

They keep their distance. Under them
     remains
a place where you found
you were human, and

10 a landscape in which you know you are
     mortal.
And a time to choose between them.
I have chosen:

Out of myth into history I move to be
part of that ordeal
whose darkness is   15

only now reaching me from those fields,
those rivers, those roads clotted as
firmaments[1] with the dead.

How slowly they die
as we kneel beside them, whisper in   20
     their ear.
And we are too late. We are always too
     late.

---

1. firmaments *n.*: Skies perceived as solid arches or vaults.

RESPONDING TO THE SELECTION

Your Response
1. Do you agree with the speaker that a choice has to be made between myth and history? Explain.

Recalling
2. What are the "iron inklings of an Irish January"?
3. What do the fields, the rivers, and the roads hold?

Interpreting
4. Why are the stars outside history?
5. What is the effect of the speaker's saying "you" in lines 8, 9, and 10?
6. What is the ordeal mentioned in line 14?

7. In what way is the darkness of the ordeal parallel to the light of the stars?

Applying
8. In what way can this poem be applied to your country's history?

LEARNING OPTION

Cross-curricular Connection. Find out more about some stars that are visible at night where you live. Make a chart that lists the names of at least ten of the stars and how many light years it takes light from each of them to reach Earth. Then subtract the number of light years from the current Earth year to find out during what Earth year the light we are now seeing left the star.

ONE WRITER'S PROCESS

Eavan Boland and "The Achill Woman"

PREWRITING

A Lasting Image Poets are often haunted by images of experiences they have had, images whose meanings they try to tease out and shape into poems. For Eavan Boland, a haunting image formed one Easter time when she was a first-year student at Trinity College in Dublin. Not having done well in her exams, she had gone to Achill Island "in a purgatorial mood" to study the English Court poets of the sixteenth century. Every evening during her stay at the tiny cottage there, the caretaker, an old woman, carried water to her in a large metal bucket. The image of the woman stayed with Boland. "I can see her still. She has a tea-towel round her waist—perhaps this is one image that has become all the images I have of her—she wears an old cardigan and her hands are blushing with cold as she puts down the bucket."

Boland and the woman often talked of what it had been like for the people of Achill during the tragic time in Irish history when the potato crop failed and thousands of people died of starvation. "She was the first person to talk to me about the famine," Boland says. "She kept repeating to me that they were great people, the people in the famine. Great people. I had never heard that before." The old woman spoke with force about the suffering of the villagers, who "had moved closer to the shore, the better to eat the seaweed."

The Meaning of the Image At the time, Boland failed to appreciate the old woman and the meaning of her words. "Yet even then," she says, "I sensed a power in the encounter. I knew, without having words

for it, that she came from a past which affected me."

DRAFTING

Image and Meaning For years the image of the Achill woman stayed with Boland, and she developed an increasing sense of the inadequacy of her earlier response to the woman's words. When she came to write a poem about the experience, she found that the chief difficulty was to find the correct balance between the image and the meaning she now saw in it. According to Boland, "This is the difficulty and strength of so much poetry. The experience is negotiated . . . into the meaning of the experience. But if the second is heavier than the first then the poem ends making meaning of an experience which is not properly set out in the earlier part of the poem."

Accuracy of Detail One way Boland strove to avoid this imbalance was to render the image of the woman and the setting as vividly and accurately as she remembered them.

Sometimes this passion for accuracy gave her trouble, as in the line about the "zinc-music of the handle on the rim." Originally, she'd written "the tin-music of the handle on the rim," but says, "I knew it wasn't right, wasn't accurate." She then remembered that zinc is the metal used on those particular buckets, and changed the line accordingly.

The Illusion of Time To express the image's meaning, Boland deliberately introduced symbols like the Easter moon and the fire as well as "a shift of time and a widening of perspective." She also wanted to get the time elements in the poem right—the way in which "the present is already becoming the future from which I look at that past."

In any poem, Boland believes, it is necessary to render time accurately. "It's important not to have it go slowly where it needs to pass by rapidly. And the other way around." She wanted her image of the old woman on Achill to be like the view from a train window: "Something that flashes by and is yet understood." To achieve this effect she used assonance—the repetition of vowel sounds found in juxtaposed words and phrases like *tuned* and *zinc-music* and *cold rosiness.*

Working Habits Despite these difficulties, the writing of "The Achill Woman" came fairly easily to Boland. She remembers writing it "right through one cold, raw Irish January," beginning just after Christmas and continuing for about five weeks. "I don't think of 'The Achill Woman' as particularly difficult to write. It took those weeks of working both morning and in the evening: sometimes for one hour, sometimes for three or four."

Like many writers, Boland has specific writing habits and is attached to certain materials, such as the ledger-type notebooks she writes in. "This was the beginning of the year so I bought a large, azure-colored one in a newsagent just outside Trinity College. 'The Achill Woman' was the first poem in it. I would begin the poems on the right-hand page—sometimes with only five or six lines on a page. I almost never used the reverse but went straight on to the right-hand page overleaf. And so on. I always wrote in ballpoint pen—not a favorite one, but preferably a light cheap pen with a yellow stem and a sharp point. I could buy them anywhere."

REVISING AND EDITING

An Important Distinction To Boland there is a distinction between revision and rewriting. "Revision is the brisk, practical amendment as you go along—the error-correcting protocol of composition. You stand back. You look. You move ahead reshaping lines, and language." Rewriting, she claims, is entirely different—almost literally a writing again in which you "seem to be moving but you are really standing still, moving through a swamp of missed intentions and hopeless amendments. Often you are rewriting a poem you never wrote in the first place." One reason "The Achill Woman" was completed fairly quickly was that it was revised rather than rewritten.

Showing the Poem To get help with the revision process, some writers show their first drafts to family or friends, but Boland rarely shows her work to anyone until it is finished. Her husband, Kevin, also a writer, was the first person to read "The Achill Woman." He liked it at once. "I was pleased," Boland says, "because he was in possession both of my telling him the story and the poem itself," which meant he was able to judge how well she had achieved her aim of balancing image and meaning—of setting an outer narrative of remembered experience against an "inner landscape in which the now of the poem becomes the retrospect of the poet."

Thinking About the Process

1. Boland doesn't show her work to anyone until it is completely finished. What are the advantages and disadvantages of this practice?
2. **Writing** Boland distinguishes between revising and rewriting. Do you make the same distinction? Write a brief paragraph explaining your approach to revision; then exchange paragraphs with a classmate.

BIOGRAPHIES

Derek Walcott (1930–   )

Among the finest poets writing in English today, Derek Walcott displays great intellectual energy and imagination. His poems may lead the reader from Trinidad to ancient Greece, then on again to Shakespeare's England, sometimes in a single line.

Walcott was born on the Caribbean island of St. Lucia and attended university in Jamaica. He published the first of his many books of poetry when he was just nineteen. His book *Omeros* won the W. H. Smith Literary Award for poetry in 1990. He is also an accomplished playwright and the founder of the Trinidad Theater Workshop. His play *The Odyssey* opened in London in 1992.

Walcott spends part of each year teaching college in Boston, Massachusetts, but he makes his home in Jamaica, where he continues to produce theater and to write. Although his plays draw on African-Caribbean traditions, his poetry often taps European ones, and in his writing Walcott wrestles with the heritage of European imperialism. British rule subjected people in the Caribbean to much suffering, but it brought with it the powerful verbal tradition that Walcott so admires and to which he has made contributions that have won him the Nobel Prize (1992). In his book *The Fortunate Traveler* (1982), he sums up his attitude toward the British Empire: "It's good that everything's gone, except their language, /which is everything."

James Berry (1925–   )

A leading Caribbean poet currently writing in Britain, James Berry draws upon the imagery and rhythm of the rural West Indies as well as the excitement and personal freedom of urban London. His poetry, which he often performs on British radio and television, is steeped in the African-Caribbean oral tradition.

Born in a small village in Jamaica, Berry grew up in a state of poverty common in the West Indies. He and each of his five siblings left school at fourteen to help support their family. During World War II, he left Jamaica for the United States to find work. After living in several places, including Harlem in New York City, Berry returned to Jamaica discouraged by the prejudice he encountered. He left in 1948 for England and began to write.

Berry is dedicated to affirming his cultural heritage. When he attended English schools as a child in Jamaica, he says, his background was disqualified or just ignored. Now he creates characters that children of African descent can look up to. His collection of stories *A Thief in the Village* was a Coretta Scott King Honor Book in 1989. In 1991 he published a book of poems, *When I Dance*.

GUIDE FOR INTERPRETING

from Midsummer, XXIII; *from* Omeros, *from* Chapter XXVIII; Thoughts on My Mother; From Lucy: Englan' Lady

Writers' Techniques

Theme. The main or central idea expressed in a literary work is its **theme.** When the theme is stated directly, as in the rhyming couplet at the end of a Shakespeare sonnet, it is rather clear what meaning the author intends. Usually, however, theme is implied. In Tennyson's "Ulysses," for example, the theme is that life should be a constant striving for new experience, but the speaker in the poem never makes that exact statement.

None of these four poems by West Indian poets Derek Walcott and James Berry have directly stated themes; the complex history of the Caribbean region eludes an easy distillation of meaning. Since the British presence in the West Indies was originally a colonial one, the multiracial makeup of the islands is largely a result of the slave trade. Seeking a better life, many West Indians have emigrated to the United Kingdom. By 1990 the British citizenry included over 3 million people of African–West Indian heritage.

West Indian communities in Britain have suffered from both racial prejudice and economic hardship, and frustrations finally erupted in violence. In April 1981 the riots in the West Indian neighborhood of Brixton, a suburb of London, inspired several other violent protests that summer. Walcott refers to only the Brixton riots by name in *XXIII* from *Midsummer,* but the title suggests a theme developed from the riots as a whole. Alienation, indignation, and loss set against a love for the English language and a pride in one's heritage create the ambivalence expressed in the themes of these two poets.

Focus

What do the names West Indies and Caribbean make you think of? Imagine you grew up on one of the islands, and write about how you would react if you moved to a colder, damper climate.

Primary Source

When asked how he sees himself in the poetic tradition of the English language, Derek Walcott has said the following:

> I am primarily, absolutely a Caribbean writer. The English language is nobody's special property. It is the property of the imagination. . . . [E]very culture has its particular emphasis and obviously the Caribbean's poetry, talent, and genius is in its music. But then again the modern Caribbean is a very young thing. I consider myself at the beginning, rather than at the end, of a tradition.

from Midsummer
XXIII

Derek Walcott

With the stampeding hiss and scurry of green lemmings,
midsummer's leaves race to extinction like the roar
of a Brixton riot[1] tunneled by water hoses;
they seethe towards autumn's fire—it is in their nature,
5   being men as well as leaves, to die for the sun.
The leaf stems tug at their chains, the branches bending
like Boer cattle under Tory whips that drag every wagon
nearer to apartheid.[2] And, for me, that closes
the child's fairy tale of an antic England—fairy rings,
10   thatched cottages fenced with dog roses,
a green gale lifting the hair of Warwickshire.
I was there to add some color to the British theater.
"But the blacks can't do Shakespeare, they have no experience."
This was true. Their thick skulls bled with rancor
15   when the riot police and the skinheads exchanged quips
you could trace to the Sonnets, or the Moor's eclipse.
Praise had bled my lines white of any more anger,
and snow had inducted me into white fellowships,
while Calibans howled down the barred streets of an empire
20   that began with Caedmon's raceless dew,[3] and is ending
in the alleys of Brixton, burning like Turner's ships.[4]

---

1. Brixton riot: Residents of the South London district of Brixton
rioted in April 1981 to protest racial prejudice and economic
disadvantage.
2. Boer (boͧor) **cattle . . . apartheid:** In the seventeenth century,
the Boers, people of Dutch descent, colonized a portion of what is
now South Africa. The Tories, members of a political party in
Britain, held power when the Boer War (1899–1902) resulted in
British control of South Africa. The system of apartheid was
established by the Boers when South Africa became a republic.
3. Caedmon's (kad′ mənz) **raceless dew:** Poetry written by the
earliest known English poet, Caedmon, who lived in the seventh
century.
4. Turner's ships: British artist J.M.W. Turner (1775–1851)
painted atmospheric canvases of ships burning in battle.

REVOLUTION IS CHANGE,
CHANGE IS LIFE, 1988
Jean Patrick Icart-Pierre
The Bronx Musuem of the Arts, New York

RESPONDING TO THE **S**ELECTION

Your Response

1. Which of the images in the poem do you find the most vivid? Why?

Recalling

2. To what are midsummer's leaves compared?
3. How is "antic England" described?
4. Who were involved in the riots?

Interpreting

5. The speaker recalls his presence in England during the Brixton riots. (a) What was his response at the time? (b) How has his attitude changed?
6. How was the speaker's experience of Shakespeare different from the rioters'?
7. What congruence does Walcott see between the leaves' "race to extinction" and the condition of the British Empire? What image does he use to draw this parallel?

Applying

8. Interracial conflict is a serious problem wherever it occurs. How does the poem affect your attitude toward prejudice?

ANALYZING **L**ITERATURE

Understanding Theme

As in much poetry, the **theme** in this poem is not stated directly. No single statement sums up Walcott's feelings about his visit to England or about the Brixton riots. However, all of the poem's elements are linked to one central idea.

1. Identify three references in the poem to conflicts over race in Britain.
2. Why is the allusion to the Boer War in lines 7 and 8 appropriate to the theme?
3. The Moor in Shakespeare's play *Othello* (line 16) is an African. The island-born Caliban (line 19) in *The Tempest* is enslaved by a European. How do these allusions enhance the theme?
4. How does the irony in Walcott's knowing about British cultural history—shown in his references to Shakespeare, Caedmon, and Turner—contribute to the theme of the poem?
5. How do you think the speaker feels about the prospects for race relations in Britain? Explain.

from Omeros

from Chapter XXVIII
Derek Walcott

Now he heard the griot[1] muttering his prophetic song
of sorrow that would be the past. It was a note, long-drawn
and endless in its winding like the brown river's tongue:

"We were the color of shadows when we came down
5 with tinkling leg-irons to join the chains of the sea,
for the silver coins multiplying on the sold horizon,

and these shadows are reprinted now on the white sand
of antipodal coasts, your ashen ancestors
from the Bight of Benin, from the margin of Guinea.[2]

10 There were seeds in our stomachs, in the cracking pods
of our skulls on the scorching decks, the tubers
withered in no time. We watched as the river-gods

changed from snakes into currents. When inspected,
our eyes showed dried fronds in their brown irises,
15 and from our curved spines, the rib-cages radiated

like fronds from a palm-branch. Then, when the dead
palms were heaved overside, the ribbed corpses
floated, riding, to the white sand they remembered,

to the Bight of Benin, to the margin of Guinea.
20 So, when you see burnt branches riding the swell,
trying to reclaim the surf through crooked fingers,

after a night of rough wind by some stone-white hotel,
past the bright triangular passage of the windsurfers,
remember us to the black waiter bringing the bill."

25 But they crossed, they survived. There is the epical splendor.

---

1. griot (grē′ ō) *n.*: In West African cultures, a poet/historian/performer who preserves and passes on the oral tradition.
2. the Bight (bīt) **of Benin** (be nēn′) **. . . Guinea** (gin′ ē): Area of west central Africa that came to be known as the Slave Coast.

Multiply the rain's lances, multiply their ruin,
the grace born from subtraction as the hold's iron door

rolled over their eyes like pots left out in the rain,
and the bolt rammed home its echo, the way that thunder-
30 claps perpetuate their reverberation.

So there went the Ashanti one way, the Mandingo another,
the Ibo another, the Guinea.³ Now each man was a nation
in himself, without mother, father, brother.

---

3. the Ashanti (ə shän′ tə) . . . the Mandingo (man diŋ′ gō . . . the
Ibo (ē′ bō′) . . . the Guinea: Names of West African peoples.

RESPONDING TO THE SELECTION

Your Response
1. How does the tone of this poem make you feel? Explain.

Recalling
2. Who is speaking in lines 4 through 24?
3. What happens to the members of the different West African peoples once they cross the sea?

Interpreting
4. Why is the horizon described as "sold" in line 6?
5. What are the dead palms of lines 16 and 17?
6. Describe the shift in time that begins at line 20.
7. What does it mean that "Now each man was a nation in himself . . . "?

Applying
8. This poetic account of the slave trade gives a voice to those who were enslaved. What else does this poem do that a prose historical account cannot?

ANALYZING LITERATURE

Understanding Theme
This selection is an excerpt from Walcott's book-length poem *Omeros*. Omeros is the Greek name for Homer, who created his epics, the *Iliad* and the *Odyssey,* in about the eighth century B.C. In Walcott's book, Homer serves as a guide,
teaching the speaker about both the past and the present.
1. Homer's epics were recited for many years before they were written down. What oral tradition is referred to in Walcott's poem?
2. In the *Odyssey,* Odysseus, the king of Ithaca, endures a ten-year, danger-fraught sea voyage on his way home from fighting in the Trojan War. Upon his return, order and unity are restored to his kingdom. How is the ordeal suffered by the Africans taken in slavery different?
3. Find evidence in the poem that for Walcott, this investigation of his African heritage serves as a bittersweet homecoming.

THINKING AND WRITING

Writing About Images
An image is a word or phrase that appeals to one or more of the five senses. Both Homer and Walcott use vivid imagery in their poems. For example, Homer's most famous image is "the winedark sea," which he repeats throughout the *Odyssey.* Write an essay discussing the imagery in this excerpt from Walcott's *Omeros.* Identify and make a list of as many of the images as you can. To which sense or senses does each image appeal? In your draft discuss how the images are related to one another. When you revise, make sure you have used appropriate transitional words and phrases.

Thoughts on My Mother

James Berry

Bare trees turn the mind
to palm leaves a-rattle round
an open house with shadows wild
about a boy stretching sinews
5   in the stings and wash
of your voice your hands your eyes

Your oiled hand makes a cross
on my belly, and all
pain goes

10   Caretaker of my beginnings your echoes
pull me in and out from where many
bare feet slap earth floor,
secure, under the thatch cured in smoke
old as granpuppa, your domain
15   wattled in, with smells mixed with
ginger, nutmeg and pimento berries[1]
and old sweat of donkey padding

And your pestle a-crush woodfired
coffeebeans and cocoabeans
20   with cinnamon, and corn and cassava,[2]
and no food is ever the same
after your salted pepper spice-up
from a sapling table

December is stuck in gardens
25   and bed blankets here
but red hibiscus[3] opens up

---

1. pimento berries: The fruit of a West Indian tree
that when dried is called allspice.
2. cassava (kə sä′ və) *n*.: The starchy, edible root of a
tropical American plant.
3. hibiscus (hī bis′ kəs) *n*.: A plant of the mallow
family whose large, usually red flowers can be used to
make tea.

the playmates' wood-and-straw
place, and the song in your hair
like your patience I could
30 never have, with your luxury
iced water in a calabash[4]

Woman
you hang no accomplishments:
it's one late gold ring a-flash
35 your only jewel, yet eight people's
habits and clothes-fabric were
like a map in your palm

Frost winds in England try
to skin me white: you are
40 warm, your face
wet in sweat, black in sunlight
as you dig, chop or stitch,
with feet bare like
the scorpions and centipedes,
45 that I may let go my tasseled roots
the sun pulls upward.

CARIBBEAN MADONNA (detail)
David Wilson
Courtesy of the Artist

---

4. calabash *n.*: A receptacle made from a dried,
hollowed-out gourd.

RESPONDING TO THE SELECTION

Your Response

1. What thoughts do you have about home when
you are away from it?

Recalling

2. Where is the speaker? Where is his mother?

Interpreting

3. What is the speaker's attitude toward his
mother? Explain.
4. What images does the speaker use to contrast
his life as a youth and his current life?

Applying

5. People often remember things from their early
childhood more vividly than recent events. Why
do you think this is so?

CRITICAL THINKING AND READING

Appreciating Regional Words

The landscape and culture of Jamaica, where
James Berry grew up, have had a strong influence on the way English is spoken there. Names
for foods, such as *cassava* and *calabash,* may
be unfamiliar to North Americans, and sentences
are formed in unusual ways.

1. What regional spelling does Berry use for
grandfather? What North American terms are
like it?
2. What part of speech does "a-crush" in line 18
serve as? How is it more vivid than words that
might be used in its place?
3. What do you think the meaning of the phrase
"hang no accomplishments" is?

LEARNING OPTION

Multicultural Activity. Find out more about
plants used as food in Jamaica. In particular,
investigate the spices for which the island is
famous. What dishes are they used in? What
medicinal properties do they have? Report your
findings or prepare a Jamaican dish for class.

From Lucy: Englan' Lady

James Berry

You ask me 'bout the lady. Me dear,
old center here still shine
with Queen. She affec' the place
like the sun: not comin' out oft'n
5   an' when it happ'n everybody's out
smilin', as she wave a han'
like a seagull flyin' slow slow.

An' you know she come from
dust free rooms an' velvet
10 an' diamond. She make you feel
this on-an'-on[1] town, London,
where long long time deeper than mind.[2]
An' han's after han's[3] die away,
makin' streets, putt'n' up bricks,
15 a piece of brass, a piece of wood
an' plantin' trees: an' it give
a car a halfday job gett'n' through.

An' Leela, darlin', no, I never
meet the Queen in flesh. Yet
20 sometimes, deep deep, I sorry for her.

---

1. on-an'-on: Extraordinary.
2. deeper . . . mind: More than can be
comprehended.
3. han's after han's: Many generations.

Everybody expec' a show
from her, like she a space touris'
on earth. An' darlin', unless
you can go home an' scratch up⁴
25   you' husban', it mus' be hard
strain keepin' good graces for
all hypocrite faces.

Anyhow, me dear, you know what
ole time people say,
30   "Bird sing sweet for its nest."⁵

---

4. scratch up: Lose your temper at.
5. "Bird . . . nest": Jamaican proverb, referring to
the nightingale's habit of singing loudest near its
nest. It means, "Those closest to home are the most
contented."

RESPONDING TO THE SELECTION

Your Response
1. What kind of person do you imagine Lucy to be?
2. Do you find her description of Queen Elizabeth insightful? Explain.

Recalling
3. To whom is the poem addressed?
4. Where is the speaker of the poem?
5. According to Lucy, how is the Queen like the sun?

Interpreting
6. What problems does Lucy think the Queen has as a result of her position?
7. What perception of the Queen does Lucy illustrate by quoting the proverb in line 30?
8. This poem is one of several in which Berry employs Lucy as his speaker. A recent immigrant in England, she writes letters home to Jamaica. What West Indian sensibilities are expressed in this "letter"?

9. What does Berry's attitude toward Lucy seem to be?

Applying
10. Lucy uses an old Jamaican proverb to make a point to her friend Leela. What common sayings do you use when trying to get your meaning across?

LEARNING OPTION

Speaking and Listening. Much of the charm in this poem comes from Berry's evocation of Lucy's Jamaican dialect. In fact, this is a poem that should be read aloud to be fully appreciated. You might want to listen to a recording of West Indian poetry or fiction to hear the sound of the dialect before practicing the poem yourself. Berry himself offers the following advice for reading a poem in Jamaican dialect: ". . . Feel out the rhythms. Feel it re-created. Then express it with your own easy natural voice." After you have practiced, read the poem aloud in class.

CROSS CURRENTS

London Moves to Broadway

THE BRITISH INVASION

Although it's commonly supposed that the British have invaded the American stage only recently, they've actually been treading our boards from the very beginning. Take musicals, for example—those entertaining productions in which a story is told by a combination of spoken dialogue and musical numbers. America claims the first musical —*The Black Crook* (1866)—but England says hers were better. Perhaps we can't settle that dispute, but no one can argue that British musicals were not exported to America from the very beginning. For example, only five years after England's first musical comedy—Osmond Carr's 1892 *In Town*—debuted in London, it was staged in New York.

The balance of trade leveled out somewhat in the next few years, as musical comedy became more firmly established. *The Belle of New York* premiered in New York in 1897, but achieved its major success a year later in London, where it became the first American musical to run for over a year. On the other hand, *Florodora* was a hit in London in 1899 but ran even longer in New York after opening there in 1900. The balance was still tipped in England's favor, however. Although the American stage prospered during the next few years, musicals imported from England (and Vienna!) continued to hold sway here in the early years of the twentieth century.

A SUDDEN SHIFT

Things shifted suddenly with the outbreak of World War I. Swollen with anti-German feeling, Americans no longer wanted European musicals. At the same time, English playwrights suffered a dry spell, and American playwrights and composers flowered as never before. Jerome Kern, Cole Porter, and Irving Berlin set Broadway ablaze with a series of magnificent productions. Oscar Hammerstein II set toes tapping on both sides of the Atlantic with his catchy lyrics. Al Jolson crooned the smash hits from George Gershwin's musicals. Many of these productions found their way to British shores.

After a slow start in the early twenties, American musicals stormed American and British footlights. Fred Astaire and his sister Adele hoofed their way through the first musical collaboration of brothers George and Ira Gershwin; the team of Richard Rodgers and Lorenzo Hart debuted in 1925. In 1927 and 1928 more than fifty musicals opened on Broadway. Paul Robeson sang the haunting song "Ol' Man River" in the 1928 London production of the hit *Show Boat.* The heyday of the American musical continued into the thirties, with the first Pulitzer Prize awarded to a musical (*Of Thee I Sing,* 1931). The American musical continued to grow in the forties and fifties with such hits as Rodgers and Hammerstein's *South Pacific* (1949) and *The King and I* (1951), and Lerner and Loewe's *My Fair Lady* (1956).

SIGNS OF REVIVAL

Meanwhile, the English musical had been showing signs of revival, most notably with the 1960 hit *Oliver!*, seen in New York in 1963. The heyday of the American musical was over; the stage was set for London's invasion of Broadway. Critics—and audiences—agree that England produced the only major theatrical talent of the seventies and eighties.

In an interesting reversal, a number of British musical hits debuted in America and then traveled back home. The most famous of these is the remarkable *Jesus Christ Superstar*, a musical based on the life of Christ. The smash team of lyricist Tim Rice and composer Andrew Lloyd Webber opened the play first in New York in 1971, then journeyed back with it to London a year later. But for their next success, *Evita*, the duo returned to the old pattern: This musical opened first in London in 1978, then a year later in New York. In the same decade, the American stage also imported England's *Billy*, a musical based on the play *Billy Liar*; *The Good Companions*; *Joseph and the Amazing Technicolor Dreamcoat*; and *The Moony Shapiro Songbook* as well as a number of excellent dramas. Lloyd Webber scored big again in 1981 when he brought *Cats* to the New York stage. Based on T. S. Eliot's *Old Possum's Book of Practical Cats*, this dazzling production is marked by extravagant makeup, costumes, and creative staging.

THE 1980's

By the eighties, England had become seemingly the only source of successful musicals; of the twenty-one shows on Broadway at the beginning of 1983, more than a third came from England's theater district, the West End. And these shows were good, too:

In 1987, for example, twelve of Broadway's nineteen Tony Awards went to musicals that originated on the London stage. The musical *Me and My Girl*, for example, catapulted English actor Robert Lindsay to stardom. But the brightest light on Broadway belongs to Andrew Lloyd Webber.

Webber added to his string of commercial successes when he exported his musical wonderland *Starlight Express*; more noted for its roller skating and clever set than for its plot, it nonetheless delighted packed audiences. His astonishingly successful *Phantom of the Opera* is a quasi-operatic retelling of the monster-meets-girl melodrama.

Perhaps the most striking example of the way London has moved to Broadway is *Follies*, not so much an import from the West End as a complete restaging of American Stephen Sondheim's 1971 musical. Although the original version won five Tony Awards during its Broadway run, it lost nearly its entire investment. British producer Cameron Mackintosh's invitation to Sondheim to "have a wee think" about the play resulted in an entirely revamped show. The three-million-dollar London production opened to huge advance sales, and Mackintosh hopes to bring *Follies* back to Broadway, a rare reverse transfer that would be both welcome yet humbling.

As one British paper put it, "The Great White Way seems to have become an overseas colony of the West End."

YOUR WRITING PROCESS

RETELLING A STORY

How would you give a well-known story a new twist? Novelist John Gardner decided to retell the Anglo-Saxon epic *Beowulf* from the monster's point of view rather than the hero's! (See the feature on Gardner's novel *Grendel*, pages 50–51.) He also could have updated this old tale by turning it into a science-fiction saga. Which of the stories in this unit can you imagine retelling from a different point of view or with an updated setting?

> **Focus**
> **Assignment:** Update a story or tell it from a different point of view.
> **Purpose:** To find new meaning in an existing story.
> **Audience:** Readers of a student literary magazine.

Prewriting

1. Recall and reflect. Skim the stories in this unit. Make a mental note of the setting and point of view in each, especially in the ones you remember most vividly. How could you update them or tell them from a different point of view? Jot down notes as you skim. Then choose the story that you would like to retell.

2. What could change? For each possible retelling, do some freewriting to determine how you might alter the original story. If you get stuck, simply rewrite the question to spark new thoughts.

> **Student Model**
> "The Rocking-Horse Winner": What could change? The rocking horse could be a video game that the boy plays again and again. Instead of playing the horse races, the older characters could be playing the lottery. What else could change? The boy could get lucky numbers from his video game. The story could still be about luck and obsession, gambling and money. The time and place would change. And the characters' names and the things they say and do would change, too.

3. Review the story. Don't rely exclusively on your memory of the story. Once you have developed a general idea for your retelling, carefully review each paragraph. As you do so, make notes about how you can creatively change its details.

Drafting

1. Leave room to revise. Give yourself plenty of white space to make changes. Whether you are handwriting, typing, or word processing, leave space between lines and allow wide margins. This extra space will enable you to edit your new version of the story more easily.

2. Use the original story as a pattern. Refer to your freewriting notes for ideas, but also use the story itself as a pattern. As you go through it, change key details to update the story or to reflect another point of view.

Student Model

Updating of "The Rocking-Horse Winner": Natalie Morgan was cute, but she was unlucky. She thought she felt love for Vincent when they got married, but soon she realized that it must have been indigestion. She even had trouble loving her three children, but she never let on. She went to PTA meetings, baked chocolate chip cookies every week, and took the children to the art museum once a month, but she did not love them.

Student Model

"Araby" from Mangan's sister's point of view rather than the boy's: I used to live on North Richmond Street with my brother Mangan. He would play noisily with his friends, and in the evening I would have to go out and call him in to tea. When I did, there was always a shy boy who stood by the railings and watched me.

Revising and Editing

1. Read dialogue with a classmate. Ask a classmate to read through the dialogue with you to check its believability and smoothness. Often our ears can hear what our eyes miss.

2. Use words that carry meaning. Work hard to choose the most precise words possible. For example, don't just settle for "He sat in the chair." Find a word or phrase that conveys a more specific image and a richer connotation: *white wicker rocking chair, worn-out recliner, bar stool,* or *leather ottoman.* And *how* did he *sit?* Did he *slump, lounge,* or *perch?*

3. Pay attention to pronouns. A pronoun that does not agree with its antecedent can stop your readers in their tracks and make you look like a clumsy, careless writer. Question each pronoun, and make sure that it agrees with its antecedent in gender, number, and case. Remember that certain indefinite pronouns such as *no one* and *everybody* are always singular.

Grammar Tip

Pay particular attention to your use of *who* and *whom.* *Who,* nominative case, replaces words such as *he, she,* or *they. Whom,* objective case, replaces words such as *him, her,* or *them.* [For more on *who* and *whom,* see the Handbook of Grammar and Revising Strategies.]

Options for Publishing

• Submit your retelling to your school's literary magazine. Accompany it with a letter explaining that you have retold a well-known story.

• Read your version of the story aloud to the class. Have them comment on the way in which you have altered the original.

• Find a piece of fine art to accompany your retold story and display both on the bulletin board of your classroom. After you have shared your story, keep it in your portfolio.

Reviewing Your Writing Process

1. Which editing suggestion helped you the most as you revised your story? Could you use this tip for other assignments? Why or why not?

2. Did retelling the story give you a better appreciation for the work that went into writing it? Explain.

Literary Map of Great Britain

N

Outer Hebrides

Isle of Skye

Inner Hebrides

SCOTTISH HIGHLANDS

Johnson and
Boswell tour
Hebrides, 1773

ATLANTIC OCEAN

King Duncan's palace (Macbeth)

● Macbeth's castle

Loch Ness

Dunsinane
(Macbeth slain)

SCOTLAND

NORTH SEA

Sir Patrick Spens
and Scottish lords drown:
"The Seafarer"

Loch
Lomond

Dumferling *"Sir Patrick Spens"*

● **Ayshire**
Burn's "Sweet Afton,"
"To a Mouse"

English-Scottish border.
Setting of many early ballads

**NORTHERN
IRELAND**

Sligo
Yeat's
"Lake Isle
of Innisfree"

IRISH SEA

Kelloe
E.B. Browning born

Lake District
Wordsworth's poetry

Whitby
Caedmon's hymns

Haworth Moor
● Setting of *Jane Eyre*

Humberside
Marvell lives, writes

Dublin ✪
Birthplace of Steele,
Swift, Shaw, Wilde,
Yeats, Joyce

IRELAND

Wakefield
Medieval mystery
and morality plays

Gawain vs.
Green Knight

A Shropshire Lad,
Housman

Lichfield
Samuel Johnson
born

Kilcolman ●
Spenser composes
Fairie Queene

Stratford-on-Avon
Shakespeare

ENGLAND

WALES

Cambridge*

Swansea
Dylan Thomas's poetry

Wordsworth's Tintern Abbey

Stonehenge

● **Oxford***

Thames River

● **London** ✪

Canterbury
Destination of
Chaucer's pilgrims;
Marlowe born

Salisbury
Geo. Herbert's
Temple

Route of
Chaucer's pilgrims

Dorset
Hardy's Wessex
("Three Strangers")

Tintagel
Legendary birthplace
of King Arthur

Dean Prior
Herrick a
country parson
here

Portsmouth
Dickens born

Dover
Arnold's
"Dover Beach"

ENGLISH CHANNEL

FRANCE

Rulers of England and Great Britain (including dates of reign)

This chart presents the rulers of England and Great Britain from Anglo-Saxon times to the present. The earliest English kings were rulers not of England in its entirety but of kingdoms within England. The first of an unbroken succession of kings or queens of England was William I (1066-87). In 1707, upon the passage of the Act of Union, which united England and Scotland, Queen Anne became the first monarch of Great Britain.

[Kingdom of Kent]
Ethelbert, 560-616

[Kingdom of Northumbria]
Ethelfrith, 593-617
Edwin, 617-633
Oswald, 635-642
Oswy, 642-670
Ecgfrith, 670-685

[Kingdom of Mercia]
Penda, 626-655
Ethelbald, 716-757
Offa II, 757-796
Cenulf, 796-821

[Kingdom of Wessex]
Ine, 688-726

Saxons and Danes
Egbert, 802-39
Æthelwulf, 839-58
Æthelbald, 858-60
Æthelbert, 860-65
Æthelred, 865-71
Alfred, 871-99
Edward 899-924
Athelstan, 924-39
Edmund, 946-55
Edred, 946-55
Edway, 955-59
Edgar, 959-78
Edward (the Martyr), 978-1016
Æthelred (the Unready), 978-1016
Edmund (Ironside), son of Æthelred 1016
Canute, by conquest, 1016-35
Harold I (Harefoot), 1037-40
Harthacunute, 1040-42
Edward (the Confessor), 1042-66
Harold II, 1066

House of Normandy
William I The Conquerer, 1066-87
William II, 1087-1100
Henry I, 1100-1135

House of Blois
Stephen, 1135-54

House of Plantagenet
Henry II, 1154-89
Richard I, (Coeur de Lion) 1189-99
John, 1199-1216
Henry III, 1216-72
Edward I, 1272-1307
Edward II, 1302-27
Edward III, 1327-77
Richard II, 1327-99

House of Lancaster
Henry IV, 1399-1413
Henry V, 1413-22
Henry VI, 1422-61, 1470-99

House of York
Edward IV, 1461-70, 1471-83
Edward V, 1483
Richard III, 1483-85

House of Tudor
Henry VII, 1485-1509
Henry VIII, 1509-47
Edward VI, 1547-53
Mary I, 1553-58
Elizabeth I, 1558-1603

House of Stuart
James I (James VI of Scotland), 1603-25
Charles I, 1625-49

Commonwealth and Protectorate
Council of State, 1649-53
Cromwell, Oliver, lord protector, 1653-58
Cromwell, Richard, lord protector, 1658-59

House of Stuart (restored)
Charles II, 1660-85
James II, 1685-88
William III, ruled jointly with Mary II, 1689-94; ruled alone, 1694-1702
Mary II, ruled jointly with William III, 1689-94
Anne, 1702-14

House of Hanover
George I, 1714-27
George II, 1727-60
George III, 1760-1820
George IV, 1820-30
William IV, 1830-37
Victoria, 1837-1901

House of Saxe-Coburg-Gotha
Edward VII, 1901-10

House of Windsor
(family name changed during World War I)
George V, 1910-36
Edward VIII, 1936
George VI, 1936-1952
Elizabeth II, 1952

HANDBOOK OF THE WRITING PROCESS
Lesson 1: Prewriting

You may wish that you could just sit down, spend a few minutes, and magically write a polished paragraph or essay. Unfortunately, most writing is not so easy. It takes time and hard work. Nevertheless, you can write more confidently if you understand that writing is a process, not a single step. Most writers go through these stages.

1. *Prewriting:* getting and organizing ideas for writing
2. *Drafting:* writing down ideas in a rough first draft
3. *Revising:* reworking and improving the written draft
4. *Proofreading:* finding and correcting errors in spelling, punctuation, capitalization, grammar, usage, and manuscript form
5. *Publishing:* sharing the writing with other people

STEP 1: ANALYZE THE SITUATION

Instead of immediately starting to write your paper, begin by thinking through what you need and want to accomplish. Ask yourself the following questions.

1. *Assignment:* To what extent does the assignment define what you should do? Does it specify a topic? Does it require a paragraph or an essay? Does the assignment contain any key words such as *explain, compare, identify, retell, discuss, contrast, describe, cite, analyze, define, develop,* or *show*?
2. *Topic:* What will you write about? How can you state your subject precisely? Is your topic exact and narrow enough? Can you sum it up

in a topic sentence or thesis statement that suggests your position or viewpoint?
3. *Purpose:* What is your goal? Will you explain, describe, tell, or argue? Do you want your reader to react by understanding, imagining, being entertained, or being persuaded?
4. *Audience:* Who will read your writing? What should you assume about the reader's background and knowledge?
5. *Voice:* How should your writing sound to a reader? Should it sound informal, formal, calm, emotional, logical, ironic, or straightforward?
6. *Content:* What information will you need to provide about the topic? Can you gather all the information you need by analyzing your reading or by thinking about the topic? Do you need to do research? If so, what resources should you draw on?
7. *Form:* How will you shape your writing? Is it to be creative—a play, a poem, or a story? Is it to be an essay, a paragraph, a report, or a term paper? What parts will the writing include? What plan will you use to arrange the parts? What will come first, second, third, and so on?

STEP 2: MAKE A PLAN

After analyzing your writing situation, you can plan what to do next. Often you will need to find a topic or to narrow the one assigned. Then you can return to any unresolved questions that remain. For example, suppose that you are assigned an informal essay explaining to your classmates three techniques used in a poem of your choice. Your assignment defines your purpose (to explain), audience (classmates), and voice (informal). Your essay's topic (the poem and your point about it), content (your explanation and examples of three techniques), and form (the order of the paragraphs) will be clearer after you select and analyze a specific poem.

STEP 3: GATHER INFORMATION

Your assignment may or may not tell you exactly what topic to work on. Either way, instead of just hoping for a brilliant idea, try one of these prewriting methods to get ideas for or about a topic.

1. *Freewriting:* Write about the topic for several minutes. Don't worry about spelling, punctuation, or logical connections between ideas. Simply get down on paper everything that comes to mind about the topic. Later you can rephrase your best ideas.
2. *Clustering:* On a blank piece of paper, write and circle your topic. Add other ideas, circling them and using lines to connect them to the topic.
3. *Questioning:* Act like a reporter and ask questions about your topic. Begin your questions with *who, what, where, when, why,* and *how.*
4. *Listing:* Make a list of events in sequence, pro and con arguments, differences, similarities, subtypes, examples, or causes.
5. *Analyzing:* Identify the parts of your topic. That is, look for subtopics and for relationships among the parts and the whole.
6. *Researching:* Look up terms, details, or whatever background you need to know.

STEP 4: ORGANIZE YOUR NOTES

After gathering ideas, you are ready to organize your material and to work out a rough outline. Whatever order you choose should suit your topic, be logical, build from idea to idea, and interest a reader. Try one of these patterns or the reverse of one of these patterns.

1. *Chronological order:* first to last
2. *Spatial order:* nearest to farthest, topmost to bottommost, and so on
3. *Order of complexity:* simplest to most elaborate
4. *Order of familiarity:* best to least understood
5. *Order of frequency:* most to least numerous
6. *Order of importance:* least to most significant
7. *Order of effectiveness:* least to most convincing

CASE STUDY: PREWRITING

Brian's English teacher assigned an informal paragraph. Brian was to pick a reading that he found especially interesting and then explain briefly how and why he reacted to it as he did.

Brian decided to write about Mary Shelley's Introduction to *Frankenstein.* First he analyzed the writing situation.

- Assignment: paragraph—explain reaction

- Topic: Shelley's Introduction to *Frankenstein*—but what about it?

- Purpose: explain so reader understands

- Audience: Ms. Burton—maybe class? all have read Shelley's essay

- Voice: informal, personal reactions

- Content: why like it? why interesting?

- Form: paragraph—needs topic sentence and examples—which ones? what order?

Brian decided to try freewriting to figure out what to say about his topic.

Shelley wrote this famous story. It is also famous in movies. I thought she must of been a natural writer. Didn't expect her to have trouble writing. Byron and Shelley wrote OK stories even tho they are famous poets. But she can't get an idea. After hearing about these experiments she gets this vision. She still doesn't think she can write a story, then she sees its her story.

Brian saw two main ideas in his freewriting: Mary Shelley had written a famous story, and she had trouble writing, just as he did. He did not know how to develop the first idea but he thought he could figure out a topic sentence about the second. He made this rough outline, using details from the essay.

- Topic: I did not expect Shelley to have trouble writing.
    She can't get an idea—others can
    She gets a vision
    Finally she sees that it's her story
    conclusion?

ACTIVITIES AND ASSIGNMENTS

A. Answer these questions about the case study:

1. Review Brian's freewriting and rough outline. Did he finally resolve all the questions about his writing situation? Revise his first chart to include his later decisions.

2. Review Brian's freewriting. What mistakes in grammar or phrasing did Brain make? Why didn't he take the time to correct these at this stage?

3. What order did Brian use to arrange the three details in his rough outline?

B. Choose a selection that interests you. Follow these prewriting steps to prepare for writing an informal paragraph about it:

1. Make notes to analyze your writing situation.

2. Decide what your next step should be. Use one of the prewriting techniques explained above to gather ideas.

3. Work out a rough outline, using your prewriting notes. Make sure that you have a specific topic and an idea about how to organize your ideas. Save all of your notes.

Lesson 2: Drafting and Revising

DRAFTING YOUR PAPER

Drafting is the process of putting ideas down on paper. The following guidelines will help you with the drafting stage of the writing process:

1. Choose a drafting method that is right for you. Some people like to make a detailed outline or prewriting plan and then write a slow, meticulous draft based on this outline or plan. Other people like to write a very quick and very rough draft and then revise this draft several times.

2. Whichever drafting method you choose, it is a good idea to do at least some planning before writing. In other words, you should have some idea about what you are going to say and in what order. You may wish to make a rough outline before you begin drafting.

3. Concentrate on getting your ideas down on paper. You can revise and proofread your work later.

4. Be open to new ideas that occur to you as you write. If necessary, change your writing plan to accommodate these new ideas.

REVISING YOUR DRAFT

Revising is the process of reworking and refining your draft. To revise a paper, read it over carefully and ask yourself the questions in the Checklist for Revision.

If your answer to any of the questions is "no," rework your draft until you can answer "yes." You may find that you need to revise your draft several times.

CASE STUDY: DRAFTING AND REVISING

Brian used his prewriting notes to begin writing his informal paragraph on Mary Shelley's Introduction to *Frankenstein*. After reviewing the assignment, his freewriting, and his rough out-

---

CHECKLIST FOR REVISION

Topic and Purpose
- [ ] Is my topic clear?
- [ ] Does the writing have a specific purpose?
- [ ] Does the writing achieve its purpose?

Audience
- [ ] Will everything I have written be clear to my audience?
- [ ] Will my audience find the writing interesting?
- [ ] Will my audience respond in the way I would like?

Voice and Word Choice
- [ ] Is the impression my writing conveys the one I intended it to convey?
- [ ] Is my language appropriately formal or informal?
- [ ] Have I avoided vague, undefined terms?
- [ ] Have I used vivid, specific nouns, verbs, and adjectives?
- [ ] Have I avoided jargon that my audience will not understand?
- [ ] Have I avoided clichés?
- [ ] Have I avoided slang, odd connotations, euphemisms, and gobbledygook (except for novelty or humor)?

Content/Development
- [ ] Have I avoided including unnecessary or unrelated ideas?
- [ ] Have I developed my topic completely?
- [ ] Have I supplied examples or details that support the statements that I have made?
- [ ] Are my sources of information unbiased, up-to-date, and authoritative?
- [ ] Are my quotations verbatim, or word for word?

Form
- [ ] Have I followed a logical method of organization?
- [ ] Have I used transitions, or connecting words, to make the organization clear?
- [ ] Does the writing have a clear introduction, body, and conclusion?

line, Brian decided that he needed to work on a topic sentence. Here's how he drafted and revised that topic sentence:

- Topic idea: I did not expect Shelley to have trouble writing.

- Topic sentence: I enjoyed reading it because I found out about her trouble writing which was not what I expected.

- Revised version: I enjoyed reading Mary Shelley's Introduction to *Frankenstein* because I found out about something I didn't expect—that she had trouble coming up with ideas for writing.

Next Brian used this topic sentence to get started drafting his paragraph, shown at right.

ACTIVITIES AND ASSIGNMENTS

A. Answer the following questions about Brian's revisions of his rough draft:

1. What transitions did Brian add to his paragraph?
2. Why did Brian delete the sentence, "She is just real terrified"?
3. Why did Brian change some of the wording in his sentence about Mary Shelley's vision?
4. Why did he add the last sentences?
5. What other changes did Brian make? Why did he make these changes?

B. Using your notes from the preceding lesson, draft and revise your own paragraph. Follow these steps:

1. Review your notes and your rough outline.
2. Work on your topic sentence, refining it so that your specific topic and your approach to or attitude toward the topic is clear.
3. If necessary, revise your rough outline. Note your subtopics (the parts of your main topic),

and add any new significant details that occur to you.

4. Use your revised topic sentence to start your paragraph.
5. Write the body of your paragraph, presenting the subtopics and details from your outline.
6. Write a conclusion.
7. Revise your draft using the Checklist for Revision on page 1169. Keep all of your notes and drafts.

I enjoyed reading Mary Shelley's Introduction to Frankenstein because I found out about something I didn't expect—that she had trouble coming up with ideas for writing Since Her story has become so famous, I thought Instead, that Shelley was just a natural writer. I found out, she had trouble getting an idea for a story. Even though her husband, Shelley, Byron, and Polidori had wrote theres. She could not think of an idea. imaginative a terrifying Finally she has this weird vision about an ex- creating life. periment in science. She is just real terrified. At first, recognize She just does not see this as her story she just wishes she did write something just as frightening creepy. Then she realizes that she has her this is idea for a story. Her problem surprised me but they also reassured me. I hadn't expected to find out that a writer like her had the same writing problem I usually do.

Lesson 3: Proofreading and Publishing

USING EDITORIAL SYMBOLS

The last lesson discussed reorganizing, adding, cutting, and otherwise revising your writing. Once you have made these major revisions, you are ready to make more detailed changes such as adding punctuation, correcting capitalization, and refining word order. The editorial symbols on the right are especially helpful for marking such changes on your final draft.

PROOFREADING YOUR FINAL DRAFT

Proofreading is your last careful review of your paper. As you proofread, look for minor errors and for rough passages that you missed earlier. If possible, let your revised draft sit for a few hours or a day before going over it. Taking a break from your manuscript should make it easier for you to see flaws. Ask yourself the questions listed on the next page as you proofread.

Use a dictionary, a style manual, or a writing textbook to check spellings and rules for punctuation, capitalization, and manuscript form. Once your paper has been proofread, make a clean final copy, if necessary. Check your final version carefully to catch any errors in copying.

PUBLISHING, OR SHARING YOUR WORK WITH OTHERS

After proofreading your paper, you are ready to share it with readers. When you write papers for school, your teachers will be your primary readers. Nevertheless, you or your class can expand your audience in the following ways:
1. Exchange papers with a small group of students from your class.
2. Read your paper aloud to your class or to another class.
3. Share your writing with your friends and relatives.
4. Make a booklet of your writing at the end of the semester or year.
5. Make a class booklet with a paper by every student.
6. Contribute some of your writing to the school literary magazine.

EDITORIAL SYMBOLS		
Symbol	Meaning	Example
(move symbol)	move text	She never again published because of this
ℓ or —	delete	in this ~~this~~ book
∧	insert	the poem's *rhyme* scheme
⌒	no space	mono logue
⊙	add period	a line ends It
∧	add comma	sonnets, odes and other lyric poems
∨	add apostrophe	writers style
∨	add quotation marks	The Train from Rhodesia
∼	transpose	to wildly run
¶	begin paragraph	the stanza. The next image
/	lower case	The Poet writes
≡	capitalize	in "Shore woman"

7. If your school does not have a literary magazine, start one.
8. Contribute your writing to your school or community newspaper.
9. Enter writing contests for student writers sponsored by community groups or by magazines.

10. Send your writing to magazines that publish student writing.

CASE STUDY: PROOFREADING AND PUBLISHING

Brian revised his draft paragraph and made a new copy, including all his additions and changes. Then he used the Checklist for Proofreading on the left to locate any remaining problems. This is Brian's proofread draft:

CHECKLIST FOR PROOFREADING

Grammar and Usage
- ☐ Are all of my sentences complete? That is, have I avoided sentence fragments?
- ☐ Do all of my sentences express only one complete thought? That is, have I avoided run-on sentences?
- ☐ Do the verbs I have used agree with their subjects?
- ☐ Have all the words in my paper been used correctly? Am I sure about the meanings of all these words?
- ☐ Is the thing being referred to by each pronoun (*I, me, this, each,* etc.) clear?
- ☐ Have I used adjectives and adverbs correctly?

Spelling
- ☐ Am I absolutely sure that each word has been spelled correctly?

Punctuation
- ☐ Does every sentence end with a punctuation mark?
- ☐ Have I used commas, semicolons, colons, hyphens, dashes, parentheses, quotation marks, and apostrophes correctly?

Capitalization
- ☐ Have I capitalized any words that should not be capitalized?
- ☐ Should I capitalize any words that I have not capitalized?

Manuscript Form
- ☐ Have I indented the first line(s) of my paragraph(s)?
- ☐ Have I written my name and the page number in the top right-hand corner of each page?
- ☐ Have I double-spaced the manuscript?
- ☐ Is my manuscript neat and legible?

I enjoyed reading Mary Shelley's Introduction to <u>Frankenstein</u> because I found out about ~~something I didn't expect~~ that she had trouble coming up with ideas for writing. Since her story ∧*about Frankenstein* has become so famous, I thought Shel*e*ly was just a natural writer. Instead, I found out that she had trouble getting an idea for ~~a~~ *her* story. Even though her husband, Byron, and Polidori had ∧*written* ~~wrote theres~~ ∧*their stories*, she could not think of an idea. Finally she *had an* ~~has this~~ imaginative vision about a terrifying experiment in creating life. At first, she ~~does~~ *did* not recognize this as her story, she just ~~wish~~ *wished* ~~es~~ she ~~old~~ *could* write something as frightening. Then she ~~realizes~~ *realized* that this ~~is~~ *was* her idea for a story. Her problems surprised me, but they also reassured me. I hadn't expected to find out that a writer like her had the same writing problem I usually do.

Brian recopied his paper, read it through for careless errors, and then exchanged papers with a small group in class.

ACTIVITIES AND ASSIGNMENTS

A. Answer the following questions about Brian's proofreading in the case study.

1. Explain why Brian made each change that he did.
2. What other changes do you think Brian might have made? Explain why you would have made those changes.

B. Proofread and publish your draft from the preceding lesson on Drafting and Revising. Follow these steps:

1. Use the Checklist for Proofreading on page 1172 to review your draft. Correct any problems that the checklist helps you to identify.
2. Recopy your corrected paper. Read through this final version to make sure that you copied everything correctly.
3. Share your draft with your teacher and with the other students in class.

HANDBOOK OF GRAMMAR AND REVISING STRATEGIES

STRATEGIES FOR REVISING PROBLEMS IN GRAMMAR AND STANDARD USAGE

Problems of Sentence Structure

■ Run-on Sentences

GUIDE FOR REVISING: A run-on sentence results when no punctuation or coordinating conjunction separates two or more independent clauses. A run-on sentence also occurs when only a comma is used to join two or more independent clauses.

Strategy 1: Form two sentences by using a period to separate independent clauses.

First Draft At Cambridge University Margaret Drabble concentrated on the theater, after graduation she joined the Royal Shakespeare Company.

Revision At Cambridge University Margaret Drabble concentrated on the theater. After graduation she joined the Royal Shakespeare Company.

Strategy 2: Separate independent clauses with a semicolon.

First Draft Beowulf is a typical epic hero he embodies the highest ideals of his culture: loyalty, courage, and generosity.

Revision Beowulf is a typical epic hero; he embodies the highest ideals of his culture: loyalty, courage, and generosity.

Model From Literature The breeze freshened; a great brilliance burst upon the lagoon, sparkled on the rippling water. —*Conrad, p. 836*

Strategy 3: Use a comma and a coordinating conjunction (*and, but, or, for, yet, so*) to join the two sentences.

First Draft Nadine Gordimer has long been one of the most celebrated contemporary novelists writing in English in 1991 she won a Nobel Prize.

Revision Nadine Gordimer has long been one of the most celebrated contemporary novelists writing in English, and in 1991 she won a Nobel Prize.

Strategy 4: Make one clause subordinate by adding a subordinating conjunction.

First Draft His novel *The Rainbow* was declared obscene D. H. Lawrence felt he could no longer remain in England and left the country for extended travels overseas.

Revision   After his novel *The Rainbow* was declared obscene, D. H. Lawrence felt he could no longer remain in England and left the country for extended travels overseas.

■ Fragments

GUIDE FOR REVISING: A fragment is a group of words that does not express a complete thought. Although a fragment may begin with a capital letter and end with a period, it is only part of a sentence because it lacks a subject, a verb, or both.

Strategy: **Add the necessary sentence parts to make a phrase fragment into a complete sentence with a subject and a verb.**

First Draft   Much of metaphysical poetry focuses on religious themes. In their verse used complex, intellectual metaphors called conceits.

Revision   Much of metaphysical poetry focuses on religious themes. In their verse, poets such as John Donne and George Herbert used complex, intellectual metaphors called conceits.

■ Mixed Constructions

GUIDE FOR REVISING: A mixed construction results when a sentence begins with one pattern and ends with another.

Strategy: **Make sure that you use a single structural pattern consistently throughout each sentence.**

First Draft   Boswell's *The Life of Samuel Johnson* pioneers the form of the literary biography, and also many intriguing insights into eighteenth-century life in London are offered by the work.

Revision   Boswell's *The Life of Samuel Johnson* pioneers the form of the literary biography and also offers many insights into eighteenth-century life in London.

Model From Literature   Thy voice is on the rolling air;
   I hear thee where the waters run;
   Thou standest in the rising sun,
And in the setting thou art fair.   —*Tennyson, p. 709*

Problems of Clarity and Coherence

■ Effective Transitions

GUIDE FOR REVISING: Transitions are words or phrases that help the reader by signaling connections between words, sentences, and paragraphs.

Strategy 1:	Use transitions to indicate chronological order. Transitions may be used to indicate frequency, duration, or a particular time.
First Draft	Macbeth heard the witches' prophecy and began to reflect on his future prospects.
Revision	When Macbeth heard the witches' prophecy, he began to reflect on his future prospects.
Model From Literature	"But since the sun of today rose she hears nothing. She hears not me—me!" —*Conrad, p. 830*

Strategy 2:	Use transitions to indicate spatial relationships. Transitions may be used to show closeness, distance, or direction.
First Draft	In "The Lagoon," Joseph Conrad describes the trees and the river.
Revision	At the beginning of "The Lagoon," Joseph Conrad describes the trees and the river.
Model From Literature	Near it, two tall nibong palms, that seemed to come out of the forests in the background, leaned slightly over the ragged roof, with a suggestion of sad tenderness and care in the droop of their leafy and soaring heads. —*Conrad, p. 829*

Strategy 3:	Use transitions to indicate comparison or contrast, or cause and effect.
First Draft	Tennyson's "The Lady of Shalott" may seem like a simple ballad; the poet's emphasis on the web and the mirror suggests that this work contains some sophisticated symbolic meanings.
Revision	Tennyson's "The Lady of Shalott" may seem like a simple ballad; the poet's emphasis on the web and the mirror, however, suggests that this work contains some sophisticated symbolic meanings.

■ Incomplete and Illogical Comparisons

GUIDE FOR REVISING: When something is omitted from a comparison or only implied, the comparison may be incomplete or illogical.

Strategy 1:	Be sure that a comparison contains only items of a similar kind.
First Draft	The structure of a villanelle is even tighter and more demanding than a sonnet.
Revision	The structure of a villanelle is even tighter and more demanding than that of a sonnet.

Model From Literature	"There's no worse enemy and no better friend than a brother, Tuan, for one brother knows another, and in perfect knowledge is strength for good or evil." —*Conrad, p. 832*

Strategy 2:	**Be sure to include the words *other* or *else* in comparisons that compare one of a group with the rest of the group.**
First Draft	Megan thought that Elizabeth Bowen's "The Demon Lover" was more suspenseful than any contemporary short story she'd read.
Revision	Megan thought that Elizabeth Bowen's "The Demon Lover" was more suspenseful than any other contemporary short story she'd read.
Model From Literature	"I felt that you were more lonely than anybody else in the world," he went on, "and yet, perhaps, that you were the only person in the world who was really, truly alive." —*Mansfield, p. 875*

■ Revising for Pronoun-Antecedent Agreement

GUIDE FOR REVISING: Personal pronouns must agree with their antecedents in number (singular or plural), person (first, second, or third), and gender (masculine, feminine, or neuter).

Strategy 1:	**Make sure that a pronoun used to stand for a noun that appears somewhere else in the sentence agrees in number (singular or plural) with that noun.**
First Draft	Third-world settings and the psychology of human character consistently intrigued Graham Greene, and it often appears in his fiction.
Revision	Third-world settings and the psychology of human character consistently intrigued Graham Greene, and they often appear in his fiction.
Model From Literature	People should not leave looking glasses hanging in their rooms any more than they should leave open checkbooks or letters confessing some hideous crime. —*Woolf, p. 850*

Strategy 2:	**When you use a pronoun to stand for two or more nouns joined by *or* or *nor*, make sure that it is singular. Use a plural personal pronoun if any part of a compound antecedent joined by *or* or *nor* is plural.**
First Draft	Neither Samuel Johnson nor Charles Dickens had their roots in London.

Revision	Neither Samuel Johnson nor Charles Dickens had his roots in London.

Strategy 3:	**When you use a personal pronoun to stand for a singular indefinite pronoun, make sure that it is also singular. Use a plural personal pronoun when the antecedent is a plural indefinite pronoun.**

First Draft	Both Philip Larkin and Ted Hughes are important contemporary voices in British poetry; however, each displays a quite different style in their verse.
Revision	Both Philip Larkin and Ted Hughes are important contemporary voices in British poetry; however, each displays a quite different style in his verse.
Model From Literature	All of Beowulf's Band had jumped from their beds, ancestral Swords raised and ready, determined To protect their prince if they could. *—Beowulf, p. 30*

Strategy 4:	**Do not use a pronoun to stand for a noun unless it is obvious which noun is its antecedent.**

First Draft	Both Daniel Defoe and Samuel Pepys described the Great Plague of 1665, but he wrote a firsthand account.
Revision	Both Daniel Defoe and Samuel Pepys described the Great Plague of 1665, but Pepys wrote a firsthand account.

■ Dangling Modifiers

GUIDE FOR REVISING: A dangling phrase or clause either seems to modify the wrong word or no word at all, because the word it should logically modify has been omitted from the sentence.

Strategy 1:	**Fix a participial phrase by adding the word that the phrase should modify, usually right after or before the phrase.**

First Draft	Having grown up in an age of social ferment, his plays should address the problems of class barriers and "middle-class morality."
Revision	Having grown up in an age of social ferment, Shaw felt that his plays should address the problems of class barriers and "middle-class morality."
Model From Literature	The white man, turning his back upon the setting sun, looked along the empty and broad expanse of the sea-reach. *—Conrad, p. 828*

Strategy 2:	Fix a dangling clause by rewording the sentence.
First Draft	When he was a boy, D. H. Lawrence's father worked in the coal mines near Nottingham.
Revision	When D. H. Lawrence was a boy, his father worked in the coal mines near Nottingham.

■ Misplaced Modifiers

GUIDE FOR REVISING: A modifier placed too far away from the word it modifies is called a misplaced modifier. Misplaced modifiers may seem to modify the wrong word in a sentence. Always place a modifier as close as possible to the word it modifies.

Strategy:	Move the modifying word, phrase, or clause closer to the word it should logically modify.
First Draft	Sir Gawain admits his greed and cowardice to the Green Knight, embarrassed at his failure to live up to the code of chivalry.
Revision	Embarrassed at his failure to live up to the code of chivalry, Sir Gawain admits his greed and cowardice to the Green Knight.
Model From Literature	Recognizing the name, she opened it and read on the top sheet inside: "Reasons for believing G. to be born in 1409." —*Forster, p. 845*

Problems of Consistency

■ Subject-Verb Agreement

GUIDE FOR REVISING: Subject and verb must agree in number. A singular subject needs a singular verb, and a plural subject needs a plural verb.

Strategy 1:	A phrase or clause that interrupts a subject and its verb does not affect subject-verb agreement.
First Draft	The decline of religion and of human values such as loyalty and love are Matthew Arnold's major theme in "Dover Beach."
Revision	The decline of religion and of human values such as loyalty and love is Matthew Arnold's major theme in "Dover Beach."
Model From Literature	My plenteous joys, Wanton in fullness, seek to hide themselves In drops of sorrow. —*Shakespeare, p. 255*

Strategy 2:	**Use a singular verb with two or more singular subjects joined by _or_ or _nor_. When singular and plural subjects are joined by _or_ or _nor_, the verb must agree with the subject closest to it.**
First Draft	Neither Wordsworth nor the other major Romantic poets uses the form of rhymed couplets often.
Revision	Neither Wordsworth nor the other major Romantic poets use the form of rhymed couplets often.
Model From Literature	Great strength or great wisdom is of much value to an individual. —_Boswell, p. 524_

Strategy 3:	**A linking verb must agree with its subject, regardless of the number of its predicate nominative.**
First Draft	Allusions to both the pagan and the Christian religious traditions is a prominent feature of _Beowulf_.
Revision	Allusions to both the pagan and the Christian religious traditions are a prominent feature of _Beowulf_.
Model From Literature	Days are where we live. —_Larkin, p. 1128_

Strategy 4:	**Indefinite pronouns such as _all_, _any_, _more_, _most_, _none_, and _some_ can agree with either a singular or plural verb. The correct usage depends on the meaning given to the pronoun.**
Models From Literature	It was about one o'clock when Paul's mother and father drove up to their house. All was still. —_Lawrence, p. 865_
	Behind them were the servants. All were crawling all over with insects. —_Lessing, p. 925_

■ Inconsistencies in Verb Tense

GUIDE FOR REVISING: Verb tenses should not shift unnecessarily from sentence to sentence or within a single sentence.

Strategy:	**In sentences describing two actions that occurred at different times in the past, the past perfect tense is used for the earlier action.**
First Draft	By the time Milton was born in 1608, the plays of Shakespeare were popular favorites for many years.
Revision	By the time Milton was born in 1608, the plays of Shakespeare had been popular favorites for many years.

| Model From Literature | They hadn't been across the bridge two hours when everybody knew that there were two foreign detectives in town looking for Mr. Calloway—everybody knew, that is to say, except Mr. Calloway, who couldn't talk Spanish. —*Greene, p. 898* |

■ Faulty Parallelism

GUIDE FOR REVISING: Parallel grammatical structures can be two or more words of the same part of speech, two or more phrases of the same type, or two or more clauses of the same type. Correct a sentence containing faulty parallelism by rewording it so that each parallel idea is expressed in the same grammatical structure.

Strategy:	Check to see that the words, phrases, and clauses in series are parallel.
First Draft	In the "General Prologue," Chaucer describes the setting, introduces the pilgrims, and the stage is set for the telling of the Canterbury tales.
Revision	In the "General Prologue," Chaucer describes the setting, introduces the pilgrims, and sets the stage for the telling of the Canterbury tales.
Model From Literature	"You'd like almost everything about Russian life," he said warmly. "It's so informal, so impulsive, so free without question." —*Mansfield, p. 873*

Problems With Incorrect Words or Phrases

■ Nonstandard Pronoun Cases

GUIDE FOR REVISING: Use the nominative case of a personal pronoun for the subject of a sentence, for a predicate nominative, and for the pronoun in a nominative absolute. Use the objective case for the object of any verb or preposition or for the subject of an infinitive.

Strategy 1:	Be sure to identify the case of a personal pronoun correctly when the pronoun is part of a compound construction. You will often find it helpful to confirm the cases of pronouns by rewording the sentence mentally.
First Draft	Seeing a production of *Macbeth* on television helped Ray and I to understand the play better.
Revision	Seeing a production of *Macbeth* on television helped Ray and me to understand the play better.

Model From Literature	We became friends, B. Wordsworth and I. —*Naipaul, p. 961*

Strategy 2:	**Personal pronouns in the possessive case show possession before nouns. The possessive case is also regularly used when a pronoun precedes a gerund.**
First Draft	I thought that me reading "Sir Gawain and the Green Knight" aloud brought the poem to life.
Revision	I thought that my reading "Sir Gawain and the Green Knight" aloud brought the poem to life.
Model From Literature	Upon my going into the church, I entertained myself with the digging of a grave; . . . —*Addison and Steele, p. 487*

Strategy 3:	**In elliptical clauses with *than* or *as,* use the form of the pronoun that you would use if the clause were fully stated.**
First Draft	Ramon knows more about Anglo-Saxon literature and customs than me.
Revision	Ramon knows more about Anglo-Saxon literature and customs than I [know].

■ Wrong Words or Phrases

GUIDE FOR REVISING: Words or phrases that are suitable in one context may be inappropriate in another.

Strategy 1:	**Make sure that the literal meaning of a word or phrase expresses your meaning precisely.**
First Draft	In her introduction to *Frankenstein,* Mary Shelley tells how it all began.
Revision	In her introduction to *Frankenstein,* Mary Shelley describes the circumstances of the novel's genesis.

Strategy 2:	**Be sure that your language is appropriately formal or informal, depending on your writing context.**
First Draft	The speaker in "Do Not Go Gentle into That Good Night" urges his father not to accept death like a wimp.
Revision	The speaker in "Do Not Go Gentle into That Good Night" urges his father not to accept death meekly.

GUIDE FOR REVISING: A double negative is the use of two or more negative words in one clause to express a negative meaning.

Strategy:	**Do not use *but* in its negative sense with another negative. Do not use *barely, hardly,* and *scarcely* with another negative word.**
First Draft	Gerard Manley Hopkins wasn't but a grammar school student when he started to write poetry.
Revision	Gerard Manley Hopkins was but a grammar school student when he started to write poetry.

Problems of Readability

GUIDE FOR REVISING: Varying the length and structure of your sentences will help you to hold your readers' attention.

Strategy 1:	**Combine short, related sentences by using compound, complex, or compound-complex sentences.**
First Draft	Robert Herrick was apprenticed to a wealthy uncle. His uncle was a goldsmith. Herrick went to Cambridge. He was twenty-two years old at the time. He graduated from Cambridge with a master's degree seven years later. He was then ordained as a minister.
Revision	Robert Herrick was apprenticed to a wealthy uncle, who was a goldsmith. When Herrick was twenty-two, he went to Cambridge, from which he graduated seven years later with a master's degree. He was then ordained as a minister.
Model From Literature	After tea in summer while it was still light and warm he would sit in his back garden playing the fiddle, and when he did everybody else came out to listen. —*Sillitoe, p. 940*

Strategy 2:	**Simplify rambling sentences by separating them into simpler sentences or by regrouping ideas.**
First Draft	After Elizabeth Bowen published her first novel, which was called *The Hotel,* in 1927, she wrote for a number of years perfecting her skills during the 1930's, until in 1938 she published, on the eve of World War II, one of her best-known works, *The Death of the Heart,* a novel that traces the interlocking fortunes of a group of Londoners during the 1930's.

Revision	After Elizabeth Bowen published her first novel, *The Hotel,* in 1927, she spent the next decade perfecting her writing skills. In 1938, on the eve of World War II, she published *The Death of the Heart,* one of her best-known works. This novel traced the interlocking fortunes of a group of Londoners during the 1930's.
Model From Literature	Out ran Margaret to join them, looking at the hills. Out came the servants from the kitchen. They all stood and gazed. Over the rocky levels of the mountain was a streak of rust-colored air.

                                                               —Lessing, p. 922

Strategy 3:	**Avoid a series of monotonous sentence openers or a series of sentences that overuse any one particular sentence structure. Vary the sentence openers in a passage.**
First Draft	Gray's theme in these stanzas is that many good people go unnoticed. The humble villagers buried in the churchyard might have been heroic or famous. Many wonderful things in nature remain undiscovered. Many potentially great people never develop their talents.
Revision	In these stanzas Gray's theme is that many good people go unnoticed. For example, he speculates that the humble villagers buried in the churchyard might have been heroic or famous. Just as many wonderful things in nature remain undiscovered, so many potentially great people never develop their talents.

■ Stringy Sentences

GUIDE FOR REVISING: Too many prepositional phrases can make writing wordy and monotonous.

Strategy:	**Eliminate some prepositional phrases to reduce the number of words and make the meaning clearer.**
First Draft	In "My Last Duchess" by Robert Browning, the speaker of the poem is a duke of the Renaissance period in Italy.
Revision	In Robert Browning's "My Last Duchess," the speaker is an Italian Renaissance duke.

■ Overuse of Passive Voice

GUIDE FOR REVISING: Strengthen your writing by using the active voice whenever possible. Passive verbs usually force the reader to wait until the end of the sentence to identify who or what is doing the action.

Strategy:	Change passive verbs to active verbs whenever possible.
First Draft	Greek and Latin were studied at night by Housman, and scholarly articles on classical philology were written by him for academic journals.
Revision	Housman studied Greek and Latin at night, and he wrote scholarly articles on classical philology for academic journals.

Problems of Conciseness

■ Redundancy

GUIDE FOR REVISING: Redundancy is the unnecessary repetition of an idea. It makes writing heavy and dull.

Strategy:	Eliminate redundant words, phrases, and clauses.
First Draft	During the turbulent, unsettled years of the fifteenth century, a novel type of dramatic presentation emerged: the morality play.
Revision	During the turbulent fifteenth century, a new type of drama emerged: the morality play.

■ Unnecessary Intensifiers

GUIDE FOR REVISING: Intensifiers such as *really, very, truly,* and *of course* should be used to strengthen statements. Overuse of these words may weaken a sentence.

Strategy:	Eliminate unnecessary intensifiers from your writing.
First Draft	V. S. Naipaul has acknowledged the really significant influence of Joseph Conrad on his work.
Revision	V. S. Naipaul has acknowledged the significant influence of Joseph Conrad on his work.

Problems of Appropriateness

■ Inappropriate Diction

GUIDE FOR REVISING: Problems of inappropriate diction occur when words or phrases that are generally accepted in informal conversation or writing are inappropriately used in formal writing.

Strategy:	Choose the appropriate level of diction based on your subject, audience, and writing occasion.

First Draft	When Dryden takes a crack at both Ben Jonson and Shake-speare, Shakespeare comes up the winner.
Revision	In his comparison of the two playwrights, Dryden acknowl-edges that he admires Ben Jonson but loves Shakespeare.

■ Inappropriate Imagery

GUIDE FOR REVISING: An image, or a figure of speech, is inap-propriate when the comparison seems overly exaggerated or when the reader cannot easily understand the connection.

Strategy:	**Do not mix metaphors. A comparison that contains many unlike objects may become ludicrous.**
First Draft	After he hears the news of Lady Macbeth's death, Macbeth real-izes that the game is over and that his uphill fight to fend off the opposing forces will probably go up in flames.
Revision	After he hears the news of Lady Macbeth's death, Macbeth real-izes that his desperate struggle to fend off the enemy is a battle he will probably lose.

■ Clichés

GUIDE FOR REVISING: Clichés are expressions that were once fresh and vivid but through overuse now lack force and appeal.

Strategy:	**When you recognize a cliché, you should substitute a fresh expression of your own.**
First Draft	According to A. E. Housman, time flies.
Revision	According to A. E. Housman, we can never recapture our fleet-ing youth.

SUMMARY OF GRAMMAR

Nouns A **noun** is the name of a person, place, or thing. A **common noun** names any one of a class of people, places, or things. A **proper noun** names a specific person, place, or thing.

Common nouns	Proper nouns
writer	Margaret Drabble, E. M. Forster
country	India, Great Britain

Pronouns Pronouns are words that stand for nouns or for words that take the place of nouns. **Personal pronouns** refer to the person speaking; the person spoken to; or the person, place, or thing spoken about.

First Person	I, me, my, mine	we, us, our, ours
Second Person	you, your, yours	you, your, yours
Third Person	he, him, his she, her, hers it, its	they, them, their, theirs

A **reflexive pronoun** ends in -self or -selves and adds information to a sentence by referring to a noun or pronoun near the beginning of the sentence.

An **intensive pronoun** ends in -self or -selves and adds emphasis to a noun or pronoun in a sentence.

> He reminded *himself* that facts are universal property, . . . (reflexive) —*Forster, p. 844*

> The raven *himself* is hoarse
> That croaks the fatal entrance of Duncan
> Under my battlements. (intensive)
> —*Shakespeare, p. 257*

Demonstrative pronouns direct attention to specific people, places, or things.

> *this* cup   *these* cats   *that* saucer   *those* dogs

A **relative pronoun** begins a subordinate clause and connects it to another idea in the sentence.

> Annoyed, she picked up the letter, *which* bore no stamp.   —*Bowen, p. 889*

Interrogative pronouns are used to begin questions.

> "And to *whom* have you written?"
> —*Forster, p. 846*

Indefinite pronouns refer to people, places, or things, often without specifying which ones.

> *Nought's* had, *all's* spent,
> Where our desire is got without content: . . .
> —*Shakespeare, p. 283*

Verbs A **verb** is a word or group of words that expresses time while showing an action, a condition, or the fact that something exists. An **action verb** tells what action someone or something is performing. An action verb is **transitive** if it directs action toward someone or something named in the same sentence.

> *Gather* ye rosebuds while ye may, . . .
> —*Herrick, p. 394*

An action verb is **intransitive** if it does not direct action toward something or someone named in the same sentence.

> The thought *served* as a challenge.
> —*Woolf, p. 853*

A **linking verb** is a verb that connects its subject with a word generally found near the end of the sentence. All linking verbs are intransitive.

> But after some time that order *was* more necessary, . . .   —*Defoe, p. 469*

Helping verbs are verbs that can be added to another verb to make a single verb phrase.

> Nothing but an extreme love of truth *could have hindered* me from concealing this part of my story.
> —*Swift, p. 479*

Adjectives An **adjective** is a word used to describe a noun or pronoun or to give a noun or pronoun a more specific meaning. Adjectives answer these questions:

What kind?	*purple* hat, *happy* face
Which one?	*this* bowl, *those* cameras
How many?	*three* cars, *several* dishes
How much?	*less* attention, *enough* food

The articles *the, a,* and *an* are adjectives. *An* is used before a word beginning with a vowel sound.

A noun may sometimes be used as an adjective:

> *language* lesson   *chemistry* book

Adverbs An **adverb** is a word that modifies a verb, an adjective, or another adverb. Adverbs answer the questions *Where? When? In what manner? To what extent?*

> She answered *soon*. (modifies verb *answered*)
> *Afterward* they ate dinner. (modifies verb *ate*)
> I was *extremely* sad. (modifies adjective *sad*)
> You called *more* often than I. (modifies adverb *often*)

Prepositions A **preposition** is a word that relates a noun or pronoun that appears with it to another word in the sentence. Prepositions are almost always followed by nouns or pronouns:

around the fire	*between* them	*in* sight
from the woods	*through* us	*till* sunrise

Conjunctions A **conjunction** is used to connect other words or groups of words. **Coordinating conjunctions** connect similar kinds or groups of words:

bread *and* wine   brief *but* powerful

Correlative conjunctions are used in pairs to connect similar words or groups of words:

both Luis *and* Rosa   *neither* you *nor* I

Subordinating conjunctions connect two ideas by placing one below the other in rank or importance:

When I am in a serious humor, I very often walk by myself in Westminster Abbey; . . .

—*Addison and Steele, p. 487*

The Count your master's known munificence
Is ample warrant *that* no one just pretense
Of mine for dowry will be disallowed; . . .

—*Browning, p. 728*

Interjections An **interjection** is a word that expresses feeling or emotion and functions independently of a sentence.

Ah, love, let us be true
To one another! . . .   —*Arnold, p. 757*

"Oh, yes, very well."   —*Mansfield, p. 871*

Sentences A **sentence** is a group of words with two main parts: a subject and a predicate. Together these parts express a complete thought.

Shadows   pointed towards the pithead: . . .

—*Larkin, p. 1129*

Poor chap, he   always loved larking . . .

—*Smith, p. 1131*

A **fragment** is a group of words that does not express a complete thought.

Phrases A **phrase** is a group of words, without subject and verb, that functions as one part of speech. A **prepositional phrase** is a group of words that includes a preposition and a noun or pronoun.

before dawn	*except* us
on account of the rain	*prior to* 1979

An **adjective phrase** is a prepositional phrase that modifies a noun or pronoun by telling what kind or which one.

The space *of sky above us* was the color *of ever-changing violet* . . .   —*Joyce, p. 880*

An **adverb phrase** is a prepositional phrase that modifies a verb, an adjective, or an adverb by pointing out where, when, in what manner, or to what extent.

Arsat came *through the doorway with noiseless steps* and squatted down *by the fire.*

—*Conrad, p. 831*

An **appositive phrase** is a noun or pronoun with modifiers, placed next to a noun or pronoun to add information and details.

Mrs. Henderson, *a devoted wife,* was turning over the leaves with a smile upon her face . . .

—*Forster, p. 842*

A **participial phrase** is a participle that is modified by an adjective or adverb phrase or that has a complement. The entire phrase acts as an adjective.

The boy gazed at his uncle from those big, hot, blue eyes, *set rather close together.*   —*Lawrence, p. 861*

A **gerund phrase** is a gerund with modifiers or a complement, all acting together as a noun.

And may there be no *moaning of the bar,*
When I put out to sea, . . .   —*Tennyson, p. 722*

An **infinitive phrase** is an infinitive with modifiers, complements, or a subject, all acting together as a single part of speech.

On the supernatural side of the letter's entrance she was not permitting her mind *to dwell.*

—*Bowen, p. 891*

Clauses A **clause** is a group of words with its own subject and verb. An **independent clause** can stand by itself as a complete sentence. A **subordinate clause** cannot stand by itself as a complete sentence; it can only be part of a sentence. An **adjective clause** is a subordinate clause that modifies a noun or pronoun by telling what kind or which one.

Mr. Thomas Davies the actor, *who then kept a bookseller's shop in Russell Street, Covent Garden,* told me that Johnson was very much his friend . . .   —*Boswell, p. 522*

Subordinate **adverb clauses** modify verbs, adjectives, adverbs, or verbals by telling where, when, in what manner, to what extent, under what condition, or why.

As soon as I saw the dead man I sent an orderly to a friend's house nearby . . .   —*Orwell, p. 908*

Subordinate **noun clauses** act as nouns.

. . . I can't invent *what I haven't seen—* . . .

—*Greene, p. 898*

SUMMARY OF CAPITALIZATION AND PUNCTUATION

CAPITALIZATION

Capitalize the first word in sentences, interjections, and incomplete questions. Also capitalize the first word in a quotation if the quotation is a complete sentence.

> Then, still holding the letter, he said to her, "Where do you live?" —*Drabble, p. 952*

Capitalize all proper nouns and adjectives.

> A. E. Housman   Thames River   Trinidadian

Capitalize titles showing family relationships when they refer to a specific person unless they are preceded by a possessive noun or pronoun.

> Uncle Oscar   Mangan's sister

Capitalize the first word and all other key words in the titles of books, periodicals, poems, stories, plays, paintings, and other works of art.

> *Frankenstein*   "Shooting an Elephant"
> "The Fiddle"   "Naming of Parts"

PUNCTUATION

End Marks   Use a **period** to end a declarative sentence, a mild imperative sentence, an indirect question, and most abbreviations.

> This tale is true, and mine.
> —*"The Seafarer," trans. by Raffel, p. 13*

> Let me not to the marriage of true minds
> Admit impediments.   —*Shakespeare, p. 230*

> She asked me was I going to *Araby.*
> —*Joyce, p. 881*
> Mrs. Drover

Use a **question mark** to end an interrogative sentence or an incomplete question.

> Sent he to Macduff?   —*Shakespeare, p. 292*

> What love of thine own kind? What ignorance of pain?   —*Shelley, p. 646*

Use an **exclamation mark** after an exclamatory sentence, a forceful imperative sentence, or an interjection expressing strong emotion.

> "Hold off! unhand me, graybeard loon!"
> —*Coleridge, p. 597*

> "Ah-ah-ah-ow-ow-ow-oo!"   —*Shaw, p. 976*

COMMAS

Use a comma before the conjunction to separate two independent clauses in a compound sentence.

> My heart aches, and a drowsy numbness pains
> My sense, . . .   —*Keats, p. 657*

Use commas to separate three or more words, phrases, or clauses in a series.

> Daffodil came in first, Lancelot second, Mirza third.   —*Lawrence, p. 861*

Use commas to separate adjectives of equal rank. Do not use commas to separate adjectives that must stay in a specific order.

> His big, soft eyes stared eagerly at the white man, . . .   —*Conrad, p. 830*

> And each slow dusk a drawing-down of blinds.
> —*Owen, p. 1077*

Use a comma after an introductory word, phrase, or clause.

> When Lady Anstey's book on Giovanni da Empoli was published, Mr. Henderson found in it much that needed forgiveness.   —*Forster, p. 842*

Use commas to set off parenthetical and nonessential expressions.

> "Only you'd have to promise, honor bright, uncle, not to let it go beyond us three."
> —*Lawrence, p. 862*

Use commas with places, dates, and titles.

> Coventry, England   September 1, 1939
> Reginald Farrars, M.P.

Use commas after items in addresses, after the salutation in a personal letter, after the closing in all letters, and in numbers of more than three digits.

> Hull Crescent, Dorchester   Dear Randolph,
> Yours faithfully,   9,744

Use a comma to indicate words left out of an elliptical sentence, to set off a direct quotation, and to prevent a sentence from being misunderstood.

> In Tennyson's poetry, I admire the music; in Browning's, the sentiments.

> "There isn't a soul here," I said, "who doesn't talk English."   —*Greene, p. 900*

SEMICOLONS

Use a semicolon to join independent clauses that are not already joined by a conjunction.

> He had been a very charitable priest; in his will he had left all his money to institutions . . .
> —*Joyce, p. 880*

Use a semicolon to join independent clauses separated by either a conjunctive adverb or a transitional expression.

He had the use only of one eye; yet so much does mind govern and even supply the deficiency of organs, that his visual perceptions, as far as they extended, were uncommonly quick . . .
—*Boswell, p. 525*

Use semicolons to avoid confusion when independent clauses or items in a series already contain commas.

The Emperor concluded me to be drowned, and that the enemy's fleet was approaching in a hostile manner; but he was soon eased of his fears; for, the channel growing shallower every step I made, I came in a short time within hearing, . . .
—*Swift, p. 477*

COLONS

Use a colon before a list of items following an independent clause.

Notable Victorian poets include the following: Tennyson, Browning, Arnold, Housman, and Hopkins.

Use a colon to introduce a formal or lengthy quotation.

And on the pedestal these words appear:
"My name is Ozymandias, king of kings: . . . "
—*Shelley, p. 638*

Use a colon to introduce a sentence that summarizes or explains the sentence before it.

The third day of the illness was critical: they were waiting for a change.
—*Lawrence, p. 866*

QUOTATION MARKS

A direct quotation represents a person's exact speech or thoughts and is enclosed within quotation marks.
"If I go," I said, "I will bring you something."
—*Joyce, p. 882*

An indirect quotation reports only the general meaning of what a person said or thought and does not require quotation marks.

Mother said he never considered me.
—*Bowen, p. 892*

Always place a comma or a period inside the final quotation mark.

"We will each write a ghost story," said Lord Byron; . . .
—*Shelley, p. 673*

Place a question mark or an exclamation mark inside the final quotation mark if the end mark is part of the quotation; if it is not part of the quotation, place it outside the final quotation mark.

"You dear thing!" she cried, embracing him; "you're too good to be alive!"
—*Forster, p. 845*

Use single quotation marks for a quotation within a quotation.

"As fine as ever. 'A little less imagination in archaeology and a little more in art' was his advice to Sir William yesterday."
—*Forster, p. 845*

Underline the titles of long written works, movies, television and radio shows, lengthy works of music, paintings, and sculptures. Also underline foreign words not yet accepted into English and words you wish to stress.

| <u>Pygmalion</u> | <u>Howards End</u> | <u>Guernica</u> |
| <u>60 Minutes</u> | <u>Parsifal</u> | <u>déjà vu</u> |

Use quotation marks around the titles of short written works, episodes in a series, songs, and titles of works mentioned as parts of collections.

"The Lagoon" "The Tiger" "Shooting an Elephant"
"Afton Water" "Boswell Meets Johnson"

PARENTHESES

Use parentheses to set off asides and explanations only when the material is not essential or when it consists of one or more sentences.

My eyes were often full of tears (I could not tell why) and at times a flood from my heart seemed to pour itself out into my bosom.
—*Joyce, p. 882*

HYPHENS

Use a hyphen with certain numbers, after certain prefixes, with two or more words used as one word, with a compound modifier and within a word when a combination of letters might otherwise be confusing.

twenty-nine   pre-Romantic   re-create
brother-in-law   once-in-a-lifetime

APOSTROPHES

Add an apostrophe and an -s to show the possessive case of most singular nouns.

Blake's poems   an editor's pencil

Add an apostrophe to show the possessive case of plural nouns ending in -s and -es.

the girls' songs   the Ortizes' car

Add an apostrophe and an -s to show the possessive case of plural nouns that do not end in -s or -es.

the children's games   the mice's whiskers

Use an apostrophe in a contraction to indicate the position of the missing letter or letters.

"You wouldn't have asked me if you'd thought I minded."
—*Drabble, p. 952*

Use an apostrophe and an -s to write the plurals of numbers, symbols, letters, and words used to name themselves.

the 1890's   five a's   no *if*'s or *but*'s

GLOSSARY OF COMMON USAGE

among, between
Among is generally used with three or more items. *Between* is generally used with only two items.

> *Among* Chaucer's characters, my favorite has always been the Wife of Bath.

> The ballad "Get Up and Bar the Door" consists largely of a dialogue *between* a man and his wife.

amount, number
Amount refers to quantity or a unit, whereas *number* refers to individual items that can be counted. Therefore, *amount* generally appears with a singular noun, and *number* appears with a plural noun.

> The *amount* of attention that great writers have paid to the Faust legend is remarkable.

> A considerable *number* of important English writers have been fascinated by the legend of King Arthur.

as, because, like, as to
The word *as* has several meanings and can function as several parts of speech. To avoid confusion, use *because* rather than *as* when you want to indicate cause and effect.

> *Because* the narrator of Joyce's "Araby" is infatuated with Mangan's sister, he cannot see that he is driven by vanity.

Do not use the preposition *like* to introduce a clause that requires the conjunction *as*.

> *As* we might expect in a story by Graham Greene, the death of Mr. Calloway in "Across the Bridge" contains elements of both tragedy and comedy.

The use of *as to* for *about* is awkward and should be avoided.

> Roberto's essay compared Browning's aggressive optimism *about* the future in "Prospice" with Tennyson's quieter outlook on the afterlife in "Crossing the Bar."

bad, badly
Use the predicate adjective *bad* after linking verbs such as *feel, look,* and *seem.* Use *badly* whenever an adverb is required.

> In "My Last Duchess," the Duke of Ferrara does not seem to feel *bad* about the death of his wife; on the contrary, he eagerly contemplates the prospect of remarriage.

> The announcement of Lady Macbeth's death *badly* unnerves Macbeth; in his famous soliloquy, he compares life to a "walking shadow" and a "tale told by an idiot."

because of, due to
Use *due to* if it can logically replace the phrase *caused by.* In introductory phrases, however, *because of* is better usage than *due to.*

> The numerous classical allusions in Milton's *Paradise Lost* may be *due to* the poet's ambition to imitate and, if possible, surpass the epics of Homer and Virgil.

> *Because of* the expansion of the reading public and the rise of publishers, booksellers, and royalties, writers during the eighteenth century became less dependent on a small number of wealthy patrons.

compare, contrast
The verb *compare* can involve both similarities and differences. The verb *contrast* always involves differences. Use *to* or *with* after *compare.* Use *with* after *contrast.*

> In "Silent Noon" Dante Gabriel Rossetti paradoxically *compares* the lovers' "twofold silence" *to* a song of love.

> Denise's report *compared* Shelley's style in "To a Skylark" *with* that of Keats in "Ode to a Nightingale."

> In Conrad's "The Lagoon," Arsat's point of view in the narration of his "story within a story" *contrasts with* the more detached, third-person point of view that the author uses for most of the tale.

continual, continuous
Continual means "occurring again and again in succession." *Continuous* means "occurring without interruption."

> In "The Seafarer" the speaker's description of *continual* hailstorms at sea contributes to the poem's melancholy atmosphere.

> The speaker's white-hot fervor in "Ode to the West Wind" suggests that Shelley may have written the poem in a single *continuous* burst of poetic inspiration.

different from, different than
The preferred usage is *different from.*

> In its simple, precise language, Housman's style is different from that of many other Victorian poets, including Tennyson, Hopkins, and the Rossettis.

farther, further
Use *farther* when you refer to distance. Use *further* when you mean "to a greater degree" or "additional."

> Although the sexton tries to persuade him to go no *farther,* Defoe is determined to enter the churchyard.

Boswell *further* illustrates Johnson's conversation by quoting his opinions of Sheridan and Derrick.

fewer, less

Use *fewer* for things that can be counted. Use *less* for amounts or quantities that cannot be counted.

In "Tintern Abbey" Wordsworth uses *fewer* end-stopped lines than Pope does in *The Rape of the Lock.*

At the beginning of Luke's parable, the prodigal son shows *less* respect than the older son for the father.

just, only

When you use *just* as an adverb meaning "no more than," be sure that you place it directly before the word it modifies logically. Likewise, be sure you place *only* before the word it logically modifies.

The form of the villanelle allows a poet to use *just* two rhymes.

John Keats was *only* twenty-four when he wrote some of his greatest poems, including many of the odes and "The Eve of St. Agnes."

lay, lie

Do not confuse these verbs. *Lay* is a transitive verb meaning "to set or put something down." Its principal parts are *lay, laying, laid, laid. Lie* is an intransitive verb meaning "to recline." Its principal parts are *lie, lying, lay, lain.*

Coleridge implies that the mariner's reckless act of killing the albatross *lays* a curse on the crew.

As Paul *lies* dead at the end of D. H. Lawrence's story, his Uncle Oscar sadly comments that the boy may be better off "gone out of a life where he rides his rocking horse to find a winner."

plurals that do not end in -s

The plurals of certain nouns from Greek and Latin are formed as they were in their original language. Words such as *criteria, media,* and *phenomena* are plural and should not be treated as if they were singular *(criterion, medium, phenomenon).*

Are the electronic *media* of the twentieth century contributing to the death of literature?

raise, rise

Raise is a transitive verb that usually takes a direct object. *Rise* is intransitive and never takes a direct object.

"In Musée des Beaux Arts," W. H. Auden *raises* the question of our insensitivity to other people's suffering.

As Doolittle *rises* to leave in Act II of *Pygmalion,* Higgins offers him ten pounds.

that, which, who

Use the relative pronoun *that* to refer to things or people. Use *which* only for things and *who* only for people.

The contemporary poet *that* I most enjoy reading is James Berry.

"Fern Hill," *which* reflects Dylan Thomas's brilliant ability to evoke emotional response, plays on the connotations of words.

Addison and Steele, *who* were close friends for most of their lives, had very different personalities and careers.

when, where

Do not directly follow a linking verb with *when* or *where.* Also be careful not to use *where* when your context requires *that.*

Faulty: Evaluation is *when* you make a judgment about the quality or value of something.

Revised: Evaluation is the process of making a judgment about the quality or value of something.

Faulty: Nottingham in the English Midlands is *where* both D. H. Lawrence and Alan Sillitoe were born.

Revised: Both D. H. Lawrence and Alan Sillitoe were born in Nottingham in the English Midlands.

Faulty: Sandy read *where,* after the Brownings eloped to Italy, they spent most of their married life in Florence.

Revised: Sandy read *that,* after the Brownings eloped to Italy, they spent most of their married life in Florence.

who, whom

Remember to use *who* only as a subject in clauses and sentences and *whom* only as an object.

Henry Higgins treats Liza with brutal sarcasm; two characters *who* seem far more sensitive to her feelings are Mrs. Higgins and Colonel Pickering.

V. S. Naipaul, *whom* many critics have praised as one of the best contemporary writers in English, was born and raised in Trinidad.

HANDBOOK OF LITERARY TERMS AND TECHNIQUES

ALLEGORY An *allegory* is a literary work with two or more levels of meaning—one literal level and one or more symbolic levels. The events, settings, objects, or characters in an allegory stand for ideas or qualities beyond themselves. Allegorical writing was common in the Middle Ages. Thereafter, the popularity of allegory declined, but Spenser revived the form in *The Faerie Queene,* and John Bunyan revived it yet again in *The Pilgrim's Progress.* Some modern novels, such as Joseph Conrad's *Heart of Darkness,* can be read allegorically. When reading a work allegorically, one tries to match every element at the literal level with a corresponding element at the symbolic level.

ALLITERATION *Alliteration* is the repetition of initial consonant sounds. Emily Brontë used alliteration of *l* sounds in "The Old Stoic":

> Riches I hold in *l*ight esteem,
>   And *L*ove I *l*augh to scorn;
> And *l*ust of fame was but a dream
>   That vanished with the morn

Alliteration is often used, especially in poetry, to emphasize and to link words as well as to create pleasing, musical sounds. Alliteration of stressed syllables was one of the characteristic features of Anglo-Saxon poetry.
See *Anglo-Saxon Poetry.*

ALLUSION An *allusion* is a reference to a well-known person, place, event, literary work, or work of art. Writers often make allusions to tales from the Bible, classical Greek and Roman myths, plays by Shakespeare, historical or political events, and other materials with which they expect their readers to be familiar. An allusion appears in Shakespeare's *A Midsummer Night's Dream,* when Hermia swears "by Cupid's strong-

est bow," thus referring to the god of love in Roman mythology. Writers sometimes use allusions as a sort of shorthand to suggest ideas in a simple and concise manner.

ANAPEST See *Meter.*

ANGLO-SAXON POETRY *Anglo-Saxon poetry* is the rhythmic poetry composed in Old English before A.D.1100. It generally has four accented syllables and an indefinite number of unaccented syllables in each line. Each line is divided in half by a caesura, or pause, and the halves are linked by the alliteration of two or three of the accented syllables. The following lines from "Wulf and Eadwacer" show the alliteration and caesuras used in Anglo-Saxon poetry:

> I *w*aited for my *W*ulf//with far-*W*andering
>   yearnings,
> *Wh*en it was rainy *w*eather//and I sat *w*eeping.

Anglo-Saxon poetry was originally composed orally and then sung or chanted to the accompaniment of a primitive harp.
See *Alliteration, Caesura,* and *Kenning.*

ANTAGONIST An *antagonist* is a character or force in conflict with the main character, or protagonist, in a literary work. In *Beowulf,* on page 20, the protagonist faces two antagonists—Grendel and Grendel's mother.
See *Character* and *Protagonist.*

APHORISM An *aphorism* is a general truth or observation about life, usually stated concisely and pointedly. Often witty or wise, memorable aphorisms appear in the works of Chaucer, Shakespeare, Pope, Johnson, and many other writers. An essay writer may have an *aphoristic style*—a style characterized by use of such statements—as does Francis Bacon. The following aphorism comes from Bacon's "Of Studies":

> Crafty men condemn studies, simple men admire them, and wise men use them.

In an essay, an aphorism can be used to sum up or reinforce a point or argument.

APOSTROPHE   An *apostrophe* is a figure of speech in which a speaker directly addresses an absent person or a personified quality, object, or idea. Shelley opens his poem "Ode to the West Wind" with an apostrophe that addresses the wind. Apostrophe is often used in poetry and in speeches to add emotional intensity.
See *Figurative Language.*

ASIDE   An *aside* is a statement delivered by an actor to an audience in such a way that other characters on stage are presumed not to hear what is said. In an aside the character reveals his or her private thoughts, reactions, or motivations.

ASSONANCE   *Assonance* is the repetition of vowel sounds in stressed syllables containing dissimilar consonant sounds. Robert Browning used assonance in the following famous line from his poem "Andrea del Sarto":

> Ah, but a man's reach should exceed his grasp

The long *e* sound is repeated in the words *reach* and *exceed* in stressed syllables containing these consonants: *r–ch* and *c–d.*
See *Consonance.*

AUTOBIOGRAPHY   *Autobiography* is a form of nonfiction in which a person tells his or her own life story. Unlike a diary or a letter, an autobiography is written for a public audience. George Orwell's "Shooting an Elephant," on page 906, is an example of the autobiographical essay.

BALLAD   A *ballad* is a songlike poem that tells a story, often one dealing with adventure or romance. Most ballads have the following charac-teristics: four- or six-line stanzas, rhyme, simple language, and dramatic action.

Many ballads employ repetition of a refrain. Some have incremental repetition, in which a refrain is varied slightly each time it appears.

The British Isles have a rich tradition of *folk ballads*—songs that originated among illiterate peoples and were passed from singer to singer by word of mouth. Examples in your text include "Sir Patrick Spens" and "Barbara Allan." Many English, Scottish, Welsh, and Irish writers have created *literary ballads*—sophisticated poems in the style of folk ballads. One such literary ballad is Samuel Taylor Coleridge's *The Rime of the Ancient Mariner,* on page 596.

BIOGRAPHY   A *biography* is a form of nonfiction in which a writer tells the life story of another person. A good biographer uses many sources of information, including, perhaps, the subject's letters and journals, interviews with the subject or with people who know the subject, personal knowledge about the subject, and books and other works about the subject. James Boswell's *The Life of Samuel Johnson,* an excerpt from which appears on page 522, is one of the most famous of all biographies. Boswell's work has been widely praised for its accuracy of reporting and its liveliness of style.

BLANK VERSE   *Blank verse* is poetry written in unrhymed iambic pentameter lines. Each iambic foot has one weakly stressed syllable followed by one strongly stressed syllable. A pentameter line has five of these feet. Blank verse usually contains occasional variations in rhythm that are introduced to create emphasis, variety, and naturalness of sound. Because blank verse sounds much like ordinary spoken English, it is often used in drama and in poetry. Great English writers of blank verse include Shakespeare, Wordsworth, Browning, and Auden. The following lines come from Wordsworth's blank-verse poem

"Lines Composed a Few Miles Above Tintern Abbey," on page 580:

Fŏr thóu | aŕt wíth | mĕ hére | ŭpón | t̆he bánks
Ŏf thís | faĭr rív|ĕr; thóu |mў déar|ĕst Fríend

See *Meter.*

CAESURA   A *caesura* is a natural pause, or break, in the middle of a line of poetry. In Anglo-Saxon poetry a caesura divides each four-stress line in half and thus is essential to the rhythm. See *Anglo-Saxon Poetry.*

CARPE DIEM   *Carpe diem* is a Latin phrase meaning "seize the day." Many great literary works have been written with the *carpe diem* theme. All have in common the fact that they urge people to enjoy life in the present. One of the best-known poems on this theme is Robert Herrick's "To the Virgins, to Make Much of Time," on page 394, which begins with the line, "Gather ye rosebuds while ye may."

CHARACTER   A *character* is a person or animal who takes part in the action of a literary work. Characters are described in different ways:
1. In terms of their significance: A character who plays an important role is called a *major character.* A character who does not play an important role is called a *minor character.*
2. In terms of their roles: A character who plays the central role in a story is called the *protagonist.* A character who opposes the protagonist is called the *antagonist.*
3. In terms of their complexity: A complex character is called *round,* a simple character *flat.*
4. In terms of the degree to which they change: A character who changes is called *dynamic;* a character who does not change is called *static.*

   Character types that readers recognize easily, such as the hard-boiled detective or the wicked stepmother, are called *stereotypes,* or *stock characters.*
See *Characterization* and *Motivation.*

CHARACTERIZATION   *Characterization* is the act of creating and developing a character. A writer uses *direct characterization* when he or she states a character's traits explicitly. *Indirect characterization* occurs when the writer reveals a character's traits by some other means. A character's traits can be revealed indirectly by means of what he or she says, thinks, or does; by means of a description of his or her appearance; or by means of the statements, thoughts, or actions of other characters. When using indirect characterization, the writer depends on the reader to infer a character's traits from the clues provided.
See *Character.*

CLASSICISM   *Classicism* is an approach to literature and to the other arts that stresses reason, harmony, balance, proportion, clarity, and idealism in imitation of the philosophers and artists of ancient Greece and Rome. Classicism is often contrasted with Romanticism, which places a premium on imagination and emotion, sometimes at the expense of reason and proportion. Classicism also differs from Realism, which concentrates on the actual rather than on the ideal.
See *Neoclassicism, Realism,* and *Romanticism.*

CLIMAX   The *climax* is the high point of interest or suspense in a literary work. Often the climax is also the *crisis* in the plot, the point at which the protagonist changes his or her understanding or situation. Sometimes the climax coincides with the *resolution,* the point at which the central conflict is ended. In a story the climax generally occurs near the end. For example, Charles Dickens's "The Signalman," on page 740, reaches its climax with the signalman's death. In a play the climax often falls close to the middle, marking the end of the rising action and the beginning of the falling action. For example, in William Shakespeare's *Macbeth,* the climax is the banquet scene, in Act III. This scene begins the movement toward Macbeth's downfall.
See *Plot.*

COMEDY A *comedy* is a literary work, especially a play, that has a happy ending. Comedies often show ordinary characters in conflict with their societies. Problems are resolved through laughter, reconciliation, and correction of moral faults or social wrongs. Types of comedy include *romantic comedy,* which involves problems among lovers, and the *comedy of manners,* which satirically challenges the social customs of a sophisticated society. Bernard Shaw's *Pygmalion,* on page 968, is a modern comedy of manners. Many comedies feature humorous physical action and witty dialogue. Comedy is often contrasted with tragedy, in which the protagonist meets an unfortunate end.

See *Drama* and *Tragedy.*

CONCEIT A *conceit* is an unusual and surprising comparison between two very different things. This special kind of metaphor or complicated analogy is often the basis for a whole poem. During the Elizabethan period, sonnets commonly included *Petrarchan conceits,* ones that extravagantly compared the beloved's beauty or the speaker's suffering to something else. Shakespeare satirizes such overblown conceits in his Sonnet 130:

> I love to hear her speak; yet well I know
> That music hath a far more pleasing sound:
> I grant I never saw a goddess go;
> My mistress, when she walks, treads on the
>   ground.
> And yet, by heaven, I think my love as rare
> As any she belied with false compare.

Seventeenth-century metaphysical poets were fond of elaborate, unusual, highly intellectual conceits. For example, in "Love's Alchemy," John Donne compares the unreliability of love to the unreliability of alchemy to make gold.

See *Metaphor.*

CONCRETE POEM A *concrete poem* is one with a shape that suggests its subject. An example in this text is George Herbert's "Easter Wings," on page 374.

See *Emblematic Image.*

CONFLICT A *conflict* is a struggle between opposing forces. Sometimes this struggle is *internal,* or within a character. At other times the struggle is *external,* or between the character and some outside force. The outside force may be another character, nature, or some element of society such as a custom or a political institution. Often the conflict in a work is complicated and combines several of these possibilities. For example, Macbeth struggles against the better parts of his own nature, against Banquo and Fleance, against fate, and against the forces led by Malcolm, Macduff, and Siward.

See *Antagonist, Plot,* and *Protagonist.*

CONNOTATION A *connotation* is an association that a word calls to mind in addition to its dictionary meaning. For example, the words *home* and *domicile* have the same dictionary meaning. However, the first has positive connotations of warmth and security while the second does not. A writer who wants to convey a sense of warmth and security will be more likely to use the word *home* than the word *domicile.* Because the connotations of words are so powerful, writers choose words with connotations that suggest the shades of meaning they intend.

See *Denotation.*

CONSONANCE *Consonance* is the repetition of consonant sounds in stressed syllables containing dissimilar vowel sounds. D. H. Lawrence uses consonance in these lines from "Snake":

> A snake came to my water-trough
> On a *hot, hot,* day, and I in pajamas for the heat,
> To drink there.

The words *hot* and *heat* have the same consonants but different vowels. When used at the

ends of lines, consonance can create *approximate* or *slant rhyme.*
See *Assonance.*

COUPLET A *couplet* is a pair of rhyming lines written in the same meter. These iambic tetrameter couplets come from John Milton's "L'Allegro":

And if I give thee honor due,
Mirth, admit me of the crew
To live with her, and live with thee,
In unreproved pleasures free.

A *heroic couplet* is a rhymed pair of iambic pentameter lines. During the Neoclassical Period, the popular heroic couplet was often also a *closed couplet,* with its meaning and grammar complete within two lines. These lines from Alexander Pope's *An Essay on Criticism* illustrate the closed heroic couplet:

True ease in writing comes from art, not chance,
As those move easiest who have learned to
    dance.

Sonnets written in the English, or Shakespearean, style usually end with heroic couplets.
See *Sonnet.*

CRISIS The *crisis* in the plot of a story or play is the turning point for the protagonist—the point at which his or her situation or understanding is changed. This point often coincides with the *climax,* or emotional high point, of the story.
See *Climax* and *Plot.*

DACTYL See *Meter.*

DENOTATION The *denotation* of a word is its objective meaning, that to which the word refers, independent of other associations the word calls to mind. Dictionaries list the denotative meanings of words. Another term for denotative meaning is *referential meaning.*
See *Connotation.*

DENOUEMENT The *denouement* in a literary work is anything that happens after the resolution of the plot. At this point the central conflict is resolved, and the consequences for the protagonist are already decided. Essentially, a denouement is a tying up of loose ends.
See *Plot.*

DIALECT A *dialect* is the form of a language spoken by people in a particular region or group. Dialects differ from one another in grammar, vocabulary, and pronunciation. Robert Burns used a Scots dialect in poems like "Auld Lang Syne":

Should auld acquaintance be forgot,
And never brought to min'?
Should auld acquaintance be forgot,
And days o' lang syne?

Dialect is sometimes used as a part of characterization. For example, the social status of each character in Bernard Shaw's *Pygmalion,* on page 968, is revealed by the dialect the character speaks. The central character, Eliza Doolittle, is trained to speak Received Standard English—a dialect with high social prestige—rather than her native Cockney dialect.

DIALOGUE A *dialogue* is a conversation between characters. Writers use dialogue to reveal character, to present events, to add variety to narratives, and to interest readers. The dialogue in a story or play is usually set off by quotation marks and paragraphing. The dialogue in a play script generally follows the characters' names.

DIARY A *diary* is a personal record of daily events, usually written in prose. Most diaries are not written for publication; sometimes, however, interesting diaries or diaries by influential people do find their way into print. One example of a published diary is that of Samuel Pepys, a selection from which appears on page 460.
See *Journal.*

DICTION   *Diction* is word choice. A writer's diction can be a major determinant of his or her style. Diction can be described as formal or informal, abstract or concrete, plain or ornate, ordinary or technical.
See *Style.*

DIMETER   See *Meter.*

DRAMA   A *drama* is a story written to be performed by actors. It may consist of one or more large sections called *acts,* which are made up of any number of smaller sections called *scenes.*

Drama originated in the religious rituals and symbolic re-enactments of primitive peoples. The ancient Greeks developed drama into a sophisticated art and created such dramatic forms as tragedy and comedy.

The first dramas in England were the miracle plays and morality plays of the Middle Ages. *Miracle plays* told Biblical stories. *Morality plays,* such as *Everyman,* on page 178, dealt with personified virtues and vices. The English Renaissance saw a great flowering of drama in England, culminating in the works of William Shakespeare, who wrote many of the world's greatest comedies, tragedies, histories, and romances. During the Neoclassical Age, English drama turned to witty, satirical comedies of manners that probed the virtues of upper-class society. Superb examples of Neoclassical comedy include Goldsmith's *She Stoops to Conquer* and Congreve's *The Way of the World.* The Romantic and Victorian ages were not great periods for drama in England. However, a few good verse plays were written, including Percy Bysshe Shelley's *The Cenci* and *Prometheus Unbound* and Robert Browning's *Pippa Passes.* The end of the nineteenth and beginning of the twentieth centuries saw a resurgence of the drama in England and throughout the English-speaking world. Great plays of the Modern Period include Bernard Shaw's *Pygmalion,* on page 968, and plays by William Butler Yeats, John Millington Synge, Christopher Fry, T. S. Eliot, Harold Pinter, and Samuel Beckett.

DRAMATIC MONOLOGUE   A *dramatic monologue* is a poem in which an imaginary character speaks to a silent listener. During the monologue, the speaker reveals his or her personality, usually at a moment of crisis. Examples of dramatic monologues in this text are Robert Browning's "My Last Duchess," on page 726 and Alfred, Lord Tennyson's "Ulysses," on page 718.

ELEGY   An *elegy* is a solemn and formal lyric poem about death. It may mourn a particular person or reflect on a serious or tragic theme, such as the passing of youth, beauty, or a way of life. See Thomas Gray's "Elegy Written in a Country Churchyard," on page 532.
See *Lyric Poem.*

EMBLEMATIC IMAGE   An *emblematic image* is a symbolic figure or shape presented through the arrangement of the lines of a poem. For example, George Herbert's "Easter Wings," on page 374, is shaped like a pair of wings.
See *Concrete Poem.*

END-STOPPED LINE   An *end-stopped line* of poetry concludes with a break in the meter and in the meaning. This pause at the end of a line often is punctuated by a period, comma, dash, or semicolon. These lines from "Away, Melancholy," by Stevie Smith, are end-stopped:

> Are not the trees green,
> The earth as green?
> Does not the wind blow,
> Fire leap and the rivers flow?
> Away melancholy.

See *Run-on Line.*

EPIC   An *epic* is a long narrative poem about the adventures of gods or of a hero. *Beowulf,* on page 20, is a *folk epic,* one that was composed orally and passed from storyteller to storyteller. The ancient Greek epics attributed to Homer—the *Iliad* and the *Odyssey*—are also folk epics. The *Aeneid,* by the Roman poet Virgil, and *The Divine Comedy,* by the Italian poet Dante Alighieri, are examples of literary epics from the Classical and Medieval periods, respectively. John Milton's *Paradise Lost,* a selection from which appears on page 411, is also a literary epic. Milton's goal in creating *Paradise Lost* was to write a Christian epic similar in form and equal in value to the great epics of antiquity. Because of an epic's length and seriousness of theme, it presents an encyclopedic portrait of the culture in which it was produced.

Epic conventions are traditional characteristics of epic poems, including an opening statement of the theme; an appeal for supernatural help in telling the story; a beginning *in medias res* (Latin: "in the middle of things"); long lists, or catalogs, of people and things; accounts of past events; and descriptive phrases such as kennings, Homeric similes, and Homeric epithets. See *Epithet, In Medias Res, Invocation,* and *Kenning.*

EPIGRAM   An *epigram* is a brief, pointed statement in prose or in verse. The concluding couplet in an English sonnet may be epigrammatic. An essay may be written in an *epigrammatic style,* one characterized by use of epigrams.

EPIGRAPH   An *epigraph* is a quotation that appears at the beginning of a literary work, like Rainer Maria Rilke's lines at the beginning of Margaret Drabble's "A Voyage to Cythera," on page 946. An epigraph generally introduces a motif or theme developed in the work itself.

EPIPHANY   *Epiphany* is a term introduced by James Joyce to describe a moment of revelation or insight in which a character recognizes some truth. In Joyce's "Araby," the boy's epiphany comes at the end of the story, on page 880, when he recognizes the falsity of his dream.

EPITAPH   An *epitaph* is an inscription written on a tomb or burial place. In literature, epitaphs include serious or humorous lines written as if intended for such use. Examples are the epitaph in Thomas Gray's "Elegy Written in a Country Churchyard," which appears on page 532.

EPITHET   An *epithet* is a word or phrase that states a characteristic quality of a person or thing. A. E. Housman uses epithets like "golden friends" and "lightfoot lad" in "With Rue My Heart Is Laden." *Homeric epithets,* such as "wide-wayed city," "clear-voiced heralds," and "high-hearted princes" in the *Iliad,* were common in classical epics and in later imitations of such. See *Epic.*

ESSAY   An *essay* is a short, nonfiction work about a particular subject. Essays are of many types but may be classified by tone or style as formal or informal. An essay is often classed by its main purpose as descriptive, narrative, expository, argumentative, or persuasive.

EXEMPLUM   An *exemplum* is a short tale or anecdote with a moral, especially one used in a medieval sermon. Geoffrey Chaucer's "The Pardoner's Tale," on page 159, illustrates the moral that "love of wealth is the root of all evil."

EXPOSITION   In a story or drama, the *exposition* is the part of the plot that introduces the characters, the setting, and the basic situation. For example, in William Shakespeare's *A Midsummer Night's Dream,* the first scene introduces the lovers and their problems, locates the action in the palace at Athens near a wood, and establishes the light mood of a romantic comedy. See *Plot.*

EXPRESSIONISM   *Expressionism* was an artistic movement of the early twentieth century. The Expressionists emphasized the inner experiences of individuals, not objective realities.

EXTENDED METAPHOR   See *Metaphor.*

FALLING ACTION   The *falling action* is all of the action that takes place after the climax in a literary work. During this time, the conflict is resolved and the suspense decreases.
See *Plot* and *Rising Action.*

FANTASY   *Fantasy* is highly imaginative writing that contains elements not found in real life. Elizabeth Bowen's "The Demon Lover," on page 888, is a fantasy. Writers use fantasies to entertain readers and sometimes to make serious points about reality.

FICTION   *Fiction* is prose writing about imaginary characters and events. Some writers of fiction base their stories on real people and events, while others rely solely on their imaginations.
See *Narration, Nonfiction,* and *Prose.*

FIGURATIVE LANGUAGE   *Figurative language* is writing or speech not meant to be interpreted literally. Poets and other writers use figurative language to create vivid word pictures, to make their writing emotionally intense and concentrated, and to state their ideas in new and unusual ways that satisfy readers' imaginations.
See *Figure of Speech.*

FIGURE OF SPEECH   A *figure of speech* is an expression or a word used imaginatively rather than literally. Among the types of figurative language are apostrophe, hyperbole, irony, metaphor, metonymy, oxymoron, paradox, personification, simile, and synecdoche.
See *Figurative Language.* See also the entries for individual figures of speech.

FLASHBACK   A *flashback* is a section of a literary work that interrupts the sequence of events to relate an event from an earlier time. The writer may present the flashback as a character's memory or recollection, as part of an account or story told by a character, or as a dream or daydream.

For example, in Elizabeth Bowen's "The Demon Lover," on page 888, Mrs. Drover remembers saying farewell to her fiancé twenty-five years earlier. Writers use flashbacks to show what motivates a character and to supply background information in a dramatic way.
See *Foreshadowing.*

FOIL   A *foil* is a character who provides a contrast to another character, thus intensifying the impact of that other character. For example, Banquo and Macduff act as foils for the ambitious and tyrannical Macbeth.

FOLKLORE   *Folklore* includes the stories, legends, myths, ballads, riddles, sayings, and other traditional works produced orally by illiterate or semi-literate peoples. Folklore influences written literature in many ways, as is suggested by the beheading contest in *Sir Gawain and the Green Knight,* on page 96, and the fiancé in Elizabeth Bowen's "The Demon Lover," on page 888.

FOLK TALE   A *folk tale* is a story composed orally and then passed from person to person by word of mouth. Many of Chaucer's stories were based on folk tales.
See *Folklore.*

FOOT   See *Meter.*

FORESHADOWING   *Foreshadowing* is the use, in a literary work, of clues that suggest events that have yet to occur. Writers use foreshadowing to create suspense or to prepare the audience for the eventual outcome of events.
See *Flashback.*

FREE VERSE   *Free verse* is poetry not written in a regular rhythmical pattern, or meter. Instead of having metrical feet and lines, free verse has a rhythm that suits its meaning and that uses the sounds of spoken language in lines of different lengths. Free verse has been widely used in twentieth-century poetry. An example is "The Galloping Cat," by Stevie Smith:

All the same I
Intend to go on being
A cat that likes to
Gallop about doing good
So
Now with my bald head I go,
Chopping the untidy flowers down, to and fro.

GOTHIC   *Gothic* is a term used to describe literary works that make extensive use of primitive, medieval, wild, mysterious, or natural elements. Gothic elements offended eighteenth-century Neoclassical writers but appealed to the Romantic writers who followed them. *Gothic novels,* such as Mary Wollstonecraft Shelley's *Frankenstein,* a selection from which appears on page 672, are often set in gloomy castles where horrifying, supernatural events take place.

HEPTAMETER   See *Meter.*

HERO/HEROINE   A *hero* or *heroine* is a character whose actions are inspiring or noble. Often heroes struggle to overcome foes or to escape from difficulties. The most obvious examples of heroes and heroines are the larger-than-life characters in myths and legends like Beowulf or Odysseus. However, ordinary characters can, and often do, perform heroic deeds.

HEXAMETER   See *Meter.*

HYPERBOLE   *Hyperbole* is deliberate exaggeration or overstatement. In "On Monsieur's Departure," Elizabeth I used this figure of speech:

I grieve and dare not show my discontent,
I love and yet am forced to seem to hate,
I do, yet dare not say I ever meant,
I seem stark mute but inwardly to prate.
  I am and not, I freeze and yet am burned,
  Since from myself another self I turned.

Of course, Queen Elizabeth was not turned by love into another person, she was not mute or burned, and she did not act in total opposition to her true feelings. Such excessive claims are examples of hyperbole.
See *Figurative Language.*

IAMBIC PENTAMETER   See *Meter.*

IMAGE   An *image* is a word or phrase that appeals to one or more of the senses—sight, hearing, touch, taste, or smell. In a famous essay on *Hamlet,* T. S. Eliot explained how a group of images can be used as an "objective correlative." By this phrase Eliot meant that a complex emotional state can be suggested by images that are carefully chosen to evoke this state.
See *Imagery.*

IMAGERY   *Imagery* is the descriptive language used in literature to re-create sensory experiences. The following lines from William Collins's "Ode to Evening" show how a poet can use imagery to appeal to several senses:

Now air is hushed, save where the weak-eyed bat,
With short shrill shrieks flits by on leathern wing,
Or where the beetle winds
His small but sullen horn,
As oft he rises 'midst the twilight path,
Against the pilgrim borne in heedless hum.

These lines describe the sounds, sights, and movements of evening. Imagery enriches writing by making it more vivid, setting a tone, suggesting emotions, and guiding a reader's reactions.

IN MEDIAS RES   The phrase *in medias res,* Latin for "in the middle of things," is a storytelling method used in epic poems and in other narratives. When a writer begins *in medias res,* the story starts in the middle, jumping right into the action. The background and the initial events are introduced later by means of one or more flash-

backs. John Milton's *Paradise Lost* follows this pattern. Milton's epic begins with Satan and the fallen angels on the burning lake in Chaos. Not until Books V and VI does Raphael tell Adam about the great battle that occurred just before those angels fell from heaven.
See *Epic*.

INVERSION An *inversion* is a reversal or change in the regular word order of a sentence. For instance, Anne Killigrew begins the poem "Upon the Saying That My Verses Were Made by Another" in this way:

> Next Heaven, my vows to thee, O sacred Muse!
> I offered up, nor didst thou them refuse.

These lines reverse the usual subject-verb-object order, "I offered up my vows to thee," and the usual negative construction, "nor didst thou refuse them." Poets use inversion to emphasize words and preserve the meter of a poem.

INVOCATION An *invocation* is an appeal to a Muse or other divine being for help in writing a poem. In ancient Greece and Rome, writers often began their works by calling for the aid of the Muses, who were the goddesses responsible for the various arts. In *Paradise Lost,* on page 411, John Milton appeals to his "Heavenly Muse," the Holy Spirit of the Christian trinity.
See *Epic*.

IRONY *Irony* is the general name given to literary techniques that involve surprising, interesting, or amusing contradictions. In *verbal irony,* words are used to suggest the opposite of their usual meaning. In *dramatic irony,* there is a contradiction between what a character thinks and what the reader or audience knows to be true. In *irony of situation,* an event occurs that directly contradicts the expectations of the characters, the reader, or the audience.

JOURNAL A *journal* is a daily autobiographical account of events and personal reactions. Daniel Defoe adapted this form to fictional use in his *A Journal of the Plague Year,* an excerpt from which appears on page 468.
See *Diary*.

KENNING A *kenning* is a metaphorical phrase, used in Anglo-Saxon poetry to replace a concrete noun. In "The Seafarer," on page 13, the cuckoo is called "summer's sentinel" and the sea "the whale's home."
See *Anglo-Saxon Poetry* and *Epic*.

LEGEND A *legend* is a widely told story about the past that may or may not be based in fact. A legend often reflects a people's identity or cultural values, generally with more historical truth and less emphasis on the supernatural than in a myth. English legends include the stories of King Arthur and Robin Hood.
See *Myth*.

LYRIC POEM A *lyric poem* expresses the observations and feelings of a single speaker. Unlike a narrative poem, it presents an experience or a single effect, but it does not tell a full story. Types of lyrics include the elegy, the ode, and the sonnet. The lyric flourished in the songs and sonnets of the Renaissance, was revived by the Romantic poets, and remained the most common poetic form in the nineteenth and twentieth centuries. Alfred, Lord Tennyson; Robert Browning; Elizabeth Barrett Browning; Matthew Arnold; William Butler Yeats; W. H. Auden; Dylan Thomas; and Stevie Smith all wrote great lyric poems.

MEMENTO MORI *Memento mori* is a Latin phrase meaning "remember that you must die." Many literary works have dealt with the *memento mori* theme, including Marvell's "To His Coy Mistress," on page 378, and Gray's "Elegy Written in a Country Churchyard," on page 532.

METAPHOR A *metaphor* is a figure of speech in which one thing is spoken of as though it were something else, as in "death, that long sleep." Through this identification of dissimilar things, a comparison is suggested or implied. Emily Brontë uses the following metaphor in the second stanza of her poem "Remembrance": "my thoughts no longer hover . . . resting their wings." The metaphor suggests similarities between the speaker's thoughts and the wings of a bird.

An *extended metaphor* is developed at length and involves several points of comparison.

A *mixed metaphor* occurs when two metaphors are jumbled together. For example, thorns and rain are illogically mixed in "The thorns of life rained down on him."

A *dead metaphor* is one that has been so overused that its original metaphorical impact has been lost. Examples of dead metaphors include "the foot of the bed" and "toe the line." See *Figurative Language.*

METAPHYSICAL POETRY   *Metaphysical poetry* is the term used to describe the works of such seventeenth-century English poets as Richard Crashaw, John Donne, George Herbert, Andrew Marvell, Thomas Traherne, and Henry Vaughan. The term was first used by Samuel Johnson in an attack on writers who fill their works with far-fetched conceits and who make poetry a vehicle for displays of learning. Characteristic features of metaphysical poetry include intellectual playfulness, argument, paradoxes, irony, elaborate and unusual conceits, incongruity, and the rhythms of ordinary speech. Examples of metaphysical poems in this text include Donne's "Song," on page 360, and Marvell's "To His Coy Mistress," on page 378.

METER   The *meter* of a poem is its rhythmical pattern. This pattern is determined by the number and types of stresses, or beats, in each line. To describe the meter of a poem, you must *scan* its lines. *Scanning* involves marking the stressed and unstressed syllables, as follows:

˘Wéen | thăt, whĕn | thĕ gráve's | dărk wáll
Dĭd fírst | hĕr fórm | rĕtáin,
Thĕy thóught | thĕir heárts | cŏuld ne'ér | rĕcáll
Thĕ líght | ŏf jóy | ăgáin.

    —Emily Brontë, "Song"

As you can see, each stressed syllable is marked with a slanted line (´) and each unstressed syllable with a horseshoe symbol (˘). The stresses are then divided by vertical lines into groups called *feet.* The following types of feet are common in English poetry:

1. *Iamb:* a foot with one unstressed syllable followed by one stressed syllable, as in the word "ăfráid"

2. *Trochee:* a foot with one stressed syllable followed by one unstressed syllable, as in the word "héathĕr"

3. *Anapest:* a foot with two unstressed syllables followed by one stressed syllable, as in the word "dĭsĕmbárk"

4. *Dactyl:* a foot with one stressed syllable followed by two unstressed syllables, as in the word "sólĭtŭde"

5. *Spondee:* a foot with two stressed syllables, as in the word "wórkdáy"

6. *Pyrrhic:* a foot with two unstressed syllables, as in the last foot of the word "ŭnspéak|ăblў"

7. *Amphibrach:* a foot with an unstressed syllable, one stressed syllable, and another unstressed syllable, as in the word "ănóthĕr"

8. *Amphimacer:* a foot with a stressed syllable, one unstressed syllable, and another stressed syllable, as in "úp ănd dówn"

A line of poetry is described as *iambic, trochaic, anapestic,* or *dactylic* according to what kind of foot appears most often in the line.

Lines are also described in terms of the number of feet that occur in them, as follows:

1. *Monometer:* verse written in one-foot lines:
Soúnd thĕ Flúte!
Nów it's mútĕ.
Bírds dĕlíght
Dáy ănd Níght.
    —William Blake, "Spring"

2. *Dimeter:* verse written in two-foot lines:

Ŏ Róse | thŏu ărt síck.
Thĕ invís | iblĕ wórm,
Thăt flíes | ĭn thĕ níght
Ĭn thĕ hów | lĭng stórm:
Hăs found | oŭt thy̆ béd
Ŏf crim | sŏn jóy:
Ănd hĭs dárk | sĕcrĕt lóve
Dŏes thy̆ lífe | dĕstróy.
　　　—William Blake, "The Sick Rose"

3. *Trimeter:* verse written in three-foot lines:

Ĭ wént | tŏ thĕ Gárd | ĕn ŏf Lóve
Ănd sáw | whăt ĭ név | ĕr hăd séen:
Ă Cháp | ĕl wăs buílt | ĭn thĕ mídst,
Whĕre Ĭ used | tŏ pláy | ŏn thĕ gréen.
　　　—William Blake, "The Garden of Love"

4. *Tetrameter:* verse written in four-foot lines:

Ĭ wánd | ĕr thró' | eăch chárt | er'd stréet,
Nĕar whére | thĕ chárt | er'd Thámes | dŏes flów
Ănd mărk | ĭn ev | ĕry fáce | Ĭ méet
Márks ŏf | wéaknĕss, | márks ŏf | wóe.
　　　—William Blake, "London"

5. *Pentameter:* verse written in five-foot lines:

Ănd wĕ | ăre pút | ŏn éarth | ă lítt | lĕ spáce,
Thăt wĕ | măy léarn | tŏ béar | thĕ béams | ŏf lóve
　　　—William Blake, "The Little Black Boy"

A six-foot line is called a *hexameter.* A line with seven feet is a *heptameter.*

A complete description of the meter of a line tells both how many feet there are in the line and what kind of foot is most common. Thus the stanza from Emily Brontë's poem, quoted at the beginning of this entry, would be described as being made up of alternating iambic tetrameter and iambic trimeter lines. Poetry that does not have a regular meter is called *free verse.*

METONYMY　*Metonymy* is a figure of speech that substitutes something closely related for the thing actually meant. In the opening line of "The Lost Leader," Robert Browning says, "Just for a handful of silver he left us," using silver to refer to money in the form of a government grant.
See *Figurative Language.*

MIRACLE PLAY　See *Drama.*

MOCK EPIC　A *mock epic* is a poem about a trivial matter written in the style of a serious epic. The incongruity of style and subject matter produces comic effects. Alexander Pope's *The Rape of the Lock,* on page 494, is a mock epic.
See *Epic.*

MONOLOGUE　A *monologue* is a speech or performance given entirely by one person or by one character.
See *Dramatic Monologue* and *Soliloquy.*

MOOD　*Mood,* or atmosphere, is the feeling created in the reader by a literary work or passage. Mood may be suggested by the writer's choice of words, by events in the work, or by the physical setting. Nadine Gordimer begins "The Train from Rhodesia," on page 930, with a mood-evoking description of the brick, mud, and tin buildings at the hot, sandy train station. Everyone there awaits the train, the only relief in this inactive and restricted environment.
See *Setting* and *Tone.*

MORALITY PLAY　See *Drama.*

MOTIF　A *motif* is a recurring literary convention or an element repeated within a literary work. For example, D. H. Lawrence, in "The Rocking-Horse Winner," on page 858, repeats the motif of luck throughout his story. A motif, part of the literary tradition or an author's own invention, generally unifies a work and enhances its theme.

MOTIVATION　A *motivation* is a reason that explains, at least partially, a character's thoughts, feelings, actions, or speech. Characters may be

motivated by physical needs; by wants, wishes, desires, or dreams; or by beliefs, values, and ideals. Effective characterization involves creating believable motivations.
See *Character.*

MYTH   A *myth* is a fictional tale, originally with religious significance, that explains the actions of gods or heroes, the causes of natural phenomena, or both. Allusions to characters and motifs from Greek, Roman, Norse, and Celtic myths are common in English literature. In addition, mythological stories are often retold or adapted, as Bernard Shaw's *Pygmalion,* on page 968, illustrates. Pygmalion was a character from Greek mythology who created a beautiful sculpture of a woman and then fell in love with his own creation.
See *Legend.*

NARRATION   *Narration* is writing that tells a story. The act of telling a story is also called *narration.* The *narrative,* or story, is told by a storyteller called the *narrator.* Narration is one of the major forms of discourse and appears in many guises. Biographies, autobiographies, journals, reports, novels, short stories, plays, narrative poems, anecdotes, fables, parables, myths, legends, folk tales, ballads, and epic poems are all narratives, or types of narration.

NARRATIVE POEM   A *narrative poem* tells a story in verse. Three traditional types of narrative poems include ballads, such as "Sir Patrick Spens," on page 84, and "Barbara Allan," on page 91; epics, such as *Beowulf,* on page 20; and metrical romances, such as *Sir Gawain and the Green Knight,* on page 96. Other narrative poems in this text include the selection from Spenser's *The Faerie Queene,* on page 220; the selection from Milton's *Paradise Lost,* on page 411; Coleridge's "The Rime of the Ancient Mariner," on page 596; and Tennyson's "The Lady of Shalott," on page 698.

NATURALISM   *Naturalism* was a literary movement among writers at the end of the nineteenth century and during the early decades of the twentieth century. The Naturalists, influenced by the theories of Social Darwinists like Sir Herbert Spencer, tended to view people as hopeless victims of immutable natural laws.
See *Realism.*

NEOCLASSICISM   *Neoclassicism* was a literary movement of the Restoration and the eighteenth century in which writers turned to classical Greek and Roman literary models and standards. Like the ancient Greeks, the Neoclassicists stressed reason, order, harmony, restraint, correctness, and decorum. The way these qualities took literary form is illustrated by the balanced and controlled heroic couplet, perfected by John Dryden and Alexander Pope. Much Neoclassical literature dealt with themes related to proper human conduct. The most popular literary forms of the day—essays, letters, early novels, epigrams, parodies, and satires—reflected this emphasis on society as a subject. Just as the Neoclassicists rejected the individualism and extravagance of the Renaissance in favor of classical restraint, so the nineteenth-century Romantics rejected Neoclassicism in favor of imagination, emotion, and the individual.
See *Classicism* and *Romanticism.*

NONFICTION   *Nonfiction* is prose writing that presents and explains ideas or that tells about real people, places, objects, or events.
See *Fiction.*

NOVEL   A *novel* is a long work of fiction. A novel often has a complicated plot, many major and minor characters, a significant theme, and several settings. Novels can be grouped in many ways based on the historical periods in which they are written (such as Romantic or Victorian), on the subjects and themes that they treat (such as Gothic or regional), on the techniques used in them (such as stream of consciousness), or on their debts to literary movements (such as Naturalism or Realism). Among early novels were Samuel Richardson's works *Pamela* and *Clarissa Harlowe,* and Henry Fielding's *Tom Jones.* Other classic English novels include Jane Austen's *Pride and Prejudice,* Sir Walter Scott's *Waverley,* Charles Dickens's *David Copperfield,* and George Eliot's *The Mill on the Floss.* Major twentieth-century novelists include James Joyce, Virginia Woolf, D. H. Lawrence, Henry James, Graham Greene, and Patrick White. A *novella,* for example, Joseph Conrad's *Heart of Darkness,* is not as long as a novel but is longer than a short story.

OBJECTIVE CORRELATIVE   See *Image.*

OCTAVE   See *Stanza.*

ODE   An *ode* is a long, formal lyric poem with a serious theme. It may or may not have a traditional structure with three alternating stanza patterns called the *strophe,* the *antistrophe,* and the *epode.* An ode may be written for a private occasion, as was John Keats's "Ode to a Nightingale" on page 657, or it may be prepared for a public ceremony, as was John Dryden's "A Song for St. Cecilia's Day," on page 453. Odes often honor people, commemorate events, or respond to natural scenes.
See *Lyric Poem.*

ONOMATOPOEIA   *Onomatopoeia* is the use of words that imitate sounds. Examples of such words are *buzz, hiss, murmur,* and *rustle.* Seamus Heaney uses onomatopoeia in "Churning Day" to suggest the sounds of making butter:

> My mother took first turn, set up rhythms
> that slugged and thumped for hours. Arms
>   ached.
> Hands blistered. Cheeks and clothes were
>   splattered
> with flabbymilk.

Onomatopoeia is used to create musical effects and to reinforce meaning.

ORAL TRADITION   *Oral tradition* is the passing of songs, stories, and poems from generation to generation by word of mouth. Among the many materials composed or preserved through oral tradition in Great Britain are *Beowulf,* on page 20, and the folk ballads on pages 84–92. In his *Morte d'Arthur,* Sir Thomas Malory drew on written French sources and on Arthurian legends from the oral tradition. Edmund Spenser drew on the same sources when composing *The Faerie Queene.* Shakespeare drew on materials from the oral tradition to create the *sprites* and *fairies* of *A Midsummer Night's Dream.* Folk epics, ballads, myths, legends, folk tales, folk songs, proverbs, nursery rhymes—all such products of the oral tradition were originally spoken or sung rather than written down.
See *Ballad, Folklore, Legend,* and *Myth.*

OXYMORON   *Oxymoron* is a figure of speech that fuses two contradictory or opposing ideas. An oxymoron, such as "freezing fire" or "happy grief," thus suggests a paradox in just a few words. In Book I of *Paradise Lost,* Milton uses the oxymoron "darkness visible" to describe the pit into which Satan and the other rebellious angels have been thrown.
See *Figurative Language* and *Paradox.*

PARADOX   A *paradox* is a statement that seems to be contradictory but that actually presents a truth. In "Love's Growth," John Donne presents the following paradox:

> Methinks I lied all winter, when I swore
> My love was infinite, if spring make it more.

Because a paradox is surprising or even shocking, it draws the reader's attention to what is being said.
See *Figurative Language* and *Oxymoron.*

PARALLELISM *Parallelism* is the repetition of a grammatical pattern. Stevie Smith uses parallel infinitive verbs in her poem "Is It Wise?":

Is it wise
To hug misery
To make a song of Melancholy
To weave a garland of sighs
To abandon hope wholly?
No, it is not wise.

Parallelism is used in poetry and in other writing to emphasize and to link related ideas.

PASTORAL A literary work is *pastoral* if it deals with the pleasures of a simple, rural life or with escape to a simpler place and time. The tradition of pastoral literature began in ancient Greece with the poetic idylls of Theocritus. Theocritus wrote about the simple lives of shepherds and goatherds. The Roman poet Virgil also wrote a famous collection of pastoral poems, the *Eclogues,* in imitation of Theocritus. Virgil's characters were also idealized rustics.

During the European Renaissance, pastoral writing became quite popular. One famous example of the genre is *The Countess of Pembroke's Arcadia,* by Sir Phillip Sidney. Another example is Christopher Marlowe's "The Passionate Shepherd to His Love," on page 215.

Today the term *pastoral* is commonly applied to any work in which a speaker longs to escape to a simpler, rural life. By this definition both William Wordsworth's "The World Is Too Much with Us," on page 589, and William Butler Yeats's "The Lake Isle of Innisfree," on page 1061, are pastoral poems.

PENTAMETER   See *Meter.*

PERSONIFICATION *Personification* is a type of figurative language in which a nonhuman subject is given human characteristics. Percy Bysshe Shelley used personification in these lines from "To Night":

Swiftly walk o'er the western wave,
    Spirit of the Night!
Out of the misty eastern cave
Where, all the long and lone daylight
Thou wovest dreams of joy and fear,
Which make thee terrible and dear,
    Swift be thy flight!

Effective personification of things or ideas makes them vital, as if they were human. See *Figurative Language* and *Metaphor.*

PLOT   *Plot* is the sequence of events in a literary work. The two primary elements of any plot are characters and a conflict. Most plots can be analyzed into most or all of the following parts:
1. The *exposition* introduces the setting, the characters, and the basic situation.
2. The *inciting incident* introduces the central conflict.
3. During the *development,* the conflict runs its course and usually intensifies.
4. At the *climax,* the conflict reaches a high point of interest or suspense.
5. At the *resolution,* the conflict is ended.
6. The *denouement* ties up loose ends that remain after the resolution of the conflict.

There are many variations on the standard plot structure. Some stories begin *in medias res* ("in the middle of things"), after the inciting incident has already occurred. In some stories the expository material appears toward the middle, in flashbacks. In many stories there is no denouement. Occasionally, though not often, the conflict is left unresolved.

POETRY   *Poetry* is one of the three major types, or genres, of literature, the others being prose and drama. Poetry defies simple definition because there is no single characteristic that is found in all poems and not found in all non-poems. In other words, poems are what philosophers of language call an "ill-defined set."

Often poems are divided into lines and stanzas. Many poems employ regular rhythmical patterns, or meters. However, some are written in free verse. Most poems make use of highly concise, musical, and emotionally charged language. Many also use imagery, figurative language, and devices of sound like rhyme.

Types of poetry include narrative poetry (ballads, epics, and metrical romances), dramatic poetry (dramatic monologues and dramatic dialogues), lyrics (sonnets, odes, elegies, and love poems), and concrete poetry.

POINT OF VIEW   *Point of view* is the perspective, or vantage point, from which a story is told. If a character within the story tells the story, then it is told from the *first-person* point of view. If a voice from outside the story tells it, then the story is told from the *third-person* point of view. If the knowledge of the storyteller is limited to the internal states of one character, then the storyteller has a *limited* point of view. If the storyteller's knowledge extends to the internal states of all of the characters, then the storyteller has an *omniscient* point of view. The point of view from which a story is told determines what view of events will be presented.

PROSE   *Prose* is the ordinary form of written language and one of the three major types of literature. Most writing that is not poetry, drama, or song is considered prose. Prose occurs in two major forms: fiction and nonfiction.

PROTAGONIST   The *protagonist* is the main character in a literary work. In D. H. Lawrence's "The Rocking-Horse Winner," on page 858, the protagonist is Paul.
See *Antagonist* and *Character.*

PSALM   A *psalm* is a song or hymn of praise, like those in the Book of Psalms in the Bible.

PUN   A *pun* is a play on words. A pun may involve using a word or a phrase that has two different meanings or it may involve using two different words or phrases with the same sound, as in *sun* and *son.* The title of George Herbert's poem "The Collar" is a pun that suggests both the clerical collar of an Anglican minister and "choler," or anger, the emotion expressed at the beginning of the poem. Puns are often humorous but may serve serious purposes as well, as the example from Herbert shows.

PYRRHIC   See *Meter.*

QUATRAIN   See *Stanza.*

REALISM   *Realism* is the presentation in art of details from actual life. Another term for Realism, one that derives from Aristotle's *Poetics,* is *mimesis,* the Greek word for "imitation." During the last part of the nineteenth century and the first part of the twentieth, Realism enjoyed considerable popularity among writers in the English-speaking world. Nowhere, perhaps, was Realism more evident than in the novel. Novels often dealt with grim social realities and presented realistic portrayals of the psychological states of characters. Realism also influenced the theater in the early Modern Era. During the first part of this century, for example, the most common sort of stage setting was that in which a room was presented as though one wall had been removed and the audience were peering inside.

REFRAIN   A *refrain* is a regularly repeated line or group of lines in a poem or song.

REGIONALISM   *Regionalism* is the tendency to confine one's writing to the presentation of materials drawn from a particular geographical area. For example, the Brontës wrote about Yorkshire, Thomas Hardy wrote about Dorset and Wessex, and D. H. Lawrence wrote about Nottinghamshire. A Regionalist writer presents the distinct culture of an area, including its speech, customs, landscape, and history.

RHYME *Rhyme* is the repetition of sounds at the ends of words. *End rhyme* occurs when rhyming words appear at the ends of lines. *Internal rhyme* occurs when rhyming words fall within a line. *Exact rhyme* is the use of identical rhyming sounds, as in *love* and *dove*. *Approximate,* or *slant rhyme,* is the use of sounds that are similar but not identical, as in *prove* and *glove*.

RHYME SCHEME A *rhyme scheme* is a regular pattern of rhyming words in a poem or stanza. To indicate a rhyme scheme, assign each final sound in the poem or stanza a different letter. The following lines from Charlotte Brontë's "On the Death of Anne Brontë" have been marked:

There's little joy in life for *me,*	*a*
And little terror in the *grave;*	*b*
I've lived the parting hour to *see*	*a*
Of one I would have died to *save.*	*b*

The rhyme scheme of this stanza is *abab.*

RHYTHM See *Meter*.

RISING ACTION The *rising action* is that part of a plot that leads up to the climax. During the rising action, suspense increases as the complications of the conflict develop.
See *Falling Action* and *Plot*.

ROMANCE A *romance* is a story that presents remote or imaginative incidents rather than ordinary, realistic experience. The term *romance* was originally used to refer to medieval tales of the deeds and loves of noble knights and ladies. These early romances, or tales of chivalry and courtly love, are exemplified by *Sir Gawain and the Green Knight,* on page 96, and by Malory's *Morte d'Arthur,* on page 170. During the Renaissance in England, many writers drew heavily on the romance tradition. One such writer was Edmund Spenser, whose *The Faerie Queene* combines elements of romance and elements of the epic. From the eighteenth century on, the term *romance* has been commonly used to describe sentimental novels about love.

ROMANTICISM *Romanticism* was a literary and artistic movement of the eighteenth and nineteenth centuries. In reaction to Neoclassicism, the Romantics emphasized imagination, fancy, freedom, emotion, wildness, the beauty of the untamed natural world, the rights of the individual, the nobility of the common man, and the attractiveness of pastoral life. Important figures in the Romantic movement included William Wordsworth; Samuel Taylor Coleridge; Percy Bysshe Shelley; John Keats; and George Gordon, Lord Byron.

RUN-ON LINE A *run-on line* is one that does not contain a pause or a stop at the end. A run-on line ends in the middle of a statement and of a grammatical unit, and the reader must read the next line to find the end of the statement and the completion of the grammatical unit. The beginning of Molly Holden's "The Double Nature of White" illustrates the run-on line:

> White orchards are the earliest, stunning
> the spirit resigned to winter's black, white thorn
> sprays first the bare wet branches of the hedge.

See *End-Stopped Line*.

SATIRE *Satire* is writing that ridicules or holds up to contempt the faults of individuals or of groups. A satirist may use a sympathetic tone or an angry, bitter tone. Some satire, like Jonathan Swift's *Gulliver's Travels,* an excerpt from which appears on page 474, is written in prose. Other satire, such as Henry Reed's "The Naming of Parts," on page 1114, is written in poetry. Although a satire is often humorous, its purpose is not simply to make readers laugh but also to correct the flaws and short-comings that it points out.

SCANSION *Scansion* is the process of analyzing the metrical pattern of a poem.
See *Meter*.

SESTET See *Stanza*.

SETTING The *setting* of a literary work is the time and place of the action. A setting can serve many different purposes. It can provide a backdrop for the action. It can be the force that the protagonist struggles against and thus the source of the central conflict. It can also be used to create a mood, or atmosphere. In many works the setting symbolizes some point that the author wishes to emphasize.
See *Mood* and *Symbol*.

SHORT STORY A *short story* is a brief work of fiction. The short story resembles the longer novel but generally has a simpler plot and setting. In addition, a short story tends to reveal character at a crucial moment rather than to develop it through many incidents.

SIMILE A *simile* is a figure of speech that compares two dissimilar things by using a key word such as *like* or *as*. Christina Rossetti uses simile in "Goblin Market" to describe two sisters:

> Like two blossoms on one stem,
> Like two flakes of new-fallen snow,
> Like two wands of ivory
> Tipped with gold for awful kings.

By comparing dissimilar things, the writer of a simile shocks the reader into appreciation of the qualities of the things being compared. A simile makes a description vivid and memorable.
See *Figurative Language*.

SOLILOQUY A *soliloquy* in a play or prose work is a long speech made by a character who is alone and thus reveals his or her private thoughts and feelings to the audience or reader. William Shakespeare opens Act III of *Macbeth* with a soliloquy in which Banquo speculates on Macbeth's reaction to the witches' prophecy.
See *Monologue*.

SONNET A *sonnet* is a fourteen-line lyric poem with a single theme. Sonnets vary but are usually written in iambic pentameter, following one of two traditional patterns.

The *Petrarchan* or *Italian sonnet* is divided into two parts, an eight-line octave and a six-line sestet. The octave rhymes *abba abba,* while the sestet generally rhymes *cde cde* or uses some combination of *cd* rhymes. The two parts of this sonnet work together. The octave raises a question, states a problem, or presents a brief narrative, and the sestet answers the question, solves the problem, or comments on the narrative.

The *Shakespearean* or *English sonnet* has three four-line quatrains plus a concluding two-line couplet. The rhyme scheme of such a sonnet is usually *abab cdcd efef gg*. Each of the three quatrains usually explores a different variation of the main theme. Then the couplet presents a summarizing or concluding statement.
See *Lyric Poem* and *Sonnet Sequence*.

SONNET SEQUENCE A *sonnet sequence* is a series or group of sonnets written to one person or on one theme. Although each sonnet can stand alone as a separate poem, the sequence lets the poet trace the development of a relationship or examine different aspects of a single subject. Examples of sonnet sequences are Sir Philip Sidney's *Astrophel and Stella*, Edmund Spenser's *Amoretti*, and Elizabeth Barrett Browning's *Sonnets From the Portuguese*.
See *Sonnet*.

SPEAKER The *speaker* is the imaginary voice assumed by the writer of a poem. In other words, the speaker is the character who tells the poem. This character is often not identified by name. The title of William Blake's poem "The Chimney Sweeper" identifies the speaker, a child who gives this account of his life:

> When my mother died I was very young,
> And my father sold me while yet my tongue

Could scarcely cry "'weep! 'weep! 'weep! 'weep!"
So your chimneys I sweep and in soot I sleep.

Although this speaker matter-of-factly accepts his life, the poem is ironic because the poet expects readers to have a different view of the child's situation. Recognizing the speaker and thinking about his or her characteristics are often central to interpreting a lyric poem.
See *Point of View*.

SPONDEE   See *Meter*.

SPRUNG RHYTHM   *Sprung rhythm* is the term used by Gerard Manley Hopkins to describe the idiosyncratic meters of his poems. Discovering the underlying metrical pattern of a poem written in sprung rhythm is difficult. The rhythm is quite varied and contains such violations of traditional metrical rules as several strong stresses in a row or feet containing more than two weak stresses.

STANZA   A *stanza* is a group of lines in a poem, seen as a unit. Many poems are divided into stanzas that are separated by spaces. Stanzas often function like paragraphs in prose. Each stanza states and develops one main idea.

Stanzas are commonly named according to the number of lines found in them, as follows:
1. *Couplet:* a two-line stanza
2. *Tercet:* a three-line stanza
3. *Quatrain:* a four-line stanza
4. *Cinquain:* a five-line stanza
5. *Sestet:* a six-line stanza
6. *Heptastich:* a seven-line stanza
7. *Octave:* an eight-line stanza
See *Sonnet*.

STREAM OF CONSCIOUSNESS   *Stream of consciousness* is a narrative technique that presents thoughts as if they were coming directly from a character's mind. Lacking chronological order, the events in a stream-of-consciousness narra-

tive are presented from the character's point of view, mixed in with the character's ongoing feelings and memories. Developed by writers such as James Joyce and Virginia Woolf, stream-of-consciousness writing is used to reveal a character's complex psychology and to present it in realistic detail.
See *Point of View*.

STYLE   A writer's *style* is his or her typical way of writing. Determinants of a writer's style include formality, use of figurative language, use of rhythm, typical grammatical patterns, typical sentence lengths, and typical methods of organization. John Milton is noted for a grand, heroic style that contrasts with John Keats's rich, sensory style and with T. S. Eliot's allusive, ironic style.
See *Diction*.

SUSPENSE   *Suspense* is a feeling of growing curiosity or anxious uncertainty about the outcome of events in a literary work. Writers create suspense by raising questions in the minds of their readers.

SYMBOL   A *symbol* is anything that stands for or represents something else. Thus a flag can symbolize a country, a group of letters can symbolize a spoken word, a spoken word can symbolize an object, a fine car can symbolize wealth, and so on. In literary criticism a distinction is often made between *traditional* or *conventional symbols*—ones that are part of our general cultural inheritance—and *personal symbols*—ones that are created by particular authors for use in particular works. For example, the lamb in William Blake's poem "The Lamb" is a conventional symbol for peace, gentleness, and innocence, one that Blake inherited from the Bible and from the pastoral tradition. However, the tiger in Blake's poem "The Tiger" is not a conventional or inherited symbol. Blake created this symbol of evil specifically for this poem.

Conventional symbolism is often based on elements of nature. For example, youth is often symbolized by greenery or springtime, middle age by summer, and old age by autumn or winter. Death is often symbolized by darkness or cold. The sun is often used as a symbol of power or authority. Roses are symbols of love and beauty. Doves are symbols of peace. Foxes are symbols of craftiness, and owls of wisdom.

Conventional symbols are also borrowed from the spheres of religion and politics. For example, a cross may be a symbol of Christianity or the color red a symbol of Marxist ideology.

SYMBOLISM   *Symbolism* was a literary movement of nineteenth-century France. The Symbolist writers reacted against Realism and stressed, instead, the importance of suggestion and evocation of emotional states, especially by means of symbols. The Symbolists were also quite concerned with using sound to achieve emotional effects. Important Symbolist writers included Stéphane Mallarmé, Paul Verlaine, and Arthur Rimbaud. English writers who were influenced by the Symbolist movement included William Butler Yeats and T. S. Eliot.

SYNECDOCHE   *Synecdoche* is a figure of speech in which a part of something is used to stand for the whole. In the preface to his long poem entitled *Milton,* William Blake includes these lines: "And did those feet in ancient time/ Walk upon England's mountains green?" The feet stand for the whole body, and "England's mountains green" stand for England generally. See *Figurative Language.*

TETRAMETER   See *Meter.*

THEME   The *theme* is a central idea, concern, or purpose in a literary work. In an essay the theme might be directly stated in what is known as a thesis statement. In a serious literary work, the theme is usually expressed indirectly rather than directly. A light work, one written strictly for entertainment, may not have a theme.

TONE   The *tone* of a literary work is the writer's attitude toward the readers and toward the subject. A writer's tone may be formal or informal, friendly or distant, personal or pompous. For example, William Hazlitt's tone in his essay on Macbeth, on page 328, is earnest and respectful, while James Boswell's tone in *The Life of Samuel Johnson,* which begins on page 522, is familiar and engaging.
See *Mood.*

TRAGEDY   *Tragedy* is a type of drama or literature that shows the downfall or destruction of a noble or outstanding person, traditionally one who possesses a character weakness called a *tragic flaw.* Macbeth, for example, is a brave and noble figure led astray by ambition. The *tragic hero,* through choice or circumstance, is caught up in a sequence of events that inevitably results in disaster. Because the protagonist is neither a wicked villain nor an innocent victim, the audience reacts with mixed emotions—both pity and fear, according to the Greek philosopher Aristotle, who defined tragedy in the *Poetics.* The outcome of a tragedy, in which the protagonist is isolated from society, contrasts with the happy resolution of a comedy, in which the protagonist makes peace with society.
See *Comedy* and *Drama.*

TRIMETER   See *Meter.*

TROCHEE   See *Meter.*

GLOSSARY

READING THE GLOSSARY ENTRIES

The words in this glossary are from selections appearing in your textbook. Each entry in the glossary contains the following parts:

1. Entry Word. This word appears at the beginning of the entry in boldface type.

2. Pronunciation. The symbols in parentheses tell how the entry word is pronounced. If a word has more than one possible pronunciation, the most common of these pronunciations is given first.

3. Part of Speech. Appearing after the pronunciation, in italics, is an abbreviation that tells the part of speech of the entry word. The following abbreviations have been used:

n. noun   **p.** pronoun   **v.** verb

adj. adjective   **adv.** adverb   **conj.** conjunction

4. Definition. This part of the entry follows the part-of-speech abbreviation and gives the meaning of the entry word as used in the selection in which it appears.

KEY TO PRONUNCIATION SYMBOLS USED IN THE GLOSSARY

The following symbols are used in the pronunciations that follow the entry words:

Symbol	Key Words	Symbol	Key Words
a	asp, fat, parrot	b	bed, fable, dub
ā	ape, date, play	d	dip, beadle, had
ä	ah, car, father	f	fall, after, off
		g	get, haggle, dog
e	elf, ten, berry	h	he, ahead, hotel
ē	even, meet, money	j	joy, agile, badge
		k	kill, tackle, bake
i	is, hit, mirror	l	let, yellow, ball
ī	ice, bite, high	m	met, camel, trim
		n	not, flannel, ton
ō	open, tone, go	p	put, apple, tap
ô	all, horn, law	r	red, port, dear
o͞o	ooze, tool, crew	s	sell, castle, pass
o͝o	look, pull, moor	t	top, cattle, hat
yo͞o	use, cute, few	v	vat, hovel, have
yoo	united, cure, globule	w	will, always, swear
oi	oil, point, toy	y	yet, onion, yard
ou	out, crowd, plow	z	zebra, dazzle, haze
u	up, cut, color	ch	chin, catcher, arch
ʉr	urn, fur, deter	sh	she, cushion, dash
		th	thin, nothing, truth
ə	a in ago	th	then, father, lathe
	e in agent	zh	azure, leisure
	i in sanity	ŋ	ring, anger, drink
	o in comply	'	[indicates that a
	u in focus		following l or n is a
ər	perhaps, murder		syllabic consonant,
			as in able (ā' b'l)]

FOREIGN SOUNDS

à   This symbol, representing the *a* in French *salle,* can best be described as intermediate between (a) and (ä).

ë   This symbol represents the sound of the vowel cluster in French *coeur* and can be approximated by rounding the lips as for (ō) and pronouncing (e).

ö   This symbol variously represents the sound of *eu* in French *feu* or of *ö* or *oe* in German *blöd* or *Goethe* and can be approximated by rounding the lips as for (ō) and pronouncing (ā).

ô   This symbol represents a range of sounds between (ô) and (u); it occurs typically in the sound of the *o* in French *tonne* or German *korrekt;* in Italian *poco* and Spanish *torero,* it is almost like English (ô), as in *horn.*

ü   This symbol variously represents the sound of *u* in French *duc* and in German *grun* and can be approximated by rounding the lips as for (ō) and pronouncing (ē).

kh   This symbol represents the voiceless velar or uvular fricative as in the *ch* of German *doch* or Scots English *loch.* It can be approximated by placing the tongue as for (k) but allowing the breath to escape in a stream, as in pronouncing (h).

r   This symbol represents any of various sounds used in languages other than English for the consonant *r.* It may represent the tongue-point trill or uvular trill of the *r* in French *reste* or *sur,* German *Reuter,* Italian *ricotta,* Russian *gorod,* etc.

ƀ   This symbol represents the sound made by the letter *v* between vowels. It is pronounced like a *b* sound but without letting the lips come together.

This pronunciation key is from *Webster's New World Dictionary,* Second College Edition. Copyright © 1986 by Simon & Schuster. Used by permission.

A

abasement   (ə bās' mənt)   *n.* Condition of being put down or humbled

abash   (ə bash')   *v.* To make ashamed or ill at ease

abate   (ə bāt')   *v.* To lessen; to put an end to

ablution   (ab lo͞o' shən)   *n.* Washing or cleansing of the body

abstract   (ab' strakt)   *n.* Brief summary stating main points

acanthus   (ə kan' thəs)   *n.* Thistlelike plant

accede   (ak sēd')   *v.* (With *to*) To yield to; agree upon

acrid   (ak' rid)   *adj.* Sharp; bitter

adamantine   (ad' ə man' tēn)   *adj.* Unbreakable

adjure   (a jo͝or')   *v.* To appeal to earnestly

affected   (ə fek' tid)   *adj.* In a manner not true to the person

affliction   (ə flik' shən)   *n.* State of pain or misery, pain; suffering

aggrandizement   (ə gran' diz mənt)   *n.* Increase in power

alacrity   (ə lak' rə tē)   *n.* Willingness

allure (ə loor′) *v.* To entice; charm; induce

amaranth (am′ ə ranth′) *n.* Imaginary flower that never fades or dies

amass (ə mas′) *v.* To gather together

anarchy (an′ ər kē) *n.* Absence of government; confusion, disorder, and violence

animadversion (an′ ə mad vur′ zhən) *n.* Unfavorable comment

anointed (ə noint′ id) *adj.* Declared sacred

anterior (an tir′ ē ər) *adj.* At or toward the front

antic (an′ tik) *adj.* Odd and funny; ludicrous

antipodal (an tip′ ə dəl) *adj.* Situated on opposite sides of the earth

apartheid (ə pär′ tīd; -tād) *n.* The policy of strict racial segregation, and political and economic discrimination against nonwhites in South Africa

aperture (ap′ ər chər) *n.* An opening

apostate (ə päs′ tāt′) *adj.* Denying former religious conviction

apothecary (ə päth′ ə ker ē) *n.* A pharmacist or druggist; person who formerly prepared drugs

appendage (ə pen′ dij) *n.* Something added on

application (ap′ lə kā′ shən) *n.* A specific act or case

apprehension (ap′ rə hen′ shən) *n.* Fear; concern

appropriate (ə prō′ prē āt′) *v.* To borrow without giving credit

arbiter (är′ bə tər) *n.* Judge; umpire

arboreal (är bôr′ ē əl) *adj.* Situated near or among trees

armament (är′ mə mənt) *n.* Arms, weapon

ascendancy (ə send′ ən sē) *n.* A major or dominating influence

aspire (ə spīr′) *v.* To be ambitious

asperity (as per′ ə tē) *n.* Ill temper; irritability

asphodel (as′ fə del′) *n.* Plant with yellow or white lilylike flowers

assay (a sā′) *v.* To try, attempt; prove or test

assiduity (as ə dyoo′ ə tē) *n.* Diligence

assignation (as′ ig nā′ shən) *n.* An appointment to meet

atrophy (a′ trə fē) *v.* To waste away

augment (ôg ment′) *v.* To make greater; enlarge

august (ô gust′) *adj.* Inspiring awe and reverence

avarice (av′ ər is) *n.* Greed

aver (ə vur′) *v.* To state to be true

avocation (av′ ə kā′ shən) *n.* Something that calls one away or distracts from something

avouch (ə vouch′) *v.* To assert positively; affirm

avow (ə vou′) *v.* To swear

awe (ô) *n.* Fear mixed with great respect

B

baleful (bāl′ fəl) *adj.* Of or with evil intent

balm (bäm) *n.* Anything healing or soothing

baneful (bān′ fəl) *adj.* Full of harm; destructive

barrow (bar′ ō) *n.* Heap of earth or rocks marking a grave

Beelzebub (bē el′ zə bub′) *n.* Traditionally, the chief devil, or Satan

beget (bi get′) *v.* To bring into being

belie (bi lī′) *v.* To prove false; contradict

bent (bent) *adj.* Determined; resolved

blight (blīt) *n.* Condition of withering

blithe (blīth) *adj.* Cheerful

bole (bōl) *n.* Tree trunk

boon (boon) *n.* Something good or pleasant that is given, as a blessing

brazen (brā′ z'n) *adj.* 1. Made of brass; 2. bold; shameless

burnished (bur′ nishd) *adj.* Made shiny by daily use

C

caitiff (kāt′ if) *n.* Evil person

cant (kant) *n.* Insincere talk

caprice (kə prēs′) *n.* A tendency to act on whim

careen (kə rēn′) *v.* To lean to one side

career (kə rir′) *v.* To move swiftly forward

carriage (kar′ ij) *n.* A way of bearing oneself; deportment

casement (kās′ mənt) *n.* A window that is hinged at the sides

cataract (kat′ ə rakt′) *n.* A waterfall

cavil (kav′ 'l) *v.* To raise trivial objections

certitude (sur′ tə tood) *n.* A certainty

chaffinch (chaf′ finch′) *n.* Small European songbird

chary (cher′ ē) *adj.* Not giving freely

chaste (chāst) *adj.* Pure; untainted; unblemished

chastise (chas tīz′) *v.* To condemn sharply; scold

chide (chīd) *v.* To scold; rebuke

chimerical (ki mer′ i k'l) *adj.* Imaginary; unreal

chrysalis (kris′ əl əs) *n.* A cocoon of a butterfly

churl (churl) *n.* 1. *same as* ceorl; farm laborer; peasant: 2. Surly, ill-bred person; boor

circumscribe (sur′ kəm skrīb′) *v.* To limit; confine

circumspection (sur′ kəm spek′ shən) *n.* Caution

clamorous (klam′ ər əs) *adj.* Noisy

cleave (klēv) *v.* Split apart

clotted (klät′ id) *adj.* Thickly jumbled in a mass or cluster

cloyed (kloid) *adj.* Made sick by an overdose

cluster (klus′ tər) *n.* A group, gathering; bunch, as of grapes for wine

cockle (käk′ 'l) *n.* An edible shellfish with two heart-shaped shells

colonnade (käl′ ə nād′) *n.* A series of columns set at regular intervals

colossal (kə läs′ 'l) *adj.* Enormous

compact (kəm pakt′) *v.* To put together

complaisance (kəm plā′ z'ns) *n.* A desire to be agreeable

compound (käm′ pound) *v.* To join; combine

compunctious (kəm punk′ shəs) *adj.* Sorrowful; regretful

conciliatory (kən sil′ ē ə tôr′ ē) *adj.* Agreeable

conflagration (kän′ flə grā′ shən)   *n.* A great fire
conjecture (kən jek′ chər)   *v.* To guess
constant (kän′ stənt)   *adj.* Faithful; unchanging; unceasing
consummation (kän′ sə mā′ shən)   *n.* State of fulfillment or completion
consumed (kən sōōm′d′)   *adj.* Overtaken, overwhelmed
contention (kən ten′ shən)   *n.* A controversy; dispute
contrite (kən trīt′)   *adj.* Willing to repent or atone
conviction (kən vik′ shən)   *n.* A belief in something meaningful, such as a creed
coomb (kōōm)   *n.* A deep, narrow valley
copious (kō′ pē əs)   *adj.* Abundant, plentiful
coquet (kō ket′)   *v.* To flirt
corporeal (kôr pôr′ ē əl)   *adj.* Of the body
countenance (koun′ tə nəns)   *n.* A face
coupe (kōō pā′)   *n.* A closed carriage with seats on one side
courtier (kôr′ tē ər)   *n.* An attendant at a royal court
coveted (kuv′ it əd)   *v.* Wanted eagerly
covetousness (kuv′ it əs nəs)   *n.* Greediness
coy (koi)   *adj.* Unwilling to make a commitment, *not* the modern sense of "pretending to be shy."
credulity (krə dōō′ lə tē)   *n.* Tendency to believe too readily
crimp (krimp)   *v.* To shape; crease
cryptogram (krip′ tə gram)   *n.* A coded message
cur (kʉr)   *n.* A dog of mixed breeds
curb (kʉrb)   *n.* Chain or strap around a horse's lower jaw attached to the bit to check the horse
curlew (kʉr′ lōō)   *n.* Large, brownish wading bird with long legs
cynical (sin′ i k'l)   *adj.* Distrustful; sneering

D

dah (dä)   *n.* A knife
dais (dā′ is)   *n.* A platform
dale (dāl)   *n.* A hollow; valley
dappled (dap′ 'ld)   *adj.* Speckled; having more than one color
dauntless (dônt′ lis)   *adj.* Fearless
decamp (di kamp′)   *v.* To leave suddenly
decrepitude (di krep′ ə tōōd)   *n.* State of being old and broken down
deference (def′ ər əns)   *n.* Courtesy
deign (dān)   *v.* To condescend; lower oneself
deride (di rīd′)   *v.* To make fun of; ridicule
derisive (di rī′ siv)   *adj.* Mocking
descant (des kant′)   *v.* To talk at length
desolate (des′ ə lit)   *adj.* Deserted; forlorn
despoil (di spoil′)   *v.* To take away one's possessions
despotic (de spät′ ik)   *adj.* Tyrannical
destitute (des′ tə tōōt)   *adj.* Lacking
desultory (des′ 'l tôr ē)   *adj.* Passing from point to point aimlessly
didactic (dī dak′ tik)   *adj.* Instructive

diffidence (dif′ ə dəns)   *n.* Shyness; hesitation
diffusive (di fyōō′ siv)   *adj.* Spread out
dirge (dʉrj)   *n.* A song of mourning
disabused (dis′ ə byōōzd′)   *adj.* Freed from false ideas
discourse (dis kôrs′)   *v.* To talk about; discuss
discreet (dis krēt′)   *adj.* Wise; prudent
dispensation (dis pən sā′ shən)   *n.* Religious system or belief
distemper (dis tem′ pər)   *n.* Infectious disease, in this case the plague
distill (di stil′)   *v.* To draw out the part that is essential or pure
divers (dī′ vərz)   *adj.* Varied; having many parts (archaic spelling)
divination (div′ ə nā′ shən)   *n.* A clever guess
divining (də vīn′ iŋ)   *adj.* Guessing; intuitive
doleful (dōl′ fəl)   *adj.* Filled with sadness
domain (dō mān′)   *n.* Sphere of activity or influence
dominion (də min′ yən)   *n.* A place of rule; home territory
dotage (dōt′ ij)   *n.* Second childhood, state of senility
doughty (dout′ ē)   *adj.* Brave
dower (dou′ ər)   *n.* A gift
dowry (dou′ rē)   *n.* The property that a woman brings to her husband at marriage
drear (drir)   *adj.* Dreary; melancholy
dregs (dregz)   *n.* Sediment of liquids
dryad (drī′ əd)   *n.* In classical mythology, a wood nymph
dudgeon (duj′ ən)   *n.* Angry resentment; rage
dulcimer (dul′ sə mər)   *n.* Musical instrument with metal strings which produce sounds when struck by two small hammers
dun (dun)   *adj.* Dull grayish brown
dunt (dunt)   *n.* Heavy, dull-sounding blow

E

eclipse (ē klips′)   *n.* A dimming or extinction of fame or glory
eglantine (eg′ lən tīn)   *n.* Sweetbrier or honeysuckle
elocution (el′ ə kyōō′ shən)   *n.* The art of public speaking
elongated (i lôŋ′ gāt id)   *adj.* Lengthened; stretched
eloquent (el′ ə kwənt)   *adj.* Very expressive
empyreal (em pir′ ē əl)   *adj.* Referring to the indestructible substance of which Heaven, or the empyrean, is composed
encomium (en kō′ mē əm)   *n.* The formal expression of praise or tribute
encumber (in kum′ bər)   *v.* To weigh down with a load
engender (in jen′ dər)   *v.* To bring into being; cause to exist
enisled (in īld′)   *adj.* Isolated, as if placed on an island
entreat (in trēt′)   *v.* To beg; plead
equipage (ek′ wə pij′)   *n.* Horses and carriages
equivocate (i kwiv′ ə kāt′)   *v.* To tell falsehoods

escritoire   (es′ krə twär′)   *n.* An ornamental writing desk or table

eternize   (i tur′ nīz)   *v.* To make everlasting

evanescence   (ev′ ə nes′ ′ns)   *n.* Gradual disappearance, especially from sight

even   (ē′ vən)   *adj.* Parallel; on the same level with; conforming to

exact   (ig zakt′)   *v.* To demand; compel

exorciser   (ek′ sôr sīz′ ər)   *n.* A sorcerer; magician

expanse   (ik spans′)   *n.* A wide, continuous stretch, as of land

expedient   (ik spē′ dē ənt)   *n.* Device used in an emergency

expostulate   (ik späs′ chə lāt)   *v.* To reason earnestly with

extradition   (eks′ trə dish′ ən)   *n.* The release of an accused person into the custody of one state by another state

F

faceted   (fas′ ə tid)   *adj.* Having many sides

fathom   (fa*th*′ əm)   *n.* A unit of measure for the depth of water; a fathom is six feet

fastidious   (fas tid′ ē əs)   *adj.* Hard to please

feign   (fān)   *v.* To pretend

fettered   (fet′ ər′d)   *adj.* Chained; confined

fickle   (fik′ ′l)   *adj.* Unfaithful

firmament   (fur′ mə mənt)   *n.* Sky, viewed poetically as a solid arch or vault

firth   (furth)   *n.* The narrow arm of a sea

fleur-de-lys   (flur′ də les′)   *n.* An emblem resembling a lily or iris

fold   (fōld)   *n.* Pen in which to keep sheep

foment   (fō ment′)   *v.* To stir up; incite

fond   (fänd)   *adj.* Archaic: Foolish, *not* the modern sense of having affection for someone or something

foreshortened   (fôr shor′ t′nd)   *adj.* Narrowed by observer's angle of vision

forethink   (fôr thiŋk′)   *v.* To foretell; predict

forlorn   (fər lôrn′)   *adj.* Unhappy; in a pensive mood

former   (fôr′ mər)   *adj.* Earlier; coming before

frolic   (fräl′ ik)   *adj.* Merry

frond   (fränd)   *n.* The leaf of a palm; also the leaflike part of seaweed

furbished   (fur′ bishd)   *adj.* Brightened; polished

furlong   (fur′ lôŋ)   *n.* A unit for measuring distance; a furlong is equal to one eighth of a mile

fustian   (fus′ chən)   *n.* A coarse cotton cloth

G

gaiters   (gāt′ ərz)   *n.* Cloth coverings for the instep and lower leg

gall   (gôl)   *n.* Something bitter or distasteful

galled   (gôld)   *adj.* Injured or made sore by rubbing or chafing

gang   (gaŋ)   *v.* To go or walk (Scot.)

garnished   (gär′ nisht)   *adj.* Decorated; trimmed

garrulous   (gar′ ə ləs)   *adj.* Tending to talk continuously

gaudy   (gôd′ ē)   *adj.* Showy in a tasteless way

gaunt   (gônt)   *adj.* Thin

genial   (jēn′ yəl)   *adj.* Kindly, cordial

gesticulate   (jes tik′ yə lāt′)   *v.* To communicate excitedly by gestures

gisarme   (gi zärm′)   *n.* A battle-ax

glean   (glēn)   *v.* To pick from, as crops

glen   (glen)   *n.* A valley

glimmer   (gli′ mər)   *n.* A faint manifestation or dim perception

gowden   (gou′ d′n)   *adj.* Golden

grace   (grās)   *n.* God's favor or approval

grate   (grāt)   *n.* Frame of metal bars used as a partition

gratuitous   (grə tōō′ ə təs)   *adj.* Undeservedly or without reason

guile   (gīl)   *n.* Artful trickery; cunning

H

haft   (haft)   *n.* Handle of a weapon or tool

haggard   (hag′ ərd)   *adj.* Having a worn, guant, or wild look

halcyon   (hal′ sē ən)   *adj.* Calm

haply   (hap′ le)   *adv.* By chance

harbinger   (här′ bin jər)   *n.* A forerunner

harmonious   (här mō′ nē əs)   *adj.* In a manner that is in accordance

harry   (har′ ē)   *v.* To harass

hauberk   (hô′ bərk)   *n.* A coat of armor

haughty   (hôt′ ē)   *adj.* Lofty

headrig   (hed′ rig)   *n.* The part of a plow that turns over the soil; moldboard

health   (helth)   *n.* A wish for happiness, as in drinking a series of toasts

heraldic   (hə ral′ dik)   *adj.* Resembling an English coat of arms

hermitage   (hur′ mit ij)   *n.* A retreat suitable for meditation; originally, a hermit's dwelling

hew   (hyōō)   *n.* Color; hue

hoary   (hôr′ e)   *adj.* White or gray with age

hobnailed   (häb′ nāld)   *adj.* Studded with nails to prevent wear or slipping

hospitable   (häs pit′ə bəl)   *adj.* Friendly and kind toward guests

hypocrite   (hip′ə krit)   *n.* A person who pretends to be what he or she is not

I

ignominy   (ig′ nə min′ ē)   *n.* Humiliation; dishonor; disgrace

illumine   (i lōō′ min)   *v.* To light up

imminent   (im′ ə nənt)   *adj.* Likely to happen soon

impaired   (im perd′)   *v.* Diminished

impertinence   (im pur′ t′n əns)   *n.* Rudeness

imperturbable   (im′ pər tur′ bə b′l)   *adj.* Calm; not easily ruffled

impetuous (im pech' ōō wəs) *adj.* Given to rash or hasty action; doing things on the spur of the moment; tending to act impulsively, without thinking

impious (im' pē əs) *adj.* Disrespectful; irreverent, ungodly

importuning (im' pôr tōōn' iŋ) *v.* Begging, urging

imprecation (im' prə kā' shən) *n.* A curse

impressionistic (im presh' ə nis' tik) *adj.* Conveying a quick, overall picture

impudence (im' pyōō dəns) *n.* The quality of being rash or contrary

inarticulate (in' är tik' yə lit) *adj.* Not able to speak

incessant (in ses' 'nt) *adj.* Never ceasing

incitement (in sīt' mənt) *n.* A cause to perform; encouragement

inconstancy (in kän' stən sē) *n.* A contradiction; fickleness; changeableness

incorrigible (in kôr' i jə b'l) *adj.* Not capable of being corrected or of behaving better

inculcate (in kul' kāt) *v.* To impress upon the mind by frequent repetition

indissoluble (in' di säl' yōō b'l) *adj.* Not able to be dissolved or undone

induct (in dukt') *v.* To bring formally into a society or organization; initiate; provide with knowledge or experience of something

inexorable (in ek' sər ə b'l) *adj.* Ongoing, with no sign of stopping

infirmity (in fɜr' mə tē) *n.* Physical or mental defect; illness

ingenuous (in jen' yōō wəs) *adj.* Naive; simple

inglorious (in glôr' ē əs) *adj.* Little-known

inimical (in im' i k'l) *adj.* Hostile; unfriendly

inkling (iŋk' liŋ) *n.* Indirect suggestion; hint

iniquity (in ik' wə tē) *n.* Wickedness

innumerable (in nōō' mər ə b'l) *adj.* Too many to count

inordinate (in ôr' d'n it) *adj.* Beyond reasonable limits

insipid (in sip' id) *adj.* Not exciting or interesting; dull, lifeless

intemperance (in tem' pər əns) *n.* Lack of restraint

intermit (in tər mit') *v.* To stop for a time

intimation (in' tə mā' shən) *n.* A hint

invincible (in vin' sə b'l) *adj.* Unconquerable

irony (ī' rə nē) *n.* The contrast between what is being expressed and what is known to be the truth

irremediable (ir' i mē' dē ə b'l) *adj.* Incurable; incapable of being remedied

irrepressible (ir' i pres' ə b'l) *adj.* Not able to be restrained

isthmus (is' məs) *n.* A narrow strip of land, with water on each side, connecting two larger land masses

J

japonica (jə pän' i kə) *n.* A spiny plant with pink or red flowers

judicious (jōō dish' əs) *adj.* having or showing good judgment

K

keen (kēn) *adj.* Having a sharp edge or point

ken (ken) *n.* The range of sight or knowledge

kindred (kin' drid) *n.* Relatives; relations

knave (nāv) *n.* A scoundrel; cheater

knell (nel) *n.* The sound of a bell, especially one rung slowly, as at a funeral

kraal (kräl) *n.* A fenced-in enclosure for cattle or sheep

L

laboriously (lə bôr' ē əs lē) *adv.* In a manner involving much hard work

lament (lə ment') *v.* To mourn; wail; bemoan

lamentable (lam' ən tə b'l) *adj.* Distressing

languid (laŋ' gwid) *adj.* Slow, lacking energy

languish (laŋ' gwish) *v.* To become weak or sickly looking

languor (laŋ' gər) *n.* Weakness, fatigue

largesse (lär' jes) *n.* A nobility of spirit

lark (lärk) *v.* To play around

laryngoscope (lə riŋ' gō skōp') *n.* An instrument for examining the throat

lay (lā) *n.* A short poem to be sung

lemming (lem' iŋ) *n.* A small rodent resembling a mouse; lemmings undertake mass migrations at peak population growth, ultimately drowning while trying to cross the sea

leviathan (lə vī' ə thən) *n.* A great sea monster

lexicographer (lek' sə käg' rə fər) *n.* One who compiles a dictionary

liege (lēj) *n.* A lord or king

lintel (lin' t'l) *n.* A beam over a door

litany (lit' 'n ē) *n.* A form of prayer in which a congregation repeats a fixed response

loath (lōth) *adj.* Reluctant; unwilling

lucrative (lōō' krə tiv) *adj.* Profitable

lyric (lir' ik) *n.* A poem, one of the major categories of poetry; in classical literature, a song accompanied by a lyre

M

madrigal (mad' ri gəl) *n.* A song with parts for several voices with no musical accompaniment

magnanimous (mag nan' ə məs) *adj.* Generously forgiving

mahout (mə hōōt') *n.* An elephant keeper and rider

mail (māl) *n.* A flexible body armor made of metal

maize (māz) *n.* Corn

malevolence (mə lev' ə ləns) *n.* Ill will; spitefulness

malignity (mə lig' nə tē) *n.* A strong desire to harm others; deadliness

mead-hall (mēd′ hôl) *n.* A banquet hall; mead is a beverage made from fermented honey and water

measure (mezh′ ər) *n.* A quantity, dimension, size

megalith (meg′ ə lith′) *n.* A huge stone, especially one used in prehistoric monuments

mendacity (men das′ ə tē) *n.* Lying

mestizo (mes tē′ zō) *adj.* Of Spanish and Indian parentage

metaphysical (met ə fiz′ i k′l) *adj.* Very abstract

minion (min′ yən) *n.* Attendant or agent

miscreant (mis′ crē ənt) *n.* A villain

misanthropist (mis an′ thrə pist) *n.* One who hates or mistrusts others

mockery (mäk′ ər ē) *n.* Ridicule; futile or disappointing effort

modish (mōd′ ish) *adj.* Fashionable

moleskin (mōl′ skin) *n.* Work clothes made from strong, twilled cotton fabric

molt (mōlt) *v.* Cast off; shed, as skin or feathers

moly (mō′ lē) *n.* In classical mythology, an herb of magic powers; European wild garlic

moorline (moor′ līn) *n.* The horizon where open, rolling wasteland meets the sky

morosely (mə rōs′ lē) *adv.* Sullenly; in bad humor

mortification (môr′ tə fi kā′ shən) *n.* A feeling of great shock and upset

multitudinous (mul′ tə tood′ 'n əs) *adj.* Existing in great numbers

munificence (myoo nif′ ə s'ns) *n.* Great generosity

myriad (mir′ ē əd) *n.* Ten thousand; a great number of things

myrrh (mur) *n.* A plant that produces a fragrant gum resin used in making incense and perfume

N

nativity (nə tiv′ ə tē′) *n.* A birth, especially in regard to place and time

negotiate (ni gō′ shē āt) *v.* Make arrangements for, settle, or conclude a transaction

nunnery (nun′ ər ē) *n.* A convent, a dwelling place for nuns

nymph (nimf) *n.* In classical mythology, a minor nature goddess usually shown as a lovely young girl

O

obdurate (äb′ door it, äb′ dyoor it) *adj.* Hardened against what is good or moral; stubborn, unyielding

obliquely (ə blēk′ lē) *adv.* At a slant; indirectly

obliterate (ə blit′ ə rāt) *v.* To destroy utterly

oblivious (ə bliv′ ē əs) *adj.* Forgetful or unmindful

ode (ōd) *n.* A poem of varying line lengths and usually several stanzas, often addressed to someone; in classical literature, a poem to be sung, usually in praise of someone

officious (ə fish′ əs) *adj.* Overly eager to please (obsolete meaning); offering unnecessary advice or services

opiate (ō′ pē it) *n.* Something that brings on relaxation or sleep

oppress (ə pres′) *v.* To burden

oracle (ôr′ ə k'l) *n.* In classical antiquity, the shrine in which a god spoke through a priest or priestess

orderly (ôr′ dər lē) *n.* A soldier assigned to carry out orders of a superior

ordure (ôr′ jər) *n.* Waste matter; excrement

overplus (ō′ vər plus′) *n.* A surplus, abundance; enough left over for others

overscrupulous (ō′ vər skroo′ pyə ləs) *adj.* Overly concerning about details

P

pall (pôl) *n.* A cloth, usually black, draped over a coffin

pallor (pal′ ər) *n.* An unnatural lack of color; paleness

palpable (pal′ pə b'l) *adj.* Capable of being touched or felt

panegyric (pan′ ə jir′ ik) *n.* A speech giving praise

parley (pär′ lē) *n.* A discussion

parquet (pär kā′) *n.* A flooring of inlaid woodwork in geometric forms; wooden floors

passé (pa sā′) *adj.* Stale

pastoral (pas′ tər əl) *adj.* Pertaining to country life

patron (pā′ trən) *n.* One who gives financial aid to an artist or writer

patter (pat′ ər) *v.* To speak or mumble rapidly

penetralia (pen′ ə trā′ lē ə) *n.* The innermost parts

penury (pen′ yə re) *n.* Poverty

perchance (pər chans′) *adv.* Perhaps, possibly

peremptorily (pə remp′ tə ri lē) *adv.* Decisively; without showing cause

perfidiousness (pə fid′ ē əs nis) *n.* The betrayal of trust

perfunctorily (pər funk′ tə ri lē) *adv.* Carelessly

periwig (per′ ə wig′) *n.* A type of wig often worn by men during the seventeenth and eighteenth centuries

pernicious (pər nish′ əs) *adj.* Causing serious injury; deadly; evil; wicked

perpetual (pər pech′ oo wəl) *adj.* Constant, unending

perpetuate (pər pech′ oo āt) *v.* To make perpetual; cause to continue

persistent (pər sis′ tənt) *adj.* Continuing

perturbation (pur′ tər bā′ shən) *n.* A disorder

peruke (pə rook′) *n.* A wig

perverted (pər vur′ tid) *adj.* Distorted; corrupted

pestilence (pes′ t'l əns) *n.* A highly contagious disease, such as plague

pestle (pes′ əl) *n.* A club-shaped utensil used to grind or pound substances in a receptacle called a mortar

petulance   (pech′ ə lens)   *n.* Insolent behavior; peevishness; moodiness

phantasm   (fan′ taz′m)   *n.* A supernatural form or shape

phlegm   (flem)   *n.* Sluggishness

physiognomy   (fiz′ ē äg′ nə mē)   *n.* Facial features thought to reveal character or disposition

piazza   (pē az′ ə)   *n.* An open public square

piety   (pī′ ə tē)   *n.* Devotion

pike   (pīk)   *n.* A voracious freshwater fish

pince-nez   (pans′ nā′)   *n.* Eyeglasses without sidepieces, held in place by springs gripping the bridge of the nose

pirouette   (pir′ o͞o wet′)   *v.* To dance or whirl on one foot

pithead   (pit′ hed)   *n.* The top of a mining pit or coal shaft

plagiarism   (plā′ jə riz′m)   *n.* The passing off of another's work as one's own

platitude   (plat′ ə to͞od′)   *n.* A statement lacking originality

plebian   (pli bē′ ən)   *adj.* Common; ordinary

plutocracy   (plo͞o täk′ rə sē)   *n.* The wealthy governing class

portal   (pôr′ t'l)   *n.* A door; gateway

posy   (pō′ zē)   *n.* A bouquet

prate   (prāt)   *n.* To talk much and foolishly

prau   (prau)   *n.* A swift Malayan boat with a large sail

prebendary   (preb′ ən der′ ē)   *n.* In the Church of England, honorary clergyman

precedency   (pres′ ə dən sē)   *n.* Priority because of rank

precipitate   (pri sip′ ə tit)   *adj.* Steep

predominance   (pri däm′ ə nans)   *n.* Superiority

preferment   (pri fʉr′ mənt)   *n.* An advancement in rank

pregnant   (preg′ nənt)   *adj.* Full of ideas; inventive

presumptuous   (pri zump′ cho͞o wəs)   *adj.* Unduly confident or bold

pretence   (pri tens′)   *n.* A claim (British spelling)

pretension   (pri ten′ shən)   *n.* A claim to a rank or class

pretentious   (pri ten′shəs)   *adj.* Making false claims

preternatural   (prēt′ ər nach′ ər əl)   *adj.* Outside the natural or normal order

prevarication   (pri var ə kā′ shən)   *n.* An evasion of truth

prime   (prīm)   *n.* The best stage or time; most mature period

pristine   (pris′ tēn)   *adj.* Pure; untouched; unspoiled

prodigal   (präd′ i gəl)   *adj.* Addicted to wasteful expenditure

prodigious   (prə dij′ əs)   *adj.* Enormous; huge; impressive

profuse   (prə fyo͞os′)   *adj.* Abundant, pouring out

progeny   (präj′ ə nē)   *n.* Offspring; a child

promiscuously   (prə mis′ kyo͞o wəs lē)   *adv.* Without care or thought

promontory   (präm′ ən tôr′ ē)   *n.* The land that juts out into a body of water; high point of land extending into the sea

propagator   (präp′ ə gāt′ ər)   *n.* One who causes something to happen or to spread

prophesy   (präf′ ə sī)   *v.* Predict

prophetic   (prə fet′ ik)   *adj.* Having the power to predict or foreshadow

propitiate   (prə pish′ ē āt′)   *v.* Ease the burden of; appease

prostrate   (präs′ trāt)   *adj.* Defenseless; in a prone or lying position

protracted   (prō trak′ tid)   *v.* Drawn out; prolonged

providence   (präv′ ə dens)   *n.* Divine forethought, guidance, and care; also, God

prow   (prou)   *n.* The front of a boat

puissant   (pyo͞o′ i sənt)   *adj.* Powerful

pulverous   (pul′ və rəs)   *adj.* Crumbling

pumice   (pum′ is)   *n.* A volcanic rock

punctually   (punk′ cho͞o ə lē)   *adv.* On time; promptly

Q

quay   (kē)   *n.* A wharf with facilities for loading or unloading ships

quip   (kwip)   *n.* A witty or sarcastic remark; jibe

R

raiment   (rā′ mənt)   *n.* Clothing

Raj   (raj)   *n.* Rule

rancor   (raŋ′ kər)   *n.* A continuing and bitter hate or ill will; deep spite or malice

rapture   (rap′ chər)   *n.* An expression of great joy

ravish   (rav′ ish)   *v.* To violate

recompense   (rek′ əm pens′)   *n.* A payment in return; reward

reconcile   (rek′ ən sīl′)   *v.* To make up with

recreant   (rek′ rē ənt)   *adj.* Cowardly

refractory   (ri frak′ tər ē)   *adj.* Hard to manage; stubborn

refulgent   (ri ful′ jənt)   *adj.* Shining; radiant

remonstrance   (ri män′ strəns)   *n.* A protest

remonstrate   (ri män′ strāt)   *v.* To object strongly

repose   (ri pōz′)   *v.* Lie back

repository   (ri päz′ ə tôr ē)   *n.* A center for accumulation and storage

repudiation   (ri pyo͞o′ dē ā′ shən)   *n.* A rejection; denial

respite   (res′ pit)   *n.* A postponement; delay

resplendently   (ri splen′ dənt lē)   *adj.* Splendidly, gorgeously

reticent   (ret′ ə s'nt)   *adj.* Laid back; uncommunicative

retort   (ri tôrt′)   *n.* A comeback with a smart answer or wisecrack

retreat   (ri trēt′)   *n.* A period of retirement or seclusion for prayer, religious study, and meditation

reverberation   (ri vʉr′ bə rā′ shən)   *n.* Reechoed sound; a far-reaching effect of some event or action

reverence (rev' ər əns) *n.* A great respect; deep respect or awe

righteousness (rī' chəs nis) *n.* Doing what is fair and just

rill (ril) *n.* A little brook

rime (rīm) *n.* A white frost

rioter (rī' ət ər) *n.* A loud, dissolute bully

rite (rīt) *n.* A ceremonial, formal, or solemn act performed in accordance with custom or religion

rogue (rōg) *n.* Wandering beggar or tramp; vagabond; an individual varying noticeably from the standard

rostral (räs' trəl) *adj.* Having a beaklike projection, or rostrum, as at the prow of a ship

rout (rout) *n.* An overwhelming defeat

ruminate (rōō' mə nāt) *v.* To think over; meditate

rummage (rum' ij) *v.* To search by thoroughly examining

S

sagacity (sə gas' ə tē) *n.* Wisdom: judgment

salient (sāl' yənt) *adj.* Striking; easily noticeable

salver (sal' vər) *n.* A tray usually used for the presentation of letters or visiting cards

sampan (sam' pan) *n.* A small flat-bottomed boat with a cabin formed by mats

sanguinary (saŋ' gwi ner' ē) *adj.* Bloody

sanguine (saŋ' gwin) *adj.* Of cheerful temperament

sarong (sə rôŋ') *n.* A long, brightly colored strip of cloth worn like a skirt

satiety (sə tī' ə tē) *n.* State of being filled to excess

saturnine (sat' ər nīn) *adj.* Sluggish or gloomy

schism (siz' 'm) *n.* A division into groups or factions

screed (skrēd) *n.* A long, tiresome piece of writing

scutcheon (skuch' ən) *n.* A coat of arms

segmented (seg' ment id) *adj.* Separated into parts

semblance (sem' bləns) *n.* Appearance; image

senility (si nil' ə tē) *n.* Mental and physical decay due to old age

sepulcher (sep' 'l kər) *n.* A tomb

sequacious (si kwā' shəs) *adj.* (Archaic.) Tending to follow dutifully, in service of

sequester (si kwes' tər) *v.* To keep apart from others

Seraphim (ser' ə fim) *n.* The highest order of angels

serrated (ser āt' əd) *adj.* Toothed or notched like a saw

servile (sur' v'l) *adj.* Slavelike

servitude (sur' və tōōd) *n.* The condition of a slave; subjection to a master; bondage

severance (sev' ər əns) *n.* State of being kept separate

shard (shärd) *n.* A fragment or broken pieces

sheaf (shēf) *n.* A bundle of twigs or fibers

signet (sig' nit) *n.* A seal

sinecure (sī' nə kyoor') *n.* Any office or position that brings advantage but involves little or no work

sinew (sin' yōō) *n.* Muscular power; force

sinewy (sin' yōō wē) *adj.* Tough; vigorous; powerful

slagheap (slag' hēp) *n.* A pile of waste material from mining

slumbrous (slum' brəs) *adj.* Peaceful, suggesting sleep

sock (säk) *n.* The blade of a plow

sojourn (sō' jurn) *v.* To stay for a while

solace (säl' is) *n.* A comfort in grief or trouble; relief

solicitous (sə lis' ə təs) *adj.* Showing care or concern

soliloquize (sə lil' ə kwīz') *v.* To talk to oneself

somnambulist (säm nam' byōō list) *n.* A sleepwalker

sophist (säf' ist) *n.* One who makes misleading arguments

sordid (sor' did) *adj.* Unclean, dirty

soiree (swä rā') *n.* Party held in the evening

sophistry (säf' is trē) *n.* Clever but unsound reasoning

sovereign (säv' rən) *adj.* Supreme in power, rank, or authority

specter (spek' tər) *n.* A ghost or ghost-like appearance

spectral (spek' trəl) *adj.* Ghostly

spent (spent) *adj.* Used up; gone

splaying (splā' iŋ) *v.* Spreading

sprightly (sprīt' lē) *adj.* Lively

squalid (skwäl' id) *adj.* Miserably poor; wretched

squire (skwīr) *n.* A country gentleman or landed proprietor

stealthy (stel' thē) *adj.* In a quiet, secretive way; sly; furtive

stem (stem) *v.* To stop; dam up

stile (stīl) *n.* A step or set of steps used in climbing over a fence or wall

stoic (stō' ik) *n.* A person indifferent to pleasure or pain

sublimity (sə blim' ə tē) *n.* The quality of being majestic or noble

subordinate (sə bôr' də nit) *adj.* Beneath another in rank

subtle (sut' 'l) *adj.* Cunning; ingenious

succeed (sək sēd) *v.* To follow; come after

succinct (sək siŋkt') *adj.* Belted (Archaic); terse

suffuse (sə fyōōz') *v.* To fill

sullen (sul' ən) *adj.* Gloomy; dismal

sumpitan (sump' ə tan) *n.* A Malayan blowgun which discharges poisonous darts

sundry (sun' drē) *adj.* Various; miscellaneous

superfluity (sōō' pər flōō' ə tē) *n.* An excess

suppliant (sup' lē ənt) *adj.* Beseeching prayerfully; imploring

supplication (sup' lə kā' shən) *n.* The act of praying

surmise (sər mīz') *v.* To guess, assume; to form an opinion from inconclusive evidence

swaddling (swäd' liŋ) *adj.* Long, narrow bands of cloth wrapped around newborn babies

swain (swān) *n.* A country youth

switch (swich) *n.* A light whip

sylvan (sil' vən) *adj.* Wooded

symmetry   (sim′ ə trē)   *n.* Beauty resulting from balance of form

T

taffeta   (taf′ i tə)   *n.* A fine silk fabric

talent   (tal′ ənt)   *n.* A biblical unit of money; native ability

tarry   (tar′ ē)   *v.* To delay, linger, be tardy, abide; continue in the same condition

tasseled   (tas′ əld)   *adj.* Resembling a tuft of threads or cords of equal length and gathered together in a knot

teeming   (tēm′ iŋ)   *adj.* Filled to overflowing

tempestuous   (tem pes′ chōō wəs)   *adj.* Turbulent; violently stormy

tenor   (ten′ ər)   *n.* A general tendency or course

terrestrial   (tə res′ trē əl)   *adj.* Of this world; earthly

thane   (thān)   *n.* In early England, a member of a class of freemen who held land of the king or a lord in return for military services

thatch   (thach)   *n.* Roofing material made from straw, rushes, palm trees, etc.

thrall   (thrôl)   *n.* A slave; serf

timorous   (tim′ ər əs)   *adj.* Fearful; timid

tincture   (tiŋk′ chər)   *n.* A tint

tithe   (tīth)   *n.* One tenth of a person's income, paid as a tax to support the church

tor   (tôr)   *n.* A high, rocky hill; crag

torrid   (tôr′ id)   *adj.* Hot, scorching

traffic   (traf′ ik)   *n.* Business

transcendence   (tran sen′ dəns)   *n.* A rising above

transgress   (trans gres′)   *v.* To violate a law or command; overstep or break

transient   (tran′ shənt)   *adj.* A person who passes quickly through a place

transitory   (tran′ sə tôr′ ē)   *adj.* Temporary; fleeting

tremulous   (trem′ yōō ləs)   *adj.* Trembling; timid

tress   (tres)   *n.* A lock of human hair

tryst   (trist)   *n.* A meeting

tuber   (tōō′ bər)   *n.* The thick, fleshy part of an underground stem, like a potato or yam

tuft   (tuft)   *n.* A grouping of fibers such as hair or grass

tumid   (tōō′ mid)   *adj.* Swollen

tumult   (tōō′ mult)   *n.* Commotion, disturbance; uproar; noisy confusion

tumultuous   (tōō mul′ chōō wəs)   *adj.* Disorderly; violent

turbid   (tur′ bid)   *adj.* Muddy or cloudy; confused

turret   (tur′ it)   *n.* A small tower projecting from a building

twa   (twä)   *n.* Two (Scot.)

U

uncanny   (un kan′ ē)   *adj.* Mysterious; hard to explain

unctuous   (uŋk′ chōō wəs)   *adj.* Oily

ungenial   (un jēn′ yəl)   *adj.* Unfriendly; characterized by bad weather

unravished   (un rav′ ishd)   *adj.* Undisturbed, unspoiled

usurious   (yōō zhoor′ ē əs)   *adj.* Lending money at a high rate of interest

unsurped   (yōō surp′d′)   *adj.* Wrongfully seized

V

vair   (ver)   *n.* A gray and white fur

valance   (val′ əns)   *n.* A decorative facing

vale   (vāl)   *n.* A valley

vanity   (van′ ə tē)   *n.* A trifle, knicknack, or other insignificant thing

vaunt   (vônt)   *v.* To speak boastfully

vehemence   (vē′ ə məns)   *n.* Strength of feeling and emotion

vehement   (vē′ ə mənt)   *adj.* Energetic, forceful

veldt   (velt)   *n.* Open, grassy country

verdure   (vur′ jər)   *n.* Green plants

verge   (vurj)   *n.* An edge, rim

vestige   (ves′ tij)   *n.* A trace; bit

vestry   (ves′ trē)   *n.* A church meeting room

vignettes   (vin yets′)   *n.* Decorative designs or borderless pictures in a book

vintage   (vin′ tij)   *n.* A wine or nectar of high quality

virago   (və rā′ gō)   *n.* A scolding woman

virtuous   (vur′ chōō wəs)   *adj.* Pure, righteous

virulency   (vir′ yōō lən sē)   *n.* Harmfulness

visage   (viz′ ij)   *n.* A person's face or facial expression

vis-à-vis   (vē′ zə vē′)   Face to face with

viscous   (vis′ kəs)   *adj.* Semifluid; sticky

vizard   (viz′ ərd)   *n.* A mask

W

wan   (wän)   *adj.* Sickly pale; (Archaic) gloomy, not the modern sense of sickly pale

wane   (wān)   *v.* To gradually become dimmer

wanton   (wän′ t'n)   *adj.* Luxuriant: said of vegetation; frisky; playful

wanwood   (wän′ wood)   *n.* A pale wood

wattled   (wät′ 'ld)   *adj.* Twisted or intertwined as with branches or twigs

wax   (waks)   *v.* To grow, ripen

weal   (wēl)   *n.* A discolored ridge on the skin; blister

whelk   (hwelk)   *n.* A pimple

wisteria   (wis tir′ ē ə)   *n.* Vines of shrubs with clusters of bluish, white, pink, or purplish flowers

wit   (wit)   *n.* Intelligence, wisdom

Y

yare   (yer)   *adj.* Ready; prepared

yoke   (yōk)   *n.* A wooden contrivance joining the heads of two draft animals, such as oxen, to make them capable of pulling heavier loads

ycladd   (i klad′)   [Archaic] *pp.* Clothed, dressed

yclept   (i klept′)   [Archaic] *pp.* Called; named

Z

zephyr   (zef′ ər)   *n.* A gentle wind

INDEX OF FINE ART

INDEX OF SKILLS

ANALYZING LITERATURE

CRITICAL THINKING AND READING

LEARNING OPTIONS

THINKING AND WRITING

INDEX OF TITLES BY THEMES

THE POWER OF THE MIND

SEARCH FOR MEANING

SELF-REALIZATION

VALUES AND BELIEFS

INDEX OF AUTHORS AND TITLES

Page numbers in *italics* refer to biographical information.

Macmillan London Ltd.
"A Song for St. Cecilia's Day" from *The Poetical Works of John Dryden* edited by W. D. Christie. "The Three Strangers" from *Wessex Tales* by Thomas Hardy.

Methuen & Company Ltd.
"The Passionate Shepherd to His Love" and lines from *The Tragical History of the Life and Death of Dr. Faustus from Marlowe's Poems* edited by L. C. Martin. Lines from "An Essay on Man," Canto III and lines from Canto V from *The Rape of the Lock* reprinted from *The Poems of Alexander Pope* edited by John Butt. Published by Methuen & Co. Ltd., London.

New American Library, a division of Penguin books USA Inc.
From *The Tragedy of Macbeth* by William Shakespeare, edited by Sylvan Barnet. Copyright © 1963 by Sylvan Barnet.

New Beacon Books Ltd.
"From Lucy: Englan' Lady" from *Lucy's Letters* and *Loving* by James Berry. © 1982 by James Berry. "Thoughts on My Mother" from *Fractured Circles* by James Berry. © 1979 by James Berry. Reprinted by permission of the publisher, New Beacon Books Ltd.

New Directions Publishing Corporation
Lines from "The Galloping Cat" and lines from "My Muse" from Stevie Smith, *The Collected Poems of Stevie Smith*. Copyright © 1972 by Stevie Smith. "Not Waving but Drowning" and "Pretty" from Stevie Smith, *The Collected Poems of Stevie Smith*. Copyright © 1972 by Stevie Smith. Reprinted by permission of New Directions Publishing Corporation.

New Directions Publishing Corporation, and Random House UK Ltd.
"Anthem for Doomed Youth" by Wilfred Owen, from *The Collected Poems of Wilfred Owen*, edited by C. Day Lewis. Copyright © Chatto & Windus Ltd. 1946, 1963. Reprinted by permission of New Directions Publishing Corporation and Random House UK Ltd.

New Directions Publishing Corporation and David Higham Associates Ltd.
"Do Not Go Gentle into That Good Night," "Fern Hill," and "The Force That Through the Green Fuse Drives the Flower" from Dylan Thomas, *Poems of Dylan Thomas*. Copyright 1939 by New Directions Publishing Corporation; 1945 by the Trustees for the Copyrights of Dylan Thomas; 1952 by Dylan Thomas. Published in London by J. M. Dent & Sons Ltd. Reprinted by permission.

W. W. Norton & Company, Inc.
"The Achill Woman" and "Outside History" reprinted from *Outside History, Selected Poems, 1980–1990*, by Eavan Boland, by permission of W. W. Norton & Company, Inc. Copyright © 1990 by Eavan Boland. Reprinted from *Sir Gawain and the Green Knight*, A New Verse Translation by Marie Borroff, by permission of W. W. Norton & Company, Inc. Copyright © 1967 by W. W. Norton & Company, Inc.

Oxford University Press, Inc.
"The Wanderer" from *An Anthology of Old English Poetry*, translated by Charles W. Kennedy. Copyright 1960 by Oxford University Press, Inc.; renewed 1988 by Elizabeth D. Kennedy. Reprinted by permission of Oxford University Press.

Oxford University Press, Inc. and Carcanet Press.
"One Hard Look," and "She Tells Her Love . . ." from *Collected Poems* by Robert Graves. Copyright © 1975 in this edition by Robert Graves.

Oxford University Press, England
"A Poison Tree," "Infant Sorrow," "The Human Abstract," "The Lamb," and "The Tiger" from *The Poetical Works of William Blake* edited by John Sampson. From "The Life of Samuel Johnson" in *Boswell's Life of Johnson* by James Boswell, edited by C. B. Tinker. From *Wuthering Heights* by Emily Brontë, edited by H. W. Garrod. "Sonnet 43" from *The Poetical Works of Elizabeth Barrett Browning*, Oxford Edition. "Kubla Khan" and "The Rime of the Ancient Mariner" from *The Poems of Samuel Taylor Coleridge*. "Easter Wings," "Man," and "Virtue" from *The Poems of George Herbert*, edited by Helen Gardner. "An Ode for Him" and "To the Virgins, to Make Much of Time" from *The Poems of Robert Herrick* edited by L. C. Martin. "God's Grandeur," "Pied Beauty," and "Spring and Fall" from *Poems of Gerard Manley Hopkins*, 4th edition, edited by W. H. Gardner and N. H. MacKenzie. "Letter to Lord Chesterfield" from *The Letters of Samuel Johnson*, Volume I: 1719–1774, collected and edited by R. W. Chapman. "To Althea" and "To Lucasta, on Going to the Wars" from *The Poems of Richard Lovelace* edited by C. H. Wilkinson. "Sonnet 31" and "Sonnet 39" from *The Poems of Sir Philip Sidney* edited by William A. Ringler, Jr. Lines from "The Faerie Queen," "Sonnet 1," "Sonnet 26," and "Sonnet 75" from *The Poetical Works of Edmund Spenser* edited by J. C. Smith and E. de Selincourt. "Crossing the Bar," lines from "In Memoriam, A. H. H.," "Tears, Idle Tears," "The Lady of Shalott," "The Lotos-Eaters," lines from "The Princess," and "Ulysses" from *Alfred Tennyson: Poetical Works*. "Naming of Parts" by Henry Reed. Copyright © The Executor of Henry Reed's estate 1991. Reprinted from *Collected Poems of Henry Reed* edited by Jon Stallworthy (1991) by permission of Oxford University Press. Reprinted by permission.

Pantheon Books, a division of Random House, Inc.
From "The Preface" and from "A Dictionary of the English Language" by Samuel Johnson in *Johnson's Dictionary: A Modern Selection* edited by E. L. McAdam, Jr., and George Milne.

Penguin Books Ltd.

"The Nun's Priest's Tale" from *The Canterbury Tales* by Geoffrey Chaucer, translated by Nevill Coghill (Penguin Classics, Revised edition, 1977), copyright © Nevill Coghill, 1951, 1958, 1960, 1975, 1977. Reprinted by permission of Penguin Books Ltd. From *A History of the English Church and People* by Venerable Bede, translated with an introduction by Leo Sherley-Price, revised by R. E. Latham (Penguin Classics, 1955, 1965, 1968), copyright © Leo Sherley-Price, 1955, 1965, 1968 copyright © R. E. Latham, 1968, pp. 37–40. "The Prologue" and 238 lines from "The Pardoner's Tale" from *The Canterbury Tales* by Geoffrey Chaucer, translated into modern English by Nevill Coghill (Penguin Classics 1951, 1958, 1960) copyright © Nevill Coghill, 1951, 1958, 1960, pp. 19–41, 268–274. Reprinted by permission of Penguin Books Ltd.

Peters Fraser & Dunlop Group Ltd.

"A Voyage to Cythera" by Margaret Drabble, published in *Mademoiselle* Magazine, December 1967. Reprinted by permission of the Peters Fraser & Dunlop Group Ltd.

Random House, Inc.

"Holy Sonnet 10," "Holy Sonnet 14," "Meditation 17," and "Song" from *Complete Poetry and Selected Prose of John Donne* by John Donne, edited by John Hayward. Excerpt from "Chard Whitlow" from *Parodies*, edited by Dwight Macdonald. Copyright 1960 by Dwight Macdonald.

Random House, Inc. and Faber and Faber Ltd.

"In Memory of W. B. Yeats" and "Musée des Beaux Arts" copyright 1940 and renewed 1968 by W. H. Auden. Reprinted from *W. H. Auden: Collected Poems* by W. H. Auden, edited by Edward Mendelson. "What I Expected" copyright 1955 by Stephen Spender. Reprinted from *Collected Poems* by Stephen Spender. Reprinted by permission of the publishers.

Routledge & Kegan Paul, Associated Book Publishers (U.K.) Ltd.

"The Picture of Little T.C. in a Prospect of Flowers" and "To His Coy Mistress" from *The Poems of Andrew Marvell* edited by Hugh MacDonald. Reprinted by permission.

Tessa Sayle Agency

"The Fiddle" from *The Second Chance and Other Stories* by Alan Sillitoe. Copyright © 1981 by Alan Sillitoe. First appeared in *The Nottingham Press*. Reprinted by permission.

Simon & Schuster, Inc.

"A Mild Attack of Locusts" from *African Stories* by Doris Lessing. Copyright © 1951, 1953, 1954, 1957, 1958, 1962, 1963, 1964, 1965, 1972, 1981 by Doris Lessing. Pronunciation key from *Webster's New World Dictionary*—Second College Edition. Copyright © 1984 by Simon & Schuster, Inc. Reprinted by permission of Simon & Schuster, Inc. "Ah, Are You Digging on My Grave?," "The Darkling Thrush," and "The Man He Killed" from *The Complete Poems of Thomas Hardy* edited by James Gibson (New York: Macmillan, 1978). This collection was published outside the U.S. by Macmillan

(London) Ltd. in 1976. "The Lake Isle of Innisfree" and "When You Are Old"; "An Irish Airman Foresees His Death" and "The Wild Swans at Coole," copyright 1919 by Macmillan Publishing Company, renewed 1947 by Bertha Georgie Yeats; "The Second Coming," copyright 1924 by Macmillan Publishing Company, renewed 1952 by Bertha Georgie Yeats; "Sailing to Byzantium," copyright 1928 by Macmillan Publishing Company, renewed 1956 by Bertha Georgie Yeats; and "After Long Silence," copyright 1933 by Macmillan Publishing Company, renewed 1961 by Bertha Georgie Yeats. All poems reprinted with permission of Simon & Schuster, Inc. from *The Poems of W. B. Yeats: A New Edition,* edited by Richard J. Finneran.

The Society of Authors on behalf of the Estate of Bernard Shaw

Pygmalion by Bernard Shaw. Copyright ©: 1913, 1914, 1916, 1930, 1941, 1944 George Bernard Shaw. Copyright 1957 The Public Trustee as Executor of the Estate of George Bernard Shaw. Reprinted by permission.

The University of Chicago Press and Faber and Faber Ltd.

Lines from "Positives" in *Positives: Verses* by Thom Gunn. Copyright © 1967 by Thom Gunn. Reprinted by permission of the publishers.

University of Nebraska Press

"The Seafarer" reprinted from *Poems From the Old English,* translated by Burton Raffel, by permission of the author. Copyright 1960, 1964, renewed 1988, 1992 by the University of Nebraska Press. Copyright registered 1994, in the name of Burton Raffel.

Viking Penguin, a division of Penguin Books USA Inc.

"The Train from Rhodesia" from *Selected Stories* by Nadine Gordimer. Copyright 1952 by Nadine Gordimer. "The Rocking-Horse Winner" from *The Complete Short Stories of D. H. Lawrence* Vol. III. Copyright 1933 by the Estate of D. H. Lawrence; copyright renewed © 1961 by Angelo Ravagli and C. M. Weekley, Executors of the Estate of Freida Lawrence Ravagli. "Sonnet 29," "Sonnet 73," "Sonnet 116," and "Sonnet 130" from *William Shakespeare: The Complete Works*, edited by Alfred Harbage. Copyright © 1969 by Penguin Books, Inc. Reprinted by permission of Viking Penguin, a division of Penguin Books USA Inc.

Viking Penguin, a division of Penguin Books USA Inc., and Aitken and Stone

"B. Wordsworth" from *Miguel Street* by V. S. Naipaul. Copyright © 1959 by V. S. Naipaul. Used by permission.

Viking Penguin, a division of Penguin Books USA Inc., Jonathan Cape Ltd., and the Estate of James Joyce

"Araby" from *Dubliners* by James Joyce. Copyright 1916 by B. W. Huebsch. Definitive text copyright © 1967 by the Estate of James Joyce. Reprinted by permission.

Viking Penguin, a division of Penguin Books USA Inc., and John Johnson Ltd.
"The Distant Past" from *Angels at the Ritz and Other Stories* by William Trevor. Copyright © 1973 by William Trevor. Reprinted by permission.

Viking Penguin, a division of Penguin Books USA Inc., and David Higham Associates Limited.
"Across the Bridge" from *Nineteen Stories* by Graham Greene. Copyright 1947, renewed © 1975 by Graham Greene. Published in London in *Collected Stories* by Graham

Greene by William Heinemann, Ltd., and The Bodley Head Ltd. Reprinted by permission.

Viking Penguin, a division of Penguin Books USA Inc., and George Sassoon
"Wirers" from *The Collected Poems of Siegfried Sassoon* by Siegfried Sassoon. Copyright 1918, 1920 by E. P. Dutton. Copyright 1936, 1946, 1947, 1948 by Siegfried Sassoon. Used by permission.

Note: Every effort has been made to locate the copyright owner of material reprinted in this book. Omissions brought to our attention will be corrected in subsequent editions.

ART CREDITS

Boldface numbers refer to the page on which the art is found.

Cover and Title Page: *A Highland Cottage,* Myles Birket Foster, Christie's London/Superstock; **vii:** (top) *The Oseberg Ship,* Viking, c. A.D. 850, Viking Ship Museum, Bygdoy, Oslo, Werner Forman Archive; (bottom) *Funeral of Plague Victim in House of Fitzeisulf,* Trinity Chapel Window, Canterbury Cathedral, 14th century, The Granger Collection, New York; **viii:** *Queen Elizabeth I of England,* George Gower, The Granger Collection, New York; **ix:** *The Farrier's Shop,* c. 1620–1687, Gael Barend, Guildhall Art Gallery, London, Bridgeman/Art Resource, New York; **x:** *Conversation in a Park,* Thomas Gainsborough, The Louvre, Paris, Scala/Art Resource, New York; **xi:** *John Keats,* 1821, Joseph Severn, by courtesy of the National Portrait Gallery, London; **xii:** *Bayswater Omnibus,* G. W. Joy, Museum of London; **xiii:** *The Potato Diggers,* 1912, Oil on canvas, Paul Henry, Courtesy of the National Gallery of Ireland; **xiv:** *Revolution Is Change, Change Is Life,* 1988, Jean Patrick Icart-Pierre, Soft pastel on stretched paper, Collection of the artist, Photo by Tony Velez, courtesy The Bronx Museum of the Arts, New York; **xvi:** *The Bayeux Tapestry,* The Granger Collection, New York; **2:** *Insignia of the Roman Civil Governor in Charge of Five British Provinces,* Page from an early 15th-century copy of a 4th-century list of Imperial Magistrates, The Granger Collection, New York; **4:** (left) *St. Augustine,* Giuseppe Ribera, Superstock; (center) *Charles Martel Battling the Moors,* The Granger Collection, New York; (right) *Viking Sword,* Iron, copper, and silver, The Metropolitan Museum of Art, Rogers Fund, 1955, © Copyright 1980/87 by The Metropolitan Museum of Art; **5:** (left) *King Charlemagne—jewelled gold reliquary bust,* c. 1350, Domschatz, Aachen, The Granger Collection, New York; (center), *Danes Attacking a British Town,* c. 1130, The Granger Collection, New York; (right) *The Coronation of William the Conqueror,* ms. illumination, c. 1470, The Granger Collection, New York; **6:** *Saxons, Jutes, and Angles Arriving in Britain by Sea,* English manuscript illumination, The Granger Collection, New York; **8:** *The Bayeux Tapestry,* detail, *Edward the Confessor Speaks to Harold of Wessex,* The Granger Collection, New York; **14:** Ms. Ashmole, 1511, Folio 86 verso, Bodleian Library, Oxford; **18:** *Knight's Helmet* (detail), Statens Historiska Museet, Stockholm, Werner Forman

Archive; **21:** *The Dragon for "The High Kings,"* George Sharp, Courtesy of the artist; **24:** *Arthur Going to Avalon for "The High Kings"* (detail), George Sharp, Courtesy of the artist; **31:** (left) *Head of Carved Post from the Ship Burial at Oseberg,* Werner Forman Archive; (top right), *Helmet,* Statens Historiska Museet, Stockholm, Werner Forman Archive: (bottom right), *Golden Horns* (detail), The National Museet, Copenhagen, Photo by Lennart Larsen; **37:** *Slaying of Bull on the Base of a Cauldron from Gundestrup,* 100 B.C., Celtic Artifact, National Museum, Copenhagen, Werner Forman Archive; **38:** *Celtic Style Figure from the Side of a Bowl from a Burial Mound,* 9th century, Norway, Werner Forman Archive; **39:** *Detail of Dragon Head on the Mammen Horse-Collar,* 10th century, Viking, National Museum, Denmark, Werner Forman Archive; **40:** *Gilt-Bronze Winged Dragon—Bridle Mounting,* 8th century, Swedish Artifact, Statens Historiska Museet, Stockholm, Werner Forman Archive; **43:** *Gilt-Silver Brooch,* from Gotland, Viking Migration period, Scandinavia, Statens Historiska Museet, Stockholm, Werner Forman Archive; **44:** *Silver Pendant Showing the Helmet of the Vendel,* 10th century, Swedish-Ostergotland, Viking, Statens Historiska Museet, Stockholm, Werner Forman Archive; **45:** *The Oseberg Ship,* c. A.D. 850, Viking, Viking Ship Museum, Bygdoy, Oslo, Werner Forman Archive; **49:** *Beowulf,* ms. page, The British Museum, The Bettmann Archive; **51:** *Grendel,* Frontispiece from *Beowulf,* 1908, Patten Wilson, The British Library; **53:** *Reconstructed Helmet, Sutton Hoo Ship Burial,* 7th century A.D., The Granger Collection, New York; **55:** *Serra Flying Over a Boat,* Illumination from an English bestiary, c. 1185, The Granger Collection, New York; **58:** Cotton ms.Tiberius C II Folio 5 Verso (detail), Page of Bede's *History,* The British Library; **61:** Cotton ms. Tiberius C II Folio 5 Verso, Page of Bede's *History,* The British Library; **62:** *Monks,* ms. University College 165 pii, Bodleian Library, Oxford; **65:** *The Anglo-Saxon Chronicle,* Ms. Cott TIB B1. Fol 132, The British Library; **68:** *Pilgrims to Canterbury* (detail), English illuminated manuscript, c. 1400, The Granger Collection, New York; **71:** *A Baliff Supervising the Harvest* (detail), Early 14th century, English illuminated manuscript, The Granger Collection, New York; **72:** (left) *The Murder of Thomas Becket,* Eng-

John Gilbert, The Granger Collection, New York; **314:** *Mrs. Siddons as Lady Macbeth,* G. H. Harlon, Garrick Club/ET Archive; **328:** *William Hazlitt,* 1825, William Bewick, By courtesy of the National Portrait Gallery, London; **335:** *King James Bible,* 1611, Title Page of the New Testament, By permission of the Folger Shakespeare Library; **339:** *Letters From Patent Granted by Elizabeth I to Francis Drake,* ET Archive; **342:** *The Thames at Westminster Stairs,* 1631 or 1637, Claude de Jongh, Yale Center for British Art, Paul Mellon Collection; **345:** *Portrait of Charles I,* Anthony Van Dyck, The Louvre, Paris, Art Resource, New York; **346:** (left) *New Amsterdam,* The Granger Collection, New York; (center) *Francis Bacon,* John Vanderbank, 1731 copy of painting, c. 1618, by courtesy of the National Portrait Gallery, London; (right) *The Execution of Charles I, 30 January 1649,* Contemporary painting by "Weesop," The Granger Collection, New York; **347:** (left) *John Milton,* William Faithorne, The Bettmann Archive; (center) *King Louis XIV,* Hyacinthe Rigaud, The Granger Collection, New York; (right) *Andrew Marvell,* c. 1655–1660, Artist unknown, Oil on canvas, The Granger Collection, New York; **349:** *The Execution of King Charles I of England at Whitehall,* London, January 30, 1649, Colored woodcut from Contemporary Ballad-Sheet, The Granger Collection, New York; **350:** Contemporary portrait of Oliver Cromwell, Artist unknown, The Bridgeman Art Library/Art Resource, New York; **351:** *Ben Jonson,* Abraham Van Blyenberch, The Granger Collection, New York; **352:** *John Donne,* after Isaac Oliver, Oil on canvas, The Granger Collection, New York; **353:** *George Herbert,* The Granger Collection, New York; **357:** *Greenwich Palace from the Northeast with a Man-of-War at Anchor* (detail) c. 1630, National Maritime Museum; **358:** *John Donne,* after Isaac Oliver, Oil on canvas, The Granger Collection, New York; **363:** *Sir Thomas Aston at the Deathbed of His Wife,* John Souch, Manchester City Art Galleries; **370:** *George Herbert,* The Granger Collection, New York; **373:** *The Milkmaid,* Myles Birket Foster, Victoria and Albert Museum Trustees, Bridgeman/Art Resource, New York; **376:** *Andrew Marvell,* Artist unknown, Oil on canvas, c. 1655–1660, The Granger Collection, New York; **382:** *Ben Jonson,* Abraham Van Blyenberch, The Granger Collection, New York; **387:** *Shakespeare and Ben Jonson at Chess,* Karel van Mander, Photo courtesy of William M. deHeyman, Philadelphia, Pennsylvania; **390:** *Robert Herrick,* New York Public Library; **395:** *Three Ladies Adorning a Term of Hymen,* 1773, Sir Joshua Reynolds, The Tate Gallery, London; **396:** (bottom) *Richard Lovelace,* The Granger Collection, New York; **396:** (top) *Sir John Suckling,* Anthony Van Dyck, The Granger Collection, New York; **398:** *The Interrupted Sleep,* François Boucher, The Metropolitan Museum of Art, The Jules Bache Collection, 1949, © Copyright 1984 by The Metropolitan Museum of Art; **399:** *Fair Is My Love* (detail), Edwin A. Abbey, The Harris Museum and Art Gallery, Preston; **400:** *Going to the Battle,* 1858, Edward Burne-Jones, Fitzwilliam Museum, Cambridge; **403:** *The Farrier's Shop,* c. 1620–1687, Gael Barend, Guildhall Art Gallery, London, Bridgeman/Art Resource, New York; **404:** *John Milton,* c.1629, Artist unknown, The Granger Collection, New York; **416:** *Paradise Lost,* 1688, John Milton, The British Library; **421:** *The Garden of Eden,* Erastus Salisbury Field, Superstock; **422:** *John Bunyan,* The Granger Collection, New York; **425:** *The Pilgrim's Progress, Angels/Pilgrim/Knight Figures,* John Bunyan, The British Library; **432:** *Morville Hall,* Shropshire, John Inigo Richards, Roy Miles Fine Paintings, London, Bridgeman/Art Resource, New York; **428:** *Captain John Smith,* from Smith's Map of Virginia, 1616, The Granger Collection, New York; **435:** *Queen Anne and the Knights of the Garter* (detail), 1713, Peter Angelis, The Granger Collection, New York; **436:** (left) *John Locke,* 1704, Sir G. Kneller, The Granger Collection, New York; (center) *The Great Fire of London,* 1666, Contemporary painting, Dutch School, The Granger Collection, New York; (right) Illustration from *Gulliver's Travels,* The Granger Collection, New York; **437:** (left) *The Boston Tea Party,* The Granger Collection, New York; (center) *W. A. Mozart,* Johann Peter Krafft, The Granger Collection, New York; (right) *The Storming of the Bastille,* Claude Cholat, The Granger Collection, New York; **438:** *King George III of England,* c. 1760, Allan Ramsay, The Granger Collection, New York; **439:** *Sir Isaac Newton,* c. 1726, Attributed to John Vanderbank, The Granger Collection, New York; **441:** *The Rake's Progress: No. 5, The Marriage,* William Hogarth, The Granger Collection, New York; **445:** *The Election—The Polling,* William Hogarth, Sir John Soane's Museum, London, Bridgeman/Art Resource, New York; **446:** *John Dryden,* J. Maubert, By courtesy of the National Portrait Gallery, London; **449:** *Shakespeare and His Contemporaries,* John Faed, from the Collection of Mr. and Mrs. Sandor Korein, Montgomery Museum of Fine Arts; **454:** *The Music of a Bygone Age,* John Melhuish Strudwick, The Pre-Raphaelite Trust, Bridgeman/Art Resource, New York; **458:** *Samuel Pepys* (detail), c. 1695, John Closterman, The Granger Collection, New York; **462:** *The Great Fire of London,* 1666, The Museum of London; **465:** *Conversation in a Park,* Thomas Gainsborough, The Louvre, Paris, Scala/Art Resource, New York; **466:** *Daniel Defoe,* The Bettmann Archive; **468:** *Journal of the Plague Year: the Dead Cart,* The British Library; **472:** *Jonathan Swift,* Charles Jervas, The Granger Collection, New York; **476, 480:** Illustrations for *Gulliver's Travels,* Willy Pogany; The Donnell Library Children's Room, The Research Libraries; New York Public Library; Astor, Lenox, and Tilden Foundations; **482:** (top) *Joseph Addison* (detail), Sir Godfrey Kneller, The Granger Collection, New York; (bottom) *Sir Richard Steele* (detail), 1712, Jonathan Richardson, The Granger Collection, New York; **488:** *St. Edmund's Chapel, Westminster Abbey,* John Fulleylove; **492:** *Alexander Pope* (detail), c. 1783–1843, William Hoare, The Granger Collection, New York; **495:** *The Barge,* 1895–1896, Aubrey Beardsley from "The Rape of the Lock," Smithers, 1896, from *The Best of Beardsley,* Collected and edited by R. A. Walker; ©1948 by The Bodley Head, Published in the U.S.A. by Excalibur Books, Plate 63; **498:** *The Rape of the Lock,* 1895–1896, Aubrey Beardsley, from "The Rape of the Lock," Smithers, 1896, from *The Best of Beardsley,* Collected and edited by R. A. Walker, ©1948 by The Bodley Head, Published in the U.S.A. by Excalibur

Books, Plate 64; **503:** *The Battle of the Beaux and Belles,* Aubrey Beardsley, The Barber Institute of Fine Arts, The University of Birmingham; **509:** *Oliver Smith, James Boswell, and Samuel Johnson at the Mitre Tavern,* 19th century colored engraving, The Granger Collection, New York; **510:** *Samuel Johnson* (detail), 1756, Sir Joshua Reynolds, The Granger Collection, New York; **520:** *James Boswell* (detail), 1795, Sir Joshua Reynolds, The Granger Collection, New York; **523:** *Johnson and Boswell,* © The Trustees of the British Museum; **529:** *Haymakers,* 1785, George Stubbs, The Granger Collection, New York; **530:** *Thomas Gray* (detail), 1748, J. G. Eccardt, The Granger Collection, New York; **538:** *Robert Burns,* A. Nasmyth, by courtesy of the National Portrait Gallery, London; **546:** *The River Dee Near Eton Hall,* Richard Wilson, The Barber Institute, The University of Birmingham; **550:** *William Blake,* Thomas Phillips, The Granger Collection, New York; **552:** From a Manuscript of *"The Lamb"* by William Blake, Lessing J. Rosenwald Collection, Courtesy of the Library of Congress, Washington, DC; **554:** *The Tiger,* A Page from "Songs of Innocence and Experience," William Blake, The Metropolitan Museum of Art, Rogers Fund, 1917, © Copyright 1984 By The Metropolitan Museum of Art; **558:** From a Manuscript of *"A Poison Tree,"* by William Blake, Lessing J. Rosenwald Collection, Courtesy of the Library of Congress, Washington, D.C.; **561:** *Allegory of the Royal Society by Hollar,* Mansell Collection; **564:** *View in Hampshire,* Patrick Nasmyth, Guildhall Art Gallery, City of London, Bridgeman/Art Resource, New York; **567:** *Napoleon (The Campaign in France, 1814),* Jean Louis Ernest Meissonier, The Granger Collection, New York; **568:** (left) *Rosetta Stone,* The Granger Collection, New York; (center) *Napoleon Bonaparte as First Consul,* J. A. Ingres, Musee des Beaux Arts, Belgium, Bridgeman Art Library, London/Superstock, Inc.; (right) *Jane Austen,* The Granger Collection, New York; **569:** (left) *Robert Fulton's Steamboat,* The Granger Collection, New York; (center) *John Keats,* Joseph Severn, The Granger Collection, New York; (right) *London in the 1820's,* The Granger Collection, New York; **573:** *Calais Pier: An English Packet Arriving,* J.M.W. Turner, The Granger Collection, New York; **574:** *Sketch for Hadleigh Castle,* c. 1828–1829, John Constable, The Granger Collection, New York; **575:** *Sir Walter Scott/Abbotsford Family,* 1804, Sir David Wilkie, The Granger Collection, New York; **578:** *William Wordsworth,* Benjamin Hayden, The Granger Collection, New York; **581:** *Tintern Abbey,* J.M.W. Turner, Courtesy of the Trustees of the British Museum; **586:** *Landscape with a Rainbow,* Joseph Wright of Derby, Derby Art Gallery; **591:** *Cornfield by Moonlight,* Samuel Palmer, Courtesy of the Trustees of the British Museum; **594:** *Samuel Taylor Coleridge* (detail), by courtesy of the National Portrait Gallery, London; **599, 601, 602, 609:** Engraving by Gustav Doré for *The Rime of The Ancient Mariner* by Samuel Taylor Coleridge, © 1970 by Dover Publications, Inc.; **623:** *Kublai Khan,* Chinese Silk Album Leaf, The Granger Collection, New York; **624:** *Lord Byron* (detail), William West, The Granger Collection, New York; **629:** *Shipwreck,* J.C.C. Dahl, Munich Neue Pinakothek/Kavaler/Art Resource, New York;

636: *Percy Bysshe Shelley* (detail), A. Curran, The Granger Collection, New York; **641:** *Cirrus Cloud Study,* John Constable, Victoria and Albert Museum Trustees; **645:** *Cloud Study,* 1821, John Constable, Yale Center for British Art, Paul Mellon Collection; **650:** *John Keats* (detail), Joseph Severn, The Granger Collection, New York; **653:** Frontispiece, Homer's *Iliad* and *Odyssey,* 1612, G. Chapman, The British Library; **655:** *John Keats,* 1821, Joseph Severn, by courtesy of the National Portrait Gallery, London; **658:** *Small Bird On a Flowering Plum Branch,* The Goto Museum; **666:** *Harvest Field with Gleaners, Haywood, Herefordshire,* 1815, George Robert Lewis, The Tate Gallery, London; **663:** Greek Vase, Terracotta, c. 460 B.C., Attributed to the Orchard Painter, Column Krater (called the "Orchard Vase"), Side A: Women Gathering Apples, The Metropolitan Museum of Art, Rogers Fund, 1907, © Copyright 1984 by The Metropolitan Museum of Art; **670:** *Mary Shelley* (detail), c. 1840, Richard Rothwell, by courtesy of the National Portrait Gallery, London; **673:** *A View of Chamonix and Mt. Blanc,* Julius Schnon von Carolsfeld, Austrian Gallery, Vienna; **677:** *Faust: Henry Irving as Mephistopheles,* c. 1885, Theatre Museum/ET Archive; **679:** *Sir Walter Scott,* 1824, Sir Edwin Landseer, by courtesy of the National Portrait Gallery, London/Jean-Loup Charmet; **682:** *Queen Victoria's Visit to Cherbourg,* Jules Achille Noël, Royal Academy, London, Bridgeman/Art Resource, New York; **684:** *Painting of London's Crystal Palace* (detail), done for the Great Exhibition of 1851, The British Museum; **686:** (left) *Charles Dickens,* Artist unknown, The Granger Collection, New York; (center) *Queen Victoria of England,* Sir George Hayter, The Granger Collection, New York; (right) *Richard Wagner,* Franz von Lenbach, The Granger Collection, New York; **687:** (left) *The Mad Tea Party* from the First Edition of *Alice's Adventures,* Sir John Tenniel, The Granger Collection, New York; (center) *Suez Canal,* The Granger Collection, New York; (right) *Marines Fight in The Boxer Rebellion,* John Clymer, Superstock; **688:** *Dudley Street, Seven Dials, London,* 1872, Gustave Doré, The Granger Collection, New York; **691:** *Alfred, Lord Tennyson,* 1871, Carlo Pelligrini, Caricature, The Granger Collection, New York; **692:** *Bayswater Omnibus,* G. W. Joy, Museum of London; **693:** *Hyde Park Near Grosvenor Gate,* 1842, Thomas Shotter Boys, Guildhall Art Gallery, Bridgeman/Art Resource, New York; **696:** *Baron Alfred Tennyson,* c. 1840, S. Laurence, by courtesy of the National Portrait Gallery, London; **699:** *The Lady of Shalott,* John Waterhouse, The Tate Gallery, London; **708:** *Nocturne in Grey and Gold:* Chelsea Snow, 1876, James McNeill Whistler, Courtesy of The Fogg Art Museum, Harvard University Art Museums, Bequest, Glenville L. Winthrop; **715:** *Ulysses Mourning for Home,* Roman 3rd to 2nd century B.C., Carved gem of light brown sardonyx, Staatliche Museen zu Berlin; **719:** *Ulysses,* c. 1827, Jean-Auguste-Dominique Ingres, © 1993 National Gallery of Art, Washington, Chester Dale Collection; **722:** *The Angry Sea* (detail), James McNeill Whistler, Courtesy of the Freer Gallery of Art, Smithsonian Institution, Washington, D.C.; **724:** *Robert Browning,* M. Gordiagiani, The Granger Collection, New York; **727:** *Antea (Portrait of a Lady),*

PHOTO CREDITS